Intimate Communications

HERDT

Guardians of the Flutes.

Rituals of Manhood: Male Initiation in Papua New Guinea (ed.).

Ritualized Homosexuality in Melanesia (ed.).

The Sambia: Ritual and Gender in New Guinea

STOLLER

Sex and Gender: On the Development of Masculinity and Femininity.

Splitting.

The Transsexual Experiment: Sex and Gender—Volume II.

Perversion: The Erotic Form of Hatred.

Sexual Excitement: Dynamics of Erotic Life.

Observing the Erotic Imagination.

Presentations of Gender.

Cognitive Science and Psychoanalysis. (With K. M. Colby.)

Ritual talk: one-on-one backstage preparations.

INTIMATE COMMUNICATIONS

Erotics and the Study of Culture

GILBERT HERDT
AND ROBERT J. STOLLER

Columbia University Press
New York

Cover, frontispiece photograph by Gilbert Herdt, Ritual talk: one-on-one backstage preparations.

COLUMBIA UNIVERSITY PRESS
New York   Oxford
Copyright © 1990 Columbia University Press
All rights reserved

LIBRARY OF CONGRESS CATALOGING-IN-PUBLICATION DATA
Herdt, Gilbert H., 1949–
Intimate communications : erotics and the study of culture /
Gilbert Herdt and Robert J. Stoller.
p.   cm.
Bibliography: p.
Includes index.
ISBN 0-231-06900-6
ISBN 0-231-06901-4 (pbk.)
1. Sambia (Papua New Guinea people)—Sexual behavior.
2. Sambia (Papua New Guinea people)—Rites and ceremonies.
3. Group identity—Papua New Guinea.
I. Stoller, Robert J. II. Title.
DU740.42.H445   1989
306.7′0899912—dc19
89-897
CIP

Casebound editions of Columbia University Press books are Smyth-sewn
and printed on permanent and durable acid-free paper

Printed in the United States of America
c 10 9 8 7 6 5 4 3 2 1
p 10 9 8 7 6 5 4 3 2 1

CONTENTS

Illustrations appear as a group following page 244.

PREFACE

Herdt:* Toward the end of my third and very significant field trip among the Sambia of Papua New Guinea, in 1979, Bob Stoller, a psychoanalyst and professor of psychiatry, visited my field site in the village of Nilangu. I had completed doctoral dissertation research among the Sambia between 1974 and 1976, two years' work on which I based my first book, *Guardians of the Flutes* (1981), that had been written in draft form in 1978, during a time of many dialogues with S. For the next two years, between 1977 and 1979, S. and I talked together, on clinical research, erotics, and gender identity issues, because I was fortunate enough to apprentice with him. When the opportunity came for me to return to the Sambia again in 1979, it was therefore natural for him to want to visit. He did so and the culmination of our work is this book.

Since that time, S. and I have collaborated but also continued our separate researches, which have led in several directions. For my own gender research I returned to the field for follow-up studies with the Sambia in 1981, 1983, and 1985, the total period of fieldwork being about three years. This work has been published in a series of books and papers, which the reader will find referenced in our bibliography, and the findings of which are distilled in Herdt (1987c). This body of ethnographic material backgrounds the present work that also presents a new contribution on erotics and culture, the theme that drew me to work with S. and that led him to the village as well.

Our study is motivated by the lack of material on sexuality across cultures and our concern to place erotics more centrally into anthro-

*You will find "H" or "S" at the start of sections that one or the other of us primarily wrote (though, of course, each of us corrected, added citations to, and edited all of the other's material).

pology (Herdt 1987c). We hope to explore and advance the study of subjectivity more fully by doing this. To do so we must study interviews on intimate matters and try to assess how the ethnographers' procedures help or hinder the process. In this way we try to deconstruct "sexual"—we shall use the more precise term "erotic"— meanings in cultures. We shall use data collected (almost haphazardly, because our original aim was not to produce a book) through individual interviews to show that it is only through dialogue, through interpersonal and intimate communication, that certain critical points of interest to the study of gender and erotics in culture are revealed. By use of this dialogic mode we are able to provide new kinds of cross-cultural data. Nonetheless, this mode is complicated, and we should note that this book took years to produce.

Stoller: By the end of that first morning in the village, I knew that we should write this book. The impulse still surprises me, for it was not even latent when I left Los Angeles. Though I knew H.'s findings in detail—we had been working together between his field trips—I am a psychoanalyst, not an anthropologist. I could discuss theory with him to help focus his material and could suggest questions to ask or point to hidden areas to uncover. But he is an ethnographer, not I, and these New Guinea findings were his, to be written up by him. That is still the case. The task before us, then, is not so much to describe the Sambia as to contemplate ethnographic method, which— it seemed that morning, and still does—can be strengthened by the techniques that the clinician (psychiatrist/psychoanalyst) uses: we want to report on the value of subjectivity in studying culture, erotics, and gender identity.

Many ethnographers still omit from their reports the fine details of field experience that make our behavior intelligible to ourselves and to those with whom we communicate.[1] How many ethnographic studies are there of "style"—of what is harmonious, ugly, bizarre, frightening, beautiful, exciting—in art, humor, dress, decoration, erotics? What a shame that these aesthetics are removed, for they form an unending flood of sharp and dim awareness shaping our perspective on reality, each waking moment. The psychoanalyst, living within his or her own skin and trying to do so with others, is surprised that colleagues in related disciplines do not believe such data are very significant. Erotics is a case in point (Stoller 1979, 1985a).

This, then, is a book about subjectivity in the study of people, their culture, and erotics. At its center are two principles: the way researchers experience themselves is a vital ingredient of their findings; and, equally, the way informants—subjects, patients, friends—experience themselves shapes what they communicate to us. If you know these perspectives are true, you may not believe anyone doubts them, while the doubters cannot take seriously the work of those who adhere to them.

Through our work with Sambia, we shall use our ethnographic dialogues to rethink method. We believe that these ideas apply to all disciplines that study human behavior: *what the observer feels and what is felt by those whom we observe is part of the research and not an interference to be washed out in research methodology.* The way we experience ourselves is, therefore, a necessary ingredient of our work, present whether we sense it or not. And to the extent we do not sense it, it creates even more of a mess than when we do. Such knowledge is one of the clinician's greatest strengths. Where does this knowledge lie? Whether in ourselves (intrapsychic) or between ourselves and others (interpersonal), it must be scrutinized, understood, and used if we are to understand our informants and ourselves. Unfortunately, such knowledge complicates our work, and perhaps—paradoxically—forever limits what we can know. For, of course, our understanding of ourselves will always be incomplete or biased, even for those closely connected to us, even for those who share our culture, let alone for those from other places or times. Misjudging what is happening inside another can also lead to wrong conclusions. H. and I, however, feel a new attempt can be made to study these problems. In fact we are driven to do so now, for each of us has reached a point in our separate investigations where we must more fully consider this aspect of our methodology—who we are as we do our work and who each person is whom we study—before going back to our own concerns.

If we were to practice what we preach, a good part of this book would be a description of each of us, not merely the usual curriculum vitae but a more insightful look at our personalities—at those of our attributes that influenced the way each Sambia responded to us. We have done so only to a limited extent, however. (And, without having tried, we do not know if we have the courage or the wisdom to do so.) Someday, if we are successful, books such as this—and better—will be published by others. But until readers are comfortable with a subjectively oriented report, they would fuss too much over the descriptions of each of us. Only when it becomes a given in research on human behavior can we demand that each explorer show us his half of the interpersonal equation. So let the following suffice to orient the reader; you will sense more who we are as you see the way we write and read the way we spoke in the field.

In 1975, while with the Sambia doing doctoral fieldwork, H. wrote to a friend at UCLA, also a predoctoral candidate, asking if the latter could refer him to a clinician familiar with contemporary issues in sexuality—erotic behavior and gender identity.* By coincidence, the student was at that moment helping me survey the comparative ethnography on sexual excitement. In our ensuing correspondence H. saw that I knew the field, and I found that he had gathered data on sexuality richer than any available in the anthropologic literature. In time, to further strengthen his capacity to collect and make sense of such data, and to increase his skills in using subjective information, he decided that he needed training in a clinical/research center after completing his doctorate. So, on being awarded a postdoctoral fellowship, he came to study with me at UCLA.

For my own work on the development of gender identity, H.'s findings on the Sambia, including those gathered before we met, have been among the few I have found rich enough—where the people are real enough—for cross-cultural comparison. When as an ethnographer you remove yourself (and thereby me) from your data and communicate only with normative descriptions, modal personalities, and statistics, there are no true grounds for this psychologically informed act of comparing. H. discusses this view in chapter 1.

Each of us learned about the other's literature, methods, and professional skills, our discussions built around reviewing and dissecting the data (in raw form embodied in memory, field notes, and audiotapes of conversations). Because predictions made in the office were borne out later when H. returned to the Sambia, and because suggestions for leads to follow brought forth new data, our enthusiasm persisted. So, of course, I went to visit the Sambia.

Regarding personality traits, H. and I share two qualities useful for our work. First, though each of us is "properly" (that is, classically) trained in our professions and not overly rebellious, sharp-nosed colleagues sense our territorial markers on alien hydrants. Second, for reasons probably hidden in the murk of early infantile experiences, we each need to get inside others' minds, to feel what they feel, and to know what they know (without having to suffer the misery of

---

*At all times when we write "sexuality" herein, we refer only to something in those two domains: gender identity and erotics.

really being someone else). That hunger (to use a word that points toward the primordial dynamics) underlies all rationalizations of the scientific value of studying subjectivity and guarantees the pursuit of our curiosity.

If an ethnographer and analyst work together, is it not more efficient to have them both in the same person? Though we believe it would be, as in the rare cases of Roheim and Devereux, we do not believe it easily can be. Nor have LeVine's[2] ideas about cross-cultural teams generated much enthusiasm. An analyst and anthropologist from the same culture may share similar cultural blindspots, but they have advantages as a team. Whatever similarities are shared by H. and me, there must be personality differences if we are each to fit the mold of our respective professions. Ethnographers, for instance, must want to live for long stretches in a foreign culture, should yearn to identify with people culturally different from themselves, must give up the middle-class comforts out of which they are likely to have emerged (if they are to have had the educational opportunities needed for becoming an anthropologist). The desire to stay put, to have a family, or to enjoy the pleasures of one's own culture cannot be urges in the ethnographer strong enough to disrupt his or her capacity to stay away from home.[3]

On the other hand, analysts should be, whatever else goes on in their lives, people who not only think about analysis but practice it (cannot bear not to practice it).[4] Since analyses take years and—to put it mildly—do not thrive on long, repeated absences by the analyst, we can expect that most analysts will prefer to stay home. Perhaps some day an analyst who likes to practice will find himself in life circumstances that allow him first to soak up a foreign culture until it is nonetheless his own and then to practice analysis there. (There was a bit of this process when European analysts, forced to flee, settled into new countries with new languages; but the cultural shifts were far less than what the classical ethnographer experiences.)

There are other reasons why the two disciplines are not easily combined in one person. Most analysts, with premedical training, medical school, internship, and three years of psychiatric residency before starting their analytic training, are rather aged by the time their seven to ten years of analytic training have ended and they are certified as competent to practice. To lay on top of that the requirement of a doctorate in anthropology is close to absurd. So far, almost no one has been able to combine the two disciplines; and if one should, there is the danger, as with other professional hybrids, that fellow anthropologists judge this colleague to be a lousy anthropologist but a good analyst, while fellow analysts judge him a lousy analyst but a good anthropologist.

So, since it worked easily for us, we recommend that a team—a compatible ethnographer and analyst/psychiatrist—work together.[5] When the ethnographer is accepted by people in the community in which he or she is working, the chances are good the colleague will also be. The two researchers as a team bring different personalities, life experiences, training, blind spots, and insights to their work. And, if personal and professional animosities (are they different?) are not present, the two will enjoy—as we have—how the strength of one repairs the weaknesses of the other and how what is background for one can be foreground for the other.

Hence by the time the helicopter delivered me into the Valley, except for and because of Herdt, I knew more anthropologically about the Sambia than anyone else in the world, including, in some ways, even the Sambia. And, whereas it would have been impossible for a stranger to drop in and be accepted, my arrival as the friend of H., who is so well regarded by his informants, was frictionless from the start. It was even easier, perhaps, than when I first meet a patient in our culture: the Sambia saw me so much as his extension that—as I felt and he confirmed—they spoke no less freely with me present than they had previously with him alone. (And perhaps, for some Sambia, my gray hair also made me seem safer, *hors de combat*.)

It was necessary that it be that way, for I could only stay ten days. One need be very, very cautious about the findings of an observer who spent only that fragment of time in a village (see chapter 1). (Certainly, those of us in Los Angeles are bemused by the standard East Coast journalist's report of Southern California culture based on watching the Beverly Hills Hotel poolside traffic flow.) But, after a couple of years of studying with H., I knew a lot about each of the people we interviewed and their culture. I was physically and psychologically at ease from the moment of entering the village; no barrier but language blocked communication between the Sambia and me, and with H. there, I did not have to spend years learning to communicate. (To confirm these declarations, there are our tapes.) Most important, I was not there pretending to be an ethnographer and was not aiming to discover new things about the Sambia.

What I did find, which has been well noted by others and does not require long field trips or an exquisite research plan, is that there are, in studying human behavior, many circumstances when we can neither ignore who or what it is we observe nor who or what each person is whom we observe. Psychoanalysis is, among other things, a certain kind of microethnography. [H: Well, at least the analysis that Stoller practices.] So the analyst brings a long preparation in clinical skills that lets him or her listen to others, as can any seasoned clinician, with heightened (though fallible) sensitivity.

In this work, as you will see, I was H.'s assistant; though on occasion, I could push the interview in new directions or take the lead when we were later exchanging ideas. If our experience as ethnographer and psychoanalyst working together was not a fluke of the circumstances and our personalities, we presume others can find a similar balance. What we did was certainly not psychoanalysis or psychiatry: it was Herdt doing ethnography—he has well named it "clinical ethnography"—amplified and illuminated by my suggestions about how to climb with sensitivity even further into our Sambia friends' minds. And it made us see that when ethnographers learn to use the clinical skills clinicians take for granted, anthropology is closer to the human minds it would study.

This account does not tell you who we were at *any* moment when collecting data on which we shall report: that challenge is not met by such a limited biography (of course, no biography is adequate for this task; all biographies are novels, none more so than autobiographies). We only hope you do not forget, as you read, that our reports and transcripts are not facts, hard as rock. All you will have is your impressions of our impressions. If you then carry the same skeptical but benign reading to all reports on human behavior, our book will have succeeded in one of its aims.

ACKNOWLEDGMENTS

H: One's work responds to many others, in part by context, in another part by dialogue. Stoller, both through our talk and in his work, has been the strongest consistent influence on my thought. Here in Chicago, however, the key context has been shaped by several of my friends and colleagues, of whom I wish especially to thank: Rick Shweder, Bert Cohler, Andy Boxer, and Julia Targ. In the dialogue on gender in Melanesia, and critically for anthropology as a whole, my work is responsive to Marilyn Strathern's, whose remarkable and pioneering insight has been a source of inspiration.

Anthropologists incur many debts in the course of doing field research and training. It is a pleasure to acknowledge here with grateful thanks all this assistance. For predoctoral (1974–1976) field support, Herdt thanks the Australian-American Education foundation and the Department of Anthropology, Research School of Pacific Studies, the Australian National University; and for postdoctoral funding, H. thanks the National Institute of Mental Health, and the Department of Psychiatry, Neuropsychiatric Institute, UCLA. The research reported herein is based primarily on 1979 work with the Sambia in Papua New Guinea, and H. especially wishes to thank Dr. L. Jolyon West, M.D., for the UCLA support that made this study possible. The writing of this book was made possible, in part, by a grant to Herdt from the Anne P. Lederer Research institute. Additional support came from the Spencer Foundation, which is gratefully acknowledged.

H. expresses sincere gratitude to the Department of Anthropology and Sociology, the University of Papua New Guinea, and to the government of Papua New Guinea, for research affiliation that facilitated this work.

H. warmly thanks the following people whose kind logistical and moral support made work possible: Ted Bickum, Robert and Sybil Stoller, Steven Alkus, Murray Fagg, Marielle Fuller, Clifford Barnett, JoAnna Poppink, and Lew Langness. We are also indebted to Louise Waller for her unending enthusiastic editorial commitment. Both S. and I thank again Mr. and Mrs. Dennis Best, of the New Tribes Mission, Papua New Guinea, for their kind hospitality.

Stoller thanks himself, Professor Herdt, his family, and his good luck—in ascending order of significance—for the opportunity to study the Sambia.

For their helpful comments and criticisms on parts of this manuscript we are ever grateful to James L. Gibbs, Jr., Waude Kracke, and Fitz John Poole.

We gratefully acknowledge the typing and transcription work on this book by Thelma Guffan, Jackie de Havilland, Ana Haunga, Flora Degen, Debbie A. Johnson, and Vincent Wang.

Finally, Sambia is a pseudonym adopted by Herdt to protect the true identity of these people. All names and places have also been changed for this reason. And we implore anyone having access to the true identities to protect and safeguard the trust of the people whose lives we describe below. Most of all, I regret that I cannot thank by name my Sambia friends who opened their homes and their souls to us, and trusted us to share their experiences. Perhaps someday circumstances will permit us to do so.

TEXT ACKNOWLEDGMENT

Parts of the following chapters have been excerpted herein with permission of the publishers:

G. Herdt, "Semen Transactions in Sambia Culture." In G. Herdt, ed., *Ritualized Homosexuality in Melanesia*, pp. 167–210. Berkeley: University of California Press.

G. Herdt, "Ordinary People." In *The Sambia: Ritual and Gender in New Guinea*, pp. 59–66. New York: Holt, Rinehart, and Winston.

G. Herdt and R. J. Stoller, "Der Einflub der Supervision auf die ethnographische Praxis." In Hans Peter Duerr, ed., *Die Wilde Seele: Zur Ethnopsychoanalyse von Georges Devereux*, pp. 177–199. Frankfurt: Suhrkamp Verlag.

G. Herdt and R. J. Stoller, Sakulambei—A Hermaphrodite's Secret: Example of Clinical Ethnography. *Psychoanalytic Study of Society* 11:117–158.

NOTES ON DATES IN TEXT

The events and ages of people (written primarily in the short biographic sketches of our case studies) in the following text were written up in the period of 1979–1982.
Introductory and concluding chapters were completed between 1985 and 1987. Final textual changes were completed in the copy-edit (1988). Unless stated otherwise, all ages and events refer to these periods.

Intimate Communications

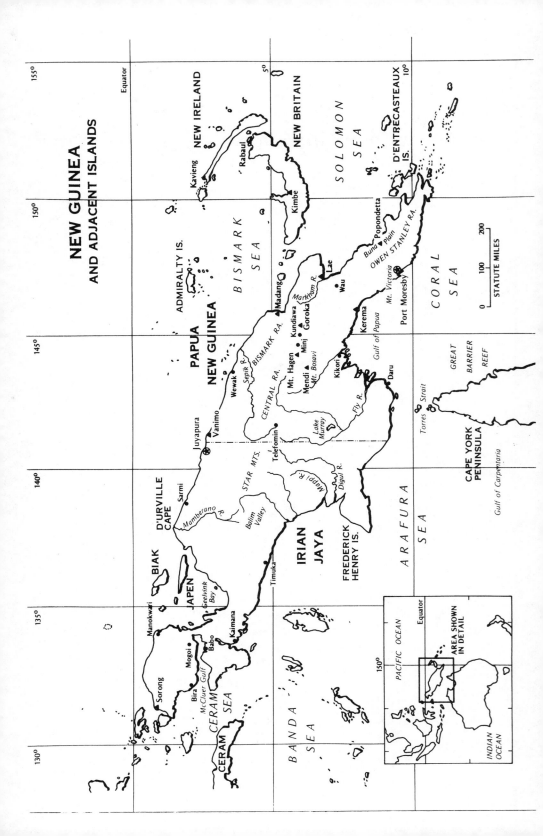

Introduction

H: This is a book that studies the personal meanings and private experiences of people in context to better and more fully understand culture. It also makes an argument for the collaboration of anthropologists and psychoanalysts, especially in the investigation of gender identity and erotics. We develop in what follows a kind of case study approach, which we call clinical ethnography.

Erotics, the study of sexual excitement, is still largely neglected in anthropology, the study of culture. Though great strides have been made in our understanding of gender—masculinity and femininity—in other cultures, erotic sexuality has been a less favored topic of study. We know about the cultural practices and symbols of men's and women's roles in other societies (reviewed in Atkinson 1982; Chodorow 1978; Herdt 1981; Ortner and Whitehead 1981; Rosaldo 1980; Rosaldo and Lamphere 1974; Rossi 1985; M. Strathern 1988). We know less about the people who embody these roles or purvey their meanings (LeVine 1982). Probably no one since Malinowski, in his *Sexual Life of Savages* (1929), has so much contributed to the systematic ethnographic study of erotics in another culture. And that was a long time ago.

Likewise, where a wealth of new material on gender in anthropology has appeared in the last few years, it seems to us that far less attention has been paid to gender identity. There is less concern with the subjectivity or phenomenology of real people's inner feelings, states of being—as in being male or female—and their related goals and representations of such. Far more has issued forth on gender roles, gender hierarchy, and the political economy of the sexual division of labor and female productivity (reviewed in M. Strathern 1988). We do not complain of this interest: does a dinner guest refuse the ap-

1

petizer? It has opened a remarkable new chapter in cross-cultural studies, whereby "gendered analysis is not merely a supplement but a *sine qua non* of social inquiry" (Atkinson 1982:256). Rather, S. and I miss more, and deeper, information on gender identity and erotics. Seldom have ethnographers pursued questions of gender identity orientation or development, as this is understood in contemporary sex research in the United States. Our work with the Sambia is a contribution toward this end.

The causes of this gap between past and present anthropology are not hard to find. On the one hand, sex has long been a tabooed topic in our society and the social sciences at large, the social context and mainstream of anthropology. Gender research has broken down this taboo, but only in part (Herdt 1984). Problems and reluctance associated with the cross-cultural study of homosexual behavior, for instance, reveal some of this old stigma and taboo (Carrier 1980; Mead 1961; Read 1980; 1984; reviewed in Blackwood 1986; Murray 1984). On the other hand, the detailed information necessary to study erotics and gender identity are usually omitted in ethnographies, at least until very recently. In part this is because of the general aims of ethnographic accounts, which are concerned with culture as a whole; and in another sense because of the theoretic treatment of gender as a cultural theme or mode, rather than as an individual construction. We shall discuss these issues later. Another cause of the gap is the sensitive, intimate nature of erotic feelings; for, as Mead (1961:1434) once said, "One characteristic of human sex behavior is the insistence on privacy." This is not quite true of all societies (Shostak 1981). Yet it is common enough that it has "serious implications for research in the field of sex" (Mead, *ibid.*). Special and sensitive attention to ethnographic rapport and interviewing is required. The overall frame of this we think of as intimate communication on sexuality.

Culture, gender identity, and erotics are our primary concerns; the Sambia of New Guinea provide our database. For this book extends the work of Herdt, the summary of which, on gender and ritual development, can be found in *The Sambia: Ritual and Gender in New Guinea* (1987c); it also continues and amplifies our collaborative work on erotics and gender identity (Herdt and Stoller 1985; Stoller and Herdt 1982, 1985); and it provides another context for Stoller's (1985a) work on the meaning of erotic excitement. For the moment we shall define our terms such that "sex" refers to biologic components, "gender" refers to masculinity and femininity, and "erotics" refers to sexual excitement.

We shall also critically examine our notions of "experience," "subjectivity," and kindred terms that emphasize the individual pole of the personal/collective spectrum in the social sciences. Our mode will not be philosophic or structural, for such formal analyses are available in the treatises of many fields, including, for psychoanalysis, that of Stoller (1979), and for anthropology, that of Herdt (1981). We prefer rather to provide an expository and didactic approach, through which we present our material as it occurred in the field. There is no hard and fast boundary between subjectivity and objectivity, and, indeed, many have rejected this dichotomy. But where such has been rejected—for reality/fantasy, and objective/subjective—the distinction between what is collective/personal has been less reanalyzed, except, perhaps, in those sensitive Third World psychoanalytic works (Doi 1973; Kakar 1983) where an awareness of the problematics involved in establishing intrapsychic meanings of cultural symbols seems more acute. These dynamic and oscillating boundaries will be charted.

For a long time, too, but often virtually in spite of itself, anthropology has pioneered the understanding of subjective states and meaning systems in other cultures. Progress in the area has been made, by design and by accident, though there is no universal agreement among anthropologists on what constitutes progress in subjectivity research. Interpretative approaches have emerged in virtually every social science and the humanities; and "experimental" ethnography is a controversial but popular genre in anthropology (see chapter 1). Some advances can be found in gender studies in this way as well, but we find, again—almost in spite of the efforts of anthropologists— that fine-grained studies of the subjectivity and meanings of erotics have been largely bypassed.

We are thus concerned in this work with deepening anthropology's long interest in the subjective dimension of people's lives. Many ethnographers have tried to reveal the thoughts and feelings of their informants, and among these workers was Malinowski, who explored the issues through his brilliant Trobriand works. British social anthropology did not, by and large, continue the effort. The approach in American cultural anthropology was more psychologic. Boas, Mead, and Benedict were pioneers in relating culture to personality orientations. Others such as Sapir, Kardiner, Kluckhohn, DuBois, Devereux, Hallowell, Spiro, LeVine, and R. Levy (to name a few) extended and enriched the psychoanalytic approach to the subjective dimension of cultural lfie. But with the eclipse of culture and personality studies and psychoanalytic interpretations in particular, anthropology withdrew its interest in culture and subjectivity. And thus the situation remained until ethnoscience and then symbolic schools of anthropology emerged in the 1960s. Now, in the 1980s, renewed interest can be seen in the relevant issues.

Ethnographers have shown a greater interest in their own subjectivity as a part of the total fieldwork project. Discussion of such concepts as "culture shock" indirectly expressed this concern, as we show in chapter 1. The design of interview schedules and questionnaires has also directly dealt with the problem of observer bias and subjectivity. The early genre of autobiographic accounts in ethnography expressed the field worker's involvement in other people's lives as well. These reports stopped short, however, of directly showing the ethnographer's thoughts and feelings during data collection. Rarely, for instance, did the ethnographer reveal his or her questions in the same context as the informants' responses, and when this was done, as in the cases of DuBois or Lewis, only limited information was reported on the fieldworker's responses to the native's responses at the time.[1] Such accounts used the fieldworker's experience, but in a chatty, peripheral way that generally humanized more formal ethnographic works published elsewhere. For S. and me, however, the ethnographer's subjectivity is of direct and nontrivial interest.

We wish to emphasize what LeVine (1982) in his well-known formulation has referred to as person-centered ethnography. As LeVine (1982:292) has noted, there is a

> growing recognition that biographical information collected in the field is inevitably filtered through the relationship between field worker and biographical subject, reflecting the personalities of both and the nature of their interaction, and that this process deserves explicit examination in research and subsequently in print.

This refers to the detailed and more personal meanings of people in society compared to the early, more normative and "nonexperimental" ethnographic accounts. Such studies are akin to what Kohut (1971) called "experience-near," or close-up, rather than impersonal accounts. They provide flesh to the skeleton of culture, subjectivity rather than the "machine" of idealized cultural actors. Our perspective is that ethnographers play a large part in constructing their accounts of a people—before and after the field: but most importantly while there and living with the Other.

Contemporary work in interpretive anthropology reveals a similar but different concern with field worker subjectivity. The goals, limits, and ramifications of this interpretive approach, perhaps best known from the works of Geertz[2] and his students, are presently the focus of hot debate in anthropology. How subjective and revealing can a fieldworker be and still remain rigorous, the authors of *Writing Culture* (Clifford and Marcus, eds., 1986), a major statement of this genre, seem to ask. Their answers are instructive. Take note, for instance, that Clifford (1986:6), who introduces the volume, lists six "determinants" of ethnographic writing, but no personal or psychologic factors are among them. The politicalization of the field is impressive, as is its debunking of the authority of ethnographic texts. How shall we evaluate these new "experimental ethnographies?"[3]

Our work shows the difficulty of drawing a hard-and-fast boundary between what is objective and what is subjective, a contrast that is becoming obsolete.[4] Depth interviews reveal better than other procedures the nuances and difficulties of showing how psychodynamic processes, such as projection, fantasy, and transference, occur across cultural boundaries. Where does projection begin and end? How can we tell someone's personal fantasy from a cultural belief? Are there no absolute boundaries between reality and fantasy? We shall try to examine such questions. And, following the leads of Devereux (1967) and LeVine (1982), we shall use a case method approach that reveals our questions, responses, and associations, so that we show how a question evokes an association in someone, which in turn leads to another question. This is not easy or apparent as a procedure in textual presentation.

We are motivated by a desire to escape pseudoscience, which still dominates many quarters of psychoanalysis and the social sciences, on the one hand, and our attempt to make the study of subjectivity more rigorous, on the other. For some, such as Tedlock (1983:322), ethnography is a "peculiar genre of fiction," the texts of which are a sort of comparative literature. Others go further and seem to suggest that ethnographic accounts should be humbled to the level (high or low?) of poetry. For us, this position goes too far. We want to find a middle ground.

S: Measuring the observer's effect on the observed and realizing that the observed affects the observer as well have, in this century, changed the nature of all research—from fundamental particle physics to my discipline, psychoanalysis. More than any other investigators of human behavior, psychoanalysts have been concerned with the distortions introduced by these subjective factors. In recent years, no clinical task has interested us more than trying to discover how aspects of the analyst's personality influence the therapeutic relationship: those that we are aware of and that can be used effectively, and those, coming from unrecognized forces within us, that produce uncontrolled effects (countertransference). H. and I believe also that these issues of self are just as important in writing reports of one's findings.

For studying human behavior, the primary instrument is not laboratory equipment, or random samples, or animals, or computers, but the researcher—ethnographer, psychologist, psychoanalyst, sociologist, or whatever. We should, therefore, know at least as much about the researcher as about the people investigated. (H: Only recently have psychologic and symbolic anthropologists emphasized this gap.) But rarely are we given that information, and readers do not much care, either. Mainstream concern lies elsewhere.

We think of Malinowski's diaries,[5] so scandalous to some anthropologists. It cannot be that his critics or defenders were surprised that, during his stay in the Trobriand Islands he was—without interruption—himself, that is, a feeling person with private experiences. In his diaries, he revealed, as he did not in his ethnographic works, that, by his own standards, he was racist, lazy, mean, tumescent with sinful desire, and under the influence of the rest of the ordinary day-to-day self-hatred that keeps ethnographers alert. Before the diaries became public, did anthropologists believe that such experiences were exceptional, that father-figures are the paragons their students fantasize, or that ethnographers leave their personalities home on setting out to the field? Do some imagine a way to study human behavior that does not filter the data through a sentient person at the time of collecting and at the time of reporting, that data are more objective—scientific—if we erase from the record the traces of the collecting process? It cannot even be that these critics did not know that the same is true of other ethnographers, at least themselves and everyone they know personally. Then surely it cannot be that these critics are unaware that this private life influences one's fieldwork at every turn and is even more pervasive when subjective life is denied or when it serves as a mat for the daily wrestle with the Devil. The critics' dismay at Malinowski's revelations marks an intuitive recognition of the same issue this book will examine more overtly and systematically: how subjectivity edits observation. We can regret that at times we participant-observers are too involved to see out through our own fog, but it is surely worse when that process goes unnoticed.

Perhaps it is too easy for those of us with medical training (forget, at this moment in the narrative, our speculative excesses) to appreciate the value of the hidden. For we benefit from innumerable advances in which the invisible was revealed. We expect that; it is our tradition. We demand that it always be part of our work. For instance, we know the uses of the blood sample, the biopsy, and the microscope in indicating the likely presence of unseen but vital phys-iology; or the power that comes with the capacity to project, in the mind's eye, the pathologic anatomy and hemodynamics of the heart from no more than the noise, interpreted as a "rub," we hear in our stethoscope; or the visualizing of a brain lesion revealed at first only in disordered speech; or the insight a reported fantasy can give into a person's hidden motives. That detective, the medical diagnostician, is forever on the edge of being wrong, for the manifest is so incom-plete, so subtle, so complexly interwoven into itself. Still, if we con-sidered only what we can see, hear, smell, and feel on the skin, we would not even be competent dermatologists.*

When it comes to the study of subjectivity—"who[†] am I," "who are we," "who are they"—the "social sciences" falter. They can mask that failure, it has often been noted, by trivializing until they find a statistically manageable task, or by analogizing on animals' behavior and brains, or by using culture-bound and oversimplified learning theory explanations, or by ignoring how fantasy moves behavior, or by denying that subjectivity even exists. (Statistics, animal research, and learning theory contribute powerfully and are invaluable for studying human behavior. I complain only of these misuses.)

We need not review here the advantages and limitations of exper-iments, those hallmarks of careful thinking. Right now, we shall note only that an experiment informs us more if the experimenter and his techniques do not contaminate the experiment. The laboratory ideal, however, is not only impossible in much behavioral research but, in the case of intimate communications, *cannot* produce the needed data. Only communication can do that, and communication requires a minimum of two interacting objects. Still, "social scientists"[‡] yearn to be scientists; science is the ideal.[6] [H: Should science aspire ulti-mately to explanation and, even more powerful, prediction? Or is it good enough, as Runciman (1983) has recently suggested, for the sci-entist to provide the highest quality *description* or, to paraphrase Taylor (1985), a better-than-average *understanding* in its own context?] Some things can be discovered—perhaps, like the Nile, can *only* be discov-

---

*A caution here as we praise the physician. Let us recall Freud's (1926) fear that medical training can threaten the kind of curiosity/empathy needed for exploring human behavior.

†Who, not "what"; "what" is a question better asked of a physiologist or computer and communications theorist.

‡This is the last time I shall use "social sciences" or "social scientists" herein. The con-tinued use of quotation marks would make for a bumpy ride, but I would not be able to talk of the social sciences without using such punctuation because, for me, there is too little science in these sciences. So, for accuracy, I shall avoid "social sciences" and instead work with such circumlocutions as: "those studying behavior."

ered—without antecedent sampling methods, controls, statistics, or an *n* of more than one.

H: Anthropology, Sapir argued fifty years ago,[7] needs the psychiatrists' skills and insights into the range of states of subjectivity. In a way, my colleague, S., still argues for this basic position.

S: This attitude will seem especially strange to those who teach that my clinical disciplines of psychiatry and psychoanalysis never have said and never will say something useful, much less true, about human behavior.[8] H., however, since beginning his training, had felt at odds with that view. No wonder we hit it off.

Herdt's kind of clinical perspective approach can transform the practice of ethnography (as it also did for Malinowski and Mead and as it is doing now for Obeyesekere, Kakar, and others). When this is offered in the universities it will bring back to anthropology the students who thought that the discipline was less interested in humans than in Structure, Syntax, and Symbolism.*

But, to equalize my complaint, consider the comparable trend, in psychoanalytic theory, that only perfunctorily acknowledges cultural factors, and that has, in over seventy years, produced only two or three psychoanalyst-ethnographers and few ethnographic works by other analysts than them.

The nondeluded psychoanalyst knows that subjectivity is still beyond the reach of scientific method, that confirming and disconfirming tests cannot be applied. Psychoanalysts' findings are notoriously open to question but closed to inspection; one can never tell, even roughly, in reading analytic reports, what happened between patient and analyst. We analysts cover the lack of such crucial data with a storm of phrases such as "further analysis unmistakably revealed . . . ," "the patient's associations proved that . . . ," "from the analysis, it appeared that this represented a . . . ," "the literature confirms the finding that . . . ," "surely," "truly," "indeed," "certainly," "without doubt," "unquestionably," "the fact was," "positively," "inevitably," "decidedly," "absolutely," "unequivocally," "fundamentally," "assuredly," "definitely," "unmistakably." Of course.

And yet, as awful as this performance is, I think that the use of subjectivity is worth the risk. And the corrective is not to retreat to

---

*The road to charisma is paved with abstractions, mysteries, italics, exclamation points, and capital letters.

the easily sketched normative surface, or to the poetic stance that all culture is merely subjective. With "subjective" ethnography, one is in danger of being duped by the invisible; but with "objective" ethnography, one is at the mercy of the visible.

These issues were forcefully presented in detailed, intense, and scholarly fashion more than twenty years ago by Devereux.[9] It is hard to judge to what extent his ideas were ignored because the audience was upset or distracted and to what extent because the ideas were simply too new and took digesting. Whatever the reasons, Devereux's insight that research can transform anxiety into research method has caused no change in either ethnography or psychoanalysis, the two disciplines he practiced. As an analyst, I find it especially surprising that he did not move psychoanalysis, given analysts' concern with how the analyst's behavior changes what happens in the treatment. So it is disappointing that when analysts publish their ideas, they almost completely omit describing who they were when the treatment events published were taking place and who they are when reporting their conclusions. I am sure that analytic theory will improve and analytic research advance from its present rudimentary state when analysts acknowledge these factors.

This text is thus (1) a communication on experiments in ethnography, (2) in itself an experiment, (3) an exploration of a new way of teaching ethnography, (4) and a preliminary presentation of an alternative approach to ethnography. Let me begin with the book as a communication. It reports experiments* in which we tried out new techniques. First, from 1975 on—initially in letters, and from 1977 on in person—a psychoanalyst supervised an ethnographer to enrich the ethnography. Second, at the same time, an ethnographer taught an analyst ethnography to enrich the analyst (but not his analytic technique). Third, the two specialists worked together in the field, extending the ethnographer's interviews but also introducing a clinician (medical practitioner: diagnostician and therapist) into the final data collecting. Fourth, as the interviews unfolded, there were at the same time (both during and between interviews) continuous discussions of the clinical findings, techniques, underlying dynamics of the participants, and the processes going on among them. We also discussed their implications for theory in ethnography and analysis, and did a bit of theory-making and breaking (braking), and problem solving (therapeutics; psychodynamics; personal histories, e.g., data on gender and erotic elements; how to interview skillfully, etc.).

*Only in the sense of trying something out, not the experiments of scientific method.

Now, the interview chapters as experiment. We are trying to create a better method of reporting clinical data—data gathered from individuals talking intimately about matters important to them, particularly regarding erotics and gender identity. (1) At the risk of boring and then losing our readers, we have presented our transcripts in fairly unadorned manner (though—after an example in chapter 4 of how it reads before cleaning up—in more bearable form), and have preserved our original tapes should a colleague want to check the printed version with that from New Guinea. (2) We have discussed and exemplified ways in which, at every step in the reporting process, we changed the raw material. (3) We have kept ourselves present, as close to the way we really were as print permits. (4) We have added commentary to the transcripts to reveal what we think was occurring that cannot be recorded on an audiotape. (5) We both together wrote the book and have indicated the parts each of us wrote. Beyond that, we have told but not shown you—that would be too lengthy and dull— that we each edited and added to the other's writing, sometimes heavily, sometimes painfully, and always openly and without much defensive compassion. We tried to do that without homogenizing our styles too much. (You should know, however, that H. was more decent in doing this than I, accepting my nit-picking and complaints more congenially than I sometimes did his.) (6) We have put in asides to each other's commentaries so the reader can share in our disagreements. (7) We have tried to create in the book the ambience of uncertainty that is the reality of field work, thinking, and theory, for we feel most everyone ignores this uncertainty.

The next category of the book's functions is teaching. We have let you see how H. taught me ethnography and I taught H. about clinical skills and psychodynamics. We later discuss how these subjects can be taught in more formal settings.

And then the last category. We have begun to create a new approach to ethnography, which we have referred to as clinical ethnography (Herdt 1981; Herdt and Stoller 1985; Stoller and Herdt 1982). Our conversations on this subject are distilled into rudimentary suggestions as to how students could be trained in these skills and what the benefits would be for ethnographers and others who study human behavior.

H: In sum, this study results from our desire to infuse erotics and gender identity more fully into cross-cultural research and to explore and advance the study of subjective experience more fully by doing so. We are trying, in the latter sense, to deconstruct sexual meanings in cultural studies. We hope to show that certain ethnographic questions can be investigated only by searching deeply into the individual, and the more individuals, the better. Our data are interviews and observations and a close look at the personal meanings of Sambia sexuality that go beyond the structural factors of their great institutions, kinship and marriage, ritual and myth. In another sense, one might say that we have chosen to focus on erotics and gender as a way of providing a common language for critically examining the means—ethnography—whereby fieldworkers study and write about culture. Our purpose is not so much to answer all the questions we raise about the study of intimate communications as to urge colleagues to agree with us that these are fundamental questions that must be answered.

PART I

Introductions

CHAPTER ONE

Clinical Ethnography

> [Ralph] Linton once quoted to me the following remark of a colleague:
>
> > "My monograph about the X-tribe is almost finished. All I have to do now is cut out the life" (i.e., all references to real people and events).
>
> Devereux, *From Anxiety to Method*

H: What makes some anthropologists cut the life from their ethnographies? How is that stance embedded in our discipline's basic concepts and techniques? Is it not a contradiction to study Man but not *a* man? This chapter is concerned with the debate between those positions, and in it we extend our arguments for the need to develop an approach in anthropology—clinical enthnography—that focuses on the reasons for and the methods of studying individuals intimately in order to better know cultures.

For almost a century anthropologists have studied the natives of exotic corners while other social scientists busily worked on pressing problems at home. Ethnography, as we know it today, emerged not by design but rather from the historical circumstances of World War I that led Malinowski to the Trobriand Islands, off the coast of New Guinea. From those years of living "as a native among the natives," as Sir James Frazer put in his preface to *Argonauts of the Western Pacific*, Malinowski defined the "subject, method, and scope of the inquiry" that was to become the classical mode of ethnography and anthropologic training. Shortly thereafter Mead went to Samoa. Other anthropologists followed. In the ensuing years Africa, Melanesia, Borneo, and the Amazon were to be sampled, bottled, and marketed at home under domestic labels. The subject was the natives' behavior; the product was the field report—the classical ethnography—about exotic places. Western civilization quickly transformed that subject matter and technique into a stable mythology about anthropology.

Since Malinowski, anthropology's supreme method has been participant–observation, a technique that structures the encounter between natives and ethnographer in a certain way. Is it an accident that Malinowski, the great ethnographer, was a poor theorist? No;

few are blessed with being great clinicians and great theorists. In no other field except, perhaps, psychoanalysis,* is theory and practice so intimately embedded in human relationships. And in no other discipline does research defy the application of objective measurements. In both fields as well, practitioners defend their methodology on the basis of special training, special talents, and special data—that "intensely personal form of knowledge"[1] characteristic of intimate communications.

The question of the relationship of subjectivity to the study of human behavior need not be restricted to anthropology. The pendulum that has swung away from psychoanalysis—the microscopic study of subjectivity—was carrying psychology, sociology, and psychiatry as well. And so these days, from a mixture of motives, many scholars in these disciplines still spurn subjectivity either as an explicit dimension of their methodology or as a subject for study. The scene is changing in anthropology, however. Interpretive approaches offer a new vision of how to handle subjectivity in ethnography. Yet, in the mainstream of anthropology, many still assume that the field worker is objective, as scientific as an experimenter in the lab. Recent statements on interpretive anthropology seem motivated by this view.[2] Other critics deride the study of individual natives in terms of their own subjective frameworks and have turned to other disciplines in trying to define the ethnographic approach.

Since its beginnings, anthropology has struggled with the question of the observer's role—of observer bias—in deciding what natives' behavior really meant. Whose interpretation (in what combination and situations) is right: the ethnographer or the native? The debate has taxed our best minds. The present consensus is: the ethnographer as observer. But even ethnographers' views are accepted only when we dress up our presence in ethnographic reports. One should, more properly, study the visible, the public, the normative; *kula* trading rings, totems, garden boundaries, marriage contracts, exogamy, kin terms and kin groups, love potions, shamanism, initiation rites, economic roles, and on and on. And yes, life histories were collected and published. But did these not leave out the author? And yes, extensive interviews were done: but among this earlier generation who besides DuBois, Devereux, and a few other clinically oriented ethnographers published their questions and findings in detail? These exceptions, older and new, are admirable. The mainstream seemed, however, to lie elsewhere: in the direction of public knowledge. Objective facts.

---

*And related fields like clinical psychology.

Public meaning—shared, formal, patterned, standardized, homogenized, itself like "culture, this acted document," for Geertz (1973:10)—is the proper stuff of the ethnographic report. Thus bent outward and emptied of their privacy, the data of field research become objective, valid. Scientific.

Participant-observation has emerged as *the* umbrella approach for anthropologic fieldwork. There are new critiques of postcolonialist anthropology and its servant, ethnography, which are reviewed in this text. We recognize these criticisms and welcome the accounts of fieldwork that have addressed them. These critiques have questioned the underlying model of scientific positivism that formed our attitudes, assumptions, and procedures in doing and writing ethnography. Our work contributes to this debate; we do not propose to eliminate participant-observation, only to question its antipsychologic framework.

Participant-observation is today best seen as an intellectual/scientific ideology. It is the shingle we hang out, the advertisement we make for anthropology's scientific status in the Academy and the granting agencies. As an ideology—shared commitments to a guiding image of research that is socialized through training—participant-observation helps integrate a growing, disparate discipline; it bridges a gap between the past and present ("intellectual history"); and it creates continuity between our founding and present-day activities (Ricoeur 1978). Every discipline has, of course, an image projected for public consumption (viz., textbooks, granting agencies, University Councils) and internal discussion (i.e., seminars, tutorials, and "private conversations" [Powdermaker 1966:9]). This is necessary. Freilich (1977:19ff.) has written well about the process. He proposes further that there are actually three cultures at work in the ethnographic process: the anthropologist's own "culture of orientation," "the native culture," and "the fieldwork culture." This last mediating concept—the heritage of modern anthropology—is Freilich's innovation, which he sees as tacit rules and assumptions about doing ethnography. He uses examples of how that cultural system permeates both professional circles (e.g., textbooks) and field research, though he concentrates on the former. Here we shall focus on the latter. We agree with Freilich, though, that participant-observation is a rationalizing ideology that shields how we construct ethnography and live in the field. A full analysis of this problem would require a review and interpretation of the signs, symbols, cultural categories, and discourses of fieldwork culture—an enormous undertaking that would require a book. In lieu of that, we offer only some first principles.

PARTICIPANT-OBSERVATION

From Malinowski on, participant-observation has been vague. The field worker's dilemmas are these. (1) *Be an objective observer* of a culture; but participate enough as a whole person that you understand all (including a people's aesthetic biases) and *become a friend*. (2) *Live with the natives* and press them enough so that their culture becomes a part of you who are alien; but in living there, *don't change them*, only observe the culture (as represented in native acts). (3) Become a *scientific authority on the culture*: in your writings don't show much of your self or your living in the field, *for that is personal, not scientific*. These dilemmas arose from the nature of anthropologic work and from our need (like psychoanalysts) to claim we are scientists. One of our basic points is that anthropologists *live* these dilemmas— in our heads, in the field, at home. The ad hoc method of field work culture developed later to help us live *with* the contradictions.

The untouched observer in this ideology is a scientist, but that kind of observer, by not participating, must observe less, possibly too much less. At the same time, the "social sciences," inventing from necessity, have wanted to be accepted as sciences less encumbered by scientific method: note such antipositivistic movements as humanism in psychology, ethnomethodology in sociology, or semiotics and hermeneutics in linguistics. Yet fieldwork *is* highly personal; without a particular fieldworker, one has no field data (Read 1965). The mythology of fieldwork culture provides recipes for "objectively" assembling and reporting fieldwork data: the ethnography. How much of the ethnographer as a whole person is admitted into one's published report?

Cultural anthropology is grounded in fieldwork: it is what distinguishes our discipline. Its methodology, participant-observation, lends itself well to anthropology's ambiguous status as one of the sciences* and also one of the humanities. It places anthropologists in the delicate position of being both a people's stranger and friend: detached, objective data-collector plus involved, trusted insider. That is how it was first heralded; only special people could manage its balancing act. However, those who pioneered field work—Malinowski and Mead, for instance—stressed, through the analogy of the laboratory experiment, the positivist science of participant-observation. Later workers

---

*In the United States, the National Institute of Mental Health classifies cultural anthropology as a "social science" and "health science," while the National Science Foundation classifies it as a "natural science." The National Endowment for the Humanities accepts anthropology also as one of its own.

such as social structuralists, culture and personality theorists, quantitative analysts and ethnosemanticists on the scientific side, and humanists, ethnohistorians, symbolists, and hermeneuts on the other, have tended to split apart this Janus. But none has rejected the ambiguity—participate but observe—of fieldwork. The fact that such divergent theoretic schools have been shielded under the same umbrella, which has also resisted change in its tried and true design, is important in understanding the mystique of fieldwork.[3]

One can see, however, important swings in the pendulum of ethnographic styles or genres. In the 1920s such fine, humanistic uses of the life history as in, say, La Farge's *Laughing Boy*, were published in the same period as material culture surveys, and institutionally focused normative ethnographies, such as Firth's *We the Tikopia*. After the 1930s, though, and such splendid rich studies as DuBois' *People of Alor*—which was published in 1944 and in itself marks a watershed of period clinical ethnography—a new trend can be noticed. Seldom do ethnographies of the 1940s and 1950s reveal much of the author. Only very limited exceptions, such as Mead's *Male and Female*, can be found, and these, by culture and personality hands, deal only very indirectly with the ethnographer's subjectivity. Institutionally focused ethnographies in the standard mode of normative social anthropology held reign until the late 1960s. Usually the authors of those texts mention individuals only in passing or in anecdotes. Usually they confine their personal experiences to a preface or the acknowledgments, or again to anecdotes. Later exceptions to this generalization are telling. A major text, Bowen's *Return To Laughter*, was published under a pseudonym, and as a novel. Read's *The High Valley* created controversy by being, in the minds of some critics, "too personal." The more recent and inflamed case of Castaneda's works has broken with past conventions, to be seen by some as a paradigm shift and by others as fairy dust. Since the 1970s symbolic and interpretive studies have brought a host of more subjective and humanistic ethnographies. These are more revealing of the author and his or her fieldwork conditions. These "experimental" accounts challenge traditional ethnography and raise new questions about the nature of knowing and the ways of interpreting ethnographic material. Yet these works remain controversial; and, as yet, they are still exceptional, not normative.

The original image of fieldwork was deceptively clear: "Living in the village with no other business but to follow native life" (Malinowski 1922:18). Within a few years, Mead (1977:4) notes, "Learning how to live in the field . . . became known as participant observation." The field was moved from the museum, armchair, or riverboat into the village.[4] The objective status of this knowledge—the ethnography—was controversial. But its aim was not, as set out in Malinowski's prospectus: "This goal is, briefly, to grasp the native's point of view, his relation to life, to realize his vision of his world" (Malinowski 1922:25;cf. Geertz 1976).

From the start this achievement was clearly difficult, requiring personal adjustment: be involved yet stay detached. Here is a textbook indication:

> A participant-observer, the anthropologist lives intimately as a member of a society. . . . He shares in the people's day-to-day activities, watches as they eat, fight, and dance, listens to their commonplace and exciting conversations, and slowly begins to live and understand life as they do. But he also remains detached from their life, at least to some degree. He is not living among another people to enjoy their way of life. He is there to understand it and then to report his understanding to others. Complete involvement, then, is incompatible with the anthropologist's primary goals, but complete detachment is incompatible with fieldwork. Successful fieldwork requires balance between the two, a balancing act which is every bit as difficult as it sounds. (Edgerton and Langness 1974:2–3)

As in any discipline, anthropologic fieldwork produces knowledge. Malinowski (1922:24) spelled out "three avenues" of this knowledge as goals for ethnography: (1) "the organization of the tribe, and the anatomy of its culture," using statistical facts; (2) "the imponderabilia of actual life," using "minute, detailed observations," a "sort of ethnographic diary;" and (3) "a collection of . . . narratives," folklore, etc., the *corpus inscriptionum* or "documents of native mentality." Eventually Malinowski attempted all these; taken together for a single society, they remain unmatched. He had no doubt that his work was scientific or that he made ethnography a Science.[5] Like Boas, Benedict, Mead, Radcliffe-Brown, and others, this ideology of science was meant to refute Social Darwinism, evolutionary speculation, shaky historical diffusionism, and bigotry in general.[6] And thus, these early workers shifted anthropology's laboratory from the museum to the village.[7]

How was the field of the village defined for doing ethnography? First, the dictum that one studied the whole tribe (its skeleton or anatomy) meant that native beliefs, behavior patterns, and social institutions were seen as parts of an abstract, functioning whole—"culture" or "society." These were to be laboratories,[8] the settings for field experiments.[9] Here lay the roots for functionalism (Malinowski, Benedict, Mead), structural-functionalism (Radcliffe-Brown, Evans-Pritchard), or modern structuralism (Lévi-Strauss). Second, this holism implied that ideally one studied in the round all of social life. "The ethnography," up until the last few years, should thus include pat chapters such as "Economy," "Religion," "Kinship," "Politics," etc. that claimed to represent the whole "culture" or "society." (We now find that effort too optimistic.) Third, present also in both Malinowski and Mead (1930, 1935) was "the individual," the study of which was contradictory. On the one hand it was easy to observe words and behavioral patterns; but on the other, it was almost impossible to study what natives thought, for they could not put their subjective states into words.[10] Therefore:

> . . . we have to study here stereotyped manners of thinking and feeling. As sociologists,* we are not interested in what A or B may feel *qua* individuals, in the accidental course of their own personal experiences—we are interested only in what they feel and think *qua* members of a given community . . . their mental states receive a certain stamp, become stereotyped by the institutions in which they live, by the influence of traditional folk-lore, by the very vehicle of thought, that is language. The social and cultural environment in which they move forces them to think and feel in a definite manner. (Malinowski 1922:23)

One abstracts "stereotypes" from observations rather than dealing with personal experience as such. And the empirical source of these social facts was clear.

> I consider that only such ethnographic sources are of unquestionable scientific value, in which we can clearly draw the line between, on the one hand, the results of direct observation and of native statements and interpretations, and on the other, the inferences of the author, based on his common sense and psychological insight. (Malinowski 1922:3)

Thus spoke Malinowski on methodology: aside from mentioning "psychological insight," his stance epitomized the mainstream in the positivist sciences of his time.

In retrospect these founding conceptions of the field were never fulfilled. (1) Few anthropologists claim to study everything anymore;

---

*Malinowski (like Mead) was slippery, sometimes claiming to be a sociologist, sometimes a psychologist.

field projects are problem-focused (as most granting agencies expect). (2) Functionalism has its limits;[11] that something functions or integrates does not make it adaptive (Alland 1970). (3) Malinowski, Radcliffe-Brown,[12] and others stressed function over meaning, despite Malinowski's pronouncements about "the native's vision of his world." (Only now is an anthropology of "meaning systems" emerging.) (4) The "functional field" of the village was defined as excluding external agents—colonial powers, missionaries, traders—even when they impinged on or devoured the natives.[13] (5) Whole segments or classes of persons and their meanings within a society, for instance, women, were virtually ignored (Ardener 1975). (6) Even granting Malinowski's dictum that we study collective categories of thinking and feeling, not personal experience, many subjects of interest have been largely ignored on those terms (e.g., the cultural context of gifts, myth, erotics or of "big men."[14] (7) Last—and of most significance—Malinowski never adhered to his own methodologic requirements. None of us has: not Malinowski or Mead, their contemporaries or students.

Had they done so more, ethnography today might be very different, nor would we be searching philosophy, semiotics, literary criticism, psychoanalysis, hermeneutics, history, etc., etc. so much for the guidelines on how to do our job: interpret our experience in other cultures, a task that we alone can tackle.

Participant-observation as a laboratory model failed, because the field is not a lab, we do not perform experiments, and tribesmen are interacted with as whole people, not experimental subjects.[15] Fieldwork was designed to make anthropology a science by ending speculation about *how* natives behave in the context of their own sociocultural institutions. (Only recently has the *why*—questions of origins—come back into cultural anthropology, but not without the criticism that this is unscientific and, the new primal sin, teleologic.) The laboratory model, even in Malinowski's works, removed the ethnographer from the native scene. Nor was it ever clear how the ethnographer was to use insight or empathy. This editing out not only removed the natives as whole people, substituting customs, institutions, and symbols in their place, but it attributed meanings and intentionality to the latter, as if such things were the people who gave them life. There are fine exceptions.[16] but they *are* exceptions.

RECENT INTERPRETIVE ANTHROPOLOGY

A flurry of critiques of cultural anthropology and its handmaiden, the ethnography that results from traditional field work in exotic cultures, has appeared in recent years. Malinowski's inheritors have been beset by various "ists": Marxists, materialists, symbolists, feminists, historicists, among others. We recognize their complaints and sympathize with some. For they have made us more aware of our colonial heritage, our disregard of the incursion of world systems into traditional societies, our not taking seriously symbolic systems or their connection to or mystification of social action, our androcentric viewpoint and sexist disregard of women, and our antihistorical (too "harmonious" and "adaptive") functionalism. Many other points could be added. Yet, until recently this intellectual debate largely stopped short of rejecting the old positivism of our umbrella approach, participant-observation, that imposes these dilemmas: be involved, but stay detached; study the Other, not yourself.[17] The same holds true for the fine anthologies on fieldwork of the past twenty years, which show anthropology's interest in reflecting on what ethnographers actually do in the field.[18] Though we applaud these efforts, they can be pushed further. For all have skimmed the surface of a basic psychodynamic problem—Devereux's (1967)—on how and why ethnographers interact with the natives.* For the reader to understand our approach to culture and experience and our handling of these issues, we shall sketch some principles.

Each culture has a somewhat unique symbolic system—signs, symbols, rules, values—that directs behavioral acts and makes for meaningful communications among its sharers. These constraints are reflected in or acted on, according to factors such as personality, sex, age, situation, and social controls. The question of how cultural ideals match actual behaviors is, relative to the person, the situation, etc., an open empirical matter.[19] The ethnographer's task is to discover those matches. In studying a native's experience, one can watch and also ask. But for many psychologic anthropologists and ourselves, depth interviewing is crucial if one expects to understand, from the native's point-of-view, how cultural ideas are perceived in his or her awareness, and how they relate to idiosyncratic ideas and feelings, or to reality. LeVine has argued such problems well.[20]

Each culture provides also a set of distinctive narratives—ways of talking—that guide who should say what to whom under what circumstances. A New Guinea big man's thumping public rhetoric differs from his private talk in a hut. Women's secret ritual talk seldom reaches the public, though its effects are felt there. A man's private

---

*In this book we follow anthropologic convention in referring to the indigines of any society (our own included) as the natives. The colonialist baggage of this term notwithstanding, 'native' helps keep us aware of who we are and are not.

feelings about his dreams and their implications may never ever be shared in public.[21] Recognizing the distinctions between these narratives (and all the knowledge to which they implicitly refer) underlies the ethnographer's interpretation of what people say. Yet, in the spontaneity of someone's communicating, these narrative distinctions may be blurred. People are different; they are idiosyncratic. So understanding those ideal types does not explain the meaning of an individual native's acts, words, or thoughts. It is thus not their culture, economy, or psychology that explains their behavior, but rather their experience—which subsumes all the above.[22]

To interpret these complex phenomena the ethnographer has only a hazy approach, participant-observation, which is vague enough to accommodate the behaviorists, ethnoscientists, marxists, feminists, symbolic and psychoanalytic-type theorists in the field. That stance seemed to work[23] in the past when those such as Benedict (1934) and Mead (1935) studied "whole cultures," or similar abstractions like "personality," "ethos," or "eidos." Ethnoscience made it work, as Geertz (1973:10–13) has argued, by ignoring the shared understandings that made the natives' mental schemas seem real. It still seemed to work for structuralists, political economists, cross-cultural psychologists, and others who, in repudiating each others' theories, seemingly accepted others' field data as scientific. But then the symbolists began to say they wanted another kind of science.

The interpretive anthropologists would have it work differently. By studying how cultural signs and symbols are constructed, and by describing how they operate in thought or are expressed in action, they hope to understand how humans construct meaning and so define their existence. Does the neologism—interpretive science—apply to what they do? In Geertz's style of this approach, culture becomes like a text in the hands of a literary critic. No need to worry over subjectivity ("mentalism," "subjectivism," "psychologism," "reductionism"), because what you see—public social action—is seemingly all there is (Geertz 1973:10). This philosophic behaviorism— "Culture is public because meaning is" (Geertz 1973:12)—has taken previous guises in anthropology to produce similar ends: configurationalism, national character studies, the life history approach, culture at a distance—that led to presumed group uniformity (the doctrine of experimental uniformity[24]). The reduction of human awareness to narrative texts—this new hermeneutics—is another maneuver by the sociocentric "social sciences" to create the illusion of objectivity without involvement (Crapanzano 1986).

Our approach differs somewhat in our interest in what flesh and blood natives do and think. We are not here mainly concerned with the cultural forms with which they think, though we shall discuss the relation between culture and experience as we go. We differ even more in attending to what the ethnographer does. The process and communications that produce ethnography are part of it, the more so when they are hidden in the final public document. To weave a culture in an ethnography by editing out the seams and stitches of its designer is to sacrifice craftmanship for mass product. When one is interested in people's meanings—not Meaning—ethnographic findings become privileged.[25] So, lacking description of what LeVine (1982:293 and also LeVine 1966) calls the "intercultural research relationship," ethnography provides the wall hangings for a mass Museum of Projective Texts. How lifeless.[26]

A variety of ethnographers is struggling to revise the fieldwork approach to give full recognition to the native's experience and the ethnographer's part in interpreting it. Ethnography is both process and product: while we are beginning to see the researchers' presence in reports, we still see little of them in the process leading to their published work. Recent works by Crapanzano, Kracke, Obeyesekere, and other pioneering clinical ethnographers provide critical and effective beacons to follow in the "experimental ethnography" genre (Marcus and Cushman 1982). Their works answer, in a sense, Sapir's[27] plea for injecting the clinical process into ethnography.[28] Here, we shall not examine further the implications for theory of our arguments. Yet we do think that the critical use of clinical ethnography will move us further in "the business of making anthropology out of fieldwork" (Bateson 1978:77).

To sum up: participant-observation commends us to study the typical, stereotypic, normal natives, and thus fieldwork is made to seem objective in the text, as if observer bias does not occur. The ideal ethnographer participates objectively, wary of real relationships with the people studied, as if the ethnographer's private experience were not what makes our field data possible. In this "public experiment"— a social contract with an implicit ideology, participant-observation— the signs of the ethnographer's and the native's subjectivity are removed. What actually happens in fieldwork is different.

THE ETHNOGRAPHY

The product of these endeavors is ethnography: fieldwork reports. The range of ethnography is enormous, in time and space, in subject matter, and in time spent in a place. In the Melanesian literature, ethnographic reports can be as brief as letters and anecdotal tidbits (Whittaker et al. 1975), as intensive as Malinowski's studies, or extensive as the many volumes of the *Cambridge Expeditions to the Torres Straits*.[29] They can come from short contacts over a few weeks' time, as with Haddon's (1901), Rivers's (1914), and Seligman's (1910) tradeboat surveys, or they may come from years in one place, as with Malinowski's (1922, 1929, 1935) Trobriand works. We have the uneven reports of missionaries, travelers, gold miners, and popularizers—with titles such as *Twenty Years in Savage New Guinea, My Father was a Cannibal, The Land that Time Forgot*, and *Adam in Oche*, some good, some bad. There are the great Papuan monographs of Williams (1936, 1940) with his biases intact, the product of a lifetime of anthropologic treks. Then there are respectable but often uninteresting monographs of the 1940s, 1950s, and 1960s on social structure, ceremonial exchange, big men, and ritual, most based on a year or two of intensive fieldwork, though a few are based on a weekend (Elkin 1953) or a few months (Blackwood 1979; Barth 1975; Fortune 1947). An overwhelming magnitude.[30]

Ethnographies are more than casual accounts of people's customs and cultures. We trust them. They are to contain little beyond objective truth.[31] Ethnographies are widely read and cited as scientific evidence in other disciplines and in anthropology, The Human Relations Area Files (established by that great quantifier, Murdock) accord ethnographies a normative, homogenized database allowing statistical correlations to be drawn from reports the world over. What do professionals think of the truth-value of ethnographies? The answer is instructive, and Evans-Pritchard once cautioned a critical attitude toward ethnographic reports.[32]

The fiction is that while anthropologists study whole societies, their reports—though only on a particular place—really concern the monolithic abstractions "society," "culture," and "personality," not the ethnographer or the natives as people. The themes and images of this fiction vary: tribal society is seen as good paradise[33] or bad paradise,[34] or degenerated paradise;[35] or it seethes with oedipal conflict,[36] or violence,[37] or paranoia,[38] or shame;[39] or it lacks oedipal conflict,[40] aggression,[41] individualism,[42] anger;[43] or it is harmonious,[44] in equilibrium,[45] gentle,[46] powerless;[47] or male dominated,[48] or female dominated,[49] or undersexed,[50] or oversexed.[51] And these findings are conveyed through different metaphors: society as a laboratory[52] or a clinic[53] or a stage[54] or a structure of Mind[55] or a structure of social roles[56] or a structure of livelihood[57] or a text for the literary critic.[58]

You name it. The "it"—society or culture—becomes the foreground; the author, whether male or female, young or old, novice or veteran, black or white, liberal or conservative, sexist or not, sinks into neutral ground.

In fact, of course, anthropologists do pass judgment on their colleagues and profession. And, for that matter, their own society.[59] We are able critics.[60] Certainly we are not a complacent group; one only need read reviews in the *American Anthropologist* or attend cocktail parties at meetings of the *American Anthropological Association* to find lively commentaries on intellectual works and resolutions about current political problems. Several kinds of criticism are made of ethnographic reports. They include questions about observer bias,[61] the competence of the reporting,[62] facts omitted or undue weight given to some facts rather than others,[63] and more than anything else, criticisms of the interpretations: theories, approaches, the style of data presentation (e.g., editing of data), familiarity with the literature, etc. What matters, for our purposes, is the human element involved in these criticisms of ethnography.

It is curious how many fieldworkers have avoided exposing themselves in their ethnography. The natives' responses, including experiencing the observer, are fated to obscurity. Seldom are the ethnographers' personal or cultural status accounted for in interpreting their findings. Some anthropologists have noted this omission,[64] but little has systematically been said about it. How odd that the highly personal knowledge of participant-observation makes so little use of one's involvement in presenting observations, through which the meanings and images of the culture of one's ethnography are also quietly voiced.[65] A few workers have used personal accounts of their experience to convey understanding. Please note, however, that with the exceptions of Lévi-Strauss's (1969) *Tristes Tropiques* and Mead's (1972) *Blackberry Winter*, our great anthropologists have not drawn explicitly on personal experience to write ethnography, nor have they published autobiographic accounts or diaries.[66] The rule in Malinowski's day was that a scientific authority edits him or herself out of the ethnography and removes other traces of life from the report.[67] This statement applies to other fields and psychoanalysis too. (Remember *The Double Helix*.)[68] Times are changing under the sign of interpretive anthropology. But not changing all that much.

What is the knowledge that claims to be ethnography? The problem may be broken down in three ways. What is ethnography? How do we know it is what it is presented as being? And what is its knowledge good for? Classical ethnography* is a special kind of investigation. It is not a lab experiment. Whatever else it is, it is primarily clinical: it studies people—flesh and blood people—with minds and motives and feelings. And these people are studied by other people, us ethnographers, who cannot search for ethnographic realities except through our motives and feelings. An ethnography that includes experience as we observe others and what we know of interpersonal interaction leads to better theories of culture and meaning systems in action. But to include our experience requires us later to reconsider how Malinowski's "psychological insight" operates in ethnography.

What is ethnography *not*? Ethnography is unlike any other discipline. Its mode of knowing, form of knowledge, its problems of accountability, and its writings set it apart from other fields. It is similar to psychoanalytic research but it is not psychoanalysis, as Ann Parsons once argued. We ethnographers are not trained to understand drives and intrapsychic conflict. We are not primarily interested in unconscious processes. (Some of us are not even trained to talk to people.) The ethnography I have published on Sambia is not applied psychoanalysis or transcultural psychiatry. Nor is it philosophy, biography, autobiography, diary, or novel, or the same as cognitive anthropology, symbolic anthropology, or psychologic anthropology. Ethnopsychiatry (Devereux 1980b) is similar, as are observational psychology[69] and ethnographic psychology (Cole 1975). Psychoanalytically oriented ethnography[70] is closer still.

Many styles of ethnography have emerged in anthropology over the past hundred years. In fact, each worker develops a particular way of doing ethnography, though the differences tend to be washed out in written reports. The "life history" was well used by an earlier generation of American students forced to do salvage ethnography with the proverbial last Indian (Nabokov 1967). Culture and personality studies added new techniques: depth interviews, projective tests, and questionnaires. Humanistic accounts—fictionalized stories and novels—are an old genre coming back to life in ethnography. First-person autobiographic accounts, such as Read's *Return To The High Valley*, have provided personal records of doing ethnography. And these have become even more frequent and visible, as the ethnographic papers in Clifford and Marcus (1986) illustrate this best.[71]

What these personalized accounts still lack, however, are *systematic* descriptions of natives interacting with the ethnographer.[72] Eth-

---

*By trained professionals, not laymen.

nographers from Malinowski on might allow a place for the life of the natives in sketches, case studies, "apt examples" (Gluckman 1967), "stereotypes" (Malinowski 1922), "fuller statistical documentation of empirical transactions" (Leach 1976), "biographies,"[73] etc., yet they generally avoided inserting their own lives into the reports. It was as if an unseen hand of Science authored the texts, rather than real people. "The whole temper of cultural anthropology," Sapir (1949:569) noted, "was impersonal to a degree." So impersonal that we rarely can picture even how the fieldworker lived. This, Crapanzano (1986) feels, still holds of even Geertz's classical ethnographic papers on the Balinese. The anthologies provide edited snapshots.[74] All the "other stuff" is put in a diary or never published.[75] (Although Mead[76] particularly described—made public—her field conditions.)

You get the picture: a powerful ideology is at work. Anthropology, in spite of its strong personal involvement, exerts a stronger pull to make research seem impersonal.

CLINICAL ETHNOGRAPHY

To give recognition to the clinical dimension of fieldwork, we suggest the term "clinical* ethnography" as a subtype and more precise form of participant-observation. Our scientific ideology can be shifted if not junked. But we cannot do without cross-cultural research, as Shweder (1984) has recently reminded us. Clinical ethnographies are reports that study the subjectivity of the researcher and the people who inform him or her. What matters are our communications with real people, one to one or one to many; people creating and exchanging meanings within interpersonal relationships.

The context counts, for cultural signs and symbols are embedded in situations. Contrary to contemporary anthropologists, we suspect that anthropologists rarely study in the field, let alone describe, whole cultural systems.[77] (At least not in one sitting.) Nor do we study only external social behavior, or its material manifestations, notwithstanding Marvin Harris. To understand meaning systems and the more private motivations and fantasies of people, we need accounts of the natives as individuals, not just as presumed spokesmen for their cultures. The natives are not slaves (i.e., "to custom"),[78] though neither

---

*The dictionary says, "*Clinical* . . . involving or depending on direct observation of the living patient; observable by clinical inspection; based on observation; applying objective or standardized methods (as interviews and personality or intelligence tests) to the description, evaluation, and modification of human behavior." The connotation of diagnosis and treatment—of the clinic—is not intended in clinical ethnography.

do they live beyond the citadel (of forces labeled "culture," "economy," "social structure," or "personality"). Other persons' meanings viewed thus in the round are our object.

How shall we use "subjectivity"? As one's private experience of experiencing—at all levels of perception, thought, speech, and action.[79] (We are not interested, for example, in sensory or motor functions, except to understand the *meanings* of a sensation or motor capacity for someone.)

We shall also stress what is true for ourself but too easily forgotten about our research subjects: barring torture, most issues with great meaning are revealed only to those one trusts, someone who will not harm you.* This desire to trust is no more a culture-bound artifact of western experience than is the capacity for insight (the power to harness subjectivity) or the need to share experience.[80] Rather, the seeds for "awareness of one's awareness—the knowledge that one knows" (Devereux 1967:23)—are essential constituents of being human. In clinical ethnography, understanding this awareness and how trust affects the study of it are crucial.

The cross-cultural study of subjectivity—a major aim of clinical ethnography—describes, interprets, and compares the ways people express feelings, beliefs, and motives. "Clinical" is meant to represent our interest in these processes—intimate communication, subjective meanings of self, others, cultural ideas and institutions, identity, and culturally patterned states of awareness. The subjective connotes skills familiar to the psychiatrist, analyst, clinical psychologist, and social worker for collecting reliable information. With the Sambia of New Guinea, our work is not therapy (though people felt better for having been able to talk in confidence); we did clinical interviewing adapted to the language and culture of Sambia.[81] To emphasize these issues in handling ethnographic data, we focus on but do not restrict our discussion to the clinical interviewing context, wherein we must accordingly interpret *all* experience. We shall argue that interpretation never stops, from home to the field and back.

Everything may potentially color the meaning of our data; so we must record as much as possible. Mead once referred to this ambitious stance as "disciplined subjectivity". At best, no matter how full our information, it is incomplete, for interpretation is always involved and is incomplete. In this process, psychoanalysis (at home) is aided by stable control of the office/analyst environment but weak-

---

*In chapter 11 we shall return to discuss interrelationships between psychoanalysis and anthropology, and in our Epilogue we take our ideas on ethics and training of clinical ethnographers further.

ened by the lack of observations of the patient beyond the office. On the other hand, anthropology (in the village) is strengthened by social observations, though we do not control the interview context in the manner of the psychoanalyst.[82] In doing clinical ethnography, therefore, time and repeated observation is a wonderful tool. Sometimes only follow-up can bring more complete data: clinical ethnography is like psychoanalysis, best done for years; and the more time one takes, the richer the observations and fuller the interpretations. A single interview, casual or not, is better than nothing. A week or a month or a year, talking with someone several times a week, provides more. But years of interviews are the test of "evidential continuity"[83] in an individual case study. What does a word mean? Why is he quiet *now*? Is that the same fantasy as two years ago? Why is she or he angry now? What about the dream fragment? Is this mood the same as the one I observed last month? Time shapes contexts and helps us interpret feelings and tacit assumptions, values, fantasy; as well as interpersonal relationships to significant others, including that alien other, the ethnographer. Clinical ethnography is not for the impatient. (Time is, of course, not time but mind. And mind, of course, is not the Mind but interpretations of subjective experience.)

There are, then, two interrelated perspectives in this clinical approach to ethnographic research. The situational one concerns the doing and reporting of interviews in longitudinal case studies. The global perspective concerns an attitude about all one's work: in order better to know what you know, study your own subjectivity and interpersonal relationships, from start to finish, that is, from the time you embark on the project until the end of your writing and editing. It may seem a paradox that the most objective means of doing this research is to explicate subjectivity. However, S. and I assume that since humans are not machines, we are biased. And so we "must use the subjectivity inherent in all observation as the royal road to authentic, rather than fictitious, objectivity" (Devereux 1967:xvii). We use our subjectivity best when we do not ignore or hide it; those deceptions distort our findings. We must, instead, show exactly who we were and are and what we did and do.

To sum up: in the "culture of fieldwork" fiction, the ethnographer is a finely tuned machine that serves as the representative of a culture of orientation to the representatives of the native culture. We shall suggest a better way: clinical ethnography. Let us now expand on this idea by looking inside the fieldwork experience to understand why we conceptualize this way.

TRAINING FOR THE FIELD

As is training in the laboratories and clinics a fundament for the medical student, fieldwork is the bedrock of training in anthropology. "Such fieldwork apprenticeship is so essential," Mead wrote (1952:344), "that I believe anthropologists should insist upon it just as medical men insist upon an internship before certifying a student as a full M.D."

But in training ethnographers, field experience has been seen as making the student totally responsible, in some intuitive way, for translating classroom theory and text into field method.

> At present we have no way of training a student to become an ethnologist other than by sending him or her into the field under conditions that make it necessary to take complete responsibility for the study of the culture. . . . On the whole the best method is to assure that a student who has had exposure to the literature and experience is to *send him into the field alone, with full responsibility for devising the appropriate applications of his graduate training to the culture of a particular people.*[84]

Whatever psychologic instruments or quantitative measures the student used, they were no substitute for "the bone-wearying labor of 'old fashioned' fieldwork" (Chapple 1952:342). And the responsibility for doing *objective* work was sacred. "The highest duty of every anthropologist," Chapple states, is in "securing accurate and objective data, as unbiased by the actions of the field man as possible."[85] But exactly how this occurred was not explained.

The result has been the tendency to see fieldwork as a magical ordeal[86] organized on a "sink or swim" principle. Nader describes it as "the principle initiation rite into the anthropological profession." Anthropologic folklore values those who have a rough time of it: "Supposedly one grows under stress, and the greater the stress, the more we grow" (Nader 1970:114).[87] Edgerton and Langness write:

> Many of the prominent anthropologists of today have criticized their professors for sending them to the field with so little formal preparation. Anthropologists have wryly recounted the frustration they felt when they asked their professors for advice [and were told] . . . "take a lot of pencils or send ahead a large supply of novels to ward off boredom." Even in more recent years some got the same sort of offhand answers to serious, anxious questions; Alan

Beals illustrates: "In 1952, on my way to India, I asked a distinguished British anthropologist to tell me his secret of success in doing fieldwork." His response was "Never accept free housing, and always carry a supply of marmalade." (1974:9)[88]

To sum up: "The student is thrown into the ethnographic ocean, and nature takes it course. If he is worth his salt, he will return from the field an anthropologist" (Nader 1970:114).

Sink or swim; nature takes it course: those who become anthropologists can adapt to other cultures. Anthropology celebrates the ability of each generation of fieldworkers to rediscover for itself this intuitive process with each culture in each "natural experiment" (Mead 1970). In the ideology of anthropology, fieldwork is a discovery process that defies formulas. Cultural relativism, a powerful piece of our ideology, underlies this attitude toward training.

There are dangers in being too explicit about how to do fieldwork, just as there are dangers in being insufficiently explicit. One cannot produce rules for doing fieldwork as if fieldwork were like a laboratory experiment. So complete and complex a human experience cannot be "programmed" in every detail. . . . An approach which might succeed admirably among gregarious Polynesians might fail altogether with the recalcitrant Nuer of the African Sudan. (Edgerton and Langness 1974:9)

Since we study whole cultures, not individuals as culture-bearers, there are limits, it is felt, to the prefield training of fieldworkers. Namely, we will not know until afterward what constitutes the experience of Anthropology (i.e., the fieldworker) studying a particular culture (i.e., as represented by the natives, their language, and material culture). That unique experiment in the special laboratories of human cultures *is* the ethnography.

This training paradigm has, from the 1920s to the early 1970s, had favorable but uneven results: relatively unconnected and basically descriptive reports, few of which were concerned with field method. Broad perspectives often stood in for theory, except in the grand sense that culture or social structure determined human behavior. What made ethnography useful was the brilliance and hard work of researchers who succeeded in bringing home remarkable truths of the Other.

Yet we fear that our bureaucratic success undermined the training of new fieldworkers.[89] "The Golden Age of American Anthropology" (Mead and Bunzel 1960) in the 1960s and early 1970s witnessed a surge of university jobs, federal grant funds, academic and public recognition, and student enrollments. This eventually slackened, but meanwhile, anthropology was almost popular, no longer a sport for the gentry. These changes democratized anthropology[90] but increasingly weakened the kind of training Mead advocated. How? Training shifted from carefully supervised apprenticeship to theory and textbooks; the teaching anthropologist became an authority and expert on a people, less a mentor and a socializer of new ethnographers. Professors had too many students and committee assignments and not enough time for individual supervision. And this bureaucratization in turn further strengthened the rise of participant-observation as a guiding fiction for the discipline. Anthropology is not to blame, of course; these structural alterations must be seen in the context of marketplace adjustments in urban America and academic life.[91] It became more difficult for anthropologists to do fieldwork. Paper work and university bureaucratic tangles grew; publish or perish pressures forced a rush to publication instead of slow immersion into one's place of study; ethnography produced few findings needed by technologically accelerating society; former colonies felt demeaned in being studied. Today, publishers have less reason to bring out large ethnographies for few readers. Ethnography, once the bizarre customs and bosoms were revealed, had as much allure as butterfly collecting.

We dislike the model of participant-observation that stands for the belief that the observer holds back participation so severely that he or she can observe only surfaces. Yet it is a fact—not a theory, a prejudice, or a fantasy—that ethnography occurs in a context of people who (just as you do now as you read) load the interaction with their subjectivity, that is, their private meanings. We also are uneasy that the culture of fieldwork ideology ignores how one's project begins at home, the instant one conceptualizes (imagines) a project. The field project is shaped by our personality, our daydreams, the texts and field reports we read, our professors' theories and anecdotes and advice, budgets, families, and friends: powerful images that move us long before we ever meet a native—and continue their effects to the end, as we make public our experience—ethnography.

The field project designed at home is obviously based on our selfhood, not just our theories or topical interests. First, of course, is the key question of personal and professional motivation: why *do* anthropology?[92] Training influences are extremely important; particular professors stimulate and guide us; certain university departments are associated with certain schools of theory or regions to be studied; and one's graduate student cohort shares interests and shapes knowledge. Then there are questions about the choice of field site: why go to the Arctic or the Amazon? How feasible or harsh and isolated is it (especially if one is Woman[93])? To match an area to one's topical interest restricts the available choices.[94] So do the needs of one's spouse or family. (Doing fieldwork can test a marriage to the limits; the many broken relationships prove the point.) Political factors are important: some Third-World countries are now closed to research; others require payments for research visas; funding agencies reward some types of research and punish others, or they rule out certain geographic areas; nor must we forget the old territorial game in anthropology, through which academic warlords claim a people as their own: 'That's Professor X's people, you can't study there.'[95]

Beyond these practical considerations, however, one's imagination figures actively in selecting a field area and subject. I chose exotic New Guinea because I wanted to study a living initiatory cult, not memories of one. We go to areas that intrigue and fascinate us;[96] perhaps the more rewarding our experiences there (research included), the more inclined we are to return.[97] Here one sees the seldom-discussed match in any field between character structure and professional research.[98]

So our work—fieldwork—begins in our heads, at home, not abroad. Vicarious participation starts there; we formulate images of the natives and of ourselves among them. Observation is grounded there: from ethnographic films or texts of related peoples, from correspondence with local missionaries or other residents in the native area, as well as (in some areas) films or discussion with professors, we take in hypotheses, field strategies, etc. (It surprises us that even clinically-oriented anthropologists ignore awareness of this prefield head work.[99]) Long before the field, an ethnography is biased, however slightly. How aware of these influences are we; of our motives and preconceptions carried into our work? Though we do not engage in old-fashioned natural history sojourns[100] (as did early European explorers[101] captivated by vulgar or romantic conceptions of "primitives") we still need to train students to be alert to this earliest fieldwork in the head.

Let us thus distinguish between several degrees of participating and observing.

First-order participation: This concerns direct interaction with others; eyewitnesses' accounts; observations of words, acts, affects—what Kardiner (1939:356) called "direct experience" in the field.

Second-order participation: indirect participation with others made while in the field; these include introspection and empathy focused on natives' experiences but going beyond what they say or do, as, for instance, when we remember the day's events and record or think about them. Here we observe our own impressions while still in the field. (Our day and night dreams in the field also belong in this category.)

Third-order participation: reading, thinking, and resonating to our fieldwork experience before and after leaving the field. How do we reach new understandings after leaving the field unless, in our heads, we are still participating in our field experience? These reworkings—interpretations—lead to our published report; they *become* the data. Without this hermeneutic approach, we forget how the acts of participating and observing begin inside of us, no matter where and when they become publicly visible.

Even in this crude schema we sense the difficulty of separating participation from observation[102] or of distinguishing between events in the world from those in the head of the ethnographer.[103] Not that there is not a vital difference between them, for there is; but it is their unity that deserves emphasis *contra* the ideology of participant-observation. To illustrate these impressions we shall rethink the field experience.

THE FIELD

Entree

What is our mental state on embarking? Are we excited and anticipating ("a great adventure"), anxious ("what will I find?"; "will I be competent?"; "it's hard to leave"), resentful ("why must I do this?"), angry ("why do they do this to me?"), or joyous ("at long last")? Or a mix of these? Shall we feel the same on stepping into the village? Why? Why not? Who helps or hinders us from getting there?

These transitional experiences modify our observations via our participations. Do we say so in our reports? Anthropology used to proudly deny that these events—this messy subjectivity—were pertinent. What do they have to do with "the culture"? ("Our subject is the village which stops at its gate.") Less so now. Mead (1977:5) wrote toward her end:

> We knew that we had been bred in our own culture and could never lose our own cultural identity; we could only learn about others through the recognition that their membership in their culture and our membership in ours, however different in substance, were alike in kind. But we did not yet recognize that every detail on reaching

the field and of interchange with those who tried to bar or facilitate our way to the field site were also part of our total field experience and so of our fieldwork.

What people help or complicate[104] our settling in: government bureaucrats, missionaries, patrol officers, linguists, native councilors, government translators? Even tourists?* How do we relate to them? What identity do we convey to each of these parties: subject, friend, student, opponent, playmate, sophisticate, fool, scholar? How are these identities conveyed back to the natives (by ourselves, by others)? Do their images make a difference in how they perceive us?

Few ethnographers will ever again work without these authorities being present, and some fieldworkers have noted their influences.[105] But in most *ethnographies* such authorities are often still absent. Why are they edited out? Perhaps politics prevents us from describing them.[106] A pity. For instance, despite rumors of antipathy between anthropologists and missionaries, field reports in New Guinea would be less advanced today were it not for the logistical assistance of various missionaries.[107]

In our first hours in the village we form and communicate indelible impressions; what do we experience and how do we behave in these initial contacts? Which people approach us? Are they friendly or hostile?[108] Who or what do they take us to be? Are we officially received by kings or chiefs? Who sponsors us? The natives press in; what motivates them: curiosity, influence-seeking, money, friendliness, anger, protection of their rights? Leaders present themselves and introduce us to their followers; or no one may come forth. Others may desire to work for us. Among the Sambia some young men and boys asked to work for me—to teach the language, to translate, to cut firewood, to cook. I hired no one at first: I didn't know what it would mean to hire them, or why they wanted to work, or how that role would alter them, or how I would or could pay them.   Only time taught me.† Textbooks advise us not to select overzealous people,[109] a preconception I remembered but which did not hold well for the Sambia, for some of my first contacts became key sponsors, teachers, translators, and friends.‡

*We are only beginning to demystify the extent to which tourism has thoroughly influenced certain ethnographic projects, as much as our view of ourselves (MacCannell 1976).
†The following allusions to my fieldwork cover my first visits (1974–76), when I spent twenty-two months with the Sambia.
‡These people included Kanteilo and Worangri, elder sponsors who were respected village leaders, and superb teachers and manipulators of me. Moondi, my best young informant, translator, and field assistant; and Weiyu, who got closer later than the others, became my best translator and closest Sambia friend. All are described in short biographies in Herdt (1987c), and see our interview chapters below.

Psychiatrists teach that the information in the first interview is very important (though we have to know ourselves well enough to trust our impressions and be practiced enough to know how to listen and observe). That first hour presents, in open or disguised forms, the characteristic elements of the ensuing interaction (i.e., treatment): signs and symptoms, moods, styles of communicating, uniqueness of personality, capacity to talk and interact, to trust and be trusted. For the anthropologist our first hours in the village reveal typical interpersonal issues that will immerse us from then on. It would be nice to have as detailed a record as possible of that time, including our personal reactions. Nicer still to place some of that diary in our later ethnography.

Culture Shock

On entering the village, we are to expect an attack of culture shock. The term conjures up images of confrontation with alien ways of life, unnatural practices: eating coagulated milk and cow's blood, women breast-feeding pigs, villagers refusing to tend their sick, infanticide, cruel treatment of women, statements that the ethnographer is a ghost or spy,[110] or that men fear their semen will dry up and they'll die. We may be stopped in our tracks, alienated, disgusted, enraged, fearful. And then we may shrink back. Depressed. We want to press down on this concept, because it is central to the objectified view of participant-observation, and because it is among the first experiences in the field. Bear with us in rethinking this problem for clinical ethnography.

Culture shock appears to be a common experience of anthropologists, however varied the specific events:

> The uneasiness brought about by living in an unpredictable social world, combined with the loss of one's comfortable social world, brings on a condition known as *culture shock*—the shock of passing from a familiar to an unknown culture. . . . In the face of culture shock the fieldworker often retreats for a period from any social interactions. (Edgerton and Langness 1974:23)

Obviously the anthropologist in the field, especially in the early period when he is not yet sure of acceptance, is subject to extreme emotional pressure. Some field situations can be frightening, raising fears for personal safety, and at the very least the anthropologist knows he is undergoing a severe professional test in which he must rely entirely on his own resources. . . . The common result of this situation is "culture shock," the same psychological malfunctioning as that experienced by most people who find themselves in strange settings, in which they recognize neither the cues of the culture nor the appropriate responses to the cues. . . . In greater or lesser degree all anthropologists experience culture shock, at least on their first field trips and not infrequently on subsequent trips as well. . . . (Foster 1969:62)

"Uneasiness," "unpredictability," "loss of one's comfortable social world," "retreat," "extreme emotional pressure," "frightening," "entirely on his own resources"—culture shock. It is expected in all of us.

Yet we are skeptical: Are we dealing with genuine anxiety or a myth? (Or a catchy phrase that hides a lot of neurosis inside the claim of appropriate fear. One person's fascination is another's fear.) If "all anthropologists experience culture shock," then why does Malinowski not describe the phenomenon? Nor do Mead, Bateson, Firth, Roheim, DuBois, Evans-Pritchard or the six editions of *Notes and Queries in Anthropology*, as far as we can figure out. What's amiss? Were these pioneers superhumans who could not be shocked? Or did they, in keeping with this book's critique, simply edit *that* life out of their disturbances in the field? As, for instance, in the infamous case of Malinowski's diaries? In both senses I think not.

Here are two other clues about our concept of culture shock. First, in *exotic cultures*, the longer one remains (or the more one returns to the same place), the less culture shock. The authors of *Long-Term Field Research in Social Anthropology* hint at the normativeness of culture shock and collectively conclude: "Not only is 'culture shock' minimized . . . [in subsequent fieldwork] . . . but often the anthropologist is fully engaged in research within a few hours of arrival."[111] Second, in urban settings—so-called urban anthropology—"culture shock" is apparently absent; one finds few references to it.[112]

"Culture shock" is a fine-sounding pop-jargon phrase that should make us cautious because of these anomalies. The idea has now been imported into western culture.[113] This fact, together with the observation that the phenomenon has been little studied except anecdotally since Oberg, even though "it" is still unselfconsciously referred to as experience and as concept, suggests that "culture shock" is exaggerated in the culture of fieldwork. This should give us pause. If one examines the anthropologic literature, allusions to the term do not appear until after World War II. Someone[114] coined the term in the late thirties or forties; by the fifties Oberg's paper helped to institutionalize it. Its origins are unimportant; what concerns me is its ideologic and psychodynamic foothold in ethnography.

Ethnographers acquire the notion of "culture shock" (like that of "informant," as we shall see), through professional socialization.[115] It helps us to maintain that tenuous balancing act: participant-observation. We can do our job—like lab workers—no matter how uncomfortable our adjustment to alien situations. The experience we call "culture shock" is thus a way of registering (objectifying) our belief that this shock occurs to ourselves as scientists, not as private persons. Intellectually mystified and psychologically rationalized in this way, it is then acceptable for the ethnographer to feel and think unacceptable things. But why use "culture shock" to cover danger, feelings of disorientation, alienation or loneliness?

First, there is our ideology. The traditional assumption is that anthropologists study primitive, static, closed systems. To adapt to these harmonious, equilibrium societies, where everyone is related (or else enemies) in face-to-face relationships, we must dislocate, even disrupt, a bit of their world. "We" penetrate, that is, some magical boundary that represents "the culture" enclosing their village. Thus, "culture shock": we are shocked in fitting in, they are jarred to accommodate us. This "we" that is shocked indexes more than the self. It is the ethnographer, bearer of the culture of fieldwork, and representative of our cultural tradition; a "normal" scientist who registers "normal" emotional/cognitive reactions vis-à-vis the "normal" representatives of the host culture. Since anthropology holds precious the doctrine of cultural relativism—whereby all customs and meaningful acts are parts of a whole pattern ("their culture") that *is* human, worthy of respect, and adaptive in some sense—we, as cultural spokesmen for the West, require some mechanism for communicating (to our culture and ourselves) that these objectionable alien practices, which we cannot object to, are understandable and eventually acceptable. Moreover, they will be made assimilable into western culture via the Science of Custom. So the ethnographer can accept (at least intellectually) the aliens' way as relative: good, natural, and human. And for all these reasons the praxis of urban anthropology should require no experience of "culture shock."[116]

On the personal side of selfhood, there are equally powerful psychodynamics compelling our use of culture shock. The mythology of culture shock convinces us that we are unbiased. Since fieldwork does not begin (as the folklore has it) until we set foot in the village, our participation with the native does not begin in our heads but rather over there; and we do not study ourselves beforehand. How we *usually* are, back home; why we unusually left it and are there; and all that transpired up to that first step in the village is ignored in the ethnography, counts as nothing. While participant-observation keeps us detached (not to be confused with objectivity), it also ensures that *we do not look inside.*

The idea of culture shock disguises our private experience in the field. "Shock" may be accurate if reality-oriented fears are involved. But if we are responding to something dangerous, such as an attack on our lives, our responses might be in the direction of, say, alertness, caution, or fear. Words like these come closer to naming our subjective states and pointing us toward knowing what we experience. But there are anxieties less immediate, with no direct danger, that more closely correspond to the popular category of culture shock. In this sense "shock" can also hide personal, idiosyncratic, neurotic* responses—legitimized as normal, expected, and nonproblematic (as in World War I victims of "shell shock"). Thus, I would rather say "I suffered from culture shock" than let myself or you know my biases, bigotries, and even racist impulses: distress that my moral, religious, or erotic sensibilities are being attacked. Or that my beliefs about what is proper demeanor or clothes or body form or personal hygiene or worship or whatever are being threatened. Here, the self's script and textual use of culture shock might be: *I did not come to this place to find (i.e., repeat) the anxieties that are so handy at home.*

Were it not for our personalities, interests, creative talents, and neurosis, we would not suffer culture shock but—in many circumstances—curiosity, delight, puzzlement, or surprise. Therefore, to place the responsibility for such experience outside of ourselves and onto culture (or nature, i.e., one's viscera) is to take a stand against insight. What we choose not to look at is a choice against learning more, ethnographically—against our recognizing that matters of taste, style, custom (to use a comfortably neutral vocabulary) may bother us a great deal and that our capacity to be bothered in such ways did not begin the moment we arrived in the strangers' land. Then, with practice, we may learn to what extent that which we feel is either our own invention or the results of outer stimuli or both.

Unless we accord personal motivation a role in the experience of culture shock we cannot account for the following folklore: that colleagues or co-workers of similar background in the same culture do

---

*By which we mean here: the invasion of one's contact with reality by unconscious conflict, either idiosyncratic or culturally shared conflicts.

not report similar culture shock; that others in our field—visitors, missionaries, traders, etc.—experience no shock where we do, or vice versa, or find instead curiosity or amusement;[117] or that, in some cases, the anthropologist's *spouse* is said to have had an easier time of it in the field. (Remember that the anthropology student is undergoing a "severe professional test.")

Some years ago, when starting work in Sambia, I experienced anxieties—shocks—of several kinds. I do not think of those experiences as culture shock, but in the old idiom they could be miscategorized that way. There was distress I felt in reaction to discrete events: helplessness at the screams of an older woman being beaten by her husband, others tensely watching outside their house—the screams intermixed with sounds of wood striking flesh, and her cries for a long dead mother. But "shock" is too vague. I felt helplessness, then pity, bitterness, sadness. (And even these words are imprecise.) Or the laughter of the initiates, who did nothing when a small boy fell from a tree on his testicles, splitting open his scrotum, blood everywhere. I was stunned for an instant and then enraged at what seemed dangerously callous complacency. Or Moondi's fearlessness, when he told me the secret practices of homosexual fellatio and thereby placed himself in grave danger. For days I feared for his life and mine, until the men accepted my knowing their secrets. Or, three months later, in the privacy of ritual initiations, when I saw the secrets become flesh in florid and open homoerotic play. I was astonished and embarrassed. (Herdt 1987c.)

Then there are emotions—they are cheapened by being called "shock"—that come from extended experiences: exhilaration with this New Guinea adventure;* loneliness for friends and family; mild depressions; malaise; sickness (malaria, dysentery); sexual frustration; rewards of friendships; and work that was an accomplishment. All these—disturbances or joys—*were* my work. I cannot afford to lose data and perspective by squashing them into the globbish "culture shock."† By staying awake, by not blurring my awareness of what I felt,[118] I sometimes found more of me and thereby allowed the ethnographer in me to find more of Sambia experience.

Malinowski, whatever else he may have felt, probably never knew of our "culture shock." He was not taught it. He did not have the luxury its distance provides, and we are unkind to forget this.[119] He was an explorer lacking the defenses of our ideologic armor. Perhaps

---

*"Culture shock" is negative. What about the wonderful surprises?

†One also loses a lot of data and perspective by the opposite extreme of going native, wherein we deny that the past is alive in our bones.

this is why his diaries revealed two people: Malinowski the Scientist, a myth his books created; and Malinowski the man, mortal as any other. The field notes and monographs were objectivity, the diaries were subjectivity. In the diaries we may have lost a hero, but anthropology gained a fuller ethnography. In the years following Malinowski, "culture shock" was created to mediate the same ideologic dilemmas that forced Malinowski into his diaries. By the 1960s, anthropology's golden age, many people, of diverse personality, social class, training, research interests, and professional motivations replaced the once small anthropology club. The pseudolanguage of culture shock allowed them to share seemingly common experiences without revealing their private biases and subjectivity. Were Malinowski alive he might now—in characteristic form—reproach us for not publishing our diaries. Either that, or better: put some of that insight where it always belonged in the first place. In our ethnography.

Identity Problems

We settle in, build a house, meet people, learn the language, learn names, make contacts, learn etiquette, learn the politics, find rapport with people, get comfortable, establish our role and identity as the anthropologist.

Supposedly, we are first like children, soaking up what is taught us.[120] Yet this analogy is flawed, for we have power—political, technologic, education—and we and our hosts know it. We know the outside. We are usually white and western, which have their power implications. Moreover, we transmit to the natives our sense of being superior, especially because we examine what they do and think and because *we* decide what about them we think is important for us to know. Thus we, going beyond their belief, believe that we become the final authorities on their reality.[121]

But do we not likewise structure the effects we have on our subjects or who they feel we are? The identity they give us, built from who knows what stories, experiences, and fantasies,[122] is confirmed and modified by our demeanor and our acts. Where do we build our hut? In the village? Away from it? Do we allow the natives inside? How do we acquire food? Do we share it? Do the natives share with us? What do we pay for? Do we work fixed hours? Do we sign off? (At night? On Sundays?) Do we establish taboos?[123] Do we make some areas off-limits: our sleeping quarters, eating quarters, toilets, storerooms, etc.? Why—what are we keeping separate from them? Do we let natives borrow? Do we borrow from them? How do we entertain ourselves when alone, with spouse, or with co-worker? How often do we travel in an area? Do we spend larger amounts of time with certain informants, friends, males, females, Europeans, on the government station, etc.? In what ways do we refuse to interact with the natives?[124]

And what meanings do people attribute to our acts? How can we unendingly respond to such factors throughout our lives at home and deny them in the field? For instance: "Though undoubtedly I feel a great debt to many villages, I thought it advisable from the point of view of academic objectivity not to get too involved in the lives of individual informants" (Epstein 1979:224).

Obviously we help shape our environment by what we do, say, and think, and our actions strongly influence the identity that the natives thereby ascribe to us. Once in motion, this identity "text" influences subsequent responses to us. A related point: do we notice if we set up modes of acculturated comportment (e.g., drinking behavior[125]) for the natives? Such issues lead to the question of who our informants are and how they choose us.

The Informant

The innocuous term "informant" emerged at the end of the nineteenth century as researchers moved off the hotel veranda to talk to "savages." "Savages" in turn became "natives," who turned into "informants." This shift was related to the emergence of the concepts of "culture" and "participant-observation." In the early part of the twentieth century the functionalists treated cultures as integrated wholes (while ignoring their own colonialist situation). The "informant" was a reaction to the early racism predating anthropology, and it represented as much as anything our intellectual progress. Where did it take us? Not too far; we did not escape our colonialist and positivistic heritage, for "the informant" is a notion that still embodies anthropology's contradictions.[126] Here, as with culture shock, let us question a key category in the culture of fieldwork.

Anthropologists know these cliches: "my informant said," "informants say," "informants argue," "informants believe," the informant stressed that," "informants could not explain," "informants denied," "it was pointed out by informants that," "informants were concerned to," "informants describe," "informants recalled." Yes: in this narrative form we see not this person in particular or that one, but rather nameless, faceless, sexless, ageless, colorless, impartial witnesses and specialists uncontaminated by who they are, precisely, or why they said what they said to us, precisely.

We needed a neutral term that made the sources of our cultural facts seem accurate and sound: objective. We needed a word to fill a gap: what does one call a category of people who tell us things and interpret them for us? They inform, provide knowledge, *become as spokesmen for their communities.* Here is a key: informants provide true knowledge about a culture that is supposedly custom-bound and homogeneous. It is not their private opinions or peculiar chunks of cultural knowledge that inform, but rather their capacity as funnels for revealing—to *anyone* who interrogates* them—the social facts as everyone else knows them, except, of course, the alien ethnographer.[127]

Anthropology's adoption of "informant" complemented the philosophic behaviorism of the time. We needed an analytic term that made our subjective data ring as scientific as that of our sister disciplines. The therapists had patients (in treatment); the academic psychologists had subjects (in experiments); the sociologists had actors and respondents (to questionnaires); the humanistic psychologists added clients; the hermeneuts use interlocutors (Reisman 1977). Are these comparisons apt? (Only clinicians—and their case is not comparable either—can claim the intensive, intimate knowledge of the ethnographer.) Only we have eyewitness accounts (Sontag 1966) coupled with the natives' point-of-view in context, the result of the live-in method that is not experimental, controlled, or abstractable. The informant, like the analytic patient, is $n = 1$.

And not only this: our informants, said Powdermaker, are thought to be friends. Here again the objective dilemma—be detached but friendly—emerges. On the one hand, our informants are like guides for the blind.[128] They are our spectacles, hearing aids, crutches, stomachs, spectographs, barometers, medical manuals, projective tests, culinary guides, drinking mates, history books, demographic files, guides in etiquette, lovers, baby-sitters, mountain-guides; they share with us their gossip, loves, hates; they interpret our dreams; become our watchdogs, cooks, servants, and even (dare we admit it?)—our sometime healers. All this humanness covered by the cold neutrality: informant. "Informant" thus admits such latitude in traditional ethnography that its promiscuous use is phony. When one term can erase the differences between individuals' age, sex, ritual status, social role, personality, context, mood, motivation, and—most important—the

---

*The dictionary gives this usage.

precise nature of one's relationship to that person, at that moment, that term is being misused (Herdt 1981). Few anthropologists operate as cold onlookers.[129] But in our ethnographic reports, in order to seem scientific, we traded one kind of racism, Social Darwinism, for another: cultural uniformity (e.g., blacks are . . . , Italians are . . . , Chinese are . . . , Sambia are . . . , doctors are . . . , farmers are . . . , ethnographers are. . . .): experiential homogeneity.

To call a person an informant is to press our audience to agree with us that we are scientific since our data are gathered in objective circumstances. But Malinowski is Malinowski: he smells of cigarettes, whisky, and concupiscence. Can we trust what he tells us about the sex lives of Trobriand girls? No, says the scientist, until his Malinowskiness is trimmed off. To the extent that you met him only in sentences that gave you no clues what sort of man he is, we could manipulate your attitudes about the validity of our ideas. Even a name, unless sufficiently foreign, can stir images; but "informant" is less likely to. The ideal informant is neutral, objective, and transmits a culture in its essence, passing the data through him or herself without the contamination of his or her subjectivity. Ideal informants selflessly tell us things, relay language and culture learning; they offer us facts, not their private interpretation of facts. This kind of informant makes us (H. and S.) flinch twice, first because no such people exist, and second because the idea supports the pretense that a culture exists in platonic forms.

Our culture of fieldwork assumes that informants yield up only true information, a belief particularly embodied in the subcategory, the "key informant." Here is, without doubt, a very close relationship. The key informant is someone known so well that his or her biography can be written.[130] But since these people are as fully subjective as anyone else, why should we assume that only truth—or the search for it—motivates them? Does truth rule out lies?[131] Don't we know that cultural knowledge is stratified, even in tribal societies, according to sex, ritual status, caste and politics? And how much more particular are the key informants' words?[132] Many of these relationships probably also contain deeper involvements—conscious and unconscious—including friendship, love, hate, attachment, and dependence: all the elements that make a relationship interesting, enjoyable, rewarding, and perishable. Are transference and countertransference involved?[133] If they are, how do we handle them?

Instead of "the informant" let us adopt the term "interpreter." After reviewing the fieldwork literature, we feel that the concept "interpreter" accurately describes and more closely approximates the methodologic role and meanings noted above than does "informant." Interpreters do nothing more than interpret things for us (which is quite a lot), offering their views and translations of their world and themselves.* Anthropology already recognizes this function in that those who inform about language can be called interpreters or translators. (See chapter 10 for a discussion.) Why should those who translate cultural conventions be more objective in doing so than interpreters of linguistic conventions? (Language and culture are equally open to interpretation; that we assume language to be more or less structured and objectively describable is another assumption of the culture of fieldwork.)

Aside from being more accurate, "interpreter" has two other advantages. One is that it is already used to describe the process of language learning. We do not need a different word to cover the process of culture learning. Moreover, the literature indicates that linguistic interpreters often serve as cultural interpreters too. (If we need to mark off these roles, we can use "linguistic" or "cultural" as modifiers, though often this description is implied in the narrative context and needs no emphasis.) The other advantage is that interpreter will sharpen the epistemologic status of our information. "The informant" carries heavy positivistic baggage; "interpreter" can hardly connote false objectivity. The term "interpreter" forces one always to be clear about what it is that is being cross-culturally negotiated. Including anonymity and privacy.[134]

What matters for ethnography is that the natives were portrayed as being disconnected from the ethnographers' experience (and vice versa). As some interpretive ethnographers have made clear, few texts reveal the native's words to us.[135] Forge (1972:296) stated this idea plainly: "No matter how friendly your informants may be, they can never understand you." No wonder some natives dislike being informants: we know[†] how it feels not to be granted that we have insight.

---

*The dictionary offers: "One who interprets or translates; especially, one who serves as oral translator between people speaking different languages."

[†]We can understand better the potential dangers for us of blandly inputting objectivity to informants when we reverse the business of being an informant. How do we perform as informants, and what do we make of our interrogators? Clifford Barnett (personal communication) tells me of anthropologists who were turned off when serving as informants to a medical research team. Why? Their interrogators only wanted certain information, not the whole story. [S: Who decides which story is the whole story?] Here the anthropologists were merely natives who could not know the whole picture and who could not therefore interpret their own experience.

Field Life: What are Data?

Having struggled with the anthropologist's dilemma in being a flawed instrument for measuring culture, we want now to ask what experiences in village living do count as data. Our answer is: all. That, however, being too much to contemplate, one must focus (and then pray that intelligence, good judgment, and originality—not to mention luck—bless our risky venture). On these terms universes of information go unused in traditional ethnography.

Example: living arrangements. I had the largest house in the village,* placing no restrictions on people coming and going. Indeed I encouraged them to. But the villagers did not want me to live alone: "You would be lonely." "Ghosts attack those who are alone." So the elder, Kanteilo, moved in. Then my cook, Kwinko, moved in. So did Moondi. And sometimes Weiyu. People called my house their hotel. So I was constantly surrounded by people. Little happened in the village that I didn't learn about eventually from people's constant talking, gossip, and everything else people do all day long. But this togetherness meant that I had no privacy. How did I experience it? I could never bear to eat alone in front of them, nor they, me; soon enough, then, the kitchen was open to food exchange.† For solitude I took walks, wrote, read, listened to the radio, sat on my porch and watched sunsets, tended my garden. Though in the swim of things, I also had ways to be by myself—pockets of aloneness, self amusement, and absorption—in this ambience of interpersonal closeness. For Sambia I was, in turn, a tourist-curiosity who became a resident; I was tutored and befriended, pampered, and deceived; I became a pseudo son, brother, and cousin, was thus fed and housed, politically and socially supported, lectured, scolded, exhorted, and extorted. I became a post office, first-aid clinic, bank, supply house—you name it. Still, I didn't merge with them; and Sambia, who are usually sensible people, probably would not have let me do so anyway.‡

---

*Sambia have small huts, and I wanted space. Did I need as much as I had? Did I need the biggest house? Did the village need me to have it? (I was and even when not there still am a political object my village uses in the local status game with its neighbors, former enemies.)

†I could afford to have large crocks of soup cooked every day, with canned meat and whatever vegetables were available. With this soup, I fed people who helped me. There was always enough for others who were around, and since food giving is so acceptable and expected, it fits my desires. (After two and a half years on soup, however, I rarely want soup anywhere, except in my village, where it is still tasty.)

‡Once, on an idle morning during a period of initiation, I was coaxed into trying on the garb of a warrior. (Until then I had never worn native dress.) I felt uncomfortable but kept quiet to get my male friends' responses. What a study in ambivalence. Some said I looked

Talking: who talks to me: Why are my friends the most verbal Sambia? Interviewing: who talks? How much, when, where, how loud or soft, about what? What topics (e.g., parents) are avoided? Does someone make eye contact? If a woman or a boy looks away or is bashful, how is this done: matter-of-factly, nervously, quietly, co-quettishly?* Why is someone quiet? What kind of silence is it—cold, warm, angry, or inviting? Why does someone only get quiet when angry? Why do I feel someone is talking too much or too little? What is the overlying mood of the interview: contentment, passivity, aggressiveness, brooding, fearfulness, or combinations of these? Joking: who makes jokes—men, boys, women? With me, too? When alone? Who laughs? With what kinds of laughter (amused, hysterical)? What do I joke about? How do I make light of events, of myself, of my anxiety? What amuses me? Appalls me? I sense someone is hiding something from me but have only empathy to go by: what are my associations (fantasies)? Do I forget names? Why don't I trust someone's dream reports? Resistance: why am I reluctant to ask something? Why do I consistently avoid some topics: What fascinates me? Bores me? Why am I afraid to ask someone about a particular experience? Why do some people altogether resist being interpreters?

Etc. . . . I need not list more in order to make the point that everything can contribute to shaping the data of clinical ethnography.

You might object that the anthropology student is ill-trained to undertake or understand this kind of interviewing. [S: It's too natural, unstilted, unscholarly.] Isn't the student in danger here, risking damage to others and him- or herself, particularly in sensitive areas such as sexual behavior, dreams, anger, and shame? Isn't fieldwork in an exotic culture demanding enough, under the circumstances of adjusting to strange life conditions—especially working alone—without adding the burden of intimate communications? Perhaps. If so, then we ought to invent training for clinically oriented ethnography and, as is done with psychiatrists, pick from our students only those most likely to be able to talk with others, and then develop the

---

"nice" and "strong" (a warrior); but others said "forget it," or "those garb are no good for you; they'll pinch and they've got lice." When I showed uneasiness, my friends told me to change back. I never wore them again.

*Sambia avoid direct eye contact with others who are defined as potential sexual partners, unless they (men to women, boys to bachelors, or vice versa) are purposely communicating erotic interest. I found that after talking with someone several times, their eye-avoidance diminished; eventually we would have regular eye contact.

seminars, practicums, and supervision that teaches students how to do such work and still comfortably live in foreign cultures.[136]

Our research aim is to understand others. Respect is a prerequisite of cross-cultural study, but where do we draw the lines for appropriate involvement with natives in the villages? When are natives, like doctors' patients, children, the mentally ill, the mentally retarded, and students, emotionally vulnerable to the fantasies they have due to our status? Mead's view (1977:7), by no means unique, is to avoid deep involvement:* "Immersing oneself in life in the field is good, but one must be careful not to drown." Ethnographers are not psychoanalysts, who, in order to allow their patients' minds full play, create a less active environment. How shall we study people's experience in another culture without ourselves knowing and experiencing the culture?

We have reached here a complex and ignored area in ethnography: the degrees of ethnographer involvement (participation and observation) with the natives and their institutions. It is amazing that these issues—psychologic, political, ethical—though basic to all fieldwork, have not been systematically discussed in the literature.

The spectrum of involvement with natives stretches from not being in the field (the armchair ethnologist), and from almost total detachment (sitting on a tractor measuring subjects' movements) in the field, to total merging into the culture (going native).

Let us take the detached fieldworker first. What is detachment? Removing one's true self from interactions? No intimate communication but only questionnaires, standardized impingements, formal interviews, structured tests, strict and technical work schedules? Is detachment avoidance? Perhaps one does not examine certain customs, behaviors, or attitudes; does not investigate beyond the limits of the village; does not look for native insights or interpretations, only for the surface of what is done or said to others; and especially, one avoids studying how the natives perceive you, what you are doing, and what your contacts with them mean to them. Such detachment is aided by believing that each native needs, hates, and loves his or her customs in the same way as others and that we should not ques-

*But those involvements occur. They are not reported. Even diaries are not published. [S: I wonder if the best ethnographic reports anywhere are not ethnographers' secret diaries. They may be full of craziness and human frailty, but less dishonest than the ethnographer's objective reports.] When ethnographers succumb [S: And sex is by no means the only sin; even the research as it is actually done—not the published deodorized account—may take cruel advantage of people; and are some missionaries guilty of soul-murder in the techniques they use to get conversions?] and edit these experiences out, are they not distorting data—on the pretext of doing science—and are their reports consequently less accurate than was the ethnographic reality?

tion what they experience. Detachment is also enhanced if one's spouse or children are there to insulate you, as does keeping your abode private. Detachment is maintained by myriad other things: language, dress, food choices, writing letters, field notes, diaries,[137] listening to music, sketching, smoking, interacting with officials, material comforts, frequency of field breaks, etc. The point is that nothing makes detachment out of these behaviors; rather, it is the ethnographers' subjectivity—a desire to keep distant—that does.

What about the other extreme, going native, becoming a pseudo-native imitating native ways?[138] We have almost no accounts of this transformation, for it is a disgrace our profession says dishonors one-self, one's professors, department, and discipline. One has failed to master the passage to professional. Too much participation has corrupted observation,[139] similar to florid states of countertransference (e.g., sexual involvement with patients) that disgrace psychiatry.

What about milder forms of acting like a native, of subliminally accepting native ways and attitudes; for instance, never show anger or never hide anger; always share food or never share food. Some may recognize similar aspects in their work but not have thought of them as examples of going native, though we know that whole teams of fieldworkers have found it necessary to appear to be closely identified with the natives.[140]

How intimately must one live with natives to present their viewpoint? There are no simple answers, though most anthropologists manage to be both participant and observer, without going native. S. and I believe that good clinical training could prepare ethnographers to approach these issues in ways that would improve their coping mechanisms and the quality of their data.

Coping in the Field

How do most fieldworkers manage to both participate and observe without going native? We just settle in and adjust. First we take time out for recreation: read, eat, sleep, photograph, sketch, swim, make a ritual out of mundane activities such as cooking or bathing, listening to the radio, write letters. Visitors—fellow anthropologists, friends, government authorities—are successful distractions. (Virtually no ethnographers actually describe personal visitors in their monographs; some do not even mention spouses or families who lived with them in the field.)[141]

When coping weakens, distracting symptoms appear. Boredom is a fine example: it substitutes for anxiety and depression but is still a terrible threat to the integrity of one's data.[142] Then there are affect-deadeners. Alcohol, especially for older generations of anthropologists who did not have psychotropic drugs, relieved boredom, anxiety, depression, anger, guilt. Nowadays marijuana, tranquilizers, and antidepressants may be used. Still, as with coping devices in any circumstance, creativity can be preserved as well as damaged by these chemical defenses. One only hopes that these defenses do not lead to more guilt and more anxiety and then a blowout.

Sometimes we need a longer respite, appropriately enough called the "field break," by a trip to the patrol post or a town for a few days. (These interludes remind us we can escape from realities natives cannot.)

These experiences, we emphasize, are part of fieldwork. But they are usually ignored in ethnographic reports. Anthropology is like surgery; not just anyone can practice it. But in advertising this, let's also tell how we do manage to do it.

The problems raised in this chapter require a clinical training anthropology students do not really receive. Without that, three factors are at risk: the natives, the ethnographer, and the data. Something's got to give if insight is blocked. In our conclusions we shall take up training issues. Our purpose, however, is not to write a textbook of clinical ethnography but only to affirm that one is needed and to urge our colleagues in anthropology to work toward this end.

CHAPTER TWO

Sambia Sexual Culture

H: This chapter introduces the Sambia and their cultural attitudes toward gender and erotics. The title, "Sexual Culture," is meant to indicate our emphasis on erotics; only here, we show structural relationships between types of persons, types of sexual transactions, and fundamental categories of culture that Sambia bring to their encounters with one another. In this sense, the sexual is but one of many domains of culture, such as politics or religion, though it is, of course, highly open to personal meanings and innovations. Sambia, by nature of their emphasis on semen, have made themselves exotic in our eyes; this was not their intention, of course, and the reader should not be unduly distracted by the exoticness of their cultural system. Rather, we hope to provide here, and to a certain extent in the following chapter, the foreground and context whereby readers can place our case studies into the normative framework of Sambia society.

Every anthropologist has certain choices when he or she sets out to write an ethnographic piece. Whether we aim to describe a behavior or belief, an institutional pattern, or something as pervasive as an ethos, these require a cultural environment in which to make sense of them. But still, we have our options: how formal or informal shall the account be? Should we keep the language and entities confined to abstractions, jargon, technical models? What features shall we omit, emphasize, or color through concrete example or personal anecdotes? What time frame do we choose? Past perfect; present tense—as indicated, for instance, by data on social change and worries about ominous or benign implications of the present? Shall we

This chapter was previously published in a slightly different form in G. Herdt, ed., *Ritualized Homosexuality in Melanesia* (Berkeley: University of California Press, 1984).

53

write in the first person singular, or plural; allow more empathy through use of the active voice? Do we need tables, diagrams, maps and charts? How much literature should be reviewed to keep our colleagues admiring or quiet? Who is our audience? Do we invite them into our accounts or keep them in the shadows? What vision of the anthropologic enterprise is drawn on, hinted at, or promoted?[1] Each time I write on Sambia these questions buzz through me, and I must make choices accordingly.

This chapter is a more or less conventional ethnographic sketch. It outlines Sambia culture, and is, in the trade, a "set piece" that summarizes more detailed accounts to be found elsewhere.[2] I, the author, am virtually invisible from the scene, in keeping with respectable ethnographic tradition. (Multiply this chapter by a few factors— add chapter titles like "kinship," "religion," "ecology"—and you have "the ethnography," a recipe that still sells). The contrast between this chapter and the following case studies are like the difference between a skeleton and its flesh. Yet each type of account needs the other, is incomplete when taken alone. And the difference between them bears as much on ethnographic styles and methods as on theories of interpreting ethnography and culture.[3]

Sambia are a fringe-area Highlands people. They inhabit isolated ranges of the southern part of the Eastern Highlands near the Papuan border. Their high forest territory is vast, while the population (around 2300) is small, with population density between five and ten people per square mile. Historically, they migrated from the Papuan hinterland around Menyama about two centuries ago. Myth and legend relate that they fled after a great war. They share in cognate cultural traditions with other Anga tribes in the area, such as the Baruya (Godelier 1986), with whom they also warred and traded. But Sambia have also been influenced by Eastern Highlands groups, especially the Fore (Lindenbaum 1979), so their society and culture embody and reflect influences and transformations of imported patterns from both Papua and the Highlands.

Social organization and economy revolve around small sedentary hamlets built atop high mountain ridges for defense. Gardening and hunting are the main economic pursuits. Sweet potatoes and taro are the chief staples. Women do most garden work. Men do all hunting, primarily for possum, cassowary, birds, and eels. Pigs are few and are of little ceremonial importance. Descent is ideally organized on the basis of patriliny. Postmarital residence is patrivirilocal, so males grow up in their father's hamlet, inherit his land, and reside there. Marriage is by infant betrothal or sister exchange; bride-wealth was introduced only in the mid-1970s. Some men, especially senior leaders, have several wives. All marriage is arranged by elders, women being traded between exogamous clans, which tend to be internally organized as an extended family. Inside hamlets, nuclear (or polygamous) families live together in small separate huts; but there are also one or two men's houses wherein all initiated, unmarried males live. The hamlet tends to function as a corporate group in matters of warfare, subsistence activities, marriage, ritual, and dispute settlements.

Sambia society is comprised of six different population clusters of hamlets in adjacent but separate river valleys. These population clusters are divided, in turn, into subgroups (phratries) believed related by ancestry, ritual, and common geographic origin. Each phratry has between two and six hamlets, situated on ridges often within sight of one another. These local hamlet groups, known as confederacies,* intermarry and engage in joint ritual initiations every three or four years. But they sometimes fight among themselves. Warfare has indeed been rife throughout the entire Highlands Anga area, taking two forms: intertribal war raids to kill and loot; and intratribal bow fights designed to bluster and get revenge for perceived wrongs. In other words, within the Sambia Valley, my fieldwork site, hamlets have intermarried, initiated, and fought—sociopolitical dynamics of the behavioral environment that are crucial for understanding social and sexual life.

Relationships between the sexes are highly polarized. One sees this polarization in virtually every social domain. A strict division of labor and ritual taboos forbids men and women from doing each other's tasks in hunting and gardening. Women are responsible for food preparation and child care. Authority rests in the hands of elders and war leaders. Men are in charge of public affairs. The hamlet itself is divided into male and female spaces and paths tabooed to the opposite sex after initiation. Men's rhetoric disparages older married women as oversexed or lecherous and younger women as prudish or shy. Men fear being contaminated and sapped of their strength (*jerungdu*) by marriageable women.

Furthermore, male/female sexual relationships are generally antagonistic, and many marital histories reveal arguments, fights, jealousies, sorcery fears, some wifebeating, and even suicide attempts. Wives (much more than female kin) are stigmatized as inferior, as

---

*Confederacy here marks the same social unit as "parish" and "subtribe" in other New Guineast typologies.

polluting and depleting to men, because of their menstrual and vaginal fluids. Sexual intercourse is supposed to be spaced to avoid depletion and premature aging or death. (Couples may have sex every three to five days, or as infrequently as once every two or three weeks, depending on their ages, length of marriage, personalities, etc.) Prolonged postpartum taboos prohibit couples from engaging in coitus for up to two and a half years following the birth of a child. These generalizations indicate trends: but Sambia are polarized compared even with other Highlands groups (Langness 1967; reviewed in Herdt and Poole 1982).

How do Sambia understand the nature and functioning of the sexes? Male is the socially preferred and valued sex. Female is perceived by men as inferior, except reproductively. Infants are assigned either to the male, female, or hermaphroditic sex, and sex-typing of behaviors and gender traits is rigid from childhood on. Females, however, are believed to mature naturally, without external aids, for their bodies contain a menstrual blood organ (*tingu*) that hastens physical and mental development, puberty, and eventually menarche, the key sign a woman is ready for marriage and procreation. (Menarche occurs late in New Guinea and is now between ages sixteen and nineteen for Sambia.) At menarche a woman is initiated in secret ceremonies in the menstrual hut forbidden to all males (see Godelier 1986:74 ff.). Males, by contrast, do not naturally mature as fast or as competently. Womb blood and maternal care not only hold them back but endanger their health. Males cannot reach puberty or other secondary sex-traits (e.g., facial hair, mature penis) without semen; their bodies, their semen organs (*keriku-keriku*), do not internally produce semen, Sambia believe. Therefore men require inseminations and magical ritual treatments over many years to catch up with females and become strong, manly men (for details, see Herdt 1980, 1981, 1982a, 1982b).

Male development and masculinization after childhood are the responsibility of the men's secret cult and its initiation system. This cult is organized and perpetuated by the confederacy of hamlets. Boys are initiated at seven to ten years of age, when they are separated from their mothers, natal households, older sisters, and younger siblings. Thereafter, they must avoid all females for many years while living in the men's house. Avoidance taboos are rigidly enforced with shaming, beatings, and ultimately death (the last used to keep boys from revealing ritual secrets). Males undergo six initiations in all over the next ten or fifteen years. First initiation (*moku*) graduates are called *choowinuku;* second-stage initiation (*imbutu*) occurs between ages eleven and thirteen; and third-stage initiation (*ipmangwi*), bachelorhood puberty rites, is for youths fourteen to sixteen years of age. These initiations are all done in sequence on large groups of agemate boys, who are from neighboring hamlets, thus making them members of a regional cohort. Initiates also become members of a warriorhood, which as local units are responsible for defending their own hamlets. Fourth-stage initiation (*nuposha*) may occur any time afterward. It is a public marriage ceremony associated with secret male rites and sexual teachings for individual youths to whom a woman has been assigned for their marriage. But genital intercourse does not yet occur between the couple. Fifth-stage initiation (*taiketnyi*) occurs when a man's wife has her menarche. The bride then has her secret initiation in the menstrual hut. Afterward, the couple can engage in coitus. The final, sixth-stage initiation (*moondangu*), is held when a man's wife bears her first child. She then undergoes a final women's secret ceremony too. Two children bring full adult manhood (*aatmwunu*) for males and personhood for both sexes.

The men's secret cult is ideally organized as a social hierarchical system according to ritual rank. Initiates are lumped into ritual categories: *kuwatni'u* is a category term for first- and second-stage prepubescent initiates (who may also be referred to as *choowinuku* or *imbutnuku,* ritual-grade titles); *ipmangwi* (or *moongenyu,* "new bamboo") bachelors are third-stage initiates of higher adolescent status. Pubescent bachelors dominate prepubescent initiates; older youths and young married men dominate them; elders are seen as politically and spiritually superior to everyone (Herdt 1982b). War leaders and shamans lead in fights and healing ceremonies, respectively. There is nothing unique about this ritual system, for many similar forms can be found in Eastern Highlands (e.g., Read 1952), Papuan Gulf (e.g., Williams 1936), and Telefomin (e.g., Barth 1975) societies. What is special, and what links Sambia and their Anga neighbors with Papuan lowland systems (e.g., Keraki, Kiwai Island, Marind-anim), is the widescale institutionalization of age-structured homosexual activities (Herdt 1984).

Sambia practice secret homosexual fellatio, which is taught and instituted in first-stage initiation. Boys learn to ingest semen from older youths through oral sexual contacts. First- and second-stage initiates may only serve as fellators; they are forbidden to reverse erotic roles with older partners. Third-stage pubescent bachelors and older youths thus act as fellateds, inseminating prepubescent boys. All males pass through both erotic stages, being first fellators, then fellated: there are no exceptions since all Sambia males are initiated and pressured to engage in homoerotic insemination.

The symbolism of the first homosexual teaching in initiation is elaborate and rich; the meaning of fellatio is related to secret bamboo flutes, and ritual equations are made between flutes, penis, and mother's breast, as between semen and breast milk (see Herdt 1982a). Boys must drink semen to grow big and strong. At third-stage initiation, bachelors may experience personal difficulty in making the erotic switch in roles (see chapter 4). Thereafter, they may continue having oral sex with boys until they father children. Essentially, youths pass from an exclusively homosexual behavioral period to a briefer bisexual period, during which they may have both homosexual and heterosexual contacts in secret, and finally to exclusive heterosexual relationships. Social and sexual inadequacies in masculine personhood are failures to achieve these transitions (see chapter 9).

SUBJECT AND OBJECTS

For the Sambia, who ritualize male obligatory homoerotic practices on a broad scale, it may be said that two forms of sexual behavior characterize their culture and developmental experience. For males, first sexual contacts are secret, transitional, male/male oral sexual behaviors; for adult males and females, the parallel form is initial male/female oral (the woman is fellator) sex in marriage. Later, heterosexual genital contacts occur. To my knowledge, no other form of sexual behavior occurs, including masturbation to orgasm. The rules and norms surrounding these two sexual modes are, in certain respects, both similar and different; I shall describe them below. But in both cases, semen acquisition is an imperative organizing principle of people's social interaction and sexual behavior. Its magical power does things to people, changing and rearranging them, as if it were a generator. They, however, can do little to affect this semen principle: it does not reflect on but merely passes through them as an electrical current through a wire, winding its way into bodies as generator coils for temporary storage. Because it is instrumental to growth, reproduction, and regeneration, semen (and its substitutes) is needed to spark and mature human life. Humans are its objects.

This view may seem upside-down to us, yet it is essential as a rational outcome of the Sambia point of view. By thus beginning with its novelty, we may hope to achieve a better understanding of the relative relationship between heterosexuality and homosexuality, subjects about which we Westerners assume so much. I shall first examine cultural ideas about semen and then study how these ideas influence sociologic types of semen transactions between males and males and males and females. Taken together, these ideas and social transactions form a system of objects of the semen. Though these two perspectives are conceptually distinct, their complementarity suggests how normative goals affect individual social action and the developmental cycle of the group. When we view all of the valuations based on this predicate, we are led to a systemic view of the structuring (but not the experience) of sexual interactions and erotism in Sambia culture.

Semen predicates two different sorts of relationships: *direct sexual transactions* between semen donors and recipients, either on the individual or group level (in the latter sense, I am speaking normatively); and *indirect semen transactions* that affect changes in a third party via the semen recipient, who is believed to serve as a transformer of semen (e.g., father to mother to baby). The concept "transformer" compares with Meigs's (1976) use of "transmitter," in which she argues that a person's body may store or deliver fluids (e.g., blood or semen) or essences to someone else. "Transformer" differs because of another dimension needed, transformation, that is, changing semen into something else, as medieval alchemists were thought to change lead into gold. I shall later disentangle these levels of description and analysis.

Cultural Ideas of Semen Value

Sambia have five main cultural categories of semen valuation. These include erotic play, procreation, growth, strength, and spirituality, all of which are connected with sexual behavior. The metaphoric and analogic uses in rhetoric and imagination of these categories can be found in other domains too (see Herdt 1981). Here, though, I shall explore their social significance for insemination.[4] The study of these categories will involve us in understanding how people (and in some ways, nonhuman entities) are represented as potential semen donors or recipients, transformers, or transmitters of semen value, in Sambia culture. This section is concerned with the cultural level of these concepts.[5]

There are two analytic senses in which I shall use the term "value." First, the anthropologic sense of conventional valuations in a culture: attributed or assumed meanings shared and assigned to people, institutions, and substances. Thus we can speak of the cultural regard for semen and the social esteem with which it thus endows persons and relationships. (There is also a libidinal value, present in conscious and unconscious thought, which will not concern us.)[6] Second, there is the Marxist sense of the value of a commodity, such as gold, which "when impressed upon products, obtains fixity only by reason of their acting and reacting upon each other as quantities of value" (Marx 1977:248).[7] Hence, we can analyze semen as a scarce resource that can be consumed and produced, conserved, invested, or otherwise spent. Persons and relationships may be valuated (as a means to an end) in regard to their status as donors or recipients of the commodity semen.

There are several tacit assumptions underlying the relation between semen information and the categories examined below, and I begin with them. (1) Semen is the most precious human fluid. Because it is believed vital for procreation and growth and is in short supply, semen is more precious than even mother's milk, its closest cultural equivalent. But precious does not necessarily mean powerful: menstrual blood is the logical antithesis of semen; it is dangerous and, in some rituals, is equally as efficacious as semen (Herdt 1982b; cf. Faithorn 1975). (2) Sambia are by character prudish people. (May I refer to them as "prudish lechers"? cf. Meggitt 1964). Semen, other body fluids, and sexuality are sensitive subjects: the data and viewpoints described below took years to assimilate, even though the presentation makes them seem obvious. (3) Sexual pleasure is seen by Sambia only in relation to another person; that is, there is no equivalent to the western category "sex" (used in relation to masturbation, pornography, etc. as an indefinite noun, e.g., "sex is . . . good, bad, fun, boring," etc.). Sex, in the Sambia sense, is only spoken of as: *duvuno* (pushing or penetrating into) a boy's mouth or a woman's vagina; or as the slackening of one's erect penis (lit., *lakelu mulu*, "penis fight") via "his bamboo orifice" (metaphor for boy's mouth) or "her thing down below" (euphemism for vagina). Again, the verb *duvuno* is not used for masturbation and only rarely for wet dreams in which the dream images concern copulating with persons (e.g., interpreted as spirits).[8] (4) When men refer to erotic desire (e.g., "I swallow my saliva [thinking about sex] with him/her") they tend to refer to their sexual outlets as if their alter's orifice (mouth or vagina) were fetishized objects like a commodity: "My penis is hungry" (i.e., they use "food" as a metaphor for their sexual needs). (5) All sexual intercourse may be defined as work (*wumdu*), play (*chemonyi*), or both. For example: it is *wumdu* to produce a baby by copulating with a woman many times; but it is *chemonyi* to copulate promiscuously with a boy once or twice knowing he will not procreate. Insemination is also an action that mediates (e.g., like ritual, *pweiyu*) between work and play, sacred and profane. Let us examine each category in turn.

EROTIC PLAY. When Sambia use *chemonyi* (play) as a noun in relation to sexual intercourse, they normatively refer to sexual release as erotic pleasure.* Semen is expended and orgasm (*imbimboogu*) achieved. I begin with this category not because it is most crucial—Sambia themselves would rank procreation first (Herdt 1981)—but because it is essential for understanding semen valuations and also because anthropologists often ignore erotic motivation as a native category.

The most general cultural attributes of erotic play may be sketched as follows. First, the factor of the sex of one's partner: erotic play symbolically typifies male/male more than male/female erotic contacts. Male/male sexual contacts are culturally defined as behaviorally promiscuous. Male/female contacts, normative only in marriage, are viewed (unless adulterous) as steady transactions aimed toward procreation. Erotic play is of course an aspect of all male/female contacts, but it is not their most important one. *Exclusive* sexual access to a person seems inversely related to erotic play: a man's wife, as his sexual property, as Sambia see it, is less exciting than a boy or woman taken at first (i.e., as a virgin), or only once, on the sly. Age is a contributing factor here: sexual partners are perceived as having more "heat" and being more exciting the younger they are. A second factor is reciprocity: the more asymmetrical the sexual partners (youth/boy), the more erotic play seems to culturally define their contact. (By contrast, I have argued elsewhere that the husband/wife dyad is the most symmetrical relationship in Sambia culture; see Herdt 1982b.) Third, sexual constancy, that is, greater frequency of sexual contacts, generally transforms sexual contacts from erotic play into something else. Husband/wife contacts are the most constant in Sambia sexual life.

Erotic play may be defined also according to the social purpose of insemination. Erotic pleasure is attached to male/male and male/

---

*There is no marked category for erotic play as such: it is signified in ideology and social intercourse by *chemonyi*, "orgasm," and several conditions of sexual excitement (e.g., erection). "Sexual" has a wide range of connotations in English; *erotic*, however, refers specifically to that which stimulates sexual desire, psychophysiologic arousal, so I prefer "erotic" in this usage.

female sexual contacts and to both oral and vaginal intercourse.* But only heterosexual genital contacts result in procreation; all other sexual contacts fulfill other quasi-reproductive functions (e.g., growth of spouse) or are for erotic play. Since homosexual fellatio cannot result in reproduction (marriage consummation), it becomes a demonstration of a fellated's psychosocial maturity, that is, of his power to masculinize a boy. But this valuation is significant only for donors: the boy-recipients value semen for their own growth. What donors value also is the fellator's mouth as a sexual outlet: the social purpose is sexual release.

Erotic play may be defined, lastly, according to the flow of a scarce commodity. Semen is viewed as a very scarce resource by Sambia, for, in reproduction, it is believed instrumental from conception to adulthood. It takes many inseminations to procreate: large expenditures of time, energy, semen. From this viewpoint, all male/female contacts may be construed as benefiting procreation (as we shall see next). Homoerotic play unevenly fits this paradigm. It is, after all, play, not work: procreative work is defined as producing babies. So how do they benefit the donor? Essentially, homoerotic play is culturally defined as an unequal exchange of commodities: recipients acquire semen, donors get sexual services. This exchange is unequal because (as Sambia see it) a man's semen is being depleted, but he gets only erotic pleasure in return ("which is insubstantial"). Homoerotic activity thus creates a dilemma for bachelors, which is perhaps why some engage in it less frequently as they approach marriage. Homoerotic play is, however, less depleting than heterosexual intercourse (work) which is, in part, why bachelors usually do not replenish the semen lost during their early homosexual activities.

PROCREATION. Procreation is defined as genital-to-genital heterosexual contacts that lead to the birth of offspring. Sambia regard vaginal intercourse as primarily focused on the production of babies. Oral insemination prepares a wife's body for making babies by strengthening her as well as by precipitating her menarche (if she has not already attained it). Fellatio also prepares her for lactation by semen being transformed into breast milk. Oral sexual contacts are not believed to make babies in anyone; only vaginal intercourse does that.

---

*All sexual contacts are symbolically defined by the norm of penetration and ejaculation into an insertee's mouth (initiate or woman) or vagina, insemination resulting from (the belief that) the full seminal emission ingested/absorbed by the recipient's body (mouth or vagina as entrance).

All heterosexual genital intercourse contributes directly to procreation in one's marriage, and *all* sexual contacts may be viewed as contributing directly to the recipients' procreative competence (wife or boy-fellator) or reproduction (wife).*

Procreation is jurally defined as resulting from genital-to-genital sexual contacts between formally married husband and wife. Since heterosexual contact is not morally or jurally allowed outside of marriage, privilege of sexual access to a woman's body is restricted by marriage; exclusive sexual rights belong to her husband. Likewise, exclusive access to a husband's body and semen, after birth of their first child, is his wife's right (which view is a key argument women use to resist polygyny). Traditionally, only infant betrothal and bride-service marriage (which was rare) required the transfer of goods or services to the donors bestowing a wife. Infant betrothal, though, required meat and small food prestations only, whereas bride-service required more wealth, in addition to the bridegroom's years-long work for his prospective affines. Sister exchange requires no exchange other than that of the women. Since infant betrothal is preferred and sister exchange marriages far outnumber those of bride-service, marriage transactions are not much related to bride-wealth in its usual anthropologic sense (cf. Collier and Rosaldo 1981).

Genital-to-genital intercourse creates a fetus by successively injecting semen into a woman's womb. After initial oral sexual contacts, a woman's body is viewed as ready to procreate. One instance of vaginal intercourse does not a fetus make: Sambia have no notion of conception in our western scientific sense. The womb is the container and transformer of semen. It changes semen into fetal tissue: primarily bone and skin but also muscle and internal organs. The semen coagulates inside the birth sac; this "biologic" process is central to fetal development, and its imagery is important in social thought (Herdt 1981:167–172 ff.). Womb and umbilical blood also become circulatory blood in the fetus; they do not produce any other parts of the child, which result only from semen. Social ideology thus defines procreation as productive work (not erotic play) in two senses: it is hard work to feed enough semen into a woman's womb to create a fetus; and it is hard work for the woman's body to change this semen into a fetus, sapping her own blood and carrying the child in her body for so long.

Blood and semen also differentially contribute to the sex of the offspring and his or her gender differentiation. First, both parents can

---

*Oral heterosexual contacts indirectly help procreation; see below under section on "growth."

magically influence the fetus's sex by ingesting various plants. They do this both because Sambia ideally prefer a boy as the firstborn and because they want to make the infant more attractive. Second, it takes more semen to create a girl than a boy. Two other beliefs explain why, and they pertain to the procreative/economic productive capacities of males versus females (i.e., in social reproduction). The most important is that females do more hard work (i.e., garden work) all the time; therefore, the female fetus pulls more semen from the mother to make itself. (A magical elaboration of this idea is that since females think about garden work constantly, their fetal thought anticipates and drains more semen strength in preparation.) The other belief is that a female fetus has a *tingu* (menstrual-blood organ), which makes the mother's vagina hot and therefore drains off more semen from the father during sexual contacts that create the fetus. During womb life, the sexes receive blood in differential amounts too. Essentially, girls have some of their mother's menstrual blood transmitted to their own menstrual-blood organs *in utero*. Later, during postnatal growth, this blood stimulates girls' psychobiologic feminization (sexual and gender differentiation). Boys, by contrast, have no blood transmitted to their inactive *tingus*. Nor do they receive any of their father's semen for use in their own semen organs: father's semen in both sexes merely creates fetal tissue. (Mystical aspects of these fetal processes are described below.)

Marriage is fully consummated after the birth of a child. Procreation results in final but distinct initiation ceremonies for the husband-father and wife-mother alike. The new father and his clan bestow a meat prestation on the wife's cognatic kin, especially patrilateral female kin, and her ritual sponsor, in public village ceremonies. Because procreation defines full adulthood for men and women, childless adults are not perceived as full persons. Nonetheless, all childlessness in marriage is attributed to barrenness in the woman or contraceptive sorcery by other men (usually thought to be envious fellow villagers who wanted the woman for themselves). Sambia men dogmatically deny the possibility of sterility in a husband (see also Read 1955); indeed, such is never discussed in social discourse, and the only category for sterility is "barren woman" (*kwoliku*). Childlessness is thus an acceptable reason for taking a second wife but not for divorce. Once a marriage is consummated, it is contracted for life; a woman is rarely taken back by the donor; when warfare occurs, a woman's ties with her natal group (i.e., enemies) are severed; divorce is thus extremely rare and usually instigated by a husband over his wife's perceived adultery; their children become jural members of the father's clan; and so only death breaks the marital bond.

GROWTH. Sambia believe that biologic growth in humans results from ingesting semen and equivalent substances (mother's milk, pandanus nuts). Sexual intercourse for growth is described as: *pinu pungooglumonjapi* ("pushing" to "grow" him/her, where *pinu* is an alternate verbal form of *duvuno*). This idiomatic form may be applied to both male/male and male/female sexual contacts.

The value of semen for human growth comes in successive stages, which differ according to the mode of semen transmission and one's sex. Initial growth for every fetus occurs through semen accumulations in the mother's womb. Postnatal growth in babies results mainly from breast-feeding. A woman's body is again treated as a biologic transformer of semen in this regard: a man's inseminations (especially oral) amass in and are transformed by his wife's breasts into mother's milk (*nu-tokeno*, breast food). After weaning, growth is aided by eating pandanus nuts, which are seasonal but are treated as nearly equal nourishment to that of mother's milk. (The productive source of this nut food is one's father's trees and his hard work in tending and scaling to procure the nuts.) Meat fed to children also contributes smaller increments to growth. Following weaning, though, girls continue to grow without further aids, whereas boys falter, staying weak and puny.

Male growth after weaning comes mostly from homosexual inseminations following initiation. This semen-nourishment form is male *monjapi'u,** which men liken to breast-feeding (Herdt 1981: 234–236). Oral sexual contacts feed semen into a boy's body, distributing semen to his maturing skin, bones, skull and producing changes toward masculinization (eventuating in puberty). The bulk of ingested semen goes to the boy's semen organ, where it accumulates as a pool. This pool is drawn on after puberty for two purposes: it produces pubescent secondary sex-traits, especially muscle, body hair, and a mature penis; and it provides semen for later sexual contacts. (The first sign of surplus semen in the body comes from wet dreams.)

Girls require and are permitted no inseminations until marriage. Postmarital oral sexual contacts in cases of marriage before menarche provide a young wife's body with semen to stimulate the final

---

*Shortened by men from *pinu pungooglumonjapi*.

changes necessary for childbearing. Men also argue, as noted above, that women need semen to create breast milk. (Some women dispute these views and argue that a woman's body naturally creates milk; however, other women disagree).

In sum, semen creates biologic growth directly in initiates and wives through sexual contact, primarily fellatio, whereas it creates growth indirectly in fetus and newborn through being transformed by a woman's body into fetal tissue and milk. For spouses, then, growth and procreation are concepts that refer to different aspects of the same sexual contacts. For the offspring, as third-party semen recipient, growth is vital after birth, and long postpartum taboos prohibit marital sexual intercourse for fear the infant will be harmed (be stunted or ugly, an outcome that would shame the parents, especially the father, who would be viewed as lacking sexual restraint). In homoerotic activity, men offer boys the normative goal that semen "grows" them. But from the donor's standpoint, though initiates' growth does provide vicarious long-term confirmation of the fellated's manhood, a fellator's growth is not of direct importance to a bachelor's personhood. Rather, homoerotic play takes precedence as the fellated's motive; the boy's growth is a latent social function of the bachelor's behavior (and is, I think, often a rationalization on the men's part).

STRENGTH. Strength (*jerungdu*) is a key concept in Sambia culture; we shall here examine only its implications for semen transmission and thereby human maturation (Herdt 1987c).

Strength is absolutely derived from semen and its equivalents: mother's milk and pandanus nuts. But more than those latter substances, semen masculinizes a male's body; there is no substitute for it. Unlike procreation or growth valuations, strength can be obtained directly only through semen. In Sambia thought, there is a tendency to play down strength and stress growth as characteristic of the breastfeeding relationship. Suckling milk makes a baby grow, but it is much less associated with strengthening it. Semen in the womb forms the skeletal fetus; nursing helps create the baby's teeth, the hardening of its skin and skull. But milk is more for growth. The strong results of milk, Sambia believe, are transformations of semen: mother ingests semen, which her breasts convert into milk. The strong part of milk is also more crucial for male infants, but it alone will not masculinize them. Thus, strength is not intrinsically produced but is rather derived from the mother/infant relationship, itself a product of marriage. In male subjectivity, however, strength is a transactional product that makes use of the father's secret sexual acquisition of semen from other men, which he feeds to his wife, whose body, in turn, has a natural capacity to store the fluid and turn it into breast food that strengthens and matures the infant.

As with growth, a father can indirectly add small amounts of strength over the years following weaning by providing meat and pandanus nuts to children. Cassowary meat, too, which may be eaten only by males, has fat (*moo-nugu*) that sometimes is treated as a second-rate semen equivalent (Herdt 1981: 110). (Other kinds of fat, e.g., from pigs or eels, are never likened to semen.) But these are small increments.

If one follows the semen cycle, we see a chain of links in which men strengthen people: husband strengthens wife through initial fellatio; father strengthens baby through mother's milk; bachelor strengthens initiate through fellatio. Symbolically, homosexual fellatio provides the key ritualized strengthening of boys' postpartum bodies. As I have emphasized elsewhere (Herdt 1981, 1982a), male insemination is chiefly seen as making a boy grow, the perceived outcome of which is strength. Culturally, the act of feeding/inseminating is equivalent to the verbal category *monjapi'u*, male nursing, the social/perceptual outcome of which is the state of being *jerungdu*, as seen in both its physical and psychosocial manifestations: large size, attractiveness, valor, forceful speech, sexual potency, and many social achievements, including progeny.

There is another secret source of strength that is important in male thought and that concerns the nonhuman sources for replenishing semen expended in sexual intercourse. Analytically, this semen valuation might be treated as separate from the "strength" concept because of its ontogenetic status in the male life cycle (adults give semen away and then must replace it to stay strong). But Sambia do not think of the matter in this way, for this replenishment is seen simply as a further extension of strength-building. Yet, since this replenishment practice is learned later in ritual life and comes from trees, not men, we shall here examine it as an auxiliary strengthening process.

In semen transactions, one person's loss is another's gain: semen, which embodies strength, depletes the donor, whose strength therefore diminishes. Fear of semen depletion is an important theme in male ritual discourse and ideology. (It is registered, too, in individual gender aberrations [Herdt 1980]). Concern with too frequent semen loss inhibits initial homosexual contacts, bachelors being cautioned to go easy. (Here, again, fellateds and fellators are at odds.) Yet bachelors' fears are not great; and the early use of ritual mechanisms for semen replenishment in fellateds is played down. Among married men, the situation is different. A key pragmatic focus of fifth- and sixth-stage initiation ceremonies is teaching about secret ingestion of white milk-sap from trees, which is believed to replace semen lost to women. (Pandanus nuts are another semen replacement, though of less importance because they are not always available.) This milk-sap comes from several forest trees and vines, and the sap is referred to as *iaamoonaalyu*, "tree mother's milk."

Trees are, in general, regarded as if they and their products were female, for example, as with pandanus trees. Myth also genderizes them this way (Herdt 1981). There seems little doubt that the imagery and symbolization of the adult man's semen replenishment is not, then, symbolic insemination but rather that of symbolic breast-feeding. This interpretation is confirmed by men's drinking sap from long aerial roots of pandanus nut trees: the trees are ritually referred to as "females," and the roots are likened to woman's breasts. We see, therefore, that semen comes at first from homosexual fellatio, later to be replaced by milk-sap (and, to a lesser extent, by pandanus nuts and cassowary fat); and semen, in turn, is transformed into milk and fetal tissue by women. At bottom, male ideology seems to postulate that these forest trees create *new* semen.

SPIRITUALITY. The final category of semen valuations I shall refer to as spirituality, though it is not a marked category in Sambia culture or language. Spirituality is, in our terms, an animistic composite of both natural and supernatural elements. These elements include most noticeably spirit familiars (*numelyu*) of various sorts, believed to be *transmitted* (not transformed) through semen for males (and through blood for females). The reproduction of spiritual elements in individuals and groups is entirely a social outcome of sexual intercourse over which individuals have little control.

Before describing spirit familiars, two other matters deserve mention. The first is the concept of soul (*koogu*), a spiritual aspect of personhood that is related to sexuality and parenting. There is no clearly formulated theory of the soul's origin in individual development. Some men attribute it only to the father's semen. Others say it is a combination of semen and material in the mother's womb (they do not specify which parts of semen and/or blood). Though the womb is important, some people attribute the birth of a child's soul not to fetal life but to postnatal socialization. Men normatively relate the father's semen to the child's soul in both sexes, especially boys. This ambiguity is no doubt an expression of all persons' normative blood ties to mother and matrilateral kin. Yet, since the soul survives death and becomes a ghost, forest spirit (big men), or hamlet spirit (prominent women) haunting its clan's territory, its patrilineal origin and after-life influence seem clear in sociopolitical organization. The skull and bones of the deceased also become powerful weapons in sorcery and are most efficacious when used by biologic kinsmen, sons especially. In both cases—souls and bones—spiritual essences of semen are thought to survive death. The other concept is "thought" or *koontu*, which I gloss as personhood. "Thought" is the totality of one's ex-perience, beliefs, and knowledge. Personhood is mainly a product of social training; its relation to body substance and biologic inheri-tance is less certain. Socialization is its chief source, however, and this means that both mother and father influence personhood.

Without question the most significant semen valuation for spirit-uality is the child's inheritance of spirit familiars. Transmission of familiars is ideologically clear and sex-linked. Boys inherit only their father's familiars via his semen. Girls inherit their mother's familiars through her blood. (Mother's milk, a semen derivative, is ignored in this domain.) Genealogic inheritance of clan familiars (i.e., totems) among males seems to derive from the semen that creates a son's body tissue. Later, males acquire other familiars attracted to them through ritual ceremonies: the nature of this attraction again implies that father's semen is instrumental. Shamanic familiars, transmitted through semen from father to son in the mother's womb, is a clear case of necessary patrilineal inheritance required for legitimate per-formance of the shamanic role (Herdt 1977), though some women shamans claim inheritance of father's familiars. Other familiars, both personal and clan-related, ensure longevity, spiritual protection, or strength. Male ideology generally denies women such blessings from their natal clan familiars. Men may have their familiars stolen un-wittingly by male children, which leads to sickness or premature death. Homosexual inseminations do not transmit familiars to semen recip-ients (cf. Schieffelin 1976, 1977). Finally, men's ingestion of milk-sap from trees is consistent with the perpetuation of their clan familiars (though this is not fully conscious in Sambia thought).

Semen Value in Social Transactions

Who may and should have sexual intercourse with what categories of persons in Sambia society? What are the principles of these social transactions? In this section I examine social action in relation to the cultural ideas of semen valuation already described. The sociology of semen transactions involves two viewpoints. First, there are direct semen transactions between persons resulting from sexual intercourse. Second, there are indirect semen transactions with a third party believed to occur by transforming semen into something else by a second party; whether the source of semen is human or nonhuman (i.e., trees), though the semen transformers are always humans. A subcategory of indirect inseminations may be seen as delayed exchanges between social groups, semen being returned to donor groups via former recipients in the subsequent generation. I shall study each of these types in turn.

DIRECT SEMEN TRANSACTIONS. All sexual contacts are restricted by exogamous taboos and social norms. Sexual contacts are permissible only between unrelated people; that is, those related through common cognatic links, especially agnates, are forbidden sexual partners. Marriage should be arranged between different clans, preferably of different villages. Statistically, though, up to fifty percent of all marriages are contracted within certain hamlets; father's sister's daughter marriage is normatively permitted in delayed-exchange marriage contracts; and mother's brother's daughter marriage, though frowned on, occurs rarely, when no alternate wife can be found (Herdt 1981). Homosexual contacts are likewise prohibited between all clansmen, matrilateral kin, age-mates, and with ritual sponsors. (Homosexual infractions occur, however, as between matrilateral cross-cousins or distant kin not normally encountered, though these are unusual.) Male initiates' ritual sponsors are called "mother's brother," a social title, since only some sponsors are actual or classificatory mother's brother. Nonetheless a boy's sponsor becomes, in effect, a pseudokinsman who combines both maternal and paternal attributes, making it very wrong for any sexual contact to occur between them. In general, all sexual contacts are highly regulated and tend to occur with people of other hamlets (who are potential or real enemies), so sexual contacts distinguish kin from nonkin and friendly from hostile persons.

In direct sexual transactions, all the above cultural ideas of semen value come into play, but the domain of erotic play is especially important. Erotic play is a social motive and goal that applies mainly to adult men. Their motive for erotic play is orgasm. Boy-fellators never have orgasms in homoerotic play. And men deny, in general, that women experience orgasm, though they believe women are lascivious and that some enjoy sexual play.

Men's enjoyment of erotic play changes through the life cycle. Some older boy-fellators do experience vicarious erotic pleasure from homosexual fellatio, as indicated by their reports (near puberty) of their own erections while fellating a bachelor, or by certain feelings or body sensations during fellation. Bachelors (fellateds) engage in homoerotic play to (in local idiom) "straighten their penises," that is, to reduce sexual tension/frustration, or to "feel *ilaiyu*" (here meaning pleasure) from orgasm. Men get erotic pleasure from copulating with their wives, first through fellatio, and then in genital-to-genital intercourse, which most men favor over fellatio. To repeat: male/female oral sexual contacts, like those with boys, are regarded more as erotic play.

Male social ideology defines both homoerotic and heteroerotic play as transactions in which the older male is *always* the inseminator. No role reversals are ever situationally permitted. The older male is viewed as the socially active party who should control the behavior interchanges that lead to the insemination. A man's control over sexual contacts is established by the social norms regulating the behavioral conditions of sexual intercourse. Men are physically bigger than boys and most women. During intercourse the man either stands over his fellator (who kneels) or lies on top of his wife (in the missionary position), methods that allow a man instant freedom to withdraw from body contact at will. Men are also usually years older than their insertees, either boys or women (even though, curiously, men regard younger wives as of like age and maturity; see Herdt 1981:177, 181). Again, these interactions are defined as asymmetric: women and boys get semen, men get erotic pleasure. Most men are (consciously) uninterested in the erotic arousal of either boys or women, so direct sexual transactions emphasize the sexual excitement of the inserter.

In spite of the men's view, the concept "erotic play" admits of some social reciprocity between all sexual partners. Men recognize that women have erotic interests; for instance, sexually experienced women are rhetorically described as lascivious harlots consumed by insatiable erotic appetites (Herdt 1981:187). Perhaps this dogma is the men's response to knowing that women favor certain men over others as mates. Men also know that boys joke about fellatio among themselves and that initiates favor some bachelors over others in regard to the amount and taste of their semen.[9] Bachelors likewise favor certain boys over others: those who are more attractive to them are either more or less sexually aggressive and/or willing to perform fellatio. These reciprocal aspects thus underscore the frame of play, and they are not found in notions of sex for procreation, growth, strength, or spirituality, all of which are passive outcomes of insemination.

Since semen is highly valued as a means to valuable social ends—personal strength, marriage, offspring, personhood—it should be conserved and wisely spent. Men assume that women and boys *desire their semen* for those social ends; no other motive is searched for in understanding why insertees engage in sexual intercourse. (*We* know the situation is more complex: for instance, boys must at first be coerced into fellatio; but men also know this.) The seeming personal conflict on men's part, at least in homoerotic contacts, is that *they get only sexual release in return for their semen.* They recognize this in idioms that depict the penis as having a mind of its own: for example, "that no good man down there [penis] gets up and we follow its nose" (euphemism for glans penis). Meaning: men inseminate from sexual impulse, almost against their will. Here, then, we may see a perceived conflict between private impulses and rational norms.

This conflict is felt in two other ways. First, women are prized as sexual outlets more than boys. Women are *owned:* this ownership is a contributing dynamic to the sexual excitement of Sambia men. Male/female relationships are, in general, filled with more power than are male/male contacts, for heterosexuality is more highly regulated. Sexually, women are also more powerful, for they can contaminate as well as deplete; and women deplete semen more than do boys. Moreover, sexual impulses leading to adultery are a tremendous social problem in Sambia society (see below). Second, when orgasm occurs it is treated as being beyond conscious control. Wet dreams are the best example.[10] For women, breast-feeding may also apply: some women report that they experience *imbimboogu*, which they liken to orgasm, when feeding, though it is not clear yet what this social labelling of their experience means (see chapter 6). All these points support the conclusion that individual sexual impulses are stronger than the need for semen constraint in heterosexual versus homosexual contacts. They also suggest that Sambia men are later motivated more toward heterosexual relationships.

Underlying this conflict is the fact that sex for erotic play is the only sexual mode that produces no social advantage to the semen donor. Because all ejaculation is debilitating and semen is a male's most valuable resource, all sexual contacts are viewed as a "careful metering of semen" (Gell 1975:252). Seen this way, erotic play represents what Gell (1975) refers to as a "nemesis of reproductivity": it makes no sense in the scheme of things, even though it is personally pleasurable. All other categories of direct sexual transactions may be defined as work, not play, for this reason: like other forms of work (e.g., gardening), sex for procreation, growth, and so forth produces social products. One's semen is spent to reproduce heirs and perpetuate one's clan. With this view in mind I will now contrast other cultural ideas pertaining to heterosexual and homosexual contacts.

The idea of procreation applies only to male/female sexual contacts. In native theory all heterosexual contacts, oral or vaginal, contribute to a woman's reproductive competence. In practice, however, only early marital contacts are treated this way: oral sex is infrequent after a woman bears children. My impression is that both men and women in later years prefer genital-to-genital contact (and I think most women always prefer vaginal sex). Though homosexual transactions are not procreative (but cf. individual boys' fears of becoming pregnant [Herdt 1981] and similar beliefs about male pregnancy elsewhere [Meigs 1976; Williams 1936]), semen in boys does assist in their reaching reproductive competence as adults.

The concepts of growth and strength are applied to both homosexual and heterosexual transactions. In theory, boy-fellators as semen recipients use sexual contact first to grow and then to get strong. Until third-stage initiation this norm holds; youths are thereafter accorded biologic maturity and may no longer serve as insertees. (By definition, a Sambia man who sought semen from another male would be terribly stigmatized as unmanly; and to do so with a boy—pederastic fellatio—would be morally unconscionable; see chapter 9.) Growth and strength apply differentially to women as semen recipients. Essentially, all heterosexual fellatio makes a woman grow and strengthens her until she is a mother. Later oral sex does not make a woman grow, for she is viewed as biologically mature. It does replenish her strength, however; a sort of perpetual fountain-of-youth men must give up after bachelorhood. Indeed, men complain that women are healthier and outlive them because of this ready source of orally ingested strength. (In this sense, a wife is like a boy-fellator.) Vaginal sex is generally believed to contribute neither growth nor strength to a woman: instead, indirectly, a man's semen creates and strengthens fetus and infant.

Finally, the concept of spirituality applies unequally to direct sexual transactions. No transmission of spirit familiars occurs between males and females. None is imparted to one's wife: she is simply *one* source of the transmission of soul and familiars to one's offspring. Again, men believe that only sons inherit father's familiars (either indirectly, through semen via mother, or directly, through cult ceremonies that call forth one's father's familiars after his death). A daughter's familiars come only from her mother; but her soul is linked (the notion is vague) to her father and his clan territory, though not irrevocably.[11] Moreover, there is absolutely no sense that a boy-fellator acquires his familiars from any bachelor-fellated; but the idea is neither here nor there, since Sambia never consider the possibility.[12] Conceptually, though, we should underline that their folk model of spiritual transmission keeps familiars discreetly in clans and firmly embedded in the genitor's procreative role. Here we see a firm separation between spirituality and sexuality, on the levels both of ideology and social action. The division between spiritual and material reproduction in marriage is especially notable (cf. Tuzin 1982).

There is one other notion, which we may define as spiritual, that involves direct homosexual transactions. *Kwolaalyuwaku*:* a multivalent concept referring to masculine decorations and ritual paraphernalia (as a category term), which is also a ritual secret pseudonym for semen. (It is also close to *kweiaalyu-waku*, which literally means "sun's white grease," an alternate for cassowary fat [*kaiouwugu moo-nugu*]). The semantic referent of the semen aspect is esoteric, yet it clearly signifies a collective semen pool. This pool is perceived as the semen contained in the bodies of all men living within neighboring hamlets: it therefore reflects the ritual cult and the confederacy. The idea is that boys have access to this pool, which they can tap into through homosexual insemination, strengthening themselves. Symbolically, then, *kwolaalyuwaku* is a metaphor for the men's collective cult.

But on the individual level, the concept is bidirectional. I was long skeptical of men's statements,that it *strengthened themselves* to inseminate many boys. How could this be? Men argue that just as a boy draws strength from numerous men, who deposit their semen in his reserve for future use, so men are kept strong by having their semen safely contained in many boys, who are likened to a sort of magical string of semen depositories for one's substance, spread throughout society. Should a man or any of his semen recipients get sick, other recipients remain strong and healthy. And since recipients harbor parts of one's semen (strength) inside them, so, too, one is kept healthy (in sympathetic-contagious magical thought). A woman lacks this protection: she is not a cult initiate, and her semen comes from only one man, her husband. Nor is a man likewise protected by inseminating women or creating children: the concept is not extended beyond homosexual contacts. Thus, semen not only bestows but maintains

---

Kwol marks male; *aalyu*, water; *waku*, a type of strong betel nut and a cover term for certain decorations. Sometimes the term is shortened to the secret name, *kweiwaku*, which men use explicitly to refer to "the semen of all men."

strength, the only evidence known to me that directly explains why homosexual insemination is felt to be less depleting than that of heterosexuality. In this ritual sense, homosexual practices are placed within a spiritual framework and are opposed to heterosexuality and marriage.

All the above sexual contacts concern normatively appropriate semen transactions between donors and recipients. *Illicit* heterosexual semen transactions (adultery) reveal the social boundary of ideas about exclusive jural claims over a man's semen. All adultery is severely condemned; a man may use violence against a wife suspected of it. Therefore, it is hidden until discovered, when the spouses fight. If a husband is accused of adultery or of wanting to take a second wife, the fight is called *kweikoonmulu*, literally "semen fight." Semen fights entail dreadful cursing and brawls. This adultery can be seen as "stealing another woman's semen," though it involves much more, of course. Accusations of a wife's adultery (which is rarer, for Sambia treat adulterous women harshly) also concern semen in two ways: fears that a husband's penis has been contaminated by intercourse with his wife's vagina after sex with another man (thought to bring him sickness); and questions about the wife's lover's semen contributions to a future child. In sum, adultery reveals that marriage bestows the right of exclusive spousal control over semen and insemination exchange as scarce resources.

What are the social effects of these direct sexual transactions on group relationship? Let us examine the most general latent and manifest functions of sexual contacts in the same generation. First, semen flow mirrors marriage transactions between groups. Semen may only be normatively transacted between persons of groups who can intermarry, that is, homosexual contact is forbidden with matrilineal kin and clansmen. The same clan that donates a wife thus has clansmen who are appropriate homosexual partners (cf. Kelly 1976). Affines of the same generation (e.g., brothers-in-law) are especially appropriate homosexual contacts. The paradigm of this affinal homoerotic bond would be a young man who marries a younger woman and who can inseminate her younger initiate brother, either consanguineal or classificatory wife's brother (cf. Serpenti 1984 and Sørum 1984). This man inseminates his wife to make her grow and strengthen her, and to procreate, and may (along with his fellow clansmen) inseminate her younger brother for erotic play, the effect of which is to help a boy grow and to strengthen him. These sexual transactions would define a man and his clan as semen donors, while his wife and brother-in-law would be recipients. Yet ego's clan is also a wife recipient from his younger homosexual partner's donor clan. This set of social transactions is common in Sambia life.

Second, marital/sexual bonds tend to create closer political ties between unrelated groups. Sambia generally engage in marriage and homosexual contacts with propinquitous groups in the same confederacy. One does not receive or give semen to intertribal enemies. Affinal ties, in particular, create closer political affiliations for mutual defense between and within hamlets. Affinal ties also establish marriage contractual obligations and sentimental bonds that persist in the next generation, influencing alignments among hamlets.

Third, semen metaphorically defines political power: inseminators are more powerful than recipients in virtually every sense. All male persons eventually serve as both direct semen donors and as recipients. All females are always direct recipients or indirect donors—to their offspring—whereas males constitute a category of both direct givers and takers. And their sexual status, of course, flip-flops during the male life cycle. Symbolically, I think, Sambia define the administration of semen as a masculine act, whereas the taking in of semen is a feminine act. One of the manifest functions of the secrecy of homosexual fellatio is to hide from women the shame men feel at having earlier performed in this feminine way (Herdt 1981: ch. 8). A latent function of homosexual secrecy is to rationalize and disguise men's use of boys as a sexual outlet. By the same token, the ritual secret of homosexual growth and strength unites all males as a category against all females. This social link, which also mystifies the nature of male/female relationships, politically reinforces male power and thereby perpetuates the men's ritual cult (Herdt 1982b).

INDIRECT SEMEN TRANSACTIONS. This mode of social transaction is based on the symbolic principle that semen is transmitted to someone whose body transforms it into something else useful to a third party. The paradigm is the nuclear family triad: father→mother→child. The alternative form of indirect insemination views men as replenishing their semen from tree sap, which their bodies turn into semen: tree→man→semen recipient. Having already described direct sexual contacts we can easily outline these semen transformations.

We have seen that sexual intercourse between spouses involves all the cultural meanings of semen value except spirituality. Now when we examine the effects of her husband's semen on her prospective infant, the woman's role as transformer is clarified at two developmental points. First, to repeat, her orally ingested semen is transformed into breast milk. This milk is stored for the infant's nourishment after birth. Subsequent semen from vaginal intercourse is stored and transformed in the woman, converted by her womb into fetal tissue, as we saw. Both the intrauterine formation of the child, as well as its postnatal breast-feeding, are indirect products of the father's semen.

In this type of indirect transaction there is a subtle application of cultural beliefs to action. Erotic play occurs between the spouses, leading to procreation; but the concept is not extended to the transformative outcome, since the father never has sexual intercourse with his offspring. Indeed the paradigm of sex as work suggests that woman, as wife/mother, is *the means of production* men need to effect children's adult reproductive competence. Semen is indispensable for reproduction, yet so is a woman's body (breasts and womb). Moreover, no matter how much the men attempt to claim procreation as solely of their production, a wife is vital for social reproduction: she not only gives birth but nourishes and cares for heirs, transforming semen into the strength of clans. She also transmits her husband's spirit familiars to sons and her own to daughters. Both parents contribute to the child's personhood or thought, but men believe only they produce its soul. Following weaning, a girl is believed to mature on her own, but a boy needs more semen for growth and strength. Thus, a boy indirectly taps the semen pool of his father through homosexual contacts with other men who substitute, in his father's place, as ritual semen donors, motivated out of erotic play. The sexual cycle is completed when this son becomes an inseminator, and his sister is traded for his wife, sister and brother having reached sexual maturity.

The other form of indirect transaction consists in men ingesting the white tree-saps. It may seem odd, here, to juxtapose this secret ritual practice with reproduction. But Sambia male ideology treats tree-sap ingestion as a part of the whole adult cycle of reproduction; and, in my experience, men directly associate tree-sap drinking as normal and regular links in a chain of psychosexual activities that are as much a part of everyday life as their own erotism. Drinking tree-sap is not actually taught until a man's last initiation, when he is a new father. Thereafter, men regularly ingest it but always in abundance after sexual intercourse with their wives. Men are thus preserving their biologic maleness (semen) and restoring their strength. Neither erotic play, growth, nor procreation as cultural ideas are applied to contacts with trees. Drinking tree sap simply regenerates semen and preserves health against depletion. So this ritual practice may be considered a defensive tactic—and the more so because it is secret—yet it is more than that.

Drinking tree-sap also has a latent creative function: creating *new* semen that flows into the societal pool of semen. Sambia men do *not* view it this way: to them, drinking tree-sap merely replaces what they have personally lost. But, besides that, they see their society as a closed system, its resources limited for reasons I shall not here detail; suffice it to say that their religion is animistic and their ethos dominated by warrior values that recognize adulthood as a personal achievement that is, nonetheless, carefully nurtured through a strict ritual system that regulates people, marriage, sexuality, and semen. This view is predicated on a cyclical model of time (cf. Leach 1961b); seasonal movements, ceremonies, and customary transactions unfold in the round. Sambia do not recognize that their population is now expanding or that the concomitant stress on their resources (means of production) may be increasing; nonetheless, men believe that they expend semen and that they get more from trees. Let us now consider the implications of this view for their use of the concept of spirituality.

The trees from which men acquire sap are on clan territory. The land itself is one's main material inheritance from previous generations; it is held in agnatic corporate estate, though men own specific tracts of it from which they exploit resources (game, pandanus nuts, milk-sap trees). Land is coveted and defended against other groups; it is central to a clan's residential and territorial organization. It is guarded also by clan spirits. Ritual practices, too, are a social heritage, customs valued in themselves and for group identity, having been handed down from previous generations. It seems obvious, therefore, that the social ideology of trees provisioning new semen through the bodies of clansmen is a latent function of the regeneration of patrilineality.

Patrifiliation thus provides land and trees, ritual practices, and the social personae needed to transform tree sap into semen. Tree sap without an adult male body is just tree sap. The male body—the product of a long process of procreation with women and homosexual insemination from men, of magical ritual treatment making it fertile and procreatively potent—is the instrument that regenerates society. Tree-sap maintains maleness and masculine personhood. It regenerates one's clan, its patriline and hamlet-based warriorhood and thus the community itself. These social identities are conceptually placed, in time and space, through concentric social networks based on a magical notion of successive degrees of purest patrilineal substance.

Hence, male ideology claims that father, son, and clansmen are of one semen substance, one common origin place, one residential location—all elements of genealogic ancestry that fan out to embrace a pool of spirit familiars, ancestral spirits, and the semen sustaining all. Whether the trees are seen as beginning or finishing this process is beside the point: Sambia have a cyclic view of their system that makes tree sap pivotal in a greater chain of being. What is the nature of semen value in this whole system? This problem forms the last part of my chapter.

DELAYED EXCHANGE. The final category of indirect semen transactions concerns exchanges across generations between groups. This subject is very complex indeed, so I shall merely sketch contours of the system of intergroup relationships. What do groups give and receive? And do their exchanges of semen balance out across time?

The key principle of delayed exchange is that groups who exchange women also exchange semen through homosexual contacts. Group A takes a woman from group B. They become affines. Their initiated males of different cohort at different life cycle stages engage in homosexual intercourse both ways (giving and receiving semen). Children of groups A and B become matrilateral kin in the following generation. In delayed exchange (infant betrothal or bride-service) marriage, group A later returns a woman to group B. In direct exchange (sister exchange) they will not. Marriage between generation 2 of these groups is frowned on, except in the case of delayed exchange infant betrothal to father's sister's daughter, that is, a daughter of group A goes back to group B. Yet actual father's sister's daughter marriage (addressed as "sister" by her mother's brother's son) is also disliked; more commonly this woman is traded for another woman from a different group. Homosexual contacts between generation 2 are also forbidden. In effect, generation 2 shares ties of blood and semen: boys of group A were formed from the blood of a woman of group B, and their body tissue came from their father, some of whose own semen may have come from males of group B. These boys (of group A) must turn to a third, unrelated group, in order to take both a wife and semen.

What do groups A and B exchange? Group A gets a woman as garden producer and maker of babies. She reproduces heirs to perpetuate group A. Group B gets food gifts and a promise of a return woman (possibly her daughter) in the next generation. Boys of group A get semen from bachelors of group B and vice versa. Homosexual insemination ensures masculinization and adult reproductive competence. Boys of groups A and B may receive ritual sponsors from each other's group (in purest form, mother's brother). This man is the boy's guardian and teacher in sexual matters (remember they are forbidden to have sex). So each group provides boys of the other group with nurturance and sexual tutorship. In generation 1, a man may copulate with both his wife and her younger brother. The man gets a wife and another homoerotic transitional sexual outlet. His wife and her younger brother both receive semen: growth, strength. And the younger brother (or, if not himself, his sons or clansmen) will eventually receive a return wife, the brother-in-law's daughter, which the latter's semen created and nourished.

What does intermarriage do to social relationships? First, marriage transforms groups from unrelated enemies to less hostile affines. Where homosexual contacts occur with groups who are politically hostile, and between which warfare and masculine competition are common, marriage places affines in a set of productive relationships where none existed before. Second, they exchange women as resources. It is in the wife-givers' best interests to ensure that the marriage is productive in every way so that they receive a woman in return. Marital sex for procreation is productive social work; it outweighs erotic play in homosexual contacts and results in social sanctions against adultery and barrenness. Third, women and semen thus become circulating commodities. Unrelated groups exchange semen, on both sides, with the wife-donors getting a wife out of the bargain. The initiated boys of both groups require semen to complete their personhood, while the men need wives as sexual outlets and procreators to step out of the adolescent stage of homosexuality into the adult stage of marriage and family. Semen, therefore, though a crucial commodity, is secondary to women as a commodity: without wives men cannot attain full personhood. Even though semen is needed to attain manhood and it strengthens the new warrior recruits a village requires to protect and expand itself, this warriorhood goes for naught unless women are available for the group's economic and biologic reproduction.

Finally, the value of semen as instigator of social reproduction at both the individual and group levels pits males against one another in symmetric competition. This competition takes two forms, intragroup and intergroup transactions (Forge 1972). The one is intrahamlet individualized competition for homosexually procured semen in order to grow and have first pick of wives needed for reproduction later. Here, boys as age-mates try to out-perform one another in a contest to achieve maturity first. (In fact, older brothers encourage their youngers toward this end.) The other competition is between hamlets, and, in a wider sense, between a confederacy of intramarrying hamlets vis-à-vis the other confederacies of Sambia society. Men aspire to make their confederacy outdo others in war and overall productivity. Hamlets also act together to find women for their bachelors so as to produce more children—potential warriors and females for the marriage trade—compared with other groups. A race is on: its outcome is social reproduction. Conflicts within hamlets erupt over men competing with one another for wives and resources. Fights with peers over women in other hamlets also occur, sometimes precipitating warfare. But intrahamlet competition is overshadowed by the normative stress on achieving social maturity in concert with the best interests of one's own village group. Ultimately, social survival requires competing neighbors too, for they provide women and semen, and are the best defense—strength in numbers—against enemies elsewhere.

CONCLUSION

In this chapter we have explored Sambia semen valuations from several points of view: what seemed esoteric, vulgar, and trivial now seems complex and symbolically significant in understanding native concepts of sexual contacts and the structure of social relations and modes of production in Sambia culture. Erotics belongs to this symbolic field and cannot be understood, either subjectively or objectively, except in relation to the meaningfulness of this field over time.

Melanesianists have often ignored erotics and its meanings, especially in constructing comparative models of social organization and culture. Even heterosexual activities have, in general, been scarcely studied; and the meaning of the temporal and symbolic structuring of heterosexuality has not been accorded much analytic value beyond the vague category "sexual antagonism," which has been implicitly used to support whatever explanatory model an author advanced (Herdt and Poole 1982). But what matters more, for my purposes, is that the fluids of sexual and reproductive acts—semen, blood, and milk—have been too narrowly studied as entities or artifacts in exchange, or as parts of the growth process in reference only to individual development or societal functioning: they have been interpreted less often as symbolic objects and commodities, expressed through concepts and social transactions, whereby the natives reproduce the identities of persons, social roles, clans, and intergroup relationships across generations.

Past analyses of semen and blood as culturally constructed concepts in New Guinea belief systems, for instance, reveal this structural–functional emphasis. These fluids have long been viewed as important in native notions of sexual temperament and gender (e.g., Mead 1935). The great interest in procreation beliefs shown in the 1920s, first by Malinowski (1913) among Aborigines, and then in Trobriand descent ideology (Malinowski 1929, 1954), illustrates this interest. Writers questioned whether natives were ignorant of procreation and what such purported ignorance of conception meant (Ashley-Montagu 1937; and see Bettelheim 1955; Leach 1966; Spiro 1968b). We see now that denial of semen valuation in kinship and procreation belongs to a broader cultural discouse on social regeneration and reproduction (Weiner 1978, 1980). In Highlands studies, since Read's (1951, 1954) work, ethnographers have noted blood and semen as cultural signs of the body, sex, and gender. Accounts of the norms of sexual contacts, dogmas about conception, sterility, and reproductive competence, and ideas about exchange of menstrual blood and semen between people as patrilineal kin and affines, all illustrate how ethnographers functionally related body fluids to sociosexual relationships and the positioning of people in networks of social groups (e.g., see Berndt 1965; Glasse and Meggitt 1969; Langness 1967; Meggitt 1964; Newman 1964; Reay 1959; A. Strathern 1972; M. Strathern 1972; Wagner 1967). Preoccupation with the exchange of sexual fluids between groups addressed western individualist concerns with "discrete acts of giving and receiving" (Weiner 1980:71; cf. for example, A. Strathern 1969, 1972). Recent theorists have gone beyond exchange constructs, or structural models that view body treatment merely as reflections of society's divisions and boundaries (Douglas 1966), to interpret semen, blood, and other entities as the culturally valued materials out of which gender and reproductivity are symbolically perpetuated (Gell 1975; Herdt 1981; Lindenbaum 1972; Meigs 1976; Panoff 1968; Poole 1981, 1982b; M. Strathern 1978, 1980; Weiner 1980).

With the Sambia, we are dealing with people whose cultural systems use sexual relationships and fluids as objects and commodities to recreate social order in successive generations, for these are among the scarcest and most vital resources in this process.

Semen and other body fluids are not just things that *are:* they have a value beyond themselves for extending one's personhood—that is, existence—beyond the present. No doubt many experiences of these material things (e.g., fluids, sex, and others' bodies) entail this transcendent attitude. Sambia spiritual concepts speak to this issue directly, just as the conflict between sex as work or sex as play addresses it indirectly. "Religion is an art of making sense out of experience, and like any other art, say, poetry, it must be taken symbolically, not literally," Firth (1981:596) has said, a view germane to the ritual meanings of semen.

The social fact of semen for Sambia is that it is a scarce resource that circulates through time. Its material and phenomenologic attributes make it usable as commodity that can be consumed, stored, and given away. Its perceived use-value derives from the fact that (1) semen can be "contained" indefinitely in bodies and (2) then be seemingly passed, from person to person, without changing its essence or efficacy; (3) it represents an investment of labor (food, care, procreation of children) acquired through direct individual sexual transaction or indirect transformation (semen into milk), that can be given or received; (4) in being transmitted semen extends its transformative value to make the recipient more reproductively and socially competent; (5) these recipients, in turn, will produce more wealth and future individuals who will fill productive roles and fill out social groups; and (6) by so doing, semen transactions recreate social links between the living and the dead, the worldly and the spiritual realms, between ego and others, and between the divisions of the society.

In Sambia imagination, individuals are born and die, but semen flows through them (along with blood) to recreate society. Individuals pass on. Growth as an aspect of these individuals dies with them. But strength persists: in the form of bones and skin tissue in offspring; in spirit familiars; in ghosts and spirits; and in the deceased's bones, which after death may be used for sorcery. Erotic play passes on too, is useless, except insofar as it has effected growth, strength, and procreation. Sex as work is far more productive, if less exciting: family and heirs result. In this model, a woman's body as sexual-procreative property belongs to her husband, as much as his semen belongs only to her. Her blood, after marriage, belongs to his clan, through his offspring, which must be paid for in birth ceremonies. Both fluids are necessary for procreation, but it is semen that men own and control best. The natural fact that semen can be drunk (passed on) like any drinkable fluid sustains the view that it is a circulating, valuable, unchanging resource that must be, nonetheless, internally transformed in certain ways by certain persons to achieve certain ends.

The most powerful social fact of homosexual contacts is that they may only occur between potential enemies who may become affines (generation 1) and then kin (generation 2). Semen transactions not only define who is related and in what salient ways, but homosexual contacts predicate the partners' relationship as prospective affines in their generation, which makes their children matrilateral kin in their own. Structurally, social ties based on blood and semen should not be mixed via sexual relationships: semen relates nonkin, who in turn, through women as links, have descendants sharing semen and blood. (A male ego may receive semen from his brother-in-law, whose children, that is the ego's sister's children, possess her husband's semen and her blood.) Ties of semen and blood (via women traded) flow in the same direction. The seeming exception is marriage to actual (not classificatory) father's sister's daughter, a marriage Sambia frown on. Such marriages are acceptable only when this woman cannot be traded for another; but in these rare marriages spouses share no blood, though they may indirectly share semen via their fathers' homosexual contacts with each other's groups. Thus, the cultural principle not to mix blood and semen is contravened, and people resist such marriages. In general, this cultural linkage (blood and semen) makes heterosexual relationships more socially important and multiplex than homosexual contacts. Both men and women, their bodies and fluids, are needed to achieve biologic and social reproduction in this model (cf. Lévi-Strauss 1949; see Pettit 1977:70–72).

The practice of homosexual behavior is embedded in a cyclical tradition of semen transactions that made one's mother and father and will define one's own future relationships with boys and women. Identities follow from this semen flow. The tempo of such an ancient practice is to be found not only in this or that day's contacts but in the last generation and the next. The system sets rigid constraints, but individuals and groups follow strategies around broad time posts to maximize the value of themselves and their resources. Time does not forget who gave and who received semen.

This view does not explain ritualized homosexuality among Sambia; it merely elucidates the phenomenon in broader terms. For to seek causes, not just of the sociocultural system of values, but of individual acts of erotic behavior, we have to examine its individual subjectivity and developmental context, according them an analytic role I have here ignored. This is the concern of the following case studies of Sambia.

PART II

Interviews

CHAPTER THREE
Interviewing Sambia

H: What do the next chapters contain? How shall we think about their contents and how they represent the natives and ourselves? Remember that we did not originally set out to do research for this or any book. I was interviewing people I'd known for years; S. joined me for a few days in the village. Since I usually tape interviews, we had a record of what happened when S. joined in. After a day or so, when we decided to do this book, we were more aware about taping and interviewing as a team. Moreover, S. got involved and became a part of the sessions as he sat with me and others. Out of this fortuitous beginning the next chapters emerged.

These studies have an anomalous position in anthropologic research. They are not biographies of people in their fullness; they are not even biographic portraits.[1] Nor are they life histories, though we briefly outlined the essentials of each individual's history; or clinical formulations, though aspects of psychodynamic functioning and character structure are mentioned in individuals' profiles and then reflected on by us. These chapters are dialogues. Aside from editing for clarity, they convey conversations, fragments of broader case studies. Presented in translation, such texts are easy to read but harder to place in their cultural context, for, as Tedlock (1983: 323) has said, they preserve the "betweenness of the dialogue." Perhaps this interpretive problem confronts all cross-cultural work, but it is especially acute in cross-cultural clinical studies.[2]

Knowing what to say about a culture and how to say it across cultural boundaries is the classical problem of anthropologic epistemology. Strange or familiar,* people, places, ideas, actions must be described to others—readers who may not have a reference point (or worse, a false one) to think with. The question: "What is Sambia marriage like?" requires subquestions such as: "How is this institution—marriage—structured in Sambia society? What are its[†] agreed-on conventions, rules, and social trappings?" Such questions lead to a metaquestion: "How is Sambia marriage different from/similar to that of the reader's culture?"—where the *institution* (marriage) becomes the focus. They require cultural background and explanation. In a word: translation. Anthropology is translation, Evans-Pritchard (1962), Geertz (1973), and others have said. But translation is evocation only; translations are interpretations, editings.[‡] Thus, in traditional ethnography, the normative perspective excludes much of life beyond the norm.

What is excluded may be of direct interest to the anthropology of self, gender, and dialogue. For some kinds of structural anthropology, the fine-grained, detailed utterances and contexts of intimate communications may not matter so much. They matter greatly to us: as S. has often said, without the *exact* details of someone's experience of erotics, your description hides more than it reveals. Thus, we have spent a great deal of time thinking about the process of writing and transcribing our interviews, and conveying them to readers. How does the editing process affect the meaning and interpretation of our interviews? To give full recognition to these oft-excluded matters we present, in the Appendix, a run-through of the entire process for interested readers.

Clinical ethnography raises special problems concerning what to say about a person's life and how to say it across cultures. The object is not the norm, yet norms must be understood in relation to the individual's thought and behavior. Here, as in what LeVine (1982) calls "person-centered ethnography," we must confront norms and rules as experienced, beliefs as internalized or deviated from in the individual's *concrete* norms. As we argued in chapter 1, clinical ethnography cannot ignore the cultural system or social settings of real people: that is the researcher's normative baseline. Yet this baseline can only be fully understood through individual case studies. How do *I* experience marriage and make it a fact in my life? The problem is

---

*We should be equally aware of the familiar: "To be 'self-evident,' a proposition or premise must be out of reach and unexaminable: it must have defenses or roots at unconscious levels" (Bateson 1976:58).

†Notice how easily we personalize social institutions in this mode of analysis: as if the institution had volition, goals—a mind of its own.

‡But there are better and worse translations. (Who informs or protects the reader?)

not quite Devereux's (1980a) problem of what is "normal and abnormal" across culture, but, more precisely, the issue of *what* a person
experiences—and *how* that is seen by self and others, that is, as normal or abnormal, normative or eccentric; at different levels of awareness. Examples (from the text that follows): What does being a shaman mean to Sakulambei? How normative is his shamanism? How
does Moondi feel shame and pleasure, and how much like our emotions are his? Does a hermaphrodite or a considerate man differ in
masculinity from other Sambia males? What form does the verb *kalu*
(sorrow, loss, sadness, depression) take in Kalutwo's feeling? And how
does Penjukwi experience her femininity when with me? These questions, in short, require particular answers for particular people through
particular communications.

Another background factor deserves mention. Our text often focuses on gender identity, the subject that first motivated us to work
together, that led me back to the Sambia, and that took S. there. We
know that our interest in erotics and in gender colors our data, writing styles, and interpretations; of course, this influence is true of all
ethnographies. In the chapters that follow we talk with people I have
seen primarily to study their masculinity and femininity.[3] Furthermore, some were seen because of anomalies in gender identity and
sexual behavior, either as biologically intersexed (Sakulambei), as abnormal in Sambia eyes (Kalutwo), or as statistically aberrant (Imano). You may object that sex and gender are clinical subjects, and
so, more than most problems that concern anthropologists, focus on
individuals. Has our clinical approach made Sambia seem like verbal, self-conscious patients in the States? No and yes. No, we do not
believe that these emphases on gender distort Sambia: the issues are
important to Sambia themselves. To ignore sex and gender would
harm one's ethnography in cultural domains as diverse as warfare,
ritual, or family life. But yes, in my field house, I create an ambience
for private reflection and discussion, an unprecedented experience
Sambia had never imagined, that permits extraordinary communications and insights.

Throughout this book we call for renewed attention to the relationship between subjectivity and culture. We have criticized the positivistic ideology and rhetoric of those schools in anthropology that
claim to do science without systematically using the subjective factors revealed herein. Our discussions of writing style, editing, jargon,
doing long-term interviewing, substituting concepts such as "culture
shock" for the observations the concepts summarize—this is our attempt to interject into doing and writing ethnography an awareness

of how we think and feel. The object of the clinical ethnography we propose is the natives' experience of self as a lens we can use for seeing their relationships, feelings, and fantasies about others, institutions, and the environment.

So far, though, in debating these issues we have not discussed our image of self, as in "oneself" or "myself." When anthropologists refer to "self," "ego," or "person" they are in as much disagreement as their psychoanalytic colleagues regarding the connotations of these concepts.[4] Is Sambia selfhood different from other New Guinea societies? How does it compare to our own western conceptions? To ground the following material on interviewing we shall first examine psychoanalytic ideas and then those of Sambia.

S: Psychoanalysts have joined others who, over millennia, have tried to define self, that essential subjective experience. Yet there is still no agreed-on view. The problem, I think, is in part due to this subjective experience of self* being so dominated by our feeling of ourself, of being present. When we psychiatrists see states of self-fragmentation—dissociation—we recognize that this sense of oneness is made up of many parts fused in what one feels to be a seamless whole. Think of more ordinary matters like the right hand versus the left in playing the piano, where it seems that a product of one's creativity is not one's own but a gift (or curse); or enthusiasm, the god within; or dreams, those that are self-created, soft—no more than a signal— or roaring; or Fate—so often no more than the refusal to accept our own responsibility; or God, the gods, the Devil, devils, saints, spirits, ghosts, forces, Mysteries—fragments we chuck up in the process of denying the fullness of our self; or hallucination and delusion, wherein one's own mental work is projected onto the outside world and is then received back by oneself (which self; there are so many in there) as alien; or inspiration; or multiple personality, in which we divide our self into several parts, each with apparent autonomy; or works of art (most obvious in writings), wherein, somewhat as with dreams, we create innumerable personages, places, and plots from out of our own self; or schizoid states in which one feels like Kafka's creatures; or physical illness, where suffering can be so intense that one feels that a part of one's body is an enemy within or when we feel that our body—the equipment that we feel, when it works smoothly, is our

---

*Theorists carefully differentiate self from sense of or experience of self; the definitions are too exquisite for me. Even after studying the texts, I am no closer to defining self, though it seems so easy to experience.

self—gives out before we do; or states of trance, hypnosis, and possession.

But for most of us most of the time, the unspoken, unquestioned sense of "I" seems so spontaneously received, so much of one piece, that we consciously know nothing of the multiple "I's."

Tracking these complexities, Freud looked at the self—he called it "Ich" (mistranslated "ego") and found it an organized, dynamically energetic, tension-filled collection of mental parts and functions, sometimes conscious, mostly not, struggling—against impulses that would disintegrate us—for synthesis.* In time, his system for the structure of the mind† shifted from the clinical (that is, what can be observed directly or indirectly): conscious, preconscious, and unconscious mentation to theoretic structures: ego, superego, and id. (In this new system, "ego" took on quite different meaning: the ego was now an "it," not an "I."‡ The word "self" disappeared from analytic rhetoric and awareness, to emerge only when analysts were dissatisfied with the gap between their clinical work, which is a matter of one's communicating with another, and their theory with its structures that, as explanations, never capture that self-essence of our lives.

During the time when the dissatisfaction with ego/superego/id was congealing, the concept of identity was elaborated. Though many subheadings of identity were listed, the reality, in what one observed in others and in oneself, was, once again, too powerful for concepts to overcome. So this effort to corral the self experience also failed, though there were gains, since "identity" reached toward connotations different from those of "self." "Identity" implies mental experiences ordered around more or less enduring social roles (such as "I am a man; husband; father; son; doctor; American") drawn in from the outside world. One might say, then, that identity refers to the sense I have of aspects of my self, while "self" has the broader meaning: all that I mean when I say "I."

We are thus led to the problem, still unsolved by philosophers, psy-

---

*In doing this conceptual work, he was demonstrating, among other things, that the academic psychologists were naive and wrong to insist that what was mental was conscious and nothing else.

†In this realm of undefinable words, "mind" is sometimes used by theorists as synonymous with "self," but they are unaware they do so, thinking they have different meanings for each. When the hair-splitting is done, it is mighty hard to tell "mind" from "self." "Self" is more stylish.

‡The self had disappeared from analytic theory but not from the treatment. Freud knew that the subjective experience—conviction—of self was at one level a precious truth, its uncovering the goal of analysis. But at another it is an illusion of free will and responsibility: where the subject feels self, the observer sees functions, fantasies, dynamics, systems (most of which are far beyond the reach of consciousness). In this sense, "I" is an "it."

choanalysts, communication theorists, and computer scientists, of who is "I." The term has two quite different meanings: the subjective, immediate experience of myself, and an objective description—in many ways described better by others than by myself—of this person, this organism, this object for which I use the pronoun "I" and they use the pronoun "he." For instance, when saying that I dream, I refer to four different "I" processes. (1) I am asleep, in some way aware that I am asleep (for instance, I know enough not to fall out of bed) and am watching my dream somewhat as I do a theater-piece. (2) I am the person in the dream living in its actions. (3) I am the writer, director, and producer of the dream that is experienced by the first two "I's" just described; that version of my "I" plots the dream's course, introduces its characters and settings, decides on the feelings that the subjective "I" shall experience when I dream my dream. I do not know this "I." (4) I am an organism, a biologic machine, especially a brain, that exudes a dream.

No ethnographer, meeting a stranger at home, would accept as single-layered the sentences the stranger spoke. And the more intimate your relationship with someone, the more completely you know and can respond to the complexity of that person's communications. In speaking of these subjective layers and intersubjective complexities, I am underlining the need for the clinician's skill in getting people to reveal what they think and feel, to tell you what motives and meanings they attach to what they do and think others are doing.

"Layers" is a limited spatial metaphor. Better is that of a microdot (Stoller 1979). In World War II, microdots were used to hide large amounts of information in a tiny, apparently innocuous space. A full page of information was photographed down, in steps smaller and smaller, until reduced to the size of a typewriter period. That spot—microdot—was then pasted onto a letter whose overt typed message contained nothing secret. The secrets were in the microdot. With this spatial metaphor we conjure up the idea of many facts compacted into a tiny area. But we must add to it dynamics, movements—meanings, motivations, feelings, memories, fantasies, themes, scripts. Only then do we approximate what our waking lives consist of any—every—moment. Surely you do not think that right now I experience only the flow of words you read, and I do not believe that as you read, these words are your only thoughts. There is more: you are interpreting the words, arguing with them, forming impressions of me. You are under the influence of the place where you sit, the binding of the book, the hunger in your stomach, the time of day, the sound outside, last night's bad experience, tomorrow's responsibilities, the fate of your grandchildren born and those yet or never to be born, what your father said that Tuesday when you were three and your mother's style of feeding you when you were five months old. And what else, what else.

So keep in mind that in interviewing Sambia we shall be constantly thinking, without overtly stating it, that every moment of everyone's life is composed of mental processes that take the form of scripts and their interwoven affects. Our main theme is that the study of these mental processes in and between people *is* the practice of ethnography, not artifacts that obstruct.

H: Let us turn now to Sambia notions of self and personhood: first to background our interviews and then to foreground the discourse style of our clinical ethnography in the village.

Let me suggest that Sambia culture entails two distinct cultural worlds: the male and the female. I have analyzed this model elsewhere (Herdt 1987c) and will not repeat the argument here, but the idea of differing gender-related world views is crucial for interpreting dialogues with Sambia men versus women. These worlds are bound together in a synergistic way: all Sambia are reared in public situations, the norms of which are shared by men and women: public culture; yet men and women have different ritual secret domains of knowledge and discourse off-limits to the opposite sex. Though children are reared in public, boys must unlearn or negate feminine cultural attributes, rules, and behaviors (i.e., they are radically resocialized into the men's cult through initiations). Adult male behavior is based on the cultural discontinuity that, as boys, they shared in the female subculture, whereas as men they must demonstrate that they no longer abide by what they shared in as children.[5] The result is conflict—social and intrapsychic—between the moral rules and directives of the women's versus the men's worlds. This internal contradiction is never resolved, because it is basic to Sambia culture; and its conflictual effects can be seen in myriad expressions of men's behavior, including concepts of self and personhood.

To understand the construction of person and gender among Sambia requires a recognition—both historical and psychocultural—that *warfare* was the key behavioral reality to which Sambia had always to address themselves and their life designs. Until the 1960s, as we noted, Sambia and their neighbors constantly were at war. How is it possible, now, to reconstruct the conditions that led to day-to-day

decisions and relationships based on such conflict, let alone to conjure up in ourselves what the *experience* of such a life was like? We
cannot (Herdt 1987c; Stephen 1987).

But we can know this—the phenomenology of much of everyday
experience was the knowledge: a war is going on. No one was untouched by that deadly stone-age warfare with its severe test in man-
to-man, brute strength combat to the death. Sambia engaged in two
types of fighting. In the Valley, bow-fighting was frequent. It was supposedly bluster—a show of strength—through displays in which
warriors lofted arrows at each other from opposite mountain sides.
This fighting was limited to straight arrows. Barbed arrows and stone
clubs were ruled out, but people were sometimes wounded, and
sometimes the wounded died. Then a real war—no holds barred—
began, until blood revenge was obtained and a truce arranged. Intertribal war-raiding was for killing and was more deadly. Men and
youths from the confederacy would go on dangerous war-parties and
journey to distant places. Sometimes this was done purely to test new
third-stage initiates, to see what they were made of. Those attacked
did the same or eventually retaliated. War was a deadly pursuit, and
personhood was constructed in response to it.

Personhood thus has its roots in the public moral norms of the
village. Sambia are gregarious; they have a strong sense of sociality
and firm ideals about what is good (*singundu*) or bad (*maatnu-maatnu*).
For children and adults these moral norms are sensible: one should
be hospitable and share food (or consumables like tobacco); one should
not steal or destroy others' property; one should not physically harm
others or shame them; one should work to provide for self and family
and not be lazy; and one should converse with others, follow parents'
instructions, be true to one's word, and not meddle too much in others' affairs. For adults, moreover, the list includes more serious in-
junctions pertaining to ritual, fighting with or killing (except in self-
defense) one's kin or affines, and never engaging in heterosexually
promiscuous or adulterous behavior. All these norms, incidentally,
apply only to one's social world (from one's village to close neighbors)
in successively weaker degrees. Enemies are not human; therefore
killing, raping, or looting them are not moral violations.[6] All Sambia
share in these morals; that is what makes them Sambia. In some ways
people are always bound by these moral rules.

The full person is defined in public culture against the norms of
esteemed adulthood. Fully masculine people are those who have been
through all initiations, who are married and have at least two children. Furthermore, men must have participated in war raids, hon-

orably defended or killed; they must be good hunters and must provide well for their families through ample gardens. They should be actively involved in ritual activities, not spend too much time with women and children. As elders, they should be actively involved in marriage and land tenure matters and stand up to be counted through sensible rhetoric when necessary. Fully feminine people should have reached menarche, been initiated, married, and have at least two children. They should be successful gardeners and generous in giving food and consumables to others. They should maintain appropriate contacts with their agnates in other hamlets, which allows them to use some of their own clans' resources. As elders, they should be involved in female ritual activities and instruct younger women in matters like sex and marriage. These normative models provide powerful rules and images of how people *ought* to behave and what they *should* strive toward.

Yet these person categories do not define selfhood, because individuals uphold them only partially, and Sambia are, like other Highlanders, rugged individualists.[7] They recognize both moral and personal differences among individuals. Common expressions of this recognition are found in folklore and casual remarks: that Kanteilo is a good story-teller or a sayer of funny things; that men such as Mon are great hunters and fearless warriors, while others are rubbishy; or that some women, such as Penjukwi, are industrious gardeners and really generous with their food, while others are lazy or stingy. Why are people this way? Eccentricity, biologic inheritance, clan differences, bad spirit influences: the accounts and stories concerning these differences vary, but they all suggest underlying recognitions of selfhood.

It is one's thought (*koontu*)*—here close to our concept of self—that is responsible for such traits. (And this sentence reflects the syntactical construction these accounts take.) When saying why so-and-so has a particular behavior pattern people add: "That's just his fashion" (*gami pasen-tokeno*) or "That's his thought." Sometimes spontaneously and at other times after being asked, people will say, "That was his father's way" (or "her mother's"). Many behaviors are alternatively attributed either to custom (*pasen-tokeno*), ritual teachings (*pweiyu koongundu*), ancestral ways (*aiyungasheru*), or myth (*pasi koongundu*). Moral and personality nuances are products of one's *koontu*. In dream reports, *koontu* is a signifier both of one's conscious

---

Koontu may be used as a reflexive nominalized verb ("I myself *think* that . . . ") or as a noun ("I had the *thought* that . . . ").

waking personhood and of self, as I have shown elsewhere (Herdt 1987d). The personal pronouns "I" and "me" mark self, whereas *koontu* refers to the norms defining the person's social role. One's thought should reflect customary moral norms that define the good person, but they do not always.

If thought, and hence, self, have origins in childhood, then it seems obvious that selfhood includes aspects of the secular—that is, profane—world of women. This view is implicit in men's *ad hoc* statements, but it contradicts male ritual dogma, and both initiates and men are ambivalent about it. (They are, however, firm in believing that one's soul, *koogu*, is mainly derived from one's same sex parent and is nourished and matured through initiation.) In private interviews some men and initiates say they did learn things from their mothers, though others flatly deny such an idea. Even so no Sambia ever denies the fact of biologic heritage or subsequent maternal care; such personal statements are never expressed in public rhetoric. This maternal bond and female world signify the mundane morals and selfhood noted above. But men loathe to acknowledge it. Here, then, are foundations of concepts of personhood and selfhood among Sambia.

What remains is to identify the boundaries of culturally constituted contexts in which communications about personhood and experience are made to others—including the ethnographer—for these normative conceptions also shape the meaning of discourse types in Sambia culture.

We can argue, consistent with the above, that Sambia people operate in three different contexts with corresponding modes of discourse noted previously: public, secret, and private.

Public situations are the most general context in which communications are made. This discourse is bounded by the public norms sketched above. These communications occur in mixed audiences of men, women, and children. Daily events, economic activities, gossip, even dream sharing belong to this category of talk. Thus people are more rule-bound and conformative here.

Secret situations entail ritual secrets, names, and other information about activities hidden from the uninitiated and the opposite sex. This male discourse occurs only in the club house, in the forest, or, on those rare initiation occasions, in ritual cult houses, whereas female secret talk occurs in the menstrual hut. Yet there are layers of ritual secrecy stratified by initiation status.[8] Thus, at the elementary level, all initiated males share in knowledge of first initiation, ritual flutes, homosexual activities, etc. More advanced secret knowledge is hidden from them until they achieve final initiations; this information concerns heterosexual purificatory rites and, ultimately, the myth of parthenogenesis—the greatest secret of all (Herdt 1981). At the highest level is esoteric ritual knowledge needed for certain ritual spells and paraphernalia; only a handful of elders—a very special audience—share in this most secret discourse (Tuzin 1980).

Finally, there are private situations, made of thoughts and activities not publicly shared but defined as not secret. Sexual activities of all kinds, because Sambia are prudish and regard them as shameful, are rarely told to others beyond one's sexual partner[9] though men brag of sexual exploits. Homosexual activities are private experiences not usually revealed except to intimates, certain agemates, and brothers. Likewise, heterosexual activities among spouses are *never* discussed with others, and adultery is carefully hidden.[10] (Children, in particular, should be kept completely in the dark about sexual activities.) Feelings of shame belong to this private domain. And so do daydreams, wet dreams, and any other nightdreams not publicly communicated. Magical knowledge about hunting, gardening, and sorcery, inherited from parents, is private information hoarded like money. Such private experience *is* selfhood; it may be shared with those one trusts most deeply, or it may not. When it is told in private situations, we may say that the communications are shaped by cultural norms and conceptions about what one *should* do, say, and think. But when such communications are made over a long time (such as to an ethnographer), these norms apply less and are transmuted by the individuals' idiosyncracies and what the interviewer does in response to them. Thus the private domain permits the person greatest freedom of expression, of selfhood.

Let me underline the distinctive nature of communication in Melanesian societies that, like Sambia, use all three modes of discourse. In western culture, by contrast, our institutionalized secrecy is poor.[11] The institutionalization of public/private/secret in Sambia life, supported by norms and taboos, is, at the same time, an obstacle to the free exchange of information between people, an obstacle to easy ethnographic interviewing, and a phenomenon in its own right worth studying (one that, incidentally, defies easy study).[12] Those, such as anthropologists or psychoanalysts, whose task is to study people's inner worlds can best appreciate the convoluted forms of talking that weave in and out of these domains, or combine them in a single statement: metaphors, circumlocutions, lies, euphemisms, double entendres, slips of the tongue, puns, stories that are half-truth or pure fiction, fictions disguised to hide the truth; many ways to say what you want to say and not say, in whatever situation, to keep the social—and oneself—intact.[13] This matrix of public/private/secret is the full medium, a code, as it were, of interpersonal communication we must keep in mind to understand Sambia talking.

But this image of Sambia derives from the past, and does not embody the signs of social change, ever-present, that make this portrait possible, dear reader. For this we have to thank the end of war. And with pacification and a gradual lessening of the tensions of intergroup competition and sorcery, we see the signs of change in personhood. Sambia, who were ever sociable, can now be more gregarious and affable. They are glad that war is gone. Pacification has removed some constraints, created more freedom. People can travel more freely. Travelers fear less that they will be attacked; children play around the hamlet and down by the river, where they never could before; women go to gardens without armed guards; the secret cult has lost some of its grip—particularly since the late seventies, when an airstrip was placed in the valley—so women have freedom and initiations are less harsh. Things are changing; our presence in the village—like that of the nearby missionaries—was a sign of another world to be reckoned with and understood.

Our Sambia interviews must be understood in the context of this change. My presence changed things: I arrived and built a house. At first, in ignorance, I interacted with people in ways (subtle or overt) that made them compromise the public/private/secret distinctions in order to accommodate me. Examples: Moondi responding to my asking about his wet dreams and then, years later, his telling me his fantasies; or other initiates discussing their homosexual experience; or Moondi and then Nilutwo revealing the secret of homosexuality; or Weiyu talking about sex with his wife; or Nilutwo reporting dreams he told no one else; or Penjukwi discussing her feelings about her body. Sambia never asked each other such questions. Only I did; only the ethnographer's outsider status permitted such out-of-place, even unthinkable, questions. But I asked in private, in my house; and, after a while, unprecedented questions and responses were accepted. And then expected.[14]

What did my unprecedented questions do? They contributed in subtle ways to the breakdown of the public/private/secret divisions, for me to move, less earlier and more later (of course), from public to secret, or from secret to private, or whatever. I could do this switching of frames (see Goffman 1974) because I had seen the secret initiations and had worked a long time with Tali on what they meant to him, a ritual expert; I had lived with Sambia and knew enough about normative public rules to predict what people should do, say, or think; and by 1979, when S. came and we conducted the interviews below, I knew my informants well.

I created thereby a new fourth category of discourse: what people said to Gilbert when alone in his house. I did not intend to do that. Yet I wanted to understand my friends in that way, too, not just how they were in rituals or in public. I wanted to understand how they made sense of their lives for themselves—in private—as shared with me.[15] What they said was constrained by Sambia culture, their ritual experience, the time of day, what had happened at breakfast that morning, of course; plus, what they thought I expected to hear them say.[16] We shall get to that.

Because Sambia culture is built for males on a contradiction—be socialized in the female subculture but be accountable only to the male subculture after initiation—the conflicts in men's and women's lives were brought into my office. This aspect of our talking may have, in retrospect, fueled people's interest in talking with me. By the time S. arrived, I was so involved in these narratives that it was no longer easy for me to reconstruct self-consciously what had happened, step-by-step, in leading up to what we label "comfortableness," "impasse," or "ambivalence" in particular case studies that follow.

Who were our subjects? All live in my field village, Nilangu, excepting Kalutwo, from the neighboring village, but who is living in Nilangu's river settlement on the valley floor, twenty minutes away. This intimate contact in the same village, in eating, healing ceremonies, gardening, gabbing, and the grand rituals, brought me close to people, spoiling the setting as objective experiment but permitting me countless, rich glimpses and understandings of people's behavior out in the light of social day. For these people are not just informants. They are also: real cronies (Tali and Weiyu), seen by me, themselves, and others as such, making them allies; translators (Weiyu); or a boy who became a research collaborator and a friend whom I supported in school (Moondi); or a frightened acquaintance who has become a faithful, still distrusting, friend (Sakulambei, who nonetheless may trust me as much as anyone else); or a neighbor (Imano); or the wife of a neurotic informant/friend, who became an informant and even better friend (Penjukwi); or, as with Kalutwo, someone in a relationship so complex that it requires a string of adjectives and nouns (stiffnecked informant who wanted to be a friend and, even more, a patient).

I know Moondi, Weiyu, and Tali best—longest and most intimately—and have watched them change over the years. I have intruded into their families and become part of their histories. From the mundane to the ritual arena, in the village and on patrols to alien tribes and on to Port Moresby, I have seen them in varied circumstances and feel that I often know what goes on inside them. The following chapters present microstudies of our dialogues with them, our first effort to put clinical ethnography into practice.

CHAPTER FOUR

Moondi's Erotism

BIOGRAPHIC SKETCH

H: Moondi is an intelligent, articulate youth of Nilangu. The eldest child of a large family, he was born about 1960, so he was nineteen at the time of these interviews. His father is unusually mild, his mother an unusually strong, renowned shaman. They are a successful couple, and their marriage is among the most important in the village. Moondi himself is somewhat short (about five feet tall), stocky and tough; he is robust and, except for occasional bouts of malaria, healthy. Unlike his peers, he has been to grade school; moreover, unlike the one percent of Sambia boys who have some schooling, he has come back to the village. He is personable and impetuous, popular and well integrated in the community. Today (1987), he lives and works in Port Moresby. But it would not surprise me—and this speculation must be seen as essential to the meaning of Moondi's life, our relationship, and his sense of himself—if he one day returned and became a leader in his area.

I first met Moondi in 1974. He was just a kid, a second-stage initiate living in the men's house. He sought me out, wanting to work as a language informant.* He was anxious to be noticed, and ingratiating; Sambia are rarely pushy. Still, he wanted to impress me that he was smart and could read and write Pidgin. These traits plus his intelligence and tattered European clothes set him somewhat apart from his peers. His initial desire to be recognized and to please—as if someone's life depended on your giving him that certain job—made

---

*Several Sambia have served as language informants to a European missionary down the valley. Moondi did so briefly; that was his only model of how I could employ and work with him.

me uneasy. Nonetheless, Moondi's behavior defied textbook wisdom ("Never use those first, too friendly informants"). Within a month his special gift for translation had become invaluable. His demeanor then returned to normal. Even now, Moondi is the best linguistic informant and interpreter I have ever found. He is insightful and verbal too; so he became an excellent informant in general, and he was at times (1975, 1979) a crucial field assistant. Through the years I have followed him closely, periodically interviewing him and exchanging letters. I know his mind better than that of any other Sambia. And we are also friends.

Because of the length and depth of our relationship, I find Moondi's life more difficult to snapshot than anyone else's. My case study of him includes hundreds of pages and scores of tapes, not to mention his letters or my observations of him in many noninterview situations. These materials are fuller than for anyone else and they include: casual or offhand remarks (e.g., jokes); casual and structured interviews; observation of him being initiated (third-stage initiation, 1975); observations of his everyday interactions with significant others and strangers; of his being ill; of traveling with him and seeing him sad and happy, etc.; and finally, occasional dream reports collected over the years. Especially, I have studied his masculinity and erotic life. Beginning in 1979 after he finished grade six, I also taught Moondi some western concepts such as fantasy, free association, and guided imagery.[1] These tools enriched our work, allowing me to go beyond conscious, especially intellectualized constructions, and to explore aspects of Moondi's imagination and unconscious processes. But because they involved insight and exposed him to disturbances from sources unconscious to him, our talking relationship—which always had therapeutic aspects—changed. I turned the talking into a kind of supportive psychotherapy to let him feel comfortable enough to discuss anything he wanted.[2] Toward the end of my visit, this talking centered on his anxieties about personality change, his impending marriage, and his plans to move to Port Moresby and work there. The remaining facts of his life can be set out in three major periods: childhood, initiation and life in the men's house, and his late schooling.

Moondi's is the last generation to have experienced warfare in their childhood; that is important. He still has vague memories of actual events (the period 1960–1965), for instance, of his mother fleeing with him into the forest when their hamlet was attacked. But his *feelings* are even more intense: of faceless enemies and dangers and of his father's absence when fighting; real, dreadful fears that scar one's soul, that initiation later compounded, and that he can never forget. For such anxieties in traditional Sambia life touched every aspect of existence; and, without doubt, they will stalk him, ghostlike, forever, awake or dreaming.[3]

His father's circumstances and his parents' marriage were more than normally caught up in war. A fight broke out in his father's natal hamlet over twenty-five years ago. His father's brother was killed by his own kin; war was set off for blood revenge. Moondi's father fled to Nilangu, where he was sheltered and offered sanctuary by his betrothed wife's clan. Hence, Moondi's father settled in his wife's village. This anomaly has thoroughly influenced their remarkable marriage. His wife, Kaiyunango—Moondi's mother—is herself an anomaly: strong-willed, outspoken, and the most powerful living female shaman.[4] She is also the good-hearted, young-looking, and vigorous mother of ten children, eight of whom are still living. Moondi is her firstborn and her favorite son. This maternal strength and love are as much a part of Moondi's optimistic character as the unusual achievement motivation that has set him above many peers. When younger, his parents squabbled and fought, but then and now their marriage is more stable than most. Perhaps the matrilocal character of the marriage helped their children be unusually emotionally robust.

Like all Sambia males, Moondi was initiated into the ritual cult. His first-stage initiation, at age eight, was in 1968. He described himself (as do others) as immature and smaller for his age than most of his agemates. So he feels he was more the object of bachelors' hazing than other boys. Initiation was terrifying. He was shocked by the ritual secrets—ritual flutes, nosebleeding, homosexual fellatio. He disliked and feared fellatio with bachelors at first;[5] it was over a year before he himself took the lead in homosexual contacts. He was lonely and sad after initiation. In actuality then—and in daydreams still— he blames his parents for his initiation: they let him be initiated against his will.

As time passed, though, Moondi adjusted to the men's house life. In 1970 he was initiated as an *imbutnuku* (second-stage initiate). He did more hunting than before. He became a more enthusiastic fellator and was sought by many bachelors as a sexual partner.* Some of these sexual relationships were temporarily exclusive: Moondi would sleep with the same youth for only a day, because he considered re-

---

*Moondi is considered handsome by Sambia, and his personality makes him equally attractive. He was expert at playing passive and seductive, and bachelors favored his willingness to pleasure them.

peated contacts with the same person unmanly (a common feeling among boys). His life might have continued thus had Moondi not decided to go to school.

In late 1971, Moondi left the Valley and went to a mission station school a day's walk away. He became a nominal convert to its religion. (He was not, however, baptized.) He was among the first Sambia boys ever formally schooled. He learned fast and advanced. A year later he was transferred to an even larger school far away. At the end of his second year he returned home for the Christmas holidays. Then fate intervened and his life changed again.

While home in the village he became gravely ill, probably a combination of malaria and bad nutrition (at school). He lay ill for weeks, into the early months of 1974, preventing him from returning to school. He felt that he had lost his chance to go on.* So he fell back into village life, healthy again because food was plentiful, helping his parents, sleeping with the bachelors, and occasionally going on short patrols with local government officers. Then I appeared on the scene.

Moondi presented himself to me as a half-literate and likeable adolescent. He proved himself invaluable, since he could read and write, at tasks like census-work, which others disliked. I also needed a dependable young interpreter to help me interview boy-initiates— someone they could trust and with whom they could identify. (An initiate could not always trust older bachelors and men.)† Moondi was perfect. He could understand, for instance, that in keeping to a formal interview schedule I had to ask exactly the same question of a cohort of boys in as similar a way as possible. But almost from the start, Moondi also talked about himself, which I encouraged, for I wanted also to understand what made him tick. I urged him to express his goals, since I was intrigued about his schooling. Eventually I learned how illness had kept him back in the village. Eventually we made a deal: if he would help me in my work for a year, I would help him get back to school.

Meanwhile, in 1975, another initiation cycle began. It was time for

---

*Why did he go to school in the first place? His parents were against it, but he went anyway. He apparently wanted to see the world, to get outside experience. At the time he was too young to go to the coast and work, which left only school. He was intelligent. What role did that play? He had enough experience with the local missionaries to see what *they* had. Thus many motives—including a job, money, and escape from the bush—were involved.

†Some information (e.g., wet dreams) is shameful to discuss with anyone, but especially with adult men. Weiyu, my adult interpreter (see chapter 5), was no different from other men. Furthermore, boys are generally intimidated by men, who regard them as ritually uneducated children who should be seen and not heard. Moondi was also discreet, and, even more than Weiyu (cf. chapter 10), kept information confidential that initiates confided to me (e.g., on dreams and sexuality).

Moondi to become a third-stage *ipmangwi*, which he greatly resisted. He said he was "not yet grown," that he needed more time, and that once initiated his "thinking would be stymied." He'd never get back to school. He ran away, hid for a bit. Others coaxed and pleaded. He considered fleeing to the coast. But he gave in to the pressure and went through the whole initiation, as I watched (Herdt 1987c). Afterward, as a fellated, he was wildly involved with boys: I have never before or since seen him so different. His passion subsided after a few weeks, and he settled into new routines. Not long after, I finished the formal interviews with initiates; his new period of schooling took him away.

Moondi had assisted me invaluably for a year; he went back to a public school in late 1975. By late 1977, through accelerated advancements, he graduated from primary school. Unfortunately, because of local quotas on school returnees, he could not continue to high school. In the meantime we exchanged letters. He seemed to mature, enjoying life more and feeling more comfortable with himself. Since then we have been friends, as close as that relationship can be with people from different worlds.

When I returned in early 1979, Moondi was back in the village. He had grown up. I was happy to have his company—not just his assistance—for many of my friends from the mid-1970s were gone, struggling to live as itinerant workers on the coast. Despite the reunion and success of that work, a cloud thus hung over my stay: so many of our friends had left the village that it was not the same place. Indeed, I found it saddening to walk by the shadowy big old men's house* in Nilangu, closed up and dusty, due to the large number of initiates who had left.[†] It took me only a few days to realize, then, that Moondi was as thankful for my company as I was for his.

Meanwhile, some weeks after I arrived, marriage negotiations were held that determined whom Moondi was to marry. A sister-exchange marriage was agreed on between M.'s parents and those of the girl— a thirteen-year-old premenarchal girl of another clan in Nilangu. This event really changed Moondi. His heterosexual fantasies increased and he was thrown into a new era of almost adult existence. Some of the ensuing changes in him are described below.

Nonetheless, Moondi made it clear from the start that he was not satisfied with village life. He had already decided before my arrival

---

*Nilangu has two men's houses, and a few new initiates (since 1977) live in the smaller one.
[†]The exodus still continued in 1981, and, I am sad to report, the village was for me lonelier than ever.

to change his life again by moving to the coast. He agreed to work with me but asked that I help him leave for Port Moresby when I left. His fiancée was too young to formally marry yet, so, meanwhile, he would try to find work and make money outside. Thus, when it came time for me to leave, both Moondi and Kwinko (my cook, and Moondi's best friend, cousin, and agemate) left too. Port Moresby took them in. And there they remain today, both busy with new lives and adult jobs. Ten thousand years passed in half their lifetime—from stoneage war to city apartments. And the wonder is that so much change still lies ahead.

This chapter concerns changes in Moondi's erotism. First are narratives of his erotic daydreams and erotic looking. This work was central to my case study of M. in 1979, and it was nearing completion when S. arrived. I have also added the fragment of a session entitled "resistance," which concerns the collecting of this erotic material. On these tapes, Moondi talks with me alone. Then S. joins us. Here and in later chapters we present our interview data in the chronologic order in which it was collected.

INTERVIEWS

What is sexually exciting to Moondi? How does he have to restrict his erotic impulses? What do his erotic daydreams look like? These are the kinds of questions motivating this session. By the time it occurred, I had nearly completed my case study, M. had spent many hours over months discussing his sense of himself and his maleness through memories, attitudes elicited through my questions, his history of his erotic behavior, dream reports, guided imagery sessions, etc. Session I occurred with M. and H. alone. His family contracted a marriage for him as is customary. M. had had a role in these negotiations. His father approached him regarding the prospective match. Without going into the details here, M. "approved" of his marriage choice after some days of heated talk.*

I was lucky to be there when this all occurred. It provided me the opportunity to examine concretely the phenomenon of erotic looking, a subject I had studied for some time. Moreover, here was a chance to record how Moondi's erotic daydreams were shifting—one of the major shifts being from homosexual to heterosexual objects. But our

---

*These omitted details include such factors as: the social upheaval already mentioned that has changed marriage arrangements; Moondi's parents' marriage; Moondi's being the eldest son, which gives him more power to be involved; and his personality—intelligence and sophistication that helped him make the best deal possible.

conversations on these topics had to be done in secret (for the reasons noted above), so we talked when no one else was around. Consequently, a previous session on erotic looking had to be cut short because other people appeared unexpectedly. Here is the transcript of our first session.

FIRST SESSION: EROTIC LOOKING

HERDT:* Last time [three days before] you and I were talking about looking† and the custom forbidding you [all initiates]‡ from looking at the women.

MOONDI: Yeah [*apprehensive*].

H: And the women too, they can't stare at you. Now I want to ask you about this . . . do you still remember where it was we stopped talking about this last time? [Reference to the fact that we had had a session earlier but were forced to stop talking about this delicate subject because Moondi felt uncomfortable with others being present outside who could overhear him.] Do you, uh . . .

M: About that? It went like this—we were talking about how the women . . . . At that time we had to stop in the middle . . . break it [our conversation] off.

H: When was that? This morning we were talking, but there were plenty of people all around. So you said, "Wait till later on."

M: [*Cuts in.*] Yeah, later on. Because you were asking me, "At the times when you look intently at women, what are you thinking then?"

H: [*Quietly.*] Um-hm.

M: [And you also asked:] "Oh, when you look very strong at women but suppose the men are watching you, too, what can you then feel?" You asked me and I said, "Oh, *Maski!*" [Pidgin word with

---

*S: Each of us did our own editing of every bit of these transcripts, after H. did the original translations. Had only one or the other of us done that editing, the transcripts would be different, and though the essense of the interviews would still be there (says who?), the interviews now to enter your mind are no longer exactly the same as they might have been.

We begin with literal transcription—as literal as can come out of a typewriter—plus description of what is happening at that moment. At this point we shall leave intact the raw, at times awkward translations, that still hover between Pidgin and colloquial American English. Then we shall switch to our cleaned-up edited style so that reading will be more bearable. In this way, our editing becomes more visible to the reader.

†Whenever I use this term it will be translated from the Pidgin *"luk luk"* or Sambia *chemdu*, which have both social and erotic connotations.

‡Throughout these transcribed texts, [ ] will be used to mark commentary inserted after New Guinea, while editing; whereas ( ) will be used only to enclose material that occurred in the original session. All narrative text and footnotes are by H. unless otherwise indicated.

no real equivalent in English that here means something like "forget it for now."] Later on. And I said, then I said, "The times when I look [at women] and all the men look at me, then I think all the men can think of me like this: I'm looking to steal [their women] or something . . . [hard to translate but something like: looking and wanting to steal what I have seen] when I am looking strong at the women. Therefore: "I want to grease [butter up] the women"; that is what they all [indefinite] can think that I want to do when I am looking too strong at all women. All the men can think that [above statement] . . . and when I realize this, then I feel shamed* when I look into their [i.e., men] eyes.

H: When you were an uninitiated boy did you know about this [looking] then too?

M: At the time I didn't understand about it. You know [as a preinitiate boy] . . . plenty of times I used to talk with all the women and I didn't feel very much shame about talking to you looking at them [sic] . . .

H: But, towards all of the girls [*tai*] is that what you also felt?

M: About the girls . . . looking at them, I didn't feel anything in particular, no, I didn't. But [*voice speeds up*] at that period, we used to—I used to be around them a lot. We used to talk and run around together[†] . . . . So I didn't feel anything in particular about them. Nor about looking at the women or the girls [*said simply and directly with no affectation*]. So we would talk a lot together and I didn't feel any particular thing about them.

H: [*Quietly.*] Um-hm.

M:[‡] When they performed the *moku* [first-stage initiation] on me, it was taboo to stare at women. They told us we can no longer get close to women. The big men made me afraid about that. But before, when I was a boy, I didn't have that fear. Only after the *moku* and then the *imbutu* and *ipmangwi*. That's when I got to be like this.

H: When you were a boy, you didn't play around [sex play] with the girls?

M: No . . . . Only because I was afraid. I wasn't afraid for no reason at all to play around with them. I was only afraid of playing around to screw them. But I didn't really understand how to actually

---

*What Sambia call "shame" (*wungulu*) is a far more powerful experience than that marked by our gentler verbs "embarrassed" or "ashamed." Therefore, to mark the difference, I use "shame" when translating directly from the vernacular.

†Sambia children can freely play in mixed sex groups until about age five when they are sexually separated.

‡We switch now to a cleaner transcript, edited to be more readable and bearable.

screw then, it was only my fantasy . . . and I thought: like our mothers and fathers do, that's how I thought of doing it. And I'd think, "If I do that, then all the men will get me," so I was afraid to do that.

H: But you didn't—or did you—look at the girls' or women's genitals when you were a boy?

M: When the girls were infants and didn't yet wear grass skirts, I saw their genitals.

H: And when they wore grass skirts?

M: Then I didn't look.

H: Is that tabooed or not?

M: No it is not taboo. But they must cover themselves. Suppose they simply went naked and the men saw them; then, in looking into the men's eyes, they would be shamed.* And it's the same with the women. We uninitiated [unclad] boys should not let women see our penises. The boy is also shamed if they all look and see him.

H: Would you have been shamed as a boy if you had looked at a woman's vagina?

M: [*Long pause; grin in voice.*] I've never looked at them. I never felt anything like that. It's their nakedness: it's not right that they should show it to you.

H: It's just down below [their genitals] that's shameful, isn't it?

M: Yeah. That part they must hide well inside their grass skirts.

H: I know that this doesn't happen here, but suppose, as a boy, one time a girl should secretly lift up her grass skirt and show you her vagina?

M: That girl [*tai*] is a real *pamuk* [whore]!

H: [*Chuckles.*] [I had never heard that word used for a girl before.] Oh, she would be a *pamuk tai*, huh?

M: Yeah. I could think, "Why is she showing me that [*a bit indignant*]? Is she a *pamuk* girl, or what?" But [*voice speeds up*] I could say to the boys [*lower voice*], "This woman, she showed me her cunt."† If I said that and the girl heard it, she could be shamed.

H: When she showed you her cunt, would your cock get tight?

M: [*Matter of fact.*] Oh, no. Not at all. I wouldn't be thinking about that with that girl. I could just say no to her, "You just don't have

---

*S: As with Americans and the interplay between a scantily covererd woman on a beach and her audience.

†This is the Pidgin term for vagina, which I leave in this form to convey its vernacular connotations.

any ·shame" [therefore, no self respect]. I wouldn't get hard. I'd just say, "You don't have any shame. You—you, ha!"

H: You could just rubbish her.

M: Yeah, curse her. Then she could feel shamed.

H: Mothers take care in fastening their little girls' grass skirts. [*Moondi looks away.*] You've got a lot of sisters and you know about this.

M: Yes. The mothers say, "You can't go and show yourselves to the boys. You must hide it [genitals] good. It is *your body.*" The mothers repeat that to all the girls and to the boys, too.

H: Now, what about the vagina: is it good or not good?

M: It's not a good thing. You [a female] could be shamed that they look at you. It's like this: they all know [*lowers voice*] that at that place [vagina] they all do it [sex]. It's not something all the men should be *looking* at. It belongs only to the two of them [spouses]. Only the man and wife should see her genitals. That's our custom. We must hide screwing. When I was a boy, if I didn't have a grass apron on, I would have felt shamed.

H: But it's your own body. Why should you be shamed by it?

M: [*Slowly.*] This is very hard for me to think more about. Why should I walk around without any clothes like a *long-long* [crazy] man?[6] They'd say to me, "You're not a small boy any more. Can you see your huge penis just hanging out there uncovered? Do you want to walk around naked like a crazy man?"

H: Now, what changed after you were initiated; what did they say at that time about looking [*purposely vague*]?

M: It concerned talking with women, and looking at women, and eating in front of women, drinking water in front of the women's eyes, eating sugar cane.* All of those things. That all changed. I thought: "Before, when I was a child, I used to just eat in front of women, but now . . . they initiated me and afterward they made me a different kind of person. They changed me and changed my thinking; and so now I can't look at women or talk with them. Or eat in front of women's eyes, either." And as I thought that, I feel afraid. It's the same as when the big men talk [exhort, threaten during the initiation]. They could hear what I said to the women, and the bachelors could come and rub stinging nettles on me [painful ritual punishment for breaking taboos].

H: And now [as a third-stage initiate]?

M: I can talk to the women sometimes. But before [pacification, when ritual was everything] we [bachelors] would have still been very

---

*These avoidances are all standard ritual taboos boys must adhere to after initiation.

shamed: we didn't do that. Now things have changed, and so we've got different ways.

H: When you were a first-stage initiate, you could not look at the women. Did you ever feel excitement when you were thinking about looking at the women?

M: No, I never felt that. Only about the bachelors.

H: Did you understand at that time that the big men were fencing you in?* That you couldn't look at the women, you could only look at the bachelors?

M: That's right. Now I can talk a little bit with the women. But I still won't ever look very strongly at them. [He does not add that he can only look at his mother, sisters, and kinswomen, and not at nubile women with whom he could have sex.] I can only glance at them, though; and talk a little bit and bow my head, and then talk looking at the ground. Before, I didn't do even that. But if you do it a little bit, more and more, some of your shame will go away. Years ago [after initiation], I used to be very ashamed of going inside my mother's house. But now I go and sit down once in a while. I want this shame to go away, so I can go and sit down sometimes. I might want to go inside of Mother's house, but if there are women inside, I don't go, thinking: "It's not good that I go inside and people all gossip that I want to look at them." Young women. (Not my sisters or my own clan, I'm not afraid about them.) Or the mother of my fiancée. They might think: "Why has he come inside here to be with me—inside the women's house? We didn't ask him to come inside here." There's plenty of people who would gossip like that if I went in there. I've heard such gossip. Sometimes when they [girls] walk around, some do this with me [*M. looks intensely at me eye-to-eye*; a seductive invitation]. They look right at me.†

[S: Does this text seem trivial, unimportant to understanding Sambia customs, subjective experience, erotism, ritual, adolescence, maleness and masculinity, styles of experiencing oneself and communicating to oneself, or capacity to communicate with a foreigner? In regard to ethnographic methodology, is this a useful way to gather data? How reliable are the data? What are H's responsibilities in regard to the transference reactions (e.g., dependency) such a conversation stirs up in Moondi, even more so since Sambia culture pro-

*This phrase—"to fence you in"—is a traditional idiom, the connotations of which here mean to sexually restrict, to ritually protect, and to keep women out of reach.
†See the third session.

vides no defense against such a powerful relationship? Are primitives' minds primitive minds?]

Second Session: Resistance

What problems arise in interviews on intimate matters? When a subject like sex is so emotionally loaded, as among Sambia, how does one deal with it? And how do its conflicts take form in the particular resistance of one person's intimate communications? Here is our starting-point.

This session occurred the morning after Session I. S. had arrived, but he did not participate here. (He joined us later, that afternoon, in the third session.)

Moondi and I are discussing the category *aambei-wutnyi* (gentle man, which has feminine connotations: see chapter 8 for more detail). Moondi is attracted to boys of this type. This subject, then, links his gender identity to erotism, especially his shift from male to female objects.

H: What about the *aambei-wutnyi*? What do you think of these men?
M: They don't say much, and they live peacefully. If you, a man, say something to them, they simply smile. I like that kind of man.
H: Can you also like this kind of initiate or like screwing with them?*
M: Yeah.
H: What kind of thoughts do you have when you think about him?
M: He doesn't say much. He just sits around. [*Pause.*] That kind of boy I can like. [*Longer pause.*] [S: H. is uh-hming: M's responses are awfully thin.] If I look at this boy, his kind of face is nice. I will like it. It's just like a girl's . . . [*pause, awkwardness*]. He doesn't have very much to say. He's not very strong. He's not strong in his ways. And when I see that [quality], I feel I like them all, that kind of man [*voice trails off*]. . . . He himself doesn't initiate conversation. He simply sits [passively].
H: Yeah, but what is it about his face that's nice, the same as a girl's?
M: [*Long pause. Searching around.*] It's like, it's not the same kind of face as other boys'.
H: Yeah. It's another kind.
M: Yeah, another kind.
H: What makes it another kind?
M: It's his looking. The way he looks at you. That's how; his way is like a girl's, he doesn't talk very much. Yeah, but even the girls—

*Moondi now takes only the fellated role in sex with boys.

they talk a lot—I know. [*Debating with himself.*] He just is the kind who doesn't say much, just sits around, and when you talk to him he smiles. [*Pause. Etc. This is getting nowhere.*]

This is resistance. Something in Moondi is gumming the works, and it bothers me, for I do not know its source. We have talked about this subject before, but Moondi is tense about it here. Others are not around, which might otherwise explain his reluctance. Is he resisting becoming *too* comfortable reflecting on these particular erotic feelings? Or is he struggling with emerging insight? He and I have discussed his sexual daydreams long enough that their covert features are emerging into consciousness. Namely, the exciting personality characteristics he attributes to his fellators are shared by his father, who is a gentle man.* Perhaps this sharedness is now transparent and Moondi cannot go further consciously without seeing the identification (thus, his resistance). [S: At any rate, observe H. as an ethnographer, with his thoughts on resistance; as he sits there with Moondi on daydreams as significant experiences; on identification; on Oedipal matters; on insight and its vicissitudes. He worries if others are around, unobserved, who might influence his informant's thoughts as well as his own. Do other ethnographers wonder what their informants experience during such data-gathering? Do they think these issues shape the data? Do they report these matters to us? Do they regret it when they do not tell us just what was going on, or do they believe that withholding information is more scientific or scholarly, more honest or fruitful?]

H: Okay. [*Switching topics.*] When, before, you were sleeping [having sex] with Weiyu, how did that come about?

M: [*A little anxious.*] I don't known . . . . At first, I didn't sleep with Weiyu. It was only after I'd slept with others. I was an *imbutu* [second-stage initiate]. [*Calmer*] . . . We were at Wopu [a nearby pig-herding place]. They were performing the third-stage [*ipmangwi*] initiations on Weiyu's age-set, and they were doing the *imbutu* on us at the same time [in 1970]. They had done the *como* eating ceremony . . . . You know, *inumdu* [a dark, shrubby, green that is eaten].[7] We all built one great big hut. And we all slept together there. The eight new *ipmangwi* and us, we just [sexually] fooled around, back and forth. And at that time, Weiyu didn't play with me. But after they performed the *ipmangwi* on him . . . [*lowers voice here*] he was sleeping in another section

*See chapter 8.

[of the Wopu house] . . . he came over at night and touched me and woke me up. And [*very low voice*] I thought, "Who is that?" So I said [*whispering*], "Who is that, who is that?" And he said, "Me, me." And I recognized Weiyu's voice. He said to me [*whispers again, very low*], "Hurry up, come on. I like you. Let's do it." [*Pause.*] And then Weiyu screwed with me. [In this sentence the quality in Moondi's voice—I've heard it before—is: "Another man who sexually used me," a feeling that lingers despite M.'s belief he is strengthened by the semen.] I was a little afraid. I was a bit crazy. And he said, "Me, me." That's what Weiyu said to me [*M. chuckles*]. Then the two of us did it.

H: Did you feel that it was [morally] all right?[8]

M: Yeah, I felt it was all right. Afterwards, when I was an *imbutu*, I used to sleep plenty of times with Weiyu. Now, Weiyu is my cousin but he [says he] didn't know I was his cousin. He was sort of crazy. He knew, all right. [*Matter-of-fact.*] He knew I was his cousin, but he didn't want to think about it. [*Pause.*]

H: And you?

M: [*Defending himself.*] At that time I was very small and I didn't know—was he my cousin or not? [*Mask of innocence.*] But it was *him*: he came to wake me up first. He was big, grown-up. And he would have known about that.

H: Did you have it with other cousins?

M: Oh, many more! [*Raised voice.*]

H: Before, huh?

M: Yeah.

H: It's not really tabooed, is it?

M: [*Quickly.*] Cousins? That's tabooed [*with some indignation*]!

H: But you play around.

M: Yeah, that's right. [*Quieter.*] It's the bachelors' badness.

H: But [what about sex with] brothers and clan brothers?

M: Oh, no no, not them. [*Pause: Trying to reason himself out again.*] And now, Weiyu is [*lower voice*]. . . . I tell him (he's shamed): "You're my cousin, and you didn't think very well." So Weiyu gets shamed, and he doesn't listen to what I say. He'll just change the subject and talk about something else. [Not much different from western folks.] But sometimes when he really listens, he'll say, "I'm sorry; I am really shamed. You mustn't say anything more about that." But I still say, "Weiyu I was your cousin, but you didn't think." And he'd say, "That's true. I was just like a pig-dog man . . . exactly." And I'd reply, "That was your craziness."

H: You said that plenty of cousins play around.

M: Yes. They're all cousins; but when they see a boy that's really nice, they think that [as a fellator] he'll feel sweet. They know he's a cousin, but still they hide it and don't say "cousin" around him. They hide it and they think, "We mustn't call him 'cousin'." Then they play around with him like he was a *birua* [man from a hostile group: an appropriate homosexual partner] so he can sleep with us.

H: You too?

M: Yeah. I know that some are my cousins, but I—uh—feel shamed if I approach them. It's like—I think like this: "They're all big; they can think for themselves that we are cousins." It's their choice. And if they like me . . . if that's what they want to do [be my fellator], it's not important.

H: And do you feel excited then?

M: [*Dully.*] Oh, no. [*Terribly dully.*] They're my cousins, it's not right to do that with them. [*Low voice.*] I won't feel excitement. [*Pause.*]

H: As a bachelor, have you played with any of your cousins?

M: No. I never was sucked off by my cousins.

[S: Is this a wrong or a right way to learn about incest taboos? Would a more formal (i.e., structural analysis) technique to better? We change subjects.]

H: [*Pause.*] I want to work with you, to talk now about you and the girl they've marked for you [his assigned fiancée]. Can we talk as we were this morning? Now, you've had a kind of fantasy. I'm concerned that we not wait too long. If too much time passes, you might forget some of your thoughts: we have stopped talking [about this subject] for three days now.*

M: It's all right. He's [S.] come, and we're all simply happy.

H: Oh, no. I wasn't talking about him blocking our work. I was thinking of how something has happened inside of you, that you're getting a new feeling, of being almost a man?

M: Yeah. I thought, "I mustn't talk too much." I must just sit down quietly.

H: But this [new manner of Moondi] is the same as your father.

M: Yeah, I thought that same thing. That's the way my father is, and now me too . . . .

H: Why should it come up now?

M: I don't know.

---

*When S. arrived, M.'s marriage concerns were temporarily forgotten.

H: Have you got some free associations?*

M: I'm not sure. I did hear that my father has gotten very sick over there, down below.[9]

H: Oh? [*News to me.*]

M: Sakulambei's woman told me. I was sorry. I wasn't just sorry, I thought about it very hard: "It's not good if he got very, very sick and he died." Around here, in these parts, we know that that is a bad place. There's lots of sickness there, and people die. My mother will go to him tomorrow . . . . She'll go to look after him.

H: Where is he?

M: At Erupmu. [*Quiet pause; then Moondi looks at me. I am waiting to see where he wants to go with this bad news.*] Oh . . . [*quickly*] that's all right. Let's go on and talk. [*Long pause. Soon after, many people enter the house. We feel it is best to stop at this point.*]

Third Session: Erotic Daydreams

The next session occurred later that afternoon, when it was quieter. At the start, S. is not in the interview, but he enters midway and joins in.

The immediate context of this discussion is as follows: during feast preparations that morning, Moondi's fiancée—accompanied by a gang of her young female friends—approached and reprimanded him in public. She had told him there was work to do (harvesting tubers for the feast?) with her parents. He felt shame and did not reply. In this situation, it is considered shameful for a youth to talk directly with his fiancée. We were never clear why *she* scolded him. But he still felt angered at being lectured—by her—in front of others. Later, Moondi mentioned that incident to Weiyu, who advised M. to talk back to her. Though seemingly trivial, this event is filled with important feelings for M: marriage, manhood, public social involvements. Here is where the tape begins. It led us into discussing his related fantasies.

H: This morning[†] we had to stop in the middle of talking about shame.

M: Yeah. It was about talking with the women.

H: Weiyu said to you, "Why don't you go talk back to her [M.'s fiancée]?" But you didn't. You told me, "I can't talk about that

---

*"Free association" is being used here as an English term; I taught it to Moondi with the concept "fantasy"; see note 1.

†Second session.

right now." [There were other people around, and he was afraid of being shamed.]

M: I thought: "It's not good that I disagree with her when we're not married yet."[10] Another thing . . . . If the men heard me being cross with that woman [fiancée], they could think: "That boy is fighting with her as if she is his *woman*," the woman who belongs to me, "as if arguing with a wife."*

H: You mean if you talk intensely with her, the men may think: "Moondi wants to marry that woman?"

M: Yeah. "He wants to marry her;" or they *could* think: "It's not time for him to talk to this woman. We [elders] haven't yet performed the *nupos* [fourth-stage initiation] on him that he can go and talk with women like that. So why has he scolded her?"

H: Is that why you get shamed?

M: Yeah. And I also feel shame when I'm near her mother and father . . . they could overhear me and think: "That boy wants our daughter too much," to screw her.

H: Would her mother and father really think that, or is that just what you think?

M: Just me. But sometimes it *is* true: people can say [*lowers voice*] "This boy is not married yet. He hasn't given a marriage feast for us. Yet he talks to her like that. Doesn't he feel shamed for talking like that?"

[*S. enters.*]

H: Let's go on to that girl they've marked for you.

M: Yeah. [*Pause.*] She really hides it when she wants to look at my face. I haven't seen her face very well, so I only can think of parts of it. I sometimes sit down and think: the nose of my woman is like this; it goes down and curves up a little bit. And I think, "Oh, that's really nice." And I think, "At night we would sleep together and do it, what all the *nupos* [married initiates] do. [*Very quickly.*] They screw in the mouth [*voice exhilarated*: the sense of a happy admission].

H: Are you talking about women? [I am surprised; I didn't realize Moondi knew the secret of the older youths: that they engage in fellatio with their young brides at or even before marriage (Herdt 1981:178–181).]

M: Of course. Weiyu told me. Though he's a little annoyed at me for telling others that he told me.

---

*Marriage always implies sexual intercourse.

H: Hm.

M: Yeah. Sometimes I think, "Suppose we constructed a house, a square house, the same kind as this one,[11] with several rooms and one bed. We'd sleep in it, and when I wanted to, I could shoot in her mouth. Because we would sleep in the same bed, I'd feel even *more* excitement. And she'd feel excitement from being with me.

H: In your daydreams* do you see her face or that of some other woman?

M: Hers. In the fantasy [M. uses this word, as taught by me, in the sense of daydream] she's got a towel and she covers up her face and her skin. She covers her breasts up completely. (I haven't yet actually seen them.) She hides them.[12] Sometimes I look at her and . . . she does that [hiding]. . . . I don't forget. So when I make up a daydream about her, I picture her face and her smile.[13] I don't forget. When I daydream about her, I imagine that.

H: When you do that, does your cock get tight?

M: Yeah! [*Said as "of course!"*] Whenever I think about her I get hard. All the time. [S: Those who believe homosexuality is caused by one's beginning erotic life with pleasurable homoerotic experiences will find this an odd homosexuality.]

Now, to see how homosexual desires compare with the heterosexual practices, I shift our conversation. I have relied on Moondi, more than anyone else, to investigate this issue, for I have watched him mature for five years (1979, by this interview) and, with our good rapport, have seen his heterosexual daydreams, underlined by the sincerity of the reported erection, overtake his homoerotic pleasures.

H: Now let us work the same way on your fantasies about X [a boy in the Yellow River Valley who used to fellate Moondi and about whom Moondi used to have daydreams].

M: Now when I'm with the initiates [potential fellators], I don't get fantasies. It's not the same as with the women, no, not at all. I'm talking only about the girl they picked for me to marry. Her only. When she is there, I feel happy about myself. When my girl looks at me, I feel she can think [*lower voice*] to herself: "My man. He's walking nearby and is seeing me." And she can look at me, and she can like me so much.

---

*I translate *koontu pookwugu* ("thought picture") as either daydream, or fantasy, depending on the situation and the speaker's meanings. Fantasies, sequences of mental images that have defined scripts, imply less recurrence and coherence than daydreams, though the two terms are experientially close. Moondi and I used only the word "fantasy," however.

H: When did you start having these kinds of feelings [a shifting from the homoerotic musings]?

M: When they chose me for marriage to her. That's when that day-dream began.

I was trying here to learn how Moondi's excitements toward boys and girls compared but didn't quite succeed. I felt he did not deal fully with his daydreams about boys because I was not clear enough.

[S: Yet the reader cannot tell that H. felt that until H. adds this paragraph above. It is in the nature of transcribed conversation that the participants' inner experience can only be inferred, and then usually not well. Novelists and poets have the advantage that they make up conversations so that the speakers reveal their intent. This is another example of our struggle with the problem of transmitting the data of subjectivity.]

H: Let's go back to your daydream. A square house.

M: Yeah. When we marry, we must build a house like this one* and construct it so one side has the fire for cooking and the other half is for sleeping. And on that side a little door. Inside is that bed; it's for two people. The two of us can sleep inside that bed.† And we can play around . . . hold her breasts. When I do that, she can feel something for herself, some kind of excitement to make her feel good. [*Pensive.*] Yeah. We can do that, and I can ask her, "Can we do it?" [have sexual intercourse]. [*He lowers his voice, which quivers slightly.*] And she says [*M. whispers*] "Oh, that's all right; we can do it." And I feel real excited; I really like sleeping with her.

H: Do you ask out loud or do you just whisper?

M: I ask her softly.

H: Because people are around or—

M: Oh, no. I'm just asking her softly, that's all. I just want to ask her softly. It's just the two of us, I shouldn't have to really make big

---

*See also note 11. A detail stands for so much. Moondi wants a square, untraditional hut: he wants change, a *new* definition of marriage, of masculine selfhood. (In fact, the pseudonym "Moondi" was chosen for this reason: it means "new [kind of] man", which is how I think of Moondi.) Does his fantasy concern identification with those Europeans who represent this change and transference to me ("similar to this hut")? Many questions that merit more data and more detailed study. But the main point is that no subjective element is meaningless.

†Extraordinary—I must repeat—to think a Sambia man will risk sleeping in the same bed as his polluting wife. What a fantasy.

noises [force her] in asking her. I just talk quietly. She's not far away. We're close together. [As he imagines this gentle love making, his voice is tender. This quality contrasts with Weiyu, who has also worked with me on his erotic daydreams. There's no tenderness there; just wham, bam, push it in: forcing a woman to have sex, a sort of rape. That's the excitement for Weiyu. Moondi, you can see, is different. Yet both are now heterosexual.] She says, "That's all right, we can do it." And when she says that, I feel my penis hard. [*Pause.*] I was thinking, "Why don't I get married quickly so I can do this." I think, "I want to sleep with her." And it gets hard.

H: In the daydream, when your cock is hard, is it [image of sexual position] in the mouth or down below?

M: [*Reflecting.*] Sometimes in the mouth and sometimes [*lowers voice*: a forbidden subject] down below.

H: Is it all right to have vaginal intercourse?

M: Yeah, she says it's all right. Then I get a tight cock in the fantasy and we screw.

H: And do you have a stiff cock while you're thinking that?

M: I get a tight cock, but for nothing. It doesn't do anything.

H: You just let it be?

M: Yeah, I just let it be . . . Oh, sometimes I have a piss, it's slack again. A fantasy does that. [*Pause.*]

H: The new kind of fantasy that you have, of women?

M: Yeah.

H: Now, the other one, about screwing initiates—

M: That belonged to before, when I was a new bachelor; then I used to imagine the boys.

H: Where is that fantasy?

M: I don't have sex much with the initiates any more. Before, yes. When we were down at Yellow Valley [during his bachelor initiation] I used to do it lots of times with that boy [X, above] who was sweet on me [the initiate with whom M. was infatuated, and vice versa]. But now? Not at all. I don't do it with the boys now.

Moondi's homoerotism has fallen off over the years. In 1975, he was regularly involved with boys. In 1976–1977, while at school, he had almost no homoerotic contacts. Since returning home, he has had infrequent homosexual play, in part, he says, because boys no longer excite him as much. He also believes he must not spend too much of his semen before marriage.

H: Could you?

M: I think that—[*pause*]. . . . No, not at all. I suppose if I felt I wanted to, I'd do it.

H: But when your cock does get tight, what do you do?

M: I just let it be, that's all.

H: Just let it be, huh? [*Long pause.*]

M: I just let it be, that's all.

Can we believe Moondi?[14] He has repeatedly denied over the years, both in words, fantasy, and actions that he masturbates. I tell this to psychoanalysts, who cannot believe it. [S: Me too, so far.] What do they doubt? That Sambia refrain? "It must be unconscious, they've just repressed it," an Australian analyst told me. [S: That's pretty silly.] Do they doubt the ethnography, or, the ethnographer's knowledge? [S: Not in H.'s case. I have pressed him twenty different ways and loaded him with my doubts so as to influence his interviews when he returned to his friends. At this point, I simply have no explanation, just doubts plus the expectation H. will someday find that some do masturbate sometimes—rarely—guiltily, secretly, never telling anyone else.] Why shouldn't they doubt? Show me one substantial report that tells what tribal people actually say and do about masturbation. [S: Roheim (1932, 1974)? Too much bend in his bias.] After seven years I still have no evidence of Moondi or anyone else masturbating to ejaculation. Here again are questions that demand in-depth clinical data. If an ethnographer says, "The Bongo Bongo do not masturbate," what are we to do with such a sweeping statement? (Beware of that weakness—few ethnographers mention masturbation in published reports.) Does such knowledge make a difference? Yes; learning about masturbation or the struggle against it can enlarge our understanding people's erotic behavior, gender identity development, self-esteem, empathy, moral outrage, religious rites, and capacity to identify with others (including those of the opposite sex). We need, in short, to study erotics, and to do so, we need deeper one-to-one study.

[S: It takes a certain innocence to think that public ritual must be more important to a culture or an individual than private fantasy. Any observer can trace the manifest content or effects of ritual. Do ethnographers know to—know how to—follow them into the individual's self-contained, secret or unconscious parts? Do ethnographers know that erotic drives, transmuted during their subterranean flow, can surface as ritual, war strategies, rules of politics, economic manifestoes, and decisions—even in Utopia—regarding woman's role at her man's side? The Leader's penis play can light the fires of crematoria and cities. And vice versa.]

H: I want to ask Dr. Stoller* if he's got anything to ask you before we stop, but it's up to you.

M: That's all right.

H: I will talk to him so he can understand. Oh . . . about S.'s work: you asked me this morning, "Does he [S.] follow your way of never telling other men about what I say?" and I said "Yes." So, likewise, if *I* talk to him, he will do the same as me [i.e., keep secrets].

M: Yeah.

S. has been sitting silently, listening. I sense both Moondi and Penjukwi as being natural and comfortable with S. I have achieved greatest trust with them: here they are generous—and courageous—with us in highly intimate interviews, like this one.

H: [*Turning to S.*] I didn't even tell you what we were doing.

S: [*Quickly.*] You were doing fantasies.

H: Yeah. This one is new during the last month—following marriage negotiations for his wife: he sees a new hut, and in the hut there is one bed. And he is in the bed with his fiancée. (She hasn't had her menarche yet.[†]) They are playing around, which he hasn't elaborated on yet, and he is excited because she has her breasts covered. He holds her breasts; and he gets more turned on; and then he gets a hard-on. And then he wants to screw her; and he asks her; and she says "yes"; and they *do* it. He gets an erection in the daydream . . . and in reality too, but he doesn't do anything with it, he says . . . I ask him, then, if this is different from the other [homosexual scenario] daydream he has, and he says it is. And I said, "Do you still have the other one sometimes?" and he said, "I do, but less and less all the time." I said, "How come you don't have sex with boys anymore?" He said, "Because I'm getting older, and I don't think about that much anymore." I asked[‡]

---

*Another detail: names and titles. Sambia call me "Gilbert," though recently (since 1979), Weiyu and Moondi have called me "Gil" (which my friends in the States call me). Before S. arrived, people asked me what to call him; Sambia are title-conscious. I told them his name was "Robert," or "Bob." Weiyu called S. "Bob." But Moondi and other called him "Dr. Stoller," apparently uncomfortable with the nickname. (And what else is involved? Power? Transference?)

†And so in reality they cannot yet be married or move further into the marriage process, that is, fourth-stage initiation, which extends over months.

‡This section has been edited for space.

if it was also because there aren't many boys available, and he said, "Yes." I said, "Is it both of those?" and he said, "Yes." I said, "Which is the most important?" He thought and said he thinks it's because there aren't any boys available. If there were, he would still screw them once in a while; but he doesn't now.

S: At this time, then, there is *no* outlet [no boys, no masturbation, no women]!

H: Right.

S: Is there an increase in the fantasy? I would think that with no outlet, it would [daydreaming] go on day and night.

H: Yeah. This is a new development: apparently he is doing it [daydreaming] quite a bit.

S: Well, it's not terribly important . . . .

H: He's hinted at this [heterosexual fantasy] to me several times before but I didn't recognize what he was talking about.*

S: Why is the girl premenarcheal? Does that turn him on?

H: Do you want me to ask him? I didn't check it out with him, since in the daydream, as in reality, she's premenarcheal.

S: But is it always a girl at that age level? For some reason that's a turn-on?

H: That's exactly correct. I hadn't thought about that. Since he thinks about screwing her in the mouth and sometimes down below, it means she's able to be screwed down below,† obviously, but I'd have to check that out with him to be sure.

S: By definition—or at least by permission—she has to be post-menarcheal . . . in order to be [vaginally] screwed by her lover. But in the daydream she's pre . . . .

H: Right. She's pre. That's very important.

S: I don't know that it is . . . it's the old story that every detail tells you something . . . but some more and some not so much.

H: This is a new version of the other daydream.

S: Why a new version today? Something about the *ceremonial* [marriage negotiations] of these past few days that you've mentioned.

H: No. [H: Yes; but I am referring to his tone. See below.]

S: Or because I'm here?

H: No. It seems related to his affect being different. We just went right into it . . . . There's something definitely different about his affect: and he found out this morning that his father is quite ill somewhere else.

---

*How much remains vague in an ethnography when the field worker—ignoring subjectivity—ignores informants' hints?
†That is, that she had her menarche.

S: Oh. And would this evening's activity [feast preparations] . . . ? If that didn't, then the news of his father would be more . . . .

H: Yeah. That's what he and I were talking about. When he first sat down, I could feel there was something different. He said, "I've been feeling different the last couple of days. Less aggressive." I said, "What does that mean? What about this afternoon?" [M.'s fiancée scolding him.] And then we talked about that. Then I said, "Does this have anything to do with you and me not having talked for three days?" He said, "No," and then he said his father is ill, which he found out this morning. That's how it went. [*Pause.*] So he and I will just continue on.

S: It's a different ambiance from the last interview. Now I'm just sitting in the midst of an on-going process and have no need to know anything. The last one [interview]* was [a tense] orientation; this one is just going—I sit and watch and it just looks very good. You get good information from both kinds, but there's more friction in the other one, which creates a different relationship. When there's less friction, you get frictionless information. They're both important. What is Moondi feeling now? My presence seems to have no [disruptive] effect. Was I present in any particular sense?

H: Well, *I'm* feeling something different in him. A flippant† quality that's not usually there but not necessarily because you're here. It may be what else is happening today. [*To Moondi:*] Dr. Stoller wants to ask you: He says that you and I are used to talking alone and now he's with us. How is that for you right now?

M: I think it's good he can listen and hear us so he can understand our talk. Your work is the same as his; when you gather secrets of one man—he [S.] won't tell that to another man. I just think it's good that he comes and listens, and if he wants to hear my secrets, that's all right. That's what I think. There's nothing wrong with it.

---

*With Kalutwo: see chapter 9.

†In the original 1979 session I said "flippant," but added: "that's not quite the right word." The dictionary defines flippant as: (1) lacking due respect of seriousness; impertinent; saucy. (2) obs. overly talkative. Now I think that neither of these connotations is apt; in fact, "lacking due respect," "impertinent," "saucy," and "overly talkative" are all wrong descriptions of what I felt in Moondi that hour. But over the course of editing, my doubts were removed, and "flippant" stuck—until I checked the dictionary. I believe now—looking back over tapes and transcription—that Moondi was lighter than usual—there was more lightness in his speech and body language. My interpretation of Moondi that moment: he felt safe and secure, less tense than normal. Somehow, our presence affected his lightness, but I cannot say quite why. The point is that my original description now seems wrong to me, and all it took was that one word. But who are we to believe—H. in 1979 or H. in 1982? I think I am more correct now, having thought about that moment a half-dozen times over three years. Here is an example of retrospective reflection changing one's description.

H: I'll tell him. [*To S.*] He thinks it's good you want to hear how the two of us talk, and he knows that you, like me, don't reveal people's secrets. And he also knows that, by doing this, you'll be able to understand better that he and I have a certain kind of work, and that you'll understand his thoughts better by being here. And I think that's correct: I don't feel any hostility at all.

S: That has to be right. It's interesting that [*struggling*] there's an awareness of his own psychology available to him; self-awareness, not just experiencing. A revolutionary idea [for a Sambia]—that you can have your own psychology—

H: [*Cuts in.*]—thoughts [that one thinks, reflects, about oneself].

S: —and be interested in doing it. And that you would sit down with someone, that someone like Moondi can make that jump. He is experiencing discovering* what we—not everyone in our culture—but what we take for granted: the past is living [intrapsychically] in the present, and not in the sense of their [Sambia] ghosts. An idea like that was just not available [before, as a fully conscious cultural understanding].

DISCUSSION

S. and H: How is the erotic manifested in Moondi? What role has culture played? Can we say that Moondi's erotism is in any way eccentric or unique, a result of his life history and personal experiences? Sexual excitement is made, not born; some combination of personal and social factors create this.

Let us review and orient this interview.[15] We are talking with Moondi, a bachelor, who is moving toward marriage. He is male, the sex preferred by parents, since only males can defend the hamlet against the unending threat of destruction in war. At age eight, he is suddenly removed from his mother's doting attention and, via brutal and terrifying initiation rites, is resocialized by the men so that he will grow up to be manly, a warrior, a husband, and a father. The process begins with the first-stage initiation, when he enters the phase of semen ingestion. He has only a few years to do so, however, for with his third-state initiation at puberty, he may no longer take in semen but is to offer his penis to the next cohort of boys. At the same time the females are forbidden to him.

Whatever reverberations lie hidden within these overt experiences,

---

*S: I.e., meaning, interpretation, belief, synthesis; not conditioning, machinery, or acetylcholinesterase (even if it takes a bucketful of enzyme to get angry at women).

we know that from the start of their erotic lives and for the years of their peak orgasmic capacity, these young men are propelled into intense, obligatory, praiseworthy, powerfully gratifying homoerotism. At the same time that males are positively reinforced as the only sex objects, females are negatively reinforced. They are not just forbidden. The taboos are nailed down by the dread created as boys now learn how vaginal fluids cause illness (if not ritually treated) and eventual death—the consequence of being infected by even a droplet of menses. Yet Moondi, who at nineteen learns the identity of the girl he will marry, begins—without deprogramming—to create powerfully erotic heterosexual daydreams. And if he is like other Sambia men, he will desire women the rest of his life, without ever forgetting his homoerotic joys. In fact, by becoming initiators and teaching about homosexual fellatio to sons and other new initiates in later years, these men are reminded of and have reinforced for them the positive value of semen and homoerotic activities.

Probably if Sambia society allowed adult married men to be homoerotic, some, as in our society, would be bisexual. But those like Moondi would not; they love their lust for women. And it is that lust—with its depth and breadth—that behavioristic explanations would say ought not be there. As Moondi exemplifies and as hundreds of hours of interviews, gossip, and bull sessions with other men revealed, desire for women is—for all its vicissitudes—as gripping for Sambia men as it is anywhere else.

Could this just be bluster by men denying that they are "really" homosexual? We doubt it as we think of their desire for multiple wives, of the occurrence of adultery despite severe taboos, and of men's drive for intercourse, so strong that even the terrors of female fluids cannot halt the heterosexual tension. And finally, were that heterosexual need weak, it would be further subdued by the men's awareness that every ejaculation of semen advances the deterioration of one's manhood. (Remember that intercourse with women is thought to be more depleting than that with boys.)

In Moondi's case, then, we see a normative gender and erotic developmental pattern. What would seem bizarre and the negation of masculinity is, here, as in other instances of age-structured homosexuality (Adam 1986; Herdt 1987b), a particularly royal road to it.

What of aberrance? An example from Moondi's narrative returns us for a moment to our data. Even in the gay community in our society, we do not hear of men who fetishize other males' mouths, comparable to the fetishizing of women's bodies by heterosexual men. In fact, despite the importance of mouths as erotic organs among homosexuals and heterosexuals in our society, one does not hear at all of the fetishizing of mouths. Yet Sambia males, in erotic reminiscing, go on and on about the shapes and aesthetics of mouths. The same point applies to the emphasis on semen among Sambia, for, as noted in chapter 2, the quality of semen is a great factor in the fellators' experience. We do not find this same preoccupation in the West, however. And though there is an aesthetic of penis appearance among many (heterosexuals and homosexuals) in our culture, there is none with the Sambia. For them the penis is a semen conveyor, a vessel. It is at these points of precise observation, where technical vocabulary and theory give way to subjective reality, that we could find the proper proportions for mixing psychodynamic and learning theories to explain a piece of behavior (see Stoller and Herdt 1985).

Later, in chapter 9, we shall examine a man—Kalutwo—for whom erotic aberrance has become a way of life, and his case will, we think, reveal even more clearly the normativeness of Moondi's erotism.

Out of particular people, in particular cultural settings, one gets particular sexual excitement. The details of this phenomenon can only come from clinical ethnography. We hope to demonstrate this more in subsequent chapters.

CHAPTER FIVE

Tali and Weiyu on Ritual and Erotics

BIOGRAPHIC SKETCHES

H: Tali and Weiyu are my two most important adult collaborators. They were essential to my research. They aided me in learning language and in understanding ritual custom, kinship, and marriage. Tali's role as a ritual expert was crucial for studying Sambia initiation and its meaning. Yet both men are far more than "informants." They are also friends and companions, cronies who helped build my house, who fed me, and became two more sets of eyes, ears, minds, and hearts. This chapter is about these men, their relationship to me, and conversations they had with S. and myself.

The following texts present these dialogues. Unlike our other interview-chapters, these data were not collected as part of individual case studies. I was working with Weiyu and Tali on various social matters, such as ritual beliefs and practices. S. joined in these conversations. He asked questions of his own that sparked unexpected responses from the men. We shall examine the themes of our talking later.

Both men have known me since 1974. Both live in Nilangu and were my neighbors. Tali was then in his late twenties, though he looked older and seemed widely experienced for his age. He was married and had a two-year-old son. Weiyu was about twenty-two years old, still a bachelor and living in the men's house. They were simply fellow-villagers then, not especially close to each other. Their relations with the outside world were as different as possible. Weiyu had worked on coastal plantations for several years in the early 1970s, he spoke Pidgin and Motu fluently, and he was relatively sophisticated (and saw himself that way) compared to his peers. Tali, on the other hand, was a traditionalist who had never been outside the local area, spoke no Pidgin, and was naive about western ways. But because they shared many personality traits and were co-workers in my research, they eventually became allies and confidants.

I knew Weiyu first. His marriage ceremony occurred only a month after my arrival in the village. He stood out from his peers: he was taller, more verbal, gregarious and (by Sambia standards and my own) handsome. He liked to show off, to be seen as acculturated when it counted; when dressed in warrior garb (which was rare, for he usually wore western clothes), he cut a dashing figure. Women liked him and he knew it: he is still a ladies' man, a Don Juan. He liked sex with boys too; in fact, he likes sex in general. He's more blatant about that than most Sambia men, and his coastal experience was a big factor in making him more sexually aggressive. Weiyu and his cohort of three fellow initiates invited me (in December 1974) to join in their initiation festivities shortly after my arrival. I was thrilled, honored, surprised: I did not see then how that single event could get me so quickly involved as their ally.[1] This experience made me, by age (I was 25, about their age), subsequent identification by other villagers, and common interests (being bachelors), their agemate.

Weiyu's childhood is unusual. (Why is this true of almost all my Sambia colleagues?[2]) His true father was a renowned and feared shaman of Pundei village (Nilangu's sister hamlet). He was said to have been a physically powerful man, too—tall and strong, impressive and reckless. Some twenty years ago (Weiyu doesn't remember him) he was murdered by his own clan brothers in an infamous massacre that set off a war between Pundei and Nilangu.[3] Weiyu's father was simply too brazen and reckless: he openly flirted with women, let it be known that he was screwing other men's wives, used his powerful sorcery knowledge to keep men afraid of him, and—the unbearable and insane sin—claimed with pride responsibility for the (sorcery) deaths of several people. He was disposed of in an ambush—hacked to death by a gang of brother-warriors. As a result, his widow fled with her two children, Weiyu and his older sister, to Nilangu, where they were given shelter by their affines. Eventually, a Nilangu big man, Chemgalo, who was himself an older widower, took Weiyu's mother as his wife. He adopted Weiyu and, with unusual kindness for that day, gave Weiyu the advantage of full social rights in the village. Shortly before his initiation, Weiyu's mother died. He has been cared for since by Chemgalo's eldest daughter (his step-sister), and Chemgalo himself, who never remarried.[4]

The wound opened by Weiyu's father's murder has never healed.

His father's only biologic brother (himself a powerful shaman) also fled Pundei and never returned. This man (now deceased) used to mutter to me that the murderers would pay eventually (i.e., through his sorcery powers). Sambia is a society that honors blood revenge, yet Weiyu's father has never been revenged. So Weiyu grew up with a fantasy, sometimes quietly expressed today, that *he*, the son, carries the burden of knowing that there has as yet been no revenge. This awareness—and quiet, romantic identification with an amazing father cut down and never known—is burned into Weiyu's masculinity.

Weiyu's marriage was also odd. He and his wife were the first couple (to my knowledge) to have chosen each other. They were mutually attracted and went against others' wishes in marrying. There is also a sense that Weiyu's wife is socially inappropriate for him.[5] They have been at each other's throats for years. Both are jealous. Weiyu is also flirtatious and an exuberant fornicator. As a bachelor he loved screwing boys (was even sometimes unscrupulous, screwing his cousins such as Moondi, Chapter 4, who are supposed to be tabooed). He outgrew boys, though, and has since concentrated on women, whom he voraciously prefers. Weiyu is, nonetheless, more a fornicator than a lover of women: he is misogynous. He has had many fights with his wife; they constantly have terrible arguments. (I know he beats his wife, but I have never seen him do it. She has also clobbered him.) Though they have a house, gardens, and now two children, their marriage is not successful or satisfying.[6] (Weiyu's mother-in-law is always telling me "I told you so"; she didn't want them to marry by choice. The mother-in-law seems to feel that their chaos is the result of marriage inspired by romance, not custom.) Tali shares feelings of misogyny with Weiyu, and though Tali and his wife fight, they do not—nor do most other couples—persist in the vicious combat that characterizes Weiyu's marriage.

Tali is older and wiser than Weiyu. He is a thinker and a planner. His life is well organized: he knows what he wants and how to get there. He was the third of four sons of a prominent man, who had three wives. He grew up in Moonunkwambi, a neighboring hamlet (of the same phratry) that no longer exits. His upbringing was otherwise ordinary. Early on he showed himself to be a gifted hunter, and he still loves to hunt. First initiated about 1955, he has since been an active ritual cult member. He also fought in several battles before pacification and was considered a good warrior.

Tali had had, however, an unusually wide range of ritual training. He likes to travel and has been to virtually every dispersed Sambia group and all surrounding tribal areas. He has trading partners in other tribes. While still a second-stage initiate he traveled with several visiting Menya tribesmen back to their villages (near Menyamya) on a trading expedition. Through this experience he made contact with ritual experts and thereby with traditions of myth beyond any most Sambia *elders* know. He had also a distant older male relative and closer half-brother, who taught him many magical spells and special secret ritual techniques. Thus, by adolescence, Tali was already well on his way to becoming a ritual expert.

What kind of man was he to become?* First, he is a traditionalist. He believes in his heritage, its customs, beliefs, and conventional wisdom about the nature of man and woman, erotic and gender development. He followed all the correct formulas for his own development, from careful attention to being a homosexual fellator to gain strength, to following elders' instructions and regulations regarding his own sexual (insertor) contacts with boys and then women. When I first knew him he dressed only in native garb. He was not an imposing figure: medium height and build, average-looking, and not an exhibitionist. But in initiation he stands out: he is an organizer, quietly in command and competent in the public rhetoric. As he has grown older, he is more prominent and he keeps people and activities steady and working. He was married rather late, in the old way of infant betrothal—the most conservative marriage—to Nashu, a very traditional woman. Today (1982), in his mid-thirties, they have been married 10 years and seem content with each other. They have two boys, aged 7 and 4. They fight and squabble, but not as much as they used to; and they seem to me, now, to be happier and more successful than ever. They are generous, well-liked people.

My relationship with Tali and older men has always been simpler for me than my relationship with other interpreters, especially youths and initiates. This was, as usual, much of my own making. For a year (1974–1975) I largely ignored Tali, something I could not do with the initiates. Having come to investigate the boys' experience of undergoing ritual initiation, I felt it a duty to attend first to that neglected topic before others, and before it was too late (after the cult had dramatically changed following westernization). Working alone, classed as a bachelor, I was more identified with bachelors and had to overcome, as much as possible, the tensions, turmoils, and one-sided dominance of that social position in my dealings with young initiates. (With some of them I never succeeded; I remained either too threa-

---

*We acknowledge permission to reprint some of this biographical material on Tali (pages 110–111) from G. Herdt, *Guardians of the Flutes*, pp. 338–341. New York: Columbia University Press, 1987.

tening or too much a rich white European, to achieve trust.) With the
bachelors, like Weiyu (until his marriage), the pressures were different, since I was perceived more as a peer (a colleague, a competitor).
With women I remained a rather distant curiosity; benign, congenial,
and eligible but much too roped off by the men to be very involved
with them. With elders I was (at least with my sponsors) adopted
affectionately, cared for, exploited and exploiting (e.g., I gave them
canned fish and small gifts) but was still seen as immature and below
them. Tali never got entangled much in these early scenarios; he was
simply there, going about his hunting (he is still an avid and successful hunter), and mentioning that he had a lot to teach me.

Two things changed our relationship in late 1975. The first was
my interest in ritual. Following the performance of collective initiations that year, I started to study myth and ritual. Before that I had
interviewed initiates, for which Moondi served as the chief interpreter. Eventually, though, I needed to interpret the texts gathered
from initiations. The men said that Tali was the one to ask. But, because of the stratification of ritual knowledge, I needed another interpreter—Weiyu—who, as a newly married man, could discuss such
matters secretly with Tali and me (the initiates and Moondi were kept
well removed at such times). Likewise, for fear of their embarrassment or shame, I had always to take care in arranging work with
Moondi and other initiates, especially on topics like dreams and sex,
when the adults were gone. I needn't belabor the obvious: that this
dual secrecy presented logistical problems, conflict in interpersonal
ties, and, after months, definitely changed my role to that of middle-
man-accomplice with initiates, who trusted me, on the neutral ground
of my house. (My acquiring ritual secrets was, sadly, not complicated
by deep involvement with women, since I remained until 1979 a spec-
tator in relation to them.)

In these circumstances, Tali took to working with me frequently,
communicating secrets about ritual and his opinions of them. He and
his little son also visited my house to pass the time in the evening. I
would offer him tea, or a cigarette, and a few disjointed pieces of
conversation; but because I spoke Sambia poorly then, we usually
said little, and he stayed only briefly. An accident then changed our
relationship.

Late in 1975, I returned from the mountain patrol station to Nilangu, hiking through the mountains with some Sambia, including
Tali. We arrived in the hamlet the day after his house had burned to
the ground. (This misfortune is not unique, since grass huts are consumed in a few minutes, once they catch fire.) Tali was devastated:

all his possessions, including his ritual items and money, were lost. He was furious at his wife, whom he blamed. As usual, he handled this event with a flurry of emotion, followed by sullenness and then quiet depression. After a day or so of detachment, feeling sympathy for him and trying to bolster his spirits, I gave him a pair of my walking shorts (he had lost all his garments too), some tobacco, and a little money. (He could use the money to help him feel better; for instance, he would have to barter or buy ritual ornaments again, and he eventually did so.) He quietly accepted the gifts with thanks, was obviously moved, but otherwise said nothing.

Over the next year, those two events—our ritual work and those gifts—came back on me in unexpected ways. More than once when I least expected it, Tali spoke of his misfortune and my kindness. Once I needed a favor; he did it without my asking. Later he said I had also helped him. At another time, while I was on patrol (1976) among the neighboring Yagwoia tribe, Tali again was invaluable: he went among his cronies, found a bilingual Sambia, and then sent word to a Yagwoia man of a distant hamlet known to hold many myths. The man arrived near midnight the next evening, to my complete surprise. But since he had to return the next day, Tali led us that very night in setting about to collect as many myths as possible (acquiring them for his own repertoire too), till the wee hours of the morning. In ways like that he made me a friend.

But most impressive of all was what occurred one evening in late 1976, after a day's work with Tali and Weiyu on ritual matters. It was near the end of my fieldwork; men knew I would leave in a few weeks. And though I told them I would return, and though they wanted to believe this, life, they know, is filled with uncertainty. Around 8:00 P.M., Tali walked into my house with his son, and we began to chat. Weiyu also arrived. After tea and some jokes, Tali said he had thought about the *tingu** again and that he wanted to say something else he had neglected that morning. This afterthought surprised me, for it happened only once before. (That is, after an interview, Tali returned later wanting to clarify a specific point.) After he shared his thoughts, I thanked him, communicating my surprise. Then he added: "You really want to know about our lives. We thought you came just to learn about the ritual customs. [*Serious.*] But you want to understand us, don't you? That's why I thought about this and told you."

Over the years Tali has become a pragmatist. He was designated the first local *komitiman* of Nilangu by its people back in the early

---

*The menstrual blood organ, important in the ritual belief system.

1970s. Since then he has been a tireless hearer of local disputes. He has slowly learned bits of Pidgin (but is still not conversant). He nearly always wears western clothes now. In recent years, he made the unprecedented decision to send his oldest son out to a mission school, instead of initiating him and having him stay close. Today he sees the ritual cult as dying and feels that his son's schooling is a decision for his family's future. Nonetheless, he continues his hunting, has broadened his social contacts, continues to make arranged marriages through infant betrothal for his sons, nose-bleeds himself and follows customary ritual ways, and runs his household as a present-day form of the household he knew and loved in his childhood.

Weiyu and Tali worked well together. I liked Weiyu; and in our several years' talking, traveling—observing initiations, visiting neighboring tribes, going to the Patrol Post to resupply—and living close by, I got to know him for himself. As you would expect, Tali and Weiyu also became closer: they were no longer just fellow villagers and cultmembers; they were also co-workers for me whose social and economic interests were allied.[7] Both are self-assertive, gregarious, high in self-esteem, verbally articulate, curious and able to enjoy new experiences, misogynous, keenly interested in ritual customs and heritage, full of enjoyment of sexual behavior, etc. From talking constantly with me they share a store of experience and cultural knowledge (about Sambia and Westerners) unusual even for elder Sambia. And so they are now intimates, whom others identify with me.

The next sessions with Stoller must be seen in the light of this history. After several months, my follow-up work with Tali on Sambia ritual was done. I was finishing up and saying goodbye. These were men with whom I am so entangled that I think of them as among the people closest to me in the world. I was ready for more challenging dialogue with them than ever before, a new kind of ethnographic experience with one's friends; a mutual exploring of interiors so as to know each other better. Stoller was our catalyst.

SUBJECT I: WIFE-STEALING

This conversation occurred spontaneously between Weiyu and Tali, with H. and S., from 10:30 until 11:30 P.M. The tone is low-key, we are alone, late at night, a bull session. As in previous days, Weiyu and Tali have again drifted to the subject of Nilutwo.[8]

Nilutwo had an accident, soon to be mortal. While hunting he fell from a tree, breaking his back. He was flown by helicopter to a distant hospital, and returned, untreatable. His legs, paralyzed, gave him constant, terrible pain. His bladder was paralyzed. The skin of his legs had terminal trophic changes. He was episodically unconscious from uremic delirium. A once powerful, driven, warm, brave, masculine man—the greatest living cassowary hunter—was reduced to a dying, invalid ward of his wife and the village. Penjukwi, his wife, managed as best she could, but the ever-present conflict in their marriage erupted again. (Nilutwo, with the men's help, had stolen Penjukwi, shrieking in rage and agony, from her natal hamlet. She was subsequently, in effect, raped into marriage by N., a legitimate though rare form of courtship nowadays; see chapter 6). Tali, who was Nilutwo's friend, took over much of his support, and eventually Penjukwi and Nilutwo began living with Tali and his wife in their house. This placed Nilutwo squarely in Tali's life, and Tali frequently expressed frustration about it, as in the following session.

The men in the village were all wondering who would get Penjukwi after Nilutwo's death. By tradition, a woman may be inherited (levirate marriage) by her deceased husband's brothers or clansmen. Penjukwi was still young and attractive, and the men were very interested in her. But she was also independent and wise, so she had pointedly avoided situations that would have compromised her future choices. Tali was, in effect, her guardian. Weiyu, who loves to talk about semen and sex anyway, let it be known that he was interested in her, would perhaps marry her. I was aghast that the men were, in a sense, already drawing straws over Penjukwi before her husband's death. Though a friend of both sides, I felt obliged to help Penjukwi and thus put myself at odds with the men.

H. fills in S. on the above. Weiyu and Tali gossip.

HERDT: [To S.] Nilutwo now [finally] is totally at his wife's mercy. They're at each other's throats. He's been so difficult for her. But Tali probably won't do it. [Tali threatened to kick Nilutwo out of T.'s house, because N. is driving everyone crazy with his incessant demands, constant pain, and screams.] Tali has a good heart. He's just shooting off steam. [*Weiyu talks in a quiet voice to Tali. Then:*]

WEIYU: Nilutwo is thinking about his woman: "Those two [Tali and Weiyu], they're sitting and watching me. They want to butter her up for when I die." [*Tali chuckles. Then Weiyu snaps to T.:*] Stop that! This is serious.*

H: [*To T. and W.*] That's what you're thinking, huh?

*Only because Weiyu wants to steal Penjukwi.

W: Yeah.

H: Oh, yeah. Because he thinks you come around to butter up Penjukwi so you can screw her? Is that why Nilutwo is angry?

W & T: [Enthusiastically] Yeah.

H: Is this true?

W: It's true that that's what he's thinking. But we're not really buttering her up. That's just what he's thinking: "I'm just sick, I'm here, they think I'm sleeping, they [Weiyu] just think to themselves, 'He's an old sick man here, he's not about to watch and see what we do.'"

H: Is it true?

W: [Broad grin.] I'm a *man!* [Meaning: of course it's true. *Tali chuckles.*]

S: [Quietly.] So they would like it, huh? [W. and T. laugh broadly.]

H: [Chuckles.] So it's really true after all; it's not just his [N.] imagination?

W: Oooooh!

S: Why not, from their point of view? [All half-serious and half-joking.]

H: Exactly [more serious]. Why not, yes! [Sarcastic.]

W: [Continues joking.] When you go back to America and come back, you may hear that your friend [W.] did this and he did that [acted lascivious] to this woman.* Everyone will tell you the story. About me. [Tries to get more serious.] But listen, it isn't like she's a man, this woman. She can't just sit around here. She can't just be unmarried here. That's no good. A woman has no strength at all. Who's to help her work her gardens and build her new outhouse, and things like that?

H: [Ironic.] Who will help her by screwing her and screwing her?

W: [Big laugh.] There, that's it! That something of hers [vagina] doesn't have a man to boss it. Now me, I must be the boss of that particular thing of hers. [Voice trails off. He's a bit excited, horny, perturbed, and joking, all at once.]

H: [To S.] He says a woman shouldn't just sit around: just sitting there is no good . . . That [sex] is all she's good for.

S: Yeah.

H: [Paraphrasing.] There'll be no one to help her; women don't have strength of their own. Who will make gardens for her or help her out? And there's no one to boss her cunt.

---

*Penjukwi outsmarted the men; Weiyu never had a chance. See chapter 6.

W: [*To H., joking.*] Tali, he's a man of the law. He doesn't think like
    this.

H: Yeah, he's a good man. But *you* . . .

T: Yes, that's right.

W: Oh, I'm all right. I am a man.

[S: Pretty funny talk. But beneath the locker-room humor is a whiff
of death. Penjukwi is not just another local lady. As H. said above,
at 18 (she is now around 24), she was kidnapped and ravished by
Nilutwo; she was also uppity, known in the Valley for her looks, independence, and a spot of schooling (in a place of sophistication: a
village by a grass airstrip three hours away). Unlike the other women,
she has too much education and speaks some Pidgin. She also has an
odd tattoo on her face. (See chapter 6.) So when her husband—he
the great hunter, far too skilled to have such an accident—fell, the
men believed she had bewitched him to get revenge after all these
years. As soon as he died, they would accost her, beat her up.

    We were in a quandary. As much as possible, and slightly cowed
by the moral dilemma involved, we had at all times—H. for years, I
for these few days—obeyed our rule not to tamper with custom, settle disputes, teach new skills (other than the search for insight), or
practice medicine. Nonetheless, we broke this rule and, before leaving, warned all concerned not to harm Penjukwi. On returning in 1981,
H. found her alive, unbeaten, unraped, unthreatened, unmarried; de-
fiantly, happily alone. Sambia culture is changing. And she is perhaps—because the men are too dispirited to force her—among the
beneficiaries.]

H: Where and when should anthropologists intervene in such situations? We join others (see Epilogue) in our concern and perplexity
over such ethical issues. Still, we feel that ethnographers should in-
sert these ethical aspects *in* their ethnographies, rather than elsewhere in field method treatises or letters to the *American Anthropologist Newsletter*. Again, such editing restricts and distorts our work.

SUBJECT II: BREAST-FEEDING OR ORGASM?

We continue without break to a second topic in the same session. This
material arises from previous conversations on women hiding their
breasts and breast-feeding. As Chapter 2 explains, this topic is powerfully linked with sex—especially fellatio—though I did not concentrate on its private manifestations until S.'s questions prompted
me to.

H: [*To Weiyu.*] I was telling him [S.] about the way we all work.

W: Uh-huh.

H: Now, I was thinking about the times you've talked about the the custom of women hiding their breasts, that it's not good for men to look at them. Last week I heard that some women say they felt *imbimboogu* [orgasm] when they breast-fed babies. Have you heard this? [*W. and T. whisper for a minute.*]*

W: No. The women don't talk about this to us. But we think our wives have felt this. I can ask my woman and find out.

H: It's taboo to look at them while they're breast-feeding?

W: [*Repeats the teachings:*] You can't look at the mother feeding the baby and can't sit around with the mother and baby. Instead, you must stay with the men in the men's house.

H: Yeah, that's [breaking post-partum taboo] no good.

W: If you watched the baby with its mouth holding on to the nipple of the breast, I'd think of my wife's mouth doing the same to my penis. If you think like that [*voice speeds up*] you won't let her be. You'll want to screw her. Then you'll ruin your child.

H: Did we ever talk before about women having *imbimboogu* with breast-feeding?

W: No. [*To T. in Sambia.*] We didn't talk about that, did we?

T: No.

W: But it's true when they breast-feed that the fluid comes out of the breast, and when that happens they feel *imbimboogu*. I think they told you the truth.

H: Did you think of this before or only now?

W: Uh, uh. Only now. You mentioned it and that's it.

H: Hmmmm. I want to tell him [S.] about this. [*To S.*] I asked them if they had ever heard that when women breast-feed they have an *imbimboogu*, and he said, "No, we'd never heard of that before."

S: Had they never *thought* of it? I'm not correcting you. They'd never heard of it, but in addition it's not part of their fantasy system? Is that right? Or you don't know? Should you ask?

H: Well, now that I've said that, Weiyu replied: "I think that when their milk comes outside that they feel *imbimboogu*." So I responded: "What do you mean that you think that?" And then I clarify: "You mean now you think that's how it is? And he said, "Yeah, that's how I think."

---

*Why are they whispering? Because this subject is illicit, secret, and filled with power for males (and females). Here, then, is an example of what elsewhere I have called "whispering secrets."[9]

S: Do they think it's possible because both organs hang from the body, have a special end, and put out a fluid?

H: Well, that's—

S: You can't ask them that . . .

H: Sure, sure, yeah.

S: Well, how could you have an organ like that where you didn't get an *imbimboogu?* Now the next question would be: is that the same as ejaculation that *they* have, or is it just that it is the appropriate word for the fluid going out, not for the feeling?* The feeling that goes with it, not the feeling that goes with it coming out. And if they believe that, then how have they never seen a woman sense that?

H: Yeah, well, one answer would be that women always hide the act. [*Pause, seeing consternation on S.'s face.*] Women always hide breast-feeding.

S: But they don't hide. I've seen them.†

H: Well, that's what I just asked him. I said, how does it go, you know, with women breast-feeding babies? And then he said the ritual teaching goes that you're not supposed to watch your wife breast-feed, because you'll think of the breast as if it were a [your] penis with the baby [wife] sucking it. He made this motion as if breasts were the penis and the nipple—

S: So the ritual teaching very consciously links breast and penis, and milk and semen . . .

H: And the baby and the mother . . .

S: Yeah; so it looks like we are getting an amplification of a peculiar detail in the daydream [seen in Moondi's case, chapter 4] and what may be central to their culture.

H: Yeah, that's right.

S: If you want to try it again anyway, you can see if they think that the woman is literally having an orgasm in our sense of the word.

H: Yeah, yeah. I'm thinking now of various possibilities [for how to ask them to clarify their thinking. *H. turns to Weiyu:*] We have now heard you say that you've never heard the women talk about this.

W: Yeah.

H: Now when women . . . what do you think women are feeling when they give milk to babies?

W: Yeah, we don't ask the women that. But we think that their water [milk], it—the water of the breast . . .

*See chapter 6.
†Further discussed in chapter 4.

H: Yeah.

W: It comes outside and—

H: What do they feel?

W: None of us think about them like that. We don't think about what they feel when the milk comes out. They just give food to babies and we just forget about thinking about it, that's all.

H: Do the men ever talk together about this?

W: No, we don't talk about this. You mustn't [taboo] look too much at them [breast-feeding]. That's what the elders say. [*Coached by Tali, whose voice is hoarse from talking so much today:*] If you look too closely, what can you do? You have no outlet, no way: what can you do [if you get sexually aroused and you want intercourse, since this is forbidden].

H: Hmmm. [*To. S.*] Here's a problem in methodology: I've just asked them again something I have already asked them before: "Do you guys have any thoughts or daydreams about women giving milk to babies?" And there's just a blank.

S: What about using guided imagery? I'm not sure whether I mean guided imagery in the sense that you use it—the more formal technique—but could you improvise something whenever you get up against a blank that you feel has something behind it?

H: Yeah.

S: Could you have offered them the opportunity to have a free-floating visual experience?

H: That's what I'm doing with Moondi.

S: So, then, that's my answer methodologically. That's the exact place to try it: where you don't feel that it's a blank just because they've run out, or are bored, or tired, or something else.

H: Yeah. I've thought about that but never made this explicit; I can now. There is still another approach: I've asked them the straightforward question and know how to get at this from a different angle.

S: Yeah. Should you now go to a more roundabout question?

H: No, what I'm saying now is that I've asked the straightforward question and I know how to get at it from another angle. One angle is to bring up the question of why in the first-stage initiation teaching, the mother's breast is equated to the penis and why men go to the trouble of equating semen with breast milk. And by doing that, I set up a train of associations which will eventually lead to the same point.

S: Oh, I see. So that's what you should do, except that they're tired and—

H: Yeah, they're tired.

S: And pick it back up tomorrow. That's what we should do then.

H: [*Chuckling.*] Enough. [*To W. and T.*] We can all work tomorrow.

S: [*To H.*] Are you noting the time of day? It may not be important, but it's an easy thing to put down.

H: No, it is important.

S: Because material gathered between 10:30 and 11:30 at night will have perhaps no explanation except the time of night.

H: I usually note the time of day in my notes because it does make a difference.

But the men refused to quit, hyped on the conversation at the moment. So we went on. During this next part of the dialogue, we get into men's private experience of ritual beliefs. These beliefs concern semen depletion, such a widely shared fear among Sambia men. Specifically, we are talking of how men, during intercourse with their wives, picture the tree sap they will drink to replace their semen.

Unfortunately, our tape broke here, and we lost about three minutes of important dialogue. S., fitting into the situation, playfully challenged Weiyu and Tali's beliefs about the growth-power in semen. He testified that while he'd never ingested semen and has drunk no milk since childhood, he nonetheless has a wife and four grown children. How could they explain that? The men took the challenge and there were several rapid interchanges, each side determined not to give in. I was apart from this conversation, having never directly challenged the men's beliefs. This led us to discussing drinking tree sap. (You will see, later, how this dialogue may have dredged up latent thoughts in the men.) [S: My purpose in challenging them was not to get information on erotic and gender issues but to investigate the style and quality of their skills in argumentation, especially logic. I found that, given their first premises plus my having nothing but my mouth for proving my assertions—no appeal to authorities and information and no technology for scientific demonstrations—they were as smart as I. I had no advantages in the debate and we all had a great time.]

S: How do they experience drinking the tree sap? Do they picture the tree?

H: They talk of it as an image of the tree. [*To W.*] Do you have a thought-image of the tree?

W: [*Enthusiastic.*] I see that all the time. When I have sex, I think about the tree. [*Spirited talk between W. and T.*]

H: [*To S.*] W. says he sees it all the time. "I never told you about this; I don't know why."

S: I'd like to hear about that. He's really talking about the cult. And your main subject of study here all these years has been the cult.

H: Yeah. There's a simple explanation for this picturing the sap. (Well, not an explanation): the tree stands for their masculinity. The tree's got their maleness in it.

S: You're suggesting that it is defensive. (We should ask them.) I was thinking that it's not only that. You get it from your mother, from the moment you're born. It represents something inside you: it represents your father or what is taught you by your father, the most primal knowledge.

H: But how could it be taught like that? Because they don't know about this use of milk sap until they're fifteen years old and more. It doesn't have to be defensive unless it's defending them against something.

S: Well, I don't know what I mean. [S: I do now, but I'm still vague: the specifics, it is true, are revealed only in adolescence, but the power of milk/semen is in some way known to everyone—male and female—from infancy on. Every object in the real world and every function of any living thing—animal or plant—is believed to be saturated with the primal power of milk/semen. So, for instance, when a mother gives her milk to her infant, the mass of microscopic movements and behaviors we summarize with the word "feeding" is just a bit different from the way mothers nurse who do not have these beliefs. The teaching, then, starts at birth, long before the knowledge takes cognitive forms.] [*Persists.*] I don't know what I mean, but I'm not going to give in to what you said.

H: [*Also persists.*] It's secret knowledge until they're seven years old or so (and in different ways, until they're sixteen or seventeen).

S: You mean it's not till then that they hear about the vital function of semen? That's not what I meant but—

H: Well, they don't need replenishing [they need to be filled up first], and if they had that [tree sap] to start with, they might not drink semen.*

S: I've got it now.

H: I wasn't thinking of it as being necessarily defensive, though it could be, because the context in which he is saying this is: when he doesn't drink sap, he has trouble ejaculating. So in the very

---

*Boys who resist homosexual insemination might drink tree sap instead, no longer comforted by the rationalization that semen is their only source.

context in which those data have emerged it leaves cause for wondering to what extent is that a defensive image. Your idea is more like what I would expect an anthropologist to give! [*Chuckle.*] This need to replace semen is a religious experience, passionate (though not erotic), as in certain rituals. Passionate and not necessarily defensive.

S: Well, let's go back. He says it happens all the time, but he doesn't mean all the time. He means that, as far as he is concerned, it can happen at times when he has no explanation? Ask him to sort of like free associate to examine when thoughts of sap come up.

H: [*To W.*] Did you say: this kind of thought [the free floating image of the tree sap] or this kind of *koontu pookwugu* [image]—is it a thought or is it a *koontu pookwugu* [image] of that tree and its milk-sap?

W: It's only thinking* (*koontu*).

H: Thinking or *koontu pookwugu?*

W: *Koontu pookwugu.*

H: Do you see a picture of the tree inside of your thoughts?

W: Yeah, yeah, yeah.

H: Does this occur at other times?

W: *All* the time I get that. *All* the time.

H: All the time.

T: All the time. Before, when you asked me—and right now, we [W. and T.] were talking among ourselves, saying, "Oh, right now, as Gilbert was asking us about that . . . we didn't think to say it— to tell him so he would understand about that."

W: Only now; we just now thought about [reflected on and verbalized] this experience. [Weiyu is saying here that he and, he says, Tali, had felt this experience many times before but simply had never verbalized it. It's not that they were hiding it, they're saying, but rather they had just never reflected on it.]

H: Yeah.

W: [*Slight pause.*] You've asked us before: "When each of you ejaculates your water, what do you feel? What do the two of you think about?" You have asked us, just like that before, but we were just crazy [*long-long*]. We didn't think about it. [*T. agrees, wistful.*] You've showed us that . . .

H: You're talking about the *imbimboogu* [orgasm]?

W: Yeah, the *imbimboogu.*

---

*This expression—"thinking"—carries the sense of idea or mentation, not image or picture, as in *koontu pookwugu,* literally "thought picture."

H: . . . about the time when you ejaculate* your water. [*Said mat-ter-of-factly;* the locker-room atmosphere is gone.]

W: Um-hm. Um-hm.

H: Does this [imagery experience] sometimes come to you? Just any old time? When you're walking around or just sitting down or—

W: [*Spontaneous.*] At times when we're sitting and singing in a song-fest in the men's club house—and we're singing and marking a song about a particular [milk-sap] tree. And then, oh—[*voice speeds up*] I think, "I will think and go [i.e., in my thoughts] to that tree. Oh, this tree, it's got—"

H: [*Breaks in*]—That kind of something . . .

W: Yeah. It's got that something [tree sap, inside], and we sing about it [tree sap], and while we're singing we think: "Sorry, this tree, it's got that particular something, it [tree] gives it to me, and its [sap] comes and sticks inside of my own good body here."

T: [*Cuts in*]—and that milk-food, it comes to us.

W: Yeah. And [W. reports he thinks], "You, only, you're [tree] the guardian of our bodies, so we mark a song for you [the tree]." [See Herdt 1988 on Sambia song-fests and masculinity.]

H: You're talking about how it controls your *jerungdu* [strength]?

W: Yeah, yeah, that's it.†

H: When you actually drink the sap?‡

W: No.

H: When you urinate?

W: No. When I drink your [canned] milk, then I think "Gilbert, let me drink your milk.§ It will go into my *keriku-keriku* [semen or-gan] here. Gilbert's helping me." [S: When I first watched these guys go for the canned milk, I did not know what was happening but nonetheless felt the power of their desire for the stuff. Polite and tense with *jerungdu* for *jerungdu*. A can, once opened, was

---

*Translation nuances: To be sure we were on the same track, I had used "orgasm" in the preceding sentence; its meaning is here unequivocal. But, in Pidgin, we rely on the verb *kap-sait* (to spill, pour out, etc.) to cover the ejaculation part of orgasm (*imbimboogu*), a term that covers both one's sexual arousal and ejaculation. Other Pidgin terms like *siutim* (to shoot, i.e., penetrate) are not used by Sambia to cover ejaculation. (Nor do Sambia use the general verb, *puspus*, "to copulate with.")

†I am surprised Weiyu could make all of this conscious. Not the thoughts about the tree sap, but that, while in the songfests singing about the tree, he can be thinking—fantasizing—about the tree and how its sap goes into his body to keep him strong. Though animistic and concrete, it still surprises me that Weiyu says he and Tali are thinking that in songfests. This statement shows, again, that Sambia social experiences have a reality unknown to the out-sider but obvious to the insider. How will one know without a technique for seeking, even when you do not suspect anything is there?

‡See Imano's account in chapter 8 about how it controls *jerungdu* [strength].

§Sambia prefer their hot drinks heavily whitened and sweetened. They would drink the canned milk straight if it were plentiful.

polished off as soon as we left the meal, one of the grand per-
quisites of helping H.]

T: [*Cuts in.*] Gilbert helps me [i.e., with his canned milk, a typical
construct like, "A man helps me be masculine and potent by giving me semen"].

H: [*Still disbelieving, to W.*] All the time? There's not one time when
you don't think about it?

W: There's not one single time when I forget it. Even when I sleep
in my house. When my wife and I screw. And when I come. The
same. The thought goes to the *itnandu* [a species of large wild
pandanus tree], the one that stands at the very top of the mountains. I think, "You, tree, you must come and hold me fast. It
would be bad if [during coitus] my soul went inside of my wife's
thing [vagina]. . . .

T: [*Cuts in.*]—the . . . uh . . . her . . . uh . . . vagina. [T. spits.
To say the word is to take its evil in one's mouth.]

W: Yes. That I know.

H: [*To S.*] As he describes it, it sounds defensive [i.e., drinking sap
defends maleness] sometimes. He has this thought when he's having an orgasm. The other time is during their songfest, when the
name of the tree comes up. He thinks then of that tree and how
he should go and drink some of its milk-sap so he will have tight
skin and stay strong. [H: That was a poor translation.]*

S: Why did you say it was defensive? [S: I do not understand now
what I was getting at, since the defensive aspects are so obvious.]

H: He also said, "There's another time when I think about this: when
I'm in my house and screwing my wife, I sometimes think about
the *itnandu* tree and how we place our head-hair at its base.† And
I think 'You, tree, you must keep me—that is, my soul—from
going into my wife's vagina when I am screwing her. Or else I'll
fall ill and die.' " [*Pause.*] This is new information for me. They've
just said, "We just never thought to tell you about this before . . . ."

S: They both have the tree come to mind when they ejaculate? Every
time?

H: That's what Weiyu says.

S: Do they believe that all the men have that same thought?

---

*I'm not sure what I'm saying here. Unless I'm talking about only the defensive function
of the fantasy. Because he has clearly said he has had pleasurable, metaphoric-type experiences in the men's house when singing about the tree. That is a positive, creative function,
not—at least not only—a defensive one. But in regard to his orgasms and the fantasy of seeing
the tree at that time, yes: the fantasy has defensive aspects.
†During later initiation rites.[10]

H: [*To W.*] Do you think that all the men have that same thought?

T: Not like that. [*They talk together rapidly about image-fantasies, about what other men had said about this, about secrets, about pandanus sap. S. and H. talk at the same time.*]

H: Well, there is some new information here for me. I think this is partly about masculine identity. They define masculinity as a system of beliefs we would see as largely defensive characture structure. They are taught: men are vulnerable since they cannot manufacture the semen they lose, the way women can with blood. But there is also the other quality you were trying to describe, a [psychodynamically] primitive sense of identification between yourself and a tree (which is so different from ourselves in that respect) with roots in early childhood and from gratifying sensual experiences.

S: [*Quiet voice.*] Can they tell us what other men have told them about this?

H: [*To W.*] Do all of the men think about that, or you two only?

W: All the *big men* [now elders]. They still think about that.

T: But the young ones have lost that kind of thinking.

W: But look: you just can't ask the men [*lowers voice*], "When you come, what do you think about?" You can ask if it feels good [*lowers voice*], but *not* about *ngoolu* [another tree sap] or *itnandu* tree-saps. You can't talk openly about those thoughts. That's just for the two of us to tell you. And you must keep it secret.*

H: [*To S.*] He says they think the elders have the same kind of thinking as they do about it.

S: What do you mean: "it"? They have the same experience, in that "it" pops into their minds in the same way, or that they also believe in the milk sap? [S. keeps me from assuming what I think they're saying, keeps me focused so I ask *exactly* what they think rather than only hitting the general area. That technique distinguishes clinical from much of ordinary ethnographic interviewing done in anthropology.]

H: Are you talking about the men having images when they ejaculate with their wives?

W: Yeah, yeah; and it's not good they all know of this—

---

*All Sambia men have favored ritual techniques for preserving health. Some are clan secrets, others are private magical practices not shared with others besides one's son. Drinking the sap of the wild pandanus is a favorite of Tali's. His paternal uncle (substitute father) taught Tali, and he has taught Weiyu. When there are secrets and secret secrets, doing ethnography can get rather sticky. Typically, in New Guinea societies, one must proceed cautiously regarding secret knowledge when asking others questions so as not to tip off interviewees to what they may not know.

H: No, no. I'm asking if, when they screw their women, and are coming, do they then picture a particular tree and its milk-sap?

W: Yeah, yeah and [*lowers voice*] the *itnandu* too.

H: [*To S.*] Yes, the big men have the same experience of seeing the
tree and the image of the tree sap when they're fucking their wives
and having an orgasm.

S: Why does he say that? Because they have said it or because it just
makes sense?

H: [*To Weiyu*] Why do you think that all the big men think that?

W: [*A bit indignant.*] I've looked at their skins, and it *never* gets loose
and slackens. Their skin and their longevity too: they have all
been around here a *long* time. All of them think those thoughts.

T: [*Cuts in.*]—because they are still here; they haven't died.

H: [*To S.*] "When you look at old men and they are still healthy, you
know they have to be doing this to keep healthy." That's what he
said.

S: I'm not asking, "Do the men drink sap?"

H: Right. He understood that. He's answering you that they must
have the same image or else they would grow ill and die. Now
listen to the second part of what they said before. They said, "This
is our secret. We think the bachelors don't have this kind of thinking. It's our secret. So you can't go and ask the other guys, 'Well,
do you have this kind of thinking?' Because if they don't know,
they'll just get weak and die and that's their problem."

S: [*Immediately.*] Tell them of course we won't tell anyone.

H: We won't tell anyone.

W: Um-hm. Yeah. Yeah. [*Pause.*] Understand: T. and I are not purposely going slow—and hiding things—so that only now we decided to speak out about this. No, no, it's not that. We wouldn't
hide something from you, no, no. Only right now did we think of
this. [*T. agrees.*] He [S.] has come and started us thinking about
this. Now that it occurs to us we're talking about it.

H: [*To S.*] He doesn't want us to think, "We've been hiding this from
you all along. We haven't. We just thought of it now. All the times
you've asked us about this before, it just never occurred to us to
tell you." Somehow, your asking them about this has jarred
something loose. [H: But why didn't I ever ask them? S: Don't
make a big deal out of it. It's no evidence of great clinical skill
that I did. The trick is to not inhibit your curiosity. If you're not
suffering your countertransference, you'll be comfortable asking
whatever you're thinking. In fact, you'll often even know what
you're thinking.]

S: Well, I've got a response. I'm not quite sure what—a "thank you" response. Like this: "The four of us, sitting around talking, have something in common despite all the bantering arguments that went before." Is that right?

H: Yes! Of course.

S: What jarred it loose would be my saying things like, "I also have children and yet I don't drink milk-sap, milk, or semen" [reference to our earlier dialogue when S. baited them by saying that even though he never drank semen, etc., etc., he was still masculine and got a logic-intact argument from them showing how that could be.] But it's not that. I think what has loosened up the information is the way we're talking: I'm talking with them as equals, because I can't do anything else. It's not an act. I talk to them the way I talk to anyone at home; because I really enjoy being here. And maybe that frees them too . . . . I don't think they're trying to impress me.

H: Well that's an interesting explanation.

S: What is?

H: Uh. [*Pause.*] I'd have to go back and think about it. It's also possible that I simply never asked them, "When you're ejaculating, do you have other thoughts or other images?" Still, it seems odd, their over-concern to tell me that this is something that just popped out, something they simply never thought of talking about before.

S: Are they telling us that the thought, not just the sap in reality, is important?

H: [*Quickly.*] Yes! They are.

S: It's very important. And they're surprised they never mentioned it before?

H: Exactly. And *I'm* surprised. That's why I'm telling it to you. I mean, that's the sense of it. That's why I pursued it when you said we should drop it and go on. I had a sense something was floating around in there that I had not seen before and that if I asked one question, that would lead into it.

S: There were Greeks who believed trees had the spirits of women inside of them. For Sambia men this sap is equivalent to milk. What's the form of the woman in the tree? We know they think women are dangerous. So what happens to men when they drink all this milk? What about women's dangerous interior? How do the men deal with that? Why is vaginal juice terribly dangerous and milk-sap isn't? The answer isn't just that milk keeps you alive and tree-sap doesn't. Do these beliefs reflect ambivalence about mother's love plus her capacity to kill you, an infantile concept that later gets projected into all their defensive masculinity?

H: Hm. [S: Not a bad response to such high-tone theory.]

S: Do they believe in any other essence of womanness that is not contaminated with the paranoia—all the poison and—

H: No.

S: [*Struggling; puzzled.*] Milk is from women, and this sap is milk. Milk is good, like semen, yet all other aspects of female interior can kill a male. It's as if the *milk* doesn't have a sex but the *vessel* in which it's contained is a female. Is that your impression?

H: Mm—yeah.

S: What's the sex of milk? It may be a senseless question.

H: No, it's not senseless.

S: I mean to them.

H: They've taught me that all milk-bearing trees are female trees.

S: But that's not the same thing as the milk being a female substance. What's the *sex* of the milk? It always comes from females.

H: You know, all of these substances, such as pandanus-nut milk or tree sap are equivalents of and compared against mother's milk. That is concrete, conscious. But beyond that, what are milk's subtle qualities? It's as if that is the conscious frame—that's the frame—and all the other things are inside of it; the tree-sap and the pandanus-nut milk and the semen.

S: There's no gentle, tender aspect, no sense of beng *grateful* about milk? Only the strong, conscious "By God, we've got to get it!" quality?

H: Right. There's not.* A good point, obvious: there is no sense of thankfulness. Rather, a frantic urgency, a need to get it inside of you, when you've lost some, get some back inside of you as soon as possible, so you can continue to be healthy and don't die.

S: In our society, someone—poet or advertiser—tells you not only that the cow is feminine, but that milk carries her feminine qualities. I get no sense here that the milk that comes out of a woman is admirable; only a necessary thing.

H: But they do feel it nourishes you.

S: Yes, but do they feel tender or grateful toward milk? Is there any poetry that implies that?

H: There doesn't seem to be. It seems they look on milk the way we look on aspirin. You don't give it credit; it just does its job.

---

*Too quick; I was referring only to adult men. For boys—fellators—their experience is more complex (less repression), but that is another story.

S: Almost like medicine. Well, you better get back to them.
H: Have you any more ideas about this?
W: [*Quickly, dully.*] No, that's it.

DISCUSSION

H: Reflecting on this material, I find that both S.'s presence and his mode of questioning brought out this new information from W. and T. He jarred loose fantasy—imagery—that the men had known but never mentioned to me. How could I have asked about semen beliefs fifty times and never gotten this image? A partial answer is that, to the men, the image is—self-evident; their experience just is; it exists but is not reflected on. And because spontaneous, the experience is felt as apart from themselves. As with the Balinese trancer whose involuntary movements in religious trance seem like: "I see my leg move but 'I' did not move it" (Bateson 1976:61), the men recall the tree while singing, without feeling they willed it.

Two methodologic points follow. First, there are beliefs, fantasies, and shared images we ethnographers will never understand unless we push our interpreters. How did Tali and Weiyu say what they felt? S. *directly* challenged them, saying, "I don't agree that semen and sap are necessary for making men" and "Prove to me that you are right." Whether or not the point is proved is beside the point: it is the confrontation with another's reality that matters. But *the* crucial question is: Who is this other person who questions? The government, missionaries, tourists intervene; and the anthropologist can too, but supposedly should not. We are there to study, not change a society (chapter 1). A sticky problem arises. Perhaps only an anthropologist (like a clinician) is enough of an insider, is trusted enough to know how to press people to manifest their latent thoughts. Ethnographers do not dispute beliefs or practices, only record them. I never openly disagreed with the men on the unity of milk and semen, for it is essential to their way of life. We clinical ethnographers face a dilemma then: never probe beliefs and risk never seeing crucial (subliminal or unconscious) aspects of them; or, dare to confront them but risk causing personal and cultural dislocation. Should we take responsibility to help people through such changes? Are we then missionaries too?

Second, the meaning of some beliefs and practices can be discovered only by prolonged interviewing such as we did. Meanings are not isolates; they can be understood only in context, illuminated by associations. The affective dimensions, in particular, will be missed or misunderstood by piecemeal or checklist questioning that is hit-or-miss, and seen as such by interviewees. (Ever try to interview someone on the telephone? Would you hang up if someone tried it on you?) Some experiences and meanings are beyond us: "What is reported by East and West alike is that, in these special states of mind, the way of knowing is precisely *not* organized in separate or separable *gestalten*" (Bateson 1976:57). Clinical ethnography done in case studies seeing someone or several people for a long time—and allowing them to talk on their own terms—is the answer (our antidote) to this perplexing ethnographic problem

CHAPTER SIX

Penjukwi: Portrait of a Woman

H: What is it like to be a woman in a society like that of the Sambia, male-biased and ridden with sexual antagonism? How does a woman experience her femaleness—in dreams, erotism, marriage, childcare? What does femininity look like in someone who was literally abducted, forcibly married, and compelled to make a life in a place not of her choosing? These questions motivated my work with Penjukwi, my friend and best woman interpreter.

This chapter carries a heavy load. I did little work with women in my first fieldwork (1974–1976), and my writings to date have been based mainly on men's views of everything, including women. At S.'s urging I worked more with women, especially with P., when I returned in 1979. The effects were striking and important, the more so in 1981, when I worked more with women than men. In this book, however, this is our only study of a woman, and we use it to show how I—a white, young, male ethnographer—worked with a woman on such intimate matters as her sexual experience, and how S.'s presence affected her.

Penjukwi was born about 1955 in Kwoli hamlet, across the Valley from Nilangu. Her father, also born in Kwoli, was an ordinary Sambia man; he belonged to its leading clan. Her mother was from Nilangu hamlet, the daughter of a well-known big man and shaman. P. was their firstborn child, one of four children still living. P.'s mother is second in the area only to Kaiyunango (Moondi's mother) in being a leading woman shaman. P.'s parents had a good marriage. She reports that they liked each other a lot and seldom quarreled. She seems to have had a relatively happy childhood until her father died.

P.'s development is a fascinating combination of both traditional and socially changing circumstances. She grew up amidst warfare, which ended around 1964 when she was nine. Kwoli was the first hamlet pacified by government patrol officers. In 1963, a government rest-hut was built there, which the people burned down. Not long after, P.'s uncle (father's brother), Jemioko, a powerful big man and leader of Kwoli, was appointed the first *lululai** in the Valley. After the last war in the area other men were jailed, which led to total pacification. Two years later missionaries appeared and began working near the village. Other social changes followed, particularly in Kwoli. Thus, by the time P. was ten, her world was shifting dramatically.

P. had good relations with both her parents, but as she grew she preferred being with her father. By six she was steadily helping in the gardens with her parents. Her parents always slept together in one hut. P. loved to go with her father, whom she describes as a wonderful, warm man, on his daily rounds to gardens and nearby hamlets. Her mother was intensely involved in shamanic activities, did healing ceremonies "all the time," and frequently reported her dreams. P. was responsible for helping her parents by babysitting and related chores. But she preferred to roam with her playmates, a group of boys and girls of the hamlet. P. says she was aware of the difference between boys and girls at an early age. She engaged in surreptitious sex play for a time (which she enjoyed) with a boy of about nine years of age (before his initiation). P. describes herself as a "strong" girl, more so than other girls her age. For instance: she disliked gardening and babysitting until she was older; she liked to climb trees (unusual) and sometimes join in boys' games. Nonetheless, these attributes were not so marked that P. would stand out from other girls as she matured. And, by about age twelve, she was more fully involved in heavy and frequent garden work, because her mother told her that "men don't like lazy wives."

P.'s father died when she was twelve, changing her life forever. Her mother went into seclusion as a widow for a year, which dampened P.'s life. During this period, another uncle—Yanduwaiko, P.'s father's brother—greatly helped the family, and he and his wife became, in effect, P.'s guardians. Eventually, still another Kwoli man (another classificatory FB) grew interested in P.'s mother. He wanted to marry her and persisted, to some extent against her will, until she gave in. They were married, P.'s mother becoming his second wife. This man, P.'s stepfather, cared for the family and was a good provider. But

---

*Government-recognized local "head man," who was given a badge, a hat, cane, and some authority to arbitrate local disputes and keep the peace.

after their marriage, P. became increasingly independent of her parents. He and P.'s mother had many arguments. Thus, P. became unhappy living in their hut, and often slept in other kinfolks' huts in Kwoli. P.'s mother continued her shamanic activities. She and her second husband had two other children until, in 1979, he hung himself.[1]

Her uncle, Yanduwaiko, was the key influence in P.'s life from then on. Yandu is interesting. He became one of two official government translators around 1965.* He still works today at the distant patrol post in the same capacity. It was thus shortly before P.'s true father died that her uncle began living away from Kwoli, on the patrol post. This life was unprecedented for the Sambia at that time (only a handful of men were then absent from the Valley, working on coastal plantations). Few Sambia had even been to the government post. Yandu is a sensible, solid citizen, well-respected and liked, sophisticated for a Sambia man of his generation. Of course, in certain ways, he has had to toe the government's party line; has, no doubt, been privy to some awful colonial events and scenes, and has had to kowtow to European authorities, becoming a bit jaded. Still, he is no fool, nor merely a government puppet;[2] and he has influence back home. Yandu also has a good marriage (and several children) with a warm, lively, and intelligent Sambia woman, who also likes P. They too began living on the patrol post in the late 1960s. And, from 1966 to 1973, when P. was married, she had many short trips to, and several periods of living on, the patrol post with her uncle's family.

Through him, then, Penjukwi got to know some western ways, after a traditionalist childhood and being sheltered by her uncle and other kin in a place not so far from home. She saw Europeans; gained limited exposure to government station people; received western clothes, food, and other items via her uncle; and all this allowed P. more freedom and movement than Sambia adolescent girls ever had had in the past (though P. herself has seldom remarked on this and seems to take it for granted). Yandu's children and wife had even greater freedom. He expressed the view that his daughters should marry whomever they wanted,† an unprecedented attitude in those days (and unusual even now). And his wife was the only Pidgin-speaking woman in the area for years.[3] Furthermore, P. began to like the qualities and potentials her uncle had—she refers to him as a "new kind" of Sambia man—suggesting that such a man was what she

---

*No doubt in part through his older brother Jemioko's influence as *lululai*.
†As long as brideprice was paid.

wanted in marriage. (P.'s parents passively allowed these developments to occur.) Still, P. spent the most time in her father's hamlet.
She became a better gardener, was otherwise involved in village life,
and continued to mature. There was no arranged marriage for her,
and the question of her marriage was never explicitly discussed until
her menarche (1973).

Two other important things happened to Penjukwi in 1971–1973,
before her marriage.

First, she attended a mission "bush" school in the Valley for a few
months in 1971. From the late 1960s on, missionaries entered the
Sambia Valley. The Seventh-day Adventists became particularly active, sending native evangelists (from other parts of New Guinea) into
the Valley with the Word. They established two beachheads: at Kwoli,
a few hundred yards above the village; and at the extreme southern
end of the Valley, at a place called Kwapalaam, where an airstrip
was later built. They proselytized and won converts. But the price for
baptism was pretty steep: strict adherence to Levitical food prohi-
bitions (no pork, no possum: hence, no meat, except rarely from cans),
"tabooing" smoking and chewing betel-nut; monogamy, forcing men
to divorce second wives; and repudiation of ritual customs. Few
Sambia could stomach these demands; fewer still could live by them.
Nonetheless, P.'s oldest uncle Jemioko, the *lululai*, nominally converted, as did a few others of her clan (more women than men). P.
herself sometimes went to Saturday services ("holiday outings"), in
the local *haus lotu*,* but she never converted or adopted the mission's
taboos. What matters is that down at Kwapalaam a mission school
was set up in 1971. P., encouraged by others, went to the school several times a week. She learned a smattering of Pidgin (but never learned
how to write). It is extraordinary that some parents associated with
the mission allowed their children to live in two adjacent, sexually-
segregated "dormitories" for a time. Soon, word got out that boys
and girls were playing around sexually. A scandal forced the school
to close.[4] P. returned home to Kwoli more acculturated.

Second was P.'s meeting at the patrol post a young Sambia man
with whom she became infatuated. He was a distant relative of her
uncle, a bachelor, handsome, travelled (he had been to the coast
briefly). They liked each other. P. says he was kind, not strong or
loud-mouthed. They flirted and socialized, but their attraction never
went further physically. By the end of 1972, P. had seen him at two

---

*The Seventh-day Adventists celebrate Sabbath on Saturdays. *Haus lotu* is Pidgin for church:
a hut with pews and a plain wooden altar.

different periods. She was fantasizing about him. (See interview.) Encouraged by her uncle's open door policy on marriage, she began to daydream about marrying him. The interest seemed mutual, and enough contact was maintained between them that it became evident they might marry. Since this man was from a different valley—another phratry—there were formidable difficulties with such a marriage,* even were her uncle and parents to approve of it. Nonetheless, P. planned for it.

Sometime in early 1973, P. had her menarche—another sign of change in her life—while out at the patrol post. She could not, therefore, go through the normal secret menarche ceremonies back in the village menstrual hut. Her uncle paid for a feast at the post. Then, her menarche over and she sexually eligible for marriage, P. returned to Kwoli.

The circumstances of P.'s marriageability were odd. She had not been betrothed as an infant. She had no older brothers to push her into a sister-exchange marriage. Her step-father had no real claims or authority over her. And her uncle had said he would allow her to choose her own partner (so long as the groom settled in payment). Her clansmen—who were few—had no strategy in mind. Thus, she was able to pursue her fantasy about marrying her sweetheart.

The men over at Nilangu, however, had a different plan. P.'s mother was from Nilangu, and she had been infant-betrothed, though Nilangu's claim to P. was for several reasons weak. But they could claim—with some justification—that if P. was to go anywhere else for a marriage, then it might be back to her mother's natal hamlet. P. was also attractive: plenty of men had an eye on her. What's more—the real key—she was available. The rumor grew that P. was going to sneak off and elope with a man from another valley. Here is where Nilutwo—my cassowary-hunter friend—entered the scene.

Nilutwo was an odd, troubled man. Born about 1942, he was much older than P.—too old, in fact, by Sambia standards. He had had a woman betrothed to him from infancy, but he spurned her (and one other) as "too strong" (i.e., aggressive) for him. He gave her to Imano, who relished her (Imano's first wife: see chapter 8). Nilutwo's development was marked by conflict. His biologic father went crazy and died in N.'s infancy, and his step-father died before he was initiated (see Herdt 1981:ch. 5). N. had bouts of "crazy" behavior in his teens, and women had rejected him as a rubbish man. After a fight with his own clan brothers over one failed marriage negotiation in the late

*.999 of all Sambia Valley marriages are transacted within in the Valley.

1960s, he left the Valley in a huff, to work on a coconut plantation near Madang. He returned in 1972 to find his prospects no better than before: no woman available, no allies to find him one. He was often getting himself in trouble over his adultery attempts. He was on the verge of despair—considering returning to the coast again—when nubile Penjukwi appeared.

Nilutwo and Penjukwi were strangers. They were not well matched—by age, personality, or past acquaintance. Yet N. had a certain claim on her: she was his true father's sister's daughter, a respectable marriage coupling. N. approached P. several times. And each time she rejected him more vehemently. P. told me N. was too old for her: she never had considered him as a mate, certainly not over her sweetheart. In early 1974 (before I arrived) N. grew desperate: he heard that P. had wised-up and was planning to run off to the Wunyu-Sambia Valley, where her sweetheart was. Actually, it was Kanteilo who told him this. The old fox had got wind of her plans and went straight to the men's house in Nilangu. There, he got the bachelors worked up—Weiyu, others, and Nilutwo—saying that P. had better be taken before Nilangu lost forever what could be had. That night, P.'s abduction was set.

Nilutwo had to lead the action. Though reluctant, it was his prerogative, his show, his wife, his manliness at stake. At dawn, he, Weiyu, Kanteilo, and two other men crept over to Kwoli and surprised P. in her mother's hut. N. plunged into the hut and grabbed P., pulling her outside. Her mother began shrieking and hitting Weiyu. People screamed, babies cried, dogs barked: chaos. P. was dragged, screaming and fighting, outside the village. But N. got scared. Weiyu took over. He grabbed P. and literally dragged her down the mountain side, she losing all her garments in the process, exposing her. Meanwhile, the other villagers were held at bay.[5] She was hauled up the other mountainside to Nilangu, and imprisoned in a hut. Nilutwo was instructed to screw her into submission. They were guarded for days. Thus began P.'s marriage.

Even by Sambia standards, this was a dreadful start. Beyond that, the usual marriage ceremony was never held. Later negotiations gained the formal acceptance of P.'s people, who were paid a small amount of bridewealth compensation. N. was told to watch P. like a hawk until she got pregnant, for fear she would run off. And he did. Soon, P. and N. were settled into life together, seeming, when I arrived in late 1974, like a long-married couple. What I did not know then was P.'s trauma and humiliation, her having to give up the fantasy of marrying her admirer, and the less-than-ordinary life she had been forced into by Nilutwo. What was done to her, no woman in years had suffered.

In 1975, P. gave birth to their first child, a girl. Nilutwo was thrilled. He was closely attached to the girl. He calmed down. He was not a bad husband, P. says. He hunted and gardened a lot, was diligent in earning money, helped others, and seldom fought with her.

N. did his best, too, to make P. happy, I am convinced. It was not so much that he loved her as that he liked her. And needed her: for his acceptance by the village as an adult man with wife and child; for food, sex, and cooking—the affection she gave that helped him endure many personal conflicts.[6] For N. was a difficult and troublesome man, and he knew it; and he did his best to make a difficult marriage work.

I saw only Nilutwo's side of this marriage for a long time. But, in 1976, at N.'s constant encouragement, I worked briefly with P. as an interpreter, though it was difficult (my Sambia wasn't very good, nor was her Pidgin). Still, it was a hapless marriage: P. made the best of a bad deal, as is typical of her. Indeed, for someone who had been through so much, she seemed cheerful, warm, and lively.

I want to underline here that Sambia marriages are based on politics, not love; fortitude, not affection. Women's lot is not good. Even today there is not much choice in marriage. Perhaps Penjukwi knew that her fantasy about marrying a handsome, traveled youth from a distant place was just a pipe-dream. Perhaps not. Her abduction was ruthless; P. never forgave Nilutwo or the men for her brutal treatment and as much as is possible for a Sambia woman, she has never let them forget it. But we need to remember that Sambia expectations are different from ours, much less romantic and prettified. When one doesn't expect much, one is less disappointed.

P. had their second child, a boy, in 1978. I returned in 1979 to find P. and N. much as before, a bit more settled, a bit happier. Penjukwi seemed to be doing fine. Then tragedy occurred. In April, Nilutwo fell from a tree, breaking his back and transecting his spinal cord. He suffered in agony for months until his death (not long after S. and I left the Valley). Until his death in September, Penjukwi had to care for N. virtually as an infant. She stuck by him, beyond Sambia expectations of a wife, until his end. (Other women said, "If I'd been stolen like you, I'd never care for him like that.") She could not travel or garden. So P. sat for weeks with him, cramped in Tali's hut where N., legs paralyzed and without bowel or bladder control, was dying. When he was cranky and nasty, she ignored him or talked back. They had bitter arguments. More than once she told him to die and be done with it. "There's other men around here." Yet she said this in anger and frustration, when no one else could bear his pain, screaming, demanding. She stayed, I think, because it was her duty; P. is honorable.

My work with P. in 1979 went well. She was warm and open. We made fine progress during the first of my two field trips that year, January through March. Her Pidgin was passable but not great. (It was far better in 1981.) Then, while I was back at UCLA, came his accident, in April. On my return (in May) we worked three months more; our talking concentrated on her having to tend N. and the resulting frustrations. My views of male–female relationships changed. But because of her onerous life, I spent much time with P. simply allowing her to express her frustrations.

P. and I worked alone some thirty times in 1979. There was a complementarity in it lacking with the men. Just as we would expect: that's in the nature of Sambia gender roles. But it was more than that. As with my other key informants, I liked P. and enjoyed being with her. Conflict *was* interjected into our relationship in four ways: by Nilutwo (who had his own reasons—namely, keeping P. away from other men); by the men (who were often jealous of P. and me); by P. herself (there were nonerotic and erotic aspects of her feelings toward me); and by myself (I never knew until I tried how much I could press P. for certain information, or how close I could get to her without her—and me—feeling uncomfortable).

By the time S. arrived, then, Nilutwo was dying and in great pain, which made P.'s life so difficult. She was also under growing pressure from the men, who, awaiting N.'s death, wondered who would get this prize, Penjukwi, as another wife, and how they would manage it. I let them know that I refused any part in these games. (See chapter 5.) An aspect of my work with her at the time, then, was anticipating what N.'s death would bring.

S. arrived and joined us. I felt no dislocation. However, toward the end, when we were discussing P.'s sexual excitement—a very sensitive matter—there were moments when I felt uneasy, we two white men alone with her asking such questions. She sensed my concern, and when we left a few days later, she went out of her way to say goodbye warmly to me.

I returned to even richer work with P. in 1981. She was alive, happy, independent, the best I had ever seen her, as she must have been before marriage. She was invaluable for my study of women and children. She seemed unscathed by those six years with Nilutwo, of whom she speaks honestly and gently. She had no husband and no plans for one, but neither would she deny the possibility. A lightness was in her.

S: This chapter, more than any other, is unbalanced as compared to what was actually said, for we have deleted two long sections; an account of an attempted rape, and a dream and its associations. These deletions intensify even more our concentration on the two erotic matters that now fill the chapter: an erotic daydream and the question does she have orgasms with breast-feeding.

It is obvious, however, that all our Sambia friends talked a lot about sex. We see three main reason for that. First (despite the paucity of such material in the ethnographic literature), sex—erotics and gender identity—is what many people think of regularly. Second, one of the main issues in H.'s research is sexuality. Third, S.'s studies are only on sexuality.

FIRST SESSION

This was our first interview together with P. She and I reestablish rapport after several days' pause following S.'s arrival. P. is at first focused on Nilutwo's pain. Then we discuss *imbimboogu*, a concept that involves us in understanding how individuals use cultural ideas.

The primary referent of *imbimboogu*, in males and females, is "orgasm." A lesser meaning is the tingling sensation in a limb that is asleep. In talking with P., I discovered that she used that term for sensual feelings she had when nursing her baby. Did her usage in that context mean that she was feeling an "orgasm" while nursing? I did not know. S. helped us find out. Early in this session, however, we discovered a man—a notorious womanizer—peeping. This had never happened before, and it angered me. When we kicked him out, P. then told how that man had accosted her three years before. We return in later sessions to the *imbimboogu* problem, which kept popping up.

HERDT We've lost quite a bit of time, haven't we? Three or four, maybe five days.

PENJUKWI [*Matter-of-factly.*] Oh, when do you leave the Valley for good?*

S: [*Enters with a kerosene lamp. Though it is still dusk, we plan to have a long session and anticipate the darkness.*] Let's put it far

---

*First P., then Kalutwo (chapter 9), open our talking with my departure. A sad feeling is in the air.

away because it's going to make a loud buzz. [*He moves across the room.*]

H: [*Echoing him.*] Yeah, as far away as possible. [*Turns to P.*] Some time yet. We don't know for sure just when we'll be leaving. A week or something like that. I've already told you about my boss, Dr. Stoller. I asked you before if it was okay for him to sit with us, and you said it is.

P: [*Raising voice, strong.*] Oh, I won't be afraid.

H: It's all right?

P: Yeah, I'm not afraid. I'm only afraid of the other men here [reference to Tali, Weiyu, and others]. Now you two have the same skin. I'm not going to be afraid of you [*a large smile in her voice that makes me know, listening to her in 1982, that she feels secure.*]

H: Good enough. [*Pause.*] Now today, what have you been doing?

P: Oh, nothing [*A little sadness in voice.*] I've just been staying in the house. My man, too [*pause*] he is in pain, and so I've stayed with him.

H: And so what if he—

P: [*Breaking in.*] What is it? He's got large sores [pressure sores] on both sides [of his buttocks], and so I've just stayed put. They [sores] aren't gone yet. They turned into really big sores, and he doesn't sit well. So I just stay around.

H: Are you getting around all right or not?

P: Me? Oh, no, no I'm not. [*Quiet, sullen despair.*]

H: How come?

P: Well, I can't go, can't walk around [to gardens, etc.], and so I have to sit around grouchy [*nervous chuckle*]. I don't sit easily; when I am able to get around then I'm fine. Whatever I need [food] I fetch and can be fine; but just sitting around the house I'm not happy. So I'm not doing well.

H: I heard that this morning the two of you [P. and Nilutwo] were sort of cross at each other. When I came along and S. was following me, [*pause*] you and Nilutwo . . .

P: Oh, not really, he wasn't cross. It was just tiredness [the sense that the argument was nothing].

H: Does he do that [*frequently*]?

P: [*Pause.*] I told him, "This master* [S.] wants to come and ex-

---

*P. uses "master" in the same way as Sakulambei, and the usage is interesting. Tali, Weiyu, and our other male subjects used it only rarely in relation to S. Saku did much more so. Why? Two things come to mind. First, P. had worked less with me in 1979 than the others. Second, women have had much less direct interaction with whites than men (many of whom have worked on the coast). In a general sense, then, the colonialist power structure is more distant

amine you. You've got to stay quiet [don't be cantankerous]. You must [*sort of smiling in her voice*] settle down so he [S.] can come and look at you."

H: Did he listen to you?

P: He didn't talk, he just listened, that's all [*amusement in her voice again*].[†]

H: Do you have any preference for what we could work on or shall I [choose it]?

P: [*Pause.*][*] This man [husband] doesn't sleep well. His sides have sores, and he turns and moves around all the time. He doesn't sleep well at night. He keeps turning at night and keeps getting me up . . . and the others did a song-fest. So we didn't sleep well [a song-fest was held last night in Tali's house, where P. and N. are living]. We were there, and so I didn't sleep well.

H: In Tali's house?

P: Yeah. Soluwulu's [Tali's brother] child wasn't well. N. told me that there wasn't anything we could do to stop the song-fest, because it wasn't our house. It's Tali's hut; so we just had to put up with it and not sleep well. Besides, they had to heal Soluwulu's baby. And Soluwulu kept going in and out, the child crying on and on; it was crying and it couldn't even take breast milk. And she [Soluwulu's wife] is pregnant again; so her milk is dry and she didn't have any to give the child [to quiet it.]**

H: Is that why it was crying?

P: Yeah [*smiling*]. An older child would simply stop, but he's too small. A child so small doesn't think. He'll just cry and cry a lot.

H: For milk?

P: For milk, but there isn't any.

H: What is it now? Has she just weaned it?

---

and more mythologized as a formal barrier to women. I would argue also that women's suppression by Sambia men is shared more by Saku, in whom hermaphroditic stigmata (and perhaps more or less conscious feminine identifications) have perpetuated distrust of whites and alienation from power figures.

[†]Here and elsewhere P. refers to Nilutwo like an ornery child to be humored and scolded, which her amusement signifies.

[*]In 1979 P.'s Pidgin was still not strong and at times like now she paused out of awkwardness as to what to say next. It was easier for her then to follow my lead. She was also, I think, intimidated by S.; she assumed S. spoke Pidgin. (What a surprise for her to find untrue the colonial stereotype that whites are omniscient.)

[**]This child, a boy, had always been very underweight and sickly. He was over three years old. Several months later Soluwulu's wife had another baby who was extremely malnourished, even though the mother did her best to feed him. He died in 1981 despite our attempts to save him. The local medical orderly said he had died of spinal meningitis compounded by pneumonia (not an easy diagnosis to make without proper training or a laboratory). I add this note to remind readers of the dreadful health problems that still take Sambia lives.

P: Just now. It's dried up [milk], but he's still crying for it, still suck-ing. But there's no milk.

H: Hmmm. And does the mother let him do that or not?

P: She just thinks, "It's not very big. So he can just suckle without [getting any milk]; that's all right. It's not so big that I should keep it off the breast."

H: Boy, but that's a pretty big child!

P: Oh, not really. That's a firstborn child, and so it doesn't grow very quickly. When it's matured and is big, then [*pause*] . . . they should not have started working yet [having sex again to make another baby].

H: Have they started walking around together yet [euphemism for having sex again]?

P: Not yet.*

H: Let me ask you about something we were talking about last time . . . about breast milk and about giving breast milk to your baby. [*P. immediately hides her face, embarrassed.*] You've got a baby now, and you're breast-feeding him. I was [began to say "surprised"] thinking about your saying that when you breast-feed him you feel *imbimboogu.*† I thought very hard about that. I was wondering, does it feel the same as when you are screwing with your man or is it another kind [of experience]?

P: [*Matter-of-fact.*] The same.

H: The same? Truly? [*Still surprised.*]

P: Just the same. [*Pause.*] When we two screw, it's the same as that. It's just the same.

H: But do you feel [with a man] hotter when screwing or when you breast-feed your baby?

P: When my man screws with me. It's only then that I feel hot.

H: Now, what about with your baby?

P: My baby, too, when it drinks milk then it can [*pause*] create that [feeling of being] hot too.

H: The same?

P: Later it can feel like [*she smiles with a nervous laugh*] *imbimboogu.*

H: Painful or sweet? [*Imbimboogu* covers both the pleasure of sexual arousal and the strange sensation of a limb "asleep."]

P: (*Quickly; natural.*) Oh, it's sweet only.

H: Is this hotness inside your breast or . . . [*voice trails off*]?

---

*P. was either ignorant or evasive here, for I had the impression from the men that Soluwulu's wife was pregnant again.
†By which I here meant orgasm.

P: Inside the breast.

H: Deep inside, the breast nipple, or what?

P: Around the nipple.

H: Can I tell Dr. S. so that he can ask you about it?

P: [*Slight anxiety, then relaxed.*] You can tell him. That's all right.

H: [*To S.*] We have been talking as we had the last two times before you came. She tells me that she *feels* the same feeling, using the term for orgasm, when she is having sex (when she is screwing with Nilutwo) as when her baby drinks her breast milk. And so I've been asking her, uh . . . how she feels *that;* and I keep asking her what are the differences, and she keeps telling me it's the same.

S: (*Quietly.*) It's been reported.

H: Really [*surprised*]?

S: It's not universal, nobody knows how often, but it is not at all unusual. Some American women [this is not to imply it happens to American women only] report that at times, when they are nursing the baby, they are not only hot and have orgasms but . . .

H: It is possible . . .

S: What I don't know is how fast does it happen, how often does it happen, where it is felt. Because there is a lot of different places: clitoral, vaginal, pelvic: how does it feel when nothing is inside of her, or when she's having coitus, etc. . . . Does she have it all the time, part of the time? Some women feel very *guilty* about it— "*Oh, my God,* what's happening?" Then try to make it into a psychological statement with their infant (just a contamination of psychoanalysis—not that analysts have not said that). At any rate, it would be interesting to find out how often; with all the babies; was it the first time: get the history of it. (I don't think it's terribly important but it's kind of: "what the hell, if that's what you're talking about.") How did the subject come up? Had you talked with her about that particular thing before or just now?

H: No, I brought that up because I wanted to ask her about it. It was, uh . . .

S: No, she told *you* because you had never heard of it before. When did she first tell you?

H: Let's see. In the last several days.

S: Another question that would be related to it would be: what happens when a man—and there's been only one man—sucks, touches or whatever [her breasts]. Could it [*imbimboogu*] happen to her with just foreplay? (I don't know whether there is any [foreplay] in her life or not.) Because there are women, who, when their breasts are stimulated, have orgasms. Whether those are the women who have it with their babies or not, I simply don't know.

H: Those all give me some questions to ask her. [*To P.*] I've been telling him, so he would understand what we're talking about this . . .

S: [*Cutting in.*] Had she heard about this from anybody else? Probably not, because they don't talk about sex.

H: Well, see, all the men believe this; all* the men say that the women feel this. That's one reason why I wanted to check it out.

S: Find out from her does she know if other women have this or not.

H: Yeah. [*To P.*] I want to ask you now about the time when you have this feeling—when you give breast milk to your baby and you feel *imbimboogu*. I was telling him about this and he was telling me his thinking about it. I want to ask you if you've heard of other women who feel *imbimboogu* when they give breast milk to their children?

P: [*Spontaneously.*] Oh, they feel that too, all of them feel that. It's not just me. I think all of them do. [Society is a useful foil even among Sambia.]

H: Do they talk about that?

P: They all say, "I give milk to my child and then I get an *imbimboogu*." Also, I see someone's water [milk] simply fall out from nothing [full breasts between feedings]. I think, "It's the same, with me." But the only time when they all get *imbimboogu* is when the baby is feeding. When my baby doesn't drink milk, then I don't feel it. At times when I leave my baby and go round the garden, don't come back quickly, when I come back slowly, then my breasts are swollen and I can get an *imbimboogu*.

H: Oh. [?]

P: Then my baby thinks, "My mother doesn't bring back my milk quickly, so I am crying and crying waiting for her." He cries and cries and waits. And when he thinks that, then my breasts have to have an *imbimboogu*. [The magical construction here is the baby wants milk, thinks of it and cries for it, and when he thinks that, it makes P.'s breasts feel *imbimboogu*, because of his thought at some distance away.] I think that when I go round, he's thinking of me like that, and so I have it.

H: You're saying that at that time, that's when you're feeling *imbimboogu*, when you walk about?

*H: That's exaggerated; see chapter 5.

P: Yeah.

H: On the path?

P: I've finished gathering food and I'm ready to come back; so at the time, when I come back walking on the path, this time it can happen [*slight laugh*]. At other times, when I don't come back quickly and I'm in my garden standing there working, I can feel *imbimboogu*.

H: When you get *imbimboogu*, you feel hot in what place [of the body]? Where do you feel hot?

P: [*Pause.*] I'm hot in the nipples, inside. That's where I feel it.

H: Down below, inside your cunt, what do you feel there?

P: Oh, no. Inside of there [*smiling*] I don't get an *imbimboogu*. At times when the two of us [husband and self] play around, that's when we [women] feel that.

H: Hmmmm.

P: And in my breasts it comes when my baby drinks from it—

H: [*Butting in.*] Wait. [At this point H. gets up after hearing a noise that suggests someone in the next room is leaning against the wall. Until this point it was absolutely quiet. I go outside into the next room, our kitchen, and am astonished and angry to find Gambakutu. He is an older, married man with two wives and many children, Nilutwo's older clan brother. He is a notorious adulterer and has for some time had his eyes on Penjukwi. It is rumored that when Nilutwo dies, he will try to take Penjukwi as another wife. Though he cannot speak Pidgin, I am outraged that he has stayed in the house, violating the confidentiality of the session, after I had asked everyone to leave. The many references to *imbimboogu* were a give-away. So I tell him in an angry but controlled voice to leave. I come back in the office to contain my anger.]

S: Why did you get up? You heard somebody?

H: Yeah [*still fuming*].

S: It was somebody who didn't belong, who shouldn't be hearing this?

H: Yeah, right. Somebody was here. That's what we were trying to avoid.

S: Should I look [to ensure that he's left]?

H: Yeah, you should.

P: [*Barely audible.*] Somebody's there in the kitchen.

H: Yeah.

S: Nope. He was just looking back to see if we were looking. Because he wants to find out what's happening here? Or he knows?

H: Yeah, he's probably ashamed now that I caught him doing it [being a voyeur].

S: Had she known he was there?

H: No. [*Turning to P.*] Did you know that he was there?

P: Who's that?

H: Gambatkutu.

P: [*Stunned.*] Oh, not at all. Didn't he go to his house [before we started]?

H: I just now removed him.

P: Oh, you go get rid of him.

H: I've already done it.

P: He shouldn't be standing there eavesdropping.

H: Yeah.

H: [*To S.*] Well, it was just—I'd have to give you the details—especially about *him*. He shouldn't have been hearing that.

S: You don't know that he did hear it.

H: Oh, yeah, I know that he heard it because that's what gave it away. He was sitting there all the time.

S: Does this damage her?

H: Well, that's it—I mean it's absolutely awful. He's been trying to screw her for months and months and we're talking about orgasms and he's probably sitting there getting a hard-on.

S: Well, I'm—now I'm just being me—but I'd kick his ass around for that,* I mean, I wouldn't just leave it at this.

H: Yeah.

S: That may not be the right thing for you [as an ethnographer] to do, but, I mean, that's just despicable.

H: It's understandable, and it's less despicable here because they think she's shit anyway, but even so—

S: I'm just being personal. So—

H: Yeah.

S: He should have been told to go, but somehow maybe you shouldn't. You'll know what to do. Is she now at risk because of this and is she now going to be troubled about this?

H: Well, yeah. [*To P.*] I've been telling him about this bad thing that he's [Gambakutu] done, sitting there listening to our talk. I always kick all the men out when you and I work. So I'm wondering whether you have any worry because he sat there and listened to us.

P: Oh, that's his way.

---

*As I would do at UCLA. Or is it none of our business to bring our morality into the ethnography, even if our beliefs are the same as P.'s?

H: Uh-uh. I'm asking you does this worry you or not? I'm saying it's not good if you're afraid he heard us talking . . .

P: Oh, no, no. He wouldn't have heard us talking about that.

H: Huh? [*Disbelieving.*]

P: No, I'm not afraid of that. I'm not afraid.

H: [*Sort of making an admission.*] Nilutwo told me that some times he [Gambakutu] comes and wants to butter you up. [We delete here—it is too complex and tangential to the chapter to follow here—a long account by P. of how Gambakutu once tried to attack her. This peeping incident led her to talk about her bad feelings regarding him. We continue from that point.] All right. I want to tell him[S.] a little bit.

P: O.K.

H: I always knew that he had at some time or other—

S: [*Cutting in.*] You mean Nilutwo?

H: No, the man who was in here, who is Nilutwo's elder brother, clan brother, and who has a claim to her after Nilutwo is dead, I knew that he had at some time tried to screw her; you know, adultery.

S: The minute you got up, that broke the discussion on breast-feeding.

H: Yeah. This is a good point to stop. Is there anything you would . . . I doubt if she'll mind if you want to ask her anything.

S: No need to keep her any more. [*To P.*] O.K., that's enough. Tomorrow. . . . [Break. H. physically accompanies P. to her house—wary of Gambakutu for her—and returns. Then:]

H: We face problems [re P.'s talking about *imbimboogu*] about semantics of the language and the culture. Do you see what I mean?

S: No. What problems?

H: This question of—you're suggesting that the women and the men (not necessarily in the same sense) believe that women have orgasms with breast-feeding; that women actually experience this— let's say "orgasm" in quotes. They use the same term for the experience in coitus and with nursing. And that men *know* that women have this experience, and that this therefore focuses men's erotism on the breast, breast-feeding, breast milk . . . you have a part of it in the public culture associated with women, and the public culture associated with men.

S: What do you mean "the public culture"?

H: The secret culture is associated with homosexuality that only boys and men know about, and which women are not supposed to know about and probably don't. There is also a secret culture that women have, in which there are ritual secrets that are hidden from men, only the women wouldn't kill the men if they were found out: what to do about breast milk, breast-feeding, and stuff like that. So you've got these different pieces of a whole phenomenology. The semantic problems would run like this—I asked her again and again, "Is it the same experience? When you're having this experience [breast] that you call orgasm what are you feeling inside your vagina?" She said, "I don't feel anything down there." And then I said, "Well, where is the heat that you're talking about?" She gave me the same answer as before. "It's in my breast." And I said, "Is it way inside, or is it at the nipple?" She says, "It's at the nipple." And then she starts to tell me this story, which is impossible; I can't believe it. When she's been in the garden all day and she hasn't breast-fed her baby and her breasts are *very* full and she feels there's a need for the breast milk to come out, she starts thinking about how she will breast-feed the baby. And as she's walking back to the hamlet, she has this experience she's calling an orgasm. I mean, it doesn't, can't . . . sound believable. I'm not doubting that she's having what she's said—the question is, what does it mean? The answer is that I need more data.

S: We'll just have to get that out of them, by some good questions, which may not succeed; you've tried for two years. If you're on to an . . . unspoken, powerful (partly because unspoken, unacknowledged) erotic communication system between the sexes, then you should investigate it further. (That's what you're doing.) If the men believe that women get erotically turned on—in our sense— by breast-feeding babies. . . . [See chapter 5 on this point.]

H: And it looks as if they are—

S: No. You're saying something different: I'm not concerned with whether the women *are* or not. If the men *believe* that, and are sending out their knowledge of this in this *particular*, complex way—of never talking about it, of sitting in corners and just snickering about it, and getting hard-ons about it, so that the women are receiving the men's knowledge from *that* complex way— then the women *must* be sending back some signals. If all the men are looking at the women's ankles, as in the nineteenth century, then the women have to find clothes in which they hide their ankles *in a certain manner*.

H: To be erotic—

S: In a manner so that when the wind blows and you step off a trolley . . . by mistake . . . In other words: it will have to be *in*

kind that the women repond with one of these hostility mechanisms which create erotic excitement.* That's what you want to
be looking for, in this. Unrelated to what we are talking about
now, you said the other day that you had once heard a very strange
[*to H.*] detail—that came up in the middle of the erotic fantasy
of a man [Imano: chapter 8] who has been defined as heterosexually mature, sexually competent—this centrally important item,
for which all the rest of the daydream is almost foreplay: [he pic-
tures] a baby at the breast and at that point he has his orgasm.[†]
Right?

H: Yeah.

S: All right. You may now have a piece of information that explains
that . . . [a fantasy] which would be impossible for a nonpsy-
chotic man in our society to have had. And you say that if you
told that to ten men here, all ten would get turned on.

H: Hm, yeah.

S: One of the *major* clues may be this potential [suggested] mechanism of the men talking about the women getting turned on: and
the women responding to that in some way. Now one of the responses the women have, is that they may in fact, a hundred percent of them, she says a lot do, but we don't know what the word
orgasm means—they may in fact get turned on by the babies. And
one of the reasons they all may be turned on in reality by the
babies is that they know that the men find it a turn on. They may
be *trained* in erotism.

H: Oh . . .

S: They've got a nipple which has some capacity—and they may be
heightening its capacity because of all this *silent*, but not absent
silent, just subtle noise—communication—going on [between the
women and men]. That would explain, in good part, why that man
[Imano] had that fantasy. Now, you may have essential pieces of
information that may be related.

H: Is it possible, that women could be having a *genuine* . . .

S: Women in our society report genuine orgasms with suckling.

H: Orgasm where?

S: Orgasm where? If you mean orgasm, there's no problem with the
word. It only has one meaning. (Unless it's misused by analysts,

---

*I believe that, rather as you need at least a whisper of hostility (to hurt, to harm, to put
down, and humiliate) for a joke, so it goes with erotic excitement. The skeptical reader will
find the argument at length in Stoller (1979 and 1985a).

[†]This session occurred before the one described in chapter 5, where Weiyu himself relays
this daydream.

who talk about gastric orgasms and bowel orgasms, [i.e.] some kind of excitement with explosiveness.) In the sense that these women are saying, women have reported that they put a baby on the breast and the baby sucks and they have a genital orgasm.

H: Genital orgasm . . .

S: That's the only orgasm there is. All the rest is fantasy.

H: Yeah, exactly. But *she's saying that she doesn't feel anything* [in her genitals].

S: Well, now—we've got to find out what she's saying.

H: Right. It's not clear yet. Well then, this is worth talking about with the men. We could talk about this tonight, because I'm going to be talking to them.

Later that night we did the main interview work in chapter 5, on men's beliefs about breast-feeding and ritual.

A LATER SESSION*

This was the longest session. [It is followed by another, starting page 192.] It lasted almost two hours. At first P. is in the next room. The previous session (unreported) ended early when men began gathering noisily in that outer room.

H: There are two things I want to ask you about. There is a dream, and then there is a daydream she has had.

S: I want some orientation. Why do you want to tell me this *now?* Then I can ask the next question. Might it not be worth the extra effort to *not* tell me, and have her review it again—and she's telling it to a new person. Perhaps it would be better for me not to have heard it before so I have nothing in my head until you translate it. And then maybe what I ask will be different than what I would ask otherwise. [*H. leaves room and brings P. in.*]

H: [*To S.*] [I'm always fascinated by] the little ways—some conscious, some unconscious—men have blocked me from working with her.

S: That would be very interesting. That belongs in methodology. That is, the ways in which—not just the translator, not just yourself,

---

*Again, unfortunately for space, we must delete our second interview with P. She began by telling a long dream about gardening, which had some anxieties in it. That led to her associating to menstrual blood; and then I asked her about the sources of semen and blood. Though valuable, these data deflect from our present focus and will be reported elsewhere. Just remember that many discussions have occurred with P. on many topics, before and after the following session.

not just this, not just that—but the ways in which *the people* will prevent you from getting data. Not just secrets; that's another story. But just because women are to be put down, and this one in particular.

H: Yeah, exactly. I thought of it now because of the guy who is in the kitchen there, who doesn't want to leave. He's lingering.

S: You're going to keep an eye on it, and if he doesn't leave, throw him out? Or he'll leave?

H: I've got to throw him out. [*H. calls out:*] Moondi, Moondi— Moondi . . . [who didn't want to be displaced.]

M: Huh?

H: Are you outside or inside?

M: Outside . . .

H: All right . . . [*To S.*] this will be difficult for her, if I ask about her daydream, because it will be with two men [H. plus S.].

S: It had gotten to be easy with you?

H: It was easy, but still difficult. [We hear Moondi leave at this point.]

S: Difficult, but her relationship with you made it possible. And now, all of a sudden, there's a stranger. But not "a member of the society" so it would be bearable. A stranger.

H: Yeah. It will probably be [awkward] for a few minutes and then pass.

S: Could you tell her anything about me to make it easier?

H: I was thinking of how I could do that. . . . [*To P.*]. We are talking about our work, and then I want to ask you about some things—

S: Tell her that you and I have shared our information for years. Not about her, but just . . . and that we are *comfortable* with each other, and keep secrets. Emphasize the sharingness so that she feels that she can share with me.

H: Um hm. [*To P.*] I want to ask you about something. But first, I want to tell you: well, you know, Dr. S. is, like my boss. The two of us share in each other's work and exchange understanding; he talks with me, and I talk to him. Even the secrets of men or women, we share those secrets too. We both follow the same rule, that you can't tell others about this; that's forbidden. You have to keep quiet, listen, and when they tell you their secrets, that becomes your secret too. I am happy that he follows this rule of mine. We're the same in that way. [*Pause.*] I want to ask you about something from before. When we started, before, on your first fantasy, you told me [some time ago] of an image you have in which you play around [sexual play] while still a *tai* [girl]. You and that *kwulai'u*

[boy] you used to play around with.* Is it okay if we talk about this?

P: Yes, that's okay.

H: When did it [daydream] first begin?

P: Oh, I was married; we were married [the abduction], and then it began.

H: When you and your man were first walking around [metaphor for sex]?

P: It was then. At the time I saw it like this: me and that boy [from her childhood], the two of us were little and we did it like this.

H: You did it like what?

P: We were together. "[I would imagine] We used to do this . . . ".

H: In the image, what can you see first? Like, his face . . . or a place, close to a tree, or see the earth or sky . . . ?

P: The edgeland forest. Close to the huts.

H: Now this place, does it have things—grass, flowers . . . [*soft voice*]?

P: [*Soft.*] Uh, huh. Grass, flowers, bamboos, pandanus fruit. And we played there [*smiles*].

H: Is it a nice place or a bad place?

P: Oh, it's a nice place.

H: And is it morning or night?

P: [*Thinking.*] Oh, morning.

H: Is it just you two, or others too?

P: Some small boys are there, and we're all carrying firewood. And we say to them, "You boys stay here; we want to go over there." Near the bush.

H: Close to them or a way off?

P: Farther away. We can't hear them. It's a long way off—we can't see them. No. Just us two. We say to each other, "We don't want them to see us. We've got to go hide in the grass." And so we go.

H: Does the boy lead or do you?

P: He pushes me [to go].

H: What does he say? He's just asking for nothing [playful foreplay talk]. Do you respond to him?

P: Yeah, I respond. I say, "We didn't come for just anything?—no; we came to search for insects and for young fern sprouts.† That's what we can find." [*Smile.*]

*The nine-year-old boy described in the introductory biographic sketch.
†Children and older adults eat these foods.

H: Um hm. When you say that, do you smile at him?*

P: Yeah.

H: Does he look strong† at you?

P: Yeah.

H: And when he looks strong at you, what do you feel—in the day-dream?

P: I think, "He wants to ask me about doing what I've heard our mommas and papas do." He mustn't want to do this. [*Smiles.*] He shouldn't look strong at me so much. So I just smile.

H: Then what happens in the image?

P: We don't talk. He says, "I want to screw you with your [P.'s slip] cock." [*Chuckles.*] . . . *He* says that: "You look at my cock"—

H: *His* cock. And what do you feel?

P: We both want that, and he's asking me . . .

H: Um hm. What do you feel inside? Happy? Afraid?

P: Just happy. [*Pause.*] Then—

H: When do you picture this? Only when screwing [with Nilutwo]?

P: At that time.

H: When you see his [Nilutwo's] face?

P: No, when I see his cock. Only then.

H: First he himself removes his trousers or grass sporran—?

P: [*Cuts in.*] *He* does that.‡

H: And when you see his *laakelu* [penis], you recall the fantasy of you and the boy playing around.

P: Right.

H: Now I want to look closer at the fantasy. The boy says, "Look at my cock." You like that.

P: Yeah.

H: Then what? Is he then forceful? Removes your grass skirt? Or what?

P: He may be forceful and . . . remove my grass skirt . . . and then we don't have . . . [*mumbles*].

H: What?

P: We do it, just play at it [screwing]. [*Smiles.*]

H: Do you see his cock in the image? His boy's cock. . . . What do you feel?

P: Happy.

*Implying seduction.
†See chapter 4, on erotic looking.
‡P. is underlining that Nilutwo makes the overture, not she. The attitude is: only a whore initiates sexual foreplay, even in marriage. And by clarifying what I had said, P. distances herself slightly from the sexual excitement that might threaten our interview. Perhaps the potential tension between us needs defusing here, keeping the talk less active, more intellectual.

H: Happy. You're not afraid of his* cock?

P: Oh, when it was new, I was a little afraid. But when he stimu-
lated† me a bit then I was really pleased. [*Chuckles.*]

H: You're talking about stimulated in your cunt or outside, the lips
of your cunt, or where stimulated?

P: Just outside. Not really inside.

H: Within this fantasy can you feel *imbimboogu?*

P: No. Only when we're done, then we feel *imbimboogu.*

H: With Nilutwo.

P: Then I get *imbimboogu.*

H: And what about in your fantasy?

P: That's . . . just my *koontu* [thought].

H: [*Surprised.*‡] What?

P: It's just *koontu.* Just thought.

H: So in your fantasy the boy stimulates the sides of your cunt with
his cock; and in truth [at that moment] Nilutwo puts his cock into
you. Is it the same moment when the boy does it and when N.
does it, that you feel *imbimboogu?*

P: The same time.

H: You won't have the fantasy *after* you feel *imbimboogu?*

P: After the fantasy I feel *imbimboogu.*§

H: Can I tell S.?

P: [*Smiles.*] You can tell him; I'll listen.

S: [*Quickly.*] Her style: when she smiled, shyly, and kept her hand
so she just barely looked at me . . . I would read it the same as
at home.

H: I think she's comfortable telling you; I think she's a bit excited
about sharing it with you; interested. And a little . . . fear, about
me telling you. But she's comfortable enough. It's fear in the form
of embarrassment, being shy, very soft, "feminine": in another

---

*I am vague here, for I was not sure how much P. was marking off her daydream from
her intercourse with N.

†*Sigerup*, the Pidgin term, is so vague (see chapter 4). Could be: aroused, buttered-up,
scratched, touched, vibrated, etc. "Stimulated" roughly translates this situation.

‡Fascinating that for the first time, here, P. refers to her experience as *koontu.* I've argued
[chapter 3, and in Herdt 1987d] that *koontu* is a metaphor for "self," specifically the public
social norms that keep people in line. May we interpret P. as meaning she has a socially
acquired script about what she *should* feel regarding orgasm with her husband, as opposed
to the private scripts she may tell no one (may not completely know herself)—except, perhaps, me?—and that may differ from what orgasm *should* be? Thanks to S., I am alert to that
possibility, and if lucky, I may learn if it's true.

§S: Our same argument put this time as rhetorical questions: is a woman's daydream to
be counted as a fit subject for ethnography; can one learn about culture this way; is the private daydream less revealing than the public myth (which probably started as a private daydream); can humans understand each other across cultures?

Sambia woman her fear would take a different form at this moment.

S: She's never looked at me, but I've never had the feeling that she was consciously cutting me out. Instead, she didn't look at me because nothing counted but you and her. And I was safe enough that she didn't even have to think about me. The pleasure she has in being with you and talking with you is the style I felt. She was concentrated on you. Not "I refuse to acknowledge the presence of this other person." It was that I wasn't important. But [she is] not hostile. Because she's so absorbed in the pleasure of being with you. And I don't even mean the affectionate but rather I think she likes the task. Okay.

H: So, I've been asking her about her favorite erotic daydream, the only one, as far as I know, she has now. This is the daydream. She's a young girl of, say eight to ten, eleven; not yet to puberty. And she is with a boy her age. They're near the village where she was born. On that side of the village there are flowers, bamboo, and grass—it's a nice place. And they've been playing with some children in the morning. They tell these others to occupy themselves while P. and the boy go off to do something. At this point she does not know what is going to happen—

S: But she does know. In this society everybody knows about sex, at an early age.

H: No, no they don't.

S: Children—

H: No.

S: They do not know about intercourse?

H: No. The implication is that the boy is stronger than she is and knows more about sex than she does. And so they go off . . . And it's the two of them alone—

S: [*Hears someone in the kitchen.*] You'd better go out there—

H: That's the old man [Chemgalo]; he's all right.* This is based on reality—

S: It sounds like it.

H: This happened several times with a boy she grew up with. And so they go out to collect ferns and insects to eat. But the boy has something different in mind. He begins to look at her sexually. That is, he is looking at her intensely, which means in this culture that he wants her, desires her.

---

*We've grown more cautious since Gambakutu's secret listening. But Chemgalo (Weiyu's step-father) is ancient, and hard-of-hearing.

S: [*Interrupts.*] This has nothing to do with her daydream but with the culture: he looks where—face, eyes ... ?

H: At her face—

S: She knows he's looking at her face and she turns her eyes down. ...

H: And smiles—

S: Because at that age she recognizes what that look means.

H: In the daydream.

S: Yeah.

H: And she smiles.

S: What smile—what kind of smile?

H: Well, I imagine, a charming smile.

S: Shy, innocent—understand, but doesn't understand.

H: It means, "I accept your desire."

S: "I do understand"—?

H: Yeah, that is, "I will be your desirable object." She started having this daydream when first having sex with her husband. She was very afraid. When she saw his penis she was very afraid. It was so big—

S: That was the first one she'd ever seen? Like that? [*Pause.*] Not crucial—

H: Yeah, I don't know* and I'd have to think it out ... That's when she had this daydream. And in it she sees a little boy's penis. First she's a bit frightened ...

S: A little boy's erect penis?

H: Yeah, a little boy's erect penis. The boy looks at her strongly, and she smiles in response. Then he says, "Look at my penis." She looks. He removes his grass skirt and she sees his erect penis ...

S: And she sees one then for the first time.

H: For the first time. And she is frightened at first, but then feels okay. ... Then, in one version he pushes her down, lays on top of her, puts his penis partly in her still immature vagina. In another version [these have been told in earlier interviews] they lay down together and it's a little less rough. The story line is that she wants him, but he's also very firm and he's pushing her. But it's not a rape, not that. She wants him [to do it that way]. And in reality she is using the daydream when she sees the [Nilutwo's] erect penis. In the past she associated to this daydream two erotic night dreams in both of which she saw a little boy's penis, not a man's penis. And in one of these, mine [a night dream seeing me]

---

*I'm 99 percent sure that as an adult woman, P. had never before seen an adult erect penis.

was the same way. It was me, my body, my face, everything was the same, but it was a little boy's penis and not a man's penis.* And *that* gets her more turned on: having this daydream when her husband is about to enter her, gets her more turned on; and the daydream is gone as soon as she has her orgasm in reality.

S: What happens? They're lying down, and he pushes in a little bit. Is there anything about a hymen?

H: That's one of the things I haven't asked about. She's a virgin [in the daydream].

S: It all seems unfinished. He *begins* pushing, he doesn't get very far. There are daydreams in which that would be the end?

H: Yeah.

S: Another thing I'd like to know, that you can't probably find out, is about women in general in this society. Here's a story. A young woman gets married in Los Angeles. And has had no real sexual experience. (Comparable to P.) She's about to have intercourse with a man who has, pretty much, raped her; that is, he has stolen her from her home, ruined all of her plans, taken her to a new place where she's got no right to do anything at all. She's never seen an erect penis on a man before. She's perhaps going to have a physically painful experience (which it is for some women).

H: And she said it was.

S: And she has an orgasm. Now it's not unheard of, but the larger question is: are the women in this culture, generally speaking, highly arousable? This would indicate it, if you were to extrapolate, like a crazy-man, which you have the right to do. But there are cultures in which women expect to have orgasms and always have orgasms. At least so it's reported (and God knows how accurate those reports are).

H: Yeah.

S: But does she represent that even in a traumatic [experience]. . . . Is she representative of all the women? Does she talk with her friends? And does she get the feeling that women expect to have orgasms always?

H: Well this is a highly personal subject. [*Sober.*]

S: Sure it is! [*Laughs.*]†

---

*I didn't deal directly with such sensitive transference reactions in P. until I returned in 1981, mainly because I wasn't able and ready to. They were worked through then in what I think was a mutually respectful way. I shall report that elsewhere.

†I want to underline here that our emotional cues to each other—my soberness, and S.'s amusement—indicate better than our words the momentary gaps between us, in our different professional experiences and emotional understanding of Sambia. Is S. not used to sexual openness in Los Angeles culture? Am I not more reticent for the Sambia?

H: She's never told this daydream to anybody else.

S: But do they talk about their experiences? People will talk about experiences sooner than they'll talk about daydreams.

H: Well, I have some idea about that, but I can ask her.*
[*To P.*] Dr. S. wants to ask us† about when you feel *imbimboogu* when screwing. He wants to ask if sometimes you talk with others about this; do you hear others sometimes talk about having *imbimboogu* with screwing? Do they talk about that?

P: No [*serious*]; they're not about to talk openly about that.

H: Women—

P: Women; no.

H: With your close friends—Nashu [Tali's wife]?

P: Not her either. She's not going to talk about *that* [*whispers*]—I've told you: only when we're asleep, and our legs are turned so that we feel *imbimboogu* [limb "asleep"; a totally different meaning of *imbimboogu*], only then can we say, "Oh, I felt *imbimboogu*." Now this other [erotism]—no, no, not at all.

H: Do you think other women feel *imbimboogu* when they play around with their men?

P: Oh, sure, only they won't talk about it. We all have *imbimboogu*, but they just don't talk about it. That would be shameful.

H: Did your mother talk about it to you?

P: No, no, she didn't ever talk about that. But I think it's not just me who gets *imbimboogu*. All of us women do. We just don't talk about it. We hide it, that's all. [*Smiles.*]

H: [*To S.*] She says what I expected (because we've talked about this before): she's never heard any women, including her best friend, tell her about having orgasms. But she believes that all women have orgasms the same way that she does. But it's *extremely*—this is a very prudish culture. People just don't talk about it. Even her mother; I asked her if she'd talk about it and she said "No."

S: The question is, "Why does she believe that they all have this?" It may just be, "Since I have this, how can anybody else not . . . ."

H: That would be the most obvious answer.

S: But they really do not [talk about it] at all. That doesn't shock me, I've heard [of other instances] before. Okay. So the other

---

*I know now (after another trip) that in general neither Sambia men nor women talk about orgasms, even in private with their closest friends.

†I do say "us" on the tape. Why not "you" instead of "us"? It was subliminal until now (1983): I am identifying with P. verbally, and thereby marking us off as a couple of insiders, vis-à-vis S. By doing so, I imply to P. that I will protect her self-respect should S. go too far in his probings.

question is whether the daydream goes any farther, beyond the point at which she's lying down and the boy begins to push.

H: Yeah. Now I have not asked her about the details of her orgasm. This is difficult . . . because of the terminology. I haven't asked her where . . . I have the sense that it's [orgasm] way inside, that is, it's vaginal—

S: Vaginal, not just clitoral.

H: Not just clitoral, if in fact that's possible.

S: What?

H: That she could have a clitoral orgasm.

S: Well it gets rubbed indirectly during intercourse and participates in women's orgasms. It either participates or it is the main part of it—depending on what's touched. It would be interesting to know—is it vaginal and to what extent. She says it is, is that right?

H: She says it is—

S: [Cutting in.] Is there a vocabulary for the anatomy, is there a word for clitoris?

H: There is a word. Boy, I tell you, I never got that from men!

S: You mean they don't know about the clitoris?

H: They know about it. But they don't want to think about it. [Pause.] It took me a long time to figure that one out.

S: Why don't they want to think about it?

H: The answer—you won't believe the answer: I can't answer you in any simple way. It would take a long time to fill you in. But [in a nutshell], my last view is that men think of it as a kind of penis.* [S: not just Sambia men.] I never got that before; I just worked on it the last few weeks. But at any rate men don't have a term for that. Now, Penjukwi gave me the term for it—

S: The women's term, or everybody's?

H: The women's term. It was a *big* secret. There may be something in that that I haven't mined yet; I think there is.

S: How do they know about it [clitoris]?

H: [Pause.]†

S: Well, I'll give you the answer: because they have experienced the sensations of it.

H: Oh.

S: All right. I mean, how else would they know of it? They're not sitting around with mirrors.

H: Yeah, obviously, sure. [To P.] First, I want to ask you: in your

*My genuine naiveté—I hail from rural Kansas—is not only a character trait but a valuable ethnographic tool.
†Another example of an obvious question I had never thought of before.

fantasy, when you see this boy, and you're playing around, and he gets on top of you, does he get on top of you while you're lying on the ground?

P: [*Pause.*] Yes.

H: Now when he puts his cock inside you, not too far inside but a ways, after you're finished, what will you both do? Inside the fantasy? Or is that the end of it?

P: At that time, I just think, "It's done."

H: It's done. After he inserts—

P: His cock—

H: Inside a bit in your cunt. And then it's done.

P: It's over—

H: Now, in truth, you feel *imbimboogu.*

P: At the same time.

H: Now I haven't asked you this before: in the fantasy you're a girl. Now in a girl, the cunt isn't opened yet.

P: Right.

H: Inside it, the opening is covered by some skin . . . covered by skin [hymen]. Does the boy break the skin and go inside?

P: [*Quickly*] Oh, no; he doesn't go completely inside. Just a tiny way.

H: This far—? [*Gestures with hand.*]

P: Yeah—when we're big, then [*pause*]. I've already told you when my breasts are still small, it's [vaginal entrance?] the same.

H: The same.

P: Yeah. When the breasts are big and mature, close to turning downwards, then at that time it [vagina] can open [i.e., menarche].

H: That was the first time, when your man screwed you—

P: Yeah, it was him, he's the one who messed me up the first time—

H: He broke it [hymen]?

P: Yeah, he broke it. It was painful then. There was no blood. Just pain.

H: Yeah. [*To S.*] She says that's the end of the daydream, the point where the boy penetrates . . .

S: Somewhat—

H: About an inch.

S: Is it stopped by her hymen?

H: [*To P.*] In the fantasy, what keeps him from going deeply inside?

P: My skin—

H: Far enough for you to just feel him, that's all?

P: I just feel him.

H: Truly inside, or just at the surface?

P: No, just the surface. We're just playing at it, that's all.

H: I've forgotten the name of it, where the skin layer is [hymen] atop your [vagina] . . . What is that—I forgot—

P: Oh, uh . . . [*thinks*] Wait . . . [she's forgotten, too]. . . . *Lakandiku.**

H: *Lakandiku.* In your fantasy, too, can you feel that inside it, there is heat?

P: Oh, not at all.

H: [*To S.*] She says that it's her hymen that prevents him from going inside. She also told me something that I guess I forgot or didn't know exactly. That she was a virgin when her husband stole her, and he was the first man who penetrated her. It was the sweetheart she had, who lives in another area, who she'd wanted to have sex with, and she was thinking of him—at the time when Nilutwo stole her.

S: Wait a minute. But not the fantasy you just told me?

H: No, no. That's about the little boy.

S: So she was not having the [little boy] fantasy when Nilutwo first came at her—

H: Oh, yeah.

S: But the sweetheart?

H: No, no.

S: What are you telling me about the sweetheart? You said it was the friend that she had in mind—

H: Oh, I'm sorry. At the time she was married, she did. She was *abducted*, and she wanted to marry her sweetheart—

S: Oh, I see—

H: And I had the impression that she may have had sex with her friend, but she didn't.

S: But she wasn't thinking of him; I thought you said she was thinking of him [sweetheart] when Nilutwo came at her—

H: She was about to marry *him*—

S: Not thinking of him at that moment—

H: Oh, no, no, not when they were having sex.

S: Okay. This was not, when she first used it, an erotic fantasy. It was a defensive fantasy—to make an erotic experience less dangerous. Do you know what I'm saying—?

H: Yeah, that's—

S: Not used for sexual excitement at all [at first]. It was used to *mas-*

---

*I had only heard this word from P. It is never used in any kind of public discourse, and not by men at all. Apparently women use it rarely in private. But at this point, I am still confused and do not realize *lakandiku* means clitoris (see p. 183).

ter an unmasterable situation. But it became an erotic fantasy—

H: Became erotic later, yeah. Let me check out one detail. [*To P.*] At first, when Nilutwo seized you and they put you in that hut, the *first* time, (when you felt pain as he went inside you) did you have this fantasy? The first time, or was it later?

P: No, it was the first time.

H: The first time. At that time did you feel *imbimboogu?* Or not?

P: Yes, At that time I felt *imbimboogu.*

H: The first time?

P: Yeah.

H: But you felt pain?

P: I felt pain; but when he screwed me the next time I had [*smiles*] *imbimboogu.*

H: Oh. [*Pause.*] The same night, or the next day, or—?

P: The next day. When he first did it, it was very painful, I didn't feel *imbimboogu.*

H: And the second night?

P: Then I got *imbimboogu.*

H: And did you have the fantasy then?

P: Yes.

H: And the first time with Nilutwo, you didn't have the fantasy?

P: Oh, no, I didn't. This here [*lakandiku*] is just the surface. Now deep inside we call it . . . *lakwuku* [vaginal vault].

H: Yeah, now when you felt *imbimboogu,* did you feel it inside the *lakwuku,* or where?

P: We feel it deep inside.

H: Where?

P: Deep inside.

H: Deep inside—in the skin . . . ?

P: There.

H: On top, where the skin is, or below in—

P: No, on top—

H: On top and inside—

P: There—

H: At the very back— . . . And when you feel your *muguchelu* [vaginal fluid] come, do you feel it in the *lakwaku*—

P: There, right there [i.e., "yes"].

H: Now, Dr. S. wants to ask you, have you ever felt *imbimboogu* in your *lakandiku* [clitoris; I finally realize P. was referring above not to the hymen but to the clitoris].

P: [*Sweeping gesture.*] *All over.* My *imbimboogu* is in all of it [genital].

H: *Lakandiku?*

P: There too. Both inside and outside.

H: Do you feel it inside first or outside first?

P: No, inside first we feel it and then outside.

H: [*To S.*] Well, this is new information to me. Let me tell you what she just said. She told me she feels her orgasm inside (and this is another term men don't have)—must be the back tissue of the vagina, the very deepest part—

S: The depth—probably nearest the cervix. What some women in our society called "deep vaginal orgasm," when there was a time when that was the measure of whether you were feminine or not, in the late fifty's and early sixty's. It was kind of joking and yet serious that you "weren't really there" unless you were capable of that. It is deep, as deep as you can get in the vagina, and it gives a whole pelvic quality to it. Not just a sharp, localized clitoral type thing—

H: Yeah. Well, it's important that this [anatomy] has a cultural category for it, that it's linguistically marked.

S: You mean this anatomical area is different from the vagina—

H: Yeah, it is marked.

S: It [vaginal vault] has no [common] name in our culture—

H: Oh—

S: It's just called vagina—

H: Well, you see, the three parts are marked. Inside this part—where she says she feels her orgasm first—she's feeling it first inside in this place. And then she feels it outside, at the clitoris—

S: What about lips?

H: [*Pause.*]

S: Do they have a name for that?

H: Yeah, they have a name for it—there's a name for it [*mugu laaku*] but this is not the same, but let me ask her. [*Turns to P. and they talk.*] The impression I get is that she feels it inside, it's not clear to what extent she's feeling—after she feels it—feels her orgasm deep inside, to what extent it becomes a generalized orgasm for everything—

S: But it spreads to all—?

H: It spreads to all. She says that she feels it first more intensely in the clitoris before she feels it on the lips of the vagina, but it seems as if it subsumes the whole area; so she's feeling generalized sensations.

S: Is there anything that sets it off besides just: the time has passed and rubbing has occurred? Is it that he or she is responding to anything [specific] that's going on in him, or is she responding to a private fantasy, or is she responding to neither of those but just to "after you rub for a while it comes," or something else?

H: [*To P. They talk at length. Back to S.*] She has an orgasm when his cock is inside of her and specifically—which she didn't tell me before—she starts to come when he has ejaculated, when she can feel the semen inside. There must be several moments when she can feel the semen start to slurp around. That's when she has her orgasm.

S: This is a statement that's a question: The thing that is exciting enough for her to finish her excitement is that he has ejaculated *his semen*, not just that he has ejaculated. That's not the same thing. Do you hear what I'm saying? Maybe—it could be the "convulsive activity" that would be the turn-on, or it could be "I possess the semen," I don't know which of those it is.

H: I think I know what it is, but let me ask her.

S: This [society having a] semen cult, it's a worthy question.

H: [*Talks with P.*] Well, *she's* putting the emphasis on feeling the fluids [hers and/or his?] or the semen inside of her. I didn't get that sense before. This is really very rewarding for me, because I *know* I've got the right terminology.

S: You never had it before?

H: No. But now I've got it, [a term] I've never used with her before: there is a category for excitement.

S: Different from the word for orgasm?

H: No, not orgasm.

S: Excitement?

H: Excitement—(the category *kalu mundereindapinu*). I've never used this term with her before. I use it with [some] men (e.g., Moondi) all the time. I ask them, "Are you feeling excitement?" It's a proof that I've got the right cultural connotation, that I can use it for the first time with her and I asked her, "When do you start to feel excitement?"*

S: It's not "excitement"—our word is too vague. We have to add "erotic" or "sexual." This is a word just for genital excitement, not any excitement?

H: This [term] is for excitement [a noun modified by various adjectives to fit the person's experience to the situation]. I say, "When you start feeling excitement, is that when he starts to ejaculate?" She says, "No, not then. It's when he starts to butter me up to

---

*Lest the reader be confused, this summary refers to material that was deleted above for space.

screw me that I start to feel excited." See, that's the correct sense of it. The correct sense—you don't get excited when he's inside of you. (It might be possible for that to happen.) But *she's* getting excited when he starts to seduce her. He wants to be inside of her, and that's when [why] she starts to get excited.

S: That's the foreplay.

H: Yeah, that's the foreplay. Then I said, "When he ejaculates, are you more excited?" and she said, "Yes." And I said, "When do you stop being excited?" "When he takes his penis out." So that's exactly what I would have predicted, but I've never [with P.] used that word [excitement]. So it's a good test that I've got the right sense of it that I can use it with her for the first time and she confirms—it's very important semantically that I've got the meanings right.

S: We've gotten quite a bit [of information]. The kinds of things if you had enough time you'd want to find out. Here's something you take for granted: She says to you, "What makes me have my orgasm is the presence of the semen in my vagina, and what gets me excited is the fact that he shows that he wants me." Those are self-evident, right?

H: Yeah.

S: No.

H: [*Laughs in surprise.*]

S: Behind those are I-don't-know-what-fantasies and life experiences. I could imagine another culture, I could imagine certainly other·women, in fact I *know* of women for whom the semen is so disgusting inside of them that they can't bear it.

H: Oh, really?

S: The question is [not only why is semen disgusting for them but] just as much why *is* it not for her. Therefore, don't take anything for granted about sexual excitement. Got it? Once you've got that clue, you'll never forget it except you always forget it and you keep getting into [twisted up by] your own definitions of normality.

H: I just recalled that every last man I've ever worked with here always says that women spit on any man who doesn't have semen. The men say that unless the women can see and feel the ejaculation—

S: All right. That's strictly not to be taken for granted.

H: I've always regarded that as a piece of men's [identity]—but now I think—

S: You don't know; you've only got one [woman's statement]—

H: But a possibility is that in many women here it [ejaculation] really is part of their excitement: it really is necessary, and if a man doesn't have a big seminal emission, it's a big deal. I never thought about it before.

S: Could this—it doesn't have to be—could this be now some of the evidence of the—you can't call it the semen cult—but the importance of semen . . . this would be the form maybe in which you get your first clue of how it shows up in the women. They may not know there's a semen cult [homosexual activities], but they may have learned that semen is big stuff, not just to produce babies. So a clue like this could be (at this point, you're just speculating wildly) your chance—you muddle along and all of a sudden you discover a doorway where you didn't know there was one—

H: Yeah.

S: And you now open that door, and it opens up into female reciprocal—reciprocating—the reciprocal of the male semen cult. In what form does that present in the women's lives? That's the way you are going. (It might not be a door.)

H: There's a whole subject that she and I have never talked about: the men's belief that women like to acquire semen either through their mouths or through their vaginas—

S: [An acquisition] which devastates the men—

H: Which devastates the men but also excites them.

S: Oh, sure.

H: And, but especially through their mouths, because it is believed to strengthen the woman's body, her tissue, her bones and to provide breast milk.

S: Are the women told this,* or is this one of the secrets of the men?

H: This is the men's belief, not necessarily a secret; it's supposed to be a public thing.

S: What do the women believe about it?

H: See, that's what I never asked her.

S: Well, ask her what do women feel—what does semen do besides—

H: I want to see if there is somebody inside here. [*Goes to check.*] I thought sure I heard some talking. He's just in there by himself [Weiyu's stepfather, Chemgalo who, uncomprehending, is sleeping out his last days in the safety of H.'s fire].

---

*Probably yes, in their secret menarche ceremonies.

S: But he's been muttering in there to himself—I saw him talking like he wasn't facing anyone else. He just shouldn't fall into the fire—

H: [*Talks to P. telling her what happened. To S.*] I was just noticing she is *so* feminine.

S: Even in our culture she would seem so. I mean, she is as feminine as any women I've ever seen in any part of the United States; Paris, France; Bergen, Norway; Rome, Italy. How come?

H: I don't know.

S: She's never learned that from the other women here. [H: She would have; there are others as feminine in demeanor.]

H: I was just noticing what she was doing with her hands and . . .

S: Her whole everywhere, those facial expressions . . .

H: Her face, and her eyes . . .

S: The sound of her voice . . .

H: Her smile, and the softness in her eyes . . . [We are enjoying ourselves.]

S: But she's very feminine by the standards here.

H: Right. Yeah, this is one of the things about gender identity. It takes you [ethnographer] so long to pick up the subtle things. Then they take on meaning. I mean the way she . . . you see the way she's using her hands [i.e., small expressive gestures]. No masculine man ever uses his hands that way.

S: But Kalutwo—

H: Yes, that's right and the other guy [Imano].

S: Up the hill—

H: Yeah. [These circumlocutions exemplify how we avoid saying people's names in front of other people, in order to preserve confidentiality.] He especially, he's [Imano] a very emotionally expressive man; that's a feminine quality.

S: Men are expressive with their hands, but it's more [*thrusts arms out, slashing at the air*] . . . fists, and uh, sharper.

H: But less than that.

S: I've seen some men doing it.

H: Weiyu will do that.

S: Yeah, that's who I was thinking about. That's who I've seen do it. He sat there gesticulating with his hands . . .

H: Yeah; but now, that other guy up the hill [Imano], he's in that [gentle masculine] category. He's an especially expressive man with his hands in a feminine way. He has soft gestures, the way he touches his face . . . (details, that are in my field notes). Like the way he'll touch his cheeks is unusual . . . . But anyway, she was saying that [collecting my thoughts] . . . I was asking her about the . . . what was the question we originally got on? I was asking her about . . . drinking semen, and she says that she thinks . . . . There for the first time, there was a little disgust in her voice. Some disgust about orally ingesting semen . . . . She said that, uh—

S: [*Butts in, lowers voice slightly and sensitively says*] Well, did she do it in her uh, uh [*groping for words*] . . .

H: She's done it a few times, and she doesn't like to do it. She thinks it's boring. Here's a fundamental difference between the men's and women's views: She thinks* it's basically baloney that semen is necessary in order to strengthen a woman, to prepare her for child bearing, and so forth. She has mixed feelings about what it is that produces breast milk. She holds out the possibility that semen *may contribute* to it, for the simple reason that she has noticed in her own body that there's no breast milk before the time she had started having sex with her husband. And she is again approaching now that period when she's about to have babies.

S: [*Inserts.*] Whoa! That might be right, but she hasn't had sex for a long time and yet she's got lots of breast milk, doesn't she? Is she feeding now?

H: Yeah, she's feeding now.

S: Where [does she believe] is it coming from?

H: Well, uh . . .

S: [*Continues.*] Other semen from other times?

H: She's got mixed opinions. She's saying that inside she feels that her breasts are making it, that there is something in her own body that's producing it. One part of her says that that part of the story is baloney too. She wouldn't reject that, but what she does specifically say is that she dislikes fellatio, and her husband has too often wanted to have fellatio with her. She will often say, "No, I don't want that, I'd rather have it down below."

S: She doesn't say why? She doesn't know why he wants it, he just wants it?

H: No, she told me why. She says that [rough translation] the old men say in the ritual teachings that the man mustn't have vaginal

---

*Now, as an adult woman. Her feeling was not as clear when younger. We ethnographers cannot be too conscious of the fact that people's gender identities and erotics may alter, as they move through the life cycle, experience more, and change.

sex too much because it is harmful to his health, and he should have fellatio more often.

S: Did the men tell the boys to tell their wives that? Or is she just inventing it?

H: No, that's true, it's a true story.

S: They did say that [*voice rising*], you mean they really do believe it?

H: That's part of the ritual teachings!

S: Oh, I thought it was "What are we going to tell the women to make sure that the women don't discover what we really do."

H: No, they [the men] really do believe that, which goes along with the view that coitus is more threatening and damaging than is fellatio. It's [coitus] closer to the source of the uterus, she's saying, (this is interesting, I hadn't thought of it like this), "Forget the mouth. I'm a bit disgusted at having your semen in my mouth. I don't believe your stories. If you want to give it to me, let's have sex in my vagina, where it's closest to my womb."

S: Also, she doesn't get any excitement from it [fellatio].

H: Yeah, exactly, but the point is that with this comment she associates sex with the womb, having semen "fed" into her womb. That's very important, because the man's view is that coitus is the most depleting act. Fellatio is definitely less depleting and dangerous because you're physically farther away from the vagina and womb. (See Herdt 1981.)

S: [*Pause.*] We don't have to give up the idea yet that we're getting the reciprocal of the men. But there's a lot more about semen in these women than in other societies' women. At least in conscious awareness.

H: Yes.

S: You want to keep looking for that. . . . You taught me that typically when the man starts into marriage, he begins fellatio with the girl as a bridge for himself toward the dangerous vagina, from the safety of the boys.

H: Right. . . . I forgot to tell you about something you asked about a while ago. When Nilutwo abducted her, and they had sex the first time, it was very [emotionally] painful for her. But she is very precise that the first time that he started to enter her, when she saw his penis, she was frightened: *that* was the first time she had the daydream. But she had *no* orgasm that time. It was the second night that she had an orgasm. She had the fantasy at the same time, and she continued to have it frequently, although not every time for the first six or so months.

S: Probably she had it frequently, meaning every time she was more frightened.

H: Yeah.

S: And less excited.

H: It's such a transparent daydream. [S: Only to us.]

S: You get what I meant when I said that is was not an erotic daydream [the first time she used it]. And it may never have been when used with her husband: [with him] it may have been an anxiety-reducing daydream. But if she's lying around all by herself and staring at the ceiling and avoiding masturbating [since Sambia all allege no one ever masturbates], and she has it, then it's an erotic daydream, and you have to understand the difference. There'll be something different in some detail between the two, says my prediction. You never did find out about another piece that we picked up. You were interrupted when we were finding out whether the word for orgasm had the same meaning as breast-feeding, and so, keep that in mind. You may want to go back.

H: Yeah, that's right.

S: At any rate, what seems more exciting [for H.'s research] than where she feels her sexual excitement—you could be on to something big, though not as big as your original discovery about the semen cult—is the ways the men's cult presents to [is filtered through] the women. It cannot present as a revealed secret. How do they absorb it [the secret], and how do they absorb it into their understanding of what it's like to be a female and a woman in this culture. Now that is probably more important in the remaining time you've got than to find out much more about what's the nature of her orgasm.

H: That sounds right.

S: So there you have some more about the semen cult, [though] we don't know *what* you've got.

H: Now that you've brought it to my attention, it seems obvious, but I wouldn't have thought of it. That's quite a thing. [*Pause.*] Well, I think we'll quit. It's been almost two hours.

S: Yeah. She's been a good help.

H: Yeah. [*To P.*] Oh, I think we'll stop now, we've finished two hours' worth now.

P: Okay.

H: I think tomorrow too, I'd like to work quite a long time with you. Is that all right?

P: Yeah, that's all right.

H: Okay. Suppose in the morning, we'll kick everybody else out and just us, we can work. Is that all right?

P: Yeah, that's good.

LAST SESSION

H: I think this is the last time that you and I will be meeting together [*quietly and slowly*].*

•   •   •

P: There's lots of people around. [*Pause. We don't know where we'll go with the interview. So S. suggests we talk about her plans for protecting herself after Nilutwo dies. How will she escape another forced marriage? Will the men beat her up? Could she be killed? We get depressed. We talk with her about her plans after N's death. Then:*]

S: If we're in a lull, then you can ask her about the tattoos. If you're not in a lull—

H: [*Depressed.*] No, I'm in a lull. [I felt down thinking about P.'s plight. We are trying to think what to do next. S. had earlier asked why P. had a light tattoo on her face, unlike other women in the village. At first—several years ago—I wondered about P.'s tattoo but had grown oblivious to it and had never asked her about it. S. reminds me now.] Dr. S. wants to ask you about that mark on your face.

P: Oh, Yanduwaiko's people—his wife—they put that on me.

H: Did you ask her for it, or did she just do it?

P: Oh, no. She did it. She said, "I want to decorate you with that" [*smiles*].

H: And you let her?

P: Yeah, I let her [*chuckles*]. She is just like my mother. I used to sleep curled up in her lap. It wasn't just me. It was Gam's wife too.

H: Do you like this?

P: [*Laughs.*] Oh . . .

S: [*Laughs.*] She covers her face with her hands. That's the first time she's done that.

H: She used to do that all the time.

S: Oh, really? Is it because of me or because of the subject? And me, or not me, or the subject, or all of us?

---

*Again we must delete a long dialogue here on sexuality to save space.

H: It's all that. [*To P.*] Do you like that mark? [*Soft humor.*]

P: Guh [*chuckles*].

H: You like it?

P: I like it.

H: What does it do for you?

P: This woman said: "We all do this. And you should have one too."

H: [*To S.*] She says it's her aunt who did it. The government translator's wife at the patrol station. She's like her mother. And at one time her aunt wanted to do it to her and to her other aunt. But then I asked her, "Do *you* like it?" And she said, "Yes, I like it."

S: But none of the women in this hamlet—

H: No.

S: None of the women in her hamlet—just the women at the patrol post. What does it mean?

H: [*To P.*] Does this mark have a meaning for you?

P: Um—no, not for me [*raises voice, squirms, chuckles*].* That's just that woman's idea. I don't have any idea about it.

H: But you like it, don't you?

P: [*Smiles.*] That's just that woman's idea. It wasn't mine.

H: Not yours?

P: They all said, "We want to put this on your skin . . . So you have to do it." That's all.

H: [*Chuckles.*] Ohhh. [*To S.*] I'm getting all kinds of new thoughts. She's very embarrassed; she wants to deny that it was her decision, "Just my aunt's." But I don't believe that.

S: Is this vanity?

H: Yeah.

S: She's caught being vain.

H: Yeah: see, this is a sign that she's a different kind of woman [from the rest in the hamlet]. She is; she regards herself that way. She speaks Pidgin and stuff like that. There's a sense that she's a little bit freer—

S: To have done this?

H: Yeah. Yeah—for sure. I'd never really thought about it much— but you see this is what women of a tribe† in the Central Highlands do. I don't want to say their name because it has a negative connotation here. They're regarded [here] as sort of promiscuous—

---

*This response, and this effect, are typically feminine, and unusual for P. with me. She seems here to resort to the womanly script, "I'm innocent."

†Chimbu. Sambia have encountered Chimbu who have body tattoos.

S: This is a custom of theirs—

H: Yeah.

S: How did it get down here? [H: It hasn't; just in P.] This is contact?

H: A lot of contact at that station. [Outside New Guineans are employed at the patrol station.]

S: And it indicates? Erotic promiscuity? A different relationship to the world?

H: Not necessarily. A different relationship—a different kind of femininity: more open. See, they kiss there; they're open about holding hands. They're more aggressive. You know the Sambia boys are afraid of those women—in Goroka and other places. [And they detest the thought of kissing.] I never thought of it before, but it matches her personality that she did that.

S: When? When was it?

H: [To P.] Did you have this done when you were a young woman [chenchorai]—

P: I was a tai [girl].

H: Oh, still a tai—were you very little, or bigger? Same as—

P: [Says a seven year old girl's name]—bigger.

H: Oh. [To S.] She was a girl still, hadn't had her menarche yet, but was within a year or two [c. 17–18 years old] of it.

S: What about the one on her arm?

H: Her arm? [Surprise. I hadn't even noticed that one.] . . . [To P.] Now what about that one on your arm?

P: [Laughs.] No, that's nothing! [H: Does the laugh signal a real choice that P. made, not the coercion she earlier described?]

H: [Another interruption from outside. This conversation is very public. Did this change P.'s behavior? To P.] There's chaos out there. What about your hand?

P: A small boy and I had them put them on us.

H: When you were still a tai?

P: Yeah, I was a tai.

H: Oh.

P: One of my [classificatory] sisters put it on us—Gam's people. I just let them.

H: [To S.] She did it when she was still a girl. She said she wasn't thinking; did it with her clan sister.

S: This is . . . most unusual.

H: Huh?

S: Most unusual.

H: Oh, it is most unusual. I never thought about it. She's really embarrassed about having it.

S: You mean, beyond the men?

H: Oh, yeah, I don't know why. I can see that she got a little angry about being asked about it.

S: Do you think it's all right [to ask about this]—I really don't know what I'm doing [*laughs*].

H: Yeah, I think it's all right. [*To P.*] When I asked you about your arm tattoo I looked at your face and I thought you felt a little anger. Why was that?

P: No—

H: You said, "No, I'm not cross about that." But I see your face, and I think there's a little anger.

P: [*Laughs.*] No, not really. It's just that you're asking me too much [about this] and that's no good.

H: Really?

P: Yeah, that's true.

H: Oh, this talk is no good?

P: Um-hm. It's not just me who's done this, plenty of other women have. I don't want to talk anymore. [*Angry.*] I'll go . . .

H: They have too; oh, yeah. [*To S.*] That's the first time in all our work she's ever done that. She says, "Don't ask me any more or I'll go outside." I don't know what it means.* First time she's ever said that.

S: The first time ever? The question is why she's so upset. . . . I guess we should quit. [Tape unintelligible for a few moments.] All right.

H: [*To P.*] That's it. . . . We want to say thank you for all you've said and for your help. We're really pleased. [*Warm smile.*]

P: Me too, I'm really pleased. It's only right now, you two have asked me too much about this [tattoo: covert way to say, "I was angry"]. So that's all—

H: Well, that's okay. We didn't know about that, and so we asked . . .

P: Well, that's okay, but you've asked me too much about this. I didn't mind until now. [H: for the first time P. wants to argue with me. She won't give it up. We really touched a sensitive spot.]

H: I can understand that. But we were just asking. You know. Dr. S. doesn't know about things here, and he just wanted to find out. You, too, do you have anything you'd like to ask him?

P: Well, I just don't understand why he kept at that. That's no good.

---

*I think that I do now (1988). Sambia never had tattoos traditionally and in 1979 only P. and her aunt did. We asked about it in a context of sexuality, and P. seemed to feel her character—moral rectitude—was challenged. She *could* get angry because S. asked the question and she felt close enough to me not to hide it.

AFTERWORD

We ended this long session in a wash, interested but tired and ready to have a break. P. had been angry and almost broke off her talk with S. Only later did I wonder if we had created in her—consciously and unconsciously—fears, doubts, and desires regarding all this sex talk, which were transformed toward the end into an angry response at S.'s surprising question about her tattoo. Unwittingly S. had pushed a button that rubbed against those anxieties, by committing a faux pas: don't ask about the aberrant (related-to-erotic) tattoo. Still, we said goodbye cordially.

And the next day, true to herself, my friend Penjukwi seemed her usual self, comfortable.*

DISCUSSION

H: This chapter illustrates the rewards for and problems in doing clinical ethnography. The rewards comes from better understanding P.'s sense of self, her view of her life experiences, and her thoughts about her sexuality. The problems include the issue of discussing such intimate topics with a woman in a male-dominated society. P's bravery is remarkable, for not only did she overcome her fears and doubts about working with two white men, but she persisted in the face of Gambakutu's ugly peeping and worries about her husband's approaching death. I underscore here again my uneasiness about the focus on erotism in this case study. Though in other chapters—on Moondi, Sakulambei, and Kalutwo—sexual and gender issues are critical, the potential for sensationalism and charges of sexism are greater here: shades of two white masters questioning one poor woman. Then, too, this chapter has been drastically shortened; the omitted materials would have decreased the artifact.

These dialogues, then, must be understood in their narrative context. Interviewing people of the opposite sex on erotic matters requires skill: trust is essential. Even that is not always enough. Many periods of interaction, sometimes therapy, may be needed to build trust before discussing sexual excitement. Respect and consideration for the other person's privacy is ever crucial. The interviewee must know—consciously and then intuitively—that the researcher is not sexually interested in the subject. Otherwise, trust is impossible, for at some level (perhaps unconscious) he or she will fear being used and therefore harmed. The researcher must know this; and that

---

*After a while she wrote to me[7] in the States, saying that things were going fine.

awareness must be made clear, explicitly or implicitly, perhaps many times. The power differential between two such people is great; only time and rapport, plus continuing respect, make such investigations possible. If this is all true for people interacting in the same society, how much more so in another culture, especially one such as Sambia, where women do not talk to men of their sexuality!

Because it has taken me years to know the importance of this last statement, I do not advise the beginning student to undertake such research prematurely. One needs beforehand so much self-under-standing, cultural and linguistic competence in the culture, and rapport with the community. In my case, I never attempted such sensitive interviews with women my first two years in the field. Perhaps the men would not have permitted me to do so anyway. Even now, as you saw, they throw up obstacles to my work with the women. Why?

We can identify these factors clearly. (1) Men never talk to women in a one-to-one, reciprocal way. (2) Women and men do not discuss their sexual experience together, and, as P. pointed out (and as we know of our own society traditionally), Sambia women do not even share with each other feelings about such intimate matters as having orgasms. (3) I suspect that men are highly interested, even jealous, of my contacts and relationships with women, though to say this is almost impossible for them. (Note Moondi's reluctance to leave us. Are the men conscious of this jealousy?) All three factors set up a context of power and status in my talking with P. This condition, and the ever-present potential for intimacy in discussing deep needs and feelings, enhance the possibilities and shape of P.'s transference. This means, for instance, that certain expectations (of her father and mother, or others) can be projected onto me, though the true source of these is not myself. The clinical ethnographer, to pursue sexuality as a long-term issue with another person, must be aware of such transference. Clinical training is necessary to attain this understanding. (See the Epilogue.)

In these sessions with P., despite the misunderstandings and the lack of more supporting data, we move closer to knowing her view of herself and her sexual experience. The link between breast-feeding sensations and genital arousal raises important questions: about the universality of certain female sexual experiences, the role of semen and milk in women's thought, and so on. We do not fully understand these experiences or their correlates—either in P.'s life history or in Sambia culture (chapter 2)—but we have more clues to follow; these are what clinical interviews can provide. Moreover, we often sense in these dialogues a pervasive *discourse* on the nature of female and male sexuality as interrelated phenomena in Sambia culture. Social reality too can be studied in a unique way via such interviews. And without the resulting dialogues, in spite of their shortcomings, an ethnographer can report on sex and gender or male/female relationships in a society, yet miss domains of information, not to mention the problem of inadequately understanding the native's viewpoint.

With subtle and intimate topics such as sexuality, surface behaviors—gestures, words, feelings, what-have-you—can mask other things. They are microdots: for instance, P.'s tattoos. What do those tattoos mean to her: femininity in general; her sense—modern, not old-fashioned, of her femaleness; sexual freedom; modernization, including travel and exposure to western ways; her social role that, in its normativeness, makes the tattoo highly visible and yet a symbol of her private self; identification with her aunt, her uncle, the customs of other New Guinea peoples; her feeling she is daring; her defiance of the men's power over women; her desire to live her own life, in spite of her fate—including the fantasy of marrying her sweetheart had it not been for Nilutwo's abduction; scripts about what men and women like and don't like; feelings about who she is and who she can never be. All compacted in a tattoo. When S. asked about it, those scripts (i.e., she—for she, her self, is those scripts) responded to S.'s question with shyness, anxiety, then anger. Her self filled the tattoo, becoming, for an instant, more important than anything—and P. was P. but not the normal P. Microdots contain all that we are and are not. Clinical ethnography is the means for studying such details.

We cannot yet answer these questions fully. The results of our work will, however, eventually bring more answers. In the meantime, our aim is to provide a means to discover better questions, and thereby enhance the discovery process in anthropology.

S: More important for me than anything else we could discuss regarding P's case is a necessary weakness in any ethnography: there is always another informant who would give more facts, a different slant, or total disagreement. Beyond that, as we emphasize, no matter how we select informants and how rich a report we generate, the story (in anthropology called "the ethnography" and in psychoanalysis "the case report") is filtered through the investigator's personality. To improve the findings, then, we would need a swarm of ethnographers. And even that would not quite work. The problem becomes worse to the extent that the above weakness is ignored.

Our interviews with Penjukwi highlight this argument: to talk only to males distorts one's view of the culture. But how does one get the women's view? Especially if you are a male ethnographer? If we recognize the inadequacy of our ethnography, at least we can imagine improvements.

Though H. sensed these issues, I hounded him, throughout the two years of our almost five-days-a-week-discussions, before we were together with the Sambia, to make the most of his good luck in having one female informant, even if that good luck was colored by her aberrance compared to the other women. He did so.

Could H. have found his ethnography in the earlier years using a woman ethnographer? Perhaps, but it would depend as well on *her* personality, skills, and relationship with H., ability to carry on in that physically hostile environment, and permission (in the subtle things, not just a gross okay) from the people—male and female—of the village. It would be as difficult to find such an ethnographer as it would have been if someone had been searching for a Herdt before 1974. The odds are not good.

Let me now underline a few points related specifically to P.

First, there is the problem of the unnatural effect the ethnographer has on the culture, especially when, with his wealth in money and technology, he introduces a community to desires never imagined. What other effects, also powerful but more subtle, do we produce when these people, unsophisticated in our ways, find themselves, like a population that has never known measles, mortally infected with a disease to which, because of their awe, admiration, envy, and love of us, they have too little resistance? What wild transference notions must inhabit them. And then this magical person—who to his colleagues is not amazing; just another ethnographer—can come and go from their land, regardless of what they want.

When planning my trip, I made up a little emergency kit, to permit, if necessary, fragmentary first aid for Gil and myself. I had wondered if I should be prepared to help Sambia as well, a problem with untold dimensions. (From H.'s teaching, I knew that one could bring in a hospital and stay busy.) Within moments of stepping off the helicopter, I learned that a man a few hours into the jungle had put a spear into his wife's back to remind her of the rules governing Sambia marriage. So I, nakedly naive, asked if I should take off down the path, cute little kit in hand, to determine whether the spear had, for instance, penetrated the peritoneum, stuck itself into a kidney, ruptured the intestine, introduced infection, could be removed without killing the woman—all this not only without my being an emergency room physician or a surgeon but without my even knowing what it meant to trot on down a path in the jungle. Had I made that house call, what promise would be in it for everyone in the valley, not just Gil's friends, about medical care? And had I done well, what goes on in people who get a glimpse of such medical care and then lose it shortly thereafter?

In P's case, we wondered, before we left the Valley, whether, when her husband died, some of the men, within the bounds of their customs, would kill her for being an uppity, disruptive female. Was it our business to prevent her murder, and, in doing so, inflict on these people our alien morality? When we decided to hell with it—we were going to protect her by warning them not to kill her or even beat her senseless—we knew we were indulging ourselves. In doing so, we perhaps saved her but pushed our friends one step further on the road to unforeseeable cultural change.

Second, what about our confusion with *imbimboogu?* Is it good ethnographic technique to press so hard and so long to understand a category? Is it proper for two men to push a vulnerable woman regarding intimate experiences, especially in a culture where men and women never talk together about such matters? Is it worth reporting even briefly, much less in so much detail, the travails of our inquiry; is this a contribution to the practice of ethnography? Is our theory strong that nonerotic psychocultural factors make up what becomes the erotic and that therefore the study of erotics is a powerful way to study a culture? If so, does it warrant what we did to P.; do we even know what we did to P? Is the absence in ethnography of reports on erotics a legitimate omission? Necessary? Worth the price? Are we correct in accusing colleagues of neurosis (countertransference) when we wonder why such data are not present in ethnography and scarcely found anywhere else in the "social sciences"?

We believe that getting details about sexual life—about any and all intimacy in individuals—is not a detour from the great issues of anthropology but is, rather, an ideal way to bring the researcher to the center of a culture. Therefore, anthropology's lack of such data, especially if it has occured because the subject is exciting, disturbing, guilt-producing, or repugnant to the ethnographer, puts the lie to anthropologists' claims of being scientists, objective, or open to understanding the people they study. This failure is thus a crime of the mind. (And no less so if ethnographers have gathered data on intimacy and then suppressed the material. Likewise when editors do the same.)

Our purpose in presenting this material, then, is not simply to inform the audience about odd Sambia folks or how odd Sambia folks are related to other peoples, but to emphasize the value of a methodology such as ours for studying people, individually or *en masse* as a culture.

CHAPTER SEVEN

Sakulambei: A Hermaphrodite's Secret

BIOGRAPHIC PORTRAIT

H: In a society that prizes maleness, in which men emphasize phallicness and exhibitionistic performances, and where ritual and myth give highest value to penis, semen, and many progeny for admission into adult masculine personhood, there could hardly be a condition more anomalous or sensitive than hermaphrodism. When I began fieldwork among the Sambia I did not know that. Nor did I know that there are intersexed Sambia: hermaphroditic males who are treated differently from birth, who are said to have microscopic penes, and who apparently suffer from 5-alpha reductase deficiency, a rare hormonal syndrome.[1] Sakulambei is such a person. This chapter reflects on his life, its public and secret stigmata; especially the private secret he never dared share with anyone, and the relationship with us that let him share it.

By 1979 Saku was in his late twenties, already established as a powerful shaman. He was married but childless. I have known him since 1974, when he was just an acquaintance who looked and acted a bit odd in the first months of our relationship. In 1975, I interviewed him several times on his shamanism. He was warm, knowledgeable, and articulate, but I felt there were things he was hiding. I was not then interested in his hermaphrodism and did not discuss it. Soon thereafter I saw him belatedly initiated into third-stage bachelorhood, years behind his agemates. A few months later he was married, surprising everyone. In early 1979, I began interviewing him in depth to understand his gender identity. After four months' constant work, we were joined by S., which produced dramatic results.

I am uneasy condensing Saku's biography. He and his history are complex and easily distorted. As with other of my friends, my materials on Saku are rich and cover years. I worked alone with him, without an interpreter. As with Nilutwo, I studied Saku's dreams, which facilitated the strong transference attachment he formed to me.[2] Saku liked me, and I, him; over the years my respect and admiration for him grew as I learned more of his struggle to be himself. He had never completely trusted me, though in his distrust, I sensed a desire to trust that was missing in, say, Kalutwo.[3] It was not until these two following sessions with S. that I understood his mistrust.

Let me now sketch Saku's history and discuss the progress of our work in 1979, when S. entered the picture.

Saku was born about 1953. Warfare was still raging throughout his childhood. During our 1979 interviews I did not know the details of his birth. I did know that, though reared in the direction of the male sex, he was sex-assigned a hermaphrodite at birth. He was so touchy discussing the subject that I could not learn the particulars from him. But once he opened up to S. and me, I was later able, in 1981, to investigate the details of his birth and even interviewed the old woman who served as midwife and who made the sex assignment.[4] He had been born with a tiny penis and an odd-looking scrotum. As are all male hermaphrodites there, he was assigned as a *kwolu-aatmwol* ("turnim-man") because people knew that sexual differentiation in the genitals would occur around puberty.[5] Hermaphrodism is a mystery to Sambia. It has magical associations. But mysterious or magical, hermaphrodites are stigmatized. No different in appearance from other hermaphrodites at birth, Saku has made himself different. He is a powerful shaman. I know of no other hermaphrodites, past or present, who became shamans, let alone great shamans. Saku's achievement is unique.

It is Sakulambei's fate to have been the son of the greatest living Sambia war leader. Mon, his father, died in 1983. But until his death, in his late sixties, he was rough and tough, and still acknowledged as *the* leading elder of Pundei hamlet. Mon killed at least eight men and was involved in countless battles. He married six times (outlived three of his wives) and fathered more than twenty children. Before his death, Mon was among the three or four oldest living Sambia in the Valley—survivor of wars, epidemics, and famines, and the last of virtually all his brothers, agemates, friends, and enemies. To the end, he was the ruthless, cold-blooded warrior, for some forty years holding leadership through bluster, guile, intelligence, threat, and his special warlike skills. For instance, he proved himself a master of treachery, not above killing a clan brother.[6] At one time he held shamanic powers, and throughout his life practiced sorcery to support his leadership. But Mon was never a successful shaman and had not practiced his arts for years. Still, longer than anyone, Mon firmly controlled his world—for nearly half a century.

Saku was the third and last child of Mon's third wife. She was much younger than M., and through a sister-exchange marriage had been traded from a distant hamlet at the other end of the Sambia Valley. Her brother, Yumalo, also a fight leader, was even more important as a great shaman. He became crucial in Saku's development. Saku's mother died many years ago, when he was five. We know little of her, except that she was frail, was a minor shaman herself, and was well liked. Her marriage to Mon was apparently not happy. She never adjusted to living in Pundei. She bore a daughter, a son, and then Saku, all of whom are still living. (From what is known,[7] all except Saku are anatomically normal.) The parents fought a lot, and Saku's mother was often ill. When she got sick, she would return to Yumalo, to be treated through his healing ceremonies. She died and was buried there in her natal hamlet (c. 1958).

In early childhood, Saku thus had an almost nonexistent relationship with his father, and his mother died early. Because of his stigma, we can presume his life would have been a disaster were it not for his maternal uncle Yumalo, who stepped in at this point. Even before his mother's death, Saku spent most of his time in his uncle's household, Yumalo already functioning as a substitute father figure. After she died, Mon ignored Saku, which was apparently fine with Yumalo, who cared for him. By that time, Saku's brother, of more interest to Mon than was Saku, had been initiated. Age was not the only reason, though; it seems that Mon saw Saku as an embarrassment, rejecting him for years.

Saku took his mother's death very hard. He says that after her funeral, her ghost came to him more than once. And something else: a few months later, he was playing alone in a garden when a young boy—a spirit being—came to him to play. The other, who looked older than Saku, befriended and talked to him and performed amazing feats. This being[8] became Saku's first and most important spirit familiar when he later practiced shamanism. A figure in Saku's dreams as a child, Saku still sees this being in his trance states now. Next to Yumalo's spirit familiars, the child familiar (who grew in imagination as Saku grew, but who manifests normal masculinity) has protected him through thick and thin. But Yumalo sensed something wrong, and when Saku told him of the child spirit's visitation, his uncle wisely told him not to pay much attention. (But not to ignore him, either.) From then on, Yumalo took an even closer interest in Saku, who became, in effect, his adopted son.

Yumalo was a curious figure. I knew him before he died, an old man, in 1977. He was a contradiction: vigorously masculine, with two wives and several children, he was nurturant and sensitive. He was a traditionalist, yet he wore funny western clothes, easily able to accommodate the accoutrements of both worlds. He was considerate, generous, never querulous—a fine, proud old wizard. Yet he was feared, some say hated, by his enemies, because of extraordinary shamanic powers and sorcery magic that surpassed others in the region. Though he liked women and had good marriages, he had his own hut apart from them; yet at the same time he felt no stigma in planting and harvesting his own sweet potatoes (female activities). In short, Yumalo was a bundle of both feminine and masculine features somehow balanced through his shamanic identity.

Saku is clear he would not have become a shaman had it not been for his uncle. True, he had all the right social ancestry to become one,* but that might have gone for naught without his uncle. From earliest years, Saku had had dreams. These dreams were crucial to his calling as a shaman. Many were prophetic. Saku gives examples of dreams he claimed to have had when only six or seven—before initiation—that people believed foretold the future. His uncle did more than encourage these dreams: he discussed them with Saku, taught him how to interpret them, and explained that they would enable Saku to become a shaman. Yumalo did not in the slightest way disparage Saku for his hermaphrodism. And because of this tolerance and his uncle's special attention to his growing preshamanic skills, Saku adored him. In short, largely due to Yumalo, Saku longed to become a great shaman like his uncle, which identity/role is laced into Saku's very being and enables him, against great odds, to surmount a difficult fate.

Saku was initiated with Weiyu's[9] age-set around 1964. He was older than the other boys, which probably helped him through the ordeals. Yet by age ten Saku was already toughened. He had been taunted by children who said he was really a girl, not a boy, or a boy who didn't have a penis. His older brother didn't help him much, but Weiyu— his cousin—always stuck up for him. There were several times when Saku got into a fight and Weiyu defended him. They were friends, not just cousins. (Years later, when Weiyu was close to death from

---

*Saku's father, father's brother, and mother were all shamans, in addition to Yumalo; and their shamanic familiars all had long genealogic validity. Thus, Saku is a primary shaman, compared to a Kalutwo, whose claim is secondary and largely contrived (see chapter 9).

malaria, Saku sat with him, performed healing ceremonies, fed him for weeks, and nurtured him back to life.) Only one thing—but an odd one—stood out in Saku's first initiation: he did not bleed when the men plunged cane-grasses down his nose.* Saku says he felt the nosebleeding was silly and not necessary for him: he would grow to be masculine quite nicely without losing any of his blood.[10] He has never bled his nose since, either.

He underwent second-stage initiation normally too, about three years later. At his first initiation, his father took more interest in him and even tried to persuade Saku to return to Pundei and live there. And though Saku did begin to spend time there—his natal hamlet and clan—he continued to spend more time at his uncle's.

Meanwhile, Saku was growing, and he was involved, like other boys, in homosexual activities. Two things should be stressed about this. First, Saku has always been known as an enthusiastic and skillful fellator, wanting to get as much semen as fast as possible. On the other hand, though, Saku (who had no trouble discussing it) told me he always felt that fellatio was a little silly. (But not silly enough not to do it.) This view, as with his refusal to nosebleed himself, carried with it the sense that his body was relatively self-contained and needed no help to mature. I didn't believe him.[11] Second, Saku's gender identity and erotic life are aberrant in that he has never been fellated. Saku did not talk about this, because he could not discuss his hermaphrodism (not just his anatomy) with me: he could not tell me that he is terrified of others seeing his genitals. Only Imano (chapter 8) resembles Saku in never having been fellated. However, their reasons were quite different: Imano wanted to save his semen for women, whereas Saku is terrified of others seeing his genitals. From all indications Saku was simply so ashamed that he could not be a sexual inserter.[12] I do not know how strong Saku's sexual impulses are, but he claims to have had several wet dreams. At the same time, he continued to be a fellator well after the normal period.[13] In part, this abnormality stems from Saku having had no third-stage—puberty—initiation until 1975 (whereas Weiyu, his agemate, had undergone that ceremony in 1970).

The main reason Saku was not elevated in the initiation cycle was his father's (and other men's) attitude that there was no sense wasting time on him. Third-stage initiation meant (among other things) that one was biologically mature and ready for marriage. "Why waste a good woman on a flawed hermaphrodite!" I have heard men say.

---

*I doubted this story, but Weiyu and others confirm it.

This attitude so hurt and enraged Saku that he finally left the Valley and went to work on the coast around 1970. He has never forgiven his father or clansmen.

So Saku left his own land. He was in Port Moresby for a while: cheap plantation labor. His dreams and some trance experiences continued. Then he moved near Goroka, the provincial capitol, where he lived on a coffee plantation for three years. He now became more sophisticated about the white man's world, seeing things he both liked and disliked. But after four years, disgusted with life there, he grew tired and homesick. He returned to Sambia to find that little had changed: he was trapped by his anatomy; to some he would always be just a freak. He worked hard, planted coffee trees, made as much money as he could (most of which he gave to his uncle and aunt), and eventually built a tin-roof house: *the* sign of westernization. He took up his healing practices, too, with more fervor, though he still had not gone through the shamanic initiation. A little later, in late 1974, I arrived on the scene.

Saku did not stand out from the crowd in those days. He alternated between traditional garb and western clothes (and still does). His height was normal but his build slight. He lacked the burly anatomy of those Sambia who look like New Guineans in racial characteristics, and his light brown skin, fair complexion, and brown frizzy hair made him look Papuan.[14] By Sambia standards, he is handsome. Closer up, though, his face is unusual.[15] I now see that it matches his personality: androgynous. His broad, intelligent forehead is faintly creased by fine horizontal worry lines. He also has creases vertical to his eyebrows, which are oddly bushy and thick on an otherwise sparsely bearded face.[16] His high cheekbones and long square nose (unusual in Sambia) give him, to me, a graceful, proud countenance. His lips are thin and gray-red, his teeth stained bright red from constant betel-nut chewing. But what strikes me most are his eyes. They are liquid, darkly beautiful, but sunken and a bit close-set. They are—I can think of no better word—chameleonic: they can seem to reflect whatever they see, and yet be expressive or dull, shallow disks, mirrors. They can be happy and sad, proud and despairing, warm and cold, dark and bright, open and mysterious. They can make him seem to be waiting, wary, suspicious, always searching for the slightest sign of disapproval or rejection. I was, consequently, more sensitive and careful with Saku than with others, as if handling crystal.

As I got to know Saku, two themes emerged. The first I observed a hundred times. His responses are highly situation–specific: Saku becomes what others do or expect him to do. He reflects his environment. (Human chameleons are hard to detect and harder to study.) For instance, it took me a long time to know that Saku makes sexual allusions or comments only in public. At first I found that, like other men, Saku made sexual allusions about women to me in private. But I felt it was contrived: there was no hostility in his slurs. (How different from the natural spontaneity with which men, such as Weiyu and Tali, frequently and vigorously insult women.) When I did not respond, did not reinforce that behavior, it stopped.

The other theme reflects a truer sense of self: "I am the shaman Saku." The shamanic identity—the trance states, dreams, identification with familiars—all are woven into himself—his core. (Cf. chapter 9.) When he was most comfortable with me, alone in my house, I saw subtle behaviors remarkable for a Sambia man. Examples: a passivity that waits for me to make a move; a quietness—quiet voice, low affect, a chronic despair—with secrecy and shame behind the quietness; an embarrassed smile as he turns his head from me, more like an initiate or woman; a way of moving his whole body when speaking or looking out the window, coupled with controlled gestural use of his hands; an almost dainty way of holding cigarettes (between the second and third fingers of his left hand), his hand propped up on his arm, the cigarette jutting out, in a way that is neither masculine nor feminine, but odd; and finally—this one baffles me—Saku is the only Sambia person I have ever seen who crosses his legs, one over the other in the British style (where did he get that!).* The sum of such traits is neither wholly masculine nor feminine; and when I am with him, his presence is unobtrusive to the point that I can feel almost alone. Strange but not unpleasant.

Saku must have known he was getting nowhere with father and clan: no woman—no masculine adult personhood—was being given, and none was in sight. His father as much as said he would not waste a woman on Saku. In 1975, this trend reached a head, and Saku disappeared. I did not know what had happened until I heard he was being initiated third-stage with distant kin of his uncle over the mountains in the Yellow River Valley. When I arrived there with friends to see their initiations, Saku stood tall in his best warrior garb. We heard a rumor that he had arranged a marriage and would return soon with his new bride. Everyone was amazed, as was I, but I was happy for him. Looking back, I believe Saku grew tired of being nothing. Something seemed to have snapped in him. So he swallowed his

---

*Perhaps from me, I'm not sure.

pride and went out to make a new life for himself—wife included—without his clan's help. He turned from what could not be—a perfect male body—to what he could have.

His uncle helped Saku again in two ways. Yumalo arranged to have his younger classificatory brother's daughter (Saku's mother's brother's daughter, a marriage frowned on by Sambia) marry Saku. Saku asked *her* for her personal permission, too—a rare gesture to a girl who had recently reached menarche. She agreed, knowing he was a hermaphrodite. Saku made bridewealth payment, equally as rare. They returned to his hamlet and took up residence. People said the marriage would never work, and they made cruel jokes about it.[17] About the same time, initiation for Moondi's cohort was held in the Valley, and a new men's house was built in Nilangu. This was a great event. A shaman's initiation—the last ever performed—was held in the new men's house. Saku was then formally confirmed as a shaman, his uncle attending the ceremony. The story of that experience is told in the session that follows.

Saku seemed happier. On returning in 1979, I wanted to get him to talk. We discussed many things, spent long hours on his dreams. But I could not get him to broach his hermaphrodism, which I wished very much to learn about as another way of understanding the origins and dynamics of Sambia gender identity. As I struggled to allow Saku to tell me—in his own way—about his early experiences in relation to being a hermaphrodite, we bogged down. He was very scared when I approached the subject, nor could he tell me details of his erotic life, for that, too, impinged on his anatomy.

By the time of S.'s arrival, we had reached an impasse, though quite different from, for instance, that with Kalutwo (see chapter 9). Saku did not resist me by staying around yet being hostile, by wearing me out, as did Kalutwo; but rather by exiting, sometimes for a day or two, or for a week. He always came back; I never scolded him. He knew, I think, that I was a friend and that I could be counted on: he wanted to trust. But I felt he had been so traumatized for so many years that it would take something great—such as patience—to lift him out of his reluctance, pain, and fear. My skills were limited.

What I could not know was that behind Saku's open secret—his hermaphroditic body—lay a deeper secret. When Stoller came, and helped Saku tell me in two hours what I had tried to have him say for years, we learned of another terrible trauma, one that had inhibited him as much as his childhood. A white man, a strange European, had years before photographed Saku's boy's nude body—in front of others—and had then left, Saku's fragile pride carried away in that photo. Since then, a humiliated Saku had despaired at what had happened that afternoon. He lived in fear that the man would return and repeat the unbearable trauma. He lived in fear of his own rage at what he would do. This is where S. helped out Saku—and me.

To conclude this introduction: Sakulambei is remarkable. His unique developmental history explains, *because* of his hermaphrodism, how a courageous person managed to survive and even prosper despite great obstacles. In creating himself, he has shown how one can, when loved enough, overcome the most terrible traumas and defy what fate seems to have in mind. But Saku's fascinating story should not obscure a point more central to our undramatic thesis: ethnographers who ignore the intimate circumstances of their work and of the lives of people with whom they work, searching for cultural structure and ignoring the aberrant are dehumanized also.

FIRST SESSION

In 1979 Sakulambei had been talking with me for several months on shamanism and its relation to other aspects of his life. I wanted also to study his gender identity. Being a hermaphrodite and so identified in the community, he provided a unique chance for understanding variations and vicissitudes in the development of masculinity. Though I several times approached the subject, he had great difficulty talking about it. I was pushing him as hard as possible, aware of his shame and anxiety that people might talk behind his back and make fun of him. In fact, people did. I was proceeding slowly and cautiously. A few days before S. arrived, I had broached the subject again, and, as he had before, Saku again exited. It wasn't that he *really* had left; he was avoiding me to avoid talking about his hermaphrodism. Since I had a lot to do and was preparing for S.'s arrival, I simply let him be during this period. But knowing S. had arrived and was important to me, Sa. returned after I had sent word that S. wanted to join me in our talking.

Saku and I were right then at a point where the information I was trying to elicit, but that I had been denied for almost five years, was most important. S.'s arrival put life back in our interviews.

The transcript begins in midstream, after I had first given S. some background and then had described the impasse in Saku's and my relationship. Saku begins by explaining how a dream of his foretold Stoller's visit.

SAKULAMBEI: No one said, "Gilbert's big man [S.] has come." The men didn't tell me. I was down in the Moonagu country.* I saw the helicopter from down there and on my own I thought, "He's [S.] come now. He's come to him [G.H.]." Then I returned and slept in my own house. I dreamed. And inside my dream I thought, "How has he come here?" And I thought, "You [myself] didn't go and see him. I hid and watched you from a way off." My body was completely shaking, and I was thinking, "How did he come here? By plane or water or what?" And the two of you, you just stood away, looking at me. You didn't come close to me. Then I went up to the master [S.] and asked him, "Where have you come from? Where have you come from?" But he didn't talk to me. He just stood there looking. So then, I said to him, "Let's go up to Nilangu and see Gilbert." I said that to him, and the man, he didn't talk, he just looked at me with his eyes, that's all. [*Ominous.*] "All right," I said to him, "you stay here. I'll go to him." And so I went and I came up to the bridge and then, after that, you called out to me. You said, "Come." And you said, "The Big One has come. I told you about him, that he would come eventually, and he's come now. Haven't you heard the news?" That's what you said to me. My response was, "I didn't know he was here." Then we shook hands. I told you that my body was very afraid and we shook hands. Then I said the same to him [S.], but he doesn't understand Pidgin. I was crazy inside my dream. So I was talking without any effect.

A little later I saw Moondi over near the bridge, and I said to him, "What are you doing here? Come on translate for me! I've never been to school." [*Through all this, Sa. is anxious, is trying to please, and feels inferior, qualities he has always had with me, though gradually less so.*] "You've been to school. What are they saying? Can you hear some English or not?" And Moondi says, "Yes, I can." Then he said to him [S.], "This man Sa. doesn't understand English; he's afraid, his skin's afraid," and I felt afraid. Then we wanted to go to Nilangu Village, but as we were approaching the bridge, the *kaunsalman's* wife called out to us. Then people woke me up and I told my wife, "I dreamed of Gilbert's boss. I saw him." I told her, "I think tomorrow he'll [S.] come," and she said, "Oh, no, he's already here. He's staying up in Ni-

---

*Moonagu phratry hamlets lie a day's walk south of us and are a different political unit from ours. Saku's wife and distant matrilateral relatives are from there.

langu. Go and see him." So I thought to myself, "Why did I stop working with Gilbert? He wants to go away now. I've got to go back." And I didn't just think that, I told her: "It's your fault. You're sick, and that's why I had to stop working." [Saku was healing her through ritual.] She said, "You're right. It's my fault." So I came back up here to see you, thinking to myself, "I'm sorry I lost my work. I'll go see him. You can see. He'll feel sorry for me. Will he take me back or not?"

H: Can I ask you about this dream? When you woke up, what did you feel?

Sa: [*Very quickly.*] Well, I hadn't seen him yet. And I thought, "He wants to kill me."

H: He wanted to *kill* you [*incredulous*]?

Sa: Yeah, that he wanted to kill me. I didn't understand him; I don't know English. Then you said to me, "That's my boss there. Why are you shaking?" A little later I shook hands with him. "I don't know you and so I was shaking." That's what I said to him.

H: In your dream what kind of face did you see?

Sa: The same as his is. The same. I had told Kerutwo's [local *kaunsalman*] wife,* "I've already seen him in my dream. His hair is white." And she said, "That's true."

Remember that Sa. is a shaman who is expected to have prophetic dreams. He is an avid dreamer who can spin long accounts of his dreams. Here he's saying he had a visionary dream before ever seeing S. In the dream he says he saw S.'s face exactly as it is. He tried out this vision on the people after he awoke from the dream. Because Sa. began this session with a dream report—one that he feels is so important—and because I feel that he is communicating his apologies and guilt, and more subtle things about what he can and cannot say and do (transference), we continue on in great detail, going over the dream. But because of lack of space, pages of the report have been cut here. We pick up where H. asks Sa. what he feels now about S.

H: Now that you're truly seeing him, what do you feel?

Sa: I'm very happy, for he didn't come here for nothing. He's the very man who sent you here. And you've come and worked and given us good food, soap, tobacco, other things. We're very happy with you. I'm very happy. Him, he alone sent you, and in that way he's really helped us. Our bodies . . .

---

*A minor shaman.

Tape runs out. While H. turns it over, S. asks him if Sa.'s full re-galia—more stylish, clean, and orderly than anyone else's—indicates Sa.'s pride in being a shaman.

H: [*Pointing at Sa.*] These are the decorations of a true shaman.
Sa: That's right. [*Wistful?*]
H: And dreaming that way happens only to a shaman.
Sa: Right.
H: And now you've come and you are wearing the decorations of a true shaman.
Sa: Right.
H: [*Turns to S.*] He says, "That's right." I hadn't paid attention to it, but these are the decorations shamans used to wear all the time. That goes with having the kind of dreams he has. So, on coming to tell us this dream—
S: —he dressed appropriately for it.
H: Yeah. [His dress is his armor for today. Somewhere, conscious and unconscious, Stoller has the power to destroy him, he thinks.]
S: And in addition, he's the carrier of the past? He's the carrier of power of being a shaman?
H: Yeah.
S: Now, you told me that he's a very good, strong shaman and knows it.
H: Uh-huh.
S: How did he get the power?
H: I know the answer, but I'll ask him . . . again.
S: I'm looking for something else [his feelings about his her-maphrodism]. He might give it to us.
H: [*To Sa.*] Dr. S. doesn't know about your shamanism. [The word I translate as "shamanism" is *kwooluku*, which has several mean-ings: the role of the shaman, the person enacting that role, and the powers of the spirit familiars that invest the particular per-son in that role (see Herdt 1977). So, when, in Sambia, I say, "your *kwooluku*," I can translate it as "your shamanism"—where "shamanism" here implies all three meanings.] He wants to ask you how its *jerungdu* [power]* came to you.
Sa: The power came as follows: shamanism doesn't come from noth-ing, just any old way. We put on all our decorations, and we sit

---

*Here and below, *jerungdu* has the usual physical and phallic connotations (Herdt 1987c) plus—for shamans—the resonance of power to control spiritual forces unavailable to other men.

down inside of the *narangu* [ceremonial cult-house where shamans are initiated (see Herdt 1987c)] and do the ceremony. It's as if we were almost dead [in a trance]. Shamanism doesn't come from nothing: if your father had a *kwooluku*, then it can come to you. And when he dies, his *kwooluku* (familiars) go to nearby spots and wait, like the base of a clump of bamboo, after he's dead. If we're still small when he dies, it won't come to us yet. It [spirit familiars] will come close to us, and watch over us and just stay there. As we grow, it is inside of the grass around the base of a bamboo clump or in a pandanus fruit tree or in nice flowers one's papa himself had planted. Now, when we're grown and we stay inside the cult-house [after initiation], then it will come back to us. Sometimes we can feel it and see it in dreams—see papa, or see him acting as a shaman. It comes up inside of us. And then we feel it. We know. We think to ourselves, "Now I'm a *kwooluku*." We hear it cry [the whistle sound the shaman emits as a sign that his spirit familiars have come inside of his person when, during a trance-state, he wants to perform as a shaman]. And that's it.

H: [*Back to S.*] Well, a pretty big mouthful but a great synopsis of the shaman's calling. He says that the decorations belong to the kind of person who becomes a shaman. The identity is associated with the decorations.

S: Does he make his own? Or did he inherit them and has he followed the tradition? Or was he *given* the tradition?

H: Let me ask him. Did you make these decorations yourself?

Sa: These here [chest band of shells] I made myself. And these [feathers], my mother's brother [Yumalo] gave them to me.

H: Oh-h. [*Surprise.*]

Sa: It was Yumalo [Saku's great shaman-uncle]. And this ass-cover, Yumalo himself made it, too, and gave it to me.

H: I hadn't realized that.

Sa: I only put it on to show him [S.]. When I'm done I'll put it back in my house.

H: Can he look at them? [*S. reaches out and touches the shell decorations draped across Sa.'s chest.*]

Sa: Yeah.

S: Are these bird-of-paradise [feathers]?

H: No, those are another kind . . . . Oh, yes, those ones there. [Sa. has several different kinds of feathers in an elaborate headdress.]

S: And he did this.

H: No. It's very interesting: his maternal uncle, the one who gave him his shamanism, gave that to him.

S: So it's giving, in a material way, not just a ceremonial tradition. OK. I interrupted you.

H: [*Repeats Saku's report.*] And that is how you are able to receive your shamanism.

S: Why is he better, stronger than other shamans?

H: Dr. S. wants to know why your shamanism is stronger than others. He heard from me that you were the strongest *kwooluku* in the Sambia valley.

Sa: You already know all that: this *kwooluku*, it doesn't belong to me. In ancient times it came to some man.* When he died, it went to another man who took his place. And he would have it, and be old, and then he would die. And so it went, until Yumalo got it. He had it. Then he died, and now I have it. It is passed along, just like that.

H: Just like that. [*A beautiful description. Repeats this for S.*]

S: [*Softly.*] Tell him something like this for me: "I am very strong, so I want to know more." Does that make sense to you?

H: Say a bit more so I get a better sense of it.

S: "There are other things, secrets." Let him know I am strong. *I am.* So I know something about secrets . . . . I can also *withstand* secrets. . . . I can also *keep* secrets. So I want to know more. But don't tell him that if it's not the right thing to say.

H: [*Reflecting.*] Um [*back to Sa.*], Dr. S. wants to tell you his thoughts before we finish: he says *he's* a strong man. He himself says this. He says he's truly pleased and fascinated with what you said, but he thinks there is more; he says, "I think this *kwooluku* also comes from something else."

Sa: Uh-huh.

H: He heard your story, but he says that he thinks it has another meaning, too, a secret [*ioolu*] that belongs to it [i.e., the hermaphrodism]. I, myself, don't know what he [S.] is pointing toward. But he says he really thinks that.

Sa: Uh-huh.

H: He thinks there is a secret in your *kwooluku*. This secret [going very slowly and carefully here] somehow helps . . . you to . . . to get some of the thinking which belongs . . . to . . . your . . . shamanism. This is what he says. He also says that in

*One of Yumalo's patrilineal putative ancestors, therefore a matrilateral ancestor of Saku.

his . . . very own . . . kind of work . . . he . . . he works with secrets all the time. With men and women in America. That's precisely his work. [For several years, S. worked with biologically intersexed patients, including some with hermaphroditic genitals, in studying origins of gender identity.] And he says that . . . he, himself, is not afraid of secrets. He has no fear of secrets. And he also says that he has strength of his own and he wants to hear more about the ways of secrets in your shamanism. Is this clear?

Sa: Uh . . .

H: Because, for myself, I'm not really clear what he's talking about.* The secrets.

Sa: Secrets here?

H: Yeah.

Sa: The secrets of a shaman? You know, there are none.†

H: No.

Sa: No. We men talk about it openly here.

H: But he doesn't mean only secrets of *kwooluku*. He means also secrets of your own. And he says he himself is not afraid of secrets.

Sa: [*Quiet, serious, apprehensive.*] Um-hm. [*A little stronger.*] I wouldn't . . . hide . . . [*Voice trails off.*]. There are no secrets in my shamanism. I'm not clear what he means.[18]

H: [*To S.*] He understands but says shamans have no secrets. Then I said, "I don't think he means just your shamanism. I think he also means you." And he said, "I have no secrets." Then I told him that you study secrets and are not afraid of secrets. Then he said, "I'm not sure that I understand what he means." It would probably be good enough to leave it at that, but you can say more.

S: Yeah. Well, that's good. Thank him. Will we be seeing him again?

H: Yeah. [*To Sa.*] Can you come back tomorrow?

Sa: [*Quietly.*] Uh-huh.

H: He says he'll be back tomorrow.

S: There may be secrets in him that he doesn't know about yet. Or something like that. Let's see if he can discover his own secrets. That'll give him power.

H: *Oh!* Yeah. [*To Sa.*] Oh, now I understand Dr. S.: He's pleased to

---

*I want S. to carry the ball.
†Even in the most superficial sense, Sa. isn't being straightforward here. Shamans are secretive people, more than any others. They have their own tricks of the trade to hide. (S. doesn't know that.) Sometimes, for their own safety, they must be sly: they have shamanic opponents who try to do them in.

talk with you. He wants to see you again, to work with you again. He says that we all have secrets in ourselves. He says that if we can find our own secrets, it can give us more strength. If we can get to the bottom of our own secrets, it helps clear away things that have a hold over us.

S: [*To Sa., via H.*] It may just come into his head, or it may come in a dream or it may not come.

H: [*To Sa.*] He's helping us some more. Saying, "This kind of secret, it can come up just any old time in thought. Or another time it can come up inside a dream. Or sometimes it won't come up at all."

S: We'll just have to watch and see.

H: [*To Sa.*] He says, "We'll just have to look and see what happens." Is that all right?

Sa: Yeah, that's good.

S: I don't know . . . but what does he feel? How does he . . . what's his experience been like with us today? What's he doing now and what's it done?

H: [*To Sa.*] He wants to ask you: all three of us have been talking. As we've been doing this, how do you feel now that we've been talking like this?

Sa: Oh, us talking here?

H: Yeah.

Sa: Oh, it's good, good. My thinking is that it's good [*a little bit forced*].

H: He says that it's good.

S: [*Quickly*] Good.

H: Did you hear him, Saku? [*He shakes his head.*] He said it's good. Well, that's it. Have you got something you want to say to me?

Sa: Only that I'm hungry for tobacco.

H: I'm sorry, but I can't help you. I'd give you some but mine's all gone. You can ask everybody else.

Sa: Yeah, they told me the same.

H: I wouldn't hide it from you if I had some.

Sa: Yeah, of course, I know. I was just asking, that's all.

S: Is he going to dress this way the next time?

H: [*To Saku.*] He wants to ask you will you be decorated the same way tomorrow too?

Sa: [*Lightly.*] Yeah, I won't change, I'm not going to change it.

H: He says—

S: I like it, I want him to wear it again.

H: [*To Saku.*] He says he really likes that a lot.

Sa: I'm not going to change, I'll go to the songfest* just like this. And tomorrow morning I can come; is that okay?

H: All right, fine.

SECOND SESSION

H: Yesterday Dr. Stoller talked to you about the kind of work he does. He said he was pleased to be with you and he was very pleased with your decorations.

Sa: [*Quietly.*] Uh-huh.

H: Yesterday he told you about his strength [*jerungdu*], which all three of us use in our work. This morning, too, you saw him use it with Nilutwo.[†]

Sa: Uh-huh.

H: What did you think of that?

Sa: No thoughts. Whatever he says, I can follow that. That's all. [*The resistance stiffens.*]

H: Hm.

Sa: Yeah. Whatever he wants to talk about is all right.

H: [*To S.*] He says he'll do whatever you want.

S: OK. Well, let's move into this, respecting the fact that he's a good shaman. I would like his impressions of my shamanistic number with Nilutwo this morning. And I don't know if I can expect this of him, but I would like the truth rather than have him butter me up or be nervous with me. You see, my view of that performance is, "Oh, God, it didn't work." They may not see it that way, but I wouldn't want him to say, "Oh, you're a great magician," in order to make me feel good. . . . I don't know how you can play that with him.

H: He wants to ask you about shamanism, his and yours. He's heard me say that you are a big shaman in this Valley. He'd be pleased to learn about your shamanism and your spirit familiars. He wants to ask you first: what do you think of what he did with Nilutwo?

Sa: I guess he wanted to look inside, to see inside his liver or something. Is a bone broken inside there? He wanted to look inside

---

*A songfest for a marriage ceremony to be held in Kwoli hamlet that night. The whole village piled out for it.

†S: Nilutwo is dying, in terrible pain because he cannot change position, is exhausted, cannot sleep, expects his friends to steal his wife when he dies, and is enraged at fate. To relieve him, I tried, before a tense audience, to hypnotize him this morning, acting like a hot-shot UCLA wizard and hoping, for his sake, that my sense of being a damn fool didn't show. He did not bat an eye. So, an honest failure, I finally stopped. No sooner had I left the hut, however, than he fell asleep and slept many hours.

of him* [S's hypnotic technique interpreted as shamanic divi-
nation for diagnosing illness].

H: What did you think of that?

Sa: It's good. It's very good. Truly good. We don't know how to do
that. He was looking hard at him.

H: Yeah. He's not a bad man [S.]. He's not someone from the ghosts.[19]
He's a good man.

Sa: Yeah, that's right.

H: So he knows how to do that kind of thing.

Sa: Yeah, that's really good. I was watching what he was doing to
Nilutwo, and I thought, "He wants to look at all of his bones or
whatever is inside of him." He looked in, and that was good.

H: [*To S.*] He thought what you did this morning was good. He
watched you carefully and felt you wanted to get inside of Nilutwo just like a shaman divinates while in a trance. It has a
magical meaning of what shamans do here.

S: So my performance is in a realm that he's familiar with.

H: Yes.

S: And I was competent, not in my results, but as a performer of it
in my own style. Is that what he's saying?

H: Yes. He said it was good and he was very glad that you did that.

S: All right. Now, let's move into his shamanism: what's it feel like
to be a shaman? How has it changed over time? What's his sense
of his power—now as compared to when he first started? Is that
enough to start?

H: Yeah. Some of these questions we've already gone over.

S: Then don't spend much time on them.

H: I don't know how this can be done, but I want to ask him the
question [I tried] before he ran away: his hermaphrodism.

S: OK, go to it. Maybe we're in good enough shape now.

H: Uh—I'm trying to think how to do it best. You've reinforced the
part in him that's most sensitive. He's not as afraid. So I've got
a good start. We were working on how he first got his powers
from his maternal uncle, the man he mentioned yesterday.

S: What do you want to know that will be difficult for him to answer unless we help him respond safely?

H: What is his sex life now?

S: You might not get that so easily.

H: [*Exasperated.*] I haven't *been* able to get it.

---

*S: I kept telling Nilutwo to stare into my eyes as I stared deeply into his. God knows
what that act means to a Sambia man. With us it means, "You are being hypnotized. So go
into a trance like you know you should."

S: He turned you away? Or you haven't dared ask?

H: I was just preparing to move into these sensitive areas when it stopped.

S: I see. Could you—uh—

H: —if somehow I could shift some of the responsibility to you . . .

S: That's what I was going to say—

H: —but do it differently—

S: —but do it differently—try this on: tell him that I put my power into you. Would that make sense? Not just taught it to you, but [*S. makes a noise here like an electric drill—"bzz": the feeling is implanted in me*] put it into you so that he is safe when he talks to you about these things. [*Emphasizes.*] "*I* will protect him because I put into *you* the capacity to protect him."

[S: By injecting my power into H., I not only let Saku know that H. now possesses my shamanic powers but I also get H. to feel it. In politer circles this is called "identification," a process we all know helps form identity—converts students to teachers or healers. It brings to life the business of education, making organic the formulating of techniques.]

H: [*To Sa.*] Do you want to say anything to him? If not, I have something to ask you. Is that all right?

Sa: Yeah. [*Quiet and a bit depressed.*] You talk. I have nothing in particular to say. [*Quiet. I feel he's holding back; he's worried where we're going.*]

H: All right. [*To S.*] To do this we need privacy, so I'm going to get rid of everyone in the house.

S: That's what he just asked you?

H: No, it's my idea. It signals him that I'm going to ask about important things.

S: Proceed, and make him know that you are *lovingly* protective. That really *is* what you're doing. Make him as comfortable as possible, and let him see you recognize how difficult this is for him. Anything you can do to make it possible, that's what you want to do. That's what you just expressed now, in fact. [H: Such simple wisdom put into practice provides a context in the field otherwise impossible to achieve but utterly essential to a Sakulambei.]

H: Yeah. [*To Sa., H. summarizes S.'s message.*]

Sa: That's your choice.

H: Is that all right?

Sa: [*Almost inaudible.*] That's all right.*

H: I don't want anyone to hear something that belongs to you only, or to your shamanism. I want to protect you.

Sa: [*Almost inaudible.*] Uh-huh.

I get up. Lots of noise, people milling around. I chase them out, fasten the door, come back into the room, and talk again.

H: He [S.] says this: he's got this strength, a power, a good power. And he wants to encircle you with protection so that, inside, you and I can talk about your shamanism and your experiences without your being afraid of me. [*Pause. No response. Now to S.*] I've said it as clearly as I can.

S: OK. Now we just have to go and see if he lets us. If he *sort* of lets us, then we can amplify.

H: You have a pretty good sense of him, his childhood, his development. But I know nothing about his sex life, and he and I have *never* discussed his hermaphrodism.

S: Well, why don't you now do it.

H: I want to ask you about your shamanism.† I want to ask you some things I haven't asked you about before. About the time you felt the spirit familiars come inside of you. Those of Yumalo. In the *narangu* [shaman's initiation] of Nilangu hamlet [1975], you still didn't have any of Yumalo's familiars, right?

Sa: Uh-huh.

H: And Yumalo told you, "I must not fall sick. If you entice my familiars away from me, I might die."

Sa: Uh-huh.

H: But later his familiars came to you, and he hadn't died yet.

Sa: Yeah . . .

H: [*Pause.*] Now, when Yumalo's familiars came to you, what did you feel?

Sa: [*Confident.*] "This mother's brother of mine, he's going to die. He's not walking around much. He just sits around his house." His familiars came to me. He wasn't visiting his gardens or anywhere else. He'd just sit around his house. And by and by he would die. He spoke out to me.

---

*S: I felt pain for him here—and more as we proceeded. I didn't want my first great shaman to be just a kid decked out in his best feathers. He was scared-trying-to-be-brave and trying to honor his identity. Quite different from Kalutwo, whose pain/resistance took the form of sullenness.

†I begin with this subject for two reasons, as I now realize. First, we are comfortable discussing it; it opens rapport again. Second, because Sa.'s sexuality is so bound up in his shamanism, which centers his identity.

H: You mean he pointed to you [the accusing finger: because Saku had taken his spirit familiars, it meant Yumalo had fallen sick].

Sa: They performed a *narangu* here and he told me, "I won't come to you now. I won't be able to stroll around from now on. This soul of mine, soon I'll give it to you* and I'll die."

H: But when did his shamanic familiars come to you: then or later?

Sa: Later. When we performed that *narangu*—

H: —Yeah—

Sa: At this time—the shamanic familiars of Yumalo—*he* sent them. He himself said he thought his familiars were choosing to go to me. So he sent his familiars to me. But I thought, and then I said, "Don't give them to me; you will get sick and die. Don't just sit around the house." I told him that. And then he said, "Oh, that's all right. I shall just become inactive." [His aged uncle was saying it was all right if he now died.]

H: Now at this time they came inside of you in the *narangu*?

Sa: Yeah—[*His voice warms; he's reaching out to try and help me understand.*]

H: I thought that it happened but you sent them all back.

Sa: Yeah, at this time I spoke out to Yumalo, "Why don't you try them out on me. Try me." [The idiom here, "Try me out," means a "test." Shamans test each other to see how powerful and disciplined they are, and so he's suggesting that he told his uncle to test him and see if he was enough of a shaman to be able to handle his uncle's spirit familiars.]

H: "You can just take back your spirit familiars afterward?"

Sa: That's what I said. [*Pause.*] And then he said, "That's all right. If I die, say, or if I really get a big sickness and can only sit around the house, then you must come and visit me." [Saku lives below, down at the river, whereas his uncle lived in a village about an hour's walk away. He's suggesting here that his uncle was saying, "It's all right for you to take my spirit familiars now, though that will eventually make me sick. So when I get sick, since you have the healing power now, you must come and perform healing ceremonies on me."] Like that. So, when I saw him afterward, I didn't just sit around [ignore and forget my uncle]. Instead, I went to him all the time. I bought fish and rice and got other foods and gave them to him. So [*voice trails off*] . . . at the time that he looked at me when he was close to dying [late 1977], it

---

*Metaphysically true, in that the spirit familiars are part of the entity of the soul, Sambia believe.

was only then his spirit familiars came to me for good. [We skip here details of Saku's shamanic trances and identifications with familiars, since this material leads us from the main course of the chapter.]

H: What do you feel then?

Sa: I feel at those times that my mother's brothers' soul hasn't gone away, not gone away.

H: It's still around. He's still around with you. He's fastened to your skin, huh?

Sa: Yeah, that's how I think; I think like that.

H: All right, I want to tell this part to Dr. Stoller so he understands, all right? [*To S.*] At the time of his shamanic initiation in 1975, his uncle's spirits wanted to come to him of their own volition. But that would have killed the old man; it would have robbed him of his soul. So Saku sent them back to him.

S: Why was his uncle willing to do it?

H: Because his uncle thought he was going to die. He was an old man. I knew Yumalo: he was a . . . strong, kindly, masculine; a presence. In some ways he resembled—had the same habits as—Saku; imitation [by Saku] mostly, I think. When he has trances now, he often sees his uncle's face. [Saku trances frequently.]

S: [*Interrupting.*] Benign?*

H: I haven't asked him that yet. Uh . . .

S: Can I ask—for orientation; it has nothing to do with the present subject but it will help me. Did he do the initiations?

H: Yes, but I don't know the details yet, because we haven't worked on that.

S: What happened when he was a [fellated] bachelor?

H: We haven't done that yet.

S: But there must be someone here who was his age.

H: Oh, yeah, I know what *they* say, but I don't know what *he* says [i.e., about screwing boys].

S: I see. Because he has testosterone, without question, in him. Do you understand what I mean? He's got appropriate facial hair and muscular build.†

H: Yeah.

---

*A question I might not have asked, at least not then. Perhaps I would have asked it later. But it seems an important point, one that might make the interview go differently now and save time later.
†Saku's facial hair only began appearing in the last several years, which is abnormal for Sambia.

S: So his testes are intact. Now does he produce—you can't answer this—does he produce semen . . . and are they [boys, women] taking it from him, or . . . ?

H: Well, the closest that I know, is rough. But pretty reliable sources say he *never* did screw any boys. The boys always wanted to, because they were curious and wanted to find out . . . but he would never do it.

S: I see.

H: But he has told me that at least once, possibly twice, he had wet dreams.

S: So that as far as you know he has only had a couple of ejaculations in his life.

H: As far as I know, right.

S: Okay, you don't need me now.

H: I've figured out a way to ask about his sex. But it would be better if you asked him. . . . This may be premature, but we don't have very much time. So, if you can somehow convey the message that *kwoolukus* are . . . if somehow it can be conveyed that strong *kwoolukus* are also masculine shamans . . . and masculine men . . . who have erections, inseminate women, who produce babies . . .

S: [*Spontaneously.*] Tell him: me.

H: Yeah.

S: Is that the approach?

H: I'm thinking now that that's how I can do it.* [*To Sa.*] Dr. Stoller wants to ask you more about your shamanism. He says, "The way of our shamans—he's talking about himself—is that a certain kind of shaman becomes a certain kind of man." [*Slowly.*] Now this kind of man develops just like everyone: first he's a child, then he grows up. Then, he [S.] says of himself, "I found a way that I became a man." And he wonders whether it was the same for you, or if it was different for you?

Sa: This shamanism here . . .

H: Yeah [*softly, almost a whisper.*]

Sa: Oh, this . . . I don't know. [*Sa. is engaged here.*] Before, did Yumalo do the same? I'm not sure.†

---

*Why could I think of that at that point? S.'s presence changed something in my relationship to Saku. Perhaps, again, as with Weiyu (chapter 10), S. put a friendly and supportive presence into our talking that gave *me* the space and perspective to free Saku from ambivalence.

†Fascinating that, in responding, Sa. has here referred us to his beloved Yumalo. This is not only defensive. Sa. modeled himself after Yumalo, using the latter in order to know what

H: [*Enthusiastic.*] Oh, but he isn't talking just about familiars, he's talking about his body too.

Sa: This *kwooluku?*

H: No, no—of his very body. [*Spontaneously to S:*] I'm going to do something that's not quite ethical, but I'm going to leave the language vague enough so that he may suspect that you are . . . you may have some hermaphroditic qualities . . . [*pause*].

S: Good. [I do, in the sense that I can work with hermaphroditic patients in such a way that a few thought I was a hermaphrodite. That is why I said "good" and felt that was not unethical.]

H: But I'm going to let him project it, if he can do it.

S: Fine.

H: [*To Sa.*] His appearance is real, but when he [S.] was born, they looked at his body and wondered: "This baby, is it another kind, or . . . ." They didn't know for sure. Now, when you see him, you see that he's become the same as a man. But now he's become a shaman. And now he's a man, too. He's the same as *you* . . . but when he was born, they thought he was a different kind. And so he wants to know if it was the same with you.*

Sa: This . . . I don't really understand you. [*Pause. Silence.*] My *kwooluku* . . . when, before, my mother gave birth. I don't understand well. [He understands precisely but is dodging. Still, compared to my earlier sessions with Saku, he is not now frantic. Rather, his voice is calm.]

H: Um-hm. [*To S.*] He says he doesn't understand.

S: What did you ask him that he doesn't understand?

H: I said, "You [S.] are now a man and a shaman; but when you were born"—and I used the neutral term for "child," not "boy" or "girl"—"they, those who first saw you when you were born—said you were a different kind." That's the language. But I left it so vague—

S: That he doesn't understand it. Or—

H: He just may be resisting—

S: He chooses not to understand it.

---

to feel and believe. Hypothesis: Sa.'s identity was not finished at initiation, unlike other males. It is still not finished. His hermaphrodism forces and allows him to pick and choose, because his aberrance has always placed him outside norms.

*I'd repressed this, until translating the tapes in 1981–82. It amounts to a lie; I as much as said S. was a hermaphrodite. I don't think it was harmful; the circumstances of the interview were extraordinary. I never lie with informants but fudged in this instance. I think it helped; but readers may disagree with this tack. [S. One should never, in doing research, lie in order to get information. Supervision corrects such mistakes.]

H: Yeah.

S: Okay, skip it. You've done what you can. Ask him what he was like when he was born. And using the same word "they" may give him a chance to get out if it's unbearable.

H: Yeah. [*To Sa.*] Now, Dr. S. wants to ask you: "When you were born, what kind of child were you?

Sa: At that time?

H: Yeah.

Sa: I don't know [*uninvolved*].

H: But, you know, what did they say . . . when you were born? What kind [of person] were you?

Sa: My father . . . mother?

H: Yeah.

Sa: I don't know—

H: You haven't heard the news [meaning: what local belief is]?

Sa: Um-hm. [*Straightfaced* and *calm.** Pause. Silence.* Saku differs from Kalutwo in that he cannot bear these silences. I know if I keep my mouth shut—something I am learning to do better—he will break the silence. He wants to please.] I heard nothing about that.

H: [*Quickly.*] You didn't hear about it. [I feel compassion for Saku's pain on this subject and try to comfort him, supporting his attempts to bridge the silences with communications.] [*Pause.*] Uh . . . [*to S.*] First he said he didn't know. And then he said he wasn't around at that time. Then he said his parents never told him.

S: About what? I'm sure you're paraphrasing him accurately. But I want to sharpen it up. They didn't say "what" about "what"?

H: [*To Sa:*] He's asking if you said, "You didn't hear well what they said?" Is that it?

Sa: I said, "That's the choice of all mommas and papas" [plural indicates all classificatory kin], that's what I said. You said to me: "Is it the same as a boy child or a girl child?"

H: Yes. [*Grateful*: breakthrough: *we're finally on the same wave-length.*]

Sa: They all said, "It's a boy child."

H: A boy child. that's what they said. [*To S.*] He said—

S: It's a male, boy.

H: A male, boy, yeah.

S: Like every other boy?

---

*Saku (like other Sambia males, who learn to lie to hide ritual secrets) is a good liar. He is more accomplished than others, because of his shamanism (doctors don't always tell patients the truth) and probably because of his hermaphrodism.

H: [*To Sa.*] He asks: "The same kind of boy as all the boys around . . . "

S: Yeah, the same.

H: [*To S.*] He says, "Yes, the same kind."

S: Now?

H: [*To Sa.*] He says, "Now too?"

Sa: Now, too, all the same.

H: He says, "Now too, the same." My feeling is he's a bit angry about this, but I think he's willing to talk about it.

S: Keep going.

H: Yeah. He's more willing to . . . you're dragging answers out of him. He's letting . . .

S: He's letting us—

H: Drag questions out of him.

S: Yeah. Should we give him support now and tell him that I'm glad he's talking with us?

H: Yeah.

S: And that I appreciate this . . . and he's helping me, who came from such a long distance, who wants to know about a shaman here.

H: Yeah, that's good.* [*Summarizes for Sa.*]

Sa: That's all right. [*Low; down.*]

S: All right but not all right.

H: Yeah. [*Pause.*] There is a danger that if we press him too much, he might get scared.

S: Yeah. [*Quiet.*]

H: There is also danger that if he's willing to answer questions we don't ask him, we may never get another chance. So it's a risk either way.† That's *always* the risk I feel about him. And I'm willing to either way, because at this point, I will do nothing to harm him. So whatever happens, I will protect him. The research comes first, and that's okay, because I *will* protect him.

S: Try this: shamans are . . . I'll just talk: this isn't what you should say; you and I know in reality that shamans the world over are different from everyone else.

---

*Understatement. One of the most important things I have learned from working with S. (and translating these tapes) is the value and need of giving support and reinforcement— especially when someone is in pain—in my talking relationships, which I'm more conscious of now.

†The first, not the second risk, seemingly endangers Saku. The second risk seemingly endangers only our research, right? Wrong: if Saku wants to unburden himself of his pain and we fail to help him do that, the chances are he may bear it alone—unsupported—the rest of his life. We would be cold not to appreciate the dual risks of this sensitive juncture.

H: Yeah.

S: He should know, and perhaps he would be interested to know, that shamans all over the world—even in my country, namely the Plains Indians, or the southwest desert groups [e.g., Devereux 1937], and the people in Siberia—all over the world, shamans are different. Nobody except someone who is different is *allowed* to be a shaman. And he should know that I come here with the information that *everywhere* shamans are different. And that's the only way they can do what they do—because they're different.

H: Yeah.

S: Start with that and then—you don't expect an answer yet—and then I want to study—and this is true when I am studying him: is he different? And if so, instead of his being afraid of it, can you let him know that he should be proud of it because he couldn't be a shaman unless he was different? Then maybe we can approach how he is different.

H: Yeah. [*To Sa.*] Did you hear him? Saku? He's been giving me knowledge: I also have never heard him say this before. He's got white hair and a lot of knowledge. [The traditional Sambia metaphors for wisdom.] And so he's told me this: he wants to talk to you about this knowledge. He says he knows about shamans in all places. They aren't the same as just plain old men and women. They're another kind. He says: "Our shamans in America aren't the same; they're not just men and women. They're different. [*Elaborates.*] Dr. Stoller is not frightening or shaming you but encouraging you to be happy about yourself. Because these powers of yours, from the *jerungdu* of your *kwooluku*, come from your being different. That different kind [of person] and your *kwoolukus* come about only from that body of yours. [*Pause.*] When I hear him say that, I feel he is only expressing his happiness toward you. He says: "I want to help you with your own thinking about yourself." And this, too, I've never heard it before. You know, I'm just a kid; he's got white hair, he's not newborn, he's old and knowledgeable. [*Pause. Long silence.*] This boss of mine, he's got friends with whom he works [i.e., patients]. Now these people, are, too, a kind of shaman. They're the same body [type] as you exactly. When they were born, people looked but couldn't make sense of their [the infants'] cocks or cunts [exact translations of the Pidgin words]. And they said: "This is a male, but it's not the same as a boy, it's another kind. It's a boy, but at the same time it's a different kind." Now this boss of mine has friends who are the same as that; they're the same, the same as you. [*Lowers voice.*] He's not afraid of them; he's not shamed for them. He's only happy about them. Why? Because they all have their own *kwoolukus*. And so he comes and is happy with you in the same way. And I have now told you all about that, that knowledge. Me, too, I don't know about this. Now he's come and taught me. [*Pause.*] Now, what do you feel when you hear this?

Throughout this long monologue, Saku and S. are silent. My speech is clear and quiet. I am trying to give a point of view radically different from that of Sambia culture. I am softly impassioned in a way I seldom am in public and have been only rarely with Saku, since I dislike monologues.

Sa: [*Quickly.*] But this is no good. [You have to hear the tape to appreciate Saku's voice, so different from before: weary, intense, and highly strained—as if these five words resonated from within the very center of his skull, uttered through clenched teeth that shred each word as it is spoken.]

H: [*Steady.*] Do you feel it's no good because of this kind [hermaphrodites] or because of this kind of talk?

Sa: The talk. [*Sullen.*]

H: Just the talk. Do you want me to say that to him?

Sa: That.

H: You want me to tell him? [*To S:*] I told him that in America you have friends who are the same kind as him. I told him they believe themselves to be males, but they're not males in the same way. They're different. And when they were born, the parents saw them and didn't understand. And that he is the same kind as them—

S: You told him, or he confirmed that—

H: I told him that he is the same kind as that. And I told him that although they're like that, you aren't afraid of them, nor do you have any feeling of shame.

S: If you try something—perhaps—this is for you to say to him, but for a beginning, for me to think. Is there any way you can find out, when he came back today, what was he hoping for . . .

H: Oh, yes . . .

S: What would he like to get? And is there any way we can open that door? Does he want to ask *me* things: I'm asking him: and he's free to. It wasn't that he came here hoping to ask me questions; he probably never thought of such a thing. What did he hope for? And what does he feel now that he's hurt and it's not going the way he'd hoped? He's been hanging around all this time because of something he wanted. What does he want? And can we help him with that?

H: Yeah. [*To Sa.*] Dr. S. says this: he sees you and thinks, at first you came back to work with us. He saw you and he was happy with our talking. And he thinks, at this time when you come here, do you yourself want to get some knowledge or understanding or feeling. . . . And now he's said to me: "I've sat here and asked you plenty, hammered your ear that way. Do you want to ask me anything?" He doesn't want to sit down and just ask you: not good that you think hard [i.e., worry] about him—

Sa: Ah, I'm not going to think hard about [fear] him. It's all right. [The first hopeful sign he's back with us, some warmth again in his voice.]

H: And he's thinking, "When you first came today, did you want to find out about something, or some feeling or such?" He wants to ask you about that.

Sa: Oh, yeah. That's clear. For myself?

H: Yeah, for yourself.

Sa: I want to say this: I'm not going to be scared or anything. And by and by I can talk to him. You know . . . here . . . they gave birth to us . . . I want to speak out to him. . . . * [Strong voice.]

H: Um-hm.

Sa: This kind here [vague], do they [whites] all understand them all completely too . . . ?

H: Yeah—[*soft*].

Sa: He wants to know—

H: Yeah . . .

Sa: So I'll tell him about it.

H: Yeah.

Sa: They all looked at us† at first—"I think it's a girl," that's what they thought. And then, later, they all looked at us and saw that we had a ball . . . they looked at us, at our ball [testes], and they all said: "I think it's a male."

H: Oh-h.

Sa: They all say that. [*Pause.*] And, likewise we've got cocks . . . and we've got balls.

H: Um-hm.

Sa: But, our water [urine] we all lose it in the middle [extreme hypospadias: urinary meatus in female position, not at the distal

---

*S.'s last comment via me turned the tide in Saku's fear and resistance. Asking Saku what he wanted acknowledged him.

†Sa. uses the plural throughout this section to refer to himself.

end of glans penis as in normal males]. Now, all the same, could they—would they fix it? [*Voice almost cracks from strain, he sounds close to tears.*] Or . . .

H: Do you want me to ask him—

Sa: Yeah . . .

H: You want me to ask him?

Sa: Yeah.

H: [*To S.*] Boy, that's really something. Whatever it was I said, it turned him all around.

S: What did he say?

H: I said . . . I gave almost a literal translation of what you said. And as you can see he loosened up and got less uptight . . .

S: Yeah.

H: And he said, "I want to tell him [S.]: 'I know you want to ask me about this, and you've come a long way to ask me about this, and so I'm not afraid, I'm going to tell you.'" I mean—that takes a tremendous amount of guts. So he says that the first time when they looked at him, they said he was a girl. Then they saw he had a penis and testes. And then later (he keeps using the first person plural to refer to himself) he says, "Now we have a penis." But also saying there's something wrong because the urine comes out wrong. I'm vague about that, what that means—

S: That's all right. . . . It's out; he's opened it up. He finally said it.

H: Now, he wants—he asked me something which astonishes me. He wants to know if you can fix . . . him. If there is something you can do, if there's some way you can fix him.

S: The chances are in reality I can't. If I were practicing medicine, even here, the thing I would have to do, before I could answer him (I'm not telling you to tell him this) is I would have to know what more is the matter [i.e., do a proper examination to arrive at a diagnosis]. It probably is something anatomical and beyond repair; I would have to determine first what is to be fixed. Is the "fix something" to make a bigger penis, to make a more naturally male appearance, or to get an erection, or is it to ejaculate or what—you know I don't even know. But before we did any of that, I would say to him what I'd say to anyone else: tell him he's brave to have said this.

H: Yeah.

S: Tell him I know that and appreciate it and respect him for what he just did.

H: [*To Sa.*] He wants to tell you about this [request]. But first, he says that you've got a lot of strength to talk out about this. Why? Because about this something many people could be afraid. You are brave to think and talk about this. And now he wants to talk to you about what you asked about. "Can this something be fixed," you ask him that?

Sa: Um-hm. That.

H: Before he answers, he must ask you more to understand what it is you want him to fix.

Sa: Yeah. . . . Before, when we were still very small. . . . [*His voice changes: quiet anger for the first time.*] Then, who came here? Gronemann. Gronemann came. They [vague] came and looked at us [me]. He looked at us [me] for nothing. And he didn't say anything [*low, quiet voice here*]. . . . They all looked inside us [me, looked at his genitals]. But you two talked [to me] and so I am telling you. [*Quiet rage.*]

H: Oh. [*Amazed.*]

Around 1965 a government patrol passed through the Sambia Valley. It was one of the early patrols, designed to assert an Australian government presence (which led, several years later, to final pacification). Gronemann, a German businessman, not a government official, accompanied this patrol. (We are not sure why he was permitted in.) He took a sexual interest in some Sambia initiated boys (prepubescents), which extended, in Saku's case, to wanting to see his genitals. He photographed Saku—a deeply humiliating experience, for Saku was ashamed of his ambiguous genitals; Sambia never appeared nude to others, and the shame was compounded by others (natives?) having witnessed the photographing. Word got out about the incident, and the resulting traumatic stigma was in Saku all these years.

I did not know until this moment about the photographing. I had heard stories of Gronemann's sexual exploits with boys, but that's all. Nor did I know until two years after this interview—1981—that Saku had had sex with Gronemann *before* the photographing (Saku sucked him). All in all a sad story.

Gronemann's business interests in New Guinea enabled him to return to the area over the years. Saku, aware of this, never felt free of threat.[20] (Discussed in the following.)

Sa: And, we [I] thought, "Later, if Gronemann comes back, we [I] want to ask him about this: 'This something here [flawed genitals]—would you [Gronemann] care enough about us [me] to . . . do something, about this [*purposely vague*]?'"

Then . . . but . . . [*scowls**] Gronemann he took our [my] picture and he looked at it, and he didn't—talk [explain why he'd
done what he did: look at and then photograph Saku's geni-
tals] . . . . So we [I] were just talking nothing about him helping us . . . . [In the last sentence, Saku seems to say—in words
and intonation—that he was a stupid son of a bitch to ever imagine being made whole by Gronemann in return for being shame-
fully photographed in the nude.]

H: Oh-h [*low*].

S: Oh, that's sad [*pain in voice on seeing Sa. now*] . . .

H: Do you want me to tell him?

Sa: Yeah, you can . . . no reason not to . . . . [Near tears.]

S: Oh—he looks like to wants to cry almost. Is that right, or am I
reading that in?

H: Yeah, that's right.[†] And that's not all. Do you know who he's been
talking about?

S: Why?

H: I've never before gotten this [secret] part of the story. Here's what
happened. Apparently, Gronemann was part of the first patrols
that ever came here. Someone must have told him of Saku.[‡] And
he must have looked at Saku and taken pictures of him. I don't
know the details. There was a hint from Saku that he hoped
Gronemann could do something to change him. But then "this"
was done to him—and I say it that way because it would have
been a terribly humiliating experience [to be photographed in
the nude[§]]. He took the picture, and—left. So here are my
thoughts: we are here, now, duplicating a similar situation; he
was humiliated before [ten years old]; he's about to cry; he had
this hope back then, that was raised and then dashed. And the

*Saku's present complex state—anger, fear, humiliation, confusion, hope, trust, distrust—
must be underlined. First is his puzzlement now, as an adult, as to what motivated this awful
stranger, Gronemann, then. Second is his still-remembered puzzlement when, as a child, he
could not understand what Gronemann was doing. Third is the mix of fear, envy, and disorientation, the result of the white men's automatic sense of superiority, even to their rights to
invade and seize Saku's body and its secret.

†Within a few moments, he did silently cry, tears falling down his cheeks, but no weeping.
I want to witness that Saku is no crybaby: in all these years I've seen him cry only once in
public, when he was deeply insulted by a clan brother. He may cry in private, because, I think,
he is compassionate (some Sambia men do not ever cry). But he is also tough; his crying here
was deeply moving: a twenty-year secret, shared. For myself, I am angry and shamed for Sa.

‡I later learned that Gronemann also interviewed and photographed other boys in the
nude.

§Sambia are prudish about exposing their genitals. They never do so, not even to bathe.
To be stripped nude and photographed in front of Europeans or other New Guineans would
have been, for a ten-year-old boy, catastrophic.

guy didn't have enough . . . compassion . . . to at least say something to *calm* him, and apparently just walked off.

S: That—we're not going to do.

H: Yeah.

S: Now the question, What's wrong?, is not an anatomical dissertation . . . . At the start tell him that; we are not going to *take* anything *away* from him; we are not going to take advantage of him. He doesn't have to answer anything. I'm not going to take any pictures of that part of him. And so forth.

H: Yeah. [*To Sa.*] Dr. S. says this: he hears this story about what Gronemann did. He's never heard this story, and I haven't either. He hears this, and he feels sorry. He wants to talk with you about your asking him if we can fix this something. But first before that he wants to say this: "Now I've come here and we're talking. I'm not going to take anything from you; not at all. I'm not going to take your picture; not at all. I'm not going to take your thoughts: if you don't want to talk, or respond to me, that's okay." It would be no good if you think he'll do the same as Gronemann before: he won't do that. He hears this and he thinks: "Oh, Gronemann didn't understand; he stood and took a picture thoughtlessly, that's all."

Sa: [*Quickly.*] And so—like this: he took our picture for no reason, and he didn't pay us for it. . . . He didn't give us good pay or anything, like clothes.

H: Yeah.

Sa: And so, I've got an angry belly about him. [*Rage.*]

H: Yeah.

Sa: Now, if he comes and asks me again—

H: Look out! huh? [I am so relieved to see Saku's anger.]

Sa: Yeah. Because before he took my picture for nothing, gave me nothing. "And you: [to Gronemann] You bring down big money in your work"—you know, that kind does.* Wait, later, the future, that's how I'd cross him.

H: Yeah. [*Thinking hard.*]

Sa: [*Reflects.*] I'm talking about Gronemann, I'm not talking about you two.

H: Yeah.

Sa: And [*raises voice, kinder*]—you can talk to me. That's all right;

---

*By talking directly to this imaginary Gronemann—who lives everyday in his insides—Saku shows he has over the years, constructed a scenario of what he would do and say to get revenge on this white man. And he knows enough of the outside to imagine that Gronemann was wealthy.

there's no shame in it. [How very different is his assurance from his mood when we began over an hour ago. He has not only revealed his secret, taken us into his confidence, and expressed his turmoil, pain, and anger, but now he says: "My anger isn't for you. Don't be afraid of the shame." He here returns S.'s earlier gift. In other words, beneath Saku's turbulence lies a warm and well-put-together man, who did not let fate burn him up.] [*Smiles.*] You know, the men who go round the coast . . . they [vague] see the cocks of Europeans.*

H: Hm. [*Pause.*]

S: [*Interrupts.*] I've really got to say this here: don't say anything; let him say everything he has to say.

H: Yeah. [*Quiet.*] Um. [*To S.*] He's very angry about what happened to him with Gronemann. I knew that's what it [emotion] was . . .

S: You knew—today?

H: Oh, no, I mean, right now. Before he said he was angry I could tell he was angry. And I said the right things to allow him to express his anger. He said he's very angry about what Gronemann did. He just took the picture and took off.

S: He's angry like you would be, and I would be, if someone did that to us. And he's in worse shape because he could never talk to anyone about it.

H: Yeah [*depressed*].

S: Till this morning.

H: Well, the most important message he left me with is that he's willing to talk with you. He's not ashamed to talk with you. Is there some other assurance that I can give—aside from all I have translated for you—that this isn't going to happen again? To make him comfortable—

S: There's no such thing as "I give you my word"? Or the equivalent?

H: Yeah, there is something like that.

S: First of all, I've got to know what word I give, because it's important to me to be honest to my word.

H: What I can do is say you will make a promise that you will not do so and so.

S: Well, what won't I do? I will *not* take a photograph; I will not ever humiliate him; I will not ever let anybody know about *him*— I might let them know about *somebody*. [And that, reader, is, in

---

*Not clear what Saku is referring to, but it may relate to stories men tell on returning from the Coast, regarding sex with white men in coastal cities.

reality, all you have been told.] That is, this story that we now have, as a piece of our methodology, might be described. There's no way we can tell him that it won't make a difference. But I promise *him*, that I will not—the most important thing—ever humiliate him.

H: [*To Sa.*] Yeah. He wants to say this to you and me. First he wants to say: he's heard this story and he feels truly sorry about what Gronemann did to you. Then he said to me, "You've got to tell Saku: I'm never going to shame Saku. I'm not going to give him more shame. I heard this story, and I'm really sorry. I won't shame him. You [H.] must tell him. I won't take his picture. I'm not going to shame him by telling people about him. I'm not going to make public some pictures or stories about him. All stories and knowledge of Saku belong only to him and to us, and I'm not to go talking around about this." And he says: "This is my promise."

S: Now after that is something positive: that he may feel better to have told somebody he trusts the terrible story he could never tell before. It may offer him some *relief*—of this burden—right now.

Terrible noise from kids screaming in the background. H. drives them off. Then:

S: This guy's been carrying an agony around inside himself. And we've got to, if we can, free him, so that he can at least go back to the starting line of what he's got the matter with him [an incompetent penis].

H: Yeah. [*To Sa.*] Dr. S. says: he's heard this bad thing Gronemann did, and he thinks, "This shame that Gronemann made in you— is connected to your fear that came from when you were first born, when your momma and papa didn't understand about how they marked you [made sex assignment at birth]—this shame has carried to the present and is stuck in your thought, and it screws up some of your thinking."

Sa: Yeah, that's right.

H: So he wants to say: you must know that he and I won't shame you or screw up your thinking; if then you can talk about it to us, then Dr. S. can expel that shame. That can make it better. You can get rid of that shame, and get rid of that bad thing Gronemann did to you before. And you can live better.

Sa: Yeah. Now I can tell you about this: if I was big, like now, and he tried to do that, sorry! He wouldn't make me shamed. But, I was just a small boy. I was the same as J. [a first-stage initiate in our village, a boy about ten years old]. They had initiated me, but that's all. I had no thought. Suppose he comes back later, I've got to tell you two. If Gronemann ever came back, I'd have said to him: "Before, you put a great shame on me. I'm not happy with you." [*Steady voice. He's back to his normal intonation now.*] Now, if he had paid me for that, paid me a lot, then I wouldn't be so angry at him. Had he done that and looked at me . . . but he didn't. He did wrong. This master.* Me, myself, from my own strength I did things—I planted a little coffee [trees] and got a little money. Now I've built my own tin-roof house. Now I work for you and make a little money. My stomach is still hot from this [*lowers voice, angry again, voice almost breaks*]. I'm just sitting down now. If you want to ask me something now—that's okay, I'm not going to get shame. I can talk.

S: The only thing I would say: you've got to give him *all the space*. Ask him the right questions . . . I don't know what to tell you: you're going to have to be a good clinician. Don't take the time to tell me what he said—just let it go. Let him run.

H: Yeah. [*To Sa.*] Do you think I should keep talking to Stoller?

Sa: [*Firm.*] You shouldn't worry; don't be afraid. You must tell him. It's my choice, if I want to tell him. So, you can go ahead and tell him [*level-headed*].

H: [*To S.*] He's identifying with me. He says you should talk with him: don't be afraid or ashamed, just tell him. [*To Sa.*] When Gronemann first got you, you were a *choowinuku* [first-stage initiate].

Sa: Yeah.

H: You didn't see him later as an *imbutu* or *ipmangwi?*

Sa: No, I didn't. [*His whole body is trembling.*]

S: Is he shaking now?

H: Yes.

S: Does he want to cry? He may.

H: I thought he was about to, on the verge.

S: Does he . . . he . . . want my permission? Is it the wrong thing to do in this society?

H: It *is* the wrong thing.

S: It's all right *with me.*

---

*Note how Saku shifts back here to the Pidgin "master," where before he used "Gronemann." He has objectified Gronemann's status to be the all-powerful white man, and he implies in this projection the reality and fantasy of the endless power-plays of life under a colonial regime.

H: It might be all right with you.

S: I'm telling you to tell him it's all right with me. But he doesn't *have* to. Can you tell him that?

H: [*To Sa.*] I was telling him [S.] this and he stopped me half-way to say that he's seeing you and he thinks that when you expressed this shame that Gronemann made in you—he sees your eyes and hands and thinks you're close to crying. You want to cry about what he did back then?

Sa: [*Quickly.*] Yeah.

H: S. says, his own way is that if you want to cry it's all right, there's nothing wrong with that. He's told me to tell you if you want to cry, it's okay.

Sa: It's like that. When I was still very small, I thought: "What does he want to *do* that he's taken off my grass sporran?"

H: He himself took off your sporran?!

Sa: Yeah. He told one of his men to do it. And at that time I thought, "He's looked at me. He wants to put nice new [western] clothes on me." But, he didn't put them on me. Now I'm big and I think to myself, "Sorry. Before, he really rubbished me, fouled me up. He took a picture of me, and maybe he showed it around to other masters." That's what I think. So, now, I think bad of him.

S: He's just shaking . . . shaking all over.

H: Yeah, I know. I think it's probably reassuring for him for us to just talk—

S: Yeah, yeah, yeah. That's what he needs [*intense whisper*].

H: So he said when he was a first-stage initiate, without his permission, an older man—not one of his kinsmen—took him to the place wherever Gronemann was, which was probably in a tent or something, and they removed his grass sporran to look at his genitals. And then, it's not clear if it was against his will—he was just ten years old—a picture was taken, and he's got a fantasy (I think you were right) that that picture is now being seen by others. And people are looking at it. And the meaning is that he was humiliated, because against his will they did something which is morally wrong here, they exposed his genitals and took the picture. So part of him is out there—floating in space. He said, tell him that—tell S. So, this is all news to me; I never got this story before.

S: I might do something, but I've got to know more. What's he feeling now? He's shaking from what?

H: Well, I can feel inside of *myself*—I am shaking.

S: Rage, humiliation, fear. What I want from him now is to get it out. Not to hold it with a shaking, but to feel free to say what the shaking is saying.

H: [*To Sa.*] I told S. what you said. He says: "I hear this, and I am thinking about this." But he also says that he sees you and you are shaking some.

Sa: Body-shaking. [He uses the Sambia, not Pidgin, word for it.]

H: Yeah. Yet he thinks that it's not good that you hold onto this shame. You must expel it, expel it through talking. Whatever you feel—anger or what—you've got to talk it out.* Talk it out to him.

S: Now what he should do is talk. To me, to you. Get it out.

H: [*To Sa.*] He says, "You talk, talk to us."

Sa: He looked[†] at me. I think about that, and I'm afraid of him. I'm not happy with him. [*Low, quiet voice.*] I'm not too afraid, but I am unhappy with him. He didn't think enough of me to give me something. That's all, that's what . . . I shake for . . . [*voice fades out*]. I'm not happy about that. I know—before, when I was small—he looked at me, but he didn't pay me for it.

H: Um-hm.

S: [*Directly to Sa.*] Talk—talk to me. Is that clear?

Sa: Yeah.

H: He says talk to him.

S: Turn to me, talk to *me*.

H: Turn around and look at him.

S: Tell me what you need to tell me.

H: Tell him what you must talk out about to S.

Sa: [*Flows.*] That's all, what I said to you. Before, he looked at me, and he didn't pay. So I'm afraid of him; afraid of only this Gronemann. This kind [of man] is no good, here. . . . He looks inside of their sporrans . . . at the pubic area of *men*. That's an altogether different kind of man[‡] [*tiredness in voice*]. So I've been afraid of him. If he had done good for me, I wouldn't think like this. Suppose he had said: "I want to do such and such, and so I'll pay you for it. And if you shake, then we can stop." If he'd said that, it would have been okay. But he looked at me, and this picture he showed to all the masters: "Here's a different kind of

---

*Talking out anger is what Sambia customarily do in moots; thus, Sa.'s talking is appropriate in that way too.

†Here and above, Sa. uses the term that can mean erotic looking. (See chapter 4.) It is a complex thing, this looking, which here carries the sense of: "I can't shake the feeling of Gronemann and others staring at me, exposed, so cheapened."

‡Saku suggests that Gronemann gets his kicks by looking at male genitals. Sa. feels that it is not right, that it is, as we would say in these circumstances, *using* the natives, perverse.

boy to look at." He thought that, he showed the picture to his friends. And so, I'm angry at him, heavy in my stomach at him. [*To S:*] I want Gilbert to understand: "Before, you [Gronemann] made me afraid and I didn't like it." So I didn't talk out to you [H.], but now I've told him all. [*Long pause.*]

It is so important to me, and to our joint work, that Sa. has acknowledged here his hiding and evasion of the subject of his hermaphrodism. This was the healthy and truly *human* thing to do. It was a way of acknowledging my struggle to reach him, and the ambivalence I felt in trying to open up this area in our dialogue. He acknowledges, that is, the open secret we could never discuss, by telling me that the dreadful secret—of Gronemann's picture-taking years ago—was a secret he could never broach. Thus, Sa. has directly responded to S.'s move above—"talk to me"—while also indirectly telling me with kindness that I am there, and that what I had tried to do was too frightening to talk about before. Not "H. is frightening," but "this deeper secret was too frightening." This acknowledgment and honesty startles me, as I think of it now (1982). Kalutwo never did that; perhaps he *cannot*. This acknowledgment is for me a sign of Sa.'s greater trust and care, of his healthy core personality.

S: What should I know?

H: He says most everything I've said before. Except he's added that he's never stopped being afraid of Gronemann . . . afraid that Gronemann will do the same thing. And in saying that, there's the sense that he didn't have the power to say "no" to Gronemann.

S: That's what I was going to say before. Now I'll say it again. [*S. repeats to Sa.*]

H: He said he was afraid to talk to me about this before, when I brought it up. But now he's told us both. [*H. repeats S.'s words to Saku.*]

Sa: I think, when I say this, I won't be afraid. If I curse him I think [*lowers voice*] I won't be afraid.

H: And you won't forget?

Sa: No. Now, what I said to Dr. S. I can't forget. [*Stronger.*] I have to put it on the front of my face [remember it easily]: I won't forget about it; I won't forget about this. I put it on my face now and I can watch and wait. I won't forget about this. [*Long pause.*] You know. When he came here and made us afraid that's not good. That's something truly no good. I always thought, suppose he would want to come here and take away [study] our customs or—that's all right, there's nothing wrong with that. But [*almost inaudible here*] when he came and did that—[*pause*] *makes us afraid* in your [sic] balls* [*sad chuckle*], that's not a good thing. So when he came here and made us afraid . . . [*pause*] that's very bad. That's what I think. You know. You masters have another kind of—a big kind of—

H: Power. [*Despair in voice.*]

Sa: Yeah. A big kind of power. Yeah. But us here—

H: You don't have any.

Sa: That's right. We don't have any [power]. [*Sad undertone throughout all this talk.*] And when he came and shamed us, that's no good, that's something that's very bad.

S: [*Cuts in.*] Is this unusual for him? What he's doing? [At this moment, Sa. is visibly shaking, his hands clasped to hold himself together. He is terrified.]

H: Yeah. Yeah, it's rare for him.

S: For him?

H: Yeah. For him.

S: And for the culture, too?

H: *Yeah. He's really tense.*

Sa: I'm really pleased with the two of you. [*Sa.'s voice breaks at this point. Pause.*]

S: [*Low voice.*] I want to hear him think out loud. Can we get him to do that now? If we can get him to, it will help me if I can know what he's experiencing.

H: [*To Sa.*] He asks what are you thinking, so he can understand. It helps him to know about you later.

Sa: [*Voice quickens.*] Oh, I am thinking he is helping me, helping me truly, I'm thinking like that. And another thing is that I'm very pleased with you. [*There's a smile in Saku's voice here. This is hard to translate. His voice is low and his words vague.*] And I was thinking no good about him [Gronemann]. I wasn't thinking good things . . . and he came along here and did that bad thing. And another [S.] has come along here to help me. And I'm very happy about that.

H: [*Repeats to S.*]

S: [*Quiet voice.*] Does he feel inside that he will be able to sleep tonight?

Sa: Well, when I go home I'll get a good sleep.

---

*An idiom: a little fear is "fear on the skin"; a lot of fear—fright—is "fear in the balls" (genitals), an allusion to the retraction of male genitals under extreme anxiety (e.g., in war).

H: You'll get a good sleep, huh?

Sa: Yeah. I think bad about Gronemann; but now he [S.] has helped me and I can forget thinking about Gronemann and all these other things, and I can go home and sleep good. And I'm very pleased with him [S.]. Very pleased. And I'm very pleased with him. That's all.

H: [*To. S.*] He says that before he was very afraid and ashamed about this and now you've helped him. And all of these feelings have gone outside of him and now he thinks that he'll be able to go and get a really good sleep.

S: That's good. If he wants to say any more, that's fine. But we don't have to have more. If he wants to do it he can tell it for *his* sake. He could—whatever the word is—deposit inside of us whatever he has to.

H: [*To Sa.*] Now, this is for later. Dr. Stoller says he is really pleased that you have talked to us and you have told us about this. That you have shared this with us. Now, suppose you want to finish here with this talk, that's all right, it's your choice. Or suppose later you want to say more, that, too, is your own choice.

Sa: I can come back later [*lower voice*] and talk.

H: Tomorrow?

Sa: Yeah. Come back later and finish with this.

S: What he tells us from now on is for his sake. We don't need more. Before, he was coming in here because Gilbert was doing research. If he wants to come in here now and talk about anything he wants, we don't need it. I don't mean "Fuck you! We don't need it." I mean he now has an opportunity to come in here and talk about *anything* he wants. He can bring it to us for his sake. And if he doesn't want to he doesn't have to.

H: [*To Sa.*] Dr. S. says: "I was working with you to get your thoughts. I, too, wanted to know about you. From now on. . . . We won't ask more about that. But if you, for yourself, want to come and talk, well, that's your own choice. We would be pleased to do that with you, to help you lose your fear. So that you won't be afraid or ashamed of this anymore."*

Sa: [*Low voice, exhausted.*] That's all right.

S: I guess that's enough work for today. Unless you've got something else that you want to ask him.

Sa: Hm. [*Long pause.*] Now what? Is that all? Is that all? Him,

---

*And this offer, this supporting relationship, I have continued with Saku ever since, across field trips in 1981, 1983, 1985, 1988.

Gronemann, that master, that's all I worry about. He shamed me, and that's it. So, I've told it *all* to you now. That's it. I wanted to tell you [H.], but I forgot about it. I wanted to say that he [Gronemann] made me shamed before, but saying that scared me. I was shaking. And so, now, I'm really happy about the two of you. That's all for now.

H: That's it. Tomorrow you must come and we'll talk again . . . .

Sa: All right, tomorrow I'll come. [*H. accompanies Sa. outside.* They say goodbye. Sa. leaves, H. returns.]

H: I was just thinking as I went out the door that I always have a compelling need when I have finished here [inside room] to go out and say a few words with the person that I have worked with to let them know I know there is another existence outside that's different from inside here, and that I am *also* out there with them, too. And that it's not good enough for me to say goodbye inside here. I have to go outside and say goodbye, too. You know, I've run that thought through my head hundreds of times—every single time I go outside that door.

S: But you would specifically *not* do that in a psychoanalysis. For different reasons, for some other thing that has to flow. [*Pause.*] *Everything* is important [*emphatic*].

H: Yeah.

S: Everything is important, including why you do that here and why I don't do that at home, with an analytic patient.

H: Well, this to me is why we are here.

AFTERWORD

The next day we were to see Saku again, but he didn't show and he sent no word. The day after that, I saw him near his house. He said he was "very sorry" for not showing; he was drained but okay. I think he was overwhelmed by our last session, needed a breathing spell to work through what happened. He offered weak excuses for not showing, which I accepted, but we both knew why he did not return. We said goodbye and kept in touch through occasional letters.

Looking back now, I realize I could never have foreseen what Saku was hiding all those years. I thought he was just ashamed of his hermaphrodism. Had I known of the trauma with Gronemann, I would have proceeded differently. But I could not know that, until S. came along. Perhaps it is a measure of how much Saku trusted me that we got as far as we did working alone. I lacked the skills to go further then. I've changed. Working with sensitive people like Saku has shown me: take nothing for granted; understand as much as possible before believing in your guesses; be supportive, and be patient.

Saku's life is better now; he is not as weighted down. In 1981, I returned to the Sambia and worked more intensely than ever with him. He was far less secretive and in two weeks was completely open. He told me more of his story, this time with less shame.

This study of Saku underscores the power of clinical ethnography for studying others' lives. A more sensitive case than that of Saku-lambei can hardly be found in the ethnographic archives. Empathy and trust made our work possible. Clinical skill helped us understand Saku's secrets. What is this skill? Why was I short on it? Did we press Saku too hard? What are the ethics of bearing down in interviews to discover something? Let me briefly review these issues.

First, to state the obvious: this material could not have been collected without remarkable trust between Saku and myself. Such rapport takes a long time to build.

Second, rapport by itself does not bring the data we collected here. That requires other clinical strengths that use focused empathy to work through someone's defenses, past their pain, if they wish to do so. You saw how S. helped Saku to feel his way through painful past experiences, sharing these with others for the first time. I could not do this before; was not experienced enough to keep Saku from getting lost in the avalanche of pain. S. got us through Saku's anxieties, to see more clearly the turmoil to which they pointed. He helped Sa. see that learning his secrets did not frighten or destroy us, and, therefore, him. S. supported Saku more tenderly than could I. With the secrets in the open, Sa. could see himself anew.

Third, training and experience create clinical technique. S.'s thirty years [1979] of interviewing and treating and formulating patient cases are available here. *That* does not bring empathy, however; empathy is more: self-image, motivation to understand other people's motivations, and interest in others are some of its characteristics. S. supplemented me here; my cultural knowledge of Sambia and my work with Saku complemented his clinical experience. Either alone could not have produced this chapter.

Most students, on beginning fieldwork, cannot undertake sensitive and intimate interviews. I could not have. Too much prior ethnographic background is required. The interviewing skills take time to develop, nor do they come naturally. Such supportive understanding requires special training. But this *can* be acquired with training. The first fieldwork is the first step.

Nilangu village. Photograph by Robert Stoller.

Nilangu children at play. Photograph by Robert Stoller.

Anguished child searches for his share of feast. Photograph by Robert Stoller.

Bridge off which Penjukwi tried to kill herself during abduction.
Photograph by Robert Stoller.

Nilangu men: afternoon gossip. Photograph by Gilbert Herdt.

A shaman leads parade of initiates. Photograph by Gilbert Herdt.

An elder teaches in Sambia male initiation.
Photograph by Gilbert Herdt.

Sambia warrior. Photograph by Gilbert Herdt.

Two men unearthing mumu feast. Photograph by Robert Stoller.

Nilangu women and girls in repose. Photograph by Gilbert Herdt.

Women and children around a fire. Photograph by Robert Stoller.

A pig kill in the bush near Nilangu. Photograph by Robert Stoller.

Feast preparations in the village. Photograph by Robert Stoller.

Small boy near a water pool. Photograph by Robert Stoller.

Intimate communications. Photograph by Robert Stoller.

S: Our discovery of Saku's secret overemphasizes Gronemann's badness. As victim, Saku experiences Gronemann as consciously malignant, while Gronemann, as is so often the case with colonialists, executives, teachers, parents, doctors, politicians, and administrators, does not realize how different it feels to be the one who delivers the power versus the one who receives it. Gronemann would probably have been surprised had he known that his whim had been an unending, awful presence for Saku. [H: Bob is being kind.] To what extent does ethnography inflict similar, though less severe, effects on the people studied? To what extent is the process by which we take information from people natural/benign/helpful and to what extent does it damage? To what extent do we researchers act in innocence and to what extent not?

Being a clinician—more precisely, a therapist—I see my work with patients as worth the pain it inflicts because the goal is therapeutic, and the intention—from moment to moment, depending on my knowledge of myself—more for the patient's good than for mine. Patients do not always experience it that way. Does this therapeutic quality hold in the ethnographer's work? Our argument is that it should, not to the extent that we, as ethnographers, are trying to remit pain, remove symptoms, or help people find happiness, but that, from moment to moment, whatever we say and think, as is true for the physician (however much it may be breeched in reality), the rule should be *primam non nocere.*

Did we press Sa. too hard? How clear are the ethics of clinical ethnography? Are they taught, practiced, monitored? Should ethnographers be as aware of the issues as, say, psychotherapists, or can the rules be as relaxed as for newspaper reporters? You saw us struggle with these problems in our interviews with Sa., where the interplay so resembled a piece of therapy.

Though not needed for every undertaking, clinical ethnography provides a way to uncover such information as Sa. gave us, with the bonus of helping people feel better about themselves.

CHAPTER EIGHT

Imano — Considerate Masculinity

H: It is well known that "strong" men are prominent in normative male comportment in Melanesia. Penetrating portraits of these are available in the literature (Read 1959; Watson 1972). "Big" men are a key to New Guinea Highlands social organization as we also know (Sahlins 1963; see also Brown 1978). And protest masculinity, in the generalized sense of defensive male-posturing to ensure against internal fears or external accusations of softness, is omnipresent too (Herdt 1987c). There has been much less attention directed to what is commonly known in Melanesia as rubbish men, antiheros who fail to live up to ideal standards of masculinity. Even here, however, there are hints of such figures around (Watson 1960). Far less is known of what Margaret Mead (1935) once called "gentle" males in New Guinea. Here, it would seem, is a very rare species indeed. In this chapter we provide a detailed report on such a man.

BIOGRAPHIC SKETCH

Imano is exceptional, perhaps the most gentle and kind Sambia man I know. Indeed, if you interview his contacts—wife and children, age-mates, extended family, friends—he emerges as one of the most considerate people in the village. What is this gentleness? I began research with Imano to understand questions like that. Why he is so considerate at first glance seems trivial but is really as important and fascinating as any manifestation of Sambia culture and erotics.

Quiet, sensitive, and intelligent, Imano is a married man in his early thirties. He is slightly older than Tali, though he looks younger and is far less socially prominent.[1] He is married with two wives; they have borne five children, of whom two are living.[2] He is a good

246

provider and able gardener. His is the second-most numerous, politically important clan in Nilangu. His father's nuclear family, moreover, is very prominent, his father having been a big man and war leader who was socially and economically very productive and lived to ripe old age. (Both parents are now dead.) The third of four sons in a family of eight children, Imano grew up well protected and strongly integrated into his natal family. This social heritage gives Imano biologic brothers and many classifactory kinsmen who are natural allies and supporters. Imano thus has lived in Nilangu his whole life, in customary arrangements that suit every ideal of masculine culture: patrician affiliation, inheritance and ancestry, patrilocal residence, and marital status. If ever one were to search for gender aberrance, you would pass Imano by; right? Wrong.

On closer examination Imano reveals—by Sambia standards—marked gender aberrance. As a child he had no wish to be a fierce warrior. When initiated he disliked (silently laughed at) homosexual practices, and compared to peers, he participated in them far less and experienced them in a different way. But his greatest aberrance is that he never served as a fellated, has never copulated with a boy. He married as quickly as possible and then took a second wife. He enjoys his wives and loves heterosexuality. Thus, Imano has deviated from several cherished social norms; and in normative terms, his form of masculinity is odd. To the western reader Imano may seem normal. But to Sambia he is almost (though not quite) as aberrant as Kalutwo (see chapter 9); Imano is to exclusive heterosexual behavior as Kalutwo is to exclusive homosexual behavior: an extreme case.

During 1974–1976 I knew Imano only slightly. He was a pleasant neighbor. I had congenial but superficial contacts with him and no special reason to interview him. It was not until 1979 that I began working with him and several other men like him to understand quiet masculinity. I did it then because I discovered belatedly that I had overlooked an important cultural category (namely, *aambei-wutnyi* "gentle" or "feminine" man) of male personhood.

In my original fieldwork I elicited, recorded, and studied the major and minor categories of masculine personhood and their symbolic attributes; so I thought. This set includes elders, war leaders, strong men, rubbish men, bachelors, initiates, and uninitiated boys.[3] (There are some similar, not identical, categorical status differentials among females.) In the 1979 work, though, I uncovered another small group of men who are quiet, married, acceptable but seen as "weak" (*wo-gaanyu*) compared to their showy peers. I had considered them ordinary (not average, and not rubbish, men, who are different). They were the men I had imagined to fight in the rear ranks during battle, compared to the rubbish men (who are said to be cowardly and, if charged, would run). Both in identity and in behavior, these gentle men reflect a masculine style that looks and feels different from, say, Weiyu, Tali, Moondi, or even Kalutwo (who is a rubbish man). Men like Moondi's father (see chapter 4), and perhaps Sakulambei (chapter 7),[4] fit this mold. They are "deviant" in Mead's terms,[5] but not so different that their presence shouts at you. Their fellows pay them no notice. A good clinician might have attended; the ethnographer didn't.

I can understand why it happened: they stay in the background. Stereotypes and category terms depend mostly on cultural context and interpersonal focus, wherein people are labeled, responded to, are given attributions, or make claims about themselves. These men are not only quiet, they are sometimes absent. Usually, men respond to others' absence—in rituals, for instance—by impugning them as weak or *wasaatu* (rubbish men). If forced, men might label as rubbishy, absentees such as Imano. However, that seldom happens; and the sense of *wasaatu* has another connotation when used for someone like Kalutwo (chapter 9, and in the following). On the other hand, *aambei-wutnyi* are not impugned, probably because in one domain that really counts today—reproductive competence—they are, if anything, eminently successful.[6] By 1979, when I began asking about the range of masculinity and femininity among Sambia, these gentle men looked different to me.

*Aambei-wutnyi** is one of those native concepts the anthropologist finds hard to translate. One rarely hears the word in everyday speech. In general, *aambei-wutnyi* is a mild slur, not used much mainly because it refers to only a few males. *Aambei-wutnyi* includes: being quiet, unshowy, socially awkward, not physically big or powerful; someone who avoids public ritual displays; who spends too much time with women and is gentle with children, liking women and family life more than do most men. It would not be quite right to gloss this noun as "feminine man" (and certainly not as "effeminate"[7]), for men such as Imano are more masculine than those Americans call feminine.[8] It was to understand the origins and dynamics of this gentle masculinity[†] that I began interviewing Imano in 1979.

**Aambei-wutnyi*: *aambei* is a transfix of *imbei*, which means "young adolescent female cassowary" and is a general metaphor for women and cassowaries; *wutnyi* marks masculine person.

[†]Whenever used, this term will be the translation of *aambei-wutnyi*; it comes closest to the meaning held by the Sambia themselves.

Let us compare rubbish men (*wusaatu*) with gentle men (*aambei-wutnyi*), for both are clearly set apart from that glorious identity, war leader (*aamooluku*). *Wusaatu* is an immediate, damning label, showing that one is weak, cowardly, irresponsible, *unmanly*. Take note that women also use *wusaatu* in reference to men, whereas *aambei-wutnyi* is used much less frequently.[9] The contrast active/passive is helpful here. The rubbish man acts as if big and showy, yet fails. Rubbish men are *wogaanyu* (weak, unmanly), a public term. *Aambei-wutnyi*, by contrast, is never used in public conversation or oratory: it is whispered. To do so would shame the men so labeled. But there is another (subliminal) reason it is not used. *Aambei-wutnyi* is a sign that a man is comfortably quiet, is more feminine than he should be; whereas *wusaatu* means that a man is uncomfortably failing to perform as masculine. *Wusaatu* is also a strong verbal social sanction to push men—the men who *can* be pushed—into being more masculine; *aambei-wutnyi* is never used that way. That difference raises a final contrast.

As stereotypes, both *wusaatu* and *aambei-wutnyi* are also social identities, stigmata. But they differ in how consistently and permanently people apply them as labels. Since the performative contexts of masculinity range so widely—from war to ritual to sex and on and on—a man's manliness may be judged according to the situation. He may be a failed warrior and a superlative hunter. A few men are *wusaatu* across the board: consistently unmanly.* For others, though, *wusaatu* is situation-specific and can later be cast off. As an identity-type, however, *aambei-wutnyi* seems invariant and predictable, Sambia say, based on personality configurations constant from childhood to old age. Yet remember that there are few of them—the label is less negative and symbolically charged than *wusaatu*; and these men—unlike rubbish men—are not out to prove anything to anyone, so they are seen less.[10] Besides, they are nice people.

I worked with Imano for a few weeks, for about twenty sessions of an hour or more each. (I also interviewed three other *aambei-wutnyi*, two adults and a pubescent initiate, but they are not discussed here.) I found Imano amazingly open; able and willing to discuss intimate feelings many Sambia men could not after months or more of interviewing. (Compare Kalutwo, from whom it took years to collect similar information. And that was like pulling teeth.) I found his frank-

---

*Kalutwo (chapter 9) is a *wusaatu* but he was not when beginning his social career twenty years ago.

ness, friendliness, and comfortableness refreshing and warm. Though I do not know Imano as well as others like Moondi, I feel my impressions are reliable. (But not complete.[11])

Weiyu, whom Imano trusts—they are close kin—always served as my translator since Imano cannot speak Pidgin. (In chapters 9 and 10 we show how Weiyu's dislike, while interpreting for Kalutwo, changes the situation.) I also interviewed Weiyu in private about his views on Imano's interviews[12] and cross-checked aspects of Imano's case study with others in the village who knew him well.

Today, Imano presents himself as an ordinary, relatively happy, traditionalist-type man. He still wears customary garb: sporran, bark cape, colored beads (but interestingly enough, he never wears the warrior's belly- or waist-bandoleers). He wears no other decorations, keeps his hair short-cropped and beard cleanly shaven (all traditional features). He has (like his brothers), an unusually high hairline, a broad forehead, bright expressive eyes, fine features, and is of medium height and build. Up close one can see fine horizontal worry-lines in his forehead, which contribute to his looking sensitive and intelligent.[13] He smiles a lot and has marked smile lines around his mouth, is fidgety and always working his hands.

Imano has told me of his development, especially childhood, in good detail. His story is confirmed by others. By any measure, whether one is Sambian or an anthropologist, what stands out is the character and presence of his father and the kind of marriage his father made. Imano describes his father as tough, fearless, a warrior quick to rise— a heavy. He was feared by men and ruled unquestionably over his wife and family. He was a main war leader in Nilangu. His speech was garbled;[14] he was a "man who didn't talk much." Even so, his children never feared him, he never hit them, and he and his wife rarely fought. The parents were often together, more than is usual. His mother was a kindly and much-loved woman, and a prolific gardener.[15] Imano's father was faithful to her, and he never took a second wife (which is extraordinary for a big man). Though he fought many battles, Imano's father was apparently not a man's man: it is said he never slept in the men's house.[16] In short, the image I have is of a tough, strict father, who was nonetheless loved and loving, who had a peaceful marriage and provided a bountiful and mostly harmonious home life.

Imano's first memory is of being breast-fed.[17] He was close to his mother until about age five. But after his mother had a new baby (he was about three), he crossed over the boundary stakes of the women's space and began sleeping closer to his father in the men's space in their house. He loved and admired his father more, as he got older. Still, he can remember in childhood being scolded for not being forceful in games and hunting. He sweated over that: his father compared him to his next older brother. (On telling this experience, Imano turned tense and looked both pained and guarded.) But he said he told his father that that was all right: his brother could be a great fighter if he wanted to while he, Imano, was different. (This remark may seem hard to believe—a five-year-old standing up to his father this way— but it is true that Sambia children have license to talk like this.* Imano reports it as a real event.) On the other hand, his mother defended him, he says, retorting that "quiet men live longer." Imano still remembers many intervillage battles of his childhood, when he hid with his mother and other children in the back of the hamlet, in fear of enemy assaults. He says he cried for his father, wishing that he would return home safely, which he always did.

Imano was glad to be initiated. He was older—ten—than his fellow initiates. He said he was happy to be "sent to the men's house" by his father, for he wanted to "grow and mature quickly." He didn't miss his mother, he said, for "I was already big and grown." He was afraid during some of the ritual ordeals but not abnormally so. His father stayed near. His response to the idea of the homosexual teaching is pure Imano: he silently laughed at the ridiculous idea of sucking another's penis.[18] But privately, he felt shame. He was afraid of fellatio, avoided it for months, being more ashamed than afraid. He sucked only two men in his life: one of them (assigned to him at initiation) once; the other—a bachelor of whom he was very fond—many times over a period of several months.[19] This fellatio, because minimal, was aberrant.

Perhaps the greater indicator that Imano's gender identity is different is his never having served as a fellated. When he first told me this I did not believe him. No man ever said that before. Imano almost boasted of it, with no shame or regret, though I checked many times. To my knowledge, no other Sambia man[†] has not been sucked by boys, for this means he is not ritually complete, has not demonstrated he is fully masculinized (Herdt 1980; 1981). But I am now convinced it is true; two other men have confirmed it of him. Though he had little homoerotic interest in boys, he was "proud to be inter-

---

*Sambia children are rarely punished, for fear it will stunt their growth. Fathers, unlike mothers, do not reprimand their children, a fact that enters into the ordeals and submission expected from initiation.

†Excepting Sakulambei (chapter 7).

ested to be initiated a bachelor" since it meant "I could marry a woman." From puberty, then, Imano has preferred women and could survive the resulting lack of sexual partners till marriage.

Imano married young, at an appropriate age, after serving two years on the coast as a plantation laborer. The experience seems to have changed him little; for example, he speaks no Pidgin. On returning he married, right away, a strong woman whose fiancé—Nilutwo— could not abide her sharp tongue and aggressive ways (see chapter 6). They have had sex a lot, more often, I think, than is usual. He enjoys this heterosexuality and is attached to his first wife. He took a second wife, another virgin, a couple of years later. This caused strife in his household, for his first wife fiercely resisted sharing him. They are all still married; but his second wife sleeps elsewhere to avoid squabbles (to be described in the session that follows). He definitely prefers his first wife sexually and otherwise.

Being a quiet man also means that Imano still attends to private ritual practices in normative ways. On the one hand, he avoids public ritual displays, seldom nosebleeding himself with the other men. On the other, it is believed he is a faithful *private* nosebleeder, regularly purging himself after his wives' periods.[20] He privately drinks milk-sap to replace semen after sex, though not always. (Indeed, he rationalizes his lack of screwing boys by saying that giving his semen to them would have used up his semen too fast. So he reserved it for women.) In short, he follows ritual procedures *after* sex to a tee, allowing him, we may speculate, more sensuous relationships with his wives (i.e., closer identification with them via these culturally-constituted defense mechanisms). The details and implications of these points are elaborated below.

How did Imano present himself during our interviews, how did he behave? First, he was often embarrassed, at times bashful, talking of himself. Other men do not express shame by bashfulness. Especially when talking about sex he was overly self-conscious.[21] After a couple of sessions, though, his shame faded, leaving only bashfulness. Once he felt easier, he alternated between being bashful and open, between uneasy and contented: smiling, with hands folded in his lap.

Second, another unusual gender trait: he expressed his emotions far more than most Sambia men. In an hour he could laugh and joke, look happy, turn somber and reflective; and these emotions moved easily on his face and body.

Third, he had lots of nervous energy, mild anxiety beyond that usually seen in men (or boys). He constantly fingered his face, touching his chin, lightly pinching his cheeks.* He shifted posture, sometimes putting his head in his hands, leaning against the table, or thoughtfully looking out the window, searching. He has an audible, soft, automatic cough, nervously clearing his throat as often as three or four times a minute. He used these anxious gestures in social interactions too.

Fourth, his habitual stance with me was: "I want to please." He smiled constantly. Even on raising his voice he smiled. He never showed me anger or disgust. He strained for approval, attentive to my questions and movements. He was affable. I never felt him to be hostile even in his anxious gestures. He thus made me feel a need to reassure him, to respond frequently, to let him know I felt him to be a good person. It was not usually that way with the other men with whom I worked, though it was when working with Penjukwi, Sakulambei, and several boys.

On the other hand, unlike the latter people, Imano did not seem fragile or easily hurt. He spoke fluidly in our interviews, and when we were done, he left easily, without loose ends. (I did not worry either that he would take what I did or said with him outside my office, because he was self-contained. That contrasted with Kalutwo, Penjukwi, and Sakulambei, with whom I did watch my behavior. For what they needed from me was never finished in interviews but spilled into other situations.)

Imano, in brief, was different, gently masculine, a personality like many of my students, colleagues, and friends in America.

THE SESSION

We interviewed Imano together only once, for an hour one morning. S. was present and fully involved. The complete edited transcript of this interview follows. What was the context of our talk?

Before S. came along, Imano was describing his life and his marriages. Because of his peculiar masculinity I was particularly interested in his heterosexuality and erotic excitement. At the start of the interview we discussed argument he had had with his wives: just one small event out of many that reveals his considerateness. In the latter part, we turned to his sexual excitement, and he discussed day-

---

*This is another idiosyncracy I have never seen in other Sambia men but have in children and some women.

dreams, replenishing his semen through drinking tree-sap, and aspects of his sexual foreplay with his first wife.

Though this range of topics may seem broad for an hour interview, it is rather typical. Readers who have done open-ended interviews know how many topics can enter an hour. Sometimes I tried to keep my interviews more focused than this one, by often returning to earlier comments of the person. Here, though, we were exploring; and our discussion opened up aspects of Imano's erotism that I had not known.

WEIYU: Imano says, "Yeah. There is a lot still to talk about, about when my [first] wife and I first started walking around" [metaphor for screwing in the forest].

HERDT: But still they argue?

W: [Quickly.] Yeah, yeah. The two of them do not talk any differently to each other.

H: She still says Imano's just a rubbish man, a soft man?*

W: Yeah, yeah, yeah.

H: And she fights with him?

W: Yeah, yeah.

H: Yesterday?

W: Yesterday. The two of them fought. Kwinko and I saw them. They had just finished fighting. Over their hand pouch [wallet] and also over . . .

I: . . . a long pair of trousers. . . . [Imano knows some Pidgin words.]

W: A long pair of trousers that was cut into halves, sewed up, and made into bilums [carrying bags]. Imano had given one to his other wife.

H: To the daughter of Kanteilo? [Imano's second wife is Kanteilo's daughter, and the old man really favors her.]

W: Yeah. Gave it to her, and so that woman [Imano's first wife] said, "Hey, does that belong to you that you are giving it away to her? That belongs to me. [The first wife had made two tote bags from the old trousers, and Imano gave one to his second wife without the first's permission.] What you own she does not look after very well."

H: What did Imano say?

W: [He turns to Imano and asks him; I. replies:] I told her, "You are big and adult." [I. talks to W., who reports:] The first wife told the

---

*When couples fight they say horrible things to each other never said otherwise. We may see his wife's epithets in this way.

second, "That bag does not belong to you. It belongs to me because my Imano gave it to me. He came back from his coastal work and gave it to me, at the same time, with some money." Now this woman [the second wife], she does not sleep there in our house. She sleeps elsewhere.* So it is not good she should lose her money. She's got to have something to put it in.

I: It's been that way.

H: Doesn't the other woman, the daughter of Kanteilo, put her money together with Imano?

I: No, no [*a feeling, half-feigned, that she is more than he can handle*].

W: Yeah, yeah, they put it together.

I: Just like that.

H: But you're saying that only the first wife and Imano put the money inside the one bag?

W: Yeah, yeah. That belongs only to that first wife—only her.

H: What of Imano?

W: He divides his money up for the two of them. He doesn't keep any for himself.

H: None? [*Surprise.*]

W: Yeah. He's a middleman, that's all. He doesn't hold it himself. When he works for money [on government patrols], he gives it to them.

H: But where does he store it?

W: He splits it down the middle and gives it to them both. He holds none at all.

H: Oh! [*Surprised throughout.*] I want to tell Dr. Stoller. Here's a good example, and just a mundane detail, of his kind of masculinity.

S: I was on the same track.

H: It's so typical. He had a fight with his wife yesterday. Kwinko and Weiyu broke it up . . . Just a yelling session, though. They had picked up sticks and were starting at it. His first wife was there when he gave a tote bag to his second wife. The first wife got jealous, typical when there's two wives. This discussion led to information that each wife has her own place for cash. Unlike most men, who hold the purse strings and dole out only pennies for their wives, he has given the money *to his wives*. When he needs money, he *asks* the wives. That's really an atypical pattern. Weiyu would never do that.

S: Why did he? When did it start? Go back to the beginning. If you want to know why, start with the first thing a person said.

---

*Because the two wives fight, they cannot live in the same house. Imano prefers to reside with his first wife.

H: [*To W.*] I want to ask him, when did he first start doing this?

W: [*For Imano.*] When he married his second wife. He used to do that with his wife and did not think more about it. So when the next wife came along, he thought to himself, "Eeegh! If I continue to give money only to the first one, the second might argue, fight with her or fight with me. It's no good to cause trouble over this."

H: But he started it when he was *first* married?

W: Yeah, the first wife.

H: All right. Let's ask him about when it all started. [*Weiyu and Imano engage in heavy conversation. Meanwhile, H. remarks to S.*] There is a really big difference between them: Imano uses his hands in a feminine style.

S: Yeah. I could see that.

H: Watch Weiyu, he doesn't use his hands to gesture the way that Imano does. You'll see it [style of mannerism] later on this afternoon when we talk with Penjukwi.*

W: [*Tugs at H.'s shirt.*] When they were first together, he wanted to butter her up—his first woman. He showed his money to her saying, "Look, look, I've got something here. You must hold onto this really good." Imano thought to himself, "I've got to give her something or she won't want me and will run away with another man." So he kind of tricked her [to get sex and to keep her]. And then she concentrated on the great pot of money he'd given her. So she really stuck close to him.

I: [*Breaks in.*] There, that's it. True, true.

W: He still thinks this way. He hasn't changed.

H: [*To S.*] This is really interesting. . . . It started when he was courting his first wife, who [formerly] was Nilutwo's fiancée. Nilutwo was trying to get rid of her and give her to him.† Imano *wanted* to marry her. He really wanted to marry her. He thought the best way to be sure that she would say yes—meaning, this is not the best way typical men[22] do—was to show her his money and say, "Look, here's what I've got; this is what I'll give you." And he gave it to her. And ever since, she's just been a great wife. Not great in that they have not fought, but—[right for him]. Still, he was afraid that if he didn't share, she would spit on him and go to another guy. This is unusual in several ways. First, rather than just saying, "You are a piece of my property; we're going to be married and that's it," he felt compelled to want her to *desire*

---

*See chapter 6.

†Nilutwo was Imano's classifactory clan brother, that is, his true father's brothers' son, making them parallel cousins, a close relationship.

him, to be attached to him. He did not just force her. That would be a major difference in masculinity compared to other men. Then—as almost no other man would do—when he married the second wife, he anticipated jealousy between the two wives *over money.* So he simply sat them down and said, "I'm going to divide up my money equally and give it to both of you." Whereas most men would hang onto it and dole it out as needed.

S: Our word—not theirs—he would be "considerate." In our society, although that [above] would not be considered nonmasculine, the phallic man is partly defined by the fact that he doesn't give a shit about other people. [*Pause.*] Having two wives is unusual?

H: No.

S: Why did he want to?

H: That's a good question; let's ask him that.

S: He loves intercourse?

H: Right. . . . [*To Imano.*] Dr. S. wants to ask you something.

W: Uh-huh.

H: Why does Imano want two wives? Why wasn't he worried at all about their having arguments?

W: [*W. and I. talk.*] He can tell you why [*smile in voice*]. Here's what he says, "If you have only one wife and she gets pregnant and has a baby, then, if you screw her, you'll harm the baby [a belief that reinforces the postpartum taboo]. Your child will be skin-and-bones and look like a flying fox [a bat: skinny, with misshapen black face, pushed-in nose, big teeth: the epitome of an ugly, nighttime creature: the dreaded ghost itself].

I: Yeah.

W: So he married both. When one has a baby, he can still screw the other. He can still screw the other one. And also, he thinks, "This one wife works hard making gardens, while the other, the second wife, is lazy."

H: [*Back to S.*] A common description and an honest answer. The post-partum custom is that when you've got a wife and screw her while she's breast-feeding, you will spoil the baby, because it's taboo. . . . It will die, it will be sickly, etc. You've got two years or more of taboo. Who are you going to screw? So: "I took another wife." And that's correct, because he really does *love* . . . heterosexual screwing.

S: Is it all right to move into that area?

H: Sure.

S: Does he do it *well,* by his standards? Does he do it well by each wife's standards? "Well" would include: hard enough (I presume);

and I don't know what else—foreplay may or may not be a part of it—you just climb on and screw and get off? Then I presume one of the criteria for the women is that it lasts long enough, etc. He's a soft man with a hard cock.

H: But he's a hard cock; that's the description [in previous work] he gives us.

S: But what is the wives' version?

H: We haven't talked about the second wife, only the first. (It would require a whole lot more work; I won't get into that.) I know the answer for the first wife: she loves screwing, and he loves screwing, and they enjoy it together even after they've had an argument, which is part of it . . . and . . .

S: What do you mean part of it? It is a turn-on?

H: I think it *is*. I think that's part of it but not the only part. He . . . says he is able, unlike some men [e.g., Weiyu]—for instance—to postpone ejaculating long enough that his wife can have an orgasm. He does that consciously because she asked him to.

S: He has no trouble doing it?

H: He doesn't seem to; most of the time he can, and he seems to enjoy prolonging it. He has made a point of telling us, many times, that when they were first married, they would screw two or three times *a day*—which is unheard of . . . *

S: Is it?

H: Yeah.

S: Why is he concerned with her pleasure? Is that typical?

H: No. It's extremely deviant.

S: Is that "considerate" again?

H: Oh, yes—it's extremely deviant.

S: Are women concerned with the men's pleasure?

H: By the men's definition.

S: But is her definition that she just spread her legs, or . . .

H: By just spreading her legs, just by allowing herself to be screwed— that is "concern" with the men's pleasure.

S: Well, he seems "concerned" in a more artistic way. Like some western men . . .

H: Oh, yes, by far. That's one of the reasons I like him. His concept (not in all of its totalities) of being with his wife is the closest thing to a relatively considerate heterosexual relationship in our culture, with give-and-take between the husband and wife, during

---

*For Sambia men, women's bodies, especially secretions, are so polluting that the danger hems in the pleasure.

sex, and where they are also. . . . He says that they talk while making love . . . about . . . making gardens, about the kids and stuff. Sometimes about erotic things.

S: At the moment they are screwing, they are talking about the gardens? [*Impressed.*]

H: No—after sex.

S: You've had the impression in the past from the men that the women don't have orgasms.

H: Yeah.

S: You seem to have a totally different body of data now.

H: That's right, because it's deeper and better. In the past I confined myself to several guys only. Now I sample different types of males.*

S: Were the first guys just holding something back from you?

H: No, no. It just happens that my two best adult informants [Tali and Weiyu] just don't recognize—in quotes—orgasms in their wives or any women. They don't; they're just phallic and that's what you'd expect.

S: Are they phallic and they also come much too soon?

H: They come very quickly, like in his [*points to Weiyu*] case. He says all the time that his wife gripes about it—that he just can't hold it, that it's just like that [*snaps fingers*].

S: Is that the cultural standard for a masculine man?

H: That's normal.

S: It's not premature ejaculation?

H: No, it's not. I checked that out, though there are a couple of men I have heard of on that level. But T. and W. do not think themselves premature ejaculators, even though they get it in and within 60 seconds [sometimes longer] they can have an ejaculation.

S: That's it [*confidently*]: "healthy attribute of a man." When they sit around talking to each other, no man who does that feels he has anything wrong with him.

H: Oh, no. The faster you get in and out, the better you are.

S: You mean, in that way you don't get poisoned?

H: Right.

S: Yet Imano's not concerned that he's in there longer than any other man in the hamlet?

---

*Studying aberrant men like Imano was important in this way. What I learned from their exceptionality gave me clues in looking again at normative men. The range of normative variation in Sambia society is thereby clearer. (I shall describe this variance elsewhere.) Warning to ethnographers: don't exclude anyone—especially deviants—from your field of study. Normative isn't all. [S. I suspect that when it comes to psychologic things—motivated behavior, affects, fantasies, etc.—no *individual* is normative, except to gross inspection. Everyone is odd around the edges.]

H: Right.

S: That means he's not concerned that what the other men call poison—intercourse—he's perfectly happy to have.

H: Right.

S: I mean: he's not worried about poison?

H: No, it's not that simple. He's also . . . he does all the ritual procedures to cleanse himself.

S: He's worried about it [*pause*], but he's not *that* worried about it?

H: He's worried about it but he still does it. Furthermore, take a for instance: the usual procedure is every time you have an ejaculation, you should go into the forest and drink milk-sap [e.g., from certain trees].

S: He does that?

H: Not always. So that's an indicator he doesn't have as much anxiety as you would expect for someone with that duration and quality of sex with his wife.

S: The hypothesis would be that he doesn't have that much anxiety because he doesn't have to prove that much about his masculinity, maleness.

H: As culturally defined and subjectively defined. That's correct. [*To Imano.*] I want to ask you about your other [second] wife. Is she happy when you put your cock inside of her? [*The two men whisper about sex and happiness.*]

W: [*Quickly.*] She'e also happy about it.

H: What is she happy about?

W: He says, "Happy with my penis" [*chuckle*]. It's big enough for her.

H: Because of its strength or its heat?

W: Its heat and [a word here I can't figure out] of it too. It goes deep inside, and her pathway [vagina] is completely filled. Big and long, up to here. She feels it, feels its sweetness; that is enough for an *imbimboogu* [orgasm]. She feels sweet. She says to him: "You can't pull it out too fast." . . . When she says that, he just lets it stay in.

H: And he, too, feels happy about letting it stay inside?

W: Yeah, yeah. That's it.

I: Happy, that's all. . . . [*to H.*]

W: [*Chuckle.*] That's how it is.

I: [*Chuckle.*] True, that's the truth. [*Imano interjects in Sambia, with an expressive voice.*] Joy. . . . [*and then goes* "whoosh," *as if to say,* "It is so pleasurable, you almost want to cry."]

H: That's true, huh?

I: That's the truth [*a little giggle*].*

H: [*To S.*] I ask him, how is your sex life with your second wife, and he says, "She likes my cock, it's hard, it's big, it's enough for her. I put it inside, really inside, she likes it, she likes me to stay inside." And I asked him, "Do you keep it inside?" And he said, "Yes, I keep it inside." And I said, "Does she have an orgasm?" And he replied, "Yes." And he said, "Yes;" and I said, "Does she usually have an orgasm?" And he said "Yes;" and then I said, "How do you feel about being inside her that long?" And he said, "I like it." And then you saw what the last response was—"I enjoy being inside of her long enough for her to have an orgasm."

S: Is her orgasm a turn-on for him?

H: That's the question I've never asked.

S: Or is it just, "I'm glad that she could have an orgasm"?

H: When your wife has an orgasm, do you also feel bodily excitement? [When I say that, Weiyu, because he and I have worked on excitement, says "*kalumundereindapinu*,"† which here refers to the erotic. He uses feeling in his voice, and expressive gestures for what those feelings would be, to also indicate having sex. Imano cues to that and responds. They set up quick exchanges that are not just words, but involve gestures and sounds associated with excitement leading to orgasm. (Incidentally, Sambia men communicate this way between themselves, too.)]

W: That's just how it is. His wife feels an orgasm, and then she says to him [*voice speeds up*]: "You mustn't take it out." And he's thinking to himself, "I want to feel the same for myself" [*excitement in Weiyu's voice*]. *Ilaiyu* [verb for pleasure, joy, happiness]!

H: I don't mean just "happy," I'm talking about feeling more. Does *he* feel more pleasure in his penis when *his wife* has an orgasm?

W: [*Coughs, embarrassed?‡ Clears his throat.*] You're asking does he feel happy?

H and W: [*together.*] . . . about his wife's orgasm.

W: Imano says, "It's very good to get an orgasm. She must get an orgasm too. [The next phrase—*hap i dia i stap*—is very hard to

---

*How very different from T. and W. (and many other men) is the tone of this talk. Despite all the sex talk, there is no dirty locker-room atmosphere. Another meaning of considerateness.

†*Kalu* is a polysemic word: as a noun, it means "liver" (body organ) associated with powerful feelings, just as we use the word "heart;" as a verb it means, sad, lonely, longing; in this construction it roughly means "liver get up," in sexual excitement. (See also chapters 5 and 6.)

‡Weiyu, my phallic friend, is unused to such a question; more important—here I speculate—he is embarrassed by such an alien thought.

translate. It connotes being overcome with the experience of *ilaiyu*, too impassioned, half-faint, spent. *I stap* means "is happening, is being;" so the whole phrase suggests "something that leaves her happily spent."] Then I'll shoot her again, more and more, and continue it more until she's finally exhausted."

H: [*To S.*] I hadn't thought of it, but it makes sense that it's a turn-on for him when his wife has orgasms. When the wife does so, he gets more excited. "When she has her orgasm, I want her to be spent and I can screw her more, and that makes me more excited. And then I want to screw her more and again and again." Now, see, that's just so peculiar. [*To W.*] You've heard about Imano's way; it is very much his own, huh?

W: Yeah. When he was talking, my thoughts went to my wife. My woman, does she get that kind of feeling? And he's talking about that, huh?

H: But you don't help your woman to have orgasm?

W: [*Interesting quality in his voice, as if defending himself against the thought that he would be the kind of—gentle—man who would want to give his wife pleasure.*] I don't think about *her* having to feel that. No, I don't feel like that.

H: When you shoot your water, do you want to screw her more?

W: [*Emphatic*] Uh-uh! No. [*Then—ambivalent.*] When the cock is loose, when I've done it, it's [sex] done. A little later, when it's tight again, [*excitement in voice and he snaps fingers*] I want to put it in and lay her back [get her worked up, and then after it's done, she'll just lay back].

H: [*Pause. To S.*] I asked Weiyu, since I hadn't before, "How do you feel about what Imano said?" He said, "I don't ever think about my wife's orgasms. That's the way he [Imano] is." I said, "Would you think about screwing her again after you've come?" He said, "No, I just pull it out." What he'll do (he has told me before) is ask her to hold his penis for a couple of minutes. That's apparently enough to get him excited again. Then he'll put it in again. And that enables her to get turned-on again, enough that the second time she may have an orgasm. [Though this isn't clear from Weiyu: he's not sure himself.] But he's not thinking about her pleasure when he does that, he's thinking about him coming again. That's a fundamental difference between him and Imano. These data are believable, I couldn't pick just anyone here off the road and ask those questions and get reliable answers. But if he (W.) says that, I believe it, because I've known him a couple of years.

I talk with him so much that when he gives me an answer, I can know if it's real. I feel it.

S: There's no reason why he should be superficial with you?

H: Right. Yet these are subjects that are normally difficult to talk about, and these are prudish guys.

S: But not in here; they're just not prudish.

H: Because it's an artificial environment. So, there you are. It's a great "natural" difference between the two of them.

S: I think you know the answer: if you ask Imano how many men are like him [*pause*] . . .

H: His answer is that he's one-of-a-kind; there's no one like him. Everyone else says the same about him; and remember he falls into the category of [*aambei-wutnyi*] gentle man. In this hamlet, there are only two other men who could be said to be that.

S: His concern for his wife is part of the proof that identifies him with that diagnostic category?

H: Yeah. It would be, but the others don't know these erotic details [and still they categorize him thus].

S: He's identifying with the woman (we would say), and the men somehow know that, even if they don't have the words?

H: Exactly. [Here I spontaneously shift topics. In previous sessions, Imano had alluded to having erections in relation to drinking tree-sap. It had not been clear to me when or why he got hard, and I wanted to clarify this. Since Sambia intensely focus on semen, in and out of sexual intercourse, and because men identify milk-sap with semen, I wanted to be sure that Imano's sensuous feelings were not fetishism: that the tree-sap, in itself, did not arouse him. (Information on semen and tree-sap in other males made such fetishism a possibility in Imano too.) So this conversation provided an opportunity for me to explore Imano's erections in this regard.] [*To Weiyu*]. I want to ask Imano about the custom of drinking milk-sap from the trees. The last time we talked, we discussed how he would go to the trees and drink their sap to replace his semen [as all men do]. First, he drinks the milk of a tree; afterwards he goes to his house and at night, when he remembers he drank the tree-sap in the afternoon, his penis is tight. What makes his penis tight then? That he drank the milk-sap, or that he is thinking of his woman?

W: [*Mid-sentence.*] . . . And he goes and drinks tree milk-sap and after that he comes and sleeps. Then he thinks to himself "Oh, I've gone and drunk the tree-sap and my water [semen] has gone to my woman. That water went into her vagina, and so I went and drank the tree-sap. Then, when he thinks this, his thinking goes to his mother [euphemism for penis] [S: *!!*] and it just gets up [erection]. And then, when he thinks that, his thoughts go to her [wife] and—

H: [*Cutting in.*] He goes to—

W: He wants to touch her [get her aroused].

H: [*Echoing Weiyu.*] He goes and wants to touch her, huh? Does he know what causes his erection?

W: Yeah, yeah. It doesn't get erect from nothing when he drinks [tree-sap]. He doesn't think of himself that he drank tree-sap and now he's got an erection. [I. thinks:] "After I've drunk the sap—did I drink it for nothing or what do I do then?" [*Weiyu whispers here, but then raises his voice to emphasize.*] "Oh, I screwed my wife's cunt and that's why I've gone and drunk it, huh?" And so he thinks this and his bugger [penis] gets tight.

H: And that's what he says just like that, huh?

W: Yeah. [*Imano agrees with W. at this point.*]

H: Now, at this time he knows that this [erection] is not simply from having to urinate* . . . . He's thinking that it's that he's seeing [fantasizing] himself drinking tree-sap—because he will later want to screw his wife. So then it gets up [he has an erection]?

W: Yeah, yeah.

H: This [erection] isn't from simply urinating?

W: Uh-uh, no, it's not from that.

H: [*Quickly.*] Now suppose he doesn't have his wife available to screw? What does he do then?

W: If he has an erection? But his wife isn't there, huh? [*Imano adds something.*]

H: That's right: she's not there or it's forbidden because she's menstruating or something.

W: Yeah, it's taboo or because his wife has a baby [postpartum taboo].

H: Yeah. [*W. turns to I. and asks him; they talk for a minute and a half. During this talking, I. clarifies what he does when his wife has a baby, is breast-feeding or otherwise caring for a baby.*]

W: He says that; "Yeah, I'm married to two women all right, and so I do that kind of thing. . . . When a baby stops me [prevents him from having sexual access to wife] and my penis is tight, then I

---

*Sambia men associate morning erections with the need to urinate. They also use urinating as a way to get rid of unwanted erections.

think to myself, 'My penis is tight here, huh? Well, I can go to the other wife who has no baby. This one here, she's got a baby and it's not good that I harm it.'" So he thinks about going to the other wife. Then, when he thinks like that but he is still sleeping in his hut with the other one [with the baby], and he gets an erection, he simply stops it, lets it be. [I. motions showing how an imaginary erection can be placed underneath one's waistband so that the penis is strapped against the abdomen and it can't move around.] And then when he's sound asleep it goes away [erection is forgotten]. He sleeps like that. In the morning he gets up and thinks to himself. "Oh, last night my cock was tight and there's that other woman who has no baby." He takes her and [they go to the forest] and he shoves it inside.

H: Oh.

W: And that's how it goes. But here's another point: suppose both of them [wives] have babies but it is still tight. When this happens he knows to come and sleep here in your house.*

H: Oh. But suppose I'm not here, then what does he do?

W: [*W. turns and asks I. and they chat. Then W. quickly says:*] Well, the men's house is always here.

H: Oh, he sleeps in the men's house, huh? [*I. is improvising: if he does sleep in the clubhouse, it's rare: I've never seen him do it.*]

W: Yeah. [*I. talks to W.*]

W: Sometimes he just goes to sleep with lots of [kin-related] women, a lot of people who are all sleeping in the same house. When he does that, he's not going to think of it [sex]—and so he can sleep peacefully.

H: Oh.

W: Now, ooh, if he and his wife sleep [*raises his voice in amusement*] in their hut, he's not going to be sleeping very well. If he sleeps alone and his cock is very, very tight, he's not going to sleep well. His cock really spoils him, spoils him greatly [he's horny]: that's the way it can harm his baby [he'll be overcome by sexual desire and want to screw his wife, which will harm the baby].

H: Okay. Now when he's talking about "all the women," who is he really talking about? Old women?

W: Oh, any of the women, the old women and his sisters and his in-laws and [I. adds "in-laws" again] . . .

H: Suppose his penis is erect for no reason. Does he simply let it alone or does he go and urinate?

---

*Imano did this only a couple of times I remember. Others did it many times.

W: [*Asks I. They talk. W. turns back and says dolefully:*] He just about comes close to hammering [hitting] his own penis [*a small chuckle in his voice*]. If his penis stands up and simply stays erect, he goes and runs away to the bush, [to hunt], that's all.

H: Oh.

W: And now when the cold gets to it, it will become slack and go down.

H: He doesn't urinate then?

W: No, he doesn't do that.

H: All right, I understand. [*Then I. begins to talk about the fact that there is very little you can say at times like this (when he has an erection). H. adds:*] Oh, sorry, there's something else, another thing I wanted to ask [choppy as if remembering something important that he had forgotten]. I need to stop here and ask . . . when he's finished drinking tree-sap and then he goes back to his house and sleeps and he has thoughts of the milk-sap of the trees . . .

W: Uh-huh.

H: [*Continuing.*] His thought then, it [semen] can go to his woman. Now sometimes can he think of—

W: [*Butting in, very firm voice*] First, he can think of the tree-sap. He can think "Oh, this tree-sap . . . here I've screwed with my woman and I screw with my wife and so, because of that, I had to go and drink, huh? Her cunt is like this [the sense that while thinking about this, he has an image of his wife's vagina] and when he thinks of that, his penis gets up.

H: But I was wondering if he sometimes thinks about his wife's breasts?

W: [*Quickly turns and immediately asks I.*] That's it, it was like before when he was younger, he would think of her papayas [a joke, a metaphor for women's breasts] and then it would be tight without any other reason.

H: Yes, but at those times when would he drink tree-sap?

W: He says at those times he doesn't think about that. He thinks to himself, "Oh, I've sent my water to my wife and so now I'm replacing it [with tree-sap]."

H: And he can also think of his wife's cunt, huh?

W: Yeah, that's right.

H: All right.

W: When he was younger and he looked at her breasts, then he got hard like that. [*I. coaches Weiyu, listening to what he is saying in Pidgin, and then adding things, which W. immediately translates.*] When he holds them [breasts], his cock is simply tight. It is tight and he thinks about this. [I. means that when he looks at her breasts and gets aroused and thinks about screwing with her, this is the image he has when he's drinking the tree-sap; and that is *what* the sap is for. I.'s voice is so heavy here that I barely hear W. I.'s voice rises to a crescendo, and he keeps repeating "my young woman, young woman"—meaning before she had her first child. This experience most aroused him—seeing her breasts. His voice has a strange quality: insistent, excitable, an intense whisper. He seems different from his usual self, with a frenetic voice, saying over and over again: "She was in this virgin period" or "She was a virgin." This thought thrills him.[23]]

H: [*To W. and I. loudly.*] Okay.

W: Uh-huh.

H: [*To S.*] Well, I'm done. If there's anything you want to ask . . . .*

S: I don't know about the last couple of things—if you could just give me a couple of sentences (so I'd know what was going on).

H: We've been talking about heterosexuality, and we have worked on this aspect before: how he goes to the forest and drinks milk-sap. He's one of the people with whom I check out the experience of how the milk-sap drinking goes. [Cf. chapter 2.] He doesn't get a hard-on [while at the tree] and there is—what he does is he drinks the sap and that night, when he goes home and is just lay-ing down, he can daydream; he gets a hard-on but it's not just any hard-on—it's a "hard-on-[concerning] the milk-sap." You see, here is where I haven't got it right yet—the sap, you see, it's like getting an injection . . . of semen, and it's inside of you—so now you can screw [because] it's inside of you. It's when you get a hard-on you've got something to give, something to ejaculate; and [he's] thinking about the sap that has gone inside of him and is, literally, [believed to be waiting] in the area of his penis. He then thinks about his wife's vagina.

S: [*Interrupting.*] Well, what form does he think about it—not pic-tures?

H: I don't know.

S: [*Continuing.*] Maybe it is, I don't know.

H: Well, he is picturing it, I mean, that's the closest I've got.

S: (*Persisting.*) Picturing what? I mean, does he say he goes around picturing her standing there—in which case he would just be seeing pubic hair or picturing her legs apart, external lips, or the whole deal [*emphasis*]? That's a different thing.

*S. was a patient listener in these sessions, and he blended in so well that at times I forgot he didn't speak the language.

H: Yeah. I haven't asked him, you see I haven't asked him those specifics.

S: [*Continuing.*] Is he picturing her doing something or is he just seeing the anatomical parts protruding or something [*voice trails off*]?

H: Let me ask him. [*H. to I. and W.*] Sometimes at night after you've taken the tree . . . . sap and at this time he thinks of his wife's cunt, his cock gets tight.

W: Uh-huh.

H: [*Continuing.*] What kind of image of his wife's cunt does he have so that his cock gets tight?

W: [*Grunting.*] Uh-huh. [*He asks Imano.*]

H: [*To S.*] *Koontu youtnu* is the native category for daydreams or fantasy. It seems to be a close-enough equivalent to our concept. He says that he thinks about her cunt, about the surrounding area of the cunt [the word W. uses means edges or sides, suggesting the lips], and inside there is its heat. And when he thinks about that, then he gets hard.

H: Does he see a picture—or?

W: [*Asks I.*] Picture, Oh, yeah, picture, a picture.

H: Now does he see the sides and its [lips] . . . at that time is his wife standing up or does he see all of her or does he just see her thing [euphemism for the vagina]?

W: [*Quickly.*] Just her thing. He just sees it, he doesn't see her face.

H: Only that [vagina]? And does he see her pubic hair?

W: Yeah, yeah, that too.

H: [*Being sure.*] Her pubic hair?

W: Yes, that.

H: And the lips of it?

W: Yes, and that too.

H: How is that—she doesn't have her grass skirt on?

W: Yeah, it's like he thinks about when they're having sex and "that's what she does to prepare for me—she makes it very easy for me," huh? That's how he thinks.

H: Yeah, now he won't think about this area here [*H. points to torso*]?

W: No, uh-uh.

H: Or about her face?

W: [*W. asks I.*] No, not that.

H: Just her thighs around the vagina, huh?

W: Yeah, he says he only thinks about that part. [*Pause.*] And also about her hotness [the heat of her vagina] . . .

H: [*To S.*] He says that he sees a—and this sounds right—he sees an image of the vagina, the lips of the vagina, the pubic hair, and the sides of the legs where they meet. He doesn't see the face, he doesn't see the lower part of the legs, he just sees that; he just sees that, sort of dislocated, and he thinks of the heat inside the vagina and that's what is exciting.

S: That's the turn-on?

H: Yeah.

S: What about the breasts?

H: I already asked him that. He says no.

S: They are not exciting?

H: [*Quickly.*] No, no. I'm sorry: breasts are exciting to him. They used to be more exciting for him when his wife's breasts were very full and tight.

S: Yeah.

H: He told me now—I asked him, "When you're getting this same image" (we were talking about when he drinks tree-sap) "Is this also [images of the breasts] exciting?" And he says, "No. Definitely not." It's only her cunt, it's not the breasts. In general, at other times, he is excited when they were full, tight breasts; whereas now, his wife is getting older.

S: Do women have—this is a gender question that applies to men and women—are women's breasts erotic to them [the women themselves]? All of them, sometimes; all of the time, some of the time?

H: [*Sigh*] Oh, boy!*

S: Do they want to be touched, kissed, fondled, or whatever on the breasts?

H: Oh, you see, I've never asked any of those questions [of I.]. I know subliminally what I think some of the answers would be, and they would go: 'Oh, women don't want to be, they don't want to have their breasts touched. It's off-limits, taboo. But you see the question is: what does that mean? It's a turn-on, subliminally: women's breasts are exciting by being hidden. [*To W.*] Are you sure this [statement] concerns only the two of you? Do you think that your women really want you to try to hold their breasts when you're screwing with them? Would your wife sometimes take your hand and put it on her breasts?

W: Uh-uh, no. [*Ambivalent.*] Yeah, a whoring woman would do that.

---

*Do you agree with me that S.'s question seems simple but is difficult to answer without extensive and intensive data? If not, how would you answer for American women? How would ethnographers answer for other societies? Sometimes, like here, S. posed questions that require years to answer.

H: Yeah, but what about your own woman?

I: He means our own [women].

W: No, not at all. Yours, yes. [W. implies white women enjoy their breasts being fondled. How does he have that fantasy?]

W: About me, holding it, like that, huh? Yeah, if you do that she can go "Aye" [*raises his voice, feigning a smile and hostility*]. "Why are you holding it like that? What are you holding me for? Do you want to screw that you're doing that or what?" And she says that to me, then I would. . . . [*I. is distracted and W. scolds him.*] Aye, cousin, you listen to this. [*Then W. talks to I., telling him to pay attention.*]

I: I'm listening, I'm listening, why are you saying that to me?

W: [*Speaking for him.*] "I'm listening!" You are thinking.

H: [*Very quickly.*] What's he thinking, what's he thinking about?

W: [*Talking for himself without checking it out with I.*] He's just thinking about what he can say next, getting ready his answers if we ask him. That's what he's thinking.

H: Is that what *he's* really thinking? [*To W.*] Right now is he daydreaming?

W: [*W. asks I.*] Yeah, yeah. [*Somewhat confused.*] Oh, he was daydreaming.

S: Let's get it! We can go to the other thing some other time. How come, right here in front of us?

H: Because we were talking about it and he was thinking "What would I say . . . ." [*I. then says, "I'm listening to them."*]

S: "What would I say" if what?

H: "If they asked me, what would I say if they asked me"—

S: "If they asked me, what would I say"?

H: [*Halting. Saying to W.*] Ask him now, right now, what's he having a fantasy about? [*W. & I. exchange for a moment.*]

W: He was thinking about his wife's breasts.

H: His wife's breasts?

W: Yeah. "When I hold them my wife says to me 'Aye!' [in the playful sense, stop that!]. My wife says that to me . . . [but it's] just play—giving me a line: 'why are you holding on to me? You're just fooling me'" [seductive, a little hostility, the sense of an amorous game].

H: Ohhhh.

W: [*Continuing.*] "Aye, you're just playing, fooling me!"

H: Playing around?

W: Yeah. He's just [wanting to be] fooling around and she's [feigning] disinterest about him trying to hold her hands . . .

H: Well what's the fooling storyline in it?

W: "You mustn't hold [amorously] me."

H: Is it that she really feels sweet about it?

W: Yeah, feels sweet, but she doesn't want him to know that she feels sweet about it, so that 's how she acts. Yeah, yeah, she [pretends] not to look and understand, not to understand it. And when she says that, you must go hold her hand and when you do, then, after that [she'll say]: "Do you want the two of us to screw?" [*Said in a light voice, as if entirely able to take the woman's line in this little drama.*] So you say, "Yes," you say it like that, and so you do it. That's what he's [I.] talking about, that's what he's picturing.

H: [*To W.*] Okay, we're just chatting. We're really happy to be talking, just talking about our work. All right. Next time, when we're working, we can go back and talk a bit longer about what you were telling us about your fantasy concerning your wife's breasts.

DISCUSSION

H: [*Echoing W.*] Oh, that's what he's thinking huh? [*To S.*] Did you get that?

S: No. I know it's about breasts and loving them or whatever it is.

H: [*Chuckle.*] He was thinking about his wife's breasts and [what happens] when they're together; this is different from what happens with Weiyu.

S: Yeah.

H: When they're together he grabs hold of his wife's breasts.

S: [*Continuing.*] Even though it's not as exciting?

H: As exciting.

S: Yeah.

H: But he holds on to her and she goes into this number where she says, "Oh, stop doing that." [*In the background Weiyu is laughing at my caricature.*] And he's getting more and more excited as she does that. And the more she does that, the more she [subliminally communicates she] wants it. The term he uses is, "She's faking at it." [*In the background I. is chuckling to himself and then begins his nervous cough.*]

S: Faking—not wanting it.

H: She's faking that she wants it. [H: That's a slip: faking that she *doesn't* want it.] And I. knows that she's faking, and she knows that I. knows that, and that's part of the game.

S: Wait a minute. She is faking that she wants him to stroke her breasts and she really doesn't want him? [H: S.'s confusion is my fault. I got it backwards.]

H: She really wants him, but she doesn't want him to know.

S: Oh, all right, it wasn't clear. She's faking *not* wanting it?

H: [*Echoing*]—Not wanting it.

S: But in fact she is getting more and more excited.

H: She does want it. Her breasts are erotic.

S: Good. And you didn't know that?

H: No, no. I did know that, but not in this way.

S: What do you mean: in what way *did* you know it?

H: I never asked him that question: "Do you . . .

S: Well, what did you know?

H: I knew that her breasts were erotic.

S: For her.

H: For him.

S: Now I'm asking . . .

H: Right. I didn't know that her breasts were erotic for *her.* I did not know that, that's right.

S: Or for anybody in this society, you didn't know that?

H: Not in this way. I knew that—

S: Well in what way did you?

H: I knew that they were erotic because they're being hidden and because—

S: No, I meant that . . . you touch them and it feels more like a "hard-on-as-you-touch-it," and feels more.

H: Right, I didn't know that.*

S: Okay. Now you still don't know if it's for anybody else except his wife.† So your next question would be, is it [that way for] two women? And if it's two women instead of one, then you begin to wonder if there aren't other women.

H: [*Quietly.*] Yeah, uh-huh.

S: So she really likes it . . .

H: Yeah, that's right. And so as she is pretending to resist him touching her breasts and getting a little bit more excited—

S: And he's getting more excited as she's excited.

H: More excited; and he has a hard-on now she's resisting him, then he holds on to her hand and says to her, "Let's screw."

---

*Here is another example of where S. helped me—through his interrogation—to clarify what I do *not* know, in order that I can ask new questions. Not only did he ask people new questions through me, but he asked me questions that brought new awareness to me, and hence new interpretations of previous data.

†As reported by her *husband.*

S: They, this couple, have foreplay.

H: [*Pause.*] Yeah.

S: That's foreplay.

H: [*Thinking and then surprised thinking it.*] That's foreplay.

S: They have foreplay and you don't know if there are other people who have foreplay.

H: No, I don't.*

S: Well, I'm also talking methodology now. It takes two of us to get this information.

H: Yeah. And that is foreplay; you see I knew that, and yet I really didn't know it, until you said, "That is foreplay." I know it [holds] for myself but I didn't think of *that* as foreplay.

S: But I'm talking about something else at the same time. I'm talking about you and me doing research and the advantage of the two of us doing it.

H: Exactly. Because you think of questions that fill out the things that are obvious, and what *you* get, you see, is what he just told *me*. What I couldn't have done was that. I asked him, "What happens when you get a hard-on and your wife has got a baby or she's not there?" [He said:] "Well, I take my cock and put it underneath the waist-bandoleers and go to sleep. In the morning I go to my [other] wife and screw her." And then I said, "What happens if you can't do that, what happens if both of them have got babies and you can't [screw them]?" And then he said, "I will go and sleep with the women." And then I said, "What do you mean by that?" And he says, "I go and sleep with the women and I don't think about it." And I said, "What women?" And he said, "My sisters."

S: So you mean he leaves his own house?

H: His own house.

S: [*Continuing.*] Because he's got a high level of horniness and he gets rid of it by [being near] forbidden—totally forbidden . . . women who are most likely to dampen his sexual excitement because he just wouldn't be excited by their breasts. They're his cure, they're his hot-cold showers.

H: Right. And that's another thing he says. "Well, sometimes I go to the men's house or sometimes I'll go and sleep with the women, namely my sisters, etc." Now that seems to me probably a normal thing to do although . . .

---

*Now after other field trips, I think Imano's kind of foreplay *is* unusual and few other couples do it this way.

S: You mean "normative"?

H: Well, certainly normative to do; it's something most men *could* do and probably don't do very frequently. I mean I need to find out about that.

S: Need to find out if he's the one that invented that technique and nobody else does it or have others done it? That's what you want to find out? Now this question you may not and shouldn't ask, and that is, does he ever want to put his hand on his cock when it's tight.

H: Now I know the answer to that. He told me and this surprised me. He told me that he would sometimes put his hand on his cock or in the area of his cock, and he said it in such a way as if to suggest that he is not masturbating but doing something similar to that. But anyway, that's the sense of it.

S: But the hand on the cock is not eventually going to start moving?

H: Right. It's going to in some way, perhaps, help him get rid of his need. . . . [*Weiyu, Imano, and I make a couple of grunts to each other without saying anything, to acknowledge each other's presence. And I say to W. and I.:*] He's [S.] pleased to be talking with you.

S: One question. In this society watching women nursing seems to be a turn-on. Now I'm not saying that idea is wrong. I'm just saying I have a feeling that there's something more about that, because I've seen women sitting around here nursing all day long. And it's not appearing to me to be something that they are hiding particularly; or as if the men are going to peek-a-boo, like if a naked girl walked down the streets in Los Angeles. So what's the story on that with him?

H: We've already gone over this: it's definitely erotic. It's a turn-on for him to watch his wife's breasts, so he leaves the house or she figures out ways to hide from him sometimes.

S: Well, what about the women sitting around [he sees] from time to time nursing?

H: I've been thinking about that.

S: [*Cutting in.*] What happens with that?

H: I've never really thought about it; but the more I do, the answer is obvious. When we were there the other night in that house—

S: [*Inserting.*] She covered up . . .

H: She covered up.*

---

*Before a healing ceremony, in someone's house, we were in a crowd where several women were nursing, one of these being Imano's first wife.

S: [*Adding.*] Sort of, but she wasn't breaking her ass to do it.

H: Yeah . . . I saw her the other afternoon—you'd have to . . .

S: [*Emphatic.*] I've seen women breast-feeding. I've been taking pictures of women breast-feeding. They're doing this whole "big thing" with these cute little babies just tugging away.

H: Let me give you the possibilities as they come to me as flashes. Number one: it's okay to breast-feed with your brothers and fathers sitting around. It's not going to be a turn-on to them. Second possibility: you know it's a turn-on and you're out in public doing that, and you *are* turning men on by doing it.

S: I can't believe that other women would let you do that.

H: Why not?

S: That the women would let you turn on the men that grossly? I mean hard-on turn-on? If that's true, then there's a whole other piece of the culture I don't know about.

H: It doesn't sound right to me either, but I can think of some of the contingencies. Maybe there's no men around. Maybe there's no men who would stand around and stare at him. [H: Slip, it should have been *her*].

S: Yesterday.

H: Yesterday?

S: At that *mumu*, there was a mob of men; as to whether they are all brothers or not [I don't know], but they couldn't have all been.

H: Yesterday; but you see I can't answer that either.

S: Is it that you only do it in a certain place? I'll give you an example.

H: [*Butting in.*] Oh, that's it, that's it exactly, that's part of the *context* factor. It means different things if you're doing it in the shopping center and different when you're doing it in the home of a man. There's going to be a couple of men sitting down there who have got their attention freed and who can watch you do this. And if there is just casual conversation you can get turned on just thinking about it, but they [women] can't give you the signals or anyway any overt signals.

S: Let's see if I've got it right. I'll translate it into our culture. A woman dressed up with, let's say, fetishistic shoes—high heels— it depends on [*chuckles to himself*] the season and fashion, with a feminine skirt in a living room, is with the men and the women after dinner. And a little bit of her thigh shows. Now the same woman, and the same people, the next day, are sitting around the swimming pool, and she's right up to her crotch with her bikini. Well, nobody's going to think [then that the thigh is erotic] though that's the same tissue. Have you got it? In other words, it's not the anatomy that's showing; and it would be a bit vague to say that it's even the situation. She is going to be sending physical signals about the skirt part of her and those signals are even better than—it's not ESP—it just happens to be her crossing her leg and moving around, and the fact that she is subtle about it makes it even more exciting. If she was gross about it, everybody would throw her out of the house. They would throw her out of their circle of friends. Is that what it is?

H: That's right, exactly, that's what it is. I never thought it out like that, but what you're saying is within certain contexts, that is—culturally defined situations—the act is subliminally loaded so that it becomes erotic.

S: Okay.

H: People are doing it. Even the word "act" is too vague. People are willing: they are willfully doing it—that is, they know what they're doing even if it is subliminal.

S: And you mean you were telling me that there isn't much about this in the anthropological literature?

H: [*Pause.*] Not in these terms, no.

S: Okay. Well I'll say no, no, it isn't true.

H: But it is true.

S: [*Still astonished, perseverating.*] But that anthropologists have never either known it or admitted it? Now that's a discovery. Why can't a discipline know that it can be done. Because therefore [if anthropology paid attention to such details] it can better describe what it is doing. It's the thing we keep talking about: what is it that you *can* measure. . . . And what are you failing to measure? And always tell people [e.g., your readers] that.

H: That is what some anthropologists said. Remember Victor Turner's argument: "We can't do what the psychoanalysts do." We can't penetrate the hoary caverns of the unconscious because we don't have the expertise.[24]

S: But I'm saying something different than that. It [listening as a psychoanalyst does] can't be done [by H.] even though you could have done it. But that's not what I was talking about. What I was saying was that even the anthropologist can't [in reality] do what the anthropologist could [in theory] do, because he'll never have enough time, because every question should lead to—well, [*gestures*]—there's the point of the pyramid: I don't know how far that pyramid spreads; not because you [anthropology] can't deal with unconscious processes, not because you're a biologist or some other discipline, just simply that every question should ask so many other questions. (But if you just stayed on the surface, it can't be done.) There isn't enough time in a lifetime. And if you could do it [describe subjectivity] with one person . . . you'd never know about the other one. That's why when you start using a word like culture or some other generalization, in some way it seems to me that you're saying it *can* be done. You do it with words that [you imagine] really encompass it all. And [then] you'll be satisfied with those words, those generalizations. What I'm saying is "No, it can't be done." Now if you really genuinely believe that, then you'd have a different anthropology.

H: Imano told us, "When I've done the thing with the tree-sap and I think about my wife's vagina, I get excited,"—and all you did was to ask him, "What do you think about then?" Such an obvious question. I should have asked that, and maybe in another six months I would have. He could respond so easily.

S: I'm just being a naturalist.

H: And it's an authentic daydream because he [Imano] was sitting there doing it just then, before us: that's an observation. It was here; he was doing it. And he was able to just say, "I see not her face, not her breasts, not her feet, but her vagina. And in seeing that I think about how inside it is hot." Now I could give you some more content which would make that more meaningful: how it's hot, and why that heat is important, and what's done with that heat, and how the heat is different from outside where your cock is and you put it inside, and stuff like that. But the central part is there. And it's still conscious and quite available. . . . And anthropologists don't ask for that data! It's just right . . . on the surface. But—it's too easy to say—it's taken me two and a half years of knowing these guys, the culture and the language and everything, to be able to sit here and just ask him that question, "What is that?" And they can just answer. It's too easy to say "no anthropologist"—there may be a few anthropologists who have my experience and my rapport and so forth. And yet *you* [not I] asked that question.

S: I think that they would ask if they wanted to be ethnographers in the best sense of the word.

H: But many were not really interested in sex and gender identity and eroticism . . .

S: But they haven't done it about *anything*. How many people have sat for two and a half years trying to establish a relationship of trust?

H: [*Yelling in background.*] Did you hear that?

S: What?

H: That loud yawning [*some muttering here between S. and H.*] Do you know what that was? That was our next subject [Kalutwo] who is giving us the signal that he is tired of waiting [i.e., two minutes]—which is typical of him. That's one of the ways that he can be overbearing. That's what I meant when I said he did that thing at the door one afternoon. The door was closed but not locked, and he comes up and interrupts a session when I am talking with somebody else. And he knows if he did that—if someone did that to him—he would be annoyed [but] he interrupts us. So he yelled out to us and says, "Open the door," and made a big deal out of it; a sarcastic joke about it, to be precise; the content was "Why are you locking me out"? And he said that in a funny but hostile way—

S: But he took some of the heat off by making a joke?

H: A joke, right. But the door was *un*locked and he hadn't pushed it to see if it would open, which is typical of his way of dealing with me in this situation.

S: Talk about anthropology . . . and let them come in. That little insignificant detail is just as important as anything. Why should you just spend your time collecting lizard songs and ignore that? Who is to say that what he just did and your description of him is of any less importance to an anthropologist, that is, the study of the psychology of mankind, than anything else? Who arbitrarily decided that that grunting yawn was to be ignored by an anthropologist, that the words to the songs are more important? What is the theory of the difference that excludes that thinking and says it's not important or "just let psychoanalysts look for it"? But— it *isn't* psychoanalytic work at all.

H: And the next question is: how is it that I, sitting here, was aware what that [yawn] indicated [whereas other] anthropologists would have missed that?

S: Right. That's just a matter of personality, what's different about you. We're talking down anthropology! Cross-cultural psychology or something [as if these things were not] related to the practice of ethnography.

H: He's very anxious so I better start. If you saw him he can't (*too much static on tape*) . . .

S: Am I a shaman from overseas?

H: My hunch is really fearful, that there's going to be fireworks going on inside of him when he is in here talking with us.

CHAPTER NINE

Kalutwo: Portrait of a Misfit

H: Kalutwo is an unremarkable-looking Sambia man in his mid-thirties whom I have periodically interviewed over the past five years.[1] He was reared as, appears to be, and lives as a biologically normal male. People first mentioned him as a man with a troubled marital history, a minor shaman of a neighboring hamlet. But marital problems are common among Sambia, and while men make fun of him, K.'s peers still acknowledge him. My first impression of K. was that as an adult he spent too much time with the small initiates around the clubhouse.

I first began working with him in 1975 on his shamanic activities, while studying individual shamans. Even then I sensed he was odd; he was sheepish when discussing his healing activities, and he avoided his own history. Those interviews unearthed fragments of his childhood and marital background. Though K. was technically married four times, each marriage prematurely failed, and he was increasingly stigmatized for those failures. The elders and his peers, as usual in such matters, tried displacing the blame onto his wives and their greedy lovers, who supposedly stole the women away.* Later interviews (in 1979) showed that such views were rationalizations: K.'s unmanly avoidance of his wives drove them, one after another, into other men's huts. This perspective led me to reconstruct more carefully K.'s family background and childhood, which began looking bizarre. I finally became aware that K. not only feared women but still preferred erotic contacts with boys. Unlike other Sambia,[2] therefore,

---

*Despite the fact that the men recognized then, and even more so now, that none of their other peers had been given and had lost four wives, without consummating a marriage or having a child.

Kalutwo comes closest to being like a homosexual in the old sense of that western label.

In the late 1950s, well before pacification, Kalutwo was traditionally reared and initiated into the male cult. He still lives in that traditionalism, which has two aspects: he was initiated into the male cult, and he is a shaman. But some pieces of his developmental history and identity in these regards are deviant. As an initiate he was a bit small for his age. Later, he fought in several battles but stayed in the back lines, no fighter. (Nor, he admits, did he aspire to be one.) He is indifferent to hunting, which adds to setting him apart from other men. Instead, he prefers gardening, a respectable pursuit, but more for middle-aged men and, of course, women. Yet he is lazy, so his gardening is lackluster. More recently (since 1975), he began assisting in shamanic healing ceremonies, which he explains he does because they help people. His involvement in gardening and healing, though, has decreased in the past few years, a period in which he has become more glaringly deviant (being unmarried and childless). He is also sadder. Since his enthusiasm for other male activities and social relationships has also decreased, his peers disparage him even more.

Still, K. presents himself as tough, stiff-lipped, a traditionalist-type: old-fashioned masculinity. He wears a grass sporran, warrior bandoliers, and bark cape, the ancient insignias of a warrior. In a time of increasing social change, he has never worked on the coast and does not want to; nor does he speak Pidgin. (By contrast, half the adult male population has now served as contract plantation laborers on the coast; they sometimes wear western garb and many speak Pidgin.)[3] Besides dressing conservatively, K. is, like Imano, scrupulous in keeping his beard shaven and hair short-cropped (both traditional masculine features). He is physically plain, short, stockier than most Sambia men, and, some say, ugly by Sambia standards.* He is stiff, distant, and uncomfortable in public; is known by his peers to be secretive; dislikes children; is often quiet, emotionally flat, and brooding; though he is watched for his sharp tongue and sarcastic wit. These traits are aberrant but not out of the range of traditional Sambia masculinity.

Below this sullen masculine appearance, however, is greater aberrance. First, he has no manly achievements: no battle scars or heroic deeds, no impressive hunting record, no female conquests (not even

---

*Sambia consider his snub nose unattractive. He told me he felt both his parents found him ugly.

one) or wives with many babies, no oratorical skills or powerful ambitions. Kalutwo, now more than ever, is shiftless, going nowhere.
Second, his marital status is abnormal: in a society anchored in its
valuing marriage as the bedrock of adulthood, he is an unmarried,
aging bachelor now and has no erotic relations with women. Third
is his physiognomy: a face controlled but deeply creased with the
heaviness of worry, suggesting that pieces of himself are at odds with
each other, making him look older than his years. These are matched
by body movements that are slow and slumped, as if he carried a
weight alone. His eyes are sad. Yet, despite this agedness, one senses
something oddly unfinished about his eyes, as if a boy lives imprisoned within. (We cannot publish our photographs of K. but believe
most readers would see these qualities.) And finally, there are his personal ties: a few companions and supporters who see him as a social
failure but not an outcast; no immediate family except for a close
relationship with his only remaining blood sibling, a widowed older
sister on whom he is dependent emotionally and for subsistence; and
the boys who fellate him, a pleasure difficult to arrange as he ages
and boys tire of him.

In short, K. imitates a tough warrior, but he cannot bring off this
performance since his own needs undermine it. So he is disparaged
as a rubbish man (*wusaatu*)—and not always behind his back—for,
in Sambia society, merely seeming tough does not prevent a man from
being stigmatized as a masculine failure when he cannot demonstrate
masculine achievements.

How did I reach these impressions? Kalutwo did not figure in my
initial research project, for that was focused on the initiations. Nor
did I use him as an adult interpreter to retrospectively study men's
past ritual experience. Though we met on the day I arrived in the
Sambia Valley (November 1974), he was only a face in the crowd; I
ignored him.[4]

Later, after interviewing him regarding shamanic healing (1975–
1976), my attitude changed; but only in 1979, while actively talking
with him for three months—mostly on erotism and his gender identity—did I try harder to understand him. Then, my empathic communication shifted greatly: Before, among the other men, I had
chuckled when they gossiped behind his back about his disgraceful
marital failures and rubbish ways. Seeing his face visibly contort with
pain as he told me of his childhood, my unthinking disparaging diminished, and I changed, for I understood better his sadness and the
helplessness he had endured alone.

The greatest methodologic problems in working with K. involved language. Like Imano, he speaks no Pidgin (though he can pick up fragments in conversation), so I had to use an interpreter. But unlike Imano, the presence of a third party (interpreter) has in part biased my data. Though K. was eager to work,[5] and such interest indicates trust, the translator's presence inhibited him. Our work would have been better, I feel, had we spoken alone. (See chapter 10.) To lessen this distortion, I have deployed the following procedures. When working on public matters (e.g., shamanic healing) where precise meanings counted, I used on different occasions one of two different interpreters. For private matters, K. himself chose Weiyu, my best translator, with whom he was cordial and felt pretty safe.[6] When possible, I cross-checked my own impressions by talking with him about the same matter at different times and from different angles. And finally, when it did not violate his confidentiality, I have sought corroboration from his friends and relatives, such as concerning his childhood circumstances. Using a translator is nonetheless a poor alternative to working alone with him, for, on the most sensitive matters and despite our rapport, K. still hides from me.[7] Here is a sketch of his masculine development.

By almost any indicator Kalutwo's childhood was unusual compared to other Sambia men. His parenting was, by Sambia standards, bizarre. Little is known about his mother, who died twenty years ago, except that she was a conscientious gardener who shunned crowds. She later avoided contact with all men. She had had three children by her first husband and was an older widow by the time Kalutwo arrived. Two of these children died, leaving an eldest sister (still alive) as her mother's chief companion. Later K.'s mother began an illicit liaison with a married man of a neighboring hamlet. (It is difficult, here, to reconstruct what such an affair entailed, but it may have involved only flirting and having had sexual intercourse several times secretly in the forest.) That man—Kalutwo's biologic father—subsequently rejected her, for reasons still not entirely clear, though he was married and already had adolescent children. This kind of rejection seldom occurs, since the product—a son—would normally be desired and claimed by the father, not left to become a fatherless bastard. (There is not even a category term in Sambia for "bastard"; that absence reflects the strong cultural basis for heterosexuality in marriage, and the wish for heirs, including adoptees.) So Sambia, who are prudish, prize virginity, expect faithfulness in marriage, and outwardly condemn promiscuity, came down hard on K.'s husbandless mother when her pregnancy became noticeable. She protested, pointing to the father, and appealed to him for marriage. In such circumstances, it would have normally been appropriate for the man to have taken K.'s mother as a second wife, but he did not do so. He disclaimed involvement or responsibility, an ominous rejection, for it labelled K.'s mother as immoral, and it meant she would have no economic support in rearing the boy. She was condemned by all, including even her brothers, who should have helped her. Instead they publicly insulted and beat her. She thus left to live in isolation with K. and another widow at a pig-herding house well removed from the hamlet.[8]

This history—of a liason that led to a morally offensive birth, humiliation, banishment, and bastardization—dominated K.'s childhood. He grew up without a father or acceptable substitute; his mother avoided all men. Unlike what should have occurred, none of his mother's brothers became substitute paternal figures. In fact, to worsen matters—and here we see how familial guilt and conflict were built into the child's environment—K. was told his father was dead, and the man's true identity was hidden from the boy. It became a family secret. Having been treated shabbily, his mother not only was bitter toward men, but withdrew from community life, including all contact with men. K., the "cause" of this unhappiness, and a male at that, became her only remaining joy (and not much of a one). Years later K. consistently described his mother to me as a whore.

K. participated, as prescribed, in all early initiations, but his response to them was strange. He feared and resisted first-stage initiation. He says, for example, that he faced the rituals wishing he had been born a *girl*, a desire unheard of from Sambia men. Though his first response to doing fellation was fear—that is how most boys respond as we have seen—within a day he was enjoying it, his pleasure made up of shame, a sense of danger—and sexual excitement. Despite his fear, K. had an erection with his *first* fellatio, he says, a remarkable response no other Sambia male has ever reported to me. He became an enthusiastic fellator for years. When, in puberty, he was initiated a bachelor, after initial embarrassment he eagerly switched to being fellated, and enjoyed copulating with boys and daydreaming about them. He did not stop using boys. He never has.

Some years later, K. was married. He was not active in the arrangements, though by custom and personal motivation he should have been enthusiastically interested. He would or could not consummate the marriage, fearing his wife sexually, even after months passed. Bored with the long wait, this wife left him (or was stolen by another man, depending on one's perspective). Three additional marriages over a period of years, went the same route, two of them to the same woman.

Only in one marriage did he have sex, and that by fellatio, at his wife's instigation.

In the mid 1970s I watched the next-to-last marriage fail. K. avoided the woman as he had his other wives; eventually an older man with other wives took her (this man was, in fact, Weiyu's only living biologic brother, much older than he was), and they married. He died in 1980. In 1981 K.'s agemates tried again to persuade him to remarry her, for his bachelorhood was an embarrassment. The couple tried; after some turmoil they had fellatio. However, by the time of my departure, the marriage ended miserably, the woman breaking away exasperated.

This one heterosexual experience so filled him with shame (a truly unmanly response for Sambia), that through a combination of self-inspired, pathetically comic circumstances, he was jailed, humiliating himself and his wife and thus rupturing the marriage. This outcome ensured bachelorhood for life.

Without question K. wants the trappings of marriage as a social institution—a wife, children (heirs), a hearth, and estate. It is just that sexually and psychologically, he cannot bear intimacy with a woman. It is not wild guessing to presume he does not like coitus (and—different from all other Sambia men—he dislikes discussing the subject).

Before 1979 I worked with K., trying mainly to glimpse the strands of his gender identity and erotic behavior. Then, as now, I thought of him as an unusual test case for understanding the origins and dynamics of Sambia masculinity. His aberrance—exclusive homosexual behavior in defiance of social norms—could shed light on the nature of Sambia heterosexuality in family and individual functioning. He was never at ease discussing his homoerotic behavior and history. Only with discomfort could he describe the type of boy who turned him on (small, unrowdy initiates with hairless upper lips).* It was harder for him to describe his erotic feelings about women, though he slurred them as dirty and dangerous. It was harder still for him to discuss feelings about me. But he could not bear discussion of—even allusions to—his rumored desire for prepubescent boys: he wanted to suck them.

I learned of this rumor only when two initiates mentioned (inde-

---

*This erotic choice in boys is common among bachelors (see Moondi, chapter 4). However, as K. gets older, he has to be less and less fussy about his fellators, whom he sometimes has to pay to service him (which is, in fact, the way in which this payment is culturally interpreted by all the parties). At thirty-five, disparaged and without the liveliness of the bachelors, K. now takes what he can get.

pendently of one another, on their own) that K. had tried to reverse fellatio roles with them. I doubted this. It is strongly tabooed but not unheard of for a married backsliding adult man to have a boy drink his semen. I know of several married bisexual men who enjoy boys, one of which cases I have substantiated.[9] But erotic reversal is fundamentally wrong for Sambia, or, to be exact, crazy.[10] No one performs fellatio on prepubescent boys; and for an adult to go for boys when they have only begun producing semen is to steal the semen society reserves for those boys, who can grow strong and manly only by its ingestion. For an adult to try and suck on a boy is simply shocking. So Kalutwo fiercely avoided this topic with me and, when I indirectly mentioned it, he fled.*

This chapter in many respects is about how K. communicated with me, how he wanted me. Not "wanted" in an erotic sense but rather a complex of needs he had—unmet by anyone else—that he came to recognize through me and then to need more. Needs like understanding, compassion, someone to talk to, someone to get sympathy from— approval that he was socially recognized and valuable because Gilbert spent hours talking with him. He needed all that plus the small amount I paid him,[11] and toward the end of our talking he could say it. But these needs were met only by revealing secrets and allowing me to ask questions that were sometimes unbearable for him. So he had profoundly ambivalent feelings toward me, far more so than that of Sakulambei (chapter 7). K. *resisted* me, then, not wanting the pain but wanting the other good things of our relationship.

FIRST SESSION: ALONE

The following text was my last session alone with Kalutwo, on July 1, before S. arrived. By persisting in asking K. about his sexual experience, I encountered more and more resistance. K. would agree to be interviewed, but when I reached into such subjects as his erotic fantasies about boys, he would clam up, turn cold, and refuse to talk. We had reached such an impasse on a couple of occasions before S. arrived. Yet K. persisted, always came back, wanting to talk again, even if he would not let me probe further. The following interview was the most intense of the final exchanges. I present it to orient the reader to the second interview, done jointly with S. five days later.

---

*The first time in 1979 I hinted at it, K. panicked, rose, and said he had to leave, which he did. (He had never done that before.) The second time, some weeks later, he left tensely, after a few minutes, when he tried to make it seem he was not running away from that subject. In subsequent years he never could discuss it.

It also provides a contrast in style to what it was like for S. to be with us.

HERDT: Last time you were telling us [H. and W.] about that first time, when you were a *kuwatni'u* [first-stage initiate, seven to eight years old], inside the cult-house, the men marked a bachelor who was to shoot [orally inseminate] you. That first time, you said, your penis was tight.

KALUTWO: [*Through W.*]* They'd put it in my mouth and I got hard.

H: What were you thinking?

K: I put it in my mouth and got hard. I put it in my mouth and it was hard.

H: Yeah. And what were you feeling? [*An effort to push through his wary perseverating.*]

K: That in the future, when my turn comes, I'll do this to boys. Later, when I'm big, they'll give me boys. Then I'll have a hard cock like now [that first time]. My cock back then was showing me what to expect later.

H: Did you have a fantasy when your cock was hard, when you were an initiate in the cult-house?

K: Yeah, that when I have a mature cock, I'll have erections just like the bachelors did when I sucked them.

H: But that first time [during the initiation, after the men told the boys about the need for boys to ingest semen], were you already thinking that later you would be able to shoot the initiates?

K: The big men told us about that: "Your turn will come. When you grow up you can screw the boys the same way the older youths had screwed you."

H: At that time was your penis tight—the first time when you held their penises,† or the first time they put their penises inside your mouth, or what?

K: [*Much tiredness in translator's voice.*] Oh, the first time that they put their penises in K.'s mouth. Then.

H: And when you held them [the bachelors' penises], was your own cock tight then?

K: No.

---

*From here on "K" indicates Weiyu translating K.'s Sambia into Pidgin. Throughout, Weiyu sounds tired, dragged out. K., on the other hand, is energetic, a bit harsh—a loud defensive, raspy whisper—as he talks of his early homosexual experiences, which he wishes to conceal from others outside the house.

†Since K. was using the plural—"Their penises, the men"—we followed him. But he did not fellate more than one youth at a time.

H: [*Perplexed. K. is giving contradictory accounts.*] Now, when they put their penises inside your mouth, what did you feel then?

K: The first time when it was new for me I felt pain on one side, inside my mouth.

H: [*Surprised.*] Pain? I think if you got some kind of pain like that, if you were to think about it, your penis wouldn't get tight. Is that true? [*Voice raises.*]

W. translates to K., and then there's a pause as K. looks for an answer. K.'s remark is the usual response men make about fellating the first few times, especially if the fellated didn't ejaculate quickly. Recall that K. was initiated small, around eight years old, so his mouth was small. And how rough or gentle was his first partner? In any case, what is striking was K.'s—the fellator's—erection.

K: [*Pause.*] The first time you do it, it can be painful. What got my cock hard was when their semen shoots in my mouth. [See Penjukwi, chapter 6.] It wasn't hard for nothing.

H: What did you feel?

K: [*W., translating, is indignant toward K.*] Well, what should I feel?* I swallowed it and I was hard, that's all.

H: [*Persists.*] What were you thinking?

K: The bachelor's semen went in and I was hard.

H: [*Irritated.*] What did you think or feel?

K: When we're done, I swallow it.

H: [*Impatient.*] Yeah, yeah, I know, but after you swallow the semen, and your cock is hard, what do you feel?

K: [*Pause.*] That in the future, I can get an erection just like any bachelor does. I'll touch the initiates, play with them. I'll be allowed.

---

*Affectless responses—"I felt nothing," or "What should I have felt"—were common for K., especially in our later work. They wore Weiyu out; they eventually wore me out. Sometimes they were said blankly, as if K. was genuinely unsure, as if he had never been taught what to feel or could not trust what he had felt. The more threatening the experiences being reported, though, the more he would turn blank, then cold. Sometimes, I think, K. consciously hid what he felt due to the translator's presence (discussed in the following). But at other times the dynamics were different. How can this difference be measured? It is true that Sambia seldom ask one another explicitly how they feel about the interior of selfhood. Even so, my observations and other men's comments about K.—in ordinary settings—confirm his low repertoire of emotional expression and his need to shy away from disclosures that reveal any of himself. On such occasions and in his relationship to me, he was more than passive; he also seemed genuinely to feel nothing, as if he were consciously empty. Interpretation: K. was subliminally aware that sometimes he must avoid probing (disclosure, insight) because it made him anxious; so he consciously resisted discussing some subjects (associated with repressed and denied conflictual feelings and their old traumas). Such interchanges in ethnographer/native awareness and their methodologic implications for transference/countertransference dynamics will be discussed further in chapters 10 and 11.

H: [*Cuts in.*] When you thought about that with a boy, did you picture their faces?

K: [*W.'s voice now is soft, sullen, downtrodden.*] I was small then. I don't remember well.

H: All the same, what made your cock erect? The cock doesn't erect by itself.

K: [*Immediately: without reflection.*] The semen goes in. That's all.

H: [*Persists.*] Well, what did you think about their semen that it made your cock hard? [*To W.*] I think he's got some thoughts about men's semen, but he's not thinking about those thoughts now.

K: My skin* isn't hard when the semen is inside. No. It's when he puts it in and the semen goes in. And that's what I'm thinking of.

H: Is it the hardness of their erections that makes yours hard?

K: When theirs is hard, then mine is [i.e., there is no other reason].†

H: Are you thinking of the whole appearance of the erection, or just its size, or the glans, or what?

K: No. It's just hard.

H: You were saying that each time they come in your mouth, you have an erection.

K: Yes, that's how it was.

H: Does it make any difference if it's a big penis or a small penis?

K: The men around here—it's small. It's [penises] small.

H: [*Puzzled.*] Huh?

K: I don't stay erect all the time, only sometimes.

H: Huh? I wasn't talking about you; I was talking about the bachelors.

K: Oh, I see.‡ The bachelors all have very, very big cocks: they become very big.

H: [*Impatient.*] I know; I know about them. You don't understand, huh [*to both W. and K.*]?

---

*K. nearly always uses euphemisms for body anatomy and fluids, more than other men. A sign of his greater prudishness?

†S: Resistance. Such resistance is fear, resentment, stubbornness. No one else was so closed off. Yet, as H. noted, K. kept returning for years, needing the love. Every psychiatrist is familiar with this opposition and the patience and insight required to hear it and then turn it to use. But what about the ethnographer without clinical skills? Does he or she record the resistance-soaked words as a true story or omit them as meaningless? Other informants, equally stiff, quit, some even the moment they are asked to help. The data they will never give may count as much as those of their garrulous colleagues. Why did K. persist? A good clinician can sometimes spring loose the information frozen in the resistance, freeing the person (patient or otherwise) and giving new dimensions to our understanding of our interpreter and of his or her culture.

‡It was not clear here if this misunderstanding was the interpreter's or Kalutwo's.

K: All the bachelors are the same. They get big, very big, like that, all of them, they get big.*

H: Uh-huh.

K: Every cock, they all do the same thing.

H: [*Disbelieving.*] They're all the same? You say they're all the same?

K: No. Only when I'm sucking them. It's the same with all of them. It happens every time.

H: [*Several further exchanges follow in the same vein; then:*] What was he thinking? There's something here that doesn't make sense to me.

K: No. There's nothing else [i.e., "That's all I have to say."] . . .

H: Me too. [*Pause; thinking hard.*] When your cock is hard, what do you feel? Happy? Angry? Do you complain? [I have the sense of butting up against a brick wall. I can't get any feeling out of him.]

K: I wasn't happy about that. [*Clears throat; a sign, I came to know, that he is indignant.*] [A moment's loss of recording here from broken tape.]

I'm really pushing K. here, belligerent. Rarely am I belligerent with Sambia or anyone else. Lest the reader become too critical of my sex questions, I offer two observations. First, no Sambia man I ever interviewed had such trouble saying why he got aroused. Second, K. himself had much less difficulty discussing screwing boys (though he resisted providing details of his excitement). K. was aberrant. I see now why I resisted translating these tapes:[†] such resistance (K.), such frustration (H.). My annoyance increases until it breaks through here and stymies the dialogue.

[*Kalutwo breaks in, louder than my voice, and talks for about thirty seconds. Weiyu asks him questions. This goes on for about a minute, and they halt. Then, to break the heaviness, I offer them tobacco. We all light up and continue.*]

H: Now, when was the first time—he was big, or a little older, or a little younger—that he started to think about [fantasize about] the faces of the initiates—about when he could start to screw them? Was that when he was a first- or second-stage initiate or what?

---

*S: Is he, in this obtuseness, playing at being the village idiot, and if so, is he conscious he is? Pseudostupidity is a technique the weak use to disarm the powerful, a masochistic gimmick that works best when it is so habitual that it is unconscious.

†More than with any other tapes, I labored over these for Kalutwo, feeling tired and bored.

[*W. translates to K., who clears his throat again. The tape is turned over and Weiyu says:*]

W: He was second-stage.

H: When did you begin to imagine the faces of the boys you could screw?

K: When the hair under my arms and the pubic hair began to grow.

H: What were you imagining about shooting the boys' mouths?

K: Nothing. It got erect, and I thought, "It gets erect."

H: [*Small voice.*] Oh. [*Pause.*] Did the bachelors ever touch your penis while screwing you?

W: [*Puzzled; doesn't know what I'm driving at: won't let himself dare to think it.*] About . . . what?

H: Did bachelors ever touch K.'s [fellator's] penis?

W: You mean, did he get hard if they touched him?

H: Yeah.

W: Do you really mean that?

H: Yeah [*nonchalant*]. I've heard that some do that sometimes. The bachelors.

W: When K. was an initiate?

H: Yeah, either younger or older.

K: [*Looks stunned, then appalled.*] No. Not at that time, no. [*Long pause. Silence.*]

I am approaching asking him, but not directly yet, about his desire as an adult to suck boys' penises. I hoped, if I touched on subjects close to that one, he would drop a hint, a signal that it was okay for me to ask about his sucking or touching boys' penises. His "No" here—with grunts of moral indignation—turns off that effort. So I search for a way to proceed. Impossible, on this dread subject, with a translator present.

H: Later, when you started to shoot the initiates . . . you knew what your penis was doing [what his erections meant]. You knew why your penis was erecting, huh? The penis got up at the [thought of] mouths of the initiates, didn't it?

K: Yeah. When older, it would get up; but I didn't know why.

H: [*Consternation.*] I'm not sure. I would like to know. You say that as a second-stage initiate your penis would get up and you didn't know why. You got an image [fantasy] of the faces of the initiates, and then your penis would get up for no reason. I'm thinking that when you got to be a bachelor you knew the reason why your penis got up.

K: Yeah, when I was a bachelor, yeah. My penis would get tight when sleeping* with the boys. Tight.

H: Oh, yeah. But before, you told us that you would get a fantasy about screwing the mouths of [fellators] boys.

K: I think about their mouths, and my penis gets tight. [*K. says this like a declaration. He starts talking to W. again. W. concludes:*]

W: Yeah. [*Quoting Kalutwo.*] The tree's way is to stand up. But you and me, us men, we're different. When we think about something, then the penis can get up, that's all.

H: That's it! That's what I'm saying. You and I have talked, on and on and on and on . . . and you say your penis just erects for no reason, at least when you were an initiate. And now what are you saying?

K: When I think about the mouth of the boys, then my penis gets tight.

H: Is that it?

K: [*Angry.*] That's it. That's all that happened. It [the penis] just gets up by itself. At that time [when you are an initiate], no, no, you won't think about anything. It just gets up by itself. [*W. chuckles.*]

W: It's just tight for no reason at that time [*chuckles again*].

K: Oh, you [W. and H.] you go back, you keep going back to where you had started talking before. [Apparent allusion to me asking him about his erections in his first fellatio experience, which he didn't like.] [*W. chuckles again.*] And so I think I'm going to go now. Tomorrow I'll come back. [Again, Kalutwo is saying, "I don't want to work on this; so if you do I'm going to leave. Beware, any time in the future, any time you bring this up, I won't talk about it, I'll leave."]

W: It's us, the two of us,   we're strong . . . strong . . . strong . . . [Weiyu's stuttering here†].

K: I've told you I can only work when I have nothing else to do. Now I have to go; there are other things to do.

So K., who must be panic stricken, tells us that he wants to leave; he's had it. He's insulting to us in his affect, makes faces, but he doesn't just leave; that would be too rude. Weiyu jokes; he is terribly embarrassed. As a last resort I confront him with my reality assessment:

---

*This euphemism for screwing (common among Sambia) K. used frequently; but I have always felt that for him the literalness of sleeping-together-skin-contact mattered more than for most Sambia homoerotic partners.
†Whenever Weiyu becomes very nervous he stutters.

"Are you afraid of me; are you running away?" I am a bit surprised that he agrees almost spontaneously; so I repeat: "Is there any way I can help you feel better?" He tries to accept that plea, recognizing somehow that I am giving him back control; he must sense that beyond his defenses I really care. Finally he says he'll leave and come back later in the afternoon, when he'll feel better about working, a positive sign. I agree; then, another odd turn. After silence he asks me what my last question was, fifteen minutes ago. I am surprised; he really doesn't want to leave. I repeat the question in context without hostility and he begins to respond, but, taking his lead, I ask another question, and he draws back again. Then he insults us by asking us if we heard he said he wanted to leave! I say yes, unsmiling, and he departs, leaving us alone; it's bizarre. He's running because I was too close.

A side note, a difficult but important methodologic issue. K.—who started working for the money—is now fleeing because, perhaps, like Galako, my other failure,* I was too close to home, confronting K. too much with the conflicts he has so long avoided, rationalized, hidden from. He knows this; except that with K. there is a translator— which makes it doubly unbearable. He must sense it better than anyone but we two. No amount of money now can lure him to reveal more unless he decides to do that for himself and me. He surely won't. How does the tired rhetoric of participation-observation explain that? At this moment I am intensely aware that I am doing unconventional ethnography.

SECOND SESSION: WITH STOLLER

The session opens with the four of us—Kalutwo, Weiyu, S., and H.— seated at the table in my house. It is mid-afternoon, we are alone. We are all within reaching distance. Except for W., we all look at each other. W. is staring out the window when we begin, seemingly bored. But K. watches us, especially me, intensely, more searching than usual. We are looking at him. I feel awkward, somewhat embarrassed because of the previous impasse with K. and because I do not know where to begin. S. and I talk about K., orienting the interview. K.

---

*Galako is now [1979] a bachelor—Moondi's agemate—whom I studied for a few weeks. His intense attachment, as fellated, to a small boy was striking and unusual. I had tried to get him to discuss this for weeks, seeing him on a regular basis. (I interviewed him three years ago, too, while he was still an initiate.) He got scared and left, and would not be interviewed again. In 1981, frightened still, he refused to be interviewed but would sit and gab with me publicly. In 1988 he lived unmarried in a coastal town.

knows this, and the more we discuss him, the more he stares at us. S. is heard first, describing his impressions of K. at this moment.

S: [*Looking at K.*] . . . and it's among the saddest faces I've ever seen—on anyone* [*pause*]. But it's not just sad, because his eyes keep turning up to look at me, to wonder what's happening. But this man—but he's not—he hasn't been able to get rid of it. Some people, when they're chronically depressed, are doing other things to their depression—to schizify it . . . so that you don't quite feel its intensity. His brow looks like he's in *today's* pain. Not just old pain that he's gotten used to. Chronic depression can take so many forms. His has taken no other form except—and it isn't depression—it's sad, hurt . . .

H: [*cuts in*]—Despair—

S: —Despair: "My God, can't you help me? What are you going to do to me next"—in the sense of a kid who is going to get hit, pleading. And now he lowers his eyes to drink his coffee and it's: "Oh, Jesus, nothing good is going to happen." All of those [*lowers voice*] looks in a *terribly* sad face. And he doesn't change? That's not a hundred percent of the day?

H: That's a lot of it [*quietly*]. Not a hundred percent, but ninety percent.

S: All right. A hundred percent is a different condition.

H: It's ninety percent. Some days maybe seventy or eighty percent.

S: That it shifts has another whole psychiatric meaning than if it's permanent. *Almost* permanent is existentially different than if it were totally permanent. And it's worse to be able to *feel* the differences [perhaps] in a way, than to just have made it fixed unchangingly like a manic-depressive depression that lasts for three years. God knows that's awful, but you learn ways of living with that. This man isn't able to live with what's happening.

H: In a sense the pain is more conscious.

S: Yeah. He's really living the true pain, not a distorted version of it.

---

*S: By saying, "*It's* among the saddest faces I've . . . " I was subliminally expressing an impression different from, "*He's* among the saddest people I've . . . " or, "*His face* is among the saddest I've. . . . " The way I said it implied more starkly that Kalutwo does not, for all his anguish, offer himself to us. We do not so fully receive his pain that we want to reach out to help him. Instead, his pain also shows anger and withdrawal—a demand for help that contains refusal at the same time. He withholds his face from us. He is doomed, for he has doomed himself. Without insight, he will never find the script in his lifelong attitude (character structure) of making demands on others, in order to test their commitment, that they will never fulfill. I am familiar with that technique in our society, where that silent, hidden demand is assuaged by daydreams of some wonderful, loving, understanding, caring person—heavenly or secular—who ends the pain. This mechanism prolongs masochism to eternity.

H: And that's the story that he gives. He doesn't put it in those words, but that's what he—

S: You mean you have data that confirm my impressions as I look at his face?

H: Yeah. [*To K. and W.*] Dr. S. and I have been talking about our work. That's all. He [S.] doesn't know about your life. Let us see how our work goes. The two of us have been talking, that's all. Now we've finished, and I'm simply letting you know, that's all. [*To S.*] I don't know where I'm going. I'll just have to do it as I go along. Because of the situation I told you about. [Reference to the above impasse in my interviewing with K. before S. arrived.] I shall try to feel him out to see how much he can talk about without getting frightened. I'll do that: I will respond to the affects and ask him accordingly. So I don't know quite how I'll go with it.

S: What about trying this route: he keeps looking at me. To go back
   . to where you were before I arrived would be to lose an opportunity. [On the other hand, opportunities are the last things we want with certain people, because it's too much for them.] Might you not be able to work your *way* into it by finding out more: what does he feel about me being here—instead of going instantly back to the place. One other thing. . . . W. is sitting here in a completely different posture.* The two of them are parallel now, instead of facing. Is that because he simply hasn't gone to work yet, or is that a response to this man?

H: Yeah. [*Cautiously.*] He is responding to him. That's how he usually sits here with K. [Listening to the tape now, I remember the suspicion growing in me that crystallized when S. asked me about Weiyu's posture. I knew something was different in Weiyu's behavior all along, but S. made it—W.'s resistance to translating for K.—fully conscious and thereby available for me to use in later work. My initial caution here—I tell W. that S. and I are talking only about work—reflects a concern that in this exchange they would sense—W. sometimes picks up on my English—that W. was resistant, which would shift his subsequent behavior.]

S: But not with others?

H: No, not with others.

S: OK. Consider this possibility: K. is aware of this totally different, unbelievable experience now there's two of us here. I'm known in

---

*Note how S. immediately picks up the body language messages of Weiyu, which I had virtually ignored: see the next chapter.

the village in some way. You might do better—wherever you're trying to go in your work with him—acknowledging that new event. Asking him what does he make of this. The more open-ended the question about my presence, the better the information you'll get.

H: Yeah. We've stopped working for four or five days. And now the three of us are talking again. But it's different; it's not just the three of us. [*To K.*] S. has come and is sitting with us. What do you feel about this? [For the first time in this session W. perks up. I think he sensed a bit of a challenge here, which interested him.]

K: [*Pause. Smile in voice.*] Nothing in particular. I'm just waiting for the two of you, that's all.

H: OK. [*To S.*] This is a typical response. He said, "I don't feel anything." He's saying, "Whatever you want to do . . . I'm just following you guys."

S: Fair enough. Caution and depression and a lot else. But I won't give up yet. I want to know who he thinks I am . . . and not just a label.

H: [*To K.*] Dr. S. wants to ask you what kind of man do you think he is?

K: You are the kind of man that would come to a place like this; you've come to watch Gilbert work.

S: Still evasive. Again: what kind of man am I? Not label, not profession, but things like "good," "bad," "interested," "kind," "dangerous," "a mixture of." I'm really pushing him for a—

H: —And he's really bad about questions like this, because I ask him all the time.

S: Maybe I shouldn't do it—

H: [*Cuts in.*]—Uh-uh! I ask him all the time, and he's just very [*searches for a word*] unresponsive. Let me ask him.

S: Also, tell him I don't want him to be unresponsive. [*Laughs.*]

H: [*To K.*] Dr. Stoller knows you don't know about him, but he still wants to ask you about your thoughts about him. What kind of man do you think he is? Is he a good man, or is he no good; is he a man who does bad, a man who talks too strong, a man who holds a grudge, a man who makes you afraid, a man who follows other men: what kind of man? Think clearly and say whatever comes up. [*I finish and W. starts to translate. W. clears his throat* taken a bit aback by the questions we pose.]

K: No, this man . . . our good man [uses first person plural] . . . has come into our hamlet. What kind of badness could he have? He has no badness. He is nice (*singundu*).

H: [*Responding immediately.*] What kind of *singundu?*

K: *Singundu.* [*No elaboration.*]

H: His skin? His habits? His meanings? Or what? On his face or in his liver [his true feelings]?

K: Uh-uh. What kind of something could be in his liver? [*Voice trails off.*]

S: [*Quietly, the objective physician.*]* He is not in as much pain as he was.

H: Yeah, I can see. [*Pause.*] But I don't know why. [*Small chuckle.*]

K: This place is the deep forest . . . and yet he's come. He is a good man, not a no-good man. I won't worry over him about anything in particular. I think only that, "Ooh, he's come along inside this great forest. He's a good man to come here to see me. This place doesn't have a road for a car or for going all the way to America or Australia. . . . Flying—and then landing here [helicopter]— that's the only way you can get here."

H: [*To S.*] You probably understand most of that. He says you're a good guy; it's really special that you've come to a place like this in the middle of the forest. And he says, "Why shouldn't I think you're a good guy. . . . You're nice, you haven't done anything bad so far, you've come to be with this other guy who's good, and . . . you know he thinks it's—

S: —Is this superficial or b.s.—or safety—or does he feel, "There's something in that face [S.'s] that shows curiosity and involvement with me?"

H: It's not just bullshit, but it's superficial, the kind of answer he usually gives. I've been working with him for months this visit, right? I rarely get more affect than that. . . . I know [hope?] there's more there . . . but it's so deeply hidden . . . that it's very hard for him to dredge up much more than that. It's genuine, but it's not the whole story. And it's also phony, in a way, because he's not telling you what he really feels, and both I and the interpreter know that.

S: Yeah. [*Quiet voice.*] That's great. And we're working out a way of talking with him as we're doing this. [*Intensifies.*] He came in so troubled and worried. Now he's engaged (though we don't know what it means that he is). And he now has a different look. The sadness is still there, but his head is both pulled back—"I'm being

---

*S: That's too ironically polite. I was just warming up before the game, a curious observer with someone I didn't know and had barely started to identify with. As yet no love, no hate, no commitment, no defenses.

so careful" and pushing forward—"I want to get into this more."
[*H. agrees.*]

H: Now he's given you a piece of himself; he's offered you his opinion of you. So now he wants a response.

S: Here's my response (but I don't know how you're going to do [put] it): "I'm glad that he is responding, but I want more."

H: Dr. S. says this: He's happy to hear your words. He feels good that Kalutwo is expressing his ideas. Now he wants to hear more about K.'s feelings about himself. [*As W. translates this, K. smiles and looks up at us. Before that his head is mostly low, in his hands, his eyes looking at the floor.*]

S: There! Look at that. Now, that was an odd smile . . . shy and—

H: [*Breaks in*]—a nervous smile—

S: Yeah . . . but not a total push-me-away smile.

H: No . . . warm . . . it was a good smile.

S: Nervous, yeah; because he's wondering what the hell is going on . . . what game am I [S.] playing. But it still seemed a little relieved. . . . Don't let me say these things if you don't agree.

H: Yeah, I know.

S: We're dropping bit by bit down to something more workable.

H: That's right. [*Pause.*] Kalutwo, have you more thoughts about Dr. S.? [*Said quietly.*]

K: No, I don't have any more thoughts. He [S.] is our man. He is our visitor, a nice man. [*Slowly.*] He is like our Gilbert here. . . . He's a good man, not in a small way, with his gift of the sheep and tinned fish and rice [S.'s gifts to the village for a feast]. Only Gilbert's kind of people care and look after us. He visits Gilbert, and he has given us sheep and a huge bag of rice and fish. But it would not be good if he came here and buttered up Gilbert . . .

H: [*To S.*] He's warming up. He says you and I are different in wanting to come inside of a jungle like this. But, he says I'm afraid you're going to steal H. away, and take him back with you to America. It's very nice to talk with you, but you're going to steal away this man who's working with me.

S: The look he had before was of a dog that had been badly whipped. Then someone petted the dog for a moment, and the dog felt a bit better—without trusting, with good reason: one pat doesn't make a whole new life. But now here's something to be stressed, that you haven't quite told me. He seems to be saying, "I love Gilbert. You're [S.] coming here, that's very nice, but I'm really frightened that you're going to take away this person that I love." If he feels that, then how the hell does he deal with the fact that he has love for—nonerotic love [*H. agrees*]—has love for, can't do anything about, has feeling for—someone you can't control, who has different skin, clothes, and comes and goes. . . . What's the point of getting yourself attached to someone like that who in the past left you, *before* the man from overseas came to take him away, and now is even *more* likely to leave.

H: That's correct. It's in his ambivalence: even when I was really pressing, half of him wanted to stay [when he would start to flee]. And now he's back.

S: He couldn't leave! Why, he's the one person who's hung around your place more than anyone else—never said a word, face to the wall, not communicating with anyone—including himself. Yet he's always *here*. He's so desperate to be attached to someone. Fill me in for one or two words. (I'm sorry it breaks into our present discussion, but I'll need it.) What whipped him, or who whipped him?

H: Briefly: he never had a father. His natural father's identity was kept a secret from him because he was a bastard. The mother hated the father. The mother brought him up feeling that he should be afraid of men, and he was brought up so that the mother didn't like him very much, either. She had a lot of resentment because it happened to her, that men (her brothers) had treated her the way that they did when she had the baby, and the father wouldn't accept it. He grew up thinking that the father disliked him. He told me that when he was going to be initiated, he said, "Why wasn't I a girl?" [*Silence.*]

S: Proceed. [*Pause.*] That's a terrible tragedy. I feel sad when I hear it. When I say, "Proceed," I'm trying to cut off my feelings, which I shouldn't do.

H: Yeah, it's just—

S: —his face looked—

H: His whole life is like that. But saying that makes it seem like it's been done to him. And it has, but the last twenty years he's done it to himself.

S: Of course. That's the story of mankind.

H: Well, I'll move it along now.

S: And I'll hang back.

H: [*To K.*] Now, before, the two of us were talking a lot about our work and about the meaning of your—what you feel about us— What does it mean—that? . . . And *now* the two of us are sitting here and talking, wondering how we can find a way of interviewing good. So that our work can go along a straight course . . . and come out on top. Now he [S.] knows what it's like [to interview] in America; and I know what it's like here, inside Sambia. But I don't know what it's like [interviewing] in America. So now the two of us have combined it. So we're just telling you. [*To W.*] Now, I'm thinking of K., and I'm thinking if, from before, if there's something—if he's got anything he wants to ask S. about, at this time, he should just talk. I'm not talking about only now, I'm not saying that I want to push him—I'm not thinking about just now. . . . Later, if he gets some thoughts and wants to talk about them or ask about them, he should just talk. He can ask him [S.]. He has white hair: he's our elder and he has a lot of knowledge and if he [K.] wants to ask him [S.] something later, that's all right. It's his choice, whatever he wants . . . and I'm not just talking about now, I'm talking about later, too. And all later times, too. [*To S.*] You're going to be his father.

S: [*Quietly.*] That's what I was thinking before.

H: That's exactly what it's going to be.*

S: This is very hard.

H: That's exactly right.

S: It must be terrifying for him. You're his father, and I'm your father.

H: Yeah. My first thought was to say to her [a slip—I meant "him"]— but I couldn't figure out how to say it—"If you ever have something you want to *ask* Dr. Stoller, ask him." But I couldn't say that to him; it puts too much of a burden on him, and he's too passive for that. So, I tried to do it by saying you're a wise old man, and you and I are trying to find a way to do this work here: I constantly ask you questions, and he should too. Part of the problem is his worry I am leaving.† And now the news has just been brought that . . . and with that clear to him, his affect will change because he is going to be aware that I am dealing with the transportation problems, that I'm probably getting what I want, and that I'll be going soon.

S: So he'll have to pull back to spare himself another agony.

H: Yeah. [*Pause.*]

K: [*Spontaneously talks about two minutes. Weiyu translates to H., who translates to S.*]

H: He says he used to think, when I first came here, that I'd probably be here a year or two and then I'd go away and they'd never see me again. But when I left, I sent letters to the people who worked

---

*S: It wasn't. Perhaps there was too little time. Or perhaps, in another sense—fear and resistance, cold anger—it was. H: More the latter, my heart says.
†We have decided that when S. goes out, H. will too, for a spot of R&R.

for me and I'd tell them how I was, and sometimes I'd send a bit of money. He watched this and realized he had been wrong; that when I left I *hadn't* forgotten the people I was with; that I didn't abandon them. So, now that I'm working with him, he's saying, "I'm sitting and I'm watching and I'm wondering; since I'm working with you, are you going to be like that with me? Will you write letters to me when you leave?"

S: What are you going to say?

H: I don't know. I'm going to have to answer.

S: No, I'm asking *you* to tell *me*. I want to know what *you* feel.

H: I feel that he has made the relationship more than I expected it to be. He has responded more than I expected. And he has shown me more care and openness than I expected he would.

S: Than you thought he had in him?

H: Yeah. Than I thought he had in him. [Surprised at the thought.]

S: You thought he was so damaged that he would never *dare* allow himself to try again?

H: And *not interested* in trying. Yeah.

S: OK. So what's your answer . . .

H: My answer is that I am going to write him.

S: You mean he reached you?

H: Yeah. [*In Pidgin to K. and W.*] I've listened to him, and I'm really happy with what he said. When I leave I won't forget. I'll send a letter back to him. Weiyu, you can tell him, too, that I'm not a man who lies. I tell the truth.

W: [*Lights up on hearing that and says to K:*] He's not the kind of man who doesn't tell the truth. He *does* look after his work-friends. He's not lying. He's telling the truth. He's not full of empty talk. He says what he thinks.

K: Yes. I've watched you, and I know you tell the truth. Some European men would think, "Well, you're not my baby. I don't have to care for you and think about you, send things to you as if you were my child. Did I give birth to you? Did you come from my semen? No. You're another man's child, not mine. I'll help you only while I'm here, only then. But I'm not really your father. Rubbish! I'm not your father. I won't send you letters." Some men would think like that.* But you think differently. Your thinking I like. [*Long pause.*]

---

*Kalutwo shows us in this vivid narrative a well-etched script about how he expects people—he says "men"—react to him. He implies a wish for the father he never had.

H: He says like this . . .

S: Excuse me. . . . Look . . . he smiles. You look at each other with full contact . . . *totally* different from the start. OK, go ahead.

H: When I told him I was going to write to him, I said, "You know I'm not a person who says things he doesn't do." And he said, "Yes, I do know that." And he says, "I watched you. Some Europeans would think like this: you're not my baby that I should send you letters or money. You're not a child—I didn't carry you, I'm not your mother—" these are his words—"some men would think like that, but you're different. You remember the people you knew before. That's a very good way to be."

S: So much for the "noble savage," or the "ignorant savage," or any other racist beliefs like that. We're doing the same psychological. . . . I don't mean the cultures are the same or the identities the same. . . . I know that they have fundamental aspects of their identity that we'll *never* comprehend, that are different from us. But the dynamics—and I'm not talking about psychodynamics— just the dynamics of our relating to each other—are no different than what happens in my office. As he sits there, his face is not alien to me. Now, there are alien looks I would not understand . . . of course. But we're working here with a different style [from what ethnographers report]; the way I work with people at home. By "work," I don't mean something cold . . . distant . . . objects. I mean a human experience with form, not just appearance. We have a whole other task here: to find what's happening beyond the words. Because the translator's (Weiyu's) experiences are also part of the ambience and help create the questions and the answers—

H: —Exactly—

S: —Not just the words he [W.] chooses. His choice of words is part of it. *But there's nothing that's not part of this.* The coffee we were drinking at first is part of it. (But not to anthropologists, apparently.)

H: He's given us a signal. He's telling W. something to say to us. And every time he does that, he responds more and opens up more and feels more—

S: —Wait a minute. He *said* this? Or you just caught something subliminal—The *word* "message"?

H: —The *behavioral* message—whether it's conscious or unconscious—is, "I am opening up and I'm feeling nice."

S: Yeah, but he didn't actually say that in words, did he?

H: No. I don't know the precise content of the message yet.

W: K. says, "Your country has good food.* But you don't think (if you come here), 'What will I be short of?' You don't think like that. You think, 'That food [etc.] can just stay there ["I won't miss it"]. That's its place.' And you come alone inside these parts where we [Sambia] are as possums, sitting in tree-holes. [This jungle place is hard to live in.] The patrol officer comes and he says to us. 'Come on, give us your tax money.' 'Oh, sorry. We don't have any.' And we say that to him and he just jails us. And you? You come along and you help us and you give us money. And the officer comes to us and he asks us about throwing away our tax money and you pay us and we give it to him. Therefore, I'm very happy. It's so good that you've come to live in our hamlet."[†]

H: And I am happy to be here in this place. [*Pause.*]

K: You're a very good man. You come here. You don't come and take our food from us. You bring your own, you cook it, and give us some, even though we have our own food. You do that. You're a very good man. We're so very pleased with you. [*Pause.*]

H: [*To S.*] He's just going over the same theme, telling me what a good father or mother I am.

S: It's probably the theme of his life. But airing it has put it into that form. Do you want to say more about this? Is this defensive repetition?

H: No. [*Thinking about this now, H. agrees with S. He doesn't know why he didn't agree then.*] This hasn't happened before. I guess your arrival provided a convenient way for him to say things he has wanted to say to me before and that may also be an effort to repair what happened when I talked with him last time.

S: Yeah. It's *got* to be repaired. He feels something terrible happened—that he had to *run*: if you're panicked, you do terrible things; and after, you think, "Why did I do that?"

H: I've felt the same, that he saw this happening but couldn't prevent it. . . . I haven't given you all the details. I'll tell you after it's done. I don't want to go on much longer; it's getting late. We haven't done *anything* [*laughs*] except talk about him.

S: What have we done for him? We should do something. Does he measure what's done for him by the amount of time you spend with him?

---

*Because Sambia use food as a metaphor for relatedness and nurturance, you may interpret these remarks of K.'s as suggesting that I have forsaken the nurturance of my own land and people to come here: an act of courage he finds difficult to comprehend.

[†]S: What a run of thoughts, so much easier—almost manic—than before.

H: Partly. This was enough time.

S: We took a lot of his time by our talking to each other. Can he be told that all our talking was for him, not just for us? It really was, though we were doing our own research. It's for his sake that you want me to understand him in the way you do.

H: OK. Now it's clear. I can get that across. [*To K.*] We should finish up, but I want to say this: Dr. S. and I have talked a lot, but we weren't just talking about nothing. I am trying to teach Dr. S. what I know about you so that he can help me help you, not just for our work.

K: All right. [*Pause.*]

S: One last question. How does he feel about what we've done here today?

H: [*To K.*] Dr. S. asks, "What do you feel about our talking today?"

K: We've sat down and we've talked. I'm just pleased, that's all.

H: [*To S.*] Same as before: he feels fine, it's been good. There's a positive feeling there. No harm done.

S: Good.

H: [*To K.*] He's pleased with talking with you. OK. That's enough. The two of us [H. and S.] haven't eaten yet.

FINAL SESSION

We met with Kalutwo on the afternoon of the next day from 1:30–4:00 P.M. The four of us gathered, sat down, and sipped coffee. We exchanged greetings and small talk. Before interviewing, S. and H. discussed where to go in this session. S. suggested that he carry the interviewing. His idea was to ask K. to teach him about his shamanism. This approach was similar to our work with Sakulambei (chapter 7), only here we used it to learn more about K.'s shamanic identity, since direct questioning on K.'s sexual behavior would be too painful for him. In the midst of this questioning, K. searched for security again—referring back to the previous session when he asked me to write letters to him. Then we went on talking about his shamanism. In order to orient the reader, I add a few words here about Sambia shamanism and Kalutwo's brand in particular.

Like the rest of his development, Kalutwo's history of shamanism is splintered and convoluted. It contains too many contradictions to be considered only a role performance or dismissed merely as a defensive maneuver. Examples: K. had his first trance experience around puberty, but he did not begin serving in healing ceremonies till recently. (That fifteen-year delay is too long and therefore culturally aberrant.) He lacks the genealogic ancestry to properly claim inheritance of shamanic spirit familiars (usually inherited from one's father or father's brothers). His trance states—which I have observed in healing ceremonies—seem shallow and forced compared to those of other shamans (Saku especially, a fact his peers recognize by disparaging K. as a weak shaman); and he cannot exorcise objects (the performative feat *par excellence* of a strong shaman). Nonetheless, K. was ritually installed as a shaman in a *narangu* shamanic initiation in our village in 1975. One suspects that his marital problems and the failure of his last marriage must then have been on his mind.

Kalutwo's shamanic status does seem to help bolster and defend his identity in several ways. The shaman's role makes him stand out somewhat from the male crowd. His spirit familiars also provide him with spiritual powers others should take note of, even if they don't fear them, as they do with Sakulambei. During healing ceremonies K. is more aggressive—exhibitionistic (what Price-Williams [1975:88] refers to as "psychopomp"). K. has several familiars, some female, some male; and these figures—voices that he experiences during trance states—seem to appeal to K.'s dimensions of female and male identification, of which I believe he is more conscious (like other shamans) than most Sambia adult men. K.'s shamanism, then, helps him to sustain, against formidable social pressures, his sense of self—especially of maleness—while lacking other manly achievements.

But Kalutwo, as I mentioned, is not a great shaman in Sambia eyes. This means that his personality does not show the spectacular intrapsychic fracture lines that I believe underlie the trance and possession episodes that get things done (and sometimes, great things *do* get done) in the leading Sambia shamans' (e.g., Saku) healing performances. Ironically, however, the same dynamic structure that can do those creative things (i.e., heal someone) and which K. lacks (his shamanism is more mechanical), places these fragile shamans at greater risk of psychotic-like episodes and grandiose behaviors (sometimes leading to personal disasters, as in the case of Weiyu's father). K.'s personality is stolid and less grandiose than those latter shamans, who seem able to *become*, in trances, the fantasized masculine and feminine figures (shamanic spirit familiar personalities) that mobilize events during ceremonies.

Indeed, people disparage K. as a weak shaman, and, compared to Sakulambei—who is more unpredictable and fragmented (i.e., recall his chameleonic trait)—K. is a no-account, insignificant healer. I have always felt that K. was rather a fraud; other Sambia suggest as much, but only in gossip. His trance-states are not quite believable; the performances seem trumped-up. Because K.'s shamanism looks and feels more artificial, intellectualized, and less integrated into his personality, I interpret his shamanism (as an identity and as a role context) as more of a conscious cultural defense than, say, Sakulambei's. Take away K.'s "secondary" shamanism and you have a loss of self-esteem, social status, leaving perhaps depression. But remove Sakulambei's "primary" shamanism and you have nothing—obliteration of self, nonexistence. Those are two very different sets of dynamics and character structure.[12]

We begin with H. talking about the affective tone of interviewing K. following yesterday's positive start.

H: Your presence has put life back into the interviewing, but just where we're going, I don't know. I know what I want in the interviews with everyone else, but I don't know what I want with him.

S: That's because *he* hasn't given shape to your work together. It takes two people to give shape to a relationship.

H: That's right: he firmly said "No" to where I was going,* but he still wants to work. Yet he hasn't given me a signal.

S: [*Cuts in.*]—He hasn't told us what *he* wants. He's only told us that he doesn't want to go the route we were talking. Where did we break off yesterday, and what broke us off?

H: Only time. We had just established rapport. And there was that response to your white hair and you being someone who might answer some of his questions . . . Remember that he too is a shaman; a weak, minor shaman. He wanted it [the shaman status], and he practices it, but he does it without enthusiasm.

S: Does anyone want it from him?

H: Probably not.[13] Unless it's his sister. His sister is his mother-substitute for his mother. Now, I know what I can do to get him talking. I can just say, "I'm going to ask you about your shamanism." That's not what I really want to know about, but I don't think I'm going to learn about that. . . .

S: Tell me in two sentences what you really want to know about.

H: I want to know about his [erotic] relationships with boys. That's what I want to know about.

S: And how much do you know?

H: Not very much. I know—

S: —You know *something*. You know he has them and desires them. . . .

*Study of K.'s sexual excitement, especially its pederastic component.

H: I know he has daydreams, and I know he desires boys—I know that it still continues and basically it's—now he wants to be married. And he's got two reasons: one, because he wants children; the other reason, because boys aren't willing to go along with him anymore. [*To Weiyu*] Let's ask Kalutwo: does he have something he'd like to talk about?

K: If I do ask him [H.] for something, or if I worry about it, I can't talk out. I'll be shamed: he's [H.] not like my kinsmen that I can say just anything to him. I might cry and make him feel sorry for me.

H: What's he talking about?

W: I think he wants to ask the two of you for something.

H: OK. Ask him what it is.

K: When you go away over there [America], will you help me with a letter?

H: Yes I will.

K: I've watched others who worked with you. You don't forget them. If you did that for me, I'd get some money like you send to the others who worked for you. While you're here, I won't ask you for something: This is my country, not your own (where you've lots to give away).

H: What would you want me to give you?

K: Could I ask for something . . . like an old blanket or something like that?*

H: OK. Well, we've already talked about that; when I go out I'll send you back letters.

K: All right. That's nice. That's nice [*matter-of-fact*].

H: Now, is there something you would like to talk about, about yourself?

K: What about my shamanism?

H: I, too, was thinking about that. [*To S.*] He'd like to work on his shamanism. That's a good idea. I know that pretty well. He—it turns out he cares more for me than I thought he did.

S: I knew that right away yesterday.

H: I didn't know it. Now, whether it was because it was so guarded, or it was me, or it's the relationship; or what is it?

S: I don't know. My impression is that it's not a defect in you that

---

*What will a few dollars or a blanket add materially to K.'s life? Something, to be sure, for K. has no means of cash income (aside from the odd government roadwork or periodic census patrol labor, or others' gifts). I don't underrate that. Yet such gifts—from me—have an added significance: security, feeling wanted. You can count dollars, hourly wages, and measure blankets; but how do you measure security? Gifts between ethnographers and their friends are a complex thing: another piece of fieldwork culture that merits attention.

you wouldn't pick up. It's just that it's easy for a third person to see. Maybe the geography—you two facing each other and I as the third point on the triangle—may let me see him differently. I seem to hear him telling you . . . doing the best he can to tell you that you're—I don't like intellectualizing,* but you're his attachment object. He's never *found* one before. And it isn't all transference (in the sense of fantasy). The fact is that you *have* served him and nobody gives a *damn* about him here. He's just rubbish, right?

H: Yeah, that's right.

S: You haven't treated him like rubbish. How could he *not* feel that— because of some reality in your relationship—for the first time in his life he's got someone. And there's no way he can articulate it—to anyone.

H: Hmm. That makes sense.

S: So, to me, it's obvious. The pain there in his face is the pain of loss; since earliest childhood, a terrible sadness. He's so desperate to get close to you; but you set the rules of a game he can't understand. All he knows is that, in order to get close to you, he has to find some technique. And it's to sit down and be interviewed. I mean [*chuckles*]—I mean, it doesn't make much sense here. It makes sense in Los Angeles. But here, he has to make sense out of a totally incomprehensible way of reaching the beloved lost mother, father, object—whatever it is. And you were there sending out clear-cut signals that you would function in that way when nobody else had.† Yet he couldn't find the path through the forest to get there. And he still doesn't know how. But sometimes he's known that he's had to do it in a way that he didn't want to do it. Sometimes you touched on things so awful to him to talk about that the hope he would get good feelings from you was nullified. So he's left at a zero-point, and he just walks away—for a while— from the whole thing. Now he's in a terrible bind, because [ground down by his resistance] you withdraw. He knows you do that, and he knows that you come back . . . but will you send him letters . . . that is, will you still be there? You said you would. Nobody's ever come through before—but you're more likely to; I think he probably does believe that. And he's not into the "miss

---

*S: The circumstances—jungle, rain, mosquitoes, dinners of taro and sweet potatoes, muck— were conducive to more modest—or is it "more honest"—discourse; so we rarely intellectualized grossly.

†Right. The special—odd—discourse I mentioned in chapter 3. Only, with people like K., who need more, the therapeutic dimension of this talking is more evident, like a fire that will not burn without kindling.

you" part of this. . . . You have him available to *you*, but he's not doing what, say, Penjukwi does: she's doing it for herself. She's getting a joy out of it. The same for some of your other friends. For him, though, it's desperate, primeval.

H: That's helpful. . . . So, he says he wants to talk about his shamanism. That is as good a subject as anything else; at this point, I don't think I'm going to learn what I want to learn. [*To K.*] Dr. Stoller and I want to learn more about your *kwooluku* [the spirit familiar that makes one a shaman]. [*K. whispers to W., again on the subject of the letter.*]

W: He's talking about the letter. He says he can't get it at Mountain Patrol Station [a few days' distance].

H: Then we'll put his name on a couple of envelopes, and they can go straight to him. When S. goes back to America, he'll send a picture inside of a letter back to Kalutwo. [*K. smiles broadly and gurgles.*]

S: Hm! Biggest smile yet. How come he understands the Pidgin? Does he want a picture of the two of you? Or is that too powerful?

H: No, it's not. Do you want a picture of the two of us?

K: All right. One of me and one of the two of us?

H: Yeah.

K: All right.

S: And I can use that as an excuse for getting a picture of this room, which I really should do anyway, with the two of you talking.

K: And if you do, I'll be very, very pleased.

H: [*To S.*] He says if we do that he'll be really pleased with us.

S: Right now?

K: Yes.

S: [*Takes snaps.*] Tell him it takes a few months and I'll send it to him.

H: He says in about two moons or three moons, he'll send them along to you.

K: Fine!

H: OK, that's all. Now, Dr. Stoller would like to say this to Kalutwo: Stoller, too, is a kind of *kwooluku* [shaman].

W: Yeah, one kind of *kwooluku*-man. I thought the same thing. I thought that about him down below there. When for—

K: [*Interrupts*]—Nilutwo. We all saw him.

W: That's right. I watched him and I thought [when S. was trying to hypnotize Nilutwo]: this man, he's a *kwooluku*-man.

H: What do you think he was doing to Nilutwo?

K: The way he was looking with his eyes at N., I thought he was acting like a shaman. And that if he looks at N. like that, N. will fall down dead.

H: Dr. Stoller would like to know about Kalutwo's *kwooluku*. How does he experience it inside himself? What changes did it cause in N.? [*K. perks up, sits up a bit; has some of his old life in him.*]

K: When my familiars come to me, they come inside, and at such times my feeling is entirely different. . . . At that time my walking is—is like speeding—running . . . like a shooting arrow and very happy. You won't walk about easy, then, you just shoot along—one, two, three . . .

H: And he's talking about—?

W: —The time when the familiars want to come inside of his body.

[We discuss K.'s shamanic calling and bring up his initial trancing.]

H: But at first, when he went and lay down in his house, did the familiars come and whistle?

W: They shake around. When he [K.] starts to shake, then they all come and whistle.

H: Had you been through the *narangu* [shaman's initiation] yet?

K: No . . . the first time, I didn't see it in a dream. I started shaking and while there, it whistled. They all whistled. And then I thought: I can become a shaman. A familiar has come and stuck itself onto me, and it's making me shake. So I can become a shaman.

H: And inside of your dream, at that time, they showed you a leaf or something?

K: Yeah. Leaves, cordyline, *pit-pit* [a tall grass].

H: [*To S.*] He believes you're a kind of shaman who wants to learn about *his* shamanism. Here is what he has chosen to tell you; he's never told me this before, and I'm trying to find out what it means. He says that when he was a third-stage initiate, which would be after age sixteen, sometimes he used to walk around and go to the gardens. Sometimes, when doing that, he'd feel a bit strange. He was usually with a kinsman and his son. They went to the gardens. Then he went back to his house and lay down and started to shake a bit. At this time there was the sound of his familiar— the whistling sound you heard the other night*—which emerged

---

*S: We were in a healing ceremony, forty or so of us crammed in a hut, while K., assisting a stronger shaman, did his number, whistling, chanting, and sprinkling us with water from sacred leaves. No one took him very seriously, but they all joined in with boisterous pleasure, especially when he spritzed H. and me. I guess I was cured, but of what I never found out. (It started hours before we arrived. We squatted there from seven to midnight and then quit. The rest carried on till dawn. I was not in a trance, say I, but the hours passed outside of time; I don't know where they went.)

of its own volition. And he knew this meant that his first spirit-familiar had come to him.

S: The whistling sound the other night at the healing ceremony was not ascribed to a person but to a familiar?

H: Yeah, a spirit-familiar. Let me give you more details. . . . The setting for this first spirit-familiar visit [trance] is: he's just reached puberty; for the first time he's expected to perform as a bachelor—that is, to screw boys; he's approaching marriageable age, is having to think about sex and women; he's on his own, his mother and [biologic] father having both died within the last two or three years; he's pretty much alone in the world except for an older sister. . . . And he is reporting a trance (or pseudotrance) experience not overtly associated with anything in particular. It just happens to him; it's happened several times. He *chooses* to interpret this experience as meaning he is being selected as a shaman, even if he is without the necessary ancestry. Something in him is choosing to be a shaman.

S: Would you say this: a man who is psychologically unprepared for the tasks ahead—that is, for enthusiastic heterosexuality—at this point chooses a different route? Is that what you mean to say?

H: Right.

S: What were his responses to this first experience: honored to be chosen? frightened to be chosen?

H: First, probably scared. Then less and less scared. [*To W.*] The first time his familiar came to him, what did he feel?

H: [*While W. asks, H. says to S:*] We have gone over this material before, but there's something special about it now because he has chosen to tell *you* about it. [*As K. answers W.*] I hear what's happening here. K.'s responding as he typically does when defensive, when he doesn't want to feel. He says, "What should I feel? What do you expect me to feel?" My question "What do you feel?" is always too direct. He really has a problem feeling. That's one of the issues here.

S: You mean that the feelings are too much for him? He hasn't enough resistance against feeling? That is, his feelings are too intense, and so he must use a blunter defense, rather than just, say, a schizoid defense in which he consciously does not feel?

H: That sounds right. He hasn't enough resistance against feeling.

S: It's a possibility. It fits.

W: He says the first time he felt the familiar and it whistled, he was frightened. And that special time—not just any old time—it shows you the leaves and such like [i.e., items used in healing ceremonies]. But when he heard the whistles again, he was only pleased, not afraid. "I can," he says, "remove people's illness."

H: [*To S.*] Here's what is happening: K. has just now rolled a ciga-rette, he smokes (remember: the thing that induces the trances is smoking) as he starts to talk about his trance. He says that when he first started shaking he felt afraid, but when he *knew* he was being possessed by a familiar—that is, as distinct from just the shaking—he felt joy. "Why," I asked; the standard response he always gives—he "would be able to heal people."

S: Look at his stance now: he's turned away. He's blocked his own head so we can't see it. He's in contact with us, but in a negative way, not out of contact.

H: So defensive.* Yet, this subject of shamanism is his baby. He says he *wants* to talk about this.

S: Would he be willing to teach me anything? I mean *anything*. About shamanism. He could be generous if he would teach me. It's really true that he could teach me. Would he be willing to put into me some of his information? *Not* so I would be a shaman like him, I don't want it for that. I just want it in order to compare it to my shamanism . . . called psychoanalysis. It would be helpful to me and generous of him, like giving a feast. I'm asking *him* for some generosity.

H: Dr. S. says this: he's come a long way and he has his own famil-iars, but his familiars are of a different kind. He would be very pleased if Kalutwo would teach him something, the same as if K. were to make a feast for Dr. Stoller. [*W. gets enthused now, for he's got the flavor of what S. is trying to say through me.*]

W: Dr. S. wants you to teach him something! To tell a story about what you know.

K: [*Quietly, puzzled.*] Story about what? Say what to him?

W: Well, it's for *you* to say. It's your story. What do you want to say to him?

K: [*Cold silence. Looks at us. I sense he is bewildered, for he is so rarely asked to share his knowledge. He shares only by performing healing ceremonies.*] No.

H: No?! [*Amazed. To W.*] Ask him why.

---

*K. was saying he is pleased to be a shaman because he can help people. The shaman wants to help people, but people also fear shamans' greater sorcery power, especially in trance states when the spirit familiars take over the shaman. I see therein a defensive maneuver the shaman (this applies to Saku too) may use, a socially accepted device for controlling people at a distance. In addition, K. can be connected to others in healing ceremonies without giving of himself in other social contexts. This shaman's (K.) succorance is, then, *also* a means against being close to others in everyday life.

K: Talk about what to Dr. Stoller?

H: That's for you to decide. It's your story.

W: [*Amused to K.*] There, I told you! Say what you want to.

H: Can you teach him one little thing about getting a familiar or not? [*W. beseeches K.*]

K: [*Cold, flat.*] No.* [*Weiyu starts again, consternation in voice, which then falls off, somewhat in despair. He gives up. Long silence.*]

S: [*Quietly.*] There's no way we can get from him an explanation why—or did you even ask him why?

H: I did ask him why, and he just said "No." He's closed. And you see I'm at a loss. I don't know what's going on inside him. This is the first time since you and I have been working together here when I feel like I'm floating, lost. It's overwhelming for him. He can do it, but he doesn't want to do it.

As we tried to decide where to go next, we paused. K. and W. rolled cigarettes. We picked up the conversation, but a technical failure occurred; the batteries in the recorder had worn down and we missed about five minutes of the conversation. During these minutes our strategy changed. Faced with the failure to get K. to teach S. about shamanism, S. asked him about something else. Out of nowhere S. asked K: "What do you feel about your semen organ (*keriku-keriku*) and menstrual-blood organ (*tingu*)?" K.'s response surprised the hell out of me: he more or less denied that he had a semen organ the way other men do.† When translated to S., it didn't surprise him at all. The tape picks up here.

K: [*Low, gruff, angry voice.*] Yes, I would teach Dr. Stoller about my shamanism. But he changed the subject and asked about my *keriku-keriku*. And so I was [*stumbling*] . . . wrong, and shall shut up. What do you really want to know? [K. whispers *keriku-keriku* to W. as if it were a secret. He usually whispers about the *keriku-keriku*.] That's all; I don't know what to do now.

H: Do you want to talk more about this?

K: No. It's unpleasant.

---

*The reader need not fear that K. is simply protecting his shamanic secrets of the trade. Having interviewed over a dozen shamans and K. on this very topic, I know another motive is at work.

†Sambia believe all humans have such organs (see chapter 2). Their functions are quite different for the sexes: females get life and strength from the *tingu*, but it is nonfunctional in males; males draw all strength and masculinity from their semen organs, which, in women, are nonfunctional. For a man to assert that he has no semen organ is madness, shocking. No one had ever done it before to me.

H: I want to finish talking about this now. But first I want to understand why you don't want to talk about the *keriku-keriku.*

K: It's something that . . . the *keriku-kerikus* won't help us with our gardens; they won't go with us when we walk around. [Note the odd but not unique construction; he has animated the *keriku-keriku.*] I don't want to talk about this. Now if a man makes something, yes: then I can talk about it, but not about this, which I haven't made. [*We do not understand K. here. So W. asks him to clarify. K. shakes his head.*] Oh, yeah, yeah. The time when you, a man, make it, then I can talk about it.*

W: Oh. [*Turns to K. for clarification. K. responds curtly.*]

H: What did you say? If you make [sexual?] movements, then it [semen organ] can do something?

K: It can't do anything by itself. It won't. You, a man [the possessor] only you could control it. You, a man, that's all, can make it do something. By itself, it can do nothing.

W: [*To H.*] Now, I think you have asked him too much about the *keriku-keriku* and he wants to leave. So he's acting this way. [*Weiyu is amused and smug.*]

K: [*Exasperated.*] That's enough work for now.

H: All right, that's good enough. Now, we [H. and S.] want to say this: we ask you about the *keriku-keriku* for a good reason; we want to understand more about you and Sambia. We know it is hard for you to see what we are trying to learn. We don't want you to think we are just rambling or that we just want to give you a headache from all our questions. We need you if we are to understand.

K: [*His typical passive surrender:*] It's my fault; I don't understand. [*Long pause.*] Tomorrow he [S.] must also ask Sakulambei about the *keriku-keriku.*

H: But this . . . [*pause*] . . . it. . . . [*Pause. I am puzzled. Why does he refer us to, and link Saku with, the keriku-keriku?*] Why should we ask *him?*

K: All the shamans have *keriku-kerikus* here. You are asking about that, and so I am telling you. [Apparently, when S. asked about the *keriku-keriku,* K. took this to mean, "Do I, a minor shaman, know something special about the *keriku-keriku?*" That subject upsets K., and so he refers us to Saku, a big shaman.]

---

*S: This disordered sentence seems a combination of an unclear statement, a thought that lost its anchor when deprived (by writing it down) of its inflections, a garbled translation from Sambia to Pidgin by Weiyu, and a final translation—to English by H—cut to death by the earlier confusion.

S: At this point I break off editing the transcript of H.'s translation of the proceedings and shall use the interruption to note a few issues about editing.

Why do I now stop giving you (my edited version of) our transcript, which covers, so far, about an hour's conversation?

1. It is, in total, almost incomprehensible because of the way the participants were having trouble understanding each other.
2. K. continued to be devious, pseudostupid.
3. Background noises overwhelmed the voices so that pieces are eaten out of some sentences, spoiling the meaning on into the following intact talk.
4. The tape machine fouled up for a few moments and then worked again; perhaps we changed the batteries. (I no longer remember.)
5. Though a lot of the discussion comes through clearly on the tape and in translation, there is so little substance that I dare not risk the reader's boredom by sticking to our resolve to approximate the microscopy of our ethnography. (We comfort our scientific consciences with the thought that the transcript, in all its frazzlement, is available to colleagues, as are our original tapes.) The discussion could have been useful. It was an effort to see how Kalutwo saw himself vis-à-vis Saku, a hermaphrodite [i.e., someone with a genuine semen organ], the most respected shaman in the area. Do they both have the same kind of aberrant *keriku-keriku?* Does K. feel he is a psychic hermaphrodite?
6. As usual when confronted with K., H.'s translation powers weaken[14] as he listens to the tape and tries to render it all into English for me.]

H: So we should ask Saku? Saku understands?
K: It's hard for you to understand. So ask Saku. He will say, "This man [Kalutwo] doesn't understand. I know what you want to know and I can show you." Saku will know.
H: Oh, yes. I've heard some say that before.* [*Weiyu breaks in:*] "True, that's true" [*agreeing with K.*]. You tried to show me in the past but I didn't understand: do you think that your *keriku-keriku* is the same as Sakulambei's?

This was a tricky question. By referring us to Sakulambei, K. was (consciously? unconsciously?) comparing himself with Saku, who is

*That is, Saku is enormously knowledgeable about shamanism.

friendly to him. What did that comparison mean? At some level, K. is identifying with Saku. On the surface, K. suggests we should ask Saku because the latter is a powerful shaman. On another level, though, every Sambia man knows he possesses a semen organ, and most could tell what it does in their sexual development. (Compare Weiyu, for instance, in the next chapter.) I was wondering at this moment, then, if somehow K. was identifying himself not just with Saku's shamanic role, but with his hermaphrodism too. Few if any Sambia men—shamans included—would refer us to a hermaphrodite to clarify questions about (normal) male sexual functioning. One might argue that K. believed this was an appropriate and efficient suggestion because he knew we were interviewing Sakulambei at this period. I disagree: the fact remains that K. resisted describing his own views about the semen organ; he was trying to fob us off by saying, "Go ask Sakulambei," and he implied thereby that Saku knew the truth we were seeking about the semen (his) organ. Other men would say that hermaphrodites are so flawed that they could say nothing about maleness (semen organs). In all these respects, K.'s presentation of himself differs from other men's.

K: They're not different. [*Now Weiyu breaks in, saying,* "They're (semen organs) the same." *K. becomes expansive.*] Everywhere, America and wherever, it [the *keriku-keriku*] is the same. There aren't other kinds.

H: Oh, he thinks that he and Sakulambei are the same? [W. translates; and as K. talks, W. lets out a great belly laugh twice; apparently Kalutwo has finally tuned in on me. He starts to whisper. Then W. adds: "Oh, you're [H.] all right," sensing the odd comparison with Saku.]

K: Now I understand a bit. I know you're asking me about—

After K. has referred us to Saku for the facts on the *keriku-keriku*, he realized the implications of his comparison: that I suspected he was comparing his maleness with that of a hermaphrodite. Now his voice changes, and he visibly struggles to clarify what he was trying to say. He whispers to W., who replies in a gruff, grudging voice, "Oh, I understand" (speaking for K.). W. to K.: "That's all right; I know." K. breaks in again here and starts to whisper to W.

K: [*Whispering now.*] Are you asking about the penis or . . . ?

H: I didn't ask you about that; I asked about the *keriku-keriku*; is it the same as his [Sakulambei] or not? [*While saying this Weiyu nods his head saying,* "Yeah, it's the same keriku-keriku; yeah, I *know, the* keriku-keriku, *yeah."*] Is that [*keriku-keriku*] the same as yours?

K: [*Emphatic now.*] No, it's not the same.

H: [*To W.*] But he first said that I must ask Saku about that. [*Weiyu breaks in and starts translating rather nervously to K. Then, in an angry voice, K. responds.*]

W: K. was just talking about him being a shaman, that's all. He's a man-shaman and you asked me [about that].

K: About me. A man, yes: the *keriku-keriku* is the same, that's all, but now we're talking about shamanism.

H: Yeah.

W: Sometime in the future, S. can ask Saku about all this.

H: What does he mean. . . . I don't understand.* [*K. breaks in and starts talking louder.*]

W: What was it? Yeah. [H:? I'm lost.]

Throughout this period K.'s voice has been soft, a gruff whisper; his voice has a lot of movement, different from before. We got him worked up asking about his semen organ. He became angry, and some of that anger was in his voice. But the quietness, the tenseness in the whispering is about the secret—the shared secret—of Sakulambei's hermaphrodism, with the implication that it is shameful for people to talk about it. Especially, one should never speak of it in front of Saku, who would be greatly shamed and humiliated, which could set off an explosion. Note, too, that Saku and K. are on good terms— shamans and members of the same great-clan—and they both have aberrant marital histories. Their identification with each other is per-haps closer than anyone has said. But we then hear denial in K.'s voice, when—at the end—he realized what he implied: that he was like Saku in his anatomy, that they both had the same *keriku-keriku,* or that K. was different from other men and more like Saku. K. con-tinues talking louder, a bit frantically, with a new quality in his voice. (I've listened to the tape several times to get it.) The sense is that K. is scowling: "nasty" best describes that scowl. It is as if he is talking to spit something out (perhaps the identification with Saku).

---

*There was no input by S. in this segment until the end. I thought perhaps he had gone out, but I double-checked and he was there. S: I was. But K. included me out, never looking at me, never even pointedly not looking. He rarely looked at H., rarely at Weiyu. Mostly his eyes look down, his face wary, sad, angry, accusatory, with sudden, appropriate moments of smiling when sharing a light remark with W. He surprises me deeply that such bone-aching misery—his face has been sculpted by it—can pass for a moment. I have no sense that his depression is just dependency, manipulation.

W: [*Emphatically.*] You and me, us men. . . .

K: Yeah, the *keriku-keriku*, yours and mine, it's the same in all of us. [K. uses the word "penis" here and also *"tai,"* meaning girl, pointing out the contrast between the two sexes. Here, the external anatomy is the visible sign of the inner state being discussed via the *keriku-keriku*.] We are talking about the shamans here. I'm not the same as a man. Shamans with their ability in a trance state can [like X-ray vision] see what is inside someone. I can't see inside his body. Ask *him* [Saku, what he has inside].

H: [*Silence.*] All right. [*Quiet voice.*] Good enough.

K: Can we see what's inside me?

W: [*Animated, mocks such magical power.*] Something inside there? Some betel nut inside? [He points to a net string bag as if one can as easily see inside the body.] There's betel nut inside of there? Let me have some! [*Otherwise*] . . . you should put it away in another place. Now, this something [semen organ] belonging to all of them—you and me, we don't know. Have they [hermaphrodites] got one? We don't know. [*Going over the same ground.*]

H: All right.

W: That's *enough*, let's stop. [*Anxious to finish.*]

H: [*To S.*] This is . . .

S: He's [W.] dying. I mean this man [K.] is tearing at the interpreter's inside. . . . We'd better close things off.

H: S. is very happy, pleased that you have told us these things. We'll work again . . .

K.'s great reluctance to leave is described above and in chapter 10. For several reasons, S. and I never did work again with him. In 1981 I found K. much the same, though sadder. And ditto in later years.

KALUTWO—FINAL THOUGHTS.*

K. was terribly difficult yesterday. Our session was long, frustrating, exciting, tedious, revealing. It taught me more about resistance, especially K.'s resistance to me and W.'s resistance to translating. And about the translator's role, how unconscious forces can constrain his behavior and ultimately the information collected in any domain, es-

---

*Written the day after this session; I usually write process notes of some kind after interviews; periodically, I review notes in the field to write summary formulations on each person studied closely.

pecially those troublesome to the translator, thereby influencing the meaning of fieldwork data.

Before Bob arrived, K. and I were at a standstill. I wanted data on K.'s homoerotic relationships with boys, and why he needed them, but he pulled back. I treated him better than anyone ever had, and K. wanted unendingly to be with me. But his way of wanting me—his prickly passivity—confused and exhausted me; so I would give up on him. (Even now—1982—immersing myself in this material for over three hours while translating, it tires me to review K.'s material as it does no other.) And, as Bob says, more than K.'s sexual aberrance, there is his interpersonal aberrance—which other people dislike. He is hostile, and people not only pull back from him, but, like W., they respond to him with hostility and humiliating putdowns. K. is doomed to his terrible self-fulfilling prophecies (a sad merry-go-round he can't get off). For all that, Bob claimed he could see in K. how much K. loved me.

Bob said to me: Is it necessary that every Sambia hamlet have a rubbish man like K.—whom men can humiliate and treat like this? I responded with Levy's (1973:471–473) suggestion about the Tahitians: the *mahu* (transvestite) is present in every village as a sign (for other men) of how *not* to be masculine. Bob then says that while K. has developed and is being perceived in this way, no one set out to do this to him; once stigmatized, however, he became a convenient target for men. Kalutwo's pain, embarrassment, and need to explain himself again—when we misunderstood K.'s statement about the hermaphrodites—results in humiliation on K.'s part because K. didn't communicate clearly that "I am a man." So, in having to clarify, he subordinated himself to W.

An important contrast can be made between K. and Imano here: though men clearly assign Imano to the category of gentle man (as they don't with K.), the passivity of each is fundamentally different. Imano communicates to me about himself without hostility; in fact he's one of the least hostile Sambia men I know. He likes himself, enjoys his life and his wives; he knows who's boss when it is necessary; he allows them to push him around in little ways and sometimes in big ways. He can laugh at himself and take other men's jokes; he will even make himself the brunt of their jokes, for example, in admitting how he likes to spend so much time with his first wife. K. could never do this; his only humor is sarcasm, which he can aim only at others. He is passive but resists being passive. When describing himself, he sees himself only as the object of what others have done to him; his marriages were disasters because his clan brothers sneaked around and "stole" his wives, or because the wives committed "adultery" and humiliated him. Yet, by Sambia standards, he was worse than a terrible husband; he was no man at all.

Bob asked K. how he felt about his semen organ: where did S. pluck that question from? It was the right button: K. smiled, got embarrassed, became defensive, then hostile, and so did W. This led to valuable information, though not so much in what K. said, as by what he denied. I was startled that K. denied that he had a semen organ; what a remarkable answer, even if by misunderstanding. His ambivalence, confusion, and associating to his spirit familiars, including the way he said it all—"unmanly," in Bob's terms—was extraordinary. But the session came to a dead halt when K., stated he would talk no more about the semen organ. We said that K. was so uptight in this session, but he was also concerned and interested. And he wanted something more, especially a promise that I would send him letters when I left. Bob says that this—trustworthy love—is what K. really wanted.

S: All of H.'s interpreters became very attached to him. Undoubtedly, he chose them and they chose him because there existed from the start the *anlagen* for strong attachment. The form these reactions took in his friends we can call, for the sake of this discussion, "transference." For the nature of his interviews with each of them was so intimate in content and feelings that a therapy-like atmosphere was established. As different from anyone they had ever experienced, he wanted to listen to them, to understand them, and therefore they felt— in fact, they *were*—important to him, in ways they had never been with anyone before. He was benign, giving, and insightful, and this was coupled with his—to them—highly aberrant state of being an outsider. So they were more vulnerable to his presence—less defended against it—than they had ever been to anyone before. Nothing in their culture gave them defenses in advance, the way we would be equipped in our culture. As far as I can tell, the only advantage he got from this was better data. (I wonder—we can never know, since the reports are silent—to what extent other ethnographer–informant relationships become intimate and lead to nonresearch payoffs.)

As we saw, however, Kalutwo's case teaches us that transference reactions not only can lead to deeper, truer information but they can— probably must—lead also to resistance about giving up one's interior to another. In the transference situation, advantage and disadvantage are not only inextricably mixed but disadvantage—if one is able to look well—is hidden advantage. For, as every analyst knows with his or her patients, in the resistance is information about how one has dealt, from infancy on, with certain situations.

H. has been immersed in this transference from the start. Then, especially but not exclusively with my supervising, he became—in my view—better able to use that situation and less at its mercy. He came to see that content is shaped by relationship, and relationship is part of content. So, since the culture both *is* and *is in* the interpreter, the relationship offers the ethnographer, at any moment, a biopsy of the culture, both its structure and its specific content.

The problem for the ethnographer in dealing with transference reactions is that, so far, most ethnographers have no sense of the concept as theory or as living experience. They are, then, as Devereux (1967) says, at its mercy, unable to deal with it and therefore prone to countering it with their own distortions (that is, countertransference). In this way, they may not only lose information but increase the resistance, so that information will be more actively withheld and even more distorted. We saw that effect in action with the translator's pain in dealing with Kalutwo's unmanliness and other aberrances.

We should not avoid these issues simply because they complicate the education of ethnographers and their data collecting.

We find another example of the value of clinical experience in H.'s coming to see Kalutwo as having a homosexual orientation and thereby different from the other men. When H. and I began working together, early in those two years before I joined him in New Guinea, he knew of no one he would label as "a homosexual." In good part, he thought this because he found no one who seemed a homosexual by the criteria of our culture. My first position with him—based on simple ignorance plus statistical inference—was that there had to be homosexual Sambia men. As he began to fill me in on his friends, K. certainly stuck out as aberrant but only in his being chronically depressed, without friends, not interested in the things that were so important to the other men. Only gradually, on absorbing H.'s reports—this, remember, being before I met Kalutwo—did I suspect that K's aberance was gender/erotic as well. Then H.'s observations fell in place, and we both saw that K.'s erotic attachment was to males, not females (in fact, to boys, though I do not believe this should be called pedophilia, since the loving of boys is not aberrant but a necessary part of Sambia culture).

H.'s technique of data gathering has the strength that one can better find what goes on inside his interpreters; in that way, he has entrée into forms—external and internal—of the culture not available to an outsider. On the other hand, his method is so slow and so dependent on the relationship between ethnographer and interpreter that one may never get an adequate account of the degree to which the *meaning* of something, for example, an erotic practice or a ritual, is shared among all the people of a community. Good ethnography, if aimed at understanding the whole of a culture, needs both the interpersonal/dynamic and the normative/statistical techniques of cultural study.

POSTSCRIPT: 1987

H: It is now many years since my study of Kalutwo was begun and ended. Nothing has changed in K.'s life since that time. He is still a gender misfit, but he is also, by Sambia lifespan ages, an older, nearly aged, man. During my last visits (1985, 1988) I found him still unmarried and unhappy. My occasional letters to him—promised years ago—have not kept us in touch, for he cannot read these without a translator, and he has never responded to them; but at least we have had contact. He seemed still shy and awkward and obtuse and trying-to-be-close to me, however; and I seemed more respectful and understanding of him and the turmoil to which I subjected him. We could be cordial with one another but nothing more.

S.'s discussion of transference and countertransference is entirely appropriate and illuminating in the case of Kalutwo. Editing this chapter one last time has been painful to me, in part because of how much better I now understand our interviews. I have always felt that alone of all the several score people I have interviewed and tried to understand, my attempts with K. were a failure.

Only through training with S. did I come to see *through* K.'s words and roles—and in this sense, his defenses against his own gender aberrance and erotic problems. And only later have I come to see better how at the time I lacked the psychologic skills to be of more help to him and to my work. This pain and feeling of failure has made me at times want to edit out whole pages of the text in which I felt I looked and acted stupid, insensitive, and uncaring. I have even felt like cutting the whole chapter and throwing it in a drawer marked: "Not to be opened until retirement."

It would of course be dishonest to do so and my integrity—not my common sense—has kept me from committing this act of ultimate censorship. Yet this is only the negative side of what I learned working with Kalutwo. The positive side is how I grew and desired never to repeat such mistakes. For we learn in this way too—looking back with more experience and perhaps, sometimes, with wisdom as well.

Unless we ethnographers are willing to make available to readers (especially our students) our failures as well as our successes, we shall profit little as a discipline from our human studies; moreover, we invite being treated badly by the next generation, who will find it hard to believe we could have always been so infallible and, in that way, inhuman.

CHAPTER TEN

The Interpreter's Discomfort

H: Usually we* think of interpreters as technical aids, language machines. Interpreters don't make waves. Even anthropologists tend toward this view. Field interpreters are not judged as whole persons but rather as: competence, reliability, and usefulness; defined as: language skills, intelligence, and facility for translation.† Though we know there are other problems, the technical view holds by and large; the other problems have often been ignored.

We know, for instance, that people vary in their capacity to learn languages and translate from them across cultural or ethnic boundaries. We know also that translators and informants may face what—for lack of a better term—one might call "identity problems" in their work. Textbooks used to recognize these problems by advising discretion in choosing interpreters corrupted[2] by too much western experience.

Most anthropologists want to work in the native language without interpreters. A few do not. (I think one's wanting to learn a foreign language measures desire for empathy and identification with those people.[3]) But probably many fieldworkers in exotic cultures rely on interpreters, for, obviously, ethnographers vary in their language-learning capacities. Language families also vary in complexity. In a place such as New Guinea, with over 1,000 languages, most of them unwritten and unrecorded, there is great variation. Malinowski quickly became proficient in Kiriwinian, because it is a straightforward Mel-

---

*S: We who are not interpreters.
†One should distinguish between *interpreters,* who change verbal statements into another language, and *translators,* who are also responsible for deciphering and setting down written texts in another language. The latter task Evans-Pritchard saw as *the* problem of anthropology.[1]

anesian language with a written grammar available. Mead usually used Pidgin, not the vernacular, in New Guinea, for she worked for brief periods among groups with difficult non-Austronesian languages.[4] Therefore, many New Guineast ethnographers have worked in trade languages or *lingua franca*, at least at first, or when working with certain subgroups (e.g., women), or on particular topics (e.g., religion). Interpreters have been widely used, probably by most of these ethnographers, for significant periods. The extent of this reliance is belied by puny acknowledgments: a sentence or two soon forgotten.[5]

More important, we have not studied the personality or motives of the interpreter in the ethnographic project. Obviously, if one is simply trying to record objective, shared patterns (norms, values, etc.), using language machines—the false idea of the anthropologist-as-scientist and his interpreter and/or informant—subjective elements such as motivations play no part. *If* ethnographers act differently, their reports should behave differently: all but a rare few reports do not.[6] This chapter concerns such neglected factors. We want to look inside one interpreter to understand better the interpreter's interpreting. Our object is Weiyu's discomfort in working with Kalutwo.

Let us begin with the way interpreters are depicted in most ethnographies: nameless, voiceless, noiseless.[7] A worse lot than the ethnographer, who is at least heard (but not seen). What of the interpreter's age, sex, intelligence, incentives, life history, social or political status, temperament? Or degree of familiarity with the ethnographer: are they (like the faceless informant) strangers or friends; how long have they worked together; under what circumstances and for what purposes? These factors influence the interpreter's interpreting. Most ethnographers recognize such factors, I suspect, in choosing interpreters, but they do not say so in print.

Distortions also occur when interpreters try to normalize or screen out what they either cannot understand, empathize with, are troubled by, or feel would embarrass the interviewer. With psychiatric studies, this translation-distortion problem is acute.

Clinician to Spanish-speaking patient: What about worries, do you have many worries?

Interpreter to patient: Is is [sic] there anything that bothers you?

Patient's response: I know, I know that God is with me, I'm not afraid, they cannot get me. [*Pause*] I'm wearing these new pants and I feel protected, I feel good, I don't get headaches anymore.

Interpreter to clinician: He says that he is not afraid, he feels good, he doesn't have headaches anymore (Marcos 1979:173).

What suffers in anthropology is the ethnographic description, our main concern here.

Perhaps it is unfair to Weiyu, subjecting him to such scrutiny in his interpreting for Kalutwo, a man so frustrating that he drove us both crazy. I might have chosen to scrutinize the process with Moondi or Penjukwi.[8] But only with Weiyu did S. and I work for any length of time. So in keeping with the book's emphasis, Weiyu will serve as our subject. I believe, however, that if we were to dissect any text produced by an interpreter anywhere, we would discover similar subjective factors—more or less overt—permeating its interpretation. Besides, Weiyu himself started the dialogue. He would let me use him here.

Weiyu and I have taught each other about interpreting. Though illiterate and limited in his knowledge of western experience, he was not a naive interpreter, as chapter 5 makes clear. He was highly motivated, enjoyed interpreting, and fitted it easily into his daily routines (e.g., gardening). He had earlier worked on coastal plantations, where he learned Pidgin and Motu, for four years in the early 1970s, before marrying. (He is more fluent in Pidgin. He also speaks a little of two language groups bordering Sambia; so his linguistic range is equal to, or greater than, mine.*) His language skills are not unique; many Sambia speak several languages. Tali, for instance, is fluent in two other Anga languages besides Sambia, and younger men speak Pidgin too. Their Pidgin, though, is colloquial (bush Pidgin), picked up through informal contacts. It is sufficiently different that you must learn each local form from scratch or miss important idiomatic variations, such as in lexical meaning.[9] The more Weiyu and I worked together, the more familiar we became with each other's personality and speech styles. [S: What a huge difference in ease and accuracy must be there when translator and ethnographer are close.]

After months of work, and wanting richer interviews, I realized that I had to teach Weiyu how I wanted him to interpret for me, a procedure that John Whiting et al. (1966:156–159) has recommended and carefully discussed in his early methodologic work. I learned this skill earlier with Moondi, when doing detailed interviews with initiates. (I had never done research in another language and had never

---

*I'm not great at learning languages. I can read French, but years of classroom Spanish are almost gone. I speak, read, and write Pidgin fluently. My Sambia is conversationally equivalent to Weiyu's knowledge of the neighboring languages of Sambia.

used an interpreter. During training, I never learned that one has to coach interpreters, much less that one has to teach them to be effective. I might not have known to, had I not worked in a psychiatric setting some years before and seen diagnostic interviewing done.) At first, I was concerned mainly with getting the interpreter to render as exactly as possible everything said. But here, both Moondi's and Weiyu's translating sacrificed *completeness*: errors of omission (leaving out words, sentences), of substitution[10] (e.g., inappropriate words or concepts or—more gross and this happened less—substituting their view for the interviewees'), and condensations (glossing whole statements with a word, odd constructions, or rendering an ambiguous construction as simply "good" or "bad," "yes" or "no," etc.).

And then of course informants—suggestible—take cues from the interpreter.* The more Sambia I learned, the more these errors decreased. My questions sharpened; I knew the areas to watch carefully; I picked up errors more quickly. I found myself pleading or demanding that Moondi or Weiyu say exactly what they felt they had heard, no matter how meaningless to them. They found this at times tedious and frustrating. So I praised their faithfulness to the translation, let them know I understood how the work could make them tense, and sometimes debriefed them after sessions.[11] I was careful but, at first (1974–1976), not dedicated enough, which led to inaccuracies in those original data.

In 1979, though, I approached the interviewing differently, less concerned with general cultural patterns and more focused on individual expressions. I tape-recorded nearly all important interviews. I had learned from S. to go for details; had learned that often, in areas such as sexual excitement, moods, or fantasy, without details, you have little useful information.

By this time Weiyu and Moondi had worked with me a long time. I knew their personalities and speech styles well and they mine. We were research collaborators, and, in our closeness, our interviewing was raised to new levels of subtlety. I concentrated on exploring meanings, as in the connotations of verbs and nouns, going for depth of a person's experience and sacrificing breadth to do it.† For the first time I also imported western concepts, like "fantasy," and uncovered

---

*I don't know that this effect has been studied in ethnographic work, but I found the following statement by a linguist: "Despite taking some precautions, in some cases I have detected an increase of up to twenty percent in the number of words cognate with the interpreter's language due to the suggestive effect the interpreter has on the informant" (Healey 1964:5).

†I could afford this loss after spending two years on more sociocultural matters.

native equivalents to ideas such as "excitement." Once Moondi and I agreed on meanings, he helped teach Weiyu (see chapter 4). So, for instance, after a few weeks' work with Kalutwo, I could use Weiyu to question K. in detail about his erotic fantasy and related sexual excitement and be reasonably sure—after a few sessions—that I knew how Kalutwo's experiences, via Weiyu's translations, were connected to my questions.

[S: We cannot be sure H.'s concern with subjectivity brings truer data than the objectivity of a pigeon-training behaviorist, but we know everyone believes it *can*—even the latter scientist when he listens to music, enjoys Shakespeare, or loses his appetite to a surly waiter.] Validity does not, ultimately, rest in those tapes. It is in me, in Weiyu, and in the particular constructions I make in the text. [S: In other words, nowhere.] If you question the validity of these texts, you should. That is the point. All texts should be subjected to such scrutiny.

This chapter consists of an interview we had with Weiyu. It follows immediately on the last session in chapter 9. (These two sessions are separated by only a couple of minutes.) After we worked with Kalutwo, Weiyu arranged to get K. out of the house so W. could talk with us alone. Why?

Chapter 9 shows how frustrating it was to work with Kalutwo. He was temperamental, touchy, ambivalent, secretive, passive–aggressive, dependent, irritable. But he would stay with it, even allow more. It was tiring: an hour with K. was more than three with Imano or Penjukwi.

Weiyu's resistance to interpreting for K. grew with the weeks. Still, Weiyu was patient.[12] He never refused to work with K., for in his status as my assistant, a man like W. could not quit. And he did other interviews for me without difficulty. But in interpreting K., he could not deny his boredom, frustration, short temper, lateness for interviews, greasing me for extra tobacco or coffee to get through it; and then immediately afterward changing the subject or heading off somewhere else. Though barely there at first, by S.'s arrival these tactics were glaring.

Meanwhile, my impatience and frustration with Kalutwo had also increased. I'd pressed him and got nowhere. To press K. was to press Weiyu. Reviewing and translating the tapes these past two years, I am surprised how hostile I was to K. (but sparing W.). Sometimes it is subtle, but S. picked it up easily. No other interviewee made me do this. (In retrospect, the tapes have taught me that only tapes give good enough records to see more fully one's own subjectivity.*) Even after months of close interviewing, you see, I was not in touch with my total experience. I did not know I was responding from unconscious sources (countertransference) to K.

S: Partly, only partly. When someone's life work is to drive others crazy, only countertransference, culture blindness, or organic brain disease could keep us who interview him or her from a spot of irritation. I would judge H.'s response to be countertransference only when he took advantage of K.'s vulnerability.

Note to psychoanalytic colleagues: I think it is a mistake to call all the therapist's/researcher's responses countertransference. It's true we forever pack our pasts with us and therefore transfer those old times into the present. Still, there are times when our behavior is dominated by such distortions (neurotic perceptions), and times not. Roughly speaking, I'd say that, when treating patients or listening to interpreters—where the task, scientifically and ethically, is to hear what the other tries to communicate—countertransference is neurosis that spoils our sense of the other. If we call everything countertransference, then we have no measure of where we end and the other begins. And that is indulgence.

H: Into this complexity stepped S. He could not know the subtleties. Yet his arrival changed the behavior of all three of us. Kalutwo, frightened and angered, ran away, then returned, wanting to talk again. My hope for working with him was renewed, and S.'s presence helped me be more empathic again.[13] In those sessions, however, Weiyu did not noticeably change, until the end. His reaction to K. after finishing was climactic. He came to us, then, cursing, expressing how he really felt about K.—months of accumulated frustration spilled out. S.'s presence allowed Weiyu to do that. His response is psychodynamically and culturally complex. It differs from an earlier session (chapter 5) in which Weiyu and Tali loosened up, challenged by S.'s questions on their beliefs. Instead, indignant at Kalutwo's responses to S., Weiyu demanded to speak with us and set the record straight. I had held Weiyu back, discouraged him from discussing K.'s aberrance. He had had only me with whom to share his frustrations, and I hadn't listened.[14] S. made Weiyu's silence more unbearable, so he spoke up.
    The episode begins here, as K. leaves (p. 330).

*I can agree with Healey (1964:18) who remarks that "Listening to such recordings is a kind of shock therapy."

H: This is a real—a real . . . [*much confusion*] discovery for me: another dimension of my relationship with Weiyu, the meaning of an interpreter, and the meaning of the data I've collected from Kalutwo. I didn't have that before now . . . . It's the right question—and now it's so obvious to me . . . it's so obvious . . . so even if the whole session came to no more than this—which it didn't—it produced something important . . .

S: . . . It's a study of the methodology of anthropology, in which we were trying to demonstrate how crucial is not just the information, but the interpreter as well.

H: And not just in general about the interpreter but specific issues about the interpreter: it's so obvious that Weiyu's hostile. Why didn't I see it all along?

S: I swear, he [W.] could not look at that man [K.] . . . and for all these hours. At times he was ready to laugh out loud and had to put his hand up like this* to prevent the—whatever it is you intend when you put your hands up to block someone out . . . . [At other times] he put his head in his hands and couldn't even go on; he couldn't translate right; he couldn't talk . . .

H: It's so obvious; why didn't I see it?[†] I've been hammering my head against him for two months [*S. chuckles*]—a *long* time. And it's so obvious, now that you've said it . . . . It's been very difficult.

S: This man [K.] is tearing at the interpreter's whole life: the ritual cult, the initiations. This guy stands as proof—threat—of what can go wrong, what the whole culture is structured to prevent, to deny.[‡] In a different way from the way a woman [for Sambia men]

---

*We were all seated around a table in my interview room. I sat on one end, Weiyu sat next to me on the adjacent side, K. sat next to him, and S. faced them (on my right adjacent side). We were all within four feet of each other; W. was seated about two feet from me, and a foot from K. W. faced S., though during the session he became increasingly worn down and would sometimes look down at the table or at the opposite wall. Half the time he sat up. During the last half he leaned against the table with his elbow propped up on it, his arm supporting his head. This was his left arm, the one closest to K. His arm was a partition between them; most of the time K. could not see W.'s face because of the arm, nor did W. turn to look at him. I don't think W. was conscious of this body language. Nor was I. But S. was.

[†]I'm being unfair to myself. I did know both consciously and subliminally that Weiyu was hostile to K.; there are many examples in my notes before S. came along. But I did not know the extent of W.'s hostility, nor did I see the gross form we are about to see. S.'s presence did something to the situation that spread the hostility. He asked K. about the semen organ, and this, I think, set W. off. My interviewing and observing many others besides K. disturbed my focus then (in a way as they would not now, because I am more aware via S. of this aspect), and perhaps I needed those others to defuse my hostility too. (All that is aside from the facts of the rain, malaria, and my too many other projects.) Last, I would add—apropos chapter 1 and what I have written elsewhere—that living in a tribal village somehow blunts certain subliminal awareness, keeping them from reaching full consciousness. We discuss this point in chapter 11.

[‡]Aberrant people constantly do that to us. Perversion is subversion.

stands as proof of what goes wrong. This—K.—is another whole category. This is a category of: a-man-doesn't-turn-into-a-woman, a-man-turns-into-*that*. Is that right?

H: That's right.

S: And Weiyu is terrified by the "nonsense" of this failed man.

A baby screams in the next room at the top of its lungs; a horrible noise. Both K. and W. rise to leave. We agree to work together again tomorrow afternoon. K. asks us if we are going to Wop, where a feast will be held soon. I say that only S. will go. K. still tarries. Silence, Then W. says, "Enough. That's enough for now." But K. is not budging. I tell W. that I want to work with him further, a signal for K. to leave, getting us all off the hook. Another silence, and then the door creaks.

S: He's still not going out the door. [*We watch.*] Is that amazing or is it amazing? Is that the way he usually leaves?

H: No. It is amazing. [*It was five minutes before K. left.*]

S: That's not the way he usually leaves?

H: I'm drained: he's just a mass of ambivalence.

W: [*Rises.*] I'll go look—

H: [*Cuts in.*] Yeah, you go look [if K. has really gone] and come back.

H: [*To S.*] He [W.] just winked at me as he went out the door [to indicate that he'd see about K.].

S: Look for what?

H: He just winked at me this moment as he went out the door; Weiyu; now, just now, this moment. [*The baby screams again.*] Hey, what's going on out there?

W: [*Thinking I am talking to him.*] No, all the others—they've got to go first—we can't talk with all this clamor.

By now my house is filled with people. Imano has his baby, who is distressed for some reason. Two small boys are raising hell amid a group of oldsters gabbing and lounging on the floor. Kwinko (my cook) is tearing out his hair trying to get some order. I shoo the boys out, leaving the elders (who understand no Pidgin) alone. K. finally leaves.

S: A complex game is being played. K., in a maneuver parents and psychiatrists in our culture would recognize, both wants to go and wants to stay. He will not continue the conversation, so he leaves the room but then hovers in the adjoining room (where before he has remained for hours), jealously concerned with the conversations that continue behind the closed doors.

But he will not stay today, for the conversation is to be about him. W. wants to unburden himself about the effort to work with K. So K.—poor, tenacious, angry, deprived, suspicious, intelligent, self-destroying, sensitive, helpless, yearning K.—must be pried loose from the hut.

H: [*To S.*] Weiyu was just doing a number so he could get rid of the informant* and we could work again. He did that as an excuse.
S: Did what?
H: What he just did. It's too complicated to explain. But—
S: The baby screaming?
H: The baby screaming is—do you want the whole story? The story is this: Imano has been waiting for his interview with us. He's got his baby with him. W. and Imano cleverly agreed to kick the baby out so it would seem Imano could be with us. But that was just a ploy to fool K. into leaving so we could talk about him. This was a conspiracy between Weiyu and the next guy to get rid of the informant [Kalutwo] who has now just left.
S: How did that get rid of the informant?
H: By making it seem like we were going to work with the next guy, when we were really not going to yet.
S: Then otherwise K. would have just hung around by the fire?
H: Right.

Let us review this scenario. For Weiyu to talk with S. and me, he wanted K. away. But K. wouldn't budge. (Did he suspect we would talk about him?) So W., on his own (without talking to me), decided to get rid of K. by making it seem we were to work with Imano, whom we were to see next.† Part of the ploy was to separate Imano from his baby. That's why the baby started screaming: the child didn't want to leave his father. Now W., S., and I are alone.

S: Where are we? We are about to sit down and talk to Weiyu. And he wanted this. He needs a session after the translation? Was that your impression?
H: Well, he's the one who got rid of everyone. We'll ask him.

---

*"Informant" is the word, not "Kalutwo," so that the latter will not know about whom we are talking.
†Imano left and returned later for an interview.

W: This work with K. on the *keriku-keriku*: [*low, embarrassed laugh*] how could I know?

H: Do you, for yourself, want to talk about that?

W: Yeah. Let's not work on anything else. Let's talk about *that* man. [*Lowers voice, with emphasis.*] What kind of thinking does he have anyway?

Note to myself, 1981, on hearing the tape: There's a vengeful quality in his voice. I hadn't realized what it meant until just now. When I allowed him the chance to talk about other things, he said, "No, let's talk about that man and what kind of a mind he has." I see S. was right: at this moment, W. needs to talk this out. K. is a thorn in his side, this man who is so aberrant.

W: [*Mimicking K. disparagingly.*] "What kind of work?" What kind of talk is this of his? What kind of *jerungdu*? [*Then regular voice.*] He doesn't have *jerungdu* [courage, prowess, balls]. This kind of thinking. It's like women's! Myself—Weiyu—yes: I understand the semen organ. I've got *jerungdu*. And yes, it's [semen organ] got its *own* strength; only it can strengthen us and make us strong men. That's it. [*He is frantic in voice to get it out and to say it as strongly as he can. He has held it in so well, during the long chore of translating.*] We don't have something else. The *keriku-keriku* is our boss. That's all there is to strengthen us so that we can say, "I'm a real man." That's how I grew up. What about him? What do you two think of him?

H: Yeah.

W: You two interviewed him about his *keriku-keriku*. I'm still thinking about what you asked him; I haven't forgotten.

H: Now, you're thinking that the *keriku-keriku* makes men strong.

W: Yeah, that's it. It's for making us mature and grow strong. If he [a male] grows up with that, he will be a strong man. When he grows up, it strengthens him, his bones. That's the function of this *keriku-keriku* [*whispers that word*]. When I go to make a child,* only that one thing growing inside will strengthen its bones. It controls that process. And later it will be inside of him, strengthening him.

H: OK. I'm going to tell Dr. Stoller now. [*To S.*] He says, "This guy's

---

*A baby is created from the substances. The father contributes semen: after many ejaculations, he has stored enough in the woman that the process begins. The semen gives the baby (male or female) strength, which is nontangible, but also bones, muscle, and the *keriku-keriku*. The woman contributes blood, which becomes the soft anatomy and, in males, a constant remnant of femaleness that personifies the unending struggle [S: to which Kalutwo succumbed] against bisexuality.

thoughts are just screwy; he talks like a woman." [*S. whistles low.*] Then he says, "Kalutwo doesn't know what he's talking about. You and everyone knows what the *keriku-keriku* does. It gives you strength; it gives you bone; it gives you manliness; it gives you semen; it's what produces babies."

S: What does he feel Kalutwo said that was like a woman?

H: [*To W.*] You said that K.'s talk is the same as a—

W: [*Interrupts*]—the same thinking as a woman's. [*Excited.*] The women don't understand much when you ask them about some things. All they say is, "Uh, uh" [*motions as if women are dumb and don't know what to say*] . . . . Only when you show them "Here, here, this something" [*he points*], only then will they understand. Only then they'll understand. [*Letting off steam.*] You two worked hard with K. asking him, asking him hard about the *keriku-keriku*. And he didn't understand! . . . I don't know. Does he understand, or doesn't he? First, he said he doesn't have a *keriku-keriku*. Then he turned around a little later, and you [H.] said, "All right, if you don't have a *keriku-keriku*, if you think you don't have semen, then . . . [*Weiyu emits a little sound and kicks, as if kicking a dog away:*] Get out! Fucking! I'm tired of this little dog here, this kind of dog! [*He scowls.*] It's not good. It doesn't make sense at all, that kind of dog! Sorry, he's just a different kind.

H: [*Confused by Weiyu's pejorative analogy.*] Huh?

W: No. I'm still thinking about that man [Kalutwo]. That man—his talk, it's not straight . . . . [*Shakes head and voice trails off, with depair.*]

H: [*Quiet voice.*] What are you sorry about, Weiyu?

W: I'm sorry about one particular thing, something.

H: Weiyu?

W: I was thinking of something you said . . . that his talking was . . . . You keep asking him . . . . He said, "I'll be sorry when you go away over there, I'd like it if you sent me a letter." Not any old letter but some particular something [*means money*]. He was thinking about this, that's all. [Weiyu means Kalutwo was playing on our sympathies, while all he really wanted was money.] That's all . . . a letter. Like that. That's all. I don't have any more to say. That's all. [*Pause.*]

H: [*Clears throat.**] Now, in your thinking—

W: [*Breaks in.*]—We don't want him to think, "I'm sitting out here,

---

*I am a little startled at Weiyu's bluntness and his sophistication, which he didn't show with K. A good actor.

and they're all in there saying bad things about me." [W. is imagining what K. might have thought had we let him stay in the other room while Weiyu spoke in private with us.] So I got rid of him. He understands Pidgin; he could be shamed.[15]

H: [*Straightens up. To S.*] Weiyu got Kalutwo out of the house so that K. wouldn't be ashamed when we were talking about this. And he says that Kalutwo's thinking is just not right . . . that he just doesn't understand what the *keriku-keriku* does. . . . That Kalutwo's thoughts about this are like a woman's. Like a woman, he says one thing and then he says another thing; first he says he doesn't have the semen organ, and then he changes his mind. And when he talks about semen, he says, "Oh, I don't want to talk about that; that's an awful subject."

S: He's saying that's typical of the way women communicate?

H: Yes, and he is also saying that Kalutwo's whole attitude toward the subject is like a woman's.

S: In what way?

H: When I asked him about semen, he said, "Forget this; I don't want to talk about that anymore; I have had enough of that." That's not the response a man would make.

S: But Weiyu knows that this is not a man who is uninformed? He's a man who went through the initiation. Therefore, Weiyu would feel K. has no right to be this way. Am I right?

H: Let me ask Weiyu. You know K. knows about this. He's been initiated. He's a grown man.

W: [*Inserts enthusiastically.*] He's a grown, older man. He even knows the married men's stories about intercourse with women.

H: Does he know about the *keriku-keriku*?

W: The *keriku-keriku*? [*Whispers.*] I think he doesn't know about it. He knows it exists but not how its tubes, its pathways go, he doesn't understand how it works.

H: But you and I, all of the rest of us men, we know about the *keriku-keriku* . . .

W: Yeah, yeah. That's right. That's it. Nothing else controls you and me. Yeah. You two talked to him on a subject, but he'd only say, "Oh, you're talking about this subject, huh? I'm trying hard to understand that. All right, this subject there? All right . . . this subject?" He didn't respond to us [meaning K. didn't engage us in a dialogue; he kept asking us to clarify further our questions, which were already clear]. I was just babbling idly about women. [W. is chastizing himself: a new feminist.] Even if you talk to women, they'd understand. Women have got their own thinking;

their thinking is clear. Only *he* doesn't have any. His thinking is really another kind. A woman will understand your questions. She'll show you. Now, Kalutwo, not at all. He doesn't have any . . . of his own; he doesn't have any at all [*lower voice, frustration.*]*

H: Doesn't he know about his own *keriku-keriku*?

W: He knows, he knows but . . . . He knows that in our insides, se-men comes through the *keriku-keriku*. It's that which I think he doesn't understand. But knowledge of the semen of possums and other animals, he knows about that. He knows *only* that [that an-imals also have semen].

H: [*To S.*] He is clarifying his comments. He says, "I, Weiyu, really used the wrong analogy. Kalutwo is not like women; his thinking is not like women's because women also—if you ask them to tell you about something, they will tell you about it—they won't squirm out of it and go along a different path. They will tell you about it; and we men are also the same way." So K. has got his own special way. So I asked him about that. He said that K. knows—this is important—he knows he has a semen organ in-side because all of us men know that the only function of the se-men organ is to supply semen to the cock.

S: —And he knows he has semen.

H: He must. Well, that's not what he says.

S: I'm saying if he's having relations with boys, he knows he's got semen. Therefore, he's got a semen organ. Or he has disconnected the concept in some way that men never do, because, we might say, of his identification with women?

H: Weiyu is saying that K. is disjointed. He must know what all men know, because he's had all the teachings that there is about that thing inside . . .

S: So his answer "no" and his answer "yes" is an approximation of fact. The answer is: "Yes, I do have one; but no, I don't have one in the sense that mine is like other people's or has the same func-tion as other people's. There is something wrong inside of me so I can't be defined as a normal male."

H: Yeah. We were intellectualizing more or less about the semen or-gan until I asked him about semen. Then he [K.] got uptight; he had anger in his voice. Weiyu noted that: he said K. wasn't doing a very good job of talking about this until you asked him about

*Weiyu implies that Kalutwo's—in our lingo—erotic neurosis has ground K. into such a mass of ambivalence that only confusion remains. Even women are better than that, the mi-sogynist admits.

semen, and then he just said, "I don't want to talk about that," as if to say: "That's awful." Now, a normal man should say, "That's my semen. I've got lots of semen! What do you want to *know about it* [*showing off*]?" It's something a man should be proud of. But that's not K.'s affect. W. is telling us that Kalutwo's attitude toward semen is not a *man's* attitude. There's something disconnected in K.'s feelings about semen. W. is not that way.

S: Why did W. have to talk with us now?* In order that we be clear [see the failure in] what this man [K.] was doing?

H: Yeah.

S: What else does Weiyu want?

H: He wants to do something else, and here's where you've got it right. Now I see that. W. wants to tell us what the real function of the semen organ is.

S: That we not be left with the wrong impression?

H: That's not the only thing. There's another sense, too: W. knows so well about the semen organ that it's easy for him to talk about it. He doesn't have any trouble talking about it. *"That comes easy to me:* let me teach you about it; it's easy for me."

S: He wants to give us the right information.

H: There's also an emotional dimension too: "You're barking up the wrong tree with this guy. So let me tell it, it's so easy for me."

S: Is there some intensity, an "Oh-my-God-I'd-better-get-this-to-them?"

H: Yes. Here's how I would have read this before, if you hadn't been here and I had had the same session with Weiyu, and I hadn't been thinking the way I'm thinking right now. Weiyu would have come in, but I wouldn't have known why he got rid of Kalutwo. Then it wouldn't have happened the same way. Maybe he would have come in and said: "I'm going to tell you about the *keriku-keriku* now." And I would have said, "I know all about it."

S: You would have put aside your question, "Why in the hell is he so insistent about telling me what was already done ten, twenty times, and I know it cold?"

H: Yes, exactly; and I would have ignored what *he* wanted to do. Because the meaning of it, I think, is that this isn't for me, *this is for him.*

S: He's *got* to have this session with you.

---

*Throughout these dialogues S.'s ability always to bring me back to the interpreter's immediate subjectivity shows a clinical attention that was missing in me.

H: Exactly. I wouldn't have thought of it before, but it's so obvious now.

S: I've suddenly got a new anxiety: I look at that dwindling pile of tapes, and I look at the calendar.

H: I told you so. [S. felt his two-dozen two-hour tapes would never be used up.]

S: I didn't believe you. We should do it for his sake, but I would also like, if I could, to probe his scornful laughter, his head down, his refusal to look at the man, his anger—

H: Will you ask him about that; it would be easier for you?*

S: Sure.

H: Ask him the questions, and I will too, as ideas come to me.

S: Do we have to release him from his pain regarding Kalutwo?

H: [*To Weiyu.*] Do you want to tell us more about the semen organ?

W: No [*emphatic*]. The two of us have completed our work. I've taught you that. It's done now. It's inside your books now. Now I just want to [*whispers*] say [my] bad feelings† about that man [K.]— and so I came to talk with the two of you. You mustn't think, "He [Weiyu] wants to come and tell more about the semen organ." [*Shakes head.*] No. There's no more talk about that. I've already taught you.

H: [*To S.*] I said, "Do you want to tell us about the semen organ? And he said, "No, I don't really want to tell you about that. I just wanted to talk about these bad things about K. I just wanted to get him out of the house so I could say bad things about him." Now, I'm thinking, it's crazy. It's getting so thick for me that I'm starting to forget pieces . . .

S: You can't hold your questions together?

H: Yeah. Weiyu's [stated] purpose in doing this was to tell us about the semen organ. But that's not really what he wanted to do. He wanted to say bad things about Kalutwo. It's more conscious than I thought, his—[*pause*]

S: —Disgust, anger, rage, whatever. Those are all so conscious and have been all along. They *are* this very minute; look at his face.

H: Something is more conscious than I had thought it was [*pause*] . . . . I know what it is. He was going to come in and give us a lecture about the semen organ to explain its function.

---

*After months of work, and so many things to do before leaving in a few days, I am feeling swamped, no longer as focused as in chapter 4. That, too, is an unspoken aspect of field method.

†In hundreds of interviews over many years with Sambia this is only one of three times I ever can remember someone saying this about someone else.

But he changed his mind and said, "Look, I have already told you about that. I don't have to go into that again. What I really want is to say bad things about Kalutwo." Now that seems bizarre. Has Weiyu ever done that before? In a thousand sessions? Well, maybe a couple of times.

S: Is he concerned that we didn't recognize it so he had to make sure that we do?

H: I hadn't thought of that, but it's so obvious, that's why he did it.

Searching my memory now, I recall at most three or four times in the last two and a half years that Weiyu, having been the interpreter, returned to talk privately about a session. And it is rare for him to say he thought someone was full of bull. Remember the powerful constraints of shame in Sambia culture. To have said such things in front of K. would have shamed him greatly; thus, it would have shamed Weiyu also to have said them. Unless you want to stir up a fight, you do not insult someone.

I think now that what wasn't quite conscious in Weiyu's thinking is this: he had never before directly communicated that he thought K. was unmasculine, an incompetent male: that is the bottom line. A man should be able to talk about his semen organ and semen without shame; but K. was embarrassed discussing both subjects. (As he had been before.) And I was amazed Weiyu could verbalize with disgust, frustration, and anger his unequivocal opinion: Kalutwo is a failure as a man.

This points up a detail about clinical technique. Why didn't I check all that out with Weiyu? What S. was saying was, "I think it's quite conscious; look at the expressions on his face, etc." S. said, "Ask him if that was the reason he returned to the subject." Here is an important difference between how I operated as an ethnographer and how S. was as a clinician: it isn't enough to presume the ideas were conscious in Weiyu, as I had thought; S. wanted to *know* if they were conscious or not and what was their exact form. Details count: God lives in details. The clinician is more a detective of the individual. Where the ethnographer is satisfied—with appearance, with the outward forms of the behavior—the trained clinician (when competent) is not.

S: OK. [*Looks at W.*] What's he thinking? Is he just waiting for us to stop talking? Does he want to say more?

H: No, I asked him. He said "no."

S: OK. He's comfortable with what he said.

H: Yeah.

S: Is he concerned we didn't recognize it so he had to make sure we did?

H: I hadn't thought of that. But it's obvious in all of his comments that that's why he did it.

S: [*Very quiet.*] Not necessarily: he may know that we know it and yet he must say it anyway.

H: Oh. [*To W.*] We are wondering why you came here to say bad things about K.?

W: [*Impassioned.*] The two of you worked so hard, and you've only gotten a headache from Kalutwo's evasions. That's why. K. knows . . . . He knows, but he doesn't talk straight.

H: [*Cuts in.*] Why doesn't he want to talk straight?

W: That's it! That's what I mean! Why *doesn't* he want to talk openly? [*Raises voice, animated, excited, exasperated. Then lowers voice.*] He's shamed. Here. [*Motions to side of abdomen.*] He's thinking, "It's no good if they ask me about that something [semen organ] inside me. If I talk I'll be shamed."

H: [*With consternation.*] What do you mean? Doesn't he have one? Or what?

W: It's not that. He's got it, but he's shamed . . . of talking about what he actually does [in sex].

H: Of what?

W: Shamed of [*drops voice*] the women, or something . . .

H: The women!

W: [*Low voice again.*] Yeah. The women—and the boys too. He sleeps with them and so . . . [*pause*]. This is a new man [S.] here. So Kalutwo's shamed.

Let me underscore two background points. First the difficulty experienced when, on beginning fieldwork, I found the secret cult. The men hid it from me. Only two people, Nilutwo and Moondi, were then my interpreters on secret matters. In time, I was accepted, but even then, when men talked of homosexual practices, semen beliefs, and sex in general, they were reluctant, hidden, secretive, and ashamed. Eventually, the secrecy lifted (Herdt 1987c). The men trusted me and became open to the point that they were able to be themselves with me. But Kalutwo here reminds me of that early period, when he and others resisted talking about these sexual matters. His present resistance is a biopsy of the greater problem I've had in getting K., as compared to other men, to talk about these things.

Second, why was K. the most resistant of my informants—always resistant, not just now? No one else, except Sakulambei, who did open up to us in the end, had K.'s sort of resistance. Was this a piece of character structure, a defense to protect gender disorder: heterosexual inhibition and homosexual preference? If the latter (though we think both hunches are right), then this poor devil, in his aberrance, points up currents—anxieties and their resolutions—the rest of the people ("the culture") handle more efficiently (e.g., with repression). Thus, in this case study, we have uncovered the Sambia man's key problem of psychosocial adjustment.

W: He's shamed of this . . . of speaking his mind . . . about women. He was married before.

H: He lost his wives?

W: Yeah. He lost them all . . . . Some* of them he screwed, but he hid it from us when he was talking. [Weiyu is upset at this reference to the further evidence of K.'s unmanly way: "What man would deny he's screwed his wives?"[16] In K.'s only admission—fellatio with his second wife—he claimed she had initiated it. Weiyu never believed it. I do.]

H: [To S.] More details. He thinks Kalutwo felt ashamed because we're asking about women and boys, about having a semen organ and screwing. Weiyu says that . . . uh—

S: —that he's a New Guinea transsexual.[†] [Pause: H. looks baffled.] You didn't understand me? He wants to be rid of his male [semen] organ.

H: [Consternation.] Go on, I'm sorry.

Stunned. Thinking, "My God, that can't be true." But on hearing S. label it, something crystallized I had known a long time, and then, I thought, "Yes, there is something in that, but he's not a transsexual. He is more masculine than a transsexual." [S: Right.] What does W. allege is different about Kalutwo? K. knows the semen organ is inside him, yet he's hiding information about it from us. He wasn't really telling us what he feels about it; that's what W. means. I asked him, "Why?" W. said, "He's afraid that you [S.]—a new presence here—

---

*Whose version is true? Weiyu's? H.'s? Since K. told us he screwed only once, we must presume people have different versions of K.'s story.

†I wasn't being literal here, only playing with an idea to stimulate my own thinking, to get myself, in an instant, to play off present observations and intuitions of this man in this culture against what I learned in ours. What I meant then is that, though transsexualism is an impossible clinical concept with the Sambia, he was the closest to it one would find. [H: Sakulambei may be closer, at least he would have been a few years ago.] It would be more accurate to think in terms of transsexual impulses and their degree of consciousness rather than trying to apply to Kalutwo the diagnosis of "transsexual," which implies an identity, a powerfully motivated commitment to become female and live appropriately as one. [H: Right. I argued something like this statement of Stoller's elsewhere.[17]]

are going to ask him about screwing boys and women." So what is different about K.? "He's got the semen organ, doesn't he?" and Weiyu said "Yes." "And he's got semen, doesn't he?" and W. said "Yes. He's got that." So I repeat, "Well, what's different?" and W. says, "It's the way he's *talking* about it. He doesn't want to talk about semen because he's shamed. He's shamed because S. is asking him questions, and K. will be shamed if he tells about it: how he used to be married, how he probably screwed a couple of women in his marriages . . . . (But I wonder.) He's shamed of telling us that." At one point K. bragged to some men that he had had sex with one of his wives twice, though K. has never told *me* that. W. thinks K. fears that we shall again dredge up this whole story—that K.'s ashamed of. Weiyu's overall message is that K. is ashamed about his masculinity, maleness . . . that's why this is bizarre for W., who is *so* heterosexual.

I don't feel I sufficiently communicated to S. my sense that K. was hiding because he was afraid I would ask him about his present homosexual relationships with initiates; that I would pursue the rumor that he has tried to suck the penises of the boys; and that this may have appalled K., who wouldn't have been able to bear the shame of talking with us about that subject now. Maybe in a year or two from now he could do that, but not yet. [In 1981 he still could not.] And he couldn't do it except under *exactly* the right circumstances. Not here, with an interpreter there, in front of whom he would be deeply ashamed and whom he could not trust. Weiyu might blab it around the hamlet. Kalutwo was not just reluctant to talk about his semen and maleness, but more: he didn't want to discuss his particular form of homosexuality.

What does K. do? Though *he* has not spoken of it, it's more than rumor. To repeat: two boys told me he tries to switch roles with them; he, an adult, wants to suck them, an incredible affront to Sambia males' masculinity. K. may have been terrified we would bring that up; he fled shortly before S. arrived *because* I was finally aiming to explore. Related to this interview now is Weiyu's marked heterosexuality. In saying above that W. is *so* heterosexual I mean also that Weiyu is extremely masculine by Sambia standards. W.'s earlier enthusiasm for boys was masculine too. When I first met W., he was in the overtly bisexual period, had just married, and was not yet—his wife had not had a baby—exclusively heterosexual. From the start, he was open and almost exhibitionistic in reporting his sexual exploits, buttering the boys up and appropriately screwing them. For a Sambia, taking pride in having been an inseminator of both boys and women is masculine. And W. was extremely proud. The difference in gender identity between them permeates the interview. It makes K. uneasy with W. and makes W. despise K. Kalutwo has never felt at ease inseminating boys and was quite put off by screwing women. The contrast with W. couldn't be greater; W. with his enjoyment of homosexual relationships, which he then gave up simply because women were a greater pleasure.

S: Our focus should still be on Weiyu. He was deeply disturbed by this interview, which—is this right?—is the most intense of all the interviews that he had to translate with K., though this problem was present each previous time. It was worse for W. this time. Is that right? He's been able to put up with your asking these questions over a long time. But K. is constantly busy refusing the full masculinity of his culture. He is trying to confuse *you*; even his not talking clearly to you was a furtive expression of the failure of his masculinity. K., in a roundabout way, is expressing a dreadful possibility: a male might be unmasculine and deny his maleness, and then, as if that weren't bad enough, the son-of-a-bitch—to paraphrase the way Weiyu feels about it—does it in an unmanly way! [*Laugh.*]

H: That's it exactly. He is talking in an unmanly way.

S: About an unmanly subject that goes on inside him. That just makes it worse. So this was a very hard time for Weiyu. He just couldn't bear it after a while. Not only that, he had to get K. off the porch, as if to say, *"Get out of here!"*

H: Right, because he has never done this before—

S: He threw him out of here!

H: —He's never physically removed him before. *I've* done that a couple of times but only because I wanted to work privately with someone else.

S: This interview was unbearable for the translator, is that right?

H: Yes.

S: I don't know how much time he can spend, but maybe it will be cathartic for him to now be free to say what he does think of having to work—not what does he think of this *man*—but what does he think of having to put up with *this* translating, what was he suffering that he had to bear somehow by laughing, by putting his hand up, by refusing to look at the man, by facing parallel with him rather than face-to-face with him, by all the twisting and turning, the mistranslations, the refusal to repeat the translation properly, etc. What was he having to put up with inside himself?

H: [*To W.*] Dr. Stoller wants to ask you about your feelings when you translated for Kalutwo.

W: [*Somewhat fatigued.*] No, look, my friend. This here—I want to talk to him [S.] about it: I didn't feel anything in particular. I only talked to him [K.], that's all. I only waited for his words. I waited and waited . . . Ssh! [*disgust*] . . . I waited and waited. It was a pain in the ass [*scowling, frustrated*]. But about him? Nothing! He didn't answer me straight. "Oh, yeah, it's all the same, it's all the same," like that. He just worked at keeping his mouth shut and then later would go back and say something about what went before. I'm tired of this kind of talk. But I didn't feel anything else. This kind of man, his talking, I don't like it. I've been sitting too long. He's given me a backache. Yeah, this kind of man . . . . His style of talking. I have a backache from sitting with him so long. Now [*brightens up*], when I'm translating for Tali or with Imano, this doesn't happen.* I'm pleased with someone like that. You ask him, "How about that?" and he tells you [*sharp, strong, punctuated voice*]. So I translate quickly; that's really good. It goes quickly, quickly! I like that kind of man.

H: Yeah. [*To S.*] He says he's tired. He's tired of Kalutwo's . . . [*searching for the right word*] . . . style. You ask K. a question, and you sit and wait and wait. Finally he gives you an answer, and usually it's not right . . . . And you wait and wait some more. "I'm tired of this kind of man because he just"—

S: —He's not a man—

H: [*Echoes S.*]—He's not a man. Then he said, "This is no good . . . it's not the same with Tali. Ask him something [*H. snaps his fingers*], he'll give you an answer just like that. Or look at Imano: whatever you ask him he'll give you a straight answer just like that. It's always straight."

S: And is that correct?

H: Yes, even in Imano's case. He feels that with that kind of man, a quiet man . . . the message is (I still haven't worked this out) that Imano is so comfortable with his wife and is a [gentle] man, and yet he is so *open* about his sex life and his—

S: —But, W. feels, he's [Imano] a man, a male. He's different from the rest of us but he has his organ and he has his semen and he uses it appropriately and uses it with women. He enjoys that but

---

*W. subliminally tells us here that it matters not whether you are a tough (Tali) or soft (Imano) guy; they're fine people. It's the bogged-down obtuseness of K. that bothers him. (And K.'s fear of marriage too.) W. isn't just being a macho bigot who hates "homosexuals." I think it's Kalutwo's depression that has Weiyu so worked up.

he's still within the category of male (this is really a question), while the other guy is acting like he's in a different category by the way he behaves and by the way he answers quetions—especially by the way you can't get a straight answer.

H: Right.

S: It's very, very painful to have to deal with someone like that and be nice instead of throwing him out at the start.

H: Yeah, that's right. And I have to say that he [W.] has got—

S: —Forbearance.

H: That's right [*chuckle*]. Far more than other men. That's why I tried to be as patient as possible. I guess I realized that all along. Subliminally he has taken a lot. [*Pause.*]

W: You know, you've been working a long time, and I am the big gainer. I understand translating now and don't have to work hard to understand.

S: Tell him: I'm indebted to him. I understand what it is like for him to have to sit here and help Gil translate and to try to make it as accurate as possible despite what Kalutwo was saying. I understand the gift that he gave us by being willing to translate for us for our research.

H: Yeah. [*To W.*] Bob says this: He knows you've worked hard at helping me translate. And he knows you don't much like to translate for K. So he's very happy you have worked hard on the translating. It has gone fine; he knows that, and he knows you have done good work.

W: [*Quickly.*] I wanted to show K. what you were aiming at. But that's not how it was.

H: We know. But we're pleased with you because you tried so hard to gather knowledge about this kind of man . . . . He's got a different kind of thinking, and we know it's hard for you to try to get that thinking.

W: You too, sometimes, you got a headache . . .

H: Yeah, you're right. [*To S.*] He says, "You got some headaches too." [*Chuckle.*]

S: You bet! [*Laugh.*] I know what poor Gil has put up with!

H: [*To W.*] Yeah, the two of us, it's the same. All right. That's enough.

W: Okay. [*Leaves. Smiles goodbye.*]

H: The least pleasure I've had is from working with Kalutwo. It has been the most difficult. For the energy invested, it has been so hard, uphill every inch. Anyone else, even the shaman [Saku]—it's not true of anyone else. Even the [evasive] shamans; I enjoy working with them, almost always. Sometimes Saku is very sensitive, but the sensitivity I don't mind because I usually know where he's at. Whereas what you were saying about him, the informant [K.] is correct. [There are now people talking in the background, where Weiyu has gone for coffee with Moondi or Kwinko. So I monitor my words—it is automatic now—using "informant" instead of "Kalutwo"; I know they're there and can overhear us.] Sometimes I feel he willfully sets out to exhaust and confuse me so I will just give up.

S: The diagnosis for him at home is "passive-aggressive," the way you get at somebody by a passive technique, not by going directly at them. You exhaust them with your passive resistance. In one sense he was not a good choice if your main purpose was (and it was) to collect data—not in the superficial sense—on maleness and masculinity and sexuality. Yet he was a fine choice, because he is the most aberrant person in the society. Therefore, anything you got was worth more, because you got the most aberrant person, even though, in his aberrancy, he brought resistance with him. If you wanted to measure something in this culture that nobody in the history of the world has ever done in an alien culture, that is, how does a person resist, then you could not have picked a better case. You have now something most anthropologists don't [don't know how to] pay attention to: psychology; the inner psychology or character structure of a human being and how it colors his behavior. And you also get a glimpse into how he maintains aberrance, not just the gross aberrance of the sexuality. For they [Sambia] respond even more to his social aberrance. You couldn't have picked a better person. You may suffer from his resistance, but your suffering—not "*you* suffered"—your suffering was your organ for *measuring* aberrance. It's a more real way of measuring it than are his words. The words do not measure his aberrant personality. Our only measuring instrument is ourself, not our cognition, but our feeling: "I can't bear this." In that sense you could not have picked anyone better. But you weren't picking him for that. You salvage something additional for your research when you recognize your suffering was a piece of anthropologic research using the only organ available. You can't measure with a tape recorder what he is doing to you [and therefore who is this conglomerate of resistances, defenses, memories, fantasies, desires, affects—this person—Kalutwo]. And you can't measure it by sitting on a tractor and counting (see chapter 1). That anthropologic methodology [ours] has never been paid attention. [Not quite. See Devereux (1951, 1978), maybe Mead (1935) too, but she was rather rudimentary clinically.] Instead of *using* their suffering, anthropologists do the same goddamn thing your tractor-sitting friend does, ignoring the internal tension his informants' resistance causes, treating it as noncommunication, as not significant, not useful, not ethnographic, as epiphenomenon, working around it, changing it into something else. Shaping their research so that they didn't have to suffer. [H: Ignore it and, exhausted by ignorance and the anger plus self-hatred, it causes you, if you are committed to learning about humans, to lock yourself away at the end of the day—as if the work was so painful it couldn't go on twenty-four hours a day, blotting out how ethnography should be in the field. And get drunk or read novels or take tranquilizers or get depressed or go home and never return or be unable to write up your data or become a department chairman or university president.] You couldn't do that. You didn't have enough sense to ignore your work and to do something superficial.

H: Right. I mean—this is also really an educational experience. That all makes so much sense to me, but I never thought of it in that way. You see, Nilutwo is like that—Nilutwo had terrible, terrible—oh, my heavens!—resistance and suffering. [But we managed to work through some of it.]

S: What we're measuring is that anthropology has made a mistake. It refused to look at the individual and thought it could get away with measuring the general. There's no such thing: there are a bunch of individuals. [Mild oxygen deficiency, marked education lack, jungle madness, beginner's enthusiasm, but—I still think—more correct than ignoring individuals and their subjectivity.] Now, the majority of those individuals agree about the *tingu* and the *keriku-keriku*, but each one is an individual still, and anthropology—I have said this to you since the first day we talked—makes a mistake ignoring the individual's psychology. If they say, as [Victor] Turner (1964) did, "It's beyond me," that is *not* a mistake; that's the right thing to say. To say, "We don't want to deal with this, and we'll pay the price," is fine. But to say it's not a part of anthropology, not part of the study of Man, that's a mistake, a historic mistake, a *great* mistake. You cannot back off from mistakes like that. Mistakes like that eventually cut your throat. Let's do something else.[18]

PART III
Conclusions

CHAPTER ELEVEN

Summing Up: Clinical Ethnography of Sambia Erotics and Gender

H: In this book we have provided our closest look at Sambia erotics and gender identity. Previous works have charted the construction of gender and sexual excitement in Sambia culture in formal and certainly more conventional accounts of these phenomena.[1] This study, by contrast, is our most exhaustive effort yet to provide the reader an experience-near[2] narrative examination of Sambia sexual culture.

To be successful, a close-up, experience-near account should make a native's world come alive to the reader. More important, it should show how the culture is experienced by its purveyors; how interpreters not only sense but act on their meaning systems. To do this without demeaning the natives or oneself in the study of erotics is not easy: sex is still a dirty subject to some. Perhaps this difficulty explains in part why anthropology—which has led the way in pioneering gender studies since the 1960s—has avoided erotics as much as any other social science, the sexologists and psychoanalysts excluded of course.[3]

We have sought to present our interviews with Sambia pretty much unadorned. Sometimes these dialogues speak for themselves, sometimes not. What is between ourselves and Sambia—our culture and theirs, sometimes a language or an interpreter as well—harms communication but not insurmountably. This inbetweenness makes for distortion but also discovery.

Our use of narratives—more often dialogues—is pathbreaking in cross-cultural studies of sex and gender. Our texts show Sambia subjectivity as well if not better than our friends' myths and rituals; but these symbolic forms (available elsewhere to the reader) are a background for these texts, which poke their heads through in the words and idioms of Sambia everywhere, both by what is said and not said.

Subtleties permeate this process, for there are many ways to mistranslate words or translate too literally and miss the speaker's intention. Then there are differences, some substantial, between the meanings of our interpreters qua individuals: not semen as such, but what this body fluid means to Moondi and not Kalutwo; to Saku who lacks it, Penjukwi whose breasts exude it, and Weiyu who is concerned about its conservation. Here are great problems in the interpretation of culture and particular persons; no wonder the book took us so long to do.

Sambia is not only animistic but a dream culture and not just a society enmeshed in war but one in which gender roles and erotic experiences are built in and through conflict and dramatic rites of masculinization. Ritualized homosexuality is a part of the heroic culture complex war leaders and great shamans created and sowed to make their neighbors respect and fear them. The self in such a culture is not our nomad individual or a lone child. Selfhood is constructed in relation to others, and *only* by relation to these others does the experience of self make sense as a construct. This "relational self"— here is another popular concept[4]—is manifested in erotics and gender too. For gender, masculinity and femininity, as Stoller (1985b) has written [S: not quite], is not born but made; it is in its essence, convention. It is also more than that, because its definition is subject to the great and sometimes humorous, othertimes dastardly whims of fate, of biology and history. Who could not feel as much in the sad fate of Sakulambei? And yet, to reflect on the issue another moment, one can see gender and erotic variations as well in Moondi, in Penjukwi and Kalutwo. The "accidents" of their lives, as Freud referred to this, exemplifies a primary goal in this book: to show that those who study this domain of culture—erotics and gender—must study culture close-up, through people's subjectivity.

We never planned to do this book: Rather, it emerged from interacting with Sambia. I hesitated when S. suggested doing it. What was worth publishing? After all, I, the ethnographer, was doing what I had done in the village for years. S. dropped in for a few days. We turned on the tape recorder; our case studies were simply another week in many interviews and observations. Nothing special except our excitement in doing this together. Stoller and I complemented each other; even our disagreements enhanced our work. Our interviews were not intended to underscore this interpersonal issue or that. Yet a week of talking with people provided a range of experiences in enough depth and breadth for us to feel, at the end, that we had something to say, with examples that brought our method to life. The book has now emerged as I could not have pictured then. It results from improvisation, for we had no precedent to follow, and the product is neither an ethnography nor a textbook on theory or method.

We mention this background because the book is unconventional. Our writing style is informal; we retain the form of our dialogues in the field, and we have not dressed up our narratives with formal theory or jargon. Though I followed Stoller's lead here, I felt at times uncomfortable: we weren't scholarly. The text seemed plain—though it was often difficult to translate our transcripts from foreign languages into ordinary English—for my colleagues in anthropology. Now, however, at the end of the years-long writing process, Stoller's aesthetic position seems correct. My resistance to his style derived from my identification with the overly formal discourse style of anthropology, compelling me to feel that unadulterated language is common and reveals you have nothing upstairs; and a subliminal feeling of propriety that some of what we revealed (e.g., ourselves) should remain invisible.

Unconventional, too, is the way we preserved the dialogic character of our work. S. proposed that we not blend ourselves in writing the book, as is typical of co-authored works. Moreover, we have reported our parenthetic remarks, doubts, misunderstandings, slips-of-the-tongue, and speculations. Each has responded to this metalanguage of our interactions, as well as on our observations about interpreters' body-language, affects, etc. This noise, normally edited out of published accounts, we left in to show that it is part of ethnography. In this way, readers see our separate ways of thinking as anthropologist and psychoanalyst.

There is discussion today about deconstructing these fields. Anthropology and psychoanalysis carry a lot of intellectual baggage. Postmodern accounts of culture try to work through this, shedding false assumptions of the Other. Analyzing Freud has also become popular. Some of the anthropologic accounts are fine endeavors, conveyed with high-sounding language. Far too seldom, however, are we shown *what actually happened* in the investigator's encounter with his or her interpreters. The accounts provided for us, from the standpoint of genre, are indeed different from those of Malinowski and Mead. But when they omit the details and interpersonal processes that made the product possible, we are still at the impasse the old positivism of participant-observation bequeathed to us from the Victorian period.

I do not dislike the positivist ideology of fieldwork because it fails to yield "psychologic data." That is not its aim, and this paradigm has not completely hindered the production of sensitive accounts of culture. Rather, I object to how it renders a field study, disguising the psychologic reality of that study, regardless of what actually occurred in the field. This is faulty science and bad method. For it blurs who did and said what; why they did so; and these distortions prevent us from being close enough to unpack the ethnographer's interpretations. Malinowski's ghost is still with us: ethnographers (and psychoanalysts) still tend to omit the subjective and intersubjective dynamics of field dialogues, behaviors, and the representations of such in the writing-up process. I know that many of us in the social sciences feel interpretive anthropology has liberated us from the dead hand of experimental/biologic models in science. One marvels at the difference in ethnographic accounts in the *American Ethnologist* compared to ten years ago. But this conceptual change in our presentations of cultures has not fully reached into our field methods. Not really. It *does* make a difference that clinical processes are left out of the training for and practice of ethnography. We still rarely see the steps—*any* of the steps—that led from the field events to a report. This is a pity, for ethnography is about people's lives and real-life problems, not just about stories.[5] And some of the excesses today not only deprive us of these real-life details in context; we are given stories of stories: the nihilism of the art critic who cares little for the opinions of his subject. And unlike works of art our ethnographies are supposed to be about the real lives of real people.

We are not implying that clinical ethnography will remedy all these problems. Let the reader be skeptical about our rhetoric on the scope of clinical ethnography.

Cultural anthropology needs clinical ethnography today more than ever. When we began this project I could not imagine the upsurge in hermeneutics and interpretive ethnography. We have seen major advances in the study of culture since then. These changes entail risks, for instance, a sliding back to epistemologic relativism, as Spiro (1986) has warned. We still so little understand how people experience their traditions and how such subjectivity interacts with the public meanings of others to produce specific outcomes. We need better ways to account for and understand stability and change in human development and group functioning across societies (Spiro 1986:278–281). We need, that is, the bifocal vision of which Sapir[6] spoke long ago, a focus on individual and group simultaneously. For the study of erotics and gender identity, cross-cultural data are still too impoverished and decontextualized to truly compare masculinity and femininity, sexual excitement, and the fantasy constructs of people from different cultures. Clinical ethnography will not do this work. It is a method for making better—richer and deeper—observations. But without that method we will lack the data necessary for enlarging our understanding of these issues.

We divide our summing-up into two major areas: the study of Sambia erotics and gender, and the nature of subjectivity in other cultures, especially as discussed by anthropology and psychoanalysis. We shall conclude by discussing transference and countertransference in the study of culture and erotics, the key issue of sex talk for clinical ethnographers.

SAMBIA EROTICS AND GENDER

"Erotics" and "gender" should be dealt with separately (Stoller 1968), but it is hard to do so with our Sambia material. This problem is revealing, theoretically and methodologically. Does one's gender identity always predict the direction of erotic excitement? Dichotomous cultures, to use Carrier's (1980) term, are built on opposition between masculinity and femininity—their exaggeration, polarization. Sambia culture is like this. Thus we should expect to find this manifested somewhat in the production and performance of sexual behavior too. Culture helps structure this. It also conditions dialogue or talk about erotics and gender, but the individual contributes too, and certain differences between our interpreters above—such as Imano's gentleness, Penjukwi's tattoo, or Moondi's erotic daydreams—are impressive.

Culture will not, ultimately, predict these differences,[7] for these are not its concern, nor are they even intended consequences of socialization. That Sambia provides its great stereotypes, war leader versus rubbish man, is of supreme developmental significance for masculinity to emerge in Sambia males; but these stereotypes alone do not determine who achieves or fails in a lifetime. They do not explain Imano's softness or Weiyu's hardness. Only the boundary conditions are thus explained. Structuring of gender and erotics by culture is therefore conditional. This seems obvious to many of our colleagues in the psychologic sciences [S: "sciences"]. The shallow concern with intracultural differences is one reason that some outside anthropology mistrust its findings.

Stoller can speak to this issue better than I.

S: In recent years the study of gender identity led me to take up the old question how masculinity and femininity relate to erotic excitement. You might have thought, as I did, that anthropology would be full of the precise data one needs for comparative study. Yet I was not able to find a single report in which one learned exactly what turned a person—a particular person—on. (The word "exactly" is a crucial redundancy, for, in the case of excitement, if you do not know *exactly*, you hardly know at all. People can hide the secrets of their erotism in every detail of their behavior and fantasies.) Dozens of papers and books in the literature took for granted qualities such as "attraction" or "beauty," as if these aesthetics were givens, rather than their being for research *the* challenge.[8] There was no awareness indicated of what inner forces make an object beautiful or exciting or disgusting or frightening. Ethnographers tend to treat, say, beauty, as if the sense of it were identically precipitated in each member of a culture by the same factors; or, even more flagrantly wrong, as if beauty were a universal, a constant across cultures; or as if beauty were a necessary ingredient in everyone's erotism (that is, beauty as a cultural norm, not as a complex, personally-plus-societally-constructed subject worth close scrutiny).

I open at random a volume of Havelock Ellis; he may be quaint when judged by today's styles of writing, but many would agree with his ideas on the dynamics of beauty (especially if the racism and sexism were disguised):

> The fact that the modern European, whose culture may be supposed to have made him especially sensitive to aesthetic beauty, is yet able to find beauty even among the women of savage races serves to illustrate the statement already made that, whatever modifying influences may have to be admitted, beauty is to a large extent an objective matter. The existence of this objective element in beauty is confirmed by the fact that it is sometimes found that the men of the lower races admire European women more than women of their own race. There is reason to believe that it is among the more intelligent men of lower race—that is to say those whose aesthetic feelings are more developed—that the admiration for white women is most likely to be found. (1936:1:153).

What a fascinating piece of ethnologica; you can sometimes read reports today in anthropologic and psychoanalytic journals (also in movie fan magazines) with comparable tacit assumptions. Remarkable: the anthropologists make the same assumptions as their culture-bound colleagues. Only if you read these ethnographic reports on beauty, spanning half a century, will you believe that the observations reported, including those written recently, tell us no more about erotic excitement than this one from Ellis. Even when giving details, the authors do not tell of individuals' subjective experiences but rather of customs, myths, rituals, ideals of beauty, and the like.

In contrast, H.'s field notes impressed me even before we met because they let one know what his friends really experienced, both as they were talking to him and regarding the events they were describing to him. And he recognized how a precise detail, as does a shard in a kitchen midden, congeals vast aspects of the culture invisible to the casual, "objective" observer. Why do thinkers in some schools of anthropology still scorn such data? (It would be too bad if, as I suspect, precise description of erotic behavior remains unacceptable in anthropologic circles because there are those who, even in these liberated days, find the descriptions pornographic. Their shame for having such impulses would in that way guide them to their roles as watchdogs of orthodoxy.[9] How many symposia on erotics have been held at meetings of the American Anthropological Association?[10])

H: It is remarkable, in retrospect, to read chapter 2 and compare its cultural/structural themes with the material of our individual case studies. Here is truly an experience—experience-far and experience-near accounts—that illuminates. We have no independent test of reliability or validity to check for in comparing these data, for I produced both accounts. There is, however, the fact that S. participated as well in our case studies, and the additional fact that chapter 2 was written well before these case materials were put together. Nonetheless, the degree of correspondence between studies of the sexual meaning system, and individual "sex talk" in our interviews, underlines the synergistic nature of the two different perspectives. Sapir (Singer 1961:63–64) called this "theoretical reversibility" in culture and personality.

This sex discourse cannot predict the precise meanings of someone's erotic excitement or the direction of their masculinity/femininity. For those sensibilities or aesthetics (Stoller 1985a: chapter 2) are highly personal, multilayered, and probably contingent on situations too. Culture can provide normative boundaries, guidelines, rules, and goals for subjective self-representation, evocation, discourse: and through these social mechanisms its image contributes to the creation of erotic excitement and gender meanings. But "no culture is ever operative except through and in human beings," even Kroeber (1948:464) admitted. A fact is not a fact unless it's first a fantasy, Stoller says.

Between the social facts of culture and the psychologic events of someone's fantasies and scripts lie desires. A desire—as Foucault (1980) and Ricoeur (1970) have scolded Freud [S: And as Freud always knew]—is socially and historically determined by language and culture. A balance, a synchrony exists, between what is necessary and what is desired or between desire and possibility. What was at one time necessity for Kalutwo, namely ritualized homosexuality, has now become (aberrant) desire. He has failed as a masculine person, his own scripts say and his peers are quick to conclude, especially Weiyu. But he succeeds when fantasizing exploits with boys. In this failure we see a challenge to the Sambia folk theory of transitional same-sex behavior and a challenge to those who believe this form of sexual contact is merely an act of ritual, of domination, of power.[11] The Sambia would find such reductionism amusing. As Dover suggested of homoerotic relationships among the Ancient Greeks, many needs and complex functions are satisfied in "homosexual eros" (Dover 1978: 203). We have written of this elsewhere (Herdt 1984; Stoller and Herdt 1985).

Problems in understanding and explaining erotics take on a special character across cultural boundaries because of the very nature of different attitudes associated with talking about sex. Here our Sambia findings raise two issues that impinge on our material from the complementary perspectives of psychoanalysis and psychologic anthropology. First, how much are our Sambia case studies determined by the mode of discourse I (we) created in the village? We anticipated this question in chapter 3; we should further examine it by comparing Sambia with other societies. Second, how deeply do our interpreters experience these erotics and gender meanings? Are similarities between them a function of social roles? Does a cultural self—a set of learned scripts about the I/me for Sambia—create these meanings? Or is there a deeper universal self, an *anlage* on which culture is overlain?

The first point concerns whether or not sex discourse is restricted to western culture, and is, as it were, privatized and individualized—Foucault's (1980) critique of Freud's repression hypothesis bears on this. Foucault is wrong. There is too much repression, secrecy, guilt to say that the meanings of sex talk among Sambia differ radically from us.[12] But whether such discourse is more widespread remains to be seen. It is too much to argue for a universality of discourse, for this would ignore great structural differences between, for instance, hunters-and-gatherers and horticultural societies.[13] We should ask also whether any and all sex talk counts in our analysis—public and private, and in ritual or myth—and if so how we should weight their signs in each domain. Clearly, the Sambia have concerns about gender and erotic experience; we did not have to import these from the West. But did we—first H. and then S.—influence this Sambia talk?

Yes. Like all ethnographers we influenced this talk about sex: its form was dialogic "inbetweenness" (to use Tedlock's term). Its emergent qualities made our talk special; they spoke to us: we spoke back. Such dialogues, in the whole corpus on sex antagonism and gender in Melanesia, are extremely rare, as Fitz Poole and I showed (Herdt and Poole 1982). Indeed, to my knowledge, ours (H. and S.) is the only work of its kind: you get to see what we asked and were told, and in this way, the context and distortions are clear. This is not the case in ethnography, where a fact can now be a fact without a prior fantasy (question), or, indeed, a prior society, among the historical structuralists.[14]

Beyond Melanesia, however, a far-reaching and in my view underappreciated understanding of the role of culture in sex discourse and therefore in cross-cultural studies of sex was long ago provided by Mead. The privacy of sex raises problems with which only psychoanalysts have tried to reckon. As Mead said:

> One characteristic of human sex behavior is the insistence on privacy. This privacy may be of many types; it may only be a demand that others who share the same dwelling may not be able to observe and there may be no objection to nonparticipants hearing what is going on . . . . In most human societies sex relations are conducted as to exclude witnesses other than couples or individuals who are engaged in comparable activities. . . . The presence of unobservable areas of sex activity presents certain barriers to research which are difficult to overcome. (1961:1434–5)

That no one ever sees sex but only hears about it* is as much a problem for anthropologists today as it was for Kinsey.

Humans, Mead suggested, are shy about their sexual activity, unlikely to discuss it with strangers. Or friends. Or relatives. Or their analysts. Even among our enlightened selves, we know, many American couples avoid discussing sex, or avoid teaching their children about sex; the situation is probably similar among some "primitives." But this is not the *main* point: certain Amazonian Indians, for instance, are enthusiastic sex talkers, their ethnographer, Gregor, tells us. Yet these Mehinaku talk about sex in stories that are distant from their intimate experience: in ribald tales, in popular sexual myths,

---

*Or at least until Masters and Johnson came along, and they saw only its signs, not the minds, of their experiments' actors.

and comparing good sex with good food, often more by men, and more often in the men's house. Their discourse, which seems so open, delivers them from their experience by referring to cultural tales and exploits: stories about stories of sex (Gregor 1985:16–17, 71–72). This does not really challenge the personal and private nature of sex talk.

We agree with Mead that such intimate matters are intimate communications. Sambia appear to agree. They could discuss sex but not just with anyone and not just at the drop of a hat. Specialists can appreciate this by comparing the Sambia data to those collected from other New Guinea societies.

The Hua of New Guinea, as Meigs describes, provide a closer example of culturally-patterned talk that bears comparison.

> While the simultaneous existence of inhibited and uninhibited styles of talking about sex is undoubtedly universal, the distribution of these styles to various contexts in cultures varies. In North American culture the uninhibited expression is most obviously appropriate in such all-male contexts as locker rooms, barracks, and bars. By contrast, the comparable context in Hua culture, the men's house, is consonant only with a relatively inhibited style, or so I was told. Talk about sex that I would regard as uninhibited is permitted in Hua informal social groups including both males and females. In Western society "mixed company" represents precisely the context in which talk about sex is generally more inhibited. (1984:96)

Here we have a nice commentary on the existence of sex talk in another New Guinea society. But again, when Meigs says "or so I was told," we wonder by whom? And why? The Sambia situation differs from that of Hua, for Sambia men often discuss sex with men in ribald ways: this is a feature of their relatedness. Other New Guinea examples could be cited, and Knauft has made a very similar observation on the Gebusi of New Guinea.[15]

My point is not that the content or situations of such sex talk are identical, but that, in New Guinea, one or another such form is common. Too common to be ignored, but alas, the ethnography of such sex talk is almost unknown. And I suspect that it is better reported for New Guinea than other culture areas.[16] For instance: ethnographic reports on same-sex erotic contacts are notoriously deficient, and one must be skeptical in evaluating them, Mead (1961), Read (1980), and others have suggested. Indeed, a whole book that I edited was concerned with establishing the facts and fictions of ritualized homosexuality in Melanesia, and given the uneven quality of sex talk

ethnography about homosexuality among anthropologists, I understand critics' dissatisfactions with our field.[17]

But to return to the Sambia, here is S.'s assessment.

S: Our interpreters, after some puzzlement, had no trouble understanding Herdt's desire to get into their heads. These people, who are
so outward-directed—how to hunt, how to war, how to placate malevolent spirits, how to observe and cheat on taboos, how to garden,
how to maneuver in the jungle: skills not enhanced by one's desire
to know oneself, to get to the root of one's own motivations, to reduce
self-deception—were far more than just informants on masculine development, customs, and myths. Though they never heard of such a
thing, they were able easily, with H., to search themselves for answers to questions about meaning. And as, over the years, the probing
became deeper and more psychodynamic, some Sambia had no trouble moving with curiosity into realms of the mind they not only had
never seen in themselves or others but for which their culture has no
concepts or intimations. Moondi's insights are an example of such.
By the time I joined the interviews, H.'s friends were so easy about
and interested in the process of investigating their minds that this,
perhaps more than anything else, made the meetings feel as familiar
as working at home. In creating such an ambience, did H. so transmute natural modes in which Sambia communicate that he distorted
the situation and things they said? Did he, that is, merely move the
confessional clinical gaze (Foucault 1973) into the Village? We think
not: his mode of interviewing was designed in culturally appropriate
ways that were innovations on, but did not revolutionize, Sambia
communication.

H: Nonetheless, Foucault has made us more cautious, lest, like psychiatrists with patients, we not respect the natives' privacy, extracting from them their guilty secrets. Malinowski may not have thought
that wanting to study the natives' vision of their world made him
their confessor. Malinowski and Freud differed in their self-consciousness about this, because while Freud saw that patients confessed to
him, he also felt that he must confess to himself how little he knew,
and how much of what he knew depended on understanding himself.
And he used the same word—confess—in describing both aspects of
the discovery process (Ornston 1982:414). (By contrast, we see little
of Foucault in his lofty critique of the rest of us; he is, like Malinowski
was—in his ethnography, not his diary—a confessor only.) Some

communications that make people feel more whole, as with Sakulam-bei, are cheapened by being labeled confessions. There are admissions that will not be made, no matter what, as with Kalutwo, or that will be made, no matter what, as with Weiyu's condemnation of Kalutwo. There are sensitive and insensitive ways of asking people what they feel and of responding to them. We should be wary that our desire to understand does not make the natives say what they think we want to hear and when they do so, we must be sure that we see this. Yes, clinical ethnography involves confessions; but it requires compassion as well—an important part of understanding how much we have to learn about others' lives. Most of all it requires a respectful empathy.

This brings us back to my first point: that sex talk is not institutionalized in some cultures or is missing in others, whereas private or informal talk is there but was never studied. It is unclear whether the anthropologists who claim the former have not in fact been the ones responsible for the latter. This dilemma may account for the impoverished material on erotics in anthropology, whereas data on normative gender codes and roles are now voluminous.[18] No doubt some anthropologists are prudish,[19] but this does not explain the problem. That is caused, rather, by ignoring a whole world of culture—subjectivity. When we open the leading college textbooks[20] on human sexuality to find that the "cross-cultural chapter" trots out Malinowski on the Trobriands and Mead on New Guinea—we cannot help but be impressed by the lack in ethnographic studies of erotism and the failure of contemporary cultural anthropology to enlighten her sister disciplines (Herdt 1987c).

This failure can be explained mainly by anthropology's disregard for the individual. Aside from the core group of culture and personality workers (Spiro 1986:279–281), problems of subjectivity, of self and personhood, were historically ignored; and hence behaviors and meanings of erotics and gender were as well. This absence is still present though transmuted. Though one can say that "anthropology thrives on a tension between the construction of theory and the practice of ethnography,"[21] the tension is less due to paradigm changes and more to fads that avoid study of subjectivity in anthropology. The fact is, the participant-observation epistemology has not fundamentally changed (chapter 1), though fads come and go. The informal and intimate study of the person—and nothing else—yields an understanding of gender sensibilities and erotic aesthetics. And these sensibilities are, as Sontag (1982:106) has said in another context, the most "perishable aspect of a culture." Excluding the person has harmed not only studies of sex and gender but anthropology at large, which is so prone, Spiro (1986) has complained, to an "ethnographic particularism" that tends to the "strange customs of exotic peoples." We find this an unsatisfactory future for anthropology. Moreover, it is not merely ethnography but the writing process that excludes the individual.[22] For anthropology to establish itself at the center of studies on erotics and gender in humans requires our reclaiming the whole person as a source of intrapsychic and interpersonal meanings.

When, therefore, we turn to the second issue on selfhood, similar research aims and problems arise. Is the self a constant, a given, an *anlage* across cultures?[23] Or is it merely a cultural construct through and within which normative meanings and random behaviors of individuals are expressed? Do we seek variation, local adaptation, or do we seek universals and the nomothetics of understanding how the self is related to and regulates erotic excitement, body imagery, developmental goals, and related gender phenomena (Stoller 1979; 1985a)? Though S. and I. disagree somewhat on the interpretation of these matters, we agree that each culture provides for a self and that the experience of the I/me can be charted in its details, through clinical ethnography. When Mead, in *Male and Female* (1949), discussed the aims of ethnographic writing, she focused on the *differences* between human groups as the key to understanding human nature and gender.[24] This heritage seems to have influenced the anthropology of sex more than she might have anticipated.

Locating the causes of sexual excitement and gender in personhood and self provides a stronger heuristic bridge into deeper meanings of our Sambia material. Gender is supposedly constructed so that "sexuality cannot be abstracted from its surrounding social layers" (Ross and Rapp 1981:54). And yet this is what Freud and psychoanalytic studies try to do. When we say gender is constructed, do we mean in its architectural entirety? When S. (1985a, ch. 2) argues that erotic tastes are made and not born, does he mean this literally? Sambia erotism is surely constituted via familial dynamics as well as the dramatic rituals of its society, which creates cultural and gender discontinuity in males, a point to which we shall return. Concomitantly, this poses fundamental difficulties in understanding selfhood among the Sambia. Here we must confront the surface and depth, fix and fluidity, of Sambia subjectivity. Shall we agree with Geertz (1973:363) that these "problems, being existential, are universal; [while] their solutions, being human, are diverse"?

It is too easy to take any number of issues from our Sambia dialogues—on semen beliefs, images of pollution, the erotics of fellatio—and conclude that the erotism and gender of Sambia are *unique*, either absolutely ("They only do it like that in the South") or conditionally ("You, too, can be President [if you try hard enough]"). Epistemologic relativism (Spiro 1986) of this kind is seductive, but we can get caught in its webs. To say, by comparison, that the Balinese self is submerged in collective conceptions of "person," "time," and "conduct,"[25] not only leaves the comparative student of selfhood with the (probably) insoluble task of finding the same webs of meaning in other cultures. It also ignores the similarities in all kinds of spiders. The universalists, including the ghostbusters (the term is Shweder's [1984]), find this unacceptable, so they look beyond collective symbols for screens and symptoms, as Freud[26] often did, to discover underlying psychic meanings: hair=penis, blood-letting=castration, ritual initiation=Oedipal resolution. The usual stuff. On the other hand, the relativists have ignored this challenge. In our search for links between Sambia and other human societies we are also tempted to these facile unconscious meanings. They help get us beyond the impasse of relativism, whereby an irreconcilable dichotomy between Sambia and western selfhood and erotics thwarts comparison.[27]

The dilemma posed by forays of psychoanalysts into the study of erotics and gender in nonwestern cultures is this: though they were often the only thinkers interested in deeper manifestations of erotics and gender, they tended to pathologize the phenomena outside the West. What deviated from the norms that analysts considered the "average expectable environment" were treated as pathologic, LeVine (in press) has suggested. This not only begs the question of a value-laden construct such as average environment, it also tends to ignore the role of culture and meaning systems in allowing for more adaptive variation in social environments than Freud, for instance, imagined when he wrote the *Three Essays on Sexuality*.[28]

Kakar takes up this problem of psychoanalytic formulations of his own culture, India. He notes that where Freud's work on neurosis* was designed for evaluating individuals, the diagnostic labels were soon applied to communities, even civilizations. "Predictably, nonwestern cultures were bunched more at the neurotic end of the spectrum while *their* soul doctors, the shamans, were evaluated as frankly psychotic" (Kakar 1985:441). When they have written of India, Kakar complains, analysts found "oral fixation and oral dependence had never been quite surmounted and the resolution of Oedipal complex has

---

*The same point would apply to erotic neuroses too.

never been quite accepted."[29] Further, a 1981 psychoanalytic commentary sees Indian behavior as

> the result of intense libidinal gratification throughout the oral, anal and phallic exhibitionistic phases . . . with stringent constraints on aggression. . . . This specific sequence requires strong defensive measures, particularly against sadism and favors reaction formation. . . . There is a pull to oral fixation. . . . Oral eroticism is seen in a cultural emphasis on generosity, especially around food, institutionalized dependency, totalism.[30]

It gets worse. No wonder Malinowski[31] railed against this reduction of culture and selfhood to the unconscious. This kind of clinical ethnography is far from what we have in mind. But it is a far cry from the marvellous works of Kakar himself, who is much more culturally sensitive. Stoller and I want to understand unconscious forces and development too but in a more reasoned, experience-near manner.

The nature of sex talk in culture is forever shaped by fantasy systems that lie somewhat apart from the time/space world of the behavioral environment. Experiences felt, reprocessed, and re-presented to self and to others are no longer experiences or memories but compromises, symbolic limbos of development. Anthropologists who ignore this history are crippled in their assessment of the meaning of sex talk *across the lifespan.* How critical this point is in a culture, such as Sambia, with such strong developmental discontinuity in the lifespan. Cohler (1982:217) writes: "This focus upon a developmentally shared fantasy world, rather than the time/space world, differentiates psychoanalytic accounts from all other accounts of human development."

Anthropology's best reason for using clinical techniques and concepts is to understand and interpret the deep but nontherapy relationships we form in the field. Questionnaires, quantitative measures, projective tests, normative observational samples and controls help systematize the data flooding us. But it is the ethnographer's personality, behavior, and communications that underlie the use of those measures, their acceptance by the natives, the responses we get to them, and how we interpret them. We can never calibrate this instrument: the ethnographer's or the clinician's personality. All information must be transformed; the bottom line, as Devereux (1967:xviii) said, is that *all this means that*: the final act of interpreting is done in the ethnographer's biased, meaning-laden head. And it is communicated via the biased, meaning-laden heads of our interpreters. How do they present to us when talking in private? Are they concerned to express normative attitudes? If their several identities are in conflict (e.g., Weiyu's position as Kalutwo's kinsman versus W. being an adult warrior and cult member), how do they in their communications handle the conflict? Such clinical issues were ignored in the past because reports homogenized groups (e.g., "all men" includes Weiyu and Kalutwo). But the new attention to the descriptions of selfhood in experience-near, person-centered ethnography, shows an advance in thinking about them.

LeVine (1982:296 ff.) suggests there are three key "domains" of self that can be understood cross-culturally: routine occasions, public occasions, and autobiographic occasions. Each domain implies a context for questions and a related set of internal scripts, social roles, and discourse rules. I have worked in all three modes, yet in our case studies above (because they came at the end of two and a half years' work), I focus mainly on the autobiographic, our sex talk. This focus restricts the data we present and influences how people revealed themselves to us. We see, for instance, not Penjukwi the typical wife/mother/woman, but P. as the object of our unique discourse, with her own values and ideas communicated somewhat idiosyncratically. She tells us she believes other women have orgasms like her, but she is unsure of this. She is not terribly interested to find out, for it was we who asked *her* what she felt. It would be easy to misrepresent what she said. Had we instead presented more interviews on women's rituals or institutional activities, one might have gotten a different picture of both Penjukwi and Sambia society. Still, there are enough routine and public occasions present in our discussions, particularly with Tali and Weiyu (chapter 5), to compare the quality and substance of our communications and differences between men and women, in relation to the autobiographic texts of others. This interplay between public routine and private dialogues provides the greatest potential for psychodynamic discovery[32] relevant to the ethnography of gender.

Here is a puzzle in normative male selfhood and gender: in everyday conversation Sambia men stress the masculine, vital, phallic quality of themselves and their male institutions. Yet one can go beyond the surface of the idioms with which men speak of these things and of their environment. On doing so, I found in private talk and in the tacit meanings within their beliefs, that the most compelling and ritually useful elements for creating masculinity are fertile, prolific, quiet, steady—what men perceive to be (and privately accept as being) feminine. These two sides of male gender attitudes reflect the contradictions of their development, which begins in the women's world and ends in the men's. Tali and Weiyu hint of this. Sakulambei and Imano exemplify it.

The point emerges more fully in the spectacular myth of parthenogenesis with which I concluded *Guardians of the Flutes* (1981:ch. 8). On the surface, the secret myth-telling among the men seems to confirm the preeminence of masculinity in their inner worlds. It does so by denying the primordial presence of females in the storied beginnings of Sambia society and by interweaving the first acts of homosexual fellatio that dominate every boy's late childhood and adolescence with the rise of the family, ritual custom, and society. Closer examination, however, shows that in the myth-telling, men feel frantic to keep women at a distance to deny the discordance between male public talk and secret myth and the shame that surrounds the setting of ritual. The ways men use their myths, plus their homosexual and heterosexual practices in creating and maintaining masculinity, belie the public ideology of the male cult: at its heart the myth speaks of men's deepest doubts that they are fully male. One's maleness and masculinity will fade away without ruthless, ritual defenses to preserve them. These findings of an earlier study that was clinically informed must make us cautious: many male ethnographers of Melanesia looked only at surface behavior and cultural ideology and misread ritual discourse as pertaining to domestic and private life without any changes necessary. Paralleling this public symbolic system—the ritual cults and signs that anthropologists had taken to be pure assertions of masculinity—is a more complex mental world.[33]

We have already argued that our interpreters went beyond normative social roles in communicating with us. Moondi's erotic daydreams, Kalutwo's strange ideas about his maleness, Saku's pain over his hermaphrodism are examples of such discordance. My house provided people a place to say odd and secret things in odd ways. To the extent that interpreters are aberrant, we should interpret their behavior accordingly. Cautiously. Yet, we also saw people privately expressing their conformity to public norms: Weiyu and Tali's defense of ritual customs, Penjukwi's reaction to S.'s tattoo question, Moondi's fantasies, Kalutwo's avoidance of discussing the pederastic rumor about him, and Weiyu's outrage at Kalutwo are examples of such. Nor can we yet tell the extent to which these normative or aberrant attitudes will eventually go public, stay quiet, be accepted or rejected by others. Only further study will reveal that. Still, being present in members of the community, such attitudes are a part of village life, whether latent or manifest, so they may eventually work their way into the culture of public symbols.[34]

And further: when I ask Moondi, Weiyu, or Penjukwi—who (unlike the aberrant Kalutwo and Sakulambei) have no need to avoid discussing sex—what they feel, am I not encouraging unprecedented conversations? Will their enthusiasms transcend their normative comportment in public? Yes, no doubt: such behavior is of course constrained as a function of social controls and public censorship.[35] Their responses must be seen in relation to what normative people usually did and said in my previous fieldwork, before our interviews. But such data are still data; there are no nondata. Such responses are as much a response of Sambia culture as anything; only, interpreting them requires understanding what is normative or not in different situations.

With the issue of normativeness and aberrance in the discourse of clinical ethnography we reach a hoary problem indeed: what bearing do such materials have on an anthropologist's representations of a public, shared ideology, social action, or culture, as in Durkheim's collective consciousness? What can the microscopic study of an eccentric or even an abnormal self tell us about the social world of normal others? In the vintage culture and personality works of the 1930s, 1940s, and 1950s, this problem was circumvented or muddled. One reads, for instance, the rich and finely textured "autobiographies" of Alorese by Cora DuBois (1944) with appreciation; the "interpretations" by Abram Kardiner that follow them seem impoverished and misguided at times. This great pothole in social theory, though stated now more sophisticatedly, is present in responses to the works of Obeyesekere and Crapanzano, the latter of whom Geertz has scolded for misreading his clinical ethnography of *Tuhami* as "culture."[36] Another reviewer has in the same way[37] chided Spiro's secondary-source reinterpretation of Trobriand culture, which rediscovered the missing oedipal complex.

These are particular instances of a more general problem: nothing in recent years has interested psychologic anthropology more than the issue of what is shared in a culture.[38] There was a time when "culture" indicated that traditional societies shared the same motives, values, rules; or that they enacted roles in the same ways; or that they performed customary practices in the same way. Patterns of culture were relative and adaptively meaningful (e.g., the doctrine of cultural relativism). This fiction was based on another fiction: that personality is isomorphic with culture. Therefore: the same thought, attitudes, biases, stereotypes, feelings, etc. In this model, it was difficult to deal with what seemed—to Westerners—pathologic: warfare, cannibalism, suicide, trance states. How can what is normative in a society be pathologic? Can a society be sick? After World War II subtle shifts occurred.* Questions were asked in a different way. Not, "What do they all share in?" but, "How much—at what levels of awareness and behavior—is shared?" Wallace, Edgerton, Schwartz, and D'Andrade among others have reviewed these problems well.[39]

In asking how much is shared, we must define sharing: correlation; equivalence; identification; association; similarity? At what level: institutional or individual? Conscious; unconscious; nonconscious (ideology)? What links exist between sharing cognitions versus affects? Can a people share in a concept (e.g., soul) and yet still feel differently about it as individuals? Is cultural knowledge uniformly distributed in a society—across age, sex, social status, ritual and other distinctions? (Probably not.[40]) People may believe in a custom, yet react emotionally to it privately in different ways, as you have seen. How much of the variance in their emotional reactions is explained by normative role attitudes (e.g., "Men should control their women and avoid too much sex," Weiyu and Tali say). How much variance results from personality differences across normative roles? (Imano is comfortable with women and enjoys frequent sex with them.) Avoiding clinical methods in gender studies hinders our understanding such issues.

Since social roles influence people's identities in private, might not their gender stereotypes do so too? Of course: stereotypes of masculinity and femininity come through our tapes in many places. Such images, idealized role models, and rule-sets are present in our narrative texts, not just in how people act—via social roles—but in how they feel and think. Important clues come from peoples' attributions about others: "All men think of drinking tree sap when screwing their wives" (Weiyu and Tali) or "All women feel *imbimboogu* when breastfeeding (Penjukwi). How do they know? Can we trust their assertions? Those questions require answers that are context-dependent (do they trust us on this matter?) and quantitatively contingent (we need more cases, perhaps a standardized questionnaire with a large enough *n* if we want to generalize). Knowing of this cultural influence on gender discourse, however, is different from agreeing—with Malinowski or now with Geertz—that cultural stereotypes[†] speak, rather than the individuals who express them. For in failing to recognize that nor-

---

*Nazi Germany, as much as anything, embarrassed this intellectual position. Anthropology was shocked.

†Cultural images ("man," "woman," "shaman") in myth or narratives, idioms or idiomatic sayings, proverbs, jokes, riddles, art, ritual, social roles, dream theories, etiquette, television commercials, psychologic tests, aesthetic styles, etc.

mative views can be combined with or replaced by private (idiosyncratic) ones—and nowhere as much as in sex talk—these scholars ignored the historical origins of stereotypes, ignored the creative element in cultures, forgot that people make errors (forget customs, magical formulas, etc.), react to their own traditions (rebellions) or those of others (cargo cults), make revolutions, and sometimes change things just for the hell of it. Stereotypes come from minds, not machines.

Example: Kalutwo. K. reveals, as no other Sambia could, the distinctive features of the rubbish man.* But that label is meaningless unless we understand its dynamics: what created him, why does he dislike hunting, why can he not bear women? Another man, Imano— nearly as rubbishy—is as normatively heterosexual (perhaps more so) as others, nor has he ever engaged in adult homosexual acts; yet both men are aberrant. Kalutwo's life reveals the critical points in the male developmental cycle that must be hurdled to attain adult masculine personhood. His failures to do so, to make the normative transitions, indicate his aberrance; but they are *not* that aberrance: that is produced by his motives, goals, fantasies. Kalutwo's communications also express normative beliefs about sex with women: he is terrified they will drain him of semen (maleness, existence). But in acting on this belief to an extreme, he has failed at marriage and his self has failed the men. Should we see his use of that belief as conscious or unconscious rationalization? We guess that the form of his semen depletion fear is shared by other men. Therefore, if we can understand its origin and conscious experience in Kalutwo, we shall understand better what makes normative Sambia masculinity. And that will clarify what energizes marriage, fatherhood, ritual, warfare, and much else. Kalutwo is a guide to a shifting but important current of Sambia culture.

But let us examine the aberrant further by using, this time, a fundamental dynamic of sexual excitement: fetishism. The concept has an odd history—of erotism in psychoanalysis and animism in religious anthropology.[41] Though fetishism is a perversion and its extremes psychopathologic, in fact, Man—(all?) humans—have a touch of this dynamic in the secrets of their erotism (Stoller 1979). Sambia are no different, as you sense in reading chapter 2 and find confirmed in Kalutwo's case study.

---

*In fifty years of New Guinea culture there are no other studies of rubbish men, though specialists frequently use that folk category. That, in itself, is a comment on New Guinea anthropology.

S: Let us say that a fetish* is either a nonhuman object someone animates with human attributes (e.g., a stone worshipped as a god, a shoe more exciting than the woman wearing it) or a part of a human that, in being admired more than the whole person, dehumanizes the person (e.g., women's ankles are craved and the women as individuals ignored). The fetish is factitious, an invention that lies between the human and the nonhuman. Fetishists are collectors (those people who humanize the nonhuman and thereby find passion where philistines see only utility).

Heterosexual Sambia men are as fascinated and erotically excited by the form of boys' mouths as are heterosexual men in our society by women's breasts. In both cultures, a particular anatomic structure has been fetishized; that is, it has been focused on with such intensity that it is more important than the person whose attribute it is. The person is—sometimes a bit, sometimes a lot—dehumanized, of interest for the moment mostly as a contraption to which the desired tissue or organ is attached and even then not for the part's physiologic functions but only for its visual or tactile effect in provoking fantasies.

Thus, Sambia bachelors use these same mechanisms of fetishizing anatomy in their strong erotic fixation on the configuration of prepubertal boys' mouths. H.'s understanding of the dynamics of fetishism allowed him to collect data that thereby illuminated work on gender and erotics. Only an ethnographer allowed to watch the most secret parts of Sambia initiation would know that the boys' mouths are fetishized and then be positioned to also ask why (Herdt 1981; 1987c). And you would have to allow "why" into your research to see how this aesthetic regarding mouths is connected to something that seems far removed, such as the warfare that was the outstanding reality of traditional Sambia society and that structured the selection of a boy's homosexual partners from hostile villages.

To return to our discussion of normativeness, there is the Mind— the Universal Mind that, supposedly, is independent of and the essence of the lifelong mental experiences that we all have all day long and that are so much less heroic than (sound the trumpets): the Mind is made up of innumerable fragments: mouths, breasts, beatings, postures, smells, decorations, taboos, music, genitals, symbols, humiliation, invasions, anxiety, danger, masquerades, foolishness, disgust,

---

*Fetishism is very rare in women; in fact, many perversions are found only in men. Can we get this clinical puzzle to excite those who believe in the Universal Mind?

hope, the dorsal but never the ventral surface of the left (much more than the right) earlobe. And people's shared or idiosyncratic ideas and fantasies about what excitement is and how it* should be expressed. There is no excitement in the absence of these particularities and therefore no such *thing* as excitement without these events. Sexual excitement *is* these experiences; it is not an abstraction but an emotion, a tangible body response. Excitement has no form, no structure, no presence, no existence except in these particularities. The *word* or *idea* "excitement" is, of course, not a perceived body state: words, and ideas are not excitement. There is no nonexcited excitement—that is not an excitement, a felt experience, though all states we call "excitement" share certain qualities or they would not be excitement but, perhaps, potatoes or elephants.

Fetishism therefore permits us to repeat and emphasize our point that fundamentals of erotic experience can be communicated across cultures while other aspects of the same experience may be difficult if not impossible to transmit. Few women ethnographers, even with a man from a most exotic place, would misread an erection despite their professors teaching them that the signs of erotic excitement are culture-bound. What may be unknown and far from universal, however, is what stimuli set off the excitement and why those stimuli set off the excitement and why those stimuli, for that man, are erotic. Too often, if the reasons why seem obvious, it is because they match our experience, not because we really know the reasons.

"I could show you many famous books on anthropology with minute details about pottery and such subjects, which do not even mention what position is normally adopted in coitus. Yet I should think that the man in the street will agree with me if I say that the sexual life of a human being is nearly as important as the chips of stone that fall off when he makes an axe," says Roheim (1932: 21). Do ethnographers still fail to get these data sixty years after Roheim because gender identity or sexual excitement are not important enough for them to study? The suspicious analyst thinks there may be other motives, other reasons why. Why ("why, 'why,'" you cry) has anthropology excluded these data and these questions?

H: Used properly, the longitudinal case study can focus our understanding of culture. My narrative sketches prefacing our chapters place each person in relation to his or her interpretations of Sambia nar-

---

*There really is no "it," the purified, spiritualized, noncorporeal essence of excitement, but for the sake of simple sentences, "it" is the needed word.

rative roles and psychosocial development. We proceeded across a spectrum from the normative side—Moondi, Tali, Weiyu and (in most respects) Penjukwi—to the aberrant—Imano and Sakulambei —and on out to the abnormal (Kalutwo). You may not agree with these assessments. Could you truly disagree—and reinterpret—without our detailed communications? The aberrant person, though unnormative and therefore not representative of the mass, also provides in his or her aberrance important clues for understanding normative behavior and experience.

We cannot shake off the feeling that ethnographers avoid methods of the sort we used in our interviews because they feel they are not interested in or able to study unconscious factors. The domain of psychoanalysis. Many anthropologists, from Kroeber to Victor Turner and Geertz, have voiced such reservations. They also may believe that clinical techniques are not really crucial in doing "standard" participant-observation. Let us review this one last time.

Our field interviews were not primarily concerned with unconscious forces. We believe that the study of conscious experience is itself a challenge, one still awaiting ethnography. The subjectivity of cultural beliefs, rules, and ideas at different levels of understanding and how particular cultural actors put them into use in social and private life is little known in comparative ethnography. We are only beginning to fathom the range of states of awareness covered by "dreaming," "daydreaming," "trancing," "desire," or "motivation" in nonwestern culture. The unfolding of awareness, morality, and acquiring rules and concepts from childhood on, including individuals' adjustments to these phenomena are scarcely known, for example, in New Guinea. The links between social roles and the personal expression of emotions are also vague and only now being studied across cultures.[42] Such problems require an understanding of *conscious* experience, and it would be some time before one needed to start tackling the unconscious.

Not that unconscious forces do not shape behavior. How else do we explain Weiyu's and Penjukwi's slips of the tongue (e.g., inverting gender pronouns)? How do we explain Moondi's avoiding discussing "quiet" men? Is resistance to self-insight (his identifying his father with desired homosexual partners) not useful here? Can we not use the concept "transference" in understanding Kalutwo's reactions better? Are not Weiyu's bodily and emotional resistances to and difficulties with translating for Kalutwo (evident to us and perhaps to him subliminally too) a key to understanding Kalutwo, or masculinity, or male–male social interaction, or translating? And of course unconscious forces motivate the ethnographer as well; unless corrected, they distort research.

The value of studying individuals' conscious experience of their institutions, beliefs, and attitudes lies in the microscopic analysis of how they internally represent these elements; how those representations contain assumptions or rules otherwise missed by an outsider; how they feel about these elements and the extent to which their feelings are hidden or expressed in public and are shared by others; why they have faith in ideas or attitudes even when other beliefs seem to contradict them or cause them anxiety or shame; or how they avoid being aware of such contradictions, or, when they are aware, how they manage to cope with their intrapsychic or interpersonal conflicts.[43]

The interplay between inner experience and public behavior is central to these issues. Though anthropologists have made much progress in studying native ideas in this process, conventional ethnographies less adequately touch on natives' feelings and fantasies. Indeed, Geertz (1968) has argued that these forms of experience—even conscious—are difficult if not impossible for ethnographers to reach. We believe our case studies support a different view. I recognize that our data are conditional and that the conceptual steps that would relate them to an analysis of social practices and symbolic forms (like ritual) have still to be worked out. But these interpretive problems (which I shall not tackle here) seem solvable. Another benefit of our view is that, in believing one can collect subjective data, ethnographers will try harder to do so. That will lead us to pay more attention to our *interpreters'* concerns; to their questions about how life is lived in other places, including that of the ethnographer. By so doing, we return to the final problem we wish to examine: the effect of the fieldworker on the process of clinical ethnography.

TRANSFERENCE IN CLINICAL ETHNOGRAPHY

We should not fear using clinical methods and aberrant case studies in studying culture. As long as observations and interpretations are open to public view, readers can decide if we relied too heavily on such or extrapolated inappropriately from them to the normative. But that, of course, is the same fear we should have of all ethnographic reports. (Perhaps ethnographers at first avoid odd people because they fear natives will think the ethnographers odd too. Or identify the outsider with the odd person he interviews. What a pity if such fears stifle research.) If studies of aberrants do nothing more than sharpen our understanding of the normative they add a lot.

Clinicians should remember that they handle the normative/aberrant spectrum less frontally than anthropologists through the use of the term "appropriate." This oft-used and ambiguous word has subliminal connotations that may block research, particularly when class or ethnicity are relevant factors. Our use of "appropriate" is just as deceptive, for I share in the normative cultural system of Sambia, as I did not five years earlier.[44]

Deciphering the normative from the idiosyncratic in my interpreters' behavior and experience becomes easier by taking the long view. I could collect observations and do interviews over the years; compare a person's ideas and feelings in many different ways to see their full manifestations; I could take my time to absorb, interpret, and thereby extend the ethnography. Such long involvement with the individuals interviewed above has, however, had two other consequences, one not expected.

These long-term case studies have led me first to better understand the range of experience in my interpreters, including their unconscious feelings and defenses. My understanding is limited. But I do feel I know enough about my friends' personalities and psychodynamics to assess the normativeness of certain unconscious feelings. Saku's sense of self is so steeped in his shamanic role that his selfhood is merged with that role, and I believe he is unconscious of how much he defends himself and denies his past through that identity. These defensive identity feelings are aberrant, compared to other shamans. Another example: Moondi's erotic attachments to boys and to his fiancée typify his development and are also normative for Sambia men. These examples only show the presence of such unconscious factors; they do not explain their origins or functions in the individual or in Sambia culture. That explanation would require much more.* But I had expected that.

Second, by talking intimately with people for so long I created in them unconscious responses to myself, which I had not foreseen. They and I communicated (consciously, subliminally, unconsciously) at sufficient depth that they experienced new things in themselves. Insight. Sometimes they wanted this insight (e.g., Moondi) and some-

---

*Nor do we know, on finding similar psychodynamic functions, whether these unconscious factors would be the same for Sambia and Westerners. (Which Westerners? Men or women, children or adults, black or white, rich or poor?)

times not (e.g., Kalutwo). I, being the agent who stimulated these feelings, also awakened in them old conflicts. People resisted insight into that process; Moondi (e.g., his hesitation to describe his fellators' sexually exciting traits), Kalutwo (e.g., his exclusive homosexual orientation), Penjukwi (e.g., her anger over S.'s tattoo-probe, which she avoided), and Weiyu (e.g., his anger at Kalutwo, with whom he could not let himself identify), all showed resistance to knowing more. How typical is such resistance in Sambia culture? And what is being resisted: the questions at hand? Telling me more? Knowing more? (Or all of these avoidances?) In short, I became someone important inside these people, a person, similar to others in their pasts they had needed, from whom they expected feelings (consciously, unconsciously) that may have had little to do with the person I was. Transference. I had not expected that when first doing ethnography. I was naive.

Of all the dynamics of a long-term intercultural research relationship, those of transference and countertransference are the most crucial and the least understood.[45] Ethnographers who cannot draw on these concepts are crippled, their work shaped by forces they do not see. Would they be able to understand Kalutwo's need to be with me even when he cannot say what he wants? K.'s passive-dependent resistance is not a thing in itself; neither is his fear of what I or Weiyu would do were he to have told us what he wants erotically from boys. K.'s behavior is a transference reaction to what he feels I will do, say, or think. How much of Moondi's openness and cooperativeness is also transference? Or Saku's inability to discuss his body? Or his and Penjukwi's use of the term "master" for S.? A clinical ethnography without transference will not be clinical; in fact, it may not be much of an ethnography. [S: It cannot even occur; transference is always there, though rarely recognized.]

The same holds for the ethnographer's countertransference reactions (see Epilogue). Here, especially, we help our research along by observing ourselves. Reality-oriented feelings and ideas that do not spring from unmet needs (e.g., internal objects) filter through our behavior all day. But it takes clinical experience—prefield—to know what part of my annoyance and frustration toward Kalutwo is sensible and necessary for the relationship and what part is my countertransference to K. Knowing such differences shifts behavior, sharpens observations, and makes for different interpretations.*

Devereux (1967; 1978) has suggested that the troubling areas in an ethnographer's response to culture—those that distress him or her

---

*All responses are not countertransference though. See the following.

most—often contain the potential for theoretic insights. Yet, by their nature—distress—we shun them. That the natives do or do not suffer from discussing such areas is also significant. Whatever the area— shame, sexuality, cannibalism, psychosis—such ethnographer reflec- tiveness offers clues about what it is like (consciously, unconsciously) for the natives to experience these same issues. We cannot afford to ignore or avoid those clues through intellectualizations like "culture shock" or "reverse culture shock" (as examined in chapter 1).

Prolonged interviewing introduces greater transference/counter- transference elements in research, at home or abroad. Interpreting these influences becomes a part of interpreting our own and our translators' identities as reviewed above, for instance, in the way peo- ple use stereotypes about sexual partners or women (e.g., Moondi in chapter 4), quiet men (i.e., Imano in chapter 8), "true men" or rub- bish men (e.g., in chapters 5 and 9). To understand these stereotypes we are safest combining their meaning in private reports with ob- servations of their use by the same people in public, to create a fuller picture. But so far, I have referred to indigenous stereotypes and im- ages. What happens to this transference process when the ethnogra- pher introduces foreign concepts into the conversation?

Example: we used "fantasy" to indicate daydreams in our inter- views. (At times, though, "fantasy" also covered "mental images," "scripts," and "free association," concepts we shall not discuss now.) By introducing this concept to interpreters we change them. One must be alert to the consequences. I saw no harmful effects. [S: That de- pends on who defines "harmful."] But we do know that Moondi— now more aware of his imagery—may change what he does, says, or thinks. Obviously the appropriateness of our use of "fantasy" hinges on how well we understand Sambia culture, language, the interview context, and the person. Quite a lot. Ethnographers working closely with someone a long time will be able to use—and trust in—such concepts and resulting data and then link those to interpretations of culture and experience at large. Readers will want demonstrations of the alien concepts being used in context, to evaluate their meaning.

Some anthropologists may be uneasy using ideas like "fantasy". But remember that many anthropologic concepts, e.g., "soul," "trance," "omen," "self" are as laden with western connotations as is "fan- tasy," though only recently have we questioned their cross-cultural validity. Clinical ethnography, if it does nothing else, can help us think more carefully about such heuristic terms.

We do not work alone, of course, and we should be remiss not to thank our language/culture interpreters and indicate the importance of understanding their transference responses too. Weiyu's has been dealt with, perhaps more than he really cared for. Whiting and his colleagues (1966:156) indicated the tasks and potential bias of the *ethnographer* here. More recently, Crapanzano's[46] remarkable Moroccan case study has opened up more far-reaching implications of transference/countertransference issues in the interpreters' situation.

When western concepts are imported from other cultures we become more aware also of the specificity of transference responses. Not "Sambia fantasy," but "Moondi's fantasy" (on Tuesday afternoon, when his father was sick his mother gone to tend his father, M. moving into heterosexual relationships, sitting with me as S. looked on). A new concept embodies no necessary stereotypes, connotations, or meanings; thus, a person's responses to it are particularly revealing of his/her inner needs at the time. Thus, in this example of imported concepts, we must raise two other problems: how do they imply trust, and what is the truth-value of such material?

Trust is not truth. People may trust us—in degrees—but still not relate the truth, i.e., give us an account narrative. It is no news that people's communications are not courtroom testimony. Yet ethnographers seldom report that natives forget, misunderstand, have contradictory views, make slips, unwittingly mix information from one mode of discourse to another, etc. Truth is not a thing; it is many experiences buried in all these tactics, as is untruth. Trusting may yield more accurate forms of what our interpreters feel, at a particular moment, to be true about something. Do we show if or how they change their opinions? Trust limits distortions, which may never disappear, only fade. Someone's truth may not be drawn within black and white boundaries. And certain issues (e.g., Saku's hermaphrotism) may hold such power that only time—patience—will bring trust and truth (but not "the truth").

How do these private meanings relate to norms and institutions of a culture? What difference does it make, a structuralist might argue, if people disguise a lie: those untruths do not fundamentally affect the interpretation of social relationships or the unconscious structure of Mind (e.g., dualism as a principle of social structure). I would not be too sure. Whether or not Sakulambei trusts me does not change the existence of shamanism as an institution or a symbolic category in Sambia culture, but it does change how I interpret the relevant beliefs, rules, behaviors, experience. The depth of my knowledge aids my interpretations and colors my view. Perhaps certain structuralists believe they are more objective with primitives. We don't think so.

Our interviews show that when the interpreters trust us, they give us more information, but that is not "the truth;" the information we receive is modified by our interest, sincerity, boredom, hostility. (Granting this, the ethnographer must still make an interpretation that goes beyond the natives' view.) Trust shows itself in many voices. When Tali told us in private of ritual cult practices, for instance, was he speaking for himself or as a representative of the ritual cult? Does he share his private views only or what he thinks Weiyu or ourselves expect to hear? (What does he expect himself to think and feel?[47]) In chapter 5 we have a glimpse of this complex talk. What we cannot see, though, are the years of similar dialogues that came before; the background knowledge to which it refers in a Tali/Weiyu/Herdt discourse that is simultaneously public/private/secret and then again something more: a gestalt of our increasing intersubjective understanding as a group of three. (S. changed this group talk, and he challenged Tali's view, which I had never done.) So much background is needed to interpret these dialogues that the ethnographer draws back in dismay at trying to present them. And yet we did. Clinical ethnography will require creative researchers.

Because our interviews are not public talk or secret ritual talk but occur in an ambience of special private discourse, the nature of trust and transference responses to the fieldworker requires attention. We ensured privacy, asking others to leave the house. (Unprecedented, except in ritual talk viz. the uninitiated.) People were often remunerated: how did that change what they said? Knowing that what they said would remain confidential changed their talk. (Would Sakulambei have agreed to open his painful history to me otherwise?) Each such tactic changes trust, creates different transference responses. This private interviewing style is pretty far removed from conventional participant-observation. In short, as Bourguignon (1979: 87) put it, "Anthropologists have often argued that studying alien, 'primitive' societies made it possible to be a good deal more 'objective' than studying one's own society." By the end of her life, Mead[48] had wavered but never really defected from this view, and yet, she more than anyone, forced us to consider its limitations. Like Freud[49] before her, she was a captive of an old scientific ideology. That view is out of place in clinical ethnography; let us seek creative solutions to the lived contradiction: participate but observe. S. and I disagree somewhat on this matter: the explanation of our difference will bring us to the end of this chapter.

S: I am still not sure why H. has fussed so hard over this participant-observation: were I an ethnographer, I would want to be intimate and yet not family. When used in analytic treatment, participant-observation assures the patient of our closest, most intense attention without the threat of personal entanglements and therefore undue influence (as is inherent in transference). It is an attitude unlike that present in other therapies, for the analyst's desire is to hear—everything, were it possible—but not to coerce: not even with love, for coercion by love too often requires corrupt love. The analyst promises nothing but to listen, and when we do it well, our patients are heard as they never have been before, down to subjective levels they scarcely could imagine. It takes a peculiar personality, however, to practice this analysis: the capacity to merge and yet be fully separate in the same instant. To walk into the fire and not be burned. I don't see why this must be seen as "contradiction lived."

H: This view departs from mine in two ways. First (the least important) is that S. here conflates my criticism of the ideology of fieldwork with what ethnographers actually do. Generally, I agree that we can be involved and still detached in fieldwork. Were this not possible, we would remain only tourists or we would all go native. Yet, the old rhetorical uses of participant-observation ignore the fact that each researcher implements this approach in different ways, dependent not only on situations but our personalities and research interests as well. Nonetheless, that approach is held to be, in some ideal sense, a uniform method that is independent of the idiosyncracies. That rhetorical uniformity is, for me, a fiction. Second, and more important, psychoanalysts do not do participant-observation, which is based primarily in normative interactions with natives in *their* social world. S. recognizes this by saying, "The analyst promises nothing but to listen," which is not a normative interaction (who, in our world, converses with us by only listening, aside from God, except those in privileged positions of authority, assessment, treatment?[50]). It is a corruption of the already corrupt notion to refer to analytic therapy as participant-observation. [S: You've convinced me.] And likewise for clinical ethnography: we need a different paradigm for the interactions and discourses that occur in our case studies above. Nonetheless, no ethnographer—even in private interviews—could only listen, because others, feeling this to be bizarre, would make tracks.

We see in our difference of opinion a major contrast between the narrative styles of analysis and ethnography. Where the analyst is primarily concerned with the patients' private feelings and fantasies, the ethnographer is concerned mainly to use these as a way to better understand what shapes cultural institutions and public behavior. The difficulty with clinical ethnography is that it *is* concerned with idio-syncracy, but it must also be culturally based. I am distressed that some analysts, psychiatrists, and clinicians—sixty years after Freud's death—continue to ignore cultural factors in their writing (not to mention their treatment and training). There are some exceptions, but the failure of analysis to take culture seriously and the fact that psychoanalytic anthropology came from outside analysis and has not affected it much, remain disturbing signs of its culture-bound design. No one has argued more intelligently or forcefully for a sophisticated union of psychoanalysis and anthropology than LeVine.[51] His careful work reveals the great possibilities inherent in cross-cultural clinical method, a promise of much to come.

We reach an end when we confront the problems and potentials of clinical ethnography. It is neither traditional analysis nor conventional anthropology; it calls for a new intellectual ground. S. is unique: we should not generalize from his ability to reach beyond psycho-analysis to engage the Other in New Guinea. In fact, S.'s trip to New Guinea—aberrant for an analyst—must be seen as a sign that he does not fit the analytic mode in the same way as his colleagues. My friends sense this, though they had not the words to say it fully. In the Epi-logue we shall consider finally how analytic supervision under this psychoanalyst influenced this particular clinical ethnographer in the early years of his adventures in Paradise.

Training Clinical Ethnographers

H: How shall we train people to be clinical ethnographers? What skills should be taught and training experiences provided, before the field? What role will the supervisor play in the process? Here are some reflections.

Anthropologists who would do clinical ethnography should learn, as do clinicians in other disciplines, that oneself is the primary instrument. Seminars, books, theories, practicums, internships, and the like help. But they cannot substitute for the personality trained for empathy, self-knowledge, and skill in observing and interviewing. The ethnographer is the instrument; all else is technology. Yet to improve the instrument, we hope at least that students are trained in elementary techniques of interviewing. There are plenty of books on that subject, but they are no substitute for experience.

For training Ph.D. students in anthropology, we do not think it practical that they undergo treatment. Nor is psychoanalytic training indicated. To lay a psychoanalysis onto four years of undergraduate work and three years of graduate training is too much.[1] Analytic training, despite its rewards, may diffuse students' focus in the field. (Postdoctoral analytic training is another matter.) But reading in analysis and participation in seminars on analysis could widen horizons. What else might help? Seminars on counseling and interpersonal relationships, courses in interviewing techniques with practical experience, introductory psychiatry courses in medical schools, etc. The more supervised experience, the better.

To let the reader know I apply the same standards to myself, let me briefly consider how clinical training has affected my ethnography. What did it do to me to return to the Sambia, after receiving my Ph.D., each time loaded not only with more ethnographic knowledge but also with the clinical perspectives learned with the psychiatrist/analyst S.? This question is not easy to approach, for, as far as I know, it has never before been studied; we are in unfamiliar territory (Herdt and Stoller 1987). I shall, therefore, only skim the subject (and in doing so, anticipate the last section wherein I examine a shadowy presence crucial to field technique: how does the ethnographer study intimate matters without harming interpreters or information?).

What is different in my ethnography since 1974? First, the obvious: Sambia society shifted significantly. My interpreters changed and aged. And I, as expected of any ethnographer, grew into my profession. But though a system (in this case ethnographer-observing-interpreters-observing-ethnographer) may alter, some elements do so faster or more significantly than others. For me, postgraduate professional change was influenced most by working with S. To show how requires examples.

I brought to New Guinea the conviction that my research required closeness and trust with Sambia. Though I generally opened up my life to my interpreters as indicated above, and I had successes, there were also holes and weaknesses, even failures* in my work, as I concluded in Kalutwo's case study.

Transference issues were involved. Nilutwo's transference to me will indicate the limits of my predoctoral fieldwork (1974–1976) before supervision with a clinician helped change it into clinical ethnography. As noted above, Nilutwo was, in 1974, a troubled married man in his early thirties. He was a renowned womanizer and cassowary hunter. I began working with N. on his hunting activities, which involved his dreaming for prophetic omens. Soon, though, we were sitting daily for an hour or more, my listening to N. tell his previous night's dreams. N. was a prolific reporter of dreams, sometimes recounting two and three different long dream sequences from a night. He was intense, needy, and affectionate, but also broody, fragile, jealous, vindictive, and a bit paranoid. In a word: neurotic. After a few weeks he began to report seeing me in his dreams. I knew that this communicated closer rapport with me. I encouraged and supported his reports and had him interpret his dreams, (as far as he

---

*Perhaps failure isn't the right term; perhaps it is. Not failure *only* in the sense of material I didn't, or did not want to, or could not, collect (e.g., not being conscious that certain phenomena are "data"). Yet failure is the right word when we consciously back off, psychologically, morally, or politically, knowing that we can or should investigate certain matters that we do not.

could). I would ask questions when he finished talking. But I never interpreted his experiences for him. (I did do that, sometimes, later, in 1979.) I encouraged his associating to the dream images. His flair for this mode increased; soon, I often could not distinguish what was dream thought or secondary elaboration. And I appeared even more in his dreams, just as he came to rely on our talking sessions for cathartic release more than ever. I began to be concerned, in 1976—a while before leaving for home—that he was becoming too attached to me. (This later led to discussions between S. and me on the nature of transference and the risks of its flowering under the influence of a naive listener-interrogator-researcher-unwitting-quasi-therapist.)

Yet I did not then know how to deal with my anxiety. I had helped promote Nilutwo's transference to me, had allowed him to be closer to me and discuss subjects (like daydreams) he never discussed with anyone else. But I didn't know what to *do* with that transference. And toward the end I wondered if it was good for him: should we have engaged in this talking—which amounted to a supportive psychotherapy of sorts? (For instance, more than once we discussed his adulterous behavior and how he wanted help in getting out of the trouble it brought him.) In my position as white, powerful, possessions-rich (e.g., tennis shoes), geographically mobile, educated researcher, the power distributions of common friendship were as swamped as in a psychoanalysis.

Looking back over Nilutwo's materials, I realize that I dealt with my anxiety in a way that seems unhelpful now. When he finished a dream report and silence grew, I asked him for a *cultural* interpretation of his dreams. In other words, I referred him back to his own adult cultural symbol system—asking him, in effect, to provide an idealized interpretation of his experience. Anthropologists have often studied the manifest content or native interpretation system of dreams. That approach fits well in New Guinea cultures, the dream interpretation codes of which tend to project the experience (e.g., anxieties) outside of the dreamer onto externalized superego figures (e.g., ghosts).[2] The problem is that when I was uneasy I unconsciously accommodated myself to this cultural defense mechanism referring his *private* experiences to *public* symbols and norms.[3] This dampened his florid associations and made him distance himself from the transference, thus allowing us to be more comfortable.[4] (On the other hand, to have given him depth interpretations without being a competent psychoanalyst and without wrapping him in the safety of formal therapy would have put him at great risk.)

This example shows a bit of my early interview style. What effects of S.'s and my working directly together can be indicated in later fieldwork?

A second example: Kalutwo. My empathy for his rubbish man characteristics and ambivalence to me was low. But once we entered this new phase of clinical research, I became fascinated with his life history. I had told myself that avoiding him was simply a lack of interest. But supervision (which, like therapy, can be a deeper, inner-active process than being given facts and tactics by one's supervisor) revealed this to be a compound of my hostility and anxiety (i.e., countertransference). Now I realize how, like my male friends in the village, I had reacted to K. with contempt, in part as defense against anxiety he caused me.

By 1979 I also was sensitive to theory that relates sexual excitement and hostility, the result of working with S. This part of my clinical training culminated in discussions we had at UCLA about Sambia gender identity in 1978, before my leaving for the field. It even went on in New Guinea, supported by S.'s visit.

So I then began serious, lively interviewing with K., and I knew that my anxiety had distanced me from him. I had learned from S. more about the various forms of hostility, one of which was in myself: like Sambia men, I was threatened by K.'s unmasculine traits and so was amused at their jokes (a tactic that helped us avoid denying our unacceptable identifications with him). By 1979, more insightful, I saw through this defensive reaction to its cruelty: I had learned not only to recognize that anxiety in myself and to see how to reach for insight in understanding its source, but—the great bonus for one's data collecting (i.e., ethnography)—to use it as a clue to comprehending the other men's hostility. (A nontrivial understanding, because such clues improve one's search for the dynamics underlying myth, ritual, initiation, erotics, and even war.) Before clinical training at UCLA, I had not known how to proceed toward insight; now it still surprises me to have been hostile like that. (As with other unconsciously motivated reactions, that surprise indicates I can still repeat that hostility, but now it is easily dissipated, for it is within conscious control.) Anthropology can be done without insight only at the expense of such distortions.

Example three, from fieldwork in 1979: I have returned to the village after two and a half years' absence. The ritual cult is deteriorating: In the last initiations (1977) the men did not uniformly nosebleed boys as they've always done. The elders and ritual leaders are losing their grip. One morning, not long after I arrive, I am in my house with Tali, Weiyu, and other men, who are discussing the scandalous behavior of an eleven-year-old boy. He was initiated in 1977, making him a first-stage initiate. I know him and his family. The men are rubbishing the boy because he was recently caught in sex play with a girl, behavior so astonishing no one knows even *how* to punish him (another sign of the men's deteriorating control). The men generalize from this boy's behavior to all the new initiates—how they are weak, unmanly, and irresponsible—as the cult falls apart ("it's a sign of the times"). Even my friend Moondi, usually moderate in such matters, condemns the boy. So do I; and here is the heart of my example.

As the men related the incident my response changed from shock (to think the society has so deteriorated) to condemnation. I sympathized with the men, found myself feeling hostile to the boy. I joined with the men, righteously identified with their moral outrage—which only increased when an impudent young initiate, who happened along, thumbed his nose at the elders, adding that "One day, up on top there (i.e., heaven), Jesus will condemn the elders" for their sins (e.g., the initiation customs). I was as angry as the other men at this youngster's rhetorical imitation of a local evangelist's preachings (a New Guinean from outside the tribe). As the rhetoric heated up (only five minutes had passed during this whole episode), I suddenly stopped, struck that I, the ethnographer, was hostile to these boys. My sympathies were with the men in this divided camp of old versus young. So I questioned my motives and was ashamed.

Why was I hostile? Obviously I identified with the men, their ritual customs, and experiences of ritual we had shared in years past. My role and status were also tied to those events: not only inside the village but outside, through my work. Reflecting on my feelings I halted. I became—had to become—an observer of myself as well as a participant-observer. My behavior was not to be denied or covered up: it was what had to be explained. My motivations, conscious and unconscious, contributed to my understanding Sambia men and their rituals; but that is another story. Clinical training, especially S.'s supervision of those of my interests concerned with hostility, changed that moment of fieldwork. My point is this: rather than merely acting and reacting, I also reflected. Understanding the dynamics of Sambia ritual, generational relationships, erotics, and authority lies as much in my subjective response that moment as anything one might otherwise learn in Sambia life.

Example four: a reluctant informant. A man I have known for years—Gorutndun—had always refused me an interview. He was married, over thirty, gregarious, well liked. He was in a position of authority, too, which he opportunistically mined. I knew from gossip and my own impressions that despite his marriage and fatherhood he continued to have sex with boys. He seemed, that is, genuinely to like sex with both women and boys, and he defied custom by his persisting homosexual activities. He was not stigmatized like Kalutwo, though, for he was married and a swashbuckler, with achievements K. lacked. He being that kind of bisexual, then, I had long hoped to talk with G., wanting to understand his family history and gender dynamics as another male case study in my research. But despite every cordial move, I could not lure him to talk with me.

Before S.'s supervision, my response to G.'s reluctance would have been annoyance or, more insightful, to worry over what in myself prevented Gorutndun's talking with me. Now I could think further: I felt that G. avoided me to avoid that part of himself that I most wanted to understand. In other words, he feared looking inside, wanted no insight. And in this sense, at least, it is correct to say that he resisted me because he felt (perhaps from stories about my interviewing others) that I might probe areas he didn't want to probe. I saw his posture that way, accepted it, and did not hassle myself for not interviewing him. A shift occurred. We were cordial, but my cordiality had a resonance—an ease never there before. Two years later (1981) I asked him for an interview, which he granted. We discussed this bisexuality. It was no big deal. I was grateful to him and to myself for having the patience to see things through.

Final example: Weiyu's misogyny. Weiyu is my closest Sambia friend. We have seen him as an interpreter; I know his family intimately, know his wife, and helped him in his payment of bride wealth in 1974. Over the years he and his wife have fought a lot, as you know. Added to this is what one might call Weiyu's culturally characterologic misogyny, his feeling that aside from being objects to screw and produce babies, women are dirty, worthless, dangerous, and capable of corrupting and ruining men. Even years ago Weiyu and his beautiful wife would regularly argue and brawl. Villagers intervened but failed to calm them down; friends like Tali even pressed Weiyu to stop exploding; I talked to him too, several times scolding him for his hardness. He ignored us all.

Over the years he, like other Sambia men, also derided women: chauvinist jokes, locker-room talk, and dirty stories. My reactions were of two sorts. On the one hand, I found it distressing to see how men treated women: nothing bothered me then or now as much about

Sambia life as this misogyny. On the other hand, because in the mid-1970s I spent 90% of my time with males, had superficial contacts with females, and needed the men's material and psychologic support—not to mention friendship—I not only abided their antifemale joking but, in a latent way, reinforced it, often by eliciting material (beliefs, idioms, stories) about women, which aroused their jokes. (Again, as with the Kalutwo jokes, these putdowns kept men from being uncomfortable talking about women.) I chuckled or laughed sometimes, too, though often as not I stood back aloof. They seemed not to care, except, perhaps, for Weiyu, who knew from my negative responses how I felt. ("White man's strange morals"?)

This situation came full circle in a 1983 trip to Sambia. I thought that by then—Weiyu was almost thirty—he would mellow out. Yet the marital chaos was fierce as ever. It surprised me: he had not grown beyond his earlier misogyny, as do other men, at least somewhat, with the passing of time and arrival of children. And this pained me. They still had dreadful fights and Weiyu would break into bitter episodes in my hut of foully cursing his wife.

During this same time I had steadily worked more and more with women. Penjukwi had had the courage to talk seriously with me and had also made me for several years aware of the victims' side of the men's jokes about women. She showed me male/female relations through new eyes and ears. And we became friends, caught in grief over Nilutwo's death. And though the sexual antagonism of traditional Sambia culture had softened, I saw more than ever the men's power plays and abuses of women. The pathos of Sambia sexual culture.

Thus I changed: now more clinically adept and self-aware I found Weiyu's behavior hard to accept. His and other men's put-downs of women appealed not at all to me. I saw Weiyu as an extreme example of a character pattern that had this bitter outcome. The phallicness of his war-leader stance was not Sambia culture in the abstract, but, rather, a cold, rigid essence of the idealized masculinity of that tradition. I saw, too, that his wife sometimes created conflicts, as he did. I saw the games in which they entangled each other. I saw the other victims. I saw Weiyu become harder and less a friend to his men friends and to me. My increased identification with Sambia women made me understand the terrible reality of the men's jokes.

What, in regard to this last vignette, has changed in me? Hadn't I always understood Weiyu or the men's misogyny? Hadn't I always empathized with the women? Not quite. Part of me had resisted fully seeing my friend's feeling toward women and Sambia women's plight. I just presumed Weiyu's was a prolonged adolescence, to be outgrown. But it is not. And I resisted knowing Sambia women deeply: the combination of my personality, my American cultural orientation, and an old-fashioned professional androcentric disregard for females as culture-bearers served to intellectualize my reactions. But when congenial supervision met inner possibilities, I was more ready to understand Sambia women. I know Penjukwi as I could not have in 1974.

So I began to learn better, for instance, of the women's desire for erotic fulfillment in their marriages and their yearning to have their achievements as economic producers and mothers recognized. This understanding results from my valuing seeing men and women as individuals; from knowing that as individuals they differ in conforming to the cultural ideals ethnographers purport to have witnessed; and from my knowing that I, the ethnographer, sometimes selectively see what I want to see and interpret it according to how well I know myself. I was lucky—and wise—to return to these people enough over the years to observe them, as individuals, changing or frozen, just as the rest of the world is changing. This understanding of my countertransference I also learned in part from S.

The ability and desire to probe and understand our countertransference reactions is, to me, a hallmark of psychoanalysis and clinical ethnography. This may not require Freud's near obsession [S.: ??] with self-analysis (Becker 1973:102ff.), yet to others it might seem so. In anthropology those who have known this are few in number, but, they have made fine contributions to the study of culture. The difficulty is that the object of reflection—culture—and the lens of reflection—the ethnographer—must be revealed within the same text; and of such achievements one thinks of Lévi-Strauss' *Tristes Tropiques*, Read's *The High Valley*, and, close to anthropology, Doi's *Anatomy of Dependence*, and Kakar's *Shamans, Mystics, and Doctors*. Most recently, however, a virtually unprecedented account of countertransference in the construction of clinical ethnography is provided by Kracke (1987). Here is a rich new field of discovery awaiting us, though its mining will be plagued with unforeseeable and unprecedented training issues.

S: From the scientist's godly perch, H. is no more correct to sympathize with the cursed women than earlier when he dimly saw their viewpoint. Science is not sympathy. For we cannot argue that there is a final, essential level of truth the researcher on human behavior can attain. To know more is never to know enough. All is always interpretation.

So when he works better with the women, H. will have to go back and reinterpret his work on the men, and that will shift his perspectives on the women; *ad infinitum.* In the meanwhile he keeps changing inside. And then he becomes excited by the ideas of other colleagues—different sorts of psychoanalysts, antianalysts, molecular biologists, limbic lobists, Marxists, Marists, eschatologists, I Chingists, ethnomethodologists, neoplatonists, and phthisists. The hints, data, belief systems, truths—the interpretations—never end, always change.

To say the obvious, the same holds for the psychoanalyst. And in his or her role as supervisor, the analyst—in this case, I—is equally influenced by the ethnographer (or his students or patients), as useful a subject of study as the one we have just aired but too lengthy for consideration here.

Nonetheless, we would be foolishly even-handed not to repeat this last time our idea that ethnography is improved when the ethnographer (just as the medical clinician), by listening well—with what Freud called a "closely hovering attention"[5]—allows his interpreters to communicate better. That there is no bottom to the individual mind need not scare us off. Nor should we fear—as researchers—that by immersing ourselves deeply in individuals we shall ruin the great philosophic effort that searches for laws ruling particular events.

These five examples are the first that came to mind for H. We want to stress to readers that there are numberless more: these intersubjective and subjective processes go on all day long. The point is not that there is something special about H., or me, or this supervision, special though it may be; nor that H. is wise or foolish, insightful or blind, wrong or right. The same basic processes occur in us all, in all research, all the time. All supervision included. What we have added is simply another piece: an ethnography of supervision.

Some readers may see H.'s responses to supervision not as movements toward insight but as confusions due to meddling. Others may see in this book something even worse: exhibitionism, narcissism, sadomasochism, whatever.[6] But remember, the point is not that clinical supervision can strengthen one's ethnography—that cannot be proven with optimistic vignettes—but that *any* supervision (or our personality, not to mention the time of day, the weather, our mood of the moment, our religious beliefs, or our "'inexplicable" liking or disliking of an interpreter) changes the ethnography; we are simply showing again that these effects *are* ethnography, not artifacts to be denied. Or hidden.* If that makes the ethnographer's job harder, messier, more demanding of better and different training, and requires a capacity to study and understand oneself, then that's just too damn bad. As with the practice of psychoanalysis, ethnography—the process of working in one's head, not the morally easy hardships of malaria, lousy food, leeches, itches, rotten weather, hostile natives, exhaustion and fear—should not be done to spare the ethnographer.

H: We guess there are students in anthropology, sociology, psychology and the like who would use clinical skills more and better if only they could learn to trust themselves as one of the sources of understanding others. As Devereux argued in *From Anxiety to Method*, the basic datum in our disciplines is what happens within the observer. This statement is complex, yet there is no magic in it. To use oneself to measure others involves no more than hard work, commitment, an odd personality, formal training, good supervision, insight, worldly experience, and the desire to do clinical ethnography. Some students have the potential; it will become manifest in the right student when there is encouragement and a good role model, as in the supervision. Is not my ethnography more sensitive to interpersonal issues because of S.'s supervision? The answer lies not in our opinions: only more and better ethnographies will allow us to make such assessments.

Students have options in selecting their training. One course in interviewing will help refine one's sensitivity to other people. Where such courses do not exist, other opportunities can be found. Perhaps we should rethink training for the Ph.D. in Anthropology which, in this regard, resembles psychoanalysis: good work requires good technique (Foulks 1977:16), which is a function of one's relationship to others.

For students who wish to develop better field research skills we should allow more time in their training for supervised fieldwork at home before beginning their Ph.D. project abroad. Training in some of these skills (e.g., interviewing techniques) is available in a few anthropology departments in the United States. However, Departments of Psychiatry are not providing the kind of cultural training we need.[8] We must be innovative and activist in developing better training programs.

A final point regarding training: we need—in respect to all the

*H: However, my uneasiness at times with the autobiography here and above is a sign of my professional socialization that we should not truly disclose our insides in publications.[7]

above—better supervision in anthropology. My guess—as an observer of anthropology departments and as a teacher—is that Ph.D. students aren't as afraid of working closely with interpreters as they are of talking to their professors about talking with the natives. Some advisors may still adhere to the sink or swim philosophy critiqued in chapter 1. They may feel it is unnecessary to teach interviewing skills. This would be a pity. They may also be overly concerned with professional boundaries, or be concerned to discuss with students an area in which they themselves are weak. And anthropology does attract the idiosyncratic; who else transplant themselves in this way among aliens?[9] If comfortable with natives, the student may encounter difficulty working intimately with others at home; yet clinical training requires such intimacy. Avoiding such training means people will not see what you are like, or what you do or do not know, or how skilled you are in communicating. The end comes full circle when the student's professors, too, do not have clinical training or skills, and, beyond teaching these subjects, resist knowing themselves what they do not want to know. We do not need a Freud to tell us that this situation will produce unwanted side-effects. Let us hope for another generation of ethnographers who will find clinical ethnography of enough value to overcome these problems.

ETHICAL ISSUES

Does clinical ethnography bring special risks to the ethnographer or the natives? Are we placing additional burdens on young adults' already strained heads in not only sending them to alien places but asking them to get inside their interpreters? The particular answers depend on the personality of the researcher and the circumstances of the research. Still, there are obvious pros and cons.[10]

First, a simple distinction: there is a difference between doing casual interviewing and intensive prolonged talking with individuals. For the latter, care and discretion should be taken in selecting clinical ethnographers. Only someone who is psychologically healthy should go to the field [S: It is not that simple; and what is "psychologically healthy"?]; but only those who are demonstrably skilled at home in one-on-one interactions should do clinical ethnography.[11]

Second, the great risk in ethnographic training is for clinical issues *never* to be dealt with. (1) We cannot know what stresses students will be exposed to, but at least we should let them know something about how to recognize and cope with stress (2) without being undone by their own conflicts, guilt, or exploitation of others in the field. (3)

Being trained to recognize anxiety—particularly disturbing experiences—is a powerful advantage to students. Rather than reacting, they can act. To repeat: what we find most disturbing in another culture is often precisely what is important to study, not avoid. Whatever the substance of these disturbances—cargo cult beliefs, homicide, dreams, whatever—such anxieties felt by a healthy researcher probably point to experiences disturbing in one way or other to the natives. (4) The ideologic baggage of culture shock in anthropology indicates our awareness that we are not adequately handling all the reality we are responsible for recording. (5) The shroud surrounding deep intimacy with the natives—for example, sexual relationships*—and the shadows that make going native so sinful indicate that our training procedures can be improved. These points underline that faulty fieldwork training at present perpetuates the risk of the past. What a pity if our shame at being subjective prevented us from knowing more when we easily could.

Nonetheless, anthropology is too injudicious when, in not giving ethnographers clinical skills, it places certain interpreters at risk. Though it may well be true that "they will live out most of their lives without our creative intervention" (M. Strathern 1981:684), we do not know what the effects of our intervention will be for the rest of their lives.

S: It is unclear, when, because of trusting feelings generated in a relationship, one person may decently, honorably, or legally take advantage of another: the concept of undue influence arises. In ethnography, as long as we seem alien to our interpreters, they may be protected by their suspicions and their lack of love for us. Even so, their envy and awe of the power that accompanies our visible technology, money, capacity to escape their environment when we wish, our education and knowledge, and our other emanations of superiority can endanger them. But they are especially susceptible when they respect and love us.

We presume many ethnographers know of these effects and recognize their power in eliciting information. We feel it is useful, nonetheless, to point explicitly to the problem of undue influence, because it may greatly tempt the ethnographer. It is considered rape to seduce

---

*It is astounding but understandable that in the whole ethnographic literature I know best—Melanesia—there is not one sentence on an ethnographer's sexual feelings for (let alone involvements with) the natives. (Exclude Malinowski's diaries since he could not rise from the grave to agree to their publication, even though, I am told, they were highly edited by others regarding this sexual content.)

or otherwise inveigle into sexual intercourse people too uninformed to know the consequence of what they are willing to do: children below a certain age, mental defectives, and those rendered incompetent by mental illness. So must the ethnographer not take (nonerotic—as well as erotic) advantage of his vulnerable subjects in order to gain advantage.

As in supervising medical students, clinical psychology predoctorals, social workers, psychiatric residents, and psychoanalytic candidates, graduate schools can choose and train ethnographers to be trusted intimates of those they study, without freezing into pseudoscientific obsessive-compulsivity or broiling to a crisp in hysterical mystical unions with their savages. Either of these extremes is unethical (not to say indicative of poor research), since the ethnographer's work is grossly distorted by his or her neurosis (countertransference).* Why should ethnographers not be bound to that fundamental ethic of the physician: *Primam non nocere?*

This stance means the student will feel, after training, that he or she will not harm others with the information they confide. The ethnographer, so removed from the university, cannot be supervised or monitored in any real sense. Working thus alone, how are we to train students in knowing the difference between a true conviction and a conviction used to rationalize things that harm? There are no simple answers to this problem, but we do have indicators we can follow.[12] First, there are tape recordings, case and field notes that can be shared with supervisors and others. Second, there is the fact of interpreters working with someone a long time. While this is no absolute assurance that the ethnographer was trusted, it is a sign of being able to work intensely with people (who, in general, will not continue talking to those they do not trust, no matter how much they are materially reimbursed). Third, there is the student's presence in the material, which offers a gauge for evaluation by others.[†] Finally, there are the communications with supervisors—letters from the field, discussions and review of material at home.

H. knows—it was latent till made manifest in supervision with me—that aspects of ethnography resemble the risks and rewards of psychoanalysis, a domain wherein patients' well-being must come first. Once that awareness is part of the ethnographer's flesh, one is free.

---

*We should not be too severe. Probably, comparable to what happened in some of the psychoanalytic pioneers, new findings and great ideas sometimes flap out of crazy ethnographers' heads: we do not need many calm, insightful people; they are often unimaginative.
†Though we depend on others to be honest in reports we can do little when someone fabricates material.

Then it is easy to ask about and explore virtually anything, knowing the information will not be used for harm: a historical, political, philosophic, ethical, and moral stand on individual freedom;[13] to be free enough inside ourself to listen so well that we finally hear. Then, when we are with others, we shall be allowed to begin to experience what they know and, beyond that, what they dare not know they know.

When we have it, our interpreters—the ethnographer's subjects and the therapist's patients—are no less able to sense this openness than can our friends. The resulting mutuality will be fine, the beginning of the end of the hatred—the refusal to listen—that still poisons most human endeavors. Including anthropology and psychoanalysis.

S. and H: You see, clinical ethnography can be done most anywhere you stick your nose. That's pretty much how it was with us. S. was to drop in on H. at the village for a few days. Yet here we are, years later, concluding a book we never intended to do, still exploring, agreeing and disagreeing. A few more visits and we would add more case studies; a better view of women, the children, the elderly; a description of the dissolution of a culture; an ethnography of supervision; more on tourists, patrol officers, and missionaries; a picture of what our doing clinical ethnography did to us; and how our clinical interventions (e.g., the coming of insight into one's motives) affect a culture and its people.

If, by doing that, others would know that clinical ethnography has to be done everywhere, then they could easily do it better. Our success will occur when we become passé.

Let us end with this: the discourse in anthropology between ethnographer and interpreters and in psychoanalysis between doctor and patient must be opened to closer scrutiny. And if we in these disciplines cannot do it, who will?

The Editing Process

S: In the introduction we examined the value of using subjectivity to learn about culture via others' subjectivity. We face another aspect of this problem in the interviews in this book: how data are infiltrated by a different subjectivity—the process of editing. When the reader reads our words, what stands between what occurred and the conclusions we draw? When we were there talking with our Sambia friends, what was happening in them and what in us that no machine can capture? How are our data thereby flawed and what are the consequences of that impairment for those who would be scientific? Our book is a study of these questions; but at this point, let us suffice with a description of the editing process that starts when the tape begins to run and ends with the published words.

One speaks. The tape does not pick up the words with their original fidelity. Some are muffled, some are overridden when more than one person talks, some are hard to retrieve if a participant sits rather far from the machine. Batteries or tape run out without our being aware. The tape ends, and we notice but lose a sentence or two every time because the process of recording stops a few moments before the tape stops. Tapes disappear in harsh living and traveling conditions (this did not happen to us). Conversation is lost when a cassette is turned onto the second side or a new one installed.

The tapes arrive home safely. H. now listens and translates onto new tapes in English. Will he miss anything due to fatigue or unconscious slips? What is the relationship between the Sambia or Pidgin spoken and the words he chooses for the English translation? (This problem was faced continuously during the interviews when Sambia was being translated to Pidgin and when H. translated and summarized in English for S.) How well—months and years later, when trying

395

to recapture exactly what was happening—do we recall the setting, the looks on people's faces, the other forms of communication that so much shape and change the meanings of words? How (in 1979) does S.'s memory (age 54 in 1979 and in a different relationship to the participants from H.) compare with H.'s (age 31 then, talking with friends he has known for several years)?

H: It may interest the reader to know I transcribed in two ways: by dictation and by writing. Most of the tapes were transcribed by listening word-for-word to the tapes, while simultaneously dictating literal translation (with punctuation, intonation remarks, etc.) onto another tape from which a secretary typed to produce a text. Some of the last tapes I transcribed by listening and writing down dialogue word-for-word in longhand. It is boring. But checking my transcriptions I find that dictating throws in more errors (slips, gaps), and the translation is much rougher than when I write it. On the other hand, the dictated text preserves better the Sambia flavor. An hour of original dialogue took about ten hours (depending on the speaker, situation, etc.) to translate, but one cannot work continuously: I am numb after four or five hours. We suffer, but not as much as the linguists. Healey (1964:19) reports that it took seventy hours to transcribe an hour of text phonemically and "to obtain a fairly accurate free translation." (He says he and his translator could only bear three hours a day.) "Fairly accurate" is all I can claim for my translations; will I think that in twenty years?

S: Now H. delivers the tapes to secretaries for transcription. This transcribing work is hard: boring, wearing. (Even H.'s tapes—his translations, not the originals—are occasionally hard to make out.) What about secretaries transposing words, leaving out fragments, misperceiving words, making slips?

Let us call the product of the above labors our "raw material." What do we do to it? From here on, the reader is completely at our mercy. We could invent conversations that never occurred, report nuances we know were not present or nuances we sensed but that other observers would deny were there. (See Stoller and Geertsma [1963] on clinicians' inability to agree on what they observe.) What if pieces were removed to win arguments rather than because they are repetitive, or garbled, or—in the mass—would bore the reader into giving up reading?

Most people would despair if confronted, in a book bought for amusement or education, with raw typescript. It is our task to edit the material to make it coherent and lively and to add commentary, hoping we can restore the experience to one that simulates, for the reader, what we believe happened.* That removes the words we publish from the category of data; they are now only approximations of the original.† (The professional reader's defense against this is the presence of our original tapes, but who will go to the effort of retracing our steps; and if you do so, you have only the verbal/aural parts of the interviews. That portion is hardly enough. Though we do not know how to solve this problem, we illustrate it with a fragment in chapter 4 to show, by example, how we did this first-stage editing: see pp. 107–108).

Once we have in place, for better or worse, the replication/simulation of interviews, we must not then fool the reader: whenever we narrate, speculate, hypothesize, and conclude, we shall somehow announce our tentativeness.

And what about style? All writing has its style, even that alleged to be pure reporting. Which style should be used? How does style get created when there are two authors?

Writing is editing (Moraitus 1981). (So, of course, is conversing, thinking, remembering, daydreaming and other forms of fantasizing.) Even choosing not to edit is to edit. And if the task is to take written typescripts and try to make them (force them to) evoke a situation where speech and presence are the vehicles of communication, then we are into creative work, perhaps comparable to that of the artist but with different constraints of honesty imposed. (Ours are more severe, though we are not necessarily less corrupt.) We must even imagine how to keep readers interested, as when we decide to throw away a piece that concerns us but would be too picayune or esoteric for the audience we imagine.

All right: we do our writing and, on each submitting a piece to the other, we force on ourselves another level of editing—framing—in our effort to agree on that we shall allow to stand.

H: Here the problem of aptness in style (formal, informal) and the

---

*May I call this true fiction? All nonfiction is fiction. All fiction is nonfiction fictionalized to hide that it is nonfiction(?). Mailer (1980:33): "No writer of serious consideration is ever honest except for those rare moments—for which we keep writing—when we become, bless us, not dishonest for an instant. . . . We are all dishonest, we exaggerate, we distort, we use our tricks, we invent. After all, it is almost impossible even writing at one's very best to come near the truth." Is this quote one of those instants; or is the liar lying?

†Analytic colleagues look puzzled or disbelieving when I say that no one has ever yet presented the data on which so much of analytic theory depends. Their reaction is even less benign when I say there has never been a psychoanalytic report—Freud's included—that is clinically accurate. (See Gill 1982; Gill and Hoffman 1982.)

choice of idioms and colloquialisms enters. If informal style, we select apt constructions for awkward ones (e.g., "let's look at" instead of "it is time to examine"). Knowing the cultural/personal load of Sambia idioms, I choose American idioms that best match the corresponding meanings in Sambia/Pidgin (e.g., Sambia "shame" for the English "ashamed," the former more powerful; English "encircles" or "fences in" for Sambia "encircle with a fence" in the sense of protecting or hemming someone in). We (H. and S.) then must decide on the appropriateness of colloquialisms: S. inserts these at places that seem awkward or wrong to me, so I remove them or suggest substitutes for them. What concerns me is not just literalness in the translation but metaphoric appropriateness. (How do you measure appropriateness?) Does our American sexual slang "screwing" cover the Sambia term, which literally says "to shoot into"? I agree with S., so the word stands. But others (the reader does not see) are changed; and some changes are so subtle that even New Guinea specialists might miss them: editings of editing without warning signs to readers. So our Americanness is always there. Again, we are concerned that as *clinical* ethnographers our clinical language style not usurp the ethnography, which must faithfully reflect the subtle meanings of the moment. Most anthropologists will regard such nuances as important but not germane to normative, institutional-oriented ethnographies. But in our work they are crucial.

S: When we have a first draft, we do it again; and again and as often as necessary till we are satisfied. That draft we submit to a publisher; which firm publishes the book helps determine its contents, too. The publisher sends the manuscript to one or more professional referees to evaluate the book. The referee gives his/her opinions, which may be sent to us for incorporation. When the manuscript is accepted, an editor (supposedly) goes over every word and mark, making suggestions of greater or lesser import and at times thereby introducing a ghostly new presence into the material. We get that feedback; on which suggestions do we agree? Then the copy editor intervenes, in some places to help and some to be bossy. And at the end of the production process are the several bouts of proofreading, which result (one hopes) in only a few more changes.

If photographs are used, verisimilitude brings dozens more distortions, from type of film used (e.g., color or black-and-white, ASA number) and camera technique (e.g., make and type of box and of lens, aperture, f-stop) to time of day, framing of the scene, or blurring for dramatic effect. These are all acts of editing, the greatest of which is, perhaps, one's decision even to take a picture. Then comes the gross editing, once the film is developed (and, by the way, which laboratory shall we use?) of choosing the shots that best illustrate our points, or of cropping, or of quality of reproduction, or placement in the text, or how many pictures to use.

And then there are attention-transformers like dust jackets, forewords, indexes, covers—hard and soft, printing type, paper used.

All that work, all that editing, all that struggle to be clear, all that strain toward accuracy. Yet we shall still be defeated, by one reader more and by another less, by our very words, syntax, even punctuation, devices that, in stirring up multiple meanings we tried to avoid, make the reader believe something we did not say. And a skeptical or angry or friendly or inexperienced or experienced or psychotic or uneducated or prejudiced or intelligent or sensitive or knowledgeable reader may understand exactly what we are saying and decide that, nonetheless, what we are saying hides rather than exposes the truth. Each page is a Rorschach card.

Another problem that infuences the editing is that of confidentiality. In order to underline the great ethical issues involved, I separate this discussion here from the more mundane matters just reviewed. In both psychoanalysis and ethnography there are, of course, innumerable situations in which our subjects are not jeopardized by what they tell us. But ethnographers know as well as analysts that they could put their informants at risk; to prevent that, one must use disguises and deletions, devices against which readers may have no defense. In the balance between scientific integrity and protecting one's subjects, our society and our consciences demand that subjects come first*—if they are our own people. How close to that decency should the ethnography of alien cultures come? In the case of the Sambia, it is not enough to tell them that we plan to release our findings to strangers. For, obviously, they cannot imagine the process of placing a book into public hands and the uncounted ways in which information can disseminate without limitation. Should ethnographers abide by the standards of informed consent applied to physicians in the United States? To do so might end the practice of ethnography. (Were the same ethical concerns enforced for newspapers, magazines, radio, and TV, these media would also shut down. And so would the First Amendment to our Constitution.)

Only a person who has never written for publication would think

---

*Which, if there were no others, is a reason why analysts can never present their data—only anecdotes; and no one knows better than an analyst how critical can be each word, each inflection, each gesture, each pause: anything left out can skew the report.

these issues of writing and editing—suffered but not publicly discussed—are trivial in research (though most who do write decide then
not to mention the matter). For us, the absence of stated concern among
psychoanalysts, psychiatrists, and anthropologists (and sociologists,
psychologists, and historians) makes it unsafe to accept anyone's descriptions in the way we usually can in the physical sciences. The
differences between the latter and our disciplines are not just those
of appropriate measuring instruments but the failure of our kind of
researchers to admit that *they* are the primary instrument, which puts
them splat in the middle of the field to be examined.

Why punish our reader with this review of the publishing process?
Because we believe that many colleagues forget and their audiences
do not realize that each of these steps is as much a part of the research as the original encounters with "the culture." At the heart of
this book is the idea that "the data" are in an unending state of change
from the instant they first pass into the researcher's mind (that is,
are perceived) until, transformed by writing and publishing, the reader
incorporates them. Since a search for accuracy—for even a truth—
can be disrupted at *any* step in the process, we want *all* to be legitimized as methodology.

Being an analyst, I am distressed that these issues are not acknowledged whenever analysts write up their clinical data. In the absence of research to find the effects of editing on the observations
reported from treatment, I must insist that psychoanalysis today has
no unique, acceptable database. (It could when analysts realize we
do not yet.) It is physically painful for me to read one more analyst's
bragging—repeated dozens of times a year in our literature—about
"our science" (Stoller 1985b). Well, "science" is only a word. Our concern is not with labels but with our desires *to trust that what is reported actually occurred.* For me (but not for the dictionary, where
even reading, writing, boxing, and theology are sciences, leaving
therefore the question what in human endeavor is *not*), that is an
essence of science; and there is a well-tested system—called "scientific method"—for protecting the trust we put in people who are reporting experiences. (The issue here is not one of discovery but of
confirmation, for the scientific method is not necessarily suited for
making discoveries. Discovery comes from exploration [first in our
mind, then in the world], which, depending on the problem, may or
may not benefit from scientific method.)

What I am discussing, then, is trust, and this long description of
the problems of editing is an aspect of the principal subject of this
book, which is about trust. In what ways are the statements made by

a researcher connected to his or her original observations? Because researchers are inevitably and manifoldly biased, their audience deserves every possible defense against these distorting tendencies. Therefore, though this is a book on ethnography, we feel that our concerns about researchers' subjectivity apply as well for all who would study behavior. Whenever research aims at understanding human behavior, researchers' personalities—idiosyncracies, styles, neurotic conflicts, cultural background, biology, social status, education, etc., etc.—become part of the data.

NOTES

Preface

1. "Why is so much anthropological writing so antiseptic, so devoid of anything that brings a people to life? There they are, pinned like butterflies in a glass case, with the difference, however, that one often cannot tell what color these specimens are; and we are never shown them in flight, never see them soar or die except in generalities. The reason for this lies in the aims of anthropology, whose concern with the particular is incidental to an understanding of the general" (Read 1965:ix).

2. LeVine (1982:220 ff.) suggested collaboration between a behavioral scientist of the host culture and one from the outside.

3. Devereux (1967, 1978); LeVine (1982:292–293); and Sullivan (1937).

4. H: Over the years I have come to realize that psychoanalysts must practice analysis and anthropologists ethnography, whether in New Guinea, Chicago or wherever, or else the strength in such fields evaporates, the practitioners transmuted.

5. La Barre (1978:70) lists a number of such teams. Also Singer (1961:65): "The culture and personality approach thus requires an alternating and almost simultaneous use of two different perspectives—that of culture and that of the individual person. The approach necessarily requires either a close collaboration between an anthropologist and a psychologist or, as in Sapir's case, the capacity for bifocal vision."

Introduction

1. DuBois (1944), Lewis (1965); reviewed in Langness and Frank (1981).

2. Especially the vintage Geertz (1973) and his lecture on anti-antirelativism (Geertz 1984), for a statement of the issues.

3. The term comes especially from Marcus and Cushman's (1982) review.

4. Especially the Shweder and LeVine (1984) volume, and Shweder's (1984) rethinking of the critical problems in cultural perspective.

5. H: Since Malinowski, the professional ethnographer has had to spend from one to two years or more in one place for his colleagues to feel comfortable that his reports are trustworthy. But certain ethnographic classics, we know, have often

come from intermittent or brief episodes of field work (e.g., Lévi-Strauss 1969; Radcliffe-Brown 1922) and some classical papers derive from just a few days' or a week's visit, and yet priceless data were collected (e.g., Elkin 1953; Read 1954).

6. One can also read the early work of Sapir (1937), Mead (1949, ch. 2; reviewed in our chapter 1), and even Benedict (1934) as illustrative of the point; but for contemporary and extraordinary demonstrations of the perspective, Crapanzano (1980) and Kracke (1987).

7. Sapir's (1938) classic essay is "Why Anthropology Needs the Psychiatrist"; see also the discussion in chapter 1.

8. Psychoanalysis is a very blurred microscope, but our enemies are wrong in attacking not only our microscopy but the idea of a microscope.

9. Again, the basic insight comes from Devereux's (1967) text, which, in spite of follow-up comments from LeVine (1982) on this same point, is still largely ignored (Kracke and Herdt 1987).

1. Clinical Ethnography

1. Stocking (1980:285). And Habermas (1971:228): "Thus psychoanalytic hermeneutics, unlike the cultural sciences, aims not at the understanding of symbolic structures in general. Rather, the act of understanding to which it leads is self-reflection."

2. Reviewed in Marcus and Cushman (1982); Singer (1980).

3. For instance: how do we—in the profession—reconcile the very different images and interpretations of the same culture? Viz. Bennett's (1946) classic paper on Pueblo ethnography; Lewis (1951) on Tepotzlan; and Feil (1978) and Meggitt (1974) on the Enga. (Reviewed in Agar 1980; Bourguignon 1979.)

4. "It began as the observer moved from the mission compound or from the rocking chair on the front porch of some inn or the office of a colonial administrator to the place where the people actually lived" (Mead 1977:4).

5. Leach(1958); Stocking (1974); Young (1979).

6. For Boas (see Stocking (1968), Benedict (1934), and Mead (1939), there was the "Science of Culture" and the "Science of Man"; for Radcliffe-Brown (1952) it was the "Science of Society"; and for Malinowski (1926) it was the "Science of Custom."

7. It is perhaps no accident that much of the earliest anthropology developed in museums, and that museums are ". . . cultural institutions in the 'marked' sense of the word. For museums . . . metaphorize ethnographic specimens and data by analyzing and preserving them, making them necessary to our own refinement although they belong to some other culture. The totem poles, Egyptian mummies, arrowheads and other relics in our museums are 'culture' in two senses: they are simultaneously products of their makers and of anthropology, which is 'cultural' in the narrow sense . . . . In this light it is scarcely astonishing that Ishi, the last surviving Yahi Indian in California, spent the years after his surrender living in a museum" (Wagner 1975:27–28).

8. "The anthropologist's laboratories are primarily primitive societies, small isolated groups of people who because of their geographical or historical isolation have remained outside of the mainstream of history . . ." (Mead 1949:23).

9. The ethnomethodologists have provided a partial repositioning of this model, minus cultural and personal intentionality (Giddens 1976:40).

10. Malinowski (1922:22); Leach (1954, 1961b, 1976) for a similar view. Stocking (1983) insightfully reviews this trend.

11. Cf., for example, Giddens (1976), Hallpike (1973), Harris (1979).

12. Malinowski (1922, 1927; but see 1935) and Radcliffe-Brown (1922:viii–ix).

13. Barnes (1967:197–199; Hymes (1974); James (1973). Asad (1973:17): "The colonial power structure made the object of anthropological study accessible and safe—because of it sustained physical proximity between the observing European and living non-European became a practical possibility. It made possible the kind of human intimacy on which anthropological fieldwork is based, but ensured that intimacy should be one-sided and provisional."

14. Reviewed in M. Strathern (1988).

15. We do not perform experiments. Even the useful idea of a "natural experiment" fudges the term "experiment." As Geertz (1973:23) says: "The famous studies purporting to show that the Oedipus complex was backwards in the Trobriands, sex roles were upside down in Tchambuli, and the Pueblo Indians lacked aggression (it is characteristic that they were all negative—'but not in the south'), are, whatever their empirical validity may or may not be, not 'scientifically tested and approved' hypotheses. They are interpretations, or misinterpretations, like any others, arrived at in the same way as any others, and the attempt to invest them with the authority of physical experimentation is but methodological sleight of hand."

16. For instance, Briggs (1970), Dumont (1978), Levy (1973), and Read (1965).

17. Indeed, Geertz's *The Religion of Java* (1960:7) opens with this statement: "But it seems to me that one of the characteristics of ethnographic reporting. . . is that the ethnographer is able to get out of the way of his data, to make himself translucent so that the reader can see for himself something of what the facts look like and so judge the ethnographer's summaries and generalizations in terms of the ethnographer's actual perceptions." Do facts speak for themselves, as Durkheim thought? How could one judge the "actual" perceptions of someone without knowing that someone? Here we see a somewhat more positivist Geertz speaking than that of his "thick description" essay (1973). Marcus and Cushman (1982) and others have critiqued this stance, but in cultural, not psychologic, terms.

18. Casagrande (1960), Freilich (1972), Golde (1970), and others.

19. LeVine (1982) and Schneider (1968:1–8) for discussion.

20. LeVine (1982:237–240, 285–304). Also Crapanzano (1980); Herdt (1981: chapter 2); Obeyesekere (1981).

21. Herdt (1987d) on this aspect of Sambia dreaming.

22. At all levels of awareness. We know, however, that powerfully felt mental states, with their inevitable conviction, may never, no matter how well conscious knowledge is brought to consciousness, reach insight regarding the effects of economic, political, or other social forces—the avalanche of history—that shape the individual's subjective sense of self with all its dynamics.

23. As a conceptual framework in its time, notwithstanding its costs or benefits.

24. Herdt (1981:328), borrowed from Wallace (1969). In having joined the critics of the so-called "privacy theories of meaning," Geertz has not, either in early (1966) or later (1976) writings, addressed the problem of how private meaning relates to the public; what role the individual plays in related cultural transformations; how anthropologists can know about the "experience near" (Kohut 1971); or what reliability symbolic interpretations have.

25. "Ethnographic findings are not privileged, just particular: another country heard from. To regard them as anything more (*or anything else*) than that distorts both them and their implications . . . " (Geertz 1973:23).

26. Are these tactics the result of our lack of real understanding, our ignorance of the vernacular (Owusu 1978)? How do—and will—natives react when they read our texts? Not too well, Tedlock (1983) argues.

27. Sapir (1938). We might have begun with Sapir's (1949:574) far-reaching advice: "Instead, therefore, of arguing from a supposed objectivity [uniformity] of culture to the problem of individual variation, we shall, for certain kinds of analysis, have to proceed in the opposite direction. We shall have to operate as though we knew nothing about culture but were interested in analyzing as well as we could what a given number of human beings accustomed to live with each other actually think and do in their day to day relationships."

28. LeVine's (1982) treatment of the subject, to repeat, is the essential text.

29. *Reports of the Cambridge Expeditions to the Torres Straits* (1901–1933).

30. See Herdt (1984) for a review of the dizzying assortment of styles, flavors, depth and breadth and fantasy in Melanesianists' accounts of ritualized homosexuality in Melanesia since the 1860s.

31. The Oxford English dictionary generously defines ethnography as the "scientific descriptions of nations or races of men, their customs, habits and differences."

32. "In his *Elementary Forms of the Religious Life* Durkeim subjects other theorists of religion to remorseless criticism, but not the writers about the Australian Aboriginals on which he bases his own. So elementary a precaution applies also to our own monographs, which we take far too much on trust" (Evans-Pritchard 1962:176). Inevitably, of course, Evans-Pritchard's criticism has been turned back on his own work (Read 1980:183).

33. Turnbull on the Ituri (1961).

34. Turnbull on the Ik (1972).

35. Lévi-Strauss (1969).

36. Freud (1913).

37. Hallpike (1977).

38. Fortune (1932).

39. Benedict (1946).

40. Malinowski (1927).

41. Benedict (1934).

42. Geertz (1966).

43. Briggs (1970).

44. Mead on Arapesh (1935).

45. Gluckman (1969); Rappaport (1968).

46. Thomas (1959).

47. Lanternari (1963).

48. Mead on Mundugumor (1935).

49. Mead on Tchambuli (1935).

50. Heider (1976).

51. Meggitt (1964).

52. Malinowski (1922); Mead (1949).

53. Roheim (1932).

54. Victor Turner (1968).

55. Lévi-Strauss (1967).

56. Radcliffe-Brown (1952).

57. Leach (1961a).

58. Geertz (1973).

59. For example, Sontag's (1966) "The anthropologist as Hero"; and see also Hymes (1974) and Bohannan (1979).

60. Mead (1970:328) believed that some of this criticism stemmed from the small world of anthropology, which involves colleagues who are "real or fictive husbands, lovers, friends, parents, or children . . . . The violence of some of the internecine in-fighting that goes on within anthropological circles can be explained by the incestuous overtones of such intense relationships. Anthropologists of my generation still regard all other anthropologists, including those whom they have never met, as kin, toward whom one may express all the ambivalence generated by close family ties and toward whom one is totally obligated to provide succor *in extremis*. As the profession grows so much larger, this sense of kinship becomes harder to establish and it may be that it will survive only in the extraordinary bad manners of anthropological reviewers who will imitate their elders' style without recognizing that that style was accompanied by the kind of unquestioning willingness to help appropriate to those who regard themselves as members of one large family."

61. Reviewed in Agar (1980), Bourguignon (1979), Devereux (1967). See Murray (1979) on the especially problematic case of Castaneda's works.

62. By 1953, Fortes could write: "What Crooke foresaw in 1910 has come to pass, and it is no longer possible for the amateur, however gifted, to make a contribution of theoretical value in social anthropology" (Fortes 1974:433). Lay ethnographers in Melanesia, whether missionaries (e.g., Chalmers 1903; Leenhardt 1979), administrators (e.g., Murray 1912), patrol officers (e.g., Sinclair 1966), aside from the government anthropologists, have made contributions, though their theoretic value is open to debate.

63. For example, Agar's (1980:43) discussion of the classic Lewis/Redfield controversy.

64. This omission is reviewed most recently in Kracke (1987).

65. Thankfully, in some work (e.g., Crapanzano 1980; Dumont 1978; Herdt 1981; Parsons 1969; Reisman 1977) this trend is changing. But these accounts make only partial use of ethnographer experience in theory building. No Freud has yet appeared.

66. "I have asked leading anthropologists who espouse this 'before and after' view of fieldwork why they have not written on the subject themselves. . . . The response I received was culturally standardized: 'Yes, I suppose I thought about it when I was young. I kept diaries, perhaps some day, but you know there are really other things which are more important' (Rabinow 1977:4). Also Freilich (1977:27, n.17).

67. This may seem bold, but if one compares the ethnographic reports of, say, Malinowski (1929), Mead (1930), and F. E. Williams (1936), where the author is clearly at the scene and sometimes even in the text, with those of Radcliffe-Brown (1922), Evans-Pritchard (1937), or Fortes (1945), where they are absent, the difference is striking. This absence fills transitional period works (Clay 1975), Geertz (1966), Hogbin (1970), Kelly (1977), Leach (1961a), Meggitt (1965), Munn (1973), Newman (1965), Rappaport (1968), A. Strathern (1972), Wagner (1972), and Young (1971).

68. J. D. Watson (1968).

69. Haddon (1924), though obscure, is close to Malinowski's ideal methodologic stance.

70. Kracke (1980); LeVine (1982); Parsons (1969).

71. Reviewed in Edgerton and Langness (1974). Also Clifford and Marcus (1986), and Read (1986).

72. Crapanzano (1980), Kracke (1987), S. LeVine (1981), and Obeyesekere (1981) are fine exceptions.

73. DuBois (1944). Bourguignon (1979:97) claims that the DuBois work made data available for the first time on the natives as people. But were these people "typical" Alorese? See our discussion in "Part Two: Interviews."

74. For examples, Casagrande (1960), Freilich (1977), Golde (1970), Kimball and Watson (1972).

75. Malinowski's (1967) diary was published posthumously by his widow. (Did he have that in mind?) Also Mead (1977).

76. In her last work, Mead (1977:12) pointed out that even in her letters, "There were limits that I myself imposed. This collection might also be called 'what I told my friends it was like to do fieldwork.' I did not tell them all of it by any means." Some of her richest material is contained in her appendices (see especially Mead 1956:Appendix I, and 1949:22–47). "I remember a sharp-tongued and very sophisticated old cousin of my mother's commenting that she preferred the appendices to the text of my books. 'They really tell you something,' she said" (1977:14).

77. Mead (1949) and Geertz (1973) are surprisingly alike in this view.

78. Here we can agree with Malinowski (1926).

79. We shall not enter here into technical questions about semantics, pragmatics, and cultural knowledge (but see Keesing 1979); we leave it to others more qualified to wrestle with problems in defining the theory of meaning. But we wish to state that our interest goes beyond word meaning, which is why we emphasize subjectivity (including the unspoken) and not just that of expressed social behavior. Better still, in Tyler's (1978) idiom, we want to describe both the said and the unsaid. In studying meaning systems this subjectivity includes one's own empathy and resonances of the other's unsaid, as well as words in relation to things (reference), words in relation to words (sense), and words in relation to deeds (function).

80. Cf. Foucault (1980).

81. Herdt (1981); Herdt and Stoller (1985); Stoller and Herdt (1982, 1985).

82. Cf. LeVine (1982:185–248); also Devereux (1980a:72–90); Parin et al. 1980:372–388.

83. Erikson (1958); cf. Levy (1973) and Ricoeur's (1977) essay on psychoanalytic proof.

84. Mead (1952:343, emphasis mine). See Agar's (1980) extended critique.

85. Chapple (1952:342). Freilich (1977:12–13, n.11) shows clearly Boas's strong influence on creating this attitude.

86. "The mystique of field work—the magical properties of the term, the mysterious aspects of the work involved, the wonderful transformations that occur through living and working 'in the field'—never disappears" (Freilich 1977:15).

87. See also Chapple (1952:341–342) and Freilich (1977:15–16 ff.).

88. Cf. Spiro's (1986) critique of relativism here and its effects upon anthropology.

89. Chapple (1952) was groaning about this years ago.

90. "Anthropology, a new science, welcomed the stranger. As a science which

accepted the psychic unity of mankind, anthropology was kinder to women, to those who came from distant disciplines, to members of minority groups in general (with American Indians assuming a special position as both the victims of injustice and the carriers of a precious and vanishing knowledge), to the 'overmature,' the idiosyncratic, and the capriciously gifted or experienced, to refugees from political or religious oppression" (Mead 1960a:5).

91. Barzun (1981:34) has singled out anthropology as an example of deleterious change in American university teaching: "Moreover, in the new ambulant university, what might have been fresh and engrossing was presented in its least engaging form, that of the specialist: not anthropology as a distinctive way of looking at peoples and nations, with examples of general import, but accumulated detail about a tribe the instructor had lived with—and apparently could not get away from."

92. "In her study of life histories of eminent scientists, Roe (1953) found that anthropologists and psychologists early showed considerable concern about social relations; open rebelliousness in the family was usual among the former, and occurred only slightly less in the latter. . . . Biologists and physicists, on the other hand, had neither rebelliousness nor family difficulties and developed ways of life with less personal interaction. All the scientists stood somewhat apart from life, in contrast to successful businessmen" (Powdermaker 1966:20). In other words: "Why should a contented and satisfied person think of standing outside his or any other society and studying it?" (*Ibid.*).

93. Mead had definite and old-fashioned ideas about women in the field. Thus: women "are more personally lonely" but also "more easily live as part of the households of others" in villages; and they are "handicapped either by an inadequate knowledge of the equipment they need to use" (e.g., typewriters) "or by a kind of reversed masculine protest that makes them resent the fact that they should have to use . . . monkey wrenches"; and "women alone in the field are more likely to be preoccupied with present or future personal relationships than are men"; they are "more personally vulnerable in the field . . . more likely to become rundown, ill, or depressed or to break off their fieldwork prematurely." And more: Mead (1970:325).

94. One professor advises his students to go to an area they'll like, regardless of their topical interest, because if they're miserable they'll wind up doing bad research no matter what subject they study.

95. Mead (1972:221) writes of her and Fortune's decision to work near Bateson in the late 1920s: "We knew that Gregory was back on the Sepik—and why, Reo demanded, should he, and not we, have that magnificent culture?"

96. "I went to New Guinea to experience a world entirely different from anything I had known before—different both in its overt features and in the reality that its residents construct" (Barth 1975:5).

97. Few anthropologists have written about this subject, though Mead (1970:317–321; 1977) is again a welcome exception. It is a constant source of informal conversation when anthropologists gather; yet few of the authors in an important work (*Long-term Field Research in Social Anthropology*, Foster et al. 1979) discuss their personal reasons for going back to do restudies. The authors, in concluding, couch their collective experience in restrained terms: "Not only is it a pleasure to renew acquaintances, to see the genuine pleasure of those who welcome the anthropologist back . . . but psychologically reentry is easier than shifting to a totally different society. . . . The return is also reaffirmation of concern and

interest in the people with whom we work and gives new validation to our right to learn" (Foster et al. 1979:330–331).

98. "Anthropology affords me an intellectual satisfaction: it rejoins at one extreme the history of the world, and at the other the history of myself, and it unveils the shared motivation of one and the other at the same moment. In suggesting Man as the object of my studies, anthropology dispelled all my doubts . . . set at rest, what is more, the anxious, and destructive curiosity of which I have written above: I was guaranteed, that is to say, a more or less inexhaustible supply of matter for reflection, in the diversity of human manners, customs, and institutions. My life and my character were reconciled" (Lévi-Strauss 1969:62).

99. "In not going to the field armed with prefigured questionnaires (which find only what they are shaped to find), culture-bound hypotheses (one is motivated to verify), models (based on what verbal analogies), and problems (whose?), anthropological fieldwork is more like the naturalism of the clinical method. Beyond the hypothesis that human beings can communicate about themselves if only one listens and watches, how much does one really know beyond a vague perception of his own somehow universal humanity? But from this he must constantly delete his own cultural presuppositions, as the clinician must constantly subtract his personal countertransference distortions" (La Barre 1978:276).

100. Watson (1972).

101. For example, Whittaker et al. 1975.

102. See Spradley (1979, 1980) for numerous and varied schemas of types of observations, interviewing, etc., mainly drawn from urban ethnographic work in America. The more complex a society, the more exact we can be in the micro-analysis and classification of situations and descriptive modes, which may say more about natives studying their own society than it does about ethnographic methodology.

103. See Agar's (1980) important discussion of ways of thinking about ethnographic techniques, which has many examples from urban research.

104. "The investigator's professional training should enable him to realize that what is more important than the ceremonial or bureaucratic delays of the administration is its power to prevent him from doing any work at all in its territory" (Barnes 1967:198).

105. On New Guinea, see Lawrence (1971); Read (1984); Reay (1964); Rodman (1979); M. Strathern (1972).

106. Barnes (1967:203–294) notes how anthropologists can stress to authorities "those aspects that seem innocuous" about their research, rather than the controversial ones. And further: "I well remember the surprise with which a District Officer greeted my naive remark that I was studying him too, and I think was more circumspect thereafter." (Also Mead 1977:13–14.) In Third World countries like Papua New Guinea, anthropologists rarely write about these touchy problems lest research be denied them later. Though tactful, this self-imposed censorship is undesirable, resulting in areas of incomplete research.

107. For example, Robin's (1982) valuable but highly critical review of missionary activity in one part of Papua New Guinea.

108. In Papua New Guinea today the government grants research visas to foreign anthropologists only after having received permission from local people and authorities. Ideally, then, an ethnographer will only work among friendly (or at least not hostile) people. It does not always turn out that way. One young anthropologist was allowed in but could not contact even whole villages for two

months: everyone vanished at his approach. For all the difficulties, he eventually did fieldwork; to my knowledge, however, in his publications he has not ever described the initial traumas.

109. For an example typical of many textbooks, see Edgerton and Langness (1974:35).

110. "As Zempleni appropriately reminds us, ethnographers are 'spies' par excellence. They are, indeed, professional detectors of secrets" (Schwimmer 1980:45).

111. Foster et al. (1979:331).

112. For example, Spradley (1980). Also Oberg's (1954) classic essay. There are many allusions to culture shock used—vis-à-vis our implicit ideology—however: see, for example, Agar's (1980:50–53) review; and Wagner (1975:7) on "anthropologist shock."

113. I have heard the term on television, and Toffler's pop book, *Future Shock*, plays on it. My optometrist (a middle-aged white American man) told me the following story: "Several years ago I was in Berlin having dinner with a German (male) friend. A beautiful woman entered the restaurant, escorted to the next table. She wore furs and a sleek dress—she was a sensation. But when she removed her cloak I could see her hairy underarms. I was instantly turned off. I told my friend, who said it turned him on (he was visibly titillated). Now that's culture shock!"

114. See Oberg's (1970:6, 10–12) discussion, which cites DuBois, who credits Ruth Benedict with the invention.

115. Typically, "culture shock" is put in quotation marks or with citations to authorities. In his widely cited textbook example (which undergraduate students love), Chagnon (1968:4) anticipates excited passages by pleading: "My first day in the field illustrated to me what my teachers meant when they spoke of culture shock. I looked up and gasped when I saw a dozen burly, naked, filthy, hideous men staring at us down the shafts of their drawn arrows! Immense wads of green tobacco were stuck between their lower teeth and lips making them look even more hideous and strands of green slime dripped or hung from their noses. We arrived at the village while the men were blowing a hallucinogenic drug up their noses. One of the side effects of the drug is a runny nose. . . . Then the stench of the decaying vegetation and filth struck me. I was horrified. What sort of welcome was this for a person who came here to live with you and learn your way of life, to become friends with you?" (Chagnon 1968:5).

116. As members of the same cultural tradition we do not have to change much or change the urban culture, which is a part of our own, is less alien, "more natural, more human." But more than this, its symbolic image is different from that of the changeless tribal order. Warner (1941:787) said it forty years ago: the anthropologist studies "the development of the personality and its maintenance of its equilibrium in the social system. . . . The urban sociologist has tended to emphasize the study of social change and social organization. . . . From the anthropologist's point of view, the smaller and larger towns where the social tradition has been little disturbed and the ways of life are more harmonious and better integrated have perhaps been neglected by the sociologist. The selection of communities to be studied by anthropologists was determined by criteria which accented harmonious adjustment, high integration, and well-organized social relations."

117. Oberg (1972:85–86) states: "I have known individuals who claimed that they had never experienced culture shock. Close examination revealed that many

of them never really lived in a different culture from their own but withdrew into a self-centered cocoon and associated only with their fellow countrymen. Missionaries also survive well over long periods in alien societies. Here the lesson is quite clear. A missionary's objective is to persuade the people to give up their religious beliefs and to adopt his belief and value system. The best adjusted individuals whom I have met in strange lands have been individuals with a strong 'missionary' motive in religion, science, or welfare programs. If one lacks this motivation, the best he can do is understand another culture and to become aware of the nature of his psychological adjustment to it."

118. "Culture shock" can be used as a way to discovery, as Meintel (1973) notes. The Japanese analyst Doi, for instance, notes how he began to realize the psychocultural significance of the concept of *amae* from his "culture shock" in America (Doi 1973).

119. Perhaps Mead knew this better than anyone, which is why she scolded Malinowski's detractors with such enthusiasm (Mead 1970:324n.). More soberly, Young (1971:12) writes: "In Malinowski's defense, it must be said that innovating as he did the social anthropologists' role of participant-observer, he was without the psychological security afforded by existing precedents." But in this regard see as well Spiro's (1982) probing questions regarding Malinowski's view of the father in Trobriand Society, which involves Malinowski's own projections from his personal and cultural background (Herdt 1985).

120. A textbook example: "Thus the first task of the ethnographer is to *learn the culture* of the group he is studying; in this respect, his task is similar to that of a child born into the group, for both must discover the categories and plans shared by other group members" (Bock 1969:325).

121. For an exposure of this elitism see Crapanzano (1980); cf. Lévi-Strauss (1969).

122. When first on patrol in Sambia territory, I was mistaken for a government patrol officer. Not until I could prove otherwise—through friends' testimonies or my actions—could I shake off the first layer of distrust. And I was never trusted elsewhere as in my village. Sometimes people thought me a missionary (a mistake dispelled when I smoked my pipe in public, for they believed missionaries do not smoke). No one ever took me for a spy or a tax collector, the bane of ethnographers (Barnes 1967).

123. One young married couple in the Highlands found they had too little privacy. So they invented the fiction that their culture required them to eat—as a ritual—in private. And the natives were not allowed inside their house after dark. (See also the anecdote in Edgerton and Langness 1974:24.)

124. While I lived in Australia a foreign student conducted a strictly behavioral study on time and motion in an Aboriginal settlement. He sat atop a tractor and observed people's movements from a distance for a few months. Apart from the theoretic problems with his study, he angered the anthropologic community by his lack of involvement with the natives; was he biased by a lack of direct interaction? His study matched his personal style: he was uncomfortable interacting with people at home.

125. See Hayano (1982), Herdt (1982c), and Poole (1982a) for examples of how New Guineans, who previously lacked alcohol, learned to drink and not drink from foreigners, including anthropologists.

126. Discussed in Herdt (1981:332–337).

127. Even hermeneuts, sensitive to the issue of seeing our material in an interpretive light, are still saddled with "the informant" (Rabinow 1977:151).

128. Geertz (1973) uses this analogy.

129. Foucault (1973) refers to a similar clinical process as "the gaze."

130. For example, Aberle (1951), Dubois (1944), La Farge (1929), Mead (1960b), and Turner (1960).

131. See Watson's (1960) "key informant" portrait on this point.

132. See Spradley (1979:46–54) on "the good informant."

133. DuBois (1944:441) reports transference in a key informant's dream report, and then she states (without further comment): "I doubt that this dream is authentic." How did she reach that conclusion? More important: how did she arrive at the point of having such a rich relationship that she received dreams and could doubt the authenticity of one?

134. Mead (1960b:189) states: "I've always given pseudonyms to informants." Sometimes whole societies—like the Sambia—have been given pseudonyms (e.g., Davenport 1965; Devereux 1951; Messenger 1969).

135. Thoughtfully reviewed in Tedlock's (1983) work.

136. See Herdt and Stoller (1987).

137. Of Malinowski's diaries, Forge (1972:294) writes that they are "not about the Trobriand Islanders and what Malinowski thought about them nor even about Malinowski. They are a partial record of the struggle that affects every anthropologist in the field: a struggle to retain a sense of his own identity as an individual and as a member of a culture."

138. After noting risks in "a high degree of participant observation," Bock (1969:319) states: "Another is the danger of 'going native' to the extent of refusing to reveal any information about the group studied: and it is obvious that anthropological science could not progress if this always happened."

139. Perhaps the most infamous example is Frank Hamilton Cushing, who is alleged to have gone native with the Zuni Indians a hundred years ago (Gronewald 1972:33).

140. Vogt (1979:33).

141. "Visitors from outside this closed circle of attention [village] are both a temptation and an interruption. Letters from home wrench one's thoughts and feelings inappropriately away" (Mead 1977:7).

142. Mead (1970:324n.), commenting on a fieldwork symposium in the 1960s, was astonished at how ethnographers "testified—I can find no better word for it—to their boredom with, aversion to, or sentimental regard for members of primitive or urban proletarian communities. One does not go to a primitive community to satisfy one's demands for sophisticated twentieth-century conversation or to find personal relationship missed among one's peers." I agree; also, though I have heard a researcher describe a society studied as "very boring," I do not believe this: boredom is inside oneself.

2. Sambia Sexual Culture

1. Mead: "But so far, in seeking to make anthropological accounts useful to the sophisticated reader, who may be psychiatrist or biologist or geologist, judge or pediatrician or banker or mother of five children, we have tried to do only two things: either to convey that some aspect of human behavior could be organized

differently—such as adolescence, or a proneness to heavy drinking, or a sensitivity to art—or to convey the extent to which cultures differ from one another" (1949:31). A generation later Geertz's (1973) essay on thick description awakened the social sciences again to the place of anthropology in the Academy through a similar but fresher rhetoric.

2. See Herdt (1977, 1980, 1981, 1982a, 1982b); and Stoller and Herdt (1982). After one has written a few set pieces they fade into each other: we plagiarize ourselves and make straw men that respond to the straw men of other disciplines (M. Strathern 1981). These false creatures are as important as the original observations.

3. What is a fact in ethnography? Where do data end and interpretations begin? Geertz (1973) has written eloquently of this problem (cf. Marcus and Fisher 1986).

4. These cultural categories cross-cut various symbolic domains and social arenas, such as taboos (*kumaaku*), ritual (*pweiyu*), food sharing, myth, etc. One certainly could abstract from action and rhetoric the normative and metaphoric operations of these categories (cf. Wagner 1967, 1972). As I indicate below, sexual interaction is a conscious though not always marked frame for acting and speaking among Sambia, but I cannot here provide a description of all its manifestations.

5. See Herdt 1981 for conceptual models. This chapter considers mainly the male viewpoint, and it is not meant to be a complete cultural analysis, by any means.

6. Sambia tend to treat and think of semen as an energy force, in individuals and society, that may be compared, by direct analogy, to Freud's concept of libido. The analogy is apt in several ways: this energy force circulates through others (e.g., as subjects), who may be taken in (e.g., as objects) via semen or its equivalents (mother's milk); and it can be dammed up or released—the imagery of the hydraulic model is apt (but cf. Heider 1979:78–79, who thinks otherwise). Translated in Freudian lingo, Federn (1952) would contrast subject-libido (energy available to self qua subject) and object-libido (energy available for investment in objects). Technically, I think, semen as a symbol among Sambia is used narcissistically (object libido invested in ego is narcissistic libido) in self/other interactions.

7. My use of the terms *commodity* and *fetishization* is not a homology with Marx's usage, which was tied, of course, to the specific analysis of capitalist production, characterized by the production of commodities that emerge in a market economy. By analogy, though, these terms are useful for my analysis. Marx argued that the results of human activity transform resources into items of use-value, which are assigned an exchange value by society; the worker's time is overshadowed by the supreme importance attached to the commodity, a process through which the capitalist extracts surplus labor as profit. The Sambia, however, acknowledge semen as a result of social relationships of production (e.g., as in marriage bonds), and they tend also to stress the importance of semen as a fluid that can transform resources into more useful reproductive items or characteristics (e.g., babies, warrior strength). Nonetheless, the way that men value semen as a circulating commodity has a mystifying effect on these social relationships of production: they deny women's essential part in the reproductive process and claim final biologic development in boys is achieved only through insemination. This mystification of the total reproductive process thus enables men to extract from others the resources needed to sustain and expand themselves and their clans and to control the related scarce resources in relation to women. Finally, I do not im-

ply by use of these terms that other Melanesian groups, or even all societies with ritualized homosexuality, use semen as a key resource in the same way as Sambia, or that they value it as a commodity in their systems of circulation in order to reproduce social entities. Elements or fluids such as semen and blood clearly have variable significance in Melanesian societies; our separable analyses of them must, in a sense, renegotiate their meaning in each cultural system.

8. For instance, Sambia men do not use *duvuno* in reference to masturbation, their term for which means "peeling away the glans from penis." Genital rubbing, in the limited sense (not necessarily erotic) of stimulation of the genitals, occurs; I have seen children do it, boys sometimes do it to bachelors (to produce erections for fellatio), and men sometimes report doing it to themselves in preparation for coitus with their wives. But what they *mean* is self-stimulation *without ejaculation*. This conceptual distinction is important and should not be misunderstood: spilling one's seed not only makes no sense to Sambia, it does not seem erotically exciting for them. Their fantasy life and erotic scripting have no place for it.

9. Sambia have invented an art we could call *semenology*: they are fascinated with the forms, textures, and tastes of semen, which they discuss frequently, like wine tasters. Among boys, a fellated's penis size is not accorded much importance, whereas his seminal fluid, amount of flow, etc., is. (Privately and unconsciously, though, penis size is sometimes important.) Among women, the situation seems the reverse: a man's penis size (and sexual prowess) is important—women prefer men with big penises—whereas semenology is less significant, or so say men.

10. Sexual behavior in the imagery of dreams is viewed as erotic play: wet dreams are pleasurable but wasteful erotic play with spirits, who may wish to harm the dreamer. Breast-feeding, even though women say they experience *imbimboogu*, is not ever conceived of as erotic play by women, as far as I know, though breast-feeding is apparently a common image and form of scripting for *men's* erotic daydreams (vis-à-vis fellatio performed on them).

11. However, there is ambiguity here, since a woman who lives in another hamlet (her husband's) long enough becomes after death a ghost or hamlet spirit who may haunt there, rather than returning to her natal hamlet or clan territory. Even so, the souls of females are not a subject in which men place much interest.

12. Cf. the Great Papuan Plateau societies, especially Kaluli (Schieffelin 1976:127f. 1982), which have institutionalized such beliefs about homosexual insemination (see also Kelly 1976; Sørum 1982). On the individual level, Sambia boys report fantasies and beliefs that make it clear that identification is a part of their homoerotic experience, including, for instance, notions that incorporating a fellated's semen may bestow his personality traits.

3. *Interviewing Sambia*

1. See especially Dubois's (1944) classic on life-histories. For recent statements of the best psychocultural biographic work in context, see Levy (1973) and Crapanzano (1980).

2. Which Freud (1900:122n.2) sensed in translating dreams between different languages. Devereux's thoughts of thirty years ago still hold: "What is particularly needed is a system of psychotherapy based not on the content of any particular culture—as the psychotherapy described in my book *Reality and Dream* (1951) was based . . . but on an understanding of the nature of Culture per se: on an insight into the meaning of cultural categories, which, as the French sociological–eth-

nological school of Durkheim and Mauss stressed long ago, are identical with the great fundamental categories of human thought. This culturally neutral—or metacultural—psychotherapy is still in the making. . . . " (1980a:90).

3. I am dismayed that many colleagues still use the terms "masculine" and "feminine" as if they were self-evident or identical experiential entities across cultures. Since gender concepts are based in part on psychodynamic (especially ego) traits, learned behaviors and attitudes that are culturally relative to the society, historical period, and status-context factors (age, sex, class) being measured, the reader should know about the baseline sample of Sambia on which the piecemeal interpretations below were made. Especially since, like virtually all anthropologists working on gender in New Guinea, I have not used random or control samples. Between 1974 and 1979, I interviewed at length (not just observed) the following people on issues directly concerning masculinity and femininity, as these framed our 1979 work: two uninitiated boys, about six years old (several casual private interviews); 45 first- and second-stage initiates, each interviewed over a three-month period before and after an initiation, using a formal interview schedule (about ten of these or other initiates were seen in private open-ended interviews between five and twenty times each, between 1974–1976); five bachelors and young married men each casually interviewed between two and five times; five adult women shamans interviewed formally between two and five times each (including Moondi's mother, seen several times more); two male elders, casually or more formally interviewed between five and about twenty times each; one female elder formally interviewed several times; Nilutwo, who was seen about 230 hours over a two and a half year period, 1974–1979 (see Herdt 1981); two "gentle" men (including Imano) and two extremely masculine men, seen about ten times each, in 1979; four newly initiated boys and several older initiates (previously seen and interviewed for follow-up studies), privately interviewed in 1979; a handful of bachelors interviewed in Port Moresby in 1979 (see Herdt 1982c); and in-depth studies of Moondi, Weiyu, Sakulambei, Kalutwo, and Penjukwi, each seen between about 30 and 100 hours. Note that I have not included Tali, whom I have seen primarily to understand ritual matters; even though I have frequently interviewed him privately on gender issues, his materials raise other problems of interpretation because, in various ways, Tali saw himself as a spokesman for the ritual cult in much more self-conscious ways than do others. Thus dogma and ritual rhetoric more fully permeate his material. The above interview data also do not include other interviews on subjects such as ritual, warfare, social organization, etc. In 1981, 1983, 1985, and 1988 I returned to New Guinea and conducted additional follow-up studies of Weiyu, Moondi, Sakulambei, Kalutwo, Penjukwi, Imano, and a few others. These data are not included; but they have helped sharpen my views of these people and clarified some of the interpretations presented here.

4. Didn't the best of the culture and personality theorists (reviewed in Honigmann [1967]) do ethnographic accounts of these same phenomena? Why have we forgotten them (Spiro 1979, 1986)? And have we really advanced so far as it might seem (LeVine 1982:ch.19)? Yes and no. Yes, these newer interpretive accounts offer more of the native's *conscious experience* and emic concepts of identity, selfhood, etc. (e.g., Crapanzano 1980; Herdt 1981; Obeyesekere 1981), whereas older accounts tended to offer normative descriptions of modal personality, or anecdotal ethnographic accounts (e.g., Malinowski 1927; Mead 1935) to validate etic constructs (e.g., temperament) of local conceptions of personality. Levy (1973) on Tahitians is clearly the remarkable exception to this tradition in the 1970s. Today

we wonder where anthropologic studies of "self," "gender," and "personhood" are headed, toward experience-near and clinical accounts of lives.

5. Herdt (1987a) details this argument.

6. See Read's (1955) classic essay.

7. Langness (1981:25); Read (1965); Watson (1964).

8. Reviewed in Herdt (1982a); and see Barth (1975), Poole (1982b), M. Strathern (1988).

9. Sambia almost never describe their *actual* sexual experience with anyone but me, and that is only because I ask about it. Men's locker-room banter is another matter. Sexual partners (homosexual and heterosexual) do so only very rarely; most never do.

10. Which is why adultery is so hard to study, unless people are caught in the act (Malinowski 1926). Adultery is a great problem in the cross-cultural study of sexuality for this reason (see Gregor 1985).

11. Ignoring secret intelligence activities (Shils 1956) and the new secret sophisticates—the computer whizzes—who speak to each other via classified information across continents. Should the secrecy of the therapist's office also be excluded (reviewed in Foucault 1973; and from the margins by Malcolm 1984)? And what of the mafia, street gangs, radical political groups, subversives, Wall Street bankers, academic tenure committees, and famous chefs? None of these examples, however, suggests the religious and supernatural overtones of New Guinea secret societies.

12. See Schwimmer's (1980) important review.

13. See, in this context, Nauta's (1972) idea of "potential meaning" that represents new syntheses of meaning.

14. I subliminally reinforced my friends to discuss sensitive subjects like sex by my curiosity. Beyond that, however, they talked of what interested them.

15. See Crapanzano's (1980) procedures and discussions of this problem area.

16. Some anthropologists have said to me, "Well, of course; what you got were individual statements, filtered through normative cultural modes (attitudes, values, beliefs) of what people expected they should say to you." I respond, "Yes, but only in part." When people sit with you for hours and discuss their lives, they do so through the only way they know possible—their language and culture; they must innovate in order to keep the dialogue going, if nothing else (Tedlock 1983; Wagner 1972). They also respond to the special understanding you have jointly constructed—ethnographic interviewing—that makes their narratives meaningful to you and the situation. Those statements reflect both their culture and their experience.

4. Moondi's Erotism

1. I taught Moondi meanings and operations of "fantasy" and "free association" and began exploring—but haven't yet succeeded in using—the idea of "insight." This work is mentioned later. The guided imagery techniques I use are a form of active imagination I learned from Marielle Fuller at UCLA. In all I did guided imagery about ten times over five months, using it to uncover feelings and experiences M. associated with childhood or early initiation (against which he had memory blocks). I also used it to explore latent aspects of his sexual fantasies and symbolic behavior (e.g., surrounding the ritual flutes: see Herdt 1982a).

2. We shall mention these issues in chapter 11, but a word about them here

will clarify what I mean. People who talk and share feelings over time tend to identify with one another, and, as for example with friends, tend to transfer needs to the other, in the hope of getting comfort and guidance. We might say that these feelings are therapeutic when they lessen our anxiety and help us to feel more at ease with the other. Many relationships have these therapeutic aspects but are not therapy. That is how I see my relationships with everyone in these case studies. Moondi, however, has had a more therapy-like relationship since he began doing guided imagery with me in 1979. There are difficulties and risks in such cross-cultural therapy; I shall describe them elsewhere. For now, what matters is that, after seven years, I felt I could use guided imagery to help M. work through mild anxieties and emotional blocks on several occasions when it was appropriate. I also gave him advice, especially concerning his impending move to the city, where I could provide information that he lacked. Eventually I provided him with logistical and financial help in making his move, which was successful.

3. Moondi is pretty well balanced. Yet he has suffered nightmares, as many Sambia men do, and he is wary of his environment. It was difficult to do guided imagery with him at first because of the fears he found inside.

4. See Herdt (1987c) for a profile of her.

5. See Herdt (1982a:69–71) on Moondi's self report.

6. People who go crazy (*abrumbru*) tear off their clothes to expose themselves to others (cf. Herdt 1986); Sambia regard this as totally ridiculous.

7. This ceremony ends the third-stage initiation, which means the end of certain taboos for Weiyu. It was then appropriate for him to inseminate boys as a fellated. Moondi was one of those boys.

8. Incest rules apply here, as in heterosexual relationships: all sex is forbidden with all patrilineal kinsmen and frowned on with all other kin, matrilateral and patrilateral, as well as with one's hamlet age-mates and ritual sponsor; both affines, especially one's brother-in-law, are appropriate homosexual partners. Weiyu is vaguely related by adoption to Moondi, and since they grew up in the same village, that proximity further relates them and makes sex inappropriate between them. Wieyu's *public* reserve that day of the night of their homosexual activity probably stemmed from their kinship and their seniors. The great majority of homosexual contacts are promiscuous and Sambia males culturally regard them that way. Some boys do form sexual liaisons with bachelors for a few weeks—an interesting formative pattern in male gender identity development (see chapters 7 and 9).

9. The day before S. arrived, Moondi's father left on a long trading expedition over the mountains. He went to exchange salt bars for dried fish at a lowland place Sambia fear, for it is swampy, has many snakes, and is believed inhabited by malevolent forms of sickness and evil spirits. For someone to fall sick there, which he did, is a bad omen. So M.'s mother went to him and performed healing ceremonies. He was soon better, eventually to return weak but healthy to the village.

10. It is immoral and shameful for a betrothed couple to interact directly. Talking or arguing in public is especially bad, for this familiarity signifies the couple are already acting like spouses—implying they have begun sexual intercourse. Moondi is too sexually moral, respectful of elders, passive, and who knows what else to do that.

11. An extraordinary fantasy since Sambia husbands and wives never sleep together, much less in the same bed. (They have no platform beds.) He tells this daydream confidently and without hesitation, expressing a well-rehearsed wish.

It may derive from rumors—I heard them—that down the valley [S: where missionaries brought the Word as well as square houses with tin roofs], several men sleep all night in bed with their wives. Most Sambia men say such behavior would be wrong and dangerous to maleness.

12. Since pacification (c. 1965) many social changes have occurred, including change in dress and the sexual code. One of the first changes was the uncovering of young women's breasts. Traditionally, maidens, like all young initiates, had to hide themselves and avoid all sexually eligible men. Since the early 1970s, young women have changed in this. It seems strange to me that this custom disappeared so rapidly, to be replaced by women wearing Western blouses. Was it that the taboo on women's breasts was fragile? Older married women, however, could always go nude from the waist up, and some still do. This subject is complex and cannot be discussed here, but we can infer that erotic hiding and excitement were always associated with the face and breasts—the breasts themselves associated with many overt and subtle features of Sambia symbolism. Moondi, thus, is not expected to see women's breasts, especially those of his fiancée. Yet while some things change, things also remain the same. Some young women still hide their breasts in this way. And, ironically, the cycle is repeating itself: the effect of the missionaries is now for most women to wear clothes, so that their breasts are now more covered than ever.

13. He is dodging here. He had once hidden on the edge of a garden, to steal a glance at her face. She turned toward him, and, realizing he was staring at her from a distance, she smiled. That is the smile that delights but also embarrasses him. [S: So much for the primitive, the simple savage; for the impossibility of understanding across cultures, the worthlessness of empathy and the pointlessness of intimate communications in ethnography.] What does that smile mean? Does it communicate desire? What complex mix of her fantasies and memories is in that desire of hers? That this woman, who is to be his wife, looks at him with desire, fills him with marvelous sensations.

14. Initiated boys, bachelors, and adult men—all say they do not masturbate to ejaculate. It is the ejaculation outcome that may help clarify the confusion, since we Westerners assume masturbation leads to orgasm. (Is this distinction not useful?) There is a ritual injunction, whose truth no man denies, not to waste one's semen (Herdt 1980). Only if necessary to arouse himself before penetrating a boy's mouth will a bachelor play with his own penis. (I have no evidence that women masturbate to orgasm. I believe my key woman informant, Penjukwi, who says they do not.) Sambia children often touch their genitals, but I do not know if this is erotic. Sambia suppress the general subject as vigilantly as any other aspect of sexuality on which I questioned them. Is this true elsewhere in New Guinea? Is this not a subject for ethnography? Do ethnographers need a Freud to tell them children and adults have erotic lives and that erotism drives and shapes culture and experience in places besides New York and Kiriwina? Will someone please study this?

15. Extracted in part from Stoller, Observing the Erotic Imagination (1985:112–114).

5. Tali and Weiyu on Ritual and Erotics

1. I was the handiest source of money and influence to Sambia then. In Weiyu's case, I chipped in (without being asked) $4.00 (Australian), and some food as

wedding gifts to his wife's family in 1974. He was appreciative, but I recently discovered he forgot. No harm. He's given me a lot over the years, which cannot be repaid.

2. Looking back, I see that my closest friends are all unusual in some respects; for instance, Weiyu and Moondi are both *bomwalyu* (men living in hamlets that are not their fathers'); Nilutwo was a neurotic dreamer; Sakulambei is a strange mixture of hermaphrodism and shamanism; Penjukwi is far more verbal and independent than most women; even people like Kanteilo (my aging sponsor), Chemgalo (Weiyu's stepfather, who before his death loved to sit around my house in his old age), Kwinko (my cook), and Kambo (my best initiate-informant)—are all verbal, gregarious, and more reflective than most Sambia. I subliminally selected them, grew close to them, because they matched traits in me. And remember: anthropologists are, themselves, marginal people (or "marginal natives," Freilich 1977): misfits. Isn't that why many tend to have key informants who are marginal in *their* own societies, such as Turner's (1960) "Muchona the hornet"? Is it methodologically wrong to have unusual informants in interpreting the usual in a culture? There are cross-checks, of course: we know and observe many other people in many social situations. But as Schwartz (1978) asks, how do we define, at this primitive stage of ethnographic theory, the usual center of a culture? It doesn't exist; we are far better describing what we really experience, not what we imagine ideally exists (the dull reality of the perfection-seeking structuralists, who have made flawless formal arrangements out of messy, but more believable, human action).

3. Strange legends survive from that time, telling how the dying man was still strong enough to wound one of his assailants; how the dead man's body was thrown in a bog and rose to the surface; how the skull (on which revenge-sorcery could be performed) mysteriously disappeared; and of strange misfortunes befalling the murderers after their death. Even in death Weiyu's father exercised great power.

4. Chemgalo, a tall, skinny man, who is tough as nails, became the first convert, in old age, to a local mission. His mission membership is the main reason he never remarried. The fact that he was the first to be missionized points again to unusual influences in Weiyu's development.

5. Weiyu's wife is his step-sister's daughter, who was, like him, reared in Nilangu. This closeness gave their marriage incestuous overtones, but Sambia pay little notice, since such close marriages are well known.

6. I thought Weiyu would mellow out, but in 1981 the chaos still persisted (see the Epilogue). It surprised and pained me. Weiyu and his wife were often at odds or not speaking. He has grown closer to his son (who is at initiation age). He talks of taking another wife, and his antics in trying to marry Penjukwi still continue (see chapter 6). Along with Moondi and others, I had tried to help him and his wife to get along, but to no avail. On working more with women (1979, 1981), I found Weiyu's misogyny harder to accept than ever. I now realized from women's viewpoint how terrible were the situations into which men like Weiyu put their wives. I changed: I found Weiyu's behavior harder to accept, though I knew some of it was of his wife's making. His jokes about women were no longer funny: I knew their side.

7. Since 1975, when working with Weiyu and Tali, I have paid the equivalent (in cash and tradegoods) of full-time local wages. They worked with me full days many times, though we usually worked in mutually-agreed-on times convenient

for us all. I compensated them for time they could have spent in other productive ways; but they both continued gardening and hunting, though on a reduced scale. (This work did not seem to affect their family's food supply much, since their wives do most of the daily gardening, and they supplemented their meat supply with foods I gave them or they purchased with cash from tradestores.)

Did I introduce a class-system into the village in this way? I don't think so, but I did exacerbate economic change already in progress. Both Tali and Weiyu used their resources to help pay school fees of children in their extended families and in contributing to kinsmen's marriage exchanges, which are changing due to local inflation. I tried to compensate for lopsidedness in this resource-flow by employing a number of people from different villages (Nilutwo, Moondi, etc.), by giving food and occasional cash gifts to others who were simply supporters or friends, by helping several other boys through school, by contributing to villagewide feasts from time-to-time, and by giving away a wide range of small gifts (pots, blankets, knives, etc.) to various families over the years. This strategy has equalized wealth in the village, I believe; but it has also contributed to a longer-term disparity I had not originally anticipated in the overall wealth of the village vis-à-vis others in the tribe.

8. Nilutwo was first sketched in Herdt 1981, chapter 5, and is discussed further here in chapter 6. In 1979 I worked with N. in January and February as I had in past years. Then I returned to the States. In March, Nilutwo suffered his fall, as I learned on returning in May. Meanwhile he had been suffering, hospitalized, carried back to the village in horrid pain, and had had weeks to sour himself and his friends with the agony of dying.

9. Herdt (1982a). We want to underline our awareness that H. previously, and H. and S. here, *have* created and then reinforced an extraordinary social experience in our talk sessions. We know that our discourse with Weiyu and Tali is special in that way; this intimate talk now concerns us as much as the traditions of Sambia society. We only wish others would acknowledge more exactly the same: see chapter 11.

10. See Herdt (1981) for a description of this technique.

6. *Penjukwi: Portrait of a Woman*

1. P's step-father was an *aambei-wutnyi* like Imano (chapter 8). He was not so quiet that he didn't fight with P.'s mother, but since I knew him only vaguely, I cannot say much about him otherwise. Years later, in 1979, he hung himself after it came out that he was discovered in adultery with a woman in the village. Apparently he was overcome with shame. And while adultery is very shameful and men have been known to commit (or attempt) suicide out of shame, such an extreme response is rare. When the news came of the suicide, Weiyu, who happened to be with me at the moment, turned and said: "He was an *aambei-wutnyi*. What other kind of *man* would hang himself!" (especially, in Weiyu's view, over adultery). P. felt sorry that this happened and did mourn—for a day or two—but she felt no great loss.

2. Yanduwaiko could play both sides of the fence—government and locals— but in private he clearly placed his loyalties with the Sambia vis-à-vis others. He once mentioned to me (in 1979) at the patrol post that the "government doesn't care about much except itself," meaning that he realized he and just about everything else was expendable compared to the central bureaucracy.

3. When I first entered the Valley (1974), there were no women speaking Pidgin. (P.'s aunt was living at the patrol post.) By 1979, P. and several other women were able to converse somewhat in Pidgin, but, shamed by the men, they rarely did. By 1981, several more women were speaking it, and they were becoming bolder.

4. Moondi attended this bush school. When it closed he was sent elsewhere to a larger and more sophisticated school. (See chapter 4.)

5. It has never been clear what P.'s father did during all this fighting. Did he stand by and watch or merely shout curses? Was he in complicity with Kanteilo? We'll probably never know. But no Sambia father, or brothers, or her uncle would ever have stood for this abduction. In past times, a war would have started over it. Unfortunately, P. had no real defenders at that moment.

6. P. is, by character, an affectionate person (a character trait shared by other Sambia women and men). In their first months, P. was angry and bitter at Nilutwo. He tried to assuage her as best as possible, and in time P. made the best of the situation. But another dynamic may have added to P's feeling affectionate: N.'s ambivalence. N. was constantly torn between ambivalent feelings of all kinds, and he was, therefore, malleable: given to pleasing others. Penjukwi—being so different (nonambivalent—assertive but cordial)—complemented N. in this regard and, in fact, probably made many of the practial, day-to-day decisions in running the family. (For which N. was grateful, though he never said this in words, only showed it in actions, like providing meat for the family from his hunting.) After their children were born, P. was stuck with N. for good, since female-initiated divorce is extremely rare among Sambia. Consequently, when N. got into trouble (e.g., adultery attempts), P. stood by him, for it was really the best way to deal with such problems—over the long haul. After N.'s accident, though, his death was imminent. P. could be affectionate in a very different way: saying goodbye. Feeling between the spouses is a very complex thing in Sambia land, not so different from us.

7. Here is a letter that came later from Penjukwi, dated December 25, 1979. (It took four months to arrive.) Her younger brother (who has some schooling) was the scribe. It is the first letter I had ever gotten from her. Since we left in July, I had waited, fearing the worst, but she seemed to be all right.

"Dear Gilbert:
"Oh, yes, Gilbert, thank you very much for your letter which I have received, and I am happy about. I am all right but I am very sorry that my man [husband] is dead and you, as if you were my father, have sent me some money. [I sent her K5.00, about $7.50.] That has come to me, and I am really happy about that. I am happy to get your letter, and I am right now visiting in Kwoli [hamlet], where I have received your letter.

Well, at the time that my husband died [shortly after we left], nothing came up and happened to me until they removed the ghost* and some women cried and hit†me. But now I am all right.

---

*At death, everyone becomes a malevolent spirit and must eventually be driven from the hamlet through rites and incantations for a week.

†The antifeminist impulse in women is not restricted to our folks. However badly they may be treated, if the society has a dependable traditional structure, most of its beneficiaries will accept some aggression in exchange for stability (safety).

The time that I got your letter I was very pleased because all of my money you had given me from before I had long finished, and I was very worried about that, and you sent me some.

So that's how it is, since you asked me: are you all right? Yes I am here, and I am all right. Nothing [bad] has come up for me. Suppose some trouble comes up for me at Nilangu hamlet. . . . All right, I will go back to my place [Kwoli, where she was born and where her mother now lives]. But I am staying with Tali at Nilangu. You asked me before and I am with him. And you sent a picture, and I'd really like another one. The picture when you and I both stood up and they took it, and I'd like you to send that when you send another letter. I have to get some grass thatching for my brother [classificatory brother] at Kwoli, who he is writing this letter for me to you. I don't know at whatever time really you will come back, and so I am asking you. You must tell us; I've already heard that you're there in America, and I am very pleased to get your letter. Gilbert, good morning."

Your friend,
Penjukwi"

7. Sakulambei: A Hermaphrodite's Secret

1. This syndrome, identified in the work of Imperato-McGinley et al. (1974) on the Dominican Republic, is a biologic disorder that causes ambiguous-looking external genitals. The ambiguity is striking enough that certain individuals are mis-categorized and assigned to the female sex. Later, at puberty, through the action of normal circulating testosterone, further androgenization of the genitals leads to shifts or changes in sex role categorization and self-perception. The issues are reviewed, with respect to Sambia data, in Herdt and Davidson (1988).

2. Saku asked to serve as my cook, and at the time I had no reason to say no, since I was not working with him. He did so for about two months. In retrospect, I regret doing this, for it complicated my relationship with him. House servants can be interpreters (Kwinko was), but Saku is more fragile, and employment introduced distortion. (Has this aspect of field relationships been studied?)

3. Both Nilutwo (see Herdt 1981) and Saku formed stronger transference relationships to me than did others; my studying their dreams played its part. Both had strong needs to talk with me, but Saku, despite his hermaphrodism, was the more psychologically healthy of the two. (Nilutwo had a short psychosis in his teens, attempted rape, and engaged in horrible arguments.) Kalutwo, I feel, was more aberrant than either Saku or Nilutwo, but I never really studied his dreams. Kalutwo was so desperate for a person to attach to that he did not need dream reporting to generate a transference.

4. I finished my case study of Saku in 1981 after seven years of interviews. The old woman (and his sister) with whom I talked confirmed that at birth he was labeled a hermaphrodite but marked "male," because his glans was just visible, protruding from the top of his scrotal area.

5. Sambia believed that further growth of the male hermaphrodites' penes and retarded secondary sex traits such as facial hair occur around puberty. They therefore assign these people to the male sex in anticipation of the later male features. (cf. Imperato-McGinley et al. 1974). Saku's development confirms these views.

6. Mon and another Pundei clan brother (also still living) conspired to kill

Weiyu's father (see chapter 5); Mon masterminded it. Still, Saku, whose mother was a biologic sister to Weiyu's mother, and Weiyu, are the closest of friends. Neither has much love for Mon.

7. Saku's sister is married and has children. His older brother, however, left for the coast in 1967, while still a second-stage initiate. He has never returned to the valley, never married, and has had only vague contacts through letters with Saku and others. Since I have never seen the brother, and his social development is definitely strange, Saku's brother must remain another puzzle in an already strange story.

8. Probably an imaginary playmate, now his symbolic double.

9. Weiyu is often present in Herdt (1981), where Saku is absent; but see Herdt (1987c).

10. Saku told me he just did not want his nose to bleed, and it did not. His nose never was bled. Now, as a married man, it is appropriate that Saku regularly nosebled himself, but he says that it is needless and he'll have no part of it (see Herdt 1982c). Saku says his uncle (a member of a clan with somewhat different ritual practice) never nosebled himself either. Saku uses that to rationalize his behavior. Perhaps the selfhood of a Sambia hermaphrodite is to too fragile (his body boundaries too tenuous) to let loose anything as precious as blood. And perhaps these hermaphrodites accept more femininity in core identity and so need not so clearly mark their maleness by bloodletting.

11. Saku felt compelled to present himself to me in this way, lying if necessary to say, in essence, "I am different but still masculine and don't need the semen other males need." Saku's sexual behavior belied that intellectualization: older men say he was an expert fellator. Since he was chameleonic (as I shall describe later), he may have felt this so as to identify with men when alone, perhaps to prove that he was, in that sense, more masculine than other men.

12. Many initiates have said they tried to get Saku to screw them out of curiosity to see what his genitals looked like. Saku was probably wise to avoid them: Sambia initiates are inveterate gossips, not above humiliating him. Saku is extraordinarily careful always to cover his genitals.

13. Weiyu says Saku continued to suck older males even on the Coast, in the early 1970s, well after his puberty; that is aberrant. Saku confirmed this report. Further, he quit being a fellator mainly because his sexual partners no longer felt comfortable screwing such an advanced youth.

14. Sambia is a racially mixed population, with both Papuan and New Guinea elements. This mixture probably results from the original migrants coming from the Papuan Lowlands but moving into Highland populations.

15. Why do ethnographers seldom describe the physical appearance of their interpreters or friends? Do we ethnographers select key interpreters who not only match our personalities, but (as with some of our friends) also resemble us physically? Would such a prototype be especially true of same-sex interpreters?

16. In 1974–1976, Sa. had no facial hair. By 1979 he had some small growth on his upper-lips, which he does not shave off.

17. At the time, jokes were being made that Saku's penis had finally—inexplicably—grown enough to copulate with women. The men said it would be fruitless and that the woman would spit on him. The women said his wife must be crazy or immature and that she'd soon grow bored with a man without much of a penis. What none reckoned on was Saku's intelligence. He has arranged his life to make

his wife as happy as possible. And, a dynamic in their marriage, his wife somewhat fears Saku's shamanic powers. By 1979 the marriage was still in good order.

18. The final secret of Saku's shamanism—still unexplained by him to me—is that his familiars are real and in control of him: Saku's bedrock.

19. Staring directly into someone else—when not engaged in sexual looking or in a trance (as a shaman) is bizarre to Sambia. But because it was S.—white-haired friend/boss of H., a western doctor—it was permitted. By Saku saying S. was not a ghost, he tells us that no one but a ghost would do what S. did (e.g., in a dream), but that it was okay, not bad. In denying S. is a ghost, Saku also rejects weirder interpretations (i.e., S. is a ghost-like figure, in the cargo cultist sense), at least for us, since he is being pressed by us (authorities) for his opinion.

20. I have disguised Gronemann's true identity. Though we have to omit some and disguise other details about him, our presentation of Gronemann fits Saku's experience and others' reports of what happened.

8. *Imano—Considerate Masculinity*

1. In the United States we equate (or at least we used to) age with experience and social influence. Sambia do too. Though Tali and Imano are peers, no one equates them: Imano is socially insignificant compared to Tali, largely because Imano looks and acts younger, lighter, less weighted-down with responsibilities.

2. Infant mortality (through malaria, pneumonia, malnutrition, etc.) is high among New Guinea Highlanders, running perhaps—there are no reliable data—as high as 50 percent in some areas some years among Sambia.

3. For more precise cultural descriptions of the following aspects of Sambia gender distinctions, see Herdt (1981; 1987c).

4. Except that Sakulambei is so aberrant (even beyond being biologically intersexed) that he should be considered differently. I have heard women refer to Sakulambei as *aambei-wutnyi;* though what really counts is that he is *kwoluaatm-wol* (male pseudohermaphrodite). As we saw, Saku is pretty successful, except that he has no children (he is probably sterile), for he is married, has property and social power, and is a top-ranking shaman. He is tough, a fighter too, attributes that make people refer to him as "strong," and he is called a "strong shaman." He does not seem, socially at least, to fit the *aambei-wutnyi* category. Nonetheless, he does subliminally: he likes women, likes to sit and gossip, is caring and nurturant in his shamanistic role. Furthermore, he actively resists doing critical male rituals (e.g., self-nosebleeding). Saku is thus one of those people who fit no category easily (see chapter 7)—a reminder that we should not forget that models are *about* but not the *same* as social reality.

5. See Mead's (1935:225–230) wonderful characterizations of what she called "mild" men in Mundugumor society on the Sepik.

6. See, for example, Moondi's father, who has produced many offspring. Obviously men who like women and enjoy sex with them will—all things being equal—produce many children (cf. Chowning 1980). Being prolific reproductively is something Sambia admire, regardless of what else comes with the package. No amount of heroic deeds or battle scars can make up for lack of progeny, which is why full masculine personhood requires prowess and many children. So here is an attribute of *aambei-wutnyi* that is (subliminally) read as intensely masculine.

7. Effeminate (see Stoller 1975a) is different, a caricature of women that ex-

aggerates stereotyped feminine qualities. Effeminacy implies gender aberrance. I know of no effeminate Sambia. *Aambei-wutnyi* men do not live out that hostile exhibition. They are comfortable being, in a few important ways, more feminine than masculine.

8. Again, we can't assume that males and females show the same behavioral acts or traits from society to society, that these are seen in all places as masculine and feminine, or are experienced everywhere as the same. Ethnographers: let us please be more specific about how we use "masculine" and "feminine."

9. These category terms all refer only to males, not females. Women use the generic nouns *wogaanyu* and *wusaatu*, never *aambei-wutnyi*, in reference to each other's weak or inappropriate social performance.

10. Caveat: Sambia have been at peace for years. With warfare gone, in everyone and in all situations much of the force behind gender differentiation has diminished. Perhaps *aambei-wutnyi* would have been pushed further, have had more demanded of them in masculine performance, or else have been treated more shabbily, before pacification. We ethnographers may be underrating such social changes on gender role behavior (see Faithorn 1976; Feil 1978; and perhaps Mead fifty years ago: see Gewertz 1983).

11. Reliability and validity are aspects of all scientific data. What about ethnography? Seldom, except in glaring cases (e.g., Castaneda: see DeMille 1976; Murray 1979), is this issue discussed, though the Samoan case created great controversy (Freeman 1983). When we deal with an *n* of 1, we need to think hard on what we expect in reliability and validity (cf. chapter 11), especially since full information in our work is impossible. As long as someone is living, our constructions of his or her experience are incomplete and interminable (Freud 1937). The same basic issue but transmuted applies to the study of cultures too.

12. Weiyu's behavior differed when interpreting for these two men. He was more anxious with Kalutwo, more comfortable with Imano. He was more interested, relaxed, spontaneous, in direct eye contact, and easy in translating with Imano, but with Kalutwo tense, bored, slumped, frustrated, with bad or no eye contact, making verbal slips, and finding it difficult to translate questions or answers. For years Weiyu has translated for me with many people; thus, this just described difference isn't an artifact of his closer relationship to Imano than to Kalutwo. Here, the translator's behavior is a kind of projective test to be studied, over time, like the ethnographer's own subjectivity (chapter 10).

13. Of Imano's three biologic brothers, the eldest is a weak shaman, another *aambei-wutnyi*, who has two wives and many children; the second is more of a fighter, has an acid-sharp tongue, three wives and many children; the youngest (an agemate of Weiyu) also is quiet and gentle; he obviously likes women, and is newly wed with two children.

14. In local idiom, such a person's speech style is called *nuvuchelu*, which refers to a mouth so stuffed with betel-nut that one's speech is slurred. Precisely what caused this condition is hard to say, but it is rare. (It made one self-conscious.)

15. I knew Imano's mother before she died in 1980; then in her seventies, she was a wonderful old lady, proud and generous. Her generosity was renowned, so much so that her nickname meant "mother of the hamlet." She also had extensive gardening and sorcery magic, and she was unquestionably the most important woman elder in Nilangu, for she did the key ritual teachings for girls.

16. A major clue that Imano's father's gender identity was different from other men's. Moreover, by the time Imano arrived, his father was middle-aged. Age may

have further diminished his father's male attachments and desire to spend time in all-male company, as it does in older men today: here is certainly an important sib-position factor in Imano's masculine development.

17. Westerners may find this hard to believe, but it is commonly stated among Sambia (as elsewhere in New Guinea). When people are breast-fed (or have access to the breast) till they are three or four, they remember. There are no great discontinuities, such as secretiveness, in this domain: children see breast-feeding all the time. Those memories are filtered, screened, and reinterpreted over the years, but they survive in consciousness.

18. Of the various things boys and men have said of their responses to the first homosexual teachings, no other has ever said he (silently) laughed at them. Most boys, from my observations of ritual, are scared and confused. When Imano said this he broke into guffaws.

19. Sambia homosexuality is structured to be promiscuous. Yet Imano's relationship with the older youth was that of lovers. In previous writings I never used this term, but rather "partners," "contacts," or "liaisons," feeling that our notion "lover" (one who is in a romantic love affair) distorted the indiscriminate, promiscuous, bump-and-grind quality of homosexual intercourse among Sambia. What Imano described is different: it was *enduring*, lasting about three months; *intense*, for they had sex just about every other night; *caring*, for they slept together, shared food, hunted together, and Imano was protected by the youth; and, for Imano, *exclusive*, for he had sex with no other man during this time or afterward. (He did continue having sporadic sexual contacts with this youth for several years after.) You could see this attachment between Sambia males only when someone was comfortable in the way Imano was.

20. For a comparison of the behavior and experiences of secret nosebleeding among men, see Herdt (1982b). Developmentally, such rituals as nosebleeding— done both in collective situations and private ones—are identity-contexts, providing the ethnographer with important clues about variations in the person's fantasy, life-history, and dynamics.

21. Why *overly* self-conscious? ("Overly" means: he laughed, giggled, and hid his face [men do not do that] when first disicussing that he had sex with his wife, that he wanted to please her, and that he was letting us know of it.) Did this self-consciousness reflect a sense of aberrant erotism? I think not. For example, he was just as embarrassed to talk of his nosebleeding and of having been a fellator. (Other men are also self-conscious in these sensitive areas, but less so. And they grow out of it after adolescence.) Imano was also unlike other Sambia men in finding women marvelously exciting to possess, while not needing to be like them (e.g., by competing with, fearing, or imitating them); he does not wish to be like his wife. Thus: where other men have no such respect for women, he is overly self-conscious.

22. Masculinity, like other patterns in Sambia culture and personality, is changing, particularly in relation to western experience (Herdt 1987c). Imano has been to the coast. Is this quirk—giving money to his wives—a result of that? It probably influenced him. But, to repeat, other men don't do this, not even other returned coastal migrants. Details in gender differences like this one should make us careful about claiming that western contact is the sole instigator of change in traditional culture, or that when western intrusion occurs, it changes everyone the same way.

23. Which "him," the gender researcher wonders? Imano ten years ago? The "true" Imano self now? Or is this just a performance for friends? Or is it all of

these? Interpretation: Imano's spontaneity makes me think this is genuine excitement, which he allows us to see because he is comfortable. Hypothesis: the only other person who sees this excitement is his wife.

24. Reference to Turner's (1964) important paper on individual and collective symbolism (reviewed in Herdt 1981, Appendix A). The reader should know that S. and I have had this conversation, in one form or another, before; we seem to suffer the same quirk in talking like this, whether it's in New Guinea, UCLA, or some Washington restaurant.

9. *Kalutwo: Portrait of a Misfit*

1. Some of this biographic material is reprinted from Herdt (1980).
2. Out of my total research population (about 150 males I can profile), only four or five adult men are known to engage in homosexual fellatio regularly (not merely on the sly and occasionally) done by (never to) boys, even though, being married, the behavior is socially inappropriate and morally wrong. These men, however, are also less deviant because they are married and have children. In addition, several older men resemble K. slightly in having failed at marriage and in being quiet, conservative, unobstructive. (One, mentally retarded, has never married and engages only in homosexual activities.) I doubt if these men, on closer examination, would look like K.
3. Half the Sambia men by 1980 between age fifteen and forty-five have worked on the coast for a year or more, usually on plantations. This is a sort of rite of passage in that coastal experience has become a substitute for warrior and ritual activities. About 25% of them speak Pidgin, only some of whom are fluent. (Women do not work on the coast, and few speak Pidgin.) Many return wearing one or another western garment, usually as status symbols. Though K. differs in these regards, he is not considered deviant on these grounds.
4. By chance I was first introduced in 1974 to K. by a local missionary. The memory stands out because he told me in English that K. was one of the strange people in the Valley: he was a "strange man" with a "weak handshake," who had an "oddly close relationship to his sister." He added that K. was one of the few Sambia he didn't care for. (Deviance theorists: I dismissed the missionary's view until, years later, Sambia repeated similar views long enough that they finally sank in. In this case I believe the missionary reached his opinion independently of the natives.)
5. He usually arrived early in my house, sometimes to spend as much as two hours before interview time. In part this was because he was not doing much garden work; he had lots of time to kill.
6. Weiyu pledged himself to confidentiality, as had I, but K. knew this wasn't good enough in a tiny hamlet. In collaborative work with others (relatives, friends), I also had to be careful not to violate K.'s trust.
7. See the next chapter, where we take up problems of the interpreter's presence and reactions in more detail. Some anthropologists think ethnographic dialogue is hindered by our not being able to speak directly to the native in the vernacular. I agree. Particularly in clinical ethnography—the one-to-one sustained dialogue of a case study—third parties, even mutually trusted translators, shift the interviewing dynamics. But another dimension of the interpreter's presence also plays a part that might be overlooked: the third party provides a legitimate

reason for the native not to reveal more than is wanted of him or herself. K., who is inherently untrusting, must have known (I asked him, but he could never directly respond) that he could not completely trust Weiyu. And so he avoided certain subjects: for instance, in working on his sexual daydreams, he could talk about the scenario but would leave out exactly what he felt.

8. So it goes in a society organized by sexual polarity: women—and ultimately men (e.g., K.)—suffer the costs. (His older sister was already married and away making a family of her own. Her husband had a cordial relationship with K. and his mother, but he died prematurely.)

9. This man—Gorutndun—is Imano's age (early thirties), married, has children, is well liked, gregarious, and in a position of some authority. I knew him for years and was friendly with him, but he steadfastly refused to be interviewed until 1981. He described then how he had always liked sex with boys as fellators and women as well. (See Epilogue.) My hunch is that this bi-erotic behavior in adulthood occurs quietly among a few men, but because it is wrong, they, like Gorutndun, are loathe to discuss it.

Incidentally, if there are any who believe anthropologists get informants to say anything if well bribed, they should know of Gorutndun, Kalutwo, and others of my acquaintance: when people fear examining their own behavior—want no insight—no amount of bribery can persuade them until they trust. See Epilogue.

10. The only reliable data I have on this adult erotic role-switching comes from Nilutwo, Penjukwi's husband. He once told me how an older bachelor had tried to switch roles with him (N. was a fellator) and suck him off. N. was frightened and fled. This bachelor was Zaito, an insane man. On mentioning it, N. laughed and spoke of the act as crazy, by a crazy man. However, it occurred before the onset of Zaito's psychotic episodes. Even so, the crazy attribution indicates how Sambia regard this inversion. I have heard fleeting rumors of attempted inversion by two other men. The details of these incidents are too complex to describe here.

11. Like other regular interpreters I paid K. with money, trade goods, and food. These items cannot be discounted as motivation. But they are not enough to make someone work unless he or she wants to (as we find with K., Sakulambei, and the reluctant interpreters mentioned previously). One hears stories of fieldworkers who buy information in New Guinea, such as paying the equivalent of ten cents to many dollars per myth or folktale that people bring them. That may occur. (I never did that.) My point is that such stories concern superficial, depersonalized information: sit someone down for a few hours, ask questions they don't like, and watch them run. No amount of money will induce answers (not even lies, if an interviewer persists) an interpreter refuses to give.

12. This contrast between "primary" and "secondary" shamans as different developmental tracks and character structure formations will be taken up elsewhere. It compares with Spiro's (1968a) distinction between the psychocultural patterns of men versus women shamans' callings in Burma but differs in that I here suggest different motivations among members of the male sex. In both Spiro's and my case, though, I believe that only a psychodynamic approach will lead us to discoveries in a field overly dominated by cultural relativism (cf. Price-Williams 1975; Peters and Price-Williams 1980) or reductionistic Freudian pathologizing.

13. This statement is only roughly correct. Every hamlet desires shamans; in general, the more, the better (but recall Weiyu's father). If this social desirability is what S. meant, then I was wrong. But if—as I suspect—he was asking me if

anyone in *particular* desired K. to be a shaman, then the answer is still no—his sister included. (Note how different Saku's situation is in this regard.) A lot of qualifications for a "simple" question.

14. S: H.'s translation of these conversations with K. was the only one hard for me to edit: untranslated words, literal translations so that the meaning is incomprehensible, persisting with Pidgin and unable to break free into English, loss of narrative sense, quite a mess. Here is an example that comes up about this point.

H: [*Pause.*] You say that you feel happy when that—

H: Kalutwo breaks in, in Sambia, louder than my talk, and he continues to talk for about thirty seconds here. And Weiyu asks him some questions. This goes on for about a minute, then the tape switches—there's no translation here. Apparently we must have reached an impasse, but I don't know why it wasn't recorded. A slight break and then we continue in another line of the interviewing.

H: Now, what was the first time when he was big or, a little bigger or a little smaller, when he started to think about [fantasize about] the faces of initiates, about when he could start to copulate with them. Was that when he was a *choowinuka* or *imbutu* or what? [*Weiyu translates to K. who clears his throat again. The tape switches.*]

W: It was at that time, then. [He was an *imbutu.*]

S: My first editing of H.'s translation takes, on the average, one half-hour per typed page of transcription. When my first is typed, I read and touch it up: two and a half hours on the second round for thirty-six pages for this piece. H. goes over that version, and then I go over his. Just to be clear and accurate.

H: During the past month, I had grown increasingly exasperated with K. Though he came regularly to work, he was evasive. My frustration, and our impasse, places Weiyu in an uncomfortable position. He never avoided translating for K. Yet, as the interviews became more intense, they were more trying for him, and he lost all enthusiasm for working with K. I was aware of this pressure on W. and tried to help him. In retrospect, I did not realize how uncomfortable he was and how much hostility toward K. (and hence, for me, since I continued the work) he had bottled up. (See chapter 10.)

10. The Interpreter's Discomfort

1. Evans-Pritchard (1956). Cf. also Whiting et al., (1966:156–159). Today, there are many and more fancy texts on the problem (Marcus and Fisher 1986; Geertz 1988; Tedlock 1983).

2. Today, in a shrinking postcolonialist world, some of these corrupted are now political leaders, the new cultural spokesmen—interpreters—who must approve foreign research visas in their countries.

3. Naroll (1970) argues that the ethnographer's ability to work in the vernacular is the key factor influencing the quality of our reports.

4. In Melanesia, there are two broad types of languages: Austronesian (or "Melanesian") languages, and non-Austronesian ("Papuan") languages. New Guinea's non-Austronesian languages are among the world's most difficult tongues. Most of them are unwritten and unrecorded; they must be learned *in situ*. Experienced

linguists, working full-time on language, have spent years learning single languages like Fore, Binamurian, or Baruya. And Eunice Pike, a noted linguist, once described the Anga language family (to which Sambia belongs) as one of the most complex in the world. When it takes five years and more to achieve competence, ethnographers cannot succeed (there are exceptions, e.g., Andrew Strathern, given enough time). Thus, many New Guinea ethnographies are constructed from materials collected in Pidgin or Motu (see Bateson 1944; Mead 1939; and Tuzin 1976:xxxiv for discussion). Probably ninety percent or more of all fieldworkers in New Guinea have used interpreters in some capacity, more or less (usually more). Nonetheless, this aspect of the hermeneutics of ethnography has been ignored (Langness 1976:100 ff.).

5. The reasons for this disengagement are pretty simple: you need only credit a technical aid once; and anthropologists are supposed to be experts working from direct, sensory experience, in the vernacular: why make a big deal out of facts that give contrary impressions. Nowhere is this message clearer than in Mead's ethnographies (e.g., 1935), as opposed to her more technical discussions (e.g., 1939; 1949; 1956).

6. Though there are allusions galore to this aspect of field methodology, from Boas (1920), Malinowski (1922; and especially 1935), Mead (1939), and on up to the present (e.g., Paul 1953; Pelto and Pelto 1973; Whiting et al. 1966:157), rarely has the interpreter's role been rigorously explicated (but see Crapanzano [1980], Owusu [1978], and Powdermaker [1966] for nice exceptions). Werner and Campbell (1970) have written on the general problem in anthropology; the other social sciences have generally ignored it (cf. e.g., Burgess 1982).

7. In the Melanesian literature, Mead's *The Mountain Arapesh* ([1968], see especially pp. 19–20), though a psychologic account, is an early and valuable exception.

8. I did little interpreting using Penjukwi in 1979. But when I returned in 1981 and worked more with women, she was crucial as my woman interpreter throughout. S. and I also used Moondi, but on a smaller scale.

9. For instance, Sambia use words with meanings completely different from dictionary glosses (such as those in the Standard Pidgin dictionaries). For a few days (in 1974) I was constantly confused because women used *sisa* (sister) to refer to two brothers (male siblings), when it formally applies only to siblings of the opposite sex. (This usage reflects a native identification in their own kinship system.)

10. This is a more serious source of distortion of the native view, which only the ethnographer's cultural and linguistic knowledge can correct. Examples: my interpreters would use Pidgin *"spirit"* or *"tebari"* (corruption of *tewel*) to gloss soul (*koogu*), shadow (*wakoogu-nambelu*), spirit familiar (*nemulyu*), and even thought (*koontu*, which can also be used pragmatically as a marker for "self"); or "growim" to cover: to expand, to get big, to make someone or something big, or to psychologically separate from someone (see Herdt 1982b). I feel that the semantic complexities of New Guinea cultures have been seriously underplayed due to such translation generalities.

11. I did not do this systematically at first but simply sat around talking about the ambience and working conditions of my house. Later, in 1979, we talked about how they felt after a particular interpreting session. I have always discouraged Weiyu and Moondi from publicly discussing an informant's private communications in public, even at my house, unless we were alone, and even then I discouraged them from talking about others in my work, for that tended to gossipy in-

terchanges. Public matters were another story. I did systematically work with Moondi to develop formal interview procedures (on tape) for studying boy-initiates' cognitive and ritual variation in two sets of interviews in 1975.

12. I know now that I made Weiyu be patient. He is, by nature, impetuous, like Moondi: quick to argue and to move toward adventure (e.g., a ritual, a trip) when wisdom counseled otherwise. Both Weiyu and Moondi have changed in this regard over the years due to age, social maturing, or, in Moondi's case, schooling.

13. S. is my mentor, a role model with whom I consciously identify (ego-ideal). This identification is deeper, because I sometimes see him in dreams (transference object). I feel that he has not only taught me but also helped me learn to stay honest in my research.

14. "The investigator himself has strong motivation to overlook the interpreter's faults. If he admits that the interpreter often makes mistakes, this amounts to admitting that much of his laboriously collected data may be unreliable or that much more checking than he had hoped to do is required to establish facts conclusively" (Whiting et al. 1966:156).

15. "No outsider could understand these multiple roles and Chinese intricacies. . . . It was not the American kind of loyalty-duplicity; in America the emotions were different somehow, perhaps thinner. Here you lead a crypto-emotional life. . . . You had no personal rights, but on the other hand, the claims of feeling were more fully acknowledged" (Bellow 1982:80).

16. Weiyu is being extreme here, showing some idiosyncracy. If I were to generalize (and it is difficult to do so on this topic) there are differences, based on three factors, in men's abilities and desire to discuss sex: generation, personality, and situation. (1) Some older men are reluctant to discuss sex due to older, more conservative, cultural values. (Very old men are too, because it is beneath their dignity, in a sense.) Weiyu's generation has been exposed to and acculturated by western attitudes toward sex. In this regard, Weiyu is an example of those wage-labor migrants who have been to the coast and tasted a more promiscuous life. (2) But even in the subset of Weiyu's peers who will have coastal experience, some are still prudish and reluctant to describe sexual exploits—not in public, which almost never occurs—but in private with peers. Weiyu is here again an extreme. (Don Juan complex? See chapter 5.) (3) Even when talking in private, in the clubhouse, older men feel shame if sex with their wives comes up, though they will, when alone with their cronies, brag and joke to some extent about sexual exploits. Younger men friends—in part because of my influence—do this more easily than their seniors. All this information is needed to set in context that remark of Weiyu's. Here again the difference between normative and idiosyncratic behavior requires attention to variance in the population with which one is working.

17. See Herdt (1981: ch. 8) and Stoller and Herdt (1982).

18. After this session we were to have seen Sakulambei. He never showed, as we noted in chapter 8. But in the minutes following our interview with W., we happened to have taped our private talk which compared them. An excerpt of that tape follows:

H: This interpreting is just . . . this is teaching me how tremendously exhausting this is. I am exhausted. I feel like I have walked five miles with Kalutwo. Yesterday the feeling was the same way. That was especially—even more so, that was far more emotional to me—than the session with Sakulambei. Yet both were the same: three hours.

S: The two interviews were similar in the intensity of the resistance, but Saku was resistant because of a post-infancy-early-childhood-reality-traumatic-experience. Kalutwo's resistance also comes from early childhood [abandoned and denied by his father] but has a different structure inside, a fundamental damage to early character structure development. But you get resistance from both. Yesterday was really tough as hell, but it was child's play compared to this.

H: Two heavy resistances, yet as you compare the two of them, it's remarkable that this man, a hermaphrodite, has the more normative sense of masculinity. Saku had the maternal uncle and his mother and father, so Saku must have got enough love from his maternal uncle whom he adored.

S: Of course. When I say to him, "Come in your greatest finery," he's proud. I would not know what to say to this guy K. . . . "get a shave?" There is no way that he would ever come looking different. But all I had to do was say it to Saku. He has the resources. This guy K., there is nothing you could say to him that would make him stand up and be a real person. The only real person is passive/resistance hopelessness. It's the only thing he's got, his only gimmick. Too bad.

11. Summing Up: Clinical Ethnography of Sambia Erotics and Gender

1. Herdt (1981, 1987c); Stoller and Herdt (1982).

2. Kohut (1971), made popular in anthropology by Geertz (1976).

3. S: Once, thinking the new generation of ethnographers—beneficiaries of our modern sexual freedom—could do it, I felt I had an antidote to the pretty useless ethnographic literature on sexual excitement: have them write up the realities of the excitements in which they personally participated with the subjects of their field studies. It did not work out. I can only guess why.

4. Doi (1973); Kakar (1985).

5. "The Other must matter in one's own self-constitution; he must not simply be an object of scientific or quasi-scientific scrutiny" (Crapanzano 1980:141).

6. Sapir (1938:9–10); cf. Singer (1961:61–65).

7. "One can predict too few of the people too much of the time" (Shweder 1979:268).

8. S: I suppose certain positions (schools) in anthropology [H: and psychoanalysis] are really metaphysical. Structuralists are Idealists, and grubbers like H. and me, with our love of the detail, are Nominalists. Were I an ethnographer, I would not seriously believe in Culture but in cultures. My belief is visceral and starts literally in the body: the ideal apple is no apple. The ideal sound is silent, beyond the sounds we experience. The ideal lizard has no legs, because the ideal leg is no leg. Then the ideal tennis has no net, and the ideal ideal has no existence:

> I swear, I swear
> I do not see
> How what is not
> Can be, can be.

9. Mead (1961) hinted of and cautioned against the same possible bias in ethnographies of sexual behavior long ago.

10. None. See note 3 above.

11. Creed (1984). Cf. Knauft (1987).

12. Foucault (1980) is critiqued in Herdt (n.d.).
13. See for example, Friedl (1975).
14. Example:

"If culture is as anthropologists claim a meaningful order, still, in action meanings are always at risk. They are risked, for example, by reference to things (i.e., in extension). Things not only have their own *raison d'être*, independently of what people may make of them, they are inevitably disproportionate to the sense of the signs by which they are apprehended. Things are contextually more particular than signs and potentially more general. They are more particular insofar as signs are meaning-classes, not bound as concepts to any particular referent (or stimulus-free). Things are thus related to their signs as empirical tokens to cultural types. Yet things are more general than signs inasmuch as they present more priorities (more reality) than the distinctions and values attended to by signs. Culture is therefore a gamble played with nature, in the course of which, wittingly or unwittingly—I paraphrase Marc Bloch—the old names that are still on everyone's lips acquire connotations that are far removed from their original meaning." (Sahlins 1985:ix)

To rescue us from such islands of Culture in the dark stream of post-structuralist theory we are going to need sturdy lifeboats.

15. See especially Knauft (1987). The most accessible review of the literature, though slanted to institutionalized homosexuality, is Herdt (1984). See also Herdt and Poole (1982), Mead (1961), Read (1986), and Whiting (1941). Far-reaching revisions will stem from M. Strathern's monumental *The Gender of the Gift* (1988).
16. This could be credited, in part, to Mead's (1935, 1949, 1961) ever-popular presence; and it is now being sustained by the important work of many excellent fieldworkers (reviewed in M. Strathern, 1988).
17. See, for instance, the divergent reviews of Adam (1986), Carrier (1980), Murray (1984), and Rubin (1975).
18. Monographs and journals, too numerous to list, are notable in one respect that supports my contention: none of the major journals on sexuality has much anthropologic input, and rare are the anthropologists who sit on their editorial boards.
19. Mead (1961) and Carrier (1980) use this argument.
20. See Katchadourian and Lunde (1980), which was, I am told, the largest selling text on human sexuality.
21. Atkinson (1982:249); cf. M. Strathern (1981).
22. "Because of the overwhelming concern of early anthropologists to establish culture or society as a legitimate focus for inquiry, the existence of the individual was usually suppressed in professional ethnographic writing" (Marcus and Cushman 1982:32).

"We are constantly under the gun to produce ethnographies, critical essays, theoretical treatises, and reviews, most of which are judged according to the theoretical contributions they make to the science of anthropology. This epistemological process of extracting the etic from the emic is scientific method par excellence and is an engrained structure in our system of scientific evaluation. And yet, how do we know that the data from which etic categories are extracted reflect the social reality of the people under study? Owusu (1978) has suggested that many classic works on African societies are fundamentally flawed, for they are based on misinterpretations of the data. In my own work (P. Stoller 1980:419), I have called attention to how what Whitehead called 'perceptual delusion' unwittingly creates ethnographic fiction (1980:419)" (P. Stoller 1982:1–2).

23. Moerman (1979) makes this argument. Cf. Shweder and Bourne (1984).

24. See Mead (1949:31); cf. Geertz (1984), who provides a modern interpretive functional relativism, which Spiro (1986) criticizes as ethnographic particularism.

25. Geertz (1966). Cf. the insightful Hallowell (1967).

26. Beginning with *Totem and Taboo* (1913).

27. Kakar's (1983) work on India is helpful here.

28. Freud (1905); see also Stoller (1975b); cf. Davidson (1987); Kakar (1985); Obeyesekere (1981).

29. Kakar (1985:442) quoting Silvan (1981:97).

30. *Ibid.*

31. Malinowski's complaint, in response to Ernest Jones' response to M.'s Trobriand work (published in an analytic journal!), was that the unconscious was always the cause, the culture the effect. "The universal occurrence of the Oedipus complex is being assumed, as if it existed independently of the type of culture, of the social organization and of the concomitant ideas" (Malinowski 1927:126). Malinowski's own "myth" of the absent Oedipal complex in the Trobriands has been exhaustively critiqued by Spiro, who draws attention to the "uncritical acceptance of the finding" (1982:179): a point that also touches on the mystification of fieldwork discussed in chapter 1. Spiro is reviewed in Herdt (1985).

32. Freud's insights from dream interpretation apply here to the meanings of erotics in cultural discourse and in private interviews: "At the same time, however, I should like to utter an express warning against overestimating the importance of symbols in dream interpretation, against restricting the work of translating dreams merely to translating symbols and against abandoning the technique of making use of the dreamer's association. The two techniques of dream-interpretation must be complementary to each other; *but both in practice and in theory the first place continues to be held by the procedure which I began by describing and which attributes the decisive significance to the comments made by the dreamer"* (1900:395, my emphasis).

33. The manifestations of this mental world are most recently reviewed in Herdt (1987c). I find increasing attention paid to the problem (Herdt and Poole 1982; M. Strathern 1988; Tuzin 1982).

34. Obeyesekere (1981) more than anyone has examined the problems of transformation of private or psychologic symbols into public shared knowledge. Cf. Wagner (1975) for a nonpsychologic view of the problem in Melanesia and more generally.

35. This aspect of the issue of discourse accounts and social/ritual controls is studied in initiates' experience, in Herdt (1987a).

36. See Crapanzano (1980), chastised in public lectures by Geertz (1988).

37. See especially Weiner (1985).

38. Reviewed in Bourguignon (1979:75–115), LeVine (1982), Schwartz (1978); cf. Marcus and Fischer (1986).

39. Wallace (1969); D'Andrade (1986); Edgerton (1985); Schwartz (1978).

40. See Keesing (1979, 1982); Pelto and Pelto (1973).

41. Reviewed in Herdt (1982a).

42. See Shweder and LeVine (eds. 1984); White and Kirkpatrick (1985).

43. See especially LeVine's (1982) seminal work on psychoanalytically oriented ethnography. Cf. Parin, Morganthaler, and Parin-Matthey (1980).

44. Most novice ethnographers cannot rely on intuitions about appropriateness. They are not knowledgeable enough, which is actually an advantage: the wisdom of knowing that one is ignorant. Because of our inability to introspect and resonate in foreign settings, classical psychoanalysis there is probably impossible. (See Brody 1980; Foulks 1977: Haldipur 1980; Littlewood 1980; Spiegel 1976.)

45. But see Parson's early work (1969).

46. Crapanzano (1980:146) remarks of his translator: "He gave me distance and protected me from direct and immediate contact and from the fears and pleasures of contact."

47. See chapter 5, and Herdt (1981: Appendix A).

48. "Through the use of such techniques—and the training of students to use these techniques reliably and confidently—the ethnographic monograph came to contain a large body of ordered information which was reasonably independent of observer bias, whether that bias was owing to ethnocentricity, temperamental preferences, research interests or applied aims" (Mead 1977:3–4).

49. "No one since has contributed as much as Freud to breaking the charm of *facts* and opening up the empire of *meaning*. Yet Freud continues to include all of his discourses in the same positivist framework which they destroy" (Ricoeur 1979:326).

50. See Doi (in press), on the analysis of psychoanalysis.

51. LeVine (1982:ix): "In my view, there is no need for more theory in this field unless it is accompanied by a sturdier method of data collection. Methodology has been the central problem of culture and personality research, its greatest stumbling block, and it claims the most searching scrutiny."

Epilogue: Training Clinical Ethnographers

1. Precisely which clinical training will work for Ph.D. students is not clear, but a psychoanalysis is not the answer. It is lengthy and expensive. [S: And unnecessary and at the wrong time. And, analysis does not work well when one seeks it primarily for training rather than primarily for inner needs.] While others (Agar 1980:42 *n.* lists them, and cf. LeVine 1982) have advocated analytic training, the advice has made no great impact (Pelto and Pelto 1973). Given the difficulties, one is tempted to throw up his hands and say, "Here are your cultural biases; for the rest of it, go to a shrink" (Agar 1980:42). That is not necessarily prescribed: read on.

2. See Tuzin (1975), who demonstrated this in his study of Ilahita Arapesh.

3. See Herdt (1981:142–144) on Nilutwo's dreaming.

4. Cf. Herdt (1987d) for an attempt to see Nilutwo's dreaming in the context of Sambian and Freudian dream theory.

5. Malcolm's (1984:18) quote concerns an analyst who is: "following Freud's directive to listen with 'closely hovering attention' in order to put himself in a position to make use of everything he is told for the purposes of recognizing the concealed unconscious material."

6. H: Perhaps nothing in a footnote, or our work, or the opinions of colleagues and friends will change such views. But as an anthropologist, I am aware enough of the culture of anthropology and of cultural rules regarding scholarly writing in

America, to be warned about this point. Such opinions, too, are culturally shaped: what Americans may regard as exuberant performance, Europeans will see as exhibitionism. (See Bateson 1972. Though remember the response to Freud's *The Interpretation of Dreams*, so long ago.)

7. The word "truly" is a necessary redundancy, because, to use today's jargon, the genre conventions and tropes of ethnography have seemed to change. Now, to be in vogue, one should self-confess without truly disclosing oneself (which would be gauche). Crapanzano (1980) and Kracke (1987) are exceptions to this. Many writing in the interpretative ethnography field (Clifford and Marcus 1985) are not: their sense of disclosure is, if I recall Umberto Eco's medieval metaphor correctly, more like viewing a tapestry from its underside.

8. A recent review of education in cultural psychiatry (Moffic et al. 1987) shows this.

9. Again: Powdermaker (1966).

10. Recent issues of the *American Anthropological Association Newsletter* discuss the ethical sides of fictitious cases.

11. Some advocate "clinical anthropology"—anthropologists doing psychotherapy and making interventions—which raises issues beyond our purview here, for we did not try for treatment. I cannot see, however, that anthropologists differ from psychologists in requiring extended and supervised clinical training in formal and supervised settings before doing treatment anywhere. (See *Open Forum: Clinical Anthropology*, 1980–81.)

12. H: Warwick (1980) suggests that the key to ethical training in social science is the building of professional responsibility in students. I would add that such responsibility is internalized when the student believes there are no pat or impersonal solutions to ethical dilemmas in fieldwork; so care and patience are wonderful assistance always in these situations.

13. Not Hegel's history. Our view of mental life is the opposite of Hegel's tub-thumping idealism: "In Hegel's philosophy, history has a purpose. It is the march of Mind toward freedom. The chief barrier to freedom is the fact that Mind does not understand that it is a unity ['Mind' here is probably the same 'Self' that is being promoted these days] and as such, master of its destiny. Instead, the individual minds of human beings—which are all really manifestations of Mind—see themselves as separate, and often opposed, entities. From this comes the alienation and unhappiness that exists in this world" (P. Singer 1980). (As Popper 1971 knows, such sentiments argue for a unitary viewpoint by all people: totalitarianism.)

BIBLIOGRAPHY

Aberle, David F. 1951. *The Psychosocial Analysis of a Hopi Life-History.* Berkeley: University of California Press
Adam, Barry D. 1986. Age, Structure, and Sexuality: Reflections on the Anthropological Evidence on Homosexual Relations. In E. Blackwood, ed., *Anthropology and Homosexual Behavior*, pp. 19–34. New York: Harrington Park Press.
Agar, Michael H. 1980. *The Professional Stranger.* New York: Academic Press.
——1982. Toward an Ethnographic Language. *American Anthropologist* 84:779–795.
Alland, Alexander Jr. 1970. *Adaptation in Cultural Evolution.* New York: Columbia University Press.
Allen, Michael R. 1967. *Male Cults and Secret Initiations in Melanesia.* Melbourne: Melbourne University Press.
Ardener, Edwin. 1975. Belief and the Problem of Women [and] the 'Problem' Revised. In S. Ardener, ed., *Perceiving Women*, pp. 1–27. London: Malaby Press.
Asad, T., ed. 1973. Introduction. *Anthropology and the Colonial Encounter*, pp. 9–19. New York: Humanities Press.
Ashley-Montagu, M. F. 1937. *Coming into Being Among the Australian Aborigines.* London: Routledge.
Atkinson, Jane M. 1982. Anthropology. *Signs* 8:236–258.
Barnes, J. A. 1967. Some Ethical Problems in Modern Field Work. In D. G. Jongmans and P. C. W. Gutkind, eds., *Anthropologists in the Field*, pp. 193–213. Assen: VanGorum.
Barth, Frederik. 1974. On Responsibility to Humanity. *Current Anthropology* 15:99–102.
——1975. *Ritual and Knowledge Among the Baktaman of New Guinea.* New Haven: Yale University Press.
Barzun, Jacques. 1981. The Wasteland of American Education. *The New York Review of Books*, 28(17):34–36.
Bateson, Gregory. 1942 (1972). Experiments in Thinking About Observed Ethnological Material. *Steps to an Ecology of Mind*, pp. 73–87. New York: Ballantine Books.
——1944. Pidgin English and Cross-Cultural Communication. *Transactions of the New York Academy of Science*, Series 2, 6:137–141.

439

440   Bibliography

——1949. Bali: The Value System of a Steady State. In M. Fortes, ed., *Social Structure: Essays Presented to A. R. Radcliffe-Brown*, pp. 35–53. Oxford: Clarendon Press.

——1958. *Naven*. 2d ed. Stanford: Stanford University Press.

——1972. *Steps to an Ecology of Mind*. San Francisco: Chandler and Sharp.

——1976. Some Components of Socialization for Trance. In T. Schwartz, ed., *Socialization as Cultural Communication*, pp. 51–63. Berkeley: University of California Press.

——1978. Toward a Theory of Cultural Coherence: Comment. *Anthropological Quarterly* 51:77–78.

Bateson, Gregory and Margaret Mead. 1942. *Balinese Character: A Photographic Analysis*. Special Publications of the New York Academy of Sciences, vol. 2.

Becker, Ernest. 1973. *The Denial of Death*. New York: Free Press.

Bellow, Saul. 1982. *The Dean's December*. New York: Pocket Books.

Benedict, Ruth. 1934. *Patterns of Culture*. Boston: Houghton Mifflin.

——1938. Continuities and Discontinuities in Cultural Conditioning. *Psychiatry* 1:161–167.

——1946. *The Chrysanthemum and the Sword*. Boston: Houghton Mifflin.

Bennett, John W. 1946. The Interpretation of Pueblo Culture: A Question of Values. *Southwestern Journal of Anthropology* 2:361–374.

Berndt, Ronald Murray. 1965. The Kamano, Usurufa, Jate and Fore of the Eastern Highlands. In P. Lawrence and M. J. Meggitt, eds., *Gods, Ghosts, and Men in Melanesia*, pp. 78–104. Melbourne: Melbourne University Press.

Bertrand, William and Charles Kleymeyer. 1977. Misapplied Cross-Cultural Research: A Case Study of an Ill Fated Family Planning Research Project. In M. Stacey, M. Reid, C. Heath, and R. Dingwall, eds., *Health and the Division of Labor*, pp. 215–236. New York: Prodist.

Bettelheim, Bruno. 1955. *Symbolic Wounds, Puberty Rites and the Envious Male*. New York: Collier Books.

——1984. *Freud and Man's Soul*. New York: Vintage Books.

Blackwood, Beatrice. 1979. *Kukukuku of the Upper Watut*. C. R. Hallpike, ed. Oxford: Pitt-Rivers Museum.

Blackwood, Evelyn, ed. 1986. *Anthropology and Homosexual Behavior*. New York: Harrington Park Press.

Boas, Franz. 1920. The Method of Ethnology. *American Anthropologist* 22:311–321.

Bock, Philip K. 1969. *Modern Cultural Anthropology: An Introduction*. New York: Knopf.

Bohannan, Paul. 1979. You Can't Do Nothing. *American Anthropologist* 82:508–524.

Bowen, Elenore S. (pseudonym). 1954. *Return to Laughter*. New York: Doubleday, Natural History Press.

Bourguignon, Erika. 1979. *Psychological Anthropology*. New York: Holt, Rinehart, and Winston.

Briggs, Jean L. 1970. *Never in Anger: Portrait of an Eskimo Family*. Cambridge: Harvard University Press.

Brody, Eugene B. 1980. The Relevance of Cultural Anthropology for Psychoanalysis. *The Academy Forum* 24:7–10.

Brown, Paula. 1978. *Highland Peoples of New Guinea*. Cambridge: Cambridge University Press.

Brown, Paula and Georgeda Buchbinder. 1976. Introduction. In P. Brown and

G. Buchbinder, eds., *Man and Woman in the New Guinea Highlands*, pp. 1–12. Washington, D.C.: American Anthropological Association.

Brown, Penelope and S. Levinson. 1978. Universals in Language Usage: Politeness Phenomena. In E. N. Goody, ed., *Questions and Politeness*, pp. 56–189. Cambridge: Cambridge University Press.

Burgess, Robert G., ed. 1982. *Field Research: A Sourcebook and Field Manual*. London: Allen and Unwin.

Carrier, Joseph. 1980. Homosexual Behavior in Cross-Cultural Perspective. In J. Marmor, ed., *Sexual Inversion*, pp. 100–122. New York: Basic Books.

Casagrande, Joseph B., ed. 1960. *In the Company of Man: Twenty Portraits of Anthropological Informants*. New York: Harper.

Chagnon, Napoleon A. 1968. *Yanomamo: The Fierce People*. New York: Holt, Rinehart, and Winston.

Chalmers, James Rev. 1903. Notes on the Bugilia, British New Guinea. *Journal of the Royal Anthropological Institute* 33:108–110.

Chapple, Eliot D. 1952. The Training of the Professional Anthropologist: Social Anthropology and Applied Anthropology. *American Anthropologist* 54:340–342.

Chodorow, Nancy. 1978. *The Reproduction of Mothering*. Berkeley: University of California Press.

Chowning, Ann. 1980. Culture and Biology Among the Sengseng of New Britain. *Journal of Polynesian Society* 89:7–31.

Clay, Brenda. 1975. *Pinikindu*. Chicago: University of Chicago Press.

Clifford, James. 1986. Introduction: Partial Truths. In J. Clifford and G. Marcus, eds., *Writing Culture*, pp. 1–26. Berkeley: University of California Press.

Clifford, James and George Marcus, eds. 1986. *Writing Culture*. Berkeley: University of California Press.

Cohler, Bertram. 1982. Personal Narrative and Life Course. In B. Baltes and O. G. Brim, Jr., eds., *Life-Span Development and Behavior*, 44:205–241. New York: Academic Press.

Cole, Michael. 1975. An Ethnographic Psychology of Cognition. In R. W. Brislin, ed., *Cross-Cultural Perspectives on Learning*, pp. 157–174. New York: Wiley.

Collier, Jane F. and Michelle Z. Rosaldo. 1981. Politics and Gender in Simple Societies. In S. B. Ortner and H. Whitehead, eds., *Sexual Meanings*, pp. 275–329. Cambridge: Cambridge University Press.

Counts, Dorothy, A. 1980. Fighting Back is not the Way: Suicide and the Women of Kaliai. *American Ethnologist* 7:332–351.

Crapanzano, Vincent. 1980. *Tuhami: Portrait of a Moroccan*. Chicago: University of Chicago Press.

——1986. "Hermes' Dilemma: The Masking of Subversion in Ethnographic Description. In J. Clifford and G. Marcus, eds., *Writing Culture*, pp. 51–76. Berkeley: University of California Press.

Creed, Gerald W. 1984. Sexual Subordination: Institutionalized Homosexuality and Social Control in Melanesia. *Ethnology* 23:157–176.

D'Andrade, Roy G. 1986. Three Scientific World Views and the Covering Law Model. In D. W. Fiske and R. A. Shweder, eds., *Metatheory in Social Science*, pp. 19–41. Chicago: University of Chicago Press.

Davenport, William H. 1965. Sexual Patterns and Their Regulation in a Society of the Southwest Pacific. In F. A. Beach, ed., *Sex and Behavior*, pp. 164–207. New York: Wiley.

Davidson, Arnold I. 1987. How to Do the History of Psychoanalysis: A Reading of

Freud's Three Essays on the Theory of Psychoanalysis. *Critical Inquiry*, 14:252–277.

DeMille, Richard. 1976. *Castaneda's Journey: The Power and the Allegory*. Santa Barbara: Capra.

Devereux, George. 1937. Institutionalized Homosexuality of the Mohave Indians. *Human Biology* 9:498–527.

——1951. *Reality and Dream: The Psychotherapy of a Plains Indian*. New York: International Universities Press.

——1957a. The Awarding of a Penis as a Compensation for Rape. *International Journal of Psycho-Analysis* 38:398–401.

——1957b. Dream Learning and Individual Ritual Differences in Mohave Shamanism. *American Anthropologist* 59:1036–1045.

——1967. *From Anxiety to Method in the Behavioral Sciences*. The Hague: Mouton.

——1978. The Works of George Devereux. In G. D. Spindler, ed., *The Making of Psychological Anthropology*, pp. 364–406. Berkeley: University of California Press.

——1980a. Normal and Abnormal. *Basic Problems of Ethno-psychiatry*, pp. 3–71. Chicago: University of Chicago Press.

——1980b. *Basic Problems of Ethno-psychiatry*. Trans. B. M. Gulati and G. Devereux. Chicago: University of Chicago Press.

Doi, Takeo. 1973. *The Anatomy of Dependence*. Tokyo: Kodansha International.

——In press. The Cultural Assumptions of Psychoanalysis. In J. Stigler et al., eds., *Cultural Psychology*. New York: Cambridge University Press.

Douglas, M. 1966. *Purity and Danger*. London: Routledge & Kegan Paul.

——1970. *Natural Symbols*. New York: Pantheon Books.

Dover, Kenneth J. 1978. *Greek Homosexuality*. Cambridge, Mass.: Harvard University Press.

Dubois, Cora. 1944. *The People of Alor. A Socio-Psychological Study of an East Indian Island*. Minneapolis: University of Minnesota Press.

Dumont, Jean-Paul. 1978. *The Headman and I*. Austin: University of Texas Press.

Durkheim, Émile. 1965. (English trans. orig. 1915). *The Elementary Forms of the Religious Life*. Trans. J. W. Swain. New York: The Free Press.

Edgerton, Robert B. 1985. *Rules, Exceptions, and Social Order*. Berkeley: University of California Press.

Edgerton, Robert B. and L. L. Langness. 1974. *Methods and Styles in the Study of Culture*. San Francisco: Chandler and Sharp.

Edsall, John T. 1981. Two Aspects of Scientific Responsibility. *Science* 212:11–14.

Elkin, A. P. 1953. Delayed Exchange in Wabag Sub-District, Central Highlands of New Guinea. *Oceania* 33:161–201.

Ellis, Havelock. 1910 (1936). *Studies in the Psychology of Sex*, vol. I. New York: Random House.

Epstein, T. Scarlett. 1979. Mysore Villages Revisited. In G. M. Foster et al., eds., *Long-Term Field Research in Social Anthropology*, pp. 209–226. New York: Academic Press.

Erikson, Erik. 1958. The Nature of Clinical Evidence. *Daedalus* 87:65–87.

Evans-Pritchard, E. E. 1937. *Witchcraft, Oracles, and Magic Among the Azande*. Oxford: Oxford University Press.

——1956. *Nuer Religion*. Oxford: Clarendon Press.

——1962. *Social Anthropology and Other Essays*. New York: Free Press.

Faithorn, Elizabeth. 1975. The Concept of Pollution Among the Kafe of Papua New

Guinea. In R. R. Reiter, ed., *Toward an Anthropology of Women*, pp. 127–140. New York: Monthly Review Press.

——1976. Women as Persons: Aspects of Female Life and Male-Female Relations Among the Kafe. In P. Brown and G. Buchbinder, eds., *Man and Woman in the New Guinea Highlands*, pp. 86–95. Washington, D.C.: American Anthropological Association.

Federn, Paul. 1952. *Ego Psychology and the Psychoses*. New York: Basic Books.

Feil, Daryl K. 1978. Women and Men in the Enga Tee. *American Ethnologist* 5:263–279.

Firth, Raymond. 1981. Spiritual Aroma: Religion and Politics. Distinguished Lecture for 1980. *American Anthropologist* 83:582–605.

Forge, Anthony. 1972. The Lonely Anthropologist. In S. Kimball and J. B. Watson, eds., *Crossing Cultural Boundaries*, pp. 292–297. San Francisco: Chandler.

Fortes, Meyer. 1945. *The Dynamics of Clanship Among the Tallensi*. Oxford University Press for the International African Institute.

——1974. Social Anthropology at Cambridge since 1900. In R. Darnell, ed., *Readings in the History of Anthropology*, pp. 426–439. London: Harper & Row.

Fortune, Reo F. 1932. *Sorcerers of Dobu*. London: George Routledge.

——1939. Arapesh Warfare. *American Anthropologist* 41:22–41.

——1947. The Rules of Relationship Behavior in One Variety of Primitive Warfare. *Man* 47:108–110.

Foster, George M. 1969. *Applied Anthropology*. Boston: Little, Brown.

Foster, George M., Elizabeth Colson, Thayer Scudder, and Robert V. Kemper. 1979. Conclusion: The Long-term Study in Perspective. In G. M. Foster et al., eds., *Long-Term Field Research in Social Anthropology* pp. 323–348. New York: Academic Press.

Foucault, Michel. 1973. *The Birth of the Clinic*. Trans. A. M. S. Smith. New York: Pantheon Books.

——1980. *The History of Sexuality*. Trans. R. Hurley. New York: Pantheon Books.

Foulks, Edward F. 1977. Anthropology and Psychiatry: A New Blending of an Old Relationship. In E.F. Foulks et al., eds., *Current Perspectives in Cultural Psychiatry*, pp. 5–18. New York: Spectrum.

Frake, Charles O. 1969. Notes on Queries in Ethnography. In S. A. Tyler, ed., *Cognitive Anthropology*, pp. 123–137. New York: Holt, Rinehart and Winston.

Freeman, J. Derek. 1970. Human Nature and Culture. In D. Slayer, ed, *Man and the New Biology*, pp. 50–75. Canberra, Australia: Australian National University Press.

——1983. *Margaret Mead and Samoa*. Cambridge: Harvard University Press.

Freilich, Morris, ed. 1977. *Marginal Natives: Anthropologists at Work*. New York: Schenkman.

Freud, A. 1965. *Normality and Pathologoy in Childhood*. New York: International Universities Press.

Freud, Sigmund. *Standard Edition of the Complete Psychological Works of Sigmund Freud*. 24 vols. James Strachey, ed. and tr. London: Hogarth Press, 1953–1974; New York: Macmillan.

——1900. *The Interpretation of Dreams*. In *Standard Edition* 4–5:339–627.

——1905. *Three Essays on the Theory of Sexuality*. In *Standard Edition* 7:125–245.

——1913. *Totem and Taboo*. In *Standard Edition* 13:ix–162.

——1926. The Question of Lay Analysis. In *Standard Edition* 20:183–250.

—— 1927. The Future of an Illusion. In *Standard Edition* 21:3–57.

—— 1937(1938). Analysis Terminable and Interminable. In *Standard Edition* 23:211–253.

Friedl, Ernestine. 1975. *Men and Women in Cross-Cultural Perspective.* New York: Holt, Rinehart and Winston.

Garfinkel, Harold. 1967. *Studies in Ethnomethodology.* Englewood Cliffs, N.J.: Prentice-Hall.

Geertz, Clifford. 1960. *The Religion of Java.* Chicago: University of Chicago Press.

—— 1966. *Person, Time and Conduct in Bali: An Essay in Cultural Analysis.* Yale Southeast Asia Program, Cultural Report No. 14. New Haven: Yale University Press.

—— 1968. *Islam Observed.* New Haven: Yale University Press.

—— 1973. Thick Description: Toward An Interpretive Theory of Cultures. In *The Interpretation of Cultures: Selected Essays by C. Geertz,* pp. 3–30. New York: Basic Books.

—— 1976. From the Native's Point of View: On the Nature of Anthropological Understanding. In K. Basso and H. Selby, eds. *Meaning in Anthropology,* pp. 221–237. Albuquerque, N.M.: School for American Research and University of New Mexico Press.

—— 1983. *Local Knowledge.* New York: Basic Books.

—— 1984. Distinguished Lecture: Anti Anti-Relativism. *American Anthropologist* 86:263–278.

—— 1988. *Works and Lives.* Stanford: Stanford University Press.

Gell, Alfred. 1975. *Metamorphosis of the Cassowaries.* London: Athlone Press.

Gewertz, Deborah. 1982. Deviance Unplaced: The Story of Kaviwon Reconsidered. In F. J. P. Poole and G. H. Herdt, eds., *Sexual Antagonism, Gender, and Social Change in Papua New Guinea, Social Analysis* 12:29–35.

—— 1983. *Sepik River Societies.* New Haven: Yale University Press.

Giddens, Anthony. 1976. *New Rules of Sociological Method: A Positive Critique of Interpretive Sociologies.* New York: Basic Books.

Gill, Merton M. 1982. *Analysis of Transference,* vol. 1. New York: International Universities Press.

Gill, Merton M. and I. Z. Hoffman. 1982. *Analysis of Transference,* vol. 2. New York: International Universities Press.

Gladwin, Thomas. 1953. The Role of Man and Woman on Truk: A Problem in Personality and Culture. *Transactions of the New York Academy of Science:* 305–309.

Glasse, R. M. and M. J. Meggitt. 1969. *Pigs, Pearlshells, and Women.* Englewood Cliffs, N.J.: Prentice-Hall.

Gluckman, Max. 1967. Introduction. In A. L. Epstein, ed., *The Craft of Social Anthropology,* pp. xi–xx. London: Tavistock Publications.

—— 1969 (1956). The License in Ritual. In *Custom and Conflict in Africa,* pp. 109–136. New York: Barnes and Noble.

Goffman, Erving. 1974. *Frame Analysis.* Cambridge: Harvard University Press.

Godelier, Maurice. 1982. Social Hierarchies Among the Baruya of New Guinea. In A. Strathern, ed., *Inequality in New Guinea Highland Societies,* pp. 3–34. Cambridge: Cambridge University Press.

—— 1986. *The Production of Great Men.* Trans. R. Swyer. Cambridge: Cambridge University Press.

Golde, Peggy, ed. 1970. *Women in the Field.* Chicago: Aldine.

Gregor, Thomas. 1985. *Anxious Pleasures*. Chicago: University of Chicago Press.

Gronewald, Sylvia. 1972. Did Frank Hamilton Cushing Go Native? In S. T. Kimball and J. B. Watson, eds., *Crossing Cultural Boundaries*, pp. 33–50. San Francisco: Chandler.

Gutkind, Peter. 1967. Orientation and Research Methods in African Urban Studies. In D. G. Jongmans and P. Gutkind, eds., *Anthropologists in the Field*. Assen: Van Gorcum.

Habermas, Jurgen. 1971. *Knowledge and Human Interests*. Trans. J. J. Shapiro. Boston: Beacon Press.

Haddon, Alfred Cort. 1901. *Headhunters: Black, White, and Brown*. London: Methuen.

——1924. Introduction. In J. Holmes, *Primitive New Guinea*, pp. i–xii. London: Macmillan.

Haldipur, C. V. 1980. The Idea of "Cultural" Psychiatry: A Comment on the Foundations of Cultural Psychiatry. *Comprehensive Psychiatry* 21:206–211.

Hallowell, A. Irving. 1967. The Self and Its Behavior Environment. In *Culture and Experience*, pp. 75–110. New York: Schocken Books.

Hallpike, C. R. Fundamentalist Interpretations of Primitive Man. *Man* 8:451–470.

Harris, Marvin. 1964. *The Nature of Cultural Things*. New York: Random House.

Hayano, David M. 1982. Models for Alcohol Use and Drunkenness Among the Awa, Eastern Highlands. In M. Marshall, ed., *Through a Glass Darkly: Beer and Modernization in Papua, New Guinea*, pp. 217–226. Port Moresby: Institute of Applied Social and Economic Research.

Healey, Alan. 1964. *Handling Unsophisticated Linguistic Informants*. Series A, Occasional Papers No. 3. Canberra: Linguistic Circle of Canberra Publications.

Heider, Karl. 1976. Dani Sexuality: A Low Energy System. *Man* 11:188–201.

——1979. *Grand Valley Dani: Peaceful Warriors*. New York: Holt, Rinehart and Winston.

Herdt, Gilbert H. 1977. The Shaman's 'Calling' Among the Sambia of New Guinea. *Journal de la Société des Océanistes* (special issue) 33:153–167.

——1980. Semen Depletion and the Sense of Maleness. *Ethnopsychiatrica* 3:79–116.

——1981. *Guardians of the Flutes*. New York: McGraw-Hill.

——1982a. Fetish and Fantasy in Sambia Initiation. In G. Herdt, ed., *Rituals of Manhood: Male Initiation in Papua New Guinea*, pp. 48–98. Berkeley: University of California Press.

——1982b. Sambia Nose-Bleeding Rites and Male Proximity to Women. *Ethos* 10(3):189–231.

——1982c. Uses and Abuses of Alcohol and the Urban Adjustment of Sambia Masculine Identity. In M. Marshall, ed., *Through A Glass Darkly: Beer and Modernization in Papua New Guinea*, pp. 227–241. Port Moresby: Institute of Applied Social and Economic Research.

——1984. Ritualized Homosexual Behavior in the Male Cults of Melanesia, 1862–1983: An Introduction. In G. Herdt, ed., *Ritualized Homosexuality in Melanesia*, pp. 1–82. Berkeley: University of California Press.

——1985. Review: *Oedipus in the Trobriands*, by Melford Spiro. In *American Anthropologist* 87:205–207.

——1986. Madness and Sexuality in the New Guinea Highlands. *Social Research* (special issue on Sexuality and Madness) 53:349–368.

——1987a. The Accountability of Sambia Initiates. In L. L. Langness and

T. E. Hays, eds., *Anthropology in the High Valleys: Essays in Honor of K. E. Read*, pp. 237–282. Novato, Calif.: Chandler and Sharp.

—— 1987b. Homosexuality. In *The Encyclopedia of Religion*, 6:445–452 (15 vols.). New York: Macmillan.

—— 1987c. *The Sambia: Ritual and Gender in New Guinea*. New York: Holt, Rinehart and Winston.

—— 1987d. Selfhood and Discourse in Sambia Dream Sharing. In B. Tedlock, ed., *Dreaming: Anthropological and Psychological Interpretations*. Albuquerque: School for American Research and University of New Mexico Press.

—— 1987e. Transitional Objects in Sambia Initiation Rites. *Ethos* 15:40–57.

—— 1988. The Ethnographer's Choices. In G. N. Appell and T. N. Madan, eds., *Choice and Morality in Anthropological Perspective*, pp. 159–192. Albany, N.Y.: State University of New York Press.

—— n.d. Sexual Repression, Social Control, and Gender Hierarchy in Sambia Culture. In Barbara Miller, ed., *Gender Hierarchies*. New York: Wenner-Gren Foundation for Anthropological Research.

Herdt, G. and J. Davidson. 1988. The Sambia "Turnim-Man": Sociocultural and Clinical Aspects of Gender Formation in Male Pseudohermaphrodites with 5-Alpha Reductase Deficiency in Papua New Guinea. *Archives of Sexual Behavior* 17(1):33–56.

Herdt, Gilbert H. and Fitz John P. Poole. 1982. Sexual Antagonism: The Intellectual History of a Concept in the Anthropology of Melanesia. In F. J. P. Poole and G. H. Herdt, eds., "Sexual Antagonism," Gender, and Social Change in Papua New Guinea. *Social Analysis* (special issue) 12:3–28.

Herdt, Gilbert H. and Robert J. Stoller. 1985. Sakulambei—A Hermaphrodite's Secret: An Example of Clinical Ethnography. *Psychoanalytic Study of Society* 11:117–158.

—— 1987. The Effect of Supervision on the Practice of Ethnography. In H. P. Duerr, ed, *Die wilde Seele Zur Ethnopsychoanalyse von Georges Devereux*. Frankfurt: Suhrkamp, pp. 177–199.

Herdt, Gilbert H., ed. 1982. *Rituals of Manhood: Male Initiation in New Guinea*. Berkeley: University of California Press.

—— 1984. *Ritualized Homosexuality in Melanesia*. Berkeley: University of California Press.

Hogbin, Ian. 1970. *The Island of Menstruating Men*. Scranton, Pa: Chandler.

Honigmann, John Joseph. 1967. *Personality in Culture*. New York: Harper and Row.

Hymes, Dell. 1974. *Reinventing Anthropology*. New York: Vintage Books.

Imperato-McGinley, Julianne, J. Guerrero, T. Gautier, et al. 1974. Steroid 5-Alpha Reductase Deficiency in Man: An Inherited Form of Male Pseudo-Hermaphroditism. *Science* 186:1213–1243.

Kaberry, Phyllis. 1957. Malinowski's Contribution to Field-Work Methods and the Writing of Ethnography. In R. Firth, ed., *Man and Culture*, pp. 71–91. New York: Humanities Press.

Kakar, Sudhir. 1983. *Shamans, Mystics and Doctors*. Boston: Beacon.

—— 1985. Psychoanalysis and Non-Western Cultures. *International Review of Psycho-Analysis* 12:441–448.

—— 1986. Psychotherapy and Culture: Healing in the Indian Culture. In M. I. White and S. Pollak, eds., *The Cultural Transition*, pp. 9–23. Boston: Routledge & Kegan Paul.

Kardiner, Abram. 1939. *The Individual and His Society*. New York: Columbia University Press.

——1945. *The Psychological Frontiers of Society*. New York: Columbia University Press.

Katchadourian, Herant A. and Donald T. Lunde. 1980. *Fundamentals of Human Sexuality*. 3rd edition. New York: Holt, Rinehart, and Winston.

Keesing, Roger M. 1979. Linguistic Knowledge and Cultural Knowledge: Some Doubts and Speculations. *American Anthropologist* 81:14–36.

——1982. Introduction. In G. H. Herdt, ed., *Rituals of Manhood*, pp. 1–43. Berkeley: University of California Press.

Kelly, Raymond. 1976. Witchcraft and Sexual Relations: An Exploration in the Social and Semantic Implications of a Structure of Belief. In P. Brown and G. Buchbinder, eds., *Man and Woman in the New Guinea Highlands*, pp. 36–53. Washington, D.C.: American Anthropological Association.

——1977. *Etoro Social Structure*. Ann Arbor: University of Michigan Press.

Kiki, Albert M. 1968. *Kiki: Ten Thousand Years in a Lifetime*. New York: Praeger.

Kimball Solon Toothaker and James Bennett Watson, eds. 1972. *Crossing Cultural Boundaries: The Anthropological Experience*. San Francisco: Chandler.

Kluckhohn, Clyde et al. 1945. *The Personal Document in History, Anthropology, and Sociology*. New York: Social Science Research Council Bulletin, no. 53, pp. 79–174.

Kleinman, Arthur. 1980. *Patients and Healers in the Context of Culture*. Berkeley: University of California Press.

Knauft, Bruce M. 1987. Homosexuality in Melanesia. *Journal of Psychoanalytic Anthropology* 10:155–191.

Koch, Klaus-F. 1974. *War and Peace in Jalemo*. Cambridge: Harvard University Press.

Kohut, Heinz. 1971. *The Analysis of the Self*. New York: International Universities Press.

Kracke, Waud H. 1980. Amazonian Interviews: Dreams of a Bereaved Father. *The Annual of Psychoanalysis* 8:249–267.

——1987. Encounter with Other Cultures: Psychological and Epistemological Aspects. *Ethos* 15:58–81.

Kracke, Waud and Gilbert Herdt. 1987. Introduction. In *Interpretation in Psychoanalytic Anthropology*. Special issue of *Ethos* 15:3–7.

Kroeber, Alfred L. 1948. *Anthropology*. Rev. ed. New York: Harcourt, Brace.

La Barre, Weston. 1978. The Clinic and the Field. In G. D. Spindler, ed., *The Making of Psychological Anthropology*, pp. 259–299. Berkeley: University of California.

La Farge, Oliver. 1929. *Laughing Boy*. Boston: Houghton Mifflin.

Langer, Suzanne K. 1951. *Philosophy in a New Key*. New York: Mentor Books.

——1967. *Mind: An Essay on Human Feeling*. Baltimore: Johns Hopkins University Press.

Langness, L. L. 1967. Sexual Antagonism in the New Guinea Highlands: A Bena Bena Example. *Oceania* 37:161–177.

——1976. Discussion. In P. Brown and G. Buchbinder, eds., *Man and Woman in the New Guinea Highlands*, pp. 96–106. Washington, D.C.: American Anthropological Association.

——1981. Child Abuse and Cultural Values: The Case of New Guinea. In Jill E.

Corbin, ed., *Child Abuse and Neglect: Cross-Cultural Perspectives*, pp. 13–34. Berkeley: University of California Press.

Langness, L. L. and Gelya Frank. 1981. *Lives*. Navato: Chandler & Sharp.

Lanternari, Vittorio. 1963. *The Religions of the Oppressed*. Trans. L. Sergis. New York: Knopf.

Lawrence, Peter. 1965–66. The Garia of the Madang District. *Anthropological Forum* 1:371–392.

Leach, E. R. 1954. *Political Systems of Highland Burma*. London: G. Bell.

——1958. The Epistemological Background of Malinowski's Empiricism. In R. Firth, ed., *Man and Culture*, pp. 119–137. New York: Humanities Press.

——1961a. *Pul Eliya*. Cambridge: Cambridge University Press.

——1961b. Two Essays Concerning the Symbolic Representation of Time. In *Rethinking Anthropology*, pp. 124–136. London: Athlone Press.

——1966. Virgin Birth. *Proceedings of the Royal Anthropological Institute for Great Britain and Northern Ireland for 1965*, pp. 39–50.

——1976. *Culture and Communication*. Cambridge: Cambridge University Press.

Leenhardt, Maurice. 1979. *Do Kamo*. Trans. B. M. Gulati. Chicago: University of Chicago Press.

Levine, F. J. 1979. On the Clinical Application of Heinz Kohut's Psychology of the Self. *Journal of the Philadelphia Association for Psychoanalysis* 6:1–19.

LeVine, Robert A. 1966. Outsider's Judgments: An Ethnographic Approach to Group Differences in Personality. *Southwestern Journal of Anthropology* 22:101–116.

——1982. (1973). *Culture, Behavior and Personality*. 2d ed. New York: Aldine.

——In press. Beyond the Average Expected Environment of Psychoanalysis: Cross-Cultural Evidence on Mother–Child Interaction. In J. Stigler, R. Shweder, and G. Herdt, eds., *Cultural Psychology*. New York: Cambridge University Press.

LeVine, Sarah. 1981. Dreams of the Informant About the Researcher: Some Difficulties Inherent in the Research Relationship. *Ethos* 9:276–293.

Lévi-Strauss, Claude. 1949. *Les Structures Elémentaires de la Parenté*. Paris: Presses Universitaires de France.

——1963. *Totemism*. Trans. R. Needham. Boston: Beacon Press.

——1966. *The Savage Mind*. Chicago: University of Chicago Press.

——1967. *Structural Anthropology*. Trans. C. Jacobson and B. G. Schoepf. Garden City, N.Y.: Anchor Books.

——1969. *Tristes Tropiques*. Trans. J. Russell. New York: Atheneum.

Levy, Robert I. 1973. *The Tahitians*. Chicago: University of Chicago Press.

Lewis, Oscar. 1951. *Life in a Mexican Village*. Urbana: University of Illinois Press.

——1965. *La Vida: A Puerto Rican Family in the Culture of Poverty—San Juan and New York*. New York: Vintage Books.

Lindenbaum, Shirley. 1972. Sorcerers, Ghosts, and Polluting Women: An Analysis of Religious Belief and Population Control. *Ethnology* 11:241–253.

——1979. *Kuru Sorcery*. Palo Alto: Mayfield.

Lipuma, E. 1981. Cosmology and Economy Among the Maring of Highland New Guinea. *Oceania* 51:266–285.

Littlewood, Roland. 1980. Anthropology and Psychiatry—An Alternative Approach. *British Journal of Medical Psychology* 53:213–225.

MacCannel, Dean. 1976. *The Tourist*. New York: Schocken.

McDowell, Nancy. 1980. The Oceanic Ethnography of Margaret Mead. *American Anthropologist* 82:278–303.

Mahapatra, S. B. and M. Hamilton. 1974. Examinations for Foreign Psychiatrists: Problems of Language. *British Journal of Medical Education* 8:271–274.

Mailer, Norman. 1980. *New York Times Book Review*, May 11.

Malcolm, Janet. 1984. The Patient Is Always Right. *New York Review of Books*. December 20:13–18.

——1985. *In the Freud Archives*. New York: Vintage Books.

Malcolm, L. A. 1969. Determination of the Growth Curve of the Kukukuku People of New Guinea From Dental Eruption in Children and Adult Height. *Archaelogy and Physical Anthropology in Oceania* 4:72–78.

——1970. Growth, Malnutrition and Mortality of the Infant and Toddler in the Asai Valley of the New Guinea Highlands. *American Journal of Clinical Nutrition* 23:1090–1095.

Malinowski, Bronislau. 1913. *The Family Among the Australian Aborigines*. London: University of London Press.

——1922. *Argonauts of the Western Pacific*. New York: E. P. Dutton.

——1926. *Crime and Custom in Savage Society*. Totowa, NJ: Littlefield, Adams.

——1927. *Sex and Repression in Savage Society*. Cleveland: Meridian Books.

——1929. *The Sexual Life of Savages in North-Western Melanesia*. New York: Harcourt, Brace and World.

——1935. *Coral Gardens and Their Magic*. 2 vols. London: Allen and Unwin.

——1954. (1948). *Magic, Science and Religion, and Other Essays*. Garden City, N.Y.: Doubleday Anchor Books.

——1967. *A Diary in the Strict Sense of the Term*. London: Routledge and Kegan Paul.

Marcos, Luis R. 1979. Effects of Interpreters on the Evaluation of Psychopathology in Non-English-Speaking Patients. *American Journal of Psychiatry* 136:171–174.

Marcus, George and D. Cushman. 1982. Ethnographies as Texts. *Annual Review of Anthropology* 11:25–69.

Marcus, George and Michael Fisher. 1986. *Anthropology as Cultural Critique*. Chicago: University of Chicago Press.

Marx, Karl. 1977. The Fetishism of Commodities and the Secret Thereof. In J. L. Dolgin, David Dolgin, S. Kemnitzer, and David M. Schneider. eds., *Symbolic Anthropology: A Reader in the Study of Symbols and Meanings*, pp. 245–253. New York: Columbia University Press.

Mead, Margaret. 1930 (1968). *Growing Up in New Guinea*. New York: Dell.

——1935. *Sex and Temperament in Three Primitive Societies*. New York: Morrow.

——1939. Native Languages as Field Work Tools. *American Anthropologist* 41:189–206.

——1949. *Male and Female: A Study of the Sexes in a Changing World*. New York: Morrow.

——1952. The Training of the Cultural Anthropologist. *American Anthropologist* 54:343–346.

——1956. *New Lives for Old, Cultural Transformation: Manus 1928–53*. New York: Morrow.

——1960a. Introduction. In M. Mead and R. Bunzel, eds. *The Golden Age of Anthropology*, pp. 1–12. New York: Braziller.

——1960b. Weaver of the Border. In J. B. Casagrande, ed., *In the Company of Man* pp. 176–210. New York: Harper.

——1961. Cultural Determinants of Sexual Behavior. In W. C. Young, ed., *Sex and Internal Secretions*, pp. 1433–79. Baltimore: Williams and Wilkins.

—— 1962. Retrospect and Prospects. In *Anthropology and Human Behavior*, pp. 115–149. Washington, D.C.: Anthropological Society of Washington.

—— 1968 (1940). *The Mountain Arapesh*. Garden City, N.Y.: Natural History Press.

—— 1970. Field Work in the Pacific Islands, 1925–1967. In Peggy Golde, ed., *Women in the Field*, pp. 293–331. Chicago: Aldine.

—— 1972. *Blackberry Winter: My Early Years*. New York: Morrow.

—— 1977. *Letters From the Field 1925–1975*. New York: Harper Colophone Books.

Mead, Margaret and Ruth Bunzel, eds. 1960. *The Golden Age of Anthropology*. New York: Braziller.

Meggitt, Mervyn. 1964. Male–Female Relationships in the Highlands of Australian New Guinea, in New Guinea: The Central Highlands. *American Anthropologist* 66 (part 2): 204–224.

—— 1965. *Desert People*. Chicago: University of Chicago Press.

—— 1974. Pigs Are Our Hearts. *Oceania* 44:165–203.

—— 1977. *Blood Is Their Argument*. Palo Alto, Calif.: Mayfield.

—— 1979. Reflections Occasioned by Continuing Anthropological Field Research Among the Enga of Papua New Guinea. In G. M. Foster, et al., *Long-Term Field Research in Social Anthropology*, pp. 107–125. New York: Academic Press.

Meigs, Anna. 1976. Male Pregnancy and the Reduction of Sexual Opposition in a New Guinea Highlands Society. *Ethnology* 25:393–407.

—— 1984. *Food, Sex, and Pollution: A New Guinea Religion*. New Brunswick: Rutgers University Press.

Meintel, Deidre A. 1973. Strangers, Homecomers, and Ordinary Men. *Anthropological Quarterly* 46:47–58.

Messenger, John C. 1969. *Inis Beag: Isle of Ireland*. New York: Holt, Rinehart, and Winston.

Milgram, Stanley. 1974. *Obedience to Authority: An Experimental View*. London: Tavistock.

Minol, Bernard. 1981. A Review of the Manus Sections of Letters From the Field 1925–1975, by Margaret Mead. *Research in Melanesia* 5:43–45.

Moerman, Daniel E. 1979. Anthropology of Symbolic Healing. *Cultural Anthropology* 20:59–80.

Moffic, H. Steven, Ernest A. Kendrick, James W. Lomax, and Kelly Reid. 1987. Education in Cultural Psychiatry in the United States. *Transcultural Psychiatric Research Review* 24:167–188.

Moraitis, G. 1981. The Psychoanalytic Study of the Editing Process: Its Application in the Interpretation of a Historical Document. *Annual of Psychoanalysis*: 237–263.

Muensterberger, Werner. 1974. Introduction. In *Children of the Desert*, by G. Roheim, pp. ix–xix. New York: Basic Books.

Munn, Nancy. 1973. *Walbiri Iconography: Graphic Representation and Cultural Symbolism in a Central Australian Society*. Ithaca: Cornell University Press.

Murray, J. H. P. 1912. *Papua or British New Guinea*. London: T. Fisher Unwin.

Murray, Stephen O. 1979. The Scientific Reception of Castaneda. *Contributions in Sociology* 8:189–196.

—— 1982. The Dissolution of "Classical Ethnoscience." *Journal of the History of the Behavioral Sciences* 18:163–175.

—— 1984. *Social Theory, Homosexual Realities*. New York: Gai Sabre Monographs.

Murphy, Jane M. and Alexander H. Leighton. 1965. *Approaches to Cross-Cultural Psychiatry*. Ithaca: Cornell University Press.

Murphy, Robert F. 1959. Social Structure and Sex Antagonism. *Southwestern Journal of Anthropology* 15:89–98.

Murphy, Yolanda and Robert F. Murphy. 1974. *Women of the Forest.* New York: Columbia University Press.

Nabokov, Peter. 1967. *Two Leggings: The Making of a Crow Warrior.* New York: Crowell.

Nader, Laura. 1970. From Anguish to Exultation. In P. Golde, ed., *Women in the Field*, pp. 97–116. Chicago: Aldine.

Naroll, Raoul. 1970. Data Quality in Cross-Cultural Surveys. In R. Naroll and R. Cohen, eds., *A Handbook of Method in Cultural Anthropology*, pp. 990–1003. New York: Columbia University Press.

Nauta, Doede. 1972. *The Meaning of Information.* Gravenhage: Mouton.

Newman, Phillip. 1964. Religious Belief and Ritual in a New Guinea Society. *American Anthropologist* 66 (part 2):257–272.

—— 1965. *Knowing the Gururumba.* New York: Holt, Rinehart and Winston.

Niles, J. 1950. The Kuman of the Chimbu Region, Central Highlands, New Guinea. *Oceania* 21:25–65.

Oberg, Kalvero. 1954. Culture Shock. *The Bobbs-Merrill Reprint Series in the Social Sciences*, no. A-329.

—— 1972. Contrasts in Field Work on Three Continents. In S. T. Kimball and J. B. Watson, eds., *Crossing Cultural Boundaries*, pp. 74–86. San Francisco: Chandler.

Obeyesekere, Gananath. 1981. *Medusa's Hair.* Chicago: University of Chicago Press.

Open Forum. 1981. Open Forum: Clinical Anthropology. *Medical Anthropology Newsletter* 12.

Ornston, D. 1982. Strachey's Influence: A Preliminary Influence. *International Journal of Psycho-Analysis* 63:409–426.

Ortner, Sherry and Harriet Whitehead, eds. 1981. *Sexual Meanings.* Cambridge: Cambridge University Press.

Owusu, Maxwell. 1978. Ethnography of Africa: The Usefulness of the Useless. *American Anthropologist* 80:310–334.

Panoff, M. 1968. The Notion of the Double-Self Among the Maenge. *Journal of Polymer Science* 77:275–295.

Parin, Paul, F. Morgenthaler, and G. Parin-Matthey. 1980. *Fear Thy Neighbors as Thyself.* Trans. Patricia Klamerth. Chicago: University of Chicago Press.

Parkinson, Richard. 1907. *Dreissig Jahre in der Sudsee: Land und Leute, sitten und Gebrauche in Bismarck Archipel und auf den deutschen Salmoninseln.* Stuttgart: Strecker and Schroder.

Parsons, Anne. 1969. On Psychoanalytic Training for Research Purposes. *Belief, Magic, and Anomie: Essays in Psychological Anthropology*, pp. 334–357. New York: Free Press.

Paul, Benjamin D. 1953. Inteview Techniques and Field Relationships. In A. L. Kroeber, ed., *Anthropology Today*, pp. 430–451. Chicago: University of Chicago Press.

Pelto, Pertti J. and Gretel H. Pelto. 1973. Ethnography: The Fieldwork Enterprise. In J. J. Honigmann, ed., *Handbook of Social and Cultural Anthropology*, pp. 241–288. Chicago: Rand-McNally.

Peters, Larry and Douglass Price-Williams. 1980. Towards An Experiential Analysis of Shamanism. *American Ethnologist* 7:397–418.

Pettit, Philip. 1977. *The Concept of Structuralism: A Critical Analysis*. Berkeley: University of California Press.

Piers, Gerhart and Milton B. Singer. 1953. *Shame and Guilt*. New York: Norton.

Polanyi, Michael. 1966. *The Tacit Dimension*. Garden City, N.Y.: Doubleday Anchor Books.

Poole, Fitz John P. 1981. Transforming "Natural" Women: Female Ritual Leaders and Gender Ideology Among Bimin-Kuskusmin. In S. B. Ortner and H. Whitehead, eds., *Sexual Meanings*, pp. 116–165. New York: Cambridge University Press.

—— 1982a. Cultural Significance of "Drunken Comportment" in a Non-Drinking Society: The Bimin-Kuskusmin of the West Sepik. In M. Marshall, ed., *Through A Glass Darkly: Beer and Modernization in Papua New Guinea*, pp. 189–210. Port Moresby: Institute of Applied Social and Economic Research.

—— 1982b. The Ritual Forging of Identity: Aspects of Person and Self in Bimin-Kuskusmin Male Initiation. In G. Herdt, ed., *Rituals of Manhood: Male Initiation in Papua New Guinea*, pp. 100–154. Berkeley: University of California Press.

Popper, Karl R. 1971. *The Open Society and Its Enemies*. Vol. 2: *Hegel and Marx*. Princeton: Princeton University Press.

Powdermaker, Hortense. 1966. *Stranger and Friend*. New York: Norton.

Price-Williams, Douglass. 1975. *Explorations in Cross-Cultural Psychology*. San Francisco: Chandler and Sharp.

Rabinow, Paul. 1977. *Reflections on Fieldwork in Morocco*. Berkeley: University of California Press.

Radcliffe-Brown, A. R. 1922. *The Andaman Islanders*. Cambridge: Cambridge University Press.

—— 1939. Taboo. Reprinted in *Structure and Function in Primitive Society*, pp. 133–152. London: Oxford University Press.

—— 1952. *Structure and Function in Primitive Society*. London: Oxford University Press.

Rappaport, Roy. 1968. *Pigs for the Ancestors*. New Haven: Yale University Press.

—— 1971. Ritual, Sanctity, and Cybernetics. *American Anthropologist* 73:59–76.

Read, K. E. 1951. The Gahuku-Gama of the Central Highlands, New Guinea. *South Pacific* 5:154–164.

—— 1952. Nama Cult of the Central Highlands, New Guinea. *Oceania* 23:1–25.

—— 1954. Cultures of the Central Highlands. *Southwestern Journal of Anthropology* 10:1–43.

—— 1955. Morality and the Concept of the Person Among the Gahuku-Gama. *Oceania* 25:233–282.

—— 1959. Leadership and Consensus in a New Guinea Society. *American Anthropologist* 61:425–436.

—— 1965. *The High Valley*. London: Allen Unwin.

—— 1980. *Other Voices*. Navato, Calif.: Chandler and Sharp.

—— 1984. The Nama Cult Recalled. In G. Herdt, ed., *Ritualized Homosexuality in Melanesia*, pp. 248–291. Berkeley: University of California Press.

—— 1986. *Return to the High Valley*. Berkeley: University of California Press.

Reay, Marie. 1959. *The Kuma*. Melbourne: Melbourne University Press.

—— 1964. Present-day Politics in the New Guinea Highlands. *American Anthropologist* 66:240–256.

—— 1966. Women in Traditional Society. In E. K. Fisk, ed., *New Guinea on the Threshold*, pp. 166–184. Canberra: Australian National University Press.

Redfield, Robert. 1930. *Tapoztlan, A Mexican Village.* Chicago: University of Chicago Press.

Reisman, Paul. 1977. *Freedom in Fulani Social Life.* Chicago: University of Chicago Press.

Reports. 1904–1935. *Reports of the Cambridge Expedition to the Torres Straits.* 6 vols. Cambridge: Cambridge University Press.

Ricoeur, Paul. 1970. *Freud and Philosophy: An Essay on Interpretation.* New Haven: Yale University Press.

—— 1977. The Question of Proof in Freud's Psychoanalytic Writings. *Journal of the American Psychoanalytic Association* 25:835–871.

—— 1978. Can There be a Scientific Concept of Ideology? In J. Bien, ed., *Phenomenology and the Social Sciences: A Dialogue*, pp. 44–59. The Hague: Martins Nijhoff.

—— 1979. Psychoanalysis and the Movement of Contemporary Culture. In P. Rabinow and William M. Sullivan, eds., *Interpretive Social Science*, pp. 301–339. Berkeley: University of California Press.

Rivers, W. H. R. 1914. *The History of Melanesian Society.* 2 vols. Cambridge: Cambridge University Press.

Robin, Robert. 1982. Revival Movements in the Southern Highlands Province of Papua New Guinea. *Oceania* 52:320–343.

Rodman, Margaret. 1979. Introduction. In M. Rodman and M. Cooper, eds., *The Pacification of Melanesia*, pp. 1–23. Ann Arbor: University of Michigan Press.

Roe, Anne. 1953. A Psychological Study of Eminent Psychologists and Anthropologists, and a Comparison with Biological and Physical Scientists. *Psychological Monographs* (American Psychological Association), no. 352:1–55.

Róheim, Geza. 1926. *Social Anthropology, A Psycho-Analytic Study and A History of Australian Totemism.* New York: Boni and Liveright.

—— 1932. Psychoanalysis of Primitive Culture Types. *International Journal of Psycho-Analysis* 13:1–224.

—— 1974. *Children of the Desert.* W. Muensterberger, ed. New York: Basic Books.

Rosaldo, Michelle Z. 1980. The Use and Abuse of Anthropology: Reflections on Feminism and Cross-Cultural Understanding. *Signs* 5:389–417.

Rosaldo, Michelle Z. and Louise Lamphere. 1974. Introduction. In M. Z. Rosaldo and L. Lamphere, eds., *Woman, Culture and Society*, pp. 1–15. Stanford: Stanford University Press.

Ross, Ellen and Rayna Rapp. 1981. Sex and Society: A Research Note From Social History and Anthropology. *Comparative Studies in Society and History* 23:51–72.

Rossi, Alice, ed. 1985. *Gender and the Life Course.* New York: Aldine.

Roustang, F. 1982. *Dire Mastery.* Baltimore and London: Johns Hopkins University Press.

Royal Anthropological Institute of Great Britain and Ireland. 1951. *Notes and Queries in Anthropology.* London: Routledge and Kegan Paul.

Rubin, Gayle. 1975. The Traffic in Women: Notes on the "Political Economy" of Sex. In Rayna R. Reiter, ed., *Toward an Anthropology of Women*, pp. 157–210. New York: Monthly Review Press.

Runciman, W. G. 1983. *A Treatise on Social Theory.* Vol. I: *The Methodology of Social Theory.* Cambridge: Cambridge University Press.

Sahlins, Marshall. 1963. Poor Man, Rich Man, Big Man, Chief. *Comparative Studies in Society and History* 5:205–213.

——1985. *Islands of History*. Chicago: University of Chicago Press.

Sapir, Edward. 1937. The Contribution of Psychiatry to an Understanding of Behavior in Society. *American Journal of Sociology* 42:862–870.

——1938. Why Cultural Anthropology Needs the Psychiatrist. *Psychiatry* 1:7–12.

——1949. *Selected Writings of Edward Sapir in Language, Culture, and Personality*, D. G. Mandelbaum, ed. Berkeley: University of California Press.

Schafer, Roy. 1976. *A New Language for Psychoanalysis*. New Haven: Yale University Press.

Schieffelin, E. L. 1976. *The Sorrow of the Lonely and the Burning of the Dancers*. New York: St. Martin's Press.

——1977. The Unseen Influence: Tranced Mediums as Historical Innovators. *Journal de la Société des Océanistes* 56–57:169–178.

——1982. The Bau'a Ceremonial Hunting Lodge: An Alternative to Initiation. In G. Herdt, ed., *Rituals of Manhood: Male Initiation in Papua New Guinea*, pp. 155–200. Berkeley: University of California Press.

Schneider, David M. 1968. *American Kinship: A Cultural Account*. Englewood Cliffs, N.J.: Prentice-Hall.

Schwartz, Theodore. 1973. Cult and Context: The Paranoid Ethos in Melanesia. *Ethos* 1:153–174.

——1978. Where Is the Culture? Personality as the Distributive Locus of Culture. In George Spindler, ed., *The Making of Psychological Anthropology*, pp. 419–441. Berkeley: University of California Press.

Schwimmer, Eric. 1980. Power, Silence and Secrecy. *Toronto Semiotic Circle, Monograph No. 2*. Toronto: Victoria University.

Seligman, C. G. 1910. *The Melanesians of British New Guinea*. Cambridge: Cambridge University Press.

Serpenti, L. 1984. The Ritual Meaning of Homosexuality and Pedophilia Among the Kimam-Papuans of South Irian Jaya. In G. Herdt, ed., *Ritualized Homosexuality in Melanesia*, pp. 292–317. Berkeley: University of California Press.

Shils, Edward. 1956. *The Torment of Secrecy*. Glencoe: The Free Press.

Shostak, Marjorie. 1981. *Nisa: the Life and Words of a !Kung Woman*. New York: Vintage Books.

Shweder, Richard A. 1979. Rethinking Culture and Personality Theory: Part I. *Ethos* 7:255–278.

——1984. Anthropology's Romantic Rebellion Against the Enlightenment, or There's More to Thinking than Reason and Evidence. In R. Shweder and R. LeVine eds., *Culture Theory*, pp. 27–66. New York: Cambridge University Press.

Shweder, Richard and E. J. Bourne. 1984. Does the Concept of the Person Vary Cross-Culturally? In *Culture Theory*, pp. 158–199. New York: Cambridge University Press.

Shweder, Richard A. and Robert A. LeVine., eds. 1984. *Culture Theory*. New York: Cambridge University Press.

Silvan, M. 1981. Reply to Alan Roland's Paper on "Psychoanalytic Perspectives on Personality Development in India. *International Review of Psycho-Analysis* 8:93–99.

Simmel, George. 1950. *The Sociology of George Simmel*, Kurt H. Wolff, ed. and trans. Glencoe, Ill: Free Press.

Sinclair, James P. 1966. *Behind the Ranges*. Melbourne: Melbourne University Press.

Singer, Milton. 1961. A Survey of Culture and Personality Theory and Research.

In Bert Kaplan, ed., *Studying Personality Cross-Culturally*, pp. 9–90. New York: Harper and Row.

——1980. Signs of the Self: An Exploration in Semiotic Anthropology. *American Anthropologist* 82:485–507.

Singer, Peter. 1980. Dictator Marx? *New York Review of Books*, September 25, pp. 62–66.

Sontag, Susan. 1966. *Against Interpretation.* New York: Farrar, Straus, Giroux.

——1982. *A Susan Sontag Reader.* London: Penguin Books.

Sørum, A. 1982. The Seeds of Power: Patterns in Bedamini Male Initiation. *Social Analysis* 10:42–62.

——1984. Growth and Decay: Bedamini Notions of Sexuality. In G. Herdt, ed., *Ritualized Homosexuality in Melanesia*, pp. 318–336. Berkeley: University of California Press.

Spiegel, John P. 1976. Cultural Aspects of Transference and Countertransference Revisited. *Journal of the American Academy of Psychoanalysis* 4:447–467.

Spindler, George D. 1970. *Being an Anthropologist: Fieldwork in Eleven Cultures.* New York: Holt, Rinehart, and Winston.

Spiro, Melford E. 1964. Religion and the Irrational. In J. Helm, ed., *Symposium on New Approaches to the Study of Religion*, pp. 102–115. Seattle: American Ethnological Society and University of Washington Press.

——1968a. *Burmese Supernaturalism.* Englewood Cliffs, New Jersey: Prentice-Hall.

——1968b. Virgin Birth, Parthenogenesis, and Physiological Paternity: An Essay in Cultural Interpretation. *Man* 3:242–261.

——1979. Whatever Happened to the Id? *American Anthropologist* 81:5–13.

——1982. *Oedipus in the Trobriands.* Chicago: University of Chicago Press.

——1986. Cultural Relativism and the Future of Anthropology. *Cultural Anthropology* 1:259–286.

Spradley, James P. 1979. *The Ethnographic Interview.* New York: Holt, Rinehart, and Winston.

——1980. *Participant Observation.* New York: Holt, Rinehart, and Winston.

Spradley, James P. and David McCurdy. 1972. *The Cultural Experience.* Chicago: Science Research Associates.

Stein, Howard F. 1982. The Ethnographic Mode of Teaching Clinical Behavioral Science. In N. J. Chrisman and T. W. Maretzki, eds., *Clinically Applied Anthropology*, pp. 61–82. Boston: Reidel.

Stephen, Michele, ed. 1987. *Sorcerer and Witch in Melanesia.* New Brunswick: Rutgers University Press.

Stocking, George W., Jr. 1968. *Race, Culture, and Evolution: Essays in the History of Anthropology.* New York: Free Press.

——1974. Empathy and Antipathy in the Heart of Darkness. In R. Darnell, ed., *Readings in the History of Anthropology*, pp. 281–287. London: Harper and Row.

——1980. Innovation in the Malinowskian Mode: An Essay Review of Long-term Field Research in Social Anthropology. *Journal of the History of the Behavioral Sciences.* 16:281–286.

——1983. The Ethnographer's Magic: Fieldwork in British Anthropology from Tylor to Malinowski. In *Observers Observed: History of Anthropology*, 1:70–120. Madison: University of Wisconsin Press.

Stoller, Paul. 1982. Beatitudes, Beasts, and Anthropological Burdens. *Medical Anthropology News.* 13:1–10.

Stoller, Robert J. 1968. *Sex and Gender*, vol. 1. New York: Science House.
—— 1973. *Splitting*. New York: Quadrangle.
—— 1975a. *Perversion*. New York: Pantheon.
—— 1975b. *Sex and Gender*, vol. 2. London: Hogarth.
—— 1979. *Sexual Excitement*. New York: Pantheon.
—— 1985a. *Observing the Erotic Imagination*. New Haven: Yale University Press.
—— 1985b. *Presentations of Gender*. New Haven: Yale University Press.
Stoller, Robert J. and R. H. Geertsma. 1963. The Consistency of Psychiatrists' Clinical Judgments. *Journal of Nervous and Mental Disease*. 137:58–66.
Stoller, Robert J. and Gilbert Herdt. 1982. The Development of Masculinity: A Cross-Cultural Contribution. *Journal of the American Psychoanalytic Association*. 30:29–59.
—— 1985. Theories of Origins of Homosexuality: A Cross:cultural Look. *Archives of General Psychiatry* 42:399–404.
Strathern, Andrew J. 1969. Descent and Alliance in the New Guinea Highlands: Some Problems of Comparison. *Proceedings of the Royal Anthropology Institute of Great Britain and Ireland for 1968*, pp. 37–52.
—— 1972. *One Father, One Blood*. Canberra: Australian National University Press.
Strathern, Marilyn. 1972. *Women in Between*. London: Seminar Press.
—— 1978. The Achievement of Sex: Paradoxes in Hagen Gender-thinking. In E. C. Schwimmer, ed., *The Yearbook of Symbolic Anthropology*, pp. 171–202. London: C. Hurst.
—— 1980. No Nature, No Culture: The Hagen Case. In C. P. MacCormack and M. Strathern, eds., *Nature, Culture, and Gender*, pp. 174–222. Cambridge: Cambridge University Press.
—— 1981. Culture in a Netbag. The Manufacture of a Subdiscipline in Anthropology. *Man* 16:665–88.
—— 1988. *The Gender of the Gift*. Berkeley: University of California Press.
Sullivan, Harry S. 1937. A Note on the Implications of Psychiatry, the Study of Interpersonal Relations, for Investigations in the Social Sciences. *American Journal of Sociology* 42:848–861.
Taylor, Charles. 1985. The Person. In M. Carrothers, S. Collins, and S. Lukes, eds., *The Category of the Person*, pp. 257–281. New York: Cambridge University Press.
Tedlock, Dennis. 1983. *The Spoken Word and the Work of Interpretation*. Philadelphia: University of Pennsylvania Press.
Thomas, Elizabeth Marshall. 1959. *The Harmless People*. New York: Knopf.
Turnbull, Colin. 1961. *The Forest People*. New York: Simon and Schuster.
—— 1972. *The Mountain People*. New York: Simon & Schuster.
Turner, Victor. 1960. Muchona the Hornet. In J. B. Casagrande, ed., *In the Company of Man*. New York: Harper.
—— 1964. Symbols in Ndembu Ritual. In M. Gluckman, ed., *Closed Systems and Open Minds: The Limits of Naiveté in Social Anthropology*, pp. 20–51. Chicago:Aldine.
—— 1967. Betwixt and Between: The Liminal Period in Rites de Passage. In *The Forest of Symbols*, pp. 93–111. Ithaca, N.Y.: Cornell University Press.
—— 1968. Mukanda: The Politics of a Non-Political Ritual. In M. Schwartz et al., eds., *Local-Level Politics*, pp. 135–150. Chicago: Aldine.
—— 1978. Encounter with Freud: The Making of a Comparative Symbologist. In

George D. Spindler, ed., *The Making of Psychological Anthropology*, pp. 58–583. Berkeley: University of California Press.

Tuzin, Donald F. 1975. The Breath of a Ghost: Dreams of the Fear of the Dead. *Ethos* 3:555–578.

——1976. *The Ilahita Arapesh*. Berkeley: University of California Press.

——1980. *The Voice of the Tamberan: Truth and Illusion in Ilahita Arapesh Religion*. Berkeley: University of California Press.

——1982. Ritual Violence Among the Ilahita Arapesh: The Dynamics of Moral and Religious Uncertainty. In G. Herdt, ed., *Rituals of Manhood: Male Initiation in Papua New Guinea*, pp. 321–355. Berkeley: University of California Press.

Tyler, Stephen A. 1978. *The Said and the Unsaid: Mind, Meaning, and Culture*. New York: Academic Press.

Vogt, Evon Z. 1979. The Harvard Chiapas Project: 1957–1975. In G. M. Foster et al., eds., *Long-Term Field Research in Social Anthropology*, pp. 279–301.

Wagner, Roy. 1967. *The Curse of Souw: Principles of Daribi Clan Definition and Alliance*. Chicago: University of Chicago Press.

——1972. *Habu: the Innovation of Meaning in Daribi Religion*. Chicago: University of Chicago Press.

——1975. *The Invention of Culture*. Englewood Cliffs, N.J.: Prentice-Hall.

Warner, W. Lloyd. 1941. Social Anthropology and the Modern Community. *American Journal of Sociology* 46:785–796.

Wallace, Anthony F. C. 1969. *Culture and Personality*. 2d ed. New York: Random House.

Warwick, Donald P. 1980. *The Teaching of Ethics in the Social Sciences*. Hastings-on-Hudson, N.Y.: The Hastings Center.

Watson, James B. 1960. A New Guinea Opening Man. In J. B. Casagrande, ed., *In the Company of Man*, pp. 127–173. New York: Harper.

——1964. Anthropology in the New Guinea Highlands. In J. B. Watson, ed., *New Guinea: The Central Highlands, American Anthropologist* (special Issue) 66, 4 (part 2): 1–19.

——1972. Epilogue: In Search of Intimacy. In S. T. Kimball and J. B. Watson, eds., *Crossing Cultural Boundaries*, pp. 299–302. San Francisco: Chandler.

Watson, James D. 1968. *The Double Helix*. New York: New American Library.

Weiner, Annette B. 1978. The Reproductive Model in Trobriand Society. In J. Specht and P. White, eds., *Trade and Exchange in Oceania and Australia. Mankind* (special issue) 11:150–174.

——1980. Reproduction: A Replacement for Reciprocity. *American Ethnologist* 7:71–85.

——1985. Oedipus and Ancestors. *American Ethnologist* 12:758–762.

Werner, Oswald and Donald T. Campbell. 1970. Translating, Working Through Interpreters, and the Problem of Decentering. In R. Naroll and R. Cohen, eds., *A Handbook of Method in Cultural Anthropology*. Chicago: Rand-McNally.

White, Geoffrey M. and J. Kirkpatrick, eds. 1985. *Persons, Self, and Experience*. Berkeley: University of California Press.

Whiting, John W. M. 1941. *Becoming Kwoma*. New Haven: Yale University Press.

Whiting, J. W. M., I. L. Child, and W. W. Lambert, et al. 1966. *Field Guide for the Study of Socialization*. Six Cultures Series, vol. 1. New York: Wiley.

Williams, F. E. 1936. *Papuans of the Trans-Fly*. Oxford: Clarendon Press.

——1940. *Drama of Orokolo*. Oxford: Oxford University Press.

Wittaker, J. L., N. G. Gash, J. F. Hokey, and R. C. Lacey. 1975. *Documents and Readings in New Guinea History: Prehistory to 1889.* Brisbane: Jacaranda Press.
Young, Michael N. 1971. *Fighting with Food.* Canberra: Australian National University Press.
——1979. *The Ethnography of Malinowski.* London: Routledge & Kegan Paul.
Zwigman, Charles. 1973. The Nostalgic Phenomenon and Its Exploitation. In C. Zwingman and M. Fister-Ammende, eds., *Uprooting and After,* pp. 19–47. New York: Springer-Verlag.

Index

459

Emily Dickinson and Her Contemporaries

EMILY DICKINSON
and Her Contemporaries

Women's Verse in America, 1820–1885

Elizabeth A. Petrino

University Press of New England

Hanover and London

University Press of New England, Hanover, NH 03755
© 1998 by University Press of New England

Printed in the United States of America
5 4 3 2 1
CIP data appear at the end of the book

For My Parents

With Love

Contents

Acknowledgments

In writing this book, I have received help from a number of people, whom I would like to mention. Joel Porte gave early and lasting advice about directions the argument was to take; Dorothy Mermin turned an attentive eye to my prose style and reading of Dickinson's poems; and Debra Fried, whose graduate seminar first introduced me to Dickinson's poetry, taught me how to read the poet carefully and like the others, embodied the highest commitment to the craft of teaching. I am permanently indebted to their example. Cheryl Walker, Martha Nell Smith, and Barton Levi St. Armand provided lengthy and generous critiques that were instrumental in revising the final manuscript. Only the author of a book and experts in the field know the value of such detailed commentary. Paula Bennett and Christanne Miller offered thoughtful criticisms, provided encouragement, and underscored for me the intellectual generosity that I have come to appreciate among Dickinson critics. Several colleagues, including Mary DeShazer, Allen Mandelbaum, and Elizabeth Phillips, read the manuscript in whole or in part and contributed to my rethinking of the project in its early stages of revision. My editor, Phyllis Deutsch, offered strong support, enthusiasm, and a determination to ensure that the book would see the light of day. I owe my largest debt to my parents and to my brother, John, whose continued interest in and support of this project have contributed to my well-being and sustained me in immeasurable ways.

Grateful acknowledgment is given to the staff and reference librarians at the following libraries who have provided congenial assistance and a clean, well-lighted place to work: the Houghton Library, Harvard University; Schlesinger Library, Radcliffe College; Jones Library, Amherst, Massachusetts; British Art Gallery and the Art and Architecture Library, and Beinecke, Yale University; Division of Rare and Manuscript Collections, Olin Library, and Hortorium Collection at Mann Library, Cornell University; Rare Books and Special Collections, Duke University; and Davis Library, University of North Carolina, Chapel Hill. I am also grateful to Wake Forest University for awarding me an Archie Grant to travel to several of the aforementioned collections and the Seguiv I. Hadari Research Leave in 1995, during which time I completed the manuscript. Parts of chapter 3 were published in *Tulsa Studies in Women's Literature* 13, no. 5 (Fall 1994): 317–38.

Finally, this book has benefited enormously from the contributions of other scholars, including those mentioned and others unnamed, who have created their own legacy—a heritage of criticism and scholarship about a poet whose affinities with other writers of her time are becoming clear.

E.A.P.

Abbreviations

Letters *The Letters of Emily Dickinson*, ed., Thomas H. Johnson and Theodora Ward, 3 vols. Cambridge: Harvard University Press, 1958.

J *The Poems of Emily Dickinson*, ed. Thomas H. Johnson, 3 vols. Cambridge, Mass.: Harvard University Press, 1953.

Leyda Leyda, Jay. *The Years and Hours of Emily Dickinson*, 2 vols. New Haven: Yale University Press, 1960.

Sewall Sewall, Richard B. *The Life of Emily Dickinson*, 2 vols. New York: Farrar, Straus and Giroux, 1974.

"PUBLICATION—IS THE AUCTION"

Chapter 1

Introduction

A Heritage of Poets and the Literary Tradition

> Music coming from under a window has many times been enhanced by its separateness; and though to converse athwart a door is not usual, it seems more un-useful to discuss such a preference than it would be to analyze the beam of light that brings personality, even in death, out of seclusion.
> —Marianne Moore, "Emily Dickinson" (1933)[1]

In her 1933 review of Mabel Loomis Todd's edition of selected *Letters of Emily Dickinson*, Marianne Moore comments about the general view of the artist: "One resents the cavil that makes idiosyncrasy out of individuality, asking why Emily Dickinson should sit in the dim hall to listen to Mrs. Todd's music" (222). That Dickinson often addressed visitors from behind a door or listened to music being played in the parlor from her upstairs bedroom, for Moore, reaches beyond the mere assigning of "idiosyncrasy" as a motive. The ambiguity of Dickinson's physical situation with respect to the music she describes aptly figures the poet's relationship to her audience. If the music comes "from under a window," is she inside listening to the music being played in her yard, or relegated to the outdoors? Moore's description dismisses forty years of criticism that portrayed Dickinson as an isolated eccentric, a girl, or a spinster. Rather than endorse the prevailing view of Dickinson as a shy recluse, Moore normalizes her willful refusal to be easily understood. In fact, the opacity and resistance of Moore's own writing question the judgment among Dickinson's heirs that the Amherst poet was socially and stylistically isolated. Not only does Dickinson literally speak "athwart a door" by standing on one side speaking to a listener on the other, but her "separateness" also contradicts any expectations concerning the transparency of literary language. The challenge to the critic, then, is to draw out and to enhance the artist's "personality" and style, almost as if they were a "beam of light" shining "out of seclusion" from her age into our own.

Focusing on the conventional attitudes of the nineteenth-century publishing world toward readers and writers, in private and in print, I wish to widen the "beam of light" that shines from Dickinson's inspired and original verse out of the dark chamber of tradition. Still the most significant fact of Dickinson's literary biography is her decision not to publish—a defiant act that rejected the standards for women writers in this period. Nevertheless, she was fully saturated in women's literary culture and shaped by what I call the "limits of expression"—the topics for women delimited by editors and critics. As Joanne Dobson has argued, Dickinson participated in a "community of expression" in which women writers used silence, deferral, and coded rhetorical gestures, and responded with her own self-protective linguistic style: "Her 'slant' expressive strategy, non-publication, and frequent use of conventional feminine images allow Dickinson a poetics in which personal disclosure is screened through a series of fail-safe devices designed to allay anxiety about nonconforming articulation."[2] Similarly, Jane Donahue Eberwein argues that Dickinson employs social and linguistic strategies of limitation in order to test the boundaries of existence.[3] Viewed against the shared culture and literary tradition of other nineteenth-century women writers, Dickinson creates a new, powerful means of expression within the prescribed limits. Rejecting the sentimentality of most women's verse, she mines the duplicity of the female writer's position in relation to her friends and family in order to undercut popular pieties about death and the afterlife, marriage and motherhood, and the power and function of consolatory verse. Having internalized feminine constraints, she still wrote lyrics that revise, parody, mimic, and explode the conventions of women's poetry and the limits of their personal lives.

In broadening the literary and cultural contexts in which Dickinson has been read, I have borrowed the techniques of cultural history and literary criticism. I have also participated in the recovery of a neglected tradition in American women's poetry, only now becoming recognized both for the light it sheds on major authors and for its intrinsic value. Nineteenth-century American women writers often manifest their discomfort with poetic norms while adopting them. As critics such as Tompkins, Fetterley, Zagarell, and others have shown, their novels and short stories reveal this discomfort in disruptions of all types—fissures, ruptures, and narrative inconsistencies.[4] Although the poetry is by and large more conservative than the fiction, I argue that many women poets also resisted the dictates of the publishing world. Negotiating between the prescribed means of expression and the desire to express themselves freely, nineteenth-century American women poets subtly altered the predominant image of women as pious and self-effacing. These writers range from conservative to moderate, working class to upper middle class, regional to urban, and they all demonstrate a reluctance to confront the restrictions of the publishing world head-on.

Although poetry by both British and American women influenced Dickinson's own, I have chosen to focus on the American poets who are much less frequently discussed than their British contemporaries. There is a bewildering array of collections, anthologies, gift books, floral handbooks, and memorial volumes for the scholar to draw from, and I have therefore chosen to focus on a representative sampling of poets and popular generic forms. In the magazines and newspapers read in Dickinson's household, such as *The Springfield Republican, The Atlantic Monthly, Scribner's, The Amherst Record*, and *The Hampshire and Franklin Express*, Helen Hunt Jackson, Lydia Sigourney, Louisa May Alcott, Julia Ward Howe, Maria Lowell, as well as Emily Brontë, Elizabeth Barrett Browning, Christina Rossetti, and countless others, made their way into the poet's conscious life. These poets create a kind of cultural palimpsest, writing and rewriting central tropes about death, femininity, and motherhood that are barely visible under the erasures of literary history. Set against a new and recently recovered tradition of female verse writing, Dickinson's central place in the canon and her position as a consummate artist are clearly affirmed. Although even as a girl she spurned the tearful emotions of much women's verse, she found a variety of sentimental poems, stories, and novels worthy of mention to her friends. Fully conversant in the popular literature of the day, Dickinson drew eclectically from a wide range of contemporary literature including novels, articles, tracts, hymn books, and poems, against which she sounded her more rebellious brand of hymnody. A list of popular literature by women either found in her library (now housed at Harvard) or referred to in her letters reveals that she read a range of popular writers: Rebecca Harding Davis's *Life in the Iron Mills* (1861); Frances Hodgson Burnett's *The Fair Barbarian* (1881), which Dickinson had read with amusement in *Scribner's* and which made such an impression on her Amherst friends and neighbors that it was staged in 1883 with Mabel Loomis Todd in the starring role (Sewall, 172), Ann Manning's *The Maiden and Married Life of Mary Powell* (1852); and Elizabeth Stuart Phelps's (A. Trusta) *The Last Leaf from Sunny Side* (1854). About other books, she could hardly contain her enthusiasm. Writing in 1848 at Mount Holyoke to her friend Abiah Root, she notes that "while at home I had a feast in the reading line" (*Letters* 1, 66), mentioning a veritable smorgasbord of popular literature: Marcella Bute Smedley's *The Maiden Aunt* (1849), Henry Wadsworth Longfellow's *Evangeline* (1847), Thomas Moore's *The Epicurean* (1835), and Martin Tupper's *The Twins* and *The Heart* (1845). In 1845, in a letter to Abiah Root, she praised a poem of the type popular in newspapers of the period by a now-forgotten author, Florence Vane: "Have you seen a beautiful piece of poetry which has been going through the papers lately? *Are we almost there?* is the title of it . . ." (*Letters* 1, 34). Like her contemporaries, Dickinson praised such "effusions," as they were called, for their heightened expression and pathetic sentiment.

Since women writers were guided by the rhetorical styles of editors and publishers, I begin with an overview of the literary marketplace and discuss its impact on Dickinson's decision not to publish. From 1820 to 1880, editors who assembled collections of female verse frequently referred to the poems as "effusions," or emotional outpourings, which they then "fathered" by publishing them under their names. Reviewers in this era often characterized women's verse as more affective and less intellectual than men's, more "natural" and unpremeditated in composition. Women were considered closer to emotions than men, and apt to express pious sentiments almost without conscious thought. Critics regularly compared women's poetic voice to a child's or to birdsong. By contending that women's poetry emerges naturally from the sentiments and the emotions, sanctioned only by publication, they prepare us to understand Dickinson's refusal to allow the bulk of her poems to be printed, lest publication reduce her "Human Spirit / To Disgrace of Price—" (J, 709). Each subsequent chapter sets Dickinson's verse in relation to one or more nineteenth-century American woman poets.

The poetry and culture of mourning, among the most common subjects for nineteenth-century American women poets, is discussed in the second section of this book. While Dickinson partook of the popular cultural myths and fictions concerning death and the afterlife, she found the premises of mid-nineteenth-century America deeply questionable. Sentimental poetry portrays women and children who embody the ideals of evangelism and education. Influenced by the vast numbers of children's deaths in this period, popular writers, such as Louisa May Alcott, Henry Wadsworth Longfellow, Thomas Hood, and Lydia Sigourney, wrote tributes on the deaths of infants, children, and adolescents. Situating Dickinson's poems in relation to those of contemporaries both dramatizes the way she transformed the elegy and promotes a profound understanding of how they adapted the tenets underlying elegiac meditations to their own advantages. A popular infant elegist, for instance, Sigourney often highlights a mother's death in childbirth by juxtaposing a mother's funeral with her infant's christening; Sigourney's elegies suggest that the mother's death returns her to an infant-like state and that her son substitutes for her on earth. Taken together, her poems maintain a pious exterior, while still expanding what a woman could express in a popular and accepted verse genre. Dickinson, however, in exploring the pain and anxiety that both adults and children suffer, rejects the prospect of a blissful gathering of the family circle after death; she suggests that such a reunion is only a fiction in the minds of the mourning family.

The representation of death in extraliterary materials—posthumous portraits, funerary sculpture, the "rural cemetery" movement, and other mourning artifacts—renders more explicit fear and anxiety about death in the culture at large. The prevalence of the motif of the huge dead child, posed against more minute backgrounds, points to the breakdown in nineteenth-century consolatory fictions that was already underway in the early 1800s. Dickinson uses epitaphs to play on the absence implicit in the act of writing and reverses the expected roles of mourner and mourned to shorten our distance from the dead. Drawing on funerary iconography and epitaphic inscriptions, her poetry readjusts perspective, either from the vantage point of the dead, who encourage the living to join them, or from the living, who are so accustomed to remembering the dead that they seem more dead than alive.

The third section of this book explores how Dickinson adapts two common female discourses, floral language and geographic imagery, to reconstruct the popular conception of femininity and its rhetorical possibilities. Dickinson's habit of presenting flowers with poems falls within the context of the language of flowers, which constructed a nonverbal system of communication based on a series of codes. Floral dictionaries proliferated in England and America, including Frances Sargent Osgood's *The Poetry of Flowers, and Flowers of Poetry* (1841), Sara Josepha Hale's *Flora's Interpreter; or, The American Book of Flowers and Sentiments* (1833), and Dorothea Dix's *The Garland Of Flora* (1829). The language of flowers afforded women, who were frequently depicted as flowers and encouraged to shy away from the harsh light of self-revelation and public scrutiny, a way to express their thoughts. Dickinson uses floral lyrics to express emotions that were deemed unacceptable for women. Adapting the divine and secular resonances of floral images as used by more conservative writers like Osgood, she undercuts the pious image of woman and instead privileges secrets, silence, and deferral over actual communication.

Nineteenth-century American women poets often used extreme geographical settings—tropical jungles and arctic locales—to convey women's isolation in their domestic lives, and Dickinson adopts the vocabulary of "zones" and "solstices" that arises in the art and poetry of this period. A popular poet, short story writer, and novelist, Helen Hunt Jackson frequently describes alienation, anger, and sarcasm and portrays an intensity of feeling that is wrenchingly physical. A friend and correspondent of Dickinson's, Jackson also defines the limits of expression to which a female author had to conform and the degree to which she could question those strictures. Betsy Erkkila argues in *The Wicked Sisters: Women Poets, Literary History & Discord* (1992) that Dickinson's and Jackson's relationship showed the constraints on women's works in publishing, and a reading of their correspondence and poems shows that Dickinson refused to submit her verse to the rigors and rewards of the literary marketplace.[5] Conversely, Jackson's poetry reveals the degree to which a woman might adopt the conventional imagery of the period and still portray women's lives as unhappy and unfulfilled. Dickinson's use of tropical and arctic settings, her evocation of Emersonian nature worship as an alternative to normative Christianity, her critique of women's roles, and of the need to suppress passion are expressed in her nature poems and perhaps in her most radical symbol—the volcano.

In the final chapter, I consider the impact on the classroom and scholarship of reading Dickinson's verse against that of other nineteenth-century American women poets. Examining critics who argue for the importance of women's poetry from two different perspectives—aesthetic achievement and social context—I contend that the emergent field of nineteenth-century American women's poetry can radically change our perspective on the artistic, intellectual, and social milieux in which Dickinson and others wrote. What comes of this repositioning of Dickinson against her female contemporaries is, I believe, a fuller historical contextualizing of a consummate poet who drew richly from a wide range of contemporary sources, both high and low. With the exception of Barton Levi St. Armand's masterful study of the poet's relation to Victorian culture and Judith Farr's discussion of Dickinson's artistic and literary sensibilities, few have placed her poems in their cultural and intellectual contexts.[6] I augment these studies by grounding Dickinson's poems in their native territory and searching for parallels among poets whose names were as familiar to her as the wildflowers and plants with which their verses were often compared. Examining conventional poetic genres and literary discourses that were more or less the province of women, such as the child elegy and the flower poem, I broach unexplored critical territory and emphasize gender and culture more strongly than previous critics.

Although critics have argued that placing Dickinson against other women writers makes her originality all the more apparent, most have only gestured at the possible directions such a study might take or its feminist implications. The recovery of neglected works by nineteenth-century American women writers has aided many scholars in reconstructing the literary tradition in America.[7] But I also wish to suggest that exploring the culture and poetry of nineteenth-century women significantly complicates our understanding both of Dickinson's "individuality," in Moore's assessment, and of the other writers' achievement. Rather than view Dickinson as the capstone of a particular theory of women's literature, I wish to explore how her "separateness," in Moore's phrase, nevertheless throws into bold relief a profound connection with the underlying topics of women's verse and allows us to see both her and her female contemporaries differently. In *The Madwoman in the Attic* (1979), Sandra Gilbert and Susan Gubar argue the poet dramatizes and enacts within her lyrics personae whose life histories share features with the lives of romantic heroines in British and American fiction. They trace a line of descent that begins with Jane Austen, who maintains an ironic detachment toward the lives of her characters, and ends with the Brontës and George Eliot, who increasingly identify their heroines' lives with their own. They claim that Dickinson dramatically enacts in her poems her own life story, "an extended fiction whose subject is the life of that supposed person who was originally called Emily Dickinson."[8] Yet Dickinson speaks to the difficulty of making such connections between life and art. She writes to Higginson in 1862, "When I state myself, as the Representative of the Verse—it does not mean—me—but a supposed person" (*Letters* 2, 412). Her remark cautions us about conflating her art and her life, the poetic model of which is more appropriately, as Elizabeth Phillips notes, the dramatic monologue than a self-referential enactment of her life.[9] If we take Moore's defense of Dickinson's behavior as a commentary on her relationship to literary convention, then we might profitably explore her most immediate relationship to a neglected female literary tradition. After receiving a copy of J. E. Cross's *The Life of George Eliot* from Thomas Wentworth Higginson in 1885, she wrote to thank him and noted, "Biography first convinces us of the fleeing of the Biographied—" (*Letters* 3, 864). As Dickinson hints concerning Eliot, biographical treatments of the lives of nineteenth-century women writers often accompanied their deaths but failed to capture their lively selves.

Although Gilbert and Gubar's approach has been instrumental in defining a female literary tradition, I would argue that we need to investigate Dickinson's poetry more fully with respect to the literary achievements of her sister poets.[10] Viewed against the backdrop of a shared cultural and literary milieu, Dickinson's poetry challenges assumptions about women's lives. Other women poets had already begun to resist publishing constraints, consolatory fictions, parental roles, and floral associations in verses, so often maligned, that subtly reflect the adaptation of traditional feminine poetic discourses. In *Stealing the Language: The Emergence of Women's Poetry in America*, Alicia Suskin Ostriker argues that women poets before the modern age contradict their outward appearance. Among all the poets she mentions, Dickinson is the most self-conscious and artful in her manipulation. Able to sustain both the conventional and radical meanings through her use of ambiguity, Dickinson is exemplary among nineteenth-century poets who betray a double-sided adherence to, and subversion of, the dictates of femininity that she terms "duplicitous."[11] According to Ostriker, the constraints of subject matter led to an overdose of sentimental rhetoric in women's poetry and a corresponding diminution of artistic power:

It is also evident that the sentimentality is a result of authors' pretending not to know, not to feel, what they do know and feel. Inflated, exclamatory rhetoric is a device employed when a poet is supposed to seem natural and impulsive but is obliged to repress awareness of her body and her ego. Flights to sublimity arrive at banality when the actual world of men, women, and manners is restricted material. Soporific meters without prosodic experimentation arise when the intention is to please and soothe. (33)

Ostriker's characterization of sentimental poetry clearly stems from an awareness that nineteenth-century American female poets had to constrain their verses to accepted modes. Ostriker mentions that sentimentality arises precisely when the author is "pretending not to know" what is perfectly obvious, and her definition underscores the way nineteenth-century female poets felt the dual responsibility to maintain respectability and to articulate concerns of national importance. Although Christian evangelism, womanhood, and the home were frequent subjects, public poetry provided a forum for their deepest concerns, such as temperance, abolition, women's rights, and Native-American activism. Under the guise of sentimentality, women wielded emotional power that had national ramifications. For all the talk of "separate spheres" in the political and social lives of men and women, nineteenth-century female poets were clearly as engaged as their male counterparts in issues of national importance. Furthermore, "flights to sublimity" that "arrive at banality" appear in some of Longfellow's (and even Whitman's) most majestic and long-winded phrases, as in "The Song of Hiawatha": "As he bore the red deer homeward, / And Iagoo and Nokomis / Hailed his coming with applauses."[12] Certainly, Whittier and Bryant at times might be accused of "soporific meters." Longfellow, too. And Frances Osgood discusses "the actual world of men, women, and manners" in her witty and irreverent poems about romantic courtship, and her most sexually charged poems, such as "The Cocoa-Nut Tree," demonstrate women's erotic selves were alive and kicking.

In her benchmark study of nineteenth-century American women's poetry, *The Nightingale's Burden: Women Poets and American Culture before 1900*, Cheryl Walker explores the generic structure of women's poetry but avoids discussing their conventional topics, such as religion and the deaths of children, in order to focus on the relation between women and the patriarchal determinants of social order. In reconstructing the social, psychological, and historical milieux in which women wrote, Walker describes several archetypes that proliferated in women's poetry of the period: the "sanctuary" poem, in which the speaker retreats to a bower of refuge to escape a violent assault upon her body or mind and experiences a feeling of freedom and creativity; the "power fantasy" poem, in which images of flight and sexual aggression precede a sense of fulfillment; the "free bird" poem, in which the speaker identifies with a confined bird and longs to be free; and the "sensibility" poem, in which the speaker defines herself in terms of an immoderate and agonized hypersensitivity.[13] Emily Stipes Watts in *The Poetry of American Women from 1632 to 1945* also surveys the tradition of women's poetry and stakes out its major authors and literary motifs.[14] In her study of nineteenth-century American women's poetry, Watts contends that although women's poetry was not impious, political, or particularly assertive, women adopted a set of tropes, many based on classical mythology, that countered the prevalent Adamic myth in American culture. Similarly, examining the "social, religious and intellectual currents of her time,"[15] Paula Bennett places Dickinson in the context of other nineteenth-century women poets and argues that Dickinson's domesticity and womanhood were crucial to her development as a poet: "Her submergence into the women's sphere and her presentation of herself as 'poetess' (a *woman* poet) was, therefore, a good deal more than simply a role she played in order to keep from playing others" (13). For Bennett, Dickinson rejects masculine authority and uses nature to transcend the masculinist tradition: "Unable to reconcile herself to the concept of a transcendent God, Dickinson presents nature as a woman-centered and materially-based alternative to established religion" (20).

If nineteenth-century women attempted in their poems to free themselves from the oppressive weight of male dominance, however, they did so by conforming to the generic characteristics and typical themes and to the image of women proposed by the publishing world. It is tempting to read a twentieth-century feminist bias into nineteenth-century genteel culture, since our tendency as critics is to assume that women were strategic in promoting their own talent, though they never actually claimed they were more talented than male writers. Rather, much as female writers pretended to accept a self-effacing demeanor in print, their resistance to established poetic norms of expression amounts not to a strategy consciously directed against an oppressive culture, as some critics have argued, but to a discomfort with topics that were not equal to the actual experiences of their lives.[16]

On 7 July 1860, an anonymous article appeared in *The Springfield Republican*, perhaps written by Dickinson's friend and editor-in-chief, Samuel Bowles, on "When Should We Write":

There is another kind of writing only too common, appealing to the sympathies of the reader without recommending itself to his judgment. It may be called the literature of misery. Its writers are chiefly women, gifted women may be, full of thought and feeling and fancy, but poor, lonely and unhappy. Alas that suffering is so seldom healthful. It may be a valuable discipline in the end, but for the time being it too often clouds, withers, distorts. It is so difficult to see objects distinctly through a mist of tears. The sketch or poem is usually the writer's photograph in miniature. It reveals a countenance we would gladly brighten, but not by exposing it to the gaze of a worthless world.[17]

It is striking how much the writer, who conflates women's writing with their lives and emotions, correspondingly denigrates the so-called "literature of misery" as sentimental, contending that such emotion "clouds, withers, distorts" and so prevents the poet from accurately representing life. His quasi-scientific desire for the poet "to see objects distinctly," not "through a mist of tears," elevates rationality over feeling. Perhaps Dickinson echoed such sentiments herself when she wrote in 1861 to Higginson about her verse, "The Mind is so near itself—it cannot see, distinctly—and I have none to ask—" (*Letters* 2,

403). Furthermore, a woman's poem is thought to mimic her nature and to serve as a "photograph in miniature," clearly a violation of the privacy cherished by the men and women of the age. As Eberwein notes, the poet's brother, Austin, consistently refused to allow photographs of himself to be published in Amherst town histories and often repeated to his daughter a dictum he had learned as a child: "Fools' names and fools' faces / Only appear in public places" (6). Bowles's statement that he would only reluctantly expose a woman's "countenance" to the "worthless gaze of the world" captures the spirit that would discourage women from publishing: if a genteel woman would not show her face all over, then shouldn't the female writer also refrain from submitting her innermost feelings to public scrutiny?

Feminist critics have ranked the "literature of misery" as an expression of female power. According to Walker, the "literature of misery" defined a poet's worth in terms of the capacity to convey grief, and women writers claimed special talent as a result of their suffering and self-sacrifice.[18] If we contend, as Walker does, that drawing on a "secret sorrow" allowed women "a sense of self-importance and an object for contemplation that they could claim as their own" (88), then we can find their poems assertive, since they frequently focus on domestic sorrows and personal trials. Placing at a high premium the ability to be moved by the dying, sentimentalists believed that the fact of sudden death was a reminder of the common bond of mortality and a means to convert the mourners. A popular New England poet, Hannah F. Gould, portrays "The Dying Child's Request" (1832) to act as a *memento mori* for others:

> "To brother—sister—playmates too,
> Some gift I'd leave behind,
> To keep me, when I've passed from view,
> Still present to their mind.

> "You'll thus to them my books divide,
> My playthings give away;
> So they'll remember how I died,
> When not so old as they."[19]

Portraying children, whose certainty of the afterlife and piety remained strong, these writers provide evidence for the nineteenth-century reader that faith persevered after death. Dickinson frequently asked the question more bluntly in letters to friends and relatives on the death of a loved one: "Did he go willingly?" Yet in the hands of the sentimentalists, stories of holy trials and patient deaths were part of a larger revolt against Calvinism, for they made the emotional "melting" of a contrite heart more central than resignation to death. The expression of boundless grief and the theme of spiritual renewal were generally thought to be elevated subjects that merited heartfelt "effusions," which could rescue the mourner from damnation if only he or she were appropriately moved. As Gould's poem demonstrates, women's elegies often idealized dying children as teachers and pious exemplars. At the same time, children's messianic calling reveals how domestic traits, such as piety and the desire to teach others, extended far beyond the home and into the culture at large. Certainly, the image of women performing their domestic duties with angelic charm and moral rectitude became part of the conservative ideology to which many women writers publicly conformed in the mid-nineteenth century. Yet they also betrayed considerable business sense and negotiated their careers with savvy. As Mary Kelley has noted, because their lives were separated into "private women" and "public stages," they seldom displayed to their editors and their reading public any self-consciousness over this disparity.[20]

These three critics—Walker, Watts, and Ostriker—demonstrate that a continuum exists in American women's poetry from its Puritan origins to the 1960s, yet they only gesture toward the importance of reading Dickinson against her female contemporaries and in their shared literary culture. They define the central images, such as the "secret sorrow" and the "free bird," that pervade women's poetry. They also demonstrate the link between women poets of the same tradition, radical and conservative, black and white, who reworked common themes concerning women's poetic creativity. Finally, each critic encourages us to read Dickinson against the spectrum of nineteenth-century women writers as either an "Individual Talent" in the midst of a women's "Tradition" (Walker), a master of the duplicitous style (Ostriker), or an exponent of a feminine poetic tradition (Watts).

Feminist critics have spawned the recovery of nineteenth-century American women's literature, an ongoing process that has profound implications for the reconstruction of the American literary canon. The doctrine of "separate spheres"—the idea that women's and men's lives were presumed to belong to the home and the larger world respectively—is a mainstay of arguments about nineteenth-century women's lives and literary careers and has itself undergone significant revision.[21] In their account of the rise of the bourgeois family in nineteenth-century America, Barbara Ehrenreich and Deidre English note that the collapse of the old-order agrarian life prompted the creation of new "public" and "private" spheres dividing the home and business world into women's and men's realms, and thus maintaining a hierarchical division of work and leisure, where women occupied a central role as purveyors of morals and primary educators of children.[22] Confined to *Kinder, Kirche, Küche*—children, church, and kitchen, in the popular prewar German formulation concerning women's lives—women of the middle classes were expected to raise children and run their households; in turn, men's roles as wage earners in the business world were confirmed. Writing in 1978, Nina Baym notes that the "domestic" is not a "fixed or neutral word in critical analysis," for it betokens to modern critics not only women's fiction set within the home but entrapment.[23] In contrast, nineteenth-century women writers did not see their lives as belonging to "separate spheres," but they saw the home as a place from which women could exert almost as much control in the world as men: "If worldly values could dominate the home, perhaps the direction of influence could be reversed so that home values dominated the world. Since they identified home with basic human values, they saw this as a reformation of America into a society at last responsive to truly human needs, a fulfillment of the original settlers' dreams" (48–49).

Among some feminist literary critics, reclaiming sentimentalism has provided a way to establish women's literature as a means of empowerment. As Shirley Samuels has argued in *The Culture of Sentiment* (1992), critics of sentimentality have often taken it to task for focusing on domestic and familial relations through which they addressed crucial national issues, such as slavery, despite their exclusion from political power.[24] Sentimentalists were at once chided for refraining from exercising power over issues of real political and social importance and, simultaneously, defined by a lack of ability to act outside the home. The doctrine of separate spheres thus embodies a "double logic of power and powerlessness": "a separation from the world of 'work' (and economic power) was compensated for by the affective power of the 'home'; in the use of sentimentality, separation from political action nonetheless meant presenting an affective alternative that not only gave political actions their emotional significance, but beyond that, intimately linked individual bodies to the national body" (4). Although Samuels does not claim that women assert themselves politically through sentimental literature, sentimentality, with its fusion of feminism and abolition, foregrounds women's concerns with the way power is managed in the culture at large.

Novels like Harriet Beecher Stowe's *Uncle Tom's Cabin* (1851–52) sowed the seeds of revolt in nineteenth-century American women's writing by advocating bonds between women. For Baym, the symbiosis between home and world is best exemplified by Stowe's novel. Stowe's Eva, for instance, is linked to a female power matrix: Mrs. Bird, Mrs. Shelby, Rachel Halliday, and Aunt Dinah manipulate men's behavior and rule from the kitchen. Eva is associated with the evangelical fervor of mothers. Desiring to convert the slaves through touch, she invokes the physical contact so common among evangelists. When she lays her hand on Topsy's shoulder, her father, the atheist St. Clare, is reminded of his mother's words: "we must be willing to do as Christ did,—call them to us, and *put our hands on them*."[25] By showing how St. Clare and other men associate Eva with the piety of their mothers, Stowe hopes to persuade the public to eliminate slavery through identification with Eva's tearful passing. For Stowe and other writers of her age, women could affect the course of history through their evangelical zeal and ability to arouse pathos.

If one considers the political and personal dimensions of women's lyrics, their self-portrayals are double-edged: they can be read either as affirming a belief in the ideology of submissive womanhood or as questioning women's roles. The satisfaction of woman's role as pious nurturer, for example, is described in Julia Ward Howe's "Woman":

> A vestal priestess, proudly pure,
>   But of a meek and quiet spirit;
> With soul all dauntless to endure,
>   And mood so calm that none can stir it,
> Save when a thought most deeply thrilling
> Her eyes with gentlest tears is filling,
> Which seem with her true words to start
> From the deep fountain at her heart.
>
> A mien that neither seeks nor shuns
>   The homage scattered in her way;
> A love that hath few favored ones,
>   And yet for all can work and pray;
> A smile wherein each mortal reads
> The very sympathy he needs;
> An eye like to a mystic book
>   Of lays that bard or prophet sings,
> Which keepeth for the holiest look
>   Of holiest love its deepest things
>
> . . . .
>
> A vestal priestess, maid, or wife—
>   Vestal, and vowed to offer up
> The innocence of a holy life
>   To Him who gives the mingled cup;
> With man its bitter sweets to share,
> To live and love, to do and dare;
> His prayer to breathe, his tears to shed,
> Breaking to him the heavenly bread
> Of hopes which, all too high for earth,
> Have yet in her a mortal birth.[26]

Howe portrays an embodiment of the womanly virtues of humility and silence. "Meek and quiet," she displays chastity as a "vestal priestess." Her association with the six priestesses who guarded the sacred flame in the temple of Vesta in ancient Rome is reinforced by Howe's characterization of her as "the fireside's dearest ornament" (l. 20) and also suggests that her role is essentially domestic. Quite as remarkable as the portrait of womanly virtue and household taskmaster, however, are its multiple contradictions: she is "proudly pure," but unprepossessing; "neither seeks nor shuns" praise; favors none, but serves all; and so on. Howe's portrait balances the qualities that a woman was ideally thought to possess, since she was not assumed to feel any actual desire, creating a two-sided portrait that preserves her ambiguity to the viewer, who can see in her placid expression "a smile wherein each mortal reads / The very sympathy he needs" (ll. 13–14). Simultaneously mirroring others and fulfilling their needs for sympathy, she is aptly summed up by the Romantic image of nature as a "mystic book" (l. 15). For Emerson and Wordsworth, the leaves of this mystic book hold the traces of God to an inspired mind. Lacking the intellectual capacity to interpret herself, woman is a symbol that must be interpreted by others, a vessel that contains all the desires projected onto her. Finally, she assumes a Christian role, sharing her husband's responsibilities and embodying the "hopes which, all too high on earth, / Have yet in her a mortal birth" (ll. 33–34). The speaker's concluding lines uncover the ambiguity:

> This is the woman I have dreamed,
> And to my childish thought she seemed
> The woman I myself should be:
> Alas! I would that I were she.
>
> (ll. 35–38)

Although these lines can be read as a straightforward acceptance of this image of femininity, they also might sardonically admit that such an ideal is undesirable: to her "childish thought" this image of woman seemed perfect, but in adulthood the speaker's wish to imitate this model is reduced to a sigh.

Elizabeth Oakes Smith's "The Wife" captures some of the same ambiguities:

> All day, like some sweet bird, content to sing
>   In its small cage, she moveth to and fro—
> And ever and anon will upward spring
>   To her sweet lips, fresh from the fount below,
> The murmured melody of pleasant thought,
>   Unconscious uttered, gentle-toned and low.
> Light household duties, evermore inwrought
>   With placid fancies of one trusting heart
> That lives but in her smile, and turns
>   From life's cold seeming and the busy mart,
> With tenderness, that heavenward ever yearns
> To be refreshed where one pure altar burns.
>   Shut out from hence, the mockery of life,
>   Thus liveth she content, the meek, fond, trusting wife.[27]

This poem adopts birdsong as a central metaphor for a woman's poetic voice that depicts her supposedly "natural" and spontaneous being. Comparing a wife to "some sweet bird" in its "small cage," Oakes Smith suggests that women resemble birds in their naive expression of "pleasant thought," which rises "from the fount below . . . / Unconscious uttered" (ll. 4–6). Furthermore, home life stands in opposition to "life's cold seeming and the busy mart," suggesting that men can be redeemed by the values and virtues of the home. In serving as the earthly repository of the "one pure altar" of heaven, wife and home become more real than the world outside, where life's "cold seeming" and "mockery" of true existence reign. Indeed, although the description in the last eight lines is of the wife, it might as easily apply to a husband, who after a long day, turns with "one trusting heart / That lives but in her smile" to the inner sanctum of the home. Paradoxically, however, the home is also sustained by her (or his) "placid fancies," and her "content" (mentioned twice in the poem) relies on a denial of reality. At the poem's end, "fond" connotes naively credulous as well as caring and implies that the wife is foolish for not realizing that her husband's ascendency over her is sustained by her confined existence.

Rather than portray a woman as placidly content, neither desirous herself nor accepting the desires of others, even Dickinson's more conventional speakers often lament the fate of unappreciated women, as in the following lyric:

> Poor little Heart!
> Did they forget thee?
> Then dinna care! Then dinna care!
>
> Proud little Heart!
> Did they forsake thee?
> Be debonnaire! Be debonnaire!
>
> Frail little Heart!
> *I* would not break thee—
> Could'st credit *me*? Could'st credit me?
>
> Gay little Heart—
> Like Morning Glory!
> Wind and Sun—wilt thee array!
>
> (J, 192)

Reminiscent of Burns's Scottish lays with its dialectic "dinna," the poem adopts the sentimental imagery and repetitive phrasing reminiscent of bird calls and typical of women's poetry. But Dickinson transforms the conventional sorrowing of a traduced women by casting the speaker as one who courageously bemoans the fate of the forgotten and ill-used "little Heart."

Rather than extol a woman's state in life as teacher and purveyor of values, Dickinson's speaker challenges the "little Heart" to be stoic in the face of abuse. If the heart is forgotten, the speaker urges forgetfulness; if forsaken, gaity; if broken, faith in a *woman* rather than a man. Dickinson overturns the romantic conventions upon which poetry is based, where a man's attention determines a woman's social role and her estimation of herself. Ultimately, the poem suggests that the "little Heart" will receive its final commendation and the fulfillment of its promises only in death. The comparison to "Morning Glory," which evokes the resurrection, suggests that the heart will find its final release in the ground, where it will be arrayed by "Wind and Sun" rather than the attributes of worldly love. Far from locating the source of women's power in an inner spiritual "fount," as do Smith and Howe, Dickinson centers women's freedom in nature and, more ambiguously, in death. Even in this early poem, she creates an allegory of romantic detachment that contradicts the hierarchies of activity and passivity upon which courtship is based.[28] More generally, her poems adapt the language of sentimentalism to question the essentializing view that women were an unthinking fount of emotions and to promote Dickinson's inclusion in a community of other women writers. As the following chapters show, Dickinson's poetry emanates from an artistic and intellectual sensibility born of her native New England and shared with other women, a recognition of whose own artistic achievement has been long overdue.

Chapter 2

"This—Was a Poet"

Emily Dickinson and Nineteenth-Century
Publishing Standards

It is the woman above all—there never have been women, save pioneer
Katies; not one in flower save some moonflower Poe may have seen, or an
unripe child. Poets? Where? They are the test. But a true woman in flower,
never. Emily Dickinson, starving of passion in her father's garden, is the
very nearest we have ever been—starving.
> —William Carlos Williams, *In the American Grain*[1]

There are women so intensely feminine that they would not write to publish
if they could; too proud, because too wise to expose their feelings to a world
made up of persons with whom they neither hold communion, nor have
sympathy.
> —Elizabeth Sheppard, *Rumors* (Leyda 2, 88)

I thought that being a Poem one's self precluded the writing Poems, but
perceive the Mistake.
> —Emily Dickinson (*Letters* 2, 525)

"The whole tendency of the age is Magazine-ward," wrote Edgar Allan Poe
concerning the proliferation of magazines and periodicals in nineteenth-century
America.[2] Perhaps referring humorously to the heavenward direction of much
pious and uplifting sentimental poetry and fiction, so popular in his era, and
written primarily by women, Poe brilliantly goes on to define a woman's relationship to her literary composition. Cannily aware of the way women's lives
and poems were often confused, he claimed that "a woman will never be
brought to admit a non-identity between herself and her book."[3] We may take
his comment that a woman writer's art will never stand apart from her life also

19

as a strategy consciously adopted by literary women. As he notes, they would never "admit" that their lives and works were not identical, because they saw the conflation of a woman's life and art as an opportunity to hide behind a shield of modest femininity. Deemed the embodiment of values, women's poems were read as extensions of the female sex, and allowing their books to represent themselves publicly entitled the poets to a greater degree of freedom in their personal lives than they might otherwise have been afforded.

Perhaps the most important fact of her literary biography is Dickinson's decision not to publish. In doing so, she distinguished herself as the only American Renaissance writer who valued her own conception so completely that she was willing to forego publication. Even Higginson, litterateur and friend, advanced her poems before the public in his 1890 "An Open Portfolio" only "with some misgiving, and almost with a sense of questionable publicity," yet he readily acknowledged the authenticity of her creative vision: "Wayward and unconventional in the last degree; defiant of form, measure, rhyme, and even grammar; she yet had an exacting standard of her own, and would wait many days for a word that satisfied."[4] In light of the history of the critical discourse surrounding women's poetry, the Dickinson-Higginson relationship might be recast in terms that highlight the dismissiveness that is a normative response of a critic to a woman writer. Like the character from Elizabeth Sheppard's novel, *Rumors*, Dickinson profited by the attitude toward the lives and careers of many female authors, deemed too "feminine" to seek notoriety in print and too "wise" to circulate their verse widely among unappreciative readers.[5] Instead, she forsook publication once she realized her artistic conception would be violated and adapted the standard of moral propriety that encouraged women to shy away from the light of public exposure. She countered the prevailing opinion that women should refrain from discussing any but pious and domestic topics and sought an alternative to publication as a means of circulating her verses.

Many critics have discussed Dickinson's fascicles—the forty stab-bound and hand-sewn packets into which she copied her verse that were discovered in her bureau after her death by her sister, Lavinia—either as a form of self-publication or as an ordering device that gives method and meaning to her poetry.[6] As Martha Nell Smith has argued in *Rowing in Eden: Rereading Emily Dickinson*, these textual exchanges between the poet and her correspondents, especially her beloved sister-in-law, Susan Gilbert, and important male friends, comprise themselves a type of "publication" and amount to a method of "workshop" composition that counters the prevailing myth about her supposed isolation as a writer.[7] Dickinson "published" her poems by circulating them in her letters; she may have circulated manuscript books to Helen Hunt Jackson. Far from mere "fair copies," the fascicles are an invaluable source for discerning the poet's intentions and her compositional techniques, as the script itself becomes a form of iconic design. These holographic performances, in which lines gain or lose intelligibility with their calligraphy, are largely defeated through conventional print reproductions of her poems.

Dickinson's circulation of manuscripts, various handwriting styles, and visual puns all suggest that she found more autonomy and room for free play in the unrestricted page, and the vein of criticism that sees her as a scribal publisher raises provocative issues about her absorption of periodicals, newspapers, and giftbooks, all of which trumpeted the standards of women's verse. Dickinson's choice not to publish was influenced by the publishing constraints to which women were subjected. As Karen Dandurand has argued, Dickinson was fully aware that her poems were "going round" the newspapers, a nineteenth-century euphemism for reprinting and circulating verses, often without permission from the original source.[8] If so, then one might assume that it was perhaps not the idea of publication that so disturbed her as the loss of control over her poems once they were in the hands of editors. As she remarks to Higginson in an early letter, "I marked a line in One Verse—because I met it after I made it—and never consciously touch a paint, mixed by another person—" (*Letters* 2, 415). Rather than submit to the legitimating strategies and dictates of editors and publishers, she chose to refrain from publishing altogether.

Why did Dickinson reject the opportunity to print her verses and make the boldest quest for poetic originality among her contemporaries? How (and to what degree) did other women serve as examples? How far were these poets able to modify, redefine, and explode the prevalent definition and presentation of women's verse in nineteenth-century America? Characterized by most nineteenth-century critics as pious, natural, and unpremeditated, women's poems and their lives were often conflated. In fact, so often were women's books and lives compared that their poems came to be referred to as "embodiments," "waifs," and "children," which needed to be "fathered" under the auspices of a male critic or editor before appearing before the public. Dickinson deemed publication "the Auction / Of the Mind of Man" (J, 709), and therefore refused to allow the bulk of her poems to be printed, lest publication reduce her "Human Spirit / To Disgrace of Price—" (J, 709).

The publishing milieu contributed greatly to the formation of a nineteenth-century reader's taste. Recently, critics have focused on reconstructing the literary milieu or print culture to ask questions about how and why authors wrote. In *Beneath the American Renaissance*, David S. Reynolds draws on and demonstrates the influences of a variety of "high" and "low" discourses in American print culture, including temperance literature, evangelical tracts, and abolition newspapers on major authors, like Dickinson, Melville, and Whitman. He underscores Dickinson's allegiance with the sensibility and political sympathies of her age, even as she transforms its materials: "If the women authors of the literature of misery sought to establish an artistic middle ground between the effetely Conventional and the openly feminist, so Emily Dickinson explicitly rejected both the 'Dimity Convictions' of traditionalists and the public methods of women's rights activists, while she made the era's boldest quest for specifically artistic exhibitions of woman's power."[9] By focusing on Dickinson's specifically "artistic exhibitions of woman's power," Reynolds privileges the aesthetic over the sociological, making it difficult for him to speak of the value of much women's poetry of this era. Wishing to maintain a distinction between "high" and "low" literature, Reynolds contends that major authors rework, modify, and, ultimately, transform subliterary genres into works of art. This argument, though, masks the intrinsic artistic value of much women's writing and, conversely, the sentimentalism with which many of Dickinson's own lyrics are imbued. The hierarchical equations upon which his and other critics' arguments rest—canonical/noncanonical, radical/conservative—are put into question when we begin to consider that Dickinson adopted many of the same fictions and myths as other women writers, cultural materials that were shaped by editors' and critics' perceived role for women.

By the 1840s, magazine publishing had become a major source of revenue for established writers, and new female writers profited by the widespread distribution of their work as well. Genteel magazines, such as *Scribner's Monthly*, *Graham's Magazine*, *Harper's*, and *The Atlantic Monthly*, set the standards of literary taste and encouraged the development of a national audience for women's domestic fiction and verse. Producing Gothic tales, Western travelogs, sentimental poetry, short stories, and novels, such writers as Harriet Prescott Spofford, Caroline Kirkland, Harriet Beecher Stowe, and Alice and Phoebe Cary reaped profits. Encouraged by the ever-widening market for sensation fiction, sentimental romance, travel pieces, and periodical literature of all types, women gained notoriety, which in turn served their financial interests. Publishers branched out to the southern and western states. From about 1790 to 1830, magazine publishing had become increasingly centralized in New York and Philadelphia, where most well-known male authors, such as Whittier, Prescott, Longfellow, Lowell, and Hawthorne, had their works distributed. As British reprints of successful authors began to diminish the American bookselling trade, however, famous writers, as well as those women who were trying to break into the market, increasingly turned to magazines to publish their works. As Charvat notes, the burgeoning of magazines created a demand for poetry by which popular poets, including Longfellow and Whittier, were to profit; others, including Julia Ward Howe, Louisa May Alcott, Celia Thaxter, and Helen Hunt Jackson, eventually did as well.[10]

While the standardizing of men's and women's literary works in magazines made publishing successful as a business venture, it also promoted a unified norm of taste and required drastic artistic compromises. Even noteworthy authors had to bow their intentions to the demands of editors at powerful publishing houses. Hawthorne, for instance, came close to ruining his career by catering to his publisher, Ticknor & Fields, when they insisted that he keep turning out new works for his audience.[11] Poe, too, railed against the magazines and newspapers that he believed lessened literature's worth by demanding light and easily digestible reading: "Whatever the talent may be brought to bear upon our daily journals, (and in many cases this talent is very great,) still the imperative necessity of catching, *currente calamo*, each topic as it flits before the eye of the public, must of course materially narrow the limits of their power."[12] Like their male counterparts, women were commercially viable and successful in being published insofar as they adapted to the expectations of the publishing world.

A woman who epitomizes success through submission to publishing constraints is Susannah Rowson. Her *Charlotte Temple* (1791), a seduction novel printed in England before her departure for America, was the most popular novel in America before Scott's historical romances. Rowson's book not only demonstrates her willingness to conform to publishers' expectations but also models the way women's literature would be published later in the nineteenth century. While her *Reuben and Rachel* (1796), a novel set in the era of Columbus on American soil, failed miserably, it is significant that she ventured outside the conventions of the strictly European seduction novel precisely to satisfy the American reading public's newfound taste for historical romance. As Charvat tells us in *The Profession of Authorship in America*, "This readiness to consult the market and adapt to it her literary stock-in-trade, which was didacticism, gives Mrs. Rowson standing as an early American writer of true professional temperament."[13] Although Charvat's comment evinces the dismissal among many critics of women's literature, he correctly surmises that, from the 1790s onward, to be a successful writer, either male or female, meant tailoring literary works to the expectations of the publishing world.

In *Doing Literary Business: American Women Writers in the Nineteenth Century*, Susan Coultrap-McQuin argues that nineteenth-century women writers were among the most widely recognized in America and the most undervalued. By 1830, fully a third of published authors were women; by 1850, female writers accounted for nearly one half of the most popular writers in the nation.[14] Despite their success, women were denied both recognition and authority for their work. Indeed, Coultrap-McQuin takes as her central question their persistence in the face of tremendous obstacles: "How can we explain women's persistence and success as writers in the face of attitudes and behaviors that could render them invisible?" (3). She explains this success in part as a result of their courtly dealings with their "Gentleman Publishers," more resembling a marriage than a professional relationship with their editors. The paternalistic attitude an editor took toward his authors was mutually beneficial and symbiotic: he provided gentlemanly services, including paying bills, performing personal favors, advancing money, and advising on investments, while the author, more often than not, responded with loyalty and trust that ensured a continued commitment to his publishing house. Gentleman Publishers "sought to develop trusting, paternalistic, personal relationships with their authors; they claimed to have personal goals beyond commercial ones to advance culture and/or to provide a public service; and they assumed the role of moral guardian for their society" (34). Undoubtedly, part of the implied rationale for an editor's fatherly behavior toward women was that he acted as a buffer between the hard financial realities of the publishing world and their delicate sensibilities, but his prevalence in all aspects of the author's life did not lessen (and perhaps even affirmed) his decision-making power and role as arbiter of taste. Female writers found their cordial and supportive relationship with editors willing to publish their work both a boon and a burden: they gained a wide audience and could earn their living as writers but only by submitting their poetry to editors' dictates and conforming to a docile and agreeable public image.

Known primarily as Poe's vindictive literary executor, Rufus Griswold set the terms by which women's verse was described in the 1848 preface to his well-known anthology, *The Female Poets of America*. When we consider that Griswold's volume was widely distributed and very influential, his preface reveals several dominant ideas about women's writing in this era. He denigrates the intellectual value of women's poetry by contending that it relies heavily on an expression of the emotions. Because he believes that feeling is all-important in women's poetry, he correspondingly gives less credence to their intellect: "It is less easy to be assured of the genuineness of literary ability in women than in men."[15] Alluding to the unspent feelings that he believes underlie women's poetry, he further claims that the "finest and richest development" of the moral rectitude that was considered most developed in women might reflect "some of the qualities of genius" (7).

Griswold implies that women who are fully occupied with a loving family have no need to write poetry. He alludes to the unspent emotions of their poems, as if they exhibit a kind of debased Wordsworthianism: they betray "a soul rapt into sympathy with a purer beauty and a higher truth than earth and space exhibit," which is revealed to be only "the natural cravings of affections, undefined and wandering" (7). Thus their actual philosophical pondering can easily be confused with the nostalgia and sentiment of women's writing, which may be the product of women who have squandered their time and energies on poetry instead of keeping their homes: "We are in danger, therefore, of mistaking for the efflorescent energy of creative intelligence, that which is only the exuberance of personal 'feelings unemployed.' We may confound the vivid dreamings of an unsatisfied heart, with the aspirations of a mind impatient of the fetters of time, and matter, and mortality" (7).

Griswold claims that female writers, whose works center on the home and family, are purveyors of virtue and serve an important function in preserving culture in the midst of an ever more demanding male business world. Women of the middle class were expected to raise children and run their households; in turn, editors and critics confirmed the prevalent ideology concerning women's domestic lives, praising them as pious teachers and bastions of values. In keeping with this attitude, Griswold remarks that the influence of women's innately moral quality "never is exerted but for good" in the culture at large (8). Women's outpourings, which he claims are characterized by "the infusion of our domestic spirit," will temper the developing national "school of art" into a state of "civil refinement" (8). He writes:

It has been suggested by foreign critics, that our citizens are too much devoted to business and politics to feel interest in pursuits which adorn but do not profit, and which beautify existence but do not consolidate power: feminine genius is perhaps destined to retrieve our public character in this respect, and our shores may yet be far resplendent with a temple of art which, while it is a glory of our land, may be a monument to the honor of the sex. (8)

In contending that women's literary activities compensate for the business ideology of men, Griswold also proposes the conservative ideals that enshrine woman as a moral exemplar and household ornament. In addition, the subtly sexualized language—the "temple of art" on "our shores" may invoke the *mons veneris*—pervades the description of women's poetry by editors. Finally, Griswold's desire to commend a woman's art for the "honor of the sex" only keeps her absent from any real power—on an idealized pedestal, in the home, and firmly in her place.

If Griswold expresses a view typical among male editors of this period, Caroline May is an example of a woman who expresses the same condescending, patriarchal attitudes toward women's poems. In her 1848 preface to *The American Female Poets*, she comments on the profusion of women's poems in newspapers and bound volumes, contending that "poetry, which is the language of affections, has been freely employed among us to express the emotions of a woman's heart."[16] She remarks that women's poetry has been underrated because of its popularity, leading many Americans to value the works of women in other countries over native female authors. "As the rare exotic," she notes,

costly because of the distance from which it is brought, will often suffer in comparison of beauty and fragrance with the abundant wild flowers of our meadows and woodland slopes, so the reader of our present volume, if ruled by an honest taste, will discover in the effusions of our gifted country-women as much grace of form, and powerful sweetness of thought and feeling, as in the blossoms of woman's genius culled from other lands. (vi)

As the comparison between American women's poems and "the abundant wild flowers of our meadows and woodland slopes" suggests, women's lyrics were often figured as flowers in a "fertile garden of literature" (vi), which emphasizes both the decorative and the spontaneous nature of their poetry. Furthermore, May's characterization of women's poems as "effusions" suggests an outpouring of emotions or spirit, a commonly accepted notion, given women's supposedly more intensely emotional natures, and it recalls the attar or perfume to which their poetry was often compared. Critics contended that women's feelings needed to be pressed out, often through personal trials and suffering, before they were incorporated in poetry; Griswold concludes about Lydia Sigourney, a popular infant elegist and author of books of etiquette and advice for women: "it is only because the flower has not been crushed that we have not a richer perfume" (93).

The very number of women's poems was also used to denigrate their achievements. In 1874, an anonymous reviewer of Stoddard's new edition of Griswold's anthology writes that seventeenth- and eighteenth-century female poets are less experimental and less prolific than women in the nineteenth century. The reviewer, who is probably a man, bases this assumption on the fewer poems extant by women poets from the two previous centuries. According to the reviewer, the smaller output of poets like Bradstreet and Wheatley proves that the female sex was at that time more "sure of its place" and more true to its duties, implying that women who published forsook their proper roles as wives and mothers.[17] Although he admits that the increase in nineteenth-century American women's writing might stem from "the increase of general intelligence" or "the genius of women," he concludes that their prolificacy probably also signals a "special restlessness . . . their part of modern discontent that wreaks itself in numbers" (120), an allusion perhaps to the first protests for women's suffrage. Clearly, this reviewer seeks not only to belittle women's literary achievement, but also to turn their productivity against them.

According to the same reviewer, the (usually male) editor's task is to weed out good from bad poems by women:

To no one else is vouchsafed the fearful vision of pyramids of portfolios asking monthly inspection, and reams of waste paper attesting the censor's wrath and justice. By the side of this garland of the accepted and approved, an anthology of the rejected— may no one be indiscreet enough to cull it!—would complete a curious commentary on the position and wants of women in our republic of letters. (120)

Like a righteous Calvinist God, the editor exercises justice over the wicked: he dominates with "wrath and justice" over "pyramids of portfolios" in order to separate the chaff of bad poetry from the few pure grains. Indeed, "indiscreet" hints that women's failures were tantamount to mishaps too embarrassing, or perhaps too revealing, to be made public. Although "republic of letters" emphasizes the supposed democracy of the literary marketplace, this reviewer would perhaps prefer an aristocracy of letters and positions himself at the top of the literary pyramid. Editors clearly felt the weight of the more cultured, older, British literary tradition bearing down on their fledgling authors and so claimed that nature had a special role in encouraging great literature. Since women were so often reduced to their bodily nature, they were thought to have a peculiar alliance with the feminized earth. In his preface to *The Female Poets of America* (1848), for example, Griswold comments on the numerous submissions of American women to magazines, which he claims develop from a majestically endowed landscape rather than a rich culture or individual talent: "In the absence from us of those great visible and formal institutions by which Europe has been educated, it seems as if Nature had designed that resources of her own providing should guide us onward to the maturity of civil refinement" (8). In ascribing to women the power to guide others toward the "maturity of civil refinement," he bolsters the idea that female verse was spontaneous and natural, and he makes the individual woman writer responsible for her entire sex's advancement.

In his 1836 review of Sigourney's *Zinzendorff, and Other Poems*, Poe joins a chorus of male editors and critics in condemning a productive woman poet. Lydia Huntley Sigourney has a reputation as a great writer solely because she is popular with the reading public, "their names *being equally in the mouths of the people*."[18] The sheer number of her published poems creates a reputation for her where none should rightfully exist:

We know it to be possible that another writer of very moderate powers may build up for himself, little by little, a reputation equally great—and, this too, merely by keeping continually in the eye, or by appealing continually with little things, to the ear, of that great, overgrown, and majestical gander, the critical and biographical rabble. (123)

Popular writers like Sigourney were considered seductresses, since they made themselves visible to the male "majestical gander." In contrast to those who have "written a great work" and "by this single effort . . . attained a certain quantum of reputation" (123), a moderately talented writer can earn an equally large reputation by submitting a large number of poems "little by little" to periodicals. Indeed, their power is enhanced according to Poe by their being "continually in the eye" of the public, much like a prostitute who exposes herself to the glance of an inquiring client or whispers invitations. Not only do these less talented writers keep "continually in the eye," but they also appeal "continually with little things, to the ear," as if they secured the attention of the public with a catchy phrase. By describing Sigourney as if she were both cheating the public and prostituting herself, he reduces women's poetry to their duplicitous nature or body.

Editors demanded the pious and morally uplifting content of women's poetry to be mirrored in a smooth and untroubled meter. In 1852, an anonymous reviewer of Alice Cary's *Lyra and Other Poems* praised her verses for their metrical correctness and their sensitivity. In claiming that women poets expressed their emotions naturally and spontaneously, critics considered their best poems to be those in which the meter is correct and which appear to issue without forethought; conversely, they disparaged metrical innovations in women's verse, claiming that they gave the impression of laborious effort. Hence, the reviewer of Cary's book objects to its title poem because it "is too curiously wrought for the subject; it seems more like an experiment in poetry, than the sincere outpouring of grief."[19]

Between 1820 and 1885, editors often characterized women's verse as more affective, "natural," and unpremeditated than men's, and their portrait of women as unconscious wellsprings of emotion is amply represented by reviews of women's poetry.[20] In an anonymous 1871 review of Helen Hunt Jackson's *Verses* (1870) in *The Nation*, for example, a critic wonders if the poetry's harshness might come from Jackson's "seeming more intellectual" than she is and sums up the effect of her compact and realistic verse with an analogy that makes the critic a voyeur: "the feeling is clothed in a somewhat enigmatic form, and one finds it almost laborious to unclothe it and discover it."[21] The reviewer complains about the poetry's complexity as if he would prefer the whore to wear less. We can see that some nineteenth-century editors took the association between a woman's book and body to its extreme in equating publishing her poems with giving them a physical existence and implying that her thoughts needed to be clothed in proper language.

Nineteenth-century editors used childbearing metaphors to describe their control over the appearance of both anonymous verse and women's poems. This language of paternity or "legitimation," as I have termed it, has a double meaning: it signifies both that the critic promotes a poem as if he were conferring a secure identity on an illegitimate child and that he gives the poem his approval or authorization. In contrast, women claimed no corresponding maternity for their works. Although their seventeenth-century ancestress, Anne Bradstreet, wittily imaged her book in her dedicatory sonnet as a bastard child about to enter the world, nineteenth-century women poets figured their verses predominantly as "effusions," bodiless spirits that were the product of a momentary fancy or passing emotion for which they asked ample patience from the reader. To some degree, women perpetuated the stereotypical language of mindless, disembodied thought in their prefaces. Yet male editors continued to claim paternity (or, in Poe's case, assumed paternity) for women's literary works as a means of gaining the upper hand in print.

In his 1845 review of *The Waif*, a collection of poetry by unnamed authors edited by Longfellow, Poe aptly figures the poet who has plagiarized as a betrayed husband who has been duped into believing that his wife's child is his own. Even the title of Longfellow's collection (from which Poe is omitted) summons up the common convention that anonymous poems were like orphaned children, sent out into the world without benefit of name or parentage. Borrowed thoughts resemble a child who, once exposed to public scrutiny, is revealed to be another man's, much to the astonishment of its nominal father:

But, in either view, he thoroughly feels [his thought] as *his own*—and this feeling is counteracted only by the sensible presence of its true, palpable origin in the volume from which he has derived it—an origin which, in the long lapse of years it is almost impossible *not* to forget—for in the mean time the thought itself is forgotten. But the frailest association will regenerate it—it springs up with all the vigor of a new birth— its absolute originality is not even a matter of suspicion—and when the poet has written it and printed it, and on its account is charged with plagiarism, there will be no one in the world more astounded than himself.[22]

Much as a duped father may be the last to realize that his wife's child is not his own, a poet who has unwittingly absorbed and repeated the words of another author in his own work may find himself suddenly under siege, so that "there will be no one in the world more astounded than himself" at the charges of literary thievery. Concluding his remarks with a defensive strategy, he claims that artistic originality is always in question, adding defensively that "all literary history demonstrates that, for the most frequent and palpable plagiarisms, we must search the works of the most eminent poets" (759). In Poe's convoluted logic, he not only places himself above other authors, but he portrays himself as the victim at the hands of an unruly woman.

Editor John Keese, in his 1843 preface to Elizabeth Oakes Smith's *The Sinless Child*, reinforces the image that women's poetic efforts are unskilled, extemporaneous, and require an editor's approval. The title of Smith's popular long poem describes the child heroine, Eva, whose father has died and who lives out her short life in her mother's care. In presenting Smith's book as if he were taking on an almost generative role, Keese seeks to combine his duties as a publisher—a figure he believes others perceive as a mere businessman, pandering to the demands of the marketplace—with the more respected "editorial labours" of the "literary fraternity."[23] Clearly, even the phrase "literary fraternity" shows that male critics dominated the literary establishment. Keese criticizes the belief that the publisher has a purely "mechanical" role in printing and distributing verse, much as man might be said to have a purely "automatic" function in reproduction. "And why, indeed," he wonders, it may be observed in passing, should not a bookseller aim at being something more than the mechanical salesman of printed paper! Are *his* pursuits, of all others, the most hostile to literary culture? Is he presumed to exercise neither judgment nor taste in furthering the ends of trade; presumed to buy and sell only according to the existing demands of the literary market; while even the enterprise of the haberdasher is denied him, in anticipating the call for an article and introducing it to "the season." (viii)

Unlike a "mechanical salesman of printed paper," an editor must be a person with "judgment" and "taste" who uses his merchandising to form the taste of his readership. In contrast to a mere supplier of goods, the bookseller will decide which literature will be distributed, creating a demand for the product he supplies to the market, much as a "haberdasher" who anticipates "the call for an article" indirectly determines what will be sold that season. By arguing that booksellers should exert the power of taste and set the "fashion" in women's writing, Keese invokes the image of women readers and writers as fashion plates while underscoring the real effect that publishers and merchants had in creating a national demand for sentimental women's writing.

Keese wishes not only to exercise his taste, but also to appropriate the creative role of author. He defends his dual role as harbinger of taste and editor of the text:

Surely, in this country, at least, no pursuit is thus conducted [which allows the bookseller to exercise taste in publishing and distribution]; for which on the one side, the producer is constantly obliged to act as his own factor; on the other, whether it be the staple of cotton, or the fabrication of pin-heads, every intelligent dealer makes himself more or less familiar with the processes of nature or of art, in the production of the article. In fact, whether the "operation," be in wheat or tobacco, in books or burlaps, it is this exercise of his own intelligence, which alone gives soul to enterprise, and distinguishes the energy of the operator from that of a mill-horse or steam-engine. (viii–ix)

Like the editor, the bookseller should both distribute goods and know how they are produced. On the one hand, Keese contends that the "producer" must be his own "factor"—literally, a commission-merchant, one who buys and sells for another person. On the other hand, he distinguishes his role as an agent for the author's literary productions from his involvement in the methods of production. Not only is "every intelligent dealer" the source of his own publicity and distribution of his goods, but he also "makes himself, more or less familiar with the processes of nature or of art, in the production of the article," exercising his "intelligence" in order to give "soul" to his enterprise.

For Keese, the publisher animates the literary enterprise, thus mimicking the role of a physician or midwife who delivers a baby. He uses two more sets of oppositions. In the first, he contrasts organic life with manufactured goods—"whether [the production] be the staple of cotton, or the fabrication of pin-heads . . . whether the 'operation,' be in wheat or tobacco, in books or burlaps"—claiming that production of either natural or man-made goods requires the dealer's intervention. In the second, he prefers "intelligence, which alone gives soul to enterprise," to the raw "energy" of an unthinking animal or machine. "Intelligent" recalls the distinction editors frequently made between a male author's or critic's reputedly superior intellect and a female author's spontaneous, affective creativity. In aligning his role with that of a soul-giver, he claims that he can animate the processes of production. In making himself into an intelligent creator who can embody women's writing in print, he reenforces the terms by which women's verse was judged throughout the nineteenth century.

In concluding, Keese endorses *The Sinless Child* by publishing it under his auspices. He distances himself from any part in the poem's first appearance, for he does not wish to trespass on the work of another editor:

The writer of this, cannot claim to have been among the first to welcome the advent of a fresh and original poem, whose inspiration seems drawn from the purest well-springs of thought and fancy; nay, as already hinted, he admits that it was only the frequent demand for the work at his publishing office, under the presumption that it had already assumed the form of a book, which induced him, in the first instance, to procure a copy, and make a personal examination of its beauties. He *does* claim, however, that in the many months which have passed away since that first perusal, no effort has been spared, upon his part, to have it brought before the public in a fitting shape. (xi–xii)

In contrast to his earlier remarks that a bookseller might exert his own taste rather than respond only to the wishes of his customers, Keese states that the already "frequent demand for the work at his publishing office" first drew his attention to it, adding carefully that "it had already assumed the form of a book" when he first "procure[d] a copy, and ma[de] a personal examination of its beauties." He treats with much more care the feelings of the other editor than of the author herself, even though he states at the beginning of the essay that the reason for "'defining his position'" as editor is to explain his almost familial role in "the existing literary fashion of one friend editing the works of another, who still lives to write" (vii).

In Keese's presentation of Smith's book, we see the extreme lengths to which an editor would go in legitimating women's poetry. Giving a "fitting shape" to a book of poems not only alters the poet's work to conform to current literary standards, but it also authorizes them before they undergo public scrutiny. Following Keese's logic, one might say his attention to the "fitting shape" of women's poetry once again places emphasis on its divergence from the expected aspects of their writing—on form rather than content, analysis rather than synthesis, idea rather than feeling. He tries to keep a rigorous standard for his own work, as he does for the women writers whose works he edits:

The hesitation and diffidence of the party chiefly interested in such a step, will be appreciated and understood by those who, living by their daily literary toil, and often giving their name to the public, with some hasty effusion, designed to meet the immediate call upon their pen, still preserve a high intellectual standard within their own minds, and distrust their best productions when put forth as the consummate effort of their literary powers. (xii)

Unlike women writers, who supposedly dash off spontaneous lyrics, Keese and other editors are at risk of producing "some hasty effusion," since they live by their more workaday "literary toil" and cater to the needs of the marketplace. Dickinson's observation with regard to publishing—"Poverty—be justifying / For so foul a thing"—applies to editors as well as writers (J, 709). Editors and publishers feared ruining their own reputations if they published an immature poem and allowed their "intellectual standard" to be lowered. Keese concludes that "it is with honest and heartfelt gratification therefore, that the writer of these remarks has availed himself of the high privilege of superintending the present volume . . . under *his own name*" (xii; emphasis original) as editor. Almost as if he were conferring a secure identity on "The Sinless Child" herself, Keese puts a stamp of approval on Smith's verse for all "those who love pure poetry and respect womanly feeling" (xii).

Nineteenth-century American women poets turned the image advanced by the publishing world to their advantages. For most, publishing verse based on the everyday experience of domestic life afforded moderate to considerable fame and monetary success. Their poems centered on holy lives, patient trials, and Christian consolation in family life. In her introduction to *The American Female Poets* (1848), May affirms that the work of women writers was considered most fitting when it paid tribute to the home and its pious values: "home, with its quiet joys, its deep pure sympathies, and its secret sorrows, with which a stranger must not intermeddle, is a sphere by no means limited for woman, whose inspiration lies more in her heart than her head. Deep emotions make good foundation for lofty and beautiful thoughts" (vi). As Walker notes, there is an erotic component hinted at in May's "with which a stranger must not intermeddle."[24] Certainly, children's deaths, domestic discord, and abolition acquired erotic overtones in women's poetry and prose. But May's comment also points to the way women's exclusivity concerning private matters stakes out a domestic territory that they wished to make only theirs. Women clung to anonymity and pseudonymity as a way to guarantee privacy. For that reason, many women give little or no actual biographical information about themselves to collections: "To say where they were born seems quite enough while they are alive. Thus, several of our correspondents declared their fancies to be their only facts; others that they had done nothing all their lives; and some,—with a modesty most extreme—that they had not lived at all" (viii).

May's description of women writers' responses to questions about their lives could be a summary of Dickinson's own modest speakers, whose self-effacing poses she undermines, as in the following lyric:

> I'm Nobody! Who are you?
> Are you—Nobody—too?
> Then there's a pair of us!
> Don't tell! they'd banish us—you know!
>
> How dreary—to be—Somebody!
> How public—like a Frog—
> To tell your name—the livelong June—
> To an admiring Bog!
>
> (J, 288)

4. banish us] *advertise*   7. your] *one's*

Far from belittling herself, the speaker of this lyric heightens her importance by calling attention to herself and conspiring with the reader as an accomplice. As Alicia Suskin Ostriker has noted, this lyric reveals Dickinson's "duplicitous" stance: the poem "means both what it says and its opposite . . . contrary meanings coexist with equal force, because they have equal force within the poet."[25] Far from simply mocking the desire to be "Somebody," the speaker deliberately differentiates and thereby calls attention to herself as a "Nobody." Furthermore, she subtly resists the meek image of nineteenth-century American women. "Nobody" accepts anonymity, yet literally lacks a physical self—no body—the opposite of the critics' contention that women were closely aligned with the body. The variant reading to "advertise" sounds dreadful to a speaker who resists publication and perhaps fears being overrun with admirers, yet "They'd banish us" suggests the alternative is even more dire (especially when one considers the possible echo of Hal's promise to "banish" Falstaff in Shakespeare's *Henry IV*, I [II.iv.456]). Nobody more boldly compares being "Somebody" to repeating one's name ad infinitum, "like a Frog," to a crowd of dull-witted flatterers, "an admiring Bog." This lyric makes anonymity a prize, shared with another, thus solidifying the speaker's relationship to the reader and rejecting the notoriety that publication could bring. The speaker embodies the duplicitous nature of women, especially writers, who demurely hid behind the shelter of initials or anonymity but widely distributed their work.

Given the critical climate in which women poets wrote, it is not surprising that they often took a publicly self-effacing attitude toward their own careers. Since the era of Bradstreet, the widespread belief that women's intellect was inferior to men's had engendered a tradition of male authentication and legitimation in the presentation of American women's verse. Thus, Bradstreet's book of poems is preceded by letters and tributes by prominent male friends, attesting to her literary talent. Black women writers endured an even more extreme authentication, as their very identity as human beings, much less as poets, was in question. Published in 1783, more than a century after Bradstreet's book, Phillis Wheatley's *Poems On Various Subjects, Religious and Moral* contains a letter by her former master attesting to her education, which made her writing credible to the public. By the nineteenth century, such legitimizing gestures had become thoroughly embedded in the editorial discourse surrounding women's poetry. Women writers in this period continued to ask the public to be tolerant in reading their poems, expressing shock and embarrassment that their verse was subject to public scrutiny, and often foregrounding the unpremeditated nature of their writing. "They have sprung up like wild flowers in the dells, or among the clefts of the rock; wherever the path of life has chanced to lead," writes Sigourney in the preface to her 1834 *Poems*.[26] She blames the short and fragmentary nature of her lyrics on pressing domestic cares:

Some of the poems contained in the present collection were written at an early age. Others interspersed themselves, at later periods, amid domestic occupations or maternal cares. The greater part were suggested by passing occasions, and partake of the nature of extemporaneous productions. All reveal, by their brevity, the narrow intervals of time which were devoted to their composition. (v)

Sigourney's claim that most of her poems are "extemporaneous productions" and her contention that their "brevity" reveals "the narrow intervals of time" in which they were written suggest to the reader that her poems are designed to commemorate the passing moment, that they are the work of an amateur rather than a professional poet. Perhaps Sigourney's tendency was to compose quickly, yet the large and ornate study she had built for herself from the profits of her poems' publication suggests an attention at least to the outward signs of her position as an established writer. Her self-effacing attitude in print contrasts strongly with the actual circumstances of her professional life and suggests that such a mode of self-presentation had become largely a posture for women writers of the day.

Women writers frequently attest to the private nature of their verses, even when they publish them. Helen Hunt Jackson compares her poetry to flowers thoughtlessly strewn about by children in the dedicatory sonnet to her 1875 *Verses*:

> When children in the summer weather play,
> Flitting like birds through sun and wind and rain,
> From road to field, from field to road again,
> Pathetic reckoning of each mile they stray

They leave in flowers forgotten by the way;
Forgotten, dying, but not all in vain,
Since, finding them, with tender smiles, half pain,
Half joy, we sigh, "Some child passed here to-day."
Dear one,—whose name I name not lest some tongue
Pronounce it roughly,—like a little child
Tired out at noon, I left my flowers among
The wayside things. I know how thou hast smiled,
And that the thought of them will always be
One more sweet secret thing 'twixt thee and me.[27]

In likening the composition of her poems to the "pathetic reckoning" of the flowers that children have carelessly strewn about, she reflects the common myth that women's versifying was thoughtless and unpremeditated. These discarded flowers, which we confront "with tender smiles, half pain, / Half joy," evoke our sense of pity and regret at the loss of childhood. Jackson then compares the appearance of her poems to this same half-careless, half-pitiful scattering, implying that she created her verses in a similarly unreflective way: she has "left [her] flowers among / The wayside things." Jackson's analogy between the children's wavering path and her own circuitous method of writing reinforces the common view that women's poems were accidents of the moment. Moreover, her disparaging remarks typify women's habit of apologizing for the fragmentary and unplanned nature of their poems. Because the code of privacy prevented women from naming others in public, Jackson refuses to identify the person to whom she dedicates her book, "whose name I name not lest some tongue / Pronounce it roughly." In fact, leaving her "flowers among / The wayside things" might refer elliptically to a sexual relationship. Not only does this person share an intimacy with the author, for she hints that he or she "hast smiled" and that this remembrance will be "one more sweet secret thing" between them, but only she and her lover share knowledge of what prompted the writing of her poems—a knowledge that affirms their secret bond. Jackson's poem describes her verses as private transmissions between a woman and her lover in keeping with the popular ethic of privacy.

As we have seen, Dickinson came of age as a poet in an era that relegated women's literary endeavors to the private and personal, even when they found their way into published form. The frequent anonymity and pseudonymity of female poets, as well as their commonly perceived status as dilettantes and amateur artists, drove them to exploit another popular venue: the literary portfolio. Like an artist's sketches, which could be worked up and revised as finished products, literary "sketches," fragments, vignettes, and other pieces not meant for publication were contained in these portfolios. In an 1840 review-essay, "New Poetry," Ralph Waldo Emerson recognized its essentially private and unfinished nature:

Is there not room then for a new department in poetry, namely, *Verses of the Portfolio*? We have fancied that we drew greater pleasure from some manuscript verses than from printed ones of equal talent. For there was herein the charm of character; they were confessions; and the faults, the imperfect parts, the fragmentary verses, the halting rhymes, had a worth beyond that of high finish; for they testified that the writer was more man than artist, more earnest than vain; that the thought was too sweet and sacred to him, than that he should suffer his ears to hear or his eyes to see a superficial defect in the expression.[28]

Emerson's essay concludes his discussion of this "new department" with William Ellery Channing's "Boat Song," yet his comments pertain to women's poetry as well. Although initiated by Washington Irving's *The Sketch Book* in 1820, the portfolio tradition takes on a distinctly feminine cast by mid-century with best sellers such as Sarah Parton's *Fern Leaves from Fanny's Portfolio* (1853). Emerson praises the "charm" and "sweet" nature of these "confessions," adopting a sentimental and feminized rhetoric and evoking the common portrait of women's writing as artless and private. For Emerson, the privacy and unfinished nature of writing stems from his belief that publication is a violation of the soul, an ethic held by many of the transcendentalists, including Dickinson, Thoreau, and other forgotten authors, like Charles Lane. The elevation of fragments over finished work, a popular trend among the Romantics, advocates the modest strains of amateur poets, like Channing, who rise above the desire to publish and so stay true to their original conception, over the "high finish" of the consummate literary professional. Although he claims the fragmentary nature of these lyrics testifies that "the writer was more man than artist," he jokingly contends that these writers believe themselves to be minor divinities, too rarefied to broadcast in print an imperfect expression of their exemplary relation to God.

Both their dilettante status and their presumed relation to the divine made the portfolio an apt genre for women writers. The idea that verse should remain private, a convention that kept genteel women from publishing in the newspapers and journals, paradoxically freed women to make themselves known through circulating their manuscripts. Perhaps it is this ethic of privacy among the transcendentalists that encouraged Emerson to praise the portfolio tradition when he writes that "we should be loath to see the wholesome conventions, to which we have alluded, broken down by a general incontinence of publication, and every man's and woman's diary flying into the bookstores, yet it is to be considered, on the other hand, that men of genius are often more incapable than others of that elaborate execution which criticism exacts" (*E&L*, 1170–71). Indeed, Emerson remarks in his preface that *Parnassus* had its origin as a type of journal or blank book for his favorite readings: "This volume took its origin from an old habit of copying any poem or lines that interested me into a blank book."[29] Even at the time Emerson was writing, in mid-nineteenth-century

America, "incontinence" connoted a lack of self-restraint, particularly in sexual relations. Although he makes no distinction between the sexes when he remarks that "every man's and woman's diary" goes "flying into the bookstores," he reserves for "men of genius" the right to produce works that may not meet the critical standards of the day. On the other hand, women were encouraged to be publicly silent and blamed for publishing, almost as if they had broken sexual mores.

Moreover, the portfolio tradition spawned numerous collections of anonymous verse, which reinforced the prominent genteel convention that authorship should not be acknowledged to the general public. Guessing the names of well known authors was a common parlor game. The popularity of these literary endeavors attests to the public's enjoyment in subverting the decorum of the publishing world by guessing the identities of the authors. Helen Hunt Jackson encouraged her friend and correspondent Dickinson in 1878 to submit the poem beginning "Success is counted sweetest" to *A Masque of Poets*, one of the popular "No-Name Series" of anonymous literary productions, to which Jackson was herself a contributor. Significantly, more than one reviewer of the collection mistakenly attributed Dickinson's poem to Emerson, an error that the series editor, Thomas Niles, observes in a letter to the poet: "You were entitled to a copy of 'A Masque of Poets' without thanks, for your valuable contribution which for want of a known sponsor Mr Emerson has generally had to father" (*Letters* 2, 626). Not only did Emerson exert a profound influence on the thought and form of Dickinson's work, as Niles's remark suggests, but the literary world also sought to ascribe a "paternity" to women's poems. In his other interchanges with Dickinson, Niles obviously values his reputation as a "Gentleman Publisher" over commercial success. In answering her query about Cross's biography of George Eliot, Niles notes that "'H.H.' once old me that she wished you could be induced to publish a volume of poems"; politely refusing to insist, however, he demurely adds, "I should not want to say how highly she praised them, but to such an extent that I wish also that you could" (*Letters* 2, 726). In 1883, after again inquiring about Cross's biography of Eliot, Dickinson received a letter from Niles admitting that there were rumors Cross was still at work, and shortly afterwards, a copy of Mathilde Blind's *Life of George Eliot*, just recently published by Roberts Brothers, arrived. In response, the poet sent him her copy of the Brontë sisters' poems, possibly to suggest that they would prove worthy of biography as well. Nevertheless, Niles returned the "precious volume," apparently without understanding its implication, and added: "I will take instead a M.S. collection of your poems, that is, if you want to give them to the world through the medium of a publisher" (*Letters* 3, 769).

In the preface to Dickinson's posthumously published *Poems* (1902), Thomas Wentworth Higginson places her squarely in this tradition of dilettante writers when he claims that her poems "belong emphatically to what Emerson long since called 'the Poetry of the Portfolio,'—something produced absolutely without the thought of publication, and solely by way of expression of the writer's own mind."[30] Although Higginson recognizes her originality, he put her unconventional poems into print apologetically, as if their unfinished surface reflected on him:

Such verse must inevitably forfeit whatever advantage lies in the discipline of public criticism and the enforced conformity to accepted ways. On the other hand, it may often gain something through the habit of freedom and the unconventional utterance of daring thoughts. In the case of the present author, there was absolutely no choice in the matter; she must write thus, or not at all. (iii)

Not subject to "the discipline of public criticism" and its "enforced conformity," Dickinson rejected poetic conventions in a way that seems to us motivated by an inner vision akin to Emerson's poet-scholar's obstinacy. Even though Higginson acknowledges the benefit one could derive by standing above more mediocre expression, such irregularities cast doubt for him on her ability as a poet. In his memories of the poet, he recalls her almost as a mythical being, beyond the realm of human comprehension: "I saw her but twice face to face, and brought away the impression of something as unique and remote as Undine or Mignon or Thekla" (v). He alludes to the seemingly rough and unfinished nature of her poems and to their metrical irregularity when he observes that they have "flashes of wholly original and profound insight into nature and life; words and phrases exhibiting an extraordinary vividness of descriptive and imaginative power, yet often set in a seemingly whimsical or even rugged frame" (v). Recalling Emerson's remark in "Self-Reliance" that "I would write on the lintels of the door-post, *Whim*," rather than "spend the day in explanation" (*E&L*, 262), "whimsical" belies the deliberate, artful, and self-possessed nature of her poetry. Rather than attribute her poems to "self-reliance," Higginson adopts the discourse surrounding women's poetry and likens them to flowers: "In many cases these verses will seem to the reader like poetry torn up by the roots, with rain and dew still clinging to them, giving a freshness and a fragrance not otherwise to be conveyed" (v–vi). Staunchly accepting the criteria by which women's verse was judged in this era, Higginson was predisposed to rate Dickinson's poems as too delicate and perhaps even abnormal to endorse their publication wholeheartedly.

To be sure, Higginson recalls criticizing her verse from a perspective common among nineteenth-century American editors, and his remarks about the poet reveal that he viewed her initially very much in the tradition of other women poets when he tried to make her conform to publishing standards. In his essay, "Emily Dickinson" (1901), he writes that she differed from the normative standards of punctuation by using "chiefly dashes," noting that "it has been thought better, in printing these letters, as with her poems, to give them the benefit in this respect of the ordinary usages."[31] Contemporary critical reflections on Dickinson's verse that attend to the placement of words on the page, punctuation, and the like have suggested how fully she relied on handwriting with its calligraphic flourishes and excesses as a means to convey her poetic intentions. As Susan Howe reminds us, "Poetry is never a personal possession. The text was a vision and gesture before it became sign and coded exchange in a political economy of value."[32] Higginson characterizes Dickinson's handwriting as "not in the slightest degree illiterate, but cultivated, quaint, and wholly unique" (250); he notes that her letter "was in a handwriting so peculiar that it seemed as if the writer might have taken her first lessons by studying the famous fossil birdtracks in the museum of that college town" (250). Thus he imagines that she mirrors the print of dead birds in her own idiosyncratic cursive. When we recall that women's poetic speech was frequently thought to resemble birdsong, his remark seems characteristic of the popular conception of women's unpremeditated versifying. Moreover, he describes the irregularity of "her habit as to capitalization, as the printers call it, in which she followed the Old English and present German method of thus distinguishing every noun substantive" (250). Apparently, he did not appreciate that she may have capitalized not only nouns, but also pronouns, adjectives, and prepositions to highlight the elements of her personal mythology. In supervising the 1890 *Poems*, which he edited with Mabel Loomis Todd, Higginson regularized Dickinson's verse by repunctuating it and eliminating capitals except at the beginnings of lines, for he claims that she manifested a "defiance of form" and valued her intent over formal correctness: "she was intent upon her thought, and it would not have satisfied her to make the change" (256). To his credit, he eventually gave up his effort at normalizing her work, even though he did so only because he deemed her to be unrepentent and lost: "she interested me more in her—so to speak—unregenerate condition" (262). Ultimately, as St. Armand has noted, Higginson's "naturalist's eye" predominated over his judgment as editor, almost as if she were one of the stuffed specimens in Amherst College's laboratory.[33] Higginson turned from hunter to observer: "I could only sit still and watch, as one does in the woods; I must name my bird without a gun, as recommended by Emerson" (276).

Dickinson sought to distinguish herself from assertive and perhaps demanding advances made by other women writers. Contemporary accounts of exchanges between women and their editors, as we will see in the following chapters, convey why she was reluctant to associate herself with their tactics. Dickinson was familiar with Henry Wadsworth Longfellow's novel, *Kavanagh* (1849). In writing to his wife shortly after his first visit with Dickinson, Higginson comments: "One day her brother brought home Kavanagh hid it under the piano cover & made signs to her & they read it: her father at last found it & was displeased" (*Letters* 2, 475). A dark, comic novel, *Kavanagh* is a tale of New England village life that portrays an exchange between a "poetess" and her editor that parallels aspects of the Dickinson-Higginson friendship. The character Mr. Churchill, a schoolmaster, represents the writing life and reveals the depth to which each character misinterprets his own calling or the reality of life around him. Like John Marcher, the unenlightened protagonist of Henry James's "The Beast in the Jungle" (1903), whose tragic fate is never to realize his destiny, Churchill yearns to write a romance but is frustrated due to his dreamy, romantic nature and to the demands of personal and professional acquaintances on his time. Intending to compile "a series of papers on Obscure Martyrs,—a kind of tragic history of the unrecorded and life-long sufferings of women, which hitherto had found no historian, save now and then a novelist," he fatally lacks a sense of perspective and overlooks, of course, the native saint of his village, Alice Archer.[34] Having never revealed her love for the minister Kavanagh (the title character) or betrayed her confidence to her bosom friend, Celia, after discovering Celia's love for him, Alice stands as a mute tribute to stoical New England womanhood: "Mr. Churchill never knew, that, while he was exploring the past for records of obscure and unknown martyrs, in his own village, one of that silent sisterhood had passed away into oblivion, unnoticed and unknown" (113–14). Churchill as hagiographer betrays the potent—and often misguided—interest men showed in writing the lives of women who were expected implicitly to exemplify the ideals of motherhood and femininity, as Longfellow dryly notes in the title to one of his character's proposed lyceum lectures: "'What Lady Macbeth Might Have Been, Had Her Energies Been Properly Directed'" (115). The joke is well taken, yet has an ounce of seriousness: had Lady Macbeth or Alice Archer been fulfilling her correct domestic duties, she would have been more successful in her role as woman or wife.

Mr. Churchill's encounter with an amateur versifier, Miss Cartwright, however, suggests the lengths to which women poets might go to see their works in print, in contrast to genteel and demure ladies whose respect for the dictates of "True Womanhood" were paramount. A "damsel sitting in his armchair" when he arrives in his study one afternoon asks for his help in publishing her verses:

"I have come to ask a great favor of you, Mr. Churchill, which I hope you will not deny me. By the advice of some friends, I have collected my poems together,"—and here she drew forth from a paper a large, thin manuscript, bound in crimson velvet,—"and think of publishing them in a volume. Now, would you not do me the favor to look them over, and give me your candid opinion, whether they are worth publishing? I should value your advice so highly!"

This simultaneous appeal to his vanity and gallantry from a fair young girl, standing

on the verge of that broad, dangerous ocean, in which so many have perished, and looking wistfully over its flashing waters to the shores of the green Isle of Palms,—such an
appeal, from such a person, it was impossible for Mr. Churchill to resist. He made,
however, a faint show of resistance,—a feeble grasping after some excuse for refusal,—
and then yielded. He received from Clarissa's delicate, trembling hand the precious volume, and from her eyes a still more precious look of thanks, and then said,—
   "What name do you propose to give the volume?"
   "Symphonies of the Soul, and other Poems," said the young lady; "and, if you like
them, and it would not be asking too much, I should be delighted to have you write a
Preface, to introduce the work to the public. The publisher says it would increase the
sale very considerably." (100–1)

Not only does this encounter satirize the demands male literati, like Longfellow, must have felt female authors made on their time, but it also records for us
an image of the poetess who both assertively pushes her interests among literary professionals and relies on meek femininity to secure her way. Furthermore,
the description of her manuscript and its title—*Symphonies of the Soul, and
Other Poems*—points to the way women's works were received in nineteenth-
century America and the bodiless, spiritual quality thought to be central to their
conception.
   Unlike the fictional Miss Cartwright, Dickinson betrayed neither the requi-
site business acuity nor the self-promotion necessary for commercial success.
Yet the scene in some respects parallels Dickinson's own strategic approach to
Higginson about her verses. Like Miss Cartwright, who flatters her mentor's
vanity and seeks his "candid opinion, whether they are worth publishing"
(100), Dickinson asks Higginson similarly to tell her what is "true" (*Letters* 2,
403). Undoubtedly, the "simultaneous appeal to his vanity and his gallantry
from a fair young girl" mixes the desire to act uprightly and the wish to please
the opposite sex, a combination of attitudes at work also in the concluding line
to Dickinson's first letter to Higginson, her "Preceptor": "That you will not betray me—it is needless to ask—since Honor is it's own pawn—" (*Letters* 2,
403). Not only does she rely on the moral rectitude of what Coultrap-McQuin
refers to as a "Christian Gentleman," the moral and intellectual counterpart to
the "True Woman" according to the doctrine of the separate spheres, but she
also assumes that as a gentleman he would sacrifice himself for a lady's benefit, like a pawn in a chess game. Although she was not above deferring to Higginson's advice and deploying genteel feminine behavior in her efforts to secure his attention, she distances herself from the commercialism of her age and
demonstrates her understanding of the limits and advantages of their relationship. Higginson writes that he received four poems with her first letter ["Safe
in their Alabaster Chambers—" (J, 216), "I'll tell you how the Sun rose—" (J,
318), "The nearest Dream recedes—unrealized—" (J, 319), and "We play at
Paste—" (J, 320)]; although his comments reveal that he thought some of her

best poetry tritely sentimental, he later learned to appreciate her originality. He classes the poem beginning "The nearest Dream recedes—unrealized" (J, 319), for example, "among the most exquisite of her productions, with a singular felicity of phrase and an aerial lift that bears the ear upward with the bee it traces" (251):

> The nearest Dream recedes—unrealized—
> The Heaven we chase,
> Like the June Bee—before the School Boy,
> Invites the Race—
> Stoops—to an easy Clover—
> Dips—evades—teases—deploys—
> Then—to the Royal Clouds
> Lifts his light Pinnace—
> Heedless of the Boy—
> Staring—bewildered—at the mocking sky—
>
> Homesick for steadfast Honey—
> Ah, the Bee flies not
> That brews that rare variety!
>
> (J, 319)

The lyric points to the uncertainty of attaining a predestined place in the ever-receding mansion of "Heaven." Like the "June Bee," which heralds the beginning of summer and the end of the school year's confinement, salvation beckons but constantly eludes us, much as the bee rises to "the Royal Clouds" and leaves the boy "Staring—bewildered—at the mocking sky." Whether or not Dickinson intended to show her awareness that Higginson might not understand her poetry, he admits his confusion at her cryptic metaphors and shrewdly recognizes that he might easily substitute for the boy in the poem, who vainly tries to capture a "June bee": "The bee himself did not evade the schoolboy more than she evaded me; and even at this day I still stand somewhat bewildered, like the boy" (252).

If, in her first tentative exchanges with Higginson, Dickinson outwardly adopts a self-effacing demeanor, she also reveals her discomfort with his criticisms of her poetry by evoking the same rhetoric of embodiment and dress that pervades the editorial discourse of the period.[35] Assuming a pose that resembles the posture other women writers took toward their editors, she only tentatively acknowledges authorship of her work in her correspondence with him. He notes that "the most curious thing about the [first] letter [that he received from her] was the total absence of a signature" (250). Instead, she includes her first and last names, written in pencil, on a separate card in its own envelope and not on the poems she included. Indeed, Dickinson may well have wanted to separate herself as far as possible from her father's and grandfather's New England renown and to establish her own fame. True to his era, however, Higginson sees only the most genteel aspects of a woman's modesty, rather than the strategy of a professional author at work: "The shy writer wished to recede as far as possible from view" (251).

Dickinson viewed Higginson's criticisms almost as if they incised her body, and her response to his request for more poems further suggests her cautious rejection of his criticism. In her first letter to Higginson, she asks him to tell her if her verse is "alive"; "Should you think it breathed—and had you the leisure to tell me, I should feel quick gratitude—" (*Letters* 2, 403). Punning on the word "quick," she implies that if the poem is alive in his estimation, she will be, too. He recalls in his essay that "I remember to have ventured on some criticism which she afterwards called 'surgery,' and on some questions, part of which she evaded, as will be seen, with a naïve skill such as the most experienced and worldly coquette might envy" (253). His metaphor of coquetry invokes the language of prostitution that has underwritten editorial discourse about women's poetry. Such language also demonstrates that he understood that she kept back as much as she told him about her poems, that she taunted him by seeming to defer to his advice while she mocked it.

Moreover, her use of the metaphor of "clothing" in her next letter to Higginson suggests how closely editors and critics associated a woman's body with her poetry. Although she responded to his tentative reproaches by sending more poems, she excuses herself in the letter that accompanied them for not being able to gratify his wish for ones that were more "orderly": "While my thought is undressed—I can make the distinction, but when I put them in the Gown—they look alike, and numb" (*Letters* 2, 404). Dickinson probably refers to dressing her poems for public view, as well as to the regulating effect that the "Gown" of form has on her thought. The importance of that regularizing "Gown" is clear in her next letter to Higginson, to whom she turns for guidance in containing the potentially explosive power of imagination: "I had no Monarch in my life, and cannot rule myself, and when I try to organize— my little Force explodes—and leaves me bare and charred—" (*Letters* 2, 414). Adopting the rhetoric of dress that proliferated in the editorial discourse surrounding women's verse of this period, she rejects the more normative sensibility that Higginson unsuccessfully tried to instill in her. Her remark also might serve as a preconceived response to a critic whose contemporaries, as we have seen, imagined that women's poetry was embodied in print and "clothed" in a regular, smooth-sounding meter.

Her next few letters to Higginson continue to stress the necessity of her poetic form, even as she maintains a conventionally submissive attitude toward him. He might have suggested, as St. Armand postulates, that she instead attempt prose fiction, like the popular sensation writer Harriet Prescott

Spofford,[36] whom Dickinson admired, since in her third letter the poet thanks Higginson for his honest criticisms and replies with a courteous but definitive refusal: "Your first—gave no dishonor, because the True—are not ashamed—I thanked you for your justice—but could not drop the Bells whose jingling cooled my Tramp—" (*Letters* 2, 408). Whether she actually anticipated his suggestion that she "delay 'to publish'" or made up her mind shortly after his discouragement, she thenceforward forsook publication as a means to disseminate her work: "I smile when you suggest that I delay 'to publish'—that being foreign to my thought, as Firmament to Fin—If fame belonged to me, I could not escape her—if she did not, the longest day would pass me on the chase—and the approbation of my Dog, would forsake me—then—My Barefoot-Rank is better—" (*Letters* 2, 408). Higginson must also have suggested that her poems lacked metrical regularity, for she punningly noted that she would continue to display her metrical "foot" despite his advice. "Barefoot" carries a range of connotations for Dickinson's speakers: a sanctified soul, a dead body, an innocent child, and, most significantly in terms of "rank," a poor person. Later, she again rejected in mock-fear his criticisms that her meter is irregular, while nevertheless maintaining a mildly self-effacing demeanor: "You think my gait 'spasmodic'—I am in danger—Sir—You think me 'uncontrolled'—I have no Tribunal" (*Letters* 2, 409). Dickinson might well have been derisively classed by Higginson as one of the neoromantic poets of the so-called "Spasmodic School," including Elizabeth Barrett Browning, who yearned toward cosmic themes while they exploited intensity and formlessness. Yet she still asks him for the occasional favor of reading her poetry to see "if I told it clear" and says "'twould be control, to me—" (*Letters* 2, 409). She resisted Higginson's suggestions to revise the form of her poems, while continuing to seek his advice.

In light of Higginson's respectful dismissal of her writing and the popular characterization of women's poetry as private, untutored, and affective, Dickinson's choice not to publish is hardly surprising. Much as the journal gave transcendentalists like Thoreau and Emerson a private forum for ideas and fragmentary sketches, the lyric provided Dickinson an unpublished daybook, an almanac of moods and feelings, that she forever transformed in the exercise of her craft. When she remarks in a letter to Higginson that "My Business is Circumference," she pointedly distances herself from the desire for commercial success and allies herself instead with Emerson, for whom "Circumference" signifies the extensiveness of divinity in his essay, "Circles": "St. Augustine described the nature of God as a circle whose centre was everywhere, and its circumference nowhere" (*E&L*, 403). Reluctant to submit to what she believed were the profiteering motives of publishers, she remarks to Higginson in 1862 that "two Editors of Journals came to my Father's House, this winter—and asked me for my Mind—and when I asked them 'Why,' they said I was penurious—and they, would use it for the World—" (*Letters* 2, 404–5). The editors in question, who may have been Samuel Bowles and Dr. Josiah Gilbert Holland, are characterized as self-righteous, designing men who wanted to profit from the publication of her "Mind." They accuse her of "penury" for not printing her poems for the good of others; she, however, indicts them for greedily wishing her to publish under the guise of charity. To Louise Norcross in 1872, she writes derisively of a woman, probably Elizabeth Stuart Phelps, who requested a similar submission under the banner of feminine "duty": "Of Miss P—I know but this, dear. She wrote me in October, requesting me to aid the world by my chirrup more. Perhaps she stated it as my duty, I don't distinctly remember, and always burn such letters, so I cannot obtain it now. I replied declining. She did not write to me again—she might have been offended, or perhaps is extricating humanity from some hopeless ditch" (*Letters* 2, 500). Unlike many of her counterparts, Dickinson refused to submit to the rigors of the publishing world, and she rejected both the constraints women especially faced and the profiteering of most successful authors, even under the guise of charity.

Although she detached herself from the careerist ambitions of many versifiers, the standard image of the meek and retiring poetess allowed Dickinson to maintain a lifelong friendship from which she could question her "preceptor's" own deeply held beliefs. Higginson might easily have classed her with other nineteenth-century women writers, whose "secret sorrows" were commonly thought to provide the basis for poems on the loss of love and the deferral of a romantic union in life. Dickinson transformed the rhetoric of "secret sorrows" and the common depiction of women's poems as delicate blooms in her poems on female creativity. Hearkening back to the common description of women's verse as flowers and its meaning as a heady perfume, for example, Dickinson transforms "Attar" to describe the way the distillation of everyday experience in poetry, its "Essential Oils," may not be the province of men alone:

> Essential Oils—are wrung—
> The Attar from the Rose
> Be not expressed by Suns—alone—
> It is the gift of Screws—
>
> The General Rose—decay—
> But this—in Lady's Drawer
> Make Summer—When the Lady lie
> In Ceaseless Rosemary—
>
> (J, 675)

In *Emily Dickinson: A Poet's Grammar*, Cristanne Miller contends that Dickinson anticipates metaphors of female creativity in the twentieth century and, through her use of paradoxes and syntactical ambiguity, produces a "multiplicity of meaning and an indeterminate reference, two characteristics that open questions of meaning but frustrate the referential or informative communication most language provides."[37] If we also contend, as does Miller, that "Dickinson plays off the century's widespread conception of woman as the ministering angel in the house and of poet as sensitive, suffering soul" (31), then we can see how Dickinson's linguistic play allows her to question the role of poet as defined by the nineteenth-century publishing establishment. Symbolic of women's beauty and passion, the rose defends a claim to her right to be both woman and poet: the linguistic overtones of "expressed" and the pun on male "Suns" suggest that women as well as men can tap the hidden resources of human suffering. The double method of extracting "Attar" from a rose—through drying under the sun and crushing its petals—amounts to passive and active forms of violence, "the gift of Screws." Given the emphasis early in the poem on the agency of the "Suns" in extracting meaning, "Attar" further redefines the role of the female poet as potent. "General Rose" serves as a type of death and femininity, since it is closely associated with woman's beauty and its transience. Although this "General Rose" decays, the "Attar" subsists and can exude the aura of summer, even after the author's body lies interred in "Ceaseless Rosemary." Indeed, the similarity between the flowers laid away in a drawer and the lady's corpse confined to its coffin conflates the poetry and its author, and these parallel images suggest that lyrics can resurrect and come to substitute for the actual poet, much as Dickinson's own lyrics were rescued from oblivion in her bureau drawer by her sister, Lavinia. Adopting images popular among nineteenth-century critics and writers alike, who were thought to have sprung up like flowers so copiously throughout New England, Dickinson suggests her lyrics can refresh and renew their reader.

Aware of the definition of women's verse pervading the literary marketplace, Dickinson elsewhere defines the role of the poet in a way that distinguishes her from other poets:

> This was a Poet—It is That
> Distills amazing sense
> From ordinary Meanings—
> And Attar so immense
>
> From the familiar species
> That perished by the Door—
> We wonder it was not Ourselves
> Arrested it—before—
>
> Of Pictures, the Discloser—

The Poet—it is He—
Entitles Us—by Contrast—
To ceaseless Poverty—

Of Portion—so unconscious—
The Robbing—could not harm—
Himself—to Him—a Fortune—
Exterior—to Time—

(J, 448)

The impersonal phrasing of the first line ("This" and "It is That") and the characterization of the poet as male deliberately set Dickinson at arm's length from the popular nineteenth-century definition of the poet. The poet distills "amazing sense" and "Attar" from "the familiar species / That perished by the Door," rather than the courtly rose or other effete plant. Like Roger Chillingworth in Nathaniel Hawthorne's *The Scarlet Letter* (1850), who states, "my old studies in alchemy . . . and my sojourn, for above a year past, among a people well versed in the kindly properties of simples, have made a better physician of me than many that claim the medical degree," the speaker could claim specialized knowledge of herbs and plants others ignore.[38] Not only Indians, of course, were familiar with the medicinal properties of wildflowers and other plants, but women also acquired knowledge about plants through folklore and other women. The poet's talent lies in "arresting" the meaning of such trivial and everyday pursuits, and the result paradoxically "entitles" us to "ceaseless Poverty," as if the poet reminded us consistently of our own deprivation. The syntactical ambiguity and inversions of the last two stanzas raise the possibility that the poet's talent is inner-directed, a sentiment shared by other transcendentalists. If we take "to Him" to modify "Portion," then the poet's talent seems central to the stanza, but if "to Him" modifies "Himself," then the poet becomes himself a "Fortune" who is "Exterior—to Time—." The radical lack of self-awareness imbedded in this final possibility supports the supposed "unconscious" nature of much women's poetry. Rather than merely subscribe to the belief that women's poetry issued freely and spontaneously, however, Dickinson contends that the poet's talent exists outside the cult of personality so popular in the nineteenth century, outside of history, and even outside of time itself.

Given the emphasis on women's appearances in nineteenth-century America, Dickinson also undoubtedly recognized the powerful symbolism of the white gown she habitually wore for the last twenty years of her life. Dress signified such basic facts as social rank and occupation; it also indicated whether the family had recently experienced a death and signified the mourner's relation to the deceased. Her most significant poem concerning publication describes the color white:

> Publication—is the Auction
> Of the Mind of Man—
> Poverty—be justifying
> For so foul a thing
>
> Possibly—but We—would rather
> From Our Garret go
> White—Unto the White Creator—
> Than invest—Our Snow—
>
> Thought belong to Him who gave it—
> Then—to Him Who bear
> Its Corporeal illustration—Sell
> The Royal Air—
>
> In the Parcel—Be the Merchant
> Of the Heavenly Grace—
> But reduce no Human Spirit
> To Disgrace of Price
>
> —(J, 709)

Remarking on the meaning of white in nineteenth-century literature, Gilbert and Gubar note that its noncolor signifies female vulnerability and madness in Dickens's Miss Havisham; mortality in Tennyson's Lady of Shalott, and the power of imagination that destroys itself in Wordsworth's Lucy Gray.[39] White is the color of spiritual election, physical virginity, and metaphysical ambiguity; and when placed in the context of publication, this color refers more obviously to a blank page. Invoking perhaps, as Galway Kinnell has noted, the slave auction, the poem plays on the registers of blackness and whiteness, as they refer not only to the abolition movement but also to the liberation of the mind from the fetters of print.[40] The only group who escapes the speaker's condemnation are those who need an income—perhaps the very women writers who often sustained themselves and their families through printing their works. Yet she dismisses such depredation of the spirit for herself, preferring to remain unsullied by the tawdry motivations of the literary marketplace. In fact, if we place her remarks in the context of the editor's wish to become a substitute creator, then she displaces the role of editor with God—she wishes to go "White—Unto the White Creator." Much as Dickinson wore white in order to show that she could not be easily interpreted by the era's standards for feminine appearance, her poetry resisted the standards of interpretation adopted by the literary world.

For Dickinson, the critical discourse about nineteenth-century American women's poetry and the persistent desire on the part of editors to legitimize women's verse determined not only the social terms of her relationship with

Higginson, but also the vocabulary in which their first tentative exchanges about her poetry were to be carried out. Even while she questioned the criteria by which Higginson judged her verse, her conventional relationship with him suggests the absence of perceived alternatives for a woman who sought to be published in the nineteenth century. It is against the backdrop of the prevalent definition of women's verse by editors and critics that we can best gauge Dickinson's own use and revision of these conventions. Rather than ignore the constraints that the publishing world would have placed on her poetry, we should consider how its striking originality, so forward-looking in its sensibility, responds to cultural pressures that shaped women's lives and works in the period—pressures that throw into even bolder relief the genius of Dickinson's art.

"A MORN BY MEN UNSEEN"

Chapter 3

"Feet So Precious Charged"
Dickinson, Sigourney, and the Child Elegy

As his mental powers unfolded, his perceptions were not strikingly acute, but his habits of fixed attention prominent, and remarkable. They gave almost a solemnity to his infant countenance, so earnestly would he regard with a full, grave eye, every speaker who addressed him. Long ere the completion of his first year, in the silent watches of the night, his mother would find, on accidentally waking, that bright eye scanning her face with strange intensity . . . Often, as with magnetic influence, that searching, prolonged gaze of the babe that knew no sound of speech, seemed to draw her soul into his own, till she almost felt awe mingling with the love that had no limit.
　　　　　　　　　　　—Lydia H. Sigourney, *The Faded Hope*[1]

The widow . . . leaves Eva to learn the wants and tendencies of the soul, by observing the harmony and beauty of the external world. Even from infancy she seems to have penetrated the spiritual through the material; to have beheld the heavenly, not through a glass darkly, but face to face, by means of that singleness and truth, that look within the veil. To the pure in heart alone is the promise, "They shall see God."
　　　　　　　　　　　—Elizabeth Oakes Smith, *The Sinless Child*[2]

Pass to thy Rendevous of Light,
Pangless except for us—
Who slowly ford the Mystery
Which thou hast leaped across!
　　　　　—Emily Dickinson (J, 1564)

Emily Dickinson's assurance of God's love was deeply troubled by the deaths of children. Ravaged by tuberculosis and childhood diseases, most children born in the nineteenth century died before reaching adolescence; of those,

53

more than half died before they reached the age of five. Neither the severe Calvinist God of Jonathan Edwards nor the merciful "Everlasting All" of Isaac Watts's hymns could rationalize adequately the death of an innocent child. "Ah! dainty—dainty Death! Ah! democratic Death!" writes Dickinson to the Hollands in fall 1876. "Grasping the proudest zinnia from my purple garden,—then deep to his bosom calling the serf's child" (*Letters* 2, 341). While she betrays the Whig politics of the elite class, who feared the loss of personal property in the leveling of social classes, as Betsy Erkkila has argued, she must acknowledge death's ultimate Jacksonian democracy: it claims both high and low, the zinnia from her "purple garden" and "the serf's child."[3]

Widely hailed as "The Sweet Singer of Hartford" and as the première infant elegist of nineteenth-century America, Lydia Sigourney was part of a widespread cult of death in nineteenth-century America. In *The Faded Hope* (1853), she memorializes her son, Andrew, whose extraordinarily idealized portrait is consonant with the terms by which dying children were depicted in this period. Like Eva, the pious and otherworldly heroine of Elizabeth Oakes Smith's popular long poem, *The Sinless Child* (1843), Andrew has a special relationship to nature, deciphering its phenomena as if they were part of a language that revealed a spiritual truth. We are told that "Among his earliest developments of character, were a strong will and great truthfulness . . . His own faults were narrated with entire simplicity."[4] Showing early a spiritual vision and nearly supernatural prescience, he uses language as a transparent medium, slowly gaining the use of words, as if too great a facility would signal the beginnings of adult sophistry: "He was not rapid in his acquisition of language, but gave close attention to the import of the words that he learned, and applied them steadfastly, and without circumlocution, to their respective images" (11). Indeed, that he depends on his older sister's speech during her daily Scripture lessons to gain his first knowledge of the Bible suggests that he is close to an unspoiled truth that is traditionally distorted by the written word.

Eva, too, interprets nature as if it were a language that manifests God's will. In one of the short prose introductions to each section of her poem, Smith writes that Eva seems unnaturally close to her mother and grows up solely in her care, since her father died before she was born. "Given to the world in the widowhood of one parent, and the angelic existence of the other . . . ," she

is gifted with the power of interpreting the beautiful mysteries of our earth . . . More than this, she beholds a divine agency in all things, carrying on the great purposes of love and wisdom by the aid of innumerable happy spirits, each delighting in the part assigned it. She sees the world, not merely with mortal eyes, but looks within to the pure internal life, of which the outward is but a type.[5]

Eva's perfect insight into the spiritual side of life allows her to see beneath the veil of existence. Perceiving the "outward" world merely as a "type" of the inner, she becomes the agent of God's supervening will. She is surrounded by the sight of ministering angels, and finds solace in the spirit world, despite her mother's blindness to their beauty. Like Andrew, Eva perceives the glimmerings of the spiritual world and communicates her vision to those around her.

Like many of Dickinson's child speakers, Andrew picks up a "crumb" of knowledge here and there to sustain himself, and ultimately builds himself into a self-proclaimed religious authority. His attention and "docility" during his sister's lessons allowed him, Sigourney writes, "to gather here and there a crumb. . . . Still, in his silent gathering of fragments, the little basket of the mind became better stored than was anticipated. Especially were moral and religious precepts accumulated, and treasured" (14–15). While still practically an infant, he revealed his spiritual precocity by transforming the animals on his father's farm into his disciples, who, as Sigourney drolly notes, "were as unique as their preceptor,—being no other than a large flock of poultry" (15). Although he related to all the animals and plants around him as if they were pupils awaiting his pious instruction, he evinced a particular fondness for the flowers in his father's garden. For the most part he gently confided in them, displaying his general "friendship for the humblest creatures" (17), yet he also "established a code of justice, not unmarked by penal statutes" (18). Exercising his sway arbitrarily over his "realm," he punished any "too aspiring plants, that overshadowed and domineered over the humbler ones," by levelling them. Even the "imagined exultation" of one plant, which stood taller than a newly felled one, brought the "usual judgment" (18).

Sigourney's description of Andrew as both a benevolent "preceptor" and a Draconian enforcer of God's will confirms for us the precarious and double-sided position the dying child had for Dickinson and her contemporaries. In writing to her sister-in-law, Susan, on the death of Susan's eight-year-old son, Gilbert, Dickinson suggests that the knowledge the child gains by dying allows him to assume the role of spiritual teacher. Privy to the mystery of death, a dead baby assumes an authority over adults, who would willingly receive his instruction. Once her nephew's "Playmate," the poet seeks a lesson in heavenly faith from a new "Preceptor": "Gilbert rejoiced in Secrets—His Life was panting with them—With what menace of Light he cried 'Don't tell, Aunt Emily!' Now my ascended Playmate must instruct *me*. Show us, prattling Preceptor, but the way to thee!" (*Letters* 3, 799). Like Gilbert's, Andrew's early death casts an aura of holiness and spiritual precocity over his life. In punishing the surrounding flowers in a way that imitates God's exercise of justice, Sigourney's Andrew fully represents a divine authority. Like Jesus in the temple, he can exhibit both righteous anger and benevolent goodness. Yet his act of arbitrary destruction also resembles the angry frustration of a child, who would tyrannically exercise control over an environment in which he is himself powerless.[6] The portrayal of him as an angry feller of flowers, moreover, echoes the frequent characterization of children as flowers, an image that captures their fragility and delicacy; like blooms, children may be felled before they have reached their full maturity. Both Dickinson and Sigourney portray a child's tragic death as well as its vengeful acts in life, suggesting that children rebelled against their fates in a world where they were never meant to survive for very long.

In the child elegy, Dickinson expresses her dissatisfaction with the contemporary consolatory myth that the child enjoys a blissful existence after death. Like Sigourney's tribute volume, her poems frequently empower the child, who revenges himself for his early death on those who are left behind. Rather than offering the grieving family reasons to let the child go, she reverses the standard consolation format by depicting a dead child who himself mourns for his family. She thus undercuts the consolation offered to the mourner by openly portraying the pain and anxiety that the child undergoes in life and death. Even in poems that do not specifically commemorate the death of an actual child, she suggests that the promise of an untroubled reunion between parents and child in heaven is ultimately delusive. In this chapter, I will selectively sketch the use of the child elegy by American women writers in the nineteenth century, looking at a number of nineteenth-century poems lamenting an infant's death, particularly by Sigourney, in order to show how Dickinson's poems adopt and revise the conventions of the child elegy. Rather than offer condolence to the bereaved parents as the typical nineteenth-century version does, her poems suggest that a reunion beyond the grave is only a fiction in the minds of the mourning family.

Although their poems set out several standard features of child elegies, American women poets of the nineteenth century tend to focus even more than their predecessors on the pious and exemplary character of the dying child.[7] Like the elegies that commemorate an infant's death in the seventeenth and eighteenth centuries, the poems of nineteenth-century female poets regularly compare the infant to withering or severed flowers, alluding to the child's truncated life, to its delicate health, and to its smeared beauty.[8] Moreover, they console parents by encouraging them to compare their child's perhaps eventually painful state on earth with its blissful existence in heaven, and they look forward to a comforting reunion between parents and child after death. Yet American women poets of the nineteenth century focus to a greater extent than before on the exemplary and pious character of the dying child. In these poems, the dying child teaches a lesson in holy living to its parents.[9] The child often departs willingly, a testament to his faith in God's promise to prepare a place for him in heaven. Often speaking at the point of death, the children in these poems confidently assure those who are left behind that they will achieve a painless and contented existence in heaven. Furthermore, they willingly give their possessions away as keepsakes, cherished objects which will preserve the memory of their holy lives and encourage loved ones to emulate their pious behavior. Possessed of a sure salvation, the children of these poems faithfully anticipate a reunion with their families in heaven.

In "The Dying Child's Request" (1832), Hannah F. Gould, a popular New England poet, depicts a child who displays an exemplary Christian attitude toward death. Assuring his mother that those he leaves behind will be more precious to him in heaven because they are absent, he foretells his own death and consoles her with the promise that they will reunite in heaven:

> "There's something tells me I must go
> Where Christ prepares a home,
> To which you all, left now below,
> In little while shall come."[10]

Although he displays an unimpeachable faith in salvation, his promise that his family and friends will join him shortly after he dies eerily hints at the mortal end of those who mourn for him. Moreover, he wants his mother to distribute his possessions as keepsakes in order to incite his family and friends to live moral lives and imitate his actions so that they might join him in heaven. He asks her first to divide his belongings among his siblings and friends, then to give the money from his small savings to a missionary:

> "Then from my money-box you'll take
> The little coins within,
> To use as means, for Jesus' sake,
> In turning souls from sin."
> (ll. 21–24)

Evangelism, like an unshakable faith in an afterlife, was a hallmark of the spiritually prescient child, who spent most of his or her short life encouraging others to follow Christ's teachings. His dying moments, with which the poem concludes, demonstrate his unwavering belief in the promise of a life after death. He remarks on the spirits he sees hovering around him, eventually losing his ability to see, yet the radiance of his soul disperses the gloom of his dying moments:

> The morning sun shone in, to light
> The chamber where he lay;
> The soul that made that form so bright,
> To Heaven had passed away.
> (ll. 37–40)

Although the child's vision darkens, the poem suggests that, just as the sun brightens the room, his soul will remain a beacon to all who look to him for moral inspiration.

Although many female poets consoled parents on a child's death with the promise of everlasting life, others found little consolation in popular myths of the afterlife. Helen Hunt Jackson's "The Prince Is Dead," for example, depicts two families, one royal and one common, who suffer equally at the death of their sons:

> A room in the palace is shut. The king
>   And the queen are sitting in black.
>   All day weeping servants will run and bring,
> But the heart of the queen will lack
> All things; and the eyes of the king will swim
> With tears which must not be shed,
> But will make all the air float dark and dim,
> As he looks at each gold and silver toy,
> And thinks how it gladdened the royal boy,
> And dumbly writhes while the courtiers read
> How all the nations his sorrows heed.
>   The Prince is dead.

> The hut has a door, but the hinge is weak,
> And to-day the wind blows it back;
> There are two sitting here who do not speak;
> They have begged a few rags of black.
> They are hard at work, though their eyes are wet
> With tears which must not be shed;
> They dare not look where the cradle is set;
> They hate the sunbeam which plays on the floor,
> But will make the baby laugh out no more;
> They feel as if they were turning to stone,
> They wish the neighbors would leave them alone.
>   The Prince is dead.[11]

Like many of her poems, this lyric contrasts two settings in order to accentuate the deaths that have taken place. Wealthy and poor suffer alike, and only the habits of mourning vary: whereas the king and queen can shut the door of the chamber where the child lies, the poor couple must continue to work and live in the same room. Remarkable for how subtly she portrays the mourners, the poem implicitly contrasts the need to contain one's grief—"With tears which must not be shed" (l. 6; l. 18)—with the bluntness of emotion and the direct-ness of expression of the poor and with the king as he "dumbly writhes" at the courtiers' announcements. Jackson's evocation of wealth and its inability to console grieving parents ultimately questions the satisfaction of consolatory fictions.

Dickinson undercuts the delusory way of thinking about death offered in child elegies such as Gould's. The excessive and prolonged grieving that the sentimental tradition relished kept the child perpetually present, a consoling reminder of reunion after death to the family who was left behind. Such practices, moreover, found their embodiment in the popular artifacts of the Victorian cult of death. Figurines, miniature portraits, locks of hair, and other keepsakes served to keep the child's image almost physically preserved. Popular female elegists consoled parents by affording them a tangible image of spiritual perfection to cherish, one nearly as real as the porcelain likeness of a crying infant placed under a glass dome in the parlor, or as the portraits of children, depicted in a familiar environment with a vase of flowers or their favorite toys in the foreground.[12] Indeed, many poets who returned again and again to the child elegy gained materially by this theme; their very lives as authors depended heavily on their writing poems on the deaths of infants. Dickinson criticizes the Victorian mourner who, overly preoccupied with the loss of the dead, may seem himself to be more dead than alive. She overturns the roles of mourner and mourned, implicitly posing the question, "Who's dead, and who's alive?" Commenting more generally on the pain that both adults and children suffer in life, she questions the underlying assumptions in the elegies of the day that promise an undisturbed heavenly reunion. For Dickinson, a child's death leads only to a very circumscribed grave:

> There was a little figure plump
> For every little knoll—
> Busy needles, and spools of thread—
> And trudging feet from school—
>
> Playmates, and holidays, and nuts—
> And visions vast and small—
> Strange that the feet so precious charged
> Should reach so small a goal!
>
> (J, 146)

The "little knolls" are mounds above children's graves. A paratactic sequence joined by "and"—including "Playmates," "holidays," "nuts," and other objects and events—conveys the breadth of each child's experience. It also hints at the "littleness" of their activities and concerns, which are cut short by their deaths. These trivial concerns are indeed "vast," especially when compared to the smallness of the graves, for they point to lives yet to be lived. Louisa May Alcott's "Our Little Ghost" (1866) sentimentally describes a child's daydreams:

> Fancies innocent and lovely
>   Shine before those baby-eyes,—
> Endless fields of dandelions,
>   Brooks, and birds, and butterflies.[13]

As the title suggests, Alcott's poem invokes the specter of child mortality but defends against its threat by portraying the living child as a playful "spirit" who haunts the family home. Like Dickinson, Alcott lists the items of the child's reverie in a paratactic sequence—"Brooks, and birds, and butterflies"—yet she renders the elements of its vision sentimentally, in contrast to Dickinson's more workaday "Busy needles," "spools of thread," and "trudging feet." Dickinson's poem, moreover, does not offer a protective guarantee against the child's death, as does Alcott's. Instead, the paratactic sequence of the final stanza describing the child's vision gives way in the last two lines to a periodic sentence, in which the speaker refrains from further enumerating the objects of the child's world. "Strange" bitterly understates the child's death, as if it betokened a God with very skewed values. Rather than claim that the dead infant has gained a satisfying heavenly reward, the speaker implies that the "small" goal of the grave does not match the child's vast value. Indeed, if we read the penultimate line as containing a pun on metrical "feet," we can better characterize Dickinson's response to the child elegies of other nineteenth-century women poets: while the infant elegies of the sentimentalists predict a blissful salvation in heaven for a dead child, the feet so precious charged of Dickinson's poem lead only to an actual grave, suggesting that the child should be valued in life, rather than sentimentalized in death.

Because of their youth, children were supposed to be linked closely to nature and supernaturally aware of the immortality they had just left behind by being born, of, as Wordsworth says, "splendour in the grass, of glory in the flower."[14] The size and appearance of children in this era's funerary portraits indicate cultural attitudes toward death. Painted in 1805 by the folk artist John Brewster, Jr., *Francis O. Watts With Bird* is one example of a popular genre of posthumous art that flourished in nineteenth-century America (Fig. 1). Many portraits and book illustrations depict a gigantic dead child who dwarfs the landscape. In Brewster's painting, a two-year-old boy holding a bird on his finger towers over an idealized background of hills and trees. As A. Bruce MacLeish notes: "The boy's good nature and delicacy are emphasized by his lacy clothes, the bird in his hand, and the light that makes him stand out from the somber background" (592). Artists often sought to capture the personality, occupation, or habits of those they portrayed in telling details, but the boy's clear and serene expression, his diaphanous nightgown and glowing figure point away from earthly pursuits toward his celestial state. Moreover, he holds the bird by a string: tethered to fate, he seems the plaything of an arbitrary God. Finally, the disproportion of the huge boy to the miniature background suggests not only the vast importance of the dead child to his family but also the fear of death among the living.

Variations in size, such as one sees in *Francis O. Watts With Bird*, occurred frequently in paintings around the turn of the nineteenth century. Another

Fig. 1. *Francis O. Watts with Bird*, by John Brewster, Jr., 1805. Oil on wood panel, $35\frac{1}{2} \times 26\frac{1}{2}$ inches. Courtesy of the New York State Historical Association, Cooperstown.

Fig. 2. *Emma Van Name*, by Joshua Johnson, c. 1805. Oil on canvas, 29 × 23 inches. Courtesy of The Alexander Gallery, New York.

painting, *Emma Van Name*, by Joshua Johnson, the first professional black portrait painter in America, reflects the artist's talent for painting large family portraits, including full-length standing figures of children. Of the eighty portraits currently attributed to Johnson, forty-six include children—outnumbering those of any other painter working in Baltimore in these years.[15] Dating from around 1805, *Emma Van Name* depicts a child whose smallness is almost surreal when compared to the huge goblet of strawberries by her side. Sacred to the Virgin Mary, strawberries may suggest innocence and ripeness for death (Fig. 2).[16] Replicated in her pink dress and shoes with coral jewelry, the color red also links her to adult female sexuality. Indeed, the phallic whistle that she carries around her neck, designed to ward off old women's curses, hints that her protectors would guard her virginity and shield her from the subsequent loss of power that motherhood and marriage entailed.

By mid-nineteenth century, paintings of oversized infants were replaced by scenes that emphasized family love and mourning customs. A posthumous portrait of 1844, *Edward W. Gorham*, by Joseph Whiting Stock, depicts a boy who mischievously sits with hammer, tacks, and string before a chair (Fig. 3). The playfulness, naturalness, and spontaneity of the scene indicate that families wished to remember children as they appeared in life. In *Sidney Grey Ford*, another posthumous portrait dating from around 1843, an unknown artist depicts the child dressed in the short frock and trousers commonly worn by both boys and girls in the first half of the nineteenth century. Posed with a favorite toy before a garden wall, the boy looks directly at the viewer, while a cemetery gate topped by funerary urns visible in the background points to the boy's early death. A tuft of morning glories ("quick to bloom and quick to fade"),[17] confirms that he is divided from the world of the living and becomes a reminder of the precariousness of life for adults as well as children.

Nineteenth-century artists and poets adopted a common cultural trope for the dying child: a withered or severed bloom. Some popular sentimental elegies give an ironic twist to this standard trope by pairing a growing child with a flower, only to portray the dead child taking revenge on the bloom by crushing it. In "Two Sundays" (1870), Helen Hunt Jackson depicts a child who tears apart the flowers around her, playfully snapping their stems, until she is herself cut down. Not only is the baby pictorially framed by the "lowly" doorway, which is made even "lower" by the flowers, but her liminal position also hints that she has barely entered the world when she dies:

I.

A baby, alone, in a lowly door,
Which climbing woodbine made still lower,
Sat playing with lilies in the sun.

The loud church-bells had just begun;
The kitten pounced in the sparkling grass
At stealthy spiders that tried to pass;
The big watch-dog kept a threatening eye
On me, as I lingered, walking by.

The lilies grew high, and she reached up
On tiny tiptoes to each gold cup;
And laughed aloud, and talked, and clapped
Her small, brown hands, as the tough stems snapped,
And flowers fell till the broad hearthstone
Was covered, and only the topmost one
Of the lilies left. In sobered glee
She said to herself, "That's older than me!"

II.

Two strong men through the lowly door,
With uneven steps, the baby bore;
They had set the bier on the lily bed;
The lily she left was crushed and dead.
The slow, sad bells had just begun,
The kitten crouched, afraid, in the sun;
And the poor watch-dog, in bewildered pain,
Took no notice of me as I joined the train.[18]

The opening two sections of Jackson's poem place the child in a natural and apparently normal environment, only to foreshadow her death. Her tanned "small, brown hands" hint she is healthy. The use of iambic tetrameter with anapestic substitutions also imitates the normal rush of events, but the couplets encourage us to see each activity as discrete and unconnected to a larger, divine plan: a baby, "alone," plays in a doorway, thus vulnerable to the intrusion of outside forces. While church bells ring, suggestive of the church's domain, a kitten "pounced" on "stealthy" spiders, and a watch-dog gazes warningly at the speaker. Both kitten and dog threaten creatures around them, as if they foretold the evil and arbitrary act of the child's destruction. Moreover, the poem's eerie solemnity is enhanced by the symbols scattered throughout that associate her with Christ's passion and death: the lilies the child plays with symbolize resurrection, the "gold cup" of the flowers recalls the chalice, and her awareness of time, her "sobered glee," brings a distinct change in mood.

The infant proves fragile as the plants around her. The second stanza begins with a trochee or spondee, whose strong, slow beats reflect the solemn mood. These beats fall on the words "Two strong men," underscoring the slowed pace of the funeral cortège, which contrasts with the more buoyant feeling of the

Fig. 3. *Edward W. Gorham*, by Joseph Whiting Stock, 1844. Oil on canvas, $30\frac{1}{8} \times 25$ inches. Courtesy of the New York State Historical Association, Cooperstown.

first two stanzas. Furthermore, their "uneven steps" mimic a toddler's tentative steps, recalling the dead infant they are carrying to the grave. In a moment in which the baby seems to enact vengeance after its death, its coffin crushes the lily that was previously out of her reach; set on the "lily bed" where she used to play, the casket smashes the last flower. Profoundly ironic, the recurrent trope of the broken flower implies that the child has been crushed in death, yet her act of control in breaking the stems is acted out again by her coffin.

Although events from the first stanza recur in the second half of the poem, they seem discrete and unconnected to the baby's demise, an irony all the more emphatic when we note that both sets of events occur on the same day of the week. Every aspect of the scene that previously registered the child's vitality now reflects its death: the "loud church-bells" become "slow, sad bells"; the once pouncing kitten now "crouched, afraid, in the sun"; and the threatening dog is "in bewildered pain." The title also underscores the irony of the child's death: God's day for sanctification, Sunday holds no blessings. Death has intruded into the baby's life, leaving the isolated speaker, who was originally treated as an intruder by the watch-dog, to join the train of mourners. God becomes the ultimate, arbitrary hunter, who devours little children even on the Sabbath and introduces an awareness of mortality into the child's world. Although the child in Jackson's poem mischievously destroys the flowers around her, her aggressive behavior naively presages the poem's more central act of destruction—her death. Yet the child's aggression and her unwitting act of revenge on the lily prove that the fear and anxiety surrounding death was not wholly redressed by nineteenth-century consolatory fictions and pious dictums in nineteenth-century America.

Many child elegies portray a dead infant's ascent to heaven as a growth in stature. An example of the disparity between a dead infant's gigantic stature and a dwarfish landscape is Emma Alice Browne's "Measuring the Baby" (1883). A child is measured periodically until its death, when it is transformed by another kind of growth:

> We measured the riotous baby
> Against the cottage wall;
> A lily grew at the threshold,
> And the boy was just so tall!
> A royal tiger lily,
> With spots of purple and gold,
> And a heart like a jeweled chalice,
> The fragrant dews to hold.
>
> His eyes were wide as blue-bells,
> His mouth like a flower unblown,
> Two little bare feet, like funny white mice,
> Peep'd out from his snowy gown;
> And we thought, with a thrill of rapture,
> That yet had a touch of pain,
> When June rolls around with her roses
> We'll measure the boy again!
>
> Ah, me! In a darkened chamber,

With the sunshine shut away,
Thro' tears that fell like a bitter rain,
    We measured the boy to-day!
And the little bare feet, that were dimpled
    And sweet as a budding rose,
Lay side by side together,
    In the hush of a long repose!

Up from the dainty pillow,
    White as the rising dawn,
The fair little face lay smiling,
    With the light of Heaven thereon!
And the dear little hands, like rose-leaves
    Dropt from a rose, lay still—
Never to snatch at the sunbeams
    That crept to the shrouded sill!

We measured the sleeping baby
    With ribbons white as snow,
For the shining rose-wood casket
    That waited him below;
And out of the darkened chamber
    We went with a childless moan:—
To the height of the sinless Angels
    Our little one has grown![19]

Like other elegies on the deaths of children in this period, this poem takes measuring the baby as its central metaphor. As in "Two Sundays," the child's height is measured against a lily that "grew at the threshold" of a cottage or other "lowly" dwelling. Popular in poetry of this type, this liminal image suggests that the baby has barely ventured out into the world when it is struck down, while framing the image of the child in memento-like fashion. Illustrations to such poems often depict these children bounded in a doorway, as here (Fig. 4). The baby's highly realistic features, in contrast to the sketched-in floral garland, gateway, and lily, suggest that the illustrator combined a photograph with an ornamental frame, a common technique of mid-nineteenth-century mortuary tributes, in which the advances of photography supplemented the handiwork of an earlier era. In comparison with his elflike surroundings, the infant's huge size emphasizes the overwhelming effect of his death on his family and the tragedy that an infant's death meant to the larger culture. Yet the towering infant also seems threatening, since he resembles a doll, an image of terror and the grotesque. Indeed, the turn in Browne's poem occurs when the boy is measured for a coffin; "we measured the baby" continues as a refrain describing the boy's preparation for burial until the end, when his death

Fig. 4. Illustration of Emma Alice Browne's "Measuring the Baby," in *What Can a Woman Do?; or, Her Position in the Business and Literary World* (Detroit, Mich.; St. Louis, Mo., Cincinnati, Ohio: F. B. Dickerson & Co., 1885), n.p.

is described as a kind of growth: "To the height of the sinless Angels / Our little one has grown!" Although the elegy promises that the child has been assumed into heaven with the "sinless Angels," his physical size gives him an ascendency over death by letting him tower over both flowers and adults alike. Like the baby in Jackson's "Two Sundays," whose overweening ego admits that another being exists, Browne's poem displays through the toddler's enormity the family's love. His enormity hints that the fear of death was not contained by nineteenth-century consolatory fictions, and the unreality of his stature, especially when compared with the illustration, hints that even for a nineteenth-century readership the child's ascension was similarly fictional.

Browne's poem resonates with Dickinson's poems about "Amplitude" or "Awe." Dickinson's lyrics invoke the invitation and envoi of gravestone inscriptions in order to undercut the Victorian myth that we can expect a blissful reunion with the dead in heaven. In one elegy, the child-speaker relates her thoughts while being carried to her grave; she imagines self-pityingly how her family might have responded to her absence during their holiday celebrations:

> And would it blur the Christmas glee
> My Stocking hang too high
> For any Santa Claus to reach
> The Altitude of me—
>
> (J, 445)

Having assumed in death the proportions of a giant or having simply moved to a higher place, the speaker has separated herself from her family's celebrations and earthly pleasures. Like the heavenly growth of the baby in Browne's poem, the child's height poignantly reminds us of its distance from earth. But unlike Browne's poem, which retells the baby's death from the perspective of her family, this elegy depicts an insider's view of the grave, one which ultimately rejects the memories of home life in favor of a reunion after death with those who are still alive. Since her first thoughts only "grieved" her, the speaker has decided to think "the other way" and to imagine her family's eventual reunion with her in heaven:

> But this sort, grieved myself,
> And so, I thought the other way,
> How just this time, some perfect year—
> Themself, should come to me—

Readers in Dickinson's era must have been familiar with references to the long-awaited reunion that was promised to mourning relatives. Rather than offer the normative consolation of other child elegies, however, the conclusion to this poem portrays the dead child's point of view instead of the grieving family's. The perspective of the mourner is shifted from living parents to dead child, partly to point out the arbitrary nature of such consolation, and partly to accord the child the power of revenge over those who are still alive. Like an epitaph that warns that the reader of the tombstone would come to the same end as the dead soul who ostensibly speaks its words, this poem implies that the entombed child beckons its parents to come. Speaking as disembodied voices from the grave, epitaphs frequently call for the onlooker to halt and contemplate the grave of a fellow mortal, only to remind the reader that—sooner or later—he will return to the same spot.[20] Just as surely as we mourn the dead here on earth, they mourn for us and expect us to join them in heaven.

Lydia Sigourney modified the belief that the entire family would be reunited by portraying a reunion after death between a mother and her son. In doing so, she helped solidify the idealization of mothers which was current at the time, depicting a relation between mother and son that excluded the father and accorded women a special role as instructors and protectors of their children.[21] Dickinson invoked many of these standard consolatory myths, but only in order to contradict the easy translation of earthly doubts into heavenly hopes by writers like Sigourney, to whom I will now turn. In her elegies, Lydia Sigourney portrays a pious and idealized bond between a mother and her infant son. She built on a consolatory fiction, which was already standard in nineteenth-century America, that forecast the gathering together of the entire family beyond the grave. Yet she consoled grieving mothers in particular with the promise that they will rejoin their dead children in heaven. No doubt Sigourney was responding in her child elegies to the deaths of three of her own infants, as well as of her son, Andrew, whose care superseded every other relationship in her life. In publishing her tribute volume, *The Faded Hope*, Sigourney memorialized her son's death, and she wrote countless poems on the deaths of male infants, although she never wrote one on the death of her husband.[22] Her poems reflect the culmination of the sentimental cult of motherhood, where women's moral purity and innocence allowed them a privileged position as the primary nurturers and teachers of their children. While Sigourney accorded mothers and their sons a privileged role in her elegies, she remained well within the conventions of the period that predicted a reunion of grieving parents and children in heaven.

One can consider Sigourney's life as an example of the contradictory lives led by women writers, whom Mary Kelley has called "literary domestics."[23] As for many other nineteenth-century American women writers, no contradiction existed for Sigourney between pursuing writing professionally and leading a conventional life as a daughter, a wife, and a mother. Her commitment to her parents led her early in life to renounce the thought of marriage in order to support them through teaching and publishing,[24] yet her literary work became more professional and less altruistic as she became increasingly successful. Once she experienced the monetary success that a sizeable readership could bring, she began to turn out a prodigious number of contributions to gift volumes, periodicals, and annuals of all types. As her biographer, Gordon S. Haight, notes, with the bias typical for critics of his generation who discuss women's writing, Sigourney displayed in private a business sense that was considered uncommon at the time for women: "It is uncertain whether she practiced sweet patience consistently at home; but with her publishers she displayed a persistent sharpness of business dealing that was scarcely to be expected from a poetess."[25] She nevertheless kept up a smooth facade in public, embodying a conciliatory attitude in her relations with her editors and exhibiting a correctly feminine demeanor to her readership.[26] In fact, Sigourney was so far from finding her professional and private lives contradictory that, even after she had attained considerable success, she continued to view writing as a domestic activity, drawing up on ledger sheets the number of visits given and received, books read, pieces of clothing sewn or knit, and the number of pages of prose or lines of poetry written over the course of a year.[27] That she apparently viewed writing as a task on a par with household ones suggests how closely "private" woman and "public" duty were intermingled.

Perhaps Sigourney's conservative viewpoint offers one reason why she could overlook any contradiction, either in her life or her poetry. She implicitly encouraged the view, which was common at the time, that the lives of women and children were inherently similar and intimately connected. Editors and authors frequently referred to an innately moral quality that they believed made women naturally fit to safeguard the moral values of society and to assume the responsibility of converting others, especially men. Prominent writers, like Sigourney, reinforced this portrayal of women as pious and holy apostles. Sigourney wrote numerous advice manuals for women and their children, including such confidential and instructive volumes as *Letters to Young Ladies* (1833), *Letters to Mothers* (1838), and *Whisper to a Bride* (1850). These books depict mothers, as well as their children, as spontaneous teachers, whose untutored intellects were conduits for moral truth and virtue. Moreover, the ideal Victorian matron was generally conceived to be sexless and desireless, much as children were presumed to be free of erotic tendencies. In one poem, Dickinson claims that these gentlewomen are "Soft—Cherubic Creatures—," whose genteel "Dimity Convictions" make them so resemble childlike angels that Christ is embarrassed to redeem them (J, 401). Frequently compared throughout this period to flowers, women and children embody a cultural ideal of decorative beauty and highly prized fragility. In portraying the continuity between the lives of mothers and their dying children, Sigourney could write fully in the knowledge that her description of mothers as faithful and childlike adhered to the conservative limits which circumscribed the era's depiction of women.

Unlike Sigourney's son, who remains a perpetual child in his mother's eyes, the saintly child heroines of novels and poems attain moral perfection only in adulthood. Having escaped the influence of civilized society, novelist Sylvester Judd's Margaret absorbs moral truth from the natural life around her at the Pond where she lives in isolation with her family. Like Pearl in *The Scarlet Letter* (1850), Margaret seems an elf-child; when she is asked doctrinal questions by parishioners after attending her first religious service, she responds quizzically, evoking cries of dismay from those around her. But Margaret's story continues into adulthood, when she meets her suitor and eventual husband, Mr. Evelyn, who provides her with a more normative religious sensibility and with whom she sets out to convert the unregenerate of the small town of Livingston.[28] Her role in saving the town's souls suggests that the prescient girl continues her saintly mission on earth into adulthood.

Even after a spotless young woman dies, she imitates the role ascribed to mothers in guarding over the spiritual fates of those who are still alive. Once grown to womanhood, Smith's Eva meets Albert Linne, "a gay youth, whose errors are those of an ardent and inexperienced nature, rather than of an assenting will . . ." (115). Destined never to consummate an earthly relationship, Eva assumes the responsibility of caring for the state of her lover's soul, a duty for which women were believed to be naturally suited in life. Indeed, Eva's mother and neighbors are baffled by her deep comprehension of life, yet they contend that she "is unlike her sex only in greater truth and elevation" (41). Her chaste passion for Albert finds its culmination in heaven, from which, having progressed from "The Sinless Child" to "The Spirit Bride" (138), she acts as his guiding-spirit and constant protector. The child heroines in these works grow up to assume the responsibility accorded adult women in saving those around them, while their male counterparts, like Andrew in Sigourney's tribute volume, *The Faded Hope* (1853), can only extend a moral influence after death through an alliance with their mother's piety.

Sigourney's portrayal of Andrew, whose resistance to organized religion especially proved an obstacle for Sigourney, reveals the extent to which she tried to control his life.[29] Unlike his sister, Andrew had not had a conversion experience, an event which Sigourney and others of her generation considered necessary for proof of salvation. Unconcerned with the state of his soul as a teenager, Andrew talked of going west and settling a tract of land he had inherited from his father, claiming there he would be judged on the merits of his character. Sigourney responded with prayers, asking her friends to join her in supplication that he might be converted after all.[30] He gradually came to accept more of his mother's dictates, as he physically weakened. When he refused to discuss his sickness, Sigourney commended his stoic resilience but reproved his behavior, especially as he resisted her attention to his needs: "There was a strange pride about him, as if yielding to sickness, or accepting nursing care, savored of effeminacy or of giving unnecessary trouble" (211). Finding that he relies on her for companionship in his illness, she exults in their hours of conversation, imagining that at these times "every veil was rent, every mist removed" from between them (212); "If from eccentricity, or waywardness, or failure in reciprocity, she had at any time doubted the depth or force of his love, that doubt was put to rest forever" (213). Although he died at nineteen, he became in sickness "an increasingly tender, trustful and child-like spirit"

(222). With a childlike dependence and despite a lifelong aversion to accepting gifts of money, he was reduced in his weakened state to accepting them thankfully, and Sigourney takes satisfaction in finally gaining her triumph: "The pride of life had passed away. His soul was humbled. Scarcely, without grateful tears could his mother perceive, that everything from her hand, was accepted with the docility of a little child" (224–25).

Andrew appears both effeminate and childlike in Sigourney's description, and his death resembles those of other nineteenth-century child prophets. Like fully one half of the adolescents who died in this period, he was plagued with a disease that by the late nineteenth century was associated with young women through its representation in drama, opera, and novels—tuberculosis.[31] Like the young English poet John Keats, he appears in sickness to have acquired a feminine delicacy which only added to his already pale, delicate features: "The burning rose on the cheek, contrasting with the pure forehead, gave to the violet eye, flashing through its long fringes, unearthly brightness and expression" (215). Moreover, Andrew's habits resemble more those a woman than of a young man: he is thankful for "neatness, and tasteful arrangement" in the presentation of his last meals, and he strictly refuses to take a daily dose of cod-liver oil mixed in a glass of brandy and water due to an "early temperance-pledge" (228). Finally, even his resigned and beatific expression at the moment of death points to his mother's continued presence. Having predicted the exact hour and minute of his death, he resembles a child angel: "As the clock struck the hour of high noon, and the hand of his own watch touched the point of twelve,—he fell asleep, like an infant on the breast of its mother" (236). Andrew's holy example is memorialized by his mother, who hears the injunction "'Write!'" from a heavenly voice after his death and whose response suggests that her writing serves to sublimate her grief: "Glorious words! floating out upon the summer air, from consecrated lips, with holy healing" (237–38).

Like the dying child in nineteenth-century literature, who often consigns cherished objects to others in order to console them through his pious example, Andrew attentively gives away keepsakes, which form an integral part of the deathbed ritual in Victorian America. Much as Eva in Harriet Beecher Stowe's *Uncle Tom's Cabin* (1851–2), who provides comfort to her father's slaves on her death by cutting off her "long, beautiful curls" as gifts,[32] Andrew gives "a colored servant woman . . . to whom in boyhood, he had so perseveringly endeavored to teach the sciences" a keepsake designed to preserve her memory of him (231). Stowe's Eva, too, fervently wishes to make the slaves literate, remarking to her shocked mother that, if she had her jewels to use as she wished, she would "'sell them, and buy a place in the free states, and take all our people there, and hire teachers, to teach them to read and write'" (263). Both he and Eva try to teach those who are less advantaged than they are: education as well as evangelism formed a part of the nineteenth-century child exemplar's standard equipment in converting souls to the good.

Sigourney's poems on the deaths of male infants promise a grieving mother that she will be reunited with her dead son in heaven. In doing so, Sigourney suggests that the bond between a boy and his mother surpasses every other family tie.[33] Indeed, I would argue that she redefines the standard consolatory format in a way that was consistent with its conservative aims but which clearly set the mother and son's bond above all other family relationships. Her 1834 *Poems* usually identify these children either as male infants or make no reference to their gender; although Sigourney periodically memorialized the deaths of young women and girls in her verse, the vast majority of the poems in this volume deal with the deaths of both infant sons and their mothers.

In her elegies, a dead mother often encourages her son to join her beyond the grave, portraying a heavenly existence as more pleasant and natural than life on earth. Or, in another variation, a speaker who looks on from outside the family circle consoles the grieving mother with the prospect of a reunion with her infant son in heaven, an idealized version of the mother and child's relationship on earth. Taken together, Sigourney's poems imply that the relation between a mother and her son was so intense that a continuity existed between their lives even after death. The more material Victorian conception that the family circle would be reconstituted in heaven allowed mothers to keep a firm hold on their dead children's lives and to continue to possess them almost as if they were cherished mementos.[34] Rather than portraying a female speaker who receives comfort only from the promise of Christian salvation, Sigourney assures mothers of a material reunion with their infants in heaven.

To gain a fuller sense of the intent of her poems, one can consider the range of speakers in Sigourney's elegies. A brief catalog of her most frequently used speakers reveals that a mother and child's bond underlies every infant elegy: a mother enjoins her dead or dying child to die in order to avoid the pain and temptation of earth; a dead mother wishes her living child a happy and moral life; a generalized speaker describes a woman's joyful reunion with her dead infant in heaven; an observer of a child's funeral discourses to the bystanders about the mother's and father's sorrow; and, most commonly, a speaker who witnesses a scene of public mourning over a mother's death predicts that her child will continue to follow her holy example. Of the dozen or so child elegies in Sigourney's 1834 *Poems*, more than half focus on the mother's bond with a male infant.[35] In general, these poems begin with a mother's or child's death and then gradually reveal the logic by which the survivors can learn to accept their loss. Occasionally, they open by presenting a mother's death and offering a consoling message to her son, only to redress that loss by suggesting that she has already gained her long-awaited reward by joining her dead infant in heaven. Finally, her poems inevitably end with an upward glance, as an infant ascends to his dead mother's embrace or a mother is enjoined to "Look up!" for the compensation she lacks on earth.

Sigourney's "To a Dying Infant," a typical poem of this genre, portrays a speaker who encourages her child to ascend to heaven so that he can avoid the pain and temptation of earth. This poem somewhat resembles elegies of the seventeenth and eighteenth centuries, which console bereaved parents and relatives with the thought that the child has achieved salvation in heaven. She draws on the consoling myth that a child will be better off in heaven by depicting death as an escape from life's pain and uncertainty. Unlike earlier elegists, however, she adopts the popular nineteenth-century consolatory fiction that death is only a form of sleep. Rather than console herself on her infant's death with the thought of salvation, the mother in this poem sends her child to its heavenly sleep so that he will not sin:

> Go to thy rest, my child!
>   Go to thy dreamless bed,
> Gentle and undefiled,
>   With blessings on thy head;
> Fresh roses in thy hand,
>   Buds on thy pillow laid,
> Haste from this fearful land,
>   Where flowers so quickly fade.
>
> Before thy heart might learn
>   In waywardness to stray,
> Before thy feet could turn
>   The dark and downward way;
> Ere sin might wound the breast,
>   Or sorrow wake the tear,
> Rise to thy home of rest,
>   In yon celestial sphere.
>
> Because thy smile was fair,
>   Thy lip and eye so bright,
> Because thy cradle-care,
>   Was such a fond delight,
> Shall Love with weak embrace
>   Thy heavenward flight detain?
> No! Angel, seek thy place
>   Amid yon cherub-train.[36]

In claiming that the infant will maintain its purity by ascending to heaven, the speaker seeks to keep her hold over it. Although this poem begins as if it were going to be a lullaby, details slowly emerge to reveal that the child is dying (as the title, of course, has already told us). The mother charges her child, who is still "undefiled," to go to its "rest" in a "dreamless bed" in the hopes that its innocence will be preserved in heaven. The image of withering blooms in the last part of the stanza evokes a familiar trope of innocence, the "sweet moral blossom," which lasts only a short while before the temptations and pitfalls of the world mar its beauty. Contending in the second stanza that the infant should ascend to its "home of rest" in order to prevent its purity from being lost, the speaker attempts to extend her influence over her child even after its death. For Sigourney, heaven was not unlike the domestic sphere, where women and children remained above the world's moral and sexual corruption. From this "celestial sphere" of chaste innocence, dead mothers continued to exert a powerful influence as their children's first and most significant teachers of moral values. Although this speaker will apparently survive her baby, her wish that it die before treading "the dark and downward way" of sin allows her to imagine that it is still hers, since it will never enter the contaminated world. In the final stanza, she relinquishes the loving "cradle-care" of her infant as if she still had control over its fate. Her fantasy that she might actually be able to prolong the infant's life even momentarily in the "weak embrace" of love indicates her wish to cling to her dying child.

If Sigourney's mothers often seek to arrest their infants' heavenward flight, other poems frame almost visually a scene of mother or child's death in an effort to present a comforting keepsake to the reader. In "Baptism of an Infant, At Its Mother's Funeral," for example, a speaker wonders at the scene of death before her, which juxtaposes a mother's funeral with an infant's christening:

> Whence is that trembling of a father's hand,
> Who to the man of God doth bring his babe,
> Asking the seal of Christ?—Why doth the voice
> That uttereth o'er its brow the Triune Name
> Falter with sympathy?—And most of all,
> Why is yon coffin-lid a pedestal
> For the baptismal font?
>
> (ll. 1–7)

The tableau of father, priest, and baby is described in stark blank verse, which focuses attention on the image of the still figures who stand around the mother's casket. The speaker describes the scene as if drawing aside a veil from a tableau, only to append an instructive or consolatory moral. Like their opening scenes, the titles of Sigourney's poems provide a verbal snapshot of the central event, as the poem gradually reveals what the title already revealed. The titles often refer to scenes of nature worship, religious drama, or human tragedy, as the following ponderous ones suggest: "Solitude," "A Cottage Scene," "The Last Supper," and the immensely popular "Death of an Infant."

In "Death of an Infant," the child assumes center stage, almost as if he were a painting or piece of statuary that attracted the observer's notice:

> Death found strange beauty on that polished brow
> And dashed it out.—
> > There was a tint of rose
> On cheek and lip.—He touched the veins with ice,
> And the rose faded.—
> > Forth from those blue eyes
> There spake a wishful tenderness, a doubt
> Whether to grieve or sleep, which innocence
> Alone may wear.—With ruthless haste he bound
> The silken fringes of those curtaining lids
> Forever.—
> > There had been a murmuring sound,
> With which the babe would claim its mother's ear,
> Charming her even to tears.—The Spoiler set
> His seal of silence.—
> > But there beamed a smile
> So fixed, so holy, from that cherub brow,
> Death gazed—and left it there.—
> > > *He dared not steal*
> *The signet-ring of Heaven.*

Joanne Dobson has argued that the use of conventional images, conversational tone, and grammatical regularity in this poem encourage us to accept the consolation offered at the end in the final, manifest metaphor: "In this lone metaphor, Heaven's promise of eventual reconciliation bridges the sentimental breach implicit in the deathbed scene. The 'wishful tenderness' of affectional desire will be rewarded with reunion in the afterlife."[37] Only the beginning of the third stanza, where the transposed syntax, archaic diction, and moderately complex sentence structure signal "the child's subjectivity, its 'wishful' desire to live" (271), impedes the easy transition from image to feeling. In addition, Sigourney's theatrical description and the images drawn from the vocabulary of sculpture and painting—the baby's "polished brow" and cheeks and lips with a "tint of rose"—add to the characterization of the dead infant as an object for public display. Like a merciless stage manager, death rings down the child's "curtaining lids" forever, yet the curtain rises triumphantly again in the poem's conclusion to enshrine the child's image permanently. Although the "Spoiler" has set "His seal of silence" (ll. 12–13) on the baby, his holy smile so awes the onlooker that "even Death gazed—and left it there.—" (l. 14). Stamped with the "*signet-ring of Heaven*" (l. 15), the baby's beatific look stops death from stealing the only cherishable memory left to the grieving parents.

A speaker who looks on a death from outside the family circle often exposes the innermost feelings of the mourners, especially important when a mother is no longer present to formulate an instructive moral for a child who survives her. Maternal mortality continued at a high rate throughout the nineteenth century, and pregnancy frequently heralded the death of the mother due to miscarriages and stillbirths, difficult or premature labor, the high incidence of puerperal fever, and medical procedures such as the cesarean section, which were almost always fatal.[38] Stepping into scenes of deathbed agony or funeral mourning, the observer in these poems laments a death that, because it occurs at home, might otherwise be overlooked. In "Baptism of an Infant, At Its Mother's Funeral," the speaker seeks in a series of questions to understand why the mother's death has occurred, only to be answered by the tears of the mourners as the mother's coffin is unveiled. She then foretells the baby's sorrowful life, almost as if she were herself speaking for its absent mother:

> ——Tears were thy baptism, thou unconscious one,
> And Sorrow took thee at the gate of life,
> Into her cradle. Thou may'st never know
> The welcome of a nursing mother's kiss,
> When in her wandering ecstasy, she marks
> A thrilling growth of new affections spread
> Fresh greenness o'er the soul.
> > Thou may'st not share
> Her hallowed teaching, nor suffuse her eye
> With joy, as the first germs of infant thought
> Unfold, in lisping sound.
>
> > > (ll. 16–26)

Although his mother has died, the child lives out his mother's pious life on earth in her place, a claim borne out by the emotional and intellectual influence she continues to have on her infant. Marking the child's entry into life, the tears of the young mother's mourners baptize him: "—Tears were thy baptism, thou unconscious one, / And Sorrow took thee at the gate of life, / Into her cradle" (ll. 16–18). "Sorrow" is itself personified as a mother who will take the child into "her cradle," as if substituting for the real mother who died. As this image suggests, the grief the child suffers as a result of his mother's death serves to counsel him through life. Although deprived of her care on earth, he will grow up more aware of God's power, and hence will emulate his mother's piety:

> > Yet may'st thou walk
> Even as she walked, breathing on all around
> The warmth of high affections, purified,
> And sublimated, by that Spirit's power

Which makes the soul fit temple for its God.
——So shalt thou in a brighter world, behold
That countenance which the cold grave did veil
Thus early from thy sight, and the first tone
That bears a mother's greeting to thine ear
Be wafted from the minstrelsy of Heaven.

(ll. 27–36)

Living in an environment imbued with "The warmth of high affections," which have been "purified, / And sublimated" by his mother's death, the infant nevertheless will imitate her pious actions and achieve a union with her in spirit until he rejoins her in heaven.

Sigourney contends that a mother influences her child as its teacher, a doctrine which she discusses at some length in her *Letters to Young Ladies* (1838):

It is in the domestick sphere, in her own native province, that woman is inevitably a teacher. There she modifies by her example, her dependants, her companions, every dweller under her own roof. Is not the infant in its cradle, her pupil? Does not her smile give the earliest lesson to its soul? Is not her prayer the first messenger for it in the court of Heaven? Does she not enshrine her own image in the sanctuary of the young child's mind, so firmly that no revulsion can displace, no idolatry supplant it? Does she not guide the daughter, until placing her hand in that of her husband, she reaches that pedestal, from whence, in her turn, she imparts to others, the stamp and colouring which she has herself received? Might she not, even upon her sons, engrave what they shall take unchanged through all the temptations of time, to the bar of the last judgment? Does not the influence of woman rest upon every member of her household, like the dew upon the tender herb, or the sunbeam silently educating the young flower? or as the shower, and the sleepless stream, cheer and invigorate the proudest tree of the forest?[39]

This passage reveals that nineteenth-century mothers fulfilled a crucial role in educating their young children in ways acceptable to society. As her infant's first teacher, a mother makes an impact on it that lasts all its life and maintains her earthly control over it even after her death. She notably erects in its mind her own "image" rather than God's as an example of holy love, the infant having completely internalized her influence, as if she were its "idol." From there, she instructs it in behavior proper for an adult, encouraging her daughter to marry and her son to adhere to the values of a moral life. Moreover, she insures that these roles be endlessly perpetuated by setting her daughter on an idealized "pedestal" from which she will instill the same values in her own children, "impart[ing] to others, the stamp and colouring which she has herself received." Significantly, she considers a mother's earthly influence to be stronger over her daughter than over her son, as her remark that she might exert her sway "even upon her sons" suggests. Sigourney's faith in a girl's extreme malleability points to her belief that women actively replicate the era's prevailing ideals of femininity. Although she depicts the "influence of woman" as a nurturing force, the way she emphasizes its pervasiveness and its persistence in the images taken from nature of the "sunbeam silently educating the young flower" and "the sleepless stream" flowing endlessly through the forest suggest just how effective she imagined this influence could be.[40]

In "Death of a Beautiful Boy," Sigourney alludes early on to the pain the child suffers as a result of his mother's early death, only to suggest that he lives out his short life in her shadow. Although his mother is absent, she is present in his life in myriad ways:

> I saw thee in thine hour of sport, beside thy father's bower,
> Amid his broad and bright parterre, thyself the fairest flower;
> I heard thy tuneful voice ring out upon the summer air,
> As though some bird of Eden poured its joyous carol there,
> And lingered with delighted gaze on happy childhood's charms,
> Which once the blest Redeemer loved, and folded in his arms.
>
> I saw thee scan the classic page, with high and glad surprise,
> And saw the sun of science beam, as on an eaglet's eyes,
> And marked thy strong and brilliant mind arouse to bold pursuit,
> And from the tree of knowledge pluck its richest, rarest fruit,
> Yet still from such precocious power I shrank with secret fear,
> A shuddering presage that thy race must soon be ended here.
>
> (ll. 7–18)

Playing beside his "father's bower," the boy lives in a garden-world dominated by the presence of his masculine parent, yet the "fairest flower" points to the continued influence of his mother. An allusion to Milton ("*Proserpin* gath'ring flow'rs / Herself a fairer Flow'r by gloomy *Dis* / Was gather'd . . ."),[41] this phrase uses the common trope of a culled flower to signify early death. Sigourney alludes to Milton's Proserpine, who, like the feminized Andrew, is fated to join the world of the dead while still young. Like the young women in numerous other nineteenth-century poems, he sings in a "tuneful voice" reminiscent of a "bird of Eden."[42] The comparison to an animal, an "eaglet" whose mind is aroused to the "bold pursuit" of knowledge, recalls the theories of the post-Enlightenment Romantic philosophers, who contended that children are primitive and unspoiled examples of human goodness, rather than depraved sinners, as the Calvinists believed.[43] With the rise of evangelical religion in the first half of the nineteenth century, the image of the spontaneous affection and untutored intellect of children became a new model of holy behavior, one which parents themselves needed to embrace in order to achieve salvation and to which mothers were thought to contribute through their roles as nurturing teachers. Sigourney adopts the motif of the Garden of Eden to develop this link between the naive mind of an infant and his mother: the boy assumes Eve's role in searching after knowledge, plucking its "richest, rarest fruit." His attachment to his mother and his reunion with her in heaven is like an Oedipal scenario, yet the violence of this conflict turns inward as both mother and child die and the father remains absent and unscathed. Foretelling that the sensitive boy will live only a short time, the speaker predicts in the last line of the poem the boy's ascent to a domestic celestial sphere, where a "sainted mother's arms" will affectionately clasp him once again (l. 24). Like the act of stanza two's "Redeemer," who maternally "loved" the boy as soon as he saw him and "folded" him in his arms (l. 12), the promised embrace of his mother after death implies that they will continue their earthly relationship in heaven. In this final phrase, the mother herself takes the place of the "Redeemer" in Sigourney's view of a feminized heaven.

For Sigourney, a mother's influence over her son takes its cue at least partly from the popular image of a maiden weeping over a willow-shaded tomb that appears as a common motif in sentimental funerary iconography. Having internalized his mother's absence, the boy often increases in emotional sensitivity as he matures, a trait which is captured in the image of the growing willow tree. The weeping willow symbolized for nineteenth-century mourners the new, gradualist doctrine that promised heavenly salvation to those who suffered emotional pain and grief on earth. As Barton Levi St. Armand explains, this conventional image aptly conveyed the consoling mythology of spiritual regeneration: "The willow . . . was a traditional emblem of Christian mourning, since it shed its leaves like tears, seemed perpetually drooped in thoughtful reverie, and had the power to regenerate itself after being cut down (thereby foretelling the resurrection of the dead)."[44] The piteous shedding of tears and the merciful act of drying them often connect mother to son, as in the first stanza of "On the Death of a Mother Soon After Her Infant Son":

> There's a cry from that cradle-bed,
>   The voice of an infant's woe;
> Hark! hark! to the mother's rushing tread,
> In her bosom's fold she hath hid his head,
>   And his wild tears cease to flow.
>   Yet he must weep again,
>   And when his eye shall know
>   The burning brine of manhood's pain
>   Or youth's unuttered woe,
>   That mother fair
> With her full tide of sympathies, alas! may not be there.
>   On earth, the tree of weeping grows
>   Fast by man's side where'er he goes,
> And o'er his brightest joys, its bitterest essence flows.
>
> (ll. 1–14)

As long as the mother lives, drying her child's tears is a show of care as well as an act of sympathetic bonding. Yet the boy may survive to experience other woes in life as an adult, which his mother will no longer be there to alleviate: although he may shed tears—"the burning brine of manhood's pain"—his mother's "full tide of sympathies" will not cleanse them. Indeed, the very shape of the stanza—with its narrow neck, wide body, and pedestal base—traces the outlines of a funerary urn, a further link to the iconography of mourning in nineteenth-century America. Rather than merely symbolize the tears shed for the dead, the "tree of weeping," like an ever-lengthening measuring stick, gauges the boy's developing spiritual maturity—the taller he grows, the more sensitive he will become to earthly woes. Even after his mother dies, the boy will adopt her sympathetic response to pain and continue to follow her example.

"On the Death of a Mother, Soon After Her Infant Son" further suggests that the close bond between mother and son prompts the mother's demise. Sigourney quickly shows in the succeeding stanzas that this faithful soul has already been rewarded with her child's company in heaven. Having completely given over her days to educating her son ("And from each rising sun / Till Night her balmy cup of silence poured, / For him the paths of knowledge she explored, / Feeding his eager mind with seraph's bread, / Till intellectual light o'er his fair features spread" [ll. 23–27]), she is subdued by his early death, and resigns herself to his fate. Her submissive posture echoes the traditional Christian attitude that encouraged adults to obey God's will as a child might a parent: "Yet she who bore him shrank not 'neath the rod, / Laying her chastened soul low at the feet of God" (ll. 32–33). In the last stanza, the speaker counsels all mothers to look forward to their children's company in heaven as compensation for their suffering on earth:

> Mothers! whose speechless care,
> Whose unrequited sigh,
> Weary arm and sleepless eye
> Change the fresh rose-bud on the cheek to paleness and despair,
> Look up! Look up to the bountiful sky,
> Earth may not pay your debt, your record is on high.
> Ye have gazed in doubt on the plants that drew
> From your gentle hand their nightly dew—
> Ye have given with trembling your morning kiss,
> Ye have sown in pain—ye shall reap in bliss;
> The mother's tear, the mother's prayer,
> In faith for her offspring given,
> Shall be counted as pearls at the judgment-bar,
> And win the gold of heaven.
>
> (ll. 46–59)

Not only do mothers influence their children by acting as their earliest and most important teachers and protectors, but they can also join them in death by making the ultimate sacrifice as their sick nurse. The "speechless care" and "unrequited sigh" of these mothers are ignored, even as their bodies tire and their faces pale with anxiety and hopelessness. They constantly worry that their children might be taken away from them, gazing "in doubt" day by day on them and "trembling" with fear in the morning when they kiss them, lest they have died during the night. Sigourney promises in the conclusion to this poem that the mother who has mourned for a child on earth will be recompensed in heaven by just as much as she has suffered. Nevertheless, caring for a dying infant might promote a woman's heavenly reunion with her child in a very literal way, and the ailing health of the mother in this poem confirms for us once more that in Sigourney's elegies a mother's weary life is in many ways only an extension of her child's.

Dickinson was familiar with the Sigourney-style elegy that promised suffering mothers a reunion with their infants in heaven. Yet she adopts these conventions after her own fashion, and frequently writes elegiac meditations, which, while they do not lament the deaths of actual infants, draw on and transform the features of other child elegies. Barton Levi St. Armand remarks that Dickinson's "appropriation of the props of the Sentimental Love Religion and the popular gospel of consolation involve a process of personalization, internalization, exaggeration, and inversion."[45] Just as the death of Sigourney's son, Andrew, seems to underlie many of her infant elegies, the death of Dickinson's nephew, Gilbert, whom she called her "own Boy" (*Letters* 3, 853), occasioned some of her most lasting meditations on death, and prompted the elegaic tone of much of her later writing. In moments of genuine grief, she sublimated her pain to transform these accepted verse forms into her own statements concerning suffering, death, and the afterlife.

Like her contemporaries, Dickinson extols the dying child as a spiritual guardian, an infant prophet whose closeness to death makes him peculiarly able to preach to adults. But rather than dwell on an imagined prescience that forms part of its short but spiritually exemplary life, she claims that the child gains its knowledge of an afterlife only after it is dead. Her nephew, Gilbert, for instance, has discovered the answer to the mystery of death, which reaches beyond the ken of a living adult: "'Open the Door, open the Door, they are waiting for me,' was Gilbert's sweet command in delirium. *Who* were waiting for him, all we possess we would give to know—Anguish at last opened it, and he ran to the little Grave at his Grandparents' feet—All this and more, though *is* there more? More than Love and Death? Then tell me it's name!" (*Letters* 3, 803)[46] Despite her desire to find a "name" for existence after death, the secret of death still baffles Dickinson, and her attempt to understand it resembles a child's desire to learn to name an experience for the first time. In adopting the naive accents of a child, Dickinson affirmed the spiritual prescience of children.[47] Yet she parted company with sentimental elegists like Sigourney, who never afforded the dead child as much time as its parents to speak. Dickinson's appropriation of the myth of a postmortem reunion and of a child's prophetic knowledge allowed her aptly to convey her frustrations as a religious outsider, whose questions concerning death and the afterlife were destined to remain unanswered.

Dickinson believed that children had special access to the spiritual world and served as fitting examples of pious behavior for adults. Her letters to friends and relatives consoling them on the loss of children stress not only the "sweet velocity" (*Letters* 3, 799) of their lives, but also their faithful adherence to God's will: "'Come unto me.' Beloved Commandment. The Darling obeyed" (*Letters* 2, 636). No other death was more traumatic or grievous to Dickinson than that of her eight-year-old nephew, Gilbert, and her description of him in her letters is consonant with the terms in which dead children were described at the time. Writing in October 1883 to Susan Gilbert Dickinson, she notes his comet-like life in terms that echo funerary iconography: "No crescent was this Creature—He traveled from the Full—Such soar, but never set—" (*Letters* 3, 799). In this moving tribute, Dickinson acknowledges Gilbert's having passed beyond the ken of the living, like a sun/soul depicted winging its way toward heaven on gravestones. Furthermore, his encompassing knowledge of life and death makes him seem larger than life: "Wherefore would he wait, wronged only of Night, which he left for us—Without a speculation, our little Ajax spans the whole—" (*Letters* 3, 799). She compares Gilbert to Ajax, famed Greek hero of great stature and prowess, who fought against the Trojans, and she implies that he has transcended death in invoking the mythological warriors physical largeness. Yet the comparison is also a tender hyperbole, since Gilbert could measure up to Ajax's stature only in the eyes of those who loved him.

Dickinson deemed Gilbert's friend, Kendall Emerson, especially knowledgeable about her nephew's heavenly state, since he was with Gilbert when both were playing in a mudhole, and Gilbert contracted a fatal case of typhoid fever. The poet commemorated her eight-year-old nephew's death in three notes to Kendall. The timing of these letters, written at Christmas rather than on the anniversary of Gilbert's death, implies that his early demise reveals for her a tragic precocity. Like the Christ child, Gilbert was fated to suffer an untimely death. In her first note, in 1883, she asks for information about Gilbert's whereabouts after death with a childlike naiveté:

Dear Kendall—
Christmas in Bethlehem means most of all, this Year, but Santa Claus still asks the way to Gilbert's little friends—Is Heaven an unfamiliar Road?

Come sometime with your Sled and tell Gilbert's

Aunt Emily.

(*Letters* 3, 804–5)

In this, the most childlike of the three notes that Dickinson sent to Kendall, the poet pretends that Santa Claus seeks out "Gilbert's little friends" in order to bring them presents, then slyly asks if heaven is an "unfamiliar Road." She implies that the way to heavenly salvation is known only to those who, like Gilbert, have taken its path or who, like Kendall, have ventured close enough to death to make that road familiar.

Both of Dickinson's other letters stress the continued loss she feels at her nephew's death. In sending these notes every year as a tribute to Gilbert's memory, she implies that death might cut short Kendall's life as quickly as it did Gilbert's. In the second message, in 1884, she hints at the possibility that Kendall himself might have died during the intervening year:

Missing my own Boy, I knock at other Trundle-Beds, and trust the Curls are in—

Little Gilbert's Aunt—

(*Letters* 3, 853)

Ostensibly written to commemorate her nephew's death, the note also serves to make sure that Kendall has not died, that he is safe in his "Trundle-Bed," unlike her "own Boy," who is absent from home in his coffin. In her final note, in 1885, Dickinson once again warns Kendall that he might die as easily as Gilbert did:

Dear Kendall.

I send you a Blossom with my love—Spend it as you will—

The Woods are too deep for your little Feet to grope for Evergreen—

Your friend,

Emily—

(*Letters* 3, 894)

In enclosing a blossom with her note, she punningly alludes to the flower as a gift of money, yet symbolic of the transience of life, the flower also suggests Gilbert's early death and the possibility of Kendall's. She discourages Kendall from making a quest similar to the one he made with her nephew, lest his "little Feet" dangerously stray too far in the broad "Woods," which are "too deep." A symbol of perpetual life commonly used on gravestones, "Evergreen" suggests that Gilbert has become immortal as well as that his memory has remained fresh for the poet. Like the child in Browne's elegy, whose "little bare feet . . . were dimpled / And sweet as a budding rose" (ll. 21–22), Kendall has "little Feet" that symbolize the ease with which he, like Gilbert, might be assumed into heaven. Time has lessened her pain, allowing her some distance from her nephew's death; unlike the other two letters, which identify Dickinson as Gilbert's aunt, this one is signed simply, "Your friend."

Dickinson elsewhere assumes the guise of a naive child who is turned away from paradise in order to question God's seeming indifference to both adults and children who are denied His care:

> Why—do they shut Me out of Heaven?
> Did I sing—too loud?
> But—I can say a little "Minor"
> Timid as a Bird!
>
> Would'nt the Angels try me—
> Just—once—more—
> Just—see—if I troubled them—
> But dont—shut the door!
>
> Oh, if I—were the Gentleman
> In the "White Robe"—
> And they—were the little Hand—that knocked—
> Could—I—forbid?
>
> (J, 248)

Assuming the pose of a disobedient child who is shut out of the family circle, the speaker asks to be let into heaven, and this request resembles Gilbert's in his dying moments, when he asks to be allowed inside the gates of eternal life. The child hesitatingly asks the angels for another chance to prove his good intentions as a denizen of heaven, then posits a hypothetical case in his own defense: imagining himself in the last stanza as God or an archangel, the child implies that he feels doubly cheated in being shut out, as he reasons that, if he were in God's powerful place—if *he* were the doorkeeper of heaven—he certainly would not forbid a child's entry. The speaker thus refutes his unjust rebuff in heaven by testing the angels against the creed of "Do unto others as you would have them do unto you." Dickinson turns the table on Sigourney's familiar theme that children occupied a privileged place in heaven by portraying a child who is abandoned on heaven's doorstep, then inverts the child's lowly position with the archangel's at the poem's end to question his unjust exile on the boundary of paradise. The poet underscores the arbitrary power that God holds over the lives of infants and adults, who are denied the heavenly care and attention that the motto "Suffer the little children to come unto me" seems to promise.

Like others of her generation, Dickinson attests to a child's contentment after death. Sentimentalism provided a legitimate and therapeutic response to death, as in the following poem in which the speaker, who unwillingly travels to the grave, testifies to the dead child's happiness:

> Trudging to Eden, looking backward,
> I met Somebody's little Boy
> Asked him his name—He lisped me "Trotwood"—
> Lady, did He belong to thee?
>
> Would it comfort—to know I met him—
> And that He did'nt look afraid?
> I could'nt weep—for so many smiling
> New Aquaintance—this Baby made—
>
> (J, 1020)

Unlike the mothers in Sigourney's poems, who enjoin their children to die or hasten to follow them to heaven, the speaker is "trudging to Eden," as if she would prefer herself to remain here on earth. Following the characterization of dead children as once cherished, now lost, possessions, the speaker here asks if the mother previously owned this boy: "Lady, did He belong to thee?" But the dead child is no longer hers, and the speaker tentatively offers her knowledge of the boy's contentment as a consolation.

Furthermore, Dickinson alludes in "Trotwood" to the protagonist of Dickens's novel, *David Copperfield*, as a way of asserting that he continues in the family circle. The speaker puns that the child "would trot" to heaven and there meet an array of cheerful companions after death. Orphaned before birth by his father's death, David grows up solely in his mother's care. A wealthy, eccentric aunt, Betsy Trotwood, refuses to extend her riches to David at birth because, as a boy, he cannot take her first name. Indeed, his mother names him "Trotwood" in an attempt to satisfy his aunt, suggesting the extent to which women lay claim to his existence, even after they are no longer present in his life. Dickinson offers the thought of a happy comradeship among the dead as a much needed consolation on children's deaths. In a letter the poet wrote about two years after her nephew's death, she recalls Gilbert's dying vision of heaven as a kind of celestial playground: "October is a mighty Month, for in it Little Gilbert died. 'Open the Door' was his last Cry—'The Boys are waiting for me!'" (*Letters* 3, 891) Playfully reversing the hierarchy between adult and child, she responds that she opened the door, but she has seen him no more: "Quite used to his Commandment, his little Aunt obeyed, and still two years and many Days, and he does not return."

The motif of the dying child's escape from earth's tribulation, which appears frequently in Sigourney's poems, undergoes in Dickinson's verse a satiric reversal. Sigourney's "A Mother in Heaven to Her Dying Babe," for

example, contends that the infant will attain salvation by dying in a pure state
and avoiding the pains and temptations of adulthood:

> Long had he dwelt below,
>   Perchance his erring path,
> Had been through bitterness and woe,
>   On to his Maker's wrath
>
> (ll. 17–20)

Dickinson does not promise the same freedom from pain for the dying child.
Instead, she invokes the very same pain and anxiety in order to assert that God
leads innocent children through agony on earth:

> Far from Love the Heavenly Father
> Leads the Chosen Child,
> Oftener through Realm of Briar
> Than the Meadow mild.
>
> Oftener by the Claw of Dragon
> Than the Hand of Friend
> Guides the Little One predestined
> To the Native Land.
>
> (J, 1021)

Rather than focus on the child's anesthetized ascent to heaven, Dickinson
counters the elegies of Sigourney and others by asserting that the infant suffers
at God's bidding on earth. While the dying child in Sigourney's elegy escapes
life's "erring path," which frequently leads "through bitterness and woe," the
"Chosen Child"'s way in Dickinson's poem often goes through a "Realm of
Briar." Before the child can commend its spirit into God's hands or submit to a
mother's loving embrace after death, the guiding and protective "Hand of
Friend," presumably God's, may convert to a "Claw of Dragon." "Predestined /
To the Native Land" rather than the promised land of heaven, the child suffers
on the ground with no sure promise of salvation.

  Dickinson could think of nature as "the Gentlest Mother" (J, 790) who wills
a peaceful "Silence" on her children, and in the following lyric she likens the
release of both children and adults from life's pain to a benevolent mother's act
of putting her children to sleep. She describes life as an unending thread, and
prepares us with this image of homekeeping for the earth's role in gently alle-
viating life's suffering and pain through death:

> The Months have ends—the Years—a knot—
> No Power can untie

To stretch a little further
A Skein of Misery—

The Earth lays back these tired lives
In her mysterious Drawers—
Too tenderly, that any doubt
An ultimate Repose—

The manner of the Children—
Who weary of the Day—
Themself—the noisy Plaything
They cannot put away—

(J, 423)

The poem perhaps refers to the elderly, who "stretch a little further" the time al-
lotted them until death ends their "tired lives." Like pieces of yarn whose ends
are bound together, the months and years form a "Skein of Misery" that we cannot sever or unfasten. This image resembles the thread produced by the legendary Fates, the three sisters who were said to spin, measure, and cut the
length of each mortal life. Dickinson elsewhere characterizes the months as an
unending spool of yarn, which she would "wind" into "balls" until her lover arrives, putting them "each in separate Drawers, / For fear the numbers fuse—"
(J, 511). In the second stanza of this poem, however, "Earth" provides an escape to the pain and tribulation that people suffer in life by putting them to their
eternal sleep. Like a caring mother, she nestles their "tired lives" in her "mysterious Drawers" in the ground. This image of domestic care leads to the suggestion in the last stanza that we are like children who, exhausted by the day's
events, cannot put away "the noisy Plaything"—life.[48] Instead, these tired souls
must wait for a tender guardian to put them to their final rest. One might also
take "Themself" to modify "They," suggesting that the children are reduced to a
toy, the bauble in their own game. Such a variation recalls Sigourney's characterization of children as precious objects, who are reclaimed by a grieving
mother sending them to their heavenly sleep. By describing our mortal lives as if
they were overseen by a mother who relieves the pain and suffering of her children by laying them to their final rest, Dickinson draws on a trope familiar to
readers of Sigourney's elegies, yet she transforms the latter's act of domestic
pity into a universal benevolence, one conferred upon adults as well as children.
Although she implies that people of all ages can benefit from the earth's gentle
care, she suggests that we are as powerless as children to alter the course of our
lives.

In the following poem, which has been read as a move away from the "literature of misery" commonly associated with Sigourney and her followers, Dickinson undercuts the sentimentalized mourning over a child's death (Sewall 2,

329 n. 5). She portrays a dead child, who, just buried in the tomb yet in a state of semi-consciousness, has been reminded by a mourner's well-meaning pity that she is no longer alive:

> I cried at Pity—not at Pain—
> I heard a Woman say
> "Poor Child"—and something in her voice
> Convinced myself of me—
>
> So long I fainted, to myself
> It seemed the common way,
> And Health, and Laughter, Curious things—
> To look at, like a Toy—
>
> To sometimes hear "Rich people" buy
> And see the Parcel rolled—
> And carried, we suppose—to Heaven,
> For children, made of Gold—
>
> But not to touch, or wish for,
> Or think of, with a sigh—
> And so and so—had been to us,
> Had God willed differently.
>
> I wish I knew that Woman's name—
> So when she comes this way,
> To hold my life, and hold my ears
> For fear I hear her say
>
> She's "sorry I am dead["]—again—
> Just when the Grave and I—
> Have sobbed ourselves almost to sleep,
> Our only Lullaby—
>
> (J, 588)

4] Convicted me—of me—   15. us] me
11. we suppose] I supposed

The speaker's attachment to life and to possessions undercuts Sigourney's conception that dead children exist in an idealized state devoid of the cravings and desires of earth. The woman's remark, "'Poor Child,'" punningly hints that the child deserves pity because she has been dispossessed of material wealth as well as of her life. For the speaker, life's pleasures have grown to resemble unfamiliar objects, "Curious Things" or a "Toy," which she can never again possess. Moreover, she covets the gifts which she has heard "'Rich people'" buy for their children, naively thinking that presents might exist in heaven as well. In confusing the talk she has heard in life with the sight of a "Parcel" being "rolled—/ And carried" away, she mistakes the bundle, which probably contains another dead body, for toys. Even the idea that heaven's well-treated occupants are "Children, made of Gold" signals that she gauges their value according to a system of exchange.[49] Indeed, the phrase "Children, made of Gold," with its ambiguous reference both to the "Parcel" being carried to the grave and to the children who are already buried there, suggests not only that these children can receive gifts from their parents, but also that in some sense they have become mere toys or baubles themselves. In fact, the speaker enviously remarks that, "Had God willed differently," she might herself have been one of these privileged children. This economy of earthly possessions exposes one of the premises of Sigourney's elegies: that the mother owns and cherishes the dead child as if it were a precious object. Confined to her recollection of life and the worldly belongings of others, the speaker is reminded of what she has been denied in life by the woman's pity, and so arrives at an unwanted sense of self-consciousness.

Yet the child's dispossession points to an even more significant lack, for to accept the woman's pity would be to remind herself of the love she has been denied in life. In the first stanza, the speaker cries "at Pity—not at Pain—"; she is hurt by the pity of a nameless mourner, not by the pain of death. Unlike the infants of Sigourney's poems, who are promised a mother's loving embrace in heaven, this speaker cradles her own abstract "life," having been dispossessed of all but her hearing in the grave. When she again imagines the woman's hurtful pity, the speaker's remark is framed in free indirect discourse, which reflects her own psychic state: the woman's words are cast within quotation marks and the object of her pity takes a first-person rather than third-person singular pronoun ("'sorry I am dead'" instead of "'I'm sorry she's dead'"), so that the speaker sounds as if she were mourning her own death rather than ventriloquizing the voice of another. Like the growing sons who are deprived of maternal care in Sigourney's elegies, the speaker in this poem has internalized a tearful sympathy for her loss. Finally, the child laments especially the lack of a mother's care in the last stanza when she claims that she and the "Grave" have "sobbed ourselves almost to sleep, / Our only Lullaby—." This image suggests that the speaker longs for the forgetfulness of death, but rather than listen to a mother's voice singing her to sleep, she will lull herself into oblivion with the sound of her own sobs. Dickinson's sentimental portrayal of the dead child's thoughts here suggests how close she was in spirit to contemporary female elegists. Yet she is far from poets like Sigourney, who depict a mother's possessive influence over her dead child. Instead, Dickinson suggests that the child, alienated from its mother's care, suffers by the excessive pity that keeps it perpetually alive, when it would gratefully resign itself to the eternal sleep of the grave.

If Sigourney's elegies hint at a heavenly bond between women's lives and their sons', poems by other nineteenth-century women poets lamenting the deaths of children point to a more mundane link between death and a woman's sphere, to which a daughter is inevitably confined. In "The Little Maid" (1830), Anna Maria Wells, an American poet who was nearly as well known at the time as her half sister, Frances Sargent Osgood, depicts a young girl who grows up to live a restricted life of loneliness and poverty after her only brother has died:

> When I was a little maid
> 　　I waited on myself;
> I washed my mother's teacups,
> 　　And set them on the shelf.
>
> I had a little garden,
> 　　Most beautiful to see;
> I wished that I had somebody
> 　　To play in it with me.
>
> Nurse was in mamma's room;
> 　　I knew her by the cap;
> She held a lovely baby boy
> 　　Asleep upon her lap.
>
> As soon as he could learn to walk,
> 　　I led him by my side,—
> My brother and my playfellow,—
> 　　Until the day he died!
>
> Now I am an old maid,
> 　　I wait upon myself;
> I only wipe one teacup,
> 　　And set it on the shelf.[50]

Written as children's verse, this poem would have been read by most girls as a fantasy about their future lives, and it dramatizes the indelible impression that a son's death could make on a family's daughters, who were bound by convention to occupy the home without the promise of a son's eventual escape. The speaker begins life as a little maid, who performs her domestic duties for herself and her family while she hopes for companionship, until her brother's death consigns her to a life of lonely grieving. Distant from the girl's childhood and absent from her adult existence, her mother hovers only vaguely in the background. Her presence dimly appears in household cares and childbirth, as suggested by the "teacups" and by the baby's birth in the third stanza, pointing to these events as central ones in a woman's life. Although the birth of "a lovely baby boy" promises the girl companionship for a while, his death marks the end of both a socially normal childhood and adulthood. Having progressed from a "little maid" to an "old maid" by the poem's end, she continues to perform the same activity of keeping house she had played at as a girl and ends life in the same lonely way she begins. In fact, the girl apparently mourns her brother, as unmarried sisters often spent a lifetime fondly recalling a young brother who died. Once beyond marriageable age, a woman could substitute a lifelong dedication to her brother's memory for an actual marriage, especially during the Civil War era, when the deaths of young soldiers grew to staggering proportions and decreased the pool of eligible young men. This eroticized scenario of family devotion apparently allowed the grieving sister to find an outlet for the passion that was stifled for unmarried women in the proper Victorian household. Wells's poem depicts with startling clarity the circumscribed life of a woman who is bound by traditional mourning behavior to pay tribute to a dead brother's memory.

Before turning to a final poem by Dickinson that criticizes a girl's fate, we might ask a broader question concerning the infant elegy: why might poems on the deaths of children be a fruitful genre in which to look for commentaries on women's roles? Several of the cultural precepts that determined women's lives underlie the traditional elegy: a mother and child's bond was primary, and a woman's domestic role was at the center of her existence. Sentimental writers, like Sigourney, enshrined women on a "pedestal," which in turn kept them from attaining power outside the home. Since the infant elegy builds on women's primary role as domestic caretakers and moral exemplars, it allows them to console themselves on their loss by claiming an almost possessive hold over their dead children, who remained under their nurturing influence. Sigourney's lamentations on the deaths of sons not only bolster a woman's importance in the culture at large, but they also comfort bereaved parents and secure the elegist's place in the national consciousness. Rather than articulate their grief through original images, however, women poets mediated their lamentations through a number of sentimental tropes, such as "curtaining lids," "polished brow," and other expressions, and employed well-worn phrases in order to evoke a stock response from their readers. As Joanne Dobson notes about sentimental discourse, "A language close 'to the conversational norm' is a language that mediates its subject matter without either foregrounding itself or erecting linguistic barriers—such as learned diction, obscure tropes, or experimental uses of language—that impede comprehension. In other words, such a language operates as an apparently transparent medium for the conveyance of its subject matter and affect."[51] Deriving their metaphors from the language of nature and domestic life with which women were intimately associated, the poets sanitize grief in conventional language and convey emotion in terms that only circumscribe once again the familiar boundaries of a woman's experience—as housewife and mother.

If Sigourney's elegies hint at a heavenly bond between women and their children, Dickinson's poems question the link between motherhood and home duties that condemns women to a life of domestic cares. Another speaker questions a girl who dies as to why she sleeps, then claims she would have helped her die, if it had been possible:

> 'Tis Sunrise—Little Maid—Hast Thou
> No Station in the Day?
> 'Twas not thy wont, to hinder so—
> Retrieve thine industry—
>
> 'Tis Noon—My little Maid—
> Alas—and art thou sleeping yet?
> The Lily—waiting to be Wed—
> The Bee—Hast thou forgot?
>
> My little Maid—'Tis Night—Alas
> That Night should be to thee
> Instead of Morning—Had'st thou broached
> Thy little Plan to Die—
> Dissuade thee, if I c'd not, Sweet,
> I might have aided—thee—
>
> (J, 908)

The speaker attempts to rouse the "Little Maid" from her lethargy, only to conclude when the girl does not respond that she is better off dead than alive. Wondering why the girl does not rise and attend to her "Station in the Day," the speaker suggests that she should instead "Retrieve" her "industry." She goes on to define the girl's life as it found its common expression in contemporary literature: the girl's total existence forms a single "Day," which encompasses the traditional roles of girl, wife, and mother in the morning, noon, and evening of her life. By not fulfilling her "Station in the Day," the "Little Maid" has relinquished both her designated task in the family and her social duties as a future wife and mother; having given up the possibility of marriage and motherhood, she has abandoned "The Lily—waiting to be wed—" and "The Bee" as the day passes. The speaker then conventionally laments the child's death in the last stanza, regretting the endless sleep of mortality that prevents the girl's awakening to the "Morning" of her still youthful life. Indeed, we might take the speaker's final suggestion that if she could not have "Dissuade[d]" the girl from her "little Plan" to die she might have "aided" her as a dictum in line with Sigourney's belief that the innocent child is better off after death. Yet when we recall the speaker's previous attention to the child's social and familial duties, we find that the last two lines in fact question the role that the girl has been assigned all along. Imagining she could reason with the girl and "Dissuade" her from her "Plan," the speaker disingenuously claims that the child willfully chose to die, and decided to keep silent about it. By implying that the child has consciously decided to die, the speaker ascribes to her a willful determination not to exist. Furthermore, the speaker's use of "aided" is ambiguous: does she mean she might have eased the girl into death while she provided sympathetic comfort? Or that she might more actively have facilitated her decision to end her life? In summary, the speaker thinks that the "Little Maid"'s position in life is so constraining that she considers her earthly end preferable to a woman's life on earth, and she claims that she might have helped the girl once she had made her decision to die, much as if it had been a reasoned—and reasonable—choice.

Sigourney's poems console mothers with the belief that women's lives were continuous with their children's, a consolatory fiction which Dickinson rejects in her more radical interpretation of the child elegy. Sigourney partakes of the culturally sanctioned image of a woman as pious and domestic, but in her very idealization of the mother-son relationship, she suggests that women will be specially compensated for the pain they have suffered in life. While she expresses the sentimental consolation that was typical in poetry of this type, she diverges from the standard child elegy to accord women a more central place in the cultural mythology that predicted a gathering together of the entire family circle after death. Her example suggests that nineteenth-century American women writers were able to alter subtly the conventions of this form, even while they remained within its conservative limits. Although Dickinson adopts some of the same conventions in her elegies, she raises questions about the consolation offered by Sigourney and other nineteenth-century American female elegists. Rather than uphold Sigourney's theory of the mother's extended influence over her son, she rejects the possessive nature of the mother's bond and criticizes Sigourney's idealized conception of motherhood. In these and other poems, Dickinson casts doubt on the apparent comfort that a heavenly reunion offered to the grieving family and to mothers in particular. Finally, she suggests that the dead may willingly invite the living to join them, but that, once we do, the reunion we were promised proves to be only a fiction.

Chapter 4

"Alabaster Chambers"

Dickinson, Epitaphs, and the Culture of Mourning

> Have you ever been to Mount Auburn? If not you can form but slight
> conception—of the "City of the dead." It seems as if Nature had formed the
> spot with a distinct idea in view of its being a resting place for her children,
> where wearied & dissappointed they might stretch themselves beneath the
> spreading cypress & close their eyes "calmly as to a nights repose or flowers
> at set of sun."
>
> —Emily Dickinson (*Letters* 1, 36)

> It was, as we have intimated, a spot without beauty or bloom, like many
> others in New England; but in New England affections are green
> remembrances and enduring monuments; tears that mausoleums cannot
> always command were freely shed on this dry orchard-grass, and the purest
> purposes of life were kindled over these unadorned graves.
>
> —Sylvester Judd, *Margaret*[1]

> Oh may our follies like the falling trees
> Be stripped ev'ry leaf by autumn's wind
> May ev'ry branch of vice embrace the breeze
> And nothing leave but virtue's fruit behind
> Then when old age life's winter shall appear
> In conscious hope all future ills we'll brave
> With fortitud our disillusion bear
> And sink forgotten in the silent grave.
>
> —Anonymous Sampler Verse (1806)[2]

For many nineteenth-century American writers, heaven was a geographical,
locatable entity, widely depicted in paintings, novels, and poetry. For Dickinson, finding its spiritual coordinates proved more difficult, as she was

grounded in the awareness of early and arbitrary death rather than in a cheerful acceptance of religious platitudes. "Contentment's quiet Suburb," she writes in one lyric, is threatened by affliction, which ranges "In Acres—It's Location / Is Illocality—" (J, 963). The Victorian cemetery was not only the earthly repository for the dead, but in its rolling hills, ornate gates, and home-like tombs, it also prefigured a comforting vision of an afterlife as material as life. Dickinson's shift of focus from heavenly salvation to earthly life may be gauged by studying posthumous art, the "rural cemetery" movement, and her adaptation of the epitaph.

Funerary art and epitaphs provide insight into the inadequacy of nineteenth-century mourning fictions. She notes in a letter to Thomas Wentworth Higginson in July 1862 about her lack of a portrait: "It often alarms Father—He says Death might occur, and he has Molds of all the rest—but has no Mold of me, but I noticed the Quick wore off those things, in a few days, and forestall the dishonor—" (*Letters* 2, 411). When Dickinson mentions her lack of a "Mold," I assume she refers not only to photographs but also more broadly to a whole panoply of Victorian *objets d'art*, including plaster casts of hands, graveyard busts, embroidery, and funerary sculpture, that reified the dead and guaranteed an image to be lovingly cherished by those who survived them. The Victorian penchant for preserving a physical reminder of the dead led both to an elevation of high "feeling" in mortuary art and to a subsequent devaluation of such images as mass-produced kitsch. Dickinson's poetry offers a readjustment of vision, both from the vantage of the dead who beckon to us to join them and the living who are so accustomed to remembering the dead that they seem more dead than alive. Much as painters, sculptors, and writers set the image of the dead in canvas, stone, or verse, Dickinson displays the "State—Endowal—Focus—" (J, 489) that death confers by manipulating both epitaphic conventions and visual perspective in her lyrics.

Closer in style and thought to the sentiments expressed on Puritan gravestones than to the tearful consolation reflected in mid-nineteenth-century funerary art, Dickinson's elegiac meditations jolt the reader into an awareness of his or her own mortality through the use of a typical funerary device: the epitaph. Dickinson invokes the logic of epitaphic inscriptions in her poetry to suggest that the living and dead can reverse the roles assigned them by nineteenth-century mourning rituals. Rather than encourage mourners to look forward to a time when they will rejoin the beloved dead in heaven, as the nineteenth-century elegy so often does, her poems portray dead who unwittingly encourage their loved ones to die and come to them. By detaching the voice of the speaker from its normal conversational context, the epitaph underscores mortality and the absence that writing itself necessarily entails. I wish to examine the reversibility of the epitaph as well as how the representation of death in funerary art, mortuary paintings, and inscriptions reminds us perpetually of our own mortality. Dickinson's lyrics play on notions of presence and absence, on the possibilities of including the reader in a circuit of meaning that presumes one party is absent. Her subtle adaptation of many of the conventions of funerary art and inscriptions uses shifts in points of view to shorten our distance from the dead.

Epitaphs always carry reminders of mortality, since the voice of the dead (an obvious and patent fiction) foretells the death of the living. Given their special function as a message conveyed to the living by the dead, these inscriptions gain force as vatic proofs of an afterlife. In their study of the epitaph, Malcolm Nelson and Diana George note that in the traditional epitaph the "voice of the dead speaks to the ear of the living, reversing their roles: the deceased lives through the voice of the stone, defying death and yet reminding the living of their own mortality."[3] An epitaph from the Old Burying Ground (1769) in Brewster, Massachusetts, provides a typical invitation and envoi:

> Some hearty friend shall drop his Tear
> On my dry Bones and say
> "These once were strong as mine appear
> And mine must be as they."
>
> Thus shall our mouldering Members teach
> What now our senses learn:
> For Dust and Ashes loudest preach
> Man's infinite Concern.
>
> (637–39)

Close in thought and format to Dickinson's lyrics, this epitaph takes an abstract, tightly reasoned, and conceptual approach to death. What is significant is the ease by which the writer slips from a traditional epitaph (with its invitation to stop and ponder the remains, its connection to the reader's life, and its eventual send-off) to a more abstract lesson. As Nelson and George note, this epitaph is unlike others in its use of an observer's voice proclaiming the idea one normally finds expressed by the posthumous speaker (637). Typically, the dead person argues logically from the ground: death will overtake the mourner's life all too soon. But the second stanza's "Members" overturns even religious hierarchy and creates a communal voice for the dead and the living by punning on churchgoers and bodily limbs. Better than a minister's words, the remains of the dead "preach" the dissolution of the body and "Man's infinite Concern"—salvation. Thus, the epitaph chides the reader into an awareness of mortality, while simultaneously implying that living and dead are already members of the same, select society.

Dickinson would have been familiar with examples of New England epitaphs from seeing them in graveyards in Amherst, South Hadley, and the farmlands of western Massachusetts, but she was also exposed to epitaphs in a book owned by the Dickinsons, Helen Hunt Jackson's *Bits of Travel at Home* (1878). Although remembered today, if at all, as the author of *Ramona* (1881), a novel about an Indian man and his half-Mexican lover set in Old California, Jackson was a prolific travel writer who traveled throughout the United States and Europe. In her collection of travel essays set in New England, California, and Colorado, Jackson provides examples of epitaphs that summarize for us the mid-nineteenth-century American approach toward death. In "A Morning in a Vermont Graveyard," she describes the graves of early settlers, whose antique epitaphs resemble the terse reminders of mortality more typical of Puritan graveyards than the mid-nineteenth-century cemetery. In a passage worthy of Thoreau she describes a scene of natural splendor, archaic tombstones, and slowly encroaching industrialization:

It is the warmest spot I have found to-day; a high wall of soft pines and willow birches breaks the force of wind on two sides, and the noon sunlight lies with the glow of fire on the brown crisp grass. The blackberry vines, which this year have brighter colors than the maple-trees, flame out all over the yard in fantastic tangled wreaths of red, and the downy films of St. John's wort and thistle seeds are flying about in the air. Half an hour ago an express train went by, on the river bank, many feet below, and the noise seemed almost unpardonable so near the graves. Since then not a sound has broken the stillness, and the fleecy clouds have seemed to come down closer and closer until they look like thin veils around bending faces.[4]

The description of nature suggests that the scene evokes a visionary state in the speaker. Appropriately, the graveyard is bordered by pines and willow trees, especially indicative of mourning. Moreover, the "fantastic" overgrowth of vines and "downy films" of St. John's wort encourage the reader to contemplate the lives of the dead. Describing clouds that look like "thin veils around bending faces," she casts the graveyard in a visionary light, imaginatively identifying with Jemima Tute, whose gravestone sparks the essay ("how well she must still recollect the day" [201]).

Primarily recounting the life of Tute, pioneer and survivor of an Indian attack that killed her husband and young daughter, the essay details her capture and the deaths of other women in the fort. In the summer of 1755, Tute and the other women of Bridgman's Fort, having been left alone all day by their husbands who were tilling the fields, were attacked by Indians. Their husbands had themselves been attacked and some killed earlier. Jackson's discussion of Tute's life and epitaph at once pays homage to the dead and criticizes the desire to memorialize them in the prevailing fashion. She praises Tute as she recounts the attack on the fort and notes, quoting from a contemporary recollection of Tute written by an aide of George Washington: "She was still young and handsome, though she had daughters of marriageable age. Distress, which had taken somewhat from the original redundancy of bloom and added a softening paleness to her cheeks, rendered her appearance the more engaging" (203). Unlike her husband who died during the attack, Tute survived, was captured and ransomed, eventually remarried, and outlived her third and final husband. Like other eighteenth-century epitaphs, Tute's emphasizes the importance of reputation and social standing, especially important for women since they lacked other position in society: we are told she was "Successively relict of Messrs. WM. PHIPPS, CALEB HOWE AND AMOS TUTE"; that her eldest daughter married a Frenchman and that her youngest child died; that "By the aid of some benevolent Gentle'n, / And her own personal heroism, / She recovered the rest" of her children; and that, "Having passed thro' more vicissitudes, / And endured more hardships, than any of her cotemporaries," she had managed to keep her reputation intact ("No more can Savage Foes annoy, / Nor aught her wide-spread Fame destroy" [203]). Turning to the epitaph of Amos Tute, Jemima Tute's last husband, Jackson notes that the gravestone, although it is fifteen years older, looks modern and the inscription is clear: "It is strange that with the white marble ready to their hands on so many hillsides, the old Vermont settlers should have put so many of their records into keeping of the short-lived slate" (203–4).

Jackson concludes with a Thoreauvian description of the surrounding field and forest as a natural, pristine gravesite:

By a round-about road through pine and beech woods, dark with the undergrowth of shining laurel, we wind down from the hill into the town below. We shall pass another curious burial-ground on our left. It is not enclosed; has no tombstones; and, so far as anybody knows, there have been no interments in it for thousands of years. (207)

Characterizing a former swamp, filled in over the years, as a "curious burial-ground" and the teeth-marks of beavers as the "traces of builders," Jackson implies that nature itself constitutes a gravesite for all creatures. Although another author might make pious references at this point, Jackson makes the humorous observation that "the most distinguished, or, at any rate, the biggest person ever buried there, was an elephant" (207). She notes that "Two years ago, some Irish laborers dug part of him up. Even in a muck bed, among the Green Mountains, he was not any safer than he would have been in Trinity Church Yard in New York" (207). Despite the prevalent assertion that the dead were at rest in their natural "home," Jackson underscores their inability to be guaranteed an undisturbed rest. With clinical detail, she notes that what remains of the animal is "only forty inches of one tusk," and that tusk has been placed "on exhibition at the State Capitol, and has been mended with glue by the State Geologist" (207). Perhaps mocking the way the dead were adorned with prominent tombstones whose epitaphs displayed family ties and predicted

their painless state in death, Jackson points to the futile attempts of human beings to repair their own mortality.

Jackson's essay exemplifies the way many nineteenth-century elegies and
mortuary tributes attempted to preserve our memories of the dead. Unlike the
inscriptions on tombs built during the eighteenth century, which emphasized
reputation and social standing, nineteenth-century epitaphs stressed the emotional tie between the dead and the family. Epitaphs changed significantly from
the Puritan to the Victorian eras, when the prolixity of the earlier epitaphs and
their didactic refrains weakened to a "felt" silence. More frequently, nineteenth-
century gravestones monumentalize the dead through elaborate imitation of
natural structures, such as logs, stumps, trees, and stones, rather than through an
epitaph. Foretelling the modern practice of recording only the names and dates
of the deceased, the high Victorian cemetery often used inscriptions that simply
identified the family relation and sometimes omitted the family name altogether: "Our Angel Boy," "Mother & Son," "My Wife & Daughter." Furthermore, the initial reverie of the dead in Jackson's essay commonly appears in
nineteenth-century women's elegiac meditations; depicting female speakers
who contemplate the dead and imaginatively commune with mothers, sisters,
friends, or children, such essays and lyrics provide a pleasant contemplation
and consoling recollection of the dead. Rather than assert that women's lives
existed outside of any meaningful social or familial context, women's elegies
draw a continuous line between their female forebears and their own lives.

In light of Jackson's description of an antique graveyard in Vermont, we
might consider briefly another contemporary description of a Puritan graveyard in order to place Dickinson within the context of mid-nineteenth-century
American mortuary tributes. Older graveyards were always located next to a
church in the middle of a town or city, as if to enforce the unity of community
and church life. Unlike the ornate Victorian cemetery, they acknowledged the
harsh, unadorned truth that death is a part of life. Such an antique graveyard
appears in Sylvester Judd's utopian novel, *Margaret* (1845). The eponymous
heroine and her friend Isabel attend a funeral at the town's cemetery, which
dates from the time of the first settlers:

This spot, chosen and consecrated by the original colonists, and used for its present
purpose more than a century, lying on the South Street, was conspicuous both for its elevation and its sterility. A sandy soil nourished the yellow orchard grass that waved
ghostlike from the mounds and filled all the intervals and the paths. No verdure, neither
flower, shrub, or tree, contributed to the agreeableness of the grounds, nor was the bleak
desolation disturbed by many marks of art. There were two marble shafts, a table of red
sandstone, several very old headstones of similar material, and more modern ones of
slate. But here lay the fathers, and here too must the children of the town ere long be
gathered, and it was a place of solemn feeling to all.[5]

In stark contrast to the graveyard in Judd's novel, changes in cultural attitudes toward death in the nineteenth century encouraged the community to isolate and monumentalize for posterity the remains of the dead. Judd's graveyard lacks the meditative woods and decorative tombstones that allowed those who passed within the rural cemeteries' gates an opportunity for mournful but pleasantly consoling reverie. Unlike the three-dimensional memorial sculptures that became increasingly popular, the tablet and tombstones "of red sandstone, now gray with moss, bearing death's heads and cherub cheeks rudely carved, and quaint epitaphs, and the whole both sinking into the earth and fading under the effects of time" (1, 270), are decaying relics of an era that conceived of death as a two-dimensional event of heavenly salvation or hellish damnation.

Furthermore, new methods of interment and changes in taste regarding funerary sculpture in mid-nineteenth-century America underwrote this sentimentalization of death. The idea that the dead were as present as if they were still alive found its contemporary expression in the "rural cemetery" movement, which became prominent in the nineteenth century.[6] Responding to epidemics of yellow fever in 1819 and 1822 in Philadelphia and Boston and to another in New York City in 1822 that killed sixteen thousand around Trinity Church burial ground alone, the proponents of the new cemetery movement sought to protect the health of the general population by removing graves to the countryside. The movement away from the slate stones that were so popular among the Puritans toward funerary sculpture accompanied a more general desire to imagine salvation as a gradual process that depended on the capacity to suffer, on feelings rather than works. The founders of one of the earliest of the rural cemeteries, Mount Auburn, were so opposed to the form and conception of the church graveyard that they banned perpendicular slate slabs. Instead, larger monuments that were variations of neoclassical architectural elements—broken columns, sarcophagi, obelisks, and steles—referred to classical themes and were associated with the Romantic idealization of relics and unfinished structures. Imitations of natural forms, including chopped tree trunks or ivy-covered boulders, fashioned entirely of marble or granite, also appeared in burial grounds. More impressive as artifacts of high Victorian feeling than as testaments to holy living in the Puritan fashion, mid-century graveyard sculpture often omitted the last names of children, referring to them only by nickname, or by familial relation. Death could thus be naturalized, and earth serve as a tomb for all.

Eventually, the emphasis on a rural and natural home for the dead gave way to high Victorian tastes that preferred the ornamental garden to an arbor-shaded retreat for mourners. By the 1860s, Mount Auburn's trees were razed, hills and steep inclines leveled, swamps filled in, and ponds trimmed with granite to form more symmetrical shapes. The "rural cemetery" was propelled by a new impulse toward mid-century: it was designed not only to insure the health of the community, but also to memorialize the dead in a setting that was consoling and aesthetically pleasing to the nineteenth-century mourner. Ann Douglas characterizes the sense of placid contentment and nostalgic reverie that such a spectacle was meant to instill in the viewer: "The mid-nineteenth-century American went to the cemetery rather in the spirit in which his twentieth-century descendant goes to the movies: with the hopefulness attendant upon the prospect of borrowed emotions."[7]

For the middle class, memorializing the dead affirmed social position and promoted religious conformity. Like the typical elegy, which assured mourners that they would rejoin their loved ones in heaven, the new cemeteries conveyed a sense of permanence and prosperity. By the end of Judd's novel, Margaret and her husband, Mr. Evelyn, transform their small town of Livingston into an ideal religious community, Mons Christi, which is laid out on the order of the new "rural" cemeteries, complete with floral plantings, verdant hills, marble statuary, and an erected cross.[8] Despite the idealistic enthusiasm of its planners, the construction of this morally uplifting fictional landscape is contingent on a much-needed bequest of money, as was the new, actual venture at Mount Auburn. Having made a large financial investment, shareholders of the cemetery protected and adorned their portion of land, much as they might have a residence. Proprietors often placed wrought or cast iron fences around their lots, a habit that derived from the older cemeteries in which cattle were allowed to graze, and heavy granite curbings in the second half of the century further segmented the cemetery grounds. Part of the popular "Domestication of Death" throughout the period, as Douglas attests, this division of lots symbolized the owners' attachment to family and property status: "Nostalgia, here as elsewhere, functioned as a spiritualized form of acquisition."[9] Perhaps even more important than displaying wealth, however, parceling off the graves of family members with a border allowed the survivors to treat the dead as if they had homes of their own; the custom of erecting fences around graves softened the awareness of death for mourners, who could console themselves with the thought that they would rejoin loved ones in a domestic setting after death.

The graves in these new cemeteries stand as testaments to the loving attachment of families to their dead. In Judd's novel, Margaret watches her neighbors, the "drunken Tapleys from No. 4," who lead a life of dissolute revelry, as they solemnly "moved in a body to a corner of the lot, where four years before was laid their youngest child, a little daughter, marked by a simple swell of dry sod scarce a span long, and there at least they were sober" (1, 270). In contrast to the unadorned graves of the Puritan churchyard of Judd's novel, Victorian ornamental tombstones for children, usually only a quarter the size of an adult's, frequently bear the figure of a lamb or sleeping infant over a tablet, with an inscription that reads simply "Our Children" or "Our Angel Boy." Despite the vast difference in aesthetic taste that these stones of different eras represent, their common lack of names points to a practice dating from the seventeenth century, which could leave children unnamed over a year after their birth.[10] Parents thereby postponed the child's official entry into the family until he had passed through the period when he was most likely to contract a fatal disease. As anonymous testaments to the vast numbers of infants who died too young to be named (or too precious to have that name mentioned in public), tombstones reflect the family's deep emotional investment in the dead.

The fiction that the dead spoke and that they were fully naturalized in their setting also appears in William Wordsworth's "Essays upon Epitaphs" (1810). Like other Romantics who sought to naturalize death, Wordsworth extols nature as the ultimate tomb. In America, only eleven years later, Bryant wrote "Thanatopsis," a similarly strong defense of the way nature joins all people in death. Wordsworth expostulates upon the appropriateness of situating a cemetery in woods or fields: "I could ruminate upon the beauty which the Monuments, thus placed, must have borrowed from the surrounding images of Nature—from the trees, the wild flowers, from a stream running perhaps within sight or hearing, from the beaten road stretching its weary length hard by."[11] For Wordsworth, monuments had a picturesque quality when set against the natural landscape, and even the "beaten road stretching its weary length" conjures up images of a vast stream of humanity or even of a corpse, deepening the nineteenth-century viewer's sympathetic associations between the cemetery and the natural world.

Wordsworth attributes the erection of monuments to a twofold desire to guard the remains of the deceased and to preserve their memories: they provide "a record to preserve the memory of the dead, as a tribute due to his individual worth, for a satisfaction to the sorrowing hearts of the Survivors, and for the common benefit of the living" (96). According to Wordsworth, epitaphs are the foundation for many basic topoi of funerary icons—"Life as a Journey—Death as a Sleep overcoming the tired Wayfarer—of Misfortune as a storm that falls suddenly upon him—of Beauty as a Flower that passeth away" (96–97). Just as Wordsworth had advised the writer in the preface to *Lyrical Ballads* (1798) to write in a plain style, he notes that the tone of epitaphs should be solemn and express their grief in a "general language of humanity" (100). Not only is an impartial tone necessary to convey grief adequately, but "the common or universal feeling of humanity" must be appealed to for the epitaph to exalt the reader (101).

According to Wordsworth, the epitaph often suspends our powers of disbelief by portraying a posthumous speaker who assures the reader that the afterlife is pleasant:

The departed Mortal is introduced telling you himself that his pains are gone; that a state of rest is come; and he conjures you to weep for him no longer. He admonishes with the voice of one experienced in the vanity of those affections which are confined to earthly objects, and gives a verdict like a superior Being . . . By this tender fiction the Survivors bind themselves to a sedater sorrow, and employ the intervention of the imagination in order that the reason may speak her own language earlier than she would otherwise have been enabled to do. (104)

Consoling the reader with the idea that the speaker exists in a realm beyond pain, the writer of an epitaph supports the "tender fiction" that the dead are still alive. Yet this fantasy remains a "tender fiction," an open secret for the mourners, who console themselves partly by creating their own fictions about the deceased's continued existence.

Women elegists in this period sought to "bind themselves to a sedater sorrow," as Wordsworth notes, through the use of posthumous voice and the evocation of specifically female scenes of mourning.[12] Like male writers, many female writers invoked the visionary state that may take place in a dream to suggest the change in perspective accompanying the death of loved ones. Lydia Huntley Sigourney's "Dream of the Dead," for instance, depicts a speaker who during sleep imagines that the dead have rejoined her:

> Sleep brought the dead to me. Their brows were kind,
> And their tones tender, and, as erst they blent
> Their sympathies with each familiar scene.
> It was my earthliness that robed them still
> In their material vestments, for they seemed
> Not yet to have put their glorious garments on.
> Methought, 'twere better thus to dwell with them,
> Than with the living.
>
> (ll. 1–8)

The dead look much as they did in life, a fact the speaker attributes to her own earthly perspective. From her vantage point, she sees them "robed . . . / In their material vestments," still clothed in the flesh rather than in the "glorious garments" of the spirit. Her remark echoes the Christian doctrine that foretells the spiritual nature of the body after death: "It is sown in corruption; it is raised in incorruption: It is sown in dishonour; it is raised in glory: it is sown in weakness; it is raised in power: It is sown a natural body; it is raised a spiritual body" (1 Corinthians 15:42–44). For the speaker, the combination of the dead's inviting humanity and their enviable immortality softens the knowledge that she must join them herself. Far from being frightening and unapproachable, the speaker's view of a material heaven is so consoling that she is prompted to remark that the dead's life seems preferable to her own.

In Sigourney's "Dream of the Dead," the speaker encounters in her dream a variety of people, some of whom she was acquainted with in life and all of whom point to her desire to recapture her youth. The first is "a chosen friend, / Beloved in school-days' happiness, who came . . . / As she was wont"; then her dead mother, "Full of fresh life, and in that beauty clad / Which charmed my earliest love"; followed by "A stranger-matron," who, "sicklied o'er and pale," disappoints the speaker's injunction to hear her mother speak and inverts the mother's healthful image; and, finally, a dead infant, laughing and smiling as if it were still alive. All of them are "gentle forms / Of faithful friendship and maternal love" (ll. 40–41); all of them are female or too young to be gendered. Upon awakening from her dream, she finds that these spirits "Did flit away, and life, with all its cares, / Stood forth in strong reality" (ll. 42–43). In fact, once her dream has evaporated, the speaker is aware once again of the disappointment of her life, another feature women's poetic dream-sequences often share. Despite her knowledge of the true state of the dead ("Upon whose lips I knew the burial-clay / Lay deep, for I had heard its hollow sound, / In hoarse reverberation, '*dust to dust!*'" [ll. 32–34]), she finds this fleeting vision consoling:

> Sweet dream!
> And solemn, let me bear thee in my soul
> Throughout the live-long day, to subjugate
> My earth-born hope. I bow me at your names,
> Sinless and passionless and pallid train!
> The seal of truth is on your breasts, ye dead!
> Ye may not swerve, nor from your vows recede,
> Nor of your faith make shipwreck. Scarce a point
> Divides you from us, though we fondly look
> Through a long vista of imagined years,
> And in the dimness of far distance, seek
> *To hide that tomb, whose crumbling verge we tread*
>
> (ll. 44–55)

The speaker will cherish in her memory this vision of the dead in order to conquer an "earth-born hope" that she might continue living, rather than willingly accept death. Her beliefs are given conviction by the unshakable faith that the dead seem to have attained in heaven. That they "may not swerve, nor from your vows recede, / Nor of your faith make shipwreck" reveals that the speaker transfers her own desire for faith onto the figures of her vision. Ascribing to the dead the apparent ability to act likens them to the living for whom the problem of faith on earth is real and pressing. Despite our wish to see death at "a long vista of imagined years," our closeness to death appears with startling clarity, a consoling yet forceful reminder for Sigourney of our future heavenly existence.

Like many other poems of the period by sentimental writers that depict—

actually or symbolically—a woman's death, Sigourney's meditation evokes a woman's nostalgic desire to recapture the carefree life of childhood, ideally upon her mother's bosom. Two extraordinary examples of poems that idealize girlhood and a mother's sway are Elizabeth Akers Allen's "Rock Me to Sleep" and Sigourney's "Last Word of the Dying."[13] Having tired of flinging away the "soul-wealth" and of "sowing for others to reap," the speaker of Allen's poem begs her mother to return from death and take her into her arms again as if she were still an infant. Despite the passage of years, she longs for her mother's loving embrace to erase the pain of her burdensome adult life:

> Mother, dear mother! the years have been long
> Since I last hushed to your lullaby song;
> Sing, then, and unto my soul it shall seem
> Womanhood's years have been but a dream;
> Clasped to your arms in a loving embrace,
> With your long lashes just sweeping my face,
> Never hereafter to wake or to weep;
> Rock me to sleep, mother, rock me to sleep![14]

Allen's poem was enormously successful, even spawning another poem in response, spoken in a mother's voice, "Answer to Rock Me to Sleep." Given women's frequent admission of forced self-denial, "Rock Me to Sleep" provides a platform from which Allen could offer other women a momentary respite, a fleeting escape. Remarkable for the speaker's wish both to regress and to die, the poem offers only modified satisfaction for the expectations of women's lives. Indeed, its powerful regression—"Backward, turn backward, O Time, in your flight" (l. 1)—and blunt admission of unhappiness make it exemplary in expressing the dissatisfaction of women's lives.

Sigourney also suggests that the strong bond between a woman and her mother promotes a desire for reunion, especially among the dying. In "The Last Word of the Dying," the speaker depicts a woman who, unable to speak, instead spells out the word "Mother" in sign-language. This last act prompts the speaker to wonder if the dying woman perceives her mother's ghostly presence ("She, whose soft hand did dry thine infant tear, / Hovereth she now, with love divine / Thy dying pillow near?" [ll. 34–36]) or if she can barely bring herself to relinquish her hold over her children ("Those three fair boys, / Lingers thy soul with them, even from heaven's perfect joys? / Say—wouldst thou teach us thus, how strong a mother's tie?" [ll. 53–55]). For Sigourney, as for Allen, a woman's wish to return to her mother's arms in heaven is almost as strong as her desire to protect her own children, a desire that recurs in elegies in which women seek the shelter of a mother's arms in heaven.

In "The Dream," Elizabeth Oakes Smith similarly portrays the way a visionary state brings us a changed perspective in life:

I dreamed last night, that I myself did lay
    Within the grave, and after stood and wept,
    My spirit sorrowed where its ashes slept!
'T was a strange dream, and yet methinks it may
    Prefigure that which is akin to truth.
    How sorrow we o'er perished dreams of youth,
High hopes and aspirations doomed to be
Crushed and o'ermastered by earth's destiny!
    Fame, that the spirit loathing turns to truth—
And that deluding faith so loath to part,
That earth will shrine for us one kindred heart!
    Oh, 't is the ashes of such things that wring
Tears from the eyes—hopes like to these depart,
    And we bow down in dread, o'ershadowed by Death's wing![15]

Rather than imagine that the grave offers consolation, Oakes Smith imagines that it represents the end of earthly hopes or fame. Life is a mournful and never-ending remembrance of the "perished dreams of youth / High hopes and aspirations." Oakes Smith's poem precisely indicts the grave's ability to preserve our fame. The speaker consigns to "dreams" both "fame" and the deluding "faith" that "one kindred heart" will be enshrined on earth. Rather than address the actual "ashes" of the dead, the speaker turns at the end of the poem to the unfulfilled aspirations of her life, a more serious subject to mourn.

The curt aphorisms and biting refrains of Puritan gravestones, whose death's-heads promise that the reader will come to the same end as the dead, were an apt model for Dickinson's own revisions of cultural beliefs about death and mourning. Whereas mid-nineteenth-century women's elegies sought to soften the realization of death and redress the disappointments and griefs women often suffered, these inscriptions typically adopt the voice of the dead to remind the reader of his fate. Jackson's essay contains a number of epitaphs that serve as apt comparisons to Dickinson's own lyrics. A popular motto invokes the language of economic loss and gain, so evident in elegies within the Puritan tradition:

Death is a debt to nature due,
Which I have paid and so must you.
(207)

Like a promissory note that has reached maturity, death is a "debt" that must be paid with exactly the price of life. As Jackson notes, "A business-like view of such events must have been a family trait throughout that community, for they found nothing more tender and solemn to say of her" (207).

Another epitaph enjoins the reader to pause and contemplate the scene, reminding her of her eventual end:

> Reader, behold and shed a tear;
> Think on the dust that slumbers here;
> And when you read the fate of me,
> Think on the glass that runs for thee.
>
> (206)

The first-person speaker enjoins the reader to consider that his or her fate will be similar. Although epitaphs often record some information about the deceased, they adopt many stock funerary conventions: the invitation to stop, the injunction to meditate on one's fate, and the envoi (or send-off). The tripartite structure of the epitaph enjoins the reader to look upon the deceased's grave and to sympathize ("Reader, behold, and shed a tear"), to ponder the remains of the dead ("Think on the dust that slumbers here"), and to equate his or her own fate with the deceased's ("And when you read the fate of me, / Think on the glass that runs for thee"). The verbs of perception, such as "behold," "think," and "read," and the direct address actively engage one's attention and foretell the similar outcomes of one's life. As Debra Fried points out, the act of reading an epitaph itself aptly summarizes and predicts the death of the reader:

the epitaph's repetitions suggest that the pair, stranger and gravestone, doubly represents both the before and after, so to speak, of both living and dead. Epitaphs make us see ourselves as doubles—perhaps incomplete or imperfect doubles—of the dead, as living dead, as readers awaiting our epitaphs.[16]

The epitaph, like the tombstone, becomes a figure for the reader, who will eventually, following the inexorable logic of the epitaph, be turned into an inscription, a read text. As Fried trenchantly notes, "to be dead is to be read" (617). Yet the consoling fiction that the dead could speak also reverses this formula, for reading the epitaph is also imaginatively to exchange places with the dead, to become so enamored of mourning as to become almost dead ourselves: to read is to be dead.

Besides mirroring the position of the reader of the inscription, epitaphs serve another function distinct from other types of poetic tributes: they create a posthumous persona. As Jonathan Culler has argued, apostrophe, or the figure of voice created through direct address in a poem, can seem to animate the natural world and to create in nature an interlocutor:

We might posit, then, a third level of reading where the vocative of apostrophe is a device which the poetic voice uses to establish with an object a relationship which helps to constitute him. The object is treated as a subject, an *I* which implies a certain type of *you* in its turn. One who successfully invokes nature is one to whom nature might, in its turn, speak.[17]

If apostrophe and the "O" that signals the creation of poetic voice can posit a constitutive relationship with the world, then epitaphs can perhaps be said to perform the reverse: they create a persona by addressing a reader who is real, but willed into silence by the speaker's voice. Indeed, the formula of the epitaph does more than create a receptive listener: it forces the reader into dead silence, as if it replicated the stillness of the tomb. Epitaphs of the "Pause, Traveller!" variety enjoin the reader to give over the moment to identifying with the speaker, who aptly foretells for the reader a future identical to his own. As Fried argues, "epitaphs predict the collapse of reader and poem and a consequent proliferation of more epitaphs" (616).

Dickinson transforms the epitaphic tradition into a ghostly reversal of living and dead that casts doubt on the apparent comfort that Victorian mourning conventions sought to offer. The dead appear unwilling to communicate, as in this brief lyric:

> Endow the Living—with the Tears—
> You squander on the Dead,
> And They were Men and Women—now,
> Around Your Fireside—
>
> Instead of Passive Creatures,
> Denied the Cherishing
> Till They—the Cherishing deny—
> With Death's Etherial Scorn—
>
> (J, 521)

2. squander on] spend upon—

This poem suggests that the living to whom one denies cherishing will scorn cherishing once they are dead. Rather than "squander" our tears in regret, we should instead hold dear the living while they are able to return our care; once "Death's Etherial Scorn" is set on their faces, they will be unresponsive to our tears, having been "Denied the Cherishing / Till They—the Cherishing Deny—." In characterizing the silence of the dead as willful, Dickinson ascribes life and agency to the dead in a way that profoundly criticizes nineteenth-century habits of mourning. The ambiguous syntax of "And they were Men and Women—now" implies that the mourners might have been to blame for the dead's disappearance. The speaker's blaming of the living for the dead's fate—and the equally ambiguous implication that the dead might be revived if the mourners are affectionate to the living—is the crux of the poem: death has the power to confer "Etherial Scorn," both celestial and impalpable. Just when the mourners would most like to "Cherish" their loved ones, the dead seem most distant and outrightly elude their grasp. In contrast to their portrait as "Passive Creatures," who can only suffer the grief of the mourners, the dead in this final image appear vengeful, willfully rejecting our attentions.

Another poem suggests that our close attachment to the dead allows us to deceive ourselves that they may return to life, until we belatedly find that our preoccupation with them has made us more dead than alive:

> The distance that the dead have gone
> Does not at first appear;
> Their coming back seems possible
> For many an ardent year.
>
> And then, that we have followed them,
> We more than half suspect,
> So intimate have we become
> With their dear retrospect.
>
> (J, 1742)

4] For many a fruitless year. / That first abandoned
year. / That first absconded year.

That the dead almost palpably live on is reinforced by the variants of the last line of the first stanza: "ardent" might be replaced by "fruitless," both words that signify the passion or gestation left unfulfilled due to the dead's disappearance. "That first abandoned year" rather than "For many an ardent year" limits the recurrent act of mourning for the dead over a number of years to the period immediately following their death; "absconded" for "abandoned" further implies that the dead are temporarily removed from sight, hidden away only for the moment. Our memory of the dead leads us to become, so the poem argues, nearly dead ourselves. Not only does "their dear retrospect" invoke our act of reviewing their lives in our minds, but it proves to be the vantage point to which the living mourner, who literally moves closer to death over time, has progressed by the poem's end.

Although Dickinson also evokes the appearance of the dead in a dreamlike vision, she discounts the comforting promise of a reunion after death. The speaker of the following poem implies that the dead appear to us only while we are in a visionary state and delude us with their reality:

> Of nearness to her sundered Things
> The Soul has special times—
> When Dimness—looks the Oddity—
> Distinctness—easy—seems—

The Shapes we buried, dwell about,
Familiar, in the Rooms—
Untarnished by the Sepulchre,
The Mouldering Playmate comes—

In just the Jacket that he wore—
Long buttoned in the Mold
Since we—old mornings, Children—played—
Divided—by a world—

The Grave yields back her Robberies—
The Years, our pilfered Things—
Bright Knots of Apparitions
Salute us, with their wings—

As we—it were—that perished
Themself—had just remained till we rejoin them—
And 'twas they, and not ourself
That mourned.

                                                    (J, 607)

8. The] Our

Like the kindly figures in Sigourney's "Dream of the Dead," the "Shapes" of
stanza two seem "Familiar" or home-like, well acquainted with the "Rooms"
they once inhabited. To the speaker, these shadowy figures appear completely
untouched by death, "Untarnished by the Sepulchre." Yet the "Mouldering
Playmate," wearing a "Jacket" "Long buttoned in the Mold," takes on in Dickinson's elegiac meditation a reality that travesties the consolatory myth that
portrayed the dead's more natural existence in heaven. Sympathetically evoking the image of a child whose jacket might have been buttoned by a parent in
life, the jacket "Long buttoned in the Mold" also comments ironically on the
supposed immortality of the body: unlike the buttons, the body has steadily
decomposed. While in Sigourney's "The Dream of the Dead" the deceased infant appears natural and human in its "material vestments," in Dickinson's
poem the child has been steadily decaying, thus differentiating the actual contents of the grave from the speaker's visionary perception of the dead
"Shapes." "Divided—by a world—," living and dead exist side by side, and
their proximity echoes Sigourney's claim that we walk a tightrope between life
and death. Dickinson undercuts the popular contention that we can take comfort in the vision of the dead in heaven as untouched and lifelike.

Although the dead child seems to return to life, the speaker's vision proves
a merely psychological event, frightening in its realism and ultimately delusive. In the first stanza, "sundered Things" appear to the "Soul" at "special

times," although this new angle of perception gives only a superficial clarity to the speaker's recollected thoughts. We might understand "Oddity" to suggest that, in the daily course of events, "Dimness" characterizes the speaker's perception of the spiritual world. Moreover, the "Distinctness" with which the speaker can discern these spirits only "easy—seems—," an all-too-tentative assertion of the speaker's actual insight. This falseness of discrimination, however, goes unnoticed by the collective adult speaker through the final two stanzas when the dead return to life. In imagining that the "Grave" yields up "her Robberies" and the "Years" return "our Pilfered Things," the poem alludes, as in the "sundered Things" of the first line, to the popular characterization of the child as a precious object stolen away by death.

Yet the wished-for reunion of living and dead that the speaker of Sigourney's poem finds consoling proves merely a fiction. "Bright Knots of Apparitions" are "nots" of being, as this pun hints. While the welcoming "Salute" of the spirits, possibly even a toast to our health, promises good will (etymologically deriving from "to preserve or wish health to"), their greeting is anything but wholesome for those who meet them. The last stanza describes a reversal between the living and the dead that allows us to experience the dying of those who have already died, and its formal oddity reflects our necessary suspension of disbelief: the pentameter line with a feminine ending, which breaks the tetrameter format, parallels our wish that we might join the dead. But our desire is cut short in the last two lines, in which the child angels who have apparently exchanged positions with us seem to be themselves the living and mourning beings. The poem suggests that the visions of the dead that were popular in nineteenth-century funerary verse provide an illusory sense of consolation, as doubtful as the consolation offered to mothers in poems on the loss of children. The dead allow us to forget our distance from them only momentarily.

Dickinson reverses the consoling expectation that we will be joined by the dead. The following lyric points to the delusory wish to substitute the memory of the dead for the companionship of the living:

> You'll find—it when you die—
> The Easier to let go—
> For recollecting such as went—
> You could not spare—you know.
>
> And though their places somewhat filled—
> As did their Marble names
> With Moss—they never grew so full—
> You chose the newer names—
>
> And when this World—sets further back—

As Dying—say it does—
The former love—distincter grows—
And supercedes the fresh—

And Thought of them—so fair invites—
It looks too tawdry Grace
To stay behind—with just the Toys
We bought—to ease their place—

(J, 610)

8. names] times—

The poem addresses the power of memory to recall the dead by adopting an important epitaphic convention: that the dead could speak. The lyric describes our wish to choose the "newer names," to substitute the living for the dead. By literalizing the voice of the dead as epitaphs on their own tombstones, whose grassy "places somewhat filled— / As did their Marble names / With Moss" (ll. 5–7), she counters the fiction of voice developed in the epitaph: that the dead could speak as if they had a voice.[18] Dickinson discusses the normal human tendency to remember the dead and contends that the memory of the dead is a welcome incentive. Normally the prospect given by the epitaph's posthumous speaker, the shift in perspective in this poem is voiced by the living speaker, who recounts the change that takes place in the dying. Indeed, as we grow older and closer to death, the "former love" of the long dead seem to beckon us to join them, and life on earth without them looks "too tawdry Grace" (l. 14). When one places this poem in the context of the elegies on children, moreover, one sees that the "Toys / We bought—to ease their place—" might refer to children or young people who substitute for those who have died as well as to the trivial aspects of life. By the end of the poem, the speaker's perspective shifts to take in not only the inviting prospect of joining the dead but also the newly vilified life on earth.

The iconography of mourning increasingly promoted the myth that the dying embodied supernatural sensitivity and virtues beyond the normal. Funerary portraits and scenes of mourning in verse and fiction grew increasingly formulaic in their representations of weeping willow motifs toward mid-century. In Judd's novel, *Margaret* (1845), the heroine and Isabel carry an uncomplaining crippled boy, appropriately named Job, to his home. There they encounter his mother and notice a decorative sampler that epitomizes the conventional mourning pictures of the era:

The bright sunlight streamed into the room, quite paling and quenching flames and coals in the fireplace. A picture hung on the walls, an embroidery, floss on white satin, representing a woman leaning mourningly on an urn, and a willow drooping over her.

The woman did not appear to be at all excited by her boy's misfortune, only the breeze of her prevailing sorrow, that sometimes lulled, seemed to blow up afresh a little, as she resumed her seat after attending to his wants. (1, 237)

An embroidery that features the popular triptych of mourning maiden, funeral urn, and weeping willow captures the home's atmosphere of melancholy resignation, one which mothers of dying children were destined to accept as their own. Barton Levi St. Armand characterizes this tearful maiden, a "veiled figure" of classical origins, as "'Woman Weeping,' in contrast to Emerson's galvanic and frankly masculine image of 'Man Thinking.'"[19] He notes that "as an allegory of unalloyed remorse, of inconsolable and perpetual grief in the pagan manner, Woman Weeping was Christianized and romanticized until she took on a Madonna-like calm" (46). Indeed, we might extend the portrait to the actual circumstances of Job's awareness of his impending death and to the description of his mother, who is "a wan, care-worn, ailing looking woman, yet having a gentle and placid tone of voice" and whose own sickly appearance and religious resignation was typified by the weeping willow motif. A widow, Mistress Luce supports her son alone through domestic handiwork, a common occupation for women with little education or other training. Brought on perhaps by the added burden of domestic chores and the care of her ailing children, her illness attests to the strain of household cares for women of the working classes in the nineteenth century.

Remarkably resigned though saddened by her son's illness, she describes Job in a way that parallels the willow's growth from sapling to mournful tree:

"He gets worse and worse," she sighed,—"we did all we could."

"Won't he grow straight and stout?" asked Margaret.

"Alas!" she answered, "a whipporwill sung on the willow over the brook four nights before he was born;—we had him drawn through a split tree, but he never got better."

"Whipporwills sing every night most at the Pond in the summer," said Margaret.

"I have heard them a great many times," added Isabel. "Ma says they won't hurt us if we are only good."

"I know, I know," responded the woman, with a quick shuddering start.

"Ma says that they only hurt wicked people," continued Isabel.

"I always knew it was a judgment on account of my sins."

"What have you done?" asked Margaret anxiously.

"I cannot tell," answered the Widow, "only I am a great sinner; if you could hear the Parson preach you would think so too. I just read in my Bible what God says, 'Because you have sinned against the Lord, this is come upon you.'"

"I saw Job at the Meeting one day," said Margaret; "he recited the catechism so well. Do you know what it meant?" she continued, turning to the boy.

"If I do not, Mammy does," replied the latter. "But I know the whipporwill's song."

"Do you?" asked Margaret; "can you say it?"

"No, only I hear it every night."

"In the winter time?"

"Yes, after I go to bed."

"Do you have dreams?"

"I don't know what it is," replied the boy, "only I hear whipporwill. It sings in the willow over the urn, and sings in here," he said, pointing to his breast. "I shall die of whipporwill."

"O Father in heaven!" groaned the mother bitterly, yet with an air of resignation, "it is just."

"It sings," added the boy, "in the moonshine, I hear it in the brook in the summer, and among the flowers, and the grasshoppers sing it to me when the sun goes down, and it sings in the Bible. I shall die of whipporwill."

(I, 237–39)

The mother's story about her struggle to cure her son's illness reveals a crossover between folk wisdom and orthodox religion that was eventually combined into a new icon of sentimental mourning by the mid-nineteenth century. Although she heeds the dictums of folklore—hearing a whipporwill sing brings tidings of death, while drawing a child through a split tree wards off illness—she also relies on the minister's interpretation of the Bible to mean that her own sins are to blame for her son's frail nature. Even the gentler influences of gradualism and evangelical Christianity, whose exponents believed feeling was evidence of salvation, could not completely erase the awareness of sin and its consequences: "They are plainly told that all whom the heavenly Father hath not been pleased to plant as sacred trees in his garden, are doomed and devoted to destruction."[20]

Like his mother, the dying boy imitates the conventional mourning attitudes represented in consolatory lithographs of the period. The hanging embroidery recalls, as I have noted, the actual moment of the mother's first awareness that her son was fated to die, and Job also acquires his foreboding knowledge of death from the needlework's suggestion. Although he learns the catechism by means of rote memorization, he knows "whipporwill" instinctively, almost as if it were a language. Moreover, this doleful music has many manifestations for him in the natural world, yet he points first to the picture within his home as evidence of the song's pervasive presence. Mother and child thus so thoroughly have internalized the conventions of grieving represented by this mourning artifact that their behavior is dictated by its represented attitudes.

Another poem suggests that despite the illusory sense of progress the dead make toward heaven, their ultimate goal is uncertain:

These tested Our Horizon
Then disappeared
As Birds before achieving
A Latitude.

Our Retrospection of Them
A fixed Delight,
But our Anticipation
A Dice—a Doubt—

               (J, 886)

Dickinson's use of optics and geography suggests that our assurance of the dead's ultimate arrival in heaven depends largely on our sense of perspective. Furthermore, the discourse of scientific inquiry reflects the speaker's desire to fix heaven as a spot in the calculable universe, where the dead test the horizon to prove that it exists. "Latitude" points to the birds' disappearance before rising above the horizon; it suggests a fixed point on a grid, a desire to locate and to predict a point in space. Given the difficulty Dickinson personally experienced in justifying the existence of heaven, "Retrospection" of the dead as they were in life provides a reassuring view of our own futures, a "fixed Delight." Yet this backward glance, though predictable and reassuring, also transfixes us as we remember the beloved dead. Similar to the image of the dead's disappearance, the last line increases our doubts exponentially. In "Anticipation" of meeting the dead, we find "A Dice—a Doubt—," as much security as in a game of chance. Moreover, the multiplication of dots on dice implies the many possible combinations in each throw, none of which can be predicted with certainty. Much as the doubled die puns on the deaths of the reader and those who have disappeared from sight, our lives are doubly circumscribed by a morbid fondness for the dead and the fear that no afterlife exists.

Dickinson partook of her era's monumentalization of the dead in "Alabaster Chambers" (J, 216) that more resemble a house than a tomb, yet her terse rejection of the mourning practices suggested in the elegies of sentimental writers reveals that she was closer to the acerbic wit of the Puritan graveyards than to the mawkishness of the nineteenth-century elegy. She criticizes the ability of tombstones to memorialize the dead, partly because of the mourners' short memories and partly because fame is itself a rhetorical construct. Often writing lyrics that themselves might have been inscribed on tombstones, she invokes the cemetery setting with its artful monuments to play on the supposed "naturalness" of the dead's resting place. Indeed, her use of the epitaph to portray death's ultimate reversal was more closely related to Puritan wit than to the Christian gradualism of her era. Included in a letter written in June 1877, perhaps on the third anniversary of her father's death, the elegy beginning "Lay this Laurel on the One" (J, 1393) is most likely devoted to him, as she notes in the accompanying letter to Higginson that his death has magnified the importance of living: "Since my Father's dying, everything sacred enlarged so—it was dim to own" (*Letters* 2, 583). Later in the letter she refers to Higginson's poem, "Decoration," which had appeared in June 1874 in

Scribner's Monthly. Higginson sent a copy of Dickinson's lyric to Mrs. Todd in 1891, while she was preparing the second series of *Poems*, and he remarked that it was the "condensed essence of [the original] & so far finer."[21]

The considerable differences between the two poems suggest how Dickinson revised epitaphic conventions. Full of clichéd sentiments, Higginson's "Decoration" ostensibly concerns a speaker's memorialization of an anonymous dead soldier to whom he cannot adequately pay tribute:

DECORATION.

"Manibus date lilia plenis."

Mid the flower-wreath'd tombs I stand
Bearing lilies in my hand.
Comrades! in what soldier-grave
Sleeps the bravest of the brave?

Is it he who sank to rest
With his colors round his breast?
Friendship makes his tomb a shrine;
Garlands veil it; ask not mine.

One low grave, yon tree beneath,
Bears no roses, wears no wreath;
Yet no heart more high and warm
Ever dared the battle-storm,

Never gleamed a prouder eye
In the front of victory,
Never foot had firmer tread
On the field where hope lay dead,

Than are hid within this tomb,
Where the untended grasses bloom;
And no stone, with feign'd distress,
Mocks the sacred loneliness.

Youth and beauty, dauntless will,
Dreams that life could ne'er fulfill,
Here lie buried; here in peace
Wrongs and woes have found release.

Turning from my comrades' eyes,
Kneeling where a woman lies,
I strew lilies on the grave
Of the bravest of the brave.

The typical encomium given to the dead soldier, "the bravest of the brave," and the tribute to his valour are thoroughly conventional; like Longfellow, Higginson attempts to achieve catharsis by putting the pain of death into common language. Yet though the speaker's language invokes the traditional praise for the dead soldier, he dismisses the need for a poetic or floral tribute—"Garlands veil it; ask not mine" (l. 8)—and turns instead to the actual object of praise, a woman whose duties within the home and grief perhaps due to the death of a loved husband or brother in battle have gone unrecognized. In contrast to the garlanded tomb, the woman's "low grave" "wears no wreath." Despite the lack of ornamentation, the implicit comparison is between the woman's survival and a soldier's valor on the battlefield. But the speaker acknowledges that an inscription could not give voice to the speaker's sorrow, making silence more appropriate: "And no stone, with feign'd distress, / Mocks the sacred loneliness." Ultimately, the speaker's recollection of the dead woman modifies the reader's expectations about the "Dreams that life could ne'er fufill"; at the end of the poem, he strews lilies, symbolic of resurrection, on the grave as a tribute.

Dickinson's poem, too, concerns the impossibility of communicating the glory of the dead. Creating posthumous speakers who threaten to exchange places with the reader, she often reverses the roles of living and dead, mourner and mourned, as in the following lyric:

> Lay this Laurel on the One
> Too intrinsic for Renown—
> Laurel—vail your deathless tree—
> Him you chasten, that is He!
>
> (J, 1393)

The laurel or bay leaf, traditionally used to crown poets and military victors, promises immortality. But the two addressees—the reader and the laurel tree—reverse one's expectations. As in the traditional epitaph, the speaker enjoins the reader to stop and ponder the remains of the dead and enforces on the reader an awareness that he or she is "chastened" by their example. "Too intrinsic for Renown—" implies that the dead soldier needs no external recognition and hence renders the use of monuments unnecessary, for he is complete within himself. Addressing the laurel, whose open display of immortality embarrasses the speaker and prompts her wish that it might be shrouded, the speaker conveys the sense that poetic immortality is perhaps the only true guarantee of remembrance after death. In invoking the images of a veiled trunk, Dickinson naturalizes the graveside scene and symbolically preserves an image of the body, itself draped in a coffin. Like the marble columns half-draped with cloths populating many Victorian cemeteries, the veiled tree modifies the Romantic image of a curtain separating life from death, the fathomable from the unknown. Rather than openly portray the dead in their monuments, the Victorians symbolized the passage from life to death with a curtain, thus preserving its secrecy and displaying the heightened theatricality surrounding death. In the light of her portrayal of the unostentatious tribute to the dead, the last line proves ambiguous: "Him you chasten" might refer to the dead soldier, or to the speaker of Higginson's poem, for whom "youth and beauty, dauntless will, / Dreams that life could ne'er fulfill" are quashed by early death, despite his wish to enhance these virtues. Finally, and perhaps most importantly, "He" applies to the reader who feels "chastened" by the example of the deceased. Dickinson adapts the epitaph in her poetry in order to modify our expectation of fame, implying that not only the deceased but also the mourner are subject to the same, moderating experience.

The laurel tree also evokes a traditional symbol in funerary iconography that combines images of celestial and earthly existence: the tree of life. At least as early as Sumerian times, the tree signified the lives of human beings: "The righteous shall flourish like the palm tree: he shall grow like a cedar in Lebanon" (Psalms 92:12). A symbol of spiritual values for many cultures, the tree of life represented for the Puritans the power of God's word to regenerate human souls, just as a twig can be replanted and grow into a new plant. As Edward Taylor writes, "Yet I shall stand thy Grafft, and Fruits that are / Fruits of the Tree of Life thy Grafft shall beare."[22] Often carved on gravestones with branches cut off to signify the number of dead or hung with anthropomorphic disks, representing the souls that have taken flight, trees symbolized the lives of the deceased as well as the promise of everlasting life from the fruit of God's word. Later, the image of the tree underwent two further transformations: first in the eighteenth century as palms (signifying victory and the garden), and second in the mid-nineteenth century as the weeping willow (which represented the regeneration of the soul, the tearful remembrance of the dead, and the belief that trees planted in cemeteries might drain hazardous swamp-filled areas).[23]

Trees also figure prominently in Victorian funerary sculpture. Cut trees, stumps, logs, and natural crosses, made of granite or white marble, naturalized the remains of the dead. Often draped with ivy signifying remembrance or sheaves of wheat symbolizing human life, these sculptures promoted the fiction that the dead were similarly felled in a natural and unremarkable way. The frequent anonymity of these graves is an important reminder that all would join in one mighty sepulcher after death. Popular in this era, too, "natural" monuments marked the spots where soldiers were killed in battle during the Civil War, though these monuments are often curiously unable to convey the significance of the loss. In Herman Melville's "An Uninscribed Monument on One of the Battle-Fields of the Wilderness," for instance, a tree or other natural landmark, "though tableted," can never convey the din of battle as well as the quiet of the wood and the silence to which the reader is condemned at the end of the poem.[24] Dickinson also contends that the gravestone's inscription cannot adequately pay tribute to a dead soldier:

> Step lightly on this narrow spot—
> The broadest Land that grows
> Is not so ample as the Breast
> These Emerald Seams enclose.
>
> Step lofty, for this name be told
> As far as Cannon dwell
> Or Flag subsist or Fame export
> Her deathless Syllable.
>
> (J, 1183)

Recalling the injunction common in funerary inscriptions to pause to consider the deceased, the poem encourages the reader to "step lightly" on the ground above the dead. Rather than extol the life of the dead person, however, the speaker emphasizes the unreadability of the gravesite. She contrasts the valour of the soldier—his "ample" "Breast"—with the "narrow" space in which the body is interred, suggesting that his courage could not be contained by the grave. Only "Emerald Seams" distinguish the grave as a site. Rather than serve as a pompous memorial to the dead, this simple grave registers the impossibility of summarizing the significant events of the dead person's life.

Furthermore, Dickinson points to the power of sound to memorialize the dead. "Step lofty" enjoins the reader to rise above the grave and its small, mundane concerns. By casting the event in the realm of the hypothetical and using the subjunctive "be" rather than "is," she suggests that the soldier's fame is sustained by the repeated remarks of others. The cannon and flag "dwell" and "subsist," almost as if they lived and carried on his name in his place. "Deathless Syllable" also connotes vocality or music, since fame exists whenever the soldier's name is pronounced. In fact, "syllable" hints at the way sound as well as sense convey the soldier's fame: it calls up both the discrete sounds of words and the "bell" of a funerary procession. Although the soldier's body is buried in the "narrow spot" of the grave, his name transcends its confines and ultimately reminds us that celebrity depends upon the poem and other verbal and written tributes, rather than on the actual monumentalized grave site.

Another poem of Dickinson's combines cemetery iconography and epitaphic conventions to undercut the professed grief of the mourners. Writing to Higginson in 1877, Dickinson explicitly referred to the following poem as "an Epitaph," and Mills Campbell states that "her notion of the stone as 'confiding' is directly related to her own style of writing and that style is directly related to the convention of the speaking monument.[25] According to Mills Campbell, every linguistic gesture is a type of "speaking monument," since it attempts to claim as fully present a moment that has already been lost. At its best, poetry expresses language's "Constancy," its ability to testify to the absence of the speaker, especially in the face of our inconstant emotions toward the dead:

> She laid her docile Crescent down
> And this confiding Stone
> Still states to Dates that have forgot
> The News that she is gone—
>
> So constant to it's stolid trust,
> The Shaft that never knew—
> It shames the Constancy that fled
> Before it's emblem flew—
>
> (J, 1396)

Cosmological figures, such as the sun, stars, and moon, depict constellations representative of heaven on gravestones; more specifically, the sun represents the flight of the soul heavenward.[26] "Crescent" thus may represent the trajectory of life toward the celestial sphere. Like the marble shafts of the antique and quaint cemetery described in Judd's novel or the cut or broken marble columns scattered throughout most Victorian cemeteries, the "Shaft" of the gravestone records with "stolid trust" the life of the dead, and it exposes the less reliable "Constancy" of the living, who forget the dead woman while the stone itself still stands. A worksheet draft of the poem reveals several changes that emphasize the way the tombstone speaks as deliberately uncertain: "subjunctive" for "confiding" conveys the idea of hypothetical or contingent action, much as the eternal stone memorializes one in a less than secure state; alternately, "mechanic" for "confiding" conveys the way the formulaic rendering of the inscription prevents the full expression of emotion. The tombstone still records the "News" of the woman's death, although its "Dates" have been forgotten by most. Far from simply recording the facts of this woman's life, Dickinson indicts the culture and the family for their short memories and erects her poem as a monument, a tribute to the beloved dead.

Moreover, the lyric's presentation situates it in the context of pictorial art and furthers its critique of the epitaph's memorialization of the dead.[27] Dickinson pasted two clippings from newspapers above the poem: in the upper lefthand corner, a crescent moon with a star between the horns, and at the right, slanting tombstones with an undecipherable inscription.[28] The crescent moon and slanting tombstones might represent Islamic and Christian powers respectively and thus undermine the preeminence of a single system of belief. Placed in the context of funerary sculpture, however, these illustrations create a visual text, an "emblem" to be interpreted. Indeed, perhaps part of the point is that both pictures instill even more obscurity into our awareness of the dead's fate. Finally, if one considers that Dickinson performs by adorning her poem with illustrations the same action the speaker describes (laying down a crescent, remembering the dead), then the poem becomes an artifact that pays tribute to the dead. Like a tombstone, which combines visual and written elements, the lyric and its arrangement on the page visibly symbolize the idea that death may be recorded yet not understood.

Dickinson invokes the common fiction that the dead are only sleeping and enjoins a peaceful silence on them, even at the Apocalypse:

> Ample make this Bed—
> Make this Bed with Awe—
> In it wait till Judgment break
> Excellent and Fair.
>
> Be it's Mattress straight—
> Be it's Pillow round—
> Let no Sunrise' yellow noise
> Interrupt this Ground—
>
> (J, 829)

Sent to Thomas Niles in 1883 and entitled by the poet "Country Burial," this lyric alludes indirectly to the epitaphic convention of posthumous speech, but rather than portray the dead predicting the demise of the living or instructing the reader in holy living, Dickinson softens the expectation that the dead will rise on the last day to a comforting wish that they might be undisturbed in death. While the speaker wishes that the dead might be comfortable as they anticipate the second coming of Christ, she exaggerates the image of an "Ample" bed by invoking death's sublime sense of "Awe." According to St. Armand, Dickinson's poems reflect a celestial day in which each time of day reflects a different state of the soul.[29] The possibility of salvation is reflected in perhaps the most important cosmological image in her poems: the sun. Anticipating the arrival of the Son of God on the dawn of the Day of Reckoning, the speaker lays the emphasis on the ecstatic and hence indescribable nature of death. Punning on "Judgment Day" in "Judgment break," the speaker implies that sunrise brings with it the end of night as well as the justice of paradise. "Excellent" derives from "to rise out of" and hints etymologically at the rising of the dead from their graves as well as the outstanding good of the light of salvation. Moreover, her off-rhyme "Fair" does not conform either to the tidy rhythms of Isaac Watts's hymns or to the comforting pictures of heaven as a wholly merciful and beautiful place provided by other elegists. In the synesthesic "Sunrise' yellow noise," Dickinson combines the wish that the dead might be left undisturbed by the blaring trumpets of the resurrection and voices and peals of thunder predicted in Revelations (4:1, 5) with the arrival of the sun-god. Even "Interrupt" implies that death is a continuum whose silence is better left undisturbed. Far from embracing the joyful awakening of the dead, Dickinson wishes a peaceful silence that contradicts the popular image of the dead's resurrection.

Adapting the symbols of funerary sculpture and gravestones in her lyrics, Dickinson displays both the inconstancy of human beings' affections and the inability of epitaphs to memorialize the dead. Consigning the dead to a trenchant silence, her poems tell us again and again instead how the memorialization of the dead foreshadows our own terse-lipped quiet in the grave. In one of the four conclusions she wrote to one of her best-known poems beginning "Safe in their Alabaster Chambers" (J, 216), Dickinson adopts the images of the "Crescent," "Arcs," and "Firmaments" to depict heaven and the crown, so often found on New England tombstones, to describe immortality.[30] Pointed, fluted, layered, ribbed, banded, beaded, and pierced, crowns signified the righteousness of God's elect: "Henceforth there is laid up for me a crown of righteousness, which the Lord, the righteous judge, shall give me at that day: and not to me only, but unto all them also that love his appearing" (2 Timothy 4:8). Given the apocalyptic imagery, it is also likely Dickinson meant to invoke the elders in Revelations (4:10) who cast down their crowns as a form of obeisance before the throne of God. Rather than give voice to their worshipful chorus, however, these "Doges" are silent. Like an abstract expressionist painting, which evokes a mood through the use of color rather than form, her lyric concludes with the color white, reminiscent of "Snow," the white marble of tombs, and the emptiness of a blank page:

> Safe in their Alabaster Chambers—
> Untouched by Morning—
> And untouched by Noon—
> Lie the meek members of the Resurrection—
> Rafter of Satin—and Roof of Stone!
>
> Grand go the Years—in the Crescent—above them—
> Worlds scoop their Arcs—
> And Firmaments—row—
> Diadems—drop—and Doges—surrender—
> Soundless as dots—on a Disc of Snow—
>
> (J, 216)

Using the epitaphic conventions popular in graveyard poetry and inscriptions, Dickinson reverses the expected formula that we should wait patiently to see the dead by showing them anticipating our arrival. Nineteenth-century American women poets, like Sigourney and others, often portray heaven as a utopia where women can reunite with female friends, mothers, and children.

Epitaphs similarly posit the existence of the dead, creating the fiction that they live on in posthumous voices. Far from rejecting these notions outright, Dickinson partakes of and enriches epitaphic conventions in her elegaic meditations. Whereas other women writers romanticize the possibility of a reunion after death, Dickinson opens the epitaph to a wide range of speakers and questions the easy consolation promised in the Victorian period.

"ANCESTOR'S BROCADES"

Chapter 5

"Paradise Persuaded"

Dickinson, Osgood, and the Language of Flowers

> The expression of this divine passion ought to be divine also, and it was to
> illustrate this that flowers were ingeniously made emblematical of our most
> delicate sentiments; they do, in fact, utter in "silent eloquence" a language
> better than writing; they are the delicate symbols of the illusions of a tender
> heart and of a lively and brilliant imagination.
> —Frances Sargent Osgood, *The Poetry of Flowers, and Flowers of Poetry*[1]

> Language of flowers. They like it because no-one can hear.
> —James Joyce, *Ulysses*[2]

> You ask me what my flowers said—then they were disobedient—I gave
> them messages.
> —Emily Dickinson (*Letters* 2, 333)

"Let me thank the little Cousin in flowers, which without lips, have language—," wrote Emily Dickinson to Eugenia Hall in 1885 (*Letters* 3, 881).
For Dickinson, as for her contemporaries, flowers were repositories of cultural
meaning and communicated emotions privately. During the 1840s and 1850s,
popular female writers were adding to a growing fund of literature: the language of flowers. "Little study is necessary in the science here taught; nature
has been before us," writes Frances Sargent Osgood, who combines a floral
dictionary, poetry, and botanical treatise in her book, *The Poetry of Flowers,
and Flowers of Poetry* (1841) [25]. Creating dictionaries that codified floral
meanings and often appending botanical treatises, these writers developed
flowers into a linguistic system that, though probably never used, reflects the
popular consciousness of the Victorian period. Of course, such communication
depended on the ethic of privacy cultivated by genteel men and women who
preferred to express their emotions in private acts rather than public displays,

in letters rather than conversations. Because women especially were expected to embody piety and domesticity and were limited to these topics in public, their passion needed to be mediated through a rhetoric of "silent eloquence"—a language of gesture that implied meaning through a series of codes rather than through overt statement. I take this phrase from a passage by a popular verse writer who also penned her own dictionaries, Frances Sargent Osgood, for it embodies the language of gesture and implied meaning through which women communicated to each other without reserve feelings that were unacceptable to a reading public and staked out new emotional territory for themselves.

For nineteenth-century women, who were frequently encouraged to shy away from the harsh light of self-revelation and public scrutiny, floral symbolism afforded a private way to express their thoughts to friends, lovers, and acquaintances. Fearing for her friend, Thomas Wentworth Higginson, who was at the time leading a Union regiment during the Civil War, Emily Dickinson alluded to the pervasive floral rhetoric: "I trust the 'Procession of Flowers' was not a premonition—" (*Letters* 2, 424). Her reference to Higginson's nature essay, which appeared in the *Atlantic Monthly* in December 1862, reminds us that seasonal change is associated with death. Part of the naturalist tradition, Higginson's essay displays the nature worship of a neo-Romantic sensibility imbued in the transcendentalist belief in the traces of the divine. Indeed, even his imagery is Emersonian, as in this allusion to "Circles": "Not in the tropics only, but even in England, whence most of our floral associations and traditions come, the march of the flowers is in an endless circle, and, unlike our experience, something is always in bloom."[3] Higginson's essay encompasses a clinical examination of plants with a more sentimental rendering of their importance as harbingers of our own impermanence. "Men are perplexed with anxieties about their own immortality," he writes,

but these catkins, which hang, almost full-formed, above the ice all winter, show no such solicitude, but when March wooes them they are ready. Once relaxing, their pollen is so prompt to fall that it sprinkles your hand as you gather them; then, for one day, they are the perfection of grace upon your table, and next day they are weary and emaciated, and their little contribution to the spring is done. (*ODP*, 320–21)

Transitory and fragile, the catkins emblematize for Higginson the course of a human life. His description also captures the moment of sexual release: the plants are "ready when March wooes them" and, "once relaxing," they disgorge their pollen, "which leaves them weary and emaciated," spent forever after a brief moment of perfection.

Redolent of change, loss, and sexuality, Higginson's essay would undoubtedly have appealed to Dickinson, for she lived in an era saturated with nature writing whose authors often did not distinguish between—or saw no reason to view as mutually exclusive—scientific observation and nostalgic reverie. She was exposed to nature writing not only through essays and journal articles, like Higginson's, but also through two other works in her family's library: Mrs. C. M. Badger's *Wild Flowers Drawn and Colored From Nature* (1859) and Edward Hitchcock's *Catalogue of Plants Growing Without Cultivation in the Vicinity of Amherst College* (1829). Given that these books were written, moreover, for male and female audiences, they show that the sexes were indoctrinated with proper behavior through floral handbooks. Badger's and Hitchcock's books demonstrate that reverie and observation were two competing, though perhaps not contradictory, approaches to the natural world in nineteenth-century America: one scientific, rational, and exploratory, the other sentimental, aesthetic, and poetic. Hitchcock's book serves as a compendium for indigenous American plants that grew in and around Amherst and lists both Latin and common English names for plants. In his preface, Hitchcock names as his audience "young gentlemen, whose disposition to promote the interests of science appears so favourably in the publication of this catalogue"; he adds that through this book "they may have a pretty complete list of the plants growing in their vicinity," and further that it also "may serve as a very convenient index to an Herbarium."[4] Dickinson notes to Higginson in 1877 that every winter Hitchcock's treatise gave her much needed consolation about the continuation of natural life: "When Flowers annually died and I was a child, I used to read Dr Hitchcock's Book on the Flowers of North America. This comforted their Absence—assuring me they lived" (*Letters* 2, 573).

With its beautifully hand-colored illustrations accompanied by poems that convey the meaning of each flower, *Wild Flowers* enforces the emblematic and didactic nature of flowers. Unlike Hitchcock's catalogue of plants' names, Badger's book conforms to the type of floral compendium frequently written and read by American women in this period. Presented to Dickinson by her father, Edward Dickinson, in 1859, the book suits his desire for her to embody traditional feminine virtues even as he remembered his daughter's fondness for flowers. Badger's book embodies the tradition of women's floral writing in its watchful care over women's moral behavior and deportment, even including an introduction and prefatory poem by Lydia Sigourney:

> —One fair hand, hath skill'd to bring
> Voice of bird, and breath of Spring,
> One fair hand, before you laid
> Flowerets that can never fade,—
> While you listen, soft and clear
> Steals her wind-harp o'er your ear,—
> While you gaze, her buds grow brighter,—
> Take the book, and bless its writer.[5]

Paula Bennett notes that Sigourney's poem captures the essence of women's floral writing, which sought to make every poem a living picture.[6] Although the pictorial representation of flowers accompanying these poems enlarges their meanings, Sigourney's poem also builds on the nineteenth-century rhetoric of flowers, proposing a secret language of seduction and "stealing" influence over the reader. Just as in Nathaniel Hawthorne's *The Scarlet Letter* (1850) the narrator plucks a rose and offers it to the reader "to symbolize some sweet moral blossom, that may be found along the track, or relieve the darkening close of a tale of human frailty and sorrow,"[7] Sigourney asks for the reader's sympathy for and acceptance of the author's efforts. More than most floral lyrics other than Dickinson's, Sigourney's poem engages the reader almost as if she were a lover and compares the act of reading to a kind of seduction: "stealing" over the ear of the listener and capturing her gaze, it encourages the reader to "take" the book—literally into her hands—rather than actual flowers. Although Sigourney adopts a submissive attitude appropriate for a woman writer in humbly asking the reader to "bless its writer," her poem initiates an erotic exchange in which Badger's book substitutes for actual flowers presented by the sender (writer) to the recipient (reader). To accept the book means to surrender oneself to its verisimilitude, to submit to the author's powers of seduction, and finally to agree tacitly to make the book come to life through one's own imagination. Furthermore, since blossoms often operate as a metonym for women, flowers symbolize the way women themselves could be traded between men and families through marriage. Sigourney's poem opens the possibility that Badger's "fair hand" offers not only "flowerets that can never fade" but, by extension, herself to other women as well as men.

Hitchcock's and Badger's books share an affinity for wild plants native to America, but their differences also suggest the ways women's floral handbooks are built on the inherent instability of language codes. Both Badger's and Hitchcock's books depict wild flowers, and both prefer native American species to European ones. They show an interest in preserving and exploring their own country's plant lore. Distinguishing American from European manners and legend was a crucial aspect of both, since most floral dictionaries began with an extended homage to floral legends abroad, especially in Europe.[8] But Hitchcock's book attempts to limit the number of botanical references and names of each plant, as the preface explains: "it presents [the reader] at once with an authority for each specimen, with the most important synonyms; and thus saves him the very great labour of comparing together the descriptions given by different writers: a work which severely tasks the powers of the most accomplished botanist" (iii). In contrast, Badger delights in the ambiguity of floral meanings, listing common names and adapting for her poems each plant's common association, habitat, or season. One can gather on the basis of her example that women's floral books adopted freely the variety of meanings and names attached to common wild flowers. Far from limiting women's writing, the multiplicity of meanings in floral dictionaries afforded women the opportunity to explore the cultural and social resonances of flowers.

Dickinson displayed a lively interest in observing nature, yet she differentiated herself from the women whose rhapsodic flights over flowers characterized much of the poetry in this period. She inquired in May 1845 of her childhood friend Abiah Root, "Have you made you an herbarium yet?" (*Letters* 1, 13), offering to send her specimens of local plants. In a September letter, however, Dickinson is tongue-in-cheek about preserving a bouquet for her friend: "I would love to send you a bouquet if I had an opportunity, and you could press it and write under it, The last flowers of summer. Wouldn't it be poetical, and you know that is what young ladies aim to be now-a-days" (*Letters* 1, 21). Distinguishing herself from these ladies, she criticizes their decorous behavior but also their desire to be "poetical" in their gifts of flowers, which had become faddish by the 1840s. Although she sent flowers to friends and relatives frequently throughout her life, she rejected the sentimental versifying that often accompanied floral missives. Writing to Dr. and Mrs. Holland in 1862, Dickinson shows her awareness of the way floral symbolism might easily substitute for written prose: "Now, you need not speak, for perhaps you are weary, and 'Herod' requires all your thought, but if you are *well*—let Annie draw me a little picture of an erect flower; if you are *ill*, she can hang the flower a little on one side!" (*Letters* 2, 413). Yet her attitude toward such communication is distinctly comical, as the lines that immediately follow these reveal: "Then, I shall understand, and you need not stop to write me a letter. Perhaps you laugh at me! Perhaps the whole United States are laughing at me too! *I* can't stop for that! *My* business is to love" (*Letters* 2, 413).

In the years immediately following her schoolhood letters to Abiah Root and others, Dickinson began to explore the connotations that flowers carried and their ability to signify human experience and emotion, as Higginson's description of the catkins suggests. In this chapter, I will explore the culture of flowers in nineteenth-century America to show how Dickinson wields this genre in her own floral poems. Many of her contemporary female poets, such as Frances Sargent Osgood, used the rhetoric of floral dictionaries. Their verses playfully adopt floral images to disclaim responsibility for their own capricious behavior or emotions. While they build on the image of women as childlike, they also implicitly enlarge the range of expression available to women through their indirect style and occasional parodies of stereotypical femininity. I will first provide a brief overview of floral dictionaries and then examine some of Osgood's floral poems, which I set against lyrics of Dickinson, exploring how she enriches floral diction. Placed in the larger social context of floral writing, Dickinson's poems not only overturn romantic conventions, but they also enlarge the range of sexual and emotional significances possible for women.

Although the language of flowers culminated in the nineteenth century, it originated much earlier. The cultural anthropologist Jack Goody writes in *The Culture of Flowers* (1993) that the symbolic use of flowers in the West was predated in China and Japan by many years.[9] Among the first Western poets to use flowers symbolically, Dante used the rose as a mystical symbol for Christ. The tradition of assigning meanings to individual flowers continued among the Elizabethans and seventeenth-century English poets, such as Herrick and Marvell. Interest in the language of flowers peaked in the nineteenth century. Inspired by Madame de la Tour's *Les Langages des Fleurs*, Victorians codified and refined the significances assigned to flowers, and a vast number of floral dictionaries appeared in the 1840s and 1850s.[10] Sarah Josepha Hale's *Flora's Interpreter, and Fortuna Flora* (1850) and Frances Sargent Osgood's *The Poetry of Flowers, and Flowers of Poetry* (1841) are only two American examples.[11] Additionally, Almira H. Lincoln's *Familiar Lectures on Botany*, one of Dickinson's textbooks, contained an appendix, "Symbolical Language of Flowers," that proves the poet had direct access to floral associations.[12]

Written primarily for and by women, these dictionaries reflect the heightened sentiment and tearful "melting" popular among the Victorians. Like the Romantics, Victorian writers saw nature as a book that could be interpreted symbolically. They thought plants were emblematic of a range of emotions. Dorothea Dix, who was later to become famous as an advocate for the mentally ill, wrote in an early work that flowers were part of a language of nature: "Oh! flowers, flowers,—we may well think them 'the alphabet of the angels.' But how coldly do we look on them; how often are we regardless of their charms here; while in other lands they almost subserve the use of writing,— expressing by a blossom, joy, grief, hope, despair, happiness, devotion, piety, and almost every other sentiment that fills the mind."[13]

But the leisured Victorians used a rigid codification of floral meanings to reaffirm their class status and to maintain their high morals. Not only does floral symbolism serve as a language of sentiments, but flowers can also inculcate the viewer with virtue, as Dix reveals: "A virtuous character is likened to an unblemished flower. Piety is a fadeless bud that half opens on earth, and expands through eternity. Sweetness of temper is the odor of fresh blooms, and the amaranth flowers of pure affection open but to bloom forever" (26). Moreover, unlike their European counterparts, who used flowers purely for decoration, Americans tended to stress their didactic value. A journalist, novelist, and poet, Sarah Josepha Hale writes in her *Flora's Interpreter* (1850) that her intent is to improve the moral standing of her readers: "May it inspire our young women to cultivate those virtues which only can be represented by the fairest flowers; and may our young men strive to be worthy of the love that these fairest flowers can so eloquently reveal."[14] In comparing women to flowers, Hale implies that they should cultivate virtues while they remain passively rooted and unresponding to events outside the home. Sometimes, to stress these virtues, the meanings of flowers were often toned down in America: the red rose signifies "volupté" or voluptuousness in French dictionaries, but in American ones is often translated as "I have seen a pretty girl." In *The Culture of Flowers*, Jack Goody notes that "While it is unlikely that the Language of Flowers would have originated in a country that paid them so little attention at that time, Americans seem to have taken it more seriously, more morally, than Europe, stressing its use to promote virtue, to stimulate education and to define the values of the new nation."[15]

The language of flowers was considered a woman's genre, as the prefaces and introductions to these works reveal. In the preface to an 1843 floral dictionary, the writer tells a number of anecdotes illustrating the use of floral language in Turkey, India, Spain, and Italy—but all the stories depict women. After a short list summarizing the meanings of flowers, the writer concludes with the hope that the book may "furnish a pleasing exercise for the ingenuity of our fair readers," a remark surely directed to women.[16] Flora, the goddess of flowers, was frequently depicted in illustrations accompanying the text or referred to in poems. Authors of nineteenth-century floral dictionaries upheld the belief that women's poems and flowers were interchangeable. Hale writes in her dictionary that since "the expression of these feelings has been, in all ages, the province of poetry," then poetry must provide a "philology of flowers" (iii).

Whatever their value as literature, floral dictionaries echo the prevailing critical discourse surrounding women's poetry in the nineteenth century. Stemming from the popular portrayal of women's writing as natural and spontaneous, women's poems and flowers were often considered interchangeable both by male critics and female authors. For instance, an anonymous 1852 reviewer of Alice Cary's *Lyra and Other Poems* in *Harper's* writes that her verse "displays a rich luxuriance of imagery; all the flowers of the season woven into the elegaic wreath; but it is too artificial, too curiously wrought for the subject."[17] Indeed, when Higginson wrote the 1890 introduction to Dickinson's posthumous *Poems*, he remarked that "In many cases these verses will seem to the reader like poetry torn up by the roots, with rain and dew and earth still clinging to them, giving a freshness and fragrance not otherwise to be conveyed."[18] Rather than compare her verse to "a lily grown in a cellar," as one writer in 1878 did the poetry of "Saxe Holm" (Helen Hunt Jackson), no doubt imagining that it was Dickinson's,[19] Higginson refers instead to their "found" quality in comparing them to wild flowers, thus absolving himself of responsibility for presenting them to the public. Given that women's verse was frequently described as unpremeditated, Higginson recognized her verse's power yet attributed its originality to "extraordinary grasp and insight, uttered with an uneven vigor sometimes exasperating, seemingly wayward, but really unsought and inevitable" (vi). Indeed, the very chapter titles of his edition of

Dickinson's poems in 1890 reflect his desire to fit her poetry to the conventional topics of women's writing: "Life," "Love," "Nature," "Time and Eternity" (Dickinson, *Poems* [1890]).

One need only glance at the titles of some popular literary works from this period to assess the pervasiveness of this floral rhetoric and plant lore in America: Elizabeth Stuart Phelps's *The Last Leaf From Sunnyside* (1854), Fanny Fern's (Sarah Parton) *Fern Leaves From Fanny's Portfolio* (1850), Laura Greenwood's *The Rural Wreath; or, Life Among the Flowers* (1853), Lydia Sigourney's *The Voice of Flowers* (1846), and, perhaps most significant, Walt Whitman's *Leaves of Grass* (1855). A mere portion of the collections in this era whose titles allude to plants, flowers, or weeds, these literary works are imbued with textual and visual puns on "leaves" as pages of a book and on "flowery" or "gemmy" prose as metaphorical. Furthermore, they associate images of nature with textuality and femininity. The title page of Walt Whitman's *Leaves of Grass*, for example, depicts the twining tendrils and sprouting leaves common in women's books of verse. Helen Hunt Jackson's 1870 *Verses* also contain emblems of sacred and secular love: a hand plucking petals from a daisy, a triptych displaying the nativity scene, decorative flowers, and twining roses. Indeed, the expression "flowers of rhetoric," as metaphorical language came to be known, epitomized the belief that figurative language is ornate and decorative, and the very vocabulary of bookmaking has continued to display its roots in floral discourse well into the twentieth century. The term "fascicle," generally the division of a book, derives from floral rhetoric, and the hand-sewn packets that Dickinson made of fair copies of her poems are also termed fascicles, which are described by Hale's floral dictionary as "flowers on little stalks variously inserted and subdivided, collected into a close bundle, level at the top" (viii). "Anthology," too, comes originally from the Greek "anthologia," meaning a collection of flowers, thus pointing to the close connection between flowers and rhetoric.

The language of flowers operates according to a series of codes that is itself open to change and interpretation.[20] Their meanings derived partly from legends and partly from arbitrary assignment, flowers could therefore have many meanings. A floral handbook published in 1913 (which is still in print), contains eight meanings for daisy and thirty-nine for rose alone.[21] Moreover, there were instructions about how to present flowers, since their meanings often depended on how they were placed. For example, a flower inclined to the right indicated the first person; to the left, the second person. An upright flower expresses a thought; upside down, its reverse. Placed upon the head, a flower signifies a thought; upon the heart, love; upon the breast, ennui. The same definitions for each flower rarely appear in any two dictionaries, except in cases where generic associations are made or the same works are reprinted in a new edition. The anonymous writer of *The Language of Flowers* in 1843 attests that the expressive power of flowers is due largely to the variety of their mean-ings: "Yes, flowers have their language. Theirs is an oratory, that speaks in per-fumed silence, and there is tenderness, and passion, and even the lighthearted-ness of mirth, in the variegated beauty of their vocabulary. To the poetical mind, they are not mute to each other; to the pious, they are not mute to their Creator."[22]

The authors of floral dictionaries link femininity and flowers. In the intro-duction to her floral dictionary, *The Flowers of Poetry, and Poetry of Flowers* (1841), Osgood belittles her work and asks the reader's indulgence, a ploy common in women's literature: "Only Fancy and Feeling have woven a wreath which may yield neither bloom nor sweetness, unless the sunshine of Indul-gence, and the kindly dew of Sympathy, be suffered to play on its leaves."[23] Women's writing was thought to be natural and unpremeditated, as the lan-guage of flowers was also thought to be natural and beyond instruction. For Osgood, each creature and plant reveals God's inspiration, a thought that can best be expressed by women due to their sensitivity and piety: "The expression of this divine passion ought to be divine also, and it was to illustrate this that flowers were ingeniously made emblematical of our most delicate sentiments; they do, in fact, utter in 'silent eloquence' a language better than writing; they are the delicate symbols of the illusions of a tender heart and of a lively and brilliant imagination" (23). The idea of the language of flowers as a fund of "silent eloquence" conveys not only the privacy of this language, but also its re-liance on tacit assumptions rather than on explicit discussion of emotions. Fur-thermore, by writing poems that expressed their thoughts, nineteenth-century women wrote a new, radical poetry. As I will show, women used the language of flowers to express ideas not otherwise considered acceptable.

When he made his first visit to Dickinson at her Amherst home in 1870, Higginson was unaware that her offering him "two day lilies" (*Letters* 2, 473) as her "introduction" was a calculated act, since according to the language of flowers, day lilies signifies, among other meanings, "Coquetry." If her gift was an intentional act of self-presentation, she meant to offer the flowers as her metonymic substitute. Rather than reveal all to Higginson during his visit, she meted out as much of her mind as she pleased. Dickinson thus transformed the common habit of enclosing flowers in a note or presenting them to others into a more complex mode of self-presentation. Given the common editorial dis-course that asserted women's poems and flowers were interchangeable, she collapses the distinction between them. Like the answer to a riddle, flowers are often the unstated subjects of her lyrics, hinted at but not fully explained. Dickinson draws on the associations about flowers in order to undercut the tra-dition of romantic courtship, and her floral lyrics exult in secrets, silence, and deferral of meaning, rather than its full expression.

In assessing Dickinson's appropriation of these forms, we might consider

more closely the work of another poet who seems to combine both the sentimentalism of her era and the growing dissatisfaction that women expressed
about their lives—Frances Sargent Osgood. Cheryl Walker has written that
"Frances Osgood is undoubtedly one of the most alluring women poets before
Emily Dickinson."[24] Praising Osgood for her wit and humor, she notes her
"pointedly arch and Millayish" persona, which was "anything but naïve."[25]
Similarly, in her groundbreaking *The Poetry of American Women from 1632 to
1945*, Emily Stipes Watts says of the period from 1800 to 1850, "Osgood is
simply the best poet of all the women who wrote during these years."[26] Recently, critics have pointed out Osgood's wit and reliance on sentimental conventions and have thrown her more rebellious, irreverent poems into bold relief when compared with less original versifiers.[27] In fact, Osgood surpasses
many of her contemporaries in her ability to play off the conventions of
women's versifying and still retain a satiric tone about the relations between
men and women. As Joanne Dobson has noted, Osgood wrote a number of
witty salon verses, which have remained unpublished perhaps due to the author's awareness that they diverged from the predominant image of women as
pious and docile beings.[28] Addressed to the worldly and sophisticated New
York society of the 1840s, these lyrics question the limits of women's sexual
lives and allow their speakers to transgress, if momentarily, the image of idealized feminine behavior. Steeped in the conventions of what Barton Levi St.
Armand has termed the "sentimental love religion"—the popular fiction that in
death lovers would be reunited—Osgood manipulates in her lyrics the possibilities for satiric points of view concerning men's and women's love relations,
as Dobson notes: "What the 'sentimental love religion' allows her here is an
imaginative arena for indulgence in playful erotic posturing."[29]

Osgood wittily adopts in her verse floral images to disclaim responsibility
for women's capricious behavior or emotions. While these images build on the
characterization of women as childlike, they also implicitly enlarge the range
of expression available to women through their indirect style and occasional
parodies of stereotypical femininity. Osgood herself publicly conformed to the
image of a poetess in the authorial portrait to her 1850 *Poems*: clad in a classical décolleté gown and facing the viewer with a full-eyed expression, she typifies the ideal, otherworldly poetess. Though by 1850 she had acquired enough
stature to be pictured authoritatively above her stamped signature on the facing title page of her *Poems*, her first collection of verses, which appeared in
1846, set a more domestic and utopian tone with the illustration of a thatched
cottage half hidden in a wood and its summary legend: "Happy at Home." A
devotee of floral poetry, she published a number of works whose titles evoke
the language of flowers: *A Wreath of Wild Flowers from New England* (1838),
Flower Gift: A Token of Friendship for All Seasons (1840), *The Poetry of
Flowers, and Flowers of Poetry* (1841), *The Floral Offering; A Token of*

Friendship (1847), and *The Flower Alphabet in Gold and Colors* (1845). Given Osgood's independent lifestyle and wit, it is perhaps not surprising that her floral poems define a range of positions taken by women with their lovers—seduced, imploring, betrayed, cast off—while they maintain decorum for the nineteenth-century reading public. In fact, Osgood surpasses many of her contemporaries in her ability to play on the conventions of women's versifying and still retain a pointed, satiric tone about the relations between men and women.

In her 1846 *Poems*, Frances Sargent Osgood includes the following adaptation from the language of flowers:

> A cold, calm star look'd out of heaven,
>   And smiled upon a tranquil lake,
> Where, pure as angel's dream at even,
>   A Lily lay but half awake.
>
> The flower felt that fatal smile
>   And lowlier bow'd her conscious head;
> "Why does he gaze on me the while?"
>   The light, deluded Lily said.
>
> Poor dreaming flower!—too soon beguiled,
>   She cast nor thought nor look elsewhere,
> Else she had known the star but smiled
>   To see himself reflected there.[30]

Written perhaps as a response to Edgar Allan Poe, Osgood's literary mentor and possibly her lover, "The Lily's Delusion" epitomizes Osgood's witty, rebellious use of floral language. Close in form and sentiment to Poe's "Evening Star," written in 1827, the poem may have been meant to comment sarcastically on her betrayal by Poe, who sought to improve his own reputation through placing her poems near his by-line.[31] The Lily's semi-consciousness hints that, not yet fully initiated into the deceptions of love, she must undergo a romantic betrayal. Furthermore, the lily symbolizes death, resurrection, and purity—the woman's eventual fate. Innocent and flattered by the "fatal smile" of a "cold, calm star," the Lily does not see the vanity of the flower until too late.

Best known as Poe's literary protégée, Frances Sargent Osgood led a short but active life as a professional writer. Born in 1811 to a Boston merchant and his second wife, she spent her childhood in Hingham, Massachusetts. The family included a brother and older half sister, Anna Maria Wells, who herself became a popular New England poet. Her engagement and eventual marriage to the American portrait artist, Charles Stillman Osgood, was no doubt founded on her love of romance, which he amply satisfied when she sat for her portrait in 1834 by telling her exotic adventure stories culled from his youth. After marrying in October 1835, they moved to England, where Frances enjoyed the literary society that would end their marriage. Summering in Provincetown in 1845, Osgood met Edgar Allan Poe, who proved to be the most enduring influence on her career. She had become estranged from her husband the year before, after nine years of marriage that produced two daughters. Sexually as well as economically independent, she lived a free life, which, coupled with her apparent infatuation with Poe, has given rise to the theory that she became his lover and may have had by him her third daughter, Fanny. Poe proved to be a powerful advocate for her in the popular press, writing a number of very complimentary reviews of her poems.

Osgood's more conventional use of floral imagery offers a touchstone for women's writing about flowers, since she combines both the sentimentalism of her era and the dissatisfaction that women increasingly expressed about their lives. Although many of her lyrics propose conservative values about women and do not radically alter poetic conventions, other poems display the dissatisfaction she must have felt with woman's position. Although "Caprice" echoes the traditional view of women as flighty, moody creatures, it also claims their right to decide their own fates without explanation:

> Reprove me not that still I change
> With every changing hour,
> For glorious Nature gives me leave
> In wave, and cloud, and flower.
>
> And you and all the world would do—
> If all but dared—the same;
> True to myself—if false to you,
> Why should I reck your blame?[32]

Osgood builds on the myth that women were closer to nature than men as well as on the transcendental belief that whim is a legitimate expression of the soul. Nature's mutability gives the speaker permission to act, and so she divests herself of responsibility for her actions, even if that freedom comes at the expense of being called "capricious." She accepts the stereotype of the flighty woman, but she also calls "caprice" women's "only right":

> Be less—thou art no love of mine,
> So leave my love in peace;
> 'Tis helpless woman's right divine—
> Her only right—caprice!
> (*Poems* [1850] 214, ll. 45–48)

The resonance of the word "only" suggests a seriousness below the poem's "helplessness": Osgood's speaker insists that women lack all other rights except one—whim—then turns this natural "right" to her advantage and uses it to excuse her behavior.

Just as flowers signified emotions and thoughts that were only expressed covertly, gems were taken by many poets to signify the metaphorical use of language. Densely metaphorical prose was frequently described as "gemmy"; hence, they were associated with rhetoric in much the same way as flowers. Osgood makes this connection explicit in her poem, "The Flowers and Gems of Genius," whose otherwise forgettable rhymes and maudlin tone might encourage us to dismiss it as yet another attempt to rend unearned tears from the reader. The poem is interesting, however, when we consider that once again Osgood addresses the subject of why women write: suffering underlies their poetry, and "gems" and "flowers," that is, metaphors, hide its origins in pain.[33] In another poem, "The Language of Gems," Osgood alludes to the way the language of flowers has overtaken the older common cultural language of gems. Many of the gems she mentions are Dickinson's favorites—the ruby, chrysolite, emerald, opal, amethyst, and, most important, the diamond and pearl.[34] Like the conservative writers of floral dictionaries, however, Osgood encourages women to wear interior gems of virtue, rather than outward displays.

An anonymous article in the March 1861 issue of the *Atlantic Monthly* proves that Dickinson had contact with materials that would have strengthened her associations between jewel, flowers, and poetry. In "Diamonds and Pearls," the author recounts the story of a pearl diver who drowns in search of an exquisite specimen, then includes a poem to a lady who is begged not to wear another pearl, "the flower of gems."[35] The pearl typifies purity and virginity, and the lady in the poem would nullify the diver's sacrifice if she were to wear another. In a poem that Thomas Johnson dates from around the same year, Dickinson uses a similar subject to describe her attachment to Mary Bowles:

> Her breast is fit for pearls,
> But I was not a "Diver"—
> Her brow is fit for thrones
> But I have not a crest.
> Her heart is fit for *home*—
> I—a Sparrow—build there
> Sweet of twigs and twine
> My perennial nest.
> (J, 84)

The speaker establishes a ground for female attachment by distinguishing between the traditional offerings of men and her own gifts. Unlike the "'Diver'" who represents active exploration, or the noble who can offer her a "crest," she extols the nest of the lowly sparrow, who constructs a shelter out of remnants of more lofty constructions—"twigs and twine"—love and perseverance. Dickinson thus offers to build in Bowles's heart a "perennial" shelter, one that promises the return of love with each returning season, rather than a single tribute to her extolling the class or bravery of her male lover.

As this poem suggests, Dickinson found in another woman's heart a suitable place to build her "perennial nest," where she might cherish the sentiments and affections of those closest to her geographically and emotionally, just as she drew from the floral rhetoric of her era in order to create her own poetics of poverty. Her poems, like those of other nineteenth-century American women writers, were fashioned of domestic materials, threads, scraps, and other left-overs, yet they provided a virtual treasure house of images that she returned to again and again. She partook of the common rhetoric of flowers that created a distinctly "feminine" style in this period, yet in her poems sent to friends and relatives she expanded these images to play on the very limits of expression, to put into words emotions previously unspoken. Women in this period addressed one another in loving terms, and this erotic strain pervades especially Dickinson's relationship with her sister-in-law, Sue Gilbert.[36] As Carroll Smith-Rosenberg points out, demonstrative language had become stylized by the middle of the nineteenth century; not only homosexual but also heterosexual women learned to value sentimental, emotional relationships with other women, for they created an outlet for emotions otherwise repressed by Victorian society.[37]

Given her way of addressing Sue as "Darling" and "dear little bud" (*Letters* I, 209–10), Dickinson's affection for her sister-in-law reaches beyond merely stylized rhetoric and shows her profound love for her, which she expressed throughout her life and often imaged in floral tributes. During a stay in Cambridge about 1864 while under a physician's care for treatment of her eyes, the poet describes her love for Sue as central to her existence:

Sweet Sue—
There is no first, or last, in Forever—It is Centre, there, all the time—
To believe—is enough, and the right of supposing—
Take back that "Bee" and "Buttercup"—I have no Field for them, though for the Woman whom I prefer, Here is Festival—Where my Hands are cut, Her fingers will be found inside—
Our beautiful Neighbor "moved" in May—It leaves an Unimportance.
Take the Key to the Lily, now, and I will lock the Rose—

(*Letters* 2, 430)

Dickinson casts her imaginative encounter with Sue as a religious and super-vening event, a "Festival," in contrast to her lack of interest in the traditional forms of marriage and motherhood symbolized by the "Bee" and "Buttercup." Furthermore, she underscores the private communication between them through floral metaphors. As Smith argues, insofar as this letter uses floral images that carry the traditional associations about male-female courtship, Dickinson "appropriates the site of crucifying wounds to rewrite the biblical myth of human creation and tell a story about relations between two women who, like Adam and Eve, are flesh of one another's flesh, limbs of one another's limbs."[38] With its echo of the story of Saint Thomas who wished to verify Christ's resurrection through probing His wounds with his fingers, the description of her "cut" hands seems instead to suggest that Dickinson would subject herself to Sue's queries about the reality of her love. When one considers the vaginal and even masochistic associations of keeping open a wound, the passage suggests the twin pleasure and pain derived from her all-encompassing love for Sue. Given the traditional associations of the lily and rose, signifying purity and passionate love respectively, Dickinson may be suggesting that Sue should keep her virginity intact, while she "locks" up her own love away from the scrutiny of prying eyes.

Like other nineteenth-century American women, Dickinson frequently sent flowers to relatives and friends, often accompanying them with a letter or a poem. Yet in poems accompanying a flower, she collapses the distinction between poetry and flowers, thus enriching and complicating the act of self-presentation. Presented along with two more poems to Higginson after her first letter, this poem demonstrates a correspondence between flowers and poems:

> South Winds jostle them—
> Bumblebees come—
> Hover—hesitate—
> Drink, and are gone—
>
> Butterflies pause
> On their passage Cashmere—
> I—softly plucking,
> Present them here!
>
> (J, 86)

Sewall writes that this lyric "presented her poems to him as she frequently had presented them to others; that is, as flowers, things of nature that had come with no practice at all" (Sewall 2, 545). Surely, Dickinson was also drawing on the nineteenth-century critical discourse that portrayed women's poems as spontaneous and decorative outgrowths of a sensitive soul. For Dickinson, selecting and presenting her poems to Higginson was like culling flowers, since she presented them as unpremeditated, "found" things, thus diminishing her activity and responsibility. Yet their elusiveness is clear if we consider that they only sketch out an unmentioned topic. By omitting the actual subject of the poem—flowers—Dickinson only elliptically renders and "presents" them.

She instead depicts how the world acts on them: "South Winds," "Bumble-bees," and "Butterflies" appear for a moment or two and then vanish. The emphasis on movement and the fleeting passage of the wind, bees, and butterflies suggest that the object of description is constantly changing and that our perception of it relies on a partial view offered by the flowers' interaction with nature. Far from Amherst, "Cashmere" symbolizes transcendence; more importantly, its association with softness and lushness also parallels the speaker's act of "softly plucking" the flowers. When one considers that women's voices were commonly described as "soft" and low and that "plucking" suggests their musicality, the speaker implies that her poems are as elusive and reticent as her act of presenting them.

In sending letters to friends and relatives, Dickinson plays on the boundary between emotions that can be expressed and those that can only be implied. In a lyric sent with a flower to her cousin Eudocia Flynt in July 1862, she encodes a message about love and its ability to be articulated:

> All the letters I can write
> Are not fair as this—
> Syllables of Velvet—
> Sentences of Plush,
> Depths of Ruby, undrained,
> Hid, Lip, for Thee—
> Play it were a Humming Bird—
> And just sipped—me—
>
> (J, 334)

Previous interpretations of this poem have stressed its sexual innuendoes. In *Emily Dickinson's Imagery* (1979), Rebecca Patterson hints that Dickinson reverses the expected roles of writer and reader: by asking the reader to pretend that the flower is a hummingbird, she coyly sends a kiss.[39] But in conflating self and flower in the last two lines, she also conveys her wish to be kissed. Paula Bennett in *Emily Dickinson: Woman Poet* (1990) argues that it is an "invitation to cunnilingus."[40] Given the close association between female genitalia and flowers, Bennett's and Patterson's arguments are persuasive, yet such interpretations ignore the emphasis speech. The lyric flirts with the possibility of both telling and refraining from telling all about the speaker's feelings; it skirts the actual expression of desire by first anticipating the act, then casting it as a hypothetical exchange of emotions between two people, and finally relishing the supposed completion of the event. Contending that letters cannot compare in beauty to flowers, Dickinson describes the meaning hidden in the flower's "Syllables of Velvet" and "Sentences of Plush." Not only do "Velvet" and "Plush" recall the softness of human flesh, but they also point to the frequent characterization of women's voices as hushed. Likewise, "Depths of Ruby" may resemble the vagina, but it also suggests the mouth, organ of speech; these realms are as yet "undrained," promising the full expression of meaning. Yet they are also "Hid, Lip, for Thee": only to be relayed covertly to the recipient. Even the phrase "Play it were a Hummingbird," when "Play you were" or "Play I were" would have fit as easily, implies that the speaker is reluctant to name either herself or her interlocutor as participants in the exchange of emotion. In addition, the use of the subjunctive and past tense in the last two lines casts this event in the realm of fantasy and possibility rather than actual occurrence. Using the flower as a token of love, the speaker avoids actually confronting the recipient with the unrestrained expression of her feelings. Finally, she enlists the recipient's aid in encouraging her to imagine the full range of emotions represented by the hummingbird's act of tasting the nectar—with the sexual innuendo all the more fully developed as a result of including the reader's own imagination in the loving exchange proposed.

For Dickinson, letters as well as flowers prefigure death, since they disembody the speaker and rely on the absence of their interlocutor: "A Letter always feels to me like immortality because it is the mind alone without corporeal friend. Indebted in our talk to attitude and accent, there seems a spectral power in thought that walks alone—" (*Letters* 2, 460). Some lyrics treat the inability of flowers and letters to span the absence of loved ones:

> By a flower—By a letter—
> By a nimble love—
> If I weld the Rivet faster—
> Final fast—above—
>
> Never mind my breathless Anvil!
> Never mind Repose!
> Never mind the sooty faces
> Tugging at the Forge!
>
> (J, 109)

Sewall notes that about this time Dickinson was sending flowers and letters to both Samuel Bowles and his wife, Mary, and this lyric may well have recorded the sense of strain and uncertainty about Bowles's lukewarm response to the poems she submitted to the *Republican* (Sewall 2, 498). Nevertheless, the central issue is faith—the conviction that the ultimate *peine forte et dure* of death will result in heavenly "Repose." Like an infernal blacksmith, the speaker "weld[s] the Rivet faster—," until it is soldered permanently in heaven, yet the "sooty faces" which are "tugging at the Forge" suggest the underworld upon which immortality rests. For Dickinson, staving off the absence of friends and loved ones through an exchange of loving sentiments could only temporarily defer the threat of mortality.

Sent to Samuel Bowles in 1858, the following lyric declares that the speaker has little to do with tradition:

> If she had been the Mistletoe
> And I had been the Rose—
> How gay upon your table
> My velvet life to close—
> Since I am of the Druid,
> And she is of the dew—
> I'll deck Tradition's buttonhole—
> And send the Rose to you.
>
> (J, 44)

Cheryl Walker contends that, when read against the normative responses of other women, like Helen Hunt Jackson, to the publishing world, this lyric might well be addressing the whole generation (of which Bowles was one) that misjudged her poems.[41] Dickinson was perhaps also commenting on tradition and possibly marriage, when she juxtaposes midsummer and midwinter blooming plants with historical and traditional connotations. According to Osgood's floral dictionary, mistletoe signifies "I surmount all Difficulties" and rose, "Beauty."[42] Perhaps she was also hinting at her affection for Bowles, since the speaker says she would have found it "gay" to decorate Bowles's table, yet the belief that she might die there just as strongly rejects the possibility. Characterizing herself instead as "Mistletoe" and Mary as the "Rose" in contending that she is of the "Druid" and Mary is of the "dew," Dickinson prefers to adorn "Tradition's buttonhole" with her challenging and unexpected literary revisions. "Druid" carries religious connotations, for Celtic priests performed rituals to herald the spring every year. Such pagan rites perhaps involved sacrifice as well as gathering of plants, suggesting the martyrdom of women such as Mary to religious and cultural beliefs. Moreover, given that a buttonhole is normally adorned with a flower in man's dress, the speaker implies that she favors adopting a man's free life and rejects the decorative functions common for women. In comparing her older, wilder spirit to Mary's younger, gentler one, Dickinson relinquishes the desire to be bound by socially defined roles and embraces instead the act of redefining women's lives.

For Emily Dickinson, as for Thomas Wentworth Higginson and others of their generation, flowers are the harbingers of the divine, fragile symbols of God's presence. Higginson believed that nature's processes parallel the progress of human life. Yet his nature essays also betray the pantheistic leanings that characterized much writing of the age, and throughout they evoke the tragic sense that writers have failed to capture the poetry of nature. Just as Whitman received as a call-to-arms Emerson's injunction to find a new poet in his essay "The Poet," Dickinson might well have taken Higginson's characterization of the state of nature writing in American letters as her *point d'appui*. In his essay "My Out-Door Study," Higginson, an amateur naturalist, encourages an aspiring writer to mirror in his prose the complexity and detail of nature, to depict like a landscape artist the shadings and monochromatic changes in the hues of the universe:

If one could learn to make his statements as firm and unswerving as the horizon-line,— his continuity of thought as marked, yet as unbroken, as yonder soft gradations by which the eye is lured upward from lake to wood, from wood to hill, from hill to heavens,—what more bracing tonic could literary culture demand? (*ODP*, 255)

In studying the details of Higginson's essay, Dickinson must have sympathized with his anti-sentimental call for a masculine and "bracing tonic" to literature, but she also was of an era that allied nature and piety with little self-questioning in women's writing. "Beauty and fragrance are poured abroad over the earth in blossoms of endless varieties, radiant evidences of the boundless benevolence of the Deity," writes Frances Sargent Osgood in the introduction to her *The Poetry of Flowers* (1848) [7]. Like the transcendentalists, Osgood sees evidence of God's plan rather than natural selection in the almost infinite variety of species in the plant and animal worlds. Not surprisingly, women might easily substitute for flowers in her description, since they perform the same function in uplifting the human soul and preserving virtue: "They are made solely to gladden the heart of man, for a light to his eyes, for a living inspiration of grace to his spirit, for a perpetual admiration" (7). Higginson's and Osgood's essays reflect the simultaneous reverence for and investigation into the processes of nature, which underlie Dickinson's subtle alteration of the pious notions embedded in the discourse of flowers.

One poem combines religious fervor with sexual ecstasy:

> Come slowly—Eden!
> Lips unused to Thee—
> Bashful—sip thy Jessamines—
> As the fainting Bee—
>
> Reaching late his flower,
> Round her chamber hums—
> Counts his nectars—
> Enters—and is lost in Balms.
>
> (J, 211)

According to the language of flowers, one of the meanings of Spanish "Jessamine" is sensuality, and Dickinson's fondness for jasmine was well known by those who visited her conservatory. Undoubtedly aware of the meanings attached to this flower, Dickinson portrays the arrival in heaven as a sexual consummation, where the "fainting Bee," worn out from his flight, arrives late, and is "lost in Balms." In contrast to the niggardly act of counting his "nectars," the bee is "lost" in the fragrant, healing oil. Invoking the Garden of Eden, she uses the intrusion of death and sexuality in order to define heaven as a place where the pleasures of human life can be enjoyed.

In contrast, Dickinson elsewhere draws on the theme of deferred consummation in love to argue for the sanctity of heaven:

> Did the Harebell loose her girdle
> To the lover Bee
> Would the Bee the Harebell *hallow*
> Much as formerly?
>
> Did the "Paradise"—persuaded—
> Yield her moat of pearl—
> Would the Eden *be* an Eden,
> Or the Earl—an *Earl*?
>
> (J, 213)

According to the language of flowers, the harebell or bluebell signifies grief and submission, and it is the second meaning that illuminates for us both the poem's romantic narrative of a refusal to consummate a love affair and its larger theological implications. Rebecca Patterson notes that this lyric "describes the poet as a beleaguered flower or a pearl-moted Eden refusing to admit the impetuous bee-earl."[43] The speaker argues that the bluebell loses the respect of the bee if she gives in to his sexual advances. The Old Testament language of "hallow," "Paradise," and "Eden" hints that the poem fundamentally concerns the denial of earthly satisfaction in exchange for an afterlife. Indeed, if we take this poem in its theological context, then we can see that Dickinson retells the fall from the Garden of Eden in such a way that sexuality is a necessary precursor to salvation. Surely, Dickinson also had in mind the pearl as a sign of virginity as well as the "pearl of great price," the kingdom of God promised to the elect (Matthew 13:46).[44] "Paradise" derives etymologically from a garden, thus situating the poem's narrative within the botanical realm. The speaker seems to ask the question: if paradise were to yield the gate of "pearl," then wouldn't it lose all value as a utopia, as a threshold of new, unending, and never-tasted pleasures? Yet our awareness that Eve was "persuaded" suggests that within the garden a constitutive element existed that produced pain and sexuality as well as the opportunity for salvation, a *felix culpa*. Dickinson implies that the familiar courtship struggles between men and women—the characteristic pursuit and chase—precisely define women's and men's roles.

Another poem uses the image of the "Heart's Ease" or pansy to convey the speaker's faith and steadfastness in love:

> I'm the little "Heart's Ease"!
> I don't care for pouting skies!
> If the Butterfly delay
> Can I, therefore, stay away?
>
> If the Coward Bumble Bee
> In his chimney corner stay,
> I, must resoluter be!
> Who'll apologize for me?
>
> Dear, Old fashioned, little flower!
> Eden is old fashioned, too!
> Birds are antiquated fellows!
> Heaven does not change her blue.
> Nor will I, the little Heart's Ease—
> Ever be induced to do!
>
> (J, 176)

This lyric develops a narrative of loyalty and affectionate attachment which aptly draws on the pansy's most common significance according to the language of flowers: "Think of me."[45] According to a popular floral lexicon of 1869, "pansy" is a corruption of the French "pensez-a-moi," and it is fittingly also called "Heart's-ease, a sure result of a confident assurance that those whom we love are not unmindful of us when present or absent; not so unmindful, that is, to be careless and thoughtless of those claims we have upon their regard and affection."[46] Adapting the romantic associations of pansies as signifiers of a beloved's remembrance, Dickinson's lyric casts the theme of religious faith in secular terms and interprets Christ's injunction that he will remember in heaven those who were faithful to Him as the basis for the pansy's steadfastness in love. Indeed, if we place this poem in the context of others concerning the Garden of Eden, we see that Dickinson rejects the patristic tradition that portrayed women, specifically Eve, as treacherous, greedy creatures. The speaker's childlike voice counters God's righteous anger, his "pouting skies," and constructs a syllogism concerning the advent of heaven: why should the flower refrain from blooming even in the face of God's negligence? Indeed, the male bee's cowardice makes the pansy more resolute, as she realizes that no one will speak on her behalf an apologia, a formal argument of the type the Christian forefathers made in explanation of their faith. Characterizing Eden as an "old fashioned" place and birds as "antiquated fellows," the speaker of the third stanza affirms that the pansy's faith will be rewarded. Unlike the tempests to which flowers and human beings are subject on earth, heaven remains "blue," serene and loyal to its faithful. Not to be misled by fatuous arguments, as was Eve, the pansy asserts that she will never be "induced" to give up her faith—and by implication her constancy to her lover. Dickinson thus counters the characterization of women as flighty, moody creatures through her adaptation of floral rhetoric.

Another lyric sent to Susan Gilbert Dickinson about 1875 celebrates the arbutus for its human virtues of humility and constancy, but the flower's apparent meekness is actually a type of boldness:

> Pink—small—and punctual—
> Aromatic—low—
> Covert—in April—
> Candid—in May—
> Dear to the Moss—
> Known to the Knoll—
> Next to the Robin
> In every human Soul—
> Bold little Beauty
> Bedecked with thee
> Nature forswears
> Antiquity—
>
> (J, 1332)

Blooming for roughly two to three weeks from about the middle of April to the middle of May in northern New England, the arbutus or "pink" is one of the earliest and most ephemeral of spring flowers and hence a "punctual" heralder of the season; its nature as a creeping vine also symbolizes its "low" and humble attitudes. In his essay "April Days," Higginson comments on the arbutus's potent fragrance: "the May-flower knows the hour, and becomes more fragrant in the darkness, so that one can then often find it in the woods without aid from the eye" (*ODP*, 227). Unlike the gentian, another of Dickinson's favorite flowers, the arbutus does not carry an awareness of death but undergoes instead a series of changes that play on one's expectations of women's roles. It begins the season as "Covert," then "Candid," until recognized and cherished both by plants and human beings alike.[47] Dickinson's use of the dactyl throughout underscores the plant's development and highlights its proximity to its neighbors: each plant and animal and their love of the arbutus are accentuated by each line's two primary stresses. Late in the season, however, this humble flower, like a woman primped for admiration, becomes a "Bold little Beauty." Adorned by this humble flower, nature is led to renounce its dull appearance and "forswears / Antiquity." Indeed, if we consider that "forswear" connotes perjury, we see that Dickinson shrewdly adopts one facet of stereotypically feminine behavior: women are untrustworthy and lead men to ruin. For Dickinson, as for Osgood, such flowers supported the normative Christian understanding of human character in which humility and lowliness are elevated, yet their images also masked their playful and questioning attitudes about the traditional modesty of women.

One of her most striking poems makes the lilac a symbol of the sunset, against which she tests the observer's faith in the existence of God:

> The Lilac is an ancient shrub
> But ancienter than that
> The Firmamental Lilac
> Upon the Hill tonight—
> The Sun subsiding on his Course
> Bequeathes this final Plant
> To Contemplation—not to Touch—
> The Flower of Occident.
> Of one Corolla is the West—
> The Calyx is the Earth—
> The Capsules burnished Seeds the Stars—
> The Scientist of Faith
> His research has but just begun—
> Above his synthesis
> The Flora unimpeachable
> To Time's Analysis—
> "Eye hath not seen" may possibly
> Be current with the Blind
> But let not Revelation
> By theses be detained—
>
> (J, 1241)

7] To spectacle, but not to Touch 20. detained]
profaned—

According to Osgood, lilacs trenchantly symbolize "First Emotion of Love," and their monochromatic hues of light violet to deep purple signified a naturally artistic visual spectacle: "The gradation of colour, from the purple bud to the almost colourless flowers, is the least charm of these beautiful groups, around which the light plays and produces a thousand shades, which, all blending together in the same teint, forms that matchless harmony which the painter despairs to imitate, and the most indifferent observer delights to behold."[48] For Dickinson, purple connotes royalty as well as the blood of Christ; when set against the horizon in the sunset, this color dramatically renders His death for the entire world to bear witness. If we consider the poem's floral imagery, moreover, we see that Dickinson uses highly technical and botanical details to describe a sunset as a flower with a precision hardly equalled in contemporary literature. We know that she was exposed to the botanical names and definitions of plants and flowers through one of her textbooks, Almira H. Lincoln's 1838 *Familiar Lectures on Botany*. Lincoln's volume has a copious listing of parts of flowers, including "calyx," "corolla," "seeds," "sepal," and "petals," all joined under the general category "organs of reproduction, or parts of fructification."[49] Like many scientific texts that sought to provide a Christian answer to the advances of science, Lincoln's book argues throughout that nature is simply the manifest thought of divinity and offers a lesson about the immortality of the soul: "How impressively is the reanimation of the vegetable world urged by St. Paul, as an argument to prove the *resurrection from the dead!* The same power, which from a dry and apparently dead seed, can bring forth a fresh and beautiful plant; can assuredly, from the ruins of our mortal frame, produce a new and glorious body, and unite it to the immortal spirit by ties never to be separated" (103). Dickinson believed such a revelation to be evident through the natural world, accessible in its minute detail rather than the theories of faith. "Corolla"—petals—derives from "crown," pointing to royalty as well as to Christ's crucifixion. While the "Capsules" or seedcases enclose "burnished Seeds" or the stars, the "Calyx" or sepal is the earth, an opposite and fitting receptacle for the play of light. This lyric conjoins religion and science to cast doubt on science as a method of spiritual investigation. "The Scientist of Faith," the spiritually doctrinaire, may conduct research on flowers, fragile and transient plants, but the "Flower of Occident" will continue "unimpeachable" forever. The Son-sun pun implies that Christ's final death and resurrection is mirrored in the heavenly display. Like the purely intellectual flower in Emerson's "The Rhodora," Dickinson's "Firmamental Lilac" is given "to Contemplation—not to Touch," and only the "Blind" in soul would need more empirical proof of God's existence in the face of such a magnificent display as the sunset: "But as it is written, Eye hath not seen, nor ear heard, neither have entered into the heart of man, the things which God hath prepared for them that love him" (1 Corinthians 2:9).

Dickinson was imbued with the sentimentalism and high "feeling" of the Victorians who were reluctant to name love and other emotions outright, instead preferring a language of gesture and innuendo. Emblems of fragile innocence, flowers bore religious and cultural significance. For Dickinson, flowers were tokens of sympathy that could be sent to friends and relatives, yet they also allowed the poet to revise many of the romantic positions women assumed in nineteenth-century verse. Among her floral poems, the lyrics depicting the rose and the daisy in particular show how Dickinson established a more mature poetic voice. Among many possible floral associations, the rose probably is the most significant, signifying in Osgood's lexicon "Beauty" and for other writers "Passionate Love." Osgood's "The Dying Rose-bud's Lament," for instance, characterizes a rosebud on the verge of blooming as an allegory of a woman's life:

> Ah me! ah! wo is me!
> That I should perish now,
> With the dear sunlight just let in
> Upon my balmy brow!
> (*The Poetry of Flowers*, 234)

This lyric captures the moment when the speaker, into whose young life love had just entered, is tragically dying. Dickinson laments, although more originally, the same fate of a nameless rose who embodies loyalty in the face of indifference:

> Nobody knows this little Rose—
> It might a pilgrim be
> Did I not take it from the ways
> And lift it up to thee.
> Only a Bee will miss it—
> Only a Butterfly,
> Hastening from far journey—
> On it's breast to lie—
> Only a Bird will wonder—
> Only a Breeze will sigh—
> Ah Little Rose—how easy
> For such as thee to die!
>
> (J, 35)

As Martha Dickinson Bianchi comments in an unfinished manuscript from the 1930s, Dickinson's garden was replete with roses of various types and shades, including the tiny Greville roses, hedgehog roses, blush roses, cinnamon roses, and calico roses, whose exuberant variety parallels the range of significances contained within references to a single flower. Associated with marriage and brides, roses had a privileged place not only in their multiple plantings but also in their central placement draping the garden-house: "In my grandmother (Emily Dickinson's mother)'s day the same little flagstones led down to the garden path that ran through plots of blossom on either side, under honeysuckle arbors to a summer house thatched with roses."[50] For Dickinson, the continuance of flowers was a crucial aspect of their pleasure, as noted in Bianchi's recollection of the poet's words: "'In childhood I never sowed a seed unless it was a perennial—and that is why my garden lasts'" (2). Thus the rose's death in this poem seems all the more evocative of the anonymous "pilgrim," who lives out her life with little notice from others except members of the same mute, neglected sisterhood, with which Bianchi associated the poet:

"'I was reared in the garden, you know,' my Aunt Emily Dickinson wrote her cousin Louisa Norcross; her mother loving and living in it a hundred years ago. And as far as inheritance goes with people like that same little Emily, who grew up a poet and mystic, her mother's love of flowers came down to her intensified only by her own spirit sisterhood with every bird and flower" (1).

Another early lyric about the rose portrays nature worship as an alternative to Christianity:

> A sepal, petal, and a thorn
> Upon a common summer's morn—
> A flask of Dew—A Bee or two—
> A Breeze—a caper in the trees—
> And I'm a Rose!
>
> (J, 19)

Like many of her nature lyrics, this poem reveres nature as an alternative to Christianity. Yet the poem also defines the ease of transformation for the speaker, who, in a nearly heretical way, becomes herself the embodiment of Christ. The association of the Holy Trinity and the triple parts of a flower—"A sepal, petal, and a thorn"—suggests that a flower prompts her to take nature as her object of worship. Indeed, the speaker stresses the transformative aspects of her imagination: a "common summer's morn" can change quickly into something extraordinary with the addition of a "flask of Dew" and other natural elements. The end and internal rhyme, moreover, emphasize the ability to change one's character rapidly and at will, especially when such changes are considered in light of the unrhymed last line. The last line points to the performative aspect of the act of self-transformation: read as a declaration of her identity ("I'm a Rose!") and as a causal explanation for becoming a rose (the "And" implies "And *so* I'm a Rose!"), the speaker depends both on the creatures around her and on her own power of imagination to transform herself. Whereas Osgood's rose poems use flowers to situate women within a moral universe in which they are often victims, Dickinson's fanciful poem revels in the speaker's ability to change identity and so to evade the most traditional associations about the self, identity, and womanhood.

Osgood uses the language of flowers to conform to the dictates for women's expression, but her poems also raise the issue of what could and could not be said in women's verse—a central preoccupation of hers. In "The Daisy's Mistake," for example, she portrays a Daisy who arises before the spring to show off its beauty, despite the knowledge that it is too early. Like a debutante, the daisy is dressed "for the show" (l. 9); the other flowers resemble *grandes dames* ("The Cowslip is crown'd with a topaz tiara! / The Crocus is flaunting in golden attire" [ll. 21–22]). The daisy's vanity dooms her. Lured by the sunbeam and zephyr's promise of outings and flattery, she blooms early, even though "Instinct" counsels her to be cautious:

> Then a still, small voice, in the heart of the flower,
>   It was Instinct, whisper'd her, "Do not go!
> You had better be quiet, and wait your hour;
>   It isn't too late even yet for snow!"

> But the little field-blossom was foolish and vain,
>   And she said to herself, "What a belle I shall be!"
> So she sprang to the light, as she broke from her chain,
>   And gaily she cried, "I am free! I am free!"
>   (*Poems* [1850] 329, ll. 33–40)

This daisy, of course, is a representation of a woman, as we can tell both from Osgood's use of the feminine pronoun and from the mention of "Instinct," which was believed to be more strongly developed in women than in men. The "still, small voice" alludes to I Kings and affirms the popular belief that women's natures were more moral and pious than men's: "And after the earthquake a fire; but the Lord was not in the fire: and after the fire a still small voice" (19:12). Rather than "be quiet" as Instinct cautions her, she forsakes the feminine virtues of restraint and modesty, imagining herself too much a "belle" to hold back any longer.

"The Daisy's Mistake" turns quickly into a parable about careless girls. After the daisy symbolically frees herself by sprouting, the wind and the sun turn against her. Osgood's speaker remarks that the wind "scolded" (l. 52) the daisy as if she were a child—a girl "brought out" too soon into the social world. In fact, one might imagine a mother trotting out a similar story to convince her daughter that entering too hastily into fashionable society has dire consequences. Exiled from the ground, she laments her fate in the last stanza:

> And so she lay with her fair head low,
>   And mournfully sigh'd in her dying hour,
> "Ah! had I courageously answer'd 'No!'
>   I had now been safe in my native bower!"
>   (*Poems*, 331, ll. 57–60)

Through the allegory of the daisy, Osgood depicts women as vain and moody creatures who are punished for their faults, but she also hints that women have little choice in what happens to them. The logic by which the zephyr and sunbeam encourage the daisy to shine is a double bind: she is "either too bashful or lazy" (l. 32), not brave enough or too indolent, if she does not appear. Innocent or coquette, Osgood's daisy occupies an untenable position that constrains her behavior no matter how she reacts.

Dickinson also wrote a cluster of poems in which the speaker styles herself as "Daisy," and the innocence that this flower traditionally connotes allows her to develop a range of positions for speakers who challenge the traditional concept of womanhood. Floral images in her poems overturn accepted doctrines of romantic place, for they provided a fund of traditional associations about womanhood and courtship against which she could subtly question these commonly held values. In a lyric probably sent to Austin about 1859, Dickinson characterizes him as "Caesar" and herself a mild "Daisy," who seeks admission into his presence:

> Great Caesar! Condescend
> The Daisy, to receive,
> Gathered by Cato's Daughter,
> With your majestic leave!
>
> (J, 102)

If Dickinson meant to send a flower with this poem, she playfully anticipates and reverses the expectations Austin might have had for refusing to accept it. She styles herself as Portia, the daughter of Cato, a Roman general and enemy of Caesar. In Shakespeare's *Julius Caesar*, Portia, in order to discover the reason for her husband Brutus's moodiness, declares herself more resilient than the average woman: "Think you I am no stronger than my sex, / Being so fathered and so husbanded?" (II.i.296–97). By styling herself as a woman with a "man's mind" (II.iv.8), as does Portia, Dickinson both asserts her independence from traditional gender stereotypes and plays on the expectation that a woman would be received gallantly by any man. Given that Cato was Caesar's opponent, a flower as a gesture of reconciliation or love from his daughter would have been rejected. Yet a flower—or the woman who presents it— would undoubtedly be allowed into his presence. Furthermore, she may allude in a more radical way to herself as the descendent of a female tradition: just as Austin as Caesar is the offspring of a line of male rulers, she hails from "Cato's Daughter," an opposing and female line. Dickinson thus plays on the romantic conventions in this period that would have made it difficult for a man to reject a woman's offering, while she elevates her brother as Caesar and casts herself in the role of the lowly and modest Daisy.

Another poem describes an indolent housewife who is made fully indolent by death until she is laid in "Daisies" at the end:

> How many times these low feet staggered—
> Only the soldered mouth can tell—
> Try—can you stir the awful rivet—
> Try—can you lift the hasps of steel!

Stroke the cool forehead—hot so often—
Lift—if you care—the listless hair—
Handle the adamantine fingers
Never a thimble—more—shall wear—

Buzz the dull flies—on the chamber window—
Brave—shines the sun through the freckled pane—
Fearless—the cobweb swings from the ceiling—
Indolent Housewife—in Daisies—lain!

(J, 187)

The poem depicts a housewife who seems lazy in giving up her home duties, thus contrasting with poems by other nineteenth-century American women poets in which women happily perform their duties. By addressing the reader directly, Dickinson highlights not only the woman's life of domestic toil but also the reader's impotence in the face of death. In the first stanza, the woman's mouth, "soldered" in death, prevents her from betraying its secrets. Given the improvements in funerary technology in this period, the "awful rivet" and "hasps of steal" of the coffin aptly convey to the reader the permanence of death. Furthermore, the editors' substitution of "can" for "care" in the sixth line in the published version of her *Poems* (1890) lessens Dickinson's understated emphasis on the general indifference over the woman's welfare and instead points to the reader's incapacity to wrest the woman from death, despite the reader's pity.

In contrast to the reader's impotence, Dickinson reveals in the last stanza the woman's own seeming willful indolence. The room, grown untidy due to the housewife's disappearance, gradually reveals in its disarray the woman's assertiveness: although "dull flies" buzz, suggesting death and corruption, a cobweb "Fearless . . . swings" from the ceiling, and the sun shines "Brave" on the pane "freckled" with dirt. The characterization of the housewife as "Indolent" is twofold, meaning both lazy and, etymologically, free of pain. In contrast to the inability of the speaker to wrest the housewife from death, the housewife seems to languish in bed, rather than in a coffin. Unlike Osgood, who uses the daisy to teach a lesson of moral rectitude, Dickinson undercuts the expectation that women perform their duties with pious and uplifted spirits.

A subservient speaker prostrates herself before a powerful "Master," the sun, in the following lyric, but she seems to assert herself by approaching him:

The Daisy follows soft the Sun—
And when his golden walk is done—
Sits shily at his feet—
He—waking—finds the flower there—
Wherefore—Marauder—art thou here?
Because, Sir, love is sweet!

We are the Flower—Thou the Sun!
Forgive us, if as days decline—
We nearer steal to Thee!
Enamored of the parting West—
The peace—the flight—the Amethyst—
Night's possibility!

(J, 106)

Echoing the "Sir" with which the heroine of Charlotte Brontë's *Jane Eyre*
(1847) addressed her beloved Rochester, the Daisy adoringly follows the sun,
shortening the distance between them. Rather than affirming her dependence
on him, her approach asserts her presence, as she embraces "Night's possibility." As Margaret Homans also has shown, the daisy derives from "day's-eye,"
a term that reflects the phototropic flower's dependence on and resemblance to
the sun.[51] A mere reflection of the sun's presence, the daisy is described by the
third-person speaker as "soft" and "shy" in the first stanza, but she assumes the
role of speaker in the second stanza and subtly reverses the expectations about
the passive/feminine behavior of women in the eyes of the active/masculine
"Sun." According to most floral dictionaries, the "Daisy" typifies innocence,
and Badger writes in *Wild Flowers* that the daisy is "a troublesome weed to
farmers, but a favorite flower with children" (v). Indeed, this flower represents
naiveté and a childlike purity, which Dickinson adopted in many of her poems.
Following the sun during his daily "golden walk," the daisy "shyly" turns her
face toward his warmth in a way that seems to confirm her passivity. Yet his
characterization of her as a "Marauder" correctly reveals that she also skillfully renegotiates her position and assertively presses forward, as "steal" hints
in the second stanza. Adopting a generalized first-person plural speaker, Dickinson allows the reader and the flower to form an "I-Thou" relationship with
the "sun," thus solidifying the daisy's relationship with the reader and setting
both against the masculine sun. Echoing Isaac Watts's hymn "Nearer My God
to Thee" in the daisy's plea for forgiveness, Dickinson not only rewrites a
more conservative scriptural intention but also reverses the expected roles for
men and women by allowing the daisy actively to approach her adored lover.

Although the path of the "enamored" daisy is toward the "parting West,"
the poem's final lines also point to a liberating "flight," an escape from the
strictures of responsibility in the realm of "Night's possibility." "Enamored" of
the sunset, the daisy desires a union with her lover that inevitably also promises
death. Yet the night is also defined as the absence of the sun, a time when the
daisy is freed from the expectations that keep her firmly in an inferior position
during the day. Recalling the deepening purple of sunset, "Amethyst" connotes
royalty and points to her accession to power. In approaching her lover, the sun,
the daisy not only seems to approach him more assertively but also opens herself to a realm of freedom.

Floral imagery covertly expresses the physical side of Daisy's love:

> I tend my flowers for thee—
> Bright Absentee!
> My Fuschzia's Coral Seams
> Rip—while the Sower—dreams—
>
> Geraniums—tint—and spot—
> Low Daisies—dot—
> My Cactus—splits her Beard
> To show her throat—
>
> Carnations—tip their spice—
> And Bees—pick up—
> A Hyacinth—I hid—
> Puts out a Ruffled Head—
> And odors fall
> From flasks—so small—
> You marvel how they held—
>
> Globe Roses—break their satin flake—
> Upon my Garden floor—
> Yet—thou—not there—
> I had as lief they bore
> No Crimson—more—
>
> Thy flower—be gay—
> Her Lord—away!
> It ill becometh me—
> I'll dwell in Calyx—Gray—
> How modestly—alway—
> Thy Daisy—
> Draped for thee!

(J, 339)

Dickinson might have had Samuel Bowles in mind as the recipient of this poem, since Johnson dates it from "early 1862," approximately the same time that the Bowleses sailed to Europe (Sewall 2, 526). Indeed, the poem seems to be addressed to a lover who is gone, the "Bright Absentee," while the speaker's garden blossoms. The poem concerns the domestic and housewifely duties of tending a garden. In light of the opening reference to sewing, the pun on "Sower" alludes both to the planting of seeds in a garden and the stitching of a housewife. Yet, as it progresses, Dickinson describes the speaker's sexual desire through the floral images as revealed in a dream. It is appropriate that this poem takes a dream as the setting for expressing pent-up longings, unraveled and exposed in sleep. The "Coral Seams" might represent a panoply of bodily and social functions, which "rip" and are reconstructed during sleep. Might Dickinson have meant by "Coral Seams" the mouth's lips? the vagina's? or housewifely duties and tasks? Like Penelope's weaving, such tapestries are broken down every night and must be reconfigured during the day.

Both the colors and the physical descriptions of the flowers point to the speaker's sexual desire. Dickinson uses a variety of flowers in an almost hallucinatory way, revealing the speaker's concern with self-exposure and gender inversion. Nearly all the flowers are red or pink and suggest some sort of sexual violation: geraniums "tint—and spot"; the cactus "splits"; carnations empty their "spice"; a hyacinth exposes a "Ruffled Head." Despite the many references to pollination and growth, the strength of the speaker's desire surprises even her, as she "marvel[s]" at the volume of perfume held by such small "flasks." Of course, odors might refer to bodily smells as well as to perfume, and even the gender confusion of "My Cactus—splits her Beard" suggests that, in the throes of the dream, the differences between men and women are conflated.

Finally, the speaker's remark in the last stanza that she "modestly" waits for her lover in nunlike "Calyx—Gray—" ironically understates the vivid, impressionistic description of the garden. Dickinson's use of archaisms such as "lief" and "becometh" associate the speaker with an old-fashioned modesty that is perhaps required by the "Lord" who may return. The speaker seems to be saying: why should my garden bloom and I be happy while my lover is absent? Yet she only pretends to shroud herself in somber hues by day, since her thoughts in sleep reveal an impatient and surging passion, contradicting the modesty and innocence that the daisy connotes.

By considering a sentimental poet like Osgood, we can see that Dickinson absorbed the conventions of nineteenth-century American women's writing, while transforming these norms in her own idiosyncratic verse. Like more conservative women writers, she sent flowers to relatives and friends in order to commemorate holidays or as tokens of friendship. Yet she complicates this tradition by writing poems that not only present flowers to a recipient but also play on the common association of poetry and flowers. Far from the formulaic rendering of feelings by Osgood and other sentimental poets, Dickinson's poems transmute floral meanings in order to comment more profoundly on change, mortality, and the afterlife. In addition, she transforms the sending of flowers to a loved one from a simple social gesture to a more significant act of self-presentation. Recovering nineteenth-century American social and literary traditions, such as the language of flowers, allows us to see Dickinson's reliance on the genteel conventions of her age as well as her originality as a poet.

Chapter 6

"Fame of Myself"

Dickinson, Jackson, and the Question
of Female Authorship

A very subtle analysis upon a very few truths pushed to their extreme
application; the morbidness, improbability, quaintness and shrinking which
would result from a lack of the sun's ripening influences, like a lily grown in
a cellar. All these lead us to the conclusion that the author may be a person
long shut out from the world and living in a world of her own; that perhaps
she is a recluse.

—"Who Is Saxe Holm?" (1878)[1]

Travel increaseth a man. But, next to going bodily, is to wander, through the
magical power of print, whithersoever one will. A good book of travel is a
summer's vacation . . . Every one is in itself a gem. Brilliant, chatty, full of
fine feminine taste and feeling,—just the letters one waits impatiently to get,
and reads till the paper has been fingered through. It has been often
observed that women are the best correspondents. We cannot analyze the
peculiar charm of their letters. It is a part of that mysterious *personnel*
which is the atmosphere of every womanly woman.

—Anonymous review of Helen Hunt Jackson, *Bits of Travel*[2]

> Most she touched me by her muteness—
> Most she won me by the way
> She presented her small figure—
> Plea itself—for Charity—
>
> Were a Crumb my whole possession—
> Were there famine in the land—
> Were it my resource from starving—
> Could I such a plea withstand—

Not upon her knee to thank me
Sank this Beggar from the Sky—
But the Crumb partook—departed—
And returned On High—

I supposed—when sudden
Such a Praise began
'Twas as Space sat singing
To herself—and men—

'Twas the Winged Beggar—
Afterward I learned
To her Benefactor
Making Gratitude
                    —Emily Dickinson (J, 760)

8. plea] face   10. this] the   20. Making] paying

In a letter of March 1885 to Helen Hunt Jackson, Dickinson expressed her admiration of her correspondent's novel: "Pity me, however, I have finished *Ramona*. Would that like Shakesphere, it were just published!" (*Letters* 3, 866). Much as for her Shakespeare was "just published," Dickinson strove for eternal fame that would keep her poetry perpetually alive. Some critics have ascribed Dickinson's high praise of Jackson to flattery or to the poet's own misguided taste for sentimental writing.[3] Yet that Dickinson read and enjoyed much women's verse, including Jackson's, suggests that she had wide-ranging and eclectic tastes. In an 1871 letter to Thomas Wentworth Higginson, she remarks on the eternal quality of Jackson's writing: "Mrs. Hunt's Poems are stronger than any written by Women since Mrs—Browning, with the exception of Mrs Lewes—but truth like Ancestor's Brocades can stand alone—" (*Letters* 2, 491).

Although Dickinson began her correspondence with Jackson about 1868, when she was already a fully mature poet, she responded almost as intensely to her as she had to Higginson after the publication of his essay, "A Letter to a Young Contributor," in the *Atlantic Monthly*, seven years earlier. If Higginson was Dickinson's literary counselor and aesthetic soul mate, Jackson was a lively correspondent and appreciative reader who demonstrated both the pleasures and perils of entering the literary marketplace. Most importantly, Jackson was the only contemporary of Dickinson's to recognize her greatness, and her appreciative inquiries about the status of her friend's "portfolios" probably encouraged Dickinson to meet with her twice and to correspond with her for the rest of her life (*Letters* 3, 841). Jackson thus characterized her friend's verse as part of the sentimental tradition of women's verse writing, and even her most thoughtful support carried with it the belief that it was a woman's responsibility to perform acts of selfless charity, as she remarks sententiously to Dickinson in mid-May, 1879: "To be busy is the best help I know of, for all sorts of discomforts" (*Letters* 2, 639).

Even though she praised Jackson's talent, Dickinson refuted both the commercialism of the popular press and the stereotypical role to which women writers were expected to conform. The duality of a nineteenth-century American woman writer's life—personal freedom and professional constraints, radical poetry and conservative beliefs—was nowhere more present than in Jackson's. To extrapolate from one of Dickinson's mid-1860s poems to Jackson's life, Jackson embodied the "Winged Beggar" whose demure, pious, and even mute approach enlisted "Charity" from editors and critics, only to allow her to sing more loudly "To herself—and men—" (J, 760). Like her views on home and the family, her correspondence with Dickinson and with her editor, Thomas Bailey Aldrich, reveals a complex relation between what she wished to express and what she was able to say according to the prescribed modes of speaking for women writers. Moreover, her *Verses* (1870), which acquired considerable praise from critics and other writers, resembles other women's works both in its use of initials to identify the author and in its physical design with emblems (located at the beginning and end of the volume and directly over the table of contents) representing Christian faith, secular love, and the decorative arts. Nevertheless, her poems often undercut the accepted sentiment of women's writing, and thus clash with the more conservative illustrations for her book. To examine Jackson and Dickinson's correspondence and poems, then, gives us a privileged glimpse into not only the workings of the publishing world for nineteenth-century American women, but also the reasons why Dickinson chose not to exchange the "futile Diadem" of worldly renown for a longer lasting fame:

> Fame of Myself, to justify,
> All other Plaudit be
> Superfluous—An Incense
> Beyond Necessity—
>
> Fame of Myself to lack—Although
> My Name be else Supreme—
> This were an Honor honorless—
> A futile Diadem—
>
> (J, 713)

Jackson was one of few contemporaries to recognize Dickinson's talent, yet she was often unable to appreciate her meaning, a short-sightedness that must have confirmed Dickinson's belief that worldly fame was not to be. Around 1868, while Jackson summered in Amherst, they reestablished contact, and their subsequent correspondence lasted the rest of their lives. After Jackson married her second husband, William Sharpless Jackson, while vacationing in New Hampshire in 1875, Dickinson sent her wedding congratulations in the form of a one-line note and a cryptic poem:

> Have I a word but joy?
> > E. Dickinson

> > Who fleeing from the Spring
> > The Spring avenging fling
> > To Dooms of Balm—
> > > (*Letters* 2, 544)

Despite saying that she has only "a word," she feels the impact and qualifies the idea of marriage in the three-line lyric that follows. In fact, the poem might as easily concern Dickinson, as the positioning of her name above the poem implies. The seasons appear to "avenge" themselves on the poet, who avoids the rites of spring with their associations of marriage. Surely, the paradoxical expression "Dooms of Balm" suggests both the detriments and advantages of being single: she is condemned to life without a husband, yet she is promised the solace of poetry. Jackson responded by sending back the poem with a request for "interpretations" (*Letters* 2, 544); Dickinson withheld it, perhaps because she lacked confidence that Jackson was her best audience. Sensing that Dickinson had momentarily withdrawn her trust, Jackson asks her to write again "when it did not bore you" (*Letters* 2, 545); she further notes that she has "a little manuscript volume with a few of your verses in it," a common habit among nineteenth-century readers who transcribed or clipped and pasted their favorite verses into a book (*Letters* 2, 545). In one of her most far-reaching and noteworthy compliments in 1868, however, she adds that "You are a great poet—and it is wrong to the day you live in, that you will not sing aloud. When you are what men call dead, you will be sorry you were so stingy" (*Letters* 2, 545).

Jackson also made the mistake of thinking she could draw Dickinson into the type of social existence she had shared with other friends: "I hope some day, somewhere I shall find you in a spot where we can know each other" (*Letters* 2, 545). Higginson, too, had written her in 1869 asking her to come down to Boston, because "All ladies do" (*Letters* 2, 462); he characterized her as a literary "lady" author of the type that populated Boston and the Northeast. To his credit, however, he also recognized the originality and acuteness of her mind, which isolated her from her contemporaries:

It is hard [for me] to understand how you can live s[o alo]ne, with thoughts of such a [quali]ty coming up in you & even the companionship of your dog withdrawn. Yet it isolates one anywhere to think beyond a certain point or have such luminous flashes as come to you—so perhaps the place does not make much difference. (*Letters* 2, 461)

The physical and social existences which Higginson and Jackson lived were outside of her domain, and despite their wish to find a common ground for meeting their friend, her originality and intense privacy separated her from others.

Although she made one of the only serious attempts to convince Dickinson to publish, Jackson, like others of her generation, preferred the sonorous rhythms and discursive phrasing of the Victorians to the short, clipped lines of Dickinson's own more metaphysical poems. Jackson included in one of her letters a circular for the "No Name Series" to be issued by Roberts Brothers, her publisher, in hopes of convincing Dickinson to publish. As was so often the case, Dickinson turned to Higginson for advice in the matter, thus avoiding responsibility herself and deferring to his opinion. She mentioned that she told Jackson she was "incapable" of submitting her poems and begs him to "give me a note saying you disapproved it" (*Letters* 2, 563). Eventually, upon rereading Dickinson's verses, Jackson calls them "more clear than I thought they were" and agrees that "Part of the dimness must have been in me" (*Letters* 2, 565). Yet she remarks that "I like your simplest and [most direct] lines best" (*Letters* 2, 565), and she thanks her for writing "such plain letters" (*Letters* 2, 564). More complex than Jackson's poetry, Dickinson's lyrics struck her as obscure, much as the poet's life seemed abnormal. She notes the originality of Dickinson's writing and her life:

[I feel] as if I ha[d been] very imperti[nent that] day [in] speaking to you [as] I did,—accusing you of living away from the sunlight—and [telling] you that you [looke]d ill, which is a [mor]tal piece of ill[ness] at all times, but re[al]ly you look[ed] so [wh]ite and [mo]th-like[!] Your [hand] felt [l]ike such a wisp in mine that you frigh[tened] me. I felt [li]ke a [gr]eat ox [tal]king to a wh[ite] moth, and beg[ging] it to come and [eat] grass with me [to] see if it could not turn itself into beef! (*Letters* 2, 565)

Jackson uses language of transformation and of flowers and butterflies, so common in descriptions of women's verse, when she notes that Dickinson was "living away from the sunlight" and appeared "[mo]th-like." While Jackson is aware of Dickinson's originality, she also acknowledges implicitly the need for women writers to become "beef" to be consumed by others. As Betsy Erkkila argues, Jackson conformed to the dictates of the literary marketplace and compromised her artistic vision: "For all her national reputation as one of the most acclaimed writers of her time, Jackson was also in some sense both the product and the victim of popular taste."[4]

Despite Jackson's awareness of her friend's originality, she placed her in the "portfolio" tradition of other sentimental female writers. Jackson assumes that writers, perhaps especially women, have a duty to "sing aloud" for the good of others. Shortly before her death, Jackson thought of herself as part of an era that was fast becoming legendary: "It is a cruel wrong to your 'day & generation' that you will not give them light" (*Letters* 3, 841). Concerned with the status of Dickinson's works after her death, she offers to be the custodian of the fame that Dickinson so long and faithfully eluded: "If such a thing should happen as that I should outlive you, I wish you would make me your literary legatee & executor" (*Letters* 3, 841). Dickinson pointedly refused to answer. Jackson fully explains in this letter the ethic of feminine helpfulness that underlies her wish to see Dickinson publish:

Surely, after you are what is called 'dead,' you will be willing that the poor ghosts you have left behind, should be cheered and pleased by your verses, will you not?—You ought to be.—I do not think we have a right to with hold from the world a word or a thought any more than a *deed*, which might help a single soul. (*Letters* 3, 841–42)

For Jackson, a woman writer is duty bound to aid others with her words, much as any woman is expected to help others with her "deeds." Even the sentimentality of "might help a single soul" points to her belief that women were responsible for the moral welfare of others. Far from Dickinson's contention that Jackson's poetry resembles "truth," Jackson's argument as to why her friend should put forth her works in print adheres to the doctrine of feminine helpfulness.

Although a highly successful poet, American Indian activist, travel writer, and novelist, Jackson expresses regret over exposing her work in print, a common remonstration in prefaces by women writers of this period. In a letter to Abigail May responding to a request that she speak before the New England Women's Club in the fall of 1873, for example, she writes that "I cannot conceive of, any emergency which could screw up my courage to the point necessary to enable me to 'make remarks,' or to read a paper of my own"; she adds, concerning her decision to publish, "It is often almost more than I can bear the slight publicity which I have brought upon myself by saying,—behind the shelter of initials, and in the crowded obscurity of print—a few of the things I have felt deeply."[5]

No mere modest gesture, Jackson's engagement in social issues, especially the American Indian's plight, as well as in her career and an energetic social life, would seem to contradict her reluctance to voice her opinions publicly.[6] From about 1881 to 1883, she was organizing the background information she needed in order to write *Ramona*, and she published several articles in support of the Indian cause during this time, such as "Father Junípero and His Work" and "The Present Condition of Mission Indians in Southern California."[7] Such political sentiments were also genuinely felt and commonly expressed by her counterparts. Women writers supported temperance, abolition, suffrage, and revivalism, among other movements, and their political activism loosened the bonds of social conformity. Many worked toward social change, speaking publicly, lobbying legislators, holding office in male organizations, and crossing the barriers of race in the service of a higher cause, but at the same time they accepted the conventional view that women should embody the virtues of restraint and modesty. According to social historian Carroll Smith-Rosenberg, "It is significant that most of these women remained rooted within a bourgeois world of marriage and motherhood."[8]

Despite her interest in bettering the world, Jackson adhered to the values of family and home. In the same 1873 letter to Abigail May, she writes:

But I thank you most cordially—and through you, the committee—for this invitation. It touches me to the heart, and gratifies me more than I can say that I should have been thought worthy to speak on that sacredest of all themes—"Little children." I should disagree with you utterly in regarding "Home and private life" as a "narrower field" than those you have previously discussed.—It is to me the one sublime point, from which the lever rightly poised, can heave the whole world:—the only point from which the world ever will be moved. All these reforms seem to me trivial, dilatory, ineffective. Give the world one generation of good just, loving, clear headed, well educated mothers,—and the men and the measures which the world needs, will follow. (A-134, May-Goddard Collection)

Like Lydia Huntley Sigourney and other nineteenth-century American women poets, Jackson was conservative about the place of women in the home and their role as protectors and teachers of their children. What might be taken for two competing interests—women can struggle to achieve real change in society or they can nurture their husbands and children in the home—are reconcilable. Bringing up children for the larger good is the "lever" by which power relationships are destabilized and new social bonds established. Although "men and the measures" may ultimately accomplish the work, Jackson clearly believed that women were the source of monumental change by educating, prodding, and guiding their children. According to Susan Coultrap-McQuin, Jackson's belief in feminine helpfulness and the desire to effect social change was not contradictory: "Though True Womanhood and individuality seem almost wholly contradictory to our contemporary thinking, for Jackson they were not. In fact, her paradoxical beliefs in True Womanhood and in her expression of individuality seem to have given her an effective approach to a marketplace in transition from the ideals of the Gentleman Publisher to those of the Businessman Publisher" (150).

Jackson's poetry received high recommendation in the literary world.

Fig. 5. Emblem, Helen Hunt Jackson's ("H.H.") *Verses* (Boston: Roberts Brothers, 1875), viii.

Emerson included five of her poems in his anthology, *Parnassus* (1874), and writes in the preface that her poems "have rare merit of thought and expression, and will reward the reader for the careful attention which they require."[9] In his journals, he further praises her for "originality, elegance, and compression" and especially admires her "Thought" and "Ariadne's Farewell."[10] According to one anecdote, he was asked to name the best woman poet in America and replied, "Jackson," adding "Why not drop the word *woman*?"[11] The abstractness and mythological references of her poems must have appealed to him, and the emblems that frame the text of her 1875 *Verses* reflect the dichotomy of holy and secular love, an issue with which Emerson was himself concerned. Two illustrations immediately following the preface—a hand holding grapes above a chalice (which appears directly below the table of contents) and a triptych of Christ with the shepherds and Magi (placed above the first poem of the volume, "A Christmas Symphony")—have Christian resonances: one recalls the sacramental wine, which, in the Christian community, becomes the blood of Christ through the rite of transubstantiation, and the other evokes the birth of Christ, whose passion and death appear symbolically in the wreath of thorns surrounding the Christ Child's picture (Figs. 5 and 6). Yet the figure also evokes wine as a source of forgetfulness and love, since "Vintage" is listed in the table of contents directly above the illustration. Rather than invoking Christian themes, "Vintage" associates wine with a mythic place:

> Before the time of grapes,
>   While they altered in the sun,
> And out of the time of grapes,
>   When the vintage songs were done,—
>
> From secret southern spot,
>   Whose warmth not a mortal knew;
> From shades which the sun forgot,
>   Or could not struggle through[12]

Emerson's "Bacchus" also describes an oxymoronic "remembering wine" that issues from a secret place:

Fig. 6. Illustration, Helen Hunt Jackson's ("H.H.") *Verses* (Boston: Roberts Brothers, 1875), 9.

> Bring me wine, but wine which never grew
> In the belly of the grape,
> Or grew on vine whose tap-roots, reaching through
> Under the Andes to the Cape,
> Suffer no savor of the earth to scape.[13]

While Emerson uses wine to revive inner-consciousness, Jackson refers to wine as a symbol of a woman's love:

> Soul of my soul, the shapes
>   Of the things of earth are one;
> Rememberest thou the grapes
>   I brought thee in the sun?
>
> And darest thou still drink
>   Wine stronger than seal can sign?
> And smilest thou to think
>   Eternal vintage thine?
>   (*Verses*, 190, ll. 13–20)

"Wine stronger than seal can sign" alludes to the Song of Solomon—"Set me as a seal upon thine heart, as a seal upon thine arm: for love is strong as death; jealousy is cruel as the grave" (8:6)—and possibly to Revelations, where a book is "sealed with seven seals" until the Lamb of God reveals it to human beings (5:1). Despite its biblical context, Jackson's verse emphasizes the secularity of love and the arbitrariness of its external signs. "Soul of my soul" suggests that her outlook is romantic rather than religious, and "the shapes / Of the things of the earth are one" implies that it is far from everlasting. Love is perilous, and when based on "things of the earth," doomed to fail. Finally, the series of rhetorical questions ending the poem underscores the ambiguity of love's outcome: the beloved's sureness of "Eternal vintage" may be based on the "sign" of love and its covenant, but that sign may be misinterpreted, much as the "shapes" of earth are delusive and based on appearances.

Other reviewers considered her a poet of genuine vision and insight, yet their assessments conform to the standards by which women's poems were commonly judged. Higginson praised her work for "an intensity of feeling un-surpassed by any woman since Elizabeth Barrett Browning"; nonetheless, he disliked their compactness and their metrical roughness—features that now make Jackson seem modern.[14] Similarly, an anonymous reviewer for *The Nation* remarked an "intenseness of feeling, or rather a tension of feeling, which is incompatible with prettiness."[15] By and large, critics disliked the metrical ir-regularity that conflicted with the sheer "prettiness" of her poems, although they praised her, as did the writer of this review, for "evidences of poetical feeling" and genuine insight (183). Underlying the vague criticisms of these reviewers was the belief that the best women's poetry was sweet and "smooth," while the worst was intellectual and "harsh": "The merely pretty things that may be found in it are very few, for, in truth, H.H. appears to be not only too ready to use—perhaps as seeming more intellectual—somewhat involved and harsh modes of expressing her thoughts and feelings" (183–84). Yet her enor-mous popularity was undeniable. Magazines so valued her work that Josiah Gilbert Holland, a friend of the Dickinsons and the editor of *Scribner's Magazine* and *The Century*, reputedly considered giving over one number entirely to Jackson's writing, a proposal that was finally dismissed only because it might have been thought too sensational.[16]

Many of Jackson's *Verses* (1870) look forward to the imagistic concision and literary experimentation of early Modernist writers such as Amy Lowell and H.D. Often employing the theme of Christian piety and self-denial com-mon among female poets, Jackson's didacticism and moralizing are worthy of other, less inventive sentimental women writers. Yet she differs from other prominent women poets, especially those who wrote in the early to middle part of the century, in depicting moral irresolution and criticizing women's do-mestic alienation. Her poetry displays more realism than those of many of her contemporaries, perhaps prompting critics to disparage her poems as too rough and unmusical. In the era immediately preceding the literary experimentation and the changing attitudes toward women's lives of the 1880s and 1890s, Jack-son registers a discomfort with social norms, both in her conflicted relation-ship with her editors and in her frequently troubled attempts to resolve ques-tions of faith or a woman's place.

First published in 1870 and subsequently reissued with additions, Helen Hunt Jackson's 1875 *Verses* and 1910 *Poems* contain illustrations that reaffirm the dictates of women's poetic expression.[17] Her *Verses* resembles other women's works both in its use of initials to identify the author and in its design, with emblems representing Christian faith, secular love, and the decorative arts (located at the beginning and end of the volume and directly over the table of contents). The title page of the 1875 edition shows a woman spinning thread, and this image reappears in the second poem, "Spinning," whose "blind spinner" valiantly confirms the speaker's faith against the passage of time and the blindness of fate. Placed at the head of this volume, the illustration hints that the female poet, like Jackson, "spins" out words for money. For a woman poet, writing amounted to a type of domestic endeavor. A "spinster" was a woman who remained single beyond the traditional age for marrying, perhaps employing herself by making thread for others. "Distaff" refers to the staff on which flax, thread, or yarn is wound and alludes to feminine toil. Jackson was unmarried when she wrote this volume, and although she was not husbandless all of her life, she supported herself with the earnings from her book, much as a spinster might have lived on the wages she earned for her domestic labor.

Preceded by "A Christmas Symphony," a poem that conventionally assures the reader of an afterlife by celebrating Christ's birth, "Spinning" provides a counterpoint to the normative Christian standpoint and prepares us for the sets of opposites that form the rest of the book. Similar to Emerson's "Days," which depicts "hypocritic" time as a series of female figures, who are "Muffled and dumb like barefoot dervishes,"[18] "Spinning" depicts a speaker who, like a "blind spinner," passes her days in work without a definite sense of purpose or direction.

> Like a blind spinner in the sun,
>   I tread my days;
> I know that all the threads will run
>   Appointed ways;
> I know each day will bring its task,
> And, being blind, no more I ask.
>   (*Verses*, 14, ll. 1–6)

The spinner here resembles Clotho, who spins the thread of human life, one of the Fates, the trio of goddesses in classical mythology who were believed to determine the span of each human life. The speaker states that, "being blind," she resigns herself to the inevitable progression of "appointed" tasks in life. Although this poem contends that one should resign oneself with Christian faith to a new life in heaven, its invocation of a figure from Greek mythology supplements the purely Christian symbolism. The poem seeks to allay suffering with the promise of an afterlife, but, unlike other women's poetry, it diverges from the formulaic rendering of life as fulfilling and untroubled by combining Greek myth and Christian symbolism.

The aura of genteel sentiment that characterized women's poetry and lives did not prevent Jackson from pursuing her interests as a professional. Although she began writing as an outlet for her grief over her son Rennie's death, she considered publishing a way of making money: "I don't write for money, I write for love—I *print* for money."[19] Her life appeared to be full of the "secret sorrows" commonly thought to form the basis for women's poetry throughout most of the nineteenth century. Women were thought particularly capable of articulating these pitiful events, which more often than not included the deaths of their children. In particular, Jackson's very first published poems, "The Key to the Casket" and "Lifted Over," profited by a lucrative and growing call for child elegies, which provided consolation to the vast number of families who lost infants and young children.

For both Dickinson and Jackson, giving up poems to charities proved to be a problem, for they were requested with very little discretion. Jackson was judicious throughout her career in choosing where and when she would be published. Anxious to let only her best lyrics represent her in print, she was reluctant to send out poems for no pay to charitable causes. "A woman wrote asking me to send her a poem on the Arbutus for a subscriber's book—or chromo gallery or something I forget what," she wrote to Aldrich in 1884. "It is odd how people that would not dream of writing and asking you for $20—will calmly ask you to write a poem to order . . . I sat down & wrote three poems on the Arbutus! The first and second seemed to me quite too good for charity poems, & I meanly kept them, and sent her the worst!—" (23 February 1884; Aldrich, Ms. 2530). The genteel conventions of authorship placed the female writer in a double bind: women were supposed to contribute poems gratis to charities. Jackson wished to receive full pay for her poems, and she hoped to control where and when the best would appear, an important consideration for a poet who wished to present herself to the public in the best light possible.

Dickinson also resisted sending poems to a charity, although she probably saw the request as an imposition more on her privacy than on her pocketbook. The request was probably made by Joseph K. Chickering, a professor of English at Amherst College, who sought support for the Annual Sale of the Mission Circle, an event designed to aid children in India and Far Eastern countries. She wrote to Higginson several times concerning the proposed submission. The first time, in 1880, she tells him that "I have promised three Hymns to a charity, but without your approval could not give them—" (*Letters* 3, 680); she further notes "They are short and I could write them quite plainly" and asks if he would tell her if they are "faithful." But does she mean "faithful" to her own conception or sufficiently pious? Perhaps she was responding to a request for a poem on a religious topic, an appropriate choice considering that the charity was the Mission Circle, as evidenced also by her next letter to Higginson: "Grateful for the kindness, I enclose those you allow, adding a fourth, lest one of them you might think profane—" (*Letters* 3, 681). Of the four she included, the poem beginning "Dare you see a Soul *at the White Heat?*" (J, 365) might most easily have offended strictly orthodox sensibilities. In the letters conclusion, she hints again at the religious dictates to which she felt these poems had to conform and to the almost pious "conviction" Higginson's criticism would engender in her: "Reprove them as your own—To punish them would please me, because the fine conviction I had so true a friend—" (*Letters* 3, 681). Rather than point to the ostensibly religious value of these poems, she commends Higginson for his devotion to her. For Dickinson, Higginson's criticisms would both prove his friendship and confirm the sanctity that she believed true poetry endows on the poet.

Although she expresses gratitude for Higginson's desire to help her and states that she will follow his advice "implicitly" (*Letters* 3, 681), her lukewarm response shows that she was not attracted to giving her poems to charity. In fact, she considered refusing Chickering's request, since it was impersonally delivered: "The one who asked me for the Lines, I had never seen—He spoke of 'a Charity'—I refused but did not inquire—He again earnestly urged, on the ground that in that way I might 'aid unfortunate Children'—The name of 'Child' was a snare to me and I hesitated—Choosing my most rudimentary, and without criterion, I inquired of you—" (*Letters* 3, 681–82). Rather than object to sending her poems to charity on the basis of a bad business venture, as Jackson did, Dickinson thought any submission of her poems as a kind of "publishing," a violation of the soul. Whereas in "Self-Reliance," Emerson condemns the "foolish philanthropist" for giving to "the thousandfold Relief Societies" when "there is a class of persons to whom by all spiritual affinity I am bought and sold,"[20] nineteenth-century American women were willing to submit poems for publication in service of a higher cause. In an era when female piety and charity were one, Dickinson might well have felt that Chickering was both intruding on her privacy as well as taking advantage of women's selflessness, a dilemma she finally resolved by deciding not to make her poems public.

In Jackson's *Poems* (1910), an illustration of the author departs from the presentation of women's sentimental verse writing. Judging from the motifs, illustrations, and designs, the editors clearly wished to place Jackson's volume in the Victorian era, but her portrait reveals a realistic and modern sensibility. The frontispiece displays Jackson's picture with her signature directly below, a common adornment that verifies the identity of the author. Although these portraits appear in works authored by men as well as women, the pictures in women's anthologies or collections of verse by a single author frequently are aimed at embodying the most prized female virtues. Frances Sargent Osgood's portrait in *Poems* (1850), for instance, is preceded by the illustrations of two figures from the poems—Zuleika, an Arabian maiden holding a rose, and an infant girl balancing a butterfly on her finger—both of which convey the

Fig. 7. Frontispiece, Helen Jackson's *Poems* (Boston: Little, Brown, and Company, 1910). "H.H." to ED: "What portfolios of verses you must have."

virtues of feminine innocence and purity. Osgood's portrait appears immediately before the poems along with a copy of her signature, and her beatific, full-eyed look suggests that she personally practices the virtues that she enjoins on her reader. Jackson's portrait seems to convey the feminine virtues of restraint and decorum, yet she appears in a much more realistic light than Osgood (Fig. 7). Rather than appear, like Osgood, in a classical-looking shoulderless tunic, which idealizes the poet by making her seem to be from some legendary time, Jackson is dressed as a conventional Victorian matron. Her eyes seem sharp yet amused, and her right hand is raised to her chin as if to suggest her meditation on the scene. Far from Osgood's tearful glance, Jackson's look conveys an acute mind that deals humanely and intelligently with the surrounding world.

Fig. 8. Illustration, Helen Jackson's *Poems* (Boston: Little, Brown, and Company, 1910), vii.

The illustration of a keepsake chest appearing directly above the table of contents, however, is squarely in the tradition of sentimental female versification, and it hearkens back to the mid-nineteenth-century portrayal of women's verses as private and untutored (Fig. 8). An ornately carved box, whose open lid reveals the initials "H.J." enclosed in a wreath, contains a protruding manuscript roll tied with ribbon, and surrounding the box are sheets of manuscript, presumably from Jackson's private cache. The roses placed behind the box correspond with the floral motif that appears elsewhere in the volume (as on the page entitled "Dedication," whose letters are interwoven with a budding rose and decorated at the bottom of the page by daisies). When coupled with manuscript rolls, the floral motif points not only to the decorative tradition of female verse, but also to the habit of enclosing pressed flowers in letters. In addition, a seal with the initials of the author suggests either that these manuscripts were included in her correspondence or that they were letters themselves, since only official documents or an envelope might be fastened with such a seal. As the designs in Jackson's volume attest, even in 1910 editors placed Jackson's verse in the prescribed categories by which women's verse was judged sixty years earlier, no matter how forward-looking it might be.

A holdover from the age of Victorian sentiment, the chest prefacing Jackson's book of poetry is synonymous with an era when women's poetry was thought to be nostalgic and sentimental. Since a chest or coffer was reserved for precious jewels, trinkets, and keepsakes, placing women's poems in a chest both elevates and trivializes them as sentimental tokens. Women's verses were popularly characterized as nostalgic trinkets or precious objects to be lovingly preserved. More generally, keeping one's poems locked away in a chest insured privacy, much as Dickinson herself placed fair copies of her poems, folded and sewn into packets, in a bureau drawer. An "Ebon Box" filled with letters and other mementos in one of Dickinson's lyrics recalls the chest filled with manuscripts adorning Jackson's book, but this chest also instills in the person who opens it an awareness of mortality:

> In Ebon Box, when years have flown
> To reverently peer,
> Wiping away the velvet dust
> Summers have sprinkled there!
>
> To hold a letter to the light—
> Grown Tawny now, with time—
> To con the faded syllables
> That quickened us like Wine!
>
> Perhaps a Flower's shrivelled cheek
> Among it's stores to find—
> Plucked far away, some morning—
> By gallant—mouldering hand!
>
> A curl, perhaps, from foreheads
> Our Constancy forgot—
> Perhaps, an Antique trinket—
> In vanished fashions set!
>
> And then to lay them quiet back—
> And go about it's care—
> As if the little Ebon Box
> Were none of our affair!
>
> (J, 169)

Not only do the trinkets in the "Ebon Box" recall the fleeting passage of time, but they also call up the memory of the beloved dead with a vividness that exposes the triteness of Victorian mourning conventions. The "Ebon Box" contains keepsakes popular in the Victorian era—a letter, a flower, a lock of hair, and a piece of jewelry—and betokens more than the popular consolatory habit of keeping mementos of the deceased, since it resembles a coffin as well as a chest filled with familiar objects from the past. Rather than simply memorializing the dead, the tokens themselves become signs of mortality: although the letter has "grown Tawny," its words, like "wine," once conveyed to the reader a hint of passion; the flower's petals resemble the "shrivelled cheek," perhaps of a suitor, whose "gallant—mouldering hand" plucked the flower at the distance of years; the curl reminds the speaker of the dead whom "our Constancy forgot"; and an "Antique trinket" is now set in "vanished fashions" of years before. Acts of politeness and gallantry are repaid with a lack of "Constancy" and inattention to the memory of the dead. Indeed, Dickinson's poem concerns the power of objects to evoke our remembrance of the dead, despite our wish to deny their continued relevance to our lives. Although we try to put aside the preserved and cherished mementos of the dead, "As if the little Ebon Box / Were none of our affair" implies that we cannot.

For Dickinson, the "Ebon Box" alerts its caretaker to the disturbing truth of mortality that putting these treacherous keepsakes in a box might be an effort to contain. As Barton Levi St. Armand explains, Dickinson revises the tradition of sentimental versifying that eventually elevated the dead into beloved objects, following from actual technological advances, as new methods of interment were developed and more sanitary cemeteries were built: "The loved dead themselves became keepsakes, as advances in embalming and the invention of waterproof tombs and airtight burial cases actually allowed sentimentalists to treat the corpse as the metaphorical gem, treasure, or idol it so often is in the lofty lamentations of mortuary verse."[21] Rather than convey a sense of the beloved dead's continued presence, keepsakes remind the reader of his or her own mortality. Dickinson placed the fair copies of her poems, folded and sewn into small packets, in a bureau drawer, and one might ask if poems placed in a chest or consigned to a drawer during the poet's life were as threatening as keepsakes: did they have the same explosive power to remind a reader years after the poet has died of the fact of human mortality?

For Dickinson, a word can infect its reader years after its author has died:

> A Word dropped careless on a Page
> May stimulate an eye
> When folded in perpetual seam
> The Wrinkled Maker lie
>
> Infection in the sentence breeds
> We may inhale Despair
> At distances of Centuries
> From the Malaria—
>
> (J, 1261)

2. stimulate] consecrate   4. Maker] Author

This lyric concerns the power of words to transmit meaning from dead author to living reader. Like a piece of paper, the "Wrinkled Maker" is "folded" and bound up, as if she were being mailed first-class to God. Even after its "Wrinkled Maker" has disappeared, a word transmits mortality's disease, "Despair." A word can live on and breathe out the "Malaria"—literally, "bad air"—as if it were the animated presence of its maker and remind us of death; we can later "inhale" it "at distances of Centuries." For Dickinson, poems have the power to "stimulate" the reader who carelessly happens upon them years later, much as keepsakes in the previous poem can convey a sense of mortality to their care-taker. In contrast to the image propagated by the publishing world that women's poems were sentimental tokens, Dickinson hints that poems can transcend the lifespan of the poet and convey the spectre of mortality to the reader years later.

Despite her early success, Jackson approached publishing carefully, and her manipulation of the publishing world is clear in her letters to her editor, Thomas Bailey Aldrich, and her mentor, Thomas Wentworth Higginson. Jackson's professional relationship with Aldrich was complex enough to allow her to express her business instincts, while she conformed to the prevalent self-effacing image. In many of her letters asking for his advice, she adopts a conventionally modest attitude toward Aldrich. She often feared that her verse was not good, asking Aldrich "Are either of these bits of verse lyrical?" (14 February 1884; Aldrich, Ms. 2529). Once she decided on writing as a profession, she adopted Higginson as her mentor. Early on, she had patterned her first prose efforts after his, parsing sentences and rewriting whole paragraphs from his *Out-Door Papers* in an effort to write more elegantly.[22] That she intended to flatter Higginson seems obvious, an intention not entirely lost on him. In the following anecdote concerning her first submission to *The Atlantic*, he notes her canny business sense:

It is certain that she was repeatedly urged to send something in that direction by a friend who then contributed largely to the magazine, but she for a long time declined; saying that the editors were overwhelmed with poor poetry, and that she would wait for something of which she felt sure. Accordingly she put into that friend's hands a poem called "Coronation," with permission to show it to Mr. Fields and let him have it if he wished, at a certain price. It was a high price for a new-comer to demand; but she was inexorable, including rather curiously among her traits that of being an excellent business woman, and generally getting for her wares the price she set upon them. Fields read it at once, and exclaimed, "It's a good poem"; then read it again, and said, "It's a *devilish* good poem," and accepted it without hesitation.[23]

Jackson modestly derides her own efforts in keeping with the belief that women should downplay their achievements, but in doing so she also secures herself a better reputation when she does send in her poem, having created an aura of interest about her work (the "friend" here who first asked Jackson to submit her poems was probably Higginson himself). Asking a "high price" for her first submission and being "inexorable" was at odds with her image as a genteel lady author, prompting Higginson to conclude that she comprised "rather curiously among her traits that of being an excellent business woman." Not expected to show an aptitude for business, Jackson's business sense appears even alongside a deferential attitude toward her publishers.

Despite her conventional attitude toward women's role in publishing, Jackson expressed herself openly with her editor, Thomas Bailey Aldrich, concerning the constraints placed on her poetry. Jackson's correspondence with Aldrich reflects many of the publishing conventions that applied to women writers in the nineteenth century. As editor of *The Atlantic Monthly*, Aldrich supervised the appearance of Jackson's pieces in his magazine from 1881 until her death in 1885. Their correspondence dates from the years when she had reached the peak of her popularity, having already published poetry, short stories, and travel pieces in *The Atlantic* and other magazines, as well as the capstone of her career, *Ramona* (1884). As an established writer, she conformed to the common image of women writers that encouraged them to ask meekly for the acceptance and encouragement of their editors. Yet she also resisted the criticisms of her proofreader when they differed from her own well-developed conception of her verse.

Although she used a self-belittling tone in sending Aldrich her poetry, Jackson sought to further her own interests by making sure that she would be published. She paid for the stereotype plates and publication of her first few volumes with Fields, Osgood and Company, until she moved to Roberts Brothers shortly afterwards. Despite a cordial relationship with her editors, she frequently felt the need to publish more often than they allowed to keep her name before the public, as she notes in sending Aldrich some unsolicited verses: "Look at the audacity of me—sending another bit of verse when you said you couldn't arrange for one more: but a sonnet doesn't take much room: and I don't want the Atlantic to go six whole months without hearing from me you know" (8 May 1882; Aldrich, Ms. 2500). Jackson expresses similar sentiments to Aldrich on at least two other occasions. She remarks on 16 October 1882, "I am always glad to have papers in the Atlantic at less rates of pay than I get elsewhere, because I consider the having them read by the Atlantic audience part of the pay" (Aldrich, Ms. 2504). In the same complimentary tone, on 22 February 1883, she again thanks Aldrich for the honor of being included in his magazine, and shows her interest in keeping her name before the public: "I consider part of the pay for an article in the Atlantic is, always, its being in the Atlantic:—at the same time, one must have some regard to one's 'market value'" (Aldrich, Ms. 2515).

Despite her desire to be remembered by the reading public, Jackson also recognized the dangers of publishing too much or too often. Successful writers were expected to turn out a great deal of publishable material for magazines. Like Lydia Sigourney, who acknowledged that churning out poetry for magazines ruined her career as a serious writer, Jackson feared that she might become a hack if she produced too quickly.[24] She responded testily to Aldrich in 1882 that she would not write to his or anyone's order: "I myself am sick of being asked,—or if not asked,—expected, to write 'magazinable' papers:—I am on the point of vowing not to write a word for magazines for a year" (29 November 1882; Aldrich, Ms. 2507). She remarks on another occasion that she dislikes the idea of being paid for each page of text she writes, although the proposal tempts her: "As for the so much per page plan, it is a vicious one—& if publishers could only see it is dead against their real interests. It is a million times easier to put your thing into twenty pages than into ten.—I confess, I wouldn't like to subject myself to the temptation of being paid by page or column" (22 February 1883; Aldrich, Ms. 2515). As a highly rated travel writer, Jackson could easily have stretched her copy for more pay. That she refused to do so is a tribute both to her skill and to her awareness of her "market value" as a well-known writer. Addressing Aldrich as her "Dear and Obdurate Editor," she nevertheless thanks him for his editorial comments, adding that his praise is worth more than money to her: "I would rather you send back a poem calling it, 'Lyrical & brook-like,' than accept it & send me a cheque silently" (14 February 1884; Aldrich, Ms. 2529).

Not only did Jackson reject the demand of publishers that she write to order, but she also ignored some of the corrections made by her proofreader. In several letters, she objects fervently to the vagueness and frequency of his comments:

And I wish you could tell the blue pencil man from me, that I think he ought to have some more colors in pencils—and let us understand the significance of them. He draws that doubtful blue line under a word—and I sit & rack my brain for half an hour to divine what he can possibly have seen to object to in that word, & then I suddenly discover—or think I do!—that all he meant by that particular blue line was that the word was not printed straight.— (4 November 1882; Aldrich, Ms. 2505)

Since the proofreader's corrections often amounted to little more than a plea for more legible handwriting, less repetitive phrasing, and the like, Jackson often found them tiresome, and sometimes agreed, sometimes ignored them. The issues underlying Jackson's dissension with her editor and proofreader varied, as did the tone she took toward them. Her arguments with her proofreader concern stylistic choices—repetitive phrases and word choice—while her discussions with Aldrich almost always refer to business negotiations— persuading him to take a piece, discussing pay scale, determining where and how frequently she would publish.

Jackson often bypassed the proofreader's stylistic comments by turning the authority for final editorial changes over to Aldrich. In another letter, for example, she refuses to yield to the corrections of the proofreader, disdaining even to call him by name: "If the underscoring came from your half of the blue pencil, I give right up: and you may put any other word in there you choose. But if it is 'the other fellow,' I stick to my (own) text" (15 January 1883; Aldrich, Ms. 2512). Concessions only went so far, and she was often unwilling to give in to another's opinion. Finally, when the recommendations of the "blue pencil man" were too abhorrent, she summarily rejected his criticisms without any attempt at conciliation: "I have not however heeded all the scornful underlinings of your Proof Reader.—Has he not a morbid aversion for the repetitions of a word? I have a liking for such repetitions in certain ways and places:—and have left some untouched, which he evidently expected me to hustle out of sight" (19 April 1881; Aldrich, Ms. 2482). The accusatory tone of "your Proof Reader" ultimately blames Aldrich for the criticism. Yet the proofreader, who is the safer object of satire and more responsible for the changes, receives all the insults. Persuade or deride: her attention to her editor's opinion and equally strong condemnation of her proofreader's comments indicates that she heaped her criticisms on the latter in order to preserve her good rapport with Aldrich.

In "The Way to Sing," Jackson testifies to a poet's need for independence of thought:

> The birds must know. Who wisely sings
> Will sing as they;
> The common air has generous wings
> Songs make their way.
> No messenger to run before,
> Devising plan;
> No mention of the place or hour
> To any man;
> No waiting till some sound betrays
> A listening ear;
> No different voice, no new delays,
> If steps draw near.
> (*Poems*, 37, ll. 1–12)

The indifference of the bird to whomever may be listening suggests that the poet must sing freely with little attention to audience or context. Jackson's literary career and public existence outside Amherst and Boston made her an attractive correspondent for Dickinson, for whom her flight from the East and unquenchable energy symbolized transcendence. Unlike the women of her sonnets, Jackson was not trapped by domestic circumstances. Upon hearing that Jackson had broken a leg, an injury that kept her infirm from January until her death from cancer in August of 1884, Dickinson made an analogy between poet and bird that conformed to the free bird image so popular among women poets: "I shall watch your passage from Crutch to Cane with jealous affection. From there to your Wings is but a stride—as was said of the convalescing Bird" (*Letters* 3, 840). Symbolizing personal freedom and the ability to transcend circumstances, the free bird contradicted the image of the caged bird, which represented the pressure of social and sexual constraints, like the parrot in a gilded cage at the opening of Kate Chopin's *The Awakening* (1900). When she alludes further to Jackson's injury shortly before her death in a letter to William Sharpless Jackson, Dickinson implies that her death provided an escape from life and a spiritual release: "Dear friend, can you walk, were the last words that I wrote her. Dear friend, I can fly—her immortal (soaring) reply" (*Letters* 3, 889). Not to be restricted simply to Christian imagery, however, she raises Jackson to classical and mythic proportions—"Helen of Troy will die, but Helen of Colorado, never" (*Letters* 3, 889). For the Dickinson of the letters, transcendence above a conventional woman's life and mutability were clearly Jackson's most admirable qualities late in her life.

Another poem of Dickinson's probably sent to Jackson conveys the same image of a bluebird's independent nature:

> Before you thought of Spring
> Except as a Surmise
> You see—God bless his suddenness—
> A Fellow in the Skies
> Of Independent Hues
> A little weather worn
> Inspiring habiliments
> Of Indigo and Brown—
> With specimens of Song
> As if for you to choose—
> Discretion in the interval
> With gay delays he goes
> To some superior Tree
> Without a single Leaf
> And shouts for joy to Nobody
> But his seraphic self—
>
> (J, 1465)

This relatively late poem of Dickinson's concerns our testing of the world with empirical hypotheses, which are proven to be perhaps too tentative in light of the bird's miraculous affirmation of self.[25] The arrival of a bluebird, which embodies independence and action, heralds the season and contrasts with the reader's belated acknowledgment of the season's arrival. We are provided "specimens," or examples, of songs that are representative of an entire class, genus, or whole, much as a scientist might provide examples of an animal or plant or a traveling salesman display samples of his wares. Indeed, "specimen" derives etymologically from specere, or *to see*; the bird, then, presents visual proof of spring. Littered with religious references ("God bless his suddenness," "Inspiriting habiliments," "seraphic self"), the description of the bird underscores the link between his sudden, gay appearance and the joyful and unforeseen existence of grace. Given that the reader foretells the appearance of the season only by "Surmise," his awareness precedes conscious thought—"before you thought of Spring"—and again implies that grace is unsought and preexisting. Finally, the words "as if for you to choose—," followed closely by "discretion," raise an interesting ambiguity: Is the speaker referring to the bird, who alights gingerly on the trees? Or is the remark directed to the reader, who may choose "discretion in the interval" rather than song? Like the bird, the reader has the opportunity to hold back from full expression, to engage in "gay delays" of singing, and perhaps withholding one's voice is evidence of freedom and independence of mind, much as the bird provides an overt vision of "Independent Hues." Given the common depiction of women's poetic voices as birdsong, this lyric may express Dickinson's attitude toward poetry and publishing her works in the literary marketplace: resisting the opinions of others and proclaiming its independence, the bird sets an example for his human counterparts as he "shouts for joy to Nobody / But his seraphic self—" (J, 1465).

Like most women of the period who published anonymously, Jackson signed her earliest pieces with initials. In her first published poem, "The Key to the Casket," she signed her name "Marah," an acronym of "Ma of Rennie Hunt," which fittingly evokes the poem's central event—the death from tuberculosis of her eight-year-old son only six weeks before. After publishing more poems under this pseudonym, including another tribute to her son entitled "Lifted Over," she began to use her initials, H.H., for all her poetry. "Saxe Holm" served as the pen name for a number of her novels and stories, prompting a series of articles aimed at deciphering the author's identity. To the end of her life, Jackson refused to acknowledge authorship, leading one columnist to speculate that perhaps she had co-authored the stories with Dickinson: "The two were intimate friends in early life and it is possible that the stories were the joint work of each, so that each could with truth deny that she had written them" (Leyda 2, 472). The so-called Saxe Holm controversy today seems a quaint exercise in the conventions of genteel authorship, yet the debate over the authorship of Jackson's writings underscores the common use of personae as a publishing strategy in nineteenth-century American women's writing. Throughout the nineteenth century, critics thought women used pseudonyms to increase their notoriety or to attaching themselves to a project that might fail, rather than to avoid the discrimination rampant in the publishing world. An anonymous 1875 article entitled "Another Woman Claims To Be Saxe Holm, Author" in *The Boston Gazette* disproves the claim of a Brooklyn woman that she was the real Saxe Holm, adding her story "is all very amusing to me, as I happen to know that the editor of Scribner's suggested these stories to the writer, who is a poet, and wrote under this signature fearing that they might not be successful, and dreading the effect of such a circumstance upon a name and reputation that already stood with the highest."[26] Reviewers like this one came to accept a woman writer's use of a pseudonym as a publishing strategy, much as they recognized her pen name as a persona—a fictional personality constructed for the benefit of the publishing community and the general readership and, ultimately, to sell more books.

Besides allowing an author to conceal her identity from the public, pseudonyms were part of constructed speakerly identities. An 1878 article called "Who is Saxe Holm?" published in *The Springfield Republican* and possibly written by editor Samuel Bowles (a close friend of the Dickinsons) implies that denying authorship is a posture agreed upon by both critics and writers: "The whole world of letters has seized upon this gospel of the new literary dispensation and circulated fibs with the most saintly countenance. It is this principle, no doubt, which has led our critics to believe that Helen Hunt could be Saxe Holm and deny it and be a very excellent woman all in the same moment. In fact, it has come to such a pass that denials of this sort are of no account whatever in the eyes of the reviewers."[27] Both acknowledging that such avowals and disavowals of authorship were only part of the publishing game and holding women to a higher moral standard than men were common among nineteenth-century critics. The writer sanctimoniously condemns the author for denying to be Saxe Holm, yet he admits that such pretense was common. Not merely a symptom of genteel reticence among women, this convention also allowed women to stimulate interest in their works among the reading public by coyly denying authorship and then creating controversy.

Furthermore, Saxe Holm's characteristics parallel those of Emily Dickinson's own personality. Bowles would have been aware of the poet's inclination early in her career to publish, and he might have hazarded a guess that she had turned to prose in the intervening years, submitting her work to be printed only under the shelter of a pseudonym. Although the writer contends that "H.H." is "open to the charge of sentimentality," he describes her primarily as a realist, "emphatically a woman of every day life," who deals in "practical home and society questions" (4). In contrast, he asserts that Saxe Holm is more imaginative, secretive, and less worldly. "The questions" that Saxe Holm "propounds," he writes, "are of a subtle, mysterious, way-side, we had almost said underground sort, so much do they smack of the cellar—questions which she gropes about with for some time and then abandons, leaving an uneasy conviction in the mind of the reader of something wrong" (4). The characterization of her poems as "way-side" and cellar-grown evokes the belief that she is beyond the pale of normal womanhood, much as Jackson's characterization of Dickinson as "moth-like" paints her as pale, timid, and abnormal.

Moreover, such characterizations might emanate from the many stories that revolved around Dickinson's life. While Jackson's poetry could flower in the full light of day, Dickinson's was most fit to be hidden away in a cellar or hothouse, too delicate to be exposed to the full light of public scrutiny. According to the author, Saxe Holm's abnormal thoughts derive from her unhealthy and reclusive living conditions:

A very subtle analysis upon a very few truths pushed to their extreme application; the morbidness, improbability, quaintness and shrinking which would result from a lack of the sun's ripening influences, like a lily grown in a cellar. All these lead us to the conclusion that the author may be a person long shut out from the world and living in a world of her own; that perhaps she is a recluse. (7)

Dickinson's habit of not admitting visitors certainly qualified her as a "recluse," and the description of Saxe Holm as "a lily grown in a cellar" suggests she is fragile and secluded from normal influences in keeping with the popular characterization of women as delicate flowers. The reviewer emphasizes the Poe-like morbidity of Saxe Holm—"always morbid, and morbid to the last degree . . . the ideal element of her poetry pushed to its extremity" (4). According to the reviewer, Jackson's writing varies from Saxe Holm's and their stylistic differences abound: Jackson's poetry is "sweet," sensitive, and pious; Saxe Holm's is "intense," jarringly emotional, and "reverent with the reverence of one stricken with admiration and awe" (5). Both these personae recall the obverse images of the sentimental and Gothic writers, and they suggest that they had largely become stylized performances, masks to be adopted and shed by the female writer depending on her intent. Saxe Holm, he writes, "seems to feel a kinship to the natural world, is as exquisitely sensitive to the feelings produced by birds and flowers and is as familiar with their ways and language as if she were, indeed, one of them" (5). Dickinson would surely have qualified as "morbid" in Bowles's mind, for he was very familiar with her secluded life and at least mildly aware of the elegaic tone of her writing, based on the few poems he had read. Furthermore, he places the writer in the class of sentimental female writers, who were described as sensitive, fearful, and lonely souls, and he calls her stories "weird and improbable" (4), comparing her poems to "strains of solemn music floating at night from some way-side church" (4). Neither her poems nor her stories, however, conformed to the dictates of Calvinism: "From the puritanical religion of New England's daughters, and especially from its cant, she is singularly free" (5).

Several more comments offer further proof that the writer probably had Dickinson in mind. The writer deems Saxe Holm's background privileged in many ways: "we may imagine her to be a member of one of those 'sleepy and dignified' New England families whom she has so vividly described; of a timid nature; separated from the outside world, devoted to literature and flowers" (7). Dickinson's family was the most distinguished in Amherst: her grandfather was a founder of Amherst College, and her father, a prominent lawyer, who served several terms in the Massachusetts State Legislature and one in Congress. Finally, the writer of the article supposes that Saxe Holm may, like Jackson, have been from Amherst, since "it may be stated in a general way that two persons capable of literary expression may have lived in the same town" (7).

The stereotypically feminine image of Saxe Holm as otherworldly, intense, and heterodox has profound implications for our understanding of Dickinson's choice of subject matter and style. Jackson's poetry is complex enough to embody the conflicting attitudes that led most nineteenth-century American editors to consider women writers saints or sinners, mothers and daughters or spinsters. The subject matter and presentation of her poetry reflect the fine line she maintained between accepting and resisting the standards for female expression: while conforming to the accepted topics of female verse—Christian love and self-denial—she reveals her dissatisfaction with these conventions. Jackson's uneasiness with the conventional role for women subtly resists the norms for women's expression, and this discomfort underscores Dickinson's more radical condemnation of women's roles. The decorative lettering and the final illustration offer a purely secular view of love. The first letter of each poem is capitalized and intertwined with flowers, which typifies Victorian floral design and makes no reference to Christian piety. The final emblem counterpoints the Christian design of a hand holding grapes over a cup. Appearing directly below the final poem, "Last Words," a pair of hands plucking a petal from a daisy points to the theme of worldly love (Fig. 9). This emblem implies that love is a game of chance, as does the poem "The Sign of the Daisy," which appears only two pages earlier. The speaker tells of a woman who, perhaps after an unhappy love affair, disregards the outcome of the children's game of plucking petals as a way of predicting affection, preferring to believe that "'One story no two daisies tell'" (*Verses*, 189, l. 6). After another summer, however, the woman has forgotten her suffering—"Her heart had lost its last year's pain" (*Verses*, 189, ll. 11–12)—and the speaker then remarks in the final stanza that self-deception is the daisy's real message.

> So never the daisy's sweet sign deceives,
>   Though no two will one story tell;
> The glad heart sees the daisy leaves,
>   But thinks not of their hidden spell,
> Heeds not which lingered and which fell.
>   "He loves me; yes, he loves me well."
> Ah, happy heart which sees, believes!
>   This is the daisy's secret spell!
>   (*Verses*, 189, ll. 17–24)

"The Sign of the Daisy" undercuts the interpretation of "signs" upon which both secular and religious love are based; while one is encouraged to "believe" without "seeing" according to Christian doctrine, the opposite dictum that

Fig. 9. Emblem, Helen Hunt Jackson's ("H.H.") *Verses* (Boston: Roberts Brothers, 1875), 191.

"seeing is believing" proves inapt in romantic love, where one might wrongly convince oneself of another's affection.

Given the disavowal of romantic love presented in "The Sign of the Daisy" (a critique reinforced by the emblem at the book's end), "Last Words" receives a different inflection due to its placement. The dying speaker reluctantly departs from life, enjoining her mourners to remember "that I am looking backward as I go, / Am lingering while I haste, and in this rain / Of tears of joy am mingling tears of pain" (*Verses*, 191, ll. 2–4). Her final words, however, are cast in doubt when juxtaposed with the emblem:

> And when, remembering me, you come some day
> And stand there, speak no praise, but only say,
> "How she loved us! It was for that she was so dear!"
> These are the only words that I shall smile to hear.
> (*Verses*, 191, ll. 11–14)

If we take seriously "The Sign of the Daisy'"s exposure of love as a fickle game, then the endearment hoped for in "Last Words" is less than secure. Expressing a conventional sentimental send-off, in which the plucked flower symbolizes mortality, the speaker wishes to obscure the humble traces of her existence ("Do not adorn with costly shrub, or tree, / Or flower, the little grave which shelters me" [*Verses*, 191, ll. 5–6]). But the placement of the poem immediately above the image of a hand plucking petals from a daisy, an emblem representing the fickleness of love, suggests that we cannot be sure of her affection or, if it is genuine, that she may not be able to trust those who have offered the same to her. By contrasting the redemptive powers of holy love with the trials and self-deceptions of its secular counterpart, Jackson implies that both are a part of her experience and perhaps of every woman's.

Dickinson found little comfort in the Victorian conventions of death, and her poems more radically critique women's roles than do those of other nineteenth-century American women poets. Her lyrics share themes of romantic and holy love, Christian self-denial, and ennobling renunciation with Jackson's, as the common use of the casket symbol shows. While Jackson's poetry was marketed as sentimental, she renounced the pressure on women's lives more strongly in her poetry than any other woman writer except Dickinson. Many of Jackson's poems embody features mentioned by Cheryl Walker and Emily Stipes Watts. Sorrow and suffering are characterized from a normative Christian standpoint as a type of richness. "My Legacy," for example, describes a fairy-tale scenario of a woman who fervently seeks a promised treasure, only to find that her inheritance is the privilege to share Christ's "sweet legacy of sorrow" (*Verses*, 18, l. 52). Jackson invokes extreme states of being and climatic conditions to describe the life of a woman who has been unduly neglected. "Found Frozen," for instance, adopts the conceit of a freezing traveler to depict a woman's slow death in her home, where her tribulations have gone unnoticed by her family. Other poems use the imagery of extreme landscapes and climates to represent the depths of passion, much as Dickinson's poems often depict a "tropic" or other exotic location to describe the experience of love. Finally, renunciation of love, food, and worldly ambition in Jackson's poems confers a royal status on the speaker, who will be rewarded with heavenly bliss for her sacrifices.

Famine in Jackson's poetry is often a metaphor for spiritual or emotional deprivation. Jackson depicts a speaker who laments the life of a woman deprived of her family's affection; that she has another woman defend the oppressed woman in her poem, rather than allowing that woman to speak, suggests that she felt too inhibited to criticize women's roles directly. Perhaps Jackson wished to prevent speculation on her own marriage, especially considering the attacks made against Saxe Holm. "In Time of Famine" defends a woman's stern behavior against the insults of a mocking crowd:

> "She has no heart," they said, and turned away,
> Then, stung so that I wished my words might be
> Two-edged swords, I answered low:—
> > "Have ye
> Not read how once when famine held fierce sway˙
> In Lydia, and men died day by day
> Of hunger, there were found brave souls whose glee
> Scarce hid their pangs, who said, 'Now we
> Can eat but once in two days; we will play
> Such games on those days when we eat no food
> That we forget our pain.'
> > "Thus they withstood
> Long years of famine; and to them we owe
> The trumpets, pipes, and balls which mirth finds good
> To-day, and little dream that of such woe
> They first were born.
> > "That woman's life I know
> Has been all famine. Mock now if ye dare,
> To hear her brave sad laughter in the air."
>
> (*Verses*, 25–26)

The poem begins with the words of observers who misjudge the woman, claiming "'She has no heart'" and condemning her for not behaving as a stereotypical woman. Hoping her words might be "two-edged swords," the speaker recounts a story about the Lydians, who suffer a famine and devise games and musical instruments to fend off their hunger pangs. Lydia, an ancient trade center in Asia Minor, was well known for its riches (the wealthy Croesus was its last king, reigning from 560–546 B.C.). Lydians are said to have invented some musical instruments and to have made many innovations in music; that musical instruments and games resulted from a long period of famine clearly conveys the poem's theme: hunger is empowering. Rather than consider famine weakening, the speaker contends that "'long years of famine'" have made the woman stronger, concluding, "'That woman's life I know / Has been all famine. Mock now if ye dare, / To hear her brave sad laughter in the air'" (*Verses*, 26, ll. 14–16).

Hunger particularly evokes the care and attention the woman has been denied. In using direct discourse to recount the Lydians' words, Jackson gives voice to an ancient language still not fully understood, implying that the speaker has a special knowledge of their plight. Perhaps writing poetry was Jackson's response to deprivation in her own life: in discussing the instruments and toys the Lydians made, "'The trumpets, pipes, and balls which mirth finds good / To-day'" (*Verses*, 25–26, ll. 12–13), she alludes to the musical origin of poetry. Even the speaker's goading remark to those mocking bystanders that they should again deride the woman's "'brave sad laughter'" after learning her story reminds us that the woman expresses pain vocally. Tinged with bitterness, her cry exudes irony—she has experienced deprivation and can laugh in her total understanding. Finally, the speaker's "'I know'" hints that she is intimately acquainted with the woman's condition—perhaps she has experienced the same lack of care in her own life. Likewise, the speaker's sense of solidarity with the woman derives from shared experience, a response to the constraints on women's lives.

Especially through its association with love, the sonnet makes this form apt for Jackson, who comments on the lack of love between husbands and wives, parents and children. First, the sonnet afforded Jackson the opportunity to develop an analogy between a woman's domestic life and an extreme geographical setting in order to convey her sense of alienation. As Alistair Fowler has noted, far from imposing a difficult set of criteria to meet, formal or generic constraints such as those posed by the sonnet are often helpful to the author: "They offer room, as one might say, for him to write in—a habitation of mediated definiteness; a proportioned mental space; a literary matrix by which to order his experience during composition."[28] The idea of "proportioned mental space" to which Fowler refers also corresponds to a geographical location established in the poem. Like many of Jackson's sonnets, this one has an extended conceit in the octave (which here describes the freezing traveler), then a sestet in which this metaphor is applied to a woman's home life.[29] For Jackson, the orderly structure of the sonnet provided her geographic analogies with a habitation and a name.

Second, the sonnet allows Jackson to develop a woman's interior state of mind by comparison with external events and locales. According to Michael Spiller, one great achievement of the sonnet as developed by the *stilnovisti* and particularly Dante is that "the fourteen-line Sicilian sonnet, without in the least losing its capacity to argue, instruct, plead and also mock, acquires the further capacity to mirror the epiphanic moments of the inner self, the moments at which an inner transformation occurs through contact with the ideal."[30] Traditionally, the sonnet allows for moments of change in point of view, reversals of opinion, and the like. Jackson profits greatly from the dramatic unveiling and then reversal of the settings, and she mines the contemplative uses of the sonnet in portraying a woman's inner psychological landscape through references to the natural world. Finally, unlike other sonnet writers such as Shakespeare, Elizabeth Barrett Browning, Emerson, and Longfellow, Jackson consistently speaks as an observer who narrates another woman's unhappy life, either in defense, subtle agreement, or even acknowledgment that she shares her beliefs. Perhaps speaking for a woman who had no voice in the public sphere, Jackson expresses another woman's silent turmoil, even as she distances herself from actually speaking out against such suffering or admitting that the same may have happened to her.

Perhaps rejecting the sonnet after Elizabeth Barrett Browning's masterful use of the form in *Sonnets From the Portuguese* (1850), Dickinson found the lyric, with its metaphorical complexity and tighter format, more congenial. Jackson, on the other hand, was at ease with the more relaxed implied simile that formed the sestet. While Jackson uses the image of a freezing traveler to depict a woman's neglected life, Dickinson uses a freezing person as a metaphor for the psychic trauma of mourning, notably in the poem beginning "After great pain, a formal feeling comes—" (J, 341). She evokes the growing numbness that accompanies mourning, until the speaker reaches a state of sheer oblivion, which is remembered later as an "Hour of Lead" that comes "As Freezing persons, recollect the Snow—/ First—Chill—then Stupor—then the letting go—" (J, 341). Finally, Dickinson extends the central experience of the poem to the speaker herself; while Jackson's "I" operates on the margins of the poem, Dickinson's "I" fully explores a state of being.

In a lyric adopting images of snow, Dickinson comments perhaps on her decision not to make her poems available for publication:

> Through the strait pass of suffering—
> The Martyrs—even—trod.

Their feet—upon Temptation—
Their faces—upon God—

A stately—shriven—Company—
Convulsion—playing round—
Harmless—as streaks of Meteor—
Upon a Planet's Bond—

Their faith—the everlasting troth—
Their Expectation—fair—
The Needle—to the North Degree—
Wades—so—thro' polar Air!

(J, 792)

While it is impossible to document Dickinson's intent or state of mind, the poem accompanies a letter that Johnson surmises was sent in early 1862 to Samuel Bowles, who had by that time received a number of her poems to which he responded lukewarmly. Sewall, too, places the lyric in the context of her frequent exchanges with Bowles over her poetry (Sewall 2, 491). Bowles had printed anonymously on 4 May 1861, the lyric beginning "I taste a liquor never brewed" (J, 214); he gave it a new title, "The May-Wine," altered two lines to get an exact rhyme, and changed one line to create a more understandable metaphor. A second poem, "Safe in their Alabaster Chambers" (J, 216) was printed in *The Republican* as "The Sleeping," on 1 March 1862, with its punctuation, capitalization, and lineation regularized.[31] Dickinson may be insisting on the importance of her vision by refusing to submit her "Snow" to the publishers: "If you doubted my Snow—for a moment—you never will—again—I know" (*Letters* 2, 394). To extrapolate to a reading of her poem, she may be describing her decision to preserve her artistic vision against all external pressures. "The Needle—to the North Degree—" describes the direction that leads to the utmost height of the physical and celestial worlds, even while the phrase implies that the ascent through "polar Air" will be agonizing. Thus she figures poetic vocation as withstanding the physical demands of an extreme geographical locale, exactly the setting that other nineteenth-century American female poets used to convey a sense of alienation in the home.

In Jackson's "Found Frozen," for example, a freezing traveler portrays a woman's gradual death in her own home, which goes unnoticed by her family:

She died, as many travellers have died,
O'ertaken on an Alpine road by night;
Numbed and bewildered by the falling snow,
Striving, in spite of failing pulse, and limbs

> Which faltered and grew feeble at each step,
> To toil up the icy steep, and bear
> Patient and faithful to the last, the load
> Which, in the sunny morn, seemed light!
>   And yet
> 'T was in the place she called her home, she died;
> And they who loved her with the all of love
> Their wintry natures had to give, stood by
> And wept some tears, and wrote across her grave
> Some common record which they thought was true;
> But I, who loved her first, and last, and best,—*I* knew.
>
>   (*Verses*, 20)

A woman's slow demise is compared to a freezing traveler overtaken by growing numbness. Worn down by a burden "which, in the sunny morn, seemed light," the freezing traveler symbolizes a woman who perhaps began her youthful married life by easily managing her duties, only to find herself more and more estranged from her family. The second stanza provides an ironic commentary on the woman's death: she died "in the place she called her home" (*Verses*, 20, l. 9), alienated by the "wintry natures" of her family (*Verses*, 20, l. 11), who expeditiously weep "some tears" after she dies and compose an epitaph. Jackson hints dissatisfaction with the prescribed role for women when she writes that the woman's family erected "some common record which they thought was true" (*Verses*, 20, l. 13), implying that the typical encomium on the deaths of wives and mothers is not equal to the actual experiences of their lives. In contrast to the largely unrhymed lines of the rest of the poem, the final couplet enforces the speaker's awareness of the woman's plight both through its rhyme and repetition. By suspending meaning until the end of the line and adding an additional beat, Jackson forces us to reconsider the woman's plight not from a distance, but from the speaker's own perspective. She further joins in solidarity with the woman's plight when she repeats and emphasizes "I" in the last line: "But I, who loved her first, and last, and best,—*I* knew." In fact, "Found Frozen" might be a new epitaph for the woman's tombstone, since its title evokes many of the Victorian monuments of the dead, which provide a short poetic record of the dead's life or a caption of only a word or two, sometimes with no name.

Jackson's "Polar Days" uses a Lapp's waiting throughout the winter for the sunrise as an analogy for a lover's anticipation of a romantic union:

> As some poor piteous Lapp., who under firs
> Which bend and break with load of arctic snows
> Has crept and crouched to watch when crimson glows
> Begin, feels in his veins the thrilling stirs

Of warmer life, e'en while his fear deters
His trust; and when the orange turns to rose
In vain, and widening to the westward goes
The ruddy beam and fades, heartsick defers
His hope, and shivers through one more long night
Of sunless day;—
                    So watching, one by one,
The faintest glimmers of the morn's gray light,
The sleepless exiled heart waits for the bright
Full day, and hopes till all its hours are done,
That the next one will bring its love, its sun.

                                        (*Verses*, 127)

Evoking the imagery of many of Dickinson's lyrics, in which a speaker anticipates the appearance of a sun-god, "Polar Days" uses the dramatic setting and
wild imagery of Jackson's other love sonnets. A Lapp who anticipates the full
day and is disappointed is a metaphor for the lover who waits for the arrival of
his beloved. The extremity of the setting matches the intensity of the speaker's
feelings; the length of the winter above the arctic circle—six long months—intensifies the lover's plight. Like the abandoned or deprived figures in Jackson's
other sonnets, the "sleepless exiled heart" here is figuratively banished to an
extreme geographical setting, even though the lover presumably exists in a setting much closer to what we know as home. Furthermore, the title, "Polar
Days," is at odds with the "full day" the lover anticipates in the second stanza;
this discrepancy implies that the "full day," which will come when all its hours
are done," may be heralded by the long-awaited sunrise or perhaps only by
death. In depicting a Lapp who waits for the sun that heralds the beginning of
summer, Jackson conjoins the time of day with the season; both the dawn and
summer symbolize awakening hopes and expectations.

Landscapes of extremes—arctic snow and polar seas, volcanoes and tropical
oceans—convey an inner, psychological landscape, in which the currents of passion are resolved only in death or the expiation of desire. "The Zone of Calms"
uses a dramatic geographical setting to convey the heights and depths of passion:

As yearning currents from the trackless snows,
And silent Polar seas, unceasing sweep
To South, to North, and linger not where leap
Red fires from glistening cones,—nor where the rose
Has triumph on the snow-fed Paramos,
In upper air,—nor yet where lifts the deep
Its silver Atolls on whose bosoms sleep
The purple sponges; and, as in repose
Meeting at last, they sink upon the breast
Of that sweet tropic sea, whose spicy balms

> And central heat have drawn them to its arms,—
> So soul seeks soul, unsatisfied, represt,
> Till in Love's tropic met, they sink to rest,
> At peace forever, in the "Zone of Calms."
> *(Verses,* 21)

A note to Jackson's 1910 *Poems* reveals that "The Zone of Calms is the space comprised between the second degree north latitude and the second degree south" (20), a broad strip of land on either side of the equator spanning Asia and Africa. This poem draws an analogy between the power of nature and of human passions, depicting the convergence of waters from opposite ends of the earth in the "Zone of Calms," which symbolizes the satisfaction of desire. Passion is like a river, originating in "yearning currents" from desolate "Polar seas," flowing ceaselessly past volcanoes and over the high, bleak plateaus of the Andes. The volcano, "where leap / Red fires from glistening cones," and the rose, which "has triumph on the snow-fed Paramos," or plains, are symbols of subterranean passion and romantic love. Like the volcano, the "Atolls" are built up from the bottom of the earth and convey the idea of submerged passion; they resemble a conjugal partner, "on whose bosoms sleep / The purple sponges," until the currents, like exhausted lovers, "sink upon the breast" of the "sweet tropic sea," whose warmth and scent have "drawn them to its arms." Jackson embellishes the conventional perception of romantic love by depicting passion in all its raw energy and elemental attraction, which continues "unsatisfied, represt" until death.

Jackson's vocabulary echoes Dickinson's in its invocation of extreme climates and distant locales, as in "zone," "tropic," "torrid," and "polar," and one sees that nineteenth-century American women used such images to depict their alienation in the home. In "Dickinson's Mystic Day," St. Armand relates the hours, seasons, hemispheres, and colors in her poems to the speaker's nearness to death and salvation.[32] Dickinson uses "polar" to refer to exile, usually in the face of death, which in one poem presents a "Polar Expiation" (J, 532). Sometimes this withdrawal is self-imposed, as when the mind turns inward to face a more fearsome solitude than death, a "polar privacy," a "Finite Infinity" (J, 1695). In contrast, South America in particular represented a land of febrile heat and intense passion for Jackson and her contemporaries. Dickinson also refers to South America and other tropical locales as the stage for passion. In one poem, she equates "Brazil" with inestimable wealth, for which the speaker "offered Being" (J, 621). In another poem, she names a famed Ecuadorian mountain as an immense height, which perhaps symbolizes worldly obstacles to romantic union and which the speaker hopes she and her lover might scale together, "Taking turns—at the Chimborazo—," until they stand "Ducal" beside "Love" (J, 453). Italy, on the other hand, represents the land of romance and the home of her most beloved poet, Elizabeth Barrett Browning. In the poem beginning "Our lives are Swiss—" (J, 80), Italy repre-sents the land of warmth and passion that stands beyond "the siren Alps," which "intervene" between the poet and her promised land.

For Dickinson, place names refer broadly to sumptuous luxury or physical striving without distinguishing one specific location from another. In "Emily Dickinson's Geography," Rebecca Patterson remarks that "Maps and geo-graphical facts were of interest to her not for themselves but as she could use them symbolically to identify and order the more subtle elements of the mind's world."[33] Patterson further explains that places form "symbol clusters, in which all the differently named oceans mean the same thing, and all the warm countries—Italy, Africa, Brazil, for example—are the same heart's country, and all the mountain ranges and individual peaks are one and the same (except her volcanoes, which are a different kind of mountain and have their own unique function)" (141–42). Feminist critics have taken the volcano mainly to represent surging emotion, suppressed beneath the mild exterior of a woman's proper demeanor. In "Vesuvius at Home: The Power of Emily Dickinson," Adrienne Rich argues that the volcano often images the speaker's relation to her *daemon* or creative force.[34] Since patriarchal culture has used the language of heterosexual love or theology to convey a woman's relationship to her imag-ination, Dickinson dons a "mask, at least, of innocuousness and of contain-ment" (169) and translates her struggle to express her conception in unortho-dox and original poetry through a central metaphor, the volcano. Images of geographical extremes and volcanic mountains convey not only the depth of passion but also repressed expression:

> A still—Volcano—Life—
> That flickered in the night—
> When it was dark enough to do
> Without erasing sight—
>
> A quiet—Earthquake Style—
> Too subtle to suspect
> By natures this side Naples—
> The North cannot detect
>
> The Solemn—Torrid—Symbol—
> The lips that never lie—
> Whose hissing Corals part—and shut—
> And Cities—ooze away—
>
> (J, 601)

3. do] show   4. erasing] endangering   6. subtle] smouldering   12. ooze] slip—/ slide—/ melt—

The poem draws an analogy between outward existence and a seething volcano to convey a tumultuous but unspoken inner life. Reminiscent of the wild landscape of Frederick Edwin Church's *Cotopaxi* (1862), which depicts a famous volcano in the Andes, this poem also shows the repressed emotion of the speaker's life. The speaker alludes to nearby Pompeii, which conveys the same idea of repressed passion. Indeed, all of Dickinson's volcano poems allude to some deeply buried passion, only obliquely expressed and often misinterpreted by others: the oxymoronic "still—Volcano—Life—" and "quiet—Earthquake Style—" of this poem point to a composure that belies seething passion. As in Jackson's "Found Frozen," where the speaker blames the "wintry natures" of the abandoned woman's family for not recognizing her demise, this speaker hints that those around her do not suspect explosiveness beneath a mild demeanor, "too subtle" for "natures this side Naples" unaccustomed to the blistering heat of strong passion. The "Solemn—Torrid—Symbol—" suggests that the volcano must be interpreted, as if the speaker had already articulated her suffering but finds her words are constantly being misapprehended by those around her. Like the "uniform hieroglyphic" of Walt Whitman's "Song of Myself,"[35] "Symbol" implies that the volcano already stands as an object used to represent something else—hence, it is a sign that must be interpreted according to a system of belief. Furthermore, "the lips that never lie" underscores both the delights and dangers of honestly expressing one's innermost feelings. Like vaginal lips, her mouth resembles "hissing Corals," whose truth-telling wrecks everything in sight: "And Cities—ooze—away—." Both in the social world and in sex, giving voice to seething passion beneath a mild exterior is dangerous and ultimately can destroy.

Jackson's "A Woman's Death-Wound," in contrast, describes the effect of one biting remark on a woman:

> It left upon her tender flesh no trace.
> The murderer is safe. As swift as light
> The weapon fell, and, in the summer night,
> Did scarce the silent, dewy air displace;
> 'Twas but a word. A blow had been less base.
> Like dumb beast branded by an iron white
> With heat, she turned in blind and helpless flight,
> But then remembered, and with piteous face
> Came back.
>   Since then the world has nothing missed
> In her, in voice or smile. But she—each day
> She counts until her dying be complete.
> One moan she makes, and ever doth repeat:
> "O lips that I have loved and kissed and kissed,
> Did I deserve to die this bitterest way?"
>
> (*Poems*, 205)

Like the other sonnets about women's lives, the speaker describes a woman who suffers throughout her life after she is psychologically "wounded" by a word; in fact, the poem might more appropriately be entitled "A Woman's Life-Wound," since she lives a slow death after perhaps a lover's rejection. After Freud, it is perhaps easy to imagine a woman's wound as the vagina. Yet even though the symbolic resonance of the "wound" may be less apt for a nineteenth-than a twentieth-century audience, the references to violence and verbal abuse suggest that the woman suffers at the hands of a lover as a sexual object. What is also striking in this poem is the hint at the woman's repressed emotion—she continues to exist in such a way that "the world has nothing missed / In her, in voice or smile" (*Poems*, 205, ll. 9–10). We are vaguely told that, after turning "in blind and helpless flight" (*Poems*, 205, l. 7), she "remembered," presumably her household duties, and "came back" (*Poems*, 205, ll. 8–9). Undoubtedly, Jackson refers to the doctrine that women should be serene, untroubled, and helpful at home. More likely than not, however, the woman is the victim of mental abuse: although we do not know the "single word" revealed, its impact is clear.

A parallel study of Jackson's "A Woman's Death-Wound" and Dickinson's "A Still—Volcano—Life—" (J, 601) reveals their syntactical and conceptual differences. Like most of her sonnets, Jackson's poem begins discursively, even conversationally: "It left upon her tender flesh no trace" (*Poems*, 205, l. 1). As the poem continues, however, the observer recounts a woman's suffering through an extravagant conceit or extended simile that emphasizes the depth of a woman's suffering: she has been mortally wounded in conversation by someone close to her. Although many of her descriptive phrases are trite and sentimental—"as swift as light" and "dewy air"—the octave develops a central idea expressed in normal syntax that strikingly conveys the woman's alienation. Repetition also highlights the key figure in the poem: "But she— each day / She counts until her dying be complete" (*Poems*, 205, l. 10–11). The initial spondee of this line arrests the reader's attention and the break in thought forces us to reassess the woman's happiness in light of her moment's pain. While her sonnets revert to a traditional notion of romantic love that supports an idealized notion of men's and women's relations, they also create a sense of implicit and political solidarity, as does "A Woman's Death-Wound," between the abused woman and the often female speaker, who recounts her tale and thus bridges the gap between her, the abused women, and, by implication, any reader.

Dickinson's lyric conveys a similar sense of extremity about women's lives, but she detaches herself from any connection with the subject, instead directing her gaze inward and emphasizing conceptual difficulty rather than the clarity of expression meant to convey meaning easily to others. In commenting on the poet's style in *Dickinson and the Strategies of Reticence*, Joanne Dobson observes that "Unlike Jackson, she does not find through her pain a connection with others; her metaphoric movement here is not a journey out into the world, but rather an exercise in conjecture."[36] Through ambiguity, paradox, and syntactical breaks, Dickinson's language offers her a privileged vantage point from which she can challenge the norms of expression for women while remaining aloof from their methods. Both lines, "A still—Volcano—Life" and "a quiet—Earthquake Style," describe through the use of paradox a woman's repressed existence, but they focus on her "style," both socially and linguistically, which allows her to subsist undetected. Unlike Jackson, Dickinson refuses to normalize her choice of adjectives and prefers combinations of noun pairs; in fact, she originally wrote "Volcanic" for "Volcano," then dismissed the choice. The use of infinitives "to do" and "to suspect" unattached to any particular subject create a sense of impersonality. Oddly, they also imply that the life and style actively escape the notice of others, rather than are simply overlooked, as the implied passive suggests. Rather than articulate her ideas in complete and coherent sentences, as do Jackson's lyrics, Dickinson's lines often lack a clearly defined grammatical subject. In fact, her stanzas often make sense only when the last line of the previous stanza is read with the one that follows: for example, "The North cannot detect / The Solemn—Torrid—Symbol—." By fracturing the sense of each stanza and forcing us to read the last line of one stanza as the beginning of the next, she undoes our expectations about the integrity of meaning inhering in the stanza form. The off-rhyme in the concluding line also opens the poem to new, radical interpretations and prevents easy closure. Reminiscent of the last line of Herman Melville's "Billy in the Darbies," "I am sleepy, and the oozy weeds about me twist,"[37] Dickinson's use of words like "ooze" reflects a wider range of lexical choices than Jackson's. Rather than appeal to the reader's sympathy or find in the expression of love an antidote to pain, Dickinson ends with the threat of destruction all the more strongly expressed for being implied in the last image.

Other poems of Dickinson's concerning volcanoes depict the power of speech to destroy. She uses Sicily's Etna to exemplify the belief that the female persona sways others more successfully through primping, caressing, and acting than aggression:

> When Etna basks and purrs
> Naples is more afraid
> Than when she shows her Garnet Tooth—
> Security is loud—
>
> (J, 1146)

In comparing the destructive force of a volcano's lava to a "Garnet Tooth," Dickinson calls attention to speech's power to disturb, dismay, and, ultimately, destroy. Rather than attribute to another the power to disturb a woman's life, the lyric presents speech as the guarantor of a woman's "Security"—the "loud" noise that is voiced and high in volume.

The following lyric, which Thomas Johnson dates as relatively late in Dickinson's career, images the power of repressed emotion as a seemingly dormant volcano, describing its power to erupt only in the final line:

> On my volcano grows the Grass
> A meditative spot—
> An acre for a Bird to choose
> Would be the General thought—
>
> How red the Fire rocks below
> How insecure the sod
> Did I disclose
> Would populate with awe my solitude
> (J, 1677)

Like Jackson's "A Woman's Death-Wound," in which a woman suffers but presents a placid exterior to the world, Dickinson's poem uses the image of the volcano to symbolize repressed emotion whose power to destroy is revealed only in the last stanza. The first line calls attention to the location where the volcano lies, "a meditative spot"; it avoids any discussion of what lies below the earth and instead focuses on its benign appearance and location. Yet the geography of Dickinson's poem is highly personal and unspecific, as she chooses to describe a "spot" and "acre" of the type dismissed as being dangerous by the "General thought." Indeed, the image of the volcano embodies the duplicity of the woman's and the female writer's life: her pious and subservient appearance belies her tumultuous inner life, just as the land might shift due to subterranean pressures. Given that her lyric adopts strict pentameter rhythm for the concluding line, Dickinson suggests that the woman's speech has such explosive power that it can easily transcend the normal bounds of her tetrameter. While Jackson portrays a woman's constrained speech through the extended analogies of the sonnet, Dickinson breaks through her tightly reined tetrameter to hint at the power of woman's speech to destroy, rather than to conform to the dictates of expression.

Although Dickinson memorialized "Helen of Colorado" in her letters, Jackson applied very different standards to her own work than did other successful nineteenth-century American women poets. Jackson's poems treat acceptable themes for women—Christian love and self-denial, romantic attachment, and seclusion from the world outside the family—in a way that confirms the beliefs of the period. Yet her poems also disrupt these norms, especially underscoring the irony of a woman's role in the home and disclosing a feeling of solidarity with a deprived woman. Several other poems wrestle with faith or question its validity outright.[38] Although most of her poems do not explicitly criticize the place of women, Jackson frequently raises questions about the satisfactoriness of their lives.

Dickinson was similar to Jackson and other women writers in voicing conventional feminine themes—renunciation, piety, and self-sacrifice—yet she does not seek an easy resolution to metaphysical problems. Instead, she openly portrays moral irresolution, which Jackson registers only indirectly. Free from the need to girdle them to public taste, Dickinson did not wish to expose her innermost thoughts to public view. Instead, she created a personal mythology that partook of the norms for women's expression and privately explored the deepest elements of individual experience. Dickinson echoes the same indifference to worldly circumstance in a lyric sent to Jackson in the same letter in 1884, where a bird's reluctance to alight except where it is free clearly conveys its independence. In contrast to its search for "a Fence without a Fare," the bird "squandered" a "Note," the very excess of which signifies its inner liberty. Perhaps Dickinson's highest compliment to Jackson is Jackson's seeming unconcern for the reactions of others, yet the impact of her poems is undeniable:

> Upon his Saddle sprung a Bird
> And crossed a thousand Trees
> Before a Fence without a Fare
> His Fantasy did please
> And then he lifted up his Throat
> And squandered such a Note
> A Universe that overheard
> Is stricken by it yet—
>
> (J, 1600)

1. sprung a Bird] sprang the Bird,
7–8] A Universe's utter Art / Could not it imitate—

Chapter 7

Seeing "New Englandly"

Dickinson and Nineteenth-Century American Women's Poetry

> A minor literature doesn't come from a minor language; it is rather that
> which a minority constructs within a major language.
> —Gilles Deleuze and Félix Guattari, *Kafka: Toward a Minor Literature*[1]

Dickinson was steeped in the culture and literature of nineteenth-century America. She exploded many of the tropes and popular myths of nineteenth-century poetry, while she made the boldest quest for poetic originality. As her poems on volcanoes, tropic seas, and arctic wastes affirm, she used images of geographical extremity that reflected her mind's alienated landscape. Her lyrics, moreover, are illuminated by a comparative study of other nineteenth-century women's poems, whose images, metaphors, and generic features trace parallel lines of descent. Set against the editorial discourse that circumscribed their verse, the reasons for Dickinson's refusal to succumb to what would have been the indignity of publication are abundantly clear. Even though she far excelled other poets of her age, the poetic careers of most nineteenth-century American women writers reveal that they agreed to conform their verse to the publishing dictates for women.

Emily Dickinson once said that her perspective differed from that of her British contemporaries, since her way of seeing was "New Englandly":

> The Robin's my Criterion for Tune—
> Because I grow—where Robins do—
> But, were I Cuckoo born—
> I'd swear by him—
> The ode familiar—rules the Noon—
> The Buttercup's, my Whim for Bloom—

> Because, we're Orchard sprung—
> But, were I Britain born,
> I'd Daisies spurn—
> None but the Nut—October fit—
> Because, through dropping it,
> The Seasons flit—I'm taught—
> Without the Snow's Tableau
> Winter, were lie—to me—
> Because I see—New Englandly—
> The Queen, discerns like me—
> Provincially—
>
> (J, 285)

9. Daisies spurn] Clovers—scorn—

When Dickinson announces, "The Robin's my Criterion for Tune—," she acknowledges a profound affinity for the landscape and culture of New England, but she also underscores her decision to choose a standard for her verse that stands apart from the criteria used to judge other women's verse. While she adopts a common nineteenth-century trope for the female poetic voice as birdsong, her definitive control over both voice and poetic materials clearly sets her apart from most other poets. Commenting on the native materials that established the "criterion" by which she judged her verse, she asserts her affinity for things from New England rather than from England. Unlike the British Romantics, who were born in the land where the "Cuckoo" reigned supreme, she adheres to the native robin, buttercup, daisy, and "Snow's Tableau." Yet she readily admits that, based on the very accident of birth or social conditioning, we are subject to bias: we may perceive a false chronology about the passage of the seasons or associate times of the year with a certain display of nature, as suggested by "The Seasons flit—I'm taught—." Seeing "provincially" therefore applies not only to aspects of her daily, rural life but also to the individual's subjective perspective, leveling social distinctions and elevating the speaker: "The Queen, discerns like me— / Provincially—." The viewpoint expressed in seeing "New Englandly," as George Monteiro and Barton Levi St. Armand suggest, refers to a way of seeing, rooted in its culture and time: "For most readers it has come to mean in the broadest sense that her work should be interpreted in the context of and as part of New England's intellectual, religious, and literary history. But New England also has a social and cultural history, and it is of course only logical that Emily Dickinson should have her own place in that history, albeit an original one."[2]

This self-conscious "provinciality" drew widely on all available sources, and, as with many great writers, eclectically. In her second letter to Higginson in 1862, Dickinson mentions a number of British prose writers' and poets' works among her "Books," including those of Keats, Robert Browning, Elizabeth Barrett Browning, Sir Thomas Browne, and Ruskin. But she names as equally important her daily "Companions" in the woods and fields: "Hills—Sir—and the Sundown—and a Dog—large as myself, that my Father bought me—They are better than Beings—because they know but do not tell—and the noise in the Pool, at Noon—excels my Piano" (*Letters* 2, 404). She notes that nature's reticence is preferable to social interchange for her and indeed exceeds her own powers of expression. She later seeks information from Higginson and Susan Gilbert Dickinson regarding American novelists and poets, including Maria Lowell, Rebecca Harding Davis, and Harriet Prescott Spofford.

If Dickinson appropriated whatever came to hand, literary critics have been more fastidious. Despite the recent fine work by a number of critics who wish to reclaim a neglected tradition of American literature that includes these writers, "sentimental" writing still requires an apologia. Against the canonized Dickinson's poetry, nineteenth-century American women's poems, with their occasionally archaic diction and heightened emotion, occupy an embattled place in the on-going reconstruction of the American literary canon. Some critics have proposed a theory of reading practices in order to recuperate already extant nineteenth-century women's writing. Taking the point of view that literature should be read depending on how it is meant to move the reader, they argue that sentimental literature is rooted in institutional conventions and relies on a deeply entrenched set of communal values.[3] As Joanne Dobson has proposed, sentimental texts employ stock literary conventions to respond to human loss and grief: "Literary sentimentalism . . . is premised on an emotional and philosophical ethos that celebrates human connection, both personal and communal, and acknowledges the shared devastation of affectional loss."[4] Part of the critic's task, then, is to uncover the verbal codes and key gestures that act as cues to the reader's emotional responses and correspond to the social and behavioral norms of the period. Formalist criticism, currently out of fashion, might be used to expose the inner workings of texts, often reflecting the original use of language when filtered through their authors' idiosyncratic imaginations, and thereby secure their place in the literary canon. According to Dobson, "As a body of literary texts, sentimental writing can be seen in a significant number of instances to process a conventional sentimental aesthetics through individual imagination, idiosyncratic personal feeling, and skilled use of language, creating engaging, even compelling fictions and lyrics—as, for example, in works by Alice Cary, Harriet Jacobs, Frances Sargent Osgood, Lydia Sigourney, and Harriet Beecher Stowe, to name a few" (265).

The project of recovering and teaching nineteenth-century American women's writing has produced a self-critique that mirrors anxieties about how we assign cultural value. In "Commentary: Nineteenth-Century American Women Writers and the Politics of Recovery," Judith Fetterley notes that although the texts of nineteenth-century American women writers have been reprinted and several exemplary biographies have been written of novelists and short story writers, there is a general lack of critical biographies and literary studies. Indeed, critical studies and biographies of poets are comparatively absent. Fetterley has proposed several reasons why women's literature has continually been relegated to an aesthetically inferior and institutionally minor position. Among the possible reasons, she speculates that critical blindness spawned by current directions in literary theory has created "the sense of impossibility currently associated with the project of American literary history."[5] In addition, the feminist critique of the "literary" as a concept that privileges texts announcing themselves as literary over non-literary and, consequently, certain writers over others, has excluded a discussion of writers who define themselves as explicitly writing literature. Finally, according to Fetterley, the pronounced emphasis on the contexts in which these works were read denies the significance they may have for today's readers. Rather than argue for their aesthetic value, critics who have embraced aesthetic relativism in the interest of recovering women's literature have also risked sealing it off from any general audience, except one thoroughly familiar with the habits of nineteenth-century readers. The study of Dickinson and her contemporaries intervenes theoretically and pragmatically at a pivotal moment when scholars and teachers are searching for new ways to define the value of "minor" writers.

Except for Dickinson's crucial example, nineteenth-century American women's poetry was thought until only recently to be more conservative and less stylistically varied than the fiction, and intellectually dull. Even sensitive readers like Louise Bogan, who in her *Achievement in American Poetry, 1900–1950* (1951) delineated an "authentic current" of emotion and technical simplicity in the poems of Lizette Woodworth Reese (1856–1935), Louise Imogen Guiney (1861–1920), and Dickinson, considered sentimental poetry a backdrop against which the early twentieth-century writers needed to define themselves. Early twentieth-century critics and modernist writers divorced themselves from the exaggerated emotion and simple narratives about domestic life of the Victorian era and advocated instead restrained feeling and a highly imagistic style. The aesthetic criteria of the nineteenth-century editors who judged women's poetry—insisting that it speak about pious and domestic topics in a smooth-flowing, untroubled meter and with full, perfect rhymes—also prompted late nineteenth-century and early twentieth-century critics' vehemence against sentimental verse. Like Mark Twain's sentimental versifier, Emmeline Grangerford, the poetess became humorists' stock-in-trade.

In reaction to the period of high Victorian "feeling," the modern era ushered in an interest in the image and aesthetic restraint. As Paula Bennett has eloquently argued, however, the imagist poem finds its roots in late nineteenth-century women's nature poems, which often reflect "a movement . . . toward greater concrete detail, more ambiguous and flexible stylistic expression, and toward a much wider—and more disturbing—range of themes and voices than sentimentalism, with its commitment to religiously-based domestic and cultural values, allowed."[6] Male poets, like Edward Arlington Robinson (1869–1935), according to Bogan, were able to "twist the clichés of sentimental poetry to a wry originality" and heralded a new era in American poetry, revealing a heightened realism, laconic speech, and dry humor.[7] On the other hand, women poets, whose methods "proved to be as strong as they seemed to be delicate," were thought responsible for the important task of "revivifying warmth of feeling in the poetry of his time" (22–23). Bogan dates the beginning of this new era of genuine feeling and technical simplicity from the publication of Wilcox's *Poems of Passion* in 1886 and Reese's *A Branch of May* in 1887. Despite their achievement, however, she deems the high emotionalism and formulaic techniques of women's verse responsible for the drop in the quality of Victorian poetry:

Women, it is true, contributed in a large measure to the general leveling, dilution, and sentimentalization of verse, as well as of prose, during the nineteenth century. Their successes in the field of the sentimental novel had been overpowering; and their "poetic" ambitions were boundless. The American literary tradition, from the time of seventeenth-century Ann Bradstreet ("The Tenth Muse Lately Sprung up in America") had never been without an outstanding American woman "singer." Mrs. Sigourney had occupied this role over a protracted period—her life extended from the year of Washington's second Presidency to that of Lincoln's death—and she had successors. Women's verse of this popular variety reflected with deadly accuracy every change in the nation's sentimental tendencies. (23)

Although in many ways she belittled the quality of women's verse by inscribing it within a sentimental frame, Bogan also paid tribute to the first appearance of genuinely realistic and adventurous poets who were contemporaries of Dickinson: "It is all the more remarkable, in view of this redoubtable and often completely ridiculous record of sentimental feminine attitudinizing in verse, that true, compelling, and sincere women's talents were able to emerge. Sentimental poetry on the middle level was never destroyed—it operates in full and unimpeded force at the present day; but an authentic current began to run beside it" (24).

Rather than consign women's poetry to the dustbin of history, however, many critics are involved in the essential work of recovering and reading primary texts, which as Judith Fetterley has observed, "must precede the writing of literary history, biography, and criticism."[8] Considering the already extensive work done to reprint women's texts, write their critical biographies, pioneer new and more useful anthologies, and compile lengthy and inclusive encyclopedias, an examination of the assumptions brought to bear in the reading and teaching of nineteenth-century women's poetry has been largely ignored. Yet these presuppositions intersect with larger debates about the values underlying our pedagogical and critical approaches to authors and their works: as historical documents or aesthetic objects, close reading or thematic study, "major" or "minor" texts, subjects or socially constructed selves. Both theoretically and pragmatically, we need a critical assessment of the values by which women's verse has been judged, for these presuppositions intersect with larger debates about how we value literature and reflect how we teach literature generally. The critical disagreement about what constitutes "value" in literary works reflects the long-established divide between literature and American studies departments. Many critics have forsaken the idea of aesthetic standards and instead justify recovery of women's literature as a way of understanding the social, psychological, and political dimensions of women's lives. Like nineteenth-century editors and critics, who lauded the affective and spontaneous in women's poetical "effusions," twentieth-century debates about value reflect how closely our shifting aesthetic criteria correspond to changes in national and ideological orientations.

In attempting to recover a neglected tradition of sentimental literature, critics have suggested we examine the criteria by which women's work was originally judged. Engaging the reader in a heightened display of feeling, sentimental texts "work" when they succeed in moving the reader, although sometimes for reasons unintended by the author. In *Sensational Designs: The Cultural Work of American Fiction, 1790–1860* (1985), Jane Tompkins contends that, unlike modernist writers, who valued unique language, sentimental novelists used commonplace and conventional language to appeal to the reader's emotions. Rather than extol the works of Stowe and other female writers over those of their male contemporaries on aesthetic grounds, she contends that the neglected tradition of women's literature should be judged according to its political or moral objectives:

I will argue that the work of sentimental writers is complex and significant in ways *other than* those that characterize the established masterpieces. I will ask the reader to set aside some familiar categories for evaluating fiction—stylistic intricacy, psychological subtlety, epistemological complexity—and to see the sentimental novel not as an artifice of eternity answerable to certain formal criteria and to certain psychological and philosophical concerns, but as a political enterprise, halfway between sermon and social theory, that both codifies and attempts to mold the values of its time.[9]

Although Tompkins's work has been instrumental in grounding us in an appreciation of women's writing, to value sentimental literature only for its political objectives rather than its "psychological and philosophical concerns" threatens to ignore the already considerable intellectual complexity and psychological subtlety of women's writing and denigrates their artistic ability. One might read such works in order to excavate political and social values, but the works also yield pleasure based on rhetorical and linguistic complexity and stylistic eloquence, certainly objectives as important as their political motivation. Doing "cultural work," as Tompkins puts it, in a way that is not reductive or crassly materialistic means we must account for the rhetorical power and artistic achievement of texts when they are precisely grounded in their historical contexts.

In his essay "Teaching Nineteenth-Century American Women Writers," Paul Lauter challenges the formal and conceptual standards we apply to canonical literary works and explains the way nineteenth-century women's literature has been traditionally devalued:

> If we accept the definitions of literary excellence constructed in significant measure from the canonical works and used to perpetuate their status, we will inevitably place most of the fiction by nineteenth-century white women and black writers at a discount, and view them as at best elegiac local colorists, at worst, domestic sentimentalists. Indeed, we will not see what these writers are attempting to accomplish, much less how well or poorly they do what Jane Tompkins calls their "cultural work."[10]

For Lauter, looking from the standpoint of a classic, a work that by definition has transcended the time in which it was written, prevents us from appreciating the qualities that make nineteenth-century women's writing distinctive. Viewing texts as historical agents, Lauter argues that they encode and transmit ideas pervading the literary works and culture of their time. If we accept only the standards of self-containment, metaphysical ambiguity, and irony extolled by the New Critics, we will appreciate neither the stated nor implicit intentions of the author, nor their relative success or failure, much less their ability to effect social change. According to the New Critics, discerning the motives of the author to justify her aesthetic achievement is fallacious. Yet ignoring the limiting topics applied to women's verse and the circumstances of its writing threatens to make us underrate their work.

Both Tompkins and Lauter make compelling arguments for including nineteenth-century American women writers in the canon based on their intellectual and historical contribution to our culture, and they separately combat innumerable obstacles raised by other critics as to the reasons why women's literature should be kept outside the classroom, including what Lauter terms "the problem of standards" (114). Even while acknowledging Dickinson's linguistic superiority to the other female poets of her era, I wish to question the definition of "greatness" that has operated so long in academic scholarship and in the classroom and has prevented us from fully awarding their due to previously neglected and long-maligned poets.

Nineteenth-century American women's poetry conforms to the dominant narratives concerning women's lives and the generic tropes and structure of women's verse. Whenever they published, these poets spoke covertly and under the shelter of initials or anonymity. Nevertheless, their poems promote a sense of social cohesion and create a forum from which to address issues of national importance, such as slavery, alcohol abuse, animal rights, children's education, women's suffrage, and the forcible removal and divestment of Indians from their lands.[11] Furthermore, ambiguity, double-voicing, common imagistic patterns, and dialect are some literary techniques that appear in both women's fiction and poetry. We might classify the speakerly voices of many women's poems as mimetic: as Mary Jacobus explains, mimetism contains a voice that imitates a traditional view of the lives of women who, unable to write outside of the patriarchal literary tradition, must even in representing a literary heroine adopt the vocabulary and stylistic techniques of the tradition in order to undo it.[12] For Osgood, Sigourney, and Jackson, the pressures to conform to a way of speaking led them frequently to adopt, sometimes posing, the voices of docile women. Yet these poets wore a mask of servility, as did Dickinson, through which they questioned, mocked, and cajoled the reader. Lydia Sigourney often promoted the interests of women in her poems on infant death, albeit sentimentally, by displacing the father and erecting the mother as her children's sole caretaker and primary teacher. Frances Sargent Osgood used floral poems, a popular feminine discourse, as a covert means to portray erotic feelings. Only Helen Hunt Jackson, who wrote many sonnets in addition to lyrics perhaps because they afforded her greater flexibility to voice a number of opinions that respectable women could not espouse, did not meld the voice of rebellion with that of subservience—she chose instead to portray a female speaker who comments on the misspent lives of women while employing a traditional verse form. Nineteenth-century American female poets chose to use a rhetoric of secrets, silence, and deferral rather than overt expression to bypass the era's norms of expression and involve the reader actively in issues of national importance.

While Dickinson rejected the manipulation, constriction, and bowdlerizing of women's verse in print culture, she also was thoroughly imbued in and shaped by it. An early lyric sent to Higginson in 1862 describes the process by which she comes to recognize great poetry from experimenting with lesser and perhaps worthless materials:

> We play at Paste—
> Till qualified, for Pearl—
> Then, drop the Paste—
> And deem ourself a fool—

The Shapes—though—were similar—
And our new Hands
Learned *Gem*-Tactics—
Practicing *Sands*—

(J, 320)

Dickinson was undoubtedly responding in this poem to Higginson's essay "Letter to a Young Contributor," published in the April 1862 *Atlantic Monthly* (which she took as an open invitation to send him her poetry), and especially to his emphasis on accepting the perpetual deferral of fame, as expressed in lines from the concluding paragraph: "we may learn humility, without learning to despair, from earth's evanescent glories. Who cannot bear a few disappointments, if the vista be so wide that the mute inglorious Miltons of this sphere may in some other sing their Paradise as Found?"[13] Sewall observes that "'We play at Paste' agreed, on one level, with his emphasis on the necessity of constant revision, or practice, in literary composition and, on a higher level, echoed the idea in his final paragraph that the whole human exercise was merely preparation for the divine" (Sewall 2, 545). Equally important to understanding Dickinson's process of composition, however, is that through these repeated efforts of trial and error she developed "*Gem*-Tactics," almost as if her poems represented near military encounters or skirmishes with an enemy. Indeed, as a woman and as a poet, Dickinson must have been aware of the restrictions placed on her verse, and her choice of "Pearl" as a metaphor for poetry confirms her familiarity with the common description of women's lyrics as gems. "*Sands*," too, not only puns on the paste commonly used to make nineteenth-century costume jewelry but also may allude to the fact that women's topics were limited, as implied in the French word *sans*, "without." Whereas the first stanza describes the actual process of writing, the second comments on the method by which she recognizes "Pearl" from dross. "*Gem*-Tactics" thus underscores her self-conscious adaptation of poetic methods her contemporaries used, while she acknowledges the tactical nature of her own poetry.

Teaching nineteenth-century American women's poetry provides thematic and formal insight into the shapes that taught "*Gem*-Tactics." Nineteenth-century female poets modify the predominant characterizations of women and subvert language from within. Like any substantial body of poetry, women's verse has its own formal intricacies and irregularities, its original lights, but even a cursory glance at a variety of women poets suggests that they possess artistic value and insight complementary and equivalent to men's. By taking into account a larger literary landscape that includes nineteenth-century women's poetry, students can both appreciate a neglected group of poets and begin to interrogate the limitations of conventional notions of greatness. Commonly exposed to only a handful of major texts, they find their presuppositions about women's weepy poetry questioned once they read more than a few central poets. Furthermore, the emphasis placed on emotion rather than intellect in many nineteenth-century women's poems may lead students to expand their sense of the range and intensity of emotions poetry can represent and allow for useful cross-referencing between male and female writers. Regularly taught to discount their emotions in college classrooms, students find that reading sentimental poetry often validates their own emotional responses to works of literature. Among the many uses of women's poetry is consolation—the public exhibition of sympathy—which promoted a sense of cohesion among members of a nineteenth-century reading community often afflicted by the deaths of relatives and friends. Indeed, its emphasis on emotion over intellect may lead us to reevaluate not only the poetry but the very way we teach. As Jane Tompkins has argued, the focus on a narrow range of intellectual pursuits in college classrooms has created a sterile and even paranoid environment in which students betray "a divided state of consciousness, a hypertrophy of the intellect and will, an undernourished heart."[14] Cultivating a balanced emotional and intellectual response, or perhaps simply taking account of our still strong affective response to many texts, might lead us to reevaluate this poetry.

Dickinson adapted the verse genres already popular among other women poets and transformed them. Her life story is in many respects a classic example of the nineteenth-century American woman writer, since it both publicly maintains and privately undermines adherence to the so-called doctrine of "True Womanhood." Nineteenth-century American women's poetry connects with their audience and repairs divisions between people. To contend that nineteenth-century American women's writing is worth reading—is, in fact, readable—we need to acknowledge its very different criteria for judging value, which are based on a desire to bridge the gap between alienated selves. Freed from the constraints on the topics of women's verse, Emily Dickinson adapts these norms to her own uses and creates poetry that transcends her age and ours. Until we examine the poetry of other nineteenth-century women as seriously as Dickinson's, it will be long before we appreciate the interrelation of both.

Notes

1. Introduction (pp. 1–18)

1. Marianne Moore, "Emily Dickinson," *Poetry* 41, no. 4 (January 1933): 222.
2. Joanne Dobson, *Dickinson and the Strategies of Reticence: The Woman Writer in Nineteenth-Century America* (Bloomington and Indianapolis: Indiana University Press, 1989), xii.
3. Jane Donahue Eberwein, *Dickinson: Strategies of Limitation* (Amherst: University of Massachusetts Press, 1985). According to Eberwein, Dickinson employed strategies, including role playing and imaginative identification with more powerful figures, in order to make her religious quest: "If she were to grow, she would do so by pressing in upon limitations and then devising those strategies for expansion that poetry encouraged" (19). Like both Dobson and Eberwein, who contend that Dickinson's linguistic habits and techniques allowed her to bypass limitations applying to women in particular, I argue that Dickinson's adaptation of specifically female poetic genres, such as the child elegy and the flower poem, responded to the condition of women's lives in nineteenth-century America.
4. See, for instance, Jane Tompkins, *Sensational Designs: The Cultural Work of American Fiction, 1790–1860* (New York: Oxford University Press, 1985); Judith Fetterley, ed., *Provisions: A Reader from 19th-Century American Women* (Bloomington: Indiana University Press, 1985); and Sandra A. Zagarell, "Expanding 'America': Lydia Sigourney's Sketch of Connecticut, Catharine Sedgwick's Hope Leslie," *Tulsa Studies in Women's Literature* 6, no. 2 (Fall 1987): 225–45.
5. For discussion of Jackson's submission to publishing dictates and Dickinson's refusal to conform, see Erkkila, "Going to Market: Helen Hunt Jackson," *The Wicked Sisters: Women Poets, Literary History & Discord* (New York: Oxford University Press, 1992), 86–98.
6. See Barton Levi St. Armand, *Emily Dickinson and Her Culture: The Soul's Society* (Cambridge: Cambridge University Press, 1984), and Judith Farr, *The Passion of Emily Dickinson* (Cambridge, Mass.: Harvard University Press, 1992).
7. See Ann Douglas, *The Feminization of American Culture* (1977; New York: Anchor Press, 1988); St. Armand, *Emily Dickinson and Her Culture*; Lawrence Buell, *New England Literary Culture: From Revolution Through Renaissance* (Cambridge: Cambridge University Press, 1986); and David S. Reynolds, *Beneath the American Renaissance: The Subversive Imagination in the Age of Emerson and Melville* (Cambridge, Mass.: Harvard University Press, 1989).
8. Sandra M. Gilbert and Susan Gubar, *The Madwoman in the Attic: The Woman Writer and the Nineteenth-Century Literary Imagination* (New Haven: Yale University Press, 1979), 583.
9. Phillips argues that Dickinson's "histrionic imagination" is represented in poems that "reveal as they enact in words situations that she thought significant or interesting. The monologues are not necessarily masks for Dickinson herself; they are

often performances that reflect the lives of people whose voices she 'supposed'" (85). See Elizabeth Phillips, *Emily Dickinson: Personae and Performance* (University Park, Penn.: The Pennsylvania State University Press, 1988).

10. Other influential Dickinson critics either approach her poetry from a feminist perspective or describe a psycho-biographical background for appreciating her work. See Margaret Homans, *Women Writers and Poetic Identity: Dorothy Wordsworth, Emily Brontë, and Emily Dickinson* (Princeton: Princeton University Press, 1980); Vivian R. Pollak, *Dickinson: The Anxiety of Gender* (Ithaca: Cornell University Press, 1984); Susan Juhasz, ed., *Feminist Critics Read Emily Dickinson* (Bloomington: Indiana University Press, 1983); and Cynthia G. Wolff, *Emily Dickinson* (Reading, Mass.: Addison-Wesley, 1986).

11. Alicia Suskin Ostriker, *Stealing the Language: The Emergence of Women's Poetry in America* (Boston: Beacon Books, 1986), 40 and *passim*.

12. Henry Wadsworth Longfellow, *Selected Poems*, ed. Lawrence Buell (New York: Penguin Books, 1988), 83.

13. For discussion of these types of poems, as well as others describing the "burden of beauty," and the experienced woman, see Cheryl Walker, *The Nightingale's Burden: Women Poets and American Culture before 1900* (Bloomington: Indiana University Press, 1982), *passim*.

14. Emily Stipes Watts, *The Poetry of American Women from 1632 to 1945* (Austin and London: University of Texas Press, 1977), 4–7.

15. Paula Bennett, *Emily Dickinson: Woman Poet* (Iowa City: University of Iowa Press, 1990), 18.

16. See, for instance, Dobson, *Dickinson and the Strategies of Reticence*. Dobson proposes that women's writing at mid-century "shows characteristics of . . . an expressive community—constituting a discourse distinctively and discernibly patterned by cultural assumptions regarding the nature of womanhood and her 'divine reticence'" (9). Although Dobson correctly defines this "community of expression" as a prescriptive and constraining set of conventions against which women defined themselves, their discomfort with these norms, I would argue, more often appears in the occasional breaks, fissures, and omissions within their texts, rather than in any strategic and conscious subversion.

17. *The Springfield Daily Republican* 17, no. 160, whole no. 4981 (July 7, 1860), 4; quoted in David S. Reynolds, *Beneath the American Renaissance: The Subversive Imagination in the Age of Emerson and Melville* (Cambridge and London: Harvard University Press, 1989), 395.

18. Walker, *Nightingale's Burden*, 88.

19. Donald Hall, ed., *The Oxford Book of Children's Verse in America* (New York and Oxford: Oxford University Press, 1985), 21, ll. 13–20.

20. Mary Kelley, *Private Woman, Public Stage: Literary Domesticity in Nineteenth-Century America* (New York and Oxford: Oxford University Press, 1984).

21. In a very influential article, Barbara Welter has argued for the existence of a "Cult of True Womanhood." Welter defines the feminine ideal during this period as pious, loyal, submissive, and, ideally, married with children. Welter, "The Cult of True Womanhood: 1820–1860," *American Quarterly* 18 (Summer 1966): 151–74. For another early and instrumental discussion of "woman's sphere," see Nancy F.

Cott, *The Bonds of Womanhood: "Woman's Sphere" in New England, 1780–1835* (New Haven: Yale University Press, 1977). For a summary of noteworthy research about the domestic lives of nineteenth-century women, see Mary P. Ryan, "In Domestic Captivity: A Decade in the Historiography of Women," in *The Empire of the Mother: American Writing about Domesticity, 1830 to 1860*, Women & History, nos. 2 and 3 (New York: The Institute for Research in History and the Haworth Press, 1982), 1–18.

22. Barbara Ehrenreich and Deirdre English, eds., *For Her Own Good: 150 Years of the Medical Profession's Advice to Women* (Garden City, N.J.: Anchor Press, 1978), esp. 5–13.

23. Nina Baym, *Women's Fiction: A Guide to Novels by and about Women in America, 1820–70* (1978; reprint: Urbana and Chicago: University of Illinois Press, 1993), 26.

24. Shirley Samuels, "Introduction," *The Culture of Sentiment: Race, Gender, and Sentimentality in Nineteenth-Century America* (New York and Oxford: Oxford University Press, 1992), 4.

25. Harriet Beecher Stowe, *Uncle Tom's Cabin* (New York: Bantam, 1981), 281.

26. Rufus Wilmot Griswold, ed., *The Female Poets of America* (New York: P. F. Collier, 1870), 322, ll. 1–18, 25–34. All further references to this poem are to the version in this edition.

27. Griswold, *Female Poets*, 187.

28. See, for example, representative arguments made by Margaret Homans, "'Oh, Vision of Language!': Dickinson's Poems of Love and Death," in Juhasz, *Feminist Critics Read Emily Dickinson*, 114–33; and Mary Loeffelholz, *Dickinson and the Boundaries of Feminist Theory* (Urbana and Chicago: University of Illinois Press, 1991).

2. "This—Was a Poet" (pp. 19–48)

1. William Carlos Williams, *In the American Grain* (1925; reprint: New York: New Directions, 1956), 178–79.

2. Quoted in Gordon S. Haight, *Mrs. Sigourney: The Sweet Singer of Hartford* (New Haven: Yale University Press, 1930), 77; quoted from Edgar Allan Poe, *Complete Works*, ed. James A. Harrison, 17 vols. (New York: Thomas Y. Crowell & Co., 1902), 16: 117.

3. Quoted in Haight, *Mrs. Sigourney*, 99; quoted from Poe, *Complete Works*, 16:12.

4. Thomas Wentworth Higginson, "An Open Portfolio," *The Christian Union* 42 (September 25, 1890): 393.

5. Quoted by Mary Clemmer Ames in a letter to *The Springfield Republican* on the death of Adelaide Procter. Leyda 2: 88.

6. There is a strong field of criticism related to Dickinson's scribal publishing that provides possible explanations as to how the poet composed and circulated manuscripts in various states of completion. For representative debates concerning the significance of the fascicles, see Sharon Cameron, *Choosing Not Choosing: Dickinson's Fascicles* (Chicago: University of Chicago Press, 1992), and Dorothy Huff Oberhaus, *Emily Dickinson's Fascicles: Method & Meaning* (University Park: The

Pennsylvania State University Press, 1995). For a discussion of the relation of the poet's handwriting to the actual page, see Susan Howe, "Some Notes on Visual Intentionality in Emily Dickinson," *HOW(ever)* 3, no. 4 (1986): 11–13; "These Flames and Generosities of the Heart: Emily Dickinson and the Illogic of Sumptuary Values," *Sulfur* 28 (1991): 134–55; and Paul Crumbley, *Inflections of the Pen: Dash and Voice in Emily Dickinson* (Lexington: The University Press of Kentucky, 1997). For a discussion of the poet's late prose fragments, including their script and relation to her canon, see Marta L. Werner, *Emily Dickinson's Open Folios: Scenes of Reading, Surfaces of Writing* (Ann Arbor: The University of Michigan Press, 1995). McGann has also argued that one should consider the poet's script as evidence of her aesthetic vision: "Her surviving manuscript texts urge us to take them at face value, to treat all her scriptural forms as potentially significant *at the aesthetic or expressive level*" (38; emphasis original). See Jerome McGann, *Black Riders: The Visible Language of Modernism* (Princeton: Princeton University Press, 1993).

7. Smith has most forcefully made this argument in *Rowing in Eden: Rereading Emily Dickinson* (Austin: The University of Texas Press, 1992). Other critics argue that the poet's relationship with Susan Gilbert Dickinson was a formative, editorial one and postulate that Sue constituted her ideal audience. See Ellen Louise Hart, "The Encoding of Homoerotic Desire: Emily Dickinson's Letters and Poems to Susan Dickinson, 1850–1886," *Tulsa Studies in Women's Literature* 9, no. 2 (1990): 251–72; and Smith, "To Fill a Gap," *San José Studies* 13 (1987): 3–25.

8. Karen Dandurand, "Dickinson and the Public," *Dickinson and Audience*, ed. Martin Orzeck and Robert Weisbuch (Ann Arbor: The University of Michigan Press, 1996), 257–58.

9. David S. Reynolds, *Beneath the American Renaissance: The Subversive Imagination in the Age of Emerson and Melville*, 414.

10. For a fuller discussion of women's and men's magazine publication, see William Charvat, *Literary Publishing in America, 1790–1850* (Philadelphia: University of Pennsylvania, 1959).

11. Other authors, however, like Longfellow, used the widespread marketing of literature to their advantage. Deemed by common readers since the Romantic era to be intellectual, artistic, and effete, poetry had fallen into disrepute by the middle part of the century. Longfellow redeemed its value by portraying the poet as a sublime prophet, philosopher, and actor in the political and social worlds, much as Emerson in "The American Scholar" called upon the scholar to shape his society. Once he established an audience for his works, Longfellow allowed cheap pamphlet and broadside editions to be published for much reduced rates in order to increase his readership. Authors could thus skillfully turn the demands of the publishing world to their advantage. In contrast, Emerson chose to be published in Boston, where publishers relied for their revenues on an extremely concentrated book-buying public. Partly as a result of his decision to be known by a regional audience, and partly because he wrote essays rather than novels or short stories, Emerson had smaller distribution of his work and arguably less impact on many authors, except for some of the most notable ones, than he otherwise might have had. See Charvat, *The Profession of Authorship in America, 1800–1870* (1968; reprint: New York: Columbia University Press, 1992), 155–67.

12. Review by Poe, *Complete Works*, 16: 118.

13. Charvat, *The Profession of Authorship in America, 1800–1870*, 24.

14. My reading of the publishing milieu has been informed by Coultrap-McQuin's argument. See Susan Coultrap-McQuin, *Doing Literary Business: American Women Writers in the Nineteenth Century* (Chapel Hill: The University of North Carolina Press, 1990), esp. 28–48.

15. Rufus W. Griswold, ed., *The Female Poets of America* (1848; reprint: Philadelphia: Moss, 1863), 7.

16. Caroline May, ed., *The American Female Poets* (Philadelphia: Lindsay & Blakiston, 1848), v.

17. Review of *The Female Poets of America, Scribner's Monthly* 8, no. 1 (May 1874): 120.

18. Poe, *Complete Works*, 8: 122.

19. Review of Alice Carey's [*sic*] *Lyra and Other Poems, Harper's New Montly Magazine* 5, no. 25 (June 1852): 138.

20. For a discussion of women's writing as more ornamental, pious, and "natural" than men's, see Ann Douglas [Wood], "The 'Scribbling Women' and Fanny Fern: Why Women Wrote," *American Quarterly* 23 (Spring 1971): 3–24.

21. "H.H.," *The Nation* 13, no. 298 (March 16, 1871): 183–84.

22. Edgar Allan Poe, *Essays and Reviews*, ed. G. R. Thompson (New York: [Literary Classics of the United States/Distributed by Viking Press] Library of America, 1984), 759.

23. Keese, Preface to Elizabeth Oakes Smith's *The Sinless Child, and Other Poems* (New York and Boston: Wiley & Putnam and W. D. Ticknor, 1843), viii.

24. Walker, *The Nightingale's Burden: Women Poets and American Culture before 1900* (Bloomington: Indiana University Press, 1982), 89.

25. Alicia Suskin Ostriker, *Stealing the Language: The Emergence of Women's Poetry in America* (Boston: Beacon Books, 1986), 40–41.

26. Lydia Sigourney, *Poems* (Philadelphia: Key & Biddle, 1834), v.

27. *Verses* [By "H.H."] (1870; reprint: Boston: Roberts Brothers & Company, 1875), iii.

28. Ralph Waldo Emerson, *Essays and Lectures*, ed. Joel Porte (New York: [Literary Classics of the United States/Distributed by the Viking Press] The Library of America, 1983), 1170. References to Emerson's essays will be abbreviated *E&L* and conform to this edition.

29. Ralph Waldo Emerson, ed., *Parnassus* (Boston: Houghton Mifflin Co., 1874), iii.

30. Emily Dickinson, *Poems*, ed. Thomas W. Higginson and Mabel Loomis Todd (1890; reprint: Boston: Little, Brown, and Company, 1902), iii.

31. Thomas W. Higginson, *Carlyle's Laugh and Other Surprises* (Boston and New York: Houghton Mifflin Co., 1909), 250.

32. Howe, "Some Notes on Visual Intentionality in Emily Dickinson," 13.

33. Barton Levi St. Armand, *Emily Dickinson and Her Culture: The Soul's Society* (Cambridge: Cambridge University Press, 1984), 213.

34. Henry Wadsworth Longfellow, *Kavanagh: A Tale* (Boston: Ticknor, Reed, and Fields, 1849); rpt. ed. Jean Downey (New Haven: College & University Press, 1965), 90.

35. I am building here on the discussion of Dickinson's professional and personal relationship with Higginson by other critics. See St. Armand, *Emily Dickinson and Her Culture*, esp. 207–16; Raymond A. Mazurek, "'I Have no Monarch in My Life': Feminism, Poetry, and Politics in Dickinson and Higginson," in *Patrons and Protégées*, 122–40; Tilden G. Edelstein, "Emily Dickinson and Her Mentor in Feminist Perspective," and Anna Mary Wells, "The Soul's Society: Emily Dickinson and Colonel Higginson," in *Nineteenth-Century Women Writers of the English Speaking World*, ed. Rhoda B. Nathan, Contributions in Women's Studies, 69 (Westport, Conn.: Greenwood Press, 1986), 37–43; 221–30; and Elizabeth Phillips, "Duplicities and Desires," *Emily Dickinson: Personae and Performance* (University Park, Penn.: The Pennsylvania State University Press, 1988), 27–41.

36. St. Armand, *Emily Dickinson and Her Culture*, 215.

37. Cristanne Miller, *Emily Dickinson: A Poet's Grammar* (Cambridge: Harvard University Press, 1987), 4–5.

38. Nathaniel Hawthorne, *The Scarlet Letter* (New York: Norton, 1988), 51.

39. For a fuller summary of the resonance of the color white among female literary characters, see Sandra M. Gilbert and Susan Gubar, *The Madwoman in the Attic: The Woman Writer and the Nineteenth-Century Literary Imagination* (New Haven: Yale University Press, 1979), 617–21.

40. Galway Kinnell, "The Deconstruction of Emily Dickinson," *American Poetry Review* 23 (1994): 40.

3. "Feet So Precious Charged" (pp. 53–93)

1. Lydia Sigourney, *The Faded Hope* (New York, 1853), 12–13.

2. Elizabeth Oakes Smith, *The Sinless Child, and Other Poems*, ed. John Keese (New York: Wiley & Putnam; and Boston: W. D. Ticknor, 1843), 52.

3. Betsy Erkkila, "Emily Dickinson and Class," *American Literary History* 4, no. 1 (Spring 1992): 4 and *passim*.

4. Sigourney, *The Faded Hope*, 11.

5. Smith, *The Sinless Child*, 40–41.

6. A suggestive reading might be that Andrew engages in an Oedipal conflict with his father: he assumes a degree of paternal authority by slaying his father's possessions and, symbolically, clearing the way for his mother's love. Whether or not Sigourney was expressing Andrew's deep-seated attachment to her in this passage, her depiction suggests that, like flowers, Andrew is subject to being cut down himself without explanation.

    Studies of the elegy have only recently begun to reinterpret this genre as harboring the author's response to his or her poetic precursors. Peter M. Sacks's *The English Elegy: Studies in the Genre from Spenser to Yeats* (Baltimore: The Johns Hopkins University Press, 1985) contends that an elegy actually effects the "work of mourning," rather than simply describing the poet's experience of loss. Other critics have pointed specifically to ways in which women poets have appropriated and revised the elegy, often considered to be a patriarchal genre. Both Celeste M. Schenck in "Feminism and Deconstruction: Re-Constructing the Elegy" [*Tulsa*

Studies in Women's Literature 5 (1) (Spring 1986): 13–27] and Joanne Feit Diehl in "'Come Slowly—Eden': An Exploration of Women Poets and Their Muse" [*Signs: Journal of Women in Culture and Society* 3, no. 3 (Spring 1978): 572–87] explore the use of the elegy by women poets who refigure their relation to female precursors in an effort to escape the imposing presence of a male authority figure or poetic tradition. Like these critics, I want to suggest that Sigourney revises the infant elegy by privileging the bond between a mother and her son, while she genuinely works through the loss of her own son in her poems.

7. For examples of this genre among American women writers in the two centuries prior to Emily Dickinson's, one might consider Anne Bradstreet's "In Memory of My Dear Grandchild Elizabeth Bradstreet, Who Deceased August, 1665, Being a Year and a Half Old" and "In Memory of My Dear Grandchild Anne Bradstreet, Who Deceased June 20, 1669, Being Three Years and Seven Months Old"; and Phillis Wheatley's "On the Death of a Young Lady of Five Years of Age." While Bradstreet's poems consider the child's death a lesson for its relatives in the transience of earthly relationships, Wheatley's elegy depicts a child who praises God in heaven while her parents listen from earth. Both poems offer normative Christian consolation that assured the child salvation in heaven, yet Wheatley's elegy looks forward to nineteenth-century poems in which the infant plays a central role in teaching its parents an exemplary lesson in resigning their fates to God.

8. This comparison of infants and adolescents (especially male ones, like Sigourney's son) to flowers derives from the legends of antiquity. In Greek mythology, the death of a young man was considered an affront to the culture's aesthetic sense. The gods regularly take pity on dead or dying youths by turning them into flowers. Hyacinth, for example, was struck by Apollo's discus, and the god was so grieved at the sight of the young man's injury that he transformed him into a flower. Narcissus, too, after pining away at the reflection of his own image in a pool of water, takes the shape of a flower. For the Greeks, early death is a disfigurement and travesty of the beauty of youth, the destruction of which is redressed in their myths with an image of equal beauty. See Edith Hamilton, *Mythology* (New York and Scarborough, Ontario: Mentor Books/New American Library, 1969), 87–91.

9. For an overview of parental attitudes toward infant mortality, including the common myth that dying children had the power to redeem others, see Sylvia D. Hoffert, "'A Very Peculiar Sorrow': Attitudes Toward Infant Death in the Urban Northeast, 1800–1860," *American Quarterly* 39, no. 4 (Winter 1987): 601–16. For a study of attitudes toward death and actual levels of mortality in early America, see Maris A. Vinovskis, "Angel's Heads and Weeping Willows: Death in Early America," *Proceedings of the American Antiquarian Society* 86 (1976) (Part 2): 273–302. Although Vinovskis argues that the overall rate of mortality was dropping in the seventeenth and eighteenth centuries, he nevertheless points out that infant mortality remained very high from the Puritan era through the nineteenth century.

10. Donald Hall, ed., *The Oxford Book of Children's Verse in America* (New York: Oxford University Press, 1985), 21, ll. 9–12.

11. In Cheryl Walker, ed., *American Women Poets of the Nineteenth Century: An Anthology* (New Brunswick: Rutgers University Press, 1992), 280–81.

12. For other examples of popular mourning artifacts, see Mary Lynn Stevens Heininger, et al., eds., *A Century of Childhood: 1820–1920* (Rochester, N.Y.: The Margaret Woodbury Strong Museum, 1984); A. Bruce MacLeish, "Paintings in the New York State Historical Association," *The Magazine Antiques* 126, no. 3 (September 1984): 590–600; Harvey Green, "A Home in Heaven: Religion, Death, and Mourning," *The Light of the Home: An Intimate View of the Lives of Women in Victorian America* (New York: Pantheon Books, 1983), 163–79; and Kenneth L. Ames, *Death in the Dining Room and Other Tales of Victorian Culture* (Philadelphia: Temple University Press, 1992).

13. Originally appeared in *The Flag of Our Union* 21, no. 37 (Sept. 15, 1866); reprinted in Hall, *The Oxford Book of Children's Verse in America*, 117, ll. 37–40.

14. William Wordsworth, "Ode: Intimations of Immortality from Recollections of Early Childhood," *Selected Poems and Prefaces*, ed. Jack Stillinger (Boston: Houghton Mifflin Co., 1965), 190, ll. 78. Other references will be noted parenthetically in the text.

15. For a discussion of Johnson's career, especially his choice of subject matter, see Carolyn J. Weekley and Stiles Tuttle Colwill, *Joshua Johnson: Freeman and Early American Portrait Painter* (Baltimore: Abby Aldrich Rockefeller Folk Art Center and the Maryland Historical Society, 1988).

16. For a discussion of *Emma Van Name*, see Anita Schorsch, *Images of Childhood: An Illustrated Social History* (New York: Mayflower Books, Inc., 1979), 66.

17. See Karin Calvert, "Cradle to Crib: The Revolution in Nineteenth-Century Children's Furniture," in *A Century of Childhood: 1820–1920*, ed. Mary Lynn Stevens Heininger (Rochester, N.Y.: Margaret Woodbury Strong Musuem, 1984), 38.

18. Jackson, *Verses*, 105–6.

19. This poem appears in Mrs. M. L. Rayne, ed., *What Can A Woman Do?; Or, Her Position in the Business and Literary World* (Detroit: F. B. Dickerson & Co., 1885), 349–51. Rayne's book is a collection of essays on occupations for women and includes a short anthology of poems. By the last two decades of the nineteenth century, professional options for women had increased dramatically. Among the careers open to women that Rayne lists are law, medicine, journalism, music, and—of course—literature.

20. For the conventions of epitaphic inscriptions, see Debra Fried, "Repetition, Refrain, and Epitaph," *ELH* 53, no. 3 (Fall 1986): 615–32; Karen Mills Campbell, "Poetry as Epitaph," *Journal of Popular Culture* 14, no. 4 (Spring 1981): 657–68; Karen Mills-Courts, *Poetry as Epitaph: Representation and Poetic Language* (Baton Rouge: Louisiana State University Press, 1990); Tarah Sage Somers, "Relict, Consort, Wife: The Use of Connecticut Valley Gravestones to Understand Concepts of Gender in the Late Eighteenth and Early Nineteenth Centuries," *Association for Gravestone Studies Newsletter* 19, no. 4 (1995): 3–4; Diana Ross McCain, "Graveyards and Gravestones," *Early American Life* 23, no. 5 (1992): 14–18; Cynthia Chase, "Reading Epitaphs," *Deconstruction Is/in America: A New Sense of the Political*, ed. Anselm Haverkamp (New York: New York University Press, 1995), 52–59; Henry Hart, "Graven Images," in *Postmodern Culture: An Electronic Journal of Interdisciplinary Criticism* 1, no 2 (1991): 7 paragraphs; and Deborah A. Smith, "'Safe in the Arms of Jesus': Consolation on Delaware Chil-

dren's Gravestones, 1840–99," *Markers: The Journal of the Association for Gravestone Studies* 4 (1987): 85–106.

21. For a discussion on the historical importance of the education that mothers gave to their children, see Nancy F. Cott, *The Bonds of Womanhood: "Woman's Sphere" in New England, 1780–1835* (New Haven: Yale University Press, 1977), 64–86 *passim*; Linda K. Kerber, "Why Should Girls Be Learnd or Wise?: Education and Intellect in the Early Republic," *Women of the Republic: Intellect and Ideology in Revolutionary America* (New York and London: W. W. Norton, 1986), 185–231; Carroll Smith-Rosenberg, "Bourgeois Discourse and the Progressive Era: An Introduction," *Disorderly Conduct: Visions of Gender in Victorian America* (New York: Oxford University Press, 1985), esp. 167–176; Mary P. Ryan, "Tying the Maternal Knot: 1830–1850," in *The Empire of the Mother: American Writing About Domesticity: 1830 to 1860*, Women & History, nos. 2 and 3 (The Institute for Research in History and the Haworth Press, 1982), 45–70; and Susan K. Harris, "Responding to the Text(s): Women Readers and the Quest for Higher Education," in *Readers in History: Nineteenth-Century American Literature and the Contexts of Response*, ed. James L. Machor (Baltimore: Johns Hopkins University Press, 1993), 259–82.

22. Sigourney's biographer, Gordon S. Haight, makes this observation in *Mrs. Sigourney: The Sweet Singer of Hartford* (New Haven: Yale University Press, 1930), 163.

23. Mary Kelley, *Private Woman, Public Stage: Literary Domesticity in Nineteenth-Century America* (Oxford: Oxford University Press, 1984), viii.

24. Haight, *Mrs. Sigourney*, 15.

25. Haight, *Mrs. Sigourney*, 44.

26. See Cheryl Walker, "A Composite Biography: Early Nineteenth-Century Women Poets," *The Nightingale's Burden: Women Poets and American Culture before 1900* (Bloomington: Indiana University Press, 1982), 67–86. In discussing the lives of professional women writers, Walker describes Sigourney as the most successful of a number of women poets publishing in this period. She portrays the poet as having a keen business sense which brought her substantial monetary success, although her pursuit of a career created serious tensions in her marriage.

27. Haight, *Mrs. Sigourney*, 45.

28. As Philip Judd Brockway notes, Judd interestingly chooses a woman as the primary source of the town's spiritual regeneration. Philip Judd Brockway, "Sylvester Judd (1813–1853): Novelist of Transcendentalism," *University of Maine Studies* 2nd ser., no. 53 (April 1941): 78. For a contemporary nineteenth-century perspective of Judd's life and times, see Arethusa Hall, *Life and Character of Sylvester Judd* (Boston: Crosby, Nichols, and Company, 1854).

29. Sigourney relates that, at the age of eighteen, Andrew returned home from college to announce that he would become a soldier. A lifelong pacifist, Sigourney was shocked by her son's intention; after long arguments, she eventually agreed to use her influence among friends to get him admitted to West Point. Despite her efforts, however, his application came too late, leaving her temporarily satisfied that she had been able to keep her son at her side a little longer. Haight, *Mrs. Sigourney*, 148–49.

30. Haight, *Mrs. Sigourney*, 150–51.

31. Haight provides this statistic and alludes to the "pale maidens who languish and die so meekly in Victorian novels" on p. 158. Sigourney wrote, of course, at a time of high infant as well as adolescent mortality. Haight also notes that one half of all children born in the nineteenth century died before reaching five years of age.

32. Harriet B. Stowe, *Uncle Tom's Cabin* (New York: Bantam Books, 1981), 286.

33. See also Ann Douglas [Wood], "Mrs. Sigourney and the Sensibility of Inner Space," *New England Quarterly* 45 (1972): 163–181. Douglas contends that Sigourney believed that women composed poetry according to a natural and spontaneous creative process that excluded men and sublimated their own sexuality. Her argument lends further support to the claim that Sigourney preferred in her poems the desexualized, less threatening male child to the man. Nina Baym has argued that although Sigourney has been noted, when she is mentioned at all, for her elegies, she also wrote a number of historical poems which should cause us to reevaluate our perception of her as a wholly private and domestic poet. See Nina Baym, "Reinventing Lydia Sigourney," *American Literature* 62, no. 3 (Sept. 1990): 385–404. In addition, Annie Finch has argued that sentimental poets, like Sigourney, who were typically allied with nature, lack the privileged central lyric self of male writers. Regularly objectified and naturalized herself as a figure, the woman poet turns to God as the ultimate lyric subject, structurally similar to concepts like nature, beauty, truth, or the beloved, against which she could prop her own lyric subjectivity: "In Sigourney's nature poems, the speaker frequently addresses, describes, or meditates alone on nature, thus providing the poetess ample opportunity to develop subjective romantic lyric 'insight' and to describe nature's transformations in relation to a central poet-self" (6). See Annie Finch, "The Sentimental Poetess in the World: Metaphor and Subjectivity in Lydia Sigourney's Nature Poetry," *Legacy* 8, no. 2 (1988): 3–18.

34. I am indebted to Shannon Minter for impressing on me the importance of this observation.

35. Even the few poems that do contain a male speaker portray the influence a mother has over her children's lives. In Sigourney's "A Father to His Motherless Children," for example, a man consoles his children on their mother's death—only to encourage them to follow her holy and virtuous example.

36. Lydia Sigourney, *Poems* (Philadelphia: Key & Biddle, 1834), 138. All further poems will be referred to by line number only within the text.

37. Joanne Dobson, "Reclaiming Sentimental Literature," *American Literature* 69, no. 2 (1997): 272.

38. For an account of the dangers that accompanied pregnancy in the nineteenth century, see "Marriage and Maternity: Introduction," *Women from Birth to Death: The Female Life Cycle in Britain, 1830–1914*, ed. Dr. Pat Jalland and Dr. John Hooper (Atlantic Highlands, N.J.: Humanities Press International, 1986), 117–23.

39. Lydia H. Sigourney, *Letters to Young Ladies* (New York: Harper Brothers, 1838), 11–12.

40. Sigourney's belief in the mother's power to educate the young appears in poems of hers that articulate a missionary zeal intended to convert the unregenerate. For Sigourney, as well as for Elizabeth Barrett Browning and for other both British and American women writers, the Greek Revolution against the Ottoman Empire

(c. 1821–31) offered an opportunity to proselytize an undereducated and needy population. In her "Intellectual Wants of Greece," Sigourney appeals directly to the generosity of all American "Sisters" and "Mothers," encouraging them to answer the "cry for knowledge" abroad with the "angel food" of their intellect. In making the desire to "feed" the mind a purely feminine task, Sigourney, as she frequently does in her poems of infant death, aligns the substantial bodily nourishment which only a mother can give to her child with the intellectual training that produces a lasting effect on children.

41. John Milton, *Paradise Lost*, Book 4, lines 269–71; in *Complete Poems and Major Prose*, ed. Merritt Y. Hughes (Indianapolis, Indiana: The Odyssey Press, 1957), 284.

42. Other poems in which children or women resemble flowers include the following: Sigourney's "Flora's Party" and "The Boy's Last Bequest"; and Frances Sargent Osgood's "'Ashes of Roses.'" Memorial sculptures of the period also frequently featured bouquets, twining wreaths of ivy, and cut lilies over the graves of women and children. One tombstone at Mt. Auburn depicts an overflowing basket of flowers and twining leaves with an inscription that reads: "My Wife & Child."

43. See Mary Lynn Stevens Heininger, "Children, Childhood, and Change in America, 1820–1920," *A Century of Childhood*, esp. 2–3, 10–11.

44. Barton Levi St. Armand, *Emily Dickinson and Her Culture: The Soul's Society* (Cambridge: Cambridge University Press, 1984), 45.

45. St. Armand, *Emily Dickinson and Her Culture*, 73.

46. Gilbert's cry to be allowed into heaven closely echoes the deathbed scenes of infants as depicted by other nineteenth-century American women poets. In "Request of a Dying Child," Sigourney records in an epigraph a dying child's plea that strikingly parallels Dickinson's own recollection of her nephew's death. She relates that a four-year-old boy "in his last moments spoke of fair green fields, and beautiful groves" (as does the dying Falstaff who "babbled of green fields" in Shakespeare's *Henry V* [II.iii.16]). Sigourney then quotes his last words: "'Let me go to them. Open the door, and let me go. Oh, *do* let me go home.'" The motif of the open door in heaven originally appears in the Book of Revelations: "behold, I have set before thee an open door, and no man can shut it" (3:8).

47. In discussing ED's use of a child's voice, I am building on previous criticism in this area, especially by feminist critics, who view her use of child speakers as a way to overturn accepted doctrines concerning women's place. See Barbara Antonina Clarke Mossberg, "Emily Dickinson's Nursery Rhymes," in *Feminist Critics Read Emily Dickinson*, ed. Suzanne Juhasz (Bloomington: Indiana University Press, 1983), 45–66; Cynthia Griffin Wolff, "The Voice of the Child," *Emily Dickinson* (Reading, Mass.: Addison-Wesley Publishing Company, 1988), 178–200; and Sandra M. Gilbert and Susan Gubar, "'A Woman—White': Emily Dickinson's Yarn of Pearl," *The Madwoman in the Attic: The Woman Writer and the Nineteenth-Century Literary Imagination* (New Haven: Yale University Press, 1979), esp. 587–94. For a discussion of Dickinson's use of the trope of the posthumous voice, see April Selley, "Satisfied Shivering: Emily Dickinson's Deceased Speakers," *ESQ: A Journal of the American Renaissance* 37, 2nd and 3rd Quarters (1991): 215–33.

48. I thank Francesca Sawaya for suggesting an alternate reading of these lines.
49. Many of Dickinson's poems image a spiritual or emotional lack as an economic deprivation. For a poem that ranks an intangible "name of Gold" over the actual, precious metal, see "It was given to me by the Gods—" (J, 454).
50. Hall, *The Oxford Book of Children's Verse in America*, 37; originally appeared in Anna Maria Wells, *Poems and Juvenile Sketches* (Boston: Carter, Hendee & Babcock, 1830).
51. Dobson, "Reclaiming Sentimental Literature," 270.

4. "Alabaster Chambers" (pp. 96–124)

1. Sylvester Judd, Jr., *Margaret: A Tale of the Real and the Ideal, Blight and Bloom; Including Sketches of a Place Not Before Described, Called Mons Christi*, 2 vols. (1845; rpt.: Boston: Philips, Sampson, and Company, 1851), 1: 269–70.
2. Reprinted in Karen L. Kilcup, ed., *Nineteenth-Century American Women Writers: An Anthology* (Oxford: Blackwell Publishers, 1997), 7.
3. Malcolm A. Nelson and Diana Hume George, "Grinning Skulls, Smiling Cherubs, Bitter Words," *Journal of Popular Culture* 15, no. 4 (Spring 1982): 171.
4. H.H. (Helen Hunt Jackson), *Bits of Travel at Home* (1878; rpt.: Boston: Roberts Brothers, 1882), 201.
5. Sylvester Judd, Jr., *Margaret*, 1, 269. Judd's novel first appeared as a one-volume edition in 1845; thus, Hawthorne may have been familiar with the work when he wrote *The Scarlet Letter* (1850), a consideration which becomes significant later in this chapter.
6. For the history of the "rural cemetery" movement, see Blanche Linden-Ward, "Putting the Past in Place: The Making of Mount Auburn Cemetery," *Cambridge Historical Society Proceedings, 1976–1979* (Rpt. 1985) 44: 171–96; Linden-Ward, *Silent City on a Hill: Landscapes of Memory & Boston's Mount Auburn Cemetery,* Urban Life & Landscapes Series (Columbus: Ohio State University Press, 1989); Stanley French, "The Cemetery as Cultural Institution: The Establishment of Mount Auburn and the 'Rural Cemetery' Movement," in *Death in America*, ed. David E. Stannard (Philadelphia: University of Pennsylvania Press, 1975), esp. 74–76; and Ann Douglas, "The Domestication of Death," *The Feminization of American Culture* (New York: Doubleday, 1988), 200–26.
7. Douglas, *Feminization*, 210.
8. Douglas, *Feminization*, 373, n.30.
9. Douglas, *Feminization*, 212.
10. See Lewis O. Saum, "Death in the Popular Mind of Pre-Civil War America," in Stannard, *Death in America*, 38.
11. William Wordsworth, "Essays Upon Epitaphs," *Literary Criticism of William Wordsworth*, ed. Paul M. Zall (Lincoln: University of Nebraska Press, 1966), 96.
12. As Ellen Louise Hart argues, Dickinson may have fantasized a relationship between herself and Susan Gilbert Dickinson that could persist beyond the grave. Rather than accept death as a stark and inevitable reality, as did their Puritan forebears, nineteenth-century writers came to view the grave increasingly as a continuation of

a bodily existence. See Ellen Louise Hart, "The Encoding of Homoerotic Desire: Emily Dickinson's Letters and Poems to Susan Dickinson, 1850–1886," *Tulsa Studies in Women's Literature* 9, no. 2 (1990): 251–72.

13. Lawrence Buell has also noted the importance and rare qualities of Allen's poem. He places her lyric in the context of others like them, including those by Whittier, Tuckerman, and Longfellow, that exemplify the fear of experience and psychological regression common in the period. See Buell, "New England Poetics: Emerson, Dickinson, and Others," *New England Literary Culture: From Revolution through Renaissance* (New York: Cambridge University Press, 1986), 124.

14. Donald Hall, ed., *Oxford Book of Children's Verse in America* (New York: Oxford University Press, 1985), 119.

15. Cheryl Walker, ed., *American Women Poets of the Nineteenth Century: An Anthology* (New Brunswick, N.J.: Rutgers University Press, 1992), 72.

16. Fried, "Repetition, Refrain, and Epitaph," *ELH* 53, no. 3 (1986): 617.

17. Jonathan Culler, "Apostrophe," *The Pursuit of Signs: Semiotics, Literature, Deconstruction* (Ithaca: Cornell University Press, 1981), 142.

18. For another poem of Dickinson's that invokes the consolatory fiction of the dead's ability to speak, see the lyric beginning "I died for Beauty—but was scarce" (J, 449).

19. Barton Levi St. Armand, *Emily Dickinson and Her Culture: The Soul's Society* (Cambridge: Cambridge University Press, 1984), 45.

20. John Calvin, *Institutes of the Christian Religion* (Edinburgh, 1845), 560; quoted in Allan I. Ludwig, *Graven Images: New England Stonecarving and its Symbols, 1650–1815* (Middletown, Conn.: Wesleyan University Press, 1966), 121.

21. Millicent Todd Bingham, *Ancestors' Brocades: The Literary Debut of Emily Dickinson* (New York: Harper & Brothers Publishers, 1945), 130.

22. Thomas H. Johnson, ed., *The Poetical Works of Edward Taylor* (Princeton: Princeton University Press, 1966), 140.

23. My interpretation of the weeping willow motif relies heavily on St. Armand's discussion in "Dark Parade: Dickinson, Sigourney, and the Victorian Way of Death," *Emily Dickinson and Her Culture*, esp. 42–46.

24. *The Poems of Herman Melville*, ed. Douglas Robillard (Albany, N.Y.: New College and University Press, 1976), 116.

25. Karen Mills Campbell, "Poetry as Epitaph," *Journal of Popular Culture* 14, no. 4 (Spring 1981): 660.

26. For a fuller discussion of cosmological symbols on gravestones and funerary iconography from the Puritans to the Victorians, see Ludwig, *Graven Images*, 187–97.

27. For a discussion of Dickinson's use of emblems and pictorial representations, especially in relation to the poem beginning "She laid her docile Crescent down" (J, 1396), see Barton Levi St. Armand and George Monteiro, "The Experienced Emblem: A Study of the Poetry of Emily Dickinson," *Prospects: An Annual Journal of American Cultural Studies* 6 (1981), esp. 197–200.

28. For the significance of Dickinson's handwriting and use of visual space, see Jerome McGann, *Black Riders: The Visible Language of Modernism* (Princeton: Princeton University Press, 1993). In addition, Susan Howe has described the typographic

ideal, so familiar to nineteenth-century audiences, that Dickinson manipulates in the presentation of her lyrics. See "These Flames and Generosities of the Heart: Emily Dickinson and the Illogic of Sumptuary Values," *Sulfur* 28 (1991): 151–52n.

29. See St. Armand, "Appendix C: Dickinson's Mystic Day," *Emily Dickinson and Her Culture*, 317.

30. Martha Nell Smith provides a full discussion of the lyric's domestic and cosmic metaphors. Reading Dickinson's poem as a prominent example of her "poetry workshop," she contends that the poet's exchanges with Susan Gilbert Dickinson about this poem's five versions alter our understanding of her reclusive writing habits. Rather than write in isolation, the poet actively sought advice and editorial criticism from her sister-in-law, whose participation leads Smith to conclude that some of her important poems are not the product of a single author but collaborative efforts. See Martha Nell Smith, "To Be Susan Is Imagination: Dickinson's Poetry Workshop," *Rowing In Eden*, esp. 180–97.

5. "Paradise Persuaded" (pp. 129–158)

1. Frances Sargent Osgood, *The Poetry of Flowers, and Flowers of Poetry, To Which Are Added, A Simple Treatise on Botany, With Familiar Examples, And A Copious Floral Dictionary* (New York: J. C. Riker, 1841), 23.

2. James Joyce, *Ulysses* (New York: Vintage Books, 1961), 78. Originally published: 1921.

3. Thomas Wentworth Higginson, "The Procession of the Flowers," *Out-Door Papers* (Boston: Ticknor and Fields, 1863), 320. All further references will be abbreviated *ODP* and appear parenthetically in the text.

4. Edward Hitchcock, "Prefatory," *Catalogue of Plants Growing Without Cultivation in the Vicinity of Amherst College* (Amherst: J. S. and C. Adams, and Co., 1829), iii.

5. Mrs. C. M. Badger, *Wild Flowers Drawn and Colored From Nature*, introduction by L. H. Sigourney (New York: Charles Scribner, 1859), 2.

6. Paula Bennett, *Emily Dickinson: Woman Poet* (Iowa City: University of Iowa, 1990), 100.

7. Nathaniel Hawthorne, *The Scarlet Letter* (New York: W. W. Norton & Co., 1988), 36. Originally published: 1850.

8. For examples of floral dictionaries that begin with lengthy synopses of European floral legends, see "Revised by the editor of 'Forget me not'" (possibly Frederic Shoberl, based on text by Louise Cortembert), *The Language of Flowers With Illustrative Poetry: To Which Is Now First Added The Calendar Of Flowers* (Philadelphia: Lea and Blanchard, 1843); and Dorothea Dix, *The Garland of Flora* (Boston: S. G. Goodrich and Co. and Carter and Hendee, 1829).

9. Jack Goody, *The Culture of Flowers* (Cambridge: Cambridge University Press, 1993). Much of my discussion of the history of floral rhetoric derives from Goody's assessment.

10. For a discussion of the language of flowers, its history, and its importance as a

cultural system, both in France and in England, see Sabine Haass, "'Speaking Flowers and Floral Emblems': The Victorian Language of Flowers," *Word and Visual Imagination: Studies in the Interaction of English and the Visual Arts*, ed. Karl Josef Höltgen, Peter M. Daly, and Wolfgang Lottes (Erlangen: Universitatsbibliothek Erlangen Nurnberg, 1988), 241–67; Brent Elliott, "The Victorian Language of Flowers," *Plant-Lore Studies: Papers Read at a Joint Conference of the Botanical Society of the British Isles and the Folklore Society Held at the University of Sussex, April 1983*, ed. Roy Vickery (London: The Folklore Society, University College of London, 1984), 61–65; Claudette Sartiliot, *Herbarium Verbarium: The Discourse of Flowers* (Lincoln: University of Nebraska Press, 1993); Beverly Seaton, "French Flower Books of the Early Nineteenth Century," *Nineteenth-Century French Studies* 11, nos. 1–2 (Fall-Winter 1982): 60–71; and Jack Goody, "The Secret Language of Flowers," *The Yale Journal of Criticism* 3, no. 2 (1990): 133–52.

11. The floral dictionaries dating from this period are numerous. Among many examples of dictionaries published both in America and England, I have consulted the following: *The Language of Flowers; With Illustrative Poetry: To Which Is Now First Added, The Calendar of Flowers*, 6th ed. (Philadelphia: Lee and Blanchard, 1843); Anna Elizabeth, ed., *The Vase of Flowers* (Boston: J. Buffum, 1851); Robert Tyas, *The Language of Flowers; or, Floral Emblems of Thoughts, Feelings, and Sentiments* (London and New York: George Routledge and Sons, 1869); J. Stevenson Bushnan, *Flowers and Their Poetry* (London: W. S. Orr & Company, 1851); M. A. (Mary Ann) Bacon, *Flowers and Their Kindred Thoughts* (London: Longman & Company, 1848); H. G. (Henry Gardiner) Adams, *Oriental Text Book and Language of Flowers* (London: Dean & Son, 1851?); *The Flowers of Shakespeare*, Plates drawn by J. E. G. (Jane Elizabeth Giraud) (London: Day & Haghe, 1845); *The Flowers of Milton*, Plates drawn by J. E. G. (Jane Elizabeth Giraud) (London: Day & Haghe, 1846); and *How to Grow Fruit and Vegetables; and The Language of Flowers* (New York: Norman L. Monro Publishers, n.d.). Osgood published several floral dictionaries that included her own floral poetry. Two examples are Frances Sargent (Locke) Osgood, *A Wreath of Wildflowers* (London: Edward Churton, 1838); and Frances Sargent Osgood, ed., *The Floral Offering, A Token of Friendship* (Philadelphia: Carey and Hart, 1847). Among the floral dictionaries available in modern reprints are Kathleen M. Gips, *The Language of Flowers: A Book of Victorian Floral Sentiments* (Chagrin Falls, Ohio: Pine Creek Press, 1990); F.W.L., *The Language of Flowers* (England: Michael Joseph, Ltd., 1968); and Sheila Pickles, ed., *The Language of Flowers* (New York: Harmony Books, 1990).

12. Almira H. Lincoln (Phelps), "Section VI. Symbolical Language of Flowers," *Familiar Lectures on Botany, Practical, Elementary, and Physiological: With an Appendix, Containing Descriptions of The Plants of the United States and Exotics, &c. For the Use of Seminaries and Private Students*, 7th ed. (New York: F. J. Huntington & Co., 1838), 171–74.

13. Dix, *The Garland of Flora*, 4.

14. Sarah Josepha Hale, *Flora's Interpreter, and Fortuna Flora* (Boston: Benjamin B. Massey and Company, 1850), iv.

15. Goody, *The Culture of Flowers*, 269–70.

16. *The Language of Flowers* (Philadelphia: Lea and Blanchard, 1843), 33.
17. [Anonymous.] Review of Alice Cary's *Lyra and Other Poems*, *Harpers New Monthly Magazine* 5, no. 25 (June 1852): 138.
18. Higginson, "Preface," *Poems of Emily Dickinson* (Boston: Roberts Brothers, 1890), v–vi.
19. "Who Is Saxe Holm?" *The Springfield Republican* (25 May 1878); rpt. *The Colorado Prospector* 15, no. 4 (April 1984): 7.
20. I am indebted to Jerome McGann for this observation.
21. For an assemblage of meanings, I consulted F. W. L., *The Language of Flowers*. According to Beverly Seaton, "there was no agreed-upon set of meanings. Instead of a universal symbolic language, the language of flowers was a vocabulary list, matching flowers with meanings, differing from book to book." See Seaton, *The Language of Flowers: A History* (Charlottesville: University of Virginia Press, 1995), 1–2. For a discussion of Dickinson's adaptation of features of floral discourse, see Elizabeth C. Stevens, "Dickinson's Language of Flowers," *Legacy* 2, no. 2 (Nov/Dec 1990), 3, 5.
22. *The Language of Flowers*, 5–6.
23. Osgood, *The Poetry of Flowers, and Flowers of Poetry*, 4.
24. Cheryl Walker, "Legacy Profile: Frances Osgood: 1811–1850," *Legacy* 1, no. 2 (Fall 1984): 5.
25. Cheryl Walker ed., *American Women Poets of the Nineteenth Century: An Anthology* (New Brunswick: Rutgers University Press, 1992), 107.
26. Watts, *The Poetry of American Women from 1632 to 1945* (Austin: University of Texas Press, 1977), 83.
27. Among the recent work by scholars concerned with recovering Osgood's fame and reputation for contemporary readers, see Dobson, "Sex, Wit, and Sentiment: Frances Osgood and the Poetry of Love," *American Literature* 65, no. 4 (December 1993): 631–50; Mary G. De Jong, "Her Fair Fame: The Reputation of Frances Sargent Osgood, Woman Poet," *Studies in the American Renaissance*, ed. Joel Myerson (Charlottesville: The University Press of Virginia, 1987), 265–84; and Paula Bennett, "'The Descent of the Angel': Interrogating Domestic Ideology in American Women's Poetry, 1858–1890," *American Literary History* 7, no. 4 (1995): 591–610. In particular, Bennett's most recent work attempts to delineate a new American women's poetic tradition which shows the protomodernism of their lyrics and disproves the belief that women's poems were written from a wholly sentimental aesthetic. See Bennett, "Late Nineteenth-Century American Women's Nature Poetry and the Evolution of the Imagist Poem," *Legacy* 9, no. 2 (1992): 89–103.
28. See Dobson, "Sex, Wit, and Sentiment," 632.
29. Dobson, "Sex, Wit, and Sentiment," 635.
30. Frances Sargent Osgood, *Poems* (New York: Clark & Austin, 1846), 67–68.
31. See Mary G. DeJong, "Lines from a Partly Published Drama: The Romance of Frances Sargent Osgood and Edgar Allan Poe," in *Patrons and Protégées: Gender, Friendship, and Writing in Nineteenth-Century America*, ed. Shirley Marchalonis (New Brunswick: Rutgers University Press, 1988), 41–42.
32. Frances Sargent Osgood, *Poems* (Philadelphia: Carey & Hart, 1850), 212, ll. 1–8.

33. Part of the poem reads:

> Ah! Thus the child of Genius pours,
> In solitude and tears,
> On one poor fleeting page, the light,
> The love of long, long years;
> And the gay world receives the ray
> Without a thought of all
> The clouds of fear and grief, through which
> Its prism'd glories fall!
> (*Poems* [1850], 109–10, ll. 17–24)

34. Patterson has tabulated the number of times jewels appear in Dickinson's work. The three most common are the pearl (thirty-one times), amber (twenty-three times), and the diamond (fourteen times). For a discussion of image clusters in Dickinson's poems and letters, see Rebecca Patterson, "The Jewel Imagery," *Emily Dickinson's Imagery* (Amherst: University of Massachusetts Press, 1979), esp. 74–93.
35. "Diamonds and Pearls," *The Atlantic Monthly*, 7, no. 41 (March 1861): 369.
36. For a discussion of erotic relations between women in nineteenth-century America, see Lillian Faderman, *Surpassing the Love of Men: Romantic Friendship and Love Between Women From the Sixteenth Century to the Present* (New York: Morrow, 1981); and Carroll Smith-Rosenberg, "The Female World of Love and Ritual: Relations Between Women in Nineteenth-Century America," *Disorderly Conduct: Visions of Gender in Victorian America* (New York: Oxford University Press, 1985), 53–76.
37. Although Smith-Rosenberg contends that a woman's letters "were but an example of the romantic rhetoric with which the nineteenth century surrounded the concept of friendship" (59), she also argues that female friendships revealed true passion and allowed women to share their pains and joys apart from men (63 *passim*).
38. Martha Nell Smith, *Rowing in Eden: Rereading Emily Dickinson* (Austin: The University of Texas Press, 1992), 143.
39. Rebecca Patterson, *Emily Dickinson's Imagery*, 83.
40. Paula Bennett, *Emily Dickinson: Woman Poet* (Iowa City: University of Iowa, 1900), 168.
41. Cherly Walker, *The Nightingale's Burden: Woman Poets and American Culture before 1900* (Bloomington: Indiana University Press, 1982), 94.
42. Osgood, *The Poetry of Flowers*, 261, 262.
43. Rebecca Patterson, *Emily Dickinson's Imagery* (Amherst: The University of Massachusetts Press, 1979), 35.
44. Patterson notes that "the pearl figures clearly and consciously as the outer defense works of virginity" (87).
45. Osgood, *The Poetry of Flowers*, 262.
46. Gips, *The Language of Flowers*, 109.
47. According to Charles R. Anderson, *Emily Dickinson's Poetry: A Stairway of Surprise* (New York: Holt, Rinehart and Winston, 1960), the poet's use of traditional subjects drawn from nature, like flowers, never fully escaped "the sentimental and

the fanciful" (98). Although for him the poem "makes a fine beginning, with its precise notations," it loses its detachment and objectivity at approximately line 5. I would argue that it is precisely the association with emotion and women's lives embedded in floral images that make them fit conveyers of her critique of stereotypical female behavior. Nevertheless, Anderson notes the centrality of the arbutus to Dickinson's circle as youths, noting that it was considered "emblematic" in men's and women's love relations, and a sprig of the same flower was pinned to Austin's earliest surviving letter to his future fiancée in 1850.

48. Osgood, *The Poetry of Flowers*, 84–85.
49. Lincoln, *Familiar Lectures on Botany*, 102.
50. Martha Dickinson Bianchi, "Emily Dickinson's Garden," *Emily Dickinson International Society Bulletin* 2, no. 2 (Nov/Dec 1990): 1.
51. Margaret Homans, "'Oh, Vision of Language!': Dickinson's Poems of Love and Death," in *Feminist Critics Read Emily Dickinson*, ed. Suzanne Juhasz (Bloomington: Indiana University Press, 1983), 118.

6. "Fame of Myself" (pp. 161–200)

1. "Who Is Saxe Holm?," *The Springfield Republican* (25 May 1878); rpt.: *The Colorado Prospector* 15, no. 4 (April 1984): 7.
2. Review from *The Boston Courier* (n.d.); rpt.: Helen Hunt Jackson [H.H.], *Bits of Travel at Home* (Boston: Roberts Brothers, 1884), n.p.
3. Several critics have condemned Jackson's verse, and few have considered it worth investigating. Michael Dorris condemns her work for being too sentimental: "Much of Mrs. Jackson's verse seems by contemporary standards overly sentimental and even saccharine. Fond of addressing the seasons, religious themes, the 'higher emotions,' and particular aspects of the landscape, her language was high Victorian, her style, arch," Dorris, "Introduction," *Ramona: A Story* (New York: Signet, 1988), vii. Other noteworthy critics, such as Richard Chase, Denis Donahue, and even one of Jackson's biographers, Evelyn Banning, have similarly disparaged her verse or have explained away ED's taste. See Michael E. Staub, "White Moth and Ox: The Friendship of ED and H. H. Jackson," *Dickinson Studies: Emily Dickinson (1830–86), U.S. Poet* 68 (1988): 19.

Nevertheless, many critics have begun to investigate Jackson's relationship with Dickinson as an index to the aesthetic standards of her age. Cheryl Walker makes the case for Jackson's importance most forcefully in "Tradition and the Individual Talent: Helen Hunt Jackson and Emily Dickinson," in *The Nightingale's Burden: Women Poets and American Culture before 1900* (Bloomington: Indiana University Press, 1982), 87–116. Walker writes: "The puzzle of Emily Dickinson's work is finally not a question of the identity of the Master or the extent of her real experience, but one of tradition and the individual talent. Although the concern with intense feeling, the ambivalence toward power, the fascination with death, the forbidden lover and secret sorrow all belong to this woman's tradition, Emily Dickinson's best work so far surpasses anything that a logical extension of that tradition's codes could have produced that the only way to explain it is by the single word, genius" (116). For a discussion of Dickinson's friendship with Jackson and its impact on her decision not to publish, see Betsy Erkkila, "Dickinson, Women Writers, and the Marketplace," *Wicked Sisters: Women Poets, Literary History & Discord* (New York: Oxford University Press, 1992), esp. 86–98; Richard B. Sewall, "Helen Hunt Jackson," *The Life of Emily Dickinson* (New York: Farrar, Straus and Giroux, 1974), 2, 577–92; and Susan Coultrap-McQuin, "'Very Serious Literary Labor': The Career of Helen Hunt Jackson," *Doing Literary Business: American Women Writers in the Nineteenth Century* (Chapel Hill: The University of North Carolina Press, 1990), 137–66. For a discussion of the differences in style and language between the two poets, see Staub; and Joanne Dobson, "'The Grieved—are Many—I am Told—': The Woman Writer and Public Discourse," *Dickinson and the Strategies of Reticence*, esp. 96–98.

4. Betsy Erkkila, *Wicked Sisters*, 98.

5. Unpublished correspondence of Jackson will be identified by date, collection, and assigned number. Manuscripts from the Thomas Baily Aldrich Papers appear courtesy of the Houghton Library, Harvard University. Manuscripts from the Abigail May-Goddard Papers appear courtesy of the Schlesinger Library, Radcliffe College. This letter is A-134, of the May-Goddard Collection.

6. Susan Coultrap-McQuin argues that Jackson's reluctance to speak out on public issues except by pleading the desire to help individuals parallels a new type of woman writer who seeks to achieve fame "by the application of individual efforts, not by advocating social change" (150). No longer wholly dependent on the Gentleman Publisher, she advocates her professional abilities "in the dress of a True Woman but with the drive of an individualistic worker" (150–51). I would agree that Jackson's desire to advance herself is accomplished through hard work, but her social advocacy, even though it is performed under the guise of feminine helpfulness, is well documented and genuinely felt. Most articles and books on Jackson focus on her Indian activism. See, for example, William Oandasan, "*Ramona*: Reflected through Indigenous Eyes," *California Courier* (Feb.–Mar. 1986): 7; Karl Keller, "Helen Hunt Jackson: Pioneer Activist of Southern California," *Seacoast* 2 (Mar. 1981): 60–65; and Michael T. Marsden, "Helen Hunt Jackson: Docudramatist of the American Indian," *Markham Review* 10 (Fall 1980–Winter 1981): 15–19.

7. "Father Junípero and His Work," by "H.H.," *Century Magazine* (May 1883); "The Present Condition of the Mission Indians in Southern California," by "H.H.," *Century Magazine* (August 1883).

8. Carroll Smith-Rosenberg *Disorderly Conduct: Visions of Gender in Victorian America* (New York and Oxford: Oxford University Press, 1985), 130–31.

9. Ralph Waldo Emerson, *Parnassus*, ed. Ralph Waldo Emerson (Boston: Houghton Mifflin, 1874), x.

10. Emerson, *Journals*, 10 vols. (Boston and New York: Houghton Mifflin Company, 1909–1914), 10: 252.

11. Quoted by Emily Pierce, "Helen Hunt Jackson (H.H.): What She Wrote, How She Lived, and Where She is Buried," *Frank Leslie's Illustrated Newspaper* (1887): 314. Courtesy of the Jones Library, Amherst, Massachusetts.

12. *Verses* [By "H.H."] (1870; rpt.: Boston: Roberts Brothers, 1875), 190, ll. 1–8. All further references are abbreviated *Verses* and included parenthetically.

13. Richard Ellmann, ed., *The New Oxford Book of American Verse* (New York: Oxford University Press, 1976), 74, ll. 1–5.

14. Thomas Wentworth Higginson, Review of *Verses* [by "H.H."], *The Atlantic Monthly*, 26, no. 161 (1871): 400.

15. *The Nation* 13, no. 298 (16 March 1871): 184.

16. Quoted in Pierce, 315; and in "Mrs. Helen Jackson ('H.H.')," attributed to Thomas W. Higginson, *Century Magazine* 31 (November 1885–April 1886): 256.

17. Helen Jackson, *Poems* (Boston: Little, Brown, and Company, 1910).

18. Ellmann, *The New Oxford Book of American Verse*, 84, l. 2.

19. See Antoinette May, *Helen Hunt Jackson: A Lonely Voice of Conscience* (San Francisco: Chronicle Books, 1987), 27. This remark of Jackson's has been quoted frequently by her biographers as well as the popular press. From the nineteenth through the early twentieth centuries, critics and editors were interested by Jackson's businesslike attitude toward publishing. For instance, the caption to a cartoon in the *New York Times Book Review* for 3 August 1930 reads as follows: "'H.H.' Neatly Splits a Hair. Helen Hunt Jackson Makes a Nice Distinction. She Began to Write Because She Needed Money. Later She Remarked, 'I Do Not Write for Money, But I Print for Money.'" Rather than explain her remark as emanating from an ethos of privacy, these editors promoted the common image of nineteenth-century women writers as hacks, an impression that has continued until today.

20. Ralph Waldo Emerson, *Essay and Lectures*, ed. Joel Porte (New York: Library of America, 1983), 262–63.

21. Barton Levi St. Armand, *Emily Dickinson and Her Culture: The Soul's Society* (Cambridge: Cambridge University Press, 1984), 63.

22. See May, *Helen Hunt Jackson*, 26.

23. "Mrs. Helen Jackson ('H.H.')," 253.

24. Sigourney poignantly acknowledged late in life that writing too much had made her a literary jack-of-all-trades: "If there is any kitchen in Parnassus, my Muse has surely officiated there as a woman of all work, and an aproned waiter." Gordon S. Haight, *Mrs. Sigourney: The Sweet Singer of Hartford* (New Haven: Yale University Press, 1930), 46; originally in Lydia H. Sigourney, *Letters of Life* (New York, 1866), 376.

25. For another of Dickinson's bluebird poems, see the lyric beginning "After all Birds have been investigated and laid aside—" (J, 1395).

26. Reprinted in *The Colorado Prospector: Historical Highlights From Early Day Newspapers* 15, no. 4 (April 1984): 6. Courtesy of the Jones Library, Amherst, Massachusetts. Page numbers correspond to this reprint and are included parenthetically in the text.

27. Reprinted in *The Colorado Prospector: Historical Highlights from Early Day Newspapers* 15, no. 4 (April 1984): 4. Courtesy of the Jones Library, Amherst, Massachusetts. Page numbers correspond to this reprint and are included parenthetically in the text.

28. Alistair Fowler, *Kinds of Literature* (Cambridge, Mass.: Harvard University Press, 1982), 31. Quoted in Michael R. G. Spiller, *The Development of the Sonnet: An Introduction* (London and New York: Routledge, 1992), 2.

29. For similar lyrics by Jackson in which a woman is abandoned or injured within the home, see "Exile" and "A Woman's Death-Wound."

30. Spiller, *Development of the Sonnet*, 43–44.

31. See Johnson, ed., *The Poems of Emily Dickinson*, 3 vols. (Cambridge, Mass.: Harvard University Press, 1955), 1, 151–55; and Sewall 2, 491.

32. St. Armand, *Emily Dickinson and Her Culture*, 317.

33. Patterson, *Emily Dickinson's Imagery* (Amherst: University of Massachusetts, 1979), 141.

34. Adrienne Rich, "Vesuvius at Home: The Power of Emily Dickinson," *On Lies, Secrets, and Silence: Selected Prose 1966–1978* (New York: W. W. Norton & Company, 1979), esp. 166–74.

35. Ellmann, *The New Oxford Book of American Verse*, 211, l. 106.

36. Joanne Dobson, *Dickinson and the Strategies of Reticence: The Woman Writer in Nineteenth-Century America* (Bloomington and Indianapolis: Indiana University Press, 1989), 96.

37. Ellmann, *The New Oxford Book of American Verse*, 310, l. 31.

38. See "When the Baby Died" and "Just Out of Sight," *Poems*, 91–92, 240–41.

7. Seeing "New Englandly" (pp. 201–210)

1. Gilles Deleuze and Félix Guattari, *Kafka: Toward a Minor Literature*, trans. Dana Polan, Theory and History of Literature (Minneapolis: University of Minnesota Press, 1986), 30: 16.

2. George Monteiro and Barton Levi St. Armand, "The Experienced Emblem: A Study of the Poetry of Emily Dickinson," *Prospects: A Journal of American Cultural Studies* 6 (1981): 187.

3. For recent critiques of sentimental literature designed to reclaim nineteenth-century American women's literature, see Joanne Dobson, "Reclaiming Sentimental Literature," *American Literature* 69, no. 2 (June 1997): 263–88; Paula Bennett, "Not Just Filler and Not Just Sentimental: Women's Poetry in American Victorian Periodicals, 1860–1900," *Periodical Literature in Nineteenth-Century America*, ed. Kenneth M. Price and Susan Belasco Smith (Charlottesville: The University Press of Virginia, 1995); and Susan K. Harris, *19th-Century American Women's Novels: Interpretive Strategies* (Cambridge: Cambridge University Press, 1990).

4. Dobson, "Reclaiming Sentimental Literature," 266.

5. Judith Fetterley, "Commentary: Nineteenth-Century American Women Writers and the Politics of Recovery," *American Literary History* 6, no. 3 (Fall 1994): 603.

6. See Paula Bennett, "Late Nineteenth-Century American Women's Nature Poetry and the Evolution of the Imagist Poem," *Legacy: A Journal of American Women Writers* 9, no. 2 (1992): 92.

7. Louise Bogan, *Achievement in American Poetry, 1900–1950* (Chicago: Henry Regnery Company, 1951), 21.

8. Fetterley, "Commentary," 600.

9. Jane Tompkins, *Sensational Designs: The Cultural Work of American Fiction, 1790–1860* (New York: Oxford University Press, 1985), 126.

10. Paul Lauter, "Teaching Nineteenth-Century American Women Writers," *Canons and Contexts* (New York: Oxford University Press, 1991), 128.

11. Often describing the setting of primeval America, in which Native-Americans figure prominently and whose dispossession and effacement from history is recounted, Sigourney, for example, undertook to address the relentless genocide in nineteenth-century America in *Zinzendorff and Other Poems* (New York and Boston, 1833) and *Pocahontas and Other Poems* (London, 1841). For a discussion of Sigourney's political and historical activism, see Nina Baym, "Reinventing Lydia Sigourney," *American Literature* 62, no. 3 (Sept. 1990): 385–404.

12. Mary Jacobus, "The Question of Language: Men of Maxims and *The Mill on the Floss*," *Critical Inquiry* 8, no. 2 (Winter 1981): 210.

13. See Sewall 2, 539. Originally appeared as Thomas Wentworth Higginson, "Letter to a Young Contributor," *The Atlantic Monthly* 9, no. 54 (April 1862): 410.

14. Jane Tompkins, *A Life in School: What the Teacher Learned* (Reading, Mass.: Addison-Wesley Publishing Company, Inc., 1996), 212.

Index

University Press of New England publishes books under its own imprint and is the publisher for Brandeis University Press, Dartmouth College, Middlebury College Press, University of New Hampshire, Tufts University, and Wesleyan University Press.

Library of Congress Cataloging-in-Publication Data
Petrino, Elizabeth A., 1962–
Emily Dickinson and her contemporaries : women's verse in America,
1820–1885 / Elizabeth A. Petrino.
    p.   cm.
    Includes bibliographical references and index.
    ISBN 0–87451–838–5 (alk. paper)
    1. Dickinson, Emily, 1830–1886—Criticism and interpretation.
2. Women and literature—United States—History—19th century.
3. American poetry—Women authors—History and criticism.
4. American poetry—19th century—History and criticism.
5. Dickinson, Emily, 1830–1886—Contemporaries.
PS1541.Z5P44   1998
811'.3099287'09034—dc21   97–44600

GRAPHICAL CALCULATORS AND THEIR DESIGN

Norman H. Crowhurst

Engineering Consultant

HAYDEN BOOK COMPANY, INC., NEW YORK
a division of HAYDEN PUBLISHING COMPANY, INC.

PREFACE

Many engineers, and others, find their job to be an all or nothing situation. When work is required, it is wanted yesterday, while at other times an effort has to be made to find work to do. Chart making is a most constructive way to fill the lean hours and, at the same time, increase efficiency when working under pressure. Carefully-planned charts can really fractionalize design time and other working time for people in almost every profession.

Although the author is not a chart maker by profession, the benefits he has gained from designing his own charts for his own purposes in engineering and technical writing have encouraged him to become a "professional" designer of graphical calculators. Designing charts that other people can use or understand without having to come to the author and ask "How do you use this . . . thing?" has presented a series of problems to the author that he has worked on over the years. The methods he has developed to surmount these problems are presented in this book.

This book is primarily about the design of calculators, but most of the features that make an effective calculator are also necessary for effective graphical communication that is intended only to inform. More than half of the graphical artwork in the author's published writings serves a merely informational purpose. The care that is necessary to develop a chart that is easily read and understood is essential in the design of calculators and charts of every type, whether they are information carriers or for manipulation.

A book of this type necessarily serves many purposes. To the person who says, "Someone should find a better way of . . ." and who thinks he does not know how himself, this book will give a very good lead in finding a way for the millions of jobs where a graphical calculator is the answer.

To the person who may already have evolved a calculator that suits his own needs, but that would be obscure to someone not familiar with it, this book will show how to dress it up so as to remove the obscurity and give it the maximum utility in its application.

v

To the technical writer who wants to make his presentation as concise and meaty as possible, this book will show how to put the more essential information in a form that is easily understood and how to make the presentation both attractive and of maximum usefulness.

Teachers of mathematics have indicated that this material would serve excellently as a source book for the development of visual aids.

It is now some years since several technical writers prepared books on technical writing, showing how to be lucid and informative in the use of language. What has been lacking for some time is an equivalent treatment for the understanding and presentation of graphical calculators. The author would have prepared it much sooner than this had he not been busy on other assignments that have seemed more pressing for much of the time. But, at last, this is it.

Here's to better graphical presentation.

Gold Beach, Oregon   NORMAN H. CROWHURST

CONTENTS

Chapter 1
CHOOSING A TYPE

When you need a calculator, or graphical illustration, for a certain purpose, the logical thing to do first would be to decide upon a general type of calculator, then adapt the broad range of that type to the particular needs of your particular purpose, lay out the design, do the detailed calculation and construction work, and make a master drawing. If the calculator is for personal or limited use, this final rendering might be the only copy. If it is for publication, then this will be a master from which hundreds, thousands, or even millions of copies are made, by whatever process is appropriate.

If you start to follow this deceptively simple procedure, however, you will find it is not that simple. All of the factors upon which successive decisions will be based are interlinked to some extent. The tentative choice of calculator type may later be rejected in favor of another, because of some factors that are not evident until some of the more detailed work is started. For this and other reasons, such idealized successive progress to a conclusion often proves impossible. However, it is useful to spell out some guides at the beginning, as many designs can be followed through in any type of calculator or presentation, according to the individual requirements. This introductory chapter will indicate the criteria on which the design is to be based, although final decisions will often have to be reserved until the appropriate chapters on individual types have been studied.

There are three basic calculator types, to which we have devoted separate chapters, following which we go into more detail about constructional methods, some features of which are common to all types, and then conclude with a summary chapter that considers how the types relate to one another.

Basic Types

The three basic calculator types are the *slide rule,* the *nomogram,* or alignment chart, and the *graphical chart.*

1

The slide rule breaks down into two types: linear (straight line) in which the sliding parts move back and forth, and circular, in which the movable scales rotate about a central pivot. Figure 1-1A shows a conventional straight slide rule (top) and one in which the movable scale appears through slots in the fixed scale, which is often made of cardboard (bottom). Fig. 1-1B shows a circular slide rule, with a radial transparent hair line.

The simplest form of nomogram uses parallel linear scales to perform functions essentially similar to those achieved with the slide rule by alignment of points on the respective scales with a straightedge (Fig. 1-1C), rather than by moving the printed scales relative to one another. Although a nomogram occupies more space (area) than do the essential components of a slide rule, both consist basically of information presented along line form scales, and it is the relation, or juxtaposition of these scales that performs the calculations.

In more complicated nomogram forms, functions are possible that cannot be embodied simply in any form of slide rule. The use of ratio scales, which are straight lines at an angle to one another or to the parallel scales already mentioned, does not directly enable new forms of calculation to be made, but alters the form of scales that may be used and thus opens the door to new presentations (Fig. 1-1D). Curved scales introduce completely new possibilities (Fig. 1-1E).

The graphical chart utilizes area in a more basic sense. It really constitutes a complete presentation of the possible calculations it covers, in graphical form, spread out on an area (Fig. 1-1F). In many respects it is the most visual form of calculator, although this visual aspect may not always be utilized in relation to the application. For example, Figs. 4-3A and B represent an instance where the design of the chart follows the visual form of the response curve it helps to plot. The visualness of the form lends itself to helping in changing the form or contour for better coverage, distribution of coverage, or readability of the range of calculations for which it is designed. Figures 4-2B and D represent an example where the change of form uses a visual concept of the chart itself to advantage, rather than the significance of the calculation, which is dominant in the charts in Figs. 4-1D and F.

Design Criteria

The main contributing factors in the choice of a calculator type are:

(a) the adaptability to the formulae or data involved in the calculation or presentation;

(b) the type of user and, possibly, his preferences in relation to calculator type;

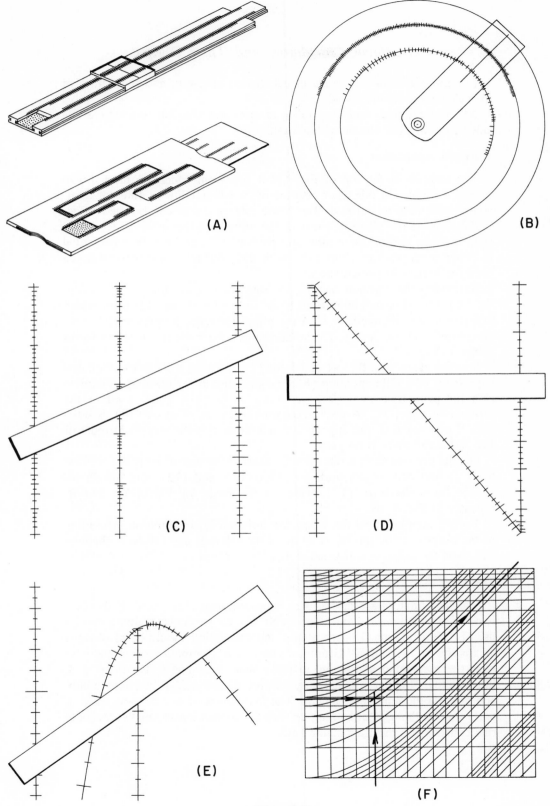

Fig. 1-1

(c) the precision and range of calculation required, and the nature of the calculation involved; and

(d) the purpose and frequency of use and the location where the calculation or presentation will be used.

Formula Adaptation

The formula at the top of Fig. 1-2 is one from which we have drawn several examples in this book because of its adaptability to different treatments, according to purpose. The phase reference (2) can be used to derive a formula for phase in terms of the arctan for the angle, which is the ratio between the imaginary and real parts of (1), and can be represented in either nomogram or chart form with little difficulty and without much need for variety in presentation.

Extracting the constant factor (3) from the original form (1), enables the frequency discriminating term to be isolated as k' in (4), from which expressions are obtained for k' at the phase reference frequency (5), converted into db form at (6). This relationship is the basis for the chart forms shown in Fig. 4-5.

Starting again with the original form (1), deriving a magnitude-squared expression (7), differentiating (8), and equating to zero to find an expression for peak frequency (9), we extract a factor e (10), used in the formula on Fig. 4-3C. A peak exists provided e, as given by (10), is positive. If e is negative, the appropriate reference uses the second formula of Fig. 4-3C and there is no peak.

For the peaking case, a reference frequency (the top of the peak) is given by (12) and making substitutions (10), (11), and (12), and the db response takes the form (13), which is the basis for Fig. 4-3A and B, repeated in Fig. 5-5B.

These examples show the scope for variation in presentation, according to the purpose to be served. A study of the relevant parts of later chapters will show the different construction aspects involved.

The User

Many calculators are designed as a promotional aid, where, if the user is not completely a layman, he probably has no particular training for the use of the calculators. In such a case, the calculation should be as obvious as possible in its method. Graphical charts are informative to people who have the mathematical training to make them meaningful, but many lack this training. Nomograms, similarly, require mathematical "reading" ability and unsettle the nonmathematical. The fascination of one or more moving parts and the "magic" of coming up with the correct answer makes the slide rule construction most appealing here.

BASIC FORMULA: $k = 1 + \dfrac{r}{R} - \omega^2 LC + j\omega\left(\dfrac{L}{R} + rC\right)$ $\qquad$ ①

Phase reference: $\omega_\phi^2 = \dfrac{r+R}{RLC}$ $\quad$ ② $\qquad\qquad$ Normalizing level: $k_{\omega=0} = 1 + \dfrac{r}{R}$ $\quad$ ③

Extracting ③ as factor:

$$k = \left(1 + \frac{r}{R}\right)\underbrace{\left[1 - \frac{\omega^2 LCR}{r+R} + j\omega\left(\frac{L + CrR}{r+R}\right)\right]}_{k'} \qquad ④$$

At ω_ϕ: $k'_{\omega_\phi} = j\omega_\phi\left(\dfrac{L + CrR}{r+R}\right) = \sqrt{\dfrac{r+R}{RLC}}\left(\dfrac{L + CrR}{r+R}\right) = \sqrt{\dfrac{L}{CR(r+R)}} + \sqrt{\dfrac{r^2 RC}{L(r+R)}}$

$$= \sqrt{\frac{r}{r+R}}\left[\sqrt{\frac{L}{CrR}} + \sqrt{\frac{CrR}{L}}\right] \qquad ⑤$$

$$f\left(\frac{r}{R}\right) \qquad f\left(\frac{L}{CrR}\right)$$

$$db_{\omega_\phi} = 20\,Log_{10}\sqrt{\frac{r}{r+R}}\left[\sqrt{\frac{L}{CrR}} + \sqrt{\frac{CrR}{L}}\right] = 10\,Log_{10}\frac{r}{r+R}\left(\frac{L}{CrR} + 2 + \frac{CrR}{L}\right) \qquad ⑥$$

$$|k|^2 = \left(1 + \frac{r}{R}\right)^2 - 2\left(1 + \frac{r}{R}\right)\omega^2 LC + \omega^4 L^2 C^2 + \omega^2\left(\frac{L}{R} + rC\right)^2 \qquad ⑦$$

$$\frac{dk^2}{d\omega^2} = 2\omega^2 L^2 C^2 - 2\left(1 + \frac{r}{R}\right)LC + \left(\frac{L}{R} + rC\right)^2 \qquad ⑧ \qquad \text{Equating to zero,}$$

$$\omega_p^2 = \left(1 + \frac{r}{R}\right)\frac{1}{LC} - \frac{1}{2}\left(\frac{L}{R} + rC\right)^2\frac{1}{L^2 C^2} = \frac{1}{LC} + \frac{r}{RLC} - \frac{1}{2R^2 C^2} - \frac{r}{RLC} - \frac{r^2}{2L^2}$$

$$= \frac{1}{LC}\left[1 - \frac{1}{2}\left(\frac{L}{CR^2} + \frac{Cr^2}{L}\right)\right] \qquad ⑨$$

Writing: $e = 1 - \dfrac{1}{2}\left(\dfrac{L}{CR^2} + \dfrac{Cr^2}{L}\right)$ ⑩ $\quad$ and $a = \dfrac{r}{R}$ ⑪ ; $\quad$ normalizing $x = \dfrac{\omega}{\omega_p}$ ⑫

$$db = 10\,Log_{10}\left[1 + \left(\frac{e}{1+a}\right)^2(x^4 - 2x^2)\right] \qquad ⑬$$

Normalizing $y = \dfrac{\omega}{\omega_\phi}$ ⑭ $\qquad db = 10\,Log_{10}\left[1 - 2\left(\dfrac{e}{1+a}\right)y^2 + y^4\right]$ $\qquad$ ⑮

Correlating: $\dfrac{\omega_p}{\omega_\phi} = \dfrac{y}{x} = \sqrt{\dfrac{e}{1+a}}$ ⑯ $\qquad db_{peak} = 10\,Log_{10}\left[1 - \left(\dfrac{e}{1+a}\right)^2\right]$ $\qquad$ ⑰

$$db_{\omega_\phi} = 10\,Log_{10}\,2\left(1 - \frac{e}{1+a}\right) \qquad ⑱$$

Fig. 1-2

If graphs are not understood, neither will graphical scales be understood, even on a slide rule. The exposure calculator on the Weston light meter discussed in Chapter 2 is an excellent example of a solution of this problem. There, the use of a scale that is basically logarithmic but uses definitely identified steps (with no intermediate values) avoids the need to understand interpolation. Such a presentation device can be used in any of the basic graphical forms, where the user may benefit from its employment.

Where the proper slide rule manipulation is not as obvious to the user as might be desirable, it is relatively simple to make its use an a, b, c procedure: the concrete calculator discussed in Chapter 2 (Fig. 2-4A) is an example of this. Although the slide rule is completely foolproof without any instructions, giving an example on the reverse side builds confidence in its use.

When the user has technical or semitechnical training, the novelty of the slide rule may still have some appeal, but there may be greater advantages to using one of the other types. This is usually dictated by the factors indicated in this chapter. However, another user-oriented factor, familiarity, is sometimes quite pertinent. Nomograms have enjoyed tremendous popularity, for reasons which appear vague. Although their derivation, at least for more than the simplest types, is not simple, their construction involves less work, which is the more probable explanation of their popularity.

Ease of construction, in itself, however, is not a justifiable reason for choice. A calculator that is worth making only has to be made once to be used many, many times. Thus, it is worth a fair amount of extra effort when it is made, to save a little effort every time it is used, whether that initial effort is directed to making it easy to use, easy to understand, or improving its accuracy. For many applications this points to the graphical type. But the fact of nomograms' popularity means their use is familiar to people who might find other types less familiar. This can be a valid reason for choosing this type.

Type and Accuracy of Calculation

It is impossible to generalize as to which type of calculator allows the best precision over the greatest range. This depends on the precise nature of the calculation—the formulae or data involved. This will become apparent as the book is studied. One calculation may lend itself readily to one type, another to a different type, and some may be impossible for certain type choices. This can only be determined by working around with a formula to see what can be done. This observation will be shown to be true, even for different constructions or arrangements within the same general type.

Chapter 2
SLIDE RULES

Slide rules form a good starting place for the consideration of graphical calculators of all kinds. Their whole operation is based on the addition and subtraction of measured distances. Figure 2-1A shows the basic rule, with linear measure, used for addition and subtraction. The upper pair of scales illustrate the process of addition. By putting the zero point (end) of the sliding scale against the length representing the quantity a, a second quantity b is measured off along the sliding scale. The sum $(a + b)$ is then read on the fixed scale opposite b on the sliding scale.

The lower part of Fig. 2-1A shows subtraction, which is the reverse process of addition. Here, the number to be subtracted, d, on the sliding scale, is put opposite the number from which it is to be subtracted, c, on the fixed scale, and the difference $(c - d)$ appears on the fixed scale opposite the zero point (end) of the sliding scale.

Logarithmic Scales

All that is needed to convert this simple addition and subtraction to multiplication and division is to alter the scales. Instead of using the basic linear gradations, we convert to logarithmic (Fig. 2-1B). The zero point (which is put a little way in from the end, so it can be more accurately aligned with a point on the other scale) is labeled 1, of which the logarithm (to any base) is zero; distances from this reference point are then measured in terms of the logarithm of the quantity named on the scale. When the 1 of the sliding scale is aligned with the scale mark a on the fixed scale (Fig. 2-1B) and a reading is taken opposite b on the sliding scale, the distance "a" along the fixed scale is log a, the distance "b" along the sliding scale is log b, so the total distance "a + b" along the fixed scale is log $a + $ log b, or log ab. The scale calibration on the fixed scale will identify the product as ab.

Division is the reverse of this process, as subtraction was the reverse of the process of addition. To divide, the scale location on the sliding scale

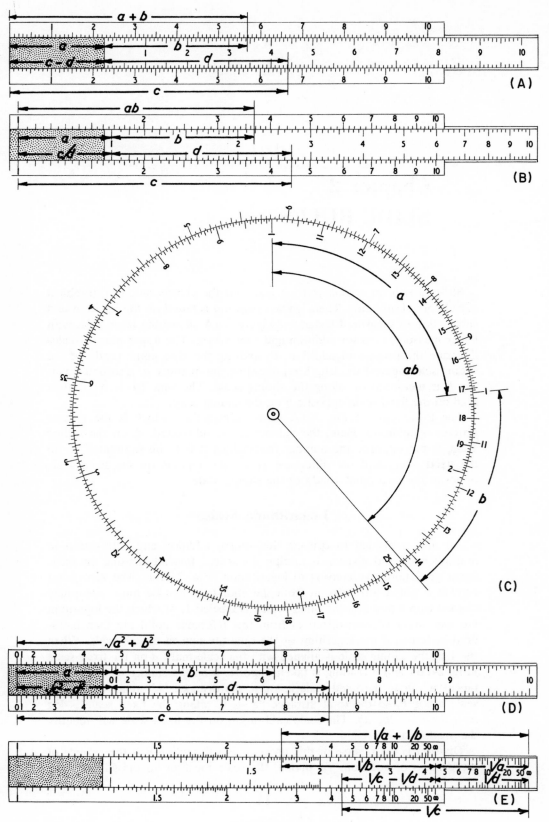

Fig. 2-1

for *d* is set opposite that for *c* on the fixed scale, and the 1 on the sliding scale points to a scale location on the fixed scale whose distance from 1 on the latter is log *c* — log *d,* or log *c/d,* so the result indicated is *c/d.*

This is the basis of the common form of slide rule. Other scales are used to enable the rule to be used for more advanced mathematical calculations, but the principle remains the same. Every calculation is reduced to a form of addition and subtraction.

Characteristics

The logarithmic scale is probably the most widely used, partly because it is repetitive, each decade (as the range between 1 and 10 is called) being a repetition of each other decade; i.e., the scale of the numbers between 1 and 10 is identical to that used for those between 10 and 100, or between 100 and 1,000, or between 0.1 and 1; and partly because multiplication and division are probably the commonest forms of mathematical calculation.

Because the logarithmic scale is repetitive, the end points may be used interchangeably. For example, if we have to multiply 3.5 by 4.5 (whatever the positions of the decimal point), we put the 1 on the sliding scale opposite 3.5 on the fixed scale and find that 4.5 on the sliding scale is beyond the top (right end) of the fixed scale. So we reverse our procedure. We put 10 of the sliding scale (on many rules this is also marked 1) opposite 3.5 on the fixed scale and read the product to the left on the fixed scale. This is opposite 4.5 on the sliding scale, which is 1.575, representing 15.75, if our original numbers had the place significance as written, because we have changed ends.

Some of the earlier slide rules were equipped with a little counter, usually mounted on the cursor, which carries the hairline, to represent the logarithm's characteristic. These were to be added and subtracted, according to whether the operation was multiplication or division and an extra 1 would be added or subtracted every time a transfer was made from end to end. If the transfer was from right to left, as in the example just described, 1 would be added; if the transfer was the opposite way, from left to right, 1 would be subtracted from the counter's indication.

Few users of slide rules bothered to keep the counter working for every calculation and most preferred to keep the decimal point "in their heads," so the device went into disuse and was discontinued on later slide rules.

Circular Rules

Reversal of rule position, however, when a product or quotient "goes over the end," can be time wasting, and even exasperating. A rule construction that avoids this is the circular slide rule (Fig. 2-1C). Also, such a construction produces a calculator that is the same size as the linear slide rule (comparing linear slide rule length with circular slide rule diameter) and has a more than threefold expansion of the straight rule's scale, with an attendant increase in precision.

In the circular slide rule, an angle is used as the logarithm base instead of a linear dimension. In Fig. 2-1C, 360° corresponds to the base 10, so log 2 is 0.30103 times 360°, or about 108°. The 1 on the scale is the zero angle reference. The illustration shows the addition of scale angles representing log a and log b, to give the angle representing log ab. If a product goes over 10 or 100, as the case may be, representing 360°, the scale continues around the circle a "second time" and there is no break, as there is on the linear type. It is as if the two ends of a linear rule had been bent round and brought together.

Although a circular slide rule has these advanatges, it is more bulky than the linear rule, which remains the more popular type for most purposes.

Special Scales

There is no limit to the kind of scales that can be put on a slide-rule form calculator. As well as the log and linear, more familiar on conventional rules, special scales have particular use in graphical calculators. We show the two most used here.

The square-law scale (Fig 2-1D) is useful for vector resolution. Distances along the scales are measured in terms of the square of the scale marking quantities. Thus the distance identified as a by the scale marking is really proportional to a^2. So the total distance resulting from graphical adding performed by the rule, as in Fig. 2-1D, is proportional to the sum of the squares, $a^2 + b^2$, but is identified by the square root of this quantity, which is the magnitude resulting from adding these two vectors in quadrature. The process can be reversed, as it is in addition and subtraction, multiplication and division, and is shown on the bottom part of Fig. 2-1D.

The other useful scale is the reciprocal scale (Fig. 2-1E). Here the zero reference point represents infinity, instead of zero (linear scale) or 1 (logarithmic scale). We have put the infinity point at the right end of the rule to enable the scales to be read from left to right in the conventional way, instead of reading "downwards," which is the natural form for this presentation.

Remember that here we are reversing the dimensional addition (from right to left, instead of left to right), but it is still addition. The sum of quantities marked on the scale as a and b is a quantity whose reciprocal is $1/a + 1/b$. This operation can be reversed as the others have been. In electrical and electronic work such a presentation finds useful application in finding equivalent values of parallel resistances and series capacitances.

Besides these more common special scales, there is an almost infinite variety of possibilities, of which Fig. 2-2 illustrates a representative range. In Fig. 2-2A two decades of logarithmic scale are shown for comparison with the other special scales, five of which use the same value range for x, which is the root variable in the calculation concerned. In Fig. 2-2B the function expressed logarithmically is $(1 + x^2)$, in part C it is $(2x + x^2)$, and so on, as noted under each scale in the figure. Note that parts E and F use functions that reach a minimum value when $x = 1$, so a double scale is needed: one part for values less than 1 and the other for values greater than 1. In a corresponding nomogram presentation, two sides of the same reference line could be used.

For part B the function is always greater than 1, so the zero reference is off the left end of the scale. For part C the function extends both below and above the zero reference. For part D the function is always less than 1, so the zero reference is off the right end of the scale. For part E and part F the function is always greater than 1, and for values of x less than 1, the function decreases as x increases, so the zero reference has been put off the right end. This was an arbitrary placement; for some applications the reverse would be more appropriate or logical.

The zero reference is marked opposite to the scale side of the line so it will be trimmed off when the scale is cut out for application to a rule. It is essential in construction, but is not needed in use of the rule. In constructing the scale, all measurements are taken from the zero reference point (to be described more fully in the nomogram chapter) and the reference point is aligned in relation to other scales on the same movable part so that the final result is correct, incorporating any constants relevant to the calculation.

The three remaining scales, parts G, H, and I of Fig. 2-2, are based on functions where the root variable x has a minimum or starting value of 1, so the lowest value shown is 1.1, rather than the 0.1 of the other scales. The functions of G and I have maximum values of 1, putting the zero reference at the right end, while the function of H goes past the zero reference.

A careful study of the scales shown in Fig. 2-2 will show how use of different functions of the root variable changes the distribution of the scale. In graphical presentations (charts), such changes in scale may be used to effect better distribution of chart area, but for slide-rule design, the adoption of these scales is invariably dictated by the relationship of the root variable to the calculation involving it. For example, the last three functions might be the attenuation constants handled in Fig. 3-5, merely by using K instead of x. In the other functions, x could be a derivative of normalized frequency, or serve a host of other purposes. Scale (C) could

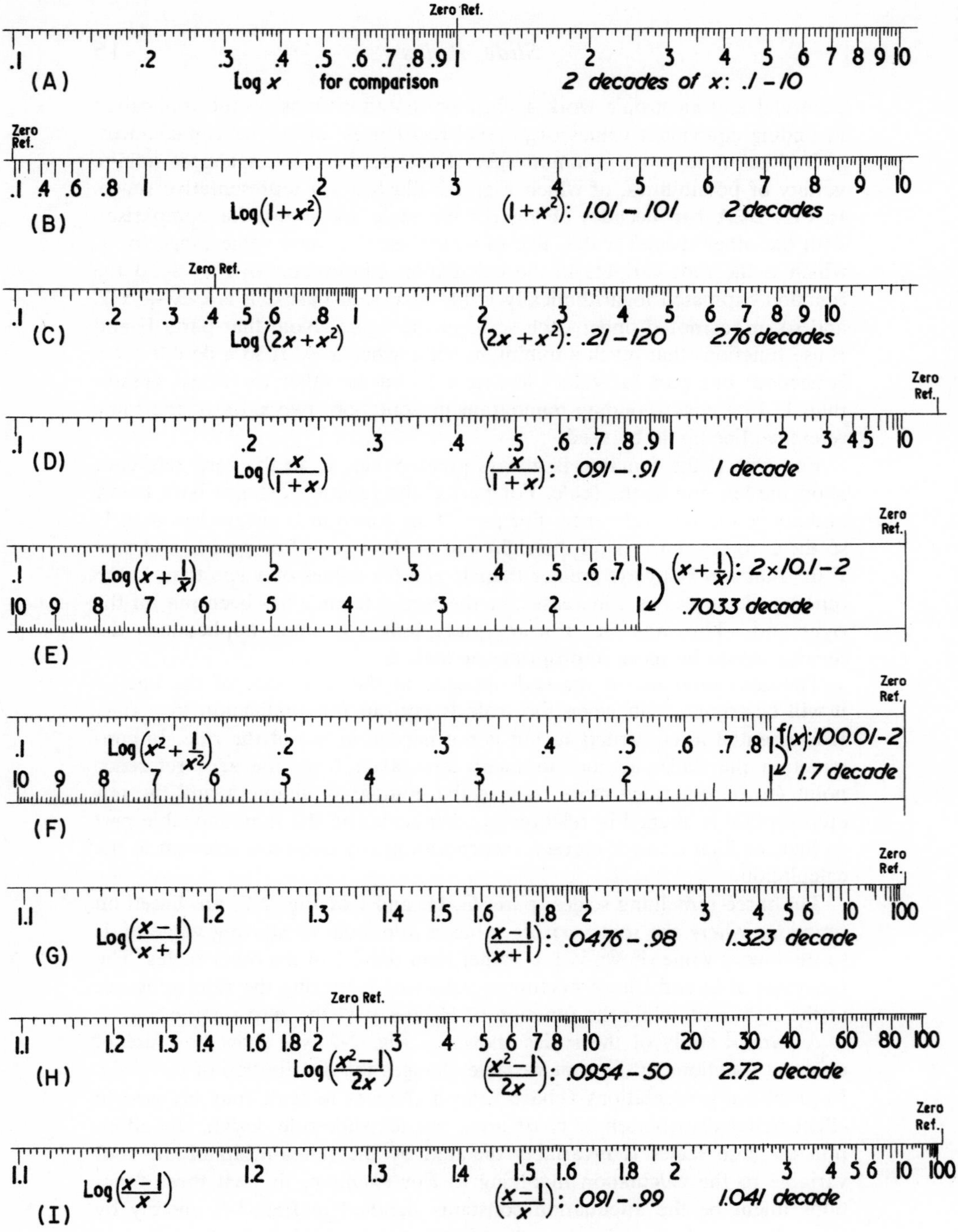

Zero Ref.

.1   (A)   .2   .3 .4 .5 .6 .7 .8 .9 1   2   3   4 5 6 7 8 9 10

Log x for comparison   *2 decades of x: .1 – 10*

Zero
Ref.

.1 .4 .6 .8 1   (B)   2   3   4   5   6   7   8   9   10

Log$(1+x^2)$ $(1+x^2)$: *1.01 – 101   2 decades*

Zero Ref.

.1   (C)   .2   .3 .4 .5 .6 .8 1   2   3   4 5 6 7 8 9 10

Log$(2x+x^2)$ $(2x+x^2)$: *.21 – 120   2.76 decades*

Zero
Ref.

.1   (D)   .2   .3   .4 .5 .6 .7 .8 .9 1   2   3 4 5   10

Log$\left(\dfrac{x}{1+x}\right)$ $\left(\dfrac{x}{1+x}\right)$: *.091 – .91   1 decade*

Zero
Ref.

.1   Log$\left(x+\dfrac{1}{x}\right)$ .2   .3   .4   .5 .6 .7 1 $\left(x+\dfrac{1}{x}\right)$: *2 × 10.1 – 2*
10 9 8 7 6   5   4   3   2   1   *.7033 decade*

(E)

Zero
Ref.

.1   Log$\left(x^2+\dfrac{1}{x^2}\right)$ .2   .3   .4   .5   .6 .7 .8 1 $f(x)$:*100.01 – 2*
10 9 8 7 6   5   4   3   2   *1.7 decade*

(F)

Zero
Ref.

1.1   Log$\left(\dfrac{x-1}{x+1}\right)$ 1.2   1.3   1.4   1.5   1.6   1.8 2   3   4 5 6   10   100

$\left(\dfrac{x-1}{x+1}\right)$: *.0476 – .98   1.323 decade*

(G)

Zero Ref.

1.1   1.2   1.3 1.4   1.6 1.8 2   3   4   5 6 7 8 10   20   30 40   60 80 100

Log$\left(\dfrac{x^2-1}{2x}\right)$ $\left(\dfrac{x^2-1}{2x}\right)$: *.0954 – 50   2.72 decade*

(H)

Zero
Ref.

1.1   Log$\left(\dfrac{x-1}{x}\right)$ 1.2   1.3   1.4   1.5 1.6 1.8 2   3   4 5 6 10   100

$\left(\dfrac{x-1}{x}\right)$: *.091 – .99   1.041 decade*

(I)

Fig. 2-2

be used for complete prediction of cases conforming to the lower part of Fig. 4-3C, or represented by values of *e* that are negative in expression (10) of Fig. 1-2. If used for this application, note that normalized frequency is *x* in equation (13) of Fig. 1-2 (where the minus sign changes to plus, with negative values of e), while in the formula of Fig. 2-2C, *x* represents normalized frequency squared.

In the relation between Fig. 2-2E and F, note that a function of $(x^2 + 1/x^2 + 2)$ would yield a scale identical with part E, the only difference in construction being that a different base is used for the logs (a different reference scale length). It should be obvious in such a case that simplification in construction will result from using the function shown in part E with the log base revised to twice the length to incorporate squaring of the function into the calculation.

More Elaborate Slide-Rule Use

Before going into features of special slide-rule calculators designed for a specific job, it will be helpful to direct a little study to some ways of using the conventional slide rule in its various forms. This diversion will serve a double purpose: short-cut methods can sometimes be applied in special slide-rule design and sometimes be useful in making necessary calculations quickly and more accurately.

The usual slide-rule instruction manual shows how to multiply and divide, from which multiplication and division can be performed as consecutive operations. One may find, or a book that gives short-cut tips may tell, how to save a movement by combining such operations into divide and multiply, in that order. For example, in Fig. 2-3A, if quantity *a* has to be multiplied by *b* and divided by *c,* the procedure is as follows: set *c* on the C scale against *a* on the D scale, to obtain the quotient on the D scale where the 1 of the C scale indicates. But this quantity is not required, so we do not read it, but proceed to read the product of this quantity multiplied by *b,* by looking on scale D opposite where *b* appears on scale C, for which we may relocate the cursor hairline. With this shortcut a movement has been saved, eliminating one possibility of error, as well as making the operation quicker.

If the slide rule possesses a reciprocal scale, the same method can be applied for successive multiplication (Fig. 2-3B). Setting the reciprocal of *b* on the C scale (found directly, with the aid of the hairline, on the CI scale) opposite *a* on the D scale (using the same position of the hairline), the C scale 1 indicates the product on the D scale. We complete the second multiplication by reading off the threefold product opposite the C scale *c* on scale D.

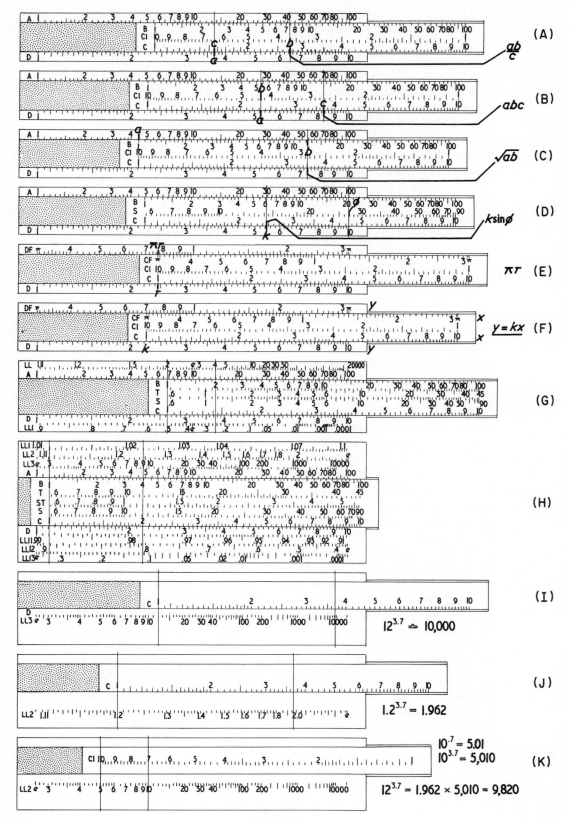

Fig. 2-3

The operation of multiplying to find a product and then extracting the square root of the product is another that would often take two settings of the rule, but can easily be simplified to one (Fig. 2-3C). Set the B scale 1 against *a* on the A scale and slide the cursor hairline to *b* on the B scale. Read off the square root of the product at the hairline on the D scale. It is important here to take care that the correct points on the A and B scales are used, taking account of decimal place in the *a* and *b* quantities:

If the quantity has an odd number of figures to the left of the decimal point, use the left half of the A or B scale.

If the quantity has an even number of figures to the left of the decimal point, use the right half of the A or B scale.

If the quantity is a fractional decimal, and the number of ciphers to the right of the decimal is zero or an even number, use the right half of the A or B scale.

If the number of ciphers to the right of the decimal is odd, use the left half of the A or B scale.

These are normal precautions to take any time a slide rule is used to find square root. Where it is used to find a product before extracting square root, the same precaution applies to the multiplier quantities in the product.

In the example shown in Fig. 2-3C the quantity *a* is about 4.5, or any quantity that is 10^{2n} times this, where *n* is any integer, positive or negative. The exponent is $2n$, because the operation is square root and an even number of places must be used to preserve the correct significant figures in the root. Similarly *b* is about 12.2, or any quantity so multiplied or divided by 10^{2n}. The result is 7.37, with the decimal point shifted according to factors (n) in the exponents of 10 used in the product terms.

A trigonometrical rule can be used with some economy, too. If the quantity $k \sin \phi$ is required, the slide rule may be set up as in Fig. 2-3D to do this in one step.

Another special feature on some rules is a "pi" scale on one face, where the normal A and B scales are on conventional rules. So the upper scales are the C and D scales, multiplied (or moved laterally) by the factor pi (a horizontal movement of log π). To calculate πr, the pi mark at one end of this scale is used instead of the usual 1 at scale end (C or D), with the aid of the hairline, to incorporate the factor pi (Fig. 2-2E). This operation can be combined to save a movement in successive multiplications, or multiplications and divisions.

Where only one such calculation, of any of these types, is involved, it may not be worth taking the time to deduce how to effect such savings. They are mentioned here because preparation of data for drawing scales for special purpose slide rules and other forms of calculator often demands the same form of calculation to be repeated a great number of times, once for each mark on a scale. As well as expediting the calculation, after taking a little time at the beginning to work out the shortest way to do it, the more direct method will produce more accurate results.

Another use of the pi scale, for which it is not specifically intended, virtually extends the conventional C and D scales without the loss of accuracy that would occur by using the A and B scales of a conventional rule instead. This is illustrated in Fig. 2-3F: a succession of quantities x has to be multiplied by a constant k to find corresponding values of a quantity y. By setting the 1 on the C scale against k on the D scale, values between x = 1 and the value of x opposite the 10 on the D scale can use the C and D scales. Above this, to complete the decade, the CF and DF scales are used, without shifting the rule setting. If this evaluation happens to be a stage of calculation, using values that move around the decade a number of times in the sequence, this method can represent a considerable saving of effort and time, as well as yielding much more consistent accuracy of result.

It is pertinent here to discuss a question not often covered in slide-rule manuals or textbooks in regard to log-log and trig scales. The manual originally issued with the rule undoubtedly explained in detail how to use the rule, but the book may not be handy, or the rule may be unfamiliar. The question is how to find which scales of the rule the trig and log scales are to be used with.

Figure 2-3G shows a rule in which both these scales are used in conjunction with the A or B scale. By setting the 1 of the B scale opposite a "round" number, such as 2, on the log-log scale (with the aid of the hairline), the square of this number, 4, is found opposite 2 on the B scale, verifying that this is the appropriate scale with which the log-log scale is intended to be used. On the sine scale, look at 30 degrees. This will correspond with 5 (representing 0.5) on one scale. In this case it is the 50 of the B scale, again verifying that the sine scale is to be used with the A or B scale. Finally, for the tangent scale, the 30 degree angle is again the most convenient, for which the tangent is 0.577. This too is 57.7 on the B scale here.

Figure 2-3H shows a type of rule where the scale to be used with all these scales is the C (or D) scale. Setting the 1 of the C scale, in this case, opposite 3 on the log-log scale, with one hairline setting, the 2 of the C scale is opposite 9 (the square of 3) on the log-log scale. Referring to the sine scale, 30° corresponds with 5 on the C scale. Finally, 30° on the tangent scale corresponds to 5.77 (or 0.577) on the C scale.

Where the C and D scales are used with log-log and trig scales, the scales usually traverse the rule more than once, an arrangement different from the type that utilizes the A and B scales. There are three log-log scales (at the top) and three inverse (or reciprocal) log-log scales (at the bottom) of

Fig. 2-3H. When the log-log value runs off the end, it continues at the opposite end, counting a decimal shift of 1 in the C or D scale significance. In Fig. 2-3G, there is just one log-log and one reciprocal log-log scale.

In Fig. 2-3H, both the sine and tangent scales are extended a full extra decade of values (of the C and D scales) by a common sine/tangent scale, because below this point (an angle of 5.74°) sine and tangent have the same value, within the readable accuracy of the rule.

We have shown, in Fig. 2-3G and H, just two types: in one, all the log-log and trig scales use the A or B scale; in the other, they all use the C or D scale. In many slide rules, some use one and some use the other. For example, one of the author's slide rules had the log-log and tangent scales use the A or B scale, while the sine scale used the C or D scale. The only way, with a strange rule, is to check each scale, as you want to use it, to be sure which is the correct scale combination.

Log-log scales are useful for calculating non-integral exponents. Where both the root, or base, and its power are within an order of magnitude of unity—between 0.1 and 10—the scale yields a degree of accuracy commensurate with the rest of the rule. But at extreme values, the accuracy becomes more critical—mainly because a tiny change in base value, or in that of the exponent, can make a relatively large change in the result, which the rule correctly shows. However, if the base and exponent are both known precisely, the rule can be used in a manner to improve the accuracy possible. For example, suppose we require a precise value of $12^{3.7}$. Direct use of the log-log scale will show only that the result is close to 10,000 (Fig. 2-3I). This can be handled more accurately by breaking the base into two factors: 1.2 and 10. Raising 1.2 to the power 3.7 (Fig. 2-3J) gives 1.962. Raising 10 to the power 3.7 can be broken down again, because 10 to the power 3 is 1,000, so we merely need 10 to the power 0.7, which is 5.01 (Fig. 2-3K). So 10 to the power 3.7 is 5,010. Finally, 12 to the power 3.7 is the product of 1.962 and 5,010, or 9,820, an operation that can be performed on the C and D scales in the normal way. This is a much more accurate result than could be obtained directly as in Fig. 2-3I.

Special Slide-Rule Calculators

Most special slide-rule calculators are made by a relatively few companies who specialize in their design. This book will limit itself to a few illustrative examples. A simple calculator that utilizes the principle introduced in Fig. 2-3B is shown in Fig. 2-4A. It illustrates two useful features. As well as inverting the B scale, so a single setting completes the calculation, it incorporates scales that are not entirely decimal, to suit the particular usage with which it is associated.

The purpose of the rule is to calculate the "yardage" (cubic yards) of concrete needed to fill a certain volume. Starting with thickness, on scale A, which may represent thickness of a wall or of a floor, and which ranges from 1¾ inches to 16 feet, we multiply by height of wall or width of floor, on scale B, to get an area. Note that thickness runs in inches up to 36, at which point the scale switches to feet, subdividing in inches or multiples, rather than the usual decimal scale. The height/width scale is in feet throughout, covering the range from 1 to 100 feet, but at the lower denominations, which normally would be subdivided in decimals, it subdivides in 12 to represent inches.

The position of the sliding scale at this point in the calculation represents the area product. The remaining scales (C and D) proportionate a third dimension against total volume. The length scale (C) is similar to the height/width scale, except that it reads from left to right, instead of right to left, and extends down to 6 inches. The cubic yards scale, D, is subdivided down to ¼ cubic yards at the lower end, with ½ as the lowest gradation, as these are normally-used measures in the ready-mix concrete business.

If we regard feet as the basic dimensions used in the basic calculation for scales A, B, and C, the D scale has to incorporate a factor of 1/27 to convert cubic feet to cubic yards. This is simply done in constructing the slide rule by sliding the scale a distance of log 27 to the right, as compared with a simple multiplication rule.

Although the use of this rule is virtually foolproof, the following instructions, printed on its reverse side, give the user, who may be untrained in this kind of thing, confidence in using it:

Example:
*How many cubic yards of material in a wall 10" thick, 13' high,
and 50' long?*

Solution:
*Find 10" on scale A, place 13' on scale B directly below, then
on scale C find 50' and read answer, 20 cubic yards, on scale D.*

In the position we have set the rule in the figure, a corresponding alignment could represent a wall 20" thick by 10' high and 60' long, which would require 37 cubic yards of material.

Figure 2-4B is a sample of a common type of calculator, made in almost endless varieties by the specialists in the calculator business. Note the simplification in the calculation made possible by eliminating the need for indicators. There are five "input" quantities and a result, all accommodated with three parts that are mutually movable, with a single relative setting of the three parts.

Every rule of this type must have some sort of "bridge." Where there are only two elements, as in Fig. 2-1C (or in linear form, in Fig. 2-4A),

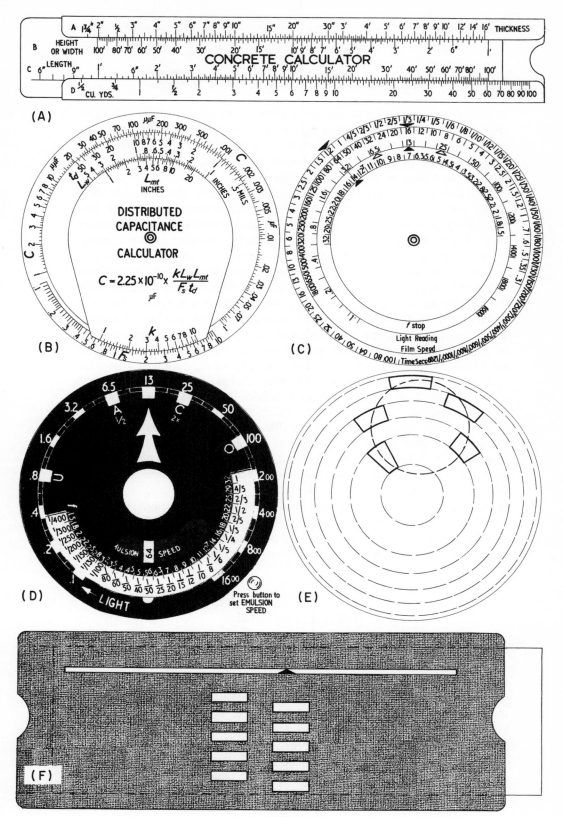

Fig. 2-4

which might be regarded as a fixed and a movable part, the only extra part that might be a convenience is a hairline cursor to aid in reading. But with more than two scale carriers, movable with respect to one another, each pair must present parallel edges. Hence the bridge, which in Fig. 2-4B enables the k scale to come alongside the F_s scale.

Calculations begin on this device by setting the respective values of k on the topmost piece and F_s on the lowest piece opposite one another and holding them together while we move the piece in between, which carries the t_d and L_w scales. Next we set the L_w value on the middle piece opposite the value of L_{mt} on the top piece, thereby carrying out all the combining of values, except the last. To complete the calculation, we read the resultant value of C against the given value of t_d. The empirical constant, given in the formula on the calculator, is incorporated in the positioning of the scale.

To construct this slide rule, a layout is chosen that enables a sequence logical to the calculation to be followed and avoids undue waste of angular "space" on scales. Here the ground, or largest piece, carries the longest total scale length: 5 decades of C and 2 decades of F_s, a total of 7 decades (all with the same base in this example). A base of 50° to the decade proves useful, being convenient to subdivide and also allowing two 5° marginal spaces.

Scale length allocated to each variable is primarily determined by the range encountered in the calculation for which it is used, or the range of "answers" that the input variables lead to. But scale length may to some extent be adjusted so the space required to accommodate them is convenient, as is done here.

Having devised the appropriate layout and checked rotational direction for each scale, these may be drawn on their respective pieces of the calculator in any order, provided the final pair (each part carries two scales) is aligned to incorporate the necessary constant correctly into the calculation.

Discrete Step Scales

Figure 2-4C shows the basic derivation of a well-known calculator—the exposure calculator on the Weston Master II exposure meter. In this case there are four variables, which could be catered for by a single movable scale carrier against a fixed one, with two scales on each. However, this would not be simple to read quickly, which is a requirement in photography. Here the same calculation uses three movable parts, excluding the cursor, which is necessary in this representation, but not in the final version.

The largest ring carries the time scale and the indicator for the film speed scale. The middle ring carries the film-speed scale and the light-reading scale. The inner ring carries the indicator for the light-reading scale and the *f*-stop scale. Setting each of these against the other will take care of all the calculation, except selecting an appropriate combination of *f* stop and time (shutter speed). This is achieved by means of the cursor, carrying indicators for these scales, which are the inner and outer ones in this presentation.

Notice that this calculator uses basically logarithmic units, although it is set out in the form of discrete steps for each quantity. The basic unit step is one tenth of a decade, and the circle is divided into 54 angles of 6⅔° each. In the scales for time, film speed, and light reading, ten steps result in a value of ten times, or one tenth of, any starting point. The numerals used may not always be precise, but are the values commonly used, or available, corresponding to this point on the scale. As only 2:1 intervals of light are identified on the meter, only every third step is identified to maintain the correct logarithmic interval on the light reading scale of the calculator.

The *f*-stop scale is different, because it has an exponent of 2 in the formula. Exposure is proportional to relative aperture diameter (which is what *f* stop measures, inversely) squared. So twenty *f* stop steps will lead to a value of one tenth, or ten times, within the accuracy of the numerals used. This is only a development to show the basic construction of the actual form used. This development of form would be difficult to use, especially in a hurry!

Figure 2-4D shows how this form physically embodies into the calculator. The intermediate scale carrier of Fig. 2-4C becomes the body of the instrument, or the fixed scale. The light readings are around the outside, in white numerals on black ground. On the same fixed body, printed concentrically underneath the other (moving) scales, is the film (emulsion) speed scale, which is viewed through a small window in the lower movable part and a larger one in the upper movable part. The window in the lower movable part allows only the indicated emulsion speed to be viewed.

Setting the emulsion speed need be done only once, when the camera is loaded, so the part that does this, the lower movable scale, is semi-fixed. It can only be moved by pressing the release clutch at lower right. This movable part carries the narrow window through which the emulsion speed is identified, and the time scale, in black figures on a white ground. The latter are in a circle immediately inside the light-reading scale, on its inside edge, to be close to the *f*-stop scale. The two lower parts are thus locked together, according to emulsion speed setting, so the remaining variables are light reading, *f* stop, and shutter speed.

The top scale, which is readily movable, carries a large arrow and some subsidiary markings for use with the light scale. The large arrow is used for average subject and lighting conditions. A and C, three basic steps to either side, represent conditions where highlight or shade detail is more important, respectively. The extreme markers, U and O, stand for underexposure and overexposure, respectivly, thus indicating a range beyond which the results would very obviously suffer from those errors.

After setting this top scale relative to the outer, completely-fixed scale for the light reading obtained on the meter, the adjacent scales for *f* stop and shutter speed display a choice of combinations that will achieve the exposure calculated for the particular occasion. By being adjacent in this way, the need of a cursor for making the selection is eliminated. Thus, what started out as a calculation that looked as if it would always be confusing is reduced to a very simple operation.

These three examples (Figs. 2-4A, B, and C) represent the main factors that can appear in specially-constructed slide rules where more than two quantities enter the calculation to make the resultant. The number of moving parts varies, according to whether scales are aligned with one another or indicators are used against scales.

While it might seem an economy to eliminate indicators, on the score of simplifying the mechanics of calculating, there are contrary arguments. For the calculators of Figs. 2-4A and B, the simplification is justified. For the exposure calculator, the same elimination would necessitate remembering, and including in every setting, the emulsion speed. By using the indicator method, this setting can be "put in and forgotten" (until the film is changed, at any rate), simplifying the rest of the job. It also allows for multiple indicators for the light scale to provide some variation for subject matter and lighting, thus enabling these additional quantities to be catered to.

"Fact Finder" Scales

A great many "calculators" of the special type are not really calculators at all, in the true sense. And many that do use true calculator scales, performing a computation by logarithms, are not as involved as those we have taken as basic examples for the more involved types. Often they provide for a number of relatively simple calculations, each involving two quantities and a result, or at most three quantities and a result (as in the concrete calculator), which can be accommodated with a single moving element. These usually use a single moving element that is revealed through one or more windows in the fixed element.

Figures 2-4E and F illustrate examples of the "fact finder" type scale. The facts presented may be a number of simple, and sometimes independent, calculations, or they may be a number of related pieces of data about different models, materials, types, etc., in a product line. Independent calculations can use different windows on the same movable parts. For example, on a calculator issued by a tape recorder manufacturer, one group of windows selects operating instructions to suit the job on hand, while another unrelated group gives playing times for different spools of tape, according to tape thickness, spool size, and transverse speed. The arrangements shown in Figs. 2-4E and F are suited to fact finding applications.

The circular calculator (Fig. 2-4E) has five windows, each occupying a 20° angle, so that, assembled in a suitable fixed casing with windows where the heavy-line outlines are, 18 such five-reading groups of facts could be accommodated. The space here has been divided into concentric rings of equal area, so that each window can have approximately equal area. The positioning has been arranged in a circle (the heavy dashed lines indicate locating circumference) to maintain association, while allowing space for appropriate identifying matter on the fixed surroundings of the holes.

This is somewhat of an idealized case and will probably be modified in almost every instance. The amount of space needed per window will not be uniform and possibly will want changing in shape or disposition for some reason associated with the facts to be presented. The unit here merely shows the basic principle to be used in planning such a design.

Figure 2-4F shows one form a linear counterpart of this calculator could take. Here the long thin slot at the top allows an indicator on the slide to identify the required grouping to be selected along the fixed frame above (or below) it. This enabels a heterogeneous group to be simultaneously visible, thus avoiding searching. The derived facts then appear in a group of windows, staggered (in virtually any pattern, the one shown here is intended as a sample) to provide spacing on the frame for appropriate identification.

Construction here is a matter of carefully calculated "doodling." Sketches are made and carefully dimensioned until an arrangement is arrived at that accommodates the information neatly and lucidly and conveniently utilizes the space. Initial doodling may be rough, with dimensions roughed in and space calculated, but it is a good idea to construct an accurate scale drawing before starting on the actual device, to be sure you have not utilized the same piece of space twice somewhere!

Combination Types

Slide rules sometimes incorporate graphs into their presentation, for purposes that become clear from the application in question. It may be to represent a relationship not readily reducible to simple slide-rule form, or it may be to achieve a more visual presentation of the represented information.

In Fig. 2-5A, a circular graphical chart, whose derivation follows a similar form to that developed in Chapter 4, uses a slide as the "scale" for one pair of variables. This is a feedback calculator chart. For those familiar

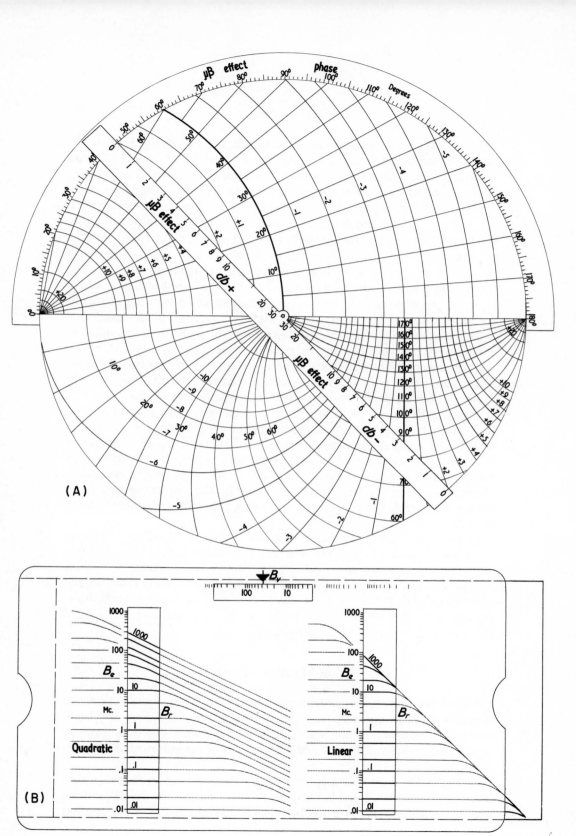

Fig. 2-5

with the subject, its basis is a derivation of the Nyquist diagram. The lower part in particular follows contours often drawn over a Nyquist diagram to give more information on overall performance.

Like the circular charts in Chapter 4, this one covers the entire range of values (from zero to infinity in absolute magnitude, although the scales are calibrated in db-logarithmic units) by transferring from the outer phase scale at a value of unity (zero db) to a point diametrically opposite. Here the outer phase scale, which is a normal angle calibration (linear), is used in conjunction with the radial markings on the rotatable arm, which uses a linear (lower half) or reciprocal (upper half) basic scale with logarithmic identification (in db). This represents a simple, vector resolution scale of the type which forms the ground for the right portion of Fig. 4-1E. The advantage of using the slide-rule method of displaying and applying this is that it avoids the need for a complete set of radial and concentric rulings on the chart, thus clarifying the presentation.

The ground of the chart, over which the slide moves, carries the other two scales, which are derived from the first in such a way as to present the rather complicated pattern developed, and which could not readily be reduced to any simple slide-rule presentation. We will not say it's impossible, because some mathematician would probably prove us wrong by doing it, but we do say it is not simple.

To derive the construction of this slide rule, we must start with the formula involved, as shown in Fig. 2-6. First note that, with the exception of a sign (which merely has the significance of direction in quantities that are complex, as here) the expression for *mu-beta* effect for which we have used the symbol *eta,* is reversible.

In Fig. 2-6A, one heavy line represents the numerator term *mu-beta* in magnitude and phase, while the other heavy line represents the denominator term. *Eta* is represented in magnitude by the *ratio* of these two sides and in phase by the angle at the apex of the triangle. In part B the reverse formula is represented. This is the form on which the slide rule is based. The heavy lines represent the numerator *eta* and the corresponding denominator term, in magnitude and phase, while *mu-beta* is represented in magnitude by the ratio of the two sides and in phase by the angle at the apex of the triangle. Because *eta* is represented by the scalar distance from the center and the angle at which this distance is measured, the movable arm can carry magnitude (converted to db) while a marker on the arm identifies angle on a peripheral scale (Fig. 2-5A).

Now, to construct the *mu-beta* scales. First (Fig. 2-6C), all points where the magnitude of *eta* and 1 minus *eta* are equal will result in *mu-beta* magnitude of 1. The locus of such points is a vertical line bisecting the distance between points 0 and 1. We have also drawn arcs to represent the loci for ratios between numerator and denominator to correspond with values of *mu-beta* magnitude of ½ and 2.

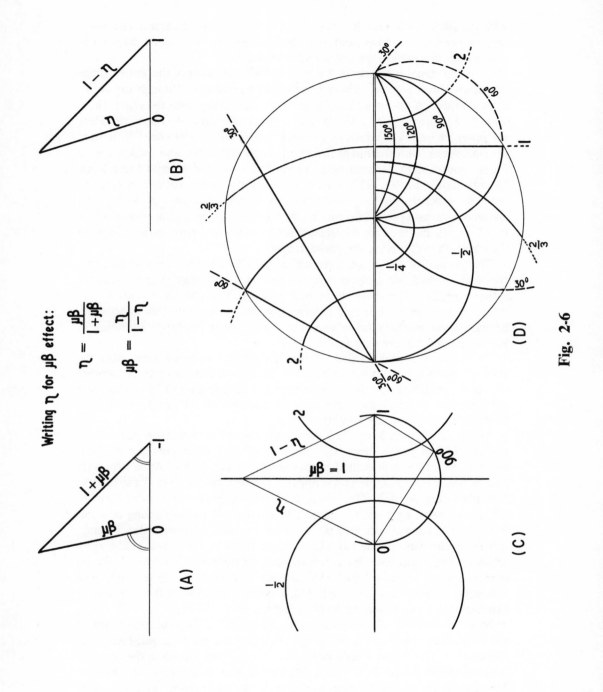

Writing η for $\mu\beta$ effect:

$$\eta = \frac{\mu\beta}{1+\mu\beta}$$

$$\mu\beta = \frac{\eta}{1-\eta}$$

Fig. 2-6

Scales for the angle of *mu-beta* are arcs passing through points 0 and 1, such that the angle in each arc is the phase value of *mu-beta* by which it is designated. We have drawn the semicircle for 90°.

As scales drawn on this basis would extend to infinity to contain all possible values and phases of *mu-beta* and *eta,* the device explained in reference to graphical charts in Fig. 4-1D-F is used. The lower half of our boundary circle (Fig. 2-6D) contains values of *eta* less than 1, while the upper half contains reciprocals of values greater than 1, extending the range to infinity within the same circle.

When magnitudes are converted to db (Fig. 2-5A) the scales on the sliding arm are identical, except for sign, the center representing zero (minus infinity db) when approached from the fractional side (minus db) and infinity (plus infinity db) when approached from the opposite direction.

When a scale marking leaves the lower semicircle (Fig. 2-6D) at its periphery, it enters the upper semicircle at a point diametrically opposite. Arcs for values of *mu-beta* magnitude less than ½ stay in the lower semicircle, as do arcs representing angles greater than 90°. Arcs for magnitude values greater than ½ and for angles less than 90° leave the lower semicircle and therefore appear as rulings of some kind in the upper one. To help establish identity at this transfer, we have used dotted lines for magnitude rulings and dashed lines for angle rulings where they pass outside either boundary. Because the straight line representing a *mu-beta* of 1 must extend to infinity (downwards), it must proceed to the center point (infinity) in the upper portion, after entering at a point diametrically opposite to where it leaves the lower part.

All the phase arcs pass through both the 0 and 1 point in the lower part. Therefore those for values less than 90° must pass through the 1 point at left extremity of the upper part, as well as a point diametrically opposite where they leave the lower part. Thus the radial and concentric pattern of rulings in the upper part is deduced and positioning of the scales established.

The other slide-rule/graphical presentation (Fig. 2-5B) uses the linear form. This undoubtedly could be reduced completely to slide-rule form, but the combination with graphical is considerably more visual. In fact, this presentation may be regarded as a facilitated means of reading a set of graphs. It relates relative bandwidths, receiver sensitivity, and noise for two types of detector (quadratic and linear). Setting video bandwidth in the long window at the top, where the indicator is on the fixed frame, corresponding values of equivalent bandwidth (on the frame) and radio bandwidth (in the window) can be read off, according to the detector type. To show the whole curves, as they might have been presented for graphical reading, we have made the frame "semi-transparent," so the complete movable slide is visible.

Chapter 3
NOMOGRAMS

In its simplest form the nomogram, or alignment chart, uses the same principles as those which form the basis for slide-rule construction and use. But instead of adding or subtracting lengths or angles by physical motion of parts of the calculator with respect to one another, all parts of the chart are fixed and the calculation is achieved by aligning points on the various scales by means of a straightedge.

The Parallel Scales Construction

The commonest form of alignment chart uses three parallel scales, uniformly spaced, and basically represents the addition $z = x + y$ (Fig. 3-1A), a fact derived from the simple geometry of the design. In this discussion and derivation of alignment charts, we shall use letter symbols to represent the quantities utilized in the calculation, here generalized as x, y, and z, while quantities with primes, in this case x', y', and z', represent the measured distances along the scales for these quantities that represent their physical values in the calculation. Thus, the quantities x', y', and z' are the physical distances measured from the zero reference intersecting all three scales to represent the values in a calculation $z = x + y$ (here the zero reference is shown at right angles to them, but this is not a necessary condition).

This equal-spaced arrangement is a special case of the more general parallel-line construction shown in Fig. 3-1B. Here we represent the spacing between lines by a and b, from which formulae are developed to give x', y', and z', so the calculation $z = x + y$ is still represented by the construction. Notice that substituting $a = b = 1$ into these formulae reduces them to the special case of Fig. 3-1A.

Mathematically, the matter of units should be explained. The quantities x, y, and z may have any dimension determined by the calculation they represent — linear dimensions, area, electrical or mechanical quantities, or

32

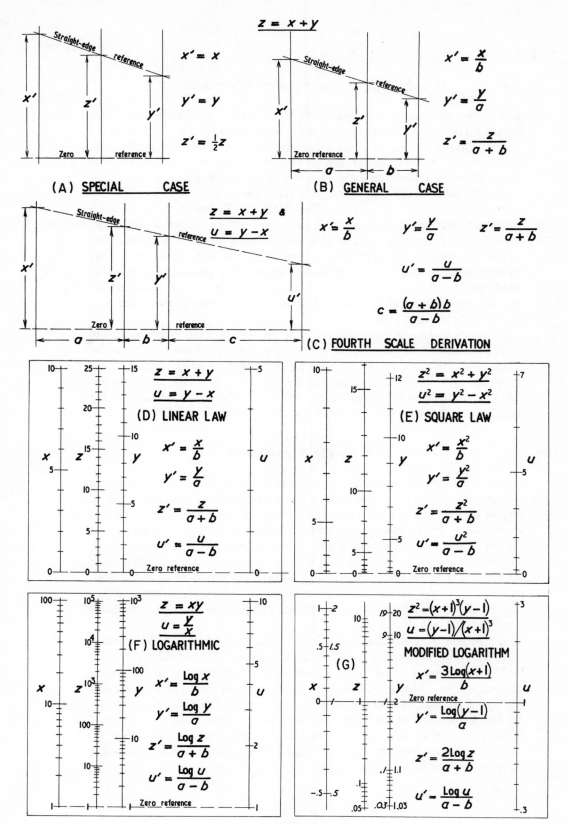

$$z = x + y$$

(A) SPECIAL CASE

$$x' = x$$
$$y' = y$$
$$z' = \tfrac{1}{2}z$$

(B) GENERAL CASE

$$x' = \frac{x}{b}$$
$$y' = \frac{y}{a}$$
$$z' = \frac{z}{a + b}$$

$$z = x + y \quad \& \quad u = y - x$$

$$x' = \frac{x}{b} \qquad y' = \frac{y}{a} \qquad z' = \frac{z}{a + b}$$

$$u' = \frac{u}{a - b}$$

$$c = \frac{(a + b)b}{a - b}$$

(C) FOURTH SCALE DERIVATION

$$z = x + y$$
$$u = y - x$$

(D) LINEAR LAW

$$x' = \frac{x}{b}$$
$$y' = \frac{y}{a}$$
$$z' = \frac{z}{a + b}$$
$$u' = \frac{u}{a - b}$$

$$z^2 = x^2 + y^2$$
$$u^2 = y^2 - x^2$$

(E) SQUARE LAW

$$x' = \frac{x^2}{b}$$
$$y' = \frac{y^2}{a}$$
$$z' = \frac{z^2}{a + b}$$
$$u' = \frac{u^2}{a - b}$$

$$z = xy$$
$$u = \frac{y}{x}$$

(F) LOGARITHMIC

$$x' = \frac{\log x}{b}$$
$$y' = \frac{\log y}{a}$$
$$z' = \frac{\log z}{a + b}$$
$$u' = \frac{\log u}{a - b}$$

$$z^2 = (x + 1)^3 (y - 1)$$
$$u = (y - 1)/(x + 1)^3$$

MODIFIED LOGARITHM

(G)

$$x' = \frac{3 \log(x + 1)}{b}$$
$$y' = \frac{\log(y - 1)}{a}$$
$$z' = \frac{2 \log z}{a + b}$$
$$u' = \frac{\log u}{a - b}$$

Fig. 3-1

just apples and pears. The quantities x', y', and z' are linear dimensions measured off in the construction of the nomogram, all to the same scale (in inches, quarter inches, or some other fixed unit of linear dimension). As measured horizontally under Fig. 3-1B, the quantities a and b are also linear dimensions, and are measured in a consistent unit that is not necessarily the same as that for the vertical scale measures.

In the formulae at the right of Fig. 3-1B, the factors a, b, and $a + b$ relate the calculation quantities x, y, and z to the chart measurements x', y', and z' that represent them. So at this point a and b do not strictly represent linear dimensions, but involve conversion units as well. What this really means is that, except in the equation representing the calculation being made (in this case, $z = x + y$), the equals sign is not strictly used within its mathematical meaning. Rather, it stands for a system of consistent proportionality within a group.

In short, to satisfy mathematical rigor the equals signs between x' and x/b, etc., should be interpreted as meaning that the dimension x', in its units, bears the same relationship to the quantity x, in whatever are its appropriate units, divided by dimension b in its units, as do the similar quantities represented in the other "equations." With this understanding of the significance of equations as we shall use them, we can proceed.

Four-Scale Nomograms

An advantage of nomogram constructions other than the equal-spaced special case is that they lend themselves to derivation of a fourth scale, as shown in Fig. 3-1C. This represents a dual calculation, $z = x + y$ and $u = y - x$. From these requirements, a value of spacing, c, is derived as shown in terms of the starting-point spacing a and b, as is a formula for u' in terms of u and the initial spacing dimensions. Notice that making $a = b$, which results in the special case, would make the values of u' and c both infinity: the hypothetical scale is infinitely expanded (represented by u'/u) and at infinite distance, represented by c. This infinite distance can be regarded as either to left or right.

If b should be larger than a, the fourth scale would be to the left, instead of to the right. This would be shown by a resulting negative value for c.

The remaining parts of Fig. 3-1 show simple derivations from the simple four-scale chart. Figure 3-1D shows actual scales for the basic formula in a particular spacing, in which a, b, and c are in the ratio 3:2:10. Notice the relative expansions of the scales. Figure 3-1E uses the same proportionate spacing applied to a square-law chart, instead of simple linear. Here the vertical ordinates are functions of the quantities squared, which enables the chart to be used to represent the two formulae shown at the top.

In these figures, the chart's zero reference line has represented zero in each of the formula quantities. The zero reference does not have to be drawn as a line, but it is important that the zero points on each scale should be aligned — in a straight line — though not necessarily in a line at right angles to the scales. Figure 3-1F shows a much more common form for this chart, where the quantities x', y', z', and u' are logarithmic functions of the calculator quantities to which they correspond. Note that in this construction, the zero reference is an alignment of the points where the *logarithm* of each quantity is zero, which means the scale markings will not be zero, but 1.

Sometimes a chart is required to incorporate more than simple multiplication or division. Numerical factors can be included by simple modification of the zero reference. For example, if the formula for the calculation is $z = kxy,$ the value on the z scale to align with $x = 1$, $y = 1$ should be $z = k$. This adaptation requires only a simple alignment during construction. The ratio of scale expansion is not changed, the z scale is merely shifted vertically to incorporate the constant factor k.

Modified Variables

Figure 3-1G shows a case where slightly more complicated modification of the variables is incorporated into the chart. First note that the zero reference is not at the bottom of the chart, as it was on the other three examples. As we shall see later, it need not be normal to the scales, but we have shown it so here for convenience.

The exponents of the various functions are represented by changing the scale expansion for these variables to incorporate them. First, the scales are to represent functions of the variables $(x + 1)$, $(y - 1)$, z, and u, which means the points to represent $(x + 1) = 1$ and $(y - 1) = 1$ will be marked 0 and 2, respectively, and, although these points are on the chart's zero reference, other points on the scales will be similarly changed. The italicized numerals on the opposite side of the x and y scales indicate the point on the decade used for that point on the scale.

Next, in the basic chart of Fig. 3-1F, from which this is a derivation, there are 2 decades of $x,$ 5 decades of $z,$ 3 decades of $y,$ and 1 decade of u. Staying with 1 decade of u and 3 of $(y - 1)$, because these have the same exponent, we go to two-thirds of a decade of $(x + 1)$ instead of 2, and 2.5 decades of z instead of 5. All scales terminate with a convenient reference number in the quantity the scale represents. As change of exponents and the shift of effective zero reference changes what may be regarded as convenient numbers in a quantity, the scale lengths do not appear to be in precisely the relationship just outlined; but in basic decade lengths they are.

For negative values of x, the usual decade markings are used, and the numerals changed by subtracting the normal (positive) number on the log scale, which is fractional in this range, from unity. On the positive side, the scale requires slight modification. The point marked 1 is at log 2 and so on. If the scale extended up a decade or two, the point marked 10 would be at log 11, the point 20 at log 21, and so on all the way up, gradually converging toward the true log scale. The difference would be very small when the point 1000 would be at log 1001.

On the y scale, the process is reversed: the mark 10 appears at log 9 and so on, while 1 is added to the normal log markings for values below the zero reference, which here is marked 2.

Ratio Scales

Here we come to the first usage of the nomogram construction that gets away from the basic addition and subtraction principle on which slide rules and simple parallel-scale nomograms are based. By inverting one of the scales for the basic variables in a parallel-line nomogram so that the zero reference is at opposite ends of the two scales, the point where the straight-edge alignment of the scale values intersects the zero reference line can be used, with an appropriate scale, as a reference which is a function of the ratio between the variables, or the function of the variables (such as arctan) that is used to plot the chart.

In Fig. 3-2A we treat the special case first (the u and z scales have been omitted for clarity). We give the intercept on the zero reference in terms of the distance r' as a fraction of the basic spacing, a. The appropriate function is shown to represent the ratio r between the independent variables x and y. The quantity u (as used in Fig. 3-1) could be plotted on a scale midway between the x and y scales, but the z scale in this case would be infinitely removed to the left or right. Such is the case where the denominator of the expression for c in Fig. 3-1C becomes zero. However, in this special case, the value of z is a function of the angle of the straightedge reference, as shown here. The fact that the z scale would be infinitely removed is shown by the substitution (into the general formula developed at the right of Fig. 3-2A) $b = \infty$.

For the general case, we place the z scale at a finite distance, shown here to the right, and use different factors (scale expansions) for the x and y scales to suit, as derived in Fig. 3-1, except that here the z scale is "outside," because the y scale has been inverted. Now we can arrive at a solution for z' on the z scale and a modified formula for r'. Note that, although r' is measured normal to the basic (x and y) scales using the spacing a as a magnitude reference, as indicated by the factor a in the numerator of the expression for r', it can equally well be measured as a corresponding magni-

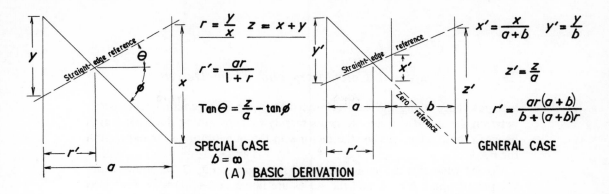

$$r = \frac{y}{x} \qquad z = x + y$$

$$r' = \frac{ar}{1+r}$$

$$\tan\Theta = \frac{z}{a} - \tan\phi$$

SPECIAL CASE
$b = \infty$

$$x' = \frac{x}{a+b} \qquad y' = \frac{y}{b}$$

$$z' = \frac{z}{a}$$

$$r' = \frac{ar(a+b)}{b+(a+b)r}$$

GENERAL CASE

(A) **BASIC DERIVATION**

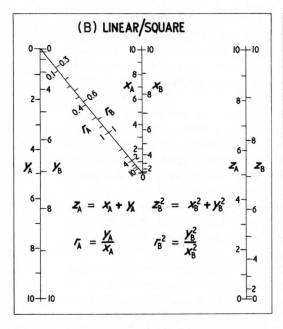

(B) **LINEAR/SQUARE**

$$z_A = x_A + y_A \qquad z_B^2 = x_B^2 + y_B^2$$

$$r_A = \frac{y_A}{x_A} \qquad r_B^2 = \frac{y_B^2}{x_B^2}$$

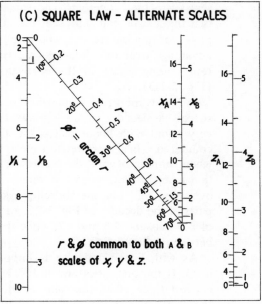

(C) **SQUARE LAW - ALTERNATE SCALES**

$\phi = \arctan r$

r & ϕ common to both A & B scales of x, y & z.

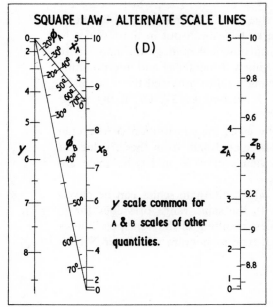

SQUARE LAW - ALTERNATE SCALE LINES

(D)

y scale common for A & B scales of other quantities.

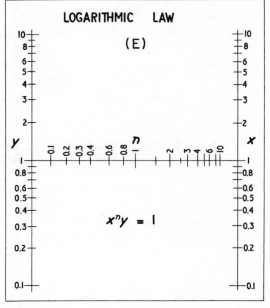

LOGARITHMIC LAW

(E)

$$x^n y = 1$$

Fig. 3-2

tude reference along the zero reference line (where the actual scale goes) between the x and y scale intercepts merely by substituting the scale length between these intercepts for the factor a in the numerator of the expression for r'.

To see what this means in an actual nomogram, Fig. 3-2B shows a development where $b = a$, and the scales are linear and square-law functions of their respective variables. The corresponding subscripts identify which scales are used together. The square-law function has the particular use that the z scale can represent the magnitude and the r scale a function of phase, of quadrature (y), and in-phase (x) component vectors. This is an advantage over the slide-rule presentation, which makes no provision for representing phase in the corresponding vector addition and resolution (Fig. 2-1D).

A disadvantage of square-law scales is that they are not repetitive for successive decades as are log-law scales. In fact, their scale distribution is very poor. With linear scales, the chief disadvantages are likely to be encountered when working too close to zero, where significance is lost, or when running beyond the highest value. With square-law scales this condition is aggravated, even low values in a decade range lose significance. To overcome this, one method employs alternate scales, working for different parts of the decade. In Fig. 3-2C, the A scales may be used where the value of z is between 5.5 and 17, while the B scales may be used for values of z between 1.7 and 5.5.

As with linear scales, it is important that all quantities use the same units. If the quantities are in 10's or 100's, or any other exponent of 10, convert them all to the same exponent of 10 as a unit. For example, in Fig. 3-2C, if x is 135 and y is 27, the value of x, being larger, determines which scale to use: 135 is represented by scale mark 13.5, which means the units, on the A scales, are 10's; the value $y = 27$ is represented by the A scale point 2.7. (Only major scale marks have been put in these scales to maintain simplicity of development; in a practical nomogram, many more will be used, as will be shown later.) Using a straightedge and interpolating, $r = 0.2$ (this is unaffected by units, being a ratio, provided the other units are correctly applied) and $z = 13.7$, representing 137. Or, if the phase angle is wanted, this is $11°$.

The angle scale is simply obtained by using the substitution $\phi = \arctan r$. To develop it, values of ϕ are first tabulated and, from these, values of $r = \tan \phi$ are derived, from which values of r' to make the scale are calculated.

Figure 3-2D shows another way in which alternate scales can be developed with this type of nomogram. With the same range of values for y, there are two possible ranges of x values, resulting in different possibilities for z. The A scales result in the normal type nomogram (the letter N configuration, as already developed), where *x, y,* and *z* scales all begin at zero. The B scales use a range of values for *x* such that *z* is always likely to be in the range from 8.7 to 10. A careful study of the configuration will show what combinations of values may be handled by each alternative and at what values the alignment straightedge will run off-scale for one of the magnitudes. This presentation may be one of several that cover the entire range of possible values, or the nature of the application may be such that those shown, or some like them, represent the entire *practical* range.

The same ratio-scale principle can be applied to logarithmic scales for the basic quantities when the ratio scale becomes a function for the exponent of one quantity, in this case *x*. Basically, this scale is a function of the exponent *ratio* between the two quantities. Note that in this case the product of the two quantities, raised to their respective exponents (the right-hand side of the formula equation) has to be 1, or whatever value of the respective quantities is used to terminate the zero reference line, which becomes the ratio scale. This can be any arbitrary constant, but it must be a specific constant for a nomogram once drawn, because this fixes where the ratio line is drawn in terms of its intercepts on the other scales.

Note that in this application the ratio scale intercepts the *x* and *y* scales at a point other than the scale ends. In linear developments, it would be possible to represent negative values of *x* and *y,* while in square-law scale developments, it would represent imaginary values. Such a continuation of the same scale (in this case curved) for real and imaginary values appears in Fig. 3-4.

Zero or Infinity Point for Zero Reference

Figures 3-3A and B show alternative ways of treating a calculation we have not so far considered. In Figure 3-3A is a development using a zero point as a common intercept for three linear scales, with the derivation, based on the formula $z = \dfrac{xy}{x + y}$, leading to scale identification. For this particular presentation, scales for *x* and *y* are direct, linear. But this form may be used with more complicated formulae that reduce to the same basic factors, just as the presentation in Fig. 3-3D is adapted for a more involved formula in Fig. 3-3E.

In the alternate treatment, the formula is rearranged to $1/z = 1/x + 1/y$. Here the basic variables are the reciprocals. The zero reference becomes infinity in the quantities *x, y,* and *z,* and the scales follow a reciprocal law. This treatment, being parallel scale, is the equivalent of the slide-rule presentation in Fig. 2-1E. In this presentation, alternate scales have again been used to improve the coverage accuracy. The rule that all values in a given calculation use the same scales (A *or* B) with the same units,

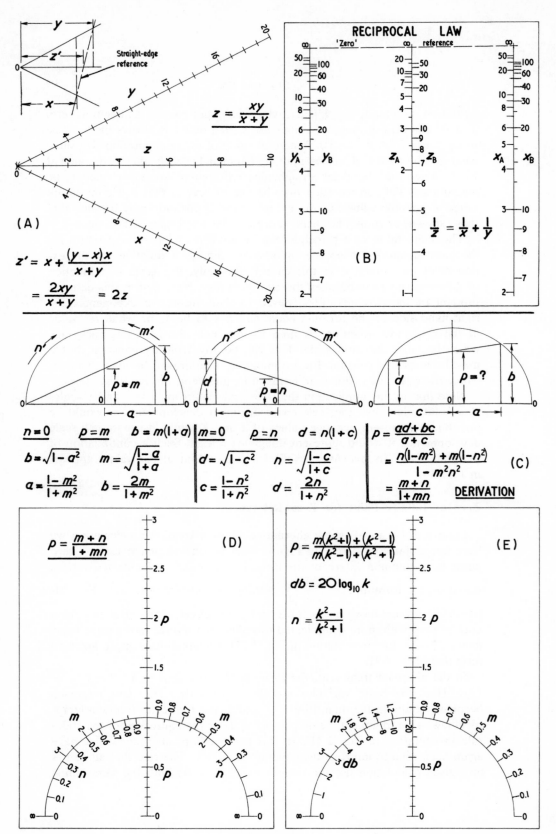

$$z = \frac{xy}{x+y}$$

(A)

$$z' = x + \frac{(y-x)x}{x+y}$$

$$= \frac{2xy}{x+y} = 2z$$

RECIPROCAL LAW

(B)

$$\frac{1}{z} = \frac{1}{x} + \frac{1}{y}$$

$$n = 0 \qquad p = m \qquad b = m(1+a)$$

$$b = \sqrt{1-a^2} \qquad m = \sqrt{\frac{1-a}{1+a}}$$

$$a = \frac{1-m^2}{1+m^2} \qquad b = \frac{2m}{1+m^2}$$

$$m = 0 \qquad p = n \qquad d = n(1+c)$$

$$d = \sqrt{1-c^2} \qquad n = \sqrt{\frac{1-c}{1+c}}$$

$$c = \frac{1-n^2}{1+n^2} \qquad d = \frac{2n}{1+n^2}$$

$$p = \frac{ad+bc}{a+c}$$

$$= \frac{n(1-m^2)+m(1-n^2)}{1-m^2 n^2}$$

$$= \frac{m+n}{1+mn}$$

(C)

DERIVATION

$$p = \frac{m+n}{1+mn}$$

(D)

$$p = \frac{m(k^2+1)+(k^2-1)}{m(k^2-1)+(k^2+1)}$$

$$db = 20 \log_{10} k$$

$$n = \frac{k^2-1}{k^2+1}$$

(E)

Fig. 3-3

discussed more fully with the square-law scale alternatives, applies here, also.

The Circular Scale

The lower part of Fig. 3-3 shows how use of the circular scale may be developed. In this case a zero reference is established along a diameter of the circle (which in this case becomes the lower boundary of the chart). An extended radius, normal to this diameter, becomes a linear reference scale for a quantity which we call p. In Fig. 3-3C, we show how to derive points along the semicircular circumference scale in two directions, for quantities we call m and n, in complementary fashion, so that when $n = 0$, $p = m$, and when $m = 0$, $p = n$. Putting the two together, with geometrical construction, we derive and simplify an expression for p in terms of m and n, as those scales have been derived.

Figure 3-3D shows the resulting chart for these basic quantities. However, these quantities may not be the ones actually required in the calculation. An example of a calculation that can use this form is the formula that gives the reflected impedance when an attenuator is incorrectly terminated. This formula appears at the top of Fig. 3-3E, where k is the attenuation factor, converted to db by taking $20 \log_{10} k$, and m is the ratio of the mismatch impedance to the design impedance of the attenuator, which may be less than or greater than 1. We have covered the range from $m = 0$ to $m = 3$ in detail, although $m = \infty$ is at the other zero reference point on the semicircular scale.

Making the substitution shown for n in terms of k reduces the rather complicated expression for p to its basic form. Thus, in the completed chart, p represents the ratio of the reflected impedance to the design value. This chart works for all two-way matched attenuators, but not for the single-way type.

Curved Scales

As an example of the method of developing a curved-scale nomogram, we consider the case of the calculation cost $(\alpha + j\beta) = p + jq$. Here, in Fig. 3-4A, we start by assuming we make two vertical scales represent linear quantities x and y, with the normal zero reference, where x and y are functions, respectively, of p and q. To resolve points on the curve, we make the construction shown, to give flexibility so the point can be anywhere it has to be, with ordinates u and z, defined as shown at the top right. The second and third lines of algebra use the geometry to eliminate the temporary reference point y' so a single equation relates x, y, z, and u in general terms.

Now, from basic mathematics, we derive expressions for p and q in terms of α and β, and equations eliminating first α and β in turn. From the latter it becomes evident that appropriate functions for u and z, in terms of α or β, will result from making x and y represent p^2 and q^2, respectively, to the same or different scales. If different scales are to be used, we would write $y = kq^2$ to reconcile the use of a different scale.

In this application, different parts of the same curve serve α and β, determined by transition from real (α) to imaginary (β) values. In some applications there may be overlap, in which case parts of the curve may have two significant values, one for each variable, as on the semicircular scale of Fig. 3-3E.

Making the substitutions developed in Fig. 3-4A leads to simple, or slightly more complicated expressions for z and u in terms of β or α. Figure 3-4B shows the uniform scale development, where values of p and q are taken from 0 to 1. Values of z are applied directly and substituted into the expression for u. For the part of the curve handling values of β, u is taken from the zero reference line at its intercept with the z ordinate for that point, as in the basic derivation (Fig. 3-4A). For the right-hand part, dealing with values of α, it is simpler to use a different reference line. By simple geometry, the distance between the new reference line (obtained by an alignment between $p = 1$ and $q = 0$ extended) and the actual zero reference is equal to z (or a simple function of it, where k is other than unity). Making these substututions, we find an expression for the new ordinate, u', used in plotting this part of the curve.

Values of β and α are tabulated in columns for points on the β part of the curve, with, successively, numerical values of $\sin^2\beta$ and z, by multiplying by the spacing between the p and q scales as unit dimension; finally the column of $\sin^2\beta$ figures is multiplied by values of $\cos^2\beta$ and by unit length on the p scale (which here is the same as the q scale) to arrive at values for dimension u. From the dimensioned columns for z and u points may be plotted and the curve drawn, using the points as markers for the scale.

Using the same dimensioning factors, values are found for z and u', in terms of $\sinh^2\alpha$ and $\sinh^4\alpha$, respectively, to plot points of the α portion of the curve. Here the unit reference for α is in nepers. The unit of β can be in either radians or degrees (we used the latter).

As with other constructions using square-law scales, the unevenness of the scales means alternate coverages are desirable. Figures 3-4C and D show two such partial coverages which are typical of the method used. In Fig. 3-4C, the zero point of the p scale is remote, a ratio of $k = 10$ is used, and the p and q scales are expanded as stated. This results in detail coverage of the range where p is between 0.95 and 1.05 and q is between 0 and 0.1. Figure 3-4D shows another expansion, in this case near zero on both p and q, between 0 and 0.32, this time keeping to $k = 1$. The derived

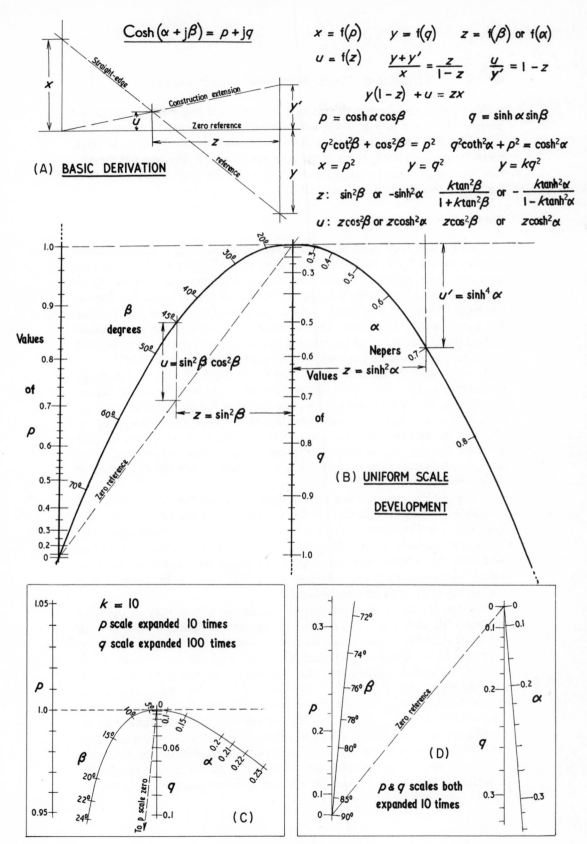

Fig. 3-4

scales look almost straight in this case, but they are really highly expanded parts of the curve in Fig. 3-4B, where it intercepts the p and q scales.

In Fig. 3-4C, the reference for the u ordinates is the $p = 1$, $q = 0$ alignment for both sections, because the zero reference quickly goes off the picture as it leaves the q scale zero. In Fig. 3-4D, the zero reference is used for both scales in deriving values of u.

Curves Not Bearing Scales

Another use sometimes made of curves in nomograms, but not recommended in this book, is illustrated in Fig. 3-5A-E. Here we have set ourselves the basic problem of covering attenuator design, the data for which appears in Fig. 3-5B. Fig. 3-5A shows the chart concept that has formed the basis of some design charts for this purpose. One way of constructing the curves would be to draw in a number of alignments for values of db (based on k) and R/Z for the specific element for which the curve is being made, and use these as tangents for the resulting curve (Fig. 3-5C).

A more accurate method of deriving the curve is shown in Fig. 3-5D. Ordinates on the curve are designated similarly to those for curve derivation in Fig. 3-4, but in this instance the fact that the straightedge used for alignment is to tangent the curve enables us to write two expressions relating to the point of contact: one in terms of the basic variables, and the other for the slope of the curve at this point. From these expressions, equations are derived for the ordinates u and z, which enable direct plotting of the curve.

Figure 3-5E shows a completed nomogram, using the latter method of construction. The second scale from the left (db) with the curves for the appropriate configuration derives values of R/Z_0 at the extreme right scale in the manner indicated in Fig. 3-5A. The extreme left scale (Z_0) is then used with the extreme right scale, using the points thus found, to calculate actual resistance values (scale slightly to right of center). In this presentation all scales (except db) are logarithmic.

Note the inversion of some scales, because the values vary in opposite manner with attenuation. The disadvantage of this construction, as with any chart applying curves in this fashion, is that at least one extra operation is involved. To illustrate, we treat the same problem by a more direct method in Fig. 3-5F. Here, only one alignment is necessary to obtain each required value. The "curves," or functions of K in the basic formula, are incorporated directly into the db scales (left), rather than by using the linear scales of Figs. 3-5A, C, and E. Values of K to correspond with db attenuation are most readily obtained from antilog tables, where each 05 of the antilog table represents 1 db. The ratios obtained from the table are substituted into the formulae for the various R values to obtain the factors by which Z_0 must be multiplied (or divided, in some cases, for convenience

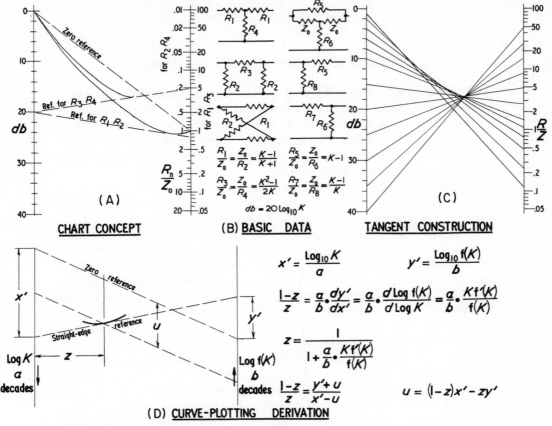

(A) **CHART CONCEPT**

(B) **BASIC DATA**

$$\frac{R_1}{Z_0} = \frac{Z_0}{R_2} = \frac{K-1}{K+1} \qquad \frac{R_5}{Z_0} = \frac{Z_0}{R_6} = K-1$$

$$\frac{R_3}{Z_0} = \frac{Z_0}{R_4} = \frac{K^2-1}{2K} \qquad \frac{R_7}{Z_0} = \frac{Z_0}{R_8} = \frac{K-1}{K}$$

$$db = 20 \, Log_{10} \, K$$

(C) **TANGENT CONSTRUCTION**

$$x' = \frac{Log_{10} \, K}{a} \qquad\qquad y' = \frac{Log_{10} \, f(K)}{b}$$

$$\frac{1-z}{z} = \frac{a}{b} \cdot \frac{dy'}{dx'} = \frac{a}{b} \cdot \frac{d \, Log \, f(K)}{d \, Log \, K} = \frac{a}{b} \cdot \frac{K f'(K)}{f(K)}$$

$$z = \frac{1}{1 + \frac{a}{b} \cdot \frac{K f'(K)}{f(K)}}$$

$$\frac{1-z}{z} = \frac{y' + u}{x' - u} \qquad\qquad u = (1-z)x' - zy'$$

(D) **CURVE-PLOTTING DERIVATION**

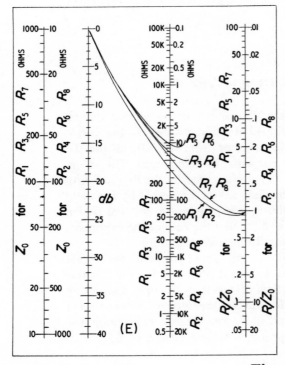

(E)

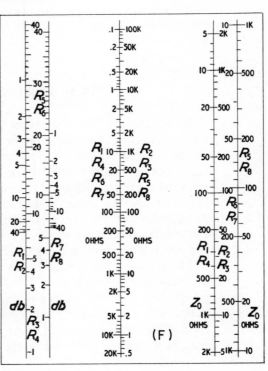

(F)

Fig. 3-5

to allow the same scale to be used for two circuit configurations). These factors are then converted to the logarithm, using the decade length required for the scale position and the zero reference point to measure from. In this case, the fact that slightly different ranges of resistance value are required for the different types of circuit has enabled us to "stagger" the scales to get separation between them.

If separation were arranged in a similar way using the equal-spaced nomogram construction, the outside scales (extreme left and right) would be used together for some circuits and the inside scales (second from left and right) would be used together for different sets of values. As we have drawn them, using asymmetrical spacing with a common central R scale, the extreme left db scales are used with the second from right Z_0 scales, and the second from left db scales are used with the extreme right Z_0 scales. Spacing is relative to the common center scale and the decade lengths used are adjusted to conform with the derivation on Fig. 3-1.

Equal spacing is used between the scales used for T, pi, and lattice networks (subscripts 1-4) so the decades on which the db and Z_0 scales are based are each twice the length of the R scale decades. For the bridged-T and L networks (subscripts 5-8), the spacing is 3:5, so the db scale is based on a decade length 1.6 times the R scale length, while the Z_0 scale is based on a decade length $2\frac{2}{3}$ times the R scale decade length.

As originally drawn (before reduction for reproduction), the scales, reading from left to right, used basic decades whose lengths were $2\frac{1}{2}''$, $2''$, $1\frac{1}{4}''$, $2\frac{1}{2}''$, and $3\frac{1}{3}''$.

Some Practical Design Aspects

In Fig. 3-6, we illustrate some practical aspects of nomogram design, using some charts the author has developed at different times. In Fig. 3-6A, the first, second, third, and fifth scales, reading from the left, all use the same unit or decade length, which is not usual in nomograms. This is because two extremes values of current (I), represented by the first and fifth scales, are used to derive design intermediate values, arrived at by exponent combinations of the extremes. The third scale provides a nominal design current, for which the formula is given. Note that the sum of the exponents is unity in both cases, which explains uniform scale expansion.

The reference line has no marks shown, but would correctly use a scale identical with the other three I scales; a scale is not provided for this reference line to avoid erroneous selection of result by reading the wrong scale. This second line is a reference for the denominator of the expression for L. The remaining scales, fourth and sixth, complete the calculation, using a regular three-scale nomogram approach, to give a value of L.

Figure 3-6B presents a similar use of exponents, with some different features. The formula is a simplification of an older method, made possible by using exponent type approximations, so that each quantity only appears once, instead of before and after application of an empirical relationship based on magnetizing force (IT/L_i), whose value is not directly required in the simplified method. The older method results in many more operations to the calculation, as well as the need for trial and error approach to any design. This direct approach, however, based on an approximation that is only valid within empirical limits (referred to IT/L_i), needs protection against misuse.

The first step in the use of this nomogram is conventional. An equally-spaced group, consisting of the right side of the extreme left reference line, the center scale, and the inner right scale, merely calculates IT from I and T, quite straightforwardly, except that the product scale is at the right instead of the center. This arrangement happens to suit this application, where T has a wider range than either I or the product, in the nature of the application. Now the left side of the left reference line, with the product scale and the extreme right scale, completes the calculation, involving the exponents 0.1, 0.9, and 1.0, in that order, left to right. The empirical constant of the formula must be included in the zero reference alignment that establishes relative position of the scales.

The decade length of the L_i scale is twice that of the IT scale (that is our arbitrary choice of relative scale) while the IT scale exponent uses nine times the L_i exponent. This means the space from the L_i scale to the L_g scale must be 18 times the spacing from the IT scale to the L_g scale, or that the spacing from the IT scale to the L_g scale is $1/17$ of that between the L_i and IT scales. Having decided this, we make a similar substitution to find the scale decade size for the L_g scale, which proves to be $20/17$ times the IT scale decade length. This is the only "odd" decade length involved, and can be set up on a slide rule with a $20/17$ ratio setting.

Now, to apply the working limits for the method, a vertical line is located which would be a reference for the quantity IT/L_i, if that quantity were used in the calculation. As the L_i scale uses twice the decade expansion of the IT scale, the position of an IT/L_i reference will divide the intervening space in a 2:1 ratio. Here we see the reason for choosing an L_i scale using greater decade length than the IT scale: to avoid having the IT/L_i location coincide with the T scale. It remains to put easily-visible markers at the extremities of this vertical reference, representing, by their vertical position, the limiting values.

Provided the second reference of the calculation (aligning L_i and IT, to find L_g) does not involve laying the straightedge so it crosses the marked areas, the method is valid. What is important, of course, is that the reference stay between the points of these areas, but marking them in this way makes the purpose clearer.

Figure 3-6C is for leakage inductance calculation, in which two physical demensions, t_w and t_d, are combined, after operating by different powers of a factor, N, that depends on sectional arrangement. This is achieved by the spacing layout between the scales for t_w, N, the integrating reference, and t_d, in that order, from left to right. Each of the first two reference lines (lowest dashed lines shown) results in the correct evaluation of the correspondingly identified parts of the formula, a and b. These are added numerically and the result re-entered at the point indicated as $a + b$, from which point, use of the chart follows straightforward, equal-spaced nomogram practice.

Apart from the special trick to get the right combination of a and b with only one N scale, thus avoiding ambiguity and possible error, this chart is typical of a many-scale variety. Every quantity has a separate reference line with its scale and the spacing is carefully figured out so that each operation uses the correct spacing, while allowing "comfortable" spacing between scales to enable them to be properly identified. In this connection, it will be realized that a full-size reproduction, instead of a greatly reduced one, as shown here for comparative purposes, will make the chart quite clear.

From the integrating reference scale through to the final L_s scale, each reference uses equal spacing reference lines, so outside scales all use the same decade lengths. So does the T scale, as it happens, because it uses an exponent of 2, as well as being a middle scale. For the t_w, N, and t_d scales, we work backwards from the integrating reference. The spacing for the t_w, N, and integrating reference group is 2:1, and the N scale in this operation uses an exponent of 2 (first expression, a, in the square brackets), so N^2 uses a decade ⅔ of the integrating reference decade, or N uses a decade 4/3 this length. The t_w scale uses a decade twice that of the integrating reference.

As for the t_d factor, the ratio of the N and integrating reference decade lengths has already been fixed at 4:3, so this is their relative distance from the t_d scale, or the spacing, in order, of N scale, integrating reference, and t_d scale, must be 1:3, and the t_d scale uses a decade 4 times that of the integrating reference. These are not the only possibilities, but were "juggled" to obtain a workable overall nomogram arrangement.

Figure 3-6D is a sample of an opposite kind from Fig. 3-6C where each reference line does at least double duty in the calculation. The calculation is basically a simple one (no unusual exponents), it just uses a lot of quantities. Starting from the L_i scale on the right of the left reference line (extra numbers spaced away from the scale) and the A_i scale on the left of the right reference line, a reference point is found on the center line. Next, from the t_L scale on the left of the left line, with this reference on the center line, a further reference point is found on the right reference line. This is used with the T scale on the center line to find a value of R_e on the right of the

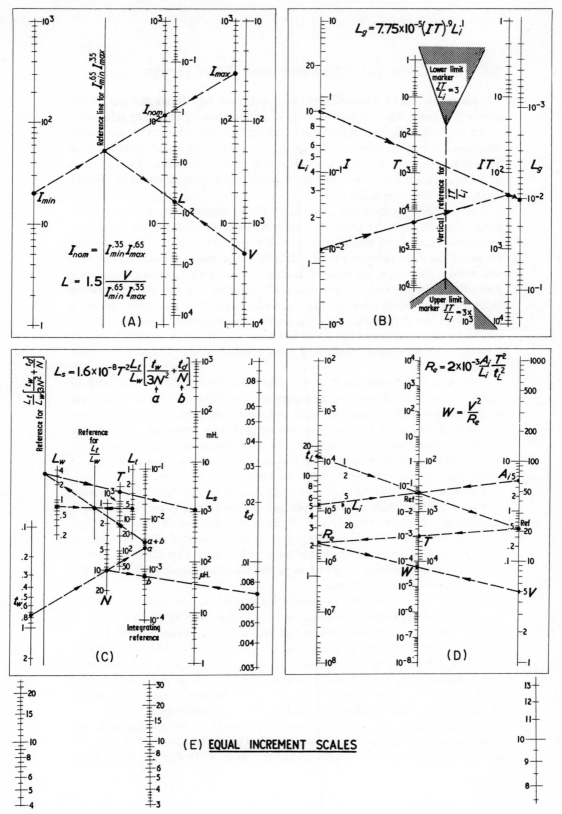

Fig. 3-6

left reference line. A further calculation will then find W on the left of the center line from this value of R_e and V on the right of the right reference.

An important feature in laying out any nomogram, whether of the multi-line type, as in Fig. 3-6C, or of this multiple-use type, is to make sure of correct zero reference follow through and of correct direction of application of successive variables. We will go over this last nomogram (Fig. 3-6D) again to see how this is done.

The quantity A_i increases upwards, with L_i downwards, as the latter is a denominator term, to make the resultant increase upwards on the center reference. Increase of this resultant, with t_L constant, results in upward increase of the right reference point. At t_L is a denominator term, its increase will reduce the result, so upward increase of t_L, with the center reference (resulting from A_i and L_i) constant, will produce the desired decrease in right reference point (downward). Upward increase of this right reference point, with the T reference constant in the center, results in downward increase for the final quantity of the first formula, R_e, at the right of the left reference. Downward increase of T on the center scale produces the same result.

The only scale to receive dual use thus far is the one that serves both L_i and R_e. Direction of increase and exponent/spacing derivation justify use of the same scale for these two, with different numbering to suit. This may be the problem: to find a way of achieving this. The empirical constant can be incorporated by positioning any of the remaining scales, A_i, t_L, or T. The final additional calculation involves no problem, as the W and V scales are separate, although using the same reference lines.

The same "up" and "down" reasoning is used for the type of nomogram in Fig. 3-6C, but there are no problems. In the example of Fig. 3-6D, it conveniently happens that L_i and R_e need the same scale expansion and direction, so the additional numbering is all that is needed. If it were otherwise, a different arrangement would have to be tried. This chart was probably evolved by shuffling the position of the variables (their scale locations) until this possibility was found.

In either type of nomogram, variables should be combined in a functional arrangement. This has been observed with both types in Fig. 3-6C and D. The first things to combine are physical dimensions A_i and L_i (referring to Fig. 3-6D). Next a material parameter, t_L, is added, after which R_e and T can be juggled, if necessary, according to the job's requirements: one problem may have fixed T and we need to know R_e; another may leave T flexible, to be chosen to achieve a satisfactory value of R_e. By its choice of sequence, the chart suits either purpose equally well.

One final thing about nomograms, which will be compared with the graphical types in Chapter 6 in more detail. This is the choice of scale spacing and expansion for intended significant accuracy. In Fig. 3-6E, we have drawn three scales with uneven lateral spacing and with scale markings at equal logarithmic increments on each of the three scales. It is quite evident that the right scale could readably be much more finely subdivided. But the density of subdivision markings carries a subconscious implication as to accuracy of result. For the right scale here, the benefit of such implied greater accuracy would be lost when referred to the other scales used in the same alignment, because the benefit of additional significance disappears: it is impossible to read either of the other scales to a corresponding accuracy.

This is a fundamental limitation of nomograms. In particular it limits the useful significance of the middle reference of a group of three. This has nothing to do with exponents in the formula for the calculation. If the quantity on one scale uses an exponent, this will change the scale expansion of that quantity, but the linear dimension that represents a certain significant accuracy in the other variables is unchanged by use of this exponent. Thus it is seen that the maximum overall significant accuracy of most nomograms will occur at, or near, the equal-spacing arrangement.

However, there is another aspect to this question. In an example where one variable has much more limited range by the nature of the application, as does L_i in Fig. 3-6B, use of wide spacing large expansion of the scale to avoid giving a false impression of significance, with widely-spaced gradations, enables the "middle" scale, which is then much closer to the opposite side (IT is close to L_g), to use a maximum significance that is almost equal to that of the opposite side scale.

As well as choosing scale spacing to make the best of space, which is discussed again in Chapter 5, these additional factors of significant accuracy should be carefully weighed in making a layout.

Chapter 4
GRAPHICAL CHARTS

The graphical chart has certain advantages over the nomogram type. Examples may be given in regard to design flexibility and relative accuracy that support either type as best for a particular case, but, in general, the graphical chart possesses a range advantage—a more consistent range of a number of variables can be accommodated, within a given standard of accuracy, and the accuracy is permanent on a graphical chart.

Distortion of the paper on which the chart is printed does not materially affect the use of a graphical chart, whereas the nomogram depends on the use of a perfect straightedge on a chart whose paper has not distorted since the chart was printed. Distortion may occur in the printing process, too. Here, too, much greater care is essential to avoid distortion of the nomogram type than the graphical type. The accuracy of the graphical type depends entirely on how accurately it is drawn in the first instance. (A disadvantage sometimes quoted for the graphical type is that it can be harder on the eyes — the pattern of lines makes the user dizzy!)

The Simple Straight-Line Chart

Figure 4-1A shows the derivation of the simplest graphical chart form, with independent variables x and y plotted linearly, horizontally and vertically, while dependent variables z and u, the sum and difference, respectively, of x and y, use diagonal rulings. In this form, the graphical chart is strictly analogous to the parallel-line nomogram. Figure 4-1B applies the same form to multiplication and division formulae with logarithmic scales for the rulings.

A problem with logarithmic rulings is that multiplication or division cannot be carried through the zero value of a variable. An alternative straight-line form (Fig. 4-1C) overcomes this, with linear scale for the input variable (x) that passes through zero and linear or reciprocal scale for the other input variable. This chart is analogous to the ratio-type nomogram

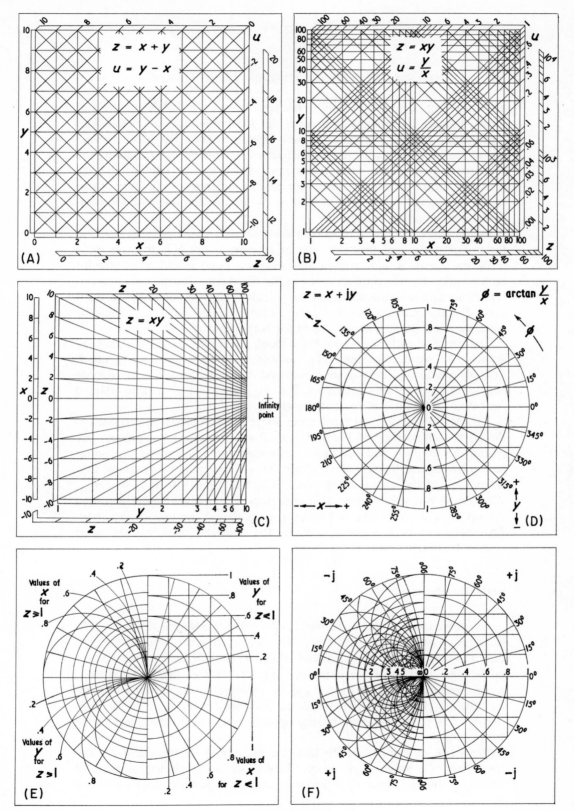

Fig. 4-1

and is, in fact, a ratio-type graphical chart. It uses the simple principle of proportionality by triangulation, with the focal point of the radial lines representing zero or infinity. The ratio-type nomogram has two "zeroes," one at each intercept with the parallel scales it connects, thus enabling the ratio scale to cover the entire ratio range from zero to infinity. But the graphical form has only one zero, representing either zero or infinity of one of the rectangularly-measured quantities, in this case the one with the horizontal scale (vertical rulings).

In Fig. 4-1C, y uses a reciprocal scale to arrive at a product function for z. For a quotient function such as $u = x/y$, which is the true ratio form, the y scale would be linear and the focal point would be at zero for both x and y. For the product function, the focal point for the radial rulings represents infinity horizontally on the y scale, and zero vertically on the x scale. For the quotient function (x/y), where a linear scale of y would be used, the focal point represents zero for both x and y.

The problem with this type is the difficult convergence, which makes the accuracy or significance extremely variable in different parts of the chart. Possibly a ratio-type nomogram, developed in Fig. 3-2, would achieve more consistent accuracy or significance. But the graphical type can be adapted for better uniformity, as we shall see shortly.

Another basic graphical type, using linear representation of variables, is the polar configuration of Fig. 4-1D. Real and imaginary components are plotted horizontally and vertically, while magnitude and phase are represented by concentric and radial rulings. This is a very literal graphical representation of the quantities involved. The limitation with it is its range. We have shown values up to 1 in quantities x, y, and z. Values less than 0.2 get close to the origin and values greater than 1 are outside the chart. The range can be changed by altering the numerals used, but the same relative limitation exists.

Scale Development

An adaptation of the same basic form can use reciprocal values. The same radial rulings represent phase (Fig. 4-1E, left side), while the magnitude (z) scale is reciprocal, instead of linear. In this way, a linear scale, in the right portion of the chart, can represent values of z from 0 to 1, while a reciprocal scale in the left portion represents values from 1 to infinity. When a changing value reaches the periphery of the chart in the right portion, it appears at a diametrically opposite point on the periphery of the left portion.

From this we can deduce the form for the rulings for the x and y scales for values of z greater than unity. They prove to be circles, or parts of circles, as shown. Figure 4-1F shows a completed skeleton chart (only first place numerals have rulings), using this construction. This extends the coverage from zero to infinity so that all possible values must be on the chart, but it does not alter the fact that the *useful* range is quite limited. Values approaching zero or infinity are too close to the origin.

A conflict in this type of chart is its discontinuity and the fact that zero and infinity are coincident at the origin. A better form would place zero and infinity at opposite points on the circumference. We will assume the real axis becomes a diameter of the chart, between the zero and infinity points on its circumference. The imaginary axis logically becomes the circumference of the circle.

A useful fact in deriving the ruling patterns is the observation that, in the reciprocal part as well as the linear part of Fig. 4-1F, all intersections of x and y rulings are mutually at right angles. Assuming this to be a property of our new chart, we derive its configuration in Fig. 4-2A. Ordinates up the x axis from the zero point we make a simple function of x that will put the value 0 at the zero point, the value 1 at the center of the circle (an arbitrary choice, with a basic significance), and the value infinity at the infinity point. This function we have designated z'. It is the ordinate of both x and z, measured along the x axis.

From geometry based on our mutual right angle assumption, we derive radii for the z rulings (u'), the x rulings (x'), and the y rulings (y'), to correspond with our initial starting point value on the x axis (z'). Note that we have based all our formulae on an outline circle of unit *radius*. An assumption of unit *diameter* could have been used, with an identical end result, but a consistent basis must be used. A reference value (e.g., R) could have been used for radius, but as it will appear as a factor in every formula, the assumption that radius is unit dimension for all calculations is more convenient. This unit dimension can have any value—5 inches, 10 inches, or whatever is a suitable size for the completed chart in the available space.

Finally, the same assumption, relative to the angle at which the phase rulings intercept the z rulings and, therefore, the angle at which they approach zero and infinity points, enables the phase mark-off points on the $z = 1$ line (a diameter at right angles to the x axis) and the radius for the phase rulings to be calculated. These are represented by d' and r', respectively.

The completed chart, which we shall call a bipolar type, is shown in Fig. 4-2B. It allows some expansion of the scale near both poles, as compared with the linear and reciprocal scales near the origin (Fig. 4-1F), thus improving the effective accuracy or significance range, as well as eliminating the unpleasant discontinuity, but the presentation is still limited.

A way to extend scale significance virtually indefinitely is to utilize logarithmic scales for the quantities x, y, and z, retaining linear for phase. This step, shown in completed (skeleton) form in Fig. 4-2D, can be visualized as a derivation from the form of Fig. 4-2B achieved by extending the zero

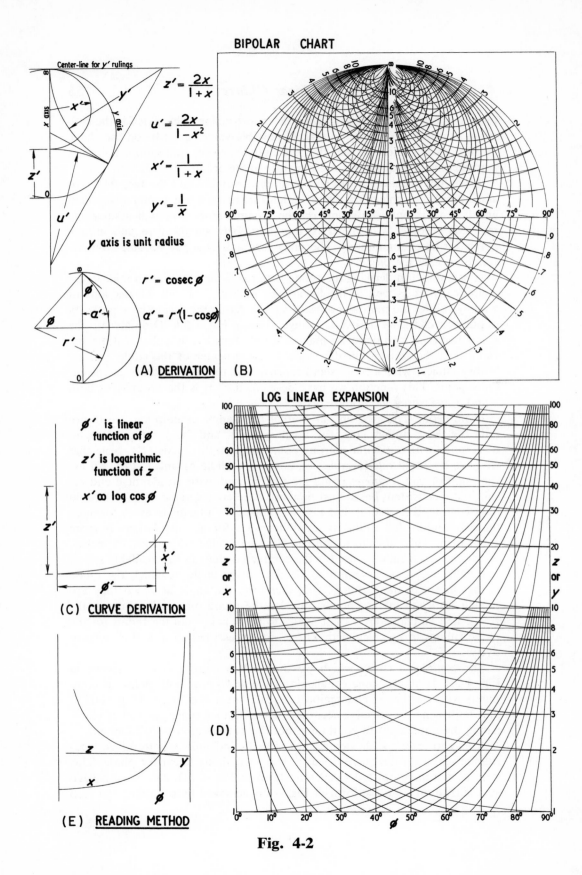

BIPOLAR CHART

$$z' = \frac{2x}{1+x}$$

$$u' = \frac{2x}{1-x^2}$$

$$x' = \frac{1}{1+x}$$

$$y' = \frac{1}{x}$$

y axis is unit radius

$$r' = \operatorname{cosec}\phi$$

$$a' = r'(1-\cos\phi)$$

(A) **DERIVATION**

(B)

LOG LINEAR EXPANSION

ϕ' is linear function of ϕ

z' is logarithmic function of z

$x' \infty \log \cos\phi$

(C) **CURVE DERIVATION**

(D)

(E) **READING METHOD**

Fig. 4-2

and infinity points downward and upward to infinity. The top and bottom of the chart are "stretched out" until we are looking at a parallel section of it taken from somewhere in the middle (there being no realizable top or bottom, because logarithms of zero and infinity are not finite).

Figure 4-2C shows the derivation of the curve that becomes the form of the x and y rulings, which are mirror images of one another, reversed from left to right. Figure 4-2E shows the method of reading such a chart. This form has the advantage common to all charts with logarithmic scales — uniform significant accuracy.

Scale Law Changes

Reverting now to the problem observed about the form of Fig. 4-1C, in Fig. 4-3A we show a chart using this form to compute the response of a peaking network relative to peak frequency, which is used as a normalizing reference. In this form, the vertical scale (horizontal rulings) is linear from top to bottom. The horizontal frequency scale (vertical rulings) in the left side portion is logarithmic. The vertical scale for the whole chart (horizontal rulings) is linear, representing the function $(x^4 - 2x^2)$ in expression (13) of Fig. 1-2, by transfer at the plotted curve from the logarithmic horizontal scale at the left. The horizontal scale (vertical rulings) for db_{peak} is derived by substituting $x = 1$ into the same expression.

To set out the db_{peak} scale, each db value is divided by 10 and subtracted from 1, for which the antilog is found from a table. For example, 10 db gives .1000, 1 db gives .7943, and 0.4 db gives .9120 at this point. These figures are subtracted from 1, giving, in the same order, .9, .2057, and .0880. Reciprocals of these figures, in an appropriate scale, give the distance of the vertical ruling from the focal point.

For the db rulings (radial) in Fig. 4-3A, a point between 0.4 and 0.5 db is found to represent a ratio of .1 (where 0.4 db represents .088). This vertical line can then be used as a reference for db rulings from top to bottom. Below the zero line, the procedure is simpler, the antilog being obtained of the db divided directly by 10, so, for 1 db minus, an antilog of 1.259 (note the decimal point position) is obtained. Subtracting 1 gives us .259. Now, because we are using the .1 vertical as reference, the intercept is 2.59 at this point. For 2 db it is 5.85, and so on, for subdivisions.

It remains to complete the radial lines that run out the bottom. For these we need reciprocals after subtracting 1 from the antilog and if we use the 8 horizontal as reference (the bottom line of the chart), these may be obtained by dividing the result into 8. Thus, to locate the 4 db radial ruling: antilog .4 is 2.512; subtract 1 leaves 1.512; divide into 8 gives 5.29 units (where the vertical reference used just now was 10 units) from the focal point, horizontally to its right.

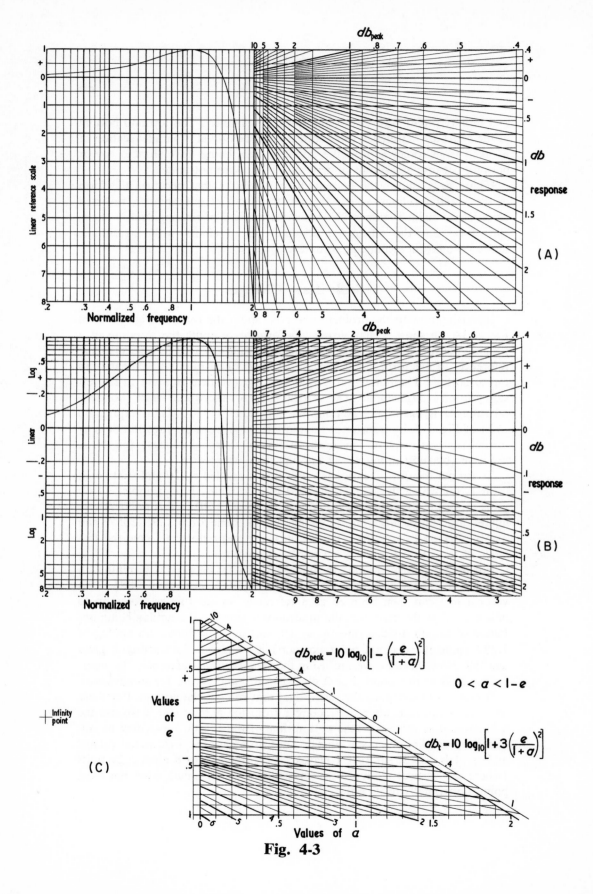

$$db_{peak} = 10 \log_{10}\left[1 - \left(\frac{e}{1+a}\right)^2\right]$$

$$0 < a < 1-e$$

$$db_t = 10 \log_{10}\left[1 + 3\left(\frac{e}{1+a}\right)^2\right]$$

Fig. 4-3

As noted, the chart still suffers from the defect observed in relation to Fig. 4-1C.

Considerable improvement may be achieved by changing the vertical scale for the whole chart (Fig. 4-3B). Only the center part is linear through the zero region, above and below which the scale switches to logarithmic. The horizontal scale (vertical rulings) is logarithmic in basis throughout. This is no change for the frequency scale at the left, but it changes the db scale at the right (marked as db$_{peak}$ along the top). Notice the improved horizontal distribution of the db scale.

In the parts of the chart where vertical and horizontal are both logarithmic scales, the resultant scale consists of straight-line parallel rulings at constant slope, determined by the relative base lengths of the vertical and horizontal logarithmic scales. As shown here, the horizontal decade (of which the chart contains a little over 1 decade) is about 3 times the vertical. Had we not been squeezing height somewhat, to make the comparison between constructions one above the other, greater relative height could have been used, resulting in a steeper angle and improving readability considerably.

In the center part of the chart (vertically), the horizontal spacing is logarithmic and the vertical spacing is linear, so the resultant rulings are a logarithmic curve, which is displaced horizontally from one ruling to the next. By making the differential coefficient of the vertical scale the same in each scale at the transition from linear to logarithmic the curve smoothly joins the straight-line part of the resulting rulings because the slope does not abruptly change at this point. This requires the distance from zero to the transition point, whatever its numerical value, to be 0.4343 decade (of the vertical logarithmic scale in this case). Note that the sequence of scale changes vertically: from logarithmic over the range from 1 down to 0.2; to linear, scaled to be equivalent to 0.8686 decade of the log scale, from 0.2 to —0.2; then logarithmic, with the same base decade but inverted (in minus values of the represented quantity), from 0.2 to 8. Thus the total height of the graph, in decades, is: top part, 0.699 decade; middle part (linear), 0.8686 decade; bottom part, 1.6021 decades. This is a total of 3.1697 (approximately 3.17) decades.

Note the relative expansion of the vertical space between rulings identified at the left as + 1 and —1: in Fig. 4-3A this is 2/9 of the total space; in Fig. 4-3B it is better than ⅔ (2.27/3.17).

Location of the db peak rulings is similar, except that a log scale is used in place of the reciprocal scale horizontally and the linear scale vertically (except between vertical values of ±0.2, where it is still linear). The curved continuation is constructed as described in Chapter 5, using the sloping lines already drawn, and terminated at the ±0.2 level, as location.

Now we turn to another chart presentation that will provide more examples in scale changing to improve coverage and scale distribution. Figure 4-3C represents, in basic linear form, the two formulae appended to the identification of the db scales. It is characteristic that the parameters' physical nature limits the combinations of values of the entities identified as *a* and *e* in this presentation, as shown in the mathematical expression; the value of *a* is always between zero and $(1 - e)$. As presented in this basic, linearly-derived chart, scale distribution is uneven and wastes space.

Because the upper and lower parts use different formulae for db at reference point, it is pertinent here to cover this application with two charts, one for each portion, rather than trying to use the approach of Fig. 4-3B. In Figure 4-4A, we show what happens to the upper part by making both quantities logarithmic. In the left-side portion, a range of *e* from 0.1 to 1 is covered. Note that it does not go down to the boundary of this section (Fig. 4-3C) $e = 0$, and that the scale congestion at the point is relatively worse in this presentation than in the top part of Fig. 4-3C. The main advantage here is that db rulings are parallel instead of converging, which does improve readability, if not distribution.

One way to handle the increasing congestion toward the point is to expand this portion, which we have done twice. The shaded portion at the top of the left-side portion is expanded to 3 times the scale at bottom left, and the portion shaded at the top of this is expanded to 10 times the original scale at top right. The shading is useful to indicate when the further expanded portions may be used to achieve greater accuracy.

This approach improves accuracy and, by virtue of the natural shape of the chart, utilizes space quite well. But it involves a virtual discontinuity. The area immediately below a shaded portion cannot be read as accurately as either the lower portion of the same section (which is gradual transition) or the part immediately inside the shading by transferring to the expansion (which is a sudden transition, or discontinuity). What would be ideal is a continuous expansion, instead of doing it in steps. This is the concept that led to the presentation of Fig. 4-4B.

Such an expansion, to execute our intent, involves the changing of variables in a way more complicated than simple log to linear, or vice versa. Changing the basic variables used to draw the chart as we have done here involves careful manipulation of formula to get a suitable form. The basic relationship used in all three forms (Fig. 4-3C and Fig. 4-4A and B) is the expression in the inner parentheses of the formulae in Fig. 4-3C. We have called this expression *b* in Fig. 4-4B, enabling us to use db as a basis for one set of reference rulings, in this case the horizontal (vertical scale). But the basic scale as measured off is neither *b* nor *log b*, but a function of it, which ultimately we derived as $\log y$, when *y* is $(1 - b)/(1 + b)$. The basis for that choice is as follows:

We want the horizontal dimension of the chart to be constant, instead of tapering to a point, so the expansion represented in steps in Fig. 4-4A takes place continuously as we move upwards. To achieve this, we want x, the horizontal ordinate, to represent the fraction that a is of the maximum value it could be for the particular db value, or value of b, represented by the vertical location in the rectangular coordinate system. Where x is 1 (its maximum value represented by the right edge of the chart), $a = y$ and, by substitution, $a = (1 - e)$ and $b = (1 - y)/(1 + y)$. Rearranging this to find y as a function of b yields the appropriate quantity for reference in deriving the vertical ordinates. Now we are ready to proceed with the construction.

The basic rectangular coordinates now represent x linearly in the horizontal direction and y logarithmically in the vertical direction. A simple substitution of y into the basic form converts this to a db scale for the vertical (horizontal rulings). Note that the expression for y leads to a scale for log y that allows b to represent values starting from zero db, and going up as far as we want to go, coming close to being a linear db scale toward the top of the chart. The bottom represents $y = 1$ with fractional decades upward (0.1, 0.01, etc.). So the bottom represents $b = 0$, while successive decades upward represent 9/11, 99/101, etc., progressively approaching unity.

It remains to produce rulings and scales for the original quantities a and e. As $a = xy$ (from the substitution at the top), and x uses a linear scale while the basic y scale is logarithmic, the a rulings are a simple logarithmic curve, displaced vertically from value to value. These may be drawn with high precision by means of a specially constructed template, or French curve (see Chapter 6).

Values of e are plotted from tabulations made at suitable interval values of x from zero to 1 (the full range of the chart). At the top of the chart, the e rulings come very close to another constant curve, displaced vertically, while toward the bottom they change from being almost straight (actually with a slight double curvature) to a slight curvature in the opposite direction, again becoming quite straight for the 0 value, which forms the bottom boundary of the chart.

Note that this construction achieves several objectives satisfactorily: the expansion of scale is uniform, instead of in steps; the chart does start from a value of $e = 0$, with a corresponding db value of zero; and good readability is achieved throughout. This is a skeleton chart for simplicity, because of its small size on the page here. The actual chart, drawn to fill a page, will have intermediate rulings and very good precision.

Figure 4-4C shows the result of converting the lower part of Fig. 4-3C to logarithmic in both directions. Readability is improved, but scale distribution, space utilization, and coverage are not. Like Fig. 4-4A, this does

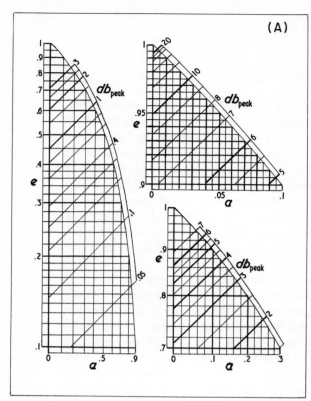

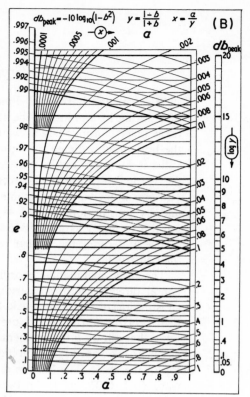

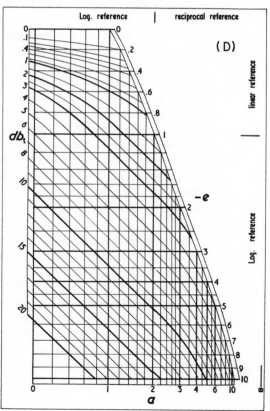

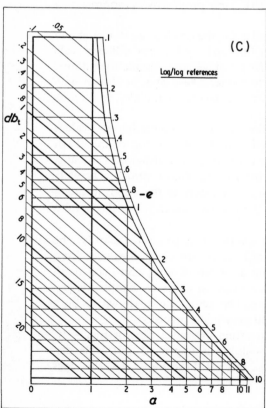

Fig. 4-4

not start at the mutual boundary condition of $e = 0$. All these defects can be improved by log/linear scale changes. In the vertical direction, values below 1 (above this point on the chart) use linear scale, enabling the chart to cover values from $e = 0$ (at the top) and at the same time expanding the space available for values greater than $e = 1$ (the lower part of the chart).

In the horizontal direction, values above $a = 2$ change to reciprocal scale, allowing an expansion of scale below this value. There is a numerical change in the scale, even in straight logarithmic presentation: the scale uses log $(1 + a)$, from the denominator of the basic expression, but is marked with values of a. The change to reciprocal scale uses an infinity reference point, which is just within the chart frame.

The vertical scale uses 0.4343 decade from 0 to 1 for the linear part and 1 decade of logarithmic below, a total of 1.4343 decade, as against 2 whole decades in Fig. 4-4C. The horizontal scale uses ¾ of the reciprocal conversion factor of 0.4343 decade. The value range used in reciprocal scale is from $a = 2$ to $a = 11$, or from $(a + 1) = 3$ to $(a + 1) = 12$, a ratio of 4:1 in reciprocal units. The conversion factor, to extend to zero at one end of a logarithmic scale or to infinity at the other, is the same. So the reciprocal part occupies ¾ of 0.4343, or 0.3257; the logarithmic part occupies 0.4771 decade (from $(a + 1) = 1$ to $(a + 1) = 3$), making a total of 0.8028, instead of 1.0792 decade (from $(a + 1) = 1$ to $(a + 1) = 12$). This allows a 25 percent expansion in this direction, as well as the 40 percent expansion in the vertical direction. A glance at the chart shows how much better the space has been utilized.

Three-Dimensional Charts

Figure 4-5 takes an example of a formula that could be given three-dimensional presentation. In Fig. 4-5A, we have given it a solid curve treatment, using a form that has the visual effect of a curve hewn out of solid material, with the graphical markings built into the material. The drawing is arduous, rather than difficult, merely using orthogonal perspective. It may not be too difficult to read, if care is taken in selecting the perspective.

A more common type of presentation is that shown in Fig. 4-5B, which represents a set of imaginary graphs for successive values of db, spaced apart in the third dimension. Often this type spaces such "cut-outs" horizontally, with each graph standing vertical (in visual effect), instead of the reverse arrangement that we have shown here. Our reason for selecting this arrangement, rather than the more common one, was to compare it with Fig. 4-5A. Here db is plotted vertically as the dependent ordinate, while the two horizontal dimensions represent jointly independent ordinates. In the solid treatment, this is the logical arrangement. In the separate contour treatment, it is no more logical to use one independent variable as the normal for the cut-out planes than the other. So we make the method less logical than the solid form. In the solid form, one can refer from the independent variables in the two horizontal directions, to find the "answer" in the vertical direction. In the separate contour form, one has to find the appropriate combination of independent variables on the edge of one of the contours, or endeavor to interpolate between them.

All in all, this makes the latter form rather difficult to read. But this really brings us back to earth, from the viewpoint of chart design. What is wrong with using a "perspective" which views either form from "vertically above"? Visually speaking, this is the basis for Fig. 4-5C. But this leads us into other considerations.

Each of the parameters, used as independent variables, is really dependent on more primary quantities. The quantities designated L and C appear only in the parameter plotted horizontally (Fig. 4-5C). The quantities designated R and r appear in both vertical and horizontal parameters. But where r is in the denominator of both, R is in the numerator of one and the denominator of the other. This means, by using logarithmic scales for the vertical and horizontal parameters directly, that varitaion of the basic quantities, L, C, r, and R can be represented as movement across the surface of the chart in a direction indicated at top right for each quantity. The arrow shows the direction for increase of that quantity in each case, a distance determined by the ratio with which the quantity changes. To illustrate, we have placed a movable scale for r on the chart in the correct direction in an arbitrary position that could represent the effect of varying the quantity r while keeping the other quantities constant in a specific problem or calculation.

This presentation could become the basis for a fairly elaborate slide-rule treatment, combined with graphical, as discussed in Chapter 2 (Fig. 2-5).

With this method of presentation, the resultant factor from which the db figure is derived is not a direct function of the parameter plotted vertically, but it is a direct function of the quantity $1 + R/r$. The net result of this fact is that changing the vertical scale to a logarithmic function of $1 + R/r$, instead of simply R/r, enables the db rulings to take up a precisely repetitive form (Fig. 4-5D).

The change of scale is made, but the identification is still in terms of R/r. Making this change also allows the value of R/r to be plotted right down to zero, without changing from logarithmic scale. This means the chart covers its full scope, instead of merely approaching it. So, for some applications, this construction is better. It expands the major portion of the R/r scale, by requiring only 1.7 decades, where previously is required 2.7 decades to go down to a value of 0.1. The rearrangement of area dis-

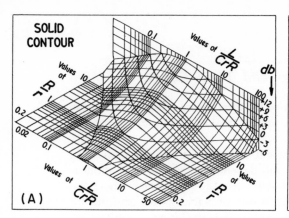

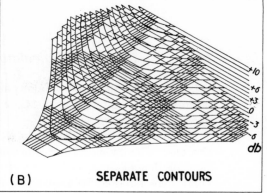

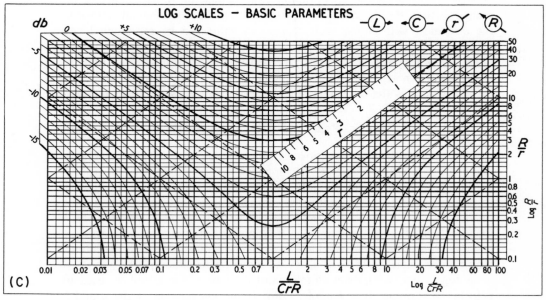

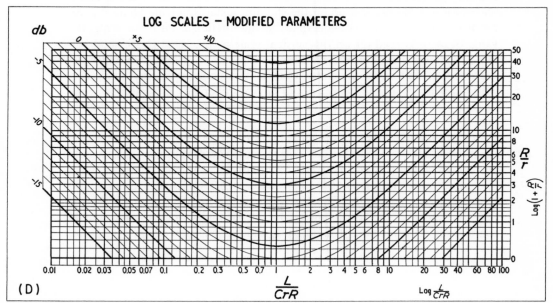

Fig. 4-5

tribution makes the upper, major part of the chart more readable and more accurate than that in Fig. 4-5C, as well as making it easier to achieve accuracy in drawing.

This does not mean there is a clear-cut advantage to either method, in this case. The choice of presentation will depend on the intended application, or that likely to be met most of the time. In applications where the chart may be used to investigate the result of varying the quantities *r* and/or *R,* or to choose an optimum value when the other quantities remain constant, the presentation of Fig. 4-5C has an obvious advantage in the directness with which such changes in value can be represented and explored.

On the other hand, if the major use will be the determination of individual results from separately predetermined quantity combinations, the chart of Fig. 4-5D has the advantage, on the score of accuracy and readability.

Some Practical Design Aspects

As with nomograms, an important thing to watch in designing a graphical chart is to avoid ambiguity which could lead to wrong use and results. In the nomogram, space economy with multiple calculations is fairly easy to achieve, because each variable uses a line, at most, and often only a scale on one side of a line, which may be shared with another variable. In a graphical chart, any operation — multiplying, dividing, or whatever — occupies space and area. We have to decide whether successive operations may use the same space over again, or move on to another area.

In Fig. 4-6A, we have a simple chart of a type that could be used to calculate a formula such as ab/c. Point 1, the intersection of the *a* and *b* scales, locates the product *ab* on the slanting scale. Referring along the appropriate ruling or interpolated space to intersection 2 on the *c* scale, the value of ab/c is read off on the vertical scale at the right (horizontal rulings). This utilizes the same area for multiplying by *b* and dividing by *c,* successively, and using the same scale (either same numerical values, or with a suitable value shift) for *b* and *c.* Any difference in numerical positioning can be cared for by using the bottom to read *b* and the top to read *c.*

For example, values of *b* might range from 1 to 100, while values of *c* range from 100 to 10,000, each 2 decades. The appropriate scales would be marked along top and bottom. Alternatively, with the same range for *b, c* could range from 5 to 500, or from 20 to 2,000. Each of these is also 2 decades, and the simple 2:1 scale relationship, in addition to the decade shift, is relatively easy to accommodate. If the scales are not conveniently commensurate, a method of handling is shown in Chapter 5 at Fig. 5-4H.

The ambiguity problem shows up if you reverse the sequence of quantity combinations. Combining *a* with *b* and then *c* is the correct order. But if you combine *a* with *c* and then *b,* which is equally possible in the configuration, the calculation becomes *ac/b* instead of *ab/c.* There may be calculations where this reversibility would be a desirable feature. In such cases, here is a way to achieve it.

But for calculations where the second alternative would always be a wrong answer, some means must be found to prevent such wrong reading. One way is to provide a clear key diagram, showing a typical calculation. In a nomogram, where a key is necessary, it is usually simple to find a relatively "empty" spot in which to put it. In a graphical chart, the whole area is often needed, leaving the alternative of putting the key on an accompanying page of text, or making a "dead" spot in the chart.

Doubling up on scale use can be used in various ways to effect space economy for different calculations. We showed multiplication and division. Where both quantities that share a scale need to use it for multiplication (numerator position), this can be achieved by inserting an arbitrary reference scale that is clearly marked. After the intersection at point 1, the sloping line or space would be followed to the reference line, which conveniently could be the vertical center line, and then a horizontal reference from this point proceeds to intersection 2 (and a third change of direction) with the result being read on the sloping scale. Space utilization and economy are precisely similar, and a key to show where the reference line is used is still needed.

In Fig. 4-6A, wrong usage resulted in reciprocal application of the affected variables. In the arrangement of Fig. 4-6B, a different kind of error occurs. In the case where reciprocal effect occurs, the mistake can be deduced by carefully checking the effect of increasing each input variable on the output quantity (answer). In the arrangement of Fig. 4-6B, this method of checking would not find the error, because any way of taking the sequence results in correct *direction* for increase, mutually.

Here the error occurs in the exponent. At first it may not be obvious that different exponents are involved, as each variable uses the same basic scale. Combination of *a* and *b* on the scale that ultimately carries *e* uses the *e* scale directly (in exponent, if not magnitude positioning) for the product. Combination at right angles with *c* results in a product on the original *a* scale, but with an exponent of one half. The reason for this is that the first combination resulted in a scale reduction of reciprocal root two in magnitude, although not in reading. The second combination results in a repeated reduction in scale of all three quantities entered thus far, making a total reduction that is one half the magnitude of the initial (*a*) scale, but still using the original scale.

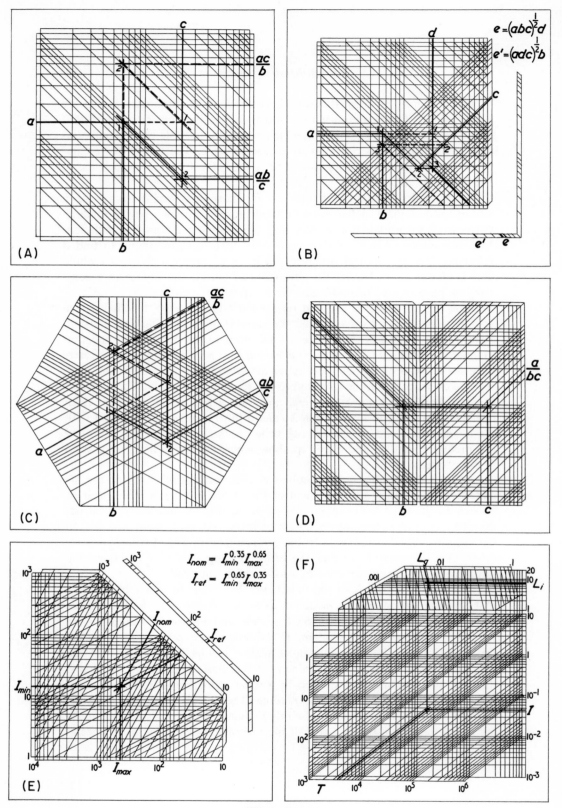

$$I_{nom} = I_{min}^{0.35} I_{max}^{0.65}$$
$$I_{ref} = I_{min}^{0.65} I_{max}^{0.35}$$

Fig. 4-6

The only variable whose exponent remains at its original value on the final *e* scale presentation is *d.* Taking the quantities in the wrong order by interchanging *b* and *d,* which use the same scale rulings, results in their also exchanging exponents, although the proper direction of increasing results is maintained on all quantities. To aid in following the two routes of calculation reference, the upright numerals, 1, 2, and 3, refer to the correct calculation using solid connecting lines, while the italic numerals, *1, 2,* and *3,* refer to the incorrect calculation using dashed lines. The formula for each result, *e* or *e',* is given at top right.

A variation of the scale magnitude situation can be illustrated by Fig. 4-6C. Careful examination will show that this chart serves a function identical with Fig. 4-6A, except that all three scales use the same decade magnitude. It has the same ambiguity as Fig. 4-6A. It is as if some special form of oblique axes were being used. Charts with this kind of derivation can use oblique axes, just as well as rectangular ones. The whole chart may be viewed as being twisted, with all rulings moving in such a way that the resulting pattern of intersections is twisted, but otherwise unchanged. The main usefulness of this device — using oblique axes — is to fit a chart whose "natural" shape is rhomboid into a more nearly rectangular shape without unnecessary waste of space.

The hexagonal shape does unify the magnitude of the three scales and thus may appear to increase the intrinsic accuracy of the chart. If only the *working* area were considered in a comparison, this would be true. But the working area is an inner hexagon, where all three sets of rulings intersect, which is only about half the size of the exterior hexagon, where the scales are read. Careful comparison, as placed on a rectangular area, shows that the diagonal scale of Fig. 4-6A uses slightly wider spacing than all the scales of Fig. 4-6C, while the vertical and horizontal scales are considerably more widely spaced. Thus, the greater accuracy inherent in the rectangular shape is evident when compared on an overall space utilization basis.

Figure 4-6D shows how ambiguity can be competely avoided so that a chart can be used without a key and the only possible way of reading it is the correct way. To give extra confidence, a key may be provided, but the presentation is foolproof. The disadvantage, of course, is that separate areas are used to combine *b* and *c,* so that either more space is required or the scales must be compressed, as compared with an arrangement of the type shown in Fig. 4-6A, a graphical chart designed for the same job.

Where necessary, this process can be repeated as many times as are necessary, either continuing across the page or moving from area to area in any way that seems to suit the application. In some cases, it may be feasible to combine the two methods, moving from area to area for some parts of the calculation and re-using the same area for others.

In calculations that do not involve exponents other than unity, the angle of slanting rulings will be determined solely by the ratio of the decade scales used for the respective vertical and horizontal rulings. Where these are equal, slanting rulings will be at 45°. Where one uses a larger scale than the other (as in the lower part of Fig. 4-6F), the angle suits the ratio.

Angle of intersection can also be used to introduce exponents other than unity into the calculation. Thus Fig. 4-6E is a graphical equivalent of part of the nomogram in Fig. 3-6A. In this case an advantage of the graphical form is evident: in the nomogram, the only safeguard against interchanging values of I_{max} and I_{min} is to be sure that the first use of the reference straightedge slopes up from left to right. In the graphical counterpart, the sloping top right edge precludes the area that would represent such a mistake: it is impossible to use the chart with such an incorrect transposition.

With both the vertical and horizontal scales using the same decade length, as shown here, the angle of the sloping rulings is determined by the arctan of the ratio between the exponents, in this case 0.35 and 0.65. Where the sum of the exponents is unity, as here, and the coefficient is also unity, so that equating the input quantities I_{max} and I_{min} results in identical output quantities also, the intercepts on this line can be the scale determination for the output quantities, which can be extended by extrapolation beyond the ends of this line.

Note that the spacing for the sloping decades is wider than either vertical or horizontal in this case. To fulfill the same purpose as that of Fig. 3-6A in a completed chart, the scale for I_{ref} would be carried on into a final section to evaluate L. If, for any reason, the vertical and horizontal scales did not use the same decade length (either to fit space, or to accommodate different ranges), the angle of the resultant output rulings would have to take the scale ratio, as well as the exponent ratio, into account. The next case illustrates this possibility.

Figure 4-6F duplicates the function of the nomogram shown in Fig. 3-6B. The scale for the IT product is horizontal (rulings vertical), with the I scale vertical and the T scale at an angle. The vertical rulings for IT carry through into the top part, which completes the calculation. The boundary conditions, represented on Fig. 3-6B by wedges to emphasize points on a vertical that must not be exceeded, are here represented by boundaries to the top part of the chart. The scale for L_i uses a slightly more compressed decade than that for I below it. Consequently the slope of the boundaries, which represent values of the quotient IT/L_i, is slightly less than that of the T rulings.

The sloping top left edge represents the value of product $IT/L_i = 3$. The sloping bottom right edge of the top part (at which the L_g rulings stop) represents the values of product $IT/L_i = 3 \times 10^3$. The scale for L_g has a slope derived from arctan $0.9/0.1 = $ arctan 9, with a modification due to the difference in vertical and horizontal scale (the horizontal in this part is twice the vertical, so the actual angle is arctan 4.5). The scale is positioned by using a sample calculation from the empirical formula, and the decade length is referred along the horizontal axis, because the rulings are nearer vertical than horizontal. The decade length, referred to the horizontal axis, will be that of the vertical rulings (horizontal scale) divided by 0.9. As in the sloping rulings of the chart in Fig. 4-6E, the decade scale spacing of the L_g rulings here is greater than that of any others on this chart.

Actually this chart has been slightly wastefully drawn. About half a decade at the left edge of the lower part is useless and could have been omitted, because it has no extension into the final stage of the calculation. A corresponding economy is not so obvious or so easy to effect in the nomogram arrangement.

Chapter 5
CONSTRUCTION DETAILS

We have covered the various types of charts and have seen what governs their shape, size, and construction. For any specific purpose, when we want to construct a chart, the problem may well be one of where to begin. The first thing, logically, if the chart's configuration has been decided upon, is to fit it into the available space. We illustrate the kind of spacing calculations involved in Fig. 5-1.

Layout

Nomograms

For a three-line nomogram to represent the calculation shown in Fig. 5-1A, with values of Z_s between 1 and 50 and values of Z_p between 200 and 60,000 (shown as 60K), we know this is 1.7 and 2.48 decades (using two-place approximations for estimation) of these respective quantities. So we choose decade lengths that will reasonably utilize the available height. A decade length of 6¼″ of Z_s takes up a total of 10⅝″, while one of 4 1/6″ takes up a total of 10⅓″ for Z_p. The frame height is 11¼″, so a ⅜″ space at the bottom of the Z_s scale will allow approximately ¼″ at the top and a ⅜″ space at the top of the Z_p scale will allow approximately 13/24″ (1/24″ more than ⅜″) at the bottom, which is comfortable spacing.

The space width in the frame is 10½″. Using the decade lengths chosen, the spacing between the Z_s and Z_p scales and the middle N scale must be in the ratio 3:2, which by using actual dimensions of 5.4″ and 3.6″, allows margins of ¾″ at the outside edges, which is comfortable spacing that way.

Now for the center scale. We can check the decade length in two ways. From the Z_s scale, it will be $2 \times 2/5$ of 6¼″, which is 5″. The factor 2 is used because N has the exponent 2 (squared) in the formula and the 2/5 is for the spacing. The check comes from the Z_p scale, from which it will be $2 \times 3/5$ of 4 1/6″, which also comes to 5″. So we use a 5″ decade,

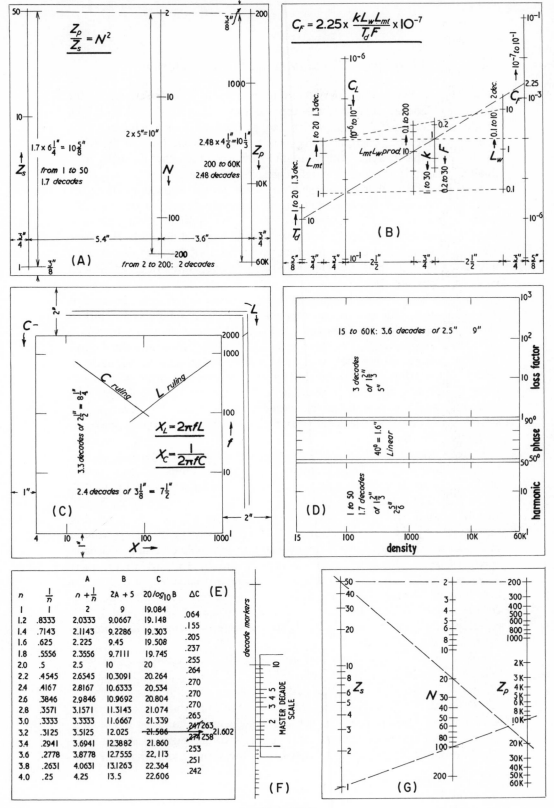

Fig. 5-1

of which 2 decades come to 10″ (using convenient terminating values for the scale). The alignment of the top values of Z_s and Z_p, 50 and 200, results in a value of $N = 2$, which can be used as a zero reference (the true zero reference, where all values are 1, runs off scale beyond the top). In this case the Z_s scale will be marked off first, then the Z_p scale, and, finally, using this top-end zero reference, the N scale.

Here it is appropriate to comment on useful decade dimensions. If necessary, any decade dimensions that prove necessary (e.g., for the L_g scale in the nomogram of Fig. 3-6B) may be used by multiplying the common logarithms of the scale numerals by the decade length dimension. But there are certain convenient dimensions that avoid the need for such calculations in making the scale and thus eliminate one possible source of error, as well as saving time and effort.

We need an accurate measuring scale (preferably of steel, because it will not distort with age, as do other materials) with subdivisions marked along different edges as follows: 1/10″, 1/20″, etc., on one edge; ¼″, ⅛″, 1/16″, etc., on another edge; and 1/12″, 1/24″, etc., on a third edge. The fourth edge will probably carry millimeters, which may occasionally be useful, but not too often, because they are not commensurate with scales using inches as a basis for measurement. The greater variety of inch subdivisions usually makes these the easier to work with. We have quite a selection of useful decade lengths to pick from that will enable scales to be plotted directly.

Using a decade length of 6¼″, the second decimal of a logarithm (0.01) is represented by 1/16″ and the first (0.1) by ⅝″. Using a decade length of 5″, the first decimal is represented by 0.5″ and the second by 1/20″. Using a decade length of 4 1/6″, the first decimal is represented by 5/12″ and the second by 1/24″. Using a decade length of 4″, the first decimal is represented by 0.4″ and measure of 0.1″ represents 0.025 in logarithmic measure, which is not quite so convenient to interpolate. Using a decade length of 3⅓″, the first decimal is represented by ⅓″, where the subdivision of 1/12″ again represents 0.025. Using a decade length of 3⅛″, a first decimal is represented by 5/16″ and a second by 1/32″. Using a decade length of 2½″, the first decimal is represented by ¼″ and 1/20″ represents 0.02 (if the scale gives 1/40″ subdivisions, these will represent the second decimal numerals).

Following this series down and up, useful decade lengths may be ⅝″, 5/6″, 1″, 1 1/24″, 1¼″, 1 9/16″, 1⅔″, 2″, 2 1/12″, 2½″, 3⅛″, 3⅓″, 4″, 4 1/16″, 5″, 6¼″, 8″, 8⅓″, 10″, and so on. Slightly less convenient are 3″, 3¾″, 7½″, and other intermediates that will subdivide conveniently for the first decimal place, but get a little awkward in handling the second and on. With common integral ratio spacings for nomogram scales, it is usually possible to pick decade lengths from the above group that will conveniently fill the space, while providing the correct relationship for the scale spacing needed to accommodate the total lengths.

A slightly more complicated nomogram example is shown in Fig. 5-1B, which is to perform the calculation represented at the top. The physical basis for this calculation makes it best suited to the separate-scale construction. A pair of scales for L_{mt} and L_w produce a central product scale. Note that these are relatively short because of the portion of final range that they represent. A T_d scale is used at the left with the reference point on this product scale to find a point on the final C_f scale that includes the empirical constant.

If both k and F are unity, this is the final result. The quantities k and F, one in the numerator and one in the denominator, use a common scale. An alignment through this scale at its unity (zero reference) point will lead to an identical value on a reference scale designated C_L. Reference through k and back through F (this sequence is important, because reversing it will interchange numerator and denominator positions of k and F) completes the calculation correctly, where these quantities are other than unity.

So much for the construction, as related to the method of use. Each combination uses the special equal-spacing nomogram. The spacing set out at the bottom correctly produces this, with convenient room for marking and identifying the scales. The L_{mt} and L_w scales are each $3\frac{1}{4}''$ from their product scale. The T_d and C_f scales are each $4''$ from the same product scale for the next step. And the C_L and C_F scales are each $3\frac{1}{4}''$ from the common k and F scale for the final steps of the calculation.

As scale length is fixed by the range required and the longest scale is that for C_F, this becomes the starting point for decade length and positioning. A convenient decade length to contain the six decades needed is selected. From there, positioning is worked backwards to include the empirical constant. The relationship between the C_L and the k and F scales is simple enough. It just requires checking that the scale directions and the final key to show the calculation sequence (which we have not shown) are correct to give the last stages of the calculation.

Now we work backwards through a product scale point of 10 and a T_d point of 10, with the point on the C_F scale that represents 2.25 in the appropriate decade of that scale for the empirical constant, to locate the T_d and product scales. The L_{mt} and L_w scales are positioned to work correctly with the product scale. The vertical staggering conveniently enables the scales to be provided with extra separation (beyond that provided by their lateral spacing) to aid in avoiding possible ambiguity of visual association.

Other nomograms are started in ways that can be deduced from these two representative examples, which represent one that fills the vertical space with all scales and one that is limited by only one scale. In some designs intermediate cases will be found. For cases involving unusual exponents, the discussion of Fig. 3-6B in Chapter 3 provides a good example. All that is necessary is to put in numbers to suit the ratios and get the "odd" scale by setting up the ratio 20/17 on a slide rule.

Slide Rules

Layout of slide-rule scales, of either type, is similar to that for nomograms. One advantage of slide rules in this connection is the fact that the relative factor, due to nomogram scale spacing, is absent. In the equally-spaced nomogram for multiplication or division operation, the middle scale has half the decade length of the two side scales. In the corresponding slide rule, all scales use the same scale expansions. In the asymmetrical nomogram, each scale has a different decade size (still assuming the same exponents in the calculation formula), but the slide rule keeps them the same. This enables the designer to concentrate on the scale length without having to be concerned about spacing.

In the linear slide rule, all scales have the same available length, and their magnitude range is only affected by any exponents in the formula. This is also basically true of the circular type, where the total available range is 360° rotation. The total number of decades needed, with reference to any of the quantities handled by the rule, determines how many degrees per decade should be used for the scale. The allocation of space around the circle may modify the basic decision to achieve readability and avoid confusing overlap between the scales.

In the circular slide rule, although the inner scales nearer the center are more compressed than the outer ones, they use the same basic decade (if they have the same exponent in the formula), which is measured in degrees of angle, not in linear distance round the edge. An example of this kind was discussed in Chapter 2 (Fig. 2-4B).

Graphical Charts

Graphical chart layout is essentially similar to that for nomograms. In Fig. 5-1C we have a simple chart with four active scales. The 2.4 decades of X and 3.3 decades of f, which will be determined by the application for which the chart is intended, form the basic rectangular dimensioning of the chart. We need scale identification for these X and f scales, plus identification for C and L, each of which extend around two sides of the chart. Two sides of the chart will need space for two sets of scales. We allow approximately 1″ for each scale. Where space is at a premium, less will do, but it so happens that exactly 1″ proves convenient here to provide decades of convenient dimension for the vertical and horizontal so the whole presentation fills the available space properly.

Having figured a size for the working area of the chart, it is only necessary to reason out the best positions for the scale identifications before we start drawing the main chart. An alternative choice to the one we have shown would put the f scale at the left, the L scale in direct contact with the chart at top and right, and the C scale spaced away at top and left.

Figure 5-1D shows how multiple section charts can be spaced out. Always allow a small space between sections, so there is no confusion as to which reference rulings carry through the boundary. Distribute the space allocation as representatively as possible, according to what they represent physically. In this case, we have two sections with logarithmic vertical scales, for which we decide to use the same decade, and one section requiring linear scale. The question is then one of choosing a decade length that will allow convenient room for a logical linear scale in that section, plus convenient outside margin for scale identification.

Scale Accuracy

Where a scale uses simple logarithmic dimensioning for its quantity, these distances can be derived directly from log tables, using either the appropriate scale to plot them or multiplying them by a factor that will enable them to be plotted with such a scale. A slide rule can be set to perform the latter operation. But many scales are encountered that are not derived so directly.

For example, in a certain feedback design chart, a set of rulings use the function $2n + 5 + 2/n$, which will need separate calculations for each scale point. Figure 5-1E shows how to set out calculations for this purpose. The scale will be identified by values of n, but will be marked off in distances proportional to the logarithm of this function. We start with numerals representing the scale markings and work out the logarithmic scale distances. Note the steps we have chosen in order to minimize writing down and rough work.

Having arrived at the final result column, it is worthwhile to add a column that represents the difference between successive markings. This will serve a dual function. First, it will indicate when the difference is small enough to change the step between scale subdivisions. Unless there is some reason for another choice, such as practical or physical limitations of usable points, subdivisions should range between certain prescribed limits of spacing, such as from $1/32''$ to $1/10''$, compatible with making the change at a convenient major scale mark. Secondly, the difference column will also provide a convenient check that will alert you to an arithmetical error in the calculations. We illustrate one here. In the value for the scale marking for 3.2, an error was made in reading the log tables. This is spotted by the erratic behavior of the difference column for adjacent values. A recheck of the calculation revealed the erroneous reading of the tables and the correct figure was substituted. It is always advisable to leave space on your worksheets for such corrections, as shown here.

There is also a method to save time and improve accuracy when a scale involves many decades. It becomes rather laborious to wade through decade after decade of a quantity, referring each point from the logarithm tables. It's bad enough when you have to calculate point by point all the way when the scale is of a non-repetitive type. For logarithmic scale, the pattern repeats every decade, so it is worth making a very accurate "master" decade on the edge of a piece of paper to use as a guide (Fig. 5-1F). Then the scale can be marked off at only the decade boundaries (powers of ten) with the steel scale, and the master decade applied, decade after decade, for the intermediate markings.

In making the master decade, first be sure to select a good, stout paper (or card) that is dimensionally stable. Then, in constructing it, pay special attention to the end marks, which must very precisely be at the correct full decade spacing so they can be used as a double check for placing the master when filling in each decade. Finally, in making the transfer, be very careful at all points to be precise. Always remember that transfer errors are additively cumulative, which on a logarithmic scale results in multiplicative error.

The same basic method is also useful in slide-rule construction. For the circular type, especially, setting off the angles and transferring them to the scale is a chore if you don't have a dividing head specially designed for this kind of work. The simplest way is to use a separate piece of paper and draw circles of the same radii (concentric) as those used for scales on the slide rule. Then, on this piece of paper, very carefully transfer a decade of scale in the angular unit decided upon, with radial markings cutting across the circular ones. Now cut out the paper along the circular lines.

The resulting pieces, with their edge markings, become master decades of the type used in Fig. 5-1F, with exactly the correct curve. Use the inner piece for an inner edge scale and vice versa, so the scales are transferred "across the line." Having the correct curve (because the radius is identical) is an aid to correct location of the decade, and previous marking off of the decade angles on the main construction enables them to be correctly fitted.

In non-repetitive scales (for any type of chart) that have to be calculated and finally converted to lengths by slide rule, accuracy can be improved by extracting fixed parts of the dimension at regular, decade-equivalent intervals. For example, distances between numerals in the range 0.1 to 1 would be calculated and measured off from the 0.1 point (which may not be inked in on the final drawing, but needs to be accurately located as a construction marker); distance between numerals in the range 1 to 10 would be calculated and measured off from the 1 point, which again must be accurately located as a construction marker.

Finally, reverting to Fig. 5-1A as an example, before starting to ink in the markings on all the scales, at least double check your nomogram or chart. You have used the top of the scales as a zero reference to position them (in this case). Check two more calculations, representing an opposite of all three scales, and one that takes an angle across the three (Fig. 5-1G). This will be a safeguard against having made a mistake in deducing scale direction, against incorrect spacing, or departure from correct spacing at some point on the scales' lengths, or some other error which may easily creep in when there are so many things to have correct for the complete chart to be accurate.

Drawing Methods

In nomograms, the step we represent here cannot be illustrated adequately in drawing. Having calculated the spacing as shown in Fig. 5-1A or B, the essential things are to ascertain that the scales are accurately spaced throughout their length, that they are straight and parallel, and that the zero reference (or other empirical positioning alignment) is accurate. In all this, it is important to have a true straightedge. Check this by ruling a line on one side, then turning over the straightedge and checking the line for "straightness" with the edge on the opposite side of the line drawn. If there is any curvature, it will not match perfectly.

Be sure all your drawing equipment is accurate. It should go without saying that the scale must have an order of accuracy at least an order of magnitude better than the resulting nomogram or chart can be read, and also that the precision of scale figures or calculations should have a similar reserve of accuracy (which can also be checked from the difference figures, as in Fig. 5-1E).

On the graphical form of chart, graphical construction can aid in achieving accuracy. Figure 5-2A illustrates how to locate each line drawn accurately. Use markers at each end of each ruling. Do not rely on a drawing machine to ensure parallelism. It may be good enough mechanically, or it may not. Keep your pen or pencil at a consistent angle, preferably normal to the paper when viewed along the line being drawn (it can slope within this normal plane to get smooth drawing).

When drawing each scale, include the extensions provided for visual ease of reading, which are at the right in Fig. 5-2A and at the bottom in Fig. 5-2B (which represents the next step, partly done).

Now comes the location of diagonal rulings. We have chosen a reactance chart for the whole development of Fig. 5-2. It is the chart whose basic

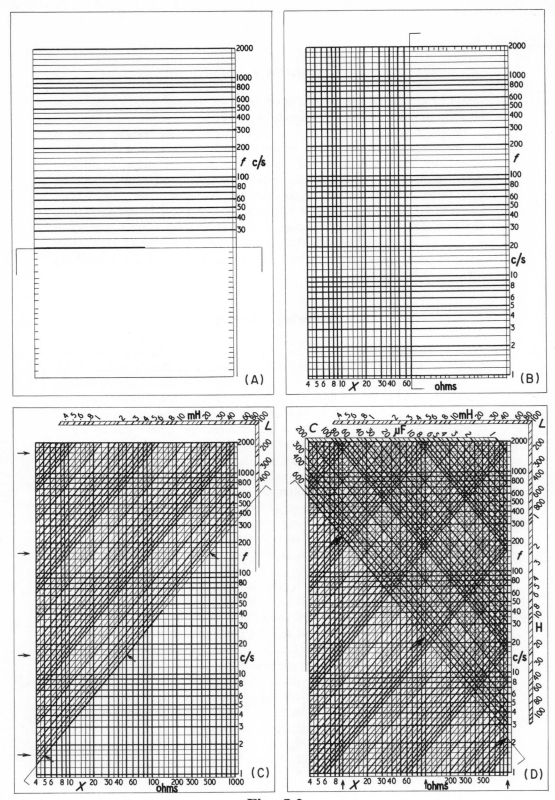

Fig. 5-2

dimensioning was shown in Fig. 5-1C, except that its proportions have been changed to fit the space in which we are now drawing it (repeated four times, to show different stages). We have the vertical and horizontal scales drawn and need the diagonals.

As correct use of the chart is more important than absolute accuracy of individual scales, the best way is to derive scales from one another in the way they will be used. As the formula gives reactance of an inductance as 2π times frequency times L, this factor of 2π has to be included. It proves useful to utilize its reciprocal, 0.15916, which can be represented well within the accuracy of the chart by 0.16, enabling a chart ruling on the frequency scale to be used as transfer reference. This means we take a frequency of 16, for example, to be equal to a pulsatance (sometimes called angular frequency) of 100, which is accurate within 0.528 percent. In a larger scale presentation, this difference could be taken into account.

Figure 5-2C shows how successive frequency lines at the 1.6 point on its decade are used to transfer L scale rulings from the X scale intercepts. The arrows at left identify the transfer reference lines. The arrows at the straightedge identify the intersections through which the line being drawn must accurately locate. Always "aim" at the widest position identifications possible, while checking intermediate ones available.

For extremities of the scale, where only one positioning marker is available, it is useful to empoly a rule with parallel markings to extrapolate. A transparent plastic straightedge, with lines drawn on its underside, parallel to its edge (so as to be in contact with the paper) will aid in maintaining parallelism to lines that have already been drawn, using more than one position identification to establish correct angle.

We have left the scale in Fig. 5-2D until last, because there is no convenient direct transfer from the X or f scales. However, when the L scale has been completed, there is a useful transfer from it, using the decade boundaries (10, 100, 1000, etc.) of the X scale as transfer reference lines. This is done in Fig. 5-2D. Again, check the intersections at the extreme transfer references available, and at intermediate points where available.

A word of caution about this derivation process. We said that the important thing is to ensure that the chart is accurate in the way it will be used, rather than to achieve absolute accuracy of scale positioning. This should not be construed to mean that any degree of laxity in drawing can be tolerated. If the chart is accurately drawn, then the two methods, absolute derivation and successive derivation, would produce coincident results. If there are minute errors, they should be such, where possible, that they do not reduce the accuracy of calculation or of scale reading.

In short, incorrect spacing on one scale cannot be corrected by incorrectly spacing another scale to correspond with it. This would minimize errors at the points where corrective derivation was made, while doubling them at other points. But if there is a uniform slight obliqueness, for example, that was not intended, using a derivation based upon perfect right angles would cause error, whereas successive derivation, as we have described it, would avoid that error by following through on the obliqueness.

Graphical Curves

Where the curves are circles, that is the way to draw them. The best procedure is to calculate the radius of each ruling as accurately as we position straight lines, together with either an identification of intercepts, or the location of its center. Remember that the important thing is the location of the final curve, not where its center is, although an accurate curve does require the center to be accurately placed. *Obliqueness cannot be compensated in a chart with circular rulings.*

For other curves, such as those in Figs. 4-2D, 4-3B, 4-4B and D, and 4-5D, a precisely-constructed template or French curve can be made. First calculate points of the curve (Fig. 5-3A) and draw them with careful precision (Fig. 5-3B). In rectangular graphs that use straight-line rulings only, precise 90° rectangularity is not vital to accuracy. If desired, oblique axes can be used without invalidating the chart's construction. But where curves are to be included in the rulings, angles assume an importance vital to accuracy. Be sure the ordinates are precisely at right angles and parallel at all times. Also be sure the chart rulings are absolutely square.

If a chart is made deliberately oblique, with curves that take that into account, double check angles at all points of construction. Where a curve is symmetrically "reflected," as in this example, such obliqueness is out of the question, of course.

Now mark off the same curve, with equal precision, on the protecting sheath paper of a piece of perspex, lucite, or other acrylic sheet. First cut the curve roughly, with adequate margin for precision shaping later, with a hacksaw or jigsaw (Fig. 5-3C). Then file it carefully to the true profile. Final shaping should be done with a square-cornered steel scraping tool (Fig. 5-3D). A precision steel rule will serve excellently. Scraping longitudinally along the edge, after it has been filed as smooth as possible to the correct contour, will produce the smoothest possible contour for easy ruling.

During the course of the final shaping, check not only the precision with which individual points conform to the original curve (Fig. 5-3G), but also the smoothness of the curve (Fig. 5-3E). This is important because it finds second-order deviations that might not show significantly in a direct examination of first-order accuracy. Roll the straightedge around the curve. Any points where a relative "corner" or "flat" occurs will be much more evident when doing this than they are to a direct examination.

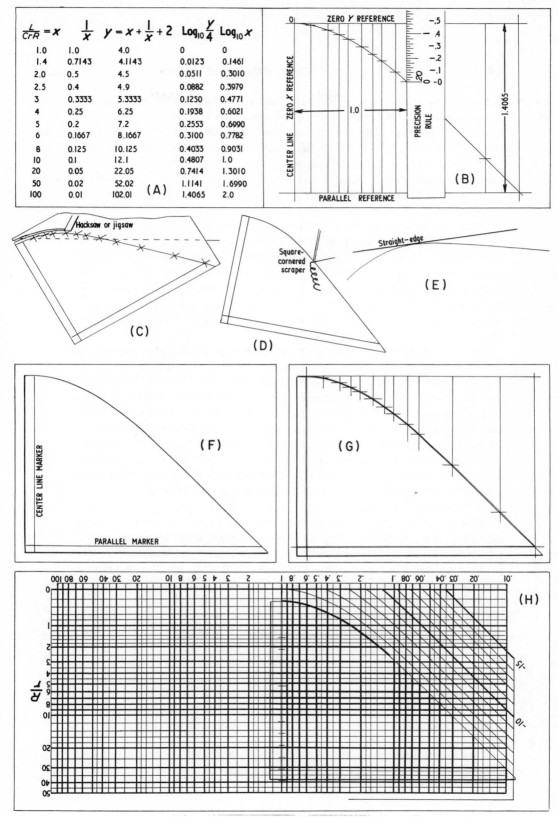

$\frac{L}{CrR} = x$	$\frac{1}{x}$	$y = x + \frac{1}{x} + 2$	$\text{Log}_{10}\frac{y}{4}$	$\text{Log}_{10}x$
1.0	1.0	4.0	0	0
1.4	0.7143	4.1143	0.0123	0.1461
2.0	0.5	4.5	0.0511	0.3010
2.5	0.4	4.9	0.0882	0.3979
3	0.3333	5.3333	0.1250	0.4771
4	0.25	6.25	0.1938	0.6021
5	0.2	7.2	0.2553	0.6990
6	0.1667	8.1667	0.3100	0.7782
8	0.125	10.125	0.4033	0.9031
10	0.1	12.1	0.4807	1.0
20	0.05	22.05	0.7414	1.3010
50	0.02	52.02	1.1141	1.6990
100	0.01	102.01	1.4065	2.0

(A)

(B) ZERO Y REFERENCE — CENTER LINE — ZERO X REFERENCE — 1.0 — PRECISION RULE — 1.4065 — PARALLEL REFERENCE

(C) Hacksaw or jigsaw

(D) Square-cornered scraper

(E) Straight-edge

(F) CENTER LINE MARKER — PARALLEL MARKER

(G)

(H)

Fig. 5-3

Second-order deviation is not important in a single curve; absolute first-order accuracy is. But when more than one curve is used, so interpolation between curves may be necessary in the use of the chart, second-order deviations become equally important. They can result in erratic change of spacing between curves, because successive curves are moved lengthwise, relative to one another, at least in some parts of themselves. This leads to false interpolation, even when the first-order accuracy of the curves may be good.

Before achieving the final precision, transfer locating markers to the perspex, carefully scoring them on both sides, exactly opposite one another (Fig. 5-3F). Then, when checking the contour against the original drawn curve (Fig. 5-3G), align the markers very accurately with the axes of the original curve. When the correct curve can be drawn quite accurately with the plastic template, it can be used for completing the curved rulings of the chart (Fig. 5-3H, which shows the chart of Fig. 4-5D partially completed).

In the case shown, vertical location is achieved by marking position on the chart's center line (1 on the horizontal scale). One side of the curves is drawn first (shown partially completed), then the curve is flipped over and the other side drawn to complete the curves. Extrapolations beyond the end of the center line may be achieved either by pencilled extension and identifying pencil markers, which can later be erased, or by using the parallel marker as identifying positioner against another set of pencil marks.

In drawing each curve, make sure the center-line marker lies precisely centered over the center line and, as a double check, see that the parallel marker is parallel with adjacent horizontal rulings on the chart.

In the case of individually-drawn curves, there is no need to make a template. For a single curve, accuracy can be improved not only by calculating an adequate number of points, but also by determining slope at certain poinst along it, notably points of maximum or transitional slope. This is also a help in drawing multiple curves, such as those in Figs. 4-4B (rulings for *e*) and 4-5C. Use of convenient French curves will always help attain smoothness, but always stop short, in following a particular template, well before visible departure from its contour is evident, and change to another curve that will help for the next part. Where curves are very slight in their curvature, a straightedge may serve better than any curved template, rocking the pen slightly to smooth the curve, so it becomes a true curve and not a succession of straight lines joined together. Some practice is needed to execute a good curve this way, but it can be very effective.

Clarity of Reading

Finally, methods must be employed in chart drawing that will render them clear to read. In nomograms, proper differentiation in the length of scale markers (Fig. 5-4A) should be used to avoid difficulty in finding the correct location of a specific value. Draw all the markers in succession down the chart, keeping track of the values they represent, so that the correct length is drawn for each. Identify sufficient markings with numerals to make reading unambiguous, without unnecessarily cluttering up the chart.

Next, identify the scales, where necessary, with designation of quantity by name, by symbol, and by units in which measured (Fig. 5-4B). It is useful to employ different lettering for each purpose, so the eye becomes accustomed to separating the information and looking for the particular piece needed at the moment.

Where a single reference line serves double or triple duty, either alternative or consecutive, make each scale clearly identifiable. Fig. 5-4C shows an example of alternative use, where the identification of the scale markings is carried in the symbols at the bottom, with units along the appropriate sets of numerals. Figure 5-4D is an example where the same reference may use different identifications in the same calculation. Here the same scale point can be identified in three different ways for the same calculation. Transfer from left to right of the scale itself is a simple relationship for which the chart may be used directly, without use of a straightedge. Detail calculation of further data is then made from this fixed reference point.

Before proceeding to full graphical type charts, Fig. 5-4E represents a compromise presentation that uses some of both. The horizontal rulings at the right of the vertical reference line for the nomogram are extended so a graphical tabulation of diameters for wire gages with different coverings can be presented. This is taken from information supplied in wire manufacturers' tables and is much easier to read, apply, and compare than having to refer to tables for use with a chart of either graphical or nomogram type. The nomogram reference line, which also carries a "turns per square inch" scale, is then used for completing the winding space calculations with the other scales. The values tabulated in this instance are manufacturers' designated maximum values.

Turning to the full graphical presentation, distinction between rulings cannot be made on a length basis, as with the nomogram. Use of different colors is a possible means of discrimination, but involves the practical difficulty that accuracy becomes dependent on the register between colors of the printing process. A more practical solution is to use lines of different thickness, or weight. Here we come to a practical drawing tip. For nomograms, because the distinction is in length of marker, it is feasible to draw them all in sequence. For charts, all lines of the same thickness should look the same thickness; the easiest way to achieve this is to set the ruling pen for each thickness in turn, and rule all the lines of that thickness, in a given scale, together.

It might seem more logical to rule the thicker, major markings first, and then "fill in" the thinner, subdivision markings. But for practical accuracy,

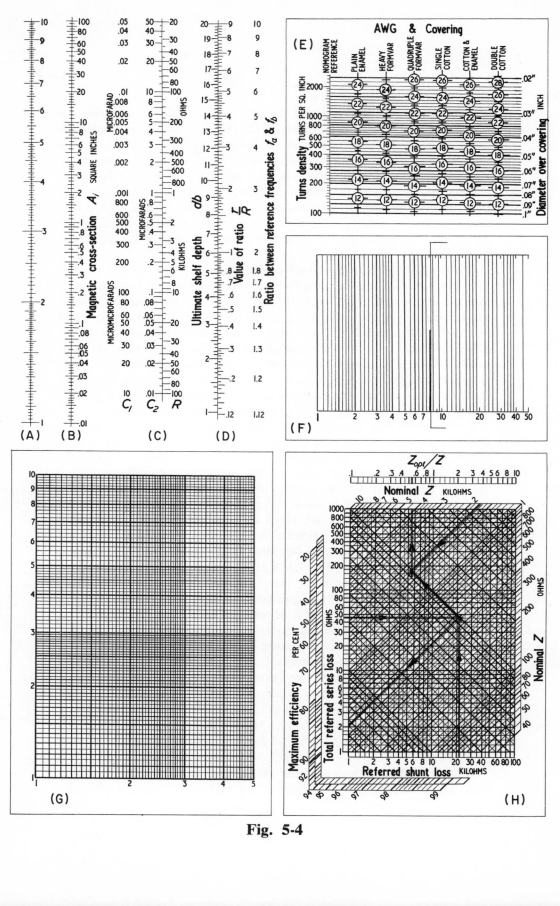

Fig. 5-4

it is best to reverse the process. First rule all the thinner lines, leaving the heavy line positions blank (Fig. 5-4F). Then go over the section again and fill in the thicker rulings. This has the double advantage that it is easier to place a thick line between appropriate thinner lines, which have been accurately positioned, than vice versa, and that less time is lost waiting for ink to dry. The heavy lines can be drawn almost immediately after the thin ones are finished, and some other work can be done while the completed set is drying. If the heavy lines are drawn first, a longer waiting time is required before the thin ones of the same scale can be added.

With very "open" scales, equivalent to the nomogram of Fig. 5-4A, more than one gradation of thickness is required (Fig. 5-4G). Here it is even more advantageous to work from thinnest to thickest, producing a very nice and easily readable finished scale.

Finally, there is the problem of readouts on graphical charts. This has been shown in almost every figure. The provision of a small margin at the edges, where values are read, in which the only rulings are those for that scale, makes graphical charts much more readable and less ambiguous. Where reference transfers from one part to another, as in Fig. 4-6D and F, a small space between scales clarifies use so the direction of reference rulings is clear. Where scales have dual use in the same calculation, scales can be provided at top for one and at bottom for the other, or at left and right, or wherever the opposite ends are located.

In Fig. 5-4H, we show another possibility, where a second use of the chart does not use a commensurate scale; i.e., the same rulings, with a different set of numerals, will serve. In such a case, the simplest thing to do is to extend the scale which serves within the chart to an outside transition reference, where (in this case) a *maximum efficiency* value is read off against the scale which is elsewhere used for *nominal Z* values. A typical use of the chart is marked over the rulings to illustrate where the double scale is used.

Readouts for graphs and good identification for nomogram scales are essential, whether or not a key is provided. Where a calculator is completely unambiguous, as in Figs. 2-4A and B, 2-5B, all of 3-1, 3-2, 3-3, 3-4, 4-4, 4-6D, E, and F, 5-1A and C, and 5-2, no key need be provided.

Where any possibility of ambiguity exists, as in Figs. 3-5E and F, 3-6A, B, C, and D, 4-2B and D, 4-3A and B, 4-6A, B, and C, 5-1B and D, and 5-4H, provision of a key, to show at a glance exactly how references are made, is virtually essential. The key should take the form of a miniature reproduction of the chart, with only enough rulings to give a skeleton impression, and thick dashed lines with directional arrows to indicate the method. Examples that could serve as keys to the fully-constructed charts they portray are Figs. 3-5A, 3-6A, B, C, and D, and 4-6A, B, and C (each of the latter without the added heavy dashed lines, which here show the wrong use).

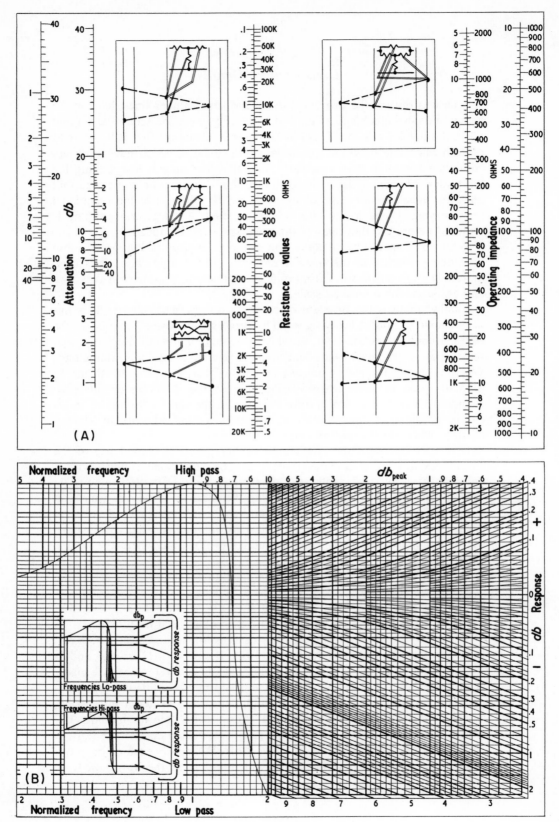

Fig. 5-5

Two examples of the use of keys in completed presentations are shown in Fig. 5-5. In Fig. 5-5A the chart of Fig. 3-5F is repeated with wider scale spacing (but maintaining the same lateral proportioning), with keys for each network for which the chart may be used indicating unambiguously where the scales need to be read to obtain each value.

In Fig. 5-5B the chart of Fig. 4-3B is repeated with only slight change in proportions (again, it is sharing a page). But another feature is shown here: duplicate frequency scales. At the bottom is the normalized frequency scale for low pass, or high frequency roll-off networks, shown previously. But the same chart may be used to predict response for high pass, or low frequency roll-off networks, merely by inverting the normalized frequency scale, which is here given along the top of the left part.

The keys are drawn in spaces made in the lower left part, which is "dead" space, because the only part of this area actually used is where the curve enables transfer to be made from the vertical frequency rulings to the horizontal rulings carrying through to the right portion of the chart.

Whether or not keys are considered necessary, any published presentation should include an example, however simple the calculator. The calculator may be completely foolproof, but an example always gives confidence, especially to someone who has not used the chart before. Where a chart is not for publication, if it needs a key, make one, even if it is only intended for your own use at later date. While the construction is fresh in mind, the method of use seems too obvious to bother to record. But given a year or so (or even less) without occasion to use it, what once seemed obvious no longer is.

Chapter 6
DUALITY BETWEEN TYPES

The information we summarize here is not vital to any type in itself, nor to their construction. However, it is useful (a) in understanding the basic properties of the types and (b) in deciding which type may best serve, in some cases. In the previous chapters, as we have gone along, we have made some comparisons, such as between slide-rule and nomogram scale relationships, the relative limitations of different types, and some analogies between nomogram and graphical chart design. For example, methods of providing limit safeguards have been fairly thoroughly compared in Chapters 3 and 4. But here we make more definite associations, in the form of a duality between the types.

In Fig. 6-1A and B, we compare a nomogram and graphical presentation of the same four quantities, side by side. The graphical chart has only been completed with all four scales, over the area served by the nomogram presentation, although both charts cover the same range in each of the four quantities. Thus it is evident that, within the same area, a graphical chart can cover a greater range in some of the quantities than is possible with the equivalent nomogram. On the other hand, a graphical chart fully occupies the area it covers, while a nomogram has spaces in which other information can be fitted.

However, it may be possible to utilize some of the "dead" area in the equivalent graphical chart for extra information (such as keys or other data) and still achieve better coverage than the nomogram.

Now notice other aspects of equivalence between the two chart forms. Changes in values of any of the quantities on the nomogram are represented by movement along the corresponding reference lines for the quantities. It is, of course, impossible to move one point of a straightedge reference, without moving at least all but one of the other points.

On the graphical chart, such movement is represented by movement in the component directions represented along the scales of x and y, and in the directions of the arrows for u and z. The alignment of four values along a straightedge in the nomogram corresponds with a point on the graphical chart.

Suppose we fix x and vary the other quantities: Fig. 6-1C shows how this is effected in both types. The reference line is pivoted around the fixed point on the x scale on the nomogram, while the reference point on the chart moves along the ruling representing the fixed x value on the graphical chart. Similar correspondencies are illustrated for each of the other quantities in Fig. 6-1D, E, and F. From this it appears that, as a line on the nomogram corresponds with a point on the graphical chart (Fig. 6-1A and B), so also a point on the nomogram corresponds with a line on the graphical chart, in terms of control of movement or change of values.

As we have already seen (Figs. 3-6B and 4-6F), a boundary on a nomogram is a point, while it is a line on a graphical chart. This equivalence is extended in Fig. 6-1G and H, where three equivalent values are marked A, B and C, as points on the nomogram and lines on the chart. Note that A and B, which are vertically aligned in the nomogram, correspond with parallel lines on the chart. The horizontal position of a point on the nomogram corresponds with an angle for the equivalent line on the graphical chart.

The point C, which occupies a different position horizontally, is equivalent to a line at quite a different angle. Note that movement across the nomogram represents rotation of the angle on the graphical chart. Check this by comparing, in order, the directions representing change of vertical value for x, C, z, y, A or B, and u, with the corresponding angle for change of equivalent values of rulings on the graphcial presentation.

While this equivalence could be developed as a complete theory — every detail of one form having an equivalence in the other — there are some practical limitations. For example, in the equal-spaced nomogram of Figs. 3-1A, 3-3B, etc., there is an equivalent direction for the xy product on the graphical chart, which will be a 45° angle to the x and y axes. But the opposite 45° angle on the chart, representing the x/y or y/x quotient, is equivalent only to a variable angle of the straightedge position in the nomogram. In more conventional nomogram terms, it is equivalent to an infinitely enlarged scale at infinite distance.

While this is more obvious for the special case, it is true of all cases. Rotation of scale angle in the graphical form is equivalent to change in both magnitude and position of the equivalent scale on the nomogram, and there is always one angle on the graphical chart that is equivalent to infinite distance, infinite magnitude expansion, on the nomogram. But this angle depends on the choice of factors on the nomogram, not on the graphical chart dimensions, where it appears as an angle. Changing the scales and spacing of the three existing scales (x, y, and product) on the nomogram will always bring the fourth quantity within finite distance and change the dimensions or relative exponents of the quantity that goes to infinity without any corresponding change in the graphical chart.

In both forms of chart, exponents are related to spacing or proportions. But, having fixed the exponent/scale relationship of two variables, the

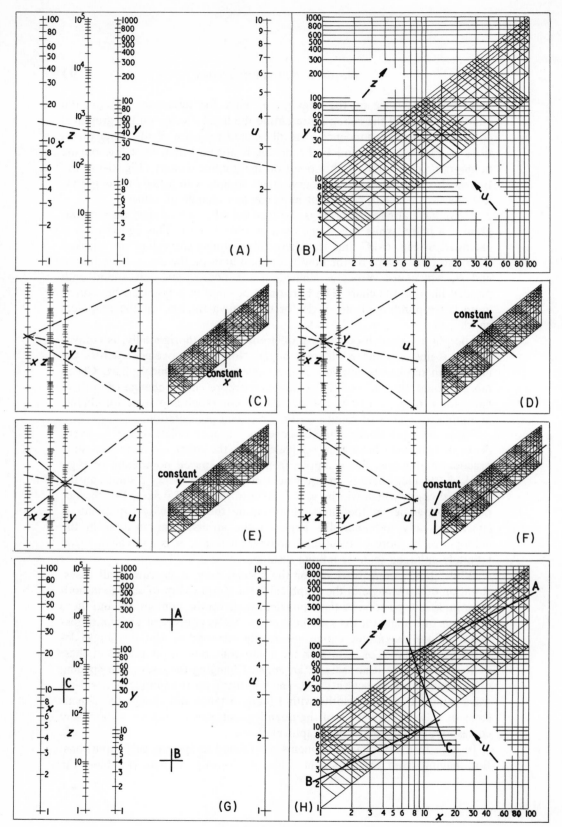

Fig. 6-1

relative exponent of these variables in a third depends on the lateral position on a nomogram type, and the scale angle on a chart type. The actual exponents can be adjusted, within the same relationship, by a change in scale magnitude.

Thus, in both types, the scale magnitude of the x and y scales and the geometry of the two relative to a z scale will determine that z is a function of $x^a y^b$, fixing the ratio $a : b$. But changing the magnitude of the z scale can vary the magnitude of a and b, in the same ratio, so the ratio $a : b$ is preserved.

The analog between slide rules and nomograms using parallel straight-line scales is obvious. Circular slide rules merely derive their scales from angular, rather than linear, measurements. As was stated in Chapter 2, slide rules avoid one complication of nomograms: that of changing the scale according to lateral spacing, as well as enabling the calculator to be read without any required aid (the straightedge).

While many so-called calculators of the slide-rule form are really fact files, rather than true calculators, they may also be combined with graphical presentation to achieve greater versatility, in which case the function of the slide is usually to replace one set of graphical rulings, either linear or circular (polar).

The two types of charts may also be combined, where a longer form of calculation seems to have its parts better adapted to different types. An ordinary slide rule can always be used in conjunction with, or as an extension to, any of the existing calculators. It should be pointed out, however, that speed of use will be achieved better where the graphical type calculator starts or completes the calculation, because this avoids the need for manipulation. With the nomogram, a straightedge needs manipulating on its surface, which must be laid down to use the slide rule and vice versa. With the graphical type, the slide rule does not have to be laid down, thus avoiding such handling motion.

It is conceivable that a slide-rule action could be combined with the nomogram into a single presentation. One possibility for this might be the equal-spaced nomogram, where a mechanical coupling of the slide-rule type could be devised to indicate the angle of the straightedge in any particular alignment, the angular indication being scaled in terms of the fourth quantity (Fig. 3-1).

Any work in the area of graphical calculators, such as we have covered in this book, is a surprising stimulator of originality, mainly because the possibilities of variation in presentation themselves have so many variables. For this reason, we have limited this presentation to marshalling the basic principles and methods that have proved successful in producing satisfactory and useful calculators, rather than attempting to give detailed coverage, which could become encyclopedic.

Index